NINETY-SEVENTH EDITION
SINCE 1912

WHO'S WHO
IN BASEBALL
2012

Official Lifetime Records
Of Major League Players

Editor
Pete Palmer

Associate Editor
Stuart Shea

Managing Editor
Rory S. Slifkin

Cover Photo By Tom DiPace

EDITOR'S NOTE: *Denotes League Leader throughout the publication.

BATTERS

ABREU, BOB KELLY (BOBBY)
Born, Maracay, Venezuela, March 11, 1974.
Bats Left. Throws Right. Height, 6 feet. Weight, 210 pounds.

Year	Club	Lea	Pos	G	AB	R	H	2B	3B	HR	RBI	SB	Avg
1991 Astros	Gulf Coast	OF-SS	56	183	21	55	7	3	0	20	10	.301
1992 Asheville	So. Atl.	OF	135	480	81	140	21	4	8	48	15	.292
1993 Osceola	Fla. St.	OF	129	474	62	134	21	17	5	55	10	.283
1994 Jackson	Texas	OF	118	400	61	121	25	9	16	73	12	.303
1995 Tucson	P.C.	OF-2B	114	415	72	126	24	17	10	75	16	.304
1996 Tucson	P.C.	OF	132	484	86	138	14	16	13	68	24	.285
1996 Houston	N.L.	OF	15	22	1	5	1	0	0	1	0	.227
1997 Jackson	Texas	OF	3	12	2	2	1	0	0	0	0	.167
1997 New Orleans	A.A.	OF	47	194	25	52	9	4	2	22	7	.268
1997 Houston a-b-c	N.L.	OF	59	188	22	47	10	2	3	26	7	.250
1998 Philadelphia	N.L.	OF	151	497	68	155	29	6	17	74	19	.312
1999 Philadelphia	N.L.	OF	152	546	118	183	35	*11	20	93	27	.335
2000 Philadelphia	N.L.	OF	154	576	103	182	42	10	25	79	28	.316
2001 Philadelphia	N.L.	OF	*162	588	118	170	48	4	31	110	36	.289
2002 Philadelphia	N.L.	OF	157	572	102	176	*50	6	20	85	31	.308
2003 Philadelphia	N.L.	OF	158	577	99	173	35	1	20	101	22	.300
2004 Philadelphia	N.L.	OF	159	574	118	173	47	1	30	105	40	.301
2005 Philadelphia	N.L.	OF	*162	588	104	168	37	1	24	102	31	.286
2006 Philadelphia	N.L.	OF	98	339	61	94	25	2	8	65	20	.277
2006 New York d	A.L.	OF	58	209	37	69	16	0	7	42	10	.330
2007 New York	A.L.	OF	158	605	123	171	40	5	16	101	25	.283
2008 New York e	A.L.	OF	156	609	100	180	39	4	20	100	22	.296
2009 Los Angeles	A.L.	OF	152	563	96	165	29	3	15	103	30	.293
2010 Los Angeles	A.L.	OF	154	573	88	146	41	1	20	78	24	.255
2011 Los Angeles	A.L.	DH-OF	142	502	54	127	30	1	8	60	21	.253
Major League Totals		16 Yrs.	2247	8128	1412	2384	554	58	284	1325	393	.293
Division Series												
1997 Houston	N.L.	PH	3	3	0	1	0	0	0	0	1	.333
2006 New York	A.L.	OF	4	15	2	5	1	0	0	4	0	.333
2007 New York	A.L.	OF	4	15	1	4	1	0	1	2	1	.267
2009 Los Angeles	A.L.	OF	3	9	4	5	2	0	0	1	0	.556
Division Series Totals			14	42	7	15	4	0	1	7	2	.357
Championship Series												
2009 Los Angeles	A.L.	OF	6	25	2	4	2	0	0	2	0	.160

a On disabled list from May 25 to July 1, 1997.
b Selected in expansion draft by Tampa Bay Devil Rays, November 18, 1997.
c Traded to Philadelphia Phillies for infielder Kevin Stocker, November 19, 1997.
d Traded to New York Yankees with pitcher Cory Lidle for infielder C.J. Henry, pitcher Matt Smith, catcher Jesus Sanchez and pitcher Carlos Monasterios, July 30, 2006.
e Filed for free agency, October 30, 2008. Signed with Los Angeles Angels, February 12, 2009.

ACKLEY, DUSTIN MICHAEL
Born, Winston-Salem, North Carolina, February 26, 1988.
Bats Left. Throws Right. Height, 6 feet, 1 inch. Weight, 185 pounds.

Year	Club	Lea	Pos	G	AB	R	H	2B	3B	HR	RBI	SB	Avg
2010 Tacoma	P.C.	2B	52	212	37	58	12	4	5	23	2	.274
2010 West Tenn	Southern	2B	82	289	42	76	21	4	2	28	8	.263
2011 Tacoma	P.C.	2B	66	271	57	82	17	3	9	35	7	.303
2011 Seattle	A.L.	2B-1B	90	333	39	91	16	7	6	36	6	.273

ALONSO, YONDER
Born, Havana, Cuba, April 8, 1987.
Bats Left. Throws Right. Height, 6 feet, 2 inches. Weight, 240 pounds.

Year	Club	Lea	Pos	G	AB	R	H	2B	3B	HR	RBI	SB	Avg
2008 Sarasota	Fla.St.	1B	6	19	1	6	1	0	0	2	0	.316
2009 Reds	Gulf Coast	1B	6	15	0	2	0	0	0	0	0	.133
2009 Sarasota	Fla.St.	1B	49	175	21	53	13	0	7	38	0	.303
2009 Carolina	Southern	1B	29	105	12	31	11	0	2	14	1	.295
2010 Carolina	Southern	1B-OF	31	101	19	27	5	0	3	13	4	.267
2010 Louisville	Int.	1B-OF	101	406	50	120	31	2	12	56	9	.296

Year Club	Lea	Pos	G	AB	R	H	2B	3B	HR	RBI	SB	Avg
2010 Cincinnati	N.L.	1B	22	29	2	6	2	0	0	3	0	.207
2011 Louisville	Int.	OF-1B	91	358	46	106	24	4	12	56	6	.296
2011 Cincinnati a	N.L.	OF-1B-3B	47	88	9	29	4	0	5	15	0	.330
Major League Totals	2 Yrs.		69	117	11	35	6	0	5	18	0	.299

a Traded to San Diego Padres with pitcher Edinson Volquez, pitcher Brad Boxberger and catcher Yasmani Grandal for pitcher Mat Latos, December 17, 2011.

ALTUVE, JOSE CARLOS

Born, Maracay, Venezuela, May 6, 1990.
Bats Right. Throws Right. Height, 5 feet, 7 inches. Weight, 170 pounds.

Year Club	Lea	Pos	G	AB	R	H	2B	3B	HR	RBI	SB	Avg
2008 Greeneville	Appal.	2B-3B	40	141	26	40	9	3	2	21	8	.284
2009 Greeneville	Appal.	2B	45	179	45	58	20	2	3	18	21	.324
2009 Tri-City	N.Y.-Penn.	2B	21	76	13	19	5	0	0	7	7	.250
2010 Lexington	So.Atl.	2B-3B	94	393	75	121	15	3	11	45	39	.308
2010 Lancaster	Calif.	2B-3B	31	116	18	32	5	2	4	22	3	.276
2011 Lancaster	Calif.	2B	52	213	38	87	13	7	5	34	19	.408
2011 Corpus Christi	Texas	2B-3B	35	144	21	52	9	3	5	25	5	.361
2011 Houston	N.L.	2B	57	221	26	61	10	.1	2	12	7	.276

ALVAREZ, PEDRO MANUEL

Born, New York, New York, February 6, 1987.
Bats Left. Throws Right. Height, 6 feet, 3 inches. Weight, 225 pounds.

Year Club	Lea	Pos	G	AB	R	H	2B	3B	HR	RBI	SB	Avg
2009 Lynchburg	Carolina	3B	66	243	38	60	14	1	14	55	1	.247
2009 Altoona	Eastern	3B	60	222	42	74	18	0	13	40	1	.333
2010 Indianapolis	Int.	3B	66	242	42	67	15	4	13	53	4	.277
2010 Pittsburgh	N.L.	3B	95	347	42	89	21	1	16	64	0	.256
2011 Pirates	Gulf Coast	3B	1	1	0	0	0	0	0	0	0	.000
2011 Bradenton	Fla.St.	3B	6	16	2	3	0	0	1	2	0	.188
2011 Indianapolis	Int.	3B	35	125	16	32	5	1	5	19	0	.256
2011 Pittsburgh a	N.L.	3B	74	235	18	45	9	1	4	19	1	.191
Major League Totals			2 Yrs. 169	582	60	134	30	2	20	83	1	.230

a On disabled list from May 20 to July 9, 2011.

ANDINO, ROBERT LAZARO

Born, Miami, Florida, April 25, 1984.
Bats Right. Throws Right. Height, 6 feet. Weight, 195 pounds.

Year Club	Lea	Pos	G	AB	R	H	2B	3B	HR	RBI	SB	Avg
2002 Marlins	Gulf Coast	SS	9	27	2	7	0	0	0	2	3	.259
2002 Jamestown	N.Y.-Penn.	SS	9	36	2	6	1	1	0	3	1	.167
2003 Greensboro	So.Atl.	SS	119	416	45	78	17	2	2	27	6	.188
2004 Jupiter	Fla.St.	SS-2B	48	196	18	55	7	2	0	15	6	.281
2004 Greensboro	So.Atl.	SS	76	295	27	83	10	1	8	46	9	.281
2005 Carolina	Southern	SS-2B	127	516	63	139	30	0	5	48	22	.269
2005 Florida	N.L.	SS	17	44	4	7	4	0	0	1	1	.159
2006 Albuquerque	P.C.	SS-2B	120	498	70	127	18	6	8	46	13	.255
2006 Florida	N.L.	SS	11	24	0	4	1	0	0	2	1	.167
2007 Albuquerque	P.C.	SS-2B	142	598	85	166	25	13	13	50	21	.278
2007 Florida	N.L.	SS	7	13	0	5	1	0	0	0	0	.385
2008 Albuquerque	P.C.	SS-2B	43	181	28	52	14	3	6	26	9	.287
2008 Florida	N.L.	2B-SS-3B-OF	44	63	7	13	2	0	2	9	0	.206
2009 Baltimore a	A.L.	SS-2B-3B-OF	78	198	31	44	7	0	2	10	3	.222
2010 Norfolk	Int.	SS-2B	132	546	72	144	30	4	13	76	16	.264
2010 Baltimore	A.L.	2B-SS-3B	16	61	6	18	4	0	2	6	1	.295
2011 Baltimore	A.L.	2B-SS-3B-OF	139	457	63	120	22	0	5	36	13	.263
Major League Totals			7 Yrs. 312	860	111	211	41	0	11	64	19	.245

a Traded to Baltimore Orioles for pitcher Hayden Penn, April 1, 2009.

ANDRUS (TORRES), ELVIS AUGUSTO

Born, Maracay, Venezuela, August 26, 1988.
Bats Right. Throws Right. Height, 6 feet. Weight, 185 pounds.

Year Club	Lea	Pos	G	AB	R	H	2B	3B	HR	RBI	SB	Avg
2005 Danville	Appal.	SS	6	18	3	5	1	0	0	1	1	.278
2005 Braves	Gulf Coast	SS-2B	46	166	26	49	6	1	3	20	7	.295

Year	Club	Lea	Pos	G	AB	R	H	2B	3B	HR	RBI	SB	Avg
2006 Rome	So.Atl.		SS	111	437	67	116	25	4	3	50	23	.265
2007 Bakersfield	Calif.		SS	27	110	19	33	2	0	2	12	15	.300
2007 Myrtle Beach a	Carolina		SS	99	385	59	94	20	3	3	37	25	.244
2008 Frisco	Texas		SS	118	482	82	142	19	2	4	65	54	.295
2009 Texas	A.L.		SS	145	480	72	128	17	8	6	40	33	.267
2010 Texas	A.L.		SS	148	588	88	156	15	3	0	35	32	.265
2011 Texas	A.L.		SS	150	587	96	164	27	3	5	60	37	.279
Major League Totals			3 Yrs.	443	1655	256	448	59	14	11	135	102	.271
Division Series													
2010 Texas	A.L.		SS	5	24	2	8	1	0	0	1	3	.333
2011 Texas	A.L.		SS	4	14	1	2	0	0	0	0	0	.143
Division Series Totals				9	38	3	10	1	0	0	1	3	.263
Championship Series													
2010 Texas	A.L.		SS	6	27	4	9	2	0	0	2	4	.333
2011 Texas	A.L.		SS	6	25	4	6	0	0	0	1	1	.240
Championship Series Totals				12	52	8	15	2	0	0	3	5	.288
World Series Record													
2010 Texas	A.L.		SS	5	17	2	3	0	0	0	1	1	.176
2011 Texas	A.L.		SS	7	29	5	8	1	0	0	0	0	.276
World Series Totals				12	46	7	11	1	0	0	1	1	.239

a Traded by Atlanta Braves to Texas Rangers with catcher Jarrod Saltalamacchia, pitcher Neftali Feliz, pitcher Matt Harrison and pitcher Beau James for infielder Mark Teixeira and pitcher Ron Mahay, July 31, 2007.

ANKIEL, RICHARD ALEXANDER (RICK)

Born, Fort Pierce, Florida, July 19, 1979.

Bats Left. Throws Left. Height, 6 feet, 1 inch. Weight, 210 pounds.

Year	Club	Lea	Pos	G	AB	R	H	2B	3B	HR	RBI	SB	Avg
1998 Peoria	Midwest		P	3	0	0	0	0	0	0	0	0	.000
1998 Pr William	Carolina		P	9	0	0	0	0	0	0	0	0	.000
1999 Arkansas	Texas		P	8	10	1	4	0	0	1	1	0	.400
1999 Memphis	P.C.		P	16	21	3	6	2	0	0	4	0	.286
1999 St. Louis	N.L.		P	9	10	0	1	0	0	0	0	0	.100
2000 St. Louis	N.L.		P	35	68	8	17	1	1	2	9	0	.250
2001 Memphis	P.C.		P	3	0	0	0	0	0	0	0	0	.000
2001 Johnson City	Appal.		P	41	105	21	30	7	0	10	35	0	.286
2001 St. Louis	N.L.		P	6	8	1	0	0	0	0	0	0	.000
2002 St. Louis a	N.L.		INJURED—Did Not Play										
2003 Tennessee	Southern		P	30	25	2	6	1	0	1	5	0	.240
2004 Tennessee	Southern		P	2	4	0	0	0	0	0	0	0	.000
2004 St. Louis b	N.L.		P	5	1	0	0	0	0	0	0	0	.000
2005 Quad Cities	Midwest		OF	51	185	33	50	10	1	11	45	0	.270
2005 Springfield	Texas		OF	34	136	18	33	7	0	10	30	0	.243
2006 St. Louis c	N.L.		INJURED—Did Not Play										
2007 Memphis	P.C.		OF	102	389	62	104	15	3	32	89	4	.267
2007 St. Louis	N.L.		OF	47	172	31	49	8	1	11	39	1	.285
2008 St. Louis	N.L.		OF	120	413	65	109	21	2	25	71	2	.264
2009 St. Louis d-e	N.L.		OF	122	372	50	86	21	2	11	38	4	.231
2010 Omaha	P.C.		OF	18	67	8	17	6	0	4	9	0	.254
2010 Kansas City	A.L.		OF	27	92	14	24	7	0	4	15	1	.261
2010 Atlanta f-g-h	N.L.		OF	47	119	17	25	6	1	2	9	2	.210
2011 Nationals	Gulf Coast		OF	1	2	0	1	0	0	0	0	0	.500
2011 Harrisburg	Eastern		OF	1	4	0	0	0	0	0	0	0	.000
2011 Syracuse	Int.		OF	2	7	2	1	1	0	0	0	1	.143
2011 Washington i-j	N.L.		OF	122	380	46	91	20	0	9	37	10	.239
Major League Totals			9 Yrs.	540	1635	232	402	84	7	64	218	20	.246
Division Series													
2000 St. Louis	N.L.		P	1	1	0	0	0	0	0	0	0	.000
2009 St. Louis	N.L.		H	2	2	0	0	0	0	0	0	0	.000
2010 St. Atlanta	N.L.		OF	4	12	1	2	0	0	1	1	0	.167
Division Series Totals				7	15	1	2	0	0	1	1	0	.133
Championship Series													
2000 St. Louis	N.L.		P	2	0	0	0	0	0	0	0	0	.000

a On disabled list from March 26 to June 5, 2002.
b On disabled list from March 25 to September 1, 2004.
c On disabled list from March 24 to November 2, 2006.
d On disabled list from May 5 to May 24, 2009.
e Filed for free agency, November 5, 2009. Signed with Kansas City Royals, January 25, 2010.

f On disabled list from May 3 to July 22, 2010.
g Traded to Atlanta Braves with pitcher Kyle Farnsworth and cash for outfielder Gregor Blanco, pitcher Jesse Chavez and pitcher Tim Collins, July 31, 2010.
h Filed for free agency, November 1, 2010. Signed with Washington Nationals, December 21, 2010.
i On disabled list from May 7 to May 24 and June 15 to July 1, 2011.
j Filed for free agency, October 30, 2011.

ARENCIBIA, JONATHAN PAUL (J.P.)
Born, Miami, Florida, January 5, 1986.
Bats Right. Throws Right. Height, 6 feet, 1 inch. Weight, 210 pounds.

Year	Club	Lea	Pos	G	AB	R	H	2B	3B	HR	RBI	SB	Avg
2007 Auburn	N.Y.-Penn.	C	63	228	31	58	17	1	3	25	0	.254
2008 Dunedin	Fla.St.	C	59	248	38	78	22	0	13	62	0	.315
2008 New Hampshire	Eastern	C	67	262	32	74	14	0	14	43	0	.282
2009 Las Vegas	P.C.	C	116	466	67	110	32	1	21	75	0	.236
2010 Las Vegas	P.C.	C	104	412	76	124	36	1	32	85	0	.301
2010 Toronto	A.L.	C	11	35	3	5	1	0	2	4	0	.143
2011 Toronto	A.L.	C	129	443	47	97	20	4	23	78	1	.219
Major League Totals	2 Yrs.	140	478	50	102	21	4	25	82	1	.213		

AVILA, ALEXANDER THOMAS (ALEX)
Born, Hialeah, Florida, January 29, 1987.
Bats Left. Throws Right. Height, 5 feet, 11 inches. Weight, 210 pounds.

Year	Club	Lea	Pos	G	AB	R	H	2B	3B	HR	RBI	SB	Avg
2008 West Michigan	Midwest	C	58	213	21	65	14	0	1	22	0	.305
2009 Erie	Eastern	C-1B	93	329	52	87	23	1	12	55	2	.264
2009 Detroit	A.L.	C	29	61	9	17	4	0	5	14	0	.279
2010 Detroit	A.L.	C	104	294	28	67	12	0	7	31	2	.228
2011 Detroit	A.L.	C-3B	141	464	63	137	33	4	19	82	3	.295
Major League Totals	3 Yrs.	274	819	100	221	49	4	31	127	5	.270		
Division Series													
2011 Detroit	A.L.	C	5	16	0	1	0	0	0	1	0	.063
Championship Series													
2011 Detroit	A.L.	C	6	25	1	2	0	0	1	1	0	.080

AVILES, MICHAEL ANTHONY (MIKE)
Born, New York, New York, March 13, 1981.
Bats Right. Throws Right. Height, 5 feet, 9 inches. Weight, 195 pounds.

Year	Club	Lea	Pos	G	AB	R	H	2B	3B	HR	RBI	SB	Avg
2003 Royals 1	Arizona	SS	52	212	51	77	19	5	6	39	11	.363
2004 Wilmington	Carolina	SS	126	463	66	139	40	4	6	68	2	.300
2005 Wichita	Texas	SS-3B-2B	133	521	79	146	33	6	14	80	11	.280
2006 Omaha	P.C.	3B-SS-2B	129	469	52	124	21	3	8	47	14	.264
2007 Omaha	P.C.	SS-3B-2B	133	538	78	159	27	6	17	77	5	.296
2008 Omaha	P.C.	2B-SS	51	214	42	72	21	6	10	42	3	.336
2008 Kansas City	A.L.	SS-2B-3B	102	419	68	136	27	4	10	51	8	.325
2009 Kansas City a	A.L.	SS-3B	36	120	10	22	3	1	1	8	1	.183
2010 Omaha	P.C.	SS-2B	17	70	8	19	3	1	1	8	0	.271
2010 Kansas City	A.L.	2B-SS-3B	110	424	63	129	16	3	8	32	14	.304
2011 Omaha	P.C.	SS-2B	35	140	21	43	8	2	9	25	6	.307
2011 Kansas City-Boston b	A.L.	3B-2B-SS-OF	91	286	31	73	17	3	7	39	14	.255
Major League Totals	4 Yrs.	339	1249	172	360	63	11	26	130	37	.288		

a On disabled list from May 24 to November 16, 2009.
b Traded to Boston Red Sox for infielder Yamaico Navarro and pitcher Kendal Volz, July 30, 2011.

AYBAR, ERICK JOHAN
Born, Bani, Dominican Republic, January 14, 1984.
Bats Both. Throws Right. Height, 5 feet, 10 inches. Weight, 170 pounds.

Year	Club	Lea	Pos	G	AB	R	H	2B	3B	HR	RBI	SB	Avg
2002 Provo	Pioneer	SS	67	273	64	89	15	6	4	29	15	.326
2003 Cedar Rapids	Midwest	SS	125	496	83	153	30	10	6	57	32	.308
2004 Rancho Cucamonga	Calif.	SS-2B	136	573	102	189	25	11	14	65	51	.330
2005 Arkansas	Texas	SS	134	535	101	162	29	10	9	54	49	.303
2006 Salt Lake	P.C.	SS	81	339	63	96	20	3	6	45	32	.283
2006 Los Angeles	A.L.	SS-2B	34	40	5	10	1	1	0	2	1	.250

Year Club	Lea	Pos	G	AB	R	H	2B	3B	HR	RBI	SB	Avg
2007 Rancho Cucamonga....Calif.		SS	2	5	3	2	0	0	0	0	3	.400
2007 Salt Lake.............P.C.		SS-2B	3	12	2	4	0	0	0	2	2	.333
2007 Los Angeles a.........A.L.		2B-SS-OF-3B	79	194	18	46	5	1	1	19	4	.237
2008 Rancho Cucamonga....Calif.		SS	3	10	2	4	1	0	0	3	2	.400
2008 Los Angeles b........A.L.		SS-2B	98	346	53	96	18	5	3	39	7	.277
2009 Los Angeles..........A.L.		SS	137	504	70	157	23	9	5	58	14	.312
2010 Los Angeles..........A.L.		SS	138	534	69	135	18	4	5	29	22	.253
2011 Salt Lake............P.C.		SS	1	4	1	1	0	0	0	0	0	.250
2011 Los Angeles c........A.L.		SS	143	556	71	155	33	8	10	59	30	.279
Major League Totals...........	6 Yrs.		629	2174	286	599	98	28	24	206	78	.276
Division Series												
2007 Los Angeles.........A.L.		OF	1	1	0	0	0	0	0	0	0	.000
2008 Los Angeles..........A.L.		SS	4	18	0	2	0	0	0	1	0	.111
2009 Los Angeles..........A.L.		SS	3	11	2	4	1	1	0	2	0	.364
Division Series Totals...........			8	30	2	6	1	1	0	3	0	.200
Championship Series												
2009 Los Angeles..........A.L.		SS	6	20	2	5	1	0	0	1	3	.250

a On disabled list from July 2 to August 6 and August 20 to September 5, 2007.
b On disabled list from May 21 to June 18, 2008.
c On disabled list from April 3 to April 20, 2011.

BAKER, JEFFREY GLEN (JEFF)
Born, Bad Kissingen, West Germany, June 21, 1981.
Bats Right. Throws Right. Height, 6 feet, 2 inches. Weight, 210 pounds.

Year Club	Lea	Pos	G	AB	R	H	2B	3B	HR	RBI	SB	Avg
2003 Asheville........So.Atl.		3B	70	263	44	76	17	0	11	44	4	.289
2004 Visalia...........Calif.		3B-SS	73	271	60	88	23	1	11	64	1	.325
2004 Tulsa..........Texas		3B	24	91	10	27	5	1	4	20	1	.297
2005 Colorado.........N.L.		3B	12	38	6	8	4	0	1	4	0	.211
2005 Colorado Springs...P.C.		3B	61	228	40	69	16	1	10	41	3	.303
2006 Colorado Springs...P.C.		OF-3B	128	482	71	147	30	4	20	108	7	.305
2006 Colorado.........N.L.		OF-1B	18	57	13	21	7	2	5	21	2	.368
2007 Colorado Springs...P.C.		1B-OF	7	26	3	6	1	0	1	2	0	.231
2007 Colorado a........N.L.		1B-OF-3B	85	144	17	32	2	2	4	12	0	.222
2008 Colorado.........N.L.		2B-1B-3B-OF	104	299	55	80	22	1	12	48	4	.268
2009 Modesto.........Calif.		2B-3B	2	5	1	2	1	0	0	1	0	.400
2009 Colorado Springs...P.C.		2B-3B	7	23	3	5	2	0	1	1	0	.217
2009 Colorado-Chicago b-c N.L.		2B-3B-1B	81	226	27	65	15	2	4	24	1	.288
2010 Chicago.........N.L.		3B-2B-1B-OF	79	206	29	56	13	2	4	21	0	.272
2011 Iowa.............P.C.		1B-2B-OF	3	10	1	3	1	1	0	1	0	.300
2011 Chicago d........N.L.		1B-2B-3B-OF	81	201	20	54	12	1	3	23	0	.269
Major League Totals...........	7 Yrs.		460	1171	167	316	75	10	33	153	8	.270
Division Series												
2007 Colorado.........N.L.		PH	1	1	0	1	0	0	0	0	0	1.000
Championship Series												
2007 Colorado.........N.L.		PH	2	2	0	1	0	0	0	0	0	.500
World Series Record												
2007 Colorado.........N.L.		PH	1	1	0	0	0	0	0	0	0	.000

a On disabled list from August 12 to September 1, 2007.
b Traded to Chicago Cubs for pitcher Al Alburquerque, July 2, 2009.
c On disabled list from April 27 to July 2, 2009.
d On disabled list from May 30 to June 13, 2011.

BARAJAS, RODRIGO RICHARD (ROD)
Born, Ontario, California, September 5, 1975.
Bats Right. Throws Right. Height, 6 feet, 2 inches. Weight, 245 pounds.

Year Club	Lea	Pos	G	AB	R	H	2B	3B	HR	RBI	SB	Avg
1996 Visalia..............Calif.		C	27	74	6	12	3	0	0	8	0	.162
1996 Lethbridge a.......Pioneer		C-1B	51	175	47	59	9	3	10	50	2	.337
1997 High Desert.........Calif.		C-1B	57	199	24	53	11	0	7	30	0	.266
1998 High Desert.........Calif.		C	113	442	67	134	26	0	23	81	1	.303
1999 El Paso...........Texas		C-1B	127	510	77	162	41	2	14	95	2	.318
1999 Arizona.............N.L.		C	5	16	3	4	1	0	1	3	0	.250
2000 Tucson.............P.C.		C-1B-3B	110	416	43	94	25	0	13	75	4	.226
2000 Arizona.............N.L.		C	5	13	1	3	0	0	1	3	0	.231
2001 Arizona.............N.L.		C	51	106	9	17	3	0	3	9	0	.160
2001 Tucson..............P.C.		1B-C-3B	45	162	23	52	13	0	9	32	3	.321

Year	Club	Lea	Pos	G	AB	R	H	2B	3B	HR	RBI	SB	Avg
2002 Arizona	N.L.	C-1B	70	154	12	36	10	0	3	23	1	.234
2002 Tucson	P.C.	C-1B	5	16	2	7	1	0	1	1	0	.438
2003 Tucson	P.C.	C	4	16	3	7	1	0	1	4	0	.438
2003 Lancaster	Calif.	C	3	12	2	5	0	0	0	3	0	.417
2003 Arizona b-c	N.L.	C	80	220	19	48	15	0	3	28	0	.218
2004 Texas d	A.L.	C-1B	108	358	50	89	26	1	15	58	0	.249
2005 Texas	A.L.	C-1B	120	410	53	104	24	0	21	60	0	.254
2006 Texas e	A.L.	C-1B	97	344	49	88	20	0	11	41	0	.256
2007 Reading	Eastern	C	2	5	0	1	0	0	0	0	0	.200
2007 Lakewood	So.Atl.	C	6	16	0	6	2	0	0	2	0	.375
2007 Philadelphia f-g	N.L.	C-1B	48	122	16	28	8	0	4	10	0	.230
2008 Toronto	A.L.	C-1B	104	349	44	87	23	0	11	49	0	.249
2009 Toronto	A.L.	C	125	429	43	97	19	0	19	71	1	.226
2010 Mets	Gulf Coast	DH	1	4	1	1	0	0	1	3	0	.250
2010 St. Lucie	Fla.St.	C	4	17	1	4	0	0	0	2	0	.235
2010 New York-LA h-i-j-k	N.L.	C	99	313	39	75	14	0	17	47	0	.240
2011 Rancho Cucamonga	Calif.	C	4	18	4	7	2	0	1	2	0	.389
2011 Los Angeles l-m	N.L.	C	98	305	29	70	13	0	16	47	0	.230
Major League Totals		13 Yrs.	1010	3139	367	746	176	1	125	449	2	.238
Division Series												
2001 Arizona	N.L.	C	1	0	0	0	0	0	0	0	0	.000
2002 Arizona	N.L.	C	2	4	1	1	0	0	1	1	0	.250
Division Series Totals			3	4	1	1	0	0	1	1	0	.250
World Series Record												
2001 Arizona	N.L.	C	2	5	1	2	0	0	1	1	0	.400

a Loaned to Oakland A's organization, April 5 to June 16, 1996.

b On disabled list from April 7 to April 28, 2003.

c On disabled list from July 5 to July 23, 2003.

d Not offered contract, December 21, 2003. Signed with Texas Rangers organization, January 12, 2004.

e Filed for free agency, October 28, 2006. Signed with Philadelphia Phillies organization, December 21, 2006.

f On disabled list from August 3 to September 1, 2007.

g Filed for free agency, October 30, 2007. Signed with Toronto Blue Jays, January 24, 2008.

h Filed for free agency, November 9, 2009. Signed with New York Mets, February 24, 2010.

i On disabled list from July 25 to August 19, 2010.

j Claimed on waivers by Los Angeles Dodgers, August 22, 2010.

k Filed for free agency, November 1, 2010, re-signed with Los Angeles Dodgers, December 3, 2010.

l On disabled list from June 19 to July 14, 2011.

m Filed for free agency, October 30, 2011. Signed with Pittsburgh Pirates, November 10, 2011.

BARMES, CLINT HAROLD

Born, Vincennes, Indiana, March 6, 1979.

Bats Right. Throws Right. Height, 6 feet. Weight, 210 pounds.

Year	Club	Lea	Pos	G	AB	R	H	2B	3B	HR	RBI	SB	Avg
2000 Portland	Northwest	SS-OF	45	181	37	51	6	4	2	16	12	.282
2000 Asheville	So.Atl.	2B-SS-3B-OF	19	81	11	14	4	0	0	4	4	.173
2001 Salem	Carolina	SS	38	121	17	30	3	3	0	9	4	.248
2001 Asheville	So.Atl.	SS	74	285	40	74	14	1	5	24	21	.260
2002 Carolina	Southern	SS	103	438	62	119	23	2	15	60	15	.272
2003 Colorado Springs	P.C.	SS-2B	136	493	63	136	35	1	7	54	12	.276
2003 Colorado	N.L.	SS	12	25	2	8	2	0	0	2	0	.320
2004 Colorado Springs	P.C.	SS-2B	125	533	104	175	42	2	16	51	20	.328
2004 Colorado	N.L.	2B-SS	20	71	14	20	3	1	2	10	0	.282
2005 Tulsa	Texas	SS	8	34	6	11	1	0	0	0	1	.324
2005 Colorado a	N.L.	SS	81	350	55	101	19	1	10	46	6	.289
2006 Colorado	N.L.	SS-2B	131	478	57	105	26	4	7	56	5	.220
2007 Colorado Springs	P.C.	SS-OF-2B-3B	108	428	68	128	20	6	11	44	8	.299
2007 Colorado	N.L.	SS-2B-OF-3B	27	37	5	8	3	0	0	1	0	.216
2008 Colorado Springs	P.C.	2B-SS	5	18	2	5	0	0	0	3	0	.278
2008 Colorado b	N.L.	2B-SS-3B-OF	107	393	47	114	25	6	11	44	13	.290
2009 Colorado	N.L.	2B-SS	154	550	69	135	32	3	23	76	12	.245
2010 Colorado c	N.L.	2B-SS-3B	133	387	43	91	21	0	8	50	3	.235
2011 Corpus Christi	Texas	SS	2	9	2	4	0	0	0	2	0	.444
2011 Oklahoma	P.C.	SS	2	6	2	2	1	0	0	1	0	.333
2011 Houston d-e	N.L.	SS	123	446	47	109	27	4	12	39	3	.244
Major League Totals		9 Yrs.	788	2737	339	691	158	15	73	324	42	.252
Division Series												
2009 Colorado	N.L.	2B	4	14	0	0	0	0	0	0	0	.000

a On disabled list from June 6 to September 2, 2005.

b On disabled list from May 24 to June 23, 2008.

c Traded to Houston Astros for pitcher Felipe Paulino, November 18, 2010.
d On disabled list from March 26 to April 29, 2011.
e Filed for free agency, October 30, 2011. Signed with Pittsburgh Pirates, November 21, 2011.

BARNEY, DARWIN JAMES KUNANE
Born, Portland, Oregon, November 8, 1985.
Bats Right. Throws Right. Height, 5 feet, 10 inches. Weight, 180 pounds.

Year Club Lea	Pos	G	AB	R	H	2B	3B	HR	RBI	SB	Avg
2007 Cubs......... Arizona	SS	5	18	6	8	3	0	0	2	0	.444
2007 Peoria........ Midwest	SS	44	176	27	48	9	3	2	21	5	.273
2008 Daytona .... Fla.St.	SS	123	409	46	107	22	4	3	51	8	.262
2009 Tennessee ....Southern	SS-2B-3B	74	252	30	80	12	0	3	32	5	.317
2009 Iowa............. P.C.	SS-2B	63	212	25	56	12	1	0	17	4	.264
2010 Iowa............. P.C.	SS-2B	114	479	72	143	24	4	2	49	11	.299
2010 Chicago .... N.L.	SS-2B-3B	30	79	12	19	4	0	0	2	0	.241
2011 Iowa............. P.C.	2B	4	14	3	5	1	0	1	3	1	.357
2011 Chicago a......... N.L.	2B-SS	143	529	66	146	23	6	2	43	9	.276
Major League Totals	2 Yrs.	173	608	78	165	27	6	2	45	9	.271

a On disabled list from June 15 to June 29, 2011.

BARTLETT, JASON ALAN
Born, Mountain View, California, October 30, 1979.
Bats Right. Throws Right. Height, 6 feet. Weight, 180 pounds.

Year Club Lea	Pos	G	AB	R	H	2B	3B	HR	RBI	SB	Avg
2001 Eugene......... Northwest	SS	68	267	49	80	12	4	3	37	12	.300
2002 Lake Elsinore ..... California	SS	75	308	57	77	14	4	1	33	24	.250
2002 Fort Myers a........Fla.St.	SS-3B-2B	39	145	24	38	7	0	2	9	11	.262
2003 New Britain ....Eastern	SS	139	548	96	162	31	8	8	48	41	.296
2004 Rochester............. Int.	SS-2B	67	269	54	89	15	7	3	29	7	.331
2004 Twins .... Gulf Coast	SS	5	14	1	5	1	0	0	1	0	.357
2004 Minnesota .... A.L.	SS-2B	8	12	2	1	0	0	0	0	2	.083
2005 Rochester............. Int.	SS	61	229	41	76	10	2	5	33	2	.332
2005 Minnesota .... A.L.	SS	74	224	33	54	10	1	3	16	4	.241
2006 Rochester............. Int.	SS	58	235	42	72	23	3	1	20	6	.306
2006 Minnesota .... A.L.	SS	99	333	44	103	18	2	2	32	10	.309
2007 Minnesota b.......... A.L.	SS	140	510	75	135	20	7	5	43	23	.265
2008 Tampa Bay c........ A.L.	SS	128	454	48	130	25	3	1	37	20	.286
2009 Charlotte ....Fla.St.	SS	3	11	2	5	0	1	0	0	0	.455
2009 Tampa Bay d .... A.L.	SS	137	500	90	160	29	7	14	66	30	.320
2010 Durham .... Int.	SS	1	3	0	2	1	0	0	0	0	.667
2010 Tampa Bay e-f ..... A.L.	SS	135	468	71	119	27	3	4	47	11	.254
2011 San Diego .... N.L.	SS	139	554	61	136	22	3	2	40	23	.245
Major League Totals	8 Yrs.	860	3055	424	838	151	26	31	282	123	.274
Division Series											
2006 Minnesota .... A.L.	SS	3	11	0	3	1	0	0	0	0	.273
2008 Tampa Bay .... A.L.	SS	4	14	3	4	1	0	0	0	0	.286
2010 Tampa Bay .... A.L.	SS	5	15	0	6	1	0	0	0	0	.400
Division Series Totals		12	40	3	13	3	0	0	0	0	.325
Championship Series											
2008 Tampa Bay .... N.L.	SS	7	23	4	5	0	1	1	1	1	.217
World Series Record											
2008 Tampa Bay .... N.L.	SS	5	14	1	3	0	0	0	2	1	.214

a Traded by San Diego Padres to Minnesota Twins for outfielder Brian Buchanan, July 12, 2002.
b Traded to Tampa Bay Devil Rays with pitcher Matt Garza and pitcher Eduardo Morlan for infielder Brendan Harris, outfielder Jason Pridie and outfielder Delmon Young, November 28, 2007.
c On disabled list from July 3 to July 24, 2008.
d On disabled list from May 25 to June 15, 2009.
e On disabled list from May 30 to June 16, 2010.
f Traded to San Diego Padres with player to be named later for pitcher Adam Russell, pitcher Brandon Gomes, pitcher Cesar Ramos and infielder Cole Figueroa, December 17, 2010. Tampa Bay Rays sent cash to complete trade, May 24, 2011.

BARTON, DARIC WILLIAM
Born, Springfield, Vermont, August 16, 1985.
Bats Left. Throws Right. Height, 6 feet. Weight, 225 pounds.

Year Club Lea	Pos	G	AB	R	H	2B	3B	HR	RBI	SB	Avg
2003 Johnson City ....Appal.	C-3B	54	172	29	50	10	0	4	29	0	.291
2004 Peoria a ...... Midwest	C	90	313	63	98	23	0	13	77	4	.313

Year	Club	Lea	Pos	G	AB	R	H	2B	3B	HR	RBI	SB	Avg
2005 Stockton.........Calif.	1B-3B-OF-C	79	292	60	93	16	2	8	52	0	.318
2005 Midland.......Texas	1B-OF	56	212	38	67	20	1	5	37	1	.316
2006 Athletics......Arizona	1B	2	5	1	1	1	0	0	2	0	.200
2006 Sacramento.......P.C.	1B	43	147	25	38	6	4	2	22	1	.259
2007 Sacramento.......P.C.	1B-3B	136	516	84	151	38	5	9	70	3	.293
2007 Oakland.........A.L.	1B	18	72	16	25	9	0	4	8	1	.347
2008 Sacramento.......P.C.	1B	8	31	4	6	0	0	1	3	0	.194
2008 Oakland b........A.L.	1B-3B	140	446	59	101	17	5	9	47	2	.226
2009 Sacramento.......P.C.	1B	70	253	48	66	21	1	9	48	1	.261
2009 Athletics......Arizona	1B	6	18	3	5	1	0	1	3	0	.278
2009 Stockton.........Calif.	1B	1	4	0	0	0	0	0	0	0	.000
2009 Oakland c........A.L.	1B	54	160	31	43	12	1	3	24	0	.269
2010 Oakland.........A.L.	1B	159	556	79	152	33	5	10	57	7	.273
2011 Sacramento.......P.C.	1B	17	61	10	12	2	0	0	4	0	.197
2011 Oakland d.......A.L.	1B	67	236	27	50	13	0	0	21	2	.212
Major League Totals	5 Yrs.	438	1470	212	371	84	11	26	157	12	.252

a Traded by St. Louis Cardinals to Oakland Athletics with pitcher Danny Haren and pitcher Kiko Calero for pitcher Mark Mulder, December 18, 2004.
b On disabled list from July 14 to August 1, 2008.
c On disabled list from July 27 to August 21, 2009.
d On disabled list from September 2 to November 2, 2011.

BAUTISTA, JOSE ANTONIO
Born, Santo Domingo, Dominican Republic, October 19, 1980.
Bats Right. Throws Right. Height, 6 feet. Weight, 190 pounds.

Year	Club	Lea	Pos	G	AB	R	H	2B	3B	HR	RBI	SB	Avg
2001 Williamsport.....N.Y.-Penn.	3B-OF	62	220	43	63	10	3	5	30	8	.286
2002 Hickory...........So.Atl.	3B-SS	129	438	72	132	26	3	14	57	3	.301
2003 Lynchburg.........Carolina	3B-2B	51	165	28	40	14	2	4	20	1	.242
2003 Pirates a.......Gulf Coast	3B	7	23	5	8	1	0	1	3	0	.348
2004 Pittsburgh.........N.L.	OF	23	40	1	8	2	0	0	0	0	.200
2004 Balt.-Tam. Bay-K.C. b-c-d-e. A.L.	3B-OF	41	48	5	10	1	0	0	2	0	.208
2005 Altoona...........Eastern	3B	117	445	63	126	27	1	23	90	7	.283
2005 Indianapolis..........Int.	3B	13	51	6	13	3	0	1	4	1	.255
2005 Pittsburgh.........N.L.	3B	11	28	3	4	1	0	0	1	1	.143
2006 Indianapolis..........Int.	3B-OF-2B	29	101	12	28	9	0	2	9	2	.277
2006 Pittsburgh.........N.L.	OF-3B-2B	117	400	58	94	20	3	16	51	2	.235
2007 Pirates.........Gulf Coast	3B	2	8	1	3	2	0	0	1	0	.375
2007 Pittsburgh f..........N.L.	3B-OF	142	532	75	135	36	2	15	63	6	.254
2008 Indianapolis..........Int.	OF-2B	9	20	6	6	2	0	2	8	1	.300
2008 Pittsburgh.........N.L.	3B	107	314	38	76	15	0	12	44	1	.242
2008 Toronto g..........A.L.	3B-1B-2B	21	56	7	12	2	0	3	10	0	.214
2009 Toronto...........A.L.	OF-3B	113	336	54	79	13	3	13	40	4	.235
2010 Toronto...........A.L.	OF-3B-1B	161	569	109	148	35	3	*54	124	9	.260
2011 Toronto...........A.L.	OF-3B	149	513	105	155	24	2	*43	103	9	.302
Major League Totals	8 Yrs.	885	2836	455	721	149	13	156	438	32	.254

a Selected by Baltimore Orioles from Pittsburgh in Rule V draft, December 15, 2003.
b Claimed on waivers by Tampa Bay Devil Rays, June 3, 2004.
c Sold to Kansas City Royals, June 28, 2004.
d Traded to New York Mets for catcher Justin Huber, July 30, 2004.
e Traded to Pittsburgh Pirates with infielder Ty Wigginton and pitcher Matt Peterson for pitcher Kris Benson and infielder Jeff Keppinger, July 30, 2004.
f On disabled list from July 15 to August 1, 2007.
g Traded to Toronto Blue Jays for player to be named later, August 21, 2008. Pittsburgh Pirates received infielder Robinson Diaz to complete trade, August 25, 2008.

BAY, JASON RAYMOND
Born, Trail, British Columbia, Canada, September 20, 1978.
Bats Right. Throws Right. Height, 6 feet, 2 inches. Weight, 205 pounds.

Year	Club	Lea	Pos	G	AB	R	H	2B	3B	HR	RBI	SB	Avg
2000 Vermont........N.Y.-Penn.	OF	35	135	17	41	5	0	2	12	17	.304
2001 Jupiter.............Fla.St.	OF-2B	38	123	12	24	4	1	1	10	10	.195
2001 Clinton...........Midwest	OF	87	318	67	115	20	4	13	61	15	.362
2002 St. Lucie...........Fla.St.	OF	69	261	48	71	12	2	9	54	22	.272
2002 Binghamton.......Eastern	OF	34	107	17	31	4	2	4	19	13	.290
2002 Mobile a-b........Southern	OF	23	81	16	25	5	2	4	12	4	.309
2003 Portland.............P.C.	OF	91	307	64	93	11	1	20	59	23	.303

Year Club	Lea	Pos	G	AB	R	H	2B	3B	HR	RBI	SB	Avg
2003 San Diego-Pittsburgh c-d-e.	N.L.	OF	30	87	15	25	7	1	4	14	3	.287
2004 Nashville	.P.C.	OF	4	10	3	4	2	0	1	3	0	.400
2004 Pittsburgh f-g.........	N.L.	OF	120	411	61	116	24	4	26	82	4	.282
2005 Pittsburgh	N.L.	OF	*162	599	110	183	44	6	32	101	21	.306
2006 Pittsburgh	N.L.	OF	159	570	101	163	29	3	35	109	11	.286
2007 Pittsburgh	N.L.	OF	145	538	78	133	25	2	21	84	4	.247
2008 Pittsburgh	N.L.	OF	106	393	72	111	23	2	22	64	7	.282
2008 Boston h	A.L.	OF	49	184	39	54	12	2	9	37	3	.293
2009 Boston i	A.L.	OF	151	531	103	142	29	3	36	119	13	.267
2010 New York j	N.L.	OF	95	348	48	90	20	6	6	47	10	.259
2011 St. Lucie...........	.Fla.St.	OF	4	12	5	6	0	0	2	4	0	.500
2011 New York k...........	N.L.	OF	123	444	59	109	19	1	12	57	11	.245
Major League Totals	9 Yrs.	1140	4105	686	1126	232	30	203	714	87	.274	
Division Series												
2008 Boston	A.L.	OF	4	17	3	7	2	0	2	5	0	.412
2009 Boston	A.L.	OF	3	8	0	1	0	0	0	0	0	.125
Division Series Totals			7	25	3	8	2	0	2	5	0	.320
Championship Series												
2008 Boston	A.L.	OF	7	24	3	7	1	0	1	4	0	.292

a Traded by Montreal Expos to New York Mets with pitcher Jim Serrano for infielder Lou Collier, March 26, 2002.
b Traded to San Diego Padres with pitcher Bobby M. Jones and pitcher Josh Reynolds for pitcher Jason Middlebrook and pitcher Steve Reed, July 31, 2002.
c On disabled list from May 26 to July 8, 2003.
d Traded to Pittsburgh Pirates with pitcher Oliver Perez and player to be named later for outfielder Brian Giles, August 26, 2003.
e Pittsburgh Pirates received pitcher Cory Stewart to complete trade, October 2, 2003.
f On disabled list from March 26 to May 7, 2004.
g Selected Rookie of the Year in National League for 2004.
h Traded to Boston Red Sox for outfielder Manny Ramirez, outfielder Brandon Moss and pitcher Craig Hansen, July 31, 2008.
i Filed for free agency, November 5, 2009. Signed with New York Mets, December 29, 2009.
j On disabled list from July 26 to November 2, 2010.
k On disabled list from March 25 to April 21, 2011.

BECKHAM, JAMES GORDON (GORDON)
Born, Atlanta, Georgia, September 16, 1986.
Bats Right. Throws Right. Height, 6 feet. Weight, 190 pounds.

Year Club	Lea	Pos	G	AB	R	H	2B	3B	HR	RBI	SB	Avg
2008 Kannapolis	So.Atl.	SS	14	58	11	18	2	0	3	8	0	.310
2009 Birmingham......	Southern	SS-2B-3B	38	147	23	44	17	0	4	22	1	.299
2009 Charlotte	Int.	3B-SS	7	28	6	13	6	0	0	3	1	.464
2009 Chicago	A.L.	3B	103	378	58	102	28	1	14	63	7	.270
2010 Chicago	A.L.	2B	131	444	58	112	25	2	9	49	4	.252
2011 Chicago	A.L.	2B	150	499	60	115	23	0	10	44	5	.230
Major League Totals	3 Yrs.	384	1321	176	329	76	3	33	156	16	.249	

BELT, BRANDON KYLE
Born, Nacogdoches, Texas, April 20, 1988.
Bats Left. Throws Left. Height, 6 feet, 5 inches. Weight, 220 pounds.

Year Club	Lea	Pos	G	AB	R	H	2B	3B	HR	RBI	SB	Avg
2010 San Jose	.Calif.	1B	77	269	62	103	28	4	10	62	18	.383
2010 Richmond	Eastern	1B-OF	46	175	26	59	11	6	9	40	2	.337
2010 Fresno	.P.C.	OF-1B	13	48	11	11	4	0	4	10	2	.229
2011 San Jose	.Calif.	1B	4	13	3	6	1	0	0	4	1	.462
2011 Fresno	.P.C.	OF-1B	49	165	32	51	12	0	8	32	4	.309
2011 San Francisco a	N.L.	OF-1B	63	187	21	42	6	1	9	18	3	.225

a On disabled list from June 1 to July 7, 2011.

BELTRAN, CARLOS IVAN
Born, Manati, Puerto Rico, April 24, 1977.
Bats Both. Throws Right. Height, 6 feet. Weight,200 pounds.

Year Club	Lea	Pos	G	AB	R	H	2B	3B	HR	RBI	SB	Avg
1995 Royals	Gulf Coast	OF	52	180	29	50	9	0	0	23	5	.278
1996 Lansing	Midwest	OF	11	42	3	6	2	0	0	0	1	.143
1996 Spokane........	Northwest	OF	59	215	29	58	8	3	7	29	10	.270

Year	Club	Lea	Pos	G	AB	R	H	2B	3B	HR	RBI	SB	Avg
1997 Wilmington	Carolina		OF	120	419	57	96	15	4	11	46	17	.229
1998 Wilmington	Carolina		OF	52	192	32	53	14	0	5	32	11	.276
1998 Wichita.............	Texas		OF	47	182	50	64	13	3	14	44	7	.352
1998 Kansas City	A.L.		OF	14	58	12	16	5	3	0	7	3	.276
1999 Kansas City a	A.L.		OF	156	663	112	194	27	7	22	108	27	.293
2000 GC Royals	Gulf Coast		PH	1	4	3	2	1	0	1	1	0	.500
2000 Wilmington	Carolina		OF	3	13	2	4	0	1	2	6	0	.308
2000 Omaha	.P.C.		OF	5	18	4	6	1	0	2	2	1	.333
2000 Kansas City b	A.L.		OF	98	372	49	92	15	4	7	44	13	.247
2001 Kansas City	A.L.		OF	155	617	106	189	32	12	24	101	31	.306
2002 Kansas City	A.L.		OF	*162	637	114	174	44	7	29	105	35	.273
2003 Wichita	Texas		OF	3	9	3	3	2	0	1	1	1	.333
2003 Kansas City c	A.L.		OF	141	521	102	160	14	10	26	100	41	.307
2004 Kansas City	A.L.		OF	69	266	51	74	19	2	15	51	14	.278
2004 Houston d-e	N.L.		OF	90	333	70	86	17	7	23	53	28	.258
2005 New York	N.L.		OF	151	582	83	155	34	2	16	78	17	.266
2006 New York	N.L.		OF	140	510	127	140	38	1	41	116	18	.275
2007 New York f	N.L.		OF	144	554	93	153	33	3	33	112	23	.276
2008 New York	N.L.		OF	161	606	116	172	40	5	27	112	25	.284
2009 Brooklyn.........	N.Y.-Penn.		OF	5	18	1	3	0	0	0	2	0	.167
2009 New York g........	N.L.		OF	81	308	50	100	22	1	10	48	11	.325
2010 St. Lucie............	Fla.St.		OF	14	49	5	18	5	0	0	5	0	.367
2010 New York h.........	N.L.		OF	64	220	21	56	11	3	7	27	3	.255
2011 New York-San Fran. i-j-k	N.L.		OF	142	520	78	156	39	6	22	84	4	.300
Major League Totals			14 Yrs.	1768	6767	1184	1917	390	73	302	1146	293	.283
Division Series													
2004 Houston..............	N.L.		OF	5	22	9	10	2	0	4	9	2	.455
2006 New York	N.L.		OF	3	9	2	2	0	0	0	1	1	.222
Division Series Totals				8	31	11	12	2	0	4	10	3	.387
Championship Series													
2004 Houston..............	N.L.		OF	7	24	12	10	1	0	4	5	4	.417
2006 New York	N.L.		OF	7	27	8	8	1	0	3	4	1	.296
Championship Series Totals				14	51	20	18	2	0	7	9	5	.353

a Selected Rookie of the Year in American League for 1999.
b On disabled list from July 4 to September 3, 2000.
c On disabled list from March 21 to April 18, 2003.
d Traded to Houston Astros for pitcher Octavio Dotel and catcher John Buck, June 24, 2004.
e Filed for free agency, October 28, 2004. Signed with New York Mets, January 11, 2005.
f On disabled list from July 25 to August 10, 2007.
g On disabled list from June 22 to September 8, 2009.
h On disabled list from March 26 to July 15, 2010.
i Traded to San Francisco Giants for pitcher Zack Wheeler, July 28, 2011.
j On disabled list from August 8 to August 23, 2011.
k Filed for free agency, October 30, 2011. Signed with St. Louis Cardinals, December 23, 2011.

BELTRE, ADRIAN
Born, Santo Domingo, Dominican Republic, April 7, 1979.
Bats Right. Throws Right. Height, 5 feet, 11 inches. Weight, 220 pounds.

Year	Club	Lea	Pos	G	AB	R	H	2B	3B	HR	RBI	SB	Avg
1995 LA-S.Domingo	Dominican		3B	62	218	56	67	15	3	8	40	2	.307
1996 Savannah	So.Atl.		3B-2B	68	244	48	75	14	3	16	59	4	.307
1996 San Berndno a	California		3B	63	238	40	62	13	1	10	40	3	.261
1997 Vero Beach..........	Fla.St.		3B-OF	123	435	95	138	24	2	26	104	25	.317
1998 San Antonio	Texas		3B	64	246	49	79	21	2	13	56	20	.321
1998 Los Angeles	N.L.		3B-SS	77	195	18	42	9	0	7	22	3	.215
1999 Los Angeles	N.L.		3B	152	538	84	148	27	5	15	67	18	.275
2000 Los Angeles b	N.L.		3B-SS	138	510	71	148	30	2	20	85	12	.290
2001 Vero Beach..........	Fla.St.		3B	3	9	0	4	1	0	0	1	0	.444
2001 Las Vegas..........	.P.C.		3B	2	5	2	3	1	0	1	2	0	.600
2001 Los Angeles c........	N.L.		3B-SS	126	475	59	126	22	4	13	60	13	.265
2002 Los Angeles	N.L.		3B	159	587	70	151	26	5	21	75	7	.257
2003 Los Angeles	N.L.		3B-SS	158	559	50	134	30	2	23	80	2	.240
2004 Los Angeles d	N.L.		3B-SS	156	598	104	200	32	0	*48	121	7	.334
2005 Seattle	A.L.		3B	156	603	69	154	36	1	19	87	3	.255
2006 Seattle	A.L.		3B-2B	156	620	88	166	39	4	25	89	11	.268
2007 Seattle	A.L.		3B	149	595	87	164	41	2	26	99	14	.276
2008 Seattle	A.L.		3B	143	556	74	148	29	1	25	77	8	.266
2009 Seattle e-f..........	A.L.		3B	111	449	54	119	27	0	8	44	13	.265
2010 Boston g	A.L.		3B	154	589	84	189	*49	2	28	102	2	.321

Year	Club	Lea	Pos	G	AB	R	H	2B	3B	HR	RBI	SB	Avg
2011 Round Rock		P.C.	3B	2	8	1	2	0	0	0	0	0	.250
2011 Texas h		A.L.	3B	124	487	82	144	33	0	32	105	1	.296
Major League Totals			14 Yrs.	1959	7361	994	2033	430	28	310	1113	114	.276
Division Series													
2004 Los Angeles		N.L.	3B	4	15	1	4	0	0	0	1	0	.267
2011 Texas		A.L.	3B	4	15	5	4	0	0	3	4	0	.267
Division Series Totals				8	30	6	8	0	0	3	5	0	.267
Championship Series													
2011 Texas		A.L.	3B	6	27	4	6	3	0	0	2	0	.222
World Series Record													
2011 Texas		A.L.	3B	7	30	5	9	2	0	2	3	0	.300

a On disabled list from June 25 to July 2, 1996.
b On disabled list from May 28 to June 16, 2000.
c On disabled list from March 23 to May 12, 2001.
d Filed for free agency, October 29, 2004. Signed with Seattle Mariners, December 17, 2004.
e On disabled list from June 29 to August 4 and August 13 to September 1, 2009.
f Filed for free agency, November 5, 2009. Signed with Boston Red Sox, January 7, 2010.
g Filed for free agency, November 2, 2010. Signed with Texas Rangers, January 5, 2011.
h On disabled list from July 23 to September 1, 2011.

BENSON, WILLIAM JOSEPH (JOE)

Born, Hinsdale, Illinois, March 5, 1988.
Bats Right. Throws Right. Height, 6 feet, 1 inch. Weight, 205 pounds.

Year	Club	Lea	Pos	G	AB	R	H	2B	3B	HR	RBI	SB	Avg
2006 Twins	Gulf Coast	OF	52	196	30	51	11	5	5	28	9	.260
2006 Beloit	Midwest	OF	8	19	2	5	0	0	0	1	1	.263
2007 Beloit	Midwest	OF	122	432	73	110	18	8	5	38	18	.255
2008 Beloit	Midwest	OF-C	69	254	39	63	16	3	4	27	17	.248
2009 Twins	Gulf Coast	OF	2	5	1	1	0	0	0	0	1	.200
2009 Fort Myers	Fla.St.	OF	80	263	46	75	10	3	5	29	14	.285
2010 Fort Myers	Fla.St.	OF	21	85	16	25	11	1	4	13	5	.294
2010 New Britain	Eastern	OF	102	374	65	94	20	7	23	49	14	.251
2011 Twins	Gulf Coast	OF	3	9	2	2	1	0	0	0	1	.222
2011 New Britain	Eastern	OF	111	400	69	114	28	4	16	67	13	.285
2011 Minnesota	A.L.	OF	21	71	3	17	6	1	0	2	2	.239

BERKMAN, WILLIAM LANCE (LANCE)

Born, Waco, Texas, February 10, 1976.
Bats Both. Throws Left. Height, 6 feet, 1 inch. Weight, 220 pounds.

Year	Club	Lea	Pos	G	AB	R	H	2B	3B	HR	RBI	SB	Avg
1997 Kissimmee	Fla.St.	OF	53	184	31	54	10	0	12	35	2	.293
1998 Jackson	Texas	OF	122	425	82	130	34	0	24	89	6	.306
1998 New Orleans	P.C.	OF	17	59	14	16	4	0	6	13	0	.271
1999 New Orleans	P.C.	OF	64	226	42	73	20	0	8	49	7	.323
1999 Houston a	N.L.	OF-1B	34	93	10	22	2	0	4	15	5	.237
2000 New Orleans	P.C.	OF	31	112	18	37	4	2	6	27	4	.330
2000 Houston	N.L.	OF-1B	114	353	76	105	28	1	21	67	6	.297
2001 Houston	N.L.	OF	156	577	110	191	*55	5	34	126	7	.331
2002 Houston	N.L.	OF	158	578	106	169	35	2	42	*128	8	.292
2003 Houston	N.L.	OF	153	538	110	155	35	6	25	93	5	.288
2004 Houston	N.L.	OF-1B	160	544	104	172	40	3	30	106	9	.316
2005 Round Rock	P.C.	OF	4	14	2	4	1	0	0	1	0	.286
2005 Houston b	N.L.	1B-OF	132	468	76	137	34	1	24	82	4	.293
2006 Houston	N.L.	1B-OF	152	536	95	169	29	0	45	136	3	.315
2007 Houston	N.L.	1B-OF	153	561	95	156	24	2	34	102	7	.278
2008 Houston	N.L.	1B	159	554	114	173	*46	4	29	106	18	.312
2009 Houston c	N.L.	1B	136	460	73	126	31	1	25	80	7	.274
2010 Trenton	Eastern	DH	2	8	1	2	0	0	0	0	0	.250
2010 Round Rock	P.C.	1B	2	6	3	3	2	0	1	3	0	.500
2010 Houston	N.L.	1B	85	298	39	73	16	1	13	49	3	.245
2010 New York d-e-f-g	A.L.	DH-1B	37	106	9	27	7	0	1	9	0	.255
2011 St. Louis	N.L.	OF-1B	145	488	90	147	23	2	31	94	2	.301
Major League Totals			13 Yrs.	1774	6154	1107	1822	405	28	358	1193	84	.296
Division Series													
2001 Houston	N.L.	OF	3	12	0	2	0	0	0	0	0	.167
2004 Houston	N.L.	OF	5	22	5	9	1	0	1	3	0	.409
2005 Houston	N.L.	1B-OF	4	14	4	5	1	0	1	5	0	.357

12

Year	Club	Lea	Pos	G	AB	R	H	2B	3B	HR	RBI	SB	Avg
2010 New York	A.L.	DH	1	4	2	2	1	0	1	2	0	.500
2011 St. Louis	N.L.	OF	5	18	4	3	1	0	1	4	1	.167
Division Series Totals			18	70	15	21	4	0	4	14	1	.300
Championship Series												
2004 Houston	N.L.	OF	7	24	7	7	2	0	3	9	1	.292
2005 Houston	N.L.	1B-OF	6	21	2	6	2	0	1	3	0	.286
2010 New York	A.L.	1B-DH	4	12	1	3	0	1	0	2	0	.250
2011 St. Louis	N.L.	OF	6	20	4	6	0	0	0	2	1	.300
Championship Series Totals			23	77	14	22	4	1	4	16	2	.286
World Series Record												
2005 Houston	N.L.	OF-1B	4	13	0	5	2	0	0	6	1	.385
2011 St. Louis	N.L.	OF-DH	7	26	9	11	1	0	1	7	0	.423
World Series Totals			11	39	9	16	3	0	1	13	1	.410

a On disabled list from April 13 to May 14, 1999.
b On disabled list from March 25 to May 6, 2005.
c On disabled list from July 23 to August 12, 2009.
d On disabled list from March 26 to April 20, 2010.
e Traded to New York Yankees with cash for pitcher Mark Melancon and infielder Jimmy Paredes, July 31, 2010.
f On disabled list from August 16 to September 1, 2010.
g Filed for free agency, November 1, 2010. Signed with St. Louis Cardinals, December 4, 2010.

BERNADINA, ROGEARVIN ARGELO (ROGER)
Born, Willemstad, Curacao, Netherlands Antilles, June 12, 1984.
Bats Left. Throws Left. Height, 6 feet, 1 inch. Weight, 200 pounds.

Year	Club	Lea	Pos	G	AB	R	H	2B	3B	HR	RBI	SB	Avg
2002 Expos	Gulf Coast	OF	57	196	22	54	7	0	3	18	1	.276
2003 Savannah	So.Atl.	OF	77	278	36	66	12	3	4	39	11	.237
2004 Savannah	So.Atl.	OF	129	450	67	107	24	7	7	66	24	.238
2005 Savannah	So.Atl.	OF	122	417	64	97	15	3	12	54	35	.233
2006 Potomac	Carolina	OF	123	434	60	117	19	3	6	42	28	.270
2007 Harrisburg	Eastern	OF	97	371	58	100	15	2	6	36	40	.270
2007 Columbus	Int.	OF	13	42	6	7	3	0	0	1	0	.167
2008 Harrisburg	Eastern	OF	73	266	47	86	11	7	5	38	26	.323
2008 Columbus	Int.	OF	47	191	33	67	13	3	4	16	15	.351
2008 Washington	N.L.	OF	26	76	10	16	1	1	0	2	4	.211
2009 Syracuse	Int.	OF	5	18	1	3	0	0	0	0	1	.167
2009 Washington	N.L.	OF	3	4	1	1	1	0	0	0	1	.250
2009 Nationals a	Gulf Coast	OF	2	4	0	1	0	0	0	0	0	.250
2010 Syracuse	Int.	OF	14	61	8	23	2	1	2	8	7	.377
2010 Washington	N.L.	OF	134	414	52	102	18	3	11	47	16	.246
2011 Syracuse	Int.	OF	46	164	26	41	9	0	6	14	14	.250
2011 Washington	N.L.	OF	91	309	40	75	12	2	7	27	17	.243
Major League Totals		4 Yrs.	254	803	103	194	32	6	18	76	38	.242

a On disabled list from April 19 to November 8, 2009.

BETANCOURT (PEREZ), YUNIESKY
Born, Santa Clara, Cuba, January 31, 1982.
Bats Right. Throws Right. Height, 5 feet, 10 inches. Weight, 190 pounds.

Year	Club	Lea	Pos	G	AB	R	H	2B	3B	HR	RBI	SB	Avg
2005 San Antonio	Texas	SS-2B	52	227	25	62	10	3	5	20	12	.273
2005 Tacoma	P.C.	SS-2B	49	183	13	54	9	6	2	30	7	.295
2005 Seattle a	A.L.	SS-2B	60	211	24	54	11	5	1	15	1	.256
2006 Seattle	A.L.	SS	157	558	68	161	28	6	8	47	11	.289
2007 Seattle	A.L.	SS	155	536	72	155	38	2	9	67	5	.289
2008 Seattle	A.L.	SS	153	559	66	156	36	3	7	51	4	.279
2009 NW Arkansas	Texas	SS	3	13	2	2	0	0	1	1	0	.154
2009 Tacoma	P.C.	2B	2	2	0	1	1	0	0	1	0	.500
2009 Seattle-Kansas City b	A.L.	SS	134	470	40	115	20	6	6	49	3	.245
2010 Kansas City c	A.L.	SS	151	556	60	144	29	2	16	78	2	.259
2011 Milwaukee d	N.L.	SS	152	556	51	140	27	3	13	68	4	.252
Major League Totals		7 Yrs.	962	3446	381	925	189	27	60	375	30	.268
Division Series												
2011 Milwaukee	N.L.	SS	5	18	5	5	1	1	0	1	0	.278
Championship Series												
2011 Milwaukee	N.L.	SS	6	24	2	8	2	0	1	5	0	.333

a Played in Cuba 2000-2004. Signed with Seattle Mariners, January 26, 2005.

b Traded to Kansas City Royals with cash for pitcher Dan Cortes and pitcher Derrick Saito, July 10, 2009.
c Traded to Milwaukee Brewers with pitcher Zack Greinke for outfielder Lorenzo Cain, infielder Alcides Escobar, pitcher Jeremy Jeffress and pitcher Jake Odorizzi, December 19, 2010.
d Filed for free agency, October 30, 2011. Signed with Kansas City Royals, December 20, 2011.

BETEMIT, WILSON
Born, Santo Domingo, Dominican Republic, November 2, 1981.
Bats Both. Throws Right. Height, 6 feet, 2 inches. Weight, 220 pounds.

Year Club	Lea	Pos	G	AB	R	H	2B	3B	HR	RBI	SB	Avg
1997 Braves	Gulf Coast	SS	32	113	12	24	6	1	0	15	0	.212
1998 Braves	Gulf Coast	SS	51	173	23	38	8	4	5	16	6	.220
1999 Danville	Appal.	SS	67	259	39	83	18	2	5	53	6	.320
2000 Jamestown	N.Y.-Penn.	SS	69	269	54	89	15	2	5	37	3	.331
2001 Myrtle Beach	Carolina	SS	84	318	38	88	20	1	7	43	8	.277
2001 Greenville	Southern	SS	47	183	22	65	14	0	5	19	6	.355
2001 Atlanta	N.L.	SS	8	3	1	0	0	0	0	0	1	.000
2002 Braves	Gulf Coast	SS	7	19	2	5	4	0	0	2	1	.263
2002 Richmond	Int.	SS	93	343	43	84	17	1	8	34	8	.245
2003 Richmond	Int.	3B-SS	127	478	55	125	23	13	8	65	8	.262
2004 Richmond	Int.	3B-SS	105	356	48	99	24	2	13	59	3	.278
2004 Atlanta	N.L.	SS-3B	22	47	2	8	0	0	0	3	0	.170
2005 Atlanta	N.L.	3B-SS-2B	115	246	36	75	12	4	4	20	1	.305
2006 Atlanta-LA a	N.L.	3B-SS-2B	143	373	49	98	23	0	18	53	3	.263
2007 Los Angeles	N.L.	3B-SS-2B-OF	84	156	22	36	8	0	10	26	0	.231
2007 New York b	A.L.	1B-SS-3B	37	84	11	19	4	0	4	24	0	.226
2008 Scranton/WB	Int.	1B-3B-2B-SS	8	27	5	9	4	0	1	5	0	.333
2008 New York c-d	A.L.	1B-3B-SS-2B	87	189	24	50	13	0	6	25	0	.265
2009 Chicago	A.L.	1B-3B	20	45	2	9	5	0	0	3	0	.200
2009 Charlotte e	Int.	3B-1B-SS	72	261	36	63	19	0	11	49	2	.241
2010 Omaha	P.C.	SS-1B-3B	29	113	9	30	6	2	2	17	1	.265
2010 Kansas City	A.L.	3B-1B-2B	84	276	36	82	20	0	13	43	0	.297
2011 Kansas City-Detroit f-g	A.L.	3B-1B-2B	97	323	40	92	22	4	8	46	4	.285
Major League Totals	9 Yrs.		697	1742	223	469	107	8	63	243	9	.269
Division Series												
2004 Atlanta	N.L.	PH	1	0	0	0	0	0	0	0	0	.000
2005 Atlanta	N.L.	PH	2	2	0	1	0	0	0	0	0	.500
2006 Los Angeles	N.L.	3B	3	8	3	4	1	0	1	1	0	.500
2011 Detroit	A.L.	3B	3	8	0	0	0	0	0	0	0	.000
Division Series Totals			9	18	3	5	1	0	1	1	0	.278
Championship Series												
2011 Detroit	A.L.	PH	1	1	0	0	0	0	0	0	0	.000

a Traded to Los Angeles Dodgers for pitcher Danys Baez, infielder Willy Aybar and cash, July 28, 2006.
b Traded to New York Yankees for pitcher Scott Proctor, July 31, 2007.
c On disabled list from April 14 to May 6 and May 11 to May 26, 2008.
d Traded to Chicago White Sox with pitcher Jeff Marquez and pitcher Jhonny Nunez for infielder Nick Swisher and pitcher Kaneoka Texeira, November 13, 2008.
e Filed for free agency, October 5, 2009. Signed with Kansas City Royals organization, November 12, 2009.
f Traded to Detroit Tigers for pitcher Antonio Cruz and catcher Julio Rodriguez, July 20, 2011.
g Filed for free agency, October 30, 2011.

BLAKE, WILLIAM CASEY (CASEY)
Born, Des Moines, Iowa, August 23, 1973.
Bats Right. Throws Right. Height, 6 feet, 2 inches. Weight, 210 pounds.

Year Club	Lea	Pos	G	AB	R	H	2B	3B	HR	RBI	SB	Avg
1996 Hagerstown	So.Atl.	3B-1B-OF	48	172	29	43	13	1	2	18	5	.250
1997 Dunedin	Fla.St.	3B-SS	129	449	56	107	21	0	7	39	19	.238
1998 Dunedin	Fla.St.	3B	88	340	62	119	28	3	11	65	9	.350
1998 Knoxville	Southern	3B	45	172	41	64	15	4	7	38	10	.372
1999 Syracuse	Int.	3B	110	387	69	95	16	2	22	75	9	.245
1999 St. Catharines	N.Y.-Penn.	3B	1	3	0	2	0	0	0	0	0	.667
1999 Toronto	A.L.	3B	14	39	6	10	2	0	1	1	0	.256
2000 Syracuse	Int.	3B-SS	30	106	10	23	6	1	2	7	0	.217
2000 Salt Lake	P.C.	3B-SS-1B	80	293	59	93	22	2	12	52	7	.317
2000 Minnesota a-b	A.L.	3B-1B	7	16	1	3	2	0	0	1	0	.188
2001 Edmonton	P.C.	3B-1B-2B-SS	94	375	64	116	24	6	10	49	14	.309
2001 Minn.-Baltimore c-d	A.L.	1B-3B	19	37	3	9	1	0	1	4	3	.243
2002 Edmonton	P.C.	3B-2B-1B-OF	126	482	87	149	25	3	19	58	24	.309
2002 Minnesota e	A.L.	3B-1B	9	20	2	4	1	0	0	1	0	.200

Year Club	Lea	Pos	G	AB	R	H	2B	3B	HR	RBI	SB	Avg
2003 Cleveland . . . . .A.L.		3B-1B	152	557	80	143	35	0	17	67	7	.257
2004 Cleveland . . . . .A.L.		3B-1B	152	587	93	159	36	3	28	88	5	.271
2005 Cleveland . . . . .A.L.		OF-3B-1B	147	523	72	126	32	1	23	58	4	.241
2006 Lake County . . . . .So.Atl.		OF	1	2	1	1	0	0	1	2	0	.500
2006 Akron . . . . Eastern		OF	1	3	0	1	1	0	0	1	0	.333
2006 Cleveland f . . . . . . .A.L.		OF-1B	109	401	63	113	20	1	19	68	6	.282
2007 Cleveland . . . . .A.L.		3B-1B-OF	156	588	81	159	36	4	18	78	4	.270
2008 Cleveland . . . . .A.L.		3B-1B-SS	94	325	46	94	24	0	11	58	2	.289
2008 Los Angeles g-h . . . . .N.L.		3B-1B-2B	58	211	25	53	12	1	10	23	1	.251
2009 Los Angeles . . . . . . .N.L.		3B-1B-OF	139	485	84	136	25	6	18	79	3	.280
2010 Los Angeles . . . . . . .N.L.		3B-1B	146	509	56	126	28	1	17	64	0	.248
2011 Rancho Cucamonga . Calif.		DH	2	8	2	3	1	0	0	1	0	.375
2011 Albuquerque. . . . . . .P.C.		3B	4	14	1	2	1	0	0	0	0	.143
2011 Los Angeles i-j . . . . .N.L.		3B-1B-OF	63	202	32	51	10	1	4	26	1	.252
Major League Totals	13 Yrs.		1265	4500	644	1186	264	18	167	616	36	.264
Division Series												
2007 Cleveland . . . . .A.L.		3B	4	17	1	2	1	0	0	2	0	.118
2008 Los Angeles . . . . . . .N.L.		3B	3	11	2	3	0	0	0	2	0	.273
2009 Los Angeles . . . . . . .N.L.		3B	3	11	1	3	0	0	0	1	0	.273
Division Series Totals			10	39	4	8	1	0	0	5	0	.205
Championship Series												
2007 Cleveland . . . . .A.L.		3B	7	26	4	9	2	0	1	2	0	.346
2008 Los Angeles . . . . . . .N.L.		3B-2B	5	19	2	5	0	0	1	2	0	.263
2009 Los Angeles . . . . . . .N.L.		3B	5	19	0	2	0	0	0	1	1	.105
Championship Series Totals			17	64	6	16	2	0	2	5	1	.250

a Claimed on waivers from Toronto Blue Jays by Minnesota Twins, May 23, 2000.
b On disabled list from June 28 to July 7, 2000.
c Claimed on waivers by Baltimore Orioles, September 21, 2001.
d Claimed on waivers by Minnesota Twins, October 12, 2001.
e Filed for free agency, October 14, 2002. Signed with Cleveland Indians, December 18, 2002.
f On disabled list from June 14 to July 13 and August 6 to August 25, 2006.
g Traded to Los Angeles Dodgers for pitcher Jonathan Meloan and catcher Carlos Santana, July 26, 2008.
h Filed for free agency, October 30, 2008, re-signed with Los Angeles Dodgers, December 9, 2008.
i On disabled list from March 22 to April 6 and April 25 to May 27 and July 3 to July 30, 2011.
j Filed for free agency, October 30, 2011. Signed with Colorado Rockies, December 20, 2011.

BLANKS, KYLE NATHANIEL

Born, Souderton, Pennsylvania, September 11, 1986.
Bats Right. Throws Right. Height, 6 feet, 6 inches. Weight, 285 pounds.

Year Club	Lea	Pos	G	AB	R	H	2B	3B	HR	RBI	SB	Avg
2005 Padres . . . . .Arizona		1B-OF	48	164	33	49	10	1	7	30	3	.299
2006 Fort Wayne. . . . . . .Midwest		1B	86	308	41	90	20	0	10	52	2	.292
2007 Lake Elsinore . . . . .Calif.		1B	119	465	94	140	31	4	24	100	11	.301
2008 San Antonio . . . . Texas		1B	132	492	75	160	23	5	20	107	5	.325
2009 San Diego . . . . N.L.		OF-1B	54	148	24	37	9	0	10	22	1	.250
2009 Portland . . . . .P.C.		1B-OF	66	233	35	66	9	1	12	38	0	.283
2010 Lake Elsinore . . . . .Calif.		DH	10	37	3	10	3	0	0	4	0	.270
2010 Portland . . . . .P.C.		OF	1	3	0	1	0	0	0	0	0	.333
2010 San Diego . . . . N.L.		OF-1B	33	102	14	16	6	1	3	15	1	.157
2011 San Antonio . . . . Texas		1B-OF	44	177	33	50	16	3	4	27	3	.282
2011 Tucson . . . . .P.C.		1B-OF	35	134	36	47	12	2	11	35	0	.351
2011 San Diego a . . . . .N.L.		OF-1B	55	170	21	39	7	1	7	26	2	.229
Major League Totals	3 Yrs.		142	420	59	92	22	2	20	63	4	.219

a On disabled list from March 30 to April 26, 2011.

BLOOMQUIST, WILLIAM PAUL (WILLIE)

Born, Bremerton, Washington, November 27, 1977.
Bats Right. Throws Right. Height, 5 feet, 11 inches. Weight, 195 pounds.

Year Club	Lea	Pos	G	AB	R	H	2B	3B	HR	RBI	SB	Avg
1999 Everett . . . . . . Northwest		2B	41	178	35	51	10	3	2	27	17	.287
2000 Lancaster . . . . California		2B-SS	64	256	63	97	19	6	2	51	22	.379
2000 Tacoma a . . . . .P.C.		2B	51	191	17	43	5	1	1	23	5	.225
2001 San Antonio . . . . Texas		SS-2B	123	491	59	125	23	2	0	28	34	.255
2002 Tacoma . . . . . . .P.C.		OF-2B-3B-SS	104	337	47	91	14	3	6	47	20	.270
2002 Seattle b. . . . . .A.L.		OF-2B	12	33	11	15	4	0	0	7	3	.455
2003 Seattle . . . . .A.L.		3B-SS-OF	89	196	30	49	7	2	1	14	4	.250

Year Club	Lea	Pos	G	AB	R	H	2B	3B	HR	RBI	SB	Avg
2004 Tacoma	P.C.	SS-OF	3	12	2	5	0	0	1	3	1	.417
2004 Seattle c	A.L.	3B-SS-1B-OF	93	188	27	46	10	0	2	18	13	.245
2005 Seattle d	A.L.	2B-SS-OF-3B	82	249	27	64	15	2	0	22	14	.257
2006 Seattle	A.L.	OF-SS-2B-3B	102	251	36	62	6	2	1	15	16	.247
2007 Seattle	A.L.	OF-2B-3B-SS	91	173	28	48	3	0	2	13	7	.277
2008 Seattle e-f	A.L.	2B-SS-2B-3B	71	165	32	46	1	0	0	9	14	.279
2009 Kansas City	A.L.	OF-SS-2B-1B	125	434	52	115	11	8	4	29	25	.265
2010 Kansas City	A.L.	OF-3B-2B	72	170	31	45	10	1	3	17	8	.265
2010 Cincinnati g-h ...	N.L.	OF-2B	11	17	0	5	0	0	0	0	0	.294
2011 Arizona i-j	N.L.	SS-OF-2B	97	350	44	93	10	2	4	26	20	.266
Major League Totals	10 Yrs.		845	2226	318	588	77	17	17	170	124	.264
Division Series												
2011 Arizona	N.L.	SS	5	22	3	7	0	0	0	1	3	.318

a On disabled list from August 6 to September 29, 2000.
b On disabled list from April 22 to May 3 and June 6 to 18, 2002.
c On disabled list from May 2 to May 21, 2004.
d On disabled list from August 30 to October 31, 2005.
e On disabled list from August 10 to September 29, 2008.
f Filed for free agency, October 30, 2008. Signed with Kansas City Royals, January 9, 2009.
g Sold to Cincinnati Reds, September 13, 2010.
h Filed for free agency, November 1, 2010. Signed with Arizona Diamondbacks, January 18, 2011.
i On disabled list from April 22 to May 18, 2011.
j Filed for free agency, October 31, 2011, re-signed with Arizona Diamondbacks, November 9, 2011.

BLUM, GEOFFREY EDWARD (GEOFF)

Born, Redwood City, California, April 26, 1973.
Bats Both. Throws Right. Height, 6 feet, 3 inches. Weight, 205 pounds.

Year Club	Lea	Pos	G	AB	R	H	2B	3B	HR	RBI	SB	Avg
1994 Vermont	N.Y.-Penn.	SS	63	241	48	83	15	1	3	38	5	.344
1995 Wst Plm Bch	Fla.St.	2B-SS-3B	125	457	54	120	20	2	1	62	6	.263
1996 Harrisburg	Eastern	2B-SS-1B-OF	120	396	47	95	22	2	1	41	6	.240
1997 Ottawa	Int.	2B-SS-3B	118	407	59	101	21	2	3	35	14	.248
1998 Ottawa	Int.	2B-SS	8	23	1	4	0	0	0	1	0	.174
1998 Expos	Gulf Coast	2B	5	18	0	3	1	1	0	1	0	.167
1998 Jupiter	Fla.St.	2B-3B-SS	17	58	13	16	6	0	0	5	1	.276
1998 Harrisburg	Eastern	3B-SS-2B	39	139	25	43	12	3	6	21	2	.309
1999 Ottawa	Int.	SS	77	268	43	71	14	1	10	37	6	.265
1999 Montreal a	N.L.	SS-2B	45	133	21	32	7	2	8	18	1	.241
2000 Montreal........	N.L.	3B-SS-2B-1B	124	343	40	97	20	2	11	45	1	.283
2001 Montreal........	N.L.	3B-OF-2B-1B	148	453	57	107	25	4	9	50	9	.236
2002 Houston b	N.L.	3B-OF-SS-1B	130	368	45	104	20	4	10	52	2	.283
2003 Houston c	N.L.	3B-2B-SS-1B	123	420	51	110	19	0	10	52	0	.262
2004 Tampa Bay d ...	A.L.	3B-2B-OF-1B	112	339	38	73	21	0	8	35	2	.215
2005 Lake Elsinore .	California	3B-OF	2	8	3	2	0	0	2	5	0	.250
2005 San Diego	N.L.	3B-2B-SS-1B	78	224	26	54	13	1	5	22	3	.241
2005 Chicago e-f-g ...	A.L.	1B-3B-SS-2B	31	95	6	19	2	1	1	3	0	.200
2006 San Diego h	N.L.	SS-3B-1B-2B	109	276	27	70	17	1	4	34	0	.254
2007 San Diego i......	N.L.	2B-3B-SS-OF	122	330	34	83	21	1	5	33	0	.252
2008 Houston	N.L.	3B-2B-1B-SS	114	325	36	78	14	1	14	53	1	.240
2009 Round Rock	P.C.	3B	2	7	0	1	1	0	0	1	0	.143
2009 Houston j......	N.L.	3B-1B-SS	120	381	34	94	14	1	10	49	0	.247
2010 Corpus Christi ...	Texas	SS	3	9	0	2	2	0	0	1	0	.222
2010 Houston k-l	N.L.	SS-1B-3B-2B	93	202	22	54	10	1	2	22	0	.267
2011 Diamomndbacks Arizona		3B	5	15	1	5	0	0	0	1	0	.333
2011 Visalia	Calif.	DH	2	5	1	3	2	0	1	2	0	.600
2011 Reno	P.C.	3B-1B	4	14	2	6	1	0	0	1	0	.429
2011 Arizona m........	N.L.	3B	23	49	8	11	3	0	2	10	0	.224
Major League Totals	13 Yrs.		1372	3938	445	986	206	15	99	478	19	.250
Division Series												
2005 Chicago	A.L.	1B	1	1	0	0	0	0	0	0	0	.000
2006 San Diego	N.L.	SS-3B	4	8	0	1	1	0	0	1	0	.125
2011 Arizona	N.L.	PH	2	2	0	0	0	0	0	0	0	.000
Division Series Totals			7	11	0	1	1	0	0	1	0	.091
World Series Record												
2005 Chicago	A.L.	2B	1	1	1	1	0	0	1	1	0	1.000

a On disabled list from May 21 to June 15, 1999.
b Traded to Houston Astros for infielder Chris Truby, March 12, 2002.
c Traded to Tampa Bay Devil Rays for pitcher Brandon Backe, December 14, 2003.

d Released by Tampa Bay Devil Rays, November 19, 2004. Signed with San Diego Padres, December 8, 2004.
e On disabled list from April 30 to May 18, 2005.
f Traded to Chicago White Sox for pitcher Ryan Meaux, July 31, 2005.
g Filed for free agency, October 31, 2005. Signed with San Diego Padres, November 16, 2005.
h Filed for free agency, October 28, 2006, re-signed with San Diego Padres, December 1, 2006.
i Filed for free agency, October 30, 2007. Signed with Houston Astros, November 20, 2007.
j On disabled list from June 13 to June 28, 2009.
k On disabled list from July 3 to August 3, 2010.
l Filed for free agency, November 1, 2010. Signed with Arizona Diamondbacks, November 15, 2010.
m On disabled list from March 22 to July 15 and July 25 to September 1, 2011.

BOESCH, BRENNAN PHILIP
Born, Santa Monica, California, April 12, 1985.
Bats Left. Throws Left. Height, 6 feet, 4 inches. Weight, 235 pounds.

Year	Club	Lea	Pos	G	AB	R	H	2B	3B	HR	RBI	SB	Avg
2006	Oneonta	N.Y.-Penn.	OF	70	292	27	85	15	6	5	54	3	.291
2007	West Michigan	Midwest	OF	126	513	52	137	19	4	10	86	15	.267
2008	Lakeland	Fla.St.	OF	111	417	46	104	17	8	7	64	3	.249
2009	Erie	Eastern	OF	131	527	89	145	26	7	28	93	11	.275
2010	Toledo	Int.	OF	15	58	6	22	3	1	3	17	2	.379
2010	Detroit	A.L.	OF	133	464	49	119	26	3	14	67	7	.256
2011	Detroit a	A.L.	OF	115	428	75	121	25	1	16	54	5	.283
Major League Totals		2 Yrs.		248	892	124	240	51	4	30	121	12	.269

a On disabled list from September 9 to October 21, 2011.

BOGUSEVIC, BRIAN THOMAS
Born, Palos Heights, Illinois, February 18, 1984.
Bats Left. Throws Left. Height, 6 feet, 3 inches. Weight, 220 pounds.

Year	Club	Lea	Pos	G	AB	R	H	2B	3B	HR	RBI	SB	Avg
2007	Corpus Christi a	Texas	PH	2	2	0	1	0	0	0	0	0	.500
2008	Salem	Carolina	OF	8	23	4	5	2	0	1	6	1	.217
2008	Corpus Christi	Texas	OF	42	124	21	46	10	2	3	20	8	.371
2009	Round Rock	P.C.	OF	138	520	68	141	25	3	6	53	22	.271
2010	Round Rock	P.C.	OF-1B	131	502	91	139	26	2	13	57	23	.277
2010	Houston	N.L.	OF	19	28	5	5	3	0	0	3	1	.179
2011	Oklahoma	P.C.	OF-1B	58	218	27	57	11	5	3	35	20	.261
2011	Houston	N.L.	OF	87	164	22	47	14	1	4	15	4	.287
Major League Totals		2 Yrs.		106	192	27	52	17	1	4	18	5	.271

a Pitched in Houston Astros organization from 2005 through 2008.

BONIFACIO, EMILIO JOSE
Born, Santo Domingo, Dominican Republic, April 23, 1985.
Bats Both. Throws Right. Height, 5 feet, 11 inches. Weight, 195 pounds.

Year	Club	Lea	Pos	G	AB	R	H	2B	3B	HR	RBI	SB	Avg
2003	Missoula	Pioneer	2B	54	146	20	29	1	1	0	16	15	.199
2004	South Bend	Midwest	2B	120	411	59	107	9	6	1	37	40	.260
2005	South Bend	Midwest	2B	127	522	81	141	14	7	1	44	55	.270
2006	Lancaster	Calif.	2B	130	546	117	175	35	7	7	50	61	.321
2007	Mobile	Southern	2B-SS	132	551	84	157	21	5	2	40	41	.285
2007	Arizona	N.L.	2B	11	23	2	5	1	0	0	2	0	.217
2008	Tucson	P.C.	2B-OF-SS	85	367	49	111	18	5	1	29	17	.302
2008	Columbus	Int.	2B	8	31	9	14	2	0	0	3	4	.452
2008	Arizona-Washington a-b	N.L.	2B-OF	49	169	29	41	6	5	0	14	7	.243
2009	Florida	N.L.	3B-SS-OF-2B	127	461	72	116	11	6	1	27	21	.252
2010	New Orleans	P.C.	OF-2B-SS	40	164	19	45	8	3	0	11	8	.274
2010	Florida	N.L.	OF-SS-3B-2B	73	180	30	47	6	3	0	10	12	.261
2011	Florida	N.L.	SS-OF-3B-2B	152	565	78	167	26	7	5	36	40	.296
Major League Totals		5 Yrs.		412	1398	211	376	50	21	6	89	80	.269

a Traded to Washington Nationals for pitcher Jon Rauch, July 22, 2008.
b Traded to Florida Marlins with pitcher P.J. Dean and infielder Jake Smolinski for pitcher Scott Olsen and outfielder Josh Willingham, November 11, 2008.

BORBON, JULIO ALBERTO
Born, Starkville, Mississippi, February 20, 1986.
Bats Left. Throws Left. Height, 6 feet, 1 inch. Weight, 180 pounds.

Year	Club	Lea	Pos	G	AB	R	H	2B	3B	HR	RBI	SB	Avg
2007 Rangers	Arizona		OF	2	8	0	2	1	0	0	0	0	.250
2007 Spokane	Northwest		OF	7	29	1	5	0	0	0	2	3	.172
2008 Bakersfield	Calif.		OF	66	291	47	89	20	0	2	36	36	.306
2008 Frisco	Texas		OF	60	255	40	86	12	2	5	22	17	.337
2009 Okla.	P.C.		OF	96	407	71	125	12	7	2	34	25	.307
2009 Texas	A.L.		DH-OF	46	157	30	49	4	0	4	20	19	.312
2010 Texas	A.L.		OF	137	438	60	121	11	4	3	42	15	.276
2011 Frisco	Texas		DH	1	4	0	0	0	0	0	0	0	.000
2011 Round Rock	P.C.		OF	32	131	27	39	10	4	0	14	16	.298
2011 Texas a	A.L.		OF	32	89	10	24	1	3	0	11	6	.270
Major League Totals		3 Yrs.	215	684	100	194	16	7	7	73	40	.284
Division Series													
2010 Texas	A.L.		OF	3	6	1	0	0	0	0	0	0	.000
Championship Series													
2010 Texas	A.L.		PH	3	1	2	0	0	0	0	0	0	.000
World Series Record													
2010 Texas	A.L.		PH	2	2	1	1	0	0	0	0	0	.500

a On disabled list from May 14 to June 3, 2011.

BOURGEOIS, JASON JERROD
Born, Houston, Texas, January 4, 1982.
Bats Right. Throws Right. Height, 5 feet, 9 inches. Weight, 190 pounds.

Year	Club	Lea	Pos	G	AB	R	H	2B	3B	HR	RBI	SB	Avg
2000 Rangers	Gulf Coast		2B	24	88	18	21	4	0	0	6	9	.239
2001 Pulaski	Appal.		2B	62	251	60	78	12	2	7	34	21	.311
2002 Charlotte	Fla.St.		2B-SS	9	27	5	5	1	0	0	4	1	.185
2002 Savannah	So.Atl.		SS-2B	127	522	72	133	21	5	8	49	22	.255
2003 Stockton	Calif.		2B-SS-3B	69	277	75	91	22	3	4	34	16	.329
2003 Frisco	Texas		2B	55	202	28	51	5	4	4	21	3	.252
2004 Frisco	Texas		2B-SS	138	530	73	135	19	7	2	58	30	.255
2005 Richmond a-b	Int.		2B-OF-SS	119	388	33	93	20	2	2	16	8	.240
2006 San Antonio	Texas		OF-2B-SS	107	411	65	114	22	7	4	38	23	.277
2007 Charlotte	Int.		2B-OF-3B	84	338	51	105	18	3	7	34	23	.311
2007 Birmingham c-d	Southern		OF-2B-3B	43	162	25	48	10	3	2	20	15	.296
2008 Charlotte	Int.		OF-2B	127	510	83	146	23	5	9	48	30	.286
2008 Chicago e	A.L.		2B	6	3	0	1	1	0	0	0	0	.333
2009 Nashville	P.C.		OF	105	424	61	134	18	6	2	41	36	.316
2009 Milwaukee f	N.L.		OF	24	37	6	7	0	0	1	3	3	.189
2010 Round Rock	P.C.		OF	65	235	37	81	10	3	5	28	18	.345
2010 Houston	N.L.		OF-2B	69	123	16	27	4	1	0	3	12	.220
2011 Astros	Gulf Coast		OF	3	10	1	3	0	0	0	4	0	.300
2011 Corpus Christi	Texas		OF	2	10	1	2	0	0	0	0	1	.200
2011 Oklahoma	P.C.		OF	4	18	4	8	3	1	0	1	0	.444
2011 Houston g	N.L.		OF-2B	93	238	30	70	8	2	1	16	31	.294
Major League Totals		4 Yrs.	192	401	52	105	13	3	2	22	46	.262

a Claimed on waivers from Texas Rangers by Atlanta Braves, March 24, 2005.
b Selected by Seattle Mariners in Rule V minor league draft, December 8, 2005.
c Filed for free agency, October 15, 2006. Signed with Chicago White Sox organization, January 19, 2007.
d Filed for free agency, October 29, 2007, re-signed with Chicago White Sox organization, November 19, 2007.
e Filed for free agency, October 17, 2008. Signed with Milwaukee Brewers organization, November 25, 2008.
f Claimed on waivers by Houston Astros, October 26, 2009.
g On disabled list from May 8 to June 4 and June 29 to July 22, 2011.

BOURJOS, PETER CHRISTOPHER
Born, Park Ridge, Illinois, March 31, 1987.
Bats Right. Throws Right. Height, 6 feet, 1 inch. Weight, 180 pounds.

Year	Club	Lea	Pos	G	AB	R	H	2B	3B	HR	RBI	SB	Avg
2006 Orem	Pioneer		OF	65	250	42	73	16	7	5	28	13	.292
2007 Angels	Arizona		OF	4	16	3	5	0	1	0	2	0	.313
2007 Cedar Rapids	Midwest		OF	63	237	37	65	9	6	5	29	19	.274
2008 Rancho Cucamonga	Calif.		OF	121	509	83	150	29	10	9	51	50	.295
2009 Arkansas	Texas		OF	110	437	72	123	16	14	6	51	32	.281
2010 Salt Lake	P.C.		OF	102	414	85	130	13	12	13	52	27	.314
2010 Los Angeles	A.L.		OF	51	181	19	37	6	4	6	15	10	.204

18

Year	Club	Lea	Pos	G	AB	R	H	2B	3B	HR	RBI	SB	Avg
2011 Los Angeles a	A.L.	OF	147	502	72	136	26	*11	12	43	22	.271
Major League Totals		2 Yrs.	198	683	91	173	32	15	18	58	32	.253

a On disabled list from July 8 to July 23, 2011.

BOURN, MICHAEL RAY
Born, Houston, Texas, December 27, 1982.
Bats Left. Throws Right. Height, 5 feet, 11 inches. Weight, 180 pounds.

Year	Club	Lea	Pos	G	AB	R	H	2B	3B	HR	RBI	SB	Avg
2003 Batavia	N.Y.-Penn.	OF	35	125	12	35	0	1	0	4	23	.280
2004 Lakewood	So.Atl.	OF	109	413	92	130	20	14	5	53	58	.315
2005 Reading	Eastern	OF	135	544	80	146	18	8	6	44	38	.268
2006 Reading	Eastern	OF	80	318	62	87	5	6	4	26	30	.274
2006 Scranton-WB	Int.	OF	38	152	34	43	5	7	1	15	15	.283
2006 Philadelphia	N.L.	OF	17	8	2	1	0	0	0	0	1	.125
2007 Philadelphia a-b	N.L.	OF	105	119	29	33	3	3	1	6	18	.277
2008 Houston	N.L.	OF	138	467	57	107	10	4	5	29	41	.229
2009 Houston	N.L.	OF	157	606	97	173	27	12	3	35	*61	.285
2010 Houston	N.L.	OF	141	535	84	142	25	6	2	38	*52	.265
2011 Houston-Atlanta c	N.L.	OF	158	656	94	193	34	10	2	50	*61	.294
Major League Totals		6 Yrs.	716	2391	363	649	99	35	13	158	234	.271
Division Series													
2007 Philadelphia	N.L.	PH	2	1	0	0	0	0	0	0	0	.000

a On disabled list from July 31 to September 10, 2007.
b Traded to Houston Astros with pitcher Geoff Geary and infielder Mike Costanzo for infielder Eric Bruntlett and pitcher Brad Lidge, November 12, 2007.
c Traded to Atlanta Braves with cash for outfielder Jordan Schafer, pitcher Juan Abreu, pitcher Paul Clemens and pitcher Brett Oberholtzer, July 31, 2011.

BRANTLEY, MICHAEL CHARLES JR.
Born, Bellevue, Washington, May 15, 1987.
Bats Left. Throws Left. Height, 6 feet, 2 inches. Weight, 200 pounds.

Year	Club	Lea	Pos	G	AB	R	H	2B	3B	HR	RBI	SB	Avg
2005 Brewers	Arizona	OF	44	173	34	60	3	1	0	19	14	.347
2005 Helena	Pioneer	OF	10	34	8	11	2	0	0	3	2	.324
2006 West Virginia	So.Atl.	OF	108	360	47	108	10	2	0	42	24	.300
2007 West Virginia	So.Atl.	1B-OF	56	218	41	73	15	1	2	32	18	.335
2007 Huntsville	Southern	OF-1B	59	187	28	47	6	1	0	21	17	.251
2008 Huntsville a	Southern	OF-1B	106	420	80	134	17	2	4	40	28	.319
2009 Columbus	Int.	OF	116	457	80	122	21	2	6	37	46	.267
2009 Cleveland	A.L.	OF	28	112	10	35	4	0	0	11	4	.313
2010 Columbus	Int.	OF	67	273	54	87	13	2	4	29	13	.319
2010 Cleveland	A.L.	OF	72	297	38	73	9	3	3	22	10	.246
2011 Cleveland b	A.L.	OF	114	451	63	120	24	4	7	46	13	.266
Major League Totals		3 Yrs.	214	860	111	228	37	7	10	79	27	.265

a Sent by Milwaukee Brewers to Cleveland Indians as player to be named later for pitcher C.C. Sabathia, October 3, 2008.
b On disabled list from August 23 to November 2, 2011.

BRANYAN, RUSSELL OLES
Born, Warner Robins, Georgia, December 19, 1975.
Bats Left. Throws Right. Height, 6 feet, 3 inches. Weight, 230 pounds.

Year	Club	Lea	Pos	G	AB	R	H	2B	3B	HR	RBI	SB	Avg
1994 Burlington	Appal.	3B	55	171	21	36	10	0	5	13	4	.211
1995 Columbus	So.Atl.	3B	76	277	46	71	8	6	19	55	1	.256
1996 Columbus	So.Atl.	3B	130	482	102	129	20	4	40	106	7	.268
1997 Kinston	Carolina	3B	83	297	59	86	26	2	27	75	3	.290
1997 Akron	Eastern	3B	41	137	26	32	4	0	12	30	0	.234
1998 Akron	Eastern	3B	43	163	35	48	11	3	16	46	1	.294
1998 Cleveland	A.L.	3B	1	4	0	0	0	0	0	0	0	.000
1999 Buffalo	Int.	3B	109	395	51	82	11	1	30	67	8	.208
1999 Cleveland	A.L.	3B	11	38	4	8	2	0	1	6	0	.211
2000 Buffalo	Int.	3B-OF	64	229	46	56	9	2	21	60	1	.245
2000 Cleveland	A.L.	OF-3B	67	193	32	46	7	2	16	38	0	.238
2001 Cleveland	A.L.	3B-OF	113	315	48	73	16	2	20	54	1	.232
2002 Cleveland	A.L.	OF-3B	50	161	16	33	4	0	8	17	1	.205

Year	Club	Lea	Pos	G	AB	R	H	2B	3B	HR	RBI	SB	Avg
2002	Cincinnati a	N.L.	OF-1B-3B	84	217	34	53	9	1	16	39	3	.244
2003	Louisville	Int.	OF-1B-3B	14	49	5	16	5	0	1	3	0	.327
2003	Cincinnati b-c	N.L.	3B-OF-1B	74	176	22	38	12	0	9	26	0	.216
2004	Richmond	Int.	OF	11	28	5	5	0	0	1	4	1	.179
2004	Buffalo	Int.	1B-3B-OF	82	313	58	90	16	2	25	75	5	.288
2004	Milwaukee d-e-f	N.L.	3B-1B	51	158	21	37	11	1	11	27	1	.234
2005	Nashville	P.C.	OF-3B	6	17	4	5	4	0	1	3	0	.294
2005	Milwaukee g	N.L.	3B-1B-OF	85	202	23	52	11	0	12	31	1	.257
2006	Tampa Bay	A.L.	OF-3B-1B	64	169	23	34	10	0	12	27	2	.201
2006	San Diego h-i	N.L.	3B	27	72	14	21	1	0	6	9	0	.292
2007	Buffalo	Int.	DH	1	4	0	0	0	0	0	0	0	.000
2007	San Diego-Phil.-St. Louis j-k-l	N.L.	3B-OF-1B	89	163	22	32	5	1	10	26	1	.196
2008	Nashville	P.C.	3B-1B-OF	45	153	24	55	15	0	12	36	4	.359
2008	Milwaukee m-n-o	N.L.	3B-1B	50	132	24	33	8	0	12	20	1	.250
2009	Seattle p-q	A.L.	1B	116	431	64	108	21	1	31	76	2	.251
2010	Akron	Eastern	1B	2	8	1	2	0	0	0	0	0	.250
2010	Columbus	Int.	1B	4	14	1	4	2	0	0	1	0	.286
2010	Cleveland-Seattle r-s-t	A.L.	DH-1B	109	376	47	89	19	0	25	57	1	.237
2011	Arizona	N.L.	1B	31	62	4	13	5	0	1	2	0	.210
2011	Los Angeles u-v	A.L.	DH-1B-3B	37	65	7	12	2	0	4	12	2	.185
Major League Totals		14 Yrs.	1059	2934	405	682	143	8	194	467	16	.232	
Division Series													
2001	Cleveland	A.L.	OF	2	3	1	1	0	0	0	0	0	.333
2006	San Diego	N.L.	3B	4	13	1	3	1	1	0	3	0	.231
Division Series Totals			6	16	2	4	1	1	0	3	0	.250	

a Traded to Cincinnati Reds for infielder Ben Broussard, June 7, 2002.

b On disabled list from March 18 to May 29, 2003.

c On disabled list from August 13 to August 28, 2003.

d Not offered contract, December 21, 2003. Signed with Atlanta Braves organization, January 21, 2004.

e Traded to Cleveland Indians for player to be named later, April 26, 2004. Milwaukee Brewers received pitcher Scott Sturkie to complete trade, May 25, 2004.

f Sold to Milwaukee Brewers, July 26, 2004.

g On disabled list from June 2 to July 4, 2005.

h Released by Milwaukee Brewers, January 17, 2006. Signed with Tampa Bay Devil Rays organization, January 31, 2006.

i Traded to San Diego Padres for pitcher Evan Meek and player to be named later, August 24, 2006. Tampa Bay Devil Rays received pitcher Dale Thayer to complete trade, September 15, 2006.

j Released by San Diego Padres, July 28, 2007. Signed with Cleveland Indians organization, August 7, 2007.

k Sold to Philadelphia Phillies, August 9, 2007.

l Traded to St. Louis Cardinals for player to be named later, August 31, 2007.

m Filed for free agency, October 30, 2007. Signed with Milwaukee Brewers organization, February 20, 2008.

n On disabled list from August 12 to September 23, 2008.

o Filed for free agency, November 1, 2008. Signed with Seattle Mariners, December 3, 2008.

p On disabled list from August 29 to September 29, 2009.

q Filed for free agency, November 9, 2009. Signed with Cleveland Indians, February 24, 2010.

r On disabled list from March 26 to April 20, 2010.

s Traded to Seattle Mariners for infielder Juan Diaz and outfielder Ezequiel Carrera, June 26, 2010.

t Filed for free agency, November 3, 2010. Signed with Arizona Diamondbacks organization, February 17, 2011.

u Released by Arizona Diamondbacks, May 21, 2011. Signed with Los Angeles Angels, May 26, 2011.

v Filed for free agency, October 30, 2011.

BRAUN, RYAN JOSEPH

Born, Mission Hills, California, November 17, 1983.

Bats Right. Throws Right. Height, 6 feet, 2 inches. Weight, 200 pounds.

Year	Club	Lea	Pos	G	AB	R	H	2B	3B	HR	RBI	SB	Avg
2005	Helena	Pioneer	3B	10	41	6	14	2	1	2	10	2	.341
2005	West Virginia	So.Atl.	3B	37	152	21	54	16	2	8	35	2	.355
2006	Brevard County	Fla.St.	3B	59	226	34	62	12	2	7	37	14	.274
2006	Huntsville	Southern	3B	59	231	42	70	19	1	15	40	12	.303
2007	Nashville	P.C.	3B	34	117	28	40	12	0	10	22	4	.342
2007	Milwaukee a	N.L.	3B	113	451	91	146	26	6	34	97	15	.324
2008	Milwaukee	N.L.	OF	151	611	92	174	39	7	37	106	14	.285
2009	Milwaukee	N.L.	OF	158	635	113	*203	39	6	32	114	20	.320
2010	Milwaukee	N.L.	OF	157	619	101	188	45	1	25	103	14	.304
2011	Milwaukee b	N.L.	OF	150	563	109	187	38	6	33	111	33	.332
Major League Totals		5 Yrs.	729	2879	506	898	187	26	161	531	96	.312	
Division Series													
2008	Milwaukee	N.L.	OF	4	16	0	5	2	0	0	2	0	.313

Year	Club	Lea	Pos	G	AB	R	H	2B	3B	HR	RBI	SB	Avg
2011 Milwaukee	N.L.	OF	5	18	5	9	4	0	1	4	1	.500
Division Series Totals			9	34	5	14	6	0	1	6	1	.412
Championship Series												
2011 Milwaukee	N.L.	OF	6	24	2	8	3	0	1	6	0	.333

a Selected Rookie of the Year in National League for 2007.
b Selected Most Valuable Player in National League for 2011.

BRIGNAC, REID MICHAEL
Born, St.Amant, Louisiana, January 16, 1986.
Bats Left. Throws Right. Height, 6 feet, 3 inches. Weight, 195 pounds.

Year	Club	Lea	Pos	G	AB	R	H	2B	3B	HR	RBI	SB	Avg
2004 Princeton	Appal.	SS	25	97	16	35	4	2	1	25	2	.361
2004 Charleston	So.Atl.	SS	3	14	3	7	1	0	0	5	0	.500
2005 SW Michigan	Midwest	SS	127	512	77	135	29	2	15	61	5	.264
2006 Visalia	Calif.	SS	100	411	82	134	26	3	21	83	12	.326
2006 Montgomery	Southern	SS	28	110	18	33	6	2	3	16	3	.300
2007 Montgomery	Southern	SS	133	527	91	137	30	5	17	81	15	.260
2008 Tampa Bay	A.L.	SS	4	10	1	0	0	0	0	0	0	.000
2008 Durham	Int.	SS-2B	97	352	43	88	26	2	9	43	5	.250
2009 Durham	Int.	SS-2B	96	415	51	117	28	2	8	44	5	.282
2009 Tampa Bay	A.L.	SS-2B	31	90	10	25	8	2	1	6	2	.278
2010 Tampa Bay	A.L.	2B-SS-OF	113	301	39	77	13	1	8	45	3	.256
2011 Durham	Int.	SS	11	39	7	9	2	1	1	4	0	.231
2011 Tampa Bay	A.L.	SS	92	249	18	48	4	0	1	15	3	.193
Major League Totals	4 Yrs.		240	650	68	150	25	3	10	66	8	.231
Division Series												
2010 Tampa Bay	A.L.	SS	2	3	0	0	0	0	0	0	0	.000
2011 Tampa Bay	A.L.	SS	3	1	0	0	0	0	0	0	0	.000
Division Series Totals			5	4	0	0	0	0	0	0	0	.000

BROWN, DOMONIC LARUN
Born, Lithonia, Georgia, September 3, 1987.
Bats Left. Throws Left. Height, 6 feet, 5 inches. Weight, 200 pounds.

Year	Club	Lea	Pos	G	AB	R	H	2B	3B	HR	RBI	SB	Avg
2006 Phillies	Gulf Coast	OF	34	117	13	25	3	0	1	7	13	.214
2007 Clearwater	Fla.St.	OF	3	9	2	4	1	0	1	7	0	.444
2007 Williamsport.....	N.Y.-Penn.	OF	74	285	43	84	11	5	3	32	14	.295
2008 Lakewood..........	So.Atl.	OF	114	444	77	129	23	3	9	54	22	.291
2009 Reading	Eastern	OF	37	147	20	41	9	4	3	20	8	.279
2009 Clearwater	Fla.St.	OF	66	238	41	72	12	3	11	44	15	.303
2009 Phillies	Gulf Coast	OF	3	10	4	5	0	2	0	0	0	.500
2010 Reading	Eastern	OF	65	236	50	75	16	3	15	47	12	.318
2010 Lehigh Valley	Int.	OF	28	107	15	37	6	1	5	21	5	.346
2010 Philadelphia	N.L.	OF	35	62	8	13	3	0	2	13	2	.210
2011 Clearwater	Fla.St.	OF	5	19	4	7	1	0	2	4	0	.368
2011 Lehigh Valley	Int.	OF	41	138	22	36	6	0	3	15	12	.261
2011 Philadelphia a.........	N.L.	OF	56	184	28	45	10	1	5	19	3	.245
Major League Totals	2 Yrs.		91	246	36	58	13	1	7	32	5	.236
Division Series												
2010 Philadelphia	N.L.	PH	1	1	1	0	0	0	0	0	0	.000
Championship Series												
2010 Philadelphia	N.L.	PH	2	2	0	0	0	0	0	0	0	.000

a On disabled list from March 22 to May 2, 2011.

BRUCE, JAY ALLEN
Born, Beaumont, Texas, April 3, 1987.
Bats Left. Throws Left. Height, 6 feet, 3 inches. Weight, 205 pounds.

Year	Club	Lea	Pos	G	AB	R	H	2B	3B	HR	RBI	SB	Avg
2005 Reds..........	Gulf Coast	OF	37	122	29	33	9	2	5	25	4	.270
2005 Billings............	Pioneer	OF	17	70	16	18	2	0	4	13	2	.257
2006 Dayton	Midwest	OF	117	444	69	129	42	5	16	81	19	.291
2007 Sarasota............	Fla.St.	OF	67	268	49	87	27	5	11	49	4	.325
2007 Louisville	Int.	OF	50	187	28	57	12	2	11	25	2	.305
2007 Chattanooga......	Southern	OF	16	66	10	22	7	1	4	15	2	.333
2008 Louisville	Int.	OF	49	184	34	67	9	5	10	37	8	.364

21

Year	Club	Lea	Pos	G	AB	R	H	2B	3B	HR	RBI	SB	Avg
2008 Cincinnati		N.L.	OF	108	413	63	105	17	1	21	52	4	.254
2009 Louisville		Int.	OF	5	18	3	5	0	0	0	0	2	.278
2009 Cincinnati a		N.L.	OF	101	345	47	77	15	2	22	58	3	.223
2010 Cincinnati		N.L.	OF	148	509	80	143	23	5	25	70	5	.281
2011 Cincinnati		N.L.	OF	157	585	84	150	27	2	32	97	8	.256
Major League Totals		4 Yrs.		514	1852	274	475	82	10	100	277	20	.256
Division Series													
2010 Cincinnati		N.L.	OF	3	8	1	2	0	0	1	1	0	.250

a On disabled list from July 12 to September 14, 2009.

BUCK, JOHNATHAN RICHARD (JOHN)

Born, Kemmerer, Wyoming, July 7, 1980.
Bats Right. Throws Right. Height, 6 feet, 3 inches. Weight, 220 pounds.

Year	Club	Lea	Pos	G	AB	R	H	2B	3B	HR	RBI	SB	Avg
1998 Astros		Gulf Coast	C	36	126	24	36	9	0	3	15	2	.286
1999 Auburn		N.Y.-Penn.	C	63	233	36	57	17	0	3	29	7	.245
1999 Michigan		Midwest	C	4	10	1	1	1	0	0	0	0	.100
2000 Michigan		Midwest	C	109	390	57	110	33	0	10	71	2	.282
2001 Lexington		So.Atl.	C	122	443	72	122	24	1	22	73	4	.275
2002 Round Rock		Texas	C	120	448	48	118	29	3	12	89	2	.263
2003 New Orleans		P.C.	C	78	274	32	70	18	2	2	39	1	.255
2004 New Orleans		P.C.	C	65	227	31	68	11	0	12	35	0	.300
2004 Kansas City a		A.L.	C	71	238	36	56	9	0	12	30	1	.235
2005 Kansas City		A.L.	C	118	401	40	97	21	1	12	47	2	.242
2006 Kansas City		A.L.	C	114	371	37	91	21	1	11	50	0	.245
2007 Kansas City		A.L.	C	113	347	41	77	18	0	18	48	0	.222
2008 Kansas City		A.L.	C	109	370	48	83	23	1	9	48	0	.224
2009 Omaha		P.C.	C	7	27	3	7	1	0	2	4	0	.259
2009 Kansas City b-c		A.L.	C	59	186	16	46	12	4	8	36	1	.247
2010 New Hampshire		Eastern	C	3	11	2	3	0	0	2	6	0	.273
2010 Toronto d-e		A.L.	C	118	409	53	115	25	0	20	66	0	.281
2011 Florida		N.L.	C	140	466	41	106	15	1	16	57	0	.227
Major League Totals		8 Yrs.		842	2788	312	671	144	8	106	382	4	.241

a Traded by Houston Astros to Kansas City Royals with pitcher Octavio Dotel for outfielder Carlos Beltran, June 24, 2004.

b On disabled list from May 31 to July 6, 2009.

c Not offered contract, December 12, 2009. Signed with Toronto Blue Jays, December 16, 2009.

d On disabled list from August 5 to August 20, 2010.

e Filed for free agency, November 1, 2010. Signed with Florida Marlins, November 16, 2010.

BURRELL, PATRICK BRIAN (PAT)

Born, Eureka Springs, Arkansas, October 10, 1976.
Bats Right. Throws Right. Height, 6 feet, 4 inches. Weight, 235 pounds.

Year	Club	Lea	Pos	G	AB	R	H	2B	3B	HR	RBI	SB	Avg
1998 Clearwater		Fla.St.	1B	37	132	29	40	7	1	7	30	2	.303
1999 Scranton-WB		Int.	1B	9	33	4	5	0	0	1	4	0	.152
1999 Reading		Eastern	1B	117	417	84	139	28	6	28	90	3	.333
2000 Scranton-WB		Int.	OF	40	143	31	42	15	1	4	25	1	.294
2000 Philadelphia		N.L.	1B-OF	111	408	57	106	27	1	18	79	2	.260
2001 Philadelphia		N.L.	OF	155	539	70	139	29	2	27	89	2	.258
2002 Philadelphia		N.L.	OF	157	586	96	165	39	2	37	116	1	.282
2003 Philadelphia		N.L.	OF	146	522	57	109	31	4	21	64	0	.209
2004 Reading		Eastern	OF	4	15	2	3	0	0	2	4	0	.200
2004 Philadelphia a		N.L.	OF	127	448	66	115	17	0	24	84	2	.257
2005 Philadelphia		N.L.	OF	154	562	78	158	27	1	32	117	0	.281
2006 Philadelphia		N.L.	OF	144	462	80	119	24	1	29	95	0	.258
2007 Philadelphia		N.L.	OF	155	472	77	121	26	0	30	97	0	.256
2008 Philadelphia b		N.L.	OF	157	536	74	134	33	3	33	86	0	.250
2009 Charlotte		Fla.St.	DH	1	4	0	0	0	0	0	0	0	.000
2009 Montgomery		Southern	DH	2	9	1	1	0	0	0	0	0	.111
2009 Tampa Bay c		A.L.	DH-OF	122	412	45	91	16	1	14	64	2	.221
2010 Fresno		P.C.	OF	5	16	4	5	1	0	1	6	0	.313
2010 Tampa Bay		A.L.	DH	24	84	9	17	5	0	2	13	0	.202
2010 San Francisco d-e		N.L.	OF	96	289	41	77	16	0	18	51	0	.266
2011 San Jose		Calif.	DH	2	8	0	3	0	0	0	2	0	.375
2011 Fresno		P.C.	OF	2	5	0	0	0	0	0	0	0	.000
2011 San Francisco f-g		N.L.	OF	92	183	17	42	9	1	7	21	0	.230
Major League Totals		12 Yrs.		1640	5503	767	1393	299	16	292	976	7	.253

Year	Club	Lea	Pos	G	AB	R	H	2B	3B	HR	RBI	SB	Avg
Division Series													
2007 Philadelphia	N.L.	OF	3	11	1	2	0	0	1	1	0	.182	
2008 Philadelphia	N.L.	OF	4	12	2	3	0	0	2	4	0	.250	
2010 San Francisco	N.L.	OF	4	10	1	2	1	0	1	3	0	.200	
Division Series Totals			11	33	4	7	1	0	4	8	0	.212	
Championship Series													
2008 Philadelphia	N.L.	OF	5	18	1	6	0	0	1	3	0	.333	
2010 San Francisco	N.L.	OF	6	19	3	4	2	0	0	1	0	.211	
Championship Series Totals			11	37	4	10	2	0	1	4	0	.270	
World Series Record													
2008 Philadelphia	N.L.	OF	5	14	0	1	1	0	0	1	0	.071	
2010 San Francisco	N.L.	OF-DH	4	13	1	0	0	0	0	0	0	.000	
World Series Totals			9	27	1	1	1	0	0	1	0	.037	

a On disabled list from August 4 to September 3, 2004.
b Filed for free agency, November 6, 2008. Signed with Tampa Bay Rays, January 5, 2009.
c On disabled list from May 12 to June 12, 2009.
d Released by Tampa Bay Rays, May 16, 2010. Signed with San Francisco Giants, May 29, 2010.
e Filed for free agency, November 1, 2010, re-signed with San Francisco Giants, December 3, 2010.
f On disabled list from July 15 to August 31, 2011.
g Filed for free agency, October 30, 2011.

BURROUGHS, SEAN PATRICK

Born, Atlanta, Georgia, September 12, 1980.
Bats Left. Throws Right. Height, 6 feet, 2 inches. Weight, 200 pounds.

Year	Club	Lea	Pos	G	AB	R	H	2B	3B	HR	RBI	SB	Avg
1999 Fort Wayne	Midwest	3B	122	426	65	153	30	3	5	80	17	.359	
1999 Rancho Cucamonga	Calif.	3B	6	23	3	10	3	0	1	5	0	.435	
2000 Mobile	Southern	3B	108	392	46	114	29	4	2	42	6	.291	
2001 Portland	P.C.	3B	104	394	60	127	28	1	9	55	9	.322	
2002 San Diego	N.L.	3B-2B	63	192	18	52	5	1	1	11	2	.271	
2002 Portland a	P.C.	2B-3B	50	179	29	54	16	2	2	23	1	.302	
2003 San Diego	N.L.	3B	146	517	62	148	27	6	7	58	7	.286	
2004 San Diego	N.L.	3B	130	523	76	156	23	3	2	47	5	.298	
2005 Portland	P.C.	3B	32	124	21	36	8	0	3	14	0	.290	
2005 San Diego b	N.L.	3B-SS-P	93	284	20	71	7	2	1	17	4	.250	
2006 Tampa Bay	A.L.	3B	8	21	3	4	1	0	0	1	1	.190	
2006 Durham c	Int.	3B	37	131	8	28	2	0	1	11	1	.214	
2007 Tacoma d	P.C.	3B	4	12	2	2	1	0	0	0	0	.167	
2008-2010					Did Not Play								
2011 Reno	P.C.	3B	34	102	19	42	11	2	2	25	0	.412	
2011 Arizona e-f	N.L.	3B	78	110	8	30	4	0	1	8	1	.273	
Major League Totals	6 Yrs.		518	1647	187	461	67	12	12	142	20	.280	
Division Series													
2005 San Diego	N.L.	PH	2	1	0	0	0	0	0	0	0	.000	
2011 Arizona	N.L.	3B	3	3	0	1	0	0	0	0	0	.333	
Division Series Totals			5	4	0	1	0	0	0	0	0	.250	

a On disabled list from May 29 to July 15, 2002.
b Traded to Tampa Bay Devil Rays for pitcher Dewon Brazelton, December 7, 2005.
c On disabled list from March 30 to April 14, 2006.
d Released by Tampa Bay Devil Rays, June 21, 2006. Signed with Seattle Mariners organization, January 3, 2007.
e Released by Seattle Mariners, June 14, 2007. Signed with Arizona Diamondbacks organization, November 22, 2010.
f Filed for free agency, November 2, 2011. Signed with Minnesota Twins organization, December 14, 2011.

BUTERA, ANDREW EDWARD (DREW)

Born, Evansville, Indiana, August 9, 1983.
Bats Right. Throws Right. Height, 6 feet, 1 inch. Weight, 195 pounds.

Year	Club	Lea	Pos	G	AB	R	H	2B	3B	HR	RBI	SB	Avg
2005 Brooklyn	N.Y.-Penn.	C	55	175	13	38	9	1	1	23	1	.217	
2006 Hagerstown	So.Atl.	C	95	295	24	55	13	0	5	38	1	.186	
2007 St. Lucie a	Fla.St.	C	52	182	22	47	14	0	5	22	0	.258	
2007 Binghamton	Eastern	C	30	117	7	22	2	0	1	4	0	.188	
2007 New Britain	Eastern	C	17	50	3	13	3	1	0	3	0	.260	
2008 New Britain	Eastern	C-1B	96	302	39	66	18	1	7	39	0	.219	
2009 Rochester	Int.	C	99	298	23	63	16	1	2	25	0	.211	
2010 Minnesota	A.L.	C	49	142	12	28	6	1	2	13	0	.197	

Year	Club	Lea	Pos	G	AB	R	H	2B	3B	HR	RBI	SB	Avg
2011 Minnesota	....	A.L.	C	93	234	19	39	9	1	2	23	0	.167
Major League Totals	....		2 Yrs.	142	376	31	67	15	2	4	36	0	.178

a Traded by New York Mets to Minnesota Twins with outfielder Dustin Martin for infielder Luis Castillo, July 30, 2007.

BUTLER, BILLY RAY
Born, Orange Park, Florida, April 18, 1986.
Bats Right. Throws Right. Height, 6 feet, 1 inch. Weight, 240 pounds.

Year	Club	Lea	Pos	G	AB	R	H	2B	3B	HR	RBI	SB	Avg
2004 Idaho Falls	.....	Pioneer	3B	72	260	74	97	22	3	10	68	5	.373
2005 High Desert	......	Calif.	3B-OF	92	379	70	132	30	2	25	91	0	.348
2005 Wichita	....	Texas	OF	29	112	14	35	9	0	5	19	0	.313
2006 Wichita	....	Texas	OF	119	477	82	158	33	1	15	96	1	.331
2007 Omaha	....	P.C.	OF-1B	57	203	40	59	10	1	13	46	1	.291
2007 Kansas City	....	A.L.	DH-1B-OF	92	329	38	96	23	2	8	52	0	.292
2008 Omaha	....	P.C.	1B	26	101	18	34	6	1	5	13	0	.337
2008 Kansas City	......A.L.		DH-1B	124	443	44	122	22	0	11	55	0	.275
2009 Kansas City	......A.L.		1B	159	608	78	183	51	1	21	93	1	.301
2010 Kansas City	......A.L.		1B	158	595	77	189	45	0	15	78	0	.318
2011 Kansas City	......A.L.		DH-1B	159	597	74	174	44	0	19	95	2	.291
Major League Totals	....		5 Yrs.	692	2572	311	764	185	3	74	373	3	.297

BYRD, MARLON JERRARD
Born, Boynton Beach, Florida, August 30, 1977.
Bats Right. Throws Right. Height, 6 feet. Weight, 235 pounds.

Year	Club	Lea	Pos	G	AB	R	H	2B	3B	HR	RBI	SB	Avg
1999 Batavia	....	N.Y.-Penn.	OF	65	239	39	70	7	6	13	49	8	.293
2000 Piedmont	....	So.Atl.	OF	133	515	104	159	29	13	17	93	41	.309
2001 Reading	....	Eastern	OF	137	510	108	161	22	8	28	89	32	.316
2002 Scranton-WB	....	Int.	OF	136	538	103	160	37	7	15	63	15	.297
2002 Philadelphia	....	N.L.	OF	10	35	2	8	2	0	1	1	0	.229
2003 Scranton-WB	....	Int.	OF	1	4	1	3	1	0	0	0	0	.750
2003 Reading	....	Eastern	OF	3	16	3	5	0	0	1	3	0	.313
2003 Philadelphia a	....	N.L.	OF	135	495	86	150	28	4	7	45	11	.303
2004 Scranton/WB	....	Int.	OF	37	152	13	40	11	1	2	17	2	.263
2004 Philadelphia	....	N.L.	OF	106	346	48	79	13	2	5	33	2	.228
2005 New Orleans	....	P.C.	OF	21	81	19	33	6	0	5	11	4	.407
2005 Scranton/WB	....	Int.	OF	5	19	4	7	1	0	3	5	0	.368
2005 Philadelphia-Washington b-c		N.L.	OF	79	229	20	61	15	2	2	26	5	.266
2006 New Orleans	....	P.C.	OF	46	155	20	42	9	0	7	29	3	.271
2006 Washington d	....	N.L.	OF	78	197	28	44	8	1	5	18	3	.223
2007 Oklahoma	....	P.C.	OF	44	176	29	63	15	2	6	32	3	.358
2007 Texas	....	A.L.	OF	109	414	60	127	17	8	10	70	5	.307
2008 Oklahoma	....	P.C.	OF	4	16	3	5	2	0	0	3	0	.313
2008 Texas e	....	A.L.	OF	122	403	70	120	28	4	10	53	7	.298
2009 Texas f	....	A.L.	OF	146	547	66	155	43	2	20	89	8	.283
2010 Chicago	....	N.L.	OF	152	580	84	170	39	2	12	66	5	.293
2011 Iowa	....	P.C.	OF	4	15	4	4	1	0	1	3	1	.267
2011 Chicago g	....	N.L.	OF	119	446	51	123	22	2	9	35	3	.276
Major League Totals	....		10 Yrs.	1056	3692	515	1037	215	27	81	436	49	.281

a On disabled list from April 14 to April 29, 2003.
b On disabled list from March 29 to May 3, 2005.
c Traded to Washington Nationals for outfielder Endy Chavez, May 14, 2005.
d Filed for free agency, October 2, 2006. Signed with Texas Rangers, December 8, 2006.
e On disabled list from April 17 to May 14, 2008.
f Filed for free agency, November 5, 2009. Signed with Chicago Cubs, December 31, 2009.
g On disabled list from May 22 to July 2, 2011.

CABRERA, ASDRUBAL JOSE
Born, Puerto La Cruz, Venezuela, November 13, 1985.
Bats Both. Throws Right. Height, 6 feet. Weight, 170 pounds.

Year	Club	Lea	Pos	G	AB	R	H	2B	3B	HR	RBI	SB	Avg
2004 Everett	......	Northwest	SS-2B-3B	63	239	44	65	16	3	5	41	7	.272
2005 Inland Empire	.....	Calif.	SS	55	225	31	64	15	6	1	26	3	.284
2005 Wisconsin	....	Midwest	2B-SS-3B	51	192	26	61	12	3	4	30	2	.318
2005 Tacoma	....	P.C.	SS	6	23	4	5	0	1	0	3	0	.217

Year	Club	Lea	Pos	G	AB	R	H	2B	3B	HR	RBI	SB	Avg
2006 Buffalo	Int.		SS	52	190	26	50	11	0	1	14	5	.263
2006 Tacoma a	P.C.		SS	60	203	27	48	12	2	3	22	7	.236
2007 Akron	Eastern		SS-2B	96	368	78	114	23	3	8	54	23	.310
2007 Buffalo	Int.		SS-2B	9	38	6	12	3	0	0	3	2	.316
2007 Cleveland	A.L.		2B-SS-3B	45	159	30	45	9	2	3	22	0	.283
2008 Buffalo	Int.		SS-2B	34	141	25	46	7	1	4	13	2	.326
2008 Cleveland	A.L.		2B-SS	114	352	48	91	20	0	6	47	4	.259
2009 Akron	Eastern		SS	4	16	5	4	1	0	0	0	2	.250
2009 Cleveland b	A.L.		SS-2B	131	523	81	161	42	4	6	68	17	.308
2010 Mahoning Valley N.Y.-Penn.			SS	2	6	0	2	1	0	0	2	0	.333
2010 Akron	Eastern		SS	4	14	4	5	2	0	1	1	2	.357
2010 Cleveland c	A.L.		SS	97	381	39	105	16	1	3	29	6	.276
2011 Cleveland	A.L.		SS	151	604	87	165	32	3	25	92	17	.273
Major League Totals			5 Yrs.	538	2019	285	567	119	10	43	258	44	.281
Division Series													
2007 Cleveland	A.L.		2B	4	17	3	3	0	0	1	2	0	.176
Championship Series													
2007 Cleveland	A.L.		2B	7	29	2	7	0	0	0	4	0	.241

a Traded to Cleveland Indians by Seattle Mariners for outfielder Eduardo Perez, June 30, 2006.

b On disabled list from June 3 to June 28, 2009.

c On disabled list from May 18 to July 20, 2010.

CABRERA, JOSE MIGUEL (MIGUEL)
Born, Maracay, Venezuela, April 18, 1983.
Bats Right. Throws Right. Height, 6 feet, 2 inches. Weight, 240 pounds.

Year	Club	Lea	Pos	G	AB	R	H	2B	3B	HR	RBI	SB	Avg
2000 Marlins	Gulf Coast		SS	57	219	38	57	10	2	2	22	1	.260
2000 Utica	N.Y.-Penn		SS	8	32	3	8	2	0	0	6	0	.250
2001 Kane County	Midwest		SS	110	422	61	134	19	4	7	66	3	.318
2002 Jupiter	Fla.St.		3B	124	478	77	134	43	1	9	75	10	.274
2003 Carolina	Southern		3B-OF	69	266	46	97	29	3	10	59	9	.365
2003 Florida	N.L.		OF-3B	87	314	39	84	21	3	12	62	0	.268
2004 Florida	N.L.		OF	160	603	101	177	31	1	33	112	5	.294
2005 Florida	N.L.		OF-3B	158	613	106	198	43	2	33	116	1	.323
2006 Florida	N.L.		3B	158	576	112	195	50	2	26	114	9	.339
2007 Florida a	N.L.		3B	157	588	91	188	38	2	34	119	2	.320
2008 Detroit	A.L.		1B-3B	160	616	85	180	36	2	*37	127	1	.292
2009 Detroit	A.L.		1B	160	611	96	198	34	0	34	103	6	.324
2010 Detroit	A.L.		1B	150	548	111	180	45	1	38	*126	3	.328
2011 Detroit	A.L.		1B	*161	572	111	197	*48	0	30	105	2	*.344
Major League Totals			9 Yrs.	1351	5041	852	1597	346	13	277	984	29	.317
Division Series													
2003 Florida	N.L.		3B	4	14	1	4	2	0	0	3	0	.286
2011 Detroit	A.L.		1B	5	15	2	3	0	0	1	3	1	.200
Division Series Totals				9	29	3	7	2	0	1	6	1	.241
Championship Series													
2003 Florida	N.L.	OF-3B-SS		7	30	9	10	0	0	3	6	0	.333
2011 Detroit	A.L.		1B	6	20	5	8	4	0	3	7	1	.400
Championship Series Totals				13	50	14	18	4	0	6	13	1	.360
World Series Record													
2003 Florida	N.L.		OF	6	24	1	4	0	0	1	3	0	.167

a Traded to Detroit Tigers with pitcher Dontrelle Willis for pitcher Burke Badenhop, pitcher Eulogio De La Cruz, pitcher Andrew Miller, catcher Mike Rabelo and outfielder Cameron Maybin, December 5, 2007.

CABRERA, MELKY
Born, Santo Domingo, Dominican Republic, August 11, 1984.
Bats Both. Throws Left. Height, 5 feet, 11 inches. Weight, 200 pounds.

Year	Club	Lea	Pos	G	AB	R	H	2B	3B	HR	RBI	SB	Avg
2003 Staten Island	N.Y.-Penn.		OF	67	279	34	79	10	2	2	31	13	.283
2004 Tampa	Fla.St.		OF	85	333	48	96	20	3	8	51	3	.288
2004 Battle Creek	Midwest		OF	42	171	35	57	16	3	0	16	7	.333
2005 New York	A.L.		OF	6	19	1	4	0	0	0	0	0	.211
2005 Columbus	Int.		OF	26	101	15	25	3	0	3	17	2	.248
2005 Trenton	Eastern		OF	106	426	57	117	22	3	10	60	11	.275
2006 Columbus	Int.		OF	31	122	19	47	6	2	4	24	3	.385
2006 New York	A.L.		OF	130	460	75	129	26	2	7	50	12	.280

Year	Club	Lea	Pos	G	AB	R	H	2B	3B	HR	RBI	SB	Avg
2007 New York	. . . .	A.L.	OF	150	545	66	149	24	8	8	73	13	.273
2008 Scranton-WB	. . . .	Int.	OF	15	57	8	19	2	0	0	5	1	.333
2008 New York	. . . .	A.L.	OF	129	414	42	103	12	1	8	37	9	.249
2009 New York a	. . . .	A.L.	OF	154	485	66	133	28	1	13	68	10	.274
2010 Atlanta b	. . . .	N.L.	OF	147	458	50	117	27	3	4	42	7	.255
2011 Kansas City c	. . . .	A.L.	OF	155	658	102	201	44	5	18	87	20	.305
Major League Totals	. . . .	7 Yrs.		871	3039	402	836	161	20	58	357	71	.275
Division Series													
2006 New York	. . . .	A.L.	OF	2	3	0	0	0	0	0	0	0	.000
2007 New York	. . . .	A.L.	OF	4	16	2	3	0	0	1	2	0	.188
2009 New York	. . . .	A.L.	OF	3	12	1	2	0	0	0	0	0	.167
2010 Atlanta	. . . .	N.L.	OF	3	8	1	0	0	0	0	1	0	.000
Division Series Totals	. . . .			12	39	4	5	0	0	1	3	0	.128
Championship Series													
2009 New York	. . . .	A.L.	OF	6	23	3	9	2	0	0	4	0	.391
World Series Record													
2009 New York	. . . .	A.L.	OF	4	13	1	2	0	0	0	0	0	.154

a Traded to Atlanta Braves with pitcher Arodys Vizcaino, pitcher Michael Dunn and cash for pitcher Javier Vazquez and pitcher Boone Logan, December 22, 2009.

b Released by Atlanta Braves, October 18, 2010. Signed with Kansas City Royals, December 10, 2010.

c Traded to San Francisco Giants for pitcher Jonathan Sanchez and pitcher Ryan Verdugo, November 7, 2011.

CABRERA, ORLANDO LUIS

Born, Cartagena, Colombia, November 2, 1974.
Bats Right. Throws Right. Height, 5 feet, 9 inches. Weight, 180 pounds.

Year	Club	Lea	Pos	G	AB	R	H	2B	3B	HR	RBI	SB	Avg
1994 Expos	. . . .	Gulf Coast	2B-SS-OF	22	73	13	23	4	1	0	11	6	.315
1995 Wst Plm Bch	. . . .	Fla. St.	SS	3	5	0	1	0	0	0	0	0	.200
1995 Vermont	. . . .	N.Y.-Penn.	2B-SS	65	248	37	70	12	5	3	33	15	.282
1996 Delmarva	. . . .	So. Atl.	SS-2B	134	512	86	129	28	4	14	65	51	.252
1997 Wst Plm Bch	. . . .	Fla. St.	SS-2B	69	279	56	77	19	2	5	26	32	.276
1997 Harrisburg	. . . .	Eastern	SS-2B	35	133	34	41	13	2	5	20	7	.308
1997 Ottawa	. . . .	Int.	SS-2B	31	122	17	32	5	2	2	14	8	.262
1997 Montreal	. . . .	N.L.	SS-2B	16	18	4	4	0	0	0	2	1	.222
1998 Ottawa	. . . .	Int.	SS-2B	66	272	31	63	9	4	0	26	19	.232
1998 Montreal	. . . .	N.L.	SS-2B	79	261	44	73	16	5	3	22	6	.280
1999 Montreal a	. . . .	N.L.	SS	104	382	48	97	23	5	8	39	2	.254
2000 Ottawa	. . . .	Int.	SS	2	6	1	4	0	0	0	0	1	.667
2000 Montreal b	. . . .	N.L.	SS-2B	125	422	47	100	25	1	13	55	4	.237
2001 Montreal	. . . .	N.L.	SS	*162	626	64	173	41	6	14	96	19	.276
2002 Montreal	. . . .	N.L.	SS	153	563	64	148	43	1	7	56	25	.263
2003 Montreal	. . . .	N.L.	SS	*162	626	95	186	47	2	17	80	24	.297
2004 Montreal	. . . .	N.L.	SS	103	390	41	96	19	2	4	31	12	.246
2004 Boston c-d-e	. . . . . .	A.L.	SS	58	228	33	67	19	1	6	31	4	.294
2005 Los Angeles f	. . . .	A.L.	SS	141	540	70	139	28	3	8	57	21	.257
2006 Los Angeles	. . . .	A.L.	SS	153	607	95	171	45	1	9	72	27	.282
2007 Los Angeles g	. . . .	A.L.	SS	155	638	101	192	35	1	8	86	20	.301
2008 Chicago h	. . . .	A.L.	SS	161	661	93	186	33	1	8	57	19	.281
2009 Oakland-Minnesota i-j	. .	A.L.	SS	160	656	83	186	36	3	9	77	13	.284
2010 Dayton	. . . .	Midwest	SS	1	3	0	0	0	0	0	0	0	.000
2010 Cincinnati k-l	. . . . . .	N.L.	SS	123	494	64	130	33	0	4	42	11	.263
2011 Cleveland	. . . .	A.L.	2B-3B-SS	91	324	35	79	13	0	4	38	6	.244
2011 San Francisco m-n	. . . .	N.L.	SS-2B-3B	39	126	4	28	3	0	1	13	2	.222
Major League Totals	. . . .	15 Yrs.		1985	7562	985	2055	459	32	123	854	216	.272
Division Series													
2004 Boston	. . . .	A.L.	SS	3	13	1	2	1	0	0	3	0	.154
2005 Los Angeles	. . . .	A.L.	SS	5	21	3	5	2	0	0	3	0	.238
2007 Los Angeles	. . . .	A.L.	SS	3	12	0	3	1	0	0	1	0	.250
2008 Chicago	. . . .	A.L.	SS	4	16	1	2	0	0	0	0	0	.125
2009 Minnesota	. . . .	A.L.	SS	3	13	1	2	0	0	0	0	1	.154
2010 Cincinnati	. . . .	N.L.	SS	3	8	0	1	0	0	0	0	0	.125
Division Series Totals	. . . .			21	83	6	15	4	0	0	7	1	.181
Championship Series													
2004 Boston	. . . .	A.L.	SS	7	29	5	11	2	0	0	5	1	.379
2005 Los Angeles	. . . .	A.L.	SS	5	20	1	4	1	0	1	3	0	.200
Championship Series Totals	. . . . . .			12	49	6	15	3	0	1	8	1	.306
World Series Record													
2004 Boston	. . . .	A.L.	SS	4	17	3	4	1	0	0	3	0	.235

a On disabled list from August 9 to October 13, 1999.
b On disabled list from July 15 to August 14, 2000.
c Traded to Chicago Cubs for infielder Alex Gonzalez, infielder Brendan Harris and pitcher Francis Beltran, July 31, 2004.
d Traded to Boston Red Sox with infielder Doug Mientkiewicz for infielder Nomar Garciaparra and outfielder Matt Murton, July 31, 2004.
e Filed for free agency, November 1, 2004. Signed with Anaheim Angels, December 20, 2004.
f On disabled list from June 27 to July 16, 2005.
g Traded to Chicago White Sox for pitcher Jon Garland, November 19, 2007.
h Filed for free agency, November 1, 2008. Signed with Oakland Athletics, March 6, 2009.
i Traded to Minnesota Twins with cash for infielder Tyler Ladendorf, July 31, 2009.
j Filed for free agency, November 9, 2009. Signed with Cincinnati Reds, February 1, 2010.
k On disabled list from August 3 to September 3, 2010.
l Filed for free agency, November 3, 2010. Signed with Cleveland Indians, February 16, 2011.
m Traded to San Francisco Giants for outfielder Thomas Neal, July 31, 2011.
n Filed for free agency, October 30, 2011.

CAIN, LORENZO LAMAR

Born, Valdosta, Georgia, April 13, 1986.
Bats Right. Throws Right. Height, 6 feet, 2 inches. Weight, 200 pounds.

Year	Club	Lea	Pos	G	AB	R	H	2B	3B	HR	RBI	SB	Avg
2005 Brewers	Arizona	OF	50	205	45	73	18	5	5	37	12	.356
2005 Helena	Pioneer	OF	6	24	4	5	0	0	0	1	0	.208
2006 West Tenn	So.Atl.	OF	132	527	91	162	36	4	6	60	34	.307
2007 Brevard County	Fla.St.	OF	126	482	67	133	21	3	2	44	24	.276
2008 Brevard County	Fla.St.	OF	80	317	50	91	22	4	7	41	19	.287
2008 Nashville	P.C.	OF	6	19	0	3	0	0	0	2	0	.158
2008 Huntsville	Southern	OF	40	148	21	41	9	5	4	17	6	.277
2009 Brewers	Arizona	OF	3	9	1	4	1	0	0	1	0	.444
2009 Wisconsin	Midwest	OF	15	52	3	10	4	0	0	3	0	.192
2009 Huntsville	Southern	OF	42	145	17	31	6	0	4	15	3	.214
2010 Huntsville	Southern	OF	62	244	45	79	6	6	3	18	21	.324
2010 Nashville	P.C.	OF	22	87	13	26	5	3	0	9	5	.299
2010 Milwaukee a	N.L.	OF	43	147	17	45	11	1	1	13	7	.306
2011 Omaha	P.C.	OF	128	487	84	152	28	7	16	81	16	.312
2011 Kansas City	A.L.	OF	6	22	4	6	1	0	0	1	0	.273
Major League Totals			2 Yrs.	49	169	21	51	12	1	1	14	7	.302

a Traded to Kansas City Royals with infielder Alcides Escobar, pitcher Jeremy Jeffress and pitcher Jake Odorizzi for outfielder Yuniesky Betancourt and pitcher Zack Greinke, December 19, 2010.

CAIRO, MIGUEL JESUS

Born, Anaco, Venezuela, May 4, 1974.
Bats Right. Throws Right. Height, 6 feet, 1 inch. Weight, 225 pounds.

Year	Club	Lea	Pos	G	AB	R	H	2B	3B	HR	RBI	SB	Avg
1992 Dodgers	Gulf Coast	SS-3B	21	76	10	23	5	2	0	9	1	.303
1992 Vero Beach	Fla.St.	2B-SS	36	125	7	28	0	0	0	7	5	.224
1993 Vero Beach	Fla.St.	2B-SS-3B	90	346	50	109	10	1	1	23	23	.315
1994 Bakersfield	Calif.	2B-SS	133	533	76	155	23	4	2	48	44	.291
1995 San Antonio a	Texas	2B-SS	107	435	53	121	20	1	1	41	33	.278
1996 Syracuse	Int.	2B-3B-SS	120	465	71	129	14	4	3	48	27	.277
1996 Toronto b	A.L.	2B	9	27	5	6	2	0	0	1	0	.222
1997 Iowa	A.A.	2B-SS	135	569	82	159	35	4	5	46	40	.279
1997 Chicago c	N.L.	2B-SS	16	29	7	7	1	0	0	1	0	.241
1998 Tampa Bay	A.L.	2B	150	515	49	138	26	5	5	46	19	.268
1999 Tampa Bay	A.L.	2B	120	465	61	137	15	5	3	36	22	.295
1999 Orlando	Southern	2B	3	13	1	5	2	0	0	1	0	.385
1999 St. Petersburg d	Fla.St.	2B	3	13	2	5	0	0	0	0	1	.385
2000 Tampa Bay	A.L.	2B	119	375	49	98	18	2	1	34	28	.261
2001 Iowa	P.C.	2B-SS-3B	34	123	22	37	7	1	3	14	3	.301
2001 Chicago-St. Louis e-f-g	N.L.	3B-2B-OF-SS	93	156	25	46	8	1	3	16	2	.295
2002 St. Louis	N.L.	OF-2B-3B-SS	108	184	28	46	9	2	2	23	1	.250
2003 Memphis	P.C.	2B	3	13	2	3	1	0	0	0	0	.231
2003 St. Louis h-i	N.L.	2B-OF-3B-SS	92	261	41	64	15	2	5	32	4	.245
2004 New York	A.L.	2B-3B-SS-1B	122	360	48	105	17	5	6	42	11	.292
2005 St. Lucie	Fla.St.	DH	1	4	0	1	0	0	0	0	0	.250
2005 Mets	Gulf Coast	2B	3	13	3	4	0	0	0	0	0	.308
2005 New York j-k	N.L.	2B-1B-3B-OF	100	327	31	82	18	0	2	19	13	.251
2006 New York l-m	A.L.	2B-1B-SS-3B	81	222	28	53	12	3	0	30	13	.239
2007 New York	A.L.	1B-SS-3B-2B	54	107	12	27	7	0	0	10	8	.252

27

Year Club	Lea	Pos	G	AB	R	H	2B	3B	HR	RBI	SB	Avg
2007 Memphis	P.C.	3B-SS-OF-1B	9	31	8	9	2	0	0	3	2	.290
2007 St. Louis n-o	N.L.	3B-2B-1B-OF	28	67	8	17	2	2	0	5	2	.254
2008 Seattle p.	A.L.	1B-3B-2B-OF	108	221	34	55	14	2	0	23	5	.249
2009 Lehigh Valley	Int.	SS-2B-3B-1B	78	296	44	85	12	2	5	33	8	.287
2009 Philadelphia q-r . . .	N.L.	2B-SS-3B	27	45	6	12	2	1	1	2	0	.267
2010 Cincinnati s	N.L.	3B-1B-2B-SS	91	200	30	58	12	0	4	28	4	.290
2011 Cincinnati	N.L.	3B-2B-1B	102	245	33	65	8	2	8	33	3	.265
Major League Totals		16 Yrs.	1420	3806	495	1016	186	32	40	381	135	.267
Division Series												
2001 St. Louis.	N.L.	OF	3	5	0	1	0	0	0	0	1	.200
2002 St. Louis.	N.L.	3B	2	4	2	4	1	0	0	3	0	1.000
2004 New York	A.L.	2B	4	14	3	3	1	0	0	1	0	.214
2009 Philadelphia	N.L.	OF-3B	2	3	0	0	0	0	0	0	0	.000
2010 Cincinnati	N.L.	PH	3	3	0	0	0	0	0	0	0	.000
Division Series Totals			14	29	5	8	2	0	0	4	1	.276
Championship Series												
2002 St. Louis.	N.L.	3B	3	13	2	5	0	0	1	2	0	.385
2004 New York	A.L.	2B	7	25	4	7	3	0	0	0	1	.280
2009 Philadelphia	N.L.	PH	2	2	0	0	0	0	0	0	0	.000
Championship Series Totals			12	40	6	12	3	0	1	2	1	.300

a Traded to Toronto Blue Jays with pitcher Bill Risley for pitcher Edwin Hurtado and pitcher Paul Menhart, December 18, 1995.
b Traded to Chicago Cubs for pitcher Jason Stevenson, November 20, 1996.
c Selected by Tampa Bay Devil Rays in expansion draft. November 18, 1997.
d On disabled list from April 24 to May 17 and July 26 to August 11, 1999.
e Released by Tampa Bay Devil Rays, November 27, 2000. Signed with Oakland Athletics organization, January 11, 2001.
f Traded to Chicago Cubs with pitcher Scott Chiasson for infielder Eric Hinske, March 28, 2001.
g Claimed on waivers by St. Louis Cardinals, August 10, 2001.
h On disabled list from June 19 to July 29, 2003.
i Filed for free agency, October 26, 2003. Signed with New York Yankees, December 19, 2003.
j Filed for free agency, October 28, 2004. Signed with New York Mets, January 10, 2005.
k On disabled list from June 15 to July 2, 2005.
l Filed for free agency, October 28, 2005. Signed with New York Yankees, January 5, 2006.
m On disabled list from August 6 to September 11, 2006.
n Filed for free agency, October 28, 2006, re-signed with New York Yankees, January 26, 2007.
o Released by New York Yankees, August 15, 2007. Signed with St. Louis Cardinals organization, August 19, 2007.
p Filed for free agency, October 29, 2007. Signed with Seattle Mariners organization, January 8, 2008.
q Filed for free agency, October 30, 2008. Signed with Philadelphia Phillies organization, February 15, 2009.
r Filed for free agency, November 6, 2009. Signed with Cincinnati Reds organization, January 27, 2010.
s Filed for free agency, November 1, 2010. Signed with Cincinnati Reds, December 8, 2010.

CALLASPO, ALBERTO JOSE
Born, Maracay, Venezuela, April 19, 1983.
Bats Both. Throws Right. Height, 5 feet, 10 inches. Weight, 180 pounds.

Year Club	Lea	Pos	G	AB	R	H	2B	3B	HR	RBI	SB	Avg
2002 Provo	Pioneer	2B-SS	70	299	70	101	16	10	3	60	13	.338
2003 Cedar Rapids . .	Midwest	2B-SS	133	514	86	168	38	4	2	67	20	.327
2004 Arkansas	Texas	SS-2B	136	550	76	156	29	2	6	48	15	.284
2005 Salt Lake	P.C.	2B	50	212	28	67	21	2	1	31	2	.316
2005 Arkansas	Texas	2B	89	350	53	104	8	0	10	49	9	.297
2006 Tucson	P.C.	2B-SS-3B-OF	114	490	93	165	24	12	7	68	8	.337
2006 Arizona a	N.L.	SS-2B-3B	23	42	2	10	1	1	0	6	0	.238
2007 Tucson	P.C.	SS-2B-3B	59	226	48	77	15	2	5	30	1	.341
2007 Arizona b	N.L.	3B-2B-OF-SS	56	144	10	31	8	0	0	7	1	.215
2008 Omaha	P.C.	2B	4	16	5	3	0	0	0	0	0	.188
2008 Kansas City c	A.L.	2B-SS-OF	74	213	21	65	8	3	0	16	2	.305
2009 Kansas City	A.L.	2B-3B-SS	155	576	79	173	41	8	11	73	2	.300
2010 Kansas City-LA d . .	A.L.	3B-2B-OF	146	562	61	149	27	2	10	56	5	.265
2011 Los Angeles	A.L.	3B	141	475	54	137	23	0	6	46	8	.288
Major League Totals		6 Yrs.	595	2012	227	565	108	14	27	204	18	.281
Championship Series												
2007 Arizona.	N.L.	PH	2	2	0	0	0	0	0	0	0	.000

a Traded by Los Angeles Angels to Arizona Diamondbacks for pitcher Jason Bulger, February 28, 2006.
b Traded to Kansas City Royals for pitcher Billy Buckner, December 14, 2007.
c On disabled list from June 28 to August 23, 2008.
d Traded to Anaheim Angels for pitcher Sean O'Sullivan and pitcher Will Smith, July 22, 2010.

CAMPANA, ANTHONY EDWARD (TONY)
Born, Kettering, Ohio, May 30, 1986.
Bats Left. Throws Left. Height, 5 feet, 8 inches. Weight, 165 pounds.

Year	Club	Lea	Pos	G	AB	R	H	2B	3B	HR	RBI	SB	Avg
2008	Cubs.............	Arizona	OF	24	83	17	23	0	0	0	10	22	.277
2008	Boise..........	Northwest	OF	1	3	0	0	0	0	0	0	0	.000
2009	Daytona...........	Fla.St.	OF	108	430	56	122	8	2	0	25	55	.284
2009	Peoria............	Midwest	OF	18	53	14	15	1	1	0	5	11	.283
2010	Tennessee	Southern	OF	131	489	76	156	22	5	0	39	48	.319
2011	Iowa................	P.C.	OF	30	120	27	41	8	2	0	9	8	.342
2011	Chicago	N.L.	OF	95	143	24	37	3	0	1	6	24	.259

CANO (MERCEDES), ROBINSON JOSE
Born, San Pedro de Macoris, Dominican Republic, October 22, 1982.
Bats Left. Throws Right. Height, 6 feet. Weight, 200 pounds.

Year	Club	Lea	Pos	G	AB	R	H	2B	3B	HR	RBI	SB	Avg
2001	Yankees........	Gulf Coast	2B-SS-3B	57	200	37	46	14	2	3	34	11	.230
2001	Staten Island	N.Y.-Penn.	3B-SS	2	8	0	2	0	0	0	2	0	.250
2002	Staten Island	N.Y.-Penn.	2B-SS	22	87	11	24	5	1	1	15	6	.276
2002	Greensboro.......	So.Atl.	SS-2B	113	474	67	131	20	9	14	66	2	.276
2003	Trenton...........	Eastern	2B-SS-C	46	164	21	46	9	1	1	13	0	.280
2003	Tampa	Fla.St.	2B	90	366	50	101	16	3	5	50	1	.276
2004	Trenton...........	Eastern	2B-3B	74	292	43	88	20	8	7	44	2	.301
2004	Columbus...........	Int.	2B	61	216	22	56	9	2	6	30	0	.259
2005	Columbus...........	Int.	2B-3B	24	108	19	36	8	3	4	24	0	.333
2005	New York...........	A.L.	2B	132	522	78	155	34	4	14	62	1	.297
2006	Yankees	Gulf Coast	DH	1	5	0	2	0	0	0	1	0	.400
2006	Trenton...........	Eastern	2B	3	10	1	5	2	0	0	2	0	.500
2006	New York a.........	A.L.	2B	122	482	62	165	41	1	15	78	5	.342
2007	New York	A.L.	2B	160	617	93	189	41	7	19	97	4	.306
2008	New York	A.L.	2B	159	597	70	162	35	3	14	72	2	.271
2009	New York	A.L.	2B	*161	637	103	204	48	2	25	85	5	.320
2010	New York	A.L.	2B	160	626	103	200	41	3	29	109	3	.319
2011	New York	A.L.	2B	159	623	104	188	46	7	28	118	8	.302
Major League Totals			7 Yrs.	1053	4104	613	1263	286	27	144	621	28	.308

Division Series

Year	Club	Lea	Pos	G	AB	R	H	2B	3B	HR	RBI	SB	Avg
2005	New York	A.L.	2B	5	19	3	5	3	0	0	5	0	.263
2006	New York	A.L.	2B	4	15	0	2	0	0	0	0	0	.133
2007	New York	A.L.	2B	4	15	3	5	1	0	2	3	0	.333
2009	New York	A.L.	2B	3	12	1	2	0	0	0	1	0	.167
2010	New York	A.L.	2B	3	12	3	4	0	1	0	1	0	.333
2011	New York	A.L.	2B	5	22	2	7	2	0	2	9	0	.318
Division Series Totals				24	95	12	25	6	1	4	19	0	.263

Championship Series

Year	Club	Lea	Pos	G	AB	R	H	2B	3B	HR	RBI	SB	Avg
2009	New York	A.L.	2B	6	23	4	6	1	2	0	4	0	.261
2010	New York	A.L.	2B	6	23	5	8	1	0	4	5	0	.348
Championship Series Totals				12	46	9	14	2	2	4	9	0	.304

World Series Record

Year	Club	Lea	Pos	G	AB	R	H	2B	3B	HR	RBI	SB	Avg
2009	New York	A.L.	2B	6	22	0	3	0	0	0	1	0	.136

a On disabled list from June 26 to August 8, 2006.

CANZLER, RUSSELL MICHAEL (RUSS)
Born, Berwick, Pennsylvania, April 11, 1986.
Bats Right. Throws Right. Height, 6 feet, 2 inches. Weight, 220 pounds.

Year	Club	Lea	Pos	G	AB	R	H	2B	3B	HR	RBI	SB	Avg
2004	Cubs..........	Arizona	3B	32	105	12	26	2	3	1	13	0	.248
2005	Cubs..........	Arizona	1B	49	157	22	47	11	3	1	20	1	.299
2006	Boise	Northwest	1B	73	280	49	74	22	4	16	61	7	.264
2007	Peoria........	Midwest	1B-OF	125	460	60	124	24	2	7	54	12	.270
2008	Daytona	Fla.St.	1B-OF	98	326	47	89	22	2	12	59	7	.273
2009	Daytona	Fla.St.	1B-OF-3B	28	100	14	27	8	1	2	14	2	.270
2009	Tennessee	Southern	1B-OF-3B	90	233	27	60	15	0	6	35	2	.258
2010	Tennessee a ...	Southern	3B-1B-OF	112	355	68	102	28	4	21	66	5	.287
2011	Durham	Int.	OF-3B-1B	131	474	78	149	40	4	18	83	5	.314
2011	Tampa Bay	A.L.	DH	3	3	0	1	0	0	0	1	0	.333

a Filed for free agency from Chicago Cubs, November 6, 2010. Signed with Tampa Bay Rays organization, November 19, 2010.

CARP, CHRISTOPHER MICHAEL (MIKE)
Born, Long Beach, California, June 30, 1986.
Bats Left. Throws Right. Height, 6 feet, 2 inches. Weight, 210 pounds.

Year	Club	Lea	Pos	G	AB	R	H	2B	3B	HR	RBI	SB	Avg
2004 Mets	Gulf Coast	1B-3B-OF	57	191	30	51	12	0	4	26	2	.267
2005 Hagerstown	So.Atl.	1B-3B	89	313	49	78	12	1	19	63	2	.249
2006 St. Lucie	Fla.St.	1B	137	491	69	141	27	1	17	88	2	.287
2007 Binghamton	Eastern	1B	97	359	55	90	16	0	11	48	2	.251
2007 St. Lucie	Fla.St.	1B	1	4	0	1	0	0	0	0	0	.250
2008 Binghamton a	Eastern	1B-OF	134	478	67	143	29	1	17	72	1	.299
2009 Tacoma	P.C.	1B-OF	110	413	66	112	25	1	15	64	0	.271
2009 Seattle	A.L.	1B	21	54	7	17	3	1	1	5	0	.315
2010 Tacoma	P.C.	1B-OF	110	409	67	105	17	1	29	76	1	.257
2010 Seattle	A.L.	1B-OF	14	37	1	7	2	0	0	0	0	.189
2011 Tacoma	P.C.	OF-1B	66	251	55	86	14	0	21	64	6	.343
2011 Seattle	A.L.	1B-OF	79	290	27	80	17	1	12	46	0	.276
Major League Totals		3 Yrs.	114	381	35	104	22	2	13	51	0	.273

a Traded by New York Mets to Seattle Mariners with pitcher Aaron Heilman, outfielder Endy Chavez, pitcher Jason Vargas, outfielder Ezequiel Carrera, pitcher Maikel Cleto and pitcher Joe Smith for pitcher J.J. Putz, pitcher Sean Green and outfielder Jeremy Reed, December 10, 2008.

CARRERA (REYES), EZEQUIEL MANUEL
Born, Guiria, Venezuela, June 11, 1987.
Bats Left. Throws Left. Height, 5 feet, 10 inches. Weight, 185 pounds.

Year	Club	Lea	Pos	G	AB	R	H	2B	3B	HR	RBI	SB	Avg
2007 Mets	Gulf Coast	OF	45	179	41	61	8	3	1	26	16	.341
2007 Brooklyn	N.Y.-Penn.	OF	20	70	11	21	2	0	0	6	6	.300
2008 St. Lucie a	Fla.St.	OF	114	430	61	113	11	12	7	29	28	.263
2009 West Tenn	Southern	OF	91	329	68	111	12	4	2	38	27	.337
2010 Columbus	Int.	OF	41	161	19	46	7	3	1	16	11	.286
2010 Tacoma	P.C.	OF	64	213	24	57	6	2	0	18	9	.268
2010 Indians b	Arizona	OF	4	14	2	6	1	0	0	4	0	.429
2011 Columbus	Int.	OF	82	328	63	94	8	3	2	25	35	.287
2011 Cleveland	A.L.	OF	68	202	27	49	8	3	0	14	10	.243

a Traded by New York Mets to Seattle Mariners with pitcher Aaron Heilman, outfielder Endy Chavez, pitcher Jason Vargas, infielder Mike Carp, pitcher Maikel Cleto and pitcher Joe Smith for pitcher J.J. Putz, pitcher Sean Green and outfielder Jeremy Reed, December 10, 2008.

b Traded to Cleveland Indians with infielder Juan Diaz for infielder Russell Branyan, June 26, 2010.

CARROLL, JAMEY BLAKE
Born, Evansville, Indiana, February 18, 1974.
Bats Right. Throws Right. Height, 5 feet, 9 inches. Weight, 170 pounds.

Year	Club	Lea	Pos	G	AB	R	H	2B	3B	HR	RBI	SB	Avg
1996 Vermont	N.Y.-Penn.	SS-2B-3B	54	203	40	56	6	1	0	17	16	.276
1997 Wst Plm Bch	Fla.St.	SS-2B-3B	121	407	56	99	19	1	0	38	17	.243
1998 Jupiter	Fla.St.	2B-SS	55	222	40	58	5	0	0	14	11	.261
1998 Harrisburg	Eastern	2B-SS	75	261	43	66	11	3	0	20	11	.253
1999 Harrisburg	Eastern	2B	141	561	78	164	34	5	5	63	21	.292
2000 Harrisburg	Eastern	3B-SS-2B	45	169	23	49	5	3	0	18	8	.290
2000 Ottawa	Int.	2B-3B-SS	91	349	53	97	17	2	2	23	6	.278
2001 Ottawa	Int.	2B-SS-3B	83	267	26	64	8	2	0	16	5	.240
2002 Harrisburg	Eastern	2B	3	9	1	4	0	0	0	1	0	.444
2002 Ottawa	Int.	3B-2B-SS	117	421	57	118	19	2	8	49	6	.280
2002 Montreal	N.L.	3B-SS-2B	16	71	16	22	5	3	1	6	1	.310
2003 Montreal	N.L.	3B-SS-2B	105	227	31	59	10	1	1	10	5	.260
2004 Montreal	N.L.	2B-3B-SS-OF	102	218	36	63	14	2	0	16	5	.289
2005 Washington	N.L.	2B-SS-3B	113	303	44	76	8	1	0	22	3	.251
2006 Colorado a	N.L.	2B-SS-3B	136	463	84	139	23	5	5	36	10	.300
2007 Colorado b	N.L.	2B-3B-SS-OF	108	227	45	51	9	1	2	22	6	.225
2008 Cleveland	A.L.	2B-3B-OF	113	347	60	96	13	4	1	36	7	.277
2009 Columbus	Int.	2B-3B	3	11	2	3	1	0	0	0	0	.273
2009 Cleveland c-d	A.L.	2B-3B-OF	93	315	53	87	10	2	2	26	4	.276
2010 Los Angeles	N.L.	SS-2B-3B-OF	133	351	48	102	15	1	0	23	12	.291
2011 Los Angeles e	N.L.	2B-SS	146	452	52	131	14	6	0	17	10	.290
Major League Totals		10 Yrs.	1065	2974	469	826	121	26	12	214	63	.278
Division Series												
2007 Colorado	N.L.	2B	1	0	0	0	0	0	0	0	0	.000
Championship Series												
2007 Colorado	N.L.	3B	2	1	0	0	0	0	0	0	0	.000

Year	Club	Lea	Pos	G	AB	R	H	2B	3B	HR	RBI	SB	Avg
	World Series Record												
2007	Colorado .........N.L.		2B	1	1	0	0	0	0	0	0	0	.000

a Sold to Colorado Rockies, February 11, 2006.
b Traded to Cleveland Indians for player to be named later, December 8, 2007. Colorado Rockies received pitcher Sean Smith to complete trade, April 22, 2008
c On disabled list from April 5 to May 12, 2009.
d Filed for free agency, November 5, 2009. Signed with Los Angeles Dodgers, December 16, 2009.
e Filed for free agency, October 30, 2011. Signed with Minnesota Twins, November 16, 2011.

CASILLA (LORA), ALEXI

Born, San Cristobal, Dominican Republic, July 20, 1984.
Bats Both. Throws Right. Height, 5 feet, 9 inches. Weight, 180 pounds.

Year	Club	Lea	Pos	G	AB	R	H	2B	3B	HR	RBI	SB	Avg
2004	Angels	Arizona	2B-SS	45	163	29	42	1	4	0	10	24	.258
2004	Cedar Rapids ..	Midwest	2B	9	29	6	9	2	1	0	1	1	.310
2004	Provo	Pioneer	2B-3B	4	12	4	4	1	1	0	1	1	.333
2005	Cedar Rapids ..	Midwest	SS-2B	78	308	62	100	11	3	3	17	47	.325
2005	Salt Lake	P.C.	2B-SS	13	39	3	10	0	0	0	1	1	.256
2005	Arkansas a	Texas	SS-2B	7	19	4	4	0	0	0	4	1	.211
2006	Fort Myers	Fla.St.	2B-SS	78	323	56	107	12	6	0	33	31	.331
2006	New Britain	Eastern	SS	45	170	28	50	10	1	1	13	19	.294
2006	Minnesota	A.L.	2B-SS	9	4	1	1	0	0	0	0	0	.250
2007	Rochester........	Int.	2B-SS	84	320	53	86	13	1	3	20	24	.269
2007	Minnesota	A.L.	2B-SS	56	189	15	42	5	1	0	9	11	.222
2008	Beloit	Midwest	2B	2	7	2	4	0	0	0	1	0	.571
2008	Rochester........	Int.	SS-2B	32	96	11	21	3	0	0	2	4	.219
2008	Minnesota b.....	A.L.	2B-SS	98	385	58	108	15	0	7	50	7	.281
2009	Rochester........	Int.	2B	40	156	21	53	3	4	2	17	9	.340
2009	Minnesota	A.L.	2B-SS	80	228	25	46	7	3	0	17	11	.202
2010	Twins	Gulf Coast	2B	5	14	1	2	1	0	0	0	0	.143
2010	Fort Myers	Fla.St.	2B-SS	3	12	0	2	0	0	0	1	1	.167
2010	New Britain	Eastern	2B-SS	6	20	1	7	0	0	0	0	1	.350
2010	Minnesota c.....	A.L.	SS-2B-3B-OF	69	152	26	42	7	4	1	20	6	.276
2011	Fort Myers	Fla.St.	2B	1	2	0	0	0	0	0	0	0	.000
2011	Minnesota d.....	A.L.	2B-SS	97	323	52	84	21	4	2	21	15	.260
Major League Totals		6 Yrs.		409	1281	177	323	55	12	10	117	50	.252

a Traded to Minnesota Twins for pitcher J.C. Romero, December 9, 2005.
b On disabled list from July 29 to August 21, 2008.
c On disabled list from June 1 to July 22, 2010.
d On disabled list from July 28 to August 12 and August 13 to October 14, 2011.

CASTRO, STARLIN DE JESUS

Born, Monte Cristi, Dominican Republic, March 24, 1990.
Bats Right. Throws Right. Height, 6 feet. Weight, 190 pounds.

Year	Club	Lea	Pos	G	AB	R	H	2B	3B	HR	RBI	SB	Avg
2008	Cubs..........	Arizona	SS-2B-3B-OF	51	196	33	61	11	5	3	22	6	.311
2009	Daytona	Fla.St.	SS	96	358	45	108	17	3	3	35	22	.302
2009	Tennessee	Southern	SS	31	111	11	32	6	3	0	14	6	.288
2010	Tennessee	Southern	SS	26	109	20	41	8	5	1	20	4	.376
2010	Chicago	N.L.	SS	125	463	53	139	31	5	3	41	10	.300
2011	Chicago	N.L.	SS	158	*674	91	*207	36	9	10	66	22	.307
Major League Totals		2 Yrs.		283	1137	144	346	67	14	13	107	32	.304

CEDENO, RONNY ALEXANDER

Born, Puerto Cabello, Venezuela, February 2, 1983.
Bats Right. Throws Right. Height, 6 feet. Weight, 180 pounds.

Year	Club	Lea	Pos	G	AB	R	H	2B	3B	HR	RBI	SB	Avg
2001	Cubs	Arizona	SS-2B-OF	52	206	36	72	13	4	1	17	17	.350
2001	Lansing	Midwest	2B-SS-3B	17	56	9	11	4	1	1	2	0	.196
2002	Lansing	Midwest	SS-2B	98	376	44	80	17	4	2	31	14	.213
2002	Boise	Northwest	SS-2B	29	110	17	24	5	2	0	6	8	.218
2003	Daytona	Fla.St.	SS-2B	107	380	43	80	18	1	4	36	19	.211
2004	West Tenn	Southern	SS	116	384	39	107	19	5	6	48	10	.279
2005	Iowa...........	P.C.	SS	65	245	42	87	14	1	8	36	11	.355
2005	Chicago	N.L.	SS-2B	41	80	13	24	3	0	1	6	1	.300
2006	Chicago	N.L.	SS-2B	151	534	51	131	18	7	6	41	8	.245

Year	Club	Lea	Pos	G	AB	R	H	2B	3B	HR	RBI	SB	Avg
2007	Iowa.............	P.C.	SS	75	287	52	103	15	3	10	37	6	.359
2007	Chicago	N.L.	SS-2B-3B	38	74	6	15	2	0	4	13	2	.203
2008	Chicago	N.L.	2B-SS-3B-OF	99	216	36	58	12	0	2	28	4	.269
2009	Seattle	A.L.	SS-2B-OF-3B	59	186	15	31	4	2	5	17	3	.167
2009	Pittsburgh a-b	N.L.	SS	46	155	17	40	4	1	5	21	2	.258
2010	Pittsburgh	N.L.	SS	139	468	42	120	29	3	8	38	12	.256
2011	Indianapolis	Int.	SS	4	15	2	4	1	1	0	1	0	.267
2011	Pittsburgh c-d	N.L.	SS-2B	128	413	43	103	25	3	2	32	2	.249
Major League Totals			7 Yrs.	701	2126	223	522	97	16	33	196	34	.246
Division Series													
2007	Chicago	N.L.	PH	2	0	0	0	0	0	0	0	0	.000
2008	Chicago	N.L.	PH	1	0	0	0	0	0	0	0	1	.000
Division Series Totals				3	0	0	0	0	0	0	0	1	.000

a Traded to Seattle Mariners with pitcher Garrett Olson for pitcher Aaron Heilman, January 28, 2009.

b Traded to Pittsburgh Pirates with outfielder Jeff Clement, pitcher Aaron Pribanic, pitcher Brett Lorin and pitcher Nathan Adcock for infielder Jack Wilson and pitcher Ian Snell, July 29, 2009.

c On disabled list from July 2 to July 22, 2011.

d Filed for free agency, October 31, 2011. Signed with New York Mets, January 10, 2012.

CERVELLI, FRANCISCO

Born, Valencia, Venezuela, March 6, 1986.
Bats Right. Throws Right. Height, 6 feet, 1 inch. Weight, 210 pounds.

Year	Club	Lea	Pos	G	AB	R	H	2B	3B	HR	RBI	SB	Avg
2005	Yankees	Gulf Coast	C-OF	24	58	10	11	2	0	1	9	1	.190
2006	Staten Island	N.Y.-Penn.	C	42	136	21	42	10	0	2	16	0	.309
2007	Tampa	Fla.St.	C	89	290	34	81	24	2	2	32	4	.279
2008	Tampa	Fla.St.	C	3	10	2	3	0	0	0	1	0	.300
2008	Yankees	Gulf Coast	C	3	8	0	2	1	0	0	0	0	.250
2008	Trenton	Eastern	C	21	73	8	23	5	0	0	8	0	.315
2008	New York	A.L.	C	3	5	0	0	0	0	0	0	0	.000
2009	Trenton	Eastern	C	16	58	8	11	1	0	2	7	0	.190
2009	Yankees	Gulf Coast	C	2	6	1	1	0	0	0	0	0	.167
2009	Scranton/WB	Int.	C	21	69	7	19	5	0	1	7	0	.275
2009	New York	A.L.	C	42	94	13	28	4	0	1	11	0	.298
2010	New York	A.L.	C-3B	93	266	27	72	11	3	0	38	1	.271
2011	Tampa	Fla.St.	C	3	10	0	3	0	0	0	1	0	.300
2011	Scranton-WB	Int.	C	3	13	2	2	0	0	0	1	0	.154
2011	New York a......	A.L.	C-3B-2B	43	124	17	33	4	0	4	22	4	.266
Major League Totals			4 Yrs.	181	489	57	133	19	3	5	71	5	.272
Division Series													
2009	New York	A.L.	C	1	0	0	0	0	0	0	0	0	.000
Championship Series													
2009	New York	A.L.	PH	1	1	0	0	0	0	0	0	0	.000
2010	New York	A.L.	C	1	2	0	0	0	0	0	0	0	.000
Championship Series Totals				2	3	0	0	0	0	0	0	0	.000

a On disabled list from March 22 to April 29 and September 13 to October 11, 2011.

CHAVEZ, ENDY DE JESUS

Born, Valencia, Venezuela, February 7, 1978.
Bats Left. Throws Left. Height, 6 feet. Weight, 170 pounds.

Year	Club	Lea	Pos	G	AB	R	H	2B	3B	HR	RBI	SB	Avg
1997	Mets..........	Gulf Coast	OF	33	119	26	33	6	3	0	15	1	.277
1997	Kingsport..........	Appal.	OF	19	73	16	22	4	0	0	4	5	.301
1998	Kingsport..........	Appal.	OF	33	114	26	33	8	4	0	16	10	.289
1999	St. Lucie..........	Fla.St.	OF	45	183	33	57	8	3	2	18	9	.311
1999	Columbia	So.Atl.	OF	73	253	40	64	8	1	0	15	20	.253
2000	St. Lucie a	Fla.St.	OF	111	433	84	129	20	2	1	43	38	.298
2001	Wichita	Texas	OF	43	168	27	50	6	1	1	13	11	.298
2001	Kansas City	A.L.	OF	29	77	4	16	2	0	0	5	0	.208
2001	Omaha b-c.........	P.C.	OF	23	104	18	35	6	0	0	4	4	.337
2002	Ottawa	Int.	OF	103	405	67	139	28	5	4	41	21	.343
2002	Montreal d-e	N.L.	OF	36	125	20	37	8	5	1	9	3	.296
2003	Montreal..........	N.L.	OF	141	483	66	121	25	5	4	47	18	.251
2004	Edmonton	P.C.	OF	14	61	9	21	3	2	0	7	5	.344
2004	Montreal..........	N.L.	OF	132	502	65	139	20	6	5	34	32	.277
2005	New Orleans	P.C.	OF	23	87	11	22	4	0	1	4	6	.253
2005	Washington-Philadelphia f-g.	N.L.	OF	98	116	19	25	4	3	0	11	2	.216

Year	Club	Lea	Pos	G	AB	R	H	2B	3B	HR	RBI	SB	Avg
2006 New York		N.L.	OF	133	353	48	108	22	5	4	42	12	.306
2007 Mets	Gulf Goast		OF	2	8	2	5	0	0	0	4	0	.625
2007 St. Lucie		Fla.St.	OF	4	16	3	8	1	0	0	2	0	.500
2007 Binghamton		Eastern	OF	1	3	0	0	0	0	0	0	0	.000
2007 New York h		N.L.	OF	71	150	20	43	7	2	1	17	5	.287
2008 New York i		N.L.	OF	133	270	30	72	10	2	1	12	6	.267
2009 Seattle j		A.L.	OF	54	161	17	44	3	1	2	13	9	.273
2010 Rangers		Arizona	OF	3	11	3	6	0	0	0	1	3	.545
2010 Oklahoma		P.C.	OF	1	5	2	1	1	0	0	0	0	.200
2010 Frisco k		Texas	OF	4	15	3	5	0	0	0	1	2	.333
2011 Round Rock		P.C.	OF	30	128	16	39	8	2	2	17	6	.305
2011 Texas l		A.L.	OF	83	256	37	77	11	3	5	27	10	.301
Major League Totals		10 Yrs.		910	2493	326	682	112	32	24	217	97	.274
Division Series													
2006 New York		N.L.	OF	3	8	1	3	0	0	0	0	0	.375
Championship Series													
2006 New York		N.L.	OF	7	27	1	5	2	0	0	0	0	.185
2011 Texas		A.L.	OF	2	4	0	0	0	0	0	0	0	.000
Championship Series Totals				9	31	1	5	2	0	0	0	0	.161
World Series Record													
2011 Texas		A.L.	OF	3	1	0	0	0	0	0	0	0	.000

a Selected by Kansas City Royals from New York Mets in Rule V draft, December 11, 2000.
b Retained by Kansas City Royals in trade for outfielder Michael Curry, March 30, 2001.
c Claimed on waivers by Detroit Tigers, December 20, 2001.
d Claimed on waivers by New York Mets, February 1, 2002.
e Claimed on waivers by Montreal Expos, February 22, 2002.
f Traded to Philadelphia Phillies for outfielder Marlon Byrd, May 14, 2005.
g Not offered contract, December 21, 2005. Signed with New York Mets, December 23, 2005.
h On disabled list from June 7 to August 28, 2007.
i Traded to Seattle Mariners with pitcher Aaron Heilman, pitcher Jason Vargas, infielder Mike Carp, outfielder Ezequiel Carrera, pitcher Maikel Cleto and pitcher Joe Smith for pitcher J.J. Putz, pitcher Sean Green and outfielder Jeremy Reed, December 10, 2008.
j On disabled list from June 20 to November 6, 2009.
k Filed for free agency, November 6, 2009. Signed with Texas Rangers organization, February 15, 2010.
l Filed for free agency, October 30, 2011. Signed with Baltimore Orioles, December 20, 2011.

CHISENHALL, LONNIE DAVID

Born, Morehead City, North Carolina, October 4, 1988.
Bats Left. Throws Right. Height, 6 feet, 1 inch. Weight, 200 pounds.

Year	Club	Lea	Pos	G	AB	R	H	2B	3B	HR	RBI	SB	Avg
2008 Mahoning Valley	N.Y.-Penn.		SS	68	276	38	80	20	3	5	45	7	.290
2009 Kinston	Carolina		3B	99	388	59	107	26	2	18	79	2	.276
2009 Akron		Eastern	3B	24	93	13	17	5	1	4	13	1	.183
2010 Akron		Eastern	3B	117	460	81	128	22	3	17	84	3	.278
2011 Columbus		Int.	3B	66	255	45	68	15	3	7	45	0	.267
2011 Cleveland		A.L.	3B-OF	66	212	27	54	13	0	7	22	1	.255

CHOO, SHIN-SOO

Born, Pusan, South Korea, July 13, 1982.
Bats Left. Throws Left. Height, 5 feet, 11 inches. Weight, 200 pounds.

Year	Club	Lea	Pos	G	AB	R	H	2B	3B	HR	RBI	SB	Avg
2001 Mariners	Arizona		OF	51	199	51	60	10	10	4	35	12	.302
2001 Wisconsin	Midwest		OF	3	13	1	6	0	0	0	3	2	.462
2002 San Bernardino	Calif.		OF	11	39	14	12	5	1	1	9	3	.308
2002 Wisconsin	Midwest		OF	119	420	69	127	24	8	6	48	34	.302
2003 Inland Empire	Calif.		OF	110	412	62	118	18	13	9	55	18	.286
2004 San Antonio	Texas		OF	132	517	89	163	17	7	15	84	40	.315
2005 Tacoma		P.C.	OF	115	429	73	121	21	5	11	54	20	.282
2005 Seattle		A.L.	OF	10	18	1	1	0	0	0	1	0	.056
2006 Tacoma		P.C.	OF	94	375	71	121	21	3	13	48	26	.323
2006 Seattle-Cleveland a		A.L.	OF	49	157	23	44	12	3	3	22	5	.280
2007 Cleveland		A.L.	OF	6	17	5	5	0	0	0	5	0	.294
2007 Indians	Gulf Coast		OF	2	5	0	1	1	0	0	2	0	.200
2007 Buffalo		Int.	OF	59	208	34	54	11	2	3	26	10	.260
2008 Buffalo		Int.	OF	12	42	1	11	2	0	1	3	1	.262
2008 Cleveland b		A.L.	OF	94	317	68	98	28	3	14	66	4	.309
2009 Cleveland		A.L.	OF	156	583	87	175	38	6	20	86	21	.300

Year	Club	Lea	Pos	G	AB	R	H	2B	3B	HR	RBI	SB	Avg
2010 Akron	Eastern		OF	3	11	1	1	0	0	0	0	1	.091
2010 Cleveland c	A.L.		OF	144	550	81	165	31	2	22	90	22	.300
2011 Lake County	So.Atl.		OF	3	8	0	0	0	0	0	1	0	.000
2011 Cleveland d	A.L.		OF	85	313	37	81	11	3	8	36	12	.259
Major League Totals		7 Yrs.		544	1955	302	569	120	17	67	306	64	.291

a Traded to Cleveland Indians with player to be named later for infielder Ben Broussard and cash, July 27, 2006. Cleveland Indians received pitcher Shawn Nottingham to complete trade, August 24, 2006.
b On disabled list from March 21 to May 30, 2008.
c On disabled list from July 3 to July 23, 2010.
d On disabled list from June 25 to August 12 and September 1 to September 15 and September 16 to November 2, 2011.

COGHLAN, CHRISTOPHER B. (CHRIS)
Born, Palm Harbor, Florida, June 18, 1985.
Bats Left. Throws Right. Height, 6 feet, 1 inch. Weight, 195 pounds.

Year	Club	Lea	Pos	G	AB	R	H	2B	3B	HR	RBI	SB	Avg
2006 Marlins	Gulf Coast		3B	2	7	2	2	0	0	0	3	0	.286
2006 Jamestown . . .	N.Y.-Penn.		3B-2B	28	94	14	28	5	1	0	12	5	.298
2007 Jupiter	Fla.St.		2B	34	130	17	26	5	3	2	18	5	.200
2007 Greensboro	So.Atl.		2B	81	305	60	99	26	4	10	64	19	.325
2008 Carolina	Southern		2B-3B	132	483	83	144	32	5	7	74	34	.298
2009 New Orleans	P.C.		2B-3B-OF	25	96	21	33	9	1	3	22	9	.344
2009 Florida a	N.L.		OF-2B	128	504	84	162	31	6	9	47	8	.321
2010 Florida b	N.L.		OF	91	358	60	96	20	3	5	28	10	.268
2011 Jupiter	Fla.St.		OF	10	35	4	12	1	0	0	2	1	.343
2011 Jacksonville . . .	Southern		OF	5	19	3	4	1	0	0	0	0	.211
2011 New Orleans	P.C.		OF	15	53	11	13	4	0	1	7	3	.245
2011 Florida c	N.L.		OF	65	269	33	62	20	1	5	22	7	.230
Major League Totals		3 Yrs.		284	1131	177	320	71	10	19	97	25	.283

a Selected Rookie of the Year in National League for 2009.
b On disabled list from July 26 to November 5, 2010.
c On disabled list from June 17 to August 19, 2011.

COLVIN, TYLER EUGENE
Born, Augusta, Georgia, September 5, 1985.
Bats Left. Throws Left. Height, 6 feet, 3 inches. Weight, 210 pounds.

Year	Club	Lea	Pos	G	AB	R	H	2B	3B	HR	RBI	SB	Avg
2006 Boise	Northwest		OF	64	265	50	71	12	6	11	53	12	.268
2007 Daytona	Fla.St.		OF	63	245	38	75	24	3	7	50	10	.306
2007 Tennessee	Southern		OF	62	247	34	72	11	2	9	31	7	.291
2008 Tennessee	Southern		OF	137	540	68	138	27	11	14	80	7	.256
2009 Daytona	Fla.St.		OF	32	112	18	28	5	2	1	10	3	.250
2009 Tennessee	Southern		OF	84	307	51	92	13	7	14	50	5	.300
2009 Chicago a	N.L.		OF	6	17	1	3	0	0	0	2	0	.176
2010 Chicago a	N.L.		OF	135	358	60	91	18	5	20	56	6	.254
2011 Iowa	P.C.		OF-1B	50	203	32	52	12	6	7	32	1	.256
2011 Chicago b	N.L.		OF-1B	80	206	17	31	8	3	6	20	0	.150
Major League Totals		3 Yrs.		221	581	78	125	26	8	26	78	6	.215

a On disabled list from September 20 to October 6, 2010.
b Traded to Colorado Rockies with infielder D.J. Le Mahieu for pitcher Casey Weathers and infielder Ian Stewart, December 8, 2011.

CONGER, HYUN CHOI (HANK)
Born, Federal Way, Washington, January 29, 1988.
Bats Both. Throws Right. Height, 6 feet, 1 inch. Weight, 220 pounds.

Year	Club	Lea	Pos	G	AB	R	H	2B	3B	HR	RBI	SB	Avg
2006 Angels	Arizona		C	19	69	11	22	3	4	1	11	1	.319
2007 Angels	Arizona		C	3	15	2	4	1	0	0	3	0	.267
2007 Cedar Rapids	Midwest		C	84	290	33	84	20	0	11	48	9	.290
2008 Rancho Cucamonga	Calif.		C	73	294	47	89	20	2	13	75	2	.303
2009 Arkansas	Texas		C	123	458	61	135	20	3	11	68	4	.295
2010 Salt Lake	P.C.		C	108	387	56	116	26	2	11	49	0	.300
2010 Los Angeles	A.L.		C	13	29	2	5	1	1	0	5	0	.172
2011 Salt Lake	P.C.		C	27	100	14	30	4	0	5	26	0	.300
2011 Los Angeles	A.L.		C	59	177	14	37	8	0	6	19	0	.209
Major League Totals		2 Yrs.		72	206	16	42	9	1	6	24	0	.204

CONRAD, BROOKS LITCHFIELD

Born, San Diego, California, January 16, 1980.
Bats Both. Throws Right. Height, 5 feet, 11 inches. Weight, 190 pounds.

Year	Club	Lea	Pos	G	AB	R	H	2B	3B	HR	RBI	SB	Avg
2001 Pittsfield.....	N.Y.-Penn.	2B-3B	65	232	41	65	16	5	4	39	14	.280
2002 Michigan	Midwest	2B	133	499	94	143	25	14	14	94	18	.287
2003 Salem........	Carolina	2B	99	345	50	98	24	3	11	61	4	.284
2003 Lexington......	So.Atl.	2B	38	140	20	26	5	2	3	11	7	.186
2004 Round Rock.....	Texas	2B	129	480	84	139	39	6	13	83	8	.290
2005 Round Rock......	P.C.	2B	113	418	84	110	22	3	21	57	12	.263
2005 Corpus Christi ...	Texas	2B	22	77	13	18	6	1	2	11	8	.234
2006 Round Rock.......	P.C.	2B-3B	138	532	100	142	40	15	24	94	15	.267
2007 Round Rock a	P.C.	2B-3B-C	139	533	85	116	36	3	22	70	12	.218
2008 Oakland	A.L.	3B-2B	6	19	0	3	1	0	0	2	0	.158
2008 Sacramento	P.C.	2B-SS-OF-3B	117	465	86	113	29	5	28	91	4	.243
2009 Gwinnett..........	Int.	2B-SS-1B-3B	110	398	66	107	25	0	12	64	13	.269
2009 Atlanta b........	N.L.	2B-3B	30	54	7	11	1	2	2	8	0	.204
2010 Atlanta..........	N.L.	3B-2B	103	156	31	39	11	1	8	33	5	.250
2011 Atlanta c........	N.L.	2B-3B-1B	92	103	11	23	5	0	4	13	2	.223
Major League Totals		4 Yrs.	231	332	49	76	18	3	14	56	7	.229
Division Series												
2010 Atlanta...........	N.L.	2B	4	11	0	1	0	0	0	0	0	.091

a Filed for free agency from Houston Astros, October 29, 2007. Signed with Oakland Athletics organization, December 8, 2007.
b Filed for free agency, October 8, 2008. Signed with Atlanta Braves organization, January 22, 2009.
c Not offered contract, December 12, 2011.

CORA, JOSE ALEXANDER (ALEX)

Born, Caguas, Puerto Rico, October 18, 1975.
Bats Left. Throws Right. Height, 6 feet. Weight, 200 pounds.

Year	Club	Lea	Pos	G	AB	R	H	2B	3B	HR	RBI	SB	Avg
1996 Vero Beach......	Fla.St.	SS-OF	61	214	26	55	5	4	0	26	5	.257
1997 San Antonio	Texas	SS	127	448	52	105	20	4	3	48	12	.234
1998 Albuquerque.......	P.C.	SS-2B	81	299	42	79	16	6	5	45	10	.264
1998 Los Angeles.......	N.L.	SS-2B	29	33	1	4	0	1	0	0	0	.121
1999 Albuquerque.......	P.C.	SS	80	302	51	93	11	7	4	37	9	.308
1999 Los Angeles a.....	N.L.	SS-2B	11	30	2	5	1	0	0	3	0	.167
2000 Albuquerque.......	P.C.	SS	30	110	18	41	8	3	0	20	5	.373
2000 Los Angeles......	N.L.	SS-2B	109	353	39	84	18	6	4	32	4	.238
2001 Los Angeles......	N.L.	SS-2B	134	405	38	88	18	3	4	29	0	.217
2002 Los Angeles.......	N.L.	SS-2B	115	258	37	75	14	4	5	28	7	.291
2003 Los Angeles......	N.L.	2B-SS	148	477	39	119	24	3	4	34	4	.249
2004 Los Angeles b	N.L.	2B	138	405	47	107	9	4	10	47	3	.264
2005 Cleveland-Boston c	A.L.	2B-SS-3B-OF	96	250	25	58	8	4	3	24	7	.232
2006 Boston d	A.L.	SS-2B-3B	96	235	31	56	7	2	1	18	6	.238
2007 Boston...........	A.L.	2B-SS-1B	83	207	30	51	10	5	3	18	1	.246
2008 Pawtucket........	Int.	2B-SS	3	11	2	3	0	0	0	0	0	.273
2008 Boston e-f	A.L.	SS-2B	75	152	14	41	8	2	0	9	1	.270
2009 Buffalo...........	Int.	SS	3	14	0	3	1	0	0	0	0	.214
2009 New York g-h.....	N.L.	SS-2B-1B	82	271	31	68	11	1	1	18	8	.251
2010 Oklahoma........	P.C.	2B-SS	6	22	5	4	1	0	1	2	1	.182
2010 New York........	N.L.	2B-SS-1B	62	169	14	35	6	3	0	20	4	.207
2010 Texas i-j.........	A.L.	2B-3B	4	7	0	2	0	0	0	0	0	.286
2011 Washington k......	N.L.	3B-SS-1B-2B	91	156	12	35	6	1	0	6	2	.224
Major League Totals		14 Yrs.	1273	3408	360	828	140	39	35	286	47	.243
Division Series												
2004 Los Angeles......	N.L.	2B	4	15	1	2	0	1	0	1	0	.133
2005 Boston...........	A.L.	SS	1	0	0	0	0	0	0	0	0	.000
2008 Boston...........	A.L.	SS	2	4	1	1	1	0	0	0	0	.250
Division Series Totals			7	19	2	3	1	1	0	1	0	.158
Championship Series												
2007 Boston...........	A.L.	2B-SS	2	0	0	0	0	0	0	0	0	.000
2008 Boston...........	A.L.	SS	2	7	0	1	0	0	0	0	0	.143
Championship Series Totals			4	7	0	1	0	0	0	0	0	.143
World Series Record												
2007 Boston...........	A.L.	2B-SS	2	0	0	0	0	0	0	0	0	.000

a On disabled list from March 25 to June 27, 1999.
b Not offered contract, December 21, 2004. Signed with Cleveland Indians, January 18, 2005.
c Traded to Boston Red Sox for infielder Ramon Vazquez, July 7, 2005.

d Filed for free agency, October 31, 2006, re-signed with Boston Red Sox, November 17, 2006.
e On disabled list from April 10 to May 11, 2008.
f Filed for free agency, October 30, 2008. Signed with New York Mets, January 22, 2009.
g On disabled list from May 18 to June 2 and August 18 to November 6, 2009.
h Filed for free agency, November 6, 2009, re-signed with New York Mets, November 30, 2009.
i Released by New York Mets, August 7, 2010. Signed with Texas Rangers organization, August 17, 2010.
j Released by Texas Rangers, September 7, 2010. Signed with Washington Nationals organization, January 17, 2011.
k Filed for free agency, October 30, 2011.

COUNSELL, CRAIG JOHN
Born, South Bend, Indiana, August 21, 1970.
Bats Left. Throws Right. Height, 6 feet. Weight, 185 pounds.

Year	Club	Lea	Pos	G	AB	R	H	2B	3B	HR	RBI	SB	Avg
1992 Bend.......	Northwest	2B-SS	18	61	11	15	6	1	0	8	1	.246
1993 Central Val ...	California	SS	131	471	79	132	26	3	5	59	14	.280
1994 New Haven.....	Eastern	SS-2B	83	300	47	84	20	1	5	37	4	.280
1995 Colo Sprngs......	P.C.	SS	118	399	60	112	22	6	5	53	10	.281
1995 Colorado	N.L.	SS	3	1	0	0	0	0	0	0	0	.000
1996 Colo Sprngs......	P.C.	2B-3B-SS	25	75	17	18	3	0	2	10	4	.240
1997 Colo Sprngs......	P.C.	2B-SS	96	376	77	126	31	6	5	63	12	.335
1997 Colorado-Florida a .	N.L.	2B	52	164	20	49	9	2	1	16	1	.299
1998 Florida b........	N.L.	2B	107	335	43	84	19	5	4	40	3	.251
1999 Florida-Los Angeles c-d	N.L.	2B-SS	87	174	24	38	7	0	0	11	1	.218
2000 Tucson...........	P.C.	2B	50	198	45	69	14	3	3	27	4	.348
2000 Arizona	N.L.	2B-3B-SS	67	152	23	48	8	1	2	11	3	.316
2001 Arizona...........	N.L.	SS-2B-3B-1B	141	458	76	126	22	3	4	38	6	.275
2002 Arizona e	N.L.	3B-SS-2B	112	436	63	123	22	1	2	51	7	.282
2003 Tucson...........	P.C.	2B-SS-3B	5	23	8	10	2	0	0	2	0	.435
2003 Arizona f-g........	N.L.	3B-SS-2B-1B	89	303	40	71	6	3	3	21	11	.234
2004 Milwaukee h.......	N.L.	SS-3B	140	473	59	114	19	5	2	23	17	.241
2005 Arizona...........	N.L.	2B-SS	150	578	85	148	34	4	9	42	26	.256
2006 Lancaster.......	Calif.	DH	1	3	1	3	1	0	0	0	0	1.000
2006 Tucson...........	P.C.	DH	2	11	2	2	0	0	0	0	0	.182
2006 Arizona i-j.......	N.L.	SS-3B-2B	105	372	56	95	14	4	4	30	15	.255
2007 Milwaukee	N.L.	3B-SS-2B	122	282	31	62	12	2	3	24	4	.220
2008 Milwaukee k.......	N.L.	3B-SS-2B	110	248	31	56	14	1	1	14	3	.226
2009 Milwaukee l	N.L.	2B-3B-SS	130	404	61	115	22	8	4	39	3	.285
2010 Milwaukee m.......	N.L.	SS-3B-2B	102	204	16	51	8	0	2	21	1	.250
2011 Milwaukee n.......	N.L.	2B-SS-3B-OF	107	157	19	28	2	1	1	9	2	.178
Major League Totals		16 Yrs.	1624	4741	647	1208	218	40	42	390	103	.255

Division Series													
1997 Florida	N.L.	2B	3	5	0	2	1	0	0	1	0	.400
2001 Arizona...........	N.L.	2B	5	16	2	3	0	0	1	3	0	.187
2008 Milwaukee	N.L.	2B-3B	4	12	0	2	0	0	0	1	0	.167
2011 Milwaukee	N.L.	2B-SS	2	2	0	0	0	0	0	0	0	.000
Division Series Totals			14	35	2	7	1	0	1	5	0	.200

Championship Series													
1997 Florida	N.L.	2B	5	14	0	6	0	0	0	2	0	.429
2001 Arizona...........	N.L.	2B-SS	5	21	5	8	3	0	0	4	1	.381
2011 Milwaukee	N.L.	2B	4	2	0	0	0	0	0	0	0	.000
Championship Series Totals			14	37	5	14	3	0	0	6	1	.378

World Series Record													
1997 Florida	N.L.	2B	7	22	4	4	1	0	0	2	1	.182
2001 Arizona...........	N.L.	2B	6	24	1	2	0	0	1	1	0	.083
World Series Totals.............			13	46	5	6	1	0	1	3	1	.130

a Traded to Florida Marlins for pitcher Mark Hutton, July 27, 1997.
b On disabled list from August 4 to September 28, 1998.
c Traded to Los Angeles Dodgers for player to be named later, June 15, 1999. Florida Marlins received pitcher Ryan Moskau to complete trade, July 15, 1999.
d Released by Los Angeles Dodgers, March 17, 2000. Signed with Arizona Diamondbacks organization, March 20, 2000.
e On disabled list from August 9 to October 14, 2002.
f On disabled list from May 7 to July 7, 2003.
g Traded to Milwaukee Brewers with infielder Junior Spivey, infielder Lyle Overbay, catcher Chad Moeller, pitcher Chris Capuano and pitcher Jorge DeRosa for infielder Richie Sexson, pitcher Shane Nance and player to be named later. Arizona Diamondbacks received outfielder Gary Varner to complete trade, December 15, 2003.
h Filed for free agency, October 29, 2004. Signed with Arizona Diamondbacks December 15, 2004.
i On disabled list from July 15 to August 22, 2006.
j Filed for free agency, October 30, 2006. Signed with Milwaukee Brewers, November 29, 2006.

k Not offered contract, October 31, 2008. re-signed with Milwaukee Brewers, January 26, 2009.
l Filed for free agency, November 9, 2009, re-signed with Milwaukee Brewers, December 14, 2009.
m Filed for free agency, November 1, 2010, re-signed with Milwaukee Brewers, December 22, 2010.
n Filed for free agency, October 30, 2011.

COWGILL, COLLIN BRANNEN

Born, Lexington, Kentucky, May 22, 1986.
Bats Right. Throws Left. Height, 5 feet, 9 inches. Weight, 185 pounds.

Year	Club	Lea	Pos	G	AB	R	H	2B	3B	HR	RBI	SB	Avg
2008 South Bend		Midwest	OF	50	201	31	50	13	3	1	17	1	.249
2008 Yakima		Northwest	OF	20	79	21	24	3	1	11	28	5	.304
2009 Visalia		Calif.	OF	61	220	39	61	9	5	6	36	11	.277
2010 Mobile		Southern	OF	131	502	89	143	34	4	16	83	25	.285
2011 Reno		P.C.	OF	98	395	95	140	24	8	13	70	30	.354
2011 Arizona a		N.L.	OF	36	92	8	22	3	0	1'	9	4	.239
Division Series													
2011 Arizona		N.L.	PH	2	1	0	1	0	0	0	2	0	1.000

a Traded to Oakland Athletics with pitcher Jarrod Parker and pitcher Ryan Cook for pitcher Craig Breslow and pitcher Trevor Cahill, December 9, 2011.

COZART, ZACHARY WARREN (ZACK)

Born, Memphis, Tennessee, August 12, 1985.
Bats Right. Throws Right. Height, 6 feet. Weight, 195 pounds.

Year	Club	Lea	Pos	G	AB	R	H	2B	3B	HR	RBI	SB	Avg
2007 Dayton		Midwest	SS-2B	53	184	28	44	7	2	2	18	3	.239
2008 Dayton		Midwest	SS-2B	109	418	57	117	20	6	14	49	3	.280
2009 Carolina		Southern	SS	131	462	72	121	29	2	10	59	10	.262
2010 Louisville		Int.	SS	136	553	91	141	30	4	17	67	30	.255
2011 Louisville		Int.	SS	77	323	57	100	26	2	7	32	9	.310
2011 Cincinnati a		N.L.	SS	11	37	6	12	0	0	2	3	0	.324

a On disabled list from July 24 to November 2, 2011.

CRAIG, ALLEN THOMAS

Born, Mission Viejo, California, July 18, 1984.
Bats Right. Throws Right. Height, 6 feet, 2 inches. Weight, 210 pounds.

Year	Club	Lea	Pos	G	AB	R	H	2B	3B	HR	RBI	SB	Avg
2006 State College		N.Y.-Penn.	3B-SS-2B	48	175	21	45	13	0	4	29	0	.257
2007 Palm Beach		Fla.St.	3B-1B	112	423	77	132	25	2	21	77	8	.312
2007 Springfield		Texas	3B	7	24	5	7	2	0	3	3	0	.292
2008 Springfield		Texas	3B-OF-1B	129	506	84	154	30	0	22	85	2	.304
2009 Memphis		P.C.	OF-1B-3B	126	472	78	152	26	1	26	83	3	.322
2010 Memphis		P.C.	OF-1B	83	306	57	98	24	2	14	81	1	.320
2010 St. Louis		N.L.	OF-1B-3B-2B	44	114	12	28	7	0	4	18	0	.246
2011 Springfield		Texas	OF	2	6	0	0	0	0	0	1	0	.000
2011 Memphis		P.C.	OF-2B	10	35	9	10	2	1	1	5	0	.286
2011 St. Louis a		N.L.	OF-2B-1B-3B	75	200	33	63	15	0	11	40	5	.315
Major League Totals			2 Yrs.	119	314	45	91	22	0	15	58	5	.290
Division Series													
2011 St. Louis		N.L.	OF	3	10	3	1	0	1	0	0	0	.100
Championship Series													
2011 St. Louis		N.L.	OF	5	8	1	3	0	0	1	3	0	.375
World Series Record													
2011 St. Louis		N.L.	OF	7	19	5	5	0	0	3	5	0	.263

a On disabled list from April 17 to May 2 and June 8 to August 10, 2011.

CRAWFORD, BRANDON MICHAEL

Born, Mountain View, California, January 21, 1987.
Bats Left. Throws Right. Height, 6 feet, 2 inches. Weight, 215 pounds.

Year	Club	Lea	Pos	G	AB	R	H	2B	3B	HR	RBI	SB	Avg
2008 Giants		Arizona	SS	4	14	3	6	1	1	0	3	0	.429
2008 Salem-Keizer		Northwest	SS	1	2	0	0	0	0	0	0	0	.000
2009 San Jose		Calif.	SS	25	105	21	39	2	2	6	17	2	.371
2009 Connecticut		Eastern	SS	108	392	38	101	26	2	4	31	11	.258
2010 San Jose		Calif.	3B-SS	5	18	4	3	1	0	0	1	0	.167
2010 Richmond		Eastern	SS	79	291	43	70	12	3	7	22	4	.241

Year Club	Lea	Pos	G	AB	R	H	2B	3B	HR	RBI	SB	Avg
2011 San Jose ....Calif.		SS	14	59	14	19	5	1	3	15	0	.322
2011 Fresno ...............P.C.		SS	29	107	13	25	5	1	1	9	5	.234
2011 San Francisco .... N.L.		SS	66	196	22	40	5	2	3	21	1	.204

CRAWFORD, CARL DEMONTE
Born, Houston, Texas, August 5, 1981.
Bats Left. Throws Left. Height, 6 feet, 2 inches. Weight, 220 pounds.

Year Club	Lea	Pos	G	AB	R	H	2B	3B	HR	RBI	SB	Avg
1999 Princeton ....Appal.		OF	60	260	62	83	14	4	0	25	17	.319
2000 Charleston-SC ...... So.Atl.		OF	135	564	99	170	21	11	6	57	55	.301
2001 Orlando .... Southern		OF	132	537	64	147	24	3	4	51	36	.274
2002 Durham ....Int.		OF	85	353	59	105	17	9	7	52	26	.297
2002 Tampa Bay .... A.L.		OF	63	259	23	67	11	6	2	30	9	.259
2003 Tampa Bay .... A.L.		OF	151	630	80	177	18	9	5	54	*55	.281
2004 Tampa Bay .... A.L.		OF	152	626	104	185	26	*19	11	55	*59	.296
2005 Tampa Bay .... A.L.		OF	156	644	101	194	33	*15	15	81	46	.301
2006 Tampa Bay .... A.L.		OF	151	600	89	183	20	*16	18	77	*58	.305
2007 Tampa Bay .... A.L.		OF	143	584	93	184	37	9	11	80	*50	.315
2008 Tampa Bay a........... A.L.		OF	109	443	69	121	12	10	8	57	25	.273
2009 Tampa Bay .... A.L.		OF	156	606	96	185	28	8	15	68	60	.305
2010 Tampa Bay b .... A.L.		OF	154	600	110	184	30	*13	19	90	47	.307
2011 Pawtucket .... Int.		OF	2	5	1	1	0	0	0	1	0	.200
2011 Boston c............. A.L.		OF	130	506	65	129	29	7	11	56	18	.255
Major League Totals	10 Yrs.		1365	5498	830	1609	244	112	115	648	427	.293
Division Series												
2008 Tampa Bay .... A.L.		OF	4	14	2	3	0	0	0	2	3	.214
2010 Tampa Bay .... A.L.		OF	5	21	1	3	0	0	1	1	1	.143
Division Series Totals			9	35	3	6	0	0	1	3	4	.171
Championship Series												
2008 Tampa Bay .... A.L.		OF	7	29	3	10	2	1	0	4	3	.345
World Series Record												
2008 Tampa Bay .... A.L.		OF	5	19	4	5	1	0	2	2	1	.263

a On disabled list from August 10 to September 26, 2008.
b Filed for free agency, November 1, 2010. Signed with Boston Red Sox, December 11, 2010.
c On disabled list from June 18 to July 18, 2011.

CRISP, COVELLI LOYCE (COCO)
Born, Los Angeles, California, November 1, 1979.
Bats Both. Throws Right. Height, 6 feet. Weight, 180 pounds.

Year Club	Lea	Pos	G	AB	R	H	2B	3B	HR	RBI	SB	Avg
1999 Johnson City ....Appal.		2B	65	229	55	59	5	4	3	22	27	.258
2000 New Jersey ...... N.Y.-Penn.		OF-2B	36	134	18	32	5	0	0	14	25	.239
2000 Peoria............. Midwest		OF	27	98	14	27	9	0	0	7	7	.276
2001 Potomac......... Carolina		OF	139	530	80	162	23	3	11	47	39	.306
2002 New Haven........Eastern		OF	89	355	61	107	16	1	9	47	26	.301
2002 Akron.............Eastern		OF	7	32	9	13	1	0	1	4	4	.406
2002 Buffalo.............. Int.		OF	4	21	3	5	1	0	0	2	1	.238
2002 Cleveland a........... A.L.		OF	32	127	16	33	9	2	1	9	4	.260
2003 Buffalo.............. Int.		OF	56	225	42	81	19	6	1	24	20	.360
2003 Cleveland .... A.L.		OF	99	414	55	110	15	6	3	27	15	.266
2004 Cleveland .... A.L.		OF	139	491	78	146	24	2	15	71	20	.297
2005 Cleveland b .... A.L.		OF	145	594	86	178	42	4	16	69	15	.300
2006 Pawtucket .... Int.		OF	1	3	0	1	0	0	0	2	0	.333
2006 Boston c-d........... A.L.		OF	105	413	58	109	22	2	8	36	22	.264
2007 Boston .... A.L.		OF	145	526	85	141	28	7	6	60	28	.268
2008 Boston e............. A.L.		OF	118	361	55	102	18	3	7	41	20	.283
2009 Kansas City f-g........ A.L.		OF	49	180	30	41	8	5	3	14	13	.228
2010 Stockton ....Calif.		OF	2	6	2	5	0	1	1	3	0	.833
2010 Sacramento .........P.C.		OF	6	22	7	13	2	1	0	5	2	.591
2010 Oakland h............ A.L.		OF	75	290	51	81	14	4	8	38	32	.279
2011 Oakland i............ A.L.		OF	136	531	69	140	27	5	8	54	*49	.264
Major League Totals	10 Yrs.		1043	3927	583	1081	207	40	75	419	218	.275
Division Series												
2007 Boston .... A.L.		OF	3	10	0	2	0	0	0	2	1	.200
2008 Boston .... A.L.		OF	2	4	2	1	0	0	0	0	1	.250
Division Series Totals			5	14	2	3	0	0	0	2	2	.214

Year	Club	Lea	Pos	G	AB	R	H	2B	3B	HR	RBI	SB	Avg
	Championship Series												
2007 Boston	A.L.	OF	7	21	2	3	1	0	0	0	1	.143
2008 Boston	A.L.	OF	5	20	2	9	2	0	0	1	0	.450
Championship Series Totals			12	41	4	12	3	0	0	1	1	.293
	World Series Record												
2007 Boston	A.L.	OF	3	2	1	1	0	0	0	0	0	.500

a Sent by St. Louis Cardinals to Cleveland Indians as player to be named later for pitcher Chuck Finley, August 6, 2002.
b On disabled list from May 18 to June 2, 2005.
c Traded to Boston Red Sox with pitcher David Riske and catcher Josh Bard for infielder Andy Marte, catcher Kelly Shoppach and pitcher Guillermo Mota, January 27, 2006.
d On disabled list from April 9 to May 28, 2006.
e Traded to Kansas City Royals for pitcher Ramon Ramirez, November 19, 2008.
f On disabled list from June 13 to November 9, 2009.
g Filed for free agency, November 9, 2009. Signed with Oakland Athletics, December 23, 2009.
h On disabled list from April 3 to May 21 and May 26 to June 22, 2010.
i Filed for free agency, October 30, 2011, re-signed with Oakland Athletics, January 5, 2012.

CROWE, TREVOR THORNTON

Born, Portland, Oregon, November 17, 1983.
Bats Both. Throws Right. Height, 6 feet. Weight, 190 pounds.

Year	Club	Lea	Pos	G	AB	R	H	2B	3B	HR	RBI	SB	Avg
2005 Akron	Eastern	OF	3	10	1	1	0	0	0	0	0	.100
2005 Mahoning Valley . .	N.Y.-Penn.	OF	12	51	9	13	2	1	1	6	4	.255
2005 Lake County	So.Atl.	OF	44	178	18	46	8	2	0	23	7	.258
2006 Kinston	Carolina	OF	60	219	51	72	15	2	4	31	29	.329
2006 Akron	Eastern	OF-2B	39	154	20	36	7	2	1	13	16	.234
2006 Lake County	So.Atl.	OF	2	5	0	0	0	0	0	0	0	.000
2007 Akron	Eastern	OF	133	518	87	134	26	4	5	50	28	.259
2008 Akron	Eastern	OF	49	198	45	64	16	2	4	28	13	.323
2008 Buffalo	Int.	OF	35	146	25	40	12	2	5	13	5	.274
2009 Columbus	Int.	OF	49	185	27	55	11	1	2	20	14	.297
2009 Cleveland a	A.L.	OF	68	183	22	43	9	3	1	17	6	.235
2010 Columbus	Int.	OF	29	119	21	29	4	1	1	13	6	.244
2010 Cleveland	A.L.	OF	122	442	48	111	24	3	2	36	20	.251
2011 Indians	Arizona	OF	6	18	9	8	3	1	2	8	2	.444
2011 Columbus	Int.	OF	5	20	1	2	0	0	0	1	2	.100
2011 Cleveland b	A.L.	OF	15	28	6	6	1	0	0	2	3	.214
Major League Totals		3 Yrs.	205	653	76	160	34	6	3	55	29	.245

a On disabled list from August 17 to September 4, 2009.
b On disabled list from March 30 to September 7, 2011.

CRUZ, NELSON RAMON

Born, Monte Cristi, Dominican Republic, July 1, 1980.
Bats Right. Throws Right. Height, 6 feet, 3 inches. Weight, 230 pounds.

Year	Club	Lea	Pos	G	AB	R	H	2B	3B	HR	RBI	SB	Avg
2001 Athletics a	Arizona	OF	23	88	11	22	3	1	3	16	6	.250
2002 Vancouver	Northwest	OF	63	214	23	59	14	0	4	25	12	.276
2003 Kane County	Midwest	OF	119	470	65	112	26	2	20	.85	10	.238
2004 Modesto	Calif.	OF	66	261	54	90	27	1	11	52	8	.345
2004 Sacramento	P.C.	OF	4	13	4	3	1	0	1	2	0	.231
2004 Midland b	Texas	OF	67	262	51	82	14	2	14	46	8	.313
2005 Huntsville	Southern	OF	68	248	45	76	19	0	16	54	10	.306
2005 Nashville	P.C.	OF	60	208	33	56	13	0	11	27	9	.269
2005 Milwaukee	N.L.	OF	8	5	1	1	1	0	0	0	0	.200
2006 Nashville	P.C.	OF	104	371	68	112	22	1	20	73	17	.302
2006 Texas c	A.L.	OF	41	130	15	29	3	0	6	22	1	.223
2007 Oklahoma	P.C.	OF	44	162	32	57	9	1	15	45	1	.352
2007 Texas	A.L.	OF	96	307	35	72	15	2	9	34	2	.235
2008 Rangers	Arizona	OF	1	4	1	1	1	0	0	1	0	.250
2008 Oklahoma	P.C.	OF	103	383	93	131	18	3	37	99	24	.342
2008 Texas	A.L.	OF	31	115	19	38	9	1	7	26	3	.330
2009 Okla	P.C.	OF	3	10	0	0	0	0	0	0	1	.000
2009 Texas d	A.L.	OF	128	462	75	120	21	1	33	76	20	.260
2010 Frisco	Texas	OF	3	11	1	4	1	0	0	1	1	.364
2010 Oklahoma	P.C.	OF	5	19	1	4	1	0	0	4	0	.211
2010 Texas e	A.L.	OF	108	399	60	127	31	3	22	78	17	.318

Year	Club	Lea	Pos	G	AB	R	H	2B	3B	HR	RBI	SB	Avg
2011 Frisco.............	Texas	OF	3	11	1	2	1	0	0	1	0	.182
2011 Round Rock..........	.P.C.	OF	3	11	3	5	0	0	3	4	0	.455
2011 Texas f	A.L.	OF	124	475	64	125	28	1	29	87	9	.263
Major League Totals	7 Yrs.		536	1893	269	512	108	8	106	323	52	.270
Division Series												
2010 Texas	A.L.	OF	5	20	5	8	2	0	3	3	1	.400
2011 Texas	A.L.	OF	4	15	1	1	0	0	0	0	0	.067
Division Series Totals			9	35	6	9	2	0	3	3	1	.257
Championship Series												
2010 Texas	A.L.	OF	6	20	6	7	3	0	2	5	0	.350
2011 Texas	A.L.	OF	6	22	7	8	2	0	6	13	0	.364
Championship Series Totals			12	42	13	15	5	0	8	18	0	.357
World Series Record												
2010 Texas	A.L.	OF	5	20	2	4	2	0	1	3	0	.200
2011 Texas	A.L.	OF	7	25	5	5	0	0	2	3	0	.200
World Series Totals.............			12	45	7	9	2	0	3	6	0	.200

a Traded by New York Mets to Oakland Athletics for infielder Jorge Velandia, August 30, 2000.
b Traded to Milwaukee Brewers with pitcher Justin Lehr for infielder Keith Ginter, December 15, 2004.
c Traded to Texas Rangers with outfielder Carlos Lee for pitcher Francisco Cordero, outfielder Kevin Mench, outfielder Laynce Nix and pitcher Julian Cordero, July 28, 2006.
d On disabled list from August 4 to August 20, 2009.
e On disabled list from April 27 to May 14 and May 29 to June 22 and August 15 to August 30, 2010.
f On disabled list from May 4 to May 23 and August 29 to September 13, 2011.

CUDDYER, MICHAEL BRENT
Born, Norfolk, Virginia, March 27, 1979.
Bats Right. Throws Right. Height, 6 feet, 2 inches. Weight, 220 pounds.

Year	Club	Lea	Pos	G	AB	R	H	2B	3B	HR	RBI	SB	Avg
1998 Fort Wayne....	Midwest	SS-2B	129	497	82	137	37	7	12	81	16	.276
1999 Fort Myers	Fla.St.	3B	130	466	87	139	24	4	16	82	14	.298
2000 New Britain	Eastern	3B	138	490	72	129	30	8	6	61	5	.263
2001 New Britain	Eastern	3B-1B-OF	141	509	95	153	36	3	30	87	5	.301
2001 Minnesota	A.L.	1B-3B	8	18	1	4	2	0	0	1	1	.222
2002 Edmonton	P.C.	OF-1B-3B	86	330	70	102	16	9	20	53	12	.309
2002 Minnesota	A.L.	OF-3B-1B	41	112	12	29	7	0	4	13	2	.259
2003 Twins	Gulf Coast	OF	2	5	1	4	0	0	1	3	0	.800
2003 Rochester.........	Int.	OF-2B-3B-1B	53	186	25	57	17	0	3	34	5	.306
2003 Minnesota	A.L.	OF-3B-1B-2B	35	102	14	25	1	3	4	8	1	.245
2004 Minnesota	A.L.	2B-3B-OF-1B	115	339	49	89	22	1	12	45	5	.263
2005 Rochester.........	Int.	3B-1B	3	9	1	1	0	0	0	0	2	.111
2005 Minnesota a	A.L.	3B-OF-2B-1B	126	422	55	111	25	3	12	42	3	.263
2006 Minnesota	A.L.	OF-1B	150	557	102	158	41	5	24	109	6	.284
2007 Minnesota b.......	A.L.	OF-1B	144	547	87	151	28	5	16	81	5	.276
2008 Rochester.........	Int.	OF	4	10	3	3	2	0	0	1	0	.300
2008 Minnesota c.......	A.L.	OF-1B	71	249	30	62	13	4	3	36	5	.249
2009 Minnesota	A.L.	OF-1B-2B	153	588	93	162	34	7	32	94	6	.276
2010 Minnesota	A.L.	1B-OF-3B-2B	157	609	93	165	37	5	14	81	7	.271
2011 Minnesota d.......	A.L.	OF-1B-2B-P	139	529	70	150	29	2	20	70	11	.284
Major League Totals	11 Yrs.		1139	4072	606	1106	239	35	141	580	52	.272
Division Series												
2002 Minnesota	A.L.	OF	5	13	1	5	1	0	0	1	0	.385
2003 Minnesota	A.L.	DH	1	4	0	1	0	0	0	1	0	.250
2004 Minnesota	A.L.	2B-1B	4	15	1	7	0	0	0	2	0	.467
2006 Minnesota	A.L.	OF	3	12	2	3	0	1	1	1	0	.250
2009 Minnesota	A.L.	1B	3	14	0	6	0	0	0	1	0	.429
2010 Minnesota	A.L.	1B	3	11	1	2	1	0	1	2	0	.182
Division Series Totals			19	69	5	24	2	1	2	8	0	.348
Championship Series												
2002 Minnesota	A.L.	OF	3	5	0	1	0	0	0	0	0	.200

a On disabled list from June 30 to July 17, 2005.
b On disabled list from July 19 to August 3, 2007.
c On disabled list from April 5 to April 25 and June 28 to September 13, 2008.
d Filed for free agency, October 30, 2011. Signed with Colorado Rockies, December 20, 2011.

DAMON, JOHNNY DAVID

Born, Fort Riley, Kansas, November 5, 1973.
Bats Left. Throws Left. Height, 6 feet, 2 Inches. Weight, 205 pounds.

Year	Club	Lea	Pos	G	AB	R	H	2B	3B	HR	RBI	SB	Avg
1992 Royals	Gulf Coast	OF	50	192	58	67	12	9	4	24	23	.349
1992 Baseball City	Fla. St.	OF	1	1	0	0	0	0	0	0	0	.000
1993 Rockford	Midwest	OF	127	511	82	148	25	13	5	50	59	.290
1994 Wilmington	Carolina	OF	119	472	96	149	25	13	6	75	44	.316
1995 Wichita	Texas	OF	111	423	83	145	15	9	16	54	26	.343
1995 Kansas City	A.L.	OF	47	188	32	53	11	5	3	23	7	.282
1996 Kansas City	A.L.	OF	145	517	61	140	22	5	6	50	25	.271
1997 Kansas City	A.L.	OF	146	472	70	130	12	8	8	48	16	.275
1998 Kansas City	A.L.	OF	161	642	104	178	30	10	18	66	26	.277
1999 Kansas City	A.L.	OF	145	583	101	179	39	9	14	77	36	.307
2000 Kansas City a	A.L.	OF	159	655	*136	214	42	10	16	88	*46	.327
2001 Oakland b	A.L.	OF	155	644	108	165	34	4	9	49	27	.256
2002 Boston	A.L.	OF	154	623	118	178	34	*11	14	63	31	.286
2003 Boston	A.L.	OF	145	608	103	166	32	6	12	67	30	.273
2004 Boston	A.L.	OF	150	621	123	189	35	6	20	94	19	.304
2005 Boston c	A.L.	OF	148	624	117	197	35	6	10	75	18	.316
2006 New York	A.L.	OF-1B	149	593	115	169	35	5	24	80	25	.285
2007 New York	A.L.	OF-1B	141	533	93	144	27	2	12	63	27	.270
2008 New York d	A.L.	OF-1B	143	555	95	168	27	5	17	71	29	.303
2009 New York e	A.L.	OF	143	550	107	155	36	3	24	82	12	.282
2010 Detroit f	A.L.	DH-OF	145	539	81	146	36	5	8	51	11	.271
2011 Tampa Bay g	A.L.	DH-OF-1B	150	582	79	152	29	7	16	73	19	.261
Major League Totals		17 Yrs.	2426	9529	1643	2723	516	107	231	1120	404	.286
Division Series												
2001 Oakland	A.L.	OF	5	22	3	9	2	1	0	0	2	.409
2003 Boston	A.L.	OF	5	19	2	6	2	0	1	3	2	.316
2004 Boston	A.L.	OF	3	15	4	7	1	0	0	0	3	.467
2005 Boston	A.L.	OF	3	13	2	3	1	0	0	0	0	.231
2006 New York	A.L.	OF	4	17	3	4	0	0	1	3	0	.235
2007 New York	A.L.	OF	4	18	2	5	0	0	2	5	0	.278
2009 New York	A.L.	OF	3	12	0	1	0	0	0	0	0	.083
2011 Tampa Bay	A.L.	DH	4	17	3	4	0	0	1	3	0	.235
Division Series Totals			31	133	19	39	6	1	5	14	7	.293
Championship Series												
2003 Boston	A.L.	OF	5	20	1	4	1	0	0	1	1	.200
2004 Boston	A.L.	OF	7	35	5	6	0	0	2	7	2	.171
2009 New York	A.L.	OF	6	30	4	9	1	0	2	5	0	.300
Championship Series Totals			18	85	10	19	2	0	4	13	3	.224
World Series Record												
2004 Boston	A.L.	OF	4	21	4	6	2	1	1	2	0	.286
2009 New York	A.L.	OF	6	22	6	8	2	0	0	4	3	.364
World Series Totals			10	43	10	14	4	1	1	6	3	.326

a Traded to Oakland Athletics with infielder Mark Ellis for pitcher Roberto Hernandez, catcher A.J. Hinch, infielder Angel Berroa and cash, January 8, 2001.
b Filed for free agency, November 5, 2001. Signed with Boston Red Sox, December 21, 2001.
c Filed for free agency, October 28, 2005. Signed with New York Yankees, December 23, 2005.
d On disabled list from July 5 to July 21, 2008.
e Filed for free agency, November 9, 2009. Signed with Detroit Tigers, February 22, 2010.
f Filed for free agency, November 1, 2010. Signed with Tampa Bay Rays, February 1, 2011.
g Filed for free agency, October 30, 2011.

DAVIS, CHRISTOPHER LYN (CHRIS)

Born, Longview, Texas, March 17, 1986.
Bats Left. Throws Right. Height, 6 feet, 4 inches. Weight, 230 pounds.

Year	Club	Lea	Pos	G	AB	R	H	2B	3B	HR	RBI	SB	Avg
2006 Spokane	Northwest	OF-1B	69	253	38	70	18	1	15	42	2	.277
2007 Bakersfield	Calif.	3B	99	386	69	115	28	3	24	93	3	.298
2007 Frisco	Texas	3B	30	109	21	32	7	0	12	25	0	.294
2008 Frisco	Texas	1B	46	186	43	62	14	0	13	42	5	.333
2008 Oklahoma	P.C.	1B	31	111	25	37	7	1	10	31	2	.333
2008 Texas	A.L.	1B-3B	80	295	51	84	23	2	17	55	1	.285
2009 Okla.	P.C.	3B-1B	44	165	27	54	12	1	6	30	0	.327
2009 Texas	A.L.	1B-3B	113	391	48	93	15	1	21	59	0	.238
2010 Oklahoma	P.C.	3B-1B-OF	103	398	67	130	31	2	14	80	3	.327
2010 Texas	A.L.	1B-3B	45	120	7	23	9	0	1	4	3	.192

Year	Club	Lea	Pos	G	AB	R	H	2B	3B	HR	RBI	SB	Avg
2011 Bowie............Eastern			1B-3B	2	6	2	3	1	0	0	0	0	.500
2011 Round Rock..........P.C.			3B-OF	48	193	39	71	14	1	24	66	1	.368
2011 Texas-Baltimore a-b.... A.L.			1B-3B	59	199	25	53	12	0	5	19	1	.266
Major League Totals............			4 Yrs.	297	1005	131	253	59	3	44	137	5	.252

a Traded to Baltimore Orioles with pitcher Tommy Hunter for pitcher Koji Uehara and cash, July 30, 2011.
b On disabled list from August 15 to September 6, 2011.

DAVIS, ISAAC BENJAMIN (IKE)
Born, Edina, Minnesota, March 22, 1987.
Bats Left. Throws Left. Height, 6 feet, 4 inches. Weight, 215 pounds.

Year	Club	Lea	Pos	G	AB	R	H	2B	3B	HR	RBI	SB	Avg
2008 Brooklyn........ N.Y.-Penn.			1B	58	215	17	55	15	0	0	17	0	.256
2009 Binghamton........Eastern			1B-OF	55	207	30	64	14	0	13	43	0	.309
2009 St. Lucie............Fla.St.			1B	59	222	28	64	17	3	7	28	0	.288
2010 Buffalo............... Int.			1B	10	33	8	12	3	0	2	4	0	.364
2010 New York...........N.L.			1B	147	523	73	138	33	1	19	71	0	.264
2011 New York a...........N.L.			1B	36	129	20	39	8	1	7	25	0	.302
Major League Totals............			2 Yrs.	183	652	93	177	41	2	26	96	3	.271

a On disabled list from May 11 to October 24, 2011.

DAVIS, RAJAI LAVAE
Born, Norwich, Connecticut, October 19, 1980.
Bats Right. Throws Right. Height, 5 feet, 11 inches. Weight, 195 pounds.

Year	Club	Lea	Pos	G	AB	R	H	2B	3B	HR	RBI	SB	Avg
2001 Pirates......... Gulf Coast			OF	26	84	19	22	1	0	0	4	11	.262
2001 Williamsport.... N.Y.-Penn.			OF-2B	6	12	1	1	0	0	0	0	0	.083
2002 Pirates......... Gulf Coast			OF	58	224	38	86	16	5	4	35	24	.384
2002 Williamsport.... N.Y.-Penn.			OF	1	4	0	0	0	0	0	0	0	.000
2002 Hickory............. So.Atl.			OF	6	14	4	6	0	0	0	3	2	.429
2003 Hickory............. So.Atl.			OF	125	478	84	146	21	7	6	54	40	.305
2004 Lynchburg....... Carolina			OF	127	509	91	160	27	7	5	38	57	.314
2005 Altoona........... Eastern			OF	123	499	82	140	22	5	4	34	45	.281
2006 Indianapolis........... Int.			OF	100	385	53	109	17	1	2	21	45	.283
2006 Pittsburgh...........N.L.			OF	20	14	1	2	1	0	0	1	1	.143
2007 Indianapolis........... Int.			OF	53	211	31	67	12	4	4	30	27	.318
2007 Pittsburgh-San Francisco a N.L.			OF	75	190	32	53	11	2	1	9	22	.279
2008 San Francisco.........N.L.			OF	12	18	2	1	0	0	0	0	4	.056
2008 Oakland b........... A.L.			OF-2B	101	196	28	51	5	4	3	19	25	.260
2009 Oakland............ A.L.			OF	125	390	65	119	27	5	3	48	41	.305
2010 Oakland c........... A.L.			OF	143	525	66	149	28	3	5	52	50	.284
2011 Dunedin............Fla.St.			OF	2	5	1	2	0	0	1	1	0	.400
2011 New Hampshire..... Eastern			OF	4	10	1	3	1	0	0	0	0	.300
2011 Toronto d........... A.L.			OF	95	320	44	76	21	6	1	29	34	.237
Major League Totals............			6 Yrs.	571	1653	238	451	93	20	13	157	177	.273

a Traded to San Francisco Giants with player to be named later for pitcher Matt Morris, July 31, 2007. San Francisco Giants received pitcher Steve MacFarland to complete trade, August 27, 2007.
b Claimed on waivers by Oakland Athletics, April 23, 2008.
c Traded to Toronto Blue Jays for pitcher Daniel Farquhar and pitcher Trystan Magnuson, November 17, 2010.
d On disabled list from April 11 to April 29 and August 14 to November 1, 2011.

DE AZA (CEDA), ALEJANDRO ALBERTO
Born, Guaymate, Dominican Republic, April 11, 1984.
Bats Left. Throws Left. Height, 6 feet. Weight, 190 pounds.

Year	Club	Lea	Pos	G	AB	R	H	2B	3B	HR	RBI	SB	Avg
2002 Dodgers........ Gulf Coast			OF-C	39	128	27	29	6	1	1	14	16	.227
2003 Ogden............Pioneer			OF	55	208	36	48	11	1	2	24	15	.231
2004 Columbus a........ So.Atl.			OF-1B	102	341	63	87	17	2	4	45	24	.255
2005 Jupiter............Fla.St.			OF	123	472	75	135	24	9	3	37	34	.286
2006 Jupiter............Fla.St.			OF	2	7	1	1	0	1	0	0	0	.143
2006 Marlins........ Gulf Coast			OF	7	24	7	11	1	0	0	4	3	.458
2006 Carolina......... Southern			OF	69	230	40	64	12	2	2	16	27	.278
2007 Marlins........ Gulf Coast			OF	4	9	2	6	2	0	0	1	2	.667
2007 Jupiter............Fla.St.			OF	2	8	1	4	1	1	0	0	0	.500
2007 Carolina......... Southern			OF	5	20	7	7	2	0	2	3	0	.350
2007 Florida.............N.L.			OF	45	144	14	33	8	2	0	8	2	.229
2008 Florida b.............N.L.						INJURED—Did Not Play							

Year	Club	Lea	Pos	G	AB	R	H	2B	3B	HR	RBI	SB	Avg
2009 Florida	N.L.	OF	22	20	6	5	1	0	0	3	0	.250
2009 New Orleans c	P.C.	OF	87	267	45	80	21	5	8	34	11	.300
2010 Charlotte	Int.	OF	79	318	53	96	21	4	5	49	16	.302
2010 Chicago	A.L.	OF	19	30	7	9	3	0	0	2	2	.300
2011 Charlotte	Int.	OF	99	385	64	124	29	5	9	37	22	.322
2011 Chicago	A.L.	OF	54	152	29	50	11	3	4	23	12	.329
Major League Totals	4 Yrs.		140	346	56	97	23	5	4	36	16	.280

a Selected Florida Marlins from Los Angeles Dodgers in Rule V draft, December 13, 2004.
b On disabled list from March 30 to October 1, 2008.
c Claimed on waivers by Chicago White Sox, October 21, 2009.

DE JESUS, DAVID CHRISTOPHER

Born, Brooklyn, New York, December 20, 1979.
Bats Left. Throws Left. Height, 6 feet. Weight, 190 pounds.

Year	Club	Lea	Pos	G	AB	R	H	2B	3B	HR	RBI	SB	Avg
2001 a					INJURED—Did Not Play								
2002 Wilmington	Carolina	OF	87	334	69	99	22	6	4	41	15	.296
2002 Wichita	Texas	OF	25	79	7	20	5	2	2	15	3	.253
2003 Wichita	Texas	OF	17	71	14	24	4	0	2	10	1	.338
2003 Omaha	P.C.	OF	59	215	49	64	16	3	5	23	8	.298
2003 Kansas City	A.L.	OF	12	7	0	2	0	1	0	0	0	.286
2004 Omaha	P.C.	OF	50	197	38	62	14	4	6	16	7	.315
2004 Kansas City	A.L.	OF	96	363	58	104	15	3	7	39	8	.287
2005 Kansas City	A.L.	OF	122	461	69	135	31	6	9	56	5	.293
2006 Omaha	P.C.	OF	3	13	0	5	0	0	0	2	0	.385
2006 Kansas City b	A.L.	OF	119	491	83	145	36	7	8	56	6	.295
2007 Kansas City	A.L.	OF	157	605	101	157	29	9	7	58	10	.260
2008 Kansas City	A.L.	OF	135	518	70	159	25	7	12	73	11	.307
2009 Kansas City	A.L.	OF	144	558	74	157	28	9	13	71	4	.281
2010 Kansas City c-d	A.L.	OF	91	352	46	112	23	3	5	37	3	.318
2011 Oakland e	A.L.	OF	131	442	60	106	20	5	10	46	4	.240
Major League Totals	9 Yrs.		1007	3797	561	1077	207	50	71	436	51	.284

a On minor league disabled list from June 19 to September 17, 2001.
b On disabled list from April 19 to May 29, 2006.
c On disabled list from July 23 to November 10, 2010.
d Traded to Oakland Athletics for pitcher Vin Mazzaro and pitcher Justin Marks, November 10, 2010.
e Filed for free agency, October 30, 2011. Signed with Chicago Cubs, November 30, 2011.

DENORFIA, CHRISTOPHER ANTHONY (CHRIS)

Born, Bristol, Connecticut, July 15, 1980.
Bats Right. Throws Right. Height, 6 feet, 1 inch. Weight, 205 pounds.

Year	Club	Lea	Pos	G	AB	R	H	2B	3B	HR	RBI	SB	Avg
2002 Reds.......	Gulf Coast	OF	57	200	38	68	9	2	0	19	18	.340
2002 Dayton	Midwest	OF	3	10	2	0	0	0	0	0	0	.000
2002 Chattanooga......	Southern	OF	3	7	0	3	2	1	0	0	0	.429
2003 Potomac.........	Carolina	OF	128	470	60	111	10	5	4	39	20	.236
2004 Potomac..........	Carolina	OF	75	269	52	84	18	4	11	51	10	.312
2004 Chattanooga......	Southern	OF	61	221	30	55	10	2	6	27	5	.249
2005 Chattanooga......	Southern	OF	46	188	40	62	17	3	7	26	4	.330
2005 Louisville	Int.	OF	91	323	50	100	12	6	13	61	8	.310
2005 Cincinnati..........	N.L.	OF	18	38	8	10	3	0	1	2	1	.263
2006 Louisville	Int.	OF	83	312	46	109	19	1	7	45	15	.349
2006 Cincinnati..........	N.L.	OF	49	106	14	30	6	0	1	7	1	.283
2007 Cincinnati...........	N.L.				INJURED—Did Not Play								
2007 Oakland a-b	A.L.				INJURED—Did Not Play								
2008 Stockton...........	Calif.	OF	2	9	1	3	0	0	0	0	0	.333
2008 Sacramento	P.C.	OF	45	189	34	57	13	1	2	20	5	.302
2008 Oakland c	A.L.	OF	29	62	10	18	3	0	1	9	2	.290
2009 Oakland	A.L.	OF	4	2	1	0	0	0	0	1	0	.000
2009 Sacramento d........	P.C.	OF	107	432	62	117	18	5	9	49	15	.271
2010 Portland	P.C.	OF	34	121	17	37	10	4	2	12	7	.306
2010 San Diego	N.L.	OF	99	284	41	77	15	2	9	36	8	.271
2011 Lake Elsinore	Calif.	OF	2	6	1	4	1	0	0	2	0	.667
2011 Tucson.............	P.C.	OF	7	17	0	2	1	0	0	0	0	.118
2011 San Diego e	N.L.	OF	111	307	38	85	13	2	5	19	11	.277
Major League Totals	6 Yrs.		310	799	112	220	40	4	17	74	23	.275

a On disabled list from March 24 to October 15, 2007.

b Traded to Oakland Athletics for pitcher Marcus McBeth and player to be named later, April 27, 2007. Cincinnati Reds received pitcher Ben Jukich to complete trade, June 12, 2007.
c On disabled list from May 7 to July 19, 2008.
d Filed for free agency, November 9, 2009. Signed with San Diego Padres organization, December 17, 2009.
e On disabled list from August 4 to September 5, 2011.

DE ROSA, MARK THOMAS
Born, Passaic, New Jersey, February 26, 1975.
Bats Right. Throws Right. Height, 6 feet, 1 inch. Weight, 205 pounds.

Year	Club	Lea	Pos	G	AB	R	H	2B	3B	HR	RBI	SB	Avg
1996 Eugene		Northwest	SS	70	255	43	66	13	1	2	28	3	.259
1997 Durham		Carolina	SS	92	346	51	93	11	3	8	37	6	.269
1998 Greenville		Southern	SS	125	461	67	123	26	2	8	49	7	.267
1998 Atlanta		N.L.	SS	5	3	2	1	0	0	0	0	0	.333
1999 Richmond		Int.	SS	105	364	41	99	16	2	1	40	7	.272
1999 Atlanta		N.L.	SS	7	8	0	0	0	0	0	0	0	.000
2000 Richmond		Int.	SS-2B-3B	101	370	62	108	22	3	3	35	13	.292
2000 Atlanta		N.L.	SS	22	13	9	4	1	0	0	3	0	.308
2001 Richmond		Int.	SS-3B-2B	49	186	31	55	18	0	2	17	7	.296
2001 Atlanta		N.L.	SS-2B-3B-OF	66	164	27	47	8	0	3	20	2	.287
2002 Myrtle Beach		Car.	2B	2	7	0	0	0	0	0	0	0	.000
2002 Richmond		Int.	2B-SS	16	55	9	14	3	0	0	6	2	.255
2002 Atlanta a		N.L.	2B-SS-OF-3B	72	212	24	63	9	2	5	23	2	.297
2003 Atlanta		N.L.	2B-3B-SS-OF	103	266	40	70	14	0	6	22	1	.263
2004 Atlanta b		N.L.	3B-SS-2B-OF	118	309	33	74	16	0	3	31	1	.239
2005 Texas		A.L.	OF-2B-SS-3B	66	148	26	36	5	0	8	20	1	.243
2006 Oklahoma		P.C.	2B-3B	3	12	2	6	1	0	0	0	0	.500
2006 Texas c-d		A.L.	OF-3B-2B-SS	136	520	78	154	40	2	13	74	4	.296
2007 Chicago		N.L.	2B-3B-OF-1B	149	502	64	147	28	3	10	72	1	.293
2008 Chicago e		N.L.	2B-OF-3B-1B	149	505	103	144	30	3	21	87	6	.285
2009 Cleveland		A.L.	3B-OF-1B	71	278	47	75	13	0	13	50	1	.270
2009 St. Louis f-g-h		N.L.	3B-1B-OF-2B	68	237	31	54	10	1	10	28	2	.228
2010 San Jose		Calif.	OF	1	4	0	0	0	0	0	0	0	.000
2010 Fresno		P.C.	2B-3B-OF	3	11	1	4	1	0	0	1	0	.364
2010 San Francisco i		N.L.	OF-2B	26	93	9	18	3	0	1	10	0	.194
2011 San Jose		Calif.	2B-3B	2	5	2	2	1	0	0	0	0	.400
2011 Fresno		P.C.	3B-2B-1B	11	42	6	13	1	0	0	3	0	.310
2011 San Francisco j-k		N.L.	3B-1B-2B	47	86	9	24	2	0	0	12	1	.279
Major League Totals		14 Yrs.		1105	3344	502	911	179	11	93	452	22	.272

Division Series

Year	Club	Lea	Pos	G	AB	R	H	2B	3B	HR	RBI	SB	Avg
2001 Atlanta		N.L.	SS	1	1	0	1	0	0	0	0	0	1.000
2002 Atlanta		N.L.	2B	4	7	2	3	1	1	0	3	0	.429
2003 Atlanta		N.L.	2B-3B	4	7	1	3	2	0	0	2	0	.429
2007 Chicago		N.L.	2B	3	9	2	3	0	0	0	0	0	.333
2008 Chicago		N.L.	2B-OF	3	12	2	4	2	0	1	4	0	.333
2009 St. Louis		N.L.	3B	3	13	1	5	1	0	0	1	0	.385
Division Series Totals				18	49	8	19	6	1	1	10	0	.388

Championship Series

Year	Club	Lea	Pos	G	AB	R	H	2B	3B	HR	RBI	SB	Avg
2001 Atlanta		N.L.	SS	4	4	0	0	0	0	0	0	0	.000

a On disabled list from May 18 to July 17, 2002.
b Not offered contract, December 20, 2004. Signed with Texas Rangers organization, January 19, 2005.
c On disabled list from April 15 to April 30, 2006.
d Filed for free agency, October 28, 2006. Signed with Chicago Cubs, November 15, 2006.
e Traded to Cleveland Indians for pitcher Jeff Stevens, pitcher Chris Archer and pitcher John Gaub, December 31, 2008.
f Traded to St. Louis Cardinals for pitcher Chris Perez and player to be named later, June 27, 2009. Cleveland Indians received pitcher Jess Todd to complete trade, July 26, 2009.
g On disabled list from July 1 to July 18, 2009.
h Filed for free agency, November 5, 2009. Signed with San Francisco Giants, December 29, 2009.
i On disabled list from May 9 to November 9, 2010.
j On disabled list from April 25 to May 10 and May 19 to August 4, 2011.
k Filed for free agency, October 30, 2011. Signed with Washington Nationals, December 28, 2011.

DESCALSO, DANIEL WILLIAM
Born, Redwood City, California, October 19, 1986.
Bats Left. Throws Right. Height, 5 feet, 10 inches. Weight, 190 pounds.

Year	Club	Lea	Pos	G	AB	R	H	2B	3B	HR	RBI	SB	Avg
2007 Batavia		N.Y.-Penn.	3B-2B	66	250	29	67	7	5	0	31	12	.268
2008 Palm Beach		Fla.St.	2B-SS-3B	115	403	57	98	24	2	8	50	7	.243

Year	Club	Lea	Pos	G	AB	R	H	2B	3B	HR	RBI	SB	Avg
2008 Springfield	Texas	2B	9	37	6	13	1	1	0	4	1	.351
2009 Memphis	.P.C.	2B-1B	46	150	23	38	4	0	2	17	3	.253
2009 Springfield	Texas	2B	73	288	46	93	26	5	8	51	0	.323
2010 Memphis	.P.C.	2B-1B	116	468	86	132	32	3	9	71	8	.282
2010 St. Louis	N.L.	3B-SS	11	34	6	9	2	0	0	4	1	.265
2011 St. Louis	N.L.	3B-2B-SS	148	326	35	86	20	3	1	28	2	.264
Major League Totals		2 Yrs.	159	360	41	95	22	3	1	32	3	.264
Division Series												
2011 St. Louis	N.L.	3B	4	3	0	0	0	0	0	0	0	.000
Championship Series												
2011 St. Louis	N.L.	3B-2B	4	3	1	1	0	0	0	0	0	.333
World Series Record												
2011 St. Louis	N.L.	3B-SS	5	3	2	2	0	0	0	0	0	.667

DESMOND, IAN M.

Born, Sarasota, Florida, September 20, 1985.
Bats Right. Throws Right. Height, 6 feet, 2 inches. Weight, 210 pounds.

Year	Club	Lea	Pos	G	AB	R	H	2B	3B	HR	RBI	SB	Avg
2004 Expos	Gulf Coast	SS	55	216	28	49	11	0	1	27	13	.227
2004 Vermont	N.Y.-Penn.	SS	4	12	2	3	0	0	1	1	0	.250
2005 Potomac	Carolina	SS	55	219	37	56	13	3	3	15	13	.256
2005 Savannah	So.Atl.	SS	73	296	37	73	10	2	4	23	20	.247
2006 Potomac	Carolina	SS	92	365	50	89	20	2	9	45	14	.244
2006 Harrisburg	Eastern	SS	37	121	8	22	4	1	0	3	4	.182
2007 Potomac	Carolina	SS	129	458	69	121	30	4	13	45	27	.264
2008 Harrisburg	Eastern	SS	93	323	42	81	14	0	12	44	12	.251
2008 Nationals	Gulf Coast	SS	3	13	1	5	1	0	0	2	3	.385
2009 Harrisburg	Eastern	SS	42	170	29	52	12	1	6	18	13	.306
2009 Syracuse	Int.	SS-OF	55	178	25	63	12	2	1	14	8	.354
2009 Washington	N.L.	SS-2B-OF	21	82	9	23	7	2	4	12	1	.280
2010 Washington	N.L.	SS-OF	154	525	59	141	27	4	10	65	17	.269
2011 Washington	N.L.	SS	154	584	65	148	27	5	8	49	25	.253
Major League Totals		3 Yrs.	329	1191	133	312	61	11	22	126	43	.262

DEWITT, BLAKE ROBERT

Born, Sarasota, Florida, August 20, 1985.
Bats Left. Throws Right. Height, 5 feet, 11 inches. Weight, 190 pounds.

Year	Club	Lea	Pos	G	AB	R	H	2B	3B	HR	RBI	SB	Avg
2004 Ogden	Pioneer	3B	70	299	61	85	19	3	12	47	1	.284
2005 Vero Beach	Fla.St.	3B	8	31	4	13	3	0	1	7	0	.419
2005 Columbus	So.Atl.	3B	120	481	61	136	31	3	11	65	0	.283
2006 Vero Beach	Fla.St.	2B-3B	106	425	61	114	18	1	18	61	8	.268
2006 Jacksonville	Southern	3B-2B	26	104	6	19	1	0	1	6	0	.183
2007 Inland Empire	Calif.	3B	83	339	48	101	29	2	8	46	2	.298
2007 Jacksonville	Southern	3B	45	178	20	50	13	1	6	20	0	.281
2008 Las Vegas	.P.C.	2B-3B-1B	27	111	16	34	4	2	4	18	1	.306
2008 Los Angeles	N.L.	3B-2B	117	368	47	97	13	2	9	52	3	.264
2009 Albuquerque	.P.C.	2B-3B-SS	92	352	64	90	21	9	7	47	2	.256
2009 Los Angeles	N.L.	3B-2B-SS	31	49	4	10	3	0	2	4	0	.204
2010 Los Angeles-Chicago a .	N.L.	2B-3B	135	440	47	115	24	5	5	52	3	.261
2011 Chicago	N.L.	OF-2B-3B	121	230	21	61	11	4	5	26	1	.265
Major League Totals		4 Yrs.	404	1087	117	283	51	11	21	134	7	.260
Division Series												
2008 Los Angeles	N.L.	2B	3	11	2	3	2	0	0	1	0	.273
Championship Series												
2008 Los Angeles	N.L.	2B	5	13	0	1	0	1	0	5	0	.077

a Traded to Chicago Cubs with pitcher Kyle Smit and pitcher Brett Wallach for pitcher Ted Lilly, infielder Ryan Theriot and cash, July 31, 2010.

DIAZ, MATTHEW EDWARD (MATT)

Born, Portland, Oregon, March 3, 1978.
Bats Right. Throws Right. Height, 6 feet, 1 inch. Weight, 205 pounds.

Year	Club	Lea	Pos	G	AB	R	H	2B	3B	HR	RBI	SB	Avg
1999 Hudson Valley . . .	N.Y.-Penn.	OF	54	208	22	51	15	2	1	20	6	.245
2000 St. Petersburg	Fla.St.	OF	106	392	37	106	21	3	6	53	2	.270

Year	Club	Lea	Pos	G	AB	R	H	2B	3B	HR	RBI	SB	Avg
2001 Bakersfield . . . . .Calif.			OF	131	524	79	172	40	2	17	81	11	.328
2002 Orlando . . . . Southern			OF-1B	122	449	71	123	28	1	10	50	31	.274
2003 Orlando . . . . Southern			OF	60	227	32	87	21	0	5	41	9	.383
2003 Durham . . . . Int.			OF	67	253	35	83	18	3	8	45	6	.328
2003 Tampa Bay . . . . A.L.			OF	4	9	2	1	0	0	0	0	0	.111
2004 Durham . . . . Int.			OF	134	503	81	167	47	5	21	93	15	.332
2004 Tampa Bay . . . . A.L.			OF	10	21	3	4	1	1	1	3	0	.190
2005 Royals . . . . .Arizona			OF	3	13	2	6	2	0	0	2	0	.462
2005 Wichita. . . . . Texas			OF	7	26	6	7	0	0	1	6	1	.269
2005 Omaha . . . . .P.C.			OF	65	259	48	96	22	4	14	56	10	.371
2005 Kansas City a-b-c. . . . . A.L.			OF	34	89	7	25	4	2	1	9	0	.281
2006 Atlanta . . . . N.L.			OF	124	297	37	97	15	4	7	32	5	.327
2007 Atlanta . . . . N.L.			OF-1B	135	358	44	121	21	0	12	45	4	.338
2008 Mississippi. . . . . . Southern			OF	7	26	5	6	0	0	1	4	1	.231
2008 Richmond . . . . Int.			OF	4	12	0	2	0	0	0	1	0	.167
2008 Atlanta d. . . . . N.L.			OF	43	135	9	33	2	0	2	14	4	.244
2009 Atlanta . . . . N.L.			OF	125	371	56	116	18	4	13	58	12	.313
2010 Gwinnett. . . . . Int.			OF	3	12	2	3	1	0	0	3	0	.250
2010 Atlanta e-f . . . . N.L.			OF	84	224	27	56	17	2	7	31	3	.250
2011 Pittsburgh-Atlanta g . . . . N.L.			OF	116	251	16	66	13	1	0	20	5	.263
Major League Totals		9 Yrs.		675	1755	201	519	91	14	43	212	33	.296
Division Series													
2010 Atlanta . . . . N.L.			OF	4	10	0	1	0	0	0	0	0	.100

a Released by Tampa Bay Devil Rays, February 18, 2005. Signed with Kansas City Royals organization, February 24, 2005.

b On disabled list from June 11 to July 18, 2005.

c Traded to Atlanta Braves for pitcher Ricardo Rodriguez, December 20, 2005.

d On disabled list from May 28 to September 24, 2008.

e On disabled list from May 15 to June 29, 2010.

f Not offered contract, December 2, 2010. Signed with Pittsburgh Pirates, December 8, 2010.

g Traded to Atlanta Braves with cash for player to be named later, August 31, 2011. Pittsburgh Pirates received pitcher Eliecer Cardenas to complete trade, September 20, 2011.

DICKERSON, CHRISTOPHER CHARLES (CHRIS)
Born, Hollywood, California, April 10, 1982.
Bats Left. Throws Left. Height, 6 feet, 3 inches. Weight, 225 pounds.

Year	Club	Lea	Pos	G	AB	R	H	2B	3B	HR	RBI	SB	Avg
2003 Billings . . . . .Pioneer			OF	58	201	36	49	6	4	6	38	9	.244
2004 Potomac . . . . Carolina			OF	15	45	5	9	2	0	0	5	3	.200
2004 Dayton . . . . Midwest			OF	84	314	50	95	15	3	4	34	27	.303
2005 Sarasota . . . . .Fla.St.			OF	119	436	68	103	17	7	11	43	19	.236
2006 Chattanooga. . . . . . Southern			OF	115	389	65	94	21	7	12	48	21	.242
2007 Louisville . . . . Int.			OF	104	354	58	92	11	6	13	44	23	.260
2007 Chattanooga. . . . . . Southern			OF	30	114	11	31	4	1	1	11	7	.272
2008 Louisville . . . . Int.			OF	97	349	65	100	16	9	11	53	26	.287
2008 Cincinnati. . . . . N.L.			OF	31	102	20	31	9	2	6	15	5	.304
2009 Louisville . . . . Int.			OF	4	12	2	3	0	0	0	1	2	.250
2009 Cincinnati a . . . . N.L.			OF	97	255	31	70	13	3	2	15	11	.275
2010 Louisville . . . . Int.			OF	13	43	12	19	5	0	3	7	6	.442
2010 Cincinnati-Milwaukee b-c. N.L.			OF	45	97	11	20	2	2	0	5	4	.206
2011 Scranton-WB . . . . Int.			OF	57	212	33	51	10	1	2	16	18	.241
2011 New York d. . . . . A.L.			OF	60	50	9	13	2	0	1	7	4	.260
Major League Totals		4 Yrs.		233	504	71	134	26	7	9	42	24	.266
Division Series													
2011 New York . . . . A.L.			OF	1	1	1	0	0	0	0	0	0	.000

a On disabled list from July 27 to August 11 and August 24 to September 30, 2009.

b On disabled list from April 30 to August 9, 2010.

c Traded to Milwaukee Brewers for outfielder Jim Edmonds, August 9, 2010.

d Traded to New York Yankees for pitcher Sergio Mitre, March 25, 2011.

DIRKS, ANDREW LEE (ANDY)
Born, Hutchinson, Kansas, January 24, 1986.
Bats Left. Throws Left. Height, 6 feet. Weight, 195 pounds.

Year	Club	Lea	Pos	G	AB	R	H	2B	3B	HR	RBI	SB	Avg
2008 Tigers . . . . Gulf Coast			OF	10	34	10	14	3	2	0	7	2	.412
2008 West Michigan . . . . . Midwest			OF	3	10	0	1	0	0	0	2	0	.100
2009 Erie. . . . . Eastern			OF	98	361	46	92	14	1	6	44	11	.255
2009 Lakeland. . . . . .Fla.St.			OF	27	103	11	34	5	0	0	18	10	.330

Year	Club	Lea	Pos	G	AB	R	H	2B	3B	HR	RBI	SB	Avg
2010 Erie..............	Eastern	OF	98	388	64	108	20	2	11	46	19	.278
2010 Toledo	Int.	OF	22	88	14	33	10	1	4	17	3	.375
2011 Toledo	Int.	OF	41	157	30	51	8	1	7	24	12	.325
2011 Detroit	A.L.	OF	78	219	34	55	13	0	7	28	5	.251
Championship Series												
2011 Detroit	A.L.	OF	2	5	1	1	0	0	0	0	1	.200

DOBBS, GREGORY STUART (GREG)

Born, Los Angeles, California, July 2, 1978.
Bats Left. Throws Right. Height, 6 feet, 1 inch. Weight, 205 pounds.

Year	Club	Lea	Pos	G	AB	R	H	2B	3B	HR	RBI	SB	Avg
2001 San Bernardino ...	Calif.	OF	3	13	2	5	1	0	1	3	0	.385
2001 Everett	Northwest	1B-OF-3B	65	249	37	80	17	2	6	41	5	.321
2002 Wisconsin	Midwest	3B	86	320	43	88	16	2	10	48	13	.275
2002 San Antonio .	Texas	OF-1B	27	96	13	35	2	0	5	15	1	.365
2003 San Antonio	Texas	3B	2	6	0	2	2	0	0	0	0	.333
2004 San Antonio	Texas	3B	51	203	25	66	14	4	5	34	5	.325
2004 Tacoma	P.C.	3B	67	255	28	69	9	2	8	31	4	.271
2004 Seattle	A.L.	3B	18	53	4	12	1	0	1	9	0	.226
2005 Tacoma	P.C.	1B-3B-OF	50	190	27	61	9	0	3	22	5	.321
2005 Seattle	A.L.	DH-1B-OF-3B	59	142	8	35	7	1	1	20	1	.246
2006 Tacoma	P.C.	3B-1B-OF	99	379	60	119	19	3	9	55	14	.314
2006 Seattle	A.L.	1B-OF-3B	23	27	4	10	3	1	0	3	0	.370
2007 Philadelphia a...	N.L.	3B-OF-1B-2B	142	324	45	88	20	4	10	55	3	.272
2008 Philadelphia	N.L.	3B-OF-1B	128	226	30	68	14	1	9	40	3	.301
2009 Philadelphia b...	N.L.	3B-OF-1B	97	154	15	38	6	0	5	20	1	.247
2010 Lehigh Valley	Int.	OF-3B	16	62	10	13	3	1	2	9	2	.210
2010 Philadelphia c...	N.L.	3B-1B-OF	88	163	13	32	7	0	5	15	1	.196
2011 Florida d.........	N.L.	3B-OF-1B	134	411	38	113	23	0	8	49	0	.275
Major League Totals		8 Yrs.	689	1500	157	396	81	7	39	211	9	.264
Division Series												
2007 Philadelphia	N.L.	3B	3	3	0	0	0	0	0	0	0	.000
2008 Philadelphia	N.L.	3B	3	5	0	3	0	0	0	0	0	.600
2009 Philadelphia	N.L.	PH	3	3	0	0	0	0	0	0	0	.000
Division Series Totals			9	11	0	3	0	0	0	0	0	.273
Championship Series												
2008 Philadelphia	N.L.	3B	3	6	2	3	1	0	0	0	0	.500
2009 Philadelphia	N.L.	PH	2	1	0	0	0	0	0	0	0	.000
Championship Series Totals			5	7	2	3	1	0	0	0	0	.429
World Series Record												
2008 Philadelphia	N.L.	DH	2	3	0	1	0	0	0	0	0	.333

a Claimed by Philadelphia Phillies on waivers, January 16, 2007.
b On disabled list from August 22 to September 16, 2009.
c Filed for free agency, October 28, 2010. Signed with Florida Marlins organization, January 31, 2011.
d Filed for free agency, October 30, 2011, re-signed with Florida Marlins, January 5, 2012.

DONALD, JASON THOMAS

Born, Clovis, California, September 4, 1984.
Bats Right. Throws Right. Height, 6 feet, 1 inch. Weight, 195 pounds.

Year	Club	Lea	Pos	G	AB	R	H	2B	3B	HR	RBI	SB	Avg
2006 Batavia.........	N.Y.-Penn.	SS	63	213	33	56	14	2	1	24	12	.263
2007 Clearwater	Fla.St.	SS	83	293	48	88	22	5	8	41	3	.300
2007 Lakewood	So.Atl.	SS	51	197	41	61	9	3	4	30	2	.310
2008 Reading	Eastern	SS	92	362	57	111	19	4	14	54	11	.307
2009 Phillies.........	Gulf Coast	SS	9	26	4	6	1	1	0	1	1	.231
2009 Columbus.........	Int.	SS	10	35	10	9	2	0	1	1	1	.257
2009 Lehigh Valley a.....	Int.	SS-2B-3B	51	208	26	49	15	1	1	16	6	.236
2010 Columbus...........	Int.	2B-SS	37	137	27	38	10	2	2	17	10	.277
2010 Cleveland	A.L.	SS-2B	88	296	39	75	19	3	4	24	5	.253
2011 Akron............	Eastern	3B-SS	9	29	4	7	0	0	0	2	1	.241
2011 Columbus...........	Int.	SS-3B	47	174	32	54	12	0	4	15	7	.310
2011 Cleveland b	A.L.	2B-SS-3B	39	132	13	42	6	1	1	8	3	.318
Major League Totals		2 Yrs.	127	428	52	117	25	4	5	32	8	.273

a Traded by Philadelphia Phillies to Cleveland Indians with catcher Lou Marson, pitcher Jason Knapp and pitcher Carlos Carrasco for pitcher Cliff Lee and outfielder Ben Francisco, July 29, 2009.
b On disabled list from March 22 to April 29, 2011.

DOUMIT, RYAN MATTHEW

Born, Moses Lake, Washington, April 3, 1981.
Bats Both. Throws Right. Height, 6 feet. Weight, 200 pounds.

Year Club	Lea	Pos	G	AB	R	H	2B	3B	HR	RBI	SB	Avg
1999 Pirates . . . . Gulf Coast	C	29	85	17	24	5	0	1	7	4	.282
2000 Williamsport . . . . . N.Y.-Penn.	C	66	246	25	77	15	5	2	40	2	.313
2001 Altoona . . . . Eastern	C	2	4	0	1	0	0	0	2	0	.250
2001 Pirates . . . . Gulf Coast	C	7	17	2	4	2	0	0	3	0	.235
2001 Hickory . . . . So.Atl.	C	39	148	14	40	6	0	2	14	2	.270
2002 Hickory . . . . So.Atl.	C	68	258	46	83	14	1	6	47	3	.322
2003 Lynchburg . . . . Carolina	C	127	458	75	126	38	1	11	77	4	.275
2004 Altoona . . . . Eastern	C	67	221	31	58	20	0	10	34	0	.262
2005 Indianapolis . . . . Int.	C-OF	51	165	41	57	11	0	12	35	1	.345
2005 Pittsburgh . . . . N.L.	C-OF	75	231	25	59	13	1	6	35	2	.255
2006 Pirates . . . . Gulf Coast	C-1B	5	14	1	0	0	0	0	0	0	.000
2006 Altoona . . . . Eastern	C-1B	4	15	4	5	3	0	0	4	0	.333
2006 Indianapolis . . . . Int.	C	6	22	3	7	1	1	0	7	0	.318
2006 Pittsburgh a . . . . N.L.	1B-C	61	149	15	31	9	0	6	17	0	.208
2007 Indianapolis . . . . Int.	C	16	53	15	22	4	0	4	20	3	.415
2007 Pittsburgh b . . . . N.L.	OF-C-1B	83	252	33	69	19	2	9	32	1	.274
2008 Altoona . . . . Eastern	C	3	7	0	3	0	0	0	0	0	.429
2008 Pittsburgh c . . . . N.L.	C-1B	116	431	71	137	34	0	15	69	2	.318
2009 Pirates . . . . Gulf Coast	C	2	7	0	0	0	0	0	0	0	.000
2009 Indianapolis . . . . Int.	C	5	17	1	2	0	0	0	0	0	.118
2009 Pittsburgh d . . . . N.L.	C-OF	75	280	31	70	16	0	10	38	4	.250
2010 Indianapolis . . . . Int.	OF-C	4	12	2	2	1	0	1	2	0	.167
2010 Pittsburgh e . . . . N.L.	C-OF-1B	124	406	42	102	22	1	13	45	1	.251
2011 Bradenton . . . . Fla.St.	C	5	14	1	2	0	0	0	1	0	.143
2011 Indianapolis . . . . Int.	C	8	26	4	6	1	1	0	3	0	.231
2011 Pittsburgh f-g . . . . N.L.	C	77	218	17	66	12	1	8	30	0	.303
Major League Totals	7 Yrs.	611	1967	234	534	125	5	67	266	10	.271

a On disabled list from April 12 to May 3 and June 5 to August 23, 2006.
b On disabled list from August 13 to September 8 and September 9 to November 13, 2007.
c On disabled list from May 14 to June 6, 2008.
d On disabled list from April 20 to July 10, 2009.
e On disabled list from July 22 to August 7, 2010.
f On disabled list from May 30 to August 3, 2011.
g Filed for free agency, October 31, 2011. Signed with Minnesota Twins, November 23, 2011.

DOWNS, RUSSELL MATT (MATT)

Born, Tuscaloosa, Alabama, March 19, 1984.
Bats Right. Throws Right. Height, 6 feet, 2 inches. Weight, 185 pounds.

Year Club	Lea	Pos	G	AB	R	H	2B	3B	HR	RBI	SB	Avg
2006 Giants . . . . Arizona	3B	46	168	34	52	16	4	0	29	6	.310
2007 Salem-Keizer . Northwest	1B-2B-3B	73	287	68	97	33	0	8	48	16	.338
2008 San Jose . . . . Calif.	2B-3B-SS-OF	109	437	74	133	30	1	17	75	24	.304
2008 Fresno . . . . P.C.	2B-OF-SS	22	86	10	21	5	0	3	7	1	.244
2009 San Francisco . . . . . N.L.	2B	17	53	6	9	2	0	1	2	1	.170
2009 Fresno . . . . P.C.	2B-3B-OF-SS	109	424	68	127	33	3	14	74	8	.300
2010 Fresno . . . . P.C.	3B-2B-SS	56	197	37	50	9	1	7	28	3	.254
2010 Giants . . . . Arizona	3B-SS	2	7	1	2	1	0	0	2	0	.286
2010 Round Rock . . . . P.C.	2B	6	19	0	2	1	0	0	2	1	.105
2010 San Fran.-Houston a N.L.	2B-3B-SS	40	97	8	21	7	0	1	7	0	.216
2011 Houston . . . . N.L.	2B-3B-1B-OF	106	199	29	55	18	0	10	41	0	.276
Major League Totals	3 Yrs.	163	349	43	85	27	0	12	50	1	.244

a Claimed on waivers by Houston Astros, August 25, 2010.

DREW, DAVID JONATHAN (J.D.)

Born, Tallahassee, Florida, November 20, 1975.
Bats Left. Throws Right. Height, 6 feet, 1 inch. Weight, 200 pounds.

Year Club	Lea	Pos	G	AB	R	H	2B	3B	HR	RBI	SB	Avg
1997 St. Paul . . . . Northern	OF	44	170	51	58	6	1	18	50	5	.341
1998 St. Paul . . . . Northern	OF	30	114	27	44	11	2	9	33	8	.386
1998 Arkansas . . . . Texas	OF	19	67	18	22	3	1	5	11	2	.328
1998 Memphis . . . . P.C.	OF	26	79	15	25	8	1	2	13	1	.316
1998 St. Louis . . . . N.L.	OF	14	36	9	15	3	1	5	13	0	.417
1999 St. Louis a . . . . N.L.	OF	104	368	72	89	16	6	13	39	19	.242
2000 St. Louis b . . . . N.L.	OF	135	407	73	120	17	2	18	57	17	.295

Year	Club	Lea	Pos	G	AB	R	H	2B	3B	HR	RBI	SB	Avg
2001 Peoria............	Midwest		OF	3	11	3	6	2	0	0	0	0	.545
2001 St. Louis c..........	N.L.		OF	109	375	80	121	18	5	27	73	13	.323
2002 St. Louis d..........	N.L.		OF	135	424	61	107	19	1	18	56	8	.252
2003 Palm Beach.........	Fla.St.		OF	8	19	4	7	0	0	1	3	0	.368
2003 St. Louis e-f..........	N.L.		OF	100	287	60	83	13	3	15	42	2	.289
2004 Atlanta g.............	N.L.		OF	145	518	118	158	28	8	31	93	12	.305
2005 Los Angeles h........	N.L.		OF	72	252	48	72	12	1	15	36	1	.286
2006 Los Angeles i.........	N.L.		OF	146	494	84	140	34	6	20	100	2	.283
2007 Boston.............	A.L.		OF	140	466	84	126	30	4	11	64	4	.270
2008 Boston j.............	A.L.		OF	109	368	79	103	23	4	19	64	4	.280
2009 Boston.............	A.L.		OF	137	452	84	126	30	4	24	68	2	.279
2010 Boston.............	A.L.		OF	139	478	69	122	24	2	22	68	3	.255
2011 Lowell........	N.Y.-Penn.		DH	1	2	1	0	0	0	0	0	0	.000
2011 Pawtucket........	Int.		SS	1	3	1	3	0	0	0	0	1	1.000
2011 Boston k-l..........	A.L.		OF	81	248	23	55	6	1	4	22	0	.222
Major League Totals...........		14 Yrs.		1566	5173	944	1437	273	48	242	795	87	.278
Division Series													
2000 St. Louis.............	N.L.		OF	2	6	1	1	0	0	0	0	2	.167
2001 St. Louis.............	N.L.		OF	5	13	1	2	0	0	1	2	0	.154
2002 St. Louis.............	N.L.		OF	2	9	1	2	0	0	1	1	0	.222
2004 Atlanta..............	N.L.		OF	5	20	1	4	0	0	0	1	1	.200
2006 Los Angeles.........	N.L.		OF	3	13	1	2	0	0	0	0	0	.154
2007 Boston.............	A.L.		OF	3	11	1	2	0	0	0	3	0	.182
2008 Boston.............	A.L.		OF	4	14	2	4	1	0	1	3	0	.286
2009 Boston.............	A.L.		OF	3	9	1	2	0	0	1	2	0	.222
Division Series Totals...........				27	95	9	19	1	0	4	12	3	.200
Championship Series													
2000 St. Louis.............	N.L.		OF	5	12	2	4	1	0	0	1	0	.333
2002 St. Louis.............	N.L.		OF	5	13	1	5	0	0	1	1	0	.385
2007 Boston.............	A.L.		OF	7	25	5	9	1	0	1	6	0	.360
2008 Boston.............	A.L.		OF	7	24	1	6	1	0	1	3	0	.250
Championship Series Totals......				24	74	9	24	3	0	3	11	0	.324
World Series Record													
2007 Boston.............	A.L.		OF	4	15	1	5	2	0	0	2	0	.333

a On disabled list from May 16 to June 17, 1999.
b On disabled list from July 8 to July 26, 2000.
c On disabled list from June 18 to July 31, 2001.
d On disabled list from June 28 to July 13, 2002.
e On disabled list from March 21 to April 20 and August 9 to September 1, 2003.
f Traded to Atlanta Braves with catcher Eli Marrero for pitcher Jason Marquis, pitcher Ray King and pitcher Adam Wainwright, December 13, 2003.
g Filed for free agency, October 28, 2004. Signed with Los Angeles Dodgers, December 23, 2004.
h On disabled list from July 4 to October 7, 2005.
i Filed for free agency, November 10, 2006. Signed with Boston Red Sox, December 5, 2006.
j On disabled list from August 18 to September 8, 2008.
k On disabled list from July 20 to September 25, 2011.
l Filed for free agency, October 30, 2011.

DREW, STEPHEN ORIS

Born, Hahira, Georgia, March 16, 1983.
Bats Left. Throws Right. Height, 6 feet, 1 inch. Weight, 185 pounds.

Year	Club	Lea	Pos	G	AB	R	H	2B	3B	HR	RBI	SB	Avg
2005 Tennessee.......	Southern		SS	27	101	11	22	5	0	4	13	2	.218
2006 Tucson..............	P.C.		SS	83	342	55	97	16	3	13	51	3	.284
2006 Arizona.............	N.L.		SS	59	209	27	66	13	7	5	23	2	.316
2007 Arizona.............	N.L.		SS	150	543	60	129	28	4	12	60	9	.238
2008 Arizona.............	N.L.		SS	152	611	91	178	44	11	21	67	3	.291
2009 Reno................	P.C.		SS	2	9	0	3	0	1	0	1	0	.333
2009 Arizona a...........	N.L.		SS	135	533	71	139	29	12	12	65	5	.261
2010 Arizona.............	N.L.		SS	151	565	83	157	33	12	15	61	10	.278
2011 Arizona b...........	N.L.		SS	86	321	44	81	21	5	5	45	4	.252
Major League Totals............		6 Yrs.		733	2782	376	750	168	51	70	321	33	.270
Division Series													
2007 Arizona.............	N.L.		SS	3	14	4	7	1	1	2	4	1	.500
Championship Series													
2007 Arizona.............	N.L.		SS	4	17	2	5	0	0	0	0	0	.294

a On disabled list from April 25 to May 12, 2009.
b On disabled list from July 21 to October 31, 2011.

DUDA, LUCAS CHRISTOPHER

Born, Fontana, California, February 3, 1986.
Bats Left. Throws Right. Height, 6 feet, 5 inches. Weight, 255 pounds.

Year	Club	Lea	Pos	G	AB	R	H	2B	3B	HR	RBI	SB	Avg
2007 Brooklyn	N.Y.-Penn.	1B-OF	67	234	32	70	20	3	4	32	3	.299
2008 St. Lucie	Fla.St.	1B-OF	133	483	58	127	26	3	11	66	2	.263
2009 Binghamton	Eastern	1B-OF	110	395	49	111	29	1	9	53	2	.281
2010 Binghamton	Eastern	OF-1B	45	161	30	46	17	0	6	34	1	.286
2010 Buffalo	Int.	OF-1B	70	264	44	83	23	2	17	53	0	.314
2010 New York	N.L.	OF	29	84	11	17	6	0	4	13	0	.202
2011 Buffalo	Int.	OF-1B	38	129	22	39	8	0	10	24	0	.302
2011 New York	N.L.	OF-1B	100	301	38	88	21	3	10	50	1	.292
Major League Totals		2 Yrs.	129	385	49	105	27	3	14	63	1	.273

DUNCAN, DAVID SHELLEY (SHELLEY)

Born, Tucson, Arizona, September 29, 1979.
Bats Right. Throws Right. Height, 6 feet, 5 inches. Weight, 225 pounds.

Year	Club	Lea	Pos	G	AB	R	H	2B	3B	HR	RBI	SB	Avg
2001 Staten Island	N.Y.-Penn.	DH	70	273	43	67	17	2	8	39	5	.245
2002 Greensboro	So.Atl.	OF	101	356	58	95	23	2	14	56	15	.267
2003 Tampa	Fla.St.	OF	91	330	42	87	19	2	8	47	5	.264
2004 Tampa	Fla.St.	1B-OF	123	424	65	105	27	1	19	78	6	.248
2005 Trenton	Eastern	1B	142	537	86	129	28	2	34	92	3	.240
2006 Trenton	Eastern	1B-OF	92	351	47	90	24	0	19	61	3	.256
2006 Columbus	Int.	OF	12	43	1	8	1	0	1	4	0	.186
2007 Scranton/WB	Int.	OF-1B	91	336	58	99	18	1	25	79	2	.295
2007 New York	A.L.	DH-OF-1B	34	74	16	19	1	0	7	17	0	.257
2008 New York	A.L.	1B-OF	23	57	7	10	3	0	1	6	0	.175
2008 Yankees	Gulf Coast	DH	2	7	0	0	0	0	0	0	0	.000
2008 Scranton/WB	Int.	OF-1B	58	205	38	49	14	0	12	44	6	.239
2009 Scranton/WB	Int.	OF-1B	123	452	85	125	30	1	30	99	2	.277
2009 New York	A.L.	OF	11	15	1	3	0	0	0	1	0	.200
2010 Columbus	Int.	OF-1B	38	146	21	44	11	0	6	34	0	.301
2010 Cleveland a	A.L.	OF-1B	85	229	29	53	10	0	11	36	1	.231
2011 Columbus	Int.	OF-1B	33	109	20	22	3	0	5	19	1	.202
2011 Cleveland	A.L.	OF-1B	76	223	29	58	17	0	11	47	0	.260
Major League Totals		5 Yrs.	229	598	82	143	31	0	30	107	1	.239
Division Series													
2007 New York	A.L.	1B	3	4	1	2	0	0	0	0	0	.500

a Filed for free agency, November 25, 2009. Signed with Cleveland Indians organization, January 4, 2010.

DUNN, ADAM TROY

Born, Houston, Texas, November 9, 1979.
Bats Left. Throws Right. Height, 6 feet, 6 inches. Weight, 275 pounds.

Year	Club	Lea	Pos	G	AB	R	H	2B	3B	HR	RBI	SB	Avg
1998 Billings	Pioneer	OF	34	125	26	36	3	1	4	13	4	.288
1999 Rockford	Midwest	OF	92	313	62	96	16	2	11	44	21	.307
2000 Dayton	Midwest	OF	122	420	101	118	29	1	16	79	24	.281
2001 Chattanooga	Southern	OF	39	140	30	48	9	0	12	31	6	.343
2001 Louisville	Int.	OF	55	210	44	69	13	0	20	53	5	.329
2001 Cincinnati	N.L.	OF	66	244	54	64	18	1	19	43	4	.262
2002 Cincinnati	N.L.	OF-1B	158	535	84	133	28	2	26	71	19	.249
2003 Cincinnati a	N.L.	OF-1B	116	381	70	82	12	1	27	57	8	.215
2004 Cincinnati	N.L.	OF-1B	161	568	105	151	34	0	46	102	6	.266
2005 Cincinnati	N.L.	OF-1B	160	543	107	134	35	2	40	101	4	.247
2006 Cincinnati	N.L.	OF-1B	160	561	99	131	24	0	40	92	7	.234
2007 Cincinnati	N.L.	OF	152	522	101	138	27	2	40	106	9	.264
2008 Cincinnati-Arizona b-c	N.L.	OF-1B	158	517	79	122	23	0	40	100	2	.236
2009 Washington	N.L.	OF-1B	159	546	81	146	29	0	38	105	0	.267
2010 Washington d	N.L.	1B	158	558	85	145	36	2	38	103	0	.260
2011 Chicago	A.L.	DH-1B-OF	122	415	36	66	16	0	11	42	0	.159
Major League Totals		11 Yrs.	1570	5390	901	1312	282	10	365	922	59	.243

a On disabled list from August 16 to October 2, 2003.
b Traded to Arizona Diamondbacks for pitcher Dallas Buck and two players to be named later, August 12, 2008.
   To complete trade, Cincinnati Reds received catcher Wilkin Castillo on August 14, 2008 and pitcher Micah Owings
   on September 10, 2008.
c Filed for free agency, November 1, 2008. Signed with Washington Nationals, February 11, 2009.
d Filed for free agency, November 1, 2010. Signed with Chicago White Sox, December 3, 2010.

ELLIS, ANDREW JAMES (A.J.)

Born, Cape Girardeau, Missouri, April 9, 1981.
Bats Right. Throws Right. Height, 6 feet, 3 inches. Weight, 225 pounds.

Year	Club	Lea	Pos	G	AB	R	H	2B	3B	HR	RBI	SB	Avg
2003 South Bend	So.Atl.	C-1B	3	6	0	0	0	0	0	0	0	.000
2004 Vero Beach	Fla.St.	C-1B	40	114	15	25	4	0	2	22	1	.219
2005 Vero Beach	Fla.St.	C	57	176	27	45	8	0	3	22	1	.256
2006 Jacksonville	Southern	C	81	252	34	63	9	1	0	21	2	.250
2007 Jacksonville	Southern	C-1B-OF	109	357	59	96	22	2	8	57	1	.269
2008 Las Vegas	P.C.	C-1B	84	274	44	88	17	4	4	59	0	.321
2008 Los Angeles	N.L.	C	4	3	1	0	0	0	0	0	0	.000
2009 Albuquerque	P.C.	C	90	283	48	89	13	2	0	39	2	.314
2009 Los Angeles	N.L.	C	8	10	0	1	0	0	0	1	0	.100
2010 Albuquerque	P.C.	C	18	61	11	16	5	1	0	7	1	.262
2010 Los Angeles	N.L.	C	44	108	6	30	5	0	0	16	0	.278
2011 Albuquerque	P.C.	C-1B	59	184	36	56	15	0	2	28	0	.304
2011 Los Angeles	N.L.	C	31	85	8	23	1	1	2	11	0	.271
Major League Totals		4 Yrs.	87	206	15	54	6	1	2	28	0	.262

ELLIS, MARK WILLIAM

Born, Rapid City, South Dakota, June 6, 1977.
Bats Right. Throws Right. Height, 5 feet, 11 inches. Weight, 195 pounds.

Year	Club	Lea	Pos	G	AB	R	H	2B	3B	HR	RBI	SB	Avg
1999 Spokane	Northwest	SS	71	281	67	92	14	0	7	47	21	.327
2000 Wilmington	Carolina	SS-2B	132	484	83	146	27	4	6	62	25	.302
2000 Wichita	Texas	2B	7	22	4	7	1	0	0	4	1	.318
2001 Sacramento a	P.C.	SS	132	472	71	129	38	0	10	53	21	.273
2002 Sacramento	P.C.	SS	21	84	14	25	10	1	0	5	4	.298
2002 Oakland	A.L.	2B-SS-3B	98	345	58	94	16	4	6	35	4	.272
2003 Oakland	A.L.	2B	154	553	78	137	31	5	9	52	6	.248
2004 Oakland b	A.L.				INJURED—Did Not Play								
2005 Oakland	A.L.	2B-SS-1B	122	434	76	137	21	5	13	52	1	.316
2006 Sacramento	P.C.	2B	4	12	1	2	0	0	0	2	0	.167
2006 Oakland c	A.L.	2B-1B	124	441	64	110	25	1	11	52	4	.249
2007 Oakland	A.L.	2B	150	583	84	161	33	3	19	76	9	.276
2008 Oakland d	A.L.	2B	117	442	55	103	20	3	12	41	14	.233
2009 Stockton	Calif.	2B	2	4	0	0	0	0	0	0	0	.000
2009 Sacramento	P.C.	2B	8	33	2	6	1	0	0	3	0	.182
2009 Oakland e	A.L.	2B	105	377	52	99	23	0	10	61	10	.263
2010 Stockton	Calif.	2B	2	5	0	1	0	0	0	1	0	.200
2010 Sacramento	P.C.	2B	1	4	0	1	0	0	0	0	0	.250
2010 Oakland f	A.L.	2B	124	436	45	127	24	0	5	49	7	.291
2011 Sacramento	P.C.	2B	3	10	0	2	1	0	0	1	0	.200
2011 Oakland	A.L.	2B-1B	62	217	21	47	11	1	1	16	7	.217
2011 Colorado g-h-i	N.L.	2B	70	263	34	72	13	0	6	25	7	.274
Major League Totals		9 Yrs.	1126	4091	567	1087	217	22	92	459	69	.266
Division Series													
2002 Oakland	A.L.	2B	5	19	1	7	2	0	1	4	0	.368
2003 Oakland	A.L.	2B	5	17	2	2	0	0	0	0	0	.118
2006 Oakland	A.L.	2B	2	7	0	2	0	0	0	0	0	.286
Division Series Totals			12	43	3	11	2	0	1	4	0	.256

a Traded to Oakland Athletics by Kansas City Royals with outfielder Johnny Damon and player to be named later for pitcher Roberto Hernandez, catcher A.J. Hinch, infielder Angel Berroa and cash, January 8, 2001.
b On disabled list from March 26 to October 20, 2004.
c On disabled list from June 1 to June 30, 2006.
d On disabled list from September 21 to November 14, 2008.
e On disabled list from April 29 to June 28, 2009.
f On disabled list from April 21 to May 22, 2010.
g On disabled list from June 7 to June 22, 2011.
h Traded to Colorado Rockies for pitcher Bruce Billings, cash and player to be named later, June 30, 2011.
i Filed for free agency, October 30, 2011. Signed with Los Angeles Dodgers, November 14, 2011.

ELLSBURY, JACOBY McCABE

Born, Madras, Oregon, September 11, 1983.
Bats Left. Throws Left. Height, 6 feet, 1 inch. Weight, 185 pounds.

Year	Club	Lea	Pos	G	AB	R	H	2B	3B	HR	RBI	SB	Avg
2005 Lowell	N.Y.-Penn.	OF	35	139	28	44	3	5	1	19	23	.317
2006 Wilmington	Carolina	OF	61	244	35	73	7	5	4	32	25	.299

Year	Club	Lea	Pos	G	AB	R	H	2B	3B	HR	RBI	SB	Avg
2006 Portland	Eastern	OF	50	198	29	61	10	3	3	19	16	.308
2007 Portland	Eastern	OF	17	73	16	33	10	2	0	13	8	.452
2007 Pawtucket	Int.	OF	87	363	66	108	14	5	2	28	33	.298
2007 Boston	A.L.	OF	33	116	20	41	7	1	3	18	9	.353
2008 Boston	A.L.	OF	145	554	98	155	22	7	9	47	*50	.280
2009 Boston	A.L.	OF	153	624	94	188	27	*10	8	60	*70	.301
2010 Red Sox	Gulf Coast	OF	3	8	3	2	0	0	0	0	1	.250
2010 Portland	Eastern	OF	2	7	2	3	1	0	0	0	1	.429
2010 Pawtucket	Int.	OF	4	17	5	8	1	0	0	2	0	.471
2010 Boston a	A.L.	OF	18	78	10	15	4	0	0	5	7	.192
2011 Boston	A.L.	OF	158	660	119	212	46	5	32	105	39	.321
Major League Totals	5 Yrs.		507	2032	341	611	106	23	52	235	175	.301
Division Series													
2007 Boston	A.L.	OF	2	1	1	0	0	0	0	0	0	.000
2008 Boston	A.L.	OF	4	18	2	6	3	0	0	6	3	.333
2009 Boston	A.L.	OF	3	12	2	3	0	1	0	0	0	.250
Division Series Totals			9	31	5	9	3	1	0	6	3	.290
Championship Series													
2007 Boston	A.L.	OF	5	8	3	2	0	0	0	1	1	.250
2008 Boston	A.L.	OF	4	14	0	0	0	0	0	1	0	.000
Championship Series Totals			9	22	3	2	0	0	0	2	1	.091
World Series Record													
2007 Boston	A.L.	OF	4	16	4	7	4	0	0	3	1	.438

a On disabled list from April 12 to May 22 and May 28 to August 4 and August 14 to November 8, 2010.

ENCARNACION, EDWIN ELPIDIO
Born, La Romana, Dominican Republic, January 7, 1983.
Bats Right. Throws Right. Height, 6 feet, 1 inch. Weight, 215 pounds.

Year	Club	Lea	Pos	G	AB	R	H	2B	3B	HR	RBI	SB	Avg
2000 Rangers	Gulf Coast	3B	51	177	31	55	6	3	0	36	3	.311
2001 Dayton	Midwest	3B	9	37	2	6	2	0	1	6	0	.162
2001 Billings	Pioneer	3B	52	211	27	55	8	2	5	26	8	.261
2001 Savannah a	So.Atl.	3B	45	170	23	52	9	2	4	25	3	.306
2002 Dayton	Midwest	3B-SS	136	517	80	146	32	4	17	73	25	.282
2003 Potomac.	Carolina	3B	58	215	40	69	15	1	6	29	7	.321
2003 Chattanooga	Southern	3B-SS	67	254	40	69	13	1	5	36	8	.272
2004 Chattanooga.	Southern	3B	120	469	73	132	35	1	13	76	17	.281
2005 Louisville	Int.	3B	78	290	44	91	23	0	15	54	7	.314
2005 Cincinnati	N.L.	3B	69	211	25	49	16	0	9	31	3	.232
2006 Louisville	Int.	3B-1B	10	36	6	11	3	0	1	1	0	.306
2006 Cincinnati b	N.L.	3B-1B	117	406	60	112	33	1	15	72	6	.276
2007 Louisville	Int.	3B	11	46	12	19	3	0	3	7	1	.413
2007 Cincinnati	N.L.	3B	139	502	66	145	25	1	16	76	8	.289
2008 Cincinnati	N.L.	3B	146	506	75	127	29	1	26	68	1	.251
2009 Louisville	Int.	3B	11	37	5	10	1	0	2	8	0	.270
2009 Cincinnati	N.L.	3B	43	139	10	29	6	1	5	16	1	.209
2009 Toronto c-d-e	A.L.	3B	42	154	25	37	5	1	8	23	1	.240
2010 Dunedin	Fla.St.	3B	3	10	2	1	0	0	1	1	0	.100
2010 Las Vegas.	P.C.	3B	7	32	9	14	2	0	3	13	0	.438
2010 Toronto f-g-h	A.L.	3B	96	332	47	81	16	0	21	51	1	.244
2011 Toronto	A.L.	DH-3B-1B	134	481	70	131	36	0	17	55	8	.272
Major League Totals	7 Yrs.		786	2731	378	711	166	5	117	392	29	.260

a Traded by Texas Rangers to Cincinnati Reds with outfielder Ruben Mateo for pitcher Rob Bell, June 15, 2001.
b On disabled list from June 7 to July 6, 2006.
c On disabled list from April 28 to July 3, 2009.
d Traded to Toronto Blue Jays with pitcher Josh Roenicke and pitcher Zach Stewart for infielder Scott Rolen, July 31, 2009.
e On disabled list from August 21 to September 5, 2009.
f On disabled list from April 15 to May 18 and August 29 to September 13, 2010.
g Claimed on waivers by Oakland Athletics, November 12, 2010.
h Not offered contract, December 2, 2010. Signed with Toronto Blue Jays, December 16, 2010.

ESCOBAR, ALCIDES

Born, Lasabana, Venezuela, December 16, 1986.
Bats Right. Throws Right. Height, 6 feet, 1 inch. Weight, 180 pounds.

Year	Club	Lea	Pos	G	AB	R	H	2B	3B	HR	RBI	SB	Avg
2004 Helena	Pioneer		SS	67	231	38	65	8	0	2	24	20	.281
2005 West Virginia	So.Atl.		SS	127	520	80	141	25	8	2	36	30	.271
2006 Brevard County	Fla.St.		SS	87	350	47	90	9	1	2	33	28	.257
2007 Brevard County	Fla.St.		SS	63	268	37	87	8	3	0	25	18	.325
2007 Huntsville	Southern		SS	62	226	27	64	5	4	1	28	4	.283
2008 Huntsville	Southern		SS	131	546	95	179	24	5	8	76	34	.328
2008 Milwaukee	N.L.		SS	9	4	2	2	0	0	0	0	0	.500
2009 Nashville	P.C.		SS-2B	109	430	76	128	24	6	4	34	42	.298
2009 Milwaukee	N.L.		SS	38	125	20	38	3	1	1	11	4	.304
2010 Milwaukee a	N.L.		SS-OF	145	506	57	119	14	10	4	41	10	.235
2011 Kansas City	A.L.		SS	158	548	69	139	21	8	4	46	26	.254
Major League Totals			4 Yrs.	350	1183	148	298	38	19	9	98	40	.252

a Traded to Kansas City Royals with outfielder Lorenzo Cain, pitcher Jeremy Jeffress and pitcher Jake Odorizzi for outfielder Yuniesky Betancourt and pitcher Zack Greinke, December 19, 2010.

ESCOBAR, YUNEL

Born, Havana, Cuba, November 2, 1982.
Bats Right. Throws Right. Height, 6 feet, 2 inches. Weight, 200 pounds.

Year	Club	Lea	Pos	G	AB	R	H	2B	3B	HR	RBI	SB	Avg
2005 Danville	Appal.		SS	8	30	9	12	2	1	2	8	0	.400
2005 Rome	So.Atl.		SS	48	198	30	62	13	3	4	19	0	.313
2006 Mississippi	Southern		SS-3B-2B	121	428	55	113	21	4	2	45	7	.264
2007 Richmond	Int.		SS	46	180	20	60	10	3	2	29	7	.333
2007 Atlanta	N.L.		SS-3B-2B	94	319	54	104	25	0	5	28	5	.326
2008 Atlanta	N.L.		SS	136	514	71	148	24	2	10	60	2	.288
2009 Atlanta	N.L.		SS	141	528	89	158	26	2	14	76	5	.299
2010 Gwinnett	Int.		SS	1	3	1	2	0	0	0	0	0	.667
2010 Atlanta	N.L.		SS	75	261	28	62	12	0	0	19	5	.238
2010 Toronto a-b	A.L.		SS	60	236	32	65	7	0	4	16	1	.275
2011 Toronto c	A.L.		SS	133	513	77	149	24	3	11	48	3	.290
Major League Totals			5 Yrs.	639	2371	351	686	118	7	44	247	21	.289

a On disabled list from April 30 to May 15, 2010.
b Traded to Toronto Blue Jays with pitcher Jo-Jo Reyes for infielder Alex Gonzalez, pitcher Tim Collins and infielder Tyler Pastornicky, July 14, 2010.
c On disabled list from September 11 to September 29, 2011.

ESPINOSA, DANIEL RICHARD (DANNY)

Born, Santa Ana, California, April 25, 1987.
Bats Both. Throws Right. Height, 6 feet. Weight, 190 pounds.

Year	Club	Lea	Pos	G	AB	R	H	2B	3B	HR	RBI	SB	Avg
2008 Vermont	N.Y.-Penn.		SS	19	64	8	21	2	0	0	4	2	.328
2009 Potomac	Carolina		SS	133	474	90	125	31	4	18	72	29	.264
2010 Harrisburg	Eastern		SS	99	386	66	101	16	4	18	54	20	.262
2010 Syracuse	Int.		SS-2B	24	95	14	28	2	1	4	15	5	.295
2010 Washington	N.L.		2B-SS	28	103	16	22	4	1	6	15	0	.214
2011 Washington	N.L.		2B	158	573	72	135	29	5	21	66	17	.236
Major League Totals			2 Yrs.	186	676	88	157	33	6	27	81	17	.232

ETHIER, ANDRE EVERETT

Born, Phoenix, Arizona, April 10, 1982.
Bats Left. Throws Left. Height, 6 feet, 1 inch. Weight, 210 pounds.

Year	Club	Lea	Pos	G	AB	R	H	2B	3B	HR	RBI	SB	Avg
2003 Kane County	Midwest		OF	40	162	23	44	10	0	0	11	2	.272
2003 Vancouver	Northwest		OF	10	41	7	16	4	1	1	7	2	.390
2004 Modesto	Calif.		OF	99	419	72	131	23	5	7	53	2	.313
2005 Sacramento	P.C.		OF	4	15	0	4	1	0	0	2	0	.267
2005 Midland a	Texas		OF	131	505	104	161	30	3	18	80	1	.319
2006 Las Vegas	P.C.		OF	25	86	15	30	4	3	1	12	2	.349
2006 Los Angeles	N.L.		OF	126	396	50	122	20	7	11	55	5	.308
2007 Los Angeles	N.L.		OF	153	447	50	127	32	2	13	64	0	.284
2008 Los Angeles	N.L.		OF	141	525	90	160	38	5	20	77	6	.305
2009 Los Angeles	N.L.		OF	160	596	92	162	42	3	31	106	6	.272
2010 Albuquerque	P.C.		OF	2	5	4	3	0	0	0	2	0	.600

Year	Club	Lea	Pos	G	AB	R	H	2B	3B	HR	RBI	SB	Avg
2010 Los Angeles b	N.L.	OF-1B	139	517	71	151	33	1	23	82	2	.292
2011 Los Angeles	N.L.	OF	135	487	67	142	30	0	11	62	0	.292
Major League Totals		6 Yrs.	854	2968	420	864	195	18	109	446	19	.291
Division Series												
2006 Los Angeles	N.L.	OF	2	1	0	0	0	0	0	0	0	.000
2008 Los Angeles	N.L.	OF	3	10	2	1	0	0	0	0	0	.100
2009 Los Angeles	N.L.	OF	3	12	5	6	2	1	2	3	0	.500
Division Series Totals			8	23	7	7	2	1	2	3	0	.304
Championship Series												
2008 Los Angeles	N.L.	OF	5	22	4	5	1	0	0	0	0	.227
2009 Los Angeles	N.L.	OF	5	19	2	5	1	0	1	3	0	.263
Championship Series Totals			10	41	6	10	2	0	1	3	0	.244

a Traded by Oakland Athletics to Los Angeles for outfielder Milton Bradley and infielder Antonio Perez, December 13, 2005.

b On disabled list from May 15 to May 31, 2010.

FIELDER, PRINCE SEMIEN
Born, Ontario, California, May 9, 1984.
Bats Left. Throws Right. Height, 6 feet. Weight, 260 pounds.

Year	Club	Lea	Pos	G	AB	R	H	2B	3B	HR	RBI	SB	Avg
2002 Beloit	Midwest	1B	32	112	15	27	7	0	3	11	0	.241
2002 Ogden	Pioneer	1B	41	146	35	57	12	0	10	40	3	.390
2003 Beloit	Midwest	1B	137	502	81	157	22	2	27	112	2	.313
2004 Huntsville	Southern	1B-OF	136	497	70	135	29	1	23	78	11	.272
2005 Nashville	P.C.	1B	103	378	68	110	21	0	28	86	8	.291
2005 Milwaukee	N.L.	1B	39	59	2	17	4	0	2	10	0	.288
2006 Milwaukee	N.L.	1B	157	569	82	154	35	1	28	81	7	.271
2007 Milwaukee	N.L.	1B	158	573	109	165	35	2	*50	119	2	.288
2008 Milwaukee	N.L.	1B	159	588	86	162	30	2	34	102	3	.276
2009 Milwaukee	N.L.	1B	*162	591	103	177	35	3	46	*141	2	.299
2010 Milwaukee	N.L.	1B	161	578	94	151	25	0	32	83	1	.261
2011 Milwaukee a	N.L.	1B	*162	569	95	170	36	1	38	120	1	.299
Major League Totals		7 Yrs.	998	3527	571	996	200	9	230	656	16	.282
Division Series												
2008 Milwaukee	N.L.	1B	4	14	1	1	0	0	1	2	0	.071
2011 Milwaukee	N.L.	1B	5	18	2	5	2	0	1	3	0	.278
Division Series Totals			9	32	3	6	2	0	2	5	0	.188
Championship Series												
2011 Milwaukee	N.L.	1B	6	20	4	4	2	0	2	3	0	.200

a Filed for free agency, October 30, 2011.

FIGGINS, DESMOND DECHONE (CHONE)
Born, Leary, Georgia, January 22, 1978.
Bats Both. Throws Right. Height, 5 feet, 7 inches. Weight, 180 pounds.

Year	Club	Lea	Pos	G	AB	R	H	2B	3B	HR	RBI	SB	Avg
1997 Rockies	Arizona	SS	54	214	41	60	5	6	1	23	30	.280
1998 Portland	Northwest	SS	69	269	41	76	9	3	1	26	25	.283
1999 Salem	Carolina	SS	123	444	65	106	12	3	0	22	27	.239
2000 Salem	Carolina	2B	134	522	92	145	26	14	3	48	37	.278
2001 Carolina	Southern	2B-SS	86	332	41	73	14	5	2	25	27	.220
2001 Arkansas a	Texas	2B-SS-3B	39	138	21	37	12	2	0	12	7	.268
2002 Salt Lake	P.C.	2B-SS	125	511	100	156	25	18	7	62	39	.305
2002 Anaheim	A.L.	2B	15	12	6	2	1	0	0	1	2	.167
2003 Salt Lake	P.C.	2B-SS-OF-3B	68	285	55	89	14	15	4	30	16	.312
2003 Anaheim	A.L.	OF-2B-SS	71	240	34	71	9	4	0	27	13	.296
2004 Anaheim	A.L.	3B-OF-2B-SS	148	577	83	171	22	17	5	60	34	.296
2005 Los Angeles	A.L.	OF-3B-2B-SS	158	642	113	186	25	10	8	57	*62	.290
2006 Los Angeles	A.L.	OF-3B-2B-SS	155	604	93	161	23	8	9	62	52	.267
2007 Salt Lake	P.C.	3B	4	14	3	5	1	0	0	1	0	.357
2007 Los Angeles b	A.L.	3B-OF-2B	115	442	81	146	24	6	3	58	41	.330
2008 Salt Lake	P.C.	3B	3	10	2	2	0	0	0	0	0	.200
2008 Los Angeles c	A.L.	3B-2B	116	453	72	125	14	1	1	22	34	.276
2009 Los Angeles d	A.L.	3B-2B-OF	158	615	114	183	30	7	5	54	42	.298
2010 Seattle	A.L.	2B	161	602	62	156	21	2	1	35	42	.259
2011 Seattle e	A.L.	3B-OF	81	288	24	54	11	1	1	15	11	.188
Major League Totals		10 Yrs.	1178	4475	682	1255	180	56	33	391	333	.280

Year	Club	Lea	Pos	G	AB	R	H	2B	3B	HR	RBI	SB	Avg
	Division Series												
2002 Anaheim..........A.L.			DH	1	0	1	0	0	0	0	0	1	.000
2004 Anaheim..........A.L.			2B-3B	3	14	0	2	0	0	0	0	1	.143
2005 Los Angeles.......A.L.			3B-OF	5	21	2	3	1	1	0	2	0	.143
2007 Los Angeles.......A.L.			OF	3	13	1	3	2	0	0	1	0	.231
2008 Los Angeles.......A.L.			3B	4	21	2	7	1	1	0	1	1	.333
2009 Los Angeles.......A.L.			3B	3	12	1	0	0	0	0	0	0	.000
Division Series Totals				19	81	7	15	4	2	0	4	3	.185
	Championship Series												
2002 Anaheim..........A.L.			PH	3	1	2	1	0	0	0	0	0	1.000
2005 Los Angeles.......A.L.			3B-OF	5	17	1	2	1	0	0	1	1	.118
2009 Los Angeles.......A.L.			3B	6	23	2	3	0	0	0	1	0	.130
Championship Series Totals				14	41	5	6	1	0	0	2	1	.146
	World Series Record												
2002 Anaheim..........A.L.			PH	2	0	1	0	0	0	0	0	0	.000

a Traded by Colorado Rockies to Anaheim Angels for outfielder Kimera Bartee, July 13, 2001.

b On disabled list from March 23 to April 30, 2007.

c On disabled list from May 4 to May 21 and May 22 to June 12, 2008.

d Filed for free agency, November 6, 2009. Signed with Seattle Mariners, December 8, 2009.

e On disabled list from August 2 to September 4, 2011.

FONTENOT, MICHAEL EUGENE (MIKE)

Born, Slidell, Louisiana, June 9, 1980.
Bats Left. Throws Right. Height, 5 feet, 8 inches. Weight, 165 pounds.

Year	Club	Lea	Pos	G	AB	R	H	2B	3B	HR	RBI	SB	Avg
2002 Frederick	Carolina		2B	122	481	61	127	16	4	8	53	13	.264
2003 Bowie.........	Eastern		2B	126	449	63	146	24	5	12	66	16	.325
2004 Ottawa	Int.		2B	136	524	73	146	30	10	8	49	14	.279
2005 Iowa.............	P.C.		2B-3B-SS-OF	111	379	60	103	22	10	6	39	3	.272
2005 Chicago a........	N.L.		PH	7	2	4	0	0	0	0	0	0	.000
2006 Iowa.............	P.C.		2B-3B-SS	111	362	54	107	28	2	8	36	5	.296
2007 Iowa.............	P.C.		SS-2B-3B-OF	55	211	46	71	17	4	6	34	3	.336
2007 Chicago	N.L.		2B-SS	86	234	32	65	12	4	3	29	5	.278
2008 Chicago	N.L.		2B-SS	119	243	42	74	22	1	9	40	2	.305
2009 Chicago	N.L.		2B-3B	135	377	38	89	22	2	9	43	4	.236
2010 Chicago-San Fran. b N.L.			2B-3B-SS	103	240	24	68	13	3	1	25	1	.283
2011 Fresno	P.C.		2B-SS	10	32	5	7	0	0	1	3	0	.219
2011 San Francisco c	N.L.		SS-2B-3B	85	220	22	50	15	3	4	21	5	.227
Major League Totals		6 Yrs.		535	1316	162	346	84	13	26	158	17	.263
	Division Series												
2007 Chicago ..........N.L.			PH	2	2	0	0	0	0	0	0	0	.000
2008 Chicago ..........N.L.			2B	3	6	0	2	0	0	0	0	0	.333
2010 San Francisco .....N.L.			3B	3	6	1	1	0	1	0	0	0	.167
Division Series Totals				8	14	1	3	0	1	0	0	0	.214
	Championship Series												
2010 San Francisco ....N.L.			3B	4	8	0	2	0	0	0	0	1	.250
	World Series Record												
2010 San Francisco .....N.L.			PH	1	0	0	0	0	0	0	0	0	.000

a Traded to Chicago Cubs by Baltimore Orioles with infielder Jerry Hairston and pitcher Dave Crouthers for outfielder Sammy Sosa, February 2, 2005.

b Traded to San Francisco Giants for outfielder Evan Crawford, August 11, 2010.

c On disabled list from May 26 to July 8, 2011.

FORSYTHE, JOHN LOGAN (LOGAN)

Born, Memphis, Tennessee, January 14, 1987.
Bats Right. Throws Right. Height, 6 feet, 1 inch. Weight, 205 pounds.

Year	Club	Lea	Pos	G	AB	R	H	2B	3B	HR	RBI	SB	Avg
2008 Eugene......	Northwest		3B	3	9	2	3	1	0	0	0	0	.333
2008 Padres	Arizona		3B	9	26	2	6	0	0	0	0	0	.231
2009 Lake Elsinore	Calif.		3B	66	236	46	76	13	3	8	30	6	.322
2009 San Antonio	Texas		3B	66	244	37	68	9	3	3	31	5	.279
2010 San Antonio	Texas		2B-3B	107	392	66	99	22	1	3	38	17	.253
2011 Tucson...........	P.C.		2B-3B-SS	46	178	41	58	12	0	8	34	8	.326
2011 San Diego ........N.L.			3B-2B-SS	62	150	12	32	9	1	0	12	3	.213

FOWLER, WILLIAM DEXTER (DEXTER)
Born, Atlanta, Georgia, March 22, 1986.
Bats Both. Throws Right. Height, 6 feet, 4 inches. Weight, 185 pounds.

Year	Club	Lea	Pos	G	AB	R	H	2B	3B	HR	RBI	SB	Avg
2005	Casper	Pioneer	OF	62	220	43	60	10	4	4	23	18	.273
2006	Asheville	So.Atl.	OF	99	405	92	120	31	6	8	46	43	.296
2007	Modesto	Calif.	OF	65	245	43	67	7	5	2	23	20	.273
2008	Tulsa	Texas	OF	108	421	92	141	31	9	9	64	20	.335
2008	Colorado	N.L.	OF	13	26	3	4	0	0	0	0	0	.154
2009	Tulsa	Texas	OF	3	10	3	4	2	0	0	3	1	.400
2009	Colorado a	N.L.	OF	135	433	73	115	29	10	4	34	27	.266
2010	Colorado Springs	P.C.	OF	27	106	23	36	10	4	2	13	1	.340
2010	Colorado	N.L.	OF	132	439	73	114	20	*14	6	36	13	.260
2011	Colorado Springs	P.C.	OF	24	97	17	23	6	1	2	9	2	.237
2011	Colorado b	N.L.	OF	125	481	84	128	35	15	5	45	12	.266
Major League Totals			4 Yrs.	405	1379	233	361	84	39	15	115	52	.262
Division Series													
2009	Colorado	N.L.	OF	4	14	1	3	0	0	0	2	0	.214

a On disabled list from August 25 to September 9, 2009.
b On disabled list from June 5 to June 20, 2011.

FRANCISCO, LOUIS BEN (BEN)
Born, Santa Ana, California, October 23, 1981.
Bats Right. Throws Right. Height, 6 feet, 1 inch. Weight, 190 pounds.

Year	Club	Lea	Pos	G	AB	R	H	2B	3B	HR	RBI	SB	Avg
2002	Mahoning Valley	N.Y.-Penn.	OF	58	235	55	82	23	2	3	23	22	.349
2003	Lake County	So.Atl.	OF	80	289	57	83	21	1	11	48	15	.287
2004	Akron	Eastern	OF	133	497	72	126	29	3	15	71	21	.254
2005	Akron	Eastern	OF	83	323	45	99	19	7	7	46	15	.307
2005	Buffalo	Int.	OF	4	16	4	8	1	0	0	3	1	.500
2006	Buffalo	Int.	OF	134	515	80	143	32	4	17	59	25	.278
2007	Buffalo	Int.	OF	95	377	60	120	27	2	12	51	22	.318
2007	Cleveland	A.L.	OF	25	62	10	17	5	0	3	12	0	.274
2008	Buffalo	Int.	OF	24	92	9	21	3	1	1	6	3	.228
2008	Cleveland	A.L.	OF	121	447	65	119	32	0	15	54	4	.266
2009	Cleveland	A.L.	OF	89	308	48	77	21	1	10	33	13	.250
2009	Philadelphia a	N.L.	OF	37	97	10	27	9	0	5	13	1	.278
2010	Philadelphia	N.L.	OF	88	179	24	48	13	0	6	28	8	.268
2011	Philadelphia b	N.L.	OF	100	250	24	61	10	1	6	34	4	.244
Major League Totals			5 Yrs.	460	1343	181	349	90	2	45	174	30	.260
Division Series													
2009	Philadelphia	N.L.	OF	3	1	0	0	0	0	0	0	0	.000
2010	Philadelphia	N.L.	PH	1	0	0	0	0	0	0	0	0	.000
2011	Philadelphia	N.L.	PH	2	2	1	1	0	0	0	1	0	.500
Division Series Totals				6	3	1	1	0	0	0	1	0	.333
Championship Series													
2009	Philadelphia	N.L.	OF	4	3	0	0	0	0	0	0	0	.000
2010	Philadelphia	N.L.	OF	3	6	1	1	0	0	0	0	0	.167
Championship Series Totals				7	9	1	1	0	0	0	0	0	.111
World Series Record													
2009	Philadelphia	N.L.	OF	4	7	0	0	0	0	0	0	0	.000

a Traded to Philadelphia Phillies with pitcher Cliff Lee for catcher Lou Marson, pitcher Jason Knapp, infielder Jason Donald and pitcher Carlos Carrasco, July 29, 2009.
b Traded to Toronto Blue Jays for pitcher Frank Gailey, December 12, 2011.

FRANCOEUR, JEFFREY BRADEN (JEFF)
Born, Atlanta, Georgia, January 8, 1984.
Bats Right. Throws Right. Height, 6 feet, 4 inches. Weight, 220 pounds.

Year	Club	Lea	Pos	G	AB	R	H	2B	3B	HR	RBI	SB	Avg
2002	Danville	Appal.	OF	38	147	31	48	12	1	8	31	8	.327
2003	Rome	So.Atl.	OF	134	524	78	147	26	9	14	68	14	.281
2004	Myrtle Beach	Carolina	OF	88	334	56	98	26	0	15	52	10	.293
2004	Greenville	Southern	OF	18	76	8	15	2	0	3	9	1	.197
2005	Mississippi	Southern	OF	84	335	40	92	28	2	13	62	13	.275
2005	Atlanta	N.L.	OF	70	257	41	77	20	1	14	45	3	.300
2006	Atlanta	N.L.	OF	*162	651	83	169	24	6	29	103	1	.260
2007	Atlanta	N.L.	OF	*162	642	84	188	40	0	19	105	5	.293

Year Club	Lea	Pos	G	AB	R	H	2B	3B	HR	RBI	SB	Avg
2008 Mississippi...... Southern		OF	3	13	3	7	0	1	0	2	0	.538
2008 Atlanta	N.L.	OF	155	599	70	143	33	3	11	71	0	.239
2009 Atlanta-New York a.....	N.L.	OF	157	593	72	166	32	4	15	76	6	.280
2010 New York	N.L.	OF	124	401	43	95	16	2	11	54	8	.237
2010 Texas b-c	A.L.	OF	15	53	9	18	2	0	2	11	0	.340
2011 Kansas City	A.L.	OF	153	601	77	171	47	4	20	87	22	.285
Major League Totals	7 Yrs.		998	3797	479	1027	214	20	121	552	45	.270
Division Series												
2005 Atlanta	N.L.	OF	4	17	2	4	1	1	0	1	0	.235
2010 Texas	A.L.	OF	2	8	1	1	1	0	0	1	0	.125
Division Series Totals			6	25	3	5	2	1	0	2	0	.200
Championship Series												
2010 Texas	A.L.	OF	4	10	0	2	0	0	0	0	0	.200
World Series Record												
2010 Texas	A.L.	OF	3	6	0	0	0	0	0	0	0	.000

a Traded to New York Mets with cash for outfielder Ryan Church, July 10, 2009.
b Traded to Texas Rangers for infielder Joaquin Arias, September 1, 2010.
c Filed for free agency, November 10, 2010. Signed with Kansas City Royals, December 8, 2010.

FREEMAN, FREDERICK CHARLES (FREDDIE)

Born, Fountain Valley, California, September 12, 1989.
Bats Left. Throws Right. Height, 6 feet, 5 inches. Weight, 225 pounds.

Year Club	Lea	Pos	G	AB	R	H	2B	3B	HR	RBI	SB	Avg
2007 Braves .... Gulf Coast		1B-3B	59	224	24	60	7	0	6	30	1	.268
2008 Rome .... So.Atl.		1B	130	491	70	155	33	7	18	95	5	.316
2009 Myrtle Beach ..... Carolina		1B	70	255	43	77	19	0	6	34	1	.302
2009 Mississippi ..... Southern		1B	41	149	15	37	8	0	2	24	0	.248
2010 Gwinnett.............. Int.		1B	124	461	73	147	35	2	18	87	6	.319
2010 Atlanta	N.L.	1B	20	24	3	4	1	0	1	1	0	.167
2011 Atlanta	N.L.	1B	157	571	67	161	32	0	21	76	4	.282
Major League Totals	2 Yrs.		177	595	70	165	33	0	22	77	4	.277

FREESE, DAVID RICHARD

Born, Corpus Christi, Texas, April 28, 1983.
Bats Right. Throws Right. Height, 6 feet, 2 inches. Weight, 220 pounds.

Year Club	Lea	Pos	G	AB	R	H	2B	3B	HR	RBI	SB	Avg
2006 Fort Wayne....... Midwest		3B	53	204	27	61	13	3	8	44	1	.299
2006 Eugene......... Northwest		3B	18	58	19	22	8	0	5	26	0	.379
2007 Lake Elsinore a........Calif.		3B	128	503	104	152	31	6	17	96	6	.302
2008 Memphis ..............P.C.		3B	131	464	83	142	29	3	26	91	5	.306
2009 Cardinals .... Gulf Coast		3B	4	11	2	5	2	0	1	6	0	.455
2009 Springfield .... Texas		3B	4	16	3	6	1	0	1	5	0	.375
2009 Memphis ..............P.C.		3B-1B	56	200	34	60	15	0	10	37	1	.300
2009 St. Louis.............	N.L.	3B-1B-C	17	31	3	10	2	0	1	7	0	.323
2010 Springfield .... Texas		DH	1	2	0	1	1	0	0	0	0	.500
2010 St. Louis b	N.L.	3B-1B	70	240	28	71	12	1	4	36	1	.296
2011 Memphis ..............P.C.		3B	4	13	1	3	1	0	0	1	0	.231
2011 St. Louis c	N.L.	3B-1B	97	333	41	99	16	1	10	55	1	.297
Major League Totals	3 Yrs.		184	604	72	180	30	2	15	98	2	.298
Division Series												
2011 St. Louis.............	N.L.	3B	5	18	1	5	2	0	1	5	0	.278
Championship Series												
2011 St. Louis.............	N.L.	3B	6	22	7	12	3	0	3	9	0	.545
World Series Record												
2011 St. Louis.............	N.L.	3B	7	23	4	8	3	1	1	7	0	.348

a Traded by San Diego Padres to St. Louis Cardinals for outfielder Jim Edmonds, December 15, 2007.
b On disabled list from June 28 to November 2, 2010.
c On disabled list from May 2 to June 27, 2011.

FUKUDOME, KOSUKE

Born, Kagoshima, Japan, April 26, 1977.
Bats Left. Throws Right. Height, 6 feet. Weight, 185 pounds.

Year Club	Lea	Pos	G	AB	R	H	2B	3B	HR	RBI	SB	Avg
1999 Chunichi....... Japan Cent.		OF	132	461	76	131	25	2	16	52	4	.284
2000 Chunichi....... Japan Cent.		OF	97	316	50	80	18	2	13	42	8	.253

Year	Club	Lea	Pos	G	AB	R	H	2B	3B	HR	RBI	SB	Avg
2001 Chunichi.......	Japan Cent.	OF	120	375	51	94	22	2	15	56	8	.251
2002 Chunichi.......	Japan Cent.	OF	140	542	85	186	42	3	19	65	4	.343
2003 Chunichi.......	Japan Cent.	OF	140	528	107	165	30	11	34	96	10	.313
2004 Chunichi.......	Japan Cent.	OF	92	350	61	97	19	7	23	81	8	.277
2005 Chunichi.......	Japan Cent.	OF	142	515	102	169	39	6	28	103	1	.328
2006 Chunichi......	Japan Cent.	OF	130	496	117	174	47	5	31	104	1	.351
2007 Chunichi a	Japan Cent.	OF	81	269	64	79	22	0	13	48	1	.294
2008 Chicago	N.L.	OF	150	501	79	129	25	3	10	58	12	.257
2009 Chicago	N.L.	OF	146	499	79	129	38	5	11	54	6	.259
2010 Chicago	N.L.	OF	130	358	45	94	20	2	13	44	7	.263
2011 Chicago	N.L.	OF	87	293	33	80	15	2	3	13	2	.273
2011 Cleveland b-c	A.L.	OF	59	237	26	59	12	1	5	22	2	.249
Major League Totals		4 Yrs.	572	1888	262	491	110	13	42	191	29	.260
Division Series												
2008 Chicago	N.L.	OF	3	10	0	1	0	0	0	0	0	.100

a Signed with Chicago Cubs, December 12, 2007.
b Traded to Cleveland Indians with cash for outfielder Abner Abreu and pitcher Carlton Smith, July 28, 2011.
c Filed for free agency, October 30, 2011.

FULD, SAMUEL BABSON (SAM)
Born, Durham, New Hampshire, November 20, 1981.
Bats Left. Throws Left. Height, 5 feet, 10 inches. Weight, 180 pounds.

Year	Club	Lea	Pos	G	AB	R	H	2B	3B	HR	RBI	SB	Avg
2005 Peoria...........	Midwest	OF	125	443	82	133	32	6	5	37	18	.300
2006 Daytona	Fla.St.	OF	89	353	63	106	19	6	4	40	22	.300
2007 Iowa..............	P.C.	OF	14	52	13	14	4	.1	1	2	2	.269
2007 Tennessee	Southern	OF	90	335	56	97	23	2	2	27	10	.290
2007 Chicago	N.L.	OF	14	6	3	0	0	0	0	0	0	.000
2008 Iowa.................	P.C.	OF	20	63	11	14	3	0	1	4	3	.222
2008 Tennessee	Southern	OF	85	339	48	92	16	3	5	48	7	.271
2009 Iowa...............	P.C.	OF	84	328	62	93	17	10	2	33	23	.284
2009 Chicago	N.L.	OF	65	97	17	29	6	1	1	2	2	.299
2010 Iowa...............	P.C.	OF	112	368	69	100	15	9	4	27	· 21	.272
2010 Chicago	N.L.	OF	19	28	3	4	1	0	0	3	0	.143
2011 Tampa Bay a	A.L.	OF	105	308	41	74	18	5	3	27	20	.240
Major League Totals		4 Yrs.	203	439	64	107	25	6	4	32	22	.244
Division Series												
2011 Tampa Bay	A.L.	OF	3	3	0	0	0	0	0	0	0	.000

a Traded to Tampa Bay Rays with infielder Hak-Ju Lee, outfielder Brandon Guyer, pitcher Chris Archer and catcher Robinson Chirinos for outfielder Fernando Perez, pitcher Matt Garza and pitcher Zachary Russcup, January 8, 2011.

FURCAL, RAFAEL
Born, Loma de Cabrera, Dominican Republic, August 24, 1977.
Bats Both. Throws Right. Height, 5 feet, 8 inches. Weight, 195 pounds.

Year	Club	Lea	Pos	G	AB	R	H	2B	3B	HR	RBI	SB	Avg
1997 Braves	Gulf Coast	2B-OF	50	190	31	49	5	4	1	9	15	.258
1998 Danville	Appal.	2B	66	268	56	88	15	4	0	23	60	.328
1999 Myrtle Beach	Carolina	SS	43	184	32	54	9	3	0	12	23	.293
1999 Macon	So.Atl.	SS	83	335	73	113	15	1	1	29	73	.337
2000 Greenville........	Southern	SS	3	10	1	2	0	0	1	3	0	.200
2000 Atlanta a-b	N.L.	SS-2B	131	455	87	134	20	4	4	37	40	.295
2001 Atlanta c............	N.L.	SS	79	324	39	89	19	0	4	30	22	.275
2002 Atlanta	N.L.	SS-2B	154	636	95	175	31	8	8	47	27	.275
2003 Atlanta	N.L.	SS	156	664	130	194	35	*10	15	61	25	.292
2004 Atlanta	N.L.	SS-2B	143	563	103	157	24	5	14	59	29	.279
2005 Atlanta d.............	N.L.	SS	154	616	100	175	31	11	12	58	46	.284
2006 Los Angeles	N.L.	SS	159	654	113	196	32	9	15	63	37	.300
2007 Inland Empire........	Calif.	SS	2	6	0	1	0	0	0	0	1	.167
2007 Los Angeles e.........	N.L.	SS	138	581	87	157	23	4	6	47	25	.270
2008 Las Vegas..........	P.C.	SS	1	3	0	1	1	0	0	1	0	.333
2008 Los Angeles f-g	N.L.	SS	36	143	34	51	12	2	5	16	8	.357
2009 Los Angeles	N.L.	SS	150	613	92	165	28	5	9	47	12	.269
2010 Inland Empire........	Calif.	SS	2	4	0	0	0	0	0	0	0	.000
2010 Albuquerque...........	P.C.	SS	2	5	3	3	1	1	1	4	0	.600
2010 Los Angeles h	N.L.	SS	97	383	66	115	23	7	8	43	22	.300
2011 Rancho Cucamonga....	Calif.	SS	6	22	10	7	0	0	0	1	1	.318
2011 Albuquerque...........	P.C.	SS	4	13	2	5	1	0	1	6	0	.385

Year	Club	Lea	Pos	G	AB	R	H	2B	3B	HR	RBI	SB	Avg
2011 Los Angeles-St. Louis i-j-k.	N.L.	SS	87	333	44	77	15	0	8	28	9	.231	
Major League Totals		12 Yrs.	1484	5965	990	1685	293	65	108	536	302	.282	
Division Series													
2000 Atlanta . . . . N.L.		SS	3	11	2	1	0	0	0	0	1	.091	
2002 Atlanta . . . . N.L.		SS	5	24	2	6	1	1	0	2	1	.250	
2003 Atlanta . . . . N.L.		SS	5	19	3	4	0	0	0	0	1	.211	
2004 Atlanta . . . . N.L.		SS	5	21	5	8	0	1	2	4	3	.381	
2005 Atlanta . . . . N.L.		SS	4	20	1	3	0	0	0	0	3	.150	
2006 Los Angeles . . . . N.L.		SS	3	11	1	2	0	0	0	1	2	.182	
2008 Los Angeles . . . . N.L.		SS	3	12	4	4	0	0	0	2	0	.333	
2009 Los Angeles . . . . N.L.		SS	3	12	2	6	0	1	0	2	0	.500	
2011 St. Louis. . . . . N.L.		SS	5	22	2	5	0	2	0	1	1	.227	
Division Series Totals			36	152	22	39	1	5	2	12	12	.257	
Championship Series													
2008 Los Angeles . . . . N.L.		SS	5	19	5	4	0	0	1	1	0	.211	
2009 Los Angeles . . . . N.L.		SS	5	21	0	3	1	0	0	1	1	.143	
2011 St. Louis. . . . . N.L.		SS	6	27	5	5	2	0	1	1	0	.185	
Championship Series Totals			16	67	10	12	3	0	2	3	1	.179	
World Series Record													
2011 St. Louis. . . . . N.L.		SS	7	28	1	5	1	0	0	1	0	.179	

a On disabled list from June 13 to June 28, 2000.
b Selected Rookie of the Year in National League for 2000.
c On disabled list from July 7 to November 6, 2001.
d Filed for free agency, October 31, 2005. Signed with Los Angeles Dodgers, December 7, 2005.
e On disabled list from March 23 to April 13, 2007.
f On disabled list from May 6 to September 24, 2008.
g Filed for free agency, November 3, 2008, re-signed with Los Angeles Dodgers, December 19, 2008.
h On disabled list from April 28 to May 25 and August 3 to September 3, 2010.
i On disabled list from April 12 to May 22 and June 4 to July 3, 2011.
j Traded to St. Louis Cardinals with cash for outfielder Alex Castellanos, July 31, 2011.
k Filed for free agency, October 31, 2011, re-signed with St. Louis Cardinals, December 10, 2011.

GARDNER, BRETT M.

Born, Holly Hill, South Carolina, August 24, 1983.
Bats Left. Throws Left. Height, 5 feet, 10 inches. Weight, 185 pounds.

Year	Club	Lea	Pos	G	AB	R	H	2B	3B	HR	RBI	SB	Avg
2005 Staten Island . . . . N.Y.-Penn.		OF-3B	73	282	62	80	9	1	5	32	19	.284	
2006 Trenton. . . . . Eastern		OF	55	217	41	59	4	3	0	13	28	.272	
2006 Tampa . . . . Fla.St.		OF	63	232	46	75	12	5	0	22	30	.323	
2007 Trenton. . . . . Eastern		OF	54	203	43	61	14	5	0	17	18	.300	
2007 Scranton/WB . . . . Int.		OF	45	181	37	47	4	3	1	9	21	.260	
2008 Scranton/WB . . . . Int.		OF	94	341	68	101	12	11	3	32	37	.296	
2008 New York . . . . A.L.		OF	42	127	18	29	5	2	0	16	13	.228	
2009 Scranton/WB . . . . Int.		OF	4	11	3	1	0	0	0	0	3	.091	
2009 New York a . . . . A.L.		OF	108	248	48	67	6	6	3	23	26	.270	
2010 New York . . . . A.L.		OF	150	477	97	132	20	7	5	47	47	.277	
2011 New York . . . . A.L.		OF	159	510	87	132	19	8	7	36	*49	.259	
Major League Totals . . , ...		4 Yrs.	459	1362	250	360	50	23	15	122	135	.264	
Division Series													
2009 New York . . . . A.L.		OF	3	0	0	0	0	0	0	0	1	.000	
2010 New York . . . . A.L.		OF	3	10	1	2	0	0	0	1	1	.200	
2011 New York . . . . A.L.		OF	5	17	3	7	1	0	0	5	0	.412	
Division Series Totals			11	27	4	9	1	0	0	6	2	.333	
Championship Series													
2009 New York . . . . A.L.		OF	6	3	2	2	0	0	0	0	0	.667	
2010 New York . . . . A.L.		OF	6	17	1	3	0	0	0	1	1	.176	
Championship Series Totals			12	20	3	5	0	0	0	1	1	.250	
World Series Record													
2009 New York . . . . A.L.		OF	5	10	1	0	0	0	0	0	0	.000	

a On disabled list from July 26 to September 7, 2009.

GENTRY, CRAIG ALAN

Born, Fort Smith, Arkansas, November 29, 1983.
Bats Right. Throws Right. Height, 6 feet, 2 inches. Weight, 190 pounds.

Year	Club	Lea	Pos	G	AB	R	H	2B	3B	HR	RBI	SB	Avg
2006 Spokane	Northwest	OF	56	221	27	62	15	4	0	13	20	.281
2007 Rangers	Arizona	OF	3	11	4	3	0	0	0	1	2	.273
2007 Clinton	Midwest	OF	55	223	40	61	15	0	3	12	24	.274
2007 Bakersfield	Calif.	OF	51	213	31	58	16	1	1	18	16	.272
2008 Frisco	Texas	OF	76	301	43	83	17	0	4	33	16	.276
2008 Oklahoma	P.C.	OF	18	59	6	12	1	0	0	1	1	.203
2009 Frisco	Texas	OF	127	512	100	155	21	7	8	53	49	.303
2009 Texas	A.L.	OF	11	17	4	2	1	0	0	1	0	.118
2010 Texas	A.L.	OF	20	33	4	7	0	0	0	3	1	.212
2010 Oklahoma a	P.C.	OF	69	259	43	80	7	4	4	35	12	.309
2011 Round Rock	P.C.	OF	30	110	21	27	5	1	1	10	5	.245
2011 Texas b	A.L.	OF	64	133	26	36	5	1	1	13	18	.271
Major League Totals		3 Yrs.	95	183	34	45	6	1	1	17	19	.246
Division Series													
2011 Texas	A.L.	OF	4	5	1	2	0	0	0	0	2	.400
Championship Series													
2011 Texas	A.L.	OF	3	5	0	2	0	0	0	1	0	.400
World Series Record													
2011 Texas	A.L.	OF	6	5	1	1	0	0	0	0	0	.200

a On disabled list from August 30 to November 5, 2010.

b On disabled list from July 28 to August 11, 2011.

GETZ, CHRISTOPHER RYAN (CHRIS)

Born, Southfield, Michigan, August 30, 1983.
Bats Left. Throws Right. Height, 6 feet. Weight, 185 pounds.

Year	Club	Lea	Pos	G	AB	R	H	2B	3B	HR	RBI	SB	Avg
2005 Great Falls	Pioneer	SS-2B	6	24	3	8	1	0	0	4	2	.333
2005 Kannapolis	So.Atl.	2B-SS	55	214	38	65	13	2	1	28	11	.304
2006 Birmingham	Southern	2B-SS	130	508	67	130	15	6	2	36	19	.256
2007 Birmingham	Southern	2B	72	278	40	83	10	2	3	29	13	.299
2008 Charlotte	Int.	2B-SS-OF-3B	111	404	60	122	24	1	11	52	11	.302
2008 Chicago	A.L.	2B	10	7	2	2	0	0	0	1	1	.286
2009 Charlotte	Int.	2B	5	15	4	4	0	0	0	0	2	.267
2009 Chicago a-b	A.L.	2B	107	375	49	98	18	4	2	31	25	.261
2010 Omaha	P.C.	2B	2	6	3	2	0	0	0	0	0	.333
2010 Kansas City c	A.L.	2B-3B	72	224	23	53	9	0	0	18	15	.237
2011 Kansas City	A.L.	2B-SS	118	380	50	97	6	3	0	26	21	.255
Major League Totals		4 Yrs.	307	986	124	250	33	7	2	76	62	.254

a On disabled list from August 12 to September 1, 2009.

b Traded to Kansas City Royals with infielder Josh Fields for infielder Mark Teahen, November 6, 2009.

c On disabled list from April 15 to April 30, 2010.

GIAMBI, JASON GILBERT

Born, West Covina, California, January 8, 1971.
Bats Left. Throws Right. Height, 6 feet, 3 inches. Weight, 230 pounds.

Year	Club	Lea	Pos	G	AB	R	H	2B	3B	HR	RBI	SB	Avg
1992 South Oregon	Northwest	3B	13	41	9	13	3	0	3	13	1	.317
1993 Modesto	California	3B	89	313	72	91	16	2	12	60	2	.291
1994 Huntsville	Southern	3B-1B	56	193	31	43	9	0	6	30	0	.223
1994 Tacoma	P.C.	3B-1B-SS	52	176	28	56	20	0	4	38	1	.318
1995 Edmonton	P.C.	3B-1B	55	190	34	65	26	1	3	41	0	.342
1995 Oakland	A.L.	3B-1B	54	176	27	45	7	0	6	25	2	.256
1996 Oakland	A.L.	1B-OF-3B	140	536	84	156	40	1	20	79	0	.291
1997 Oakland	A.L.	OF-1B	142	519	66	152	41	2	20	81	0	.293
1998 Oakland	A.L.	1B	153	562	92	166	28	0	27	110	2	.295
1999 Oakland	A.L.	1B-3B	158	575	115	181	36	1	33	123	1	.315
2000 Oakland a	A.L.	1B	152	510	108	170	29	1	43	137	2	.333
2001 Oakland b	A.L.	1B	154	520	109	178	*47	2	38	120	2	.342
2002 New York	A.L.	1B	155	560	120	176	34	1	41	122	2	.314
2003 New York	A.L.	1B	156	535	97	134	25	0	41	107	2	.250
2004 Tampa	Fla.St.	1B	2	6	0	1	0	0	0	0	0	.167
2004 New York c	A.L.	1B	80	264	33	55	9	0	12	40	0	.208
2005 New York	A.L.	1B	139	417	74	113	14	0	32	87	0	.271
2006 New York	A.L.	DH-1B	139	446	92	113	25	0	37	113	2	.253

Year	Club	Lea	Pos	G	AB	R	H	2B	3B	HR	RBI	SB	Avg
2007 Tampa	Fla.St.	DH	5	13	0	4	1	0	0	1	0	.308
2007 Scranton-WB	Int.	1B	4	9	1	1	0	0	1	1	0	.111
2007 New York d	A.L.	DH-1B	83	254	31	60	8	0	14	39	1	.236
2008 New York e	A.L.	1B	145	458	68	113	19	1	32	96	2	.247
2009 Colorado Springs	P.C.	1B	6	18	4	8	1	0	2	4	0	.444
2009 Oakland	A.L.	1B	83	269	39	52	13	0	11	40	0	.193
2009 Colorado f-g-h	N.L.	1B	19	24	4	7	1	0	2	11	0	.292
2010 Colorado i	N.L.	1B	87	176	17	43	9	0	6	35	2	.244
2011 Colorado Springs	P.C.	1B	3	7	2	3	0	0	0	3	0	.429
2011 Colorado j	N.L.	1B	64	131	20	34	6	0	13	32	0	.260
Major League Totals			17 Yrs. 2103		6932 1196		1948	391	9	428	1397	20	.281

Division Series

Year	Club	Lea	Pos	G	AB	R	H	2B	3B	HR	RBI	SB	Avg
2000 Oakland	A.L.	1B	5	14	2	4	0	0	0	1	1	.286
2001 Oakland	A.L.	1B	5	17	2	6	0	0	1	4	0	.353
2002 New York	A.L.	1B-DH	4	14	5	5	0	0	1	3	0	.357
2003 New York	A.L.	DH	4	16	1	4	2	0	0	2	0	.250
2005 New York	A.L.	1B-DH	5	19	1	8	3	0	0	2	0	.421
2006 New York	A.L.	DH-1B	3	8	1	1	0	0	1	2	1	.125
2007 New York	A.L.	1B	3	4	0	1	0	0	0	0	0	.250
2009 Colorado	N.L.	PH	3	3	1	1	0	0	0	1	0	.333
Division Series Totals			32	95	13	30	5	0	3	15	2	.316

Championship Series

Year	Club	Lea	Pos	G	AB	R	H	2B	3B	HR	RBI	SB	Avg
2003 New York	A.L.	DH	7	26	4	6	0	0	3	3	0	.231

World Series Record

Year	Club	Lea	Pos	G	AB	R	H	2B	3B	HR	RBI	SB	Avg
2003 New York	A.L.	1B	6	17	2	4	1	0	1	1	0	.235

a Selected Most Valuable Player in American League for 2000.
b Filed for free agency, November 5, 2001. Signed with New York Yankees, December 13, 2001.
c On disabled list from May 22 to June 6 and from July 26 to September 14, 2004.
d On disabled list from May 31 to August 7, 2007.
e Not offered contract, November 4, 2008. Signed with Oakland A's, January 7, 2009.
f On disabled list from July 20 to August 7, 2009.
g Released by Oakland Athletics, August 7, 2009. Signed with Colorado Rockies organization, August 24, 2009.
h Filed for free agency, November 5, 2009, re-signed with Colorado Rockies, January 28, 2010.
i Filed for free agency, November 1, 2010, re-signed with Colorado Rockies organization, January 17, 2011.
j On disabled list from July 26 to August 12, 2011.

GIAVOTELLA, JOHNNY A.

Born, Mertairie, Louisiana, July 10, 1987.
Bats Right. Throws Right. Height, 5 feet, 8 inches. Weight, 185 pounds.

Year	Club	Lea	Pos	G	AB	R	H	2B	3B	HR	RBI	SB	Avg
2008 Burlington	Midwest	2B	68	278	50	83	18	2	4	26	10	.299
2009 Wilmington	Carolina	2B	133	476	84	123	24	8	6	52	26	.258
2010 NW Arkansas	Texas	2B	134	522	92	168	35	5	9	65	13	.322
2011 Omaha	P.C.	2B-OF-3B	110	453	67	153	34	2	9	72	9	.338
2011 Kansas City	A.L.	2B	46	178	20	44	9	4	2	21	5	.247

GLOAD, ROSS PETER

Born, Brooklyn, New York, April 5, 1976.
Bats Left. Throws Left. Height, 6 feet, 1 inches. Weight, 210 pounds.

Year	Club	Lea	Pos	G	AB	R	H	2B	3B	HR	RBI	SB	Avg
1997 Utica	N.Y.-Penn.	1B	68	245	28	64	15	2	3	43	1	.261
1998 Kane County	Midwest	1B	132	501	77	157	41	3	12	92	7	.313
1999 Brevard County	Fla.St.	1B	133	490	80	146	26	3	10	74	3	.298
2000 Portland	Eastern	OF-1B	100	401	60	114	28	4	16	65	4	.284
2000 Iowa	P.C.	OF	28	104	24	42	10	2	14	39	1	.404
2000 Chicago a	N.L.	OF-1B	18	31	4	6	0	1	1	3	0	.194
2001 Iowa b	P.C.	1B	133	475	70	141	32	10	15	93	9	.297
2002 Colorado Springs	P.C.	1B-OF	104	442	69	139	28	6	16	71	9	.314
2002 Colorado c-d	N.L.	1B-OF	26	31	4	8	1	0	1	4	0	.258
2003 Charlotte e	Int.	1B-OF	133	508	72	160	40	6	18	70	6	.315
2004 Chicago	A.L.	1B-OF	110	234	28	75	16	0	7	44	0	.321
2005 Charlotte	Int.	1B-OF	60	236	45	86	22	1	15	45	0	.364
2005 Chicago f	A.L.	1B-OF	28	42	2	7	2	0	0	5	0	.167
2006 Chicago g	A.L.	1B-OF	77	156	22	51	8	2	3	18	6	.327
2007 Omaha	P.C.	DH	1	4	1	2	0	0	1	1	0	.500
2007 Kansas City h	A.L.	1B-OF	102	320	37	92	22	3	7	51	2	.287
2008 Kansas City	A.L.	1B-OF	122	388	46	106	18	1	3	37	3	.273
2009 Florida i-j	N.L.	1B-OF-P	125	230	33	60	10	2	6	30	0	.261

Year Club	Lea	Pos	G	AB	R	H	2B	3B	HR	RBI	SB	Avg
2010 Clearwater ....Fla.St.		1B	2	8	1	1	0	0	1	1	0	.125
2010 Philadelphia k.........	N.L.	1B-OF	94	128	16	36	8	0	6	22	1	.281
2011 Philadelphia l.........	N.L.	1B-OF	93	113	3	29	8	0	0	8	0	.257
Major League Totals	10 Yrs.		795	1673	195	470	93	9	34	222	12	.281
Division Series												
2011 Philadelphia	N.L.	PH	3	2	0	1	0	0	0	0	0	.500
Championship Series												
2010 Philadelphia	N.L.	PH	6	5	0	0	0	0	0	0	0	.000

a Traded to Chicago Cubs with pitcher David Noyce for outfielder Henry Rodriguez and cash, July 31, 2000.
b Claimed on waivers by Colorado Rockies, September 12, 2001.
c Traded to New York Mets with pitcher Craig House and outfielder Alex Ochoa for outfielder Benny Agbayani and infielder Todd Zeile, January 21, 2002.
d Sold to Colorado Rockies, January 26, 2002.
e Traded to Chicago White Sox for pitcher Wade Parrish, March 31, 2003.
f On disabled list from April 25 to July 17, 2005.
g Traded to Kansas City Royals for pitcher Andy Sisco, December 16, 2006.
h On disabled list from May 14 to June 30, 2007.
i Traded to Florida Marlins for player to be named later, March 31, 2009. Kansas City Royals received pitcher Eric Basurto to complete trade, May 13, 2009.
j Filed for free agency, November 5, 2009. Signed with Philadelphia Phillies, December 15, 2009.
k On disabled list from August 19 to September 3, 2010.
l Filed for free agency, October 30, 2011.

GOLDSCHMIDT, PAUL EDWARD
Born, Wilmington, Delaware, September 10, 1987.
Bats Right. Throws Right. Height, 6 feet, 3 inches. Weight, 245 pounds.

Year Club	Lea	Pos	G	AB	R	H	2B	3B	HR	RBI	SB	Avg
2009 Missoula ....Pioneer		1B-OF	72	278	48	91	26	2	17	61	4	.327
2010 Visalia ....Calif.		1B	138	525	102	165	42	3	35	108	5	.314
2011 Mobile ... Southern		1B	103	366	84	112	21	3	30	94	9	.306
2011 Arizona..............	N.L.	1B	48	156	28	39	9	1	8	26	4	.250
Division Series												
2011 Arizona..............	N.L.	1B	4	16	4	7	0	0	2	6	1	.438

GOMES, JONNY JOHNSON
Born, Petaluma, California, November 22, 1980.
Bats Right. Throws Right. Height, 6 feet, 1 inch. Weight, 225 pounds.

Year Club	Lea	Pos	G	AB	R	H	2B	3B	HR	RBI	SB	Avg
2001 Princeton ....Appal.		OF	62	206	58	60	11	2	16	44	15	.291
2002 Bakersfield .... California		OF	133	446	102	123	24	9	30	72	15	.276
2003 Orlando .... Southern		OF	120	442	68	110	28	3	17	56	23	.249
2003 Durham ....Int.		OF	5	19	2	6	2	1	0	1	0	.316
2003 Tampa Bay	A.L.	DH	8	15	1	2	1	0	0	0	0	.133
2004 Durham ....Int.		OF	114	389	73	100	27	1	26	78	8	.257
2004 Tampa Bay	A.L.	DH	5	14	0	1	0	0	0	1	0	.071
2005 Durham ....Int.		OF	45	162	34	52	13	0	14	46	7	.321
2005 Tampa Bay	A.L.	OF	101	348	61	98	13	6	21	54	9	.282
2006 Tampa Bay a..........	A.L.	DH-OF	117	385	53	83	21	1	20	59	1	.216
2007 Durham ....Int.		OF	13	43	6	13	2	0	1	7	4	.302
2007 Tampa Bay	A.L.	OF	107	348	48	85	20	2	17	49	12	.244
2008 Durham ....Int.		OF	26	107	19	27	11	0	2	14	0	.252
2008 Tampa Bay b	A.L.	DH-OF	77	154	23	28	5	1	8	21	8	.182
2009 Louisville ....Int.		OF	37	131	18	37	10	1	9	27	4	.282
2009 Cincinnati c..........	N.L.	OF	98	281	39	75	17	0	20	51	3	.267
2010 Cincinnati............	N.L.	OF	148	511	77	136	24	3	18	86	5	.266
2011 Cincinnati-Washington d-e.	N.L.	OF	120	311	41	65	12	1	14	43	7	.209
Major League Totals	9 Yrs.		781	2367	343	573	113	14	118	364	45	.242
Division Series												
2010 Cincinnati............	N.L.	OF	2	6	0	0	0	0	0	0	0	.000

a On disabled list from August 22 to October 2, 2006.
b Not offered contract, December 12, 2008. Signed with Cincinnati Reds organization, January 19, 2009.
c Not offered contract, December 12, 2009, re-signed with Cincinnati Reds, February 22, 2010.
d Traded to Washington Nationals with cash for pitcher Chris Manno and outfielder Bill Rhinehart, July 26, 2011.
e Filed for free agency, October 30, 2011.

GOMEZ (PENA), CARLOS ARGELIS

Born, Santiago, Dominican Republic, December 4, 1985.
Bats Right. Throws Right. Height, 6 feet, 4 inches. Weight, 195 pounds.

Year	Club	Lea	Pos	G	AB	R	H	2B	3B	HR	RBI	SB	Avg
2004 Kingsport	Appal.		OF	38	150	24	43	10	4	1	20	8	.287
2004 Mets	Gulf Coast		OF	19	71	10	19	7	0	0	11	9	.268
2005 Hagerstown	So.Atl.		OF	120	487	75	134	13	6	8	48	64	.275
2006 Binghamton	Eastern		OF	120	430	53	121	24	8	7	48	41	.281
2007 New Orleans	P.C.		OF	36	140	24	40	8	2	2	13	17	.286
2007 St. Lucie	Fla.St.		OF	5	13	1	2	0	0	0	0	2	.154
2007 New York a	N.L.		OF	58	125	14	29	3	0	2	12	12	.232
2008 Minnesota b	A.L.		OF	153	577	79	149	24	7	7	59	33	.258
2009 Minnesota c	A.L.		OF	137	315	51	72	15	5	3	28	14	.229
2010 Wisconsin	Midwest		OF	2	7	0	2	0	0	0	0	2	.286
2010 Nashville	P.C.		OF	8	28	7	8	0	0	0	2	2	.286
2010 Milwaukee d	N.L.		OF	97	291	38	72	11	3	5	24	18	.247
2011 Wisconsin	Midwest		OF	4	12	3	4	0	0	0	0	3	.333
2011 Milwaukee e	N.L.		OF	94	231	37	52	11	3	8	24	16	.225
Major League Totals	5 Yrs.			539	1539	219	374	64	18	25	147	93	.243
Division Series													
2009 Minnesota	A.L.		OF	1	4	1	0	0	0	0	0	0	.000
2011 Milwaukee	N.L.		OF	3	4	2	3	0	0	1	2	2	.750
Division Series Totals				4	8	3	3	0	0	1	2	2	.375
Championship Series													
2011 Milwaukee	N.L.		OF	5	10	1	2	0	0	0	0	0	.200

a On disabled list from July 5 to September 7, 2007.
b Traded to Minnesota Twins with pitcher Philip Humber, pitcher Kevin Mulvey and pitcher Deolis Garcia for pitcher Johan Santana, February 2, 2008.
c Traded to Milwaukee Brewers for infielder J.J. Hardy, November 6, 2009.
d On disabled list from May 6 to May 21 and August 3 to August 24, 2010.
e On disabled list from July 21 to September 1, 2011.

GONZALEZ, ADRIAN

Born, San Diego, California, May 8, 1982.
Bats Left. Throws Left. Height, 6 feet, 2 inches. Weight, 220 pounds.

Year	Club	Lea	Pos	G	AB	R	H	2B	3B	HR	RBI	SB	Avg
2000 Marlins	Gulf Coast		1B	53	193	24	57	10	1	0	30	0	.295
2000 Utica	N.Y.-Penn.		1B	8	29	7	9	3	0	0	3	0	.310
2001 Kane County	Midwest		1B	127	516	86	161	37	1	17	103	5	.312
2002 Portland	Eastern		1B	138	508	70	135	34	1	17	96	6	.266
2003 Albuquerque	P.C.		1B	39	139	17	30	5	1	1	18	1	.216
2003 Carolina	Southern		1B	36	137	15	42	9	1	1	16	1	.307
2003 Frisco a	Texas		1B	45	173	16	49	6	2	3	17	0	.283
2004 Oklahoma	P.C.		1B	123	457	61	139	28	3	12	88	1	.304
2004 Texas	A.L.		1B	16	42	7	10	3	0	1	7	0	.238
2005 Oklahoma	P.C.		1B	84	328	61	111	17	1	18	65	0	.338
2005 Texas	A.L.	DH-1B-OF	43	150	17	34	7	1	6	17	0	.227
2006 San Diego b	N.L.		1B	156	570	83	173	38	1	24	82	0	.304
2007 San Diego	N.L.		1B	161	646	101	182	46	3	30	100	0	.282
2008 San Diego	N.L.		1B	*162	616	103	172	32	1	36	119	0	.279
2009 San Diego	N.L.		1B	160	552	90	153	27	2	40	99	1	.277
2010 San Diego c	N.L.		1B	160	591	87	176	33	0	31	101	0	.298
2011 Boston	A.L.		1B-OF	159	630	108	*213	45	3	27	117	1	.338
Major League Totals	8 Yrs.			1017	3797	596	1113	231	11	195	642	2	.293
Division Series													
2006 San Diego	N.L.		1B	4	14	2	5	0	0	0	0	0	.357

a Traded to Texas Rangers with pitcher Ryan Snare and outfielder Will Smith for pitcher Ugueth Urbina, July 11, 2003.
b Traded to San Diego Padres with pitcher Chris Young and outfielder Termel Sledge for pitcher Adam Eaton, pitcher Akinori Otsuka and catcher Billy Killian, January 4, 2006.
c Traded to Boston Red Sox for pitcher Casey Kelly, outfielder Reymond Fuentes, infielder Anthony Rizzo and player to be named later, December 5, 2010. San Diego Padres received outfielder Eric Patterson to complete trade, December 16, 2010.

GONZALEZ, ALBERTO RAMON

Born, Maracaibo, Venezuela, April 18, 1983.
Bats Right. Throws Right. Height, 5 feet, 11 inches. Weight, 195 pounds.

Year	Club	Lea	Pos	G	AB	R	H	2B	3B	HR	RBI	SB	Avg
2004 South Bend	Midwest		SS-2B-OF	100	319	39	76	15	6	2	25	9	.238
2005 South Bend	Midwest		SS-2B-3B	95	352	60	112	21	7	1	42	12	.318

Year	Club	Lea	Pos	G	AB	R	H	2B	3B	HR	RBI	SB	Avg
2006 Tennessee	Southern		SS	129	434	67	126	20	3	6	50	5	.290
2006 Tucson	Pacific		SS	4	15	2	3	0	0	0	1	0	.200
2007 Trenton	Eastern		SS	28	109	18	36	10	1	0	16	1	.330
2007 Scranton-WB	Int.		SS-2B	106	384	44	95	21	10	1	35	11	.247
2007 New York a	A.L.		SS-3B	12	14	3	1	0	0	0	1	0	.071
2008 New York	A.L.		SS-3B-2B	28	52	4	9	2	0	0	1	0	.173
2008 Scranton-WB	Int.		SS	47	188	23	47	8	0	4	23	4	.250
2008 Columbus	Int.		SS	8	33	2	10	3	0	1	6	0	.303
2008 Washington b-c	N.L.		SS-3B	17	49	9	17	6	0	1	9	0	.347
2009 Syracuse	Int.		SS	23	90	5	28	3	1	0	8	1	.311
2009 Washington	N.L.		2B-SS-3B	105	291	31	77	16	3	1	33	1	.265
2010 Washington	N.L.		2B-3B-SS-1B	114	186	19	46	8	1	0	5	0	.247
2011 San Diego d-e	N.L.		2B-SS-3B-1B	102	247	18	53	10	2	1	32	1	.215
Major League Totals	5 Yrs.			378	839	84	203	42	6	3	81	2	.242

a Traded by Arizona Diamondbacks to New York Yankees with pitcher Steven Jackson, pitcher Ross Ohlendorf and pitcher Luis Vizcaino for pitcher Randy Johnson, January 9, 2007.
b Traded to Washington Nationals for pitcher Jhonny Nunez, July 31, 2008.
c On disabled list from August 5 to September 1, 2008.
d Traded to San Diego Padres for pitcher Erik Davis and cash, March 28, 2011.
e Released by San Diego Padres, November 16, 2011. Signed with Texas Rangers organization, December 9, 2011.

GONZALEZ, ALEXANDER (ALEX)
Born, Cagua, Venezuela, February 15, 1977.
Bats Right. Throws Right. Height, 6 feet. Weight, 200 pounds.

Year	Club	Lea	Pos	G	AB	R	H	2B	3B	HR	RBI	SB	Avg
1994 Florida	Dominican		SS	66	282	39	67	9	5	4	39	5	.238
1995 Brevard Cty	Fla.St.		SS	17	59	6	12	2	1	0	8	1	.203
1995 Marlins	Gulf Coast		SS	53	187	30	55	7	4	2	30	11	.294
1996 Marlins	Gulf Coast		SS	10	41	6	16	3	0	0	6	1	.390
1996 Kane County	Midwest		SS	4	10	2	2	0	0	0	0	0	.200
1996 Portland	Eastern		SS	11	34	4	8	0	1	0	1	0	.235
1997 Portland	Eastern		SS	133	449	69	114	16	4	19	65	4	.254
1998 Charlotte	Int.		SS	108	422	71	117	20	10	10	51	4	.277
1998 Florida	N.L.		SS	25	86	11	13	2	0	3	7	0	.151
1999 Florida	N.L.		SS	136	560	81	155	28	8	14	59	3	.277
2000 Brevard County	Fla.St.		SS	4	17	1	2	0	0	0	2	1	.118
2000 Florida a	N.L.		SS	109	385	35	77	17	4	7	42	7	.200
2001 Florida	N.L.		SS	145	515	57	129	36	1	9	48	2	.250
2002 Florida b	N.L.		SS	42	151	15	34	7	1	2	18	3	.225
2002 Marlins	Gulf Coast		SS	5	12	0	2	1	0	0	1	0	.167
2003 Florida	N.L.		SS	150	528	52	135	33	6	18	77	0	.256
2004 Florida	N.L.		SS	159	561	67	130	30	3	23	79	3	.232
2005 Florida c	N.L.		SS	130	435	45	115	30	0	5	45	5	.264
2006 Pawtucket	Int.		SS	1	3	0	1	0	0	0	0	0	.333
2006 Boston d-e	A.L.		SS	111	388	48	99	24	2	9	50	1	.255
2007 Cincinnati	N.L.		SS	110	393	55	107	27	1	16	55	0	.272
2008 Cincinnati f	N.L.		INJURED—Did Not Play										
2009 Louisville	Int.		SS	4	13	1	1	0	0	0	1	0	.077
2009 Cincinnati	N.L.		SS	68	243	16	51	12	0	3	26	0	.210
2009 Boston g-h-i	A.L.		SS	44	148	26	42	10	0	5	15	2	.284
2010 Toronto	A.L.		SS	85	328	47	85	25	1	17	50	1	.259
2010 Atlanta j	N.L.		SS	72	267	27	64	17	2	6	38	0	.240
2011 Atlanta k	N.L.		SS	149	564	59	136	27	1	15	56	2	.241
Major League Totals	13 Yrs.			1535	5552	641	1372	325	30	152	665	29	.247
Division Series													
2003 Florida	N.L.		SS	4	16	2	1	0	0	0	0	0	.063
2009 Boston	A.L.		SS	3	6	1	1	0	0	0	0	0	.167
2010 Atlanta	N.L.		SS	4	15	1	3	1	0	0	2	0	.200
Division Series Totals				11	37	4	5	1	0	0	2	0	.135
Championship Series													
2003 Florida	N.L.		SS	7	24	1	3	2	0	0	4	0	.125
World Series Record													
2003 Florida	N.L.		SS	6	22	3	6	2	0	1	2	0	.273

a On disabled list from July 28 to August 31, 2000.
b On disabled list from May 19 to November 6, 2002.
c Filed for free agency, October 27, 2005. Signed with Boston Red Sox, February 6, 2006.
d On disabled list from August 19 to September 3, 2006.
e Filed for free agency, October 30, 2006. Signed with Cincinnati Reds, November 20, 2006.
f On disabled list from March 21 to November 6, 2008.

g On disabled list from June 19 to July 24, 2009.
h Traded to Boston Red Sox for infielder Kristopher Negron, August 14, 2009.
i Filed for free agency, November 9, 2009. Signed with Toronto Blue Jays, November 26, 2009.
j Traded to Atlanta Braves with pitcher Tim Collins and infielder Tyler Pastornicky for infielder Yunel Escobar and pitcher Jo-Jo Reyes, July 14, 2010.
k Filed for free agency, October 30, 2011. Signed with Milwaukee Brewers, December 12, 2011.

GONZALEZ, CARLOS EDUARDO
Born, Maracaibo, Venezuela, October 17, 1985.
Bats Left. Throws Left. Height, 6 feet, 1 inch. Weight, 200 pounds.

Year	Club	Lea	Pos	G	AB	R	H	2B	3B	HR	RBI	SB	Avg
2003 Missoula	Pioneer	OF	72	275	45	71	14	4	6	25	12	.258
2004 South Bend	Midwest	OF	12	42	3	11	4	0	1	6	0	.262
2004 Yakima	Northwest	OF	73	300	44	83	15	2	9	44	2	.277
2005 South Bend	Midwest	OF	129	515	91	158	28	6	18	92	7	.307
2006 Lancaster	Calif.	OF	104	403	82	121	35	4	21	94	15	.300
2006 Tennessee	Southern	OF	18	61	11	13	6	0	2	5	1	.213
2007 Tucson	P.C.	OF	10	42	9	13	5	0	1	11	1	.310
2007 Mobile a	Southern	OF	120	458	63	131	33	3	16	75	9	.286
2008 Sacramento	P.C.	OF	46	173	23	49	9	1	4	28	1	.283
2008 Oakland b	A.L.	OF	85	302	31	73	22	1	4	26	4	.242
2009 Colorado Springs	P.C.	OF	48	192	43	65	12	7	10	59	6	.339
2009 Colorado	N.L.	OF	89	278	53	79	14	7	13	29	16	.284
2010 Colorado	N.L.	OF	145	587	111	*197	34	9	34	117	26	*.336
2011 Colorado Springs	P.C.	OF	3	10	1	3	0	0	0	0	0	.300
2011 Colorado c	N.L.	OF	127	481	92	142	27	3	26	92	20	.295
Major League Totals	4 Yrs.		446	1648	287	491	97	20	77	264	66	.298
Division Series													
2009 Colorado	N.L.	OF	4	17	5	10	2	0	1	1	2	.588

a Traded by Arizona Diamondbacks to Oakland Athletics with pitcher Brett Anderson, pitcher Dana Eveland, pitcher Greg Smith, infielder Chris Carter and outfielder Aaron Cunningham for pitcher Danny Haren and pitcher Connor Robertson, December 14, 2007.
b Traded to Colorado Rockies with pitcher Greg Smith and pitcher Huston Street for outfielder Matt Holliday, November 12, 2008.
c On disabled list from July 22 to August 6, 2011.

GORDON, ALEX JONATHAN
Born, Lincoln, Nebraska, February 10, 1984.
Bats Left. Throws Right. Height, 6 feet, 1 inch. Weight, 220 pounds.

Year	Club	Lea	Pos	G	AB	R	H	2B	3B	HR	RBI	SB	Avg
2006 Wichita	Texas	3B-1B	130	486	111	158	39	1	29	101	22	.325
2007 Kansas City	A.L.	3B-1B-SS	151	543	60	134	36	4	15	60	14	.247
2008 Kansas City a	A.L.	3B	134	493	72	128	35	1	16	59	9	.260
2009 Azl Royals	Arizona	3B	4	7	1	2	0	0	1	3	0	.286
2009 NW Arkansas	Texas	3B	8	30	4	11	3	0	2	10	0	.367
2009 Omaha	P.C.	3B	18	67	17	21	4	1	2	10	0	.313
2009 Kansas City b	A.L.	3B	49	164	28	38	6	0	6	22	5	.232
2010 Wilmington	Carolina	3B	7	17	7	4	3	0	0	2	1	.235
2010 Omaha	P.C.	OF	68	260	59	82	20	3	14	44	7	.315
2010 Kansas City c	A.L.	OF-3B-1B	74	242	34	52	10	0	8	20	1	.215
2011 Kansas City	A.L.	OF-1B	151	611	101	185	45	4	23	87	17	.303
Major League Totals	5 Yrs.		559	2053	295	537	132	9	68	248	46	.262

a On disabled list from August 22 to September 12, 2008.
b On disabled list from April 16 to July 16, 2009.
c On disabled list from March 26 to April 17, 2010.

GORDON, DEVARIS (DEE)
Born, Windermere, Florida, April 22, 1988.
Bats Left. Throws Right. Height, 5 feet, 11 inches. Weight, 150 pounds.

Year	Club	Lea	Pos	G	AB	R	H	2B	3B	HR	RBI	SB	Avg
2008 Ogden	Pioneer	SS	60	251	45	83	13	3	2	27	18	.331
2009 Great Lakes	Midwest	SS	131	538	96	162	17	12	3	35	73	.301
2010 Chattanooga	Southern	SS	133	555	86	154	17	10	2	39	53	.277
2011 Rancho Cucamonga	Calif.	SS	3	11	4	3	0	0	0	0	2	.273
2011 Albuquerque	P.C.	SS	70	288	51	96	10	6	0	24	30	.333
2011 Los Angeles a	N.L.	SS	56	224	34	68	9	2	0	11	24	.304

a On disabled list from August 10 to September 1, 2011.

GRANDERSON, CURTIS
Born, Blue Island, Illinois, March 16, 1981.
Bats Left. Throws Right. Height, 6 feet, 1 inch. Weight, 185 pounds.

Year	Club	Lea	Pos	G	AB	R	H	2B	3B	HR	RBI	SB	Avg
2002 Oneonta	N.Y.-Penn.	OF	52	212	45	73	15	4	3	34	9	.344
2003 Lakeland	Fla.St.	OF	127	476	71	136	29	10	11	51	10	.286
2004 Erie	Eastern	OF	123	462	89	139	19	8	21	94	14	.301
2004 Detroit	A.L.	OF	9	25	2	6	1	1	0	0	0	.240
2005 Toledo	Int.	OF	111	445	79	129	29	13	15	65	22	.290
2005 Detroit	A.L.	OF	47	162	18	44	6	3	8	20	1	.272
2006 Detroit	A.L.	OF	159	596	90	155	31	9	19	68	8	.260
2007 Detroit	A.L.	OF	158	612	122	185	38	*23	23	74	26	.302
2008 West Michigan	Midwest	OF	3	11	1	4	0	2	0	1	0	.364
2008 Toledo	Int.	OF	2	9	1	3	1	0	0	0	0	.333
2008 Detroit a	A.L.	OF	141	553	112	155	26	*13	22	66	12	.280
2009 Detroit b	A.L.	OF	160	631	91	157	23	8	30	71	20	.249
2010 Scranton/WB	Int.	OF	5	16	0	4	0	0	0	2	0	.250
2010 New York c	A.L.	OF	136	466	76	115	17	7	24	67	12	.247
2011 New York	A.L.	OF	156	583	*136	153	26	10	41	*119	25	.262
Major League Totals	8 Yrs.		966	3628	647	970	168	74	167	485	104	.267
Division Series													
2006 Detroit	A.L.	OF	4	17	3	5	0	1	2	5	1	.294
2010 New York	A.L.	OF	3	11	2	5	1	1	0	3	1	.455
2011 New York	A.L.	OF	5	20	4	5	1	1	1	3	0	.250
Division Series Totals			12	48	9	15	2	3	3	11	2	.313
Championship Series													
2006 Detroit	A.L.	OF	4	15	4	5	2	0	1	2	1	.333
2010 New York	A.L.	OF	6	17	1	5	1	0	1	3	0	.294
Championship Series Totals			10	32	5	10	3	0	2	5	1	.313
World Series Record													
2006 Detroit	A.L.	OF	5	21	1	2	1	0	0	0	0	.095

a On disabled list from March 23 to April 23, 2008.
b Traded to New York Yankees for outfielder Austin Jackson, pitcher Phil Coke and pitcher Ian Kennedy, December 9, 2009.
c On disabled list from May 2 to May 28, 2010.

GREEN, TAYLOR
Born, Comox, British Columbia, Canada, November 2, 1986.
Bats Left. Throws Right. Height, 5 feet, 11 inches. Weight, 200 pounds.

Year	Club	Lea	Pos	G	AB	R	H	2B	3B	HR	RBI	SB	Avg
2006 Helena	Pioneer	2B	62	221	36	51	12	1	1	23	0	.231
2007 West Tenn	So.Atl.	3B-1B-2B	111	397	68	130	29	2	14	86	0	.327
2008 Brevard County	Fla.St.	3B-1B	114	418	46	121	19	0	15	73	4	.289
2009 Wisconsin	Midwest	3B	6	20	6	8	1	0	1	5	0	.400
2009 Huntsville	Southern	3B-1B	87	306	34	79	15	0	5	43	0	.258
2010 Huntsville	Southern	3B-1B-2B	113	393	51	102	29	1	13	81	0	.260
2011 Huntsville	Southern	3B	3	11	2	4	1	0	0	3	0	.364
2011 Nashville	P.C.	3B-2B	120	420	74	141	36	1	22	88	1	.336
2011 Milwaukee	N.L.	2B-3B	20	37	2	10	3	0	0	1	0	.270
Division Series													
2011 Milwaukee	N.L.	PH	1	1	0	0	0	0	0	0	0	.000
Championship Series													
2011 Milwaukee	N.L.	2B	2	1	0	0	0	0	0	0	0	.000

GUERRERO, VLADIMIR NIZAO
Born, Nizao, Dominican Republic, February 9, 1976.
Bats Right. Throws Right. Height, 6 feet, 3 inches. Weight, 235 pounds.

Year	Club	Lea	Pos	G	AB	R	H	2B	3B	HR	RBI	SB	Avg
1994 Montreal	Dominican	OF	25	92	34	39	11	0	12	35	5	.424
1994 Expos	Gulf Coast	OF	37	137	24	43	13	3	5	25	0	.314
1995 Albany	So.Atl.	OF	110	421	77	140	21	10	16	63	12	.333
1996 Wst Plm Bch	Fla.St.	OF	20	80	16	29	8	0	5	18	2	.363
1996 Harrisburg	Eastern	OF	118	417	84	150	32	8	19	78	17	.360
1996 Montreal	N.L.	OF	9	27	2	5	0	0	1	1	0	.185
1997 Wst. Plm. Bch	Fla. St.	OF	3	10	0	4	2	0	0	2	1	.400
1997 Montreal a	N.L.	OF	90	325	44	98	22	2	11	40	3	.302
1998 Montreal	N.L.	OF	159	623	108	202	37	7	38	109	11	.324
1999 Montreal	N.L.	OF	160	610	102	193	37	5	42	131	14	.316

Year Club	Lea	Pos	G	AB	R	H	2B	3B	HR	RBI	SB	Avg
2000 Montreal............	N.L.	OF	154	571	101	197	28	11	44	123	9	.345
2001 Montreal............	N.L.	OF	159	599	107	184	45	4	34	108	37	.307
2002 Montreal............	N.L.	OF	161	614	106	*206	37	2	39	111	40	.336
2003 Brevard County	Fla.St.	OF	3	6	2	3	0	0	1	1	0	.500
2003 Montreal b-c	N.L.	OF	112	394	71	130	20	3	25	79	9	.330
2004 Anaheim d	A.L.	OF	156	612	*124	206	39	2	39	126	15	.337
2005 Los Angeles e........	A.L.	OF	141	520	95	165	29	2	32	108	13	.317
2006 Los Angeles	A.L.	OF	156	607	92	200	34	1	33	116	15	.329
2007 Los Angeles	A.L.	OF	150	574	89	186	45	1	27	125	2	.324
2008 Los Angeles	A.L.	OF	143	541	85	164	31	3	27	91	5	.303
2009 Rancho Cucamonga....	Calif.	DH	2	6	2	3	2	0	0	2	0	.500
2009 Los Angeles f-g	A.L.	DH-OF	100	383	59	113	16	1	15	50	2	.295
2010 Texas h...........	A.L.	DH-OF	152	593	83	178	27	1	29	115	4	.300
2011 Bowie...........	Eastern	DH	1	4	1	1	0	0	0	0	0	.250
2011 Baltimore i-j	A.L.	DH	145	562	60	163	30	1	13	63	2	.290
Major League Totals		16 Yrs.	2147	8155	1328	2590	477	46	449	1496	181	.318
Division Series												
2004 Anaheim............	A.L.	OF	3	12	1	2	0	0	1	6	0	.167
2005 Los Angeles	A.L.	OF	5	18	5	6	0	0	0	0	1	.333
2007 Los Angeles	A.L.	OF-DH	3	10	0	2	0	0	0	0	0	.200
2008 Los Angeles	A.L.	DH	4	15	2	7	1	0	0	0	1	.467
2009 Los Angeles	A.L.	DH	3	10	2	4	0	0	0	2	0	.400
2010 Texas	A.L.	DH	5	19	2	5	1	0	0	1	0	.263
Division Series Totals			23	84	12	26	2	0	1	9	2	.310
Championship Series												
2005 Los Angeles	A.L.	OF-DH	5	20	0	1	0	0	0	1	0	.050
2009 Los Angeles	A.L.	DH	6	27	3	10	3	0	1	5	0	.370
2010 Texas	A.L.	DH	6	26	2	7	2	0	0	3	0	.269
Championship Series Totals			17	73	5	18	5	0	1	9	0	.247
World Series Record												
2010 Texas	A.L.	DH-OF	4	14	0	1	0	0	0	2	0	.071

a On disabled list from April 1 to May 2 and June 6 to June 21 and July 12 to July 27, 1997.
b On disabled list from June 5 to July 21, 2003.
c Filed for free agency, October 27, 2003. Signed with Anaheim Angels, January 12, 2004.
d Selected Most Valuable Player in American League for 2004.
e On disabled list from May 21 to June 10, 2005.
f On disabled list from April 16 to May 25 and July 8 to August 4, 2009.
g Filed for free agency, November 6, 2009. Signed with the Texas Rangers, January 11, 2010.
h Filed for free agency, November 3, 2010. Signed with Baltimore Orioles, February 18, 2011.
i On disabled list from July 11 to July 26, 2011.
j Filed for free agency, October 30, 2011.

GUILLEN, CARLOS ALFONSO

Born, Maracay, Venezuela, September 30, 1975.
Bats Both. Throws Right. Height, 6 feet, 1 inch. Weight, 215 pounds.

Year Club	Lea	Pos	G	AB	R	H	2B	3B	HR	RBI	SB	Avg
1993 Houston	Domincan	SS	18	56	12	14	4	2	0	8	0	.250
1994 a.....................					INJURED—Did Not Play							
1995 Astros	Gulf Coast	DH	30	105	17	31	4	2	2	15	17	.295
1996 Quad City b	Midwest	SS	29	112	23	37	7	1	3	17	13	.330
1997 Jackson	Texas	SS	115	390	47	99	16	1	10	39	6	.254
1997 New Orleans...........	A.A.	SS	3	13	3	4	1	0	0	0	0	.308
1998 New Orleans..........	P.C.	SS	100	374	67	109	18	4	12	51	3	.291
1998 Tacoma	P.C.	2B	24	92	8	21	1	1	1	4	1	.228
1998 Seattle c-d	A.L.	2B	10	39	9	13	1	1	0	5	2	.333
1999 Seattle e.............	A.L.	SS-2B	5	19	2	3	0	0	1	3	0	.158
2000 Tacoma	P.C.	3B	24	87	19	26	4	1	2	11	4	.299
2000 Seattle f.............	A.L.	3B-SS	90	288	45	74	15	2	7	42	1	.257
2001 Seattle	A.L.	SS	140	456	72	118	21	4	5	53	4	.259
2002 Seattle	A.L.	SS	134	475	73	124	24	6	9	56	4	.261
2003 Tacoma	P.C.	3B	4	14	2	5	1	0	2	4	0	.357
2003 Seattle g-h	A.L.	SS-3B	109	388	63	107	19	3	7	52	4	.276
2004 Detroit	A.L.	SS	136	522	97	166	37	10	20	97	12	.318
2005 Detroit i.............	A.L.	SS	87	334	48	107	15	4	5	23	2	.320
2006 Detroit	A.L.	SS-1B	153	543	100	174	41	5	19	85	20	.320
2007 Detroit	A.L.	SS-1B	151	564	86	167	35	9	21	102	13	.296
2008 Detroit	A.L.	3B-1B-OF	113	420	68	120	29	2	10	54	9	.286
2009 Lakeland............	Fla.St.	OF	5	12	3	3	1	0	0	0	0	.250
2009 Toledo	Int.	DH	2	7	2	4	0	0	0	1	0	.571

Year	Club	Lea	Pos	G	AB	R	H	2B	3B	HR	RBI	SB	Avg
2009 Detroit j	....	A.L.	OF-1B	81	277	36	67	10	3	11	41	1	.242
2010 West Michigan	.....	Midwest	2B	2	6	0	2	0	0	0	0	0	.333
2010 Toledo	....	Int.	2B	5	18	5	6	3	0	1	2	0	.333
2010 Detroit k	....	A.L.	2B-OF	68	253	26	69	17	1	6	34	1	.273
2011 Lakeland	....	Fla.St.	2B	4	15	1	3	2	0	0	2	0	.200
2011 Erie	....	Eastern	DH	1	4	0	1	0	0	0	0	0	.250
2011 Toledo	....	Int.	2B	14	49	9	17	6	0	1	9	1	.347
2011 Detroit l-m	....	A.L.	2B-1B	28	95	8	22	2	1	3	13	1	.232
Major League Totals	....			14 Yrs. 1305	4673	733	1331	266	51	124	660	74	.285
Division Series													
2000 Seattle	....	A.L.	PH	1	1	0	1	0	0	0	1	0	1.000
2006 Detroit	....	A.L.	SS	4	14	3	8	3	0	1	2	0	.571
Division Series Totals	....			5	15	3	9	3	0	1	3	0	.600
Championship Series													
2000 Seattle	....	A.L.	3B	2	5	1	1	0	0	1	2	0	.200
2001 Seattle	....	A.L.	SS	3	8	1	2	0	0	0	0	0	.250
2006 Detroit	....	A.L.	1B-SS	4	16	1	3	1	0	0	0	0	.188
Championship Series Totals	......			9	29	3	6	1	0	1	2	0	.207
World Series Record													
2006 Detroit	....	A.L.	SS-1B	5	17	2	6	1	1	0	2	1	.353

a On disabled list from June 1 to September 12, 1994.
b On disabled list from May 21 to September 11, 1996.
c Traded by Houston Astros to Seattle Mariners with pitcher Freddy Garcia and player to be named later for pitcher Randy Johnson, July 31, 1998.
d Seattle Mariners received pitcher John Halama to complete trade, October 1, 1998.
e On disabled list from April 11 to November 12, 1999.
f On disabled list from April 13 to April 27, 2000.
g On disabled list from July 29 to August 23, 2003.
h Traded to Detroit Tigers for infielder Ramon Santiago and infielder Juan Gonzalez, January 8, 2004.
i On disabled list from June 8 to June 26 and August 11 to September 23, 2005.
j On disabled list from May 5 to July 24, 2009.
k On disabled list from April 23 to May 28 and July 25 to August 9 and August 17 to October 6, 2010.
l On disabled list from March 30 to July 16 and August 13 to September 11, 2011.
m Filed for free agency, October 30, 2011.

GUTIERREZ, FRANKLIN RAFAEL

Born, Caracas, Venezuela, February 21, 1983.
Bats Right. Throws Right. Height, 6 feet, 2 inches. Weight, 180 pounds.

Year	Club	Lea	Pos	G	AB	R	H	2B	3B	HR	RBI	SB	Avg
2001 Dodgers	....	Gulf Coast	OF	56	234	38	63	16	0	4	30	9	.269
2002 Las Vegas	....	P.C.	OF	2	10	2	3	2	0	0	2	0	.300
2002 South Bend	....	So.Atl.	OF	92	361	61	102	18	4	12	45	13	.283
2003 Vero Beach	....	Fla.St.	OF	110	425	65	120	28	5	20	68	17	.282
2003 Jacksonville	......	Southern	OF	18	67	12	21	3	2	4	12	3	.313
2004 Akron	....	Eastern	OF	70	262	38	79	24	2	5	35	6	.302
2004 Buffalo a	....	Int.	DH	7	27	4	4	1	0	1	3	0	.148
2005 Akron	....	Eastern	OF	95	383	70	100	25	2	11	42	14	.261
2005 Buffalo	....	Int.	OF	19	67	10	17	6	2	0	7	2	.254
2005 Cleveland	....	A.L.	OF	7	1	2	0	0	0	0	0	0	.000
2006 Buffalo	....	Int.	OF	90	349	63	97	27	0	9	38	13	.278
2006 Cleveland	....	A.L.	OF	43	136	21	37	9	0	1	8	0	.272
2007 Buffalo	....	Int.	OF	30	129	29	44	7	0	4	16	7	.341
2007 Cleveland b	....	A.L.	OF	100	271	41	72	13	2	13	36	8	.266
2008 Cleveland c	....	A.L.	OF	134	399	54	99	26	2	8	41	9	.248
2009 Seattle	....	A.L.	OF	153	565	85	160	24	1	18	70	16	.283
2010 Seattle	....	A.L.	OF	152	568	61	139	25	3	12	64	25	.245
2011 Tacoma	....	P.C.	OF	11	40	7	11	2	0	0	6	0	.275
2011 Seattle d	....	A.L.	OF	92	322	26	72	13	0	1	19	13	.224
Major League Totals	....			7 Yrs. 681	2262	290	579	110	8	53	238	71	.256
Division Series													
2007 Cleveland	....	A.L.	OF	4	10	2	2	0	0	0	0	0	.200
Championship Series													
2007 Cleveland	....	A.L.	OF	6	19	3	4	0	0	1	4	0	.211

a Traded to Cleveland Indians with player to be named later for outfielder Milton Bradley, April 4, 2004. Cleveland Indians received pitcher Andrew Brown to complete trade, May 19, 2004.
b On disabled list from March 23 to April 13, 2007.
c Traded to Seattle Mariners for pitcher Luis Valbuena and pitcher Joe Smith, December 10, 2008.
d On disabled list from March 22 to May 18 and September 6 to October 31, 2011.

GUYER, BRANDON ERIC

Born, West Chester, Pennsylvania, January 28, 1986.
Bats Right. Throws Right. Height, 6 feet, 1 inch. Weight, 210 pounds.

Year	Club	Lea	Pos	G	AB	R	H	2B	3B	HR	RBI	SB	Avg
2007	Cubs..............	Arizona	OF	17	72	10	16	4	1	1	5	6	.222
2007	Boise..........	Northwest	OF	19	71	9	19	1	0	0	14	5	.268
2008	Peoria...........	Midwest	OF	88	327	55	88	27	3	14	38	22	.269
2009	Daytona............	Fla.St.	OF	73	265	40	92	16	3	2	32	23	.347
2009	Tennessee......	Southern	OF	57	189	22	36	12	2	1	14	7	.190
2010	Tennessee.......	Southern	OF	102	369	76	127	39	6	13	58	30	.344
2011	Durham.............	Int.	OF	107	388	78	121	29	5	14	61	16	.312
2011	Tampa Bay..........	A.L.	OF	15	41	7	8	1	0	2	3	0	.195

GUZMAN, JESUS ANTONIO

Born, Cumana, Venezuela, June 14, 1984.
Bats Right. Throws Right. Height, 6 feet, 1 inch. Weight, 215 pounds.

Year	Club	Lea	Pos	G	AB	R	H	2B	3B	HR	RBI	SB	Avg
2004	Inland Empire.....	Calif.	3B-SS	114	442	80	137	35	3	6	71	10	.310
2005	San Antonio.....	Texas	3B	119	453	61	117	18	8	9	53	6	.258
2006	San Antonio.....	Texas	3B-2B	115	408	57	105	18	3	9	55	7	.257
2007	High Desert a.....	Calif.	2B-3B-OF-1B	130	518	102	156	38	5	25	112	3	.301
2008	Sacramento.......	P.C.	3B	15	59	5	14	2	0	2	9	0	.237
2008	Athletics.......	Arizona	3B-SS-2B	5	15	2	7	3	0	1	3	1	.467
2008	Midland b.......	Texas	3B-2B	80	341	57	124	21	2	14	76	5	.364
2009	Fresno...........	P.C.	1B-3B	115	452	75	145	26	5	16	71	0	.321
2009	San Francisco.....	N.L.	1B	12	20	0	5	0	0	0	0	0	.250
2010	Fresno...........	P.C.	3B-OF-1B	125	445	66	143	28	1	18	72	6	.321
2011	Tucson...........	P.C.	3B-OF-1B-2B	63	244	40	81	22	1	8	57	4	.332
2011	San Diego.......	N.L.	1B-OF	76	247	33	77	22	2	5	44	9	.312
Major League Totals...			2 Yrs.	88	267	33	82	22	2	5	44	9	.307

a Filed for free agency from Seattle Mariners, October 29, 2007. Signed with Oakland Athletics organization, November 16, 2007.
b Filed for free agency, November 3, 2008. Signed with San Francisco Giants organization, November 18, 2008.

GWYNN, ANTHONY KEITH JR. (TONY)

Born, Long Beach, California, October 4, 1982.
Bats Left. Throws Right. Height, 6 feet. Weight, 195 pounds.

Year	Club	Lea	Pos	G	AB	R	H	2B	3B	HR	RBI	SB	Avg
2003	Beloit............	Midwest	OF	61	236	35	66	8	0	1	33	14	.280
2004	Huntsville.......	Southern	OF	138	534	74	130	20	5	2	37	35	.243
2005	Huntsville.......	Southern	OF	133	509	83	138	21	5	1	41	34	.271
2006	Nashville..........	P.C.	OF	112	447	73	134	21	5	4	42	30	.300
2006	Milwaukee...........	N.L.	OF	32	77	5	20	2	1	0	4	3	.260
2007	Nashville..........	P.C.	OF	32	126	19	36	3	3	0	13	4	.286
2007	Milwaukee...........	N.L.	OF	69	123	13	32	3	2	0	10	8	.260
2008	Nashville..........	P.C.	OF	93	375	47	103	9	3	2	26	20	.275
2008	Milwaukee a.......	N.L.	OF	29	42	5	8	1	0	0	1	3	.190
2009	Nashville..........	P.C.	OF	38	152	34	47	8	1	1	9	15	.309
2009	San Diego b.........	N.L.	OF	119	393	59	106	11	6	2	21	11	.270
2010	San Diego c-d......	N.L.	OF	117	289	30	59	9	3	3	20	17	.204
2011	Los Angeles..........	N.L.	OF	136	312	37	80	12	6	2	22	22	.256
Major League Totals............			6 Yrs.	502	1236	149	305	38	18	7	78	64	.247
Division Series													
2008	Milwaukee...........	N.L.	PH	3	3	0	1	0	0	0	0	0	.333

a On disabled list from April 4 to April 23, 2008.
b Traded to San Diego Padres for outfielder Jody Gerut, May 21, 2009.
c On disabled list from August 19 to September 13, 2010.
d Not offered contract, December 2, 2010. Signed with Los Angeles Dodgers, December 11, 2010.

HAFNER, TRAVIS LEE

Born, Jamestown, North Dakota, June 3, 1977.
Bats Left. Throws Right. Height, 6 feet, 3 inches. Weight, 240 pounds.

Year	Club	Lea	Pos	G	AB	R	H	2B	3B	HR	RBI	SB	Avg
1997	Rangers........	Gulf Coast	1B-OF	55	189	38	54	14	0	5	24	7	.286
1998	Savannah..........	So.Atl.	1B-3B-OF	123	405	62	96	15	4	16	84	7	.237
1999	Savannah..........	So.Atl.	1B	134	480	94	140	30	4	28	111	5	.292
2000	Charlotte a..........	Fla.St.	1B-3B	122	436	90	151	34	1	22	109	6	.346

69

Year	Club	Lea	Pos	G	AB	R	H	2B	3B	HR	RBI	SB	Avg
2001 Tulsa b	Texas		1B	88	323	59	91	25	0	20	74	3	.282
2002 Oklahoma	P.C.		1B	110	401	79	137	22	1	21	77	2	.342
2002 Texas c	A.L.		DH-1B	23	62	6	15	4	1	1	6	0	.242
2003 Buffalo	Int.		1B	29	100	15	27	4	0	2	10	2	.270
2003 Cleveland d	A.L.		DH-1B	91	291	35	74	19	3	14	40	2	.254
2004 Cleveland	A.L.		DH-1B	140	482	96	150	41	3	28	109	3	.311
2005 Akron	Eastern		DH	3	9	0	0	0	0	0	0	0	.000
2005 Cleveland e	A.L.		DH-1B	137	486	94	148	42	0	33	108	0	.305
2006 Cleveland	A.L.		DH-1B	129	454	100	140	31	1	42	117	0	.308
2007 Cleveland	A.L.		DH-1B	152	545	80	145	25	2	24	100	1	.266
2008 Buffalo	Int.		DH	7	22	4	7	3	0	0	4	0	.318
2008 Cleveland f	A.L.		DH	57	198	21	39	10	0	5	24	1	.197
2009 Columbus	Int.		DH	12	39	6	13	4	0	1	8	0	.333
2009 Cleveland g	A.L.		DH	94	338	46	92	19	0	16	49	0	.272
2010 Cleveland h	A.L.		DH	118	396	46	110	29	0	13	50	2	.278
2011 Akron	Eastern		DH	2	6	2	3	1	0	0	0	0	.500
2011 Cleveland i	A.L.		DH	94	325	41	91	16	0	13	57	0	.280
Major League Totals		10 Yrs.		1035	3577	565	1004	236	10	189	660	9	.281
Division Series													
2007 Cleveland	A.L.		DH	4	16	4	4	0	0	1	2	0	.250
Championship Series													
2007 Cleveland	A.L.		DH	7	27	2	4	1	0	1	2	0	.148

a On disabled list from August 6 to 22, 2000.
b On disabled list from April 5 to May 11, 2001.
c Traded to Cleveland Indians with pitcher Aaron Myette for catcher Einar Diaz and pitcher Ryan Drese, December 6, 2002.
d On disabled list from May 10 to May 26, 2003.
e On disabled list from July 17 to August 4, 2005.
f On disabled list from May 26 to September 9, 2008.
g On disabled list from April 29 to June 5, 2009.
h On disabled list from July 29 to August 15, 2010.
i On disabled list from May 18 to June 17 and August 22 to September 11, 2011.

HAIRSTON, JERRY WAYNE JR.

Born, Naperville, Illinois, May 29, 1976.
Bats Right. Throws Right. Height, 5 feet, 10 inches. Weight, 185 pounds.

Year	Club	Lea	Pos	G	AB	R	H	2B	3B	HR	RBI	SB	Avg
1997 Bluefield	Appal.		SS	59	221	44	73	13	4	2	36	13	.330
1998 Frederick	Carolina		SS-2B	80	293	56	83	22	3	5	33	13	.283
1998 Bowie	Eastern		2B-SS	55	221	42	72	12	3	5	37	6	.326
1998 Baltimore	A.L.		2B	6	7	2	0	0	0	0	0	0	.000
1999 Rochester	Int.		2B	107	413	65	120	24	5	7	48	19	.291
1999 Baltimore	A.L.		2B	50	175	26	47	12	1	4	17	9	.269
2000 Rochester	Int.		2B-SS	58	201	43	59	15	1	4	21	6	.294
2000 Orioles	Gulf Coast		2B	4	10	3	3	2	0	0	3	4	.300
2000 Frederick	Carolina		2B	2	8	1	3	2	0	0	1	0	.375
2000 Baltimore a	A.L.		2B	49	180	27	46	5	0	5	19	8	.256
2001 Baltimore	A.L.		2B	159	532	63	124	25	5	8	47	29	.233
2002 Baltimore	A.L.		2B	122	426	55	114	25	3	5	32	21	.268
2003 Aberdeen	N.Y.-Penn.		2B	2	3	2	1	0	0	0	0	1	.333
2003 Bowie	Eastern		2B	6	20	4	6	1	0	1	2	0	.300
2003 Baltimore b	A.L.		2B	58	218	25	59	12	2	2	21	14	.271
2004 Bowie	Eastern		2B	5	13	4	2	1	0	0	2	2	.154
2004 Baltimore c	A.L.		OF-2B-3B	86	287	43	87	19	1	2	24	13	.303
2005 Iowa	P.C.		2B-OF	5	22	3	7	0	1	0	2	3	.318
2005 Chicago d-e	N.L.		OF-2B-SS	114	380	51	99	25	2	4	30	8	.261
2006 Chicago	N.L.		2B-OF-1B	38	82	8	17	3	0	0	4	3	.207
2006 Texas f-g	A.L.		OF-SS-2B-3B	63	88	17	18	3	1	0	6	2	.205
2007 Frisco	Texas		DH	3	12	2	2	1	0	1	2	0	.167
2007 Oklahoma	P.C.		SS-OF	4	15	2	2	0	0	1	1	0	.133
2007 Texas h-i	A.L.		OF-2B-3B-SS	73	159	22	30	7	0	3	16	5	.189
2008 Louisville	Int.		OF-SS-3B-2B	20	79	11	30	8	2	4	19	1	.380
2008 Cincinnati j-k	N.L.		OF-SS-2B-3B	80	261	47	85	20	2	6	36	15	.326
2009 Cincinnati	N.L.		3B-SS-OF-2B	86	307	47	78	18	1	8	27	7	.254
2009 New York l-m	N.L.		OF-3B-SS-2B	45	76	15	18	5	0	2	12	0	.237
2010 San Diego n-o	N.L.		SS-2B-OF-3B	119	430	53	105	13	2	10	50	9	.244
2011 Harrisburg	Eastern		SS	2	6	1	1	0	0	0	0	0	.167
2011 Washington-Milwaukee p-q-r	N.L.		3B-OF-2B-SS	120	337	43	91	21	1	5	31	3	.270
Major League Totals		14 Yrs.		1268	3945	544	1018	213	21	64	372	146	.258

Year	Club	Lea	Pos	G	AB	R	H	2B	3B	HR	RBI	SB	Avg
	Division Series												
2009 New York ........A.L.			PH	1	0	0	0	0	0	0	0	0	.000
2011 Milwaukee .......N.L.			3B	5	16	2	6	2	0	0	3	0	.375
Division Series Totals				6	16	2	6	2	0	0	3	0	.375
	Championship Series												
2009 New York ........A.L.			OF	2	2	1	1	0	0	0	0	0	.500
2011 Milwaukee ........N.L.			3B	6	23	6	9	4	0	0	1	0	.391
Championship Series Totals				8	25	7	10	4	0	0	1	0	.400
	World Series Record												
2009 New York ........A.L.			OF	3	6	0	1	0	0	0	0	0	.167

a On disabled list from May 16 to July 4, 2000.
b On disabled list from May 21 to September 4, 2003.
c On disabled list from March 31 to May 11 and from August 18 to November 3, 2004.
d Traded to Chicago Cubs with infielder Mike Fontenot and pitcher Dave Crouthers for outfielder Sammy Sosa, February 2, 2005.
e On disabled list from August 4 to August 19, 2005.
f Traded to Texas Rangers for infielder Phil Nevin, May 31, 2006.
g Filed for free agency, October 13, 2006. re-signed with Texas Rangers organization, January 5, 2007.
h On disabled list from May 17 to June 5 and August 8 to August 29, 2007.
i Filed for free agency, October 30, 2007. Signed with Cincinnati Reds organization, March 3, 2008.
j On disabled list from June 10 to June 26 and July 14 to August 1 and August 18 to September 8, 2008.
k Filed for free agency, October 31, 2008, re-signed with Cincinnati Reds, January 7, 2009.
l Traded to New York Yankees for catcher Chase Weems, July 31, 2009.
m Filed for free agency, November 10, 2009. Signed with the San Diego Padres, January 18, 2010.
n On disabled list from August 28 to September 12, 2010.
o Filed for free agency, November 1, 2010. Signed with Washington Nationals, January 19, 2011.
p On disabled list from June 30 to July 18, 2011.
q Traded to Milwaukee Brewers for outfielder Erik Komatsu, July 30, 2011.
r Filed for free agency, October 30, 2011. Signed with Los Angeles Dodgers, December 5, 2011.

HAIRSTON, SCOTT ALEXANDER
Born, Fort Worth, Texas, May 25, 1980.
Bats Right. Throws Right. Height, 6 feet. Weight, 190 pounds.

Year	Club	Lea	Pos	G	AB	R	H	2B	3B	HR	RBI	SB	Avg
2001 Missoula	Pioneer		2B	74	291	81	101	16	6	14	65	2	.347
2002 Lancaster...........	Calif.		2B-3B	18	79	20	32	11	1	6	26	1	.405
2002 South Bend	Midwest		2B-3B	109	394	79	131	35	4	16	72	9	.332
2003 Tucson...............	P.C.		DH	1	0	0	0	0	0	0	1	0	.000
2003 El Paso............	Texas		2B	88	337	53	93	21	7	10	47	6	.276
2004 Tucson..............	P.C.		2B-OF	28	115	29	36	8	3	5	20	0	.313
2004 Arizona..............	N.L.		2B-OF	101	339	39	84	15	6	13	29	3	.248
2005 Arizona..............	N.L.		OF	15	20	0	2	1	0	0	0	0	.100
2005 Tucson a............	P.C.		OF-2B	58	209	45	65	8	3	16	40	3	.311
2006 Tucson b............	P.C.		OF	98	381	83	123	22	1	26	81	3	.323
2006 Arizona b	N.L.		OF	9	15	2	6	2	0	0	2	0	.400
2007 Arizona-San Diego c-d ..	N.L.		OF	107	263	37	64	18	2	11	36	2	.243
2008 San Diego e	N.L.		OF-2B	112	326	42	81	18	3	17	31	3	.248
2009 Lake Elsinore	Calif.		OF	3	10	1	1	0	0	0	0	0	.100
2009 San Diego	N.L.		OF	56	197	26	59	14	1	10	29	8	.299
2009 Oakland f-g-h.........	A.L.		OF	60	233	24	55	13	1	7	35	3	.236
2010 Lake Elsinore	Calif.		OF	3	7	1	4	1	0	0	1	0	.571
2010 San Diego i-j	N.L.		OF	104	295	34	62	10	0	10	36	6	.210
2011 New York k-l..........	N.L.		OF-2B	79	132	20	31	8	1	7	24	1	.235
Major League Totals			8 Yrs.	643	1820	224	444	99	14	75	222	26	.244

a On disabled list from September 2 to November 14, 2005.
b On disabled list from June 20 to July 29, 2006.
c Traded to San Diego Padres for pitcher Leo Rosales, July 27, 2007.
d On disabled list from August 10 to September 8, 2007.
e On disabled list from August 28 to October 2, 2008.
f On disabled list from June 3 to June 23, 2009.
g Traded to Oakland Athletics for pitcher Ryan Webb, pitcher Craig Italiano and player to be named later, July 5, 2009. San Diego Padres received pitcher Sean Gallagher to complete trade, July 28, 2009.
h Traded to San Diego Padres with outfielder Aaron Cunningham for third baseman Kevin Kouzmanoff and infielder Eric Sogard, January 16, 2010.
i On disabled list from May 16 to June 2, 2010.
j Not offered contract, December 2, 2010. Signed with New York Mets, January 20, 2011.
k On disabled list from August 24 to September 30, 2011.
l Filed for free agency, October 30, 2011, re-signed with New York Mets, January 6, 2012.

HAMILTON, JOSHUA HOLT (JOSH)
Born, Raleigh, North Carolina, May 21, 1981.
Bats Left. Throws Left. Height, 6 feet, 4 inches. Weight, 235 pounds.

Year	Club	Lea	Pos	G	AB	R	H	2B	3B	HR	RBI	SB	Avg
1999 Princeton	Appal.	OF	56	236	49	82	20	4	10	48	17	.347
1999 Hudson Valley	N.Y.-Penn.	OF	16	72	7	14	3	0	0	7	1	.194
2000 Charleston-SC	So.Atl.	OF	96	391	62	118	23	3	13	61	14	.302
2001 Charleston-SC	So.Atl.	OF	4	11	3	4	1	0	1	2	0	.364
2001 Orlando	Southern	OF	23	89	5	16	5	0	0	4	2	.180
2002 Bakersfield	Calif.	OF	56	211	32	64	14	1	9	44	10	.303
2003-05					Did Not Play								
2006 Hudson Valley a	N.Y.-Penn.	OF	15	50	7	13	3	1	0	5	0	.260
2007 Louisville	Int.	OF	11	40	9	14	1	0	4	8	3	.350
2007 Cincinnati b-c	N.L.	OF	90	298	52	87	17	2	19	47	3	.292
2008 Texas	A.L.	OF	156	624	98	190	35	5	32	*130	9	.304
2009 Frisco	Texas	DH	1	4	1	1	0	0	0	1	1	.250
2009 Okla.	P.C.	OF	7	28	3	5	2	1	0	0	1	.179
2009 Texas d	A.L.	OF	89	336	43	90	19	2	10	54	8	.268
2010 Texas e	A.L.	OF	133	518	95	186	40	3	32	100	8	*.359
2011 Frisco	Texas	DH	2	7	3	2	0	0	1	3	0	.286
2011 Round Rock	P.C.	DH	3	11	2	2	1	0	1	3	0	.182
2011 Texas f	A.L.	OF	121	487	80	145	31	5	25	94	8	.298
Major League Totals	5 Yrs.		589	2263	368	698	142	17	118	425	36	.308
Division Series													
2010 Texas	A.L.	OF	5	18	1	2	0	0	0	1	1	.111
2011 Texas	A.L.	OF	4	15	1	4	1	0	0	2	0	.267
Division Series Totals			9	33	2	6	1	0	0	3	1	.182
Championship Series													
2010 Texas	A.L.	OF	6	20	6	7	1	0	4	7	3	.350
2011 Texas	A.L.	OF	6	26	4	8	4	0	0	5	0	.308
Championship Series Totals			12	46	10	15	5	0	4	12	3	.326
World Series Record													
2010 Texas	A.L.	OF	5	20	2	2	0	0	1	1	0	.100
2011 Texas	A.L.	OF	7	29	4	7	2	0	1	6	0	.241
World Series Totals			12	49	6	9	2	0	2	7	0	.184

a Selected by Chicago Cubs from Tampa Bay Devil Rays in Rule V draft, December 7, 2006. Sold to Cincinnati Reds, December 7, 2006.
b On disabled list from May 19 to June 4 and July 8 to August 12, 2007.
c Traded to Texas Rangers for pitcher Edinson Volquez and pitcher Danny Herrera, December 21, 2007.
d On disabled list from April 27 to May 12 and June 1 to July 6, 2009.
e Selected Most Valuable Player in American League for 2010.
f On disabled list from April 13 to May 23, 2011.

HANIGAN, RYAN M.
Born, Washington, District of Columbia, August 16, 1980.
Bats Right. Throws Right. Height, 6 feet. Weight, 195 pounds.

Year	Club	Lea	Pos	G	AB	R	H	2B	3B	HR	RBI	SB	Avg
2002 Dayton	Midwest	C	6	11	1	3	1	0	0	0	0	.273
2003 Louisville	Int.	C	1	3	1	1	0	0	0	0	0	.333
2003 Dayton	Midwest	C	92	311	43	86	12	0	1	31	3	.277
2004 Potomac	Carolina	C	119	429	58	127	21	0	5	56	6	.296
2005 Chattanooga	Southern	1B-C	100	333	45	107	14	1	4	29	4	.321
2006 Louisville	Int.	C-1B	8	13	2	2	0	0	0	1	0	.154
2006 Chattanooga	Southern	C-1B-OF	56	126	17	31	2	0	0	14	0	.246
2007 Chattanooga	Southern	C-1B	60	197	30	59	14	1	3	27	0	.299
2007 Louisville	Int.	C-1B	41	127	16	32	5	0	1	9	0	.252
2007 Cincinnati	N.L.	C	5	10	3	3	1	0	0	2	0	.300
2008 Louisville	Int.	C-1B	75	272	37	88	14	0	4	35	1	.324
2008 Cincinnati	N.L.	C	31	85	9	23	2	0	2	9	0	.271
2009 Louisville	Int.	C	5	18	4	7	2	0	0	2	0	.389
2009 Cincinnati a	N.L.	C	90	251	22	66	6	1	3	11	0	.263
2010 Louisville	Int.	C	13	46	6	11	3	0	0	2	0	.239
2010 Cincinnati b	N.L.	C	70	203	25	61	11	0	5	40	0	.300
2011 Cincinnati	N.L.	C	91	266	27	71	6	0	6	31	0	.267
Major League Totals	5 Yrs.		287	815	86	224	26	1	16	93	0	.275
Division Series													
2010 Cincinnati	N.L.	C	2	4	0	0	0	0	0	0	0	.000

a On disabled list from August 24 to September 9, 2009.
b On disabled list from May 29 to July 9, 2010.

HANNAHAN, JOHN JOSEPH (JACK)
Born, St.Paul, Minnesota, March 4, 1980.
Bats Left. Throws Right. Height, 6 feet, 2 inches. Weight, 210 pounds.

Year	Club	Lea	Pos	G	AB	R	H	2B	3B	HR	RBI	SB	Avg
2001	Oneonta	N.Y.-Penn.	3B	14	55	11	16	4	1	0	8	2	.291
2001	West Michigan	Midwest	3B	46	170	24	54	11	0	1	27	4	.318
2002	Lakeland	Fla.St.	3B	66	246	28	67	11	1	6	42	9	.272
2002	Erie	Eastern	3B	65	226	17	54	12	1	3	20	2	.239
2003	Erie	Eastern	3B	135	471	64	121	18	0	9	45	2	.257
2004	Erie	Eastern	3B-SS	108	374	48	102	21	1	8	39	7	.273
2005	Erie	Eastern	3B	7	22	1	3	0	0	0	1	0	.136
2005	Toledo	Int.	3B-1B-2B	68	238	31	64	15	0	4	28	6	.269
2006	Detroit	A.L.	1B	3	9	0	0	0	0	0	0	0	.000
2006	Toledo	Int.	2B-3B-1B	119	415	59	117	27	0	9	62	9	.282
2007	Toledo	Int.	2B-3B-1B	101	336	56	99	20	1	13	63	5	.295
2007	Oakland a	A.L.	3B	41	144	16	40	12	0	3	24	1	.278
2008	Oakland	A.L.	3B-1B	143	436	48	95	27	0	9	47	2	.218
2009	Sacramento	P.C.	3B-2B	21	81	8	18	7	0	2	11	0	.222
2009	Oakland-Seattle b	A.L.	3B-1B-SS-2B	103	267	27	57	14	2	4	19	1	.213
2010	Pawtucket	Int.	3B-2B-1B	33	110	15	28	8	0	4	12	2	.255
2010	Tacoma c	P.C.	2B-3B-SS	63	224	32	51	9	1	5	33	1	.228
2011	Cleveland	A.L.	3B-1B	110	320	38	80	16	2	8	40	2	.250
Major League Totals			5 Yrs.	400	1176	129	272	69	4	24	130	6	.231

a Traded by Detroit Tigers to Oakland Athletics for outfielder Jason Perry, August 13, 2007.
b Traded to Seattle Mariners for pitcher Justin Souza, July 11, 2009.
c On disabled list from March 26 to April 30, 2010.

HARDY, JAMES JERRY (J.J.)
Born, Tucson, Arizona, August 19, 1982.
Bats Right. Throws Right. Height, 6 feet, 2 inches. Weight, 190 pounds.

Year	Club	Lea	Pos	G	AB	R	H	2B	3B	HR	RBI	SB	Avg
2001	Brewers	Arizona	SS	5	20	6	5	2	1	0	1	0	.250
2001	Ogden	Pioneer	SS	35	125	20	31	5	0	2	15	1	.248
2002	High Desert	California	SS	84	335	53	98	19	1	6	48	9	.293
2002	Huntsville	Southern	SS	38	145	14	33	7	0	1	13	1	.228
2003	Huntsville	Southern	SS	114	416	67	116	26	0	12	62	6	.279
2004	Indianapolis	Int.	SS	26	101	17	28	10	0	4	20	0	.277
2005	Milwaukee	N.L.	SS	124	372	46	92	22	1	9	50	0	.247
2006	Milwaukee a	N.L.	SS	35	128	13	31	5	0	5	14	1	.242
2007	Milwaukee	N.L.	SS	151	592	89	164	30	1	26	80	2	.277
2008	Milwaukee	N.L.	SS	146	569	78	161	31	4	24	74	2	.283
2009	Nashville	P.C.	SS	18	71	7	18	2	0	4	12	0	.254
2009	Milwaukee b	N.L.	SS	115	414	53	95	16	2	11	47	0	.229
2010	Beloit	Midwest	SS	3	10	0	2	0	0	0	0	0	.200
2010	Minnesota c-d	A.L.	SS	101	340	44	91	19	3	6	38	1	.268
2011	Norfolk	Int.	SS	3	9	2	2	0	0	0	0	0	.222
2011	Baltimore e	A.L.	SS	129	527	76	142	27	0	30	80	0	.269
Major League Totals			7 Yrs.	801	2942	399	776	150	11	111	383	6	.264
Division Series													
2008	Milwaukee	N.L.	SS	4	14	2	6	1	0	0	2	0	.429
2010	Minnesota	A.L.	SS	3	10	0	1	1	0	0	0	0	.100
Division Series Totals				7	24	2	7	2	0	0	2	0	.292

a On disabled list from May 17 to October 31, 2006.
b Traded to Minnesota Twins for outfielder Carlos Gomez, November 6, 2009.
c On disabled list from May 5 to May 25 and June 7 to July 3, 2010.
d Traded to Baltimore Orioles with infielder Brendan Harris and cash for pitcher Jim Hoey and pitcher Brett Jacobson, December 9, 2010.
e On disabled list from April 10 to May 10, 2011.

HARRIS, WILLIAM CHARLES (WILLIE)
Born, Cairo, Georgia, June 22, 1978.
Bats Left. Throws Right. Height, 5 feet, 9 inches. Weight, 175 pounds.

Year	Club	Lea	Pos	G	AB	R	H	2B	3B	HR	RBI	SB	Avg
1999	Bluefield	Appal.	2B	5	22	3	6	1	0	0	3	1	.273
1999	Delmarva	So.Atl.	2B-OF	66	272	42	72	13	3	2	32	17	.265
2000	Delmarva	So.Atl.	2B-OF-SS	133	474	106	130	27	10	6	60	38	.274
2001	Bowie	Eastern	2B-OF	133	525	83	160	27	4	9	49	54	.305
2001	Baltimore	A.L.	OF	9	24	3	3	1	0	0	0	0	.125

Year	Club	Lea	Pos	G	AB	R	H	2B	3B	HR	RBI	SB	Avg
2002 Charlotte	....	Int.	2B-OF	89	360	54	102	16	5	5	33	32	.283
2002 Chicago a	....	A.L.	2B-OF	49	163	14	38	4	0	2	12	8	.233
2003 Charlotte	....	Int.	2B-OF	28	100	22	38	6	1	6	13	9	.380
2003 Chicago b	....	A.L.	OF-2B	79	137	19	28	3	1	0	5	12	.204
2004 Chicago	....	A.L.	2B-OF	129	409	68	107	15	2	2	27	19	.262
2005 Charlotte	....	Int.	2B	28	109	21	29	11	1	1	10	10	.266
2005 Chicago	....	A.L.	2B-SS	56	121	17	31	2	1	1	8	10	.256
2006 Boston c-d	....	A.L.	OF-2B	47	45	17	7	2	0	0	1	6	.156
2006 Pawtucket	....	Int.	OF-2B	60	218	32	48	6	1	8	17	11	.220
2007 Richmond	....	Int.	3B-2B-OF	17	58	17	21	7	2	1	7	7	.362
2007 Atlanta e	....	N.L.	OF-3B	117	344	56	93	20	8	2	32	17	.270
2008 Washington	....	N.L.	OF-2B-3B-SS	140	367	58	92	14	4	13	43	13	.251
2009 Syracuse	....	Int.	OF-2B	5	18	2	4	1	0	0	1	0	.222
2009 Washington f	......	N.L.	OF-2B-3B	137	323	47	76	18	6	7	27	11	.235
2010 Washington g	......	N.L.	OF-3B	132	224	25	41	6	2	10	32	5	.183
2011 New York h	....	N.L.	OF-2B-3B	126	240	36	59	11	0	2	23	5	.246
Major League Totals	....		11 Yrs.	1021	2397	360	575	96	24	39	210	106	.240
Division Series													
2005 Chicago	....	A.L.	2B	1	1	0	1	0	0	0	1	0	1.000
World Series Record													
2005 Chicago	....	A.L.	2B	2	1	1	1	0	0	0	0	1	1.000

a Traded to Chicago White Sox for outfielder Chris Singleton, January 29, 2002.
b On disabled list from May 22 to June 16, 2003.
c Not offered contract, December 21, 2005. Signed with Boston Red Sox organization, January 19, 2006.
d Filed for free agency, October 2, 2006. Signed with Atlanta Braves organization, December 9, 2006.
e Released by Atlanta Braves, December 12, 2007. Signed with Washington Nationals, December 13, 2007.
f On disabled list from April 13 to April 28, 2009.
g Filed for free agency, November 1, 2010. Signed with New York Mets organization, January 17, 2011.
h Filed for free agency, October 30, 2011.

HARRISON, JOSH ISAIAH
Born, Cincinnati, Ohio, July 8, 1987.
Bats Right. Throws Right. Height, 5 feet, 8 inches. Weight, 185 pounds.

Year	Club	Lea	Pos	G	AB	R	H	2B	3B	HR	RBI	SB	Avg
2008 Boise	....	Northwest	2B-OF	33	114	27	40	11	2	1	25	12	.351
2008 Peoria	....	Midwest	2B-OF	31	122	15	32	4	1	1	4	6	.262
2009 Peoria	....	Midwest	OF-2B-3B	79	303	51	102	17	7	4	33	16	.337
2009 Daytona a	....	Fla.St.	OF-3B-3B	18	70	10	20	3	1	1	9	10	.286
2009 Lynchburg	...	Carolina	3B-2B-OF	34	141	15	38	8	1	1	13	4	.270
2010 Altoona	....	Eastern	3B-2B	135	520	74	156	33	3	4	75	19	.300
2011 Indianapolis	....	Int.	3B-2B-SS	62	226	35	70	15	2	5	23	13	.310
2011 Pittsburgh	....	N.L.	3B-2B	65	195	21	53	13	2	1	16	4	.272

a Traded by Chicago Cubs to Pittsburgh Pirates with pitcher Kevin Hart and pitcher Jose Ascanio for pitcher John Grabow and pitcher Tom Gorzelanny, July 30, 2009.

HART, JON COREY (COREY)
Born, Bowling Green, Kentucky, March 24, 1982.
Bats Right. Throws Right. Height, 6 feet, 6 inches. Weight, 215 pounds.

Year	Club	Lea	Pos	G	AB	R	H	2B	3B	HR	RBI	SB	Avg
2000 Ogden	....	Pioneer	1B	57	216	32	62	9	1	2	30	6	.287
2001 Ogden	....	Pioneer	1B-OF	69	262	53	89	18	1	11	62	14	.340
2002 High Desert	....	Calif.	3B-1B	100	393	76	113	26	10	22	84	24	.288
2002 Huntsville	....	Southern	3B-1B	28	94	16	25	3	0	2	15	3	.266
2003 Huntsville	....	Southern	3B-OF	130	493	70	149	40	1	13	94	25	.302
2004 Indianapolis	....	Int.	OF-1B	121	440	68	124	29	8	15	67	17	.282
2004 Milwaukee	....	N.L.	DH	1	1	0	0	0	0	0	0	0	.000
2005 Milwaukee	....	N.L.	OF	21	57	9	11	2	1	2	7	2	.193
2005 Nashville	....	P.C.	OF-1B	113	429	85	132	29	9	17	69	31	.308
2006 Milwaukee	....	N.L.	OF-1B	87	237	32	67	13	2	9	33	5	.283
2007 Milwaukee	....	N.L.	OF	140	505	86	149	33	9	24	81	23	.295
2008 Milwaukee	....	N.L.	OF	157	612	76	164	45	6	20	91	23	.268
2009 Nashville	....	P.C.	OF	4	10	5	5	1	0	1	3	0	.500
2009 Milwaukee a	....	N.L.	OF	115	419	64	109	24	3	12	48	11	.260
2010 Milwaukee	....	N.L.	OF	145	558	91	158	34	4	31	102	7	.283
2011 Nashville	....	P.C.	OF	5	15	1	2	2	0	0	1	0	.133
2011 Milwaukee b	....	N.L.	OF	130	492	80	140	25	4	26	63	7	.285
Major League Totals	....		8 Yrs.	796	2881	438	798	176	29	124	425	78	.277

Year	Club	Lea	Pos	G	AB	R	H	2B	3B	HR	RBI	SB	Avg
Division Series													
2008 Milwaukee	N.L.	OF	4	13	0	3	0	0	0	0	0	.231	
2011 Milwaukee	N.L.	OF	5	21	4	5	0	0	1	3	0	.238	
Division Series Totals			9	34	4	8	0	0	1	3	0	.235	
Championship Series													
2011 Milwaukee	N.L.	OF	5	20	2	5	0	0	1	2	0	.250	

a On disabled list from August 2 to September 8, 2009.
b On disabled list from March 22 to April 26, 2011.

HAWPE, BRADLEY BONTE (BRAD)

Born, Fort Worth, Texas, June 22, 1979.
Bats Left. Throws Left. Height, 6 feet, 3 inches. Weight, 205 pounds.

Year	Club	Lea	Pos	G	AB	R	H	2B	3B	HR	RBI	SB	Avg
2000 Portland	Northwest	OF-1B	62	205	38	59	19	2	7	29	2	.288
2001 Asheville	So.Atl.	OF-1B	111	393	78	105	22	3	22	72	7	.267
2002 Salem	Carolina	1B	122	450	87	156	38	2	22	97	1	.347
2003 Tulsa	Texas	OF-1B	93	346	52	96	27	0	17	68	1	.277
2004 Colorado Springs	P.C.	OF	92	345	62	111	19	1	31	86	3	.322
2004 Colorado	N.L.	OF	42	105	12	26	3	2	3	9	1	.248
2005 Colorado Springs	P.C.	OF	7	28	7	13	3	0	3	11	0	.464
2005 Colorado a	N.L.	OF	101	305	38	80	10	3	9	47	2	.262
2006 Colorado	N.L.	OF	150	499	67	146	33	6	22	84	5	.293
2007 Colorado	N.L.	OF	152	516	80	150	33	4	29	116	0	.291
2008 Colorado Springs	P.C.	OF	3	11	1	1	0	0	0	0	0	.091
2008 Colorado b	N.L.	OF	138	488	69	138	24	3	25	85	2	.283
2009 Colorado	N.L.	OF	145	501	82	143	42	3	23	86	1	.285
2010 Charlotte	Fla.St.	DH	3	6	0	1	0	0	0	0	0	.167
2010 Modesto	Calif.	OF	1	4	0	1	1	0	0	1	0	.250
2010 Colorado Springs	P.C.	OF	2	9	2	2	1	0	0	0	0	.222
2010 Colorado	N.L.	OF-1B	88	259	24	66	21	2	7	37	2	.255
2010 Tampa Bay c-d-e	A.L.	1B-OF	15	39	7	7	0	0	2	7	0	.179
2011 San Diego f-g	N.L.	1B-OF	62	195	19	45	10	0	4	19	0	.231
Major League Totals	8 Yrs.		893	2907	398	801	176	23	124	490	13	.276	
Division Series													
2007 Colorado	N.L.	OF	3	11	1	3	0	0	0	0	0	.273
2009 Colorado	N.L.	OF	2	4	0	0	0	0	0	0	0	.000
Division Series Totals			5	15	1	3	0	0	0	0	0	.200	
Championship Series													
2007 Colorado	N.L.	OF	4	12	2	4	0	0	0	2	0	.333
World Series Record													
2007 Colorado	N.L.	OF	4	16	1	4	0	1	1	2	0	.250

a On disabled list from July 12 to September 2, 2005.
b On disabled list from May 21 to June 6, 2008.
c On disabled list from April 25 to May 10, 2010.
d Released by Colorado Rockies, August 24, 2010. Signed with Tampa Bay Rays organization, August 29, 2010.
e Filed for free agency, November 1, 2010. Signed with San Diego Padres, January 3, 2011.
f On disabled list from June 19 to October 30, 2011.
g Filed for free agency, October 31, 2011.

HAYES, BRETT GREGORY

Born, Pasadena, California, February 13, 1984.
Bats Right. Throws Right. Height, 6 feet, 1 inch. Weight, 205 pounds.

Year	Club	Lea	Pos	G	AB	R	H	2B	3B	HR	RBI	SB	Avg
2005 Marlins	Gulf Coast	C	3	12	2	5	1	0	0	2	0	.417
2005 Jamestown	N.Y.-Penn.	C-SS-OF	36	117	11	28	6	1	1	12	3	.239
2006 Greensboro	So.Atl.	C-1B	82	278	39	68	13	1	9	38	4	.245
2007 Jupiter	Fla.St.	C	17	65	10	22	3	1	1	11	2	.338
2007 Carolina	Southern	C-1B	74	273	22	64	16	0	3	31	2	.234
2008 Carolina	Southern	C-1B	54	181	19	42	8	0	6	18	1	.232
2008 Albuquerque	P.C.	C	37	116	21	34	3	1	5	17	1	.293
2009 New Orleans	P.C.	C-1B-2B	90	322	27	77	15	0	4	37	2	.239
2009 Florida	N.L.	1B	14	11	5	3	1	0	1	2	0	.273
2010 New Orleans	P.C.	C	16	59	7	13	3	0	1	5	0	.220
2010 Jupiter	Fla.St.	C	7	23	6	5	1	0	2	7	0	.217
2010 Florida a	N.L.	C	26	77	6	16	6	1	2	6	0	.208
2011 Florida	N.L.	C-OF-1B	64	130	19	30	9	0	5	16	0	.231
Major League Totals	3 Yrs.		104	218	30	49	16	1	8	24	0	.225	

a On disabled list from July 21 to August 5, 2010.

HEADLEY, CHASE JORDAN

Born, Fountain, Colorado, May 9, 1984.
Bats Both. Throws Right. Height, 6 feet, 2 inches. Weight, 195 pounds.

Year	Club	Lea	Pos	G	AB	R	H	2B	3B	HR	RBI	SB	Avg
2005	Fort Wayne	Midwest	3B	4	15	2	3	0	0	0	1	0	.200
2005	Eugene	Northwest	3B	57	220	29	59	14	3	6	33	1	.268
2006	Lake Elsinore	Calif.	3B	129	484	79	141	33	0	12	73	4	.291
2007	San Antonio	Texas	3B	121	433	82	143	38	5	20	78	1	.330
2007	San Diego	N.L.	3B	8	18	1	4	1	0	0	0	0	.222
2008	Portland	P.C.	OF-3B	65	259	49	79	24	1	13	40	0	.305
2008	San Diego	N.L.	OF-3B	91	331	34	89	19	2	9	38	4	.269
2009	San Diego	N.L.	OF-3B-1B	156	543	62	142	31	2	12	64	10	.262
2010	San Diego	N.L.	3B	161	610	77	161	29	3	11	58	17	.264
2011	San Diego a	N.L.	3B	113	381	43	110	28	1	4	44	13	.289
Major League Totals		5 Yrs.		529	1883	217	506	108	8	36	204	44	.269

a On disabled list from August 7 to September 19, 2011.

HEISEY, CHRISTOPHER J. (CHRIS)

Born, Lancaster, Pennsylvania, December 14, 1984.
Bats Right. Throws Right. Height, 6 feet. Weight, 215 pounds.

Year	Club	Lea	Pos	G	AB	R	H	2B	3B	HR	RBI	SB	Avg
2006	Billings	Pioneer	OF	70	245	46	70	10	0	6	37	11	.286
2007	Sarasota	Fla.St.	OF	12	43	6	15	1	0	1	5	3	.349
2007	Dayton	Midwest	OF	104	374	60	108	24	2	9	46	19	.289
2008	Sarasota	Fla.St.	OF	117	436	77	125	31	7	7	51	27	.287
2008	Chattanooga	Southern	OF	19	79	11	25	6	1	2	10	5	.316
2009	Louisville	Int.	OF	63	245	37	68	17	1	9	37	8	.278
2009	Carolina	Southern	OF	71	271	54	94	18	2	13	40	13	.347
2010	Louisville	Int.	OF	20	79	6	19	3	0	4	13	2	.241
2010	Cincinnati	N.L.	OF	97	201	33	51	10	1	8	21	1	.254
2011	Louisville	Int.	OF	4	12	1	1	0	0	1	2	0	.083
2011	Cincinnati a	N.L.	OF	120	279	44	71	9	1	18	50	6	.254
Major League Totals		2 Yrs.		217	480	77	122	19	2	26	71	7	.254
Division Series													
2010	Cincinnati	N.L.	OF	1	2	0	0	0	0	0	0	0	.000

a On disabled list from August 6 to September 1, 2011.

HELTON, TODD LYNN

Born, Knoxville, Tennessee, August 20, 1973.
Bats Left. Throws Left. Height, 6 feet, 2 inches. Weight, 210 pounds.

Year	Club	Lea	Pos	G	AB	R	H	2B	3B	HR	RBI	SB	Avg
1995	Asheville	So. Atl.	1B	54	201	24	51	11	1	1	15	1	.254
1996	New Haven	Eastern	1B	93	319	46	106	24	2	7	51	2	.332
1996	Colo Sprngs	P.C.	1B-OF	21	71	13	25	4	1	2	13	0	.352
1997	Colo Sprngs	P.C.	1B-OF	99	392	87	138	31	2	16	88	3	.352
1997	Colorado	N.L.	OF-1B	35	93	13	26	2	1	5	11	0	.280
1998	Colorado	N.L.	1B	152	530	78	167	37	1	25	97	3	.315
1999	Colorado	N.L.	1B	159	578	114	185	39	5	35	113	7	.320
2000	Colorado	N.L.	1B	160	580	138	*216	*59	2	42	*147	5	*.372
2001	Colorado	N.L.	1B	159	587	132	197	54	2	49	146	7	.336
2002	Colorado	N.L.	1B	156	553	107	182	39	4	30	109	5	.329
2003	Colorado	N.L.	1B	160	583	135	209	49	5	33	117	0	.358
2004	Colorado	N.L.	1B	154	547	115	190	49	2	32	96	3	.347
2005	Colo Sprngs	P.C.	2B	2	5	1	3	2	0	0	1	0	.600
2005	Colorado a	N.L.	1B	144	509	92	163	45	2	20	79	3	.320
2006	Colorado Springs	P.C.	1B	2	6	0	2	0	0	0	0	0	.333
2006	Colorado b	N.L.	1B	145	546	94	165	40	5	15	81	3	.302
2007	Colorado	N.L.	1B	154	557	86	178	42	2	17	91	0	.320
2008	Colorado c	N.L.	1B	83	299	39	79	16	0	7	29	0	.264
2009	Colorado	N.L.	1B	151	544	79	177	38	3	15	86	0	.325
2010	Casper	Pioneer	1B	3	10	1	5	1	0	0	5	0	.500
2010	Colorado d	N.L.	1B	118	398	48	102	18	1	8	37	0	.256
2011	Colorado	N.L.	1B	124	421	59	127	27	0	14	69	0	.302
Major League Totals		15 Yrs.		2054	7325	1329	2363	554	35	347	1308	36	.323
Division Series													
2007	Colorado	N.L.	1B	3	12	1	1	0	1	0	0	0	.083
2009	Colorado	N.L.	1B	4	16	5	3	0	0	0	2	0	.188
Division Series Totals				7	28	6	4	0	1	0	2	0	.143

Year	Club	Lea	Pos	G	AB	R	H	2B	3B	HR	RBI	SB	Avg
	Championship Series												
2007 Colorado	N.L.		1B	4	14	3	3	0	0	0	1	0	.214
	World Series Record												
2007 Colorado	N.L.		1B	4	15	2	5	2	0	0	1	0	.333

a On disabled list from July 26 to August 10, 2005.
b On disabled list from April 20 to May 5, 2006.
c On disabled list from July 3 to September 12, 2008.
d On disabled list from July 7 to August 3, 2010.

HERNANDEZ (MARIN), RAMON JOSE
Born, Caracas, Venezuela, May 20, 1976.
Bats Right. Throws Right. Height, 6 feet. Weight, 225 pounds.

Year	Club	Lea	Pos	G	AB	R	H	2B	3B	HR	RBI	SB	Avg
1994 Oakland	Dominican	C	42	134	24	33	2	0	2	18	1	.246
1995 Athletics	Arizona	C-1B-3B	48	143	37	52	9	6	4	37	6	.364
1996 W Michigan	Midwest	C-1B	123	447	62	114	26	2	12	68	2	.255
1997 Visalia	California	C-1B	86	332	57	120	21	2	15	85	2	.361
1997 Huntsville........	Southern	C-1B-3B	44	161	27	31	3	0	4	24	0	.193
1998 Huntsville........	Southern	DH-C-1B	127	479	83	142	24	1	15	98	4	.296
1999 Vancouver	.P.C.	C	77	291	38	76	11	3	13	55	1	.261
1999 Oakland a...........	A.L.	C	40	136	13	38	7	0	3	21	1	.279
2000 Oakland	A.L.	C	143	419	52	101	19	0	14	62	1	.241
2001 Oakland	A.L.	C-1B	136	453	55	115	25	0	15	60	1	.254
2002 Oakland	A.L.	C	136	403	51	94	20	0	7	42	0	.233
2003 Oakland b...........	A.L.	C	140	483	70	132	24	1	21	78	0	.273
2004 Portland	.P.C.	C	7	19	2	6	1	0	0	6	0	.316
2004 San Diego c	N.L.	C	111	384	45	106	23	0	18	63	1	.276
2005 San Diego d-e	N.L.	C	99	369	36	107	19	2	12	58	1	.290
2006 Baltimore	A.L.	C-1B	144	501	66	138	29	2	23	91	1	.275
2007 Aberdeen	N.Y.-Penn.	C	2	4	2	2	1	0	0	0	1	.500
2007 Frederick	Carolina	C	2	6	0	2	1	0	0	0	0	.333
2007 Baltimore f........	A.L.	C-1B	106	364	40	94	18	0	9	62	1	.258
2008 Baltimore g	A.L.	C-1B	133	463	49	119	22	1	15	65	0	.257
2009 Cincinnati h	N.L.	C-1B-3B	81	287	25	74	13	1	5	37	1	.258
2010 Cincinnati i-j.........	N.L.	C-1B	97	313	30	93	18	1	7	48	0	.297
2011 Cincinnati k	N.L.	C-1B	91	298	28	84	13	0	12	36	0	.282
Major League Totals		13 Yrs.	1457	4873	560	1295	250	8	161	723	8	.266
	Division Series												
2000 Oakland	A.L.	C	5	16	3	6	2	0	0	3	0	.375
2001 Oakland	A.L.	C	5	10	0	0	0	0	0	0	0	.000
2002 Oakland	A.L.	C	5	17	0	1	0	0	0	0	0	.059
2003 Oakland	A.L.	C	4	15	1	3	0	0	0	2	0	.200
2005 San Diego	N.L.	C	3	11	2	5	0	0	1	1	0	.455
2010 Cincinnati............	N.L.	C	3	7	0	1	1	0	0	0	0	.143
Division Series Totals			25	76	6	16	3	0	1	6	0	.211

a On disabled list from July 26 to August 27, 1999.
b Traded to San Diego Padres with outfielder Terrence Long for outfielder Mark Kotsay, November 26, 2003.
c On disabled list from June 21 to July 26, 2004.
d On disabled list from June 18 to July and July 25 to September 2, 2005.
e Filed for free agency, October 27, 2005. Signed with Baltimore Orioles, December 13, 2005.
f On disabled list from March 31 to April 26 and June 7 to June 22, 2007.
g Traded to Cincinnati Reds with cash for outfielder Ryan Freel, infielder Brandon Waring and infielder Justin Turner, December 9, 2008.
h On disabled list from July 17 to September 19, 2009.
i On disabled list from July 5 to July 22, 2010.
j Filed for free agency, November 1, 2010, re-signed with Cincinnati Reds, November 15, 2010.
k Filed for free agency, October 30, 2011. Signed with Colorado Rockies, November 30, 2011.

HERRERA, JONATHAN ALEJANDRO
Born, Maracaibo, Venezuela, November 3, 1984.
Bats Both. Throws Right. Height, 5 feet, 9 inches. Weight, 150 pounds.

Year	Club	Lea	Pos	G	AB	R	H	2B	3B	HR	RBI	SB	Avg
2003 Casper	Pioneer	2B	39	159	27	49	7	1	1	25	12	.308
2004 Asheville........	So.Atl.	SS	95	380	71	106	20	2	6	35	21	.279
2005 Modesto........	Calif.	SS-2B	73	310	48	80	9	4	2	30	9	.258
2005 Asheville........	So.Atl.	SS-2B	19	87	17	27	2	0	0	5	6	.310
2006 Modesto........	Calif.	SS-2B-3B	127	487	87	151	20	8	7	77	34	.310
2007 Tulsa	Texas	SS	131	509	65	131	24	4	3	40	18	.257

77

Year Club	Lea	Pos	G	AB	R	H	2B	3B	HR	RBI	SB	Avg
2008 Colorado . . . . .N.L.		2B-SS	28	61	5	14	1	1	0	3	1	.230
2008 Colorado Springs a .P.C.		SS-2B	66	226	40	70	7	0	3	31	15	.310
2009 Colorado Springs . . .P.C.		SS-2B	119	381	63	102	11	5	2	33	16	.268
2010 Colorado Springs . . .P.C.		SS-2B-3B	58	222	30	58	6	1	2	17	3	.261
2010 Colorado . . . . .N.L.		2B-3B-SS	76	222	34	63	6	2	1	21	2	.284
2011 Colorado b . . . . . . .N.L.		2B-SS-3B	104	281	28	68	5	1	3	14	4	.242
Major League Totals		3 Yrs.	208	564	67	145	12	4	4	38	7	.257

a Not offered contract, December 12, 2008, re-signed with Colorado Rockies, December 13, 2008.

b On disabled list from September 6 to October 31, 2011.

HEYWARD, JASON ADENOLITH

Born, Ridgewood, New Jersey, August 9, 1989.
Bats Left. Throws Left. Height, 6 feet, 5 inches. Weight, 240 pounds.

Year Club	Lea	Pos	G	AB	R	H	2B	3B	HR	RBI	SB	Avg
2007 Danville . . . . .Appal.		OF	4	16	3	5	1	0	0	1	0	.313
2007 Braves . . . . Gulf Coast		OF	8	27	1	8	4	0	1	5	1	.296
2008 Myrtle Beach . . . . . . Carolina		OF	7	22	3	4	2	0	0	4	0	.182
2008 Rome . . . . So.Atl.		OF	120	449	88	145	27	6	11	52	15	.323
2009 Myrtle Beach . . . . . . Carolina		OF	49	189	34	56	12	0	10	31	4	.296
2009 Gwinnett. . . . . Int.		OF	3	11	3	4	0	0	0	2	1	.364
2009 Mississippi . . . . . . Southern		OF	47	162	32	57	13	4	7	30	5	.352
2010 Atlanta a . . . . N.L.		OF	142	520	83	144	29	5	18	72	11	.277
2011 Gwinnett. . . . . Int.		OF	2	6	1	1	1	0	0	0	0	.167
2011 Atlanta b . . . . N.L.		OF	128	396	50	90	18	2	14	42	9	.227
Major League Totals		2 Yrs.	270	916	133	234	47	7	32	114	20	.255
Division Series												
2010 Atlanta . . . . N.L.		OF	4	16	0	2	0	0	0	0	0	.125

a On disabled list from June 27 to July 15, 2010.

b On disabled list from May 22 to June 15, 2011.

HILL, AARON WALTER

Born, Visalia, California, March 21, 1982.
Bats Right. Throws Right. Height, 5 feet, 11 inches. Weight, 195 pounds.

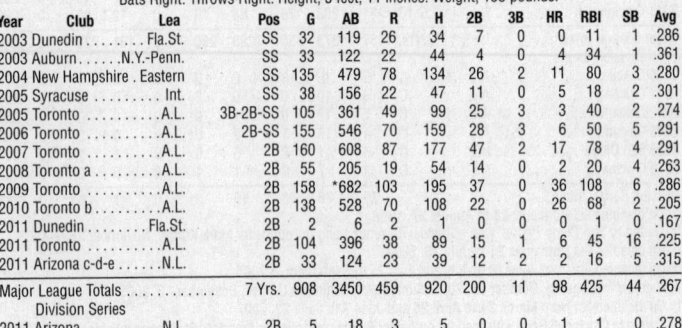

Year Club	Lea	Pos	G	AB	R	H	2B	3B	HR	RBI	SB	Avg
2003 Dunedin . . . . Fla.St.		SS	32	119	26	34	7	0	0	11	1	.286
2003 Auburn. . . . . .N.Y.-Penn.		SS	33	122	22	44	4	0	4	34	1	.361
2004 New Hampshire . Eastern		SS	135	479	78	134	26	2	11	80	3	.280
2005 Syracuse . . . . Int.		SS	38	156	22	47	11	0	5	18	2	.301
2005 Toronto . . . . .A.L.		3B-2B-SS	105	361	49	99	25	3	3	40	4	.274
2006 Toronto . . . . .A.L.		2B-SS	155	546	70	159	28	3	6	50	5	.291
2007 Toronto . . . . .A.L.		2B	160	608	87	177	47	2	17	78	4	.291
2008 Toronto a . . . . .A.L.		2B	55	205	19	54	14	0	2	20	4	.263
2009 Toronto . . . . .A.L.		2B	158	*682	103	195	37	0	36	108	6	.286
2010 Toronto b . . . . .A.L.		2B	138	528	70	108	22	0	26	68	2	.205
2011 Dunedin . . . . Fla.St.		2B	2	6	2	1	0	0	0	1	0	.167
2011 Toronto . . . . .A.L.		2B	104	396	38	89	15	1	6	45	16	.225
2011 Arizona c-d-e . . . . . .N.L.		2B	33	124	23	39	12	2	2	16	5	.315
Major League Totals		7 Yrs.	908	3450	459	920	200	11	98	425	44	.267
Division Series												
2011 Arizona. . . . . N.L.		2B	5	18	3	5	0	0	1	1	0	.278

a On disabled list from June 5 to November 14, 2008.

b On disabled list from April 8 to April 23, 2010.

c On disabled list from April 20 to May 8, 2011.

d Traded to Arizona Diamondbacks with infielder John McDonald for infielder Kelly Johnson, August 23, 2011.

e Filed for free agency, October 31, 2011, re-signed with Arizona Diamondbacks, November 15, 2011.

HINSKE, ERIC SCOTT

Born, Menasha, Wisconsin, August 5, 1977.
Bats Left. Throws Right. Height, 6 feet, 2 inches. Weight, 235 pounds.

Year Club	Lea	Pos	G	AB	R	H	2B	3B	HR	RBI	SB	Avg
1998 Williamsprt. . . . . . N.Y.-Penn.		1B	68	248	46	74	20	0	9	57	19	.298
1998 Rockford . . . . Midwest		1B-OF	6	20	8	9	4	0	1	4	1	.450
1999 Daytona . . . . Fla.St.		3B	130	445	76	132	28	6	19	79	16	.297
1999 Iowa. . . . . .P.C.		1B	4	15	3	4	0	1	1	2	0	.267
2000 West Tenn . . . . . . Southern		3B-1B-OF	131	436	76	113	21	9	20	73	14	.259
2001 Sacramento a-b-c . . . . . .P.C.		3B-2B	121	436	71	123	27	1	25	79	20	.282

Year	Club	Lea	Pos	G	AB	R	H	2B	3B	HR	RBI	SB	Avg
2002 Toronto d	A.L.	3B	151	566	99	158	38	2	24	84	13	.279
2003 Syracuse	Int.	3B	2	8	2	4	1	0	1	2	0	.500
2003 Toronto e	A.L.	3B	124	449	74	109	45	3	12	63	12	.243
2004 Toronto	A.L.	3B	155	570	66	140	23	3	15	69	12	.246
2005 Toronto	A.L.	1B	147	477	79	125	31	2	15	68	8	.262
2006 Toronto-Boston f	A.L.	OF-1B-3B	109	277	43	75	17	2	13	34	2	.271
2007 Boston g	A.L.	1B-OF	84	186	25	38	12	3	6	21	3	.204
2008 Tampa Bay h	A.L.	OF-1B-3B	133	381	59	94	21	1	20	60	10	.247
2009 Pittsburgh	N.L.	OF-1B-3B	54	106	18	27	9	0	1	11	0	.255
2009 New York i-j	A.L.	OF-3B	39	84	13	19	3	0	7	14	1	.226
2010 Atlanta k.	N.L.	OF-1B-3B	131	281	38	72	21	1	11	51	0	.256
2011 Atlanta	N.L.	OF-1B	117	236	24	55	10	0	10	28	0	.233
Major League Totals			10 Yrs.	1244	3613	538	912	230	17	134	503	61	.252
Division Series													
2007 Boston	A.L.	PH	1	1	0	0	0	0	0	0	0	.000
2010 Atlanta	N.L.	PH	4	3	1	1	0	0	1	2	0	.333
Division Series Totals			5	4	1	1	0	0	1	2	0	.250
Championship Series													
2007 Boston	A.L.	PH	1	0	1	0	0	0	0	0	0	.000
World Series Record													
2007 Boston	A.L.	PH	1	1	0	0	0	0	0	0	0	.000
2008 Tampa Bay	N.L.	PH	2	2	1	1	0	0	1	1	0	.500
2009 New York	A.L.	PH	1	0	1	0	0	0	0	0	0	.000
World Series Totals			4	3	2	1	0	0	1	1	0	.333

a Traded by Chicago Cubs with pitcher Scott Chiasson to Oakland A's for infielder Miguel Cairo, March 28, 2001.
b On disabled list from May 1 to 12, 2001.
c Traded by Oakland A's to Toronto Blue Jays with pitcher Justin Miller for pitcher Billy Koch, December 7, 2001.
d Selected Rookie of the Year in American League for 2002.
e On disabled list from May 2 to June 26, 2003.
f Sold to Boston Red Sox, August 17, 2006.
g Filed for free agency, October 30, 2007. Signed with Tampa Bay Rays organization, February 7, 2008.
h Filed for free agency, November 1, 2008. Signed with Pittsburgh Pirates, January 30, 2009.
i Traded to New York Yankees for outfielder Eric Fryer and pitcher Casey Erickson, June 30, 2009.
j Filed for free agency, November 9, 2009. Signed with Atlanta Braves, January 12, 2010.
k Filed for free agency, November 1, 2010, re-signed with Atlanta Braves, December 2, 2010.

HOLLIDAY, MATTHEW THOMAS (MATT)
Born, Stillwater, Oklahoma, January 15, 1980.
Bats Right. Throws Right. Height, 6 feet, 4 inches. Weight, 235 pounds.

Year	Club	Lea	Pos	G	AB	R	H	2B	3B	HR	RBI	SB	Avg
1998 Rockies	Arizona	3B	32	117	20	40	4	1	5	23	2	.342
1999 Asheville.	So.Atl.	3B	121	444	76	117	28	0	16	64	10	.264
2000 Salem.	Carolina	3B	123	460	64	126	28	2	7	72	11	.274
2001 Salem.	Carolina	OF	72	255	36	70	16	1	11	52	11	.275
2002 Carolina	Southern	OF	130	463	79	128	19	2	10	64	16	.276
2003 Tulsa	Texas	OF	135	522	65	132	28	5	12	72	15	.253
2004 Colorado Springs	P.C.	OF	6	22	8	8	5	0	2	4	2	.364
2004 Colorado	N.L.	OF	121	400	65	116	31	3	14	57	3	.290
2005 Tulsa	Texas	OF	7	26	6	14	3	0	1	6	1	.538
2005 Colorado a	N.L.	OF	125	479	68	147	24	7	19	87	14	.307
2006 Colorado	N.L.	OF	155	602	119	196	45	5	34	114	10	.326
2007 Colorado	N.L.	OF	158	636	120	*216	*50	6	36	*137	11	*.340
2008 Colorado Springs	P.C.	OF	3	10	4	6	1	0	1	3	0	.600
2008 Colorado b-c	N.L.	OF	139	539	107	173	38	2	25	88	28	.321
2009 Oakland	A.L.	OF	93	346	52	99	23	1	11	54	12	.286
2009 St. Louis d-e	N.L.	OF	63	235	42	83	16	2	13	55	2	.353
2010 St. Louis.	N.L.	OF	158	596	95	186	45	1	28	103	9	.312
2011 St. Louis f	N.L.	OF	124	446	83	132	36	0	22	75	2	.296
Major League Totals			8 Yrs.	1136	4279	751	1348	308	27	202	770	91	.315
Division Series													
2007 Colorado	N.L.	OF	3	13	2	3	0	0	2	3	0	.231
2009 St. Louis.	N.L.	OF	3	12	1	2	0	0	1	1	0	.167
2011 St. Louis.	N.L.	OF	4	9	2	2	0	0	0	0	0	.222
Division Series Totals			10	34	5	7	0	0	3	4	0	.206
Championship Series													
2007 Colorado	N.L.	OF	4	15	3	5	0	0	2	4	0	.333
2011 St. Louis.	N.L.	OF	6	23	6	10	2	0	1	5	0	.435
Championship Series Totals			10	38	9	15	2	0	3	9	0	.395

Year	Club	Lea	Pos	G	AB	R	H	2B	3B	HR	RBI	SB	Avg
	World Series Record												
2007 Colorado	N.L.		OF	4	17	1	5	0	0	1	3	0	.294
2011 St. Louis.............	N.L.		OF	6	19	5	3	1	0	0	0	0	.158
World Series Totals.............				10	36	6	8	1	0	1	3	0	.222

a On disabled list from June 9 to July 19, 2005.
b On disabled list from May 25 to June 10, 2008.
c Traded to Oakland Athletics for outfielder Carlos Gonzalez, pitcher Greg Smith and pitcher Huston Street, November 12, 2008.
d Traded to St. Louis Cardinals for pitcher Clayton Mortensen, infielder Brett Wallace and outfielder Shane Peterson, July 24, 2009.
e Filed for free agency, November 5, 2009, re-signed with St. Louis Cardinals, January 5, 2010.
f On disabled list from June 1 to June 16, 2011.

HOSMER, ERIC JOHN

Born, South Miami, Florida, October 24, 1989.
Bats Left. Throws Left. Height, 6 feet, 4 inches. Weight, 230 pounds.

Year	Club	Lea	Pos	G	AB	R	H	2B	3B	HR	RBI	SB	Avg
2008 Idaho Falls	Pioneer	1B	3	11	2	4	2	0	0	2	0	.364
2009 Burlington	Midwest	1B	79	280	31	71	17	2	5	49	3	.254
2009 Wilmington	Carolina	1B	27	97	9	20	2	2	1	10	0	.206
2010 Wilmington	Carolina	1B	87	325	48	115	29	6	7	51	11	.354
2010 NW Arkansas	Texas	1B	50	195	39	61	14	3	13	35	3	.313
2011 Omaha	P.C.	1B	26	98	21	43	5	0	3	15	3	.439
2011 Kansas City	A.L.	1B	128	523	66	153	27	3	19	78	11	.293

HOWARD, RYAN JAMES

Born, St. Louis, Missouri, November 19, 1979.
Bats Left. Throws Left. Height, 6 feet, 4 inches. Weight, 250 pounds.

Year	Club	Lea	Pos	G	AB	R	H	2B	3B	HR	RBI	SB	Avg
2001 Batavia	N.Y.-Penn.	1B	48	169	26	46	7	3	6	35	0	.272
2002 Lakewood	So.Atl.	1B	135	493	56	138	20	6	19	87	5	.280
2003 Clearwater	Fla.St.	1B	130	490	67	149	32	1	23	82	0	.304
2004 Reading	Eastern	1B	102	374	73	111	18	1	37	102	1	.297
2004 Scranton/WB	Int.	1B	29	111	21	30	10	0	9	29	0	.270
2004 Philadelphia	N.L.	1B	19	39	5	11	5	0	2	5	0	.282
2005 Scranton/WB.........	Int.	1B	61	210	38	78	19	0	16	54	0	.371
2005 Philadelphia a.......	N.L.	1B	88	312	52	90	17	2	22	63	0	.288
2006 Philadelphia b	N.L.	1B	159	581	104	182	25	1	*58	*149	0	.313
2007 Lakewood	So.Atl.	1B	2	6	1	2	1	0	1	4	0	.333
2007 Philadelphia c.......	N.L.	1B	144	529	94	142	26	0	47	136	1	.268
2008 Philadelphia	N.L.	1B	*162	610	105	153	26	4	*48	*146	1	.251
2009 Philadelphia	N.L.	1B	160	616	105	172	37	4	45	*141	8	.279
2010 Lakewood.........	So.Atl.	1B	1	2	0	1	1	0	0	1	0	.500
2010 Philadelphia d	N.L.	1B	143	550	87	152	23	5	31	108	1	.276
2011 Philadelphia	N.L.	1B	152	557	81	141	30	1	33	116	0	.253
Major League Totals		8 Yrs.	1027	3794	633	1043	189	17	286	864	12	.275
	Division Series												
2007 Philadelphia	N.L.	1B	3	12	1	3	0	0	1	1	0	.250
2008 Philadelphia	N.L.	1B	4	11	1	2	1	0	0	1	0	.182
2009 Philadelphia	N.L.	1B	4	16	3	6	3	0	0	6	0	.375
2010 Philadelphia	N.L.	1B	3	11	0	3	0	0	0	0	0	.273
2011 Philadelphia	N.L.	1B	5	19	1	2	0	0	1	6	0	.105
Division Series Totals				19	69	6	16	4	0	2	14	0	.232
	Championship Series												
2008 Philadelphia	N.L.	1B	5	20	4	6	1	0	0	2	0	.300
2009 Philadelphia	N.L.	1B	5	15	5	5	1	1	2	8	0	.333
2010 Philadelphia	N.L.	1B	6	22	1	7	4	0	0	0	0	.318
Championship Series Totals				16	57	10	18	6	1	2	10	0	.316
	World Series Record												
2008 Philadelphia	N.L.	1B	5	21	3	6	1	0	3	6	0	.286
2009 Philadelphia	N.L.	1B	6	23	3	4	2	0	1	3	1	.174
World Series Totals.............				11	44	6	10	3	0	4	9	1	.227

a Selected Rookie of the Year in National League for 2005.
b Selected Most Valuable Player in National League for 2006.
c On disabled list from May 10 to May 25, 2007.
d On disabled list from August 2 to August 21, 2010.

HUDSON, ORLANDO THILL

Born, Darlington, South Carolina, December 12, 1977.
Bats Both. Throws Right. Height, 6 feet. Weight, 185 pounds.

Year	Club	Lea	Pos	G	AB	R	H	2B	3B	HR	RBI	SB	Avg
1998	Medicine Hat	Pioneer	2B	65	242	50	71	18	1	8	42	6	.293
1999	Hagerstown	So.Atl.	3B	132	513	66	137	36	6	7	74	8	.267
2000	Dunedin	Fla.St.	3B-2B-SS	96	358	54	102	16	2	7	48	9	.285
2000	Tennessee	Southern	3B	39	134	17	32	4	3	2	15	3	.239
2001	Syracuse	Int.	2B-3B	55	194	31	59	14	3	4	27	11	.304
2001	Tennessee	Southern	2B-3B	84	306	51	94	22	8	4	52	8	.307
2002	Syracuse	Int.	2B	100	417	63	127	27	3	10	37	8	.305
2002	Toronto	A.L.	2B	54	192	20	53	10	5	4	23	0	.276
2003	Toronto	A.L.	2B	142	474	54	127	21	6	9	57	5	.268
2004	Toronto a	A.L.	2B	135	489	73	132	32	7	12	58	7	.270
2005	Toronto b	A.L.	2B	131	461	62	125	25	5	10	63	7	.271
2006	Arizona.............	N.L.	2B	157	579	87	166	34	9	15	67	9	.287
2007	Arizona.............	N.L.	2B	139	517	69	152	28	9	10	63	10	.294
2008	Arizona c-d........	N.L.	2B	107	407	54	124	29	3	8	41	4	.305
2009	Los Angeles	N.L.	2B	149	551	74	156	35	6	9	62	8	.283
2010	Minnesota f-g.......	A.L.	2B	126	497	80	133	24	5	6	37	10	.268
2011	Lake Elsinore	Calif.	2B	4	7	6	4	0	0	1	3	2	.571
2011	Tucson	P.C.	2B	2	4	4	3	2	0	0	1	0	.750
2011	San Diego h	N.L.	2B	119	398	54	98	15	3	7	43	19	.246
Major League Totals			10 Yrs.	1259	4565	627	1266	253	58	90	514	79	.277

Division Series

Year	Club	Lea	Pos	G	AB	R	H	2B	3B	HR	RBI	SB	Avg
2009	Los Angeles	N.L.	2B	3	0	0	0	0	0	0	0	0	.000
2010	Minnesota	A.L.	2B	3	12	2	4	0	0	1	2	0	.333
Division Series Totals				6	12	2	4	0	0	1	2	0	.333

Championship Series

Year	Club	Lea	Pos	G	AB	R	H	2B	3B	HR	RBI	SB	Avg
2009	Los Angeles	N.L.	2B	5	4	1	1	0	0	1	1	0	.250

a On disabled list from May 24 to June 16, 2004.
b Traded to Arizona Diamondbacks with pitcher Miguel Batista for infielder Troy Glaus and infielder Sergio Santos, December 27, 2005.
c On disabled list from August 10 to November 1, 2008.
d Filed for free agency, November 1, 2008. Signed with Los Angeles Dodgers, February 21, 2009.
e Filed for free agency, November 5, 2009. Signed with Minnesota Twins, February 4, 2010.
f On disabled list from May 31 to June 18 and July 24 to August 8, 2010.
g Filed for free agency, November 1, 2010. Signed with San Diego Padres, December 20, 2010.
h On disabled list from May 4 to May 19 and May 26 to June 19, 2011.

HUFF, AUBREY LEWIS

Born, Marion, Ohio, December 20, 1976.
Bats Left. Throws Right. Height, 6 feet, 4 inches. Weight, 230 pounds.

Year	Club	Lea	Pos	G	AB	R	H	2B	3B	HR	RBI	SB	Avg
1998	Chston-SC	So.Atl.	3B	69	265	38	85	19	1	13	54	3	.321
1999	Orlando	Southern	3B	133	491	85	148	40	3	22	78	2	.301
2000	Durham	Int.	3B	108	408	73	129	36	3	20	76	2	.316
2000	Tampa Bay	A.L.	3B	39	122	12	35	7	0	4	14	0	.287
2001	Durham	Int.	3B	17	66	14	19	6	0	3	10	0	.288
2001	Tampa Bay	A.L.	3B-1B	111	411	42	102	25	1	8	45	1	.248
2002	Durham	Int.	1B	32	126	18	41	9	0	3	20	0	.325
2002	Tampa Bay	A.L.	DH-1B-3B	113	454	67	142	25	0	23	59	4	.313
2003	Tampa Bay	A.L.	OF-1B-3B	162	636	91	198	47	3	34	107	2	.311
2004	Tampa Bay	A.L.	3B-1B-OF	157	600	92	178	27	2	29	104	5	.297
2005	Tampa Bay	A.L.	OF-1B-3B	154	575	70	150	26	2	22	92	8	.261
2006	Visalia	Calif.	3B	2	8	2	2	1	0	0	1	0	.250
2006	Tampa Bay	A.L.	3B	63	230	26	65	15	1	8	28	0	.283
2006	Houston a-b-c	N.L.	OF-1B-3B	68	224	31	56	10	1	13	38	0	.250
2007	Baltimore	A.L.	DH-1B-3B	151	550	68	154	34	5	15	72	1	.280
2008	Baltimore	A.L.	DH-3B-1B	154	598	96	182	48	2	32	108	4	.304
2009	Baltimore-Detroit d-e	A.L.	1B	150	536	59	129	30	1	15	85	0	.241
2010	San Francisco f	N.L.	1B-OF	157	569	100	165	35	5	26	86	7	.290
2011	San Francisco	N.L.	1B-OF	150	521	45	128	27	1	12	59	5	.246
Major League Totals			12 Yrs.	1629	6026	799	1684	356	24	241	897	37	.279

Division Series

Year	Club	Lea	Pos	G	AB	R	H	2B	3B	HR	RBI	SB	Avg
2010	San Francisco	N.L.	1B	4	15	1	4	0	0	0	1	0	.267

Championship Series

Year	Club	Lea	Pos	G	AB	R	H	2B	3B	HR	RBI	SB	Avg
2010	San Francisco	N.L.	1B	6	24	3	6	0	0	0	3	0	.250

World Series Record

Year	Club	Lea	Pos	G	AB	R	H	2B	3B	HR	RBI	SB	Avg
2010	San Francisco	N.L.	1B-DH	5	17	3	5	2	0	1	4	0	.294

a On disabled list from April 12 to May 5, 2006.
b Traded to Houston Astros with cash for pitcher Mitch Talbot and infielder Ben Zobrist, July 12, 2006.
c Filed for free agency, October 28, 2006. Signed with Baltimore Orioles, December 30, 2006.
d Traded to Detroit Tigers for pitcher Brett Jacobson, August 17, 2009.
e Filed for free agency, November 5, 2009. Signed with San Francisco Giants, January 13, 2010.
f Filed for free agency, November 1, 2010, re-signed with San Francisco Giants, November 23, 2010.

HUGHES, LUKE TREVOR

Born, Perth, Australia, August 2, 1984.
Bats Right. Throws Right. Height, 5 feet, 11 inches. Weight, 205 pounds.

Year Club	Lea	Pos	G	AB	R	H	2B	3B	HR	RBI	SB	Avg
2003 Twins . . . . Gulf Coast		SS-3B	54	190	22	58	9	4	2	25	5	.305
2004 Elizabethton . . . . . Appal.		2B-1B	44	141	20	40	8	1	3	19	1	.284
2005 Beloit . . . . Midwest		2B	72	292	42	75	14	2	7	42	4	.257
2005 Fort Myers . . . . . Fla.St.		2B	23	84	9	17	3	1	0	7	0	.202
2006 Fort Myers . . . . . Fla.St.		3B-2B-1B-SS	95	333	31	77	15	0	4	37	6	.231
2007 New Britain . . . . Eastern		2B-OF-3B-1B	92	315	56	89	18	2	9	43	4	.283
2008 New Britain . . . Eastern		3B-2B-OF	70	285	53	91	15	3	15	40	4	.319
2008 Rochester . . . . . . Int.		3B-2B	29	106	17	30	7	1	3	21	2	.283
2009 Rochester . . . . Int.		3B	37	135	19	35	8	2	6	28	2	.259
2009 Twins . . . . Gulf Coast		3B	4	11	0	3	0	0	0	0	0	.273
2009 New Britain . . . . Eastern		3B-2B-OF	56	200	22	50	15	3	6	36	1	.250
2010 Minnesota . . . . .A.L.		3B	2	7	1	2	0	0	1	1	0	.286
2010 Rochester. . . . . Int.		2B-3B	22	74	12	19	8	0	1	7	2	.257
2011 Rochester . . . . Int.		2B-3B	30	117	16	27	6	1	4	11	2	.231
2011 Minnesota . . . . . . .A.L.		2B-1B-3B	96	287	31	64	12	0	7	30	3	.223
Major League Totals		2 Yrs.	98	294	32	66	12	0	8	31	3	.224

HUNDLEY, NICHOLAS JOHN (NICK)

Born, Corvallis, Oregon, September 8, 1983.
Bats Right. Throws Right. Height, 6 feet, 1 inch. Weight, 210 pounds.

Year Club	Lea	Pos	G	AB	R	H	2B	3B	HR	RBI	SB	Avg
2005 Fort Wayne. . . . . . . Midwest		C	10	36	2	8	2	0	0	5	0	.222
2005 Eugene. . . . . Northwest		C	43	148	30	37	7	1	7	22	1	.250
2006 Lake Elsinore . . . . Calif.		C	47	176	18	49	13	0	3	23	1	.278
2006 Fort Wayne. . . . . Midwest		C	57	215	29	59	19	0	8	44	1	.274
2007 San Antonio . . . . Texas		C	101	373	55	92	23	1	20	72	0	.247
2008 Portland . . . . .P.C.		C	58	224	33	52	13	0	12	39	0	.232
2008 San Diego . . . . N.L.		C	60	198	21	47	7	1	5	24	0	.237
2009 Portland . . . . .P.C.		C	5	16	2	4	1	0	1	2	0	.250
2009 San Diego a . . . . N.L.		C-OF	78	256	23	61	15	2	8	30	5	.238
2010 San Diego . . . . N.L.		C	85	273	33	68	18	2	8	43	0	.249
2011 San Antonio . . . . Texas		C	7	23	1	4	0	0	0	1	0	.174
2011 Tucson . . . . .P.C.		C	4	11	3	3	2	0	1	5	0	.273
2011 San Diego b . . . . N.L.		C	82	281	34	81	16	5	9	29	1	.288
Major League Totals		4 Yrs.	305	1008	111	257	56	10	30	126	6	.255

a On disabled list from June 18 to August 12, 2009.
b On disabled list from May 5 to June 8 and July 6 to August 12, 2011.

HUNTER, TORII KEDAR

Born, Pine Bluff, Arkansas, July 18, 1975.
Bats Right. Throws Right. Height, 6 feet, 2 inches. Weight, 215 pounds.

Year Club	Lea	Pos	G	AB	R	H	2B	3B	HR	RBI	SB	Avg
1993 Twins . . . . Gulf Coast		OF	28	100	6	19	3	0	0	8	4	.190
1994 Fort Wayne. . . . . Midwest		OF	91	335	57	98	17	1	10	50	8	.293
1995 Fort Myers . . . . .Fla.St.		OF	113	391	64	96	15	2	7	36	7	.246
1996 Fort Myers . . . . .Fla.St.		OF	4	16	1	3	0	0	0	1	1	.188
1996 New Britain . . . . . .Eastern		OF	99	342	49	90	20	3	7	33	7	.263
1997 New Britain . . . . . .Eastern		OF	127	471	57	109	22	2	8	56	8	.231
1997 Minnesota . . . . A.L.		OF	1	0	0	0	0	0	0	0	0	.000
1998 New Britain . . . . . . .Eastern		OF	82	308	42	87	24	3	6	32	11	.282
1998 Salt Lake . . . . .P.C.		OF	26	92	15	31	7	0	4	20	2	.337
1998 Minnesota . . . . A.L.		OF	6	17	0	4	1	0	0	2	0	.235
1999 Minnesota . . . . A.L.		OF	135	384	52	98	17	2	9	35	10	.255
2000 Salt Lake . . . . .P.C.		OF	55	209	58	77	17	2	18	61	11	.368
2000 Minnesota . . . . A.L.		OF	99	336	44	94	14	7	5	44	4	.280
2001 Minnesota a . . . . A.L.		OF	148	564	82	147	32	5	27	92	9	.261

Year	Club	Lea	Pos	G	AB	R	H	2B	3B	HR	RBI	SB	Avg
2002 Minnesota	A.L.	OF	148	561	89	162	37	4	29	94	23	.289
2003 Minnesota	A.L.	OF	154	581	83	145	31	4	26	102	6	.250
2004 Minnesota b	A.L.	OF	138	520	79	141	37	0	23	81	21	.271
2005 Minnesota c	A.L.	OF	98	372	63	100	24	1	14	56	23	.269
2006 Fort Myers d	A.L.	OF	147	557	86	155	21	2	31	98	12	.278
2007 Minnesota e	A.L.	OF	160	600	94	172	45	1	28	107	18	.287
2008 Los Angeles	A.L.	OF	146	551	85	153	37	2	21	78	19	.278
2009 Rancho Cucamonga	Calif.	OF	3	9	3	3	0	0	1	3	1	.333
2009 Los Angeles f	A.L.	OF	119	451	74	135	26	1	22	90	18	.299
2010 Los Angeles	A.L.	OF	152	573	76	161	36	0	23	90	9	.281
2011 Los Angeles	A.L.	OF	156	580	80	152	24	2	23	82	5	.262
Major League Totals	15 Yrs.		1807	6647	987	1819	382	31	281	1051	177	.274
Division Series												
2002 Minnesota	A.L.	OF	5	20	4	6	4	0	0	2	0	.300
2003 Minnesota	A.L.	OF	4	14	3	6	0	1	1	2	0	.429
2004 Minnesota	A.L.	OF	4	17	5	6	1	0	1	2	2	.353
2006 Minnesota	A.L.	OF	3	11	1	3	1	0	1	2	0	.273
2008 Los Angeles	A.L.	OF	4	18	0	7	0	0	0	5	0	.389
2009 Los Angeles	A.L.	OF	3	10	2	2	1	0	1	3	0	.200
Division Series Totals			23	90	15	30	7	1	4	16	2	.333
Championship Series												
2002 Minnesota	A.L.	OF	5	18	2	3	2	0	0	0	0	.167
2009 Los Angeles	A.L.	OF	6	23	2	7	1	0	0	2	1	.304
Championship Series Totals			11	41	4	10	3	0	0	2	1	.244

a On disabled list from April 6 to April 21, 2001.
b On disabled list from April 7 to April 25, 2004.
c On disabled list from July 30 to October 6, 2005.
d On disabled list from July 16 to July 31, 2006.
e Filed for free agency, October 29, 2007. Signed with Los Angeles Angels, November 21, 2007.
f On disabled list from July 8 to August 16, 2009.

IANNETTA, CHRISTOPHER DOMENIC (CHRIS)
Born, Providence, Rhode Island, April 8, 1983.
Bats Right. Throws Right. Height, 5 feet, 11 inches. Weight, 225 pounds.

Year	Club	Lea	Pos	G	AB	R	H	2B	3B	HR	RBI	SB	Avg
2004 Asheville	So.Atl.	C	36	121	23	38	5	1	5	17	0	.314
2005 Tulsa	Texas	C	19	60	7	14	3	1	2	11	0	.233
2006 Tulsa	Texas	C	44	156	38	50	10	2	11	26	1	.321
2006 Colorado Springs	P.C.	C	47	151	23	53	11	2	3	22	0	.351
2006 Colorado	N.L.	C	21	77	12	20	4	0	2	10	0	.260
2007 Colorado Springs	P.C.	C	16	54	8	16	3	0	1	7	0	.296
2007 Colorado	N.L.	C	67	197	22	43	8	3	4	27	0	.218
2008 Colorado	N.L.	C-3B	104	333	50	88	22	2	18	65	0	.264
2009 Colorado Springs	P.C.	C	4	15	3	5	2	0	1	3	0	.333
2009 Colorado a	N.L.	C	93	289	41	66	15	2	16	52	0	.228
2010 Colorado Springs	P.C.	C-1B	17	63	17	22	7	0	5	21	0	.349
2010 Colorado	N.L.	C-1B-3B	61	188	20	37	6	1	9	27	1	.197
2011 Colorado b	N.L.	C-1B-3B	112	345	51	82	17	1	14	55	6	.238
Major League Totals	6 Yrs.		458	1429	196	336	72	9	63	236	7	.235

a On disabled list from May 24 to June 9, 2009.
b Traded to Los Angeles Angels for pitcher Tyler Chatwood, November 30, 2011.

IBANEZ, RAUL JAVIER
Born, New York, New York, June 2, 1972.
Bats Left. Throws Right. Height, 6 feet, 2 inches. Weight, 220 pounds.

Year	Club	Lea	Pos	G	AB	R	H	2B	3B	HR	RBI	SB	Avg
1992 Mariners	Arizona	DH-1B-C-OF	33	120	25	37	8	2	1	16	1	.308
1993 Appleton	Midwest	DH-1B-OF-C	52	157	26	43	9	0	5	21	0	.274
1993 Bellingham	Northwest	C	43	134	16	38	5	2	0	15	0	.284
1994 Appleton	Midwest	DH-C-1B-OF	91	327	55	102	30	3	7	59	10	.312
1995 Riverside	California	C-1B	95	361	59	120	23	9	20	108	4	.332
1996 Port City	Southern	OF-1B-C	19	76	12	28	8	1	1	13	3	.368
1996 Seattle	A.L.	DH	4	5	0	0	0	0	0	0	0	.000
1996 Tacoma	P.C.	OF-1B	111	405	59	115	20	3	11	47	7	.284
1997 Tacoma	P.C.	OF	111	438	84	133	30	5	15	84	7	.304
1997 Seattle	A.L.	OF	11	26	3	4	0	1	1	4	0	.154
1998 Tacoma	P.C.	OF	52	190	24	41	8	1	6	25	1	.216

Year Club Lea	Pos	G	AB	R	H	2B	3B	HR	RBI	SB	Avg
1998 Seattle ..........A.L.	OF-1B	37	98	12	25	7	1	2	12	0	.255
1999 Tacoma ..........P.C.	OF	8	31	6	11	1	0	3	5	1	.355
1999 Seattle a .........A.L.	OF-1B-C	87	209	23	54	7	0	9	27	5	.258
2000 Tacoma ..........P.C.	OF	10	40	3	10	4	0	0	6	0	.250
2000 Seattle b-c ........A.L.	OF-1B	92	140	21	32	8	0	2	15	2	.229
2001 Omaha ...........P.C.	OF-SS	8	27	3	4	1	0	2	5	0	.148
2001 Kansas City .......A.L.	OF-1B-3B	104	279	44	78	11	5	13	54	0	.280
2002 Kansas City ......A.L.	OF-1B	137	497	70	146	37	6	24	103	5	.294
2003 Kansas City d .....A.L.	OF-1B	157	608	95	179	33	5	18	90	8	.294
2004 Tacoma ..........P.C.	OF	4	17	2	4	1	0	0	1	0	.235
2004 Seattle e.........A.L.	OF-1B	123	481	67	146	31	1	16	62	1	.304
2005 Seattle ...........A.L.	DH-OF-1B	*162	614	92	172	32	2	20	89	9	.280
2006 Seattle ...........A.L.	OF	159	626	103	181	33	5	33	123	2	.289
2007 Seattle ...........A.L.	OF	149	573	80	167	35	5	21	105	0	.291
2008 Seattle f .........A.L.	OF	162	635	85	186	43	3	23	110	2	.293
2009 Reading ......Eastern	OF	1	2	1	0	0	0	0	0	0	.000
2009 Lehigh Valley ......Int.	OF	2	5	1	2	1	0	0	2	0	.400
2009 Philadelphia g ....N.L.	OF	134	500	93	136	32	3	34	93	4	.272
2010 Philadelphia .......N.L.	OF-1B	155	561	75	154	37	5	16	83	4	.275
2011 Philadelphia h .....N.L.	OF	144	535	65	131	31	1	20	84	2	.245
Major League Totals	16 Yrs.	1817	6387	928	1791	377	43	252	1054	44	.280
Division Series											
2000 Seattle ...........A.L.	OF	3	8	2	3	0	0	0	0	0	.375
2009 Philadelphia .......N.L.	OF	4	13	2	4	1	0	0	5	0	.308
2010 Philadelphia .......N.L.	OF	3	12	0	3	1	0	0	0	0	.250
2011 Philadelphia .......N.L.	OF	4	15	1	3	0	0	1	4	0	.200
Division Series Totals		14	48	5	13	2	0	1	9	0	.271
Championship Series											
2000 Seattle ...........A.L.	OF	6	9	0	0	0	0	0	0	0	.000
2009 Philadelphia .......N.L.	OF	5	18	4	3	1	0	1	4	0	.167
2010 Philadelphia .......N.L.	OF	5	19	1	4	1	0	0	0	0	.211
Championship Series Totals		16	46	5	7	2	0	1	4	0	.152
World Series Record											
2009 Philadelphia .......N.L.	OF-DH	6	23	2	7	4	0	1	4	0	.304

a On disabled list from May 18 to June 3, 1999.
b On disabled list from August 7 to August 21, 2000.
c Not offered contract, December 21, 2000. Signed with Kansas City Royals organization, January 13, 2001.
d Filed for free agency, October 27, 2003. Signed with Seattle Mariners, November 19, 2003.
e Filed for free agency, October 30, 2008. Signed with Philadelphia Phillies, December 16, 2008.
f Filed for free agency, October 30, 2008. Signed with Philadelphia Phillies, December 16, 2008.
g On disabled list from June 18 to July 10, 2009.
h Filed for free agency, October 30, 2011.

INFANTE, OMAR RAFAEL
Born, Puerto La Cruz, Venezuela, December 26, 1981.
Bats Right. Throws Right. Height, 6 feet. Weight, 180 pounds.

Year Club Lea	Pos	G	AB	R	H	2B	3B	HR	RBI	SB	Avg
1999 Tigers.......Gulf Coast	SS	21	75	9	20	0	0	0	4	4	.267
2000 Lakeland........Fla.St.	SS	79	259	35	71	11	0	2	24	11	.274
2000 West Michigan . Midwest	SS-2B	12	48	7	11	0	0	0	5	1	.229
2001 Erie........... Eastern	SS	132	540	86	163	21	4	2	62	27	.302
2002 Toledo ....Int.	SS	120	436	49	117	16	8	4	51	19	.268
2002 Detroit ...........A.L.	SS-2B	18	72	4	24	3	0	1	6	0	.333
2003 Toledo ....Int.	SS	64	224	28	50	10	0	2	18	22	.223
2003 Detroit ...........A.L.	SS-3B-2B	69	221	24	49	6	1	0	8	6	.222
2004 Detroit ...........A.L.	2B-SS-3B-OF	142	503	69	133	27	9	16	55	13	.264
2005 Detroit ...........A.L.	2B-SS	121	406	36	90	28	2	9	43	8	.222
2006 Detroit ...........A.L.	2B-SS-3B	78	224	35	62	11	4	4	25	3	.277
2007 Toledo ....Int.	SS-2B	10	38	3	14	2	0	0	4	1	.368
2007 Detroit a-b ........A.L.	2B-OF-SS-3B	66	166	24	45	6	1	2	17	4	.271
2008 Richmond ....Int.	OF	3	11	3	4	1	0	0	3	0	.364
2008 Atlanta c.........N.L.	OF-3B-SS-2B	96	317	45	93	24	3	3	40	0	.293
2009 Rome..........So.Atl.	2B-3B-SS-OF	5	17	1	5	0	0	0	0	1	.294
2009 Gwinnett..........Int.	SS	1	3	1	1	0	0	0	2	0	.333
2009 Atlanta d.........N.L.	2B-OF-3B-SS	70	203	24	62	9	1	2	27	2	.305
2010 Atlanta e.........N.L.	2B-3B-OF-SS	134	471	65	151	15	3	8	47	7	.321
2011 Jupiter.........Fla.St.	2B	1	5	0	3	0	0	0	0	0	.600
2011 Florida f .........N.L.	2B	148	579	55	160	24	8	7	49	4	.276
Major League Totals	10 Yrs.	942	3162	381	869	153	32	52	317	47	.275

84

Year	Club	Lea	Pos	G	AB	R	H	2B	3B	HR	RBI	SB	Avg
Division Series													
2010 Atlanta ...........N.L.		3B-2B	4	18	1	4	1	0	0	0	0	.222
Championship Series													
2006 Detroit ...........A.L.		DH	1	2	0	1	0	0	0	0	1	.500
World Series Record													
2006 Detroit ...........A.L.		PH	1	1	0	0	0	0	0	0	0	.000

a Traded to Chicago Cubs for outfielder Jacque Jones, November 12, 2007.
b Traded to Atlanta Braves with pitcher Will Ohman for pitcher Jose Ascanio, December 4, 2007.
c On disabled list from March 21 to May 8 and July 7 to July 22, 2008.
d On disabled list from May 21 to August 11, 2009.
e Traded to Florida Marlins with pitcher Michael Dunn for infielder Dan Uggla, November 16, 2010.
f On disabled list from August 5 to August 20, 2011.

INGE, CHARLES BRANDON (BRANDON)

Born, Lynchburg, Virginia, May 19, 1977.
Bats Both. Throws Right. Height, 5 feet, 11 inches. Weight, 190 pounds.

Year	Club	Lea	Pos	G	AB	R	H	2B	3B	HR	RBI	SB	Avg
1998 Jamestown......	N.Y.-Penn.	C	51	191	24	44	10	1	8	29	8	.230
1999 West Michigan.....	Midwest	C	100	352	54	86	25	2	9	46	15	.244
2000 Toledo	Int.	C	55	190	24	42	9	3	5	20	2	.221
2000 Jacksonville	Southern	C-OF	78	298	39	77	25	1	6	53	10	.258
2001 Tigers..........	Gulf Coast	C	3	10	1	1	0	0	1	2	0	.100
2001 West Michigan.....	Midwest	C	4	16	3	3	1	0	0	2	0	.188
2001 Toledo	Int.	C	27	90	11	26	11	1	2	15	1	.289
2001 Detroit a..........	A.L.	C	79	189	13	34	11	0	0	15	1	.180
2002 Toledo	Int.	C	21	65	10	17	2	4	3	13	1	.262
2002 Detroit b.............	A.L.	C	95	321	27	65	15	3	7	24	1	.202
2003 Toledo	Int.	C	39	142	15	39	9	0	5	15	3	.275
2003 Detroit	A.L.	C	104	330	32	67	15	3	8	30	4	.203
2004 Detroit c.............	A.L.	3B-C-OF	131	408	43	117	15	7	13	64	5	.287
2005 Detroit	A.L.	3B-OF	160	616	75	161	31	9	16	72	7	.261
2006 Detroit	A.L.	3B	159	542	83	137	29	2	27	83	7	.253
2007 Detroit	A.L.	3B	151	508	64	120	25	2	14	71	9	.236
2008 Toledo	Int.	C-3B	3	10	2	3	0	0	1	4	0	.300
2008 Detroit d.............	A.L.	C-3B-OF	113	347	41	71	16	4	11	51	4	.205
2009 Detroit	A.L.	3B	*161	562	71	129	16	1	27	84	2	.230
2010 West Michigan.....	Midwest	3B	1	5	0	2	2	0	0	1	0	.400
2010 Detroit e.............	A.L.	3B	144	514	47	127	28	5	13	70	4	.247
2011 Toledo	Int.	3B	29	108	18	31	4	0	7	19	0	.287
2011 Detroit f.............	A.L.	3B	102	269	29	53	10	2	3	23	1	.197
Major League Totals		11 Yrs.	1399	4606	525	1081	211	38	139	587	45	.235
Division Series													
2006 Detroit	A.L.	3B	4	15	1	2	0	0	0	0	0	.133
2011 Detroit	A.L.	3B	4	7	3	3	1	0	0	0	0	.429
Division Series Totals			8	22	4	5	1	0	0	0	0	.227
Championship Series													
2006 Detroit	A.L.	3B	4	12	3	4	1	0	1	3	0	.333
2011 Detroit	A.L.	3B	6	15	3	4	0	0	1	1	0	.267
Championship Series Totals			10	27	6	8	1	0	2	4	0	.296
World Series Record													
2006 Detroit	A.L.	3B	5	17	0	6	2	0	0	1	0	.353

a On disabled list from June 25 to August 6, 2001.
b On disabled list from May 12 to May 27, 2002.
c On disabled list from June 26 to July 15, 2004.
d On disabled list from June 23 to July 10, 2008.
e On disabled list from July 20 to August 4, 2010.
f On disabled list from June 2 to June 23, 2011.

IZTURIS, CESAR DAVID

Born, Barquisimeto, Venezuela, February 10, 1980.
Bats Both. Throws Right. Height, 5 feet, 9 inches. Weight, 190 pounds.

Year	Club	Lea	Pos	G	AB	R	H	2B	3B	HR	RBI	SB	Avg
1997 St.Cathrnes	N.Y.-Penn.	2B-SS	70	231	32	44	3	0	1	11	6	.190
1998 Hagerstown	So.Atl.	SS-2B-3B	130	413	56	108	13	1	1	38	20	.262
1999 Dunedin	Fla.St.	SS-2B-3B	131	536	77	165	28	12	3	77	32	.308
2000 Syracuse	Int.	SS	132	435	54	95	16	5	0	27	21	.218
2001 Syracuse	Int.	SS-2B	87	342	32	100	16	3	2	35	24	.292

Year	Club	Lea	Pos	G	AB	R	H	2B	3B	HR	RBI	SB	Avg
2001 Toronto a	A.L.	2B-SS	46	134	19	36	6	2	2	9	8	.269
2002 Los Angeles	N.L.	SS-2B	135	439	43	102	24	2	1	31	7	.232
2003 Los Angeles	N.L.	SS	158	558	47	140	21	6	1	40	10	.251
2004 Los Angeles	N.L.	SS	159	670	90	193	32	9	4	62	25	.288
2005 Los Angeles b	N.L.	SS	106	444	48	114	19	2	2	31	8	.257
2006 Las Vegas	.P.C.	SS-2B	15	59	9	16	3	0	0	3	0	.271
2006 Los Angeles-Chicago c-d-e .	N.L.	3B-SS-2B	54	192	14	47	9	1	1	18	1	.245
2007 Chicago-Pittsburgh f-g..	N.L.	SS-3B	110	314	31	81	14	2	0	16	3	.258
2008 St. Louis h-i	N.L.	SS-3B	135	414	50	109	10	3	1	24	24	.263
2009 Bowie	Eastern	SS	2	6	2	2	0	0	0	0	1	.333
2009 Baltimore j...........	A.L.	SS	114	387	34	99	14	4	2	30	12	.256
2010 Baltimore k...........	A.L.	SS	150	473	42	109	13	1	1	28	11	.230
2011 Orioles	Gulf Coast	2B	1	2	0	0	0	0	0	0	0	.000
2011 Bowie	Eastern	2B-SS-3B	7	25	3	6	1	0	0	3	0	.240
2011 Baltimore l-m........	A.L.	SS-2B-3B	18	30	4	6	0	0	0	1	0	.200
Major League Totals		11 Yrs.	1185	4055	422	1036	162	32	15	290	109	.255
Division Series												
2004 Los Angeles	N.L.	SS	4	17	1	3	1	0	0	0	0	.176

a Traded to Los Angeles Dodgers with pitcher Paul Quantrill for pitcher Luke Prokopec and pitcher Chad Ricketts, December 13, 2001.
b On disabled list from June 30 to July 15 and August 23 to October 7, 2005.
c On disabled list from March 28 to June 20, 2006.
d Traded to Chicago Cubs for pitcher Greg Maddux, July 31, 2006.
e On disabled list from August 22 to September 6, 2006.
f Sold to Pittsburgh Pirates, July 19, 2007.
g Filed for free agency, November 12, 2007. Signed with St. Louis Cardinals, November 30, 2007.
h On disabled list from June 21 to July 6, 2008.
i Filed for free agency, October 30, 2008. Signed with Baltimore Orioles, December 15, 2008.
j On disabled list from June 4 to July 10, 2009.
k Filed for free agency, November 1, 2010, re-signed with Baltimore Orioles, January 5, 2011.
l On disabled list from May 13 to August 5 and August 8 to September 29, 2011.
m Filed for free agency, October 30, 2011. Signed with Milwaukee Brewers organization, December 21, 2011.

IZTURIS, MAICER

Born, Barquisimeto, Venezuela, September 12, 1980.
Bats Both. Throws Right. Height, 5 feet, 8 inches. Weight, 160 pounds.

Year	Club	Lea	Pos	G	AB	R	H	2B	3B	HR	RBI	SB	Avg
1998 Burlington	Appal.	SS	55	217	33	63	8	2	2	33	16	.290
1999 Columbus.......	So.Atl.	SS	57	220	46	66	5	3	4	23	14	.300
2000 Columbus.......	So.Atl.	SS	10	29	4	8	1	0	0	1	0	.276
2001 Kinston.......	Carolina	2B	114	433	47	104	16	6	1	39	32	.240
2002 Kinston.......	Carolina	2B	58	233	28	61	13	1	1	30	24	.262
2002 Akron........	Eastern	2B	67	253	34	70	12	7	0	32	8	.277
2003 Akron........	Eastern	2B-SS-OF	54	218	31	61	11	5	1	20	14	.280
2003 Buffalo	Int.	SS-2B	85	301	43	79	16	4	2	29	14	.262
2004 Edmonton	P.C.	SS-2B	99	376	65	127	19	2	3	36	14	.338
2004 Montreal a-b	N.L.	2B	32	107	10	22	5	2	1	4	4	.206
2005 Salt Lake	P.C.	SS-3B-2B	10	31	10	14	4	0	0	2	4	.452
2005 Los Angeles c......	A.L.	3B-SS-2B-OF	77	191	18	47	8	4	1	15	9	.246
2006 Salt Lake	P.C.	SS-3B-2B	9	36	5	11	5	1	0	5	1	.306
2006 Los Angeles d	A.L.	3B-SS-2B	104	352	64	103	21	3	5	44	14	.293
2007 Rancho Cucamonga	Calif.	3B	7	22	5	7	1	0	0	3	0	.318
2007 Salt Lake	P.C.	2B-SS	5	17	3	6	1	0	0	0	0	.353
2007 Los Angeles e......	A.L.	3B-2B-SS	102	336	47	97	17	2	6	51	7	.289
2008 Rancho Cucamonga	Calif.	2B	1	2	0	1	0	0	0	0	0	.500
2008 Los Angeles f......	A.L.	SS-2B-3B	79	290	44	78	14	2	3	37	11	.269
2009 Los Angeles	A.L.	2B-SS-3B-OF	114	387	74	116	22	3	8	65	13	.300
2010 Salt Lake	P.C.	3B-SS	2	7	1	2	0	0	0	1	0	.286
2010 Los Angeles g	A.L.	3B-2B-SS	61	212	27	53	13	1	3	27	7	.250
2011 Los Angeles	A.L.	2B-3B-SS	122	449	51	124	35	0	5	38	9	.276
Major League Totals		8 Yrs.	691	2324	335	640	135	17	32	281	74	.275
Division Series												
2007 Los Angeles.......A.L.		3B	3	12	1	4	2	0	0	0	2	.333
2009 Los Angeles.......A.L.		2B	2	7	1	1	0	0	0	1	1	.143
Division Series Totals			5	19	2	5	2	0	0	1	3	.263
Championship Series												
2005 Los Angeles.......A.L.		SS	1	0	0	0	0	0	0	0	0	.000
2009 Los Angeles.......A.L.		2B	4	10	1	1	1	0	0	1	0	.100
Championship Series Totals			5	10	1	1	1	0	0	1	0	.100

a Traded by Cleveland Indians to Montreal Expos with outfielder Ryan Church for pitcher Scott Stewart, January 5, 2004.
b Traded to Anaheim Angels with outfielder Juan Rivera for outfielder Jose Guillen, November 19, 2004.
c On disabled list from April 26 to June 18, 2005.
d On disabled list from April 24 to June 9, 2006.
e On disabled list from April 30 to May 15 and May 21 to July 3, 2007.
f On disabled list from April 28 to May 13 and August 14 to October 9, 2008.
g On disabled list from May 6 to May 25 and June 16 to July 18 and August 20 to September 27, 2010.

JACKSON, AUSTIN JARRIEL

Born, Denton, Texas, February 1, 1987.
Bats Right. Throws Right. Height, 6 feet, 1 inch. Weight, 185 pounds.

Year	Club	Lea	Pos	G	AB	R	H	2B	3B	HR	RBI	SB	Avg
2005 Yankees	Gulf Coast		OF	40	148	32	45	11	2	0	14	11	.304
2006 Charleston	So.Atl.		OF	134	535	90	139	24	5	4	47	37	.260
2007 Tampa	Fla.St.		OF	67	258	53	89	15	6	10	34	13	.345
2007 Scranton/WB	Int.		OF	1	3	2	1	1	0	0	0	1	.333
2007 Charleston	So.Atl.		OF	60	235	33	61	16	1	3	25	19	.260
2008 Trenton	Eastern		OF	131	520	75	148	33	5	9	69	19	.285
2009 Scranton/WB a	Int.		OF	132	504	67	151	23	9	4	65	24	.300
2010 Detroit	A.L.		OF	151	618	103	181	34	10	4	41	27	.293
2011 Detroit	A.L.		OF	153	591	90	147	22	11	10	45	22	.249
Major League Totals	2 Yrs.			304	1209	193	328	56	21	14	86	49	.271
Division Series													
2011 Detroit	A.L.		OF	5	16	3	2	1	0	0	0	1	.125
Championship Series													
2011 Detroit	A.L.		OF	6	25	3	6	1	0	1	4	0	.240

a Traded by New York Yankees to Detroit Tigers with pitcher Phil Coke and pitcher Ian Kennedy for outfielder Curtis Granderson, December 9, 2009.

JACKSON, CONOR SIMS

Born, Austin, Texas, May 7, 1982.
Bats Right. Throws Right. Height, 6 feet, 2 inches. Weight, 225 pounds.

Year	Club	Lea	Pos	G	AB	R	H	2B	3B	HR	RBI	SB	Avg
2003 Yakima	Northwest		OF	68	257	44	82	35	1	6	60	3	.319
2004 Lancaster	Calif.		OF	67	258	64	89	19	2	11	54	4	.345
2004 El Paso	Texas		OF-3B	60	226	33	68	13	2	6	37	3	.301
2005 Tucson	P.C.		1B-OF	93	333	66	118	38	2	8	73	3	.354
2005 Arizona	N.L.		1B-OF	40	85	8	17	3	0	2	8	0	.200
2006 Arizona	N.L.		1B	140	485	75	141	26	1	15	79	1	.291
2007 Arizona	N.L.		1B-3B-OF	130	415	56	118	29	1	15	60	2	.284
2008 Arizona	N.L.		OF-1B	144	540	87	162	31	6	12	75	10	.300
2009 Visalia	Calif.		OF	3	10	1	0	0	0	0	1	0	.000
2009 Arizona a	N.L.		OF-1B	30	99	8	18	4	0	1	14	5	.182
2010 Athletics	Arizona		OF	3	7	0	0	0	0	0	1	0	.000
2010 Stockton	Calif.		OF	2	7	1	2	1	0	0	2	0	.286
2010 Reno	P.C.		OF	3	11	4	3	0	0	1	2	0	.273
2010 Sacramento	P.C.		OF	2	8	1	0	0	0	0	0	0	.000
2010 Arizona	N.L.		OF-1B	42	151	19	36	11	0	1	11	4	.238
2010 Oakland b-c-d	A.L.		OF	18	57	6	13	2	0	1	5	2	.228
2011 Oakland-Boston e-f	A.L.		1B-OF-3B	114	352	32	86	17	1	5	43	3	.244
Major League Totals	7 Yrs.			658	2184	291	591	123	9	52	295	27	.271
Division Series													
2007 Arizona	N.L.		1B	3	8	0	1	1	0	0	1	0	.125
Championship Series													
2007 Arizona	N.L.		1B	3	9	1	3	0	0	0	1	0	.333

a On disabled list from May 12 to November 20, 2009.
b On disabled list from April 19 to May 8, 2010.
c Traded to Oakland Athletics with cash for pitcher Sam Demel, June 15, 2010.
d On disabled list from July 1 to August 16 and August 20 to November 4, 2010.
e Traded to Boston Red Sox with cash for pitcher Jason Rice, August 31, 2011.
f Filed for free agency, October 30, 2011.

JANISH, PAUL RYAN
Born, Houston, Texas, October 12, 1982.
Bats Right. Throws Right. Height, 6 feet, 2 inches. Weight, 195 pounds.

Year	Club	Lea	Pos	G	AB	R	H	2B	3B	HR	RBI	SB	Avg
2004	Billings	Pioneer	SS	66	205	39	54	11	0	2	22	7	.263
2005	Dayton	Midwest	SS	55	208	30	51	10	2	5	29	5	.245
2006	Sarasota	Fla.St.	SS	91	335	53	93	17	2	9	55	8	.278
2006	Dayton	Midwest	SS	26	98	19	39	6	0	5	18	0	.398
2006	Chattanooga	Southern	SS	4	15	1	4	1	0	0	2	0	.267
2007	Louisville	Int.	SS	55	199	20	44	8	1	3	19	2	.221
2007	Chattanooga	Southern	SS-2B-3B	88	324	46	79	21	2	1	20	10	.244
2008	Louisville	Int.	SS-2B	92	318	45	80	20	1	7	42	2	.252
2008	Cincinnati	N.L.	SS	38	80	5	15	2	0	1	6	0	.188
2009	Cincinnati	N.L.	SS-P-3B	90	256	36	54	21	0	1	16	2	.211
2010	Cincinnati	N.L.	SS-3B-2B	82	200	23	52	10	0	5	25	1	.260
2011	Louisville	Int.	SS	13	43	9	11	2	0	1	3	1	.256
2011	Cincinnati	N.L.	SS-3B-2B	114	336	27	72	14	1	0	23	3	.214
Major League Totals		4 Yrs.	324	872	91	193	47	1	7	70	6	.221
Division Series													
2010	Cincinnati	N.L.	SS	1	1	0	0	0	0	0	0	0	.000

JASO, JOHN EDWARD
Born, Chula Vista, California, September 19, 1983.
Bats Left. Throws Right. Height, 6 feet, 2 inches. Weight, 205 pounds.

Year	Club	Lea	Pos	G	AB	R	H	2B	3B	HR	RBI	SB	Avg
2003	Hudson Valley	N.Y.-Penn.	C	47	154	20	34	7	0	2	20	2	.221
2004	Hudson Valley	N.Y.-Penn.	C-1B-SS	57	199	34	60	17	2	2	35	1	.302
2005	SW Michigan	Midwest	C-1B	92	332	61	102	25	1	14	50	3	.307
2006	Visalia	Calif.	C	95	366	58	113	22	0	10	55	1	.309
2007	Montgomery	Southern	C	109	380	62	120	24	2	12	71	2	.316
2008	Montgomery	Southern	C	85	284	51	77	13	2	7	43	1	.271
2008	Durham	Int.	C	31	108	14	30	7	0	5	24	1	.278
2008	Tampa Bay	A.L.	C	5	10	2	2	0	0	0	0	0	.200
2009	Durham	Int.	C	104	331	42	88	14	2	5	30	1	.266
2010	Durham	Int.	C	3	11	1	4	1	0	0	2	0	.364
2010	Tampa Bay	A.L.	C-1B	109	339	57	89	18	3	5	44	4	.263
2011	Durham	Int.	C	6	20	2	6	2	0	0	4	0	.300
2011	Tampa Bay a-b	A.L.	C	89	246	26	55	15	1	5	27	1	.224
Major League Totals		3 Yrs.	203	595	85	146	33	4	10	71	5	.245
Division Series													
2010	Tampa Bay	A.L.	C	3	10	0	3	0	0	0	1	0	.300
2011	Tampa Bay	A.L.	C	2	4	0	0	0	0	0	0	0	.000
Division Series Totals			5	14	0	3	0	0	0	1	0	.214

a On disabled list from July 15 to August 19, 2011.
b Traded to Seattle Mariners for pitcher Josh Lueke, November 27, 2011.

JAY, JONATHAN HENRY (JON)
Born, Miami, Florida, March 15, 1985.
Bats Left. Throws Left. Height, 5 feet, 11 inches. Weight, 200 pounds.

Year	Club	Lea	Pos	G	AB	R	H	2B	3B	HR	RBI	SB	Avg
2006	Quad Cities	Midwest	OF	60	234	42	80	13	3	3	45	9	.342
2007	Palm Beach	Fla.St.	OF	32	126	19	36	8	0	2	10	5	.286
2007	Cardinals	Gulf Coast	DH	1	2	0	1	0	0	0	0	0	.500
2007	Springfield	Texas	OF	26	102	17	24	4	2	2	11	4	.235
2008	Memphis	P.C.	OF	16	58	8	20	4	1	1	10	0	.345
2008	Springfield	Texas	OF	96	372	57	114	17	3	11	47	10	.306
2009	Memphis	P.C.	OF-1B	136	505	72	142	23	2	10	54	20	.281
2010	Memphis	P.C.	OF-1B	42	165	31	53	16	0	4	32	13	.321
2010	St. Louis	N.L.	OF	105	287	47	86	19	2	4	27	2	.300
2011	St. Louis	N.L.	OF	159	455	56	135	24	2	10	37	6	.297
Major League Totals		2 Yrs.	264	742	103	221	43	4	14	64	8	.298
Division Series													
2011	St. Louis	N.L.	OF	5	12	0	2	0	0	0	2	0	.167
Championship Series													
2011	St. Louis	N.L.	OF	6	25	7	6	2	0	0	1	1	.240
World Series Record													
2011	St. Louis	N.L.	OF	7	18	1	2	0	0	0	0	0	.111

JENNINGS, DESMOND DELANE

Born, Birmingham, Alabama, October 30, 1986.
Bats Right. Throws Right. Height, 6 feet, 2 inches. Weight, 200 pounds.

Year	Club	Lea	Pos	G	AB	R	H	2B	3B	HR	RBI	SB	Avg
2006	Princeton	Appal.	OF	56	213	48	59	10	1	4	20	32	.277
2007	Columbus	So.Atl.	OF	99	387	75	122	21	5	9	37	45	.315
2008	Vero Beach	Fla.St.	OF	24	85	17	22	5	1	2	6	5	.259
2009	Montgomery	Southern	OF	100	383	69	121	25	8	8	45	37	.316
2009	Durham	Int.	OF	32	114	23	37	6	2	3	17	15	.325
2010	Durham	Int.	OF	109	399	82	111	25	6	3	36	37	.278
2010	Tampa Bay	A.L.	OF	17	21	5	4	1	1	0	2	2	.190
2011	Durham	Int.	OF	89	338	68	93	19	3	12	39	17	.275
2011	Tampa Bay	A.L.	OF	63	247	44	64	9	4	10	25	20	.259
Major League Totals		2 Yrs.		80	268	49	68	10	5	10	27	22	.254
Division Series													
2010	Tampa Bay	A.L.	OF	2	2	1	0	0	0	0	0	0	.000
2011	Tampa Bay	A.L.	OF	4	15	3	5	1	0	2	2	0	.333
Division Series Totals				6	17	4	5	1	0	2	2	0	.294

JETER, DEREK SANDERSON

Born, Pequannock, New Jersey, June 26, 1974.
Bats Right. Throws Right. Height, 6 feet, 3 inches. Weight, 195 pounds.

Year	Club	Lea	Pos	G	AB	R	H	2B	3B	HR	RBI	SB	Avg
1992	Tampa Yankees	Gulf C.	SS	47	173	19	35	10	1	3	25	2	.202
1992	Greensboro	So. Atl.	SS	11	37	4	9	0	0	1	4	0	.243
1993	Greensboro	So. Atl.	SS	128	515	85	152	14	11	5	71	18	.295
1994	Tampa	Fla. St.	SS	69	292	61	96	13	8	0	39	28	.329
1994	Albany	Eastern	SS	34	122	17	46	7	2	2	13	12	.377
1994	Columbus	Int.	SS	35	126	25	44	7	1	3	16	10	.349
1995	Columbus	Int.	SS	123	486	96	154	27	9	2	45	20	.317
1995	New York	A.L.	SS	15	48	5	12	4	1	0	7	0	.250
1996	New York a	A.L.	SS	157	582	104	183	25	6	10	78	14	.314
1997	New York	A.L.	SS	159	654	116	190	31	7	10	70	23	.291
1998	Columbus	Int.	SS	1	5	2	2	2	0	0	0	0	.400
1998	New York b	A.L.	SS	149	626	*127	203	25	8	19	84	30	.324
1999	New York	A.L.	SS	158	627	134	219	37	9	24	102	19	.349
2000	Tampa	Fla.St.	SS	1	3	2	2	1	0	0	0	0	.667
2000	New York c	A.L.	SS	148	593	119	201	31	4	15	73	22	.339
2001	New York d	A.L.	SS	150	614	110	191	35	3	21	74	27	.311
2002	New York	A.L.	SS	157	644	124	191	26	0	18	75	32	.297
2003	Trenton	Eastern	SS	5	18	2	8	1	1	0	5	0	.444
2003	New York e	A.L.	SS	119	482	87	156	25	3	10	52	11	.324
2004	New York	A.L.	SS	154	643	111	188	44	1	23	78	23	.292
2005	New York	A.L.	SS	159	654	122	202	25	5	19	70	14	.309
2006	New York	A.L.	SS	154	623	118	214	39	3	14	97	34	.343
2007	New York	A.L.	SS	156	639	102	206	39	4	12	73	15	.322
2008	New York	A.L.	SS	150	596	88	179	25	3	11	69	11	.300
2009	New York	A.L.	SS	153	634	107	212	27	1	18	66	30	.334
2010	New York f	A.L.	SS	157	663	111	179	30	3	10	67	18	.270
2011	Trenton	Eastern	SS	2	4	1	2	0	0	0	0	0	.500
2011	New York g	A.L.	SS	131	546	84	162	24	4	6	61	16	.297
Major League Totals		17 Yrs.		2426	9868	1769	3088	492	65	240	1196	339	.313
Division Series													
1996	New York	A.L.	SS	4	17	2	7	1	0	0	1	0	.412
1997	New York	A.L.	SS	5	21	6	7	1	0	2	2	1	.333
1998	New York	A.L.	SS	3	9	0	1	0	0	0	0	0	.111
1999	New York	A.L.	SS	3	11	3	5	1	1	0	0	0	.455
2000	New York	A.L.	SS	5	19	1	4	0	0	0	2	0	.211
2001	New York	A.L.	SS	5	18	2	8	1	0	0	1	0	.444
2002	New York	A.L.	SS	4	16	6	8	0	0	2	3	0	.500
2003	New York	A.L.	SS	4	14	2	6	0	0	1	1	1	.429
2004	New York	A.L.	SS	4	19	3	6	1	0	1	4	1	.316
2005	New York	A.L.	SS	5	21	4	7	0	0	2	5	1	.333
2006	New York	A.L.	SS	4	16	4	8	4	0	1	1	0	.500
2007	New York	A.L.	SS	4	17	0	3	0	0	0	1	0	.176
2009	New York	A.L.	SS	3	10	4	4	2	0	1	2	0	.400
2010	New York	A.L.	SS	3	14	0	4	0	0	0	1	1	.286
2011	New York	A.L.	SS	5	24	6	6	1	0	0	2	1	.250
Division Series Totals				61	246	43	84	12	1	10	26	6	.341

Year Club	Lea	Pos	G	AB	R	H	2B	3B	HR	RBI	SB	Avg
Championship Series												
1996 New York	A.L.	SS	5	24	5	10	2	0	1	1	2	.417
1998 New York	A.L.	SS	6	25	3	5	1	1	0	2	3	.200
1999 New York	A.L.	SS	5	20	3	7	1	0	1	3	0	.350
2000 New York	A.L.	SS	6	22	6	7	0	0	2	5	1	.318
2001 New York	A.L.	SS	5	17	0	2	0	0	0	2	0	.118
2003 New York	A.L.	SS	7	30	3	7	2	0	1	2	1	.233
2004 New York	A.L.	SS	5	30	5	6	1	0	0	5	1	.200
2009 New York	A.L.	SS	6	27	5	7	0	0	2	3	0	.259
2010 New York	A.L.	SS	6	26	2	6	3	1	0	1	0	.231
Championship Series Totals			53	221	32	57	10	2	7	24	8	.258
World Series												
1996 New York	A.L.	SS	6	20	5	5	0	0	0	1	1	.250
1998 New York	A.L.	SS	4	17	4	6	0	0	0	1	0	.353
1999 New York	A.L.	SS	4	17	4	6	1	0	0	1	3	,353
2000 New York	A.L.	SS	5	22	6	9	2	1	2	2	0	.409
2001 New York	A.L.	SS	7	27	3	4	0	0	1	1	0	.148
2003 New York	A.L.	SS	6	26	5	9	3	0	0	2	0	.346
2009 New York	A.L.	SS	6	27	5	11	3	0	0	1	0	.407
World Series Totals.			38	156	32	50	9	1	3	9	4	.321

a Selected Rookie of the Year in American League for 1996.
b On disabled list from June 4 to June 19, 1998.
c On disabled list from May 12 to May 26, 2000.
d On disabled list from March 23 to April 7, 2001.
e On disabled list from April 1 to May 13, 2003.
f Filed for free agency, November 1, 2010, re-signed with New York Yankees, December 7, 2010.
g On disabled list from June 14 to July 4, 2011.

JOHNSON, CHRISTOPHER DALTON (CHRIS)
Born, Naples, Florida, October 1, 1984.
Bats Right. Throws Right. Height, 6 feet, 3 inches. Weight, 220 pounds.

Year Club	Lea	Pos	G	AB	R	H	2B	3B	HR	RBI	SB	Avg
2006 Tri-City	N.Y.-Penn.	3B-1B	60	222	18	47	7	1	1	29	7	.212
2007 Salem.	Carolina	3B-1B	60	224	24	59	11	0	6	38	1	.263
2007 Lexington	So.Atl.	3B-SS-1B	64	255	37	66	14	0	8	44	3	.259
2008 Round Rock	P.C.	3B	30	101	10	22	2	1	1	9	0	.218
2008 Corpus Christi	Texas	3B	84	330	43	107	24	0	12	58	5	.324
2009 Lancaster	Calif.	3B	4	16	5	7	5	0	0	6	0	.438
2009 Round Rock	P.C.	3B	104	384	48	108	20	5	13	42	2	.281
2009 Houston	N.L.	3B	11	22	1	2	0	0	0	1	0	.091
2010 Round Rock	P.C.	3B	38	149	26	49	10	1	8	33	0	.329
2010 Houston a	N.L.	3B	94	341	40	105	22	2	11	52	3	.308
2011 Oklahoma.	P.C.	3B	21	81	18	22	7	0	4	15	1	.272
2011 Houston	N.L.	3B	107	378	32	95	21	3	7	42	2	.251
Major League Totals	3 Yrs.		212	741	73	202	43	5	18	95	5	.273

a On disabled list from April 18 to May 8, 2010.

JOHNSON, ELLIOT TYLER
Born, Safford, Arizona, March 9, 1984.
Bats Both. Throws Right. Height, 6 feet. Weight, 190 pounds.

Year Club	Lea	Pos	G	AB	R	H	2B	3B	HR	RBI	SB	Avg
2002 Princeton	Appal.	2B-SS	42	152	21	40	10	1	1	13	14	.263
2003 Charleston	So.Atl.	2B-SS-OF	54	151	22	32	4	0	0	15	8	.212
2004 Charleston	So.Atl.	2B	126	503	92	132	22	7	6	41	43	.262
2005 Visalia	Calif.	2B	56	227	42	62	10	3	8	33	28	.273
2005 Montgomery . .	Southern	2B-SS	63	264	31	69	9	6	3	21	15	.261
2006 Montgomery . .	Southern	2B	122	494	69	139	21	10	15	50	20	.281
2007 Durham	Int.	2B	129	463	56	96	17	6	11	45	16	.207
2008 Tampa Bay	A.L.	SS-OF-2B	7	19	0	3	0	0	0	0	0	.158
2008 Durham	Int.	2B-SS-OF	107	387	49	101	26	5	9	50	15	.261
2009 Rays.	Gulf Coast	2B	5	16	2	5	2	0	0	2	0	.313
2009 Durham	Int.	2B-3B-SS-OF	63	233	31	61	9	1	11	35	7	.262
2010 Durham	Int.	SS-OF-2B	109	427	72	136	24	5	11	56	30	.319
2011 Durham	Int.	SS	2	9	1	2	0	0	0	0	0	.222
2011 Tampa Bay a	A.L.	SS-2B-1B-OF	70	160	20	31	7	2	4	17	6	.194
Major League Totals	2 Yrs.		77	179	20	34	7	2	4	17	6	.190

Year	Club	Lea	Pos	G	AB	R	H	2B	3B	HR	RBI	SB	Avg
	Division Series												
2011 Tampa Bay.......A.L.			PH	1	0	0	0	0	0	0	0	0	.000

a On disabled list from May 22 to June 12, 2011.

JOHNSON, KELLY ANDREW

Born, Austin, Texas, February 22, 1982.
Bats Left. Throws Right. Height, 6 feet, 1 inch. Weight, 205 pounds.

Year	Club	Lea	Pos	G	AB	R	H	2B	3B	HR	RBI	SB	Avg
2000 Braves.........	Gulf Coast		SS-3B	53	193	27	52	12	3	4	29	6	.269
2001 Macon...........	So.Atl.		SS	124	415	75	120	22	1	23	66	25	.289
2002 Myrtle Beach......	Carolina		SS-3B	126	482	62	123	21	5	12	49	12	.255
2003 Braves.........	Gulf Coast		SS	6	26	10	10	1	1	1	3	1	.385
2003 Greenville.......	Southern		SS	98	334	46	92	22	5	6	45	10	.275
2004 Greenville.......	Southern		OF-3B-2B	135	479	70	135	35	3	16	50	9	.282
2005 Richmond............	Int.		OF-3B-SS	44	155	35	48	12	3	8	22	7	.310
2005 Atlanta..............	N.L.		OF	87	290	46	70	12	3	9	40	2	.241
2006 Richmond............	Int.		OF	10	39	3	13	4	0	1	7	1	.333
2006 Rome a...........	So.Atl.		OF	5	19	5	9	2	1	1	3	2	.474
2007 Atlanta..............	N.L.		2B	147	521	91	144	26	10	16	68	9	.276
2008 Atlanta..............	N.L.		2B	150	547	86	157	39	6	12	69	11	.287
2009 Gwinnett.............	Int.		2B	13	52	9	16	2	2	3	16	1	.308
2009 Atlanta b-c..........	N.L.		2B	106	303	47	68	20	3	8	29	7	.224
2010 Arizona..............	N.L.		2B	154	585	93	166	36	5	26	71	13	.284
2011 Arizona..............	N.L.		2B	114	430	59	90	23	5	18	49	13	.209
2011 Toronto d-e..........	A.L.		2B	33	115	16	31	4	2	3	9	3	.270
Major League Totals............			6 Yrs.	791	2791	438	726	160	34	92	335	58	.260
	Division Series												
2005 Atlanta..............	N.L.		PH	4	2	0	0	0	0	0	0	0	.000

a On disabled list from March 24 to November 1, 2006.

b On disabled list from July 3 to July 23, 2009.

c Not offered contract, December 12, 2009. Signed with Arizona Diamondbacks, December 30, 2009.

d Traded to Toronto Blue Jays for infielder Aaron Hill and infielder John McDonald, August 23, 2011.

e Filed for free agency, October 30, 2011. Accepted arbitration, December 7, 2011.

JOHNSON, REED CAMERON

Born, Riverside, California, December 8, 1976.
Bats Right. Throws Right. Height, 5 feet, 10 inches. Weight, 180 pounds.

Year	Club	Lea	Pos	G	AB	R	H	2B	3B	HR	RBI	SB	Avg
1999 St. Catharines....	N.Y.-Penn.		OF	60	189	24	44	8	2	2	23	5	.233
2000 Dunedin...........	Fla.St.		OF	36	133	26	42	9	2	4	28	3	.316
2000 Hagerstown........	So.Atl.		OF	95	324	66	94	24	5	8	70	14	.290
2001 Tennessee.......	Southern		OF	136	554	104	174	29	4	13	74	42	.314
2002 Dunedin...........	Fla.St.		OF	8	33	7	9	3	0	0	6	0	.273
2002 Syracuse..............	Int.		OF	44	159	27	37	8	3	2	10	1	.233
2003 Syracuse..............	Int.		OF	26	101	14	33	4	1	2	16	3	.327
2003 Toronto.............	A.L.		OF	114	412	79	121	21	2	10	52	5	.294
2004 Toronto.............	A.L.		OF	141	537	68	145	25	2	10	61	6	.270
2005 Toronto.............	A.L.		OF	142	398	55	107	21	6	8	58	5	.269
2006 Toronto.............	A.L.		OF	134	461	86	147	34	2	12	49	8	.319
2007 Dunedin...........	Fla.St.		OF	4	12	1	4	1	0	1	1	0	.333
2007 Syracuse..............	Int.		OF	2	8	1	3	0	0	0	1	0	.375
2007 Toronto a..........	A.L.		OF	79	275	31	65	13	2	2	14	4	.236
2008 Chicago b-c..........	N.L.		OF	109	333	52	101	21	0	6	50	5	.303
2009 Peoria...........	Midwest		OF	3	6	2	2	0	0	0	0	0	.333
2009 Chicago d-e..........	N.L.		OF	65	165	23	42	10	2	4	22	2	.255
2010 Inland Empire........	Calif.		OF	2	6	2	3	1	0	0	0	0	.500
2010 Los Angeles f-g.......	N.L.		OF	102	202	24	53	11	2	2	15	2	.262
2011 Iowa.............	P.C.		OF	3	6	0	0	0	0	0	0	0	.000
2011 Chicago h-i..........	N.L.		OF	111	246	33	76	22	1	5	28	2	.309
Major League Totals............			9 Yrs.	997	3029	451	857	178	19	59	349	39	.283

a On disabled list from April 12 to July 6, 2007.

b Released by Toronto Blue Jays, March 23, 2008. Signed with Chicago Cubs, March 25, 2008.

c On disabled list from June 18 to July 3, 2008.

d On disabled list from June 21 to July 6 and July 30 to September 21, 2009.

e Filed for free agency, November 5, 2009. Signed with Los Angeles Dodgers, February 1, 2010.

f On disabled list from July 9 to August 4, 2010.

g Filed for free agency, November 1, 2010. Signed with Chicago Cubs organization, January 12, 2011.

h On disabled list from May 29 to June 14, 2011.

i Filed for free agency, October 30, 2011, re-signed with Chicago Cubs, January 3, 2012.

JOHNSON, ROBERT JAMES (ROB)
Born, Anaconda, Montana, July 22, 1983.
Bats Right. Throws Right. Height, 6 feet, 1 inch. Weight, 215 pounds.

Year Club	Lea	Pos	G	AB	R	H	2B	3B	HR	RBI	SB	Avg
2004 Mariners............Arizona		DH	8	27	4	6	1	0	0	1	1	.222
2004 Everett.........Northwest		C-OF	20	77	17	18	3	1	1	7	6	.234
2005 Inland Empire........Calif.		C	19	70	15	22	3	0	2	12	2	.314
2005 Wisconsin.........Midwest		C-OF	77	305	41	83	19	1	9	51	10	.272
2006 Tacoma..............P.C.		C-OF	97	337	28	78	9	4	4	33	14	.231
2007 Tacoma..............P.C.		C	112	422	57	113	26	0	6	40	7	.268
2007 Seattle..............A.L.		C	6	3	1	1	0	0	0	0	1	.333
2008 Tacoma..............P.C.		C-OF	112	417	55	127	30	0	9	49	7	.305
2008 Seattle..............A.L.		C	14	31	2	4	0	0	1	2	0	.129
2009 Seattle..............A.L.		C	80	258	21	55	19	2	2	27	1	.213
2010 Tacoma..............P.C.		C	19	64	9	19	7	0	1	8	0	.297
2010 Seattle a............A.L.		C	61	178	24	34	10	0	2	13	1	.191
2011 San Diego b..........N.L.		C	67	179	9	34	6	1	3	16	3	.190
Major League Totals...........	5 Yrs.		228	649	57	128	35	3	8	58	6	.197

a Traded to San Diego Padres for player to be named later, December 21, 2010.
b Filed for free agency, October 25, 2011. Signed with New York Mets organization, December 22, 2011.

JONES, ADAM LA MARQUE
Born, San Diego, California, August 1, 1985.
Bats Right. Throws Right. Height, 6 feet, 2 inches. Weight, 200 pounds.

Year Club	Lea	Pos	G	AB	R	H	2B	3B	HR	RBI	SB	Avg
2003 Mariners...........Arizona		SS	28	109	18	31	5	1	0	8	5	.284
2003 Everett.........Northwest		SS	3	13	2	6	1	0	0	4	0	.462
2004 Wisconsin.........Midwest		SS-3B	130	510	76	136	23	7	11	72	8	.267
2005 Inland Empire........Calif.		SS	68	271	43	80	20	5	8	46	4	.295
2005 San Antonio.........Texas		SS-OF	63	228	33	68	10	3	7	20	9	.298
2006 Tacoma..............P.C.		OF	96	380	69	109	19	4	16	62	13	.287
2006 Seattle..............A.L.		OF	32	74	6	16	4	0	1	8	3	.216
2007 Tacoma..............P.C.		OF	101	420	75	132	27	6	25	84	8	.314
2007 Seattle..............A.L.		OF	41	65	16	16	2	1	2	4	2	.246
2008 Baltimore a-b.........A.L.		OF	132	477	61	129	21	7	9	57	10	.270
2009 Baltimore c...........A.L.		OF	119	473	83	131	22	3	19	70	10	.277
2010 Baltimore...........A.L.		OF	149	581	76	165	25	5	19	69	7	.284
2011 Baltimore...........A.L.		OF	151	567	68	159	26	2	25	83	12	.280
Major League Totals...........	6 Yrs.		624	2237	310	616	100	18	75	291	44	.275

a Traded to Baltimore Orioles with pitcher Tony Butler, pitcher Kam Mickolio, pitcher George Sherrill and pitcher Chris Tillman for pitcher Erik Bedard, February 8, 2008.
b On disabled list from August 3 to September 1, 2008.
c On disabled list from September 2 to November 6, 2009.

JONES, ANDRUW RUDOLF
Born, Willemstad, Curacao, Netherlands Antillies, April 23, 1977.
Bats Right. Throws Right. Height, 6 feet, 1 inch. Weight, 240 pounds.

Year Club	Lea	Pos	G	AB	R	H	2B	3B	HR	RBI	SB	Avg
1994 Braves.........Gulf Coast		OF	27	95	22	21	5	1	2	10	5	.221
1994 Danville............Appal.		OF	36	143	20	48	9	2	1	16	16	.336
1995 Macon............So.Atl.		OF	139	537	104	149	41	5	25	100	56	.277
1996 Durham..........Carolina		OF	66	243	65	76	14	3	17	43	16	.313
1996 Greenville........Southern		OF	38	157	39	58	10	1	12	37	12	.369
1996 Richmond............Int.		OF	12	45	11	17	3	1	5	12	2	.378
1996 Atlanta..............N.L.		OF	31	106	11	23	7	1	5	13	3	.217
1997 Atlanta..............N.L.		OF	153	399	60	92	18	1	18	70	20	.231
1998 Atlanta..............N.L.		OF	159	582	89	158	33	8	31	90	27	.271
1999 Atlanta..............N.L.		OF	162	592	97	163	35	5	26	84	24	.275
2000 Atlanta..............N.L.		OF	161	*656	122	199	36	6	36	104	21	.303
2001 Atlanta..............N.L.		OF	161	625	104	157	25	2	34	104	11	.251
2002 Atlanta..............N.L.		OF	154	560	91	148	34	0	35	94	8	.264
2003 Atlanta..............N.L.		OF	156	595	101	165	28	2	36	116	4	.277
2004 Atlanta..............N.L.		OF	154	570	85	149	34	4	29	91	6	.261
2005 Atlanta..............N.L.		OF	160	586	95	154	24	3	*51	*128	5	.263
2006 Atlanta..............N.L.		OF	156	565	107	148	29	0	41	129	4	.262
2007 Atlanta a............N.L.		OF	154	572	83	127	27	2	26	94	5	.222
2008 Las Vegas..........P.C.		1B-OF	11	31	7	10	0	0	4	11	2	.323
2008 Los Angeles b-c.......N.L.		OF	75	209	21	33	8	1	3	14	0	.158

Year	Club	Lea	Pos	G	AB	R	H	2B	3B	HR	RBI	SB	Avg
2009 Frisco............	Texas		1B	3	9	0	2	0	0	0	0	1	.222
2009 Texas d-e........		A.L.	DH-OF-1B	82	281	43	60	18	0	17	43	5	.214
2010 Chicago f.........		A.L.	OF	107	278	41	64	12	1	19	48	9	.230
2011 New York g........		A.L.	OF	77	190	27	47	8	0	13	33	0	.247
Major League Totals..........	16 Yrs.			2102	7366	1177	1887	376	36	420	1255	152	.256
Division Series													
1996 Atlanta............	N.L.		OF	3	0	0	0	0	0	0	0	0	.000
1997 Atlanta............	N.L.		OF	3	5	1	0	0	0	0	1	0	.000
1998 Atlanta............	N.L.		OF	3	9	2	0	0	0	0	1	2	.000
1999 Atlanta............	N.L.		OF	4	18	1	4	1	0	0	2	0	.222
2000 Atlanta............	N.L.		OF	3	9	3	1	0	0	1	1	0	.111
2001 Atlanta............	N.L.		OF	3	12	2	6	0	0	1	1	0	.500
2002 Atlanta............	N.L.		OF	5	19	4	6	1	0	0	2	0	.316
2003 Atlanta............	N.L.		OF	5	17	1	1	0	0	0	1	0	.059
2004 Atlanta............	N.L.		OF	5	19	4	10	2	0	2	5	1	.526
2005 Atlanta............	N.L.		OF	4	17	5	8	3	0	1	5	0	.471
2011 New York.........	A.L.		OF	1	0	0	0	0	0	0	1	0	.000
Division Series Totals..........				39	125	23	36	7	0	5	20	3	.288
Championship Series													
1996 Atlanta............	N.L.		OF	5	9	3	2	0	0	1	3	0	.222
1997 Atlanta............	N.L.		OF	5	9	0	4	0	0	0	1	0	.444
1998 Atlanta............	N.L.		OF	6	22	3	6	0	0	1	2	1	.273
1999 Atlanta............	N.L.		OF	6	23	5	5	0	0	0	1	0	.217
2001 Atlanta............	N.L.		OF	5	17	4	3	0	0	1	1	0	.176
Championship Series Totals......				27	80	15	20	0	0	3	8	1	.250
World Series													
1996 Atlanta............	N.L.		OF	6	20	4	8	1	0	2	6	1	.400
1999 Atlanta............	N.L.		OF	4	13	1	1	0	0	0	0	0	.077
World Series Totals............				10	33	5	9	1	0	2	6	1	.273

a Filed for free agency, October 31, 2007. Signed with Los Angeles Dodgers, December 12, 2007.
b On disabled list from May 24 to July 4 and August 10 to September 1 and September 13 to November 4, 2008.
c Released, January 15, 2009. Signed with Texas Rangers organization, February 8, 2009.
d On disabled list from August 24 to September 8, 2009.
e Filed for free agency, November 6, 2009. Signed with Chicago White Sox, November 25, 2009.
f Filed for free agency, November 1, 2010. Signed with New York Yankees, February 14, 2011.
g Filed for free agency, October 30, 2011, re-signed with New York Yankees December 30, 2011.

JONES, GARRETT THOMAS

Born, Harvey, Illinois, June 21, 1981.
Bats Left. Throws Left. Height, 6 feet, 4 inches. Weight, 245 pounds.

Year	Club	Lea	Pos	G	AB	R	H	2B	3B	HR	RBI	SB	Avg
1999 Braves.........	Gulf Coast		1B	46	170	17	41	3	0	3	18	1	.241
2000 Danville...........	Appal.		1B	40	138	12	24	7	2	0	16	0	.174
2001 Danville...........	Appal.		1B	40	149	13	43	11	0	3	23	0	.289
2002 Quad Cities a......	Midwest		1B-OF	63	223	21	45	8	0	10	32	3	.202
2003 Fort Myers.........	Fla.St.		1B-OF	117	404	52	89	12	5	18	67	5	.220
2004 New Britain........	Eastern		1B	122	450	68	140	33	2	30	92	11	.311
2004 Fort Myers.........	Fla.St.		1B	19	66	6	16	5	0	1	6	2	.242
2005 Rochester...........	Int.		1B-OF	134	488	71	119	22	2	24	72	5	.244
2006 Rochester...........	Int.		1B-OF	140	525	72	125	32	3	21	92	3	.238
2007 Rochester...........	Int.		OF-1B	107	400	57	112	32	3	13	70	2	.280
2007 Minnesota...........	A.L.		DH-1B-OF	31	77	7	16	2	1	2	5	1	.208
2008 Rochester b.........	Int.		1B-OF	138	527	82	147	33	3	23	92	9	.279
2009 Indianapolis..........	Int.		OF-1B	72	277	44	85	18	0	12	49	14	.307
2009 Pittsburgh..........	N.L.		OF-1B	82	314	45	92	21	1	21	44	10	.293
2010 Pittsburgh..........	N.L.		1B-OF	158	592	64	146	34	1	21	86	7	.247
2011 Pittsburgh..........	N.L.		OF-1B	148	423	51	103	30	1	16	58	6	.243
Major League Totals...........	4 Yrs.			419	1406	167	357	87	4	60	193	24	.254

a Released by Atlanta Braves, May 21,2002. Signed with Minnesota Twins organization, May 24, 2002.
b Filed for free agency, November 3, 2008. Signed with Pittsburgh Pirates organization, December 16, 2008.

JONES, LARRY WAYNE (CHIPPER)

Born, Deland, Florida, April 24, 1972.
Bats Both. Throws Right. Height, 6 feet, 4 inches. Weight, 210 pounds.

Year	Club	Lea	Pos	G	AB	R	H	2B	3B	HR	RBI	SB	Avg
1990 Bradenton Braves....	Gulf C.		SS	44	140	20	32	1	1	1	18	5	.229
1991 Macon.............	So. Atl.		SS	136	473	*104	154	24	11	15	98	40	.326

Year	Club	Lea	Pos	G	AB	R	H	2B	3B	HR	RBI	SB	Avg
1992 Durham	Carolina	SS	70	264	43	73	22	1	4	31	10	.277
1992 Greenville	Southern	SS	67	266	43	92	17	11	9	42	14	.346
1993 Richmond	Int.	SS	139	536	97	174	31	12	13	89	23	.325
1993 Atlanta	N.L.	SS	8	3	2	2	1	0	0	0	0	.667
1994 Atlanta a	N.L.					INJURED—Did Not Play						
1995 Atlanta	N.L.	3B-OF	140	524	87	139	22	3	23	86	8	.265
1996 Atlanta b	N.L.	3B-SS-OF	157	598	114	185	32	5	30	110	14	.309
1997 Atlanta	N.L.	3B-OF	157	597	100	176	41	3	21	111	20	.295
1998 Atlanta	N.L.	3B	160	601	123	188	29	5	34	107	16	.313
1999 Atlanta c	N.L.	3B-SS	157	567	116	181	41	1	45	110	25	.319
2000 Atlanta	N.L.	3B-SS	156	579	118	180	38	1	36	111	14	.311
2001 Atlanta	N.L.	3B-OF	159	572	113	189	33	5	38	102	9	.330
2002 Atlanta	N.L.	OF	158	548	90	179	35	1	26	100	8	.327
2003 Atlanta	N.L.	OF	153	555	103	169	33	2	27	106	2	.305
2004 Rome	So.Atl.	OF	1	4	0	0	0	0	0	0	0	.000
2004 Atlanta d	N.L.	3B-OF	137	472	69	117	20	1	30	96	2	.248
2005 Rome	So.Atl.	3B	3	6	1	3	0	0	0	2	0	.500
2005 Atlanta e	N.L.	3B	109	358	66	106	30	0	21	72	5	.296
2006 Mississippi	Southern	3B	2	6	1	1	0	0	0	0	0	.167
2006 Atlanta f	N.L.	3B	110	411	87	133	28	3	26	86	6	.324
2007 Atlanta g	N.L.	3B-SS	134	513	108	173	42	4	29	102	5	.337
2008 Atlanta h	N.L.	3B	128	439	82	160	24	1	22	75	4	*.364
2009 Atlanta i	N.L.	3B	143	488	80	129	23	2	18	71	4	.264
2010 Atlanta i	N.L.	3B	95	317	47	84	21	0	10	46	5	.265
2011 Rome	So.Atl.	3B	2	3	0	1	0	0	0	1	0	.333
2011 Atlanta j	N.L.	3B	126	455	56	125	33	1	18	70	2	.275
Major League Totals		18 Yrs.	2387	8597	1561	2615	526	38	454	1561	149	.304
Division Series												
1995 Atlanta	N.L.	3B	4	18	4	7	2	0	2	4	0	.389
1996 Atlanta	N.L.	3B	3	9	2	2	0	0	1	2	1	.222
1997 Atlanta	N.L.	3B	3	8	3	4	0	0	1	2	1	.500
1998 Atlanta	N.L.	3B	3	10	2	2	0	0	0	1	0	.200
1999 Atlanta	N.L.	3B	4	13	2	3	0	0	0	1	0	.231
2000 Atlanta	N.L.	3B	3	12	2	4	1	0	0	1	0	.333
2001 Atlanta	N.L.	3B	3	9	2	4	0	0	2	5	0	.444
2002 Atlanta	N.L.	OF	5	17	3	5	0	0	0	2	0	.294
2003 Atlanta	N.L.	OF	5	18	3	3	0	0	2	6	0	.167
2004 Atlanta	N.L.	3B	5	20	4	4	0	0	0	0	0	.200
2005 Atlanta	N.L.	3B	4	17	3	3	2	0	1	2	0	.176
Division Series Totals			42	151	30	41	5	0	9	26	2	.272
Championship Series												
1995 Atlanta	N.L.	3B	4	16	3	7	0	0	1	3	1	.438
1996 Atlanta	N.L.	3B	7	25	6	11	2	0	0	4	1	.440
1997 Atlanta	N.L.	3B	6	24	5	7	1	0	2	4	0	.292
1998 Atlanta	N.L.	3B	6	24	2	5	1	0	0	1	0	.208
1999 Atlanta	N.L.	3B	6	19	3	5	2	0	0	1	3	.263
2001 Atlanta	N.L.	3B	5	19	1	5	1	0	0	2	0	.263
Championship Series Totals			34	127	20	40	7	0	3	15	5	.315
World Series Record												
1995 Atlanta	N.L.	3B	6	21	3	6	3	0	0	1	0	.286
1996 Atlanta	N.L.	3B-SS	6	21	3	6	3	0	0	3	1	.286
1999 Atlanta	N.L.	3B	4	13	2	3	0	0	1	2	0	.231
World Series Totals			16	55	8	15	6	0	1	6	1	.273

a On disabled list from March 20 to end of 1994 season.
b On disabled list from April 1 to April 6, 1996.
c Selected Most Valuable Player in National League for 1999.
d On disabled list from April 19 to May 8, 2004.
e On disabled list from June 6 to July 18, 2005.
f On disabled list from April 10 to April 25 and July 30 to August 13 and September 4 to September 19, 2006.
g On disabled list from May 24 to June 13, 2007.
h On disabled list from July 24 to August 8, 2008.
i On disabled list from August 11 to October 19, 2010.
j On disabled list from July 9 to July 25, 2011.

JOYCE, MATTHEW R. (MATT)
Born, Tampa, Florida, August 3, 1984.
Bats Left. Throws Right. Height, 6 feet, 2 inches. Weight, 205 pounds.

Year Club	Lea	Pos	G	AB	R	H	2B	3B	HR	RBI	SB	Avg
2005 Oneonta . . . . N.Y.-Penn.		OF	65	245	51	81	10	4	4	45	9	.331
2006 West Michigan . . . . . Midwest		OF	122	465	75	120	30	5	11	86	5	.258
2007 Erie. . . . . Eastern		OF	130	456	61	117	33	3	17	70	4	.257
2008 Toledo . . . . Int.		OF	56	200	36	54	13	2	13	41	2	.270
2008 Detroit a . . . . A.L.		OF	92	242	40	61	16	3	12	33	0	.252
2009 Tampa Bay . . . . A.L.		OF	11	32	3	6	1	0	3	7	1	.188
2009 Durham . . . . Int.		OF	111	417	73	114	35	2	16	66	14	.273
2010 Charlotte . . . . .Fla.St.		OF	10	29	6	11	5	0	2	8	1	.379
2010 Durham . . . . Int.		OF	25	92	18	27	8	0	3	12	1	.293
2010 Tampa Bay b . . . . A.L.		OF	77	216	30	52	15	3	10	40	2	.241
2011 Tampa Bay . . . . A.L.		OF	141	462	69	128	32	2	19	75	13	.277
Major League Totals	4 Yrs.		321	952	142	247	64	8	44	155	16	.259
Division Series												
2010 Tampa Bay . . . . A.L.		OF	4	9	0	2	0	0	0	0	1	.222
2011 Tampa Bay . . . . A.L.		OF	4	15	1	3	1	0	1	4	0	.200
Division Series Totals			8	24	1	5	1	0	1	4	1	.208

a Traded to Tampa Bay Rays for pitcher Edwin Jackson, December 10, 2008.
b On disabled list from March 26 to May 31, 2010.

KELLY, DONALD THOMAS (DON)
Born, Butler, Pennsylvania, February 15, 1980.
Bats Left. Throws Right. Height, 6 feet, 4 inches. Weight, 190 pounds.

Year Club	Lea	Pos	G	AB	R	H	2B	3B	HR	RBI	SB	Avg
2001 Oneonta . . . . . N.Y.-Penn.		SS	67	262	41	75	8	3	0	25	8	.286
2002 West Michigan . Midwest		SS	128	455	72	130	21	5	1	59	9	.286
2003 Erie. . . . . Eastern		SS-1B	22	83	14	22	5	1	1	13	0	.265
2003 Lakeland. . . . . . . .Fla.St.		3B-SS-1B-2B	87	303	48	96	17	4	1	38	15	.317
2004 Erie. . . . . Eastern		SS	28	101	17	23	6	2	0	9	3	.228
2004 Tigers . . . . . . Gulf Coast		SS	3	10	2	4	0	0	0	0	1	.400
2005 Erie. . . . . Eastern		3B-SS	82	329	54	112	22	3	9	54	10	.340
2005 Toledo . . . . Int.		SS-3B-OF	43	160	22	40	8	0	1	13	8	.250
2006 Erie. . . . . Eastern		2B-SS-3B-1B	58	207	30	57	11	1	0	24	5	.275
2006 Toledo . . . . Int.		SS-1B-2B	66	237	23	54	14	3	0	19	18	.228
2007 Pittsburgh . . . . .N.L.		SS-2B-OF	25	27	2	4	0	0	0	0	0	.148
2007 Indianapolis a-b . . . . Int.		OF-SS-2B-3B	52	150	20	37	5	2	0	11	6	.247
2008 Tucson . . . . P.C.		2B-SS-3B-OF	124	436	61	120	24	5	8	55	2	.275
2009 Toledo . . . . Int.		OF-1B-3B-2B	105	372	57	123	20	6	6	40	27	.331
2009 Detroit c . . . . .A.L.		OF-3B-1B-2B	31	56	8	14	3	1	0	3	1	.250
2010 Detroit . . . . .A.L.		OF-1B-3B	119	238	30	58	4	0	9	27	3	.244
2011 Detroit . . . . .A.L.		OF-3B-1B-C	113	257	35	63	8	3	7	28	2	.245
Major League Totals	4 Yrs.		288	578	75	139	15	4	16	58	6	.240
Division Series												
2011 Detroit . . . . .A.L.		OF-3B	4	11	3	4	0	0	1	2	0	.364
Championship Series												
2011 Detroit . . . . .A.L.		OF-3B	5	9	0	2	1	0	0	0	0	.222

a Filed for free agency from Detroit Tigers, October 3, 2006. Signed with Pittsburgh Pirates organization, November 16, 2006.
b Filed for free agency, October 4, 2007. Signed with Arizona Diamondbacks organization, November 24, 2007.
c Filed for free agency, November 3, 2008. Signed with Detroit Tigers organization, January 14, 2009.

KEMP, MATTHEW RYAN (MATT)
Born, Midwest City, Oklahoma, September 23, 1984.
Bats Right. Throws Right. Height, 6 feet, 2 inches. Weight, 230 pounds.

Year Club	Lea	Pos	G	AB	R	H	2B	3B	HR	RBI	SB	Avg
2003 Dodgers . . . . Gulf Coast		OF	42	159	11	43	5	2	1	17	2	.270
2004 Vero Beach. . . . . .Fla.St.		OF	11	37	5	13	5	0	1	9	2	.351
2004 Columbus. . . . . So.Atl.		OF	112	423	67	122	22	8	17	66	8	.288
2005 Vero Beach. . . . . .Fla.St.		OF	109	418	76	128	21	4	27	90	23	.306
2006 Jacksonville . . . . . Southern		OF	48	199	38	65	15	2	7	34	11	.327
2006 Las Vegas . . . . .P.C.		OF	44	182	37	67	14	6	3	36	14	.368
2006 Los Angeles . . . . N.L.		OF	52	154	30	39	7	1	7	23	6	.253
2007 Las Vegas . . . . .P.C.		OF	39	161	32	53	16	3	4	20	9	.329
2007 Los Angeles a . . . . N.L.		OF	98	292	47	100	12	5	10	42	10	.342
2008 Los Angeles . . . . N.L.		OF	155	606	93	176	38	5	18	76	35	.290

Year Club	Lea	Pos	G	AB	R	H	2B	3B	HR	RBI	SB	Avg
2009 Los Angeles	N.L.	OF	159	606	97	180	25	7	26	101	34	.297
2010 Los Angeles	N.L.	OF	*162	602	82	150	25	6	28	89	19	.249
2011 Los Angeles	N.L.	OF	161	602	*115	195	33	4	*39	*126	40	.324
Major League Totals		6 Yrs.	787	2862	464	840	140	28	128	457	144	.294
Division Series												
2008 Los Angeles	N.L.	OF	3	13	0	2	2	0	0	1	0	.154
2009 Los Angeles	N.L.	OF	3	14	2	2	0	0	1	2	0	.143
Division Series Totals			6	27	2	4	2	0	1	3	0	.148
Championship Series												
2008 Los Angeles	N.L.	OF	5	15	1	5	1	0	0	0	0	.333
2009 Los Angeles	N.L.	OF	5	20	2	5	0	0	1	2	0	.250
Championship Series Totals			10	35	3	10	1	0	1	2	0	.286

a On disabled list from April 10 to April 27, 2007.

KENDRICK, HOWARD JOSEPH
Born, Jacksonville, Florida, July 12, 1983.
Bats Right. Throws Right. Height, 5 feet, 10 inches. Weight, 195 pounds.

Year Club	Lea	Pos	G	AB	R	H	2B	3B	HR	RBI	SB	Avg
2002 Angels	Arizona	2B	42	157	24	50	6	4	0	13	12	.318
2003 Provo	Pioneer	2B	63	234	65	86	20	3	3	36	8	.368
2004 Angels	Arizona	2B	3	12	1	3	1	0	0	0	2	.250
2004 Cedar Rapids	Midwest	2B	75	313	66	115	24	6	10	49	15	.367
2005 Rancho Cucamonga....	Calif.	2B	63	279	69	107	23	6	12	47	13	.384
2005 Arkansas	Texas	2B	46	190	35	65	20	2	7	42	12	.342
2006 Salt Lake	P.C.	2B-3B	69	290	57	107	25	6	13	62	11	.369
2006 Los Angeles	A.L.	1B-2B-3B	72	267	25	76	21	1	4	30	6	.285
2007 Rancho Cucamonga....	Calif.	DH	1	4	0	1	0	0	0	0	0	.250
2007 Salt Lake	P.C.	2B	13	50	9	15	1	0	3	11	1	.300
2007 Los Angeles a.........	A.L.	2B	88	338	55	109	24	2	5	39	5	.322
2008 Rancho Cucamonga....	Calif.	2B	2	6	3	5	0	0	2	2	1	.833
2008 Salt Lake	P.C.	2B	2	5	0	1	0	0	0	1	0	.200
2008 Los Angeles b	A.L.	2B	92	340	43	104	26	2	3	37	11	.306
2009 Salt Lake	P.C.	2B	20	78	11	27	6	1	2	11	4	.346
2009 Los Angeles	A.L.	2B	105	374	61	109	21	3	10	61	11	.291
2010 Los Angeles	A.L.	2B-1B-OF	158	616	67	172	41	4	10	75	14	.279
2011 Los Angeles c.........	A.L.	2B-OF-1B	140	537	86	153	30	6	18	63	14	.285
Major League Totals		6 Yrs.	655	2472	337	723	163	18	50	305	61	.292
Division Series												
2007 Los Angeles	A.L.	2B	3	10	0	2	0	0	0	1	2	.200
2008 Los Angeles	A.L.	2B	4	17	0	2	0	0	0	0	0	.118
2009 Los Angeles	A.L.	2B	2	5	1	1	0	0	0	0	1	.200
Division Series Totals			9	32	1	5	0	0	0	1	3	.156
Championship Series												
2009 Los Angeles	A.L.	2B	4	14	3	4	0	1	1	1	0	.286

a On disabled list from April 18 to May 23 and July 8 to August 20, 2007.
b On disabled list from April 14 to May 30 and August 28 to September 22, 2008.
c On disabled list from May 20 to June 4, 2011.

KENNEDY, ADAM THOMAS
Born, Riverside, California, January 10, 1976.
Bats Left. Throws Right. Height, 6 feet. Weight, 185 pounds.

Year Club	Lea	Pos	G	AB	R	H	2B	3B	HR	RBI	SB	Avg
1997 New Jersey ..	N.Y.-Penn.	SS	29	114	20	39	6	3	0	19	9	.342
1997 Pr William	Carolina	SS	35	154	24	48	9	3	1	27	4	.312
1998 Pr William	Carolina	2B-SS	17	69	9	18	6	0	0	7	5	.261
1998 Arkansas	Texas	SS-2B	52	205	35	57	11	2	6	24	6	.278
1998 Memphis	P.C.	SS-2B	74	305	36	93	22	7	4	41	15	.305
1999 Memphis	P.C.	2B	91	367	69	120	22	4	10	63	20	.327
1999 St. Louis.	N.L.	2B	33	102	12	26	10	1	1	16	0	.255
2000 Anaheim a	A.L.	2B	156	598	82	159	33	11	9	72	22	.266
2001 Rancho Cucamonga.	Calif.	2B	3	8	3	3	2	0	0	1	3	.375
2001 Anaheim b	A.L.	2B	137	478	48	129	25	3	6	40	12	.270
2002 Anaheim...........	A.L.	2B-OF	144	474	65	148	32	6	7	52	17	.312
2003 Rancho Cucamonga.	Calif.	2B	3	11	3	3	1	0	1	1	0	.273
2003 Anaheim c	A.L.	2B	143	449	71	121	17	1	13	49	22	.269
2004 Anaheim...........	A.L.	2B	144	468	70	130	20	5	10	48	15	.278
2005 Rancho Cucamonga..	Calif.	2B	2	5	1	2	0	0	0	1	1	.400

Year	Club	Lea	Pos	G	AB	R	H	2B	3B	HR	RBI	SB	Avg
2005 Salt Lake	P.C.		2B	4	17	4	7	1	0	0	4	2	.412
2005 Los Angeles d	. . . .	A.L.	2B	129	416	49	125	23	0	2	37	19	.300
2006 Los Angeles e	. . . .	A.L.	2B	139	451	50	123	26	6	4	55	16	.273
2007 St. Louis f	. . . .	N.L.	2B-SS-OF	87	279	27	61	9	1	3	18	6	.219
2008 St. Louis.	. . . .	N.L.	2B-OF-1B	115	339	42	95	17	4	2	36	7	.280
2009 Durham	Int.		2B-1B-3B	23	82	11	23	4	0	3	9	2	.280
2009 Oakland g-h-i	. . . . . .	A.L.	3B-2B-1B-OF	129	529	65	153	29	1	11	63	20	.289
2010 Washington j	. . . . .	N.L.	2B-1B-3B	135	342	43	85	16	1	3	31	14	.249
2011 Seattle k	A.L.		1B-2B-3B	114	380	36	89	23	1	7	38	8	.234
Major League Totals			13 Yrs.	1605	5305	660	1444	280	41	78	555	178	.272
Division Series													
2002 Anaheim.	A.L.		2B	4	8	4	4	1	0	1	3	1	.500
2005 Los Angeles	A.L.		2B	5	17	0	4	0	1	0	2	0	.235
Division Series Totals				9	25	4	8	1	1	1	5	1	.320
Championship Series													
2002 Anaheim.	A.L.		2B	4	14	5	5	0	0	3	5	0	.357
2005 Los Angeles	A.L.		2B	5	14	3	4	0	0	0	1	0	.286
Championship Series Totals				9	28	8	9	0	0	3	6	0	.321
World Series Record													
2002 Anaheim.	A.L.		2B	7	25	1	7	2	0	0	2	0	.280

a Traded to Anaheim Angels with pitcher Kent Bottenfield for outfielder Jim Edmonds, March 23, 2000.
b On disabled list from March 23 to April 13, 2001.
c On disabled list from April 7 to April 22, 2003.
d On disabled list from March 25 to May 2, 2005.
e Filed for free agency, October 29, 2006. Signed with St. Louis Cardinals, November 28, 2006.
f On disabled list from August 12 to November 2, 2007.
g Released by St. Louis Cardinals, February 9, 2009. Signed with Tampa Bay Rays organization, February 17, 2009.
h Traded to Oakland Athletics for player to be named later, May 8, 2009. Tampa Bay Rays received infielder Joe Dillon to complete trade, May 9, 2009.
i Filed for free agency, November 5, 2009. Signed with Washington Nationals, February 12, 2010.
j Filed for free agency, November 3, 2010. Signed with Seattle Mariners organization, January 10, 2011.
k Filed for free agency, October 30, 2011. Signed with Los Angeles Dodgers, November 30, 2011.

KEPPINGER, JEFFREY SCOTT (JEFF)

Born, Miami, Florida, April 21, 1980.
Bats Right. Throws Right. Height, 6 feet. Weight, 180 pounds.

Year	Club	Lea	Pos	G	AB	R	H	2B	3B	HR	RBI	SB	Avg
2002 Hickory.	So.Atl.		2B	126	478	75	132	23	4	10	73	6	.276
2003 Lynchburg	Carolina		2B-3B-1B	92	342	55	111	21	2	3	51	3	.325
2004 Altoona.	Eastern		2B	82	323	45	108	17	2	1	33	10	.334
2004 Binghamton	Eastern		2B-3B	14	47	14	17	3	1	0	5	2	.362
2004 Norfolk.	Int.		2B	6	19	1	6	1	0	0	2	0	.316
2004 New York a.	N.L.		2B	33	116	9	33	2	0	3	9	2	.284
2005 Norfolk b	Int.		2B-3B-SS	64	255	40	86	15	3	3	29	5	.337
2006 Norfolk.	Int.		2B-OF-3B	87	323	36	97	13	0	2	26	0	.300
2006 Omaha	P.C.		2B-3B-1B-SS	32	127	21	45	6	1	2	17	0	.354
2006 Kansas City c	A.L.		3B-1B-2B-OF	22	60	11	16	2	0	2	8	0	.267
2007 Sarasota.	Fla.St.		3B-2B	3	12	1	4	2	0	0	1	0	.333
2007 Louisville	Int.		3B-2B-OF-1B	57	228	31	84	15	1	2	18	1	.368
2007 Cincinnati d-e	N.L.		SS-3B-2B-OF	67	241	39	80	16	2	5	32	2	.332
2008 Sarasota.	Fla.St.		3B	2	7	1	2	0	0	0	1	0	.286
2008 Louisville	Int.		3B-SS	6	22	3	11	2	0	1	2	0	.500
2008 Cincinnati f	N.L.		SS-3B-1B-2B	121	459	45	122	24	2	3	43	3	.266
2009 Houston g	N.L.		3B-2B-SS-OF	107	305	35	78	13	3	7	29	0	.256
2010 Corpus Christi . . .	Texas		2B	2	5	0	2	0	0	0	1	0	.400
2010 Houston h	N.L.		2B-SS	137	514	62	148	34	1	6	59	4	.288
2011 Corpus Christi . . .	Texas		2B	4	16	4	7	1	0	1	2	0	.438
2011 Oklahoma	Int.		2B	7	28	2	7	0	0	0	1	0	.250
2011 Houston-San Fran. i-j-k	N.L.		2B	99	379	39	105	20	0	6	35	0	.277
Major League Totals			7 Yrs.	586	2074	240	582	111	8	32	215	11	.281

a Traded to New York Mets with pitcher Kris Benson for infielder Ty Wigginton, pitcher Matt Peterson and infielder Jose Bautista, July 30, 2004.
b On disabled list from September 9 to October 31, 2005.
c Traded to Kansas City Royals for infielder Ruben Gotay, July 19, 2006.
d Traded to Cincinnati Reds for pitcher Russ Haltiwanger, January 11, 2007.
e On disabled list from March 23 to April 22, 2007.
f On disabled list from May 14 to June 22, 2008.
g Traded to Houston Astros for player to be named later, March 31, 2009. Cincinnati Reds received infielder Drew Sutton to complete trade, April 16, 2009.

h On disabled list from August 17 to September 1, 2010.
i On disabled list from March 22 to May 27, 2011.
j Traded to San Francisco Giants for pitcher Henry Sosa and pitcher Jason Stoffel, July 19, 2011.
k Not offered contract, December 12, 2011.

KINSLER, IAN MICHAEL
Born, Tucson, Arizona, June 22, 1982.
Bats Right. Throws Right. Height, 6 feet. Weight, 200 pounds.

Year Club	Lea	Pos	G	AB	R	H	2B	3B	HR	RBI	SB	Avg
2003 Spokane.....Northwest		SS	51	188	32	52	10	6	1	15	11	.277
2004 Clinton.......Midwest		SS	60	227	52	91	30	1	11	53	16	.401
2004 Frisco..........Texas		SS	71	277	51	83	21	1	9	46	7	.300
2005 Oklahoma........P.C.		2B-SS-3B	131	530	102	145	28	2	23	94	19	.274
2006 Oklahoma........P.C.		2B	10	39	7	10	3	0	2	6	1	.256
2006 Texas a..........A.L.		2B	120	423	65	121	27	1	14	55	11	.286
2007 Oklahoma........P.C.		2B	3	13	1	5	0	0	0	3	2	.385
2007 Texas b..........A.L.		2B	130	483	96	127	22	2	20	61	23	.263
2008 Texas c..........A.L.		2B	121	518	102	165	41	4	18	71	26	.319
2009 Frisco..........Texas		2B	2	7	1	0	0	0	0	0	0	.000
2009 Texas d..........A.L.		2B	144	566	101	143	32	4	31	86	31	.253
2010 Frisco..........Texas		2B	6	19	3	5	0	1	0	6	2	.263
2010 Texas e..........A.L.		2B	103	391	73	112	20	1	9	45	15	.286
2011 Texas..........A.L.		2B	155	620	121	158	34	4	32	77	30	.255
Major League Totals	6 Yrs.		773	3001	558	826	176	16	124	395	136	.275
Division Series												
2010 Texas ............A.L.		2B	5	18	5	8	0	0	3	6	0	.444
2011 Texas ............A.L.		2B	4	16	2	4	2	0	1	3	1	.250
Division Series Totals			9	34	7	12	2	0	4	9	1	.353
Championship Series												
2010 Texas ............A.L.		2B	6	20	1	5	1	1	0	3	2	.250
2011 Texas ............A.L.		2B	6	24	6	7	2	0	0	6	1	.292
Championship Series Totals			12	44	7	12	3	1	0	9	3	.273
World Series Record												
2010 Texas ............A.L.		2B	5	16	1	3	1	0	0	0	1	.188
2011 Texas ............A.L.		2B	7	25	2	9	1	0	0	2	1	.360
World Series Totals............			12	41	3	12	2	0	0	2	2	.293

a On disabled list from April 12 to May 25, 2006.
b On disabled list from July 2 to July 31, 2007.
c On disabled list from August 18 to November 14, 2008.
d On disabled list from July 29 to August 14, 2009.
e On disabled list from March 26 to April 30 and July 28 to September 1, 2010.

KIPNIS, JASON MICHAEL
Born, Northbrook, Illinois, April 3, 1987.
Bats Left. Throws Right. Height, 5 feet, 11 inches. Weight, 185 pounds.

Year Club	Lea	Pos	G	AB	R	H	2B	3B	HR	RBI	SB	Avg
2009 Mahoning Valley.. N.Y.-Penn.		OF	29	111	19	34	8	3	1	19	3	.306
2010 Kinston..........Carolina		2B	54	203	33	61	12	3	6	31	2	.300
2010 Akron.............Eastern		2B	79	315	63	98	20	5	10	43	7	.311
2011 Columbus..........Int.		2B	92	343	65	96	16	9	12	55	12	.280
2011 Cleveland a...........A.L.		2B	36	136	24	37	9	1	7	19	5	.272

a On disabled list from August 14 to September 6, 2011.

KONERKO, PAUL HENRY
Born, Providence, Rhode Island, March 5, 1976.
Bats Right. Throws Right. Height, 6 feet, 2 inches. Weight, 220 pounds.

Year Club	Lea	Pos	G	AB	R	H	2B	3B	HR	RBI	SB	Avg
1994 Yakima.........Northwest		C	67	257	25	74	15	2	6	58	1	.288
1995 San Berndno.....California		C	118	448	77	124	21	1	19	77	3	.277
1996 San Antonio.........Texas		1B	133	470	78	141	23	2	29	86	1	.300
1996 Albuquerque..........P.C.		1B	4	14	2	6	0	0	1	2	0	.429
1997 Albuquerque..........P.C.	3B-1B-2B	130	483	97	156	31	1	37	127	2	.323
1997 Los Angeles..........N.L.		1B-3B	6	7	0	1	0	0	0	0	0	.143
1998 Albuquerque..........P.C.	OF-1B-3B	24	87	16	33	10	0	6	26	0	.379
1998 Indianapols ....Int.		3B	39	150	25	49	8	0	8	39	1	.327
1998 Los Angeles-Cinc. a-b .. N.L.	1B-3B-OF	75	217	21	47	4	0	7	29	0	.217

Year	Club	Lea	Pos	G	AB	R	H	2B	3B	HR	RBI	SB	Avg
1999 Chicago	. . . .	A.L.	1B-3B	142	513	71	151	31	4	24	81	1	.294
2000 Chicago	. . . .	A.L.	1B-3B	143	524	84	156	31	1	21	97	1	.298
2001 Chicago	. . . .	A.L.	1B	156	582	92	164	35	0	32	99	1	.282
2002 Chicago	. . . .	A.L.	1B	151	570	81	173	30	0	27	104	0	.304
2003 Chicago	. . . .	A.L.	1B	137	444	49	104	19	0	18	65	0	.234
2004 Chicago	. . . .	A.L.	1B	155	563	84	156	22	0	41	117	1	.277
2005 Chicago c	. . . .	A.L.	1B	158	575	98	163	24	0	40	100	0	.283
2006 Chicago	. . . .	A.L.	1B	152	566	97	177	30	0	35	113	1	.313
2007 Chicago	. . . .	A.L.	1B	151	549	71	142	34	0	31	90	0	.259
2008 Charlotte	. . . .	Int.	1B	4	11	3	5	2	0	0	3	0	.455
2008 Chicago d	. . . .	A.L.	1B	122	438	59	105	19	1	22	62	2	.240
2009 Chicago	. . . .	A.L.	1B	152	546	75	151	30	1	28	88	1	.277
2010 Chicago e	. . . .	A.L.	1B	149	548	89	171	30	1	39	111	0	.312
2011 Chicago	. . . .	A.L.	1B	149	543	69	163	25	0	31	105	1	.300
Major League Totals	. . . .		15 Yrs.	1998	7185	1040	2024	364	8	396	1261	9	.282
Division Series													
2000 Chicago	. . . .	A.L.	1B	3	9	1	0	0	0	0	0	0	.000
2005 Chicago	. . . .	A.L.	1B	3	12	3	3	0	0	2	4	0	.250
2008 Chicago	. . . .	A.L.	1B	4	16	3	5	0	0	2	2	0	.313
Division Series Totals	. . . .			10	37	7	8	0	0	4	6	0	.216
Championship Series													
2005 Chicago	. . . .	A.L.	1B	5	21	2	6	1	0	2	7	0	.286
World Series Record													
2005 Chicago	. . . .	A.L.	1B	4	16	1	4	1	0	1	4	0	.250

a Traded to Cincinnati Reds with pitcher Dennis Reyes for pitcher Jeff Shaw, July 4, 1998.
b Traded to Chicago White Sox for outfielder Mike Cameron, November 11, 1998.
c Filed for free agency, October 27, 2005, re-signed with Chicago White Sox, November 30, 2005.
d On disabled list from June 15 to July 8, 2008.
e Filed for free agency, November 1, 2010, re-signed with Chicago White Sox, December 8, 2010.

KOTCHMAN, CASEY JOHN

Born, St. Petersburg, Florida, February 22, 1983.
Bats Left. Throws Left. Height, 6 feet, 3 inches. Weight, 215 pounds.

Year	Club	Lea	Pos	G	AB	R	H	2B	3B	HR	RBI	SB	Avg
2001 Angels	. . . .	Arizona	1B	4	15	5	9	1	0	1	5	0	.600
2001 Provo	. . . .	Pioneer	1B	7	22	6	11	3	0	0	7	0	.500
2002 Cedar Rapids	. . . . . .	Midwest	1B	81	288	42	81	30	1	5	50	2	.281
2003 Angels	. . . .	Arizona	1B	7	27	5	9	1	0	2	6	0	.333
2003 Rancho Cucamonga	. . . .	Calif.	1B	57	206	42	72	12	0	8	28	2	.350
2004 Arkansas	. . . .	Texas	1B	28	114	19	42	11	0	3	18	0	.368
2004 Anaheim	. . . .	A.L.	1B	38	116	7	26	6	0	0	15	3	.224
2004 Salt Lake	. . . .	P.C.	1B	49	199	32	74	22	0	5	38	0	.372
2005 Salt Lake	. . . .	P.C.	1B	94	363	62	105	23	1	10	58	0	.289
2005 Los Angeles	. . . .	A.L.	1B	47	126	16	35	5	0	7	22	1	.278
2006 Salt Lake	. . . .	P.C.	1B	3	7	0	0	0	0	0	1	0	.000
2006 Los Angeles a	. . . .	A.L.	1B	29	79	6	12	2	0	1	6	0	.152
2007 Los Angeles	. . . .	A.L.	1B	137	443	64	131	37	3	11	68	2	.296
2008 Los Angeles	. . . .	A.L.	1B	100	373	47	107	24	0	12	54	2	.287
2008 Atlanta b	. . . .	N.L.	1B	43	152	18	36	4	1	2	20	0	.237
2009 Gwinnett	. . . .	Int.	1B	2	3	2	0	0	0	0	3	0	.000
2009 Atlanta	. . . .	N.L.	1B	87	298	28	84	20	0	6	41	0	.282
2009 Boston c-d-e	. . . .	A.L.	1B	39	87	9	19	3	0	1	7	1	.218
2010 Seattle f	. . . .	A.L.	1B	125	414	37	90	20	1	9	51	0	.217
2011 Durham	. . . .	Int.	1B	1	4	0	1	0	0	0	0	0	.250
2011 Tampa Bay g	. . . .	A.L.	1B	146	500	44	153	24	2	10	48	2	.306
Major League Totals	. . . .		8 Yrs.	791	2588	276	693	145	7	59	332	11	.268
Division Series													
2004 Anaheim	. . . .	A.L.	PH	2	1	0	0	0	0	0	0	0	.000
2005 Los Angeles	. . . .	A.L.	PH	2	2	0	0	0	0	0	0	0	.000
2007 Los Angeles	. . . .	A.L.	1B	2	5	1	0	0	0	0	0	0	.000
2009 Boston	. . . .	A.L.	1B	3	1	0	0	0	0	0	0	0	.000
2011 Tampa Bay	. . . .	A.L.	1B	4	16	1	4	1	0	0	2	0	.250
Division Series Totals	. . . .			13	25	2	4	1	0	0	2	0	.160
Championship Series													
2005 Los Angeles	. . . .	A.L.	DH	2	7	0	2	1	0	0	1	0	.286

a On disabled list from May 9 to October 2, 2006.
b Traded to Atlanta Braves with pitcher Steve Marek for infielder Mark Teixeira, July 29, 2008.
c On disabled list from June 1 to June 16, 2009.

d Traded to Boston Red Sox for infielder Adam LaRoche, July 31, 2009. Boston Red Sox received pitcher Miguel Celestino to complete trade, March 18, 2010.
e Traded to Seattle Mariners for infielder Bill Hall and cash, January 7, 2010.
f Filed for free agency, November 4, 2010. Signed with Tampa Bay Rays organization, January 28, 2011.
g Filed for free agency, October 30, 2011.

KOTSAY, MARK STEVEN
Born, Whittier, California, December 2, 1975.
Bats Left. Throws Left. Height, 6 feet. Weight, 205 pounds.

Year Club	Lea	Pos	G	AB	R	H	2B	3B	HR	RBI	SB	Avg
1996 Kane County	Midwest	OF	17	60	16	17	5	0	2	8	3	.283
1997 Florida	N.L.	OF	14	52	5	10	1	1	0	4	3	.192
1997 Portland	Eastern	OF	114	438	103	134	27	2	20	77	17	.306
1998 Florida	N.L.	OF-1B	154	578	72	161	25	7	11	68	10	.279
1999 Florida	N.L.	OF-1B	148	495	57	134	23	9	8	50	7	.271
2000 Florida	N.L.	OF-1B	152	530	87	158	31	5	12	57	19	.298
2001 San Diego a-b	N.L.	OF	119	406	67	118	29	1	10	58	13	.291
2002 San Diego	N.L.	OF	153	578	82	169	27	7	17	61	11	.292
2003 San Diego c-d	N.L.	OF	128	482	64	128	28	4	7	38	6	.266
2004 Oakland	A.L.	OF	148	606	78	190	37	3	15	63	8	.314
2005 Oakland	A.L.	OF	139	582	75	163	35	1	15	82	5	.280
2006 Oakland	A.L.	OF-1B	129	502	57	138	29	3	7	59	6	.275
2007 Sacramento	P.C.	OF	10	37	2	10	1	0	0	2	2	.270
2007 Oakland e-f	A.L.	OF	56	206	20	44	14	0	1	20	1	.214
2008 Mississippi	Southern	OF	5	18	4	6	1	0	0	1	0	.333
2008 Atlanta	N.L.	OF	88	318	39	92	17	3	6	37	2	.289
2008 Boston g-h-i	A.L.	OF-1B	22	84	6	19	8	1	0	12	0	.226
2009 Pawtucket	Int.	OF-1B	10	33	2	10	1	0	0	5	1	.303
2009 Boston-Chicago j-k	A.L.	1B-OF	67	187	16	52	9	0	4	23	3	.278
2010 Chicago l	A.L.	DH-1B-OF	107	327	30	78	17	2	8	31	1	.239
2011 Milwaukee m	N.L.	OF-1B	104	233	18	63	13	1	3	31	3	.270
Major League Totals	15 Yrs.		1728	6166	773	1717	343	48	124	694	98	.278
Division Series												
2006 Oakland	A.L.	OF	3	14	2	2	0	0	1	2	0	.143
2008 Boston	A.L.	1B	3	10	1	3	0	0	0	0	0	.300
2011 Milwaukee	N.L.	PH	4	3	1	0	0	0	0	0	0	.000
Division Series Totals			10	27	4	5	0	0	1	2	0	.185
Championship Series												
2006 Oakland	A.L.	OF	4	16	3	4	2	0	0	0	0	.250
2008 Boston	A.L.	1B	7	30	1	7	3	0	0	0	0	.233
2011 Milwaukee	N.L.	OF	5	9	1	1	0	0	1	1	0	.111
Championship Series Totals			16	55	5	12	5	0	1	1	0	.218

a Traded to San Diego Padres with outfielder Cesar Crespo for pitcher Matt Clement, pitcher Omar Ortiz and outfielder Eric Owens, March 28, 2001.
b On disabled list from April 16 to May 1, 2001.
c On disabled list from May 19 to June 5, 2003.
d Traded to Oakland Athletics for catcher Ramon Hernandez and outfielder Terrence Long, November 26, 2003.
e On disabled list from March 23 to June 1 and August 15 to October 8, 2007.
f Traded to Atlanta Braves for pitcher Joey Devine, pitcher Jamie Richmond and cash, January 14, 2008.
g On disabled list from May 26 to July 1, 2008.
h Traded to Boston Red Sox for outfielder Luis Sumoza, August 29, 2008.
i Filed for free agency, November 1, 2008, re-signed with Boston Red Sox, January 15, 2009.
j On disabled list from March 27 to June 2, 2009.
k Traded to Chicago White Sox for outfielder Brian Anderson, July 28, 2009.
l Filed for free agency, November 1, 2010. Signed with Milwaukee Brewers, February 4, 2011.
m Filed for free agency, October 30, 2011. Signed with San Diego Padres, November 16, 2011.

KOTTARAS, GEORGE
Born, Scarborough, Ontario, Canada, May 16, 1983.
Bats Left. Throws Right. Height, 6 feet. Weight, 185 pounds.

Year Club	Lea	Pos	G	AB	R	H	2B	3B	HR	RBI	SB	Avg
2003 Idaho Falls	Pioneer	C-1B	42	143	27	37	8	1	7	24	1	.259
2004 Fort Wayne	Midwest	C	78	271	40	84	18	1	7	46	0	.310
2005 Lake Elsinore	Calif.	C	91	337	54	102	29	0	9	50	2	.303
2005 Mobile	Southern	C	29	101	16	29	7	0	2	15	0	.287
2006 Portland	P.C.	C	33	119	14	25	10	1	2	17	0	.210
2006 Mobile a	Southern	C	78	257	40	71	19	1	8	33	0	.276
2007 Pawtucket	Int.	C	87	294	32	71	22	0	9	39	1	.241

Year Club	Lea	Pos	G	AB	R	H	2B	3B	HR	RBI	SB	Avg
2008 Pawtucket	Int.	C	107	395	63	96	18	0	22	65	0	.243
2008 Boston	A.L.	C	3	5	1	1	1	0	0	0	0	.200
2009 Pawtucket	Int.	C	10	24	1	7	3	0	0	0	0	.292
2009 Boston b-c	A.L.	C-3B	45	93	15	22	11	0	1	10	0	.237
2010 Milwaukee	N.L.	C-1B-OF	67	212	24	43	12	1	9	26	2	.203
2011 Nashville	P.C.	C	29	102	19	35	8	1	4	21	0	.343
2011 Milwaukee	N.L.	C	49	111	15	28	6	1	5	17	0	.252
Major League Totals		4 Yrs.	164	421	55	94	30	2	15	53	2	.223
Division Series												
2011 Milwaukee	N.L.	C	1	3	0	0	0	0	0	1	0	.000
Championship Series												
2011 Milwaukee	N.L.	C	2	5	0	0	0	0	0	1	0	.000

a Sent by San Diego Padres to Boston Red Sox as player to be named later for pitcher David Wells, September 5, 2006.
b On disabled list from July 30 to September 1, 2009.
c Claimed on waivers by Milwaukee Brewers, November 18, 2009.

KOUZMANOFF, KEVIN
Born, Newport Beach, California, July 25, 1981.
Bats Right. Throws Right. Height, 6 feet, 1 inch. Weight, 210 pounds.

Year Club	Lea	Pos	G	AB	R	H	2B	3B	HR	RBI	SB	Avg
2003 Mahoning Valley. .	N.Y.-Penn.	3B	54	206	31	56	8	1	8	33	2	.272
2004 Akron	Eastern	3B	7	24	3	5	1	1	1	6	0	.208
2004 Lake County	So.Atl.	3B	123	473	74	156	35	5	16	87	5	.330
2005 Kinston.	Carolina	3B	68	254	47	86	20	4	12	58	3	.339
2005 Mahoning Valley. .	N.Y.-Penn.	3B	3	7	0	1	0	0	0	0	0	.143
2006 Akron	Eastern	3B	67	244	46	95	19	1	15	55	2	.389
2006 Buffalo	Int.	3B-1B	27	102	22	36	9	0	7	20	2	.353
2006 Cleveland a.	A.L.	DH-3B	16	56	4	12	2	0	3	11	0	.214
2007 San Diego	N.L.	3B	145	484	57	133	30	2	18	74	1	.275
2008 San Diego	N.L.	3B	154	624	71	162	31	4	23	84	0	.260
2009 San Diego b	N.L.	3B	141	529	50	135	31	1	18	88	1	.255
2010 Oakland	A.L.	3B	143	551	59	136	32	1	16	71	2	.247
2011 Sacramento	P.C.	3B	61	262	41	79	24	1	13	58	1	.302
2011 Oakland	A.L.	3B	46	136	13	30	6	0	4	17	2	.221
2011 Colorado c-d	N.L.	3B	27	98	11	25	5	0	3	16	0	.255
Major League Totals		6 Yrs.	672	2478	265	633	137	8	85	361	6	.255

a Traded to San Diego Padres with pitcher Andrew Brown for infielder Josh Barfield, November 8, 2006.
b Traded to Oakland Athletics with infielder Eric Sogard for outfielders Scott Hairston and Aaron Cunningham, January 16, 2010.
c Sold to Colorado Rockies, August 23, 2011.
d Filed for free agency, October 5, 2011. Signed with Kansas City Royals organization, January 14, 2012.

KUBEL, JASON JAMES
Born, Belle Fourche, South Dakota, May 25, 1982.
Bats Left. Throws Right. Height, 5 feet, 11 inches. Weight, 200 pounds.

Year Club	Lea	Pos	G	AB	R	H	2B	3B	HR	RBI	SB	Avg
2000 Twins	Gulf Coast	OF	23	78	17	22	3	2	0	13	0	.282
2001 Twins	Gulf Coast	OF	37	124	14	41	10	4	1	30	3	.331
2002 Quad Cities	Midwest	OF	115	424	60	136	26	4	17	69	3	.321
2003 Fort Myers	Fla.St.	OF	116	420	56	125	20	4	5	82	4	.298
2004 New Britain	Eastern	OF	37	138	25	52	14	4	6	29	0	.377
2004 Rochester.	Int.	OF	90	350	71	120	28	0	16	71	16	.343
2004 Minnesota	A.L.	OF	23	60	10	18	2	0	2	7	1	.300
2005 Minnesota a	A.L.				INJURED—Did Not Play							
2006 Rochester.	Int.	OF	30	120	18	34	7	2	4	22	2	.283
2006 Minnesota	A.L.	OF	73	220	23	53	8	0	8	26	2	.241
2007 Minnesota	A.L.	OF	128	418	49	114	31	2	13	65	5	.273
2008 Minnesota	A.L.	DH-OF	141	463	74	126	22	5	20	78	0	.272
2009 Minnesota	A.L.	DH-OF	146	514	73	154	35	2	28	103	1	.300
2010 Minnesota	A.L.	OF	143	518	68	129	23	3	21	92	0	.249
2011 Fort Myers	Fla.St.	OF	2	3	0	0	0	0	0	1	0	.000
2011 Rochester.	Int.	OF	5	18	3	6	1	0	1	2	0	.333
2011 Minnesota b-c	A.L.	OF	99	366	37	100	21	1	12	58	1	.273
Major League Totals		7 Yrs.	753	2559	334	694	142	13	104	429	10	.271
Division Series												
2004 Minnesota	A.L.	DH	2	7	0	1	1	0	0	0	0	.143

Year Club	Lea	Pos	G	AB	R	H	2B	3B	HR	RBI	SB	Avg
2009 Minnesota	A.L.	OF-DH	3	14	0	1	0	0	0	0	0	.071
2010 Minnesota	A.L.	OF	3	8	0	0	0	0	0	0	0	.000
Division Series Totals			8	29	0	2	1	0	0	0	0	.069

a On disabled list from March 15 to October 14, 2005.
b On disabled list from May 31 to July 22, 2011.
c Filed for free agency, October 30, 2011. Signed with Arizona Diamondbacks, December 20, 2011.

LA HAIR, BRYAN ALLAN
Born, Worcester, Massachusetts, November 5, 1982.
Bats Left. Throws Right. Height, 6 feet, 5 inches. Weight, 240 pounds.

Year Club	Lea	Pos	G	AB	R	H	2B	3B	HR	RBI	SB	Avg
2003 Everett	Northwest	1B-OF	57	201	26	49	14	0	2	20	4	.244
2004 Everett	Northwest	1B	7	25	5	11	6	0	1	7	0	.440
2004 Wisconsin	Midwest	1B-OF	67	262	30	73	24	0	5	28	0	.279
2005 Inland Empire........	Calif.	1B	126	509	81	158	28	2	22	113	0	.310
2006 San Antonio	Texas	1B	60	222	22	65	12	0	6	30	0	.293
2006 Tacoma	P.C.	1B-OF	54	202	36	66	10	0	10	44	3	.327
2007 Tacoma	P.C.	1B	138	552	79	152	46	2	12	81	0	.275
2008 Tacoma	P.C.	1B-OF	86	316	39	83	26	1	12	53	1	.263
2008 Seattle	A.L.	1B	45	136	15	34	4	0	3	10	0	.250
2009 Tacoma	P.C.	OF-1B	121	457	72	132	28	2	26	85	0	.289
2010 Iowa a-b.............	P.C.	OF-1B	125	422	71	130	30	0	25	81	3	.308
2011 Iowa	P.C.	1B-OF	129	456	91	151	38	0	38	109	2	.331
2011 Chicago	N.L.	OF-1B	20	59	9	17	5	1	2	6	0	.288
Major League Totals	2 Yrs.		65	195	24	51	9	1	5	16	0	.262

a Filed for free agency, November 9, 2009. Signed with Chicago Cubs organization, January 10, 2010.
b Filed for free agency, November 6, 2010, re-signed with Chicago Cubs organization, November 18, 2010.

LA PORTA, MATTHEW VINCENT (MATT)
Born, Port Charlotte, Florida, January 8, 1985.
Bats Right. Throws Right. Height, 6 feet, 2 inches. Weight, 210 pounds.

Year Club	Lea	Pos	G	AB	R	H	2B	3B	HR	RBI	SB	Avg
2007 Helena	Pioneer	OF	7	27	4	7	1	0	2	4	0	.259
2007 West Virginia	So.Atl.	OF	23	88	18	28	8	0	10	27	0	.318
2008 Akron	Eastern	OF	17	60	6	14	1	0	2	8	0	.233
2008 Huntsville a	Southern	OF-1B	84	302	56	87	23	2	20	66	2	.288
2009 Columbus............	Int.	1B-OF	93	338	63	101	23	2	17	60	1	.299
2009 Cleveland	A.L.	OF-1B	52	181	29	46	13	0	7	21	2	.254
2010 Columbus............	Int.	OF-1B	18	69	7	25	4	0	5	16	0	.362
2010 Cleveland	A.L.	1B-OF	110	376	41	83	15	1	12	41	0	.221
2011 Columbus............	Int.	1B	2	9	2	4	0	0	1	3	0	.444
2011 Cleveland b	A.L.	1B	107	352	34	87	23	1	11	53	1	.247
Major League Totals	3 Yrs.	269	909	104	216	51	2	30	115	3	.238

a Traded by Milwaukee Brewers to Cleveland Indians with pitcher Zach Jackson, pitcher Rob Bryson and player to be named later for pitcher C.C. Sabathia, July 7, 2008. Cleveland Indians received outfielder Michael Brantley to complete trade, October 3, 2008.
b On disabled list from June 18 to July 6, 2011.

LA ROCHE, DAVID ADAM (ADAM)
Born, Orange Co., California, November 6, 1979.
Bats Left. Throws Left. Height, 6 feet, 3 inches. Weight, 200 pounds.

Year Club	Lea	Pos	G	AB	R	H	2B	3B	HR	RBI	SB	Avg
2000 Danville	Appal.	1B	56	201	38	62	13	3	7	45	4	.308
2001 Myrtle Beach	Carolina	1B-OF	126	471	49	118	31	0	7	47	10	.251
2002 Myrtle Beach	Carolina	1B	69	250	30	84	17	0	9	53	0	.336
2002 Greenville	Southern	1B	45	173	17	50	9	0	4	19	1	.289
2003 Greenville........	Southern	1B	61	219	42	62	12	1	12	37	1	.283
2003 Richmond	Int.	1B	72	264	33	78	21	0	8	35	1	.295
2004 Richmond	Int.	1B	4	11	1	2	0	0	1	2	0	.182
2004 Atlanta a............	N.L.	1B	110	324	45	90	27	1	13	45	0	.278
2005 Atlanta	N.L.	1B	141	451	53	117	28	0	20	78	0	.259
2006 Atlanta b............	N.L.	1B	149	492	89	140	38	1	32	90	0	.285
2007 Pittsburgh	N.L.	1B	152	563	71	153	42	0	21	88	1	.272
2008 Hickory.............	So.Atl.	1B	3	10	2	6	1	0	1	4	0	.600
2008 Pittsburgh c..........	N.L.	1B	136	492	66	133	32	3	25	85	1	.270
2009 Boston	A.L.	1B	6	19	2	5	2	0	1	3	0	.263

Year	Club	Lea	Pos	G	AB	R	H	2B	3B	HR	RBI	SB	Avg
2009 Pittsburgh-Atlanta d-e-f.	N.L.	1B	144	536	76	149	36	2	24	80	2	.278
2010 Arizona g	N.L.	1B	151	560	75	146	37	2	25	100	0	.261
2011 Washington h	N.L.	1B	43	151	15	26	4	0	3	15	1	.172
Major League Totals		8 Yrs.	1032	3588	492	959	246	9	164	584	5	.267
Division Series												
2004 Atlanta	N.L.	1B	5	17	1	4	1	0	1	4	0	.235
2005 Atlanta	N.L.	1B	3	8	2	4	1	0	1	6	0	.500
Division Series Totals			8	25	3	8	2	0	2	10	0	.320

a On disabled list from May 29 to July 2, 2004.
b Traded to Pittsburgh Pirates with outfielder Jamie Romak for pitcher Mike Gonzalez and infielder Brent Lillibridge, January 17, 2007.
c On disabled list from July 28 to August 14, 2008.
d Traded to Boston Red Sox for infielder Argenis Diaz and pitcher Hunter Strickland, July 22, 2009.
e Traded to Atlanta Braves for infielder Casey Kotchman, July 31, 2009.
f Filed for free agency, November 5, 2009. Signed with Arizona Diamondbacks, January 15, 2010.
g Filed for free agency, November 2, 2010. Signed with Washington Nationals, January 7, 2011.
h On disabled list from May 22 to October 31, 2011.

LAWRIE, BRETT R.
Born, Langley, British Columbia, Canada, January 18, 1990.
Bats Right. Throws Right. Height, 6 feet. Weight, 215 pounds.

Year	Club	Lea	Pos	G	AB	R	H	2B	3B	HR	RBI	SB	Avg
2009 Wisconsin	Midwest	2B	105	372	48	102	18	5	13	65	19	.274
2009 Huntsville	Southern	2B	13	52	6	14	0	1	0	0	0	.269
2010 Huntsville a	Southern	2B	135	554	90	158	36	16	8	63	30	.285
2011 Dunedin	Fla.St.	3B	4	8	0	1	0	0	0	1	0	.125
2011 Las Vegas	P.C.	3B	69	292	64	103	24	6	18	61	13	.353
2011 Toronto b	A.L.	3B	43	150	26	44	8	4	9	25	7	.293

a Traded by Milwaukee Brewers to Toronto Blue Jays for pitcher Shaun Marcum, December 6, 2010.
b On disabled list from September 22 to September 29, 2011.

LEE, CARLOS
Born, Aguadulce, Panama, June 20, 1976.
Bats Right. Throws Right. Height, 6 feet, 2 inches. Weight, 240 pounds.

Year	Club	Lea	Pos	G	AB	R	H	2B	3B	HR	RBI	SB	Avg
1994 White Sox	Gulf Coast	3B	29	56	6	7	1	0	0	1	0	.125
1995 Hickory	So.Atl.	3B-SS	63	218	18	54	9	1	4	30	1	.248
1995 Bristol	Appal.	3B-1B	67	269	43	93	17	1	7	45	17	.346
1996 Hickory	So.Atl.	3B-1B	119	480	65	150	23	6	8	70	18	.313
1997 Winston-Sal	Carolina	3B	139	546	81	173	50	4	17	82	11	.317
1998 Birmingham	Southern	3B	138	549	77	166	33	2	21	106	11	.302
1999 Charlotte	Int.	3B	25	94	16	33	5	0	4	20	2	.351
1999 Chicago	A.L.	OF-1B	127	492	66	144	32	2	16	84	4	.293
2000 Chicago	A.L.	OF	152	572	107	172	29	2	24	92	13	.301
2001 Chicago	A.L.	OF	150	558	75	150	33	3	24	84	17	.269
2002 Chicago	A.L.	OF	140	492	82	130	26	2	26	80	1	.264
2003 Chicago	A.L.	OF	158	623	100	181	35	1	31	113	18	.291
2004 Chicago a	A.L.	OF	153	591	103	180	37	0	31	99	11	.305
2005 Milwaukee	N.L.	OF	*162	618	85	164	41	0	32	114	13	.265
2006 Milwaukee	N.L.	OF	102	388	60	111	18	0	28	81	12	.286
2006 Texas b-c	A.L.	OF	59	236	42	76	19	1	9	35	7	.322
2007 Houston	N.L.	OF	*162	627	93	190	43	1	32	119	10	.303
2008 Houston d	N.L.	OF	115	436	61	137	27	0	28	100	4	.314
2009 Houston	N.L.	OF-1B	160	610	65	183	35	1	26	102	5	.300
2010 Houston	N.L.	OF-1B	157	605	67	149	29	1	24	89	3	.246
2011 Houston	N.L.	OF-1B	155	585	66	161	38	4	18	94	4	.275
Major League Totals		13 Yrs.	1952	7433	1072	2128	442	18	349	1286	122	.286
Division Series												
2000 Chicago	A.L.	OF	3	11	0	1	1	0	0	1	0	.091

a Traded to Milwaukee Brewers for outfielder Scott Podsednik, pitcher Luis Vizcaino and player to be named later, December 13, 2004. Chicago White Sox received infielder Travis Hinton to complete trade, January 10, 2005.
b Traded to Texas Rangers with outfielder Nelson Cruz for pitcher Francisco Cordero, outfielder Kevin Mench, outfielder Laynce Nix and pitcher Julian Cordero, July 28, 2006.
c Filed for free agency, October 30, 2006. Signed with Houston Astros, November 24, 2006.
d On disabled list from August 10 to September 30, 2008.

LEE, DERREK LEON

Born, Sacramento, California, September 6, 1975.
Bats Right. Throws Right. Height, 6 feet, 5 inches. Weight, 245 pounds.

Year Club	Lea	Pos	G	AB	R	H	2B	3B	HR	RBI	SB	Avg
1993 Padres .... Arizona		1B	15	52	11	17	1	1	2	5	4	.327
1993 Rancho Cucamonga.... Calif.		1B	20	73	13	20	5	1	1	10	0	.274
1994 Rancho Cucamonga.... Calif.		3B-1B	126	442	66	118	19	2	8	53	18	.267
1995 Rancho Cucamonga.... Calif.		1B	128	502	82	151	25	2	23	95	14	.301
1995 Memphis .... Southern		1B	2	9	0	1	0	0	0	1	0	.111
1996 Memphis .... Southern		1B-3B	134	500	98	140	39	2	34	104	13	.280
1997 Las Vegas........... .P.C.		1B	124	468	85	152	29	2	13	64	17	.325
1997 San Diego a .... N.L.		1B	22	54	9	14	3	0	1	4	0	.259
1998 Florida .... N.L.		1B	141	454	62	106	29	1	17	74	5	.233
1999 Calgary............... .P.C.		1B	89	339	60	96	20	1	19	73	3	.283
1999 Florida .... N.L.		1B	70	218	21	45	9	1	5	20	2	.206
2000 Florida .... N.L.		1B	158	477	70	134	18	3	28	70	0	.281
2001 Florida .... N.L.		1B	158	561	83	158	37	4	21	75	4	.282
2002 Florida .... N.L.		1B	*162	581	95	157	35	7	27	86	19	.270
2003 Florida b............. N.L.		1B	155	539	91	146	31	2	31	92	21	.271
2004 Chicago .... N.L.		1B	161	605	90	168	39	1	32	98	12	.278
2005 Chicago .... N.L.		1B	158	594	120	*199	*50	3	46	107	15	* .335
2006 Iowa................ .P.C.		1B	1	4	0	1	0	0	0	1	0	.250
2006 Chicago c............ N.L.		1B	50	175	30	50	9	0	8	30	8	.286
2007 Chicago .... N.L.		1B	150	567	91	180	43	1	22	82	6	.317
2008 Chicago .... N.L.		1B	155	623	93	181	41	3	20	90	8	.291
2009 Chicago .... N.L.		1B	141	532	91	163	36	2	35	111	1	.306
2010 Chicago-Atlanta d-e .... N.L.		1B	148	547	80	142	35	0	19	80	1	.260
2011 Bowie.............. Eastern		DH	1	3	0	2	0	0	0	0	0	.667
2011 Baltimore .... A.L.		1B	85	334	39	82	15	1	12	41	2	.246
2011 Pittsburgh f-g-h....... N.L.		1B	28	101	16	34	2	1	7	18	0	.337
Major League Totals	15 Yrs.		1942	6962	1081	1959	432	30	331	1078	104	.281
Division Series												
2003 Florida .... N.L.		1B	4	16	2	4	1	0	0	2	1	.250
2007 Chicago .... N.L.		1B	3	12	1	4	0	0	0	0	0	.333
2008 Chicago .... N.L.		1B	3	11	2	6	3	0	0	0	0	.545
2010 Atlanta .... N.L.		1B	4	16	2	2	0	0	0	0	0	.125
Division Series Totals			14	55	7	16	4	0	0	2	1	.291
Championship Series												
2003 Florida .... N.L.		1B	7	32	2	6	2	0	1	4	1	.188
World Series Record												
2003 Florida .... N.L.		1B	6	24	2	5	0	0	0	2	0	.208

a Traded to Florida Marlins with pitcher Rafael Medina and pitcher Steve Hoff for pitcher Kevin Brown, December 15, 1997.

b Traded to Chicago Cubs for infielder Hee Seop Choi and player to be named later, November 25, 2003. Florida Marlins received pitcher Mike Nannini to complete trade, December 15, 2003.

c On disabled list from April 20 to June 25 and July 24 to August 28, 2006.

d Traded to Atlanta Braves with cash for pitcher Tyrelle Harris, pitcher Robinson Lopez and pitcher Jeffrey Lorick, August 18, 2010.

e Filed for free agency, November 1, 2010. Signed with Baltimore Orioles, January 6, 2011.

f Traded to Pittsburgh Pirates for infielder Aaron Baker, July 31, 2011.

g On disabled list from May 17 to June 4 and August 10 to September 3, 2011.

h Filed for free agency, October 30, 2011.

LEWIS, FREDERICK DESHAUN (FRED)

Born, Hattiesburg, Mississippi, December 9, 1980.
Bats Left. Throws Right. Height, 6 feet, 2 inches. Weight, 190 pounds.

Year Club	Lea	Pos	G	AB	R	H	2B	3B	HR	RBI	SB	Avg
2002 Salem-Keizer .... Northwest		OF	58	239	43	77	9	3	1	23	9	.322
2003 Hagerstown .... So.Atl.		OF	114	420	61	105	17	8	1	27	30	.250
2004 San Jose .... .Calif.		OF	115	439	88	132	20	11	8	57	33	.301
2004 Fresno .... .P.C.		OF	6	23	3	7	1	0	1	2	1	.304
2005 Norwich .... Eastern		OF	137	512	79	140	28	7	7	47	30	.273
2006 Fresno .... .P.C.		OF	120	439	85	121	20	11	12	56	18	.276
2006 San Francisco .... N.L.		OF	13	11	5	5	1	0	0	2	0	.455
2007 Fresno .... .P.C.		OF	42	171	31	50	8	6	8	32	9	.292
2007 San Francisco a ...... N.L.		OF	58	157	34	45	6	2	3	19	5	.287
2008 San Francisco .... N.L.		OF	133	468	81	132	25	11	9	40	21	.282
2009 San Francisco .... N.L.		OF	122	295	49	76	21	3	4	20	8	.258
2010 Fresno .... .P.C.		OF	7	22	6	9	3	1	1	6	2	.409
2010 Toronto b-c-d......... A.L.		OF	110	428	70	112	31	5	8	36	17	.262

Year Club	Lea	Pos	G	AB	R	H	2B	3B	HR	RBI	SB	Avg
2011 Carolina	Southern	OF	7	23	3	6	3	0	0	1	1	.261
2011 Louisville	Int.	OF	8	20	6	6	1	1	1	3	1	.300
2011 Cincinnati e	N.L.	OF	81	183	20	42	7	0	3	19	2	.230
Major League Totals		6 Yrs.	517	1542	259	412	91	21	27	136	53	.267

a On disabled list from June 9 to June 30, 2007.
b On disabled list from March 27 to April 15, 2010.
c Sold to Toronto Blue Jays, April 16, 2010.
d Not offered contract, December 2, 2010. Signed with Cincinnati Reds, January 10, 2011.
e On disabled list from March 27 to May 4, 2011.

LILLIBRIDGE, BRENT STUART
Born, Everett, Washington, September 18, 1983.
Bats Right. Throws Right. Height, 5 feet, 11 inches. Weight, 190 pounds.

Year Club	Lea	Pos	G	AB	R	H	2B	3B	HR	RBI	SB	Avg
2005 Williamsport.	.N.Y.-Penn.	SS	42	169	19	41	12	4	4	18	10	.243
2006 Lynchburg	Carolina	SS	54	201	47	63	10	3	2	28	24	.313
2006 Hickory.	So.Atl.	SS-2B	74	274	59	82	18	5	11	43	29	.299
2007 Richmond	Int.	SS	87	321	47	92	14	2	10	41	28	.287
2007 Mississippi a . .	Southern	SS	52	204	31	56	8	3	3	17	14	.275
2008 Richmond	Int.	SS	90	355	46	78	18	7	4	39	23	.220
2008 Atlanta b.	N.L.	SS-3B	29	80	9	16	6	1	1	8	2	.200
2009 Charlotte	Int.	SS-OF-2B	67	246	34	62	9	4	3	24	17	.252
2009 Chicago	.A.L.	2B-OF-SS-3B	46	95	9	15	2	0	0	3	6	.158
2010 Charlotte	Int.	SS-2B-OF	48	185	26	50	8	0	4	16	19	.270
2010 Chicago	.A.L.	2B-OF-SS	64	98	19	22	5	2	2	16	5	.224
2011 Chicago c.	.A.L.	OF-1B-2B	97	186	38	48	5	1	13	29	10	.258
Major League Totals		4 Yrs.	236	459	75	101	18	4	16	56	23	.220

a Traded by Pittsburgh Pirates to Atlanta Braves with pitcher Mike Gonzalez for infielder Adam LaRoche and outfielder Jamie Romak, January 18, 2007.
b Traded to Chicago White Sox with catcher Tyler Flowers, infielder Jonathan Gilmore and pitcher Santos Rodriguez for pitcher Javier Vazquez and pitcher Boone Logan, December 4, 2008.
c On disabled list from September 9 to September 30, 2011.

LIND, ADAM ALAN
Born, Anderson, Indiana, July 17, 1983.
Bats Left. Throws Left. Height, 6 feet, 2 inches. Weight, 195 pounds.

Year Club	Lea	Pos	G	AB	R	H	2B	3B	HR	RBI	SB	Avg
2004 Auburn.	N.Y.-Penn.	OF	70	266	43	82	23	0	7	50	1	.308
2005 Dunedin	Fla.St.	OF	126	495	80	155	42	4	12	84	2	.313
2006 New Hampshire	Eastern	OF	91	348	43	108	24	0	19	71	2	.310
2006 Syracuse	Int.	OF	34	109	20	43	7	0	5	18	1	.394
2006 Toronto	A.L.	DH-OF	18	60	8	22	8	0	2	8	0	.367
2007 Syracuse	Int.	OF	46	174	20	52	8	2	6	28	0	.299
2007 Toronto	A.L.	OF	89	290	34	69	14	0	11	46	1	.238
2008 Syracuse	Int.	OF-1B	51	189	24	62	17	2	6	50	1	.328
2008 Toronto	A.L.	OF	88	326	48	92	16	4	9	40	2	.282
2009 Toronto	A.L.	DH-OF	151	587	93	179	46	0	35	114	1	.305
2010 Toronto	A.L.	DH-OF-1B	150	569	57	135	32	3	23	72	0	.237
2011 Dunedin	Fla.St.	1B	3	10	2	6	3	0	0	4	2	.600
2011 Toronto a	A.L.	1B	125	499	56	125	16	0	26	87	1	.251
Major League Totals		6 Yrs.	621	2331	296	622	132	7	106	367	5	.267

a On disabled list from May 8 to June 4, 2011.

LONEY, JAMES ANTHONY
Born, Houston, Texas, May 7, 1984.
Bats Left. Throws Left. Height, 6 feet, 3 inches. Weight, 220 pounds.

Year Club	Lea	Pos	G	AB	R	H	2B	3B	HR	RBI	SB	Avg
2002 Vero Beach.	Fla.St.	1B	17	67	6	20	6	0	0	5	0	.299
2002 Great Falls	Pioneer	1B	47	170	33	63	22	3	5	30	5	.371
2003 Vero Beach	Fla.St.	1B-OF	125	468	64	129	31	3	7	46	9	.276
2004 Jacksonville	Southern	1B	104	395	39	94	19	2	4	35	6	.238
2005 Jacksonville	Southern	1B-OF	138	504	74	143	31	2	11	65	1	.284
2006 Las Vegas	.P.C.	1B-OF	98	366	64	139	33	2	8	67	9	.380
2006 Los Angeles	N.L.	1B-OF	48	102	20	29	6	5	4	18	1	.284
2007 Las Vegas.	.P.C.	1B-OF	58	233	28	65	19	1	1	32	2	.279
2007 Los Angeles	N.L.	1B-OF	96	344	41	114	18	4	15	67	0	.331

Year	Club	Lea	Pos	G	AB	R	H	2B	3B	HR	RBI	SB	Avg
2008 Los Angeles	N.L.		1B	161	595	66	172	35	6	13	90	7	.289
2009 Los Angeles	N.L.		1B	158	576	73	162	25	2	13	90	7	.281
2010 Los Angeles	N.L.		1B	161	588	67	157	41	2	10	88	10	.267
2011 Los Angeles	N.L.		1B	158	531	56	153	30	1	12	65	4	.288
Major League Totals	6 Yrs.			782	2736	323	787	155	20	67	418	29	.288
Division Series													
2006 Los Angeles	N.L.		1B	1	4	0	3	0	0	0	3	0	.750
2008 Los Angeles	N.L.		1B	3	14	2	3	1	0	1	6	0	.214
2009 Los Angeles	N.L.		1B	3	12	0	3	0	0	0	0	0	.250
Division Series Totals				7	30	2	9	1	0	1	9	0	.300
Championship Series													
2008 Los Angeles	N.L.		1B	5	16	0	7	2	0	0	2	0	.438
2009 Los Angeles	N.L.		1B	5	17	3	6	0	0	2	3	0	.353
Championship Series Totals				10	33	3	13	2	0	2	5	0	.394

LONGORIA, EVAN MICHAEL
Born, Downey, California, October 7, 1985.
Bats Right. Throws Right. Height, 6 feet, 2 inches. Weight, 210 pounds.

Year	Club	Lea	Pos	G	AB	R	H	2B	3B	HR	RBI	SB	Avg
2006 Visalia	Calif.		3B	28	110	22	36	8	0	8	28	1	.327
2006 Hudson Valley	N.Y.-Penn.		3B	8	33	5	14	1	1	4	11	1	.424
2006 Montgomery	Southern		3B	26	105	14	28	5	0	6	19	2	.267
2007 Durham	Int.		3B	31	104	19	28	8	0	5	19	0	.269
2007 Montgomery	Southern		3B	105	381	78	117	21	0	21	76	4	.307
2008 Durham	Int.		3B	7	25	2	5	0	0	0	1	0	.200
2008 Tampa Bay a-b	A.L.		3B-SS	122	448	67	122	31	2	27	85	7	.272
2009 Tampa Bay	A.L.		3B	157	584	100	164	44	0	33	113	9	.281
2010 Tampa Bay	A.L.		3B	151	574	96	169	46	5	22	104	15	.294
2011 Montgomery	Southern		3B	4	15	5	4	0	0	3	3	0	.267
2011 Tampa Bay c	A.L.		3B	133	483	78	118	26	1	31	99	3	.244
Major League Totals	4 Yrs.			563	2089	341	573	147	8	113	401	34	.274
Division Series													
2008 Tampa Bay	A.L.		3B	4	15	2	4	0	0	2	3	1	.267
2010 Tampa Bay	A.L.		3B	5	20	2	4	2	0	1	2	0	.200
2011 Tampa Bay	A.L.		3B	4	16	2	3	0	0	1	3	0	.188
Division Series Totals				13	51	6	11	2	0	4	8	1	.216
Championship Series													
2008 Tampa Bay	A.L.		3B	7	27	8	7	3	0	4	8	0	.259
World Series Record													
2008 Tampa Bay	A.L.		3B	5	20	0	1	0	0	0	2	0	.050

a On disabled list from August 8 to September 6, 2008.
b Selected Rookie of the Year in American League for 2008.
c On disabled list from April 3 to May 3, 2011.

LOPEZ, JOSE CELESTINO
Born, Barcelona, Venezuela, November 24, 1983.
Bats Right. Throws Right. Height, 6 feet. Weight, 200 pounds.

Year	Club	Lea	Pos	G	AB	R	H	2B	3B	HR	RBI	SB	Avg
2001 Everett	Northwest		SS-2B	70	289	42	74	15	0	2	20	13	.256
2002 San Bernardino	Calif.		SS-2B	123	522	82	169	39	5	8	60	31	.324
2003 San Antonio	Texas		SS-2B-3B	132	538	82	139	35	2	13	69	18	.258
2004 Tacoma	P.C.		SS-3B-2B	74	275	40	81	19	0	13	39	5	.295
2004 Mariners	Arizona		3B-SS-2B	4	12	3	2	1	0	0	1	1	.167
2004 Seattle	A.L.		SS-3B	57	207	28	48	13	0	5	22	0	.232
2005 Tacoma	P.C.		2B	44	182	29	58	19	0	5	31	2	.319
2005 Seattle	A.L.		2B-3B	54	190	18	47	19	0	2	25	4	.247
2006 Seattle	A.L.		2B	151	603	78	170	28	8	10	79	5	.282
2007 Seattle	A.L.		2B-3B	149	524	58	132	17	2	11	62	2	.252
2008 Seattle	A.L.		2B-1B	159	644	80	191	41	1	17	89	6	.297
2009 Seattle	A.L.		2B-1B	153	613	69	167	42	0	25	96	3	.272
2010 Seattle a	A.L.		3B	150	593	49	142	29	0	10	58	3	.239
2011 New Orleans	P.C.		2B-1B-3B	32	125	24	50	9	0	9	30	2	.400
2011 Colorado-Florida b-c	N.L.		3B-2B-1B	82	231	23	50	12	0	8	21	2	.216
Major League Totals	8 Yrs.			955	3605	403	947	201	11	88	452	25	.263

a Traded to Colorado Rockies for pitcher Chaz Roe, December 2, 2010.
b Released by Colorado Rockies, June 7, 2011. Signed with Florida Marlins organization, June 9, 2011.
c Filed for free agency, October 30, 2011. Signed with Cleveland Indians organization, December 16, 2011.

LOWRIE, JED CARLSON

Born, Salem, Oregon, April 17, 1984.
Bats Both. Throws Right. Height, 6 feet. Weight, 180 pounds.

Year Club	Lea	Pos	G	AB	R	H	2B	3B	HR	RBI	SB	Avg
2005 Lowell ......N.Y.-Penn.		SS-2B	53	201	36	66	12	0	4	32	7	.328
2006 Wilmington ... Carolina		SS	97	374	43	98	21	6	3	50	2	.262
2007 Portland .... Eastern		SS-2B	93	337	61	100	31	7	8	49	5	.297
2007 Pawtucket .... Int.		SS-2B-3B	40	160	21	48	16	1	5	21	0	.300
2008 Pawtucket .... Int.		SS-2B-3B	53	198	35	53	14	2	5	32	1	.268
2008 Boston ...........A.L.		SS-3B-2B	81	260	34	67	25	3	2	46	1	.258
2009 Portland ...... Eastern		SS	1	5	1	3	1	0	0	2	0	.600
2009 Lowell ......N.Y.-Penn.		SS	3	11	2	2	2	0	0	1	0	.182
2009 Pawtucket .... Int.		SS	22	68	9	12	3	0	3	8	0	.176
2009 Boston ...........A.L.		SS-3B-2B	32	68	5	10	2	0	2	11	0	.147
2010 Lowell ......N.Y.-Penn.		SS	6	15	2	6	1	0	0	5	0	.400
2010 Pawtucket .... Int.		2B-3B-SS	4	15	3	5	3	0	1	4	1	.333
2010 Boston a..........A.L.		2B-SS-1B-3B	55	171	31	49	14	0	9	24	1	.287
2011 Pawtucket .... Int.		SS	5	17	2	7	4	0	0	5	0	.412
2011 Boston b-c.......A.L.		SS-3B-1B-2B	88	309	40	78	14	4	6	36	1	.252
Major League Totals		4 Yrs.	256	808	110	204	55	7	19	117	3	.252
Division Series												
2008 Boston ...........A.L.		SS-3B	3	11	2	4	0	0	0	1	0	.364
2009 Boston ...........A.L.		SS	3	2	0	0	0	0	0	0	0	.000
Division Series Totals			6	13	2	4	0	0	0	1	0	.308
Championship Series												
2008 Boston ...........A.L.		SS	6	18	2	2	1	0	0	1	0	.111

a On disabled list from March 26 to July 21, 2010.
b On disabled list from June 17 to August 8, 2011.
c Traded to Houston Astros with pitcher Kyle Weiland for pitcher Mark Melancon, December 14, 2011.

LUCROY, JONATHAN CHARLES

Born, Eustis, Pennsylvania, June 13, 1986.
Bats Right. Throws Right. Height, 6 feet. Weight, 195 pounds.

Year Club	Lea	Pos	G	AB	R	H	2B	3B	HR	RBI	SB	Avg
2007 Helena ....Pioneer		C	61	234	35	80	18	2	4	39	0	.342
2008 Brevard County ......Fla.St.		C	64	236	31	69	12	1	10	44	1	.292
2008 West Tenn .... So.Atl.		C	65	239	45	74	16	1	10	33	8	.310
2009 Huntsville........ Southern		C	125	419	61	112	32	2	9	66	1	.267
2010 Huntsville........ Southern		C	10	42	8	19	3	0	0	5	0	.452
2010 Nashville ............P.C.		C	21	80	8	19	4	0	2	11	0	.237
2010 Milwaukee ....,.N.L.		C	75	277	24	70	9	0	4	26	4	.253
2011 Huntsville........ Southern		C	4	11	3	3	1	0	0	4	1	.273
2011 Milwaukee a.......... N.L.		C	136	430	45	114	16	1	12	59	2	.265
Major League Totals		2 Yrs.	211	707	69	184	25	1	16	85	6	.260
Division Series												
2011 Milwaukee .... N.L.		C	4	15	1	3	0	0	0	2	0	.200
Championship Series												
2011 Milwaukee .... N.L.		C	6	17	2	5	1	0	1	3	0	.294

a On disabled list from March 22 to April 11, 2011.

LUDWICK, RYAN ANDREW

Born, Satellite Beach, Florida, July 13, 1978.
Bats Right. Throws Left. Height, 6 feet, 3 inches. Weight, 220 pounds.

Year Club	Lea	Pos	G	AB	R	H	2B	3B	HR	RBI	SB	Avg
1999 Modesto............Calif.		OF	43	171	28	47	11	3	4	34	2	.275
2000 Modesto............Calif.		OF	129	493	86	130	26	3	29	102	10	.264
2001 Sacramento ..........P.C.		OF	17	57	10	13	3	0	1	7	2	.228
2001 Midland ....Texas		OF	119	443	82	119	23	3	25	96	9	.269
2002 Oklahoma.............P.C.		OF	78	305	62	87	27	4	15	52	2	.285
2002 Texas a.............A.L.		OF	23	81	10	19	6	0	1	9	2	.235
2003 Oklahoma.............P.C.		OF	81	317	51	96	24	3	17	63	1	.303
2003 Texas-Cleveland b-c.... A.L.		OF	47	162	17	40	8	1	7	26	2	.247
2004 Akron............Eastern		OF	8	26	4	7	2	0	1	5	0	.269
2004 Buffalo ....Int.		OF	44	166	25	45	15	0	8	30	0	.271
2004 Cleveland d .........A.L.		OF	15	50	3	11	2	0	2	4	0	.220
2005 Cleveland ...........A.L.		OF	19	41	8	9	0	0	4	5	0	.220
2005 Buffalo ....Int.		OF	54	188	27	36	10	2	4	16	0	.191
2006 Toledo e-f..........Int.		OF	134	508	81	135	34	2	28	80	2	.266

Year Club	Lea	Pos	G	AB	R	H	2B	3B	HR	RBI	SB	Avg
2007 Memphis ...........P.C.		OF	29	106	27	36	8	0	8	36	1	.340
2007 St. Louis............. N.L.		OF	120	303	42	81	22	0	14	52	4	.267
2008 St. Louis............. N.L.		OF	152	538	104	161	40	3	37	113	4	.299
2009 St. Louis g .... N.L.		OF	139	486	63	129	20	1	22	97	4	.265
2010 Memphis ...........P.C.		OF	3	9	2	3	1	0	2	5	0	.333
2010 St. Louis-San Diego h-i . N.L.		OF	136	490	63	123	27	2	17	69	0	.251
2011 Indianapolis .... Int.		OF	4	13	3	5	1	0	1	5	0	.385
2011 San Diego-Pittsburgh j-k-l . N.L.		OF	139	490	56	116	23	0	13	75	1	.237
Major League Totals .... 9 Yrs.			790	2641	366	689	148	7	117	450	17	.261
Division Series												
2009 St. Louis............. N.L.		OF	3	12	1	4	0	0	0	1	0	.333

a Traded to Texas Rangers by Oakland Athletics with pitcher Mario Ramos, infielder Jason Hart and catcher Gerald Laird for pitcher Mike Venafro and infielder Carlos Pena, January 14, 2002.
b Traded to Cleveland Indians for outfielder Shane Spencer and pitcher Ricardo Rodriguez, July 18, 2003.
c On disabled list from September 9 to October 28, 2003.
d On disabled list from April 2 to July 5, 2004.
e Filed for free agency, October 28, 2005. Signed with Detroit Tigers organization, January 4, 2006.
f Filed for free agency, October 15, 2006. Signed with St. Louis Cardinals organization, December 1, 2006.
g On disabled list from May 13 to May 29, 2009.
h On disabled list from June 26 to July 24, 2010.
i Traded to San Diego Padres for pitcher Nick Greenwood and pitcher Corey Kluber, July 31, 2010.
j Traded to Pittsburgh Pirates for player to be named later, July 31, 2011.
k On disabled list from August 23 to September 7, 2011.
l Filed for free agency, October 30, 2011. Signed with Cincinnati Reds, January 17, 2012.

MARKAKIS, NICHOLAS WILLIAM (NICK)
Born, Woodstock, Georgia, November 17, 1983.
Bats Left. Throws Left. Height, 6 feet, 2 inches. Weight, 195 pounds.

Year Club	Lea	Pos	G	AB	R	H	2B	3B	HR	RBI	SB	Avg
2003 Aberdeen .... N.Y.-Penn.		OF	59	205	22	58	14	3	1	28	13	.283
2004 Delmarva .... So.Atl.		OF	96	355	57	106	22	3	11	64	12	.299
2005 Frederick .... Carolina		OF	91	350	59	105	25	1	12	62	2	.300
2005 Bowie.............Eastern		OF	33	124	19	42	16	2	3	30	0	.339
2006 Baltimore .... A.L.		OF	147	491	72	143	25	2	16	62	2	.291
2007 Baltimore .... A.L.		OF	161	637	97	191	43	3	23	112	18	.300
2008 Baltimore .... A.L.		OF	157	595	106	182	48	1	20	87	10	.306
2009 Baltimore .... A.L.		OF	*161	642	94	188	45	2	18	101	6	.293
2010 Baltimore .... A.L.		OF	160	629	79	187	45	3	12	60	7	.297
2011 Baltimore .... A.L.		OF-1B	160	641	72	182	31	1	15	73	12	.284
Major League Totals .... 6 Yrs.			946	3635	520	1073	237	12	104	495	55	.295

MARSON, LOUIS GLENN (LOU)
Born, Scottsdale, Arizona, June 26, 1986.
Bats Right. Throws Right. Height, 6 feet, 1 inch. Weight, 200 pounds.

Year Club	Lea	Pos	G	AB	R	H	2B	3B	HR	RBI	SB	Avg
2004 Phillies .... Gulf Coast		C	38	113	18	29	3	0	4	8	4	.257
2005 Batavia .... N.Y.-Penn.		C	60	220	25	54	11	3	5	25	0	.245
2006 Lakewood.......... So.Atl.		C	104	350	44	85	16	5	4	39	4	.243
2007 Clearwater .... Fla.St.		C	111	393	68	113	24	1	7	63	3	.288
2008 Reading ....Eastern		C	94	322	55	101	18	0	5	46	3	.314
2008 Philadelphia .... N.L.		C	1	4	2	2	0	0	1	2	0	.500
2009 Philadelphia .... N.L.		C	7	17	3	4	1	0	0	0	0	.235
2009 Lehigh Valley .... Int.		C	63	211	32	62	13	0	1	24	3	.294
2009 Columbus............. Int.		C	28	103	10	25	5	1	1	9	1	.243
2009 Cleveland a........... A.L.		C	14	44	6	11	6	0	0	4	0	.250
2010 Columbus............. Int.		C	37	124	19	25	7	1	4	14	5	.202
2010 Cleveland .... A.L.		C	87	262	29	51	15	0	3	22	8	.195
2011 Cleveland .... A.L.		C	79	243	26	56	9	2	1	19	4	.230
Major League Totals .... 4 Yrs.			188	570	66	124	31	2	5	47	12	.218

a Traded to Cleveland Indians with pitcher Jason Knapp, infielder Jason Donald and pitcher Carlos Carrasco for pitcher Cliff Lee and outfielder Ben Francisco, July 29, 2009.

MARTIN, RUSSELL NATHAN

Born, East York, Ontario, Canada, February 15, 1983.
Bats Right. Throws Right. Height, 5 feet, 10 inches. Weight, 210 pounds.

Year Club	Lea	Pos	G	AB	R	H	2B	3B	HR	RBI	SB	Avg
2002 Dodgers	Gulf Coast	3B-SS	41	126	22	36	3	3	0	10	7	.286
2003 Ogden	Pioneer	C	52	188	25	51	13	0	6	36	3	.271
2003 South Bend	So.Atl.	C-OF-3B	25	98	15	28	4	1	3	14	5	.286
2004 Vero Beach	Fla.St.	C	122	416	74	104	24	1	15	64	9	.250
2005 Jacksonville	Southern	C-OF	129	409	83	127	17	1	9	61	15	.311
2006 Las Vegas	P.C.	C	23	74	14	22	9	0	0	9	0	.297
2006 Los Angeles	N.L.	C	121	415	65	117	26	4	10	65	10	.282
2007 Los Angeles	N.L.	C	151	540	87	158	32	3	19	87	21	.293
2008 Los Angeles	N.L.	C-3B	155	553	87	155	25	0	13	69	18	.280
2009 Los Angeles	N.L.	C-3B	143	505	63	126	19	0	7	53	11	.250
2010 Los Angeles a-b	N.L.	C	97	331	45	82	13	0	5	26	6	.248
2011 New York	A.L.	C-3B-2B	125	417	57	99	17	0	18	65	8	.237
Major League Totals	6 Yrs.		792	2761	404	737	132	7	72	365	74	.267
Division Series												
2006 Los Angeles	N.L.	C	3	12	2	4	0	0	0	0	0	.333
2008 Los Angeles	N.L.	C	3	13	2	4	3	0	1	5	0	.308
2009 Los Angeles	N.L.	C	3	9	0	1	0	0	0	1	0	.111
2011 New York	A.L.	C	5	17	3	3	1	0	0	0	0	.176
Division Series Totals			14	51	7	12	4	0	1	6	0	.235
Championship Series												
2008 Los Angeles	N.L.	C	5	17	3	2	0	0	0	1	1	.118
2009 Los Angeles	N.L.	C	5	16	2	4	1	0	0	2	0	.250
Championship Series Totals			10	33	5	6	1	0	0	3	1	.182

a On disabled list from August 4 to November 2, 2010.

b Not offered contract, December 2, 2010. Signed with New York Yankees, December 16, 2010.

MARTINEZ, JULIO DANIEL (J.D.)

Born, Miami, Florida, August 21, 1987.
Bats Right. Throws Right. Height, 6 feet, 3 inches. Weight, 200 pounds.

Year Club	Lea	Pos	G	AB	R	H	2B	3B	HR	RBI	SB	Avg
2009 Greeneville	Appal.	OF-1B	19	77	17	31	9	1	5	23	0	.403
2009 Tri-City	N.Y.-Penn.	OF-1B	53	187	25	61	15	2	7	33	1	.326
2010 Lexington	So.Atl.	OF	88	348	83	126	31	3	15	64	3	.362
2010 Corpus Christi	Texas	OF	50	189	24	57	9	1	3	25	2	.302
2011 Corpus Christi	Texas	OF	88	317	50	107	25	1	13	72	1	.338
2011 Houston	N.L.	OF	53	208	29	57	13	0	6	35	0	.274

MARTINEZ, MICHAEL GABRIEL

Born, Santo Domingo, Dominican Republic, September 16, 1982.
Bats Both. Throws Right. Height, 5 feet, 9 inches. Weight, 145 pounds.

Year Club	Lea	Pos	G	AB	R	H	2B	3B	HR	RBI	SB	Avg
2006 Savannah	So.Atl.	SS	30	87	9	15	0	0	0	4	4	.172
2006 Potomac	Carolina	2B	7	23	1	5	2	0	0	2	1	.217
2006 Vermont	N.Y.-Penn.	2B-SS-3B	45	159	26	51	5	2	1	19	6	.321
2007 Hagerstown	So.Atl.	SS-2B-3B	115	404	54	101	21	5	0	32	13	.250
2008 Potomac	Carolina	2B-SS	104	417	63	111	25	6	3	58	25	.266
2009 Harrisburg	Eastern	2B-SS	65	188	22	42	7	2	1	8	0	.223
2009 Potomac	Carolina	2B-SS	49	198	40	58	14	5	4	29	10	.293
2010 Harrisburg	Eastern	2B-OF-SS	100	359	41	91	14	6	8	37	15	.253
2010 Syracuse	Int.	OF-2B-3B	33	126	16	41	7	0	3	19	8	.325
2011 Philadelphia	N.L.	3B-2B-OF-SS	88	209	25	41	5	2	3	24	3	.196
Division Series												
2011 Philadelphia	N.L.	PH	2	0	1	0	0	0	0	0	0	.000

MARTINEZ, VICTOR JESUS

Born, Ciudad Bolivar, Venezuela, December 23, 1978.
Bats Both. Throws Right. Height, 6 feet, 2 inches. Weight, 210 pounds.

Year Club	Lea	Pos	G	AB	R	H	2B	3B	HR	RBI	SB	Avg
1997 Maracay-1	Venezuelan	C	53	122	21	42	12	0	0	26	6	.344
1998 Guacara-2	Venezuelan	C	55	160	28	43	13	0	1	27	8	.269
1999 Mahoning Valley	N.Y.-Penn.	C	64	235	37	65	9	0	4	36	0	.277
2000 Kinston	Carolina	C	26	83	9	18	7	0	0	8	1	.217

Year	Club	Lea	Pos	G	AB	R	H	2B	3B	HR	RBI	SB	Avg
2000 Columbus a	So.Atl.	C	21	70	11	26	9	1	2	12	0	.371
2001 Kinston	Carolina	C	114	420	59	138	33	2	10	57	3	.329
2002 Akron	Eastern	C	121	443	84	149	40	0	22	85	3	.336
2002 Cleveland	A.L.	C	12	32	2	9	1	0	1	5	0	.281
2003 Buffalo	Int.	C-1B	73	274	42	90	19	0	7	45	3	.328
2003 Akron	Eastern	C	3	12	1	4	2	0	0	2	0	.333
2003 Cleveland b	A.L.	C	49	159	15	46	4	0	1	16	1	.289
2004 Cleveland	A.L.	C	141	520	77	147	38	1	23	108	0	.283
2005 Cleveland	A.L.	C	147	547	73	167	33	0	20	80	0	.305
2006 Cleveland	A.L.	C-1B	153	572	82	181	37	0	16	93	0	.316
2007 Cleveland	A.L.	C-1B	147	562	78	169	40	0	25	114	0	.301
2008 Akron	Eastern	DH	2	6	1	2	0	0	1	1	0	.333
2008 Buffalo	Int.	C	6	20	2	6	2	0	0	2	0	.300
2008 Cleveland c	A.L.	C-1B	73	266	30	74	17	0	2	35	0	.278
2009 Cleveland-Boston d	A.L.	C-1B	155	588	88	178	33	1	23	108	1	.303
2010 Boston e-f	A.L.	C-1B	127	493	64	149	32	1	20	79	1	.302
2011 Toledo	Int.	DH	2	6	1	3	1	0	0	2	0	.500
2011 Detroit g	A.L.	DH-C-1B	145	540	76	178	40	0	12	103	1	.330
Major League Totals	10 Yrs.		1149	4279	585	1298	275	3	143	741	4	.303
Division Series												
2007 Cleveland	A.L.	C-1B	4	17	2	6	1	0	1	4	0	.353
2009 Boston	A.L.	C	3	11	0	2	0	0	0	2	0	.182
2011 Detroit	A.L.	DH	5	18	1	4	0	0	1	3	0	.222
Division Series Totals			12	46	3	12	1	0	2	9	0	.261
Championship Series												
2007 Cleveland	A.L.	C-1B	7	27	4	8	1	0	1	3	0	.296
2011 Detroit	A.L.	DH	6	22	3	6	0	1	1	2	0	.273
Championship Series Totals			13	49	7	14	1	1	2	5	0	.286

a On minor league disabled list from May 25 to July 19, 2000.

b On disabled list from August 9 to September 2, 2003.

c On disabled list from June 12 to August 29, 2008.

d Traded to Boston Red Sox for pitcher Justin Masterson, pitcher Nick Hagadone and pitcher Bryan Price, July 31, 2009.

e On disabled list from June 28 to July 26, 2010.

f Filed for free agency, November 1, 2010. Signed with Detroit Tigers, November 26, 2010.

g On disabled list from April 19 to May 4, 2011.

MATHIS, JEFFERY STEPHEN (JEFF)
Born, Marianna, Florida, March 31, 1983.
Bats Right. Throws Right. Height, 6 feet. Weight, 180 pounds.

Year	Club	Lea	Pos	G	AB	R	H	2B	3B	HR	RBI	SB	Avg
2001 Angels	Arizona	C-OF	7	23	1	7	1	0	0	3	0	.304
2001 Provo	Pioneer	C	22	77	14	23	6	3	0	18	1	.299
2002 Cedar Rapids	Midwest	C	128	491	75	141	41	3	10	73	7	.287
2003 Rancho Cucamonga	Calif.	C	98	378	74	122	28	3	11	54	5	.323
2003 Arkansas	Texas	C	24	95	19	27	11	0	2	14	1	.284
2004 Arkansas	Texas	C	117	432	57	98	24	3	14	55	2	.227
2005 Salt Lake	P.C.	C	112	427	78	118	26	3	21	73	4	.276
2005 Los Angeles	A.L.	C	5	3	1	1	0	0	0	0	0	.333
2006 Salt Lake	P.C.	C	99	384	57	111	33	3	5	45	3	.289
2006 Los Angeles	A.L.	C	23	55	9	8	2	0	2	6	0	.145
2007 Salt Lake	P.C.	C	66	250	39	61	14	2	5	26	3	.244
2007 Los Angeles	A.L.	C	59	171	24	36	12	0	4	23	0	.211
2008 Los Angeles	A.L.	C	94	283	35	55	8	0	9	42	2	.194
2009 Los Angeles	A.L.	C	84	237	26	50	8	0	5	28	2	.211
2010 Salt Lake	P.C.	C	9	33	6	8	1	1	1	5	0	.242
2010 Los Angeles a	A.L.	C	68	205	19	40	6	1	3	18	3	.195
2011 Los Angeles b	A.L.	C	93	247	18	43	12	0	3	22	1	.174
Major League Totals	7 Yrs.		426	1201	132	233	48	1	26	139	8	.194
Division Series												
2007 Los Angeles	A.L.	C	2	3	0	0	0	0	0	1	0	.000
2008 Los Angeles	A.L.	C	1	2	0	1	0	0	0	0	0	.500
2009 Los Angeles	A.L.	C	2	3	0	1	0	0	0	0	0	.333
Division Series Totals			5	8	0	2	0	0	0	1	0	.250
Championship Series												
2009 Los Angeles	A.L.	C	5	12	2	7	5	0	0	1	0	.583

a On disabled list from April 20 to June 17, 2010.

b Traded to Toronto Blue Jays for pitcher Brad Mills, December 3, 2011.

MATSUI, HIDEKI

Born: Ishikawa, Japan June 12, 1974
Bats Left, Throws Right, Height 6 feet two inches, Weight 230 pounds

Year	Club	Lea	Pos	G	AB	R	H	2B	3B	HR	RBI	SB	Avg
1993 Yomiuri Giants....	Japan Cent.	OF	57	184	27	41	9	0	11	27	1	.223
1994 Yomiuri Giants....	Japan Cent.	OF	130	503	70	148	23	4	20	66	6	.294
1995 Yomiuri Giants....	Japan Cent.	OF	131	501	76	142	31	1	22	80	9	.283
1996 Yomiuri Giants....	Japan Cent.	OF	130	487	97	153	34	1	38	99	7	.314
1997 Yomiuri Giants....	Japan Cent.	OF	135	484	93	144	18	0	37	103	9	.298
1998 Yomiuri Giants....	Japan Cent.	OF	135	487	103	142	24	3	34	100	3	.292
1999 Yomiuri Giants....	Japan Cent.	OF	135	471	100	143	24	2	42	95	0	.304
2000 Yomiuri Giants....	Japan Cent.	OF	135	474	116	150	32	1	42	108	5	.316
2001 Yomiuri Giants....	Japan Cent.	OF	140	481	107	160	23	3	36	104	3	.333
2002 Yomiuri Giants a	Japan Cent.	OF	140	500	112	167	27	1	50	107	3	.334
Japan Central Totals	10 years	1268	4572	901	1390	245	16	332	889	46	.304		
2003 New York	A.L.	OF	*163	623	82	179	42	1	16	106	2	.287
2004 New York	A.L.	OF	*162	584	109	174	34	2	31	108	3	.298
2005 New York	A.L.	OF	*162	629	108	192	45	3	23	116	2	.305
2006 New York b...........	A.L.	OF	51	172	32	52	9	0	8	29	1	.302
2007 Tampa	Fla.St.	OF	2	6	1	2	0	0	0	0	0	.333
2007 New York c...........	A.L.	OF	143	547	100	156	28	4	25	103	4	.285
2008 Tampa	Fla.St.	DH	3	8	1	2	0	0	1	1	0	.250
2008 New York d...........	A.L.	DH-OF	93	337	43	99	17	0	9	45	0	.294
2009 New York e...........	A.L.	DH	142	456	62	125	21	1	28	90	0	.274
2010 Los Angeles f...........	A.L.	DH-OF	145	482	55	132	24	1	21	84	0	.274
2011 Oakland g...........	A.L.	DH-OF	141	517	58	130	28	0	12	72	1	.251
Major League Totals	9 Yrs.	1202	4347	649	1239	248	12	173	753	13	.285		
Division Series													
2003 New York	A.L.	OF	4	15	2	4	1	0	1	3	0	.267
2004 New York	A.L.	OF	4	17	3	7	1	0	1	3	0	.412
2005 New York	A.L.	OF	5	20	4	4	1	0	1	1	0	.200
2006 New York	A.L.	OF-DH	4	16	1	4	1	0	0	1	0	.250
2007 New York	A.L.	DH	4	11	4	2	0	0	0	0	0	.182
2009 New York	A.L.	DH	3	9	1	2	0	0	1	2	0	.222
Division Series Totals		24	88	15	23	4	0	4	10	0	.261		
Championship Series													
2003 New York	A.L.	OF	7	26	3	8	3	0	0	4	0	.308
2004 New York	A.L.	OF	7	34	9	14	6	1	2	10	0	.412
2009 New York	A.L.	DH	6	21	1	5	1	0	0	3	0	.238
Championship Series Totals		20	81	13	27	10	1	2	17	0	.333		
World Series Record													
2003 New York	A.L.	OF	6	23	1	6	0	0	1	4	0	.261
2009 New York	A.L.	DH	6	13	3	8	1	0	3	8	0	.615
World Series Totals		12	36	4	14	1	0	4	12	0	.389		

a Reached agreement with New York Yankees on three year contract, December 19, 2002.
b On disabled list from May 12 to September 12, 2006.
c On disabled list from April 8 to April 23, 2007.
d On disabled list from June 23 to August 19 and September 22 to November 14, 2008.
e Filed for free agency, November 9, 2009. Signed with Los Angeles Angels, December 16, 2009.
f Filed for free agency, November 1, 2010. Signed with Oakland Athletics, December 14, 2010.
g Filed for free agency, October 30, 2011.

MAUER, JOSEPH PATRICK (JOE)

Born, St. Paul, Minnesota, April 19, 1983
Bats Left. Throws Right. Height, 6 feet, 4 inches. Weight, 220 pounds.

Year	Club	Lea	Pos	G	AB	R	H	2B	3B	HR	RBI	SB	Avg
2001 Elizabethton	Appal.	C	32	110	14	44	6	2	0	14	4	.400
2002 Quad Cities........	Midwest	C-1B	110	411	58	124	23	1	4	62	0	.302
2003 Fort Myers	Fla.St.	C-1B	62	233	25	78	13	1	1	44	3	.335
2003 New Britain	Eastern	C	73	276	48	94	17	1	4	41	0	.341
2004 Fort Myers	Fla.St.	C	2	6	0	4	0	0	0	2	0	.667
2004 Rochester............	Int.	C	5	19	1	6	3	0	0	2	0	.316
2004 Minnesota a..........	A.L.	C	35	107	18	33	8	1	6	17	1	.308
2005 Minnesota	A.L.	C	131	489	61	144	26	2	9	55	13	.294
2006 Minnesota	A.L.	C	140	521	86	181	36	4	13	84	8	*.347
2007 Fort Myers	Fla.St.	C	1	3	0	0	0	0	0	0	0	.000
2007 Minnesota b..........	A.L.	C	109	406	62	119	27	3	7	60	7	.293
2008 Minnesota	A.L.	C	146	536	98	176	31	4	9	85	1	*.328

Year	Club	Lea	Pos	G	AB	R	H	2B	3B	HR	RBI	SB	Avg
2009 Fort Myers . . . . .Fla.St.			C	5	15	2	6	2	0	0	4	0	.400
2009 Minnesota c-d . . . . A.L.			C	138	523	94	191	30	1	28	96	4	*.365
2010 Minnesota . . . . .A.L.			C	137	510	88	167	43	1	9	75	1	.327
2011 Fort Myers . . . . .Fla.St.			C	7	23	3	6	2	0	1	6	0	.261
2011 Minnesota e . . . . A.L.			C-1B-OF	82	296	38	85	15	0	3	30	0	.287
Major League Totals			8 Yrs.	918	3388	545	1096	216	16	84	502	35	.323
Division Series													
2006 Minnesota . . . . .A.L.			C	3	11	0	2	0	0	0	0	0	.182
2009 Minnesota . . . . .A.L.			C	3	12	1	5	1	0	0	1	0	.417
2010 Minnesota . . . . .A.L.			C	3	12	0	3	0	0	0	0	0	.250
Division Series Totals				9	35	1	10	1	0	0	1	0	.286

a On disabled list from April 7 to June 2 and from July 16 to October 11, 2004.
b On disabled list from May 5 to June 8, 2007.
c On disabled list from March 27 to May 1, 2009.
d Selected Most Valuable Player in American League for 2009.
e On disabled list from April 13 to June 17 and September 15 to October 3, 2011.

MAYBERRY, JOHN CLAIBORN JR.

Born, Kansas City, Missouri, December 21, 1983.
Bats Right. Throws Right. Height, 6 feet, 6 inches. Weight, 230 pounds.

Year	Club	Lea	Pos	G	AB	R	H	2B	3B	HR	RBI	SB	Avg
2005 Spokane	Northwest		OF	71	265	51	67	16	0	11	26	7	.253
2006 Clinton	Midwest		OF	126	459	77	123	26	4	21	77	9	.268
2007 Bakersfield . . . . .Calif.			OF	63	244	47	56	15	1	16	45	9	.230
2007 Frisco	Texas		OF	69	245	35	59	10	0	14	38	7	.241
2008 Frisco a	Texas		OF	21	82	16	22	8	0	4	13	4	.268
2008 Oklahoma . . . . .P.C.			OF-1B	114	437	49	115	30	7	16	58	6	.263
2009 Lehigh Valley . . . . Int.			OF	89	316	44	81	20	2	13	43	6	.256
2009 Philadelphia . . . . N.L.			OF	39	57	8	12	3	0	4	8	0	.211
2010 Lehigh Valley . . . . Int.			OF	128	495	75	132	25	1	15	65	20	.267
2010 Philadelphia . . . . N.L.			OF	11	12	4	4	0	0	2	6	0	.333
2011 Lehigh Valley . . . . Int.			OF-1B	28	113	16	30	8	0	4	15	2	.265
2011 Philadelphia . . . . N.L.			OF-1B	104	267	37	73	17	1	15	49	8	.273
Major League Totals			3 Yrs.	154	336	49	89	20	1	21	63	8	.265
Division Series													
2011 Philadelphia . . . . N.L.			OF	2	4	0	0	0	0	0	0	0	.000

a Traded by Texas Rangers to Philadelphia Phillies for outfielder Greg Golson, November 20, 2008.

MAYBIN, CAMERON KEITH

Born, Asheville, North Carolina, April 4, 1987.
Bats Right. Throws Right. Height, 6 feet, 4 inches. Weight, 205 pounds.

Year	Club	Lea	Pos	G	AB	R	H	2B	3B	HR	RBI	SB	Avg
2006 West Michigan . . . . . Midwest			OF	101	385	59	117	20	6	9	69	27	.304
2007 Tigers . . . . Gulf Coast			OF	2	7	1	4	0	0	0	1	0	.571
2007 Lakeland . . . . .Fla.St.			OF	83	296	58	90	14	5	10	44	25	.304
2007 Erie . . . . Eastern			OF	6	20	9	8	1	0	4	8	0	.400
2007 Detroit a . . . . A.L.			OF	24	49	8	7	3	0	1	2	5	.143
2008 Carolina . . . . Southern			OF	108	390	73	108	15	8	13	49	21	.277
2008 Florida . . . . N.L.			OF	8	32	9	16	2	0	0	2	4	.500
2009 New Orleans . . . . .P.C.			OF	82	298	44	95	18	8	3	39	8	.319
2009 Florida . . . . N.L.			OF	54	176	30	44	12	2	4	13	1	.250
2010 Marlins . . . . Gulf Coast			OF	3	11	4	4	1	0	1	5	0	.364
2010 New Orleans . . . . .P.C.			OF	33	130	21	44	6	2	4	23	5	.338
2010 Florida b . . . . N.L.			OF	82	291	46	68	7	3	8	28	9	.234
2011 Tucson . . . . .P.C.			OF	3	10	1	2	1	0	0	1	1	.200
2011 San Diego c . . . . N.L.			OF	137	516	82	136	24	8	9	40	40	.264
Major League Totals			5 Yrs.	305	1064	175	271	48	13	22	85	59	.255

a Traded to Florida Marlins with pitcher Burke Badenhop, pitcher Eulogio De La Cruz, pitcher Andrew Miller and catcher Mike Rabelo for pitcher Dontrelle Willis and infielder Miguel Cabrera, December 5, 2007.
b Traded to San Diego Padres for pitcher Edward Mujica and pitcher Ryan Webb, November 13, 2010.
c On disabled list from May 28 to June 13, 2011.

MC CANN, BRIAN MICHAEL
Born, Athens, Georgia, February 20, 1984.
Bats Left. Throws Right. Height, 6 feet, 3 inches. Weight, 230 pounds.

Year	Club	Lea	Pos	G	AB	R	H	2B	3B	HR	RBI	SB	Avg
2002 Braves	Gulf Coast	C	29	100	9	22	5	0	2	11	0	.220
2003 Rome	So.Atl.	C	115	424	40	123	31	3	12	71	7	.290
2004 Myrtle Beach	Carolina	C	111	385	45	107	35	0	16	66	2	.278
2005 Mississippi	Southern	C	48	166	27	44	13	2	6	26	2	.265
2005 Atlanta	N.L.	C	59	180	20	50	7	0	5	23	1	.278
2006 Rome	So.Atl.	DH	2	7	0	2	0	0	0	0	0	.286
2006 Atlanta a	N.L.	C	130	442	61	147	34	0	24	93	2	.333
2007 Atlanta	N.L.	C	139	504	51	136	38	0	18	92	0	.270
2008 Atlanta	N.L.	C	145	509	68	153	42	1	23	87	5	.301
2009 Myrtle Beach	Carolina	DH	2	6	1	2	2	0	0	1	0	.333
2009 Gwinnett	Int.	C	1	3	0	1	1	0	0	1	0	.333
2009 Atlanta b	N.L.	C	138	488	63	137	35	1	21	94	4	.281
2010 Atlanta	N.L.	C	143	479	63	129	25	0	21	77	5	.269
2011 Gwinnett	Int.	C	2	6	1	2	0	0	1	2	0	.333
2011 Atlanta c	N.L.	C	128	466	51	126	19	0	24	71	3	.270
Major League Totals	7 Yrs.		882	3068	377	878	200	2	136	537	20	.286
Division Series												
2005 Atlanta	N.L.	C	3	16	2	3	0	0	2	5	0	.188
2010 Atlanta	N.L.	C	4	14	2	6	1	0	1	3	0	.429
Division Series Totals			7	30	4	9	1	0	3	8	0	.300

a On disabled list from May 24 to June 9, 2006.
b On disabled list from April 23 to May 8, 2009.
c On disabled list from July 27 to August 14, 2011.

MC COY, MICHAEL HOWARD (MIKE)
Born, San Diego, California, April 2, 1981.
Bats Right. Throws Right. Height, 5 feet, 9 inches. Weight, 180 pounds.

Year	Club	Lea	Pos	G	AB	R	H	2B	3B	HR	RBI	SB	Avg
2002 Johnson City	Appal.	SS-2B	50	154	46	48	9	1	4	22	18	.312
2003 Peoria	Midwest	2B-SS	131	464	67	117	16	5	5	46	24	.252
2004 Peoria	Midwest	3B-2B-SS-OF	50	178	21	37	7	3	2	16	8	.208
2004 Palm Beach	Fla.St.	2B-3B-SS	61	176	34	53	12	1	2	23	7	.301
2004 Tennessee	Southern	2B	3	6	0	0	0	0	0	0	0	.000
2005 Springfield	Texas	SS-2B	5	14	1	2	0	0	0	1	0	.143
2005 Palm Beach	Fla.St.	2B-3B-OF-SS	86	282	47	76	13	2	1	27	18	.270
2006 Springfield	Texas	SS-OF-2B-3B	129	474	64	118	14	2	3	37	30	.249
2007 Springfield	Texas	OF-3B-SS	24	68	5	15	3	1	0	10	1	.221
2007 Memphis	P.C.	SS-2B-OF-3B	90	239	31	59	8	0	3	16	12	.247
2008 Frederick	Carolina	2B	1	5	1	3	0	0	0	1	0	.600
2008 Norfolk	Int.	2B-SS-3B-OF	53	152	25	42	6	1	2	16	6	.276
2008 Colorado Springs a-b	P.C.	2B-SS-3B-OF	39	140	32	48	7	2	4	27	7	.343
2009 Colorado Springs	P.C.	SS-OF-3B-2B	132	462	102	142	27	5	2	52	40	.307
2009 Colorado	N.L.	2B-OF	12	5	1	0	0	0	0	0	2	.000
2010 Las Vegas	P.C.	SS-OF	53	213	48	66	14	1	6	26	17	.310
2010 Toronto	A.L.	OF-2B-SS-3B	46	82	9	16	4	0	0	3	5	.195
2011 Las Vegas	P.C.	SS-OF-2B	38	148	33	46	6	0	2	20	14	.311
2011 Toronto	A.L.	SS-OF-3B-2B	80	197	26	39	8	0	2	10	12	.198
Major League Totals	3 Yrs.		138	284	36	55	12	0	2	13	19	.194

a Sold by St. Louis Cardinals to Baltimore Orioles, March 22, 2008.
b Traded to Colorado Rockies for infielder Juan Castro, July 19, 2008.

MC CUTCHEN, ANDREW STEFAN
Born, Fort Meade, Florida, October 10, 1986.
Bats Right. Throws Right. Height, 5 feet, 11 inches. Weight, 175 pounds.

Year	Club	Lea	Pos	G	AB	R	H	2B	3B	HR	RBI	SB	Avg
2005 Pirates	Gulf Coast	OF	45	158	36	47	9	3	2	30	13	.297
2005 Williamsport	N.Y.-Penn.	OF	13	52	12	18	3	1	0	5	4	.346
2006 Altoona	Eastern	OF	20	78	12	24	4	0	3	12	1	.308
2006 Hickory	So.Atl.	OF	114	453	77	132	20	4	14	62	22	.291
2007 Altoona	Eastern	OF	118	446	70	115	20	3	10	48	17	.258
2007 Indianapolis	Int.	OF	17	67	7	21	4	0	1	5	4	.313
2008 Indianapolis	Int.	OF	135	512	75	145	26	3	9	50	34	.283
2009 Indianapolis	Int.	OF	49	201	41	61	10	8	4	20	10	.303

Year	Club	Lea	Pos	G	AB	R	H	2B	3B	HR	RBI	SB	Avg
2009 Pittsburgh		N.L.	OF	108	433	74	124	26	9	12	54	22	.286
2010 Pittsburgh		N.L.	OF	154	570	94	163	35	5	16	56	33	.286
2011 Pittsburgh		N.L.	OF	158	572	87	148	34	5	23	89	23	.259
Major League Totals			3 Yrs.	420	1575	255	435	95	19	51	199	78	.276

MC DONALD, DARNELL TYRONE

Born, Fort Collins, Colorado, November 17, 1978.
Bats Right. Throws Right. Height, 5 feet, 11 inches. Weight, 205 pounds.

Year	Club	Lea	Pos	G	AB	R	H	2B	3B	HR	RBI	SB	Avg
1998 Delmarva		So.Atl.	OF	134	528	87	138	24	5	6	44	35	.261
1998 Frederick		Carolina	OF	4	18	3	4	2	0	1	2	2	.222
1999 Frederick		Carolina	OF	130	507	81	135	23	5	6	73	26	.266
2000 Bowie		Eastern	OF	116	459	59	111	13	5	6	43	11	.242
2001 Bowie		Eastern	OF	30	117	16	33	7	1	3	21	3	.282
2001 Rochester		Int.	OF	104	391	37	93	19	2	2	35	13	.238
2002 Bowie		Eastern	OF	37	144	21	42	9	1	4	15	9	.292
2002 Rochester		Int.	OF	91	332	43	96	21	6	6	35	11	.289
2003 Ottawa		Int.	OF	40	152	19	45	7	1	0	20	5	.296
2004 Ottawa		Int.	OF	107	410	44	96	32	1	7	44	12	.234
2004 Baltimore		A.L.	OF	17	32	3	5	1	0	0	1	1	.156
2005 Buffalo		Int.	OF	26	74	11	20	7	0	1	4	0	.270
2005 Durham a-b		Int.	OF	73	285	45	81	13	2	12	34	7	.284
2006 Durham c-d		Int.	OF	136	538	80	157	33	1	14	57	30	.292
2007 Columbus		Int.	OF	73	267	39	84	17	4	2	41	14	.315
2007 Minnesota		A.L.	OF	4	10	0	1	0	0	0	0	0	.100
2007 Rochester e		Int.	OF	61	224	32	62	12	2	5	32	19	.277
2008 Rochester f		Int.	OF	93	369	53	99	25	4	11	57	19	.268
2009 Louisville		Int.	OF	73	280	42	88	22	7	9	40	8	.314
2009 Cincinnati g		N.L.	OF	47	105	12	28	6	1	2	10	1	.267
2010 Pawtucket		Int.	OF	10	41	6	14	6	1	2	8	1	.341
2010 Boston		A.L.	OF	117	319	40	86	18	3	9	34	9	.270
2011 Pawtucket		Int.	OF	9	29	6	10	3	0	2	11	1	.345
2011 Boston h		A.L.	OF-P	79	157	26	37	6	1	6	24	2	.236
Major League Totals			5 Yrs.	264	623	81	157	31	5	17	69	13	.252

a Filed for free agency, October 15, 2004. Signed with Cleveland Indians organization, January 25, 2005.
b Released by Cleveland Indians, June 4, 2005. Signed with Tampa Bay Devil Rays, June 10, 2005,
c Filed for free agency, October 15, 2005, re-signed with Tampa Bay Devil Rays organization, January 4, 2006.
d Filed for free agency, October 15, 2006. Signed with Washington Nationals organization, November 6, 2006.
e Traded to Minnesota Twins for pitcher Levale Speigner, June 24, 2007.
f Filed for free agency, November 3, 2008. Signed with Cincinnati Reds organization, December 2, 2008.
g Filed for free agency, November 9, 2009. Signed with Boston Red Sox organization, November 24, 2009.

MC DONALD, JOHN JOSEPH

Born, New London, Connecticut, September 24, 1974.
Bats Right. Throws Right. Height, 5 feet, 11 inches. Weight, 175 pounds.

Year	Club	Lea	Pos	G	AB	R	H	2B	3B	HR	RBI	SB	Avg
1996 Watertown		N.Y.-Penn.	SS	75	278	48	75	11	0	2	26	11	.270
1997 Kinston		Carolina	SS	130	541	77	140	27	3	5	53	6	.259
1998 Akron		Eastern	SS	132	514	68	118	18	2	2	43	17	.230
1999 Akron		Eastern	SS	55	226	31	67	12	0	1	26	7	.296
1999 Buffalo		Int.	SS	66	237	30	75	12	1	0	25	6	.316
1999 Cleveland		A.L.	2B-SS	18	21	2	7	0	0	0	0	0	.333
2000 Buffalo		Int.	SS-2B	75	286	37	77	17	2	1	36	4	.269
2000 Mahoning Valley		N.Y.-Penn.	SS	5	17	0	2	1	0	0	1	0	.118
2000 Cleveland		A.L.	SS-2B	9	9	0	4	0	0	0	0	0	.444
2000 Kinston a		Carolina	SS	1	3	0	1	0	0	0	0	0	.333
2001 Buffalo		Int.	SS-2B-3B	116	410	52	100	17	1	2	33	17	.244
2001 Cleveland b		A.L.	SS-2B-3B	17	22	1	2	1	0	0	0	0	.091
2002 Cleveland		A.L.	2B-SS-3B	93	264	35	66	11	3	1	12	3	.250
2003 Lake County		So.Atl.	SS	1	3	0	0	0	0	0	0	0	.000
2003 Mahoning Valley		N.Y.-Penn.	SS	1	2	1	0	0	0	0	0	0	.000
2003 Cleveland c		A.L.	2B-SS-3B	82	214	21	46	9	1	1	14	3	.215
2004 Cleveland d		A.L.	SS-2B-3B	66	93	17	19	5	1	2	7	0	.204
2005 Toronto-Detroit e-f		A.L.	SS-2B-3B	68	166	18	46	6	1	0	16	6	.277
2006 Toronto g		A.L.	SS-2B-3B	104	260	35	58	7	3	3	23	7	.223
2007 Toronto		A.L.	SS-3B	123	327	32	82	20	2	1	31	7	.251
2008 Dunedin		Fla.St.	SS	3	11	2	4	0	0	0	1	0	.364

114

Year	Club	Lea	Pos	G	AB	R	H	2B	3B	HR	RBI	SB	Avg
2008 Toronto h		A.L.	SS-3B-2B	84	186	21	39	8	0	1	18	3	.210
2009 Toronto i		A.L.	SS-3B-2B-OF	73	151	18	39	7	0	4	13	0	.258
2010 Toronto		A.L.	2B-3B-SS-OF	63	152	27	38	9	2	6	23	2	.250
2011 Dunedin		Fla.St.	SS	1	4	0	1	0	0	0	0	0	.250
2011 Toronto		A.L.	3B-2B-SS	65	168	19	42	8	1	2	20	2	.250
2011 Arizona j-k-l		N.L.	SS	19	59	2	10	2	0	0	2	0	.169
Major League Totals			13 Yrs.	884	2092	248	498	93	14	21	179	33	.238
Division Series													
2011 Arizona		N.L.	SS	2	2	0	0	0	0	0	0	0	.000

a On disabled list from April 27 to May 9 and May 10 to June 22, 2000.
b On disabled list from May 10 to 17, 2001.
c On disabled list from June 30 to July 17 and August 27 to October 3, 2003.
d Traded to Toronto Blue Jays for player to be named later, December 2, 2004. Cleveland received pitcher Tom Mastny to complete deal, December 13, 2004.
e Sold to Detroit Tigers, July 22, 2005.
f Sold to Toronto Blue Jays, November 10, 2005.
g On disabled list from May 28 to June 12, 2006.
h On disabled list from May 7 to June 7, 2008.
i Filed for free agency, November 6, 2009, re-signed with Toronto Blue Jays, November 25, 2009.
j On disabled list from May 27 to June 17, 2011.
k Traded to Arizona Diamondbacks with infielder Aaron Hill for infielder Kelly Johnson, August 23, 2011.
l Filed for free agency, October 31, 2011, re-signed with Arizona Diamondbacks, November 2, 2011.

MC GEHEE, CASEY MICHAEL

Born, Santa Cruz, California, October 12, 1982.
Bats Right. Throws Right. Height, 6 feet, 1 inch. Weight, 195 pounds.

Year	Club	Lea	Pos	G	AB	R	H	2B	3B	HR	RBI	SB	Avg
2003 Lansing		Midwest	3B	64	243	24	66	18	1	3	23	2	.272
2004 Daytona		Fla.St.	3B-C	119	449	56	117	30	0	10	66	2	.261
2005 West Tenn		Southern	3B-1B-2B	124	455	67	135	31	1	8	72	2	.297
2006 Iowa		P.C.	3B-1B-2B-SS	135	497	56	139	28	1	11	68	0	.280
2007 Iowa		P.C.	3B-1B	18	52	3	9	2	0	1	5	0	.173
2007 Tennessee		Southern	3B-C-1B	105	384	53	105	26	2	9	54	1	.273
2008 Iowa		P.C.	3B-C-1B-2B	133	497	68	147	30	0	12	92	0	.296
2008 Chicago a		N.L.	3B	9	24	1	4	1	0	0	5	0	.167
2009 Milwaukee		N.L.	3B-2B-1B-OF	116	355	58	107	20	1	16	66	0	.301
2010 Milwaukee		N.L.	3B-1B	157	610	70	174	38	1	23	104	1	.285
2011 Milwaukee b		N.L.	3B-1B	155	546	46	122	24	2	13	67	0	.223
Major League Totals			4 Yrs.	437	1535	175	407	83	4	52	242	1	.265
Division Series													
2011 Milwaukee		N.L.	PH	3	3	0	1	0	0	0	0	0	.333
Championship Series													
2011 Milwaukee		N.L.	PH	3	2	0	0	0	0	0	0	0	.000

a Claimed on waivers by Milwaukee Brewers, October 29, 2008.
b Traded to Pittsburgh Pirates for pitcher Jose Veras, December 13, 2011.

MC LOUTH, NATHAN RICHARD (NATE)

Born, Muskegon, Michigan, October 28, 1981.
Bats Left. Throws Right. Height, 5 feet, 11 inches. Weight, 185 pounds.

Year	Club	Lea	Pos	G	AB	R	H	2B	3B	HR	RBI	SB	Avg
2001 Hickory		So.Atl.	OF-2B	96	351	59	100	17	5	12	54	21	.285
2002 Lynchburg		Carolina	OF	114	393	58	96	23	4	9	46	20	.244
2003 Lynchburg		Carolina	OF	117	440	85	132	27	2	6	33	40	.300
2004 Altoona		Eastern	OF	133	515	93	166	40	4	8	73	31	.322
2005 Indianapolis		Int.	OF	110	397	64	118	20	3	5	39	34	.297
2005 Pittsburgh		N.L.	OF	41	109	20	28	6	0	5	12	2	.257
2006 Pittsburgh a		N.L.	OF	106	270	50	63	16	2	7	16	10	.233
2007 Pittsburgh		N.L.	OF	137	329	62	85	21	3	13	38	22	.258
2008 Pittsburgh		N.L.	OF	152	597	113	165	*46	4	26	94	23	.276
2009 Rome		So.Atl.	OF	1	2	0	0	0	0	0	0	0	.000
2009 Mississippi		Southern	OF	2	3	1	0	0	0	0	0	0	.000
2009 Pittsburgh-Atlanta b-c		N.L.	OF	129	507	86	130	27	2	20	70	19	.256
2010 Gwinnett		Int.	OF	34	128	18	30	1	0	6	18	7	.234
2010 Atlanta d		N.L.	OF	85	242	30	46	12	1	6	24	7	.190
2011 Gwinnett		Int.	OF	3	6	2	3	0	0	0	1	0	.500
2011 Atlanta e-f		N.L.	OF	81	267	35	61	12	2	4	16	4	.228
Major League Totals			7 Yrs.	731	2321	396	578	140	14	81	270	87	.249

Year	Club	Lea	Pos	G	AB	R	H	2B	3B	HR	RBI	SB	Avg
Division Series													
2010 Atlanta		N.L.	OF	3	2	0	1	0	0	0	0	0	.500

a On disabled list from August 12 to October 3, 2006.
b Traded to Atlanta Braves for outfielder Gorkys Hernandez, pitcher Jeff Locke and pitcher Charlie Morton, June 3, 2009.
c On disabled list from August 16 to September 4, 2009.
d On disabled list from June 10 to July 21, 2010.
e On disabled list from May 23 to June 19 and July 29 to October 30, 2011.
f Filed for free agency, October 31, 2011. Signed with Pittsburgh Pirates, December 7, 2011.

MESORACO, DEVIN DOUGLAS
Born, Dubois, Pennsylvania, June 19, 1988.
Bats Right. Throws Right. Height, 6 feet, 1 inch. Weight, 220 pounds.

Year	Club	Lea	Pos	G	AB	R	H	2B	3B	HR	RBI	SB	Avg
2007 Reds..........	Gulf Coast		C	40	137	16	30	4	0	1	8	2	.219
2008 Dayton	Midwest		C	83	306	29	80	13	1	9	42	2	.261
2009 Sarasota............	Fla.St.		C	92	312	32	71	22	1	8	37	0	.228
2010 Lynchburg	Carolina		C	43	158	24	53	11	2	10	31	2	.335
2010 Louisville	Int.		C	14	52	5	12	3	0	3	13	0	.231
2010 Carolina	Southern		C	56	187	42	55	11	3	13	31	1	.294
2011 Louisville	Int.		C	120	436	60	126	36	2	15	71	1	.289
2011 Cincinnati............	N.L.		C	18	50	5	9	3	0	2	6	0	.180

MICHAELS, JASON DREW
Born, Tampa, Florida, May 4, 1976.
Bats Right. Throws Right. Height, 6 feet. Weight, 205 pounds.

Year	Club	Lea	Pos	G	AB	R	H	2B	3B	HR	RBI	SB	Avg
1998 Batavia........	N.Y.-Penn.		OF	67	235	45	63	14	3	11	49	4	.268
1999 Clearwater..........	Fla.St.		OF	122	452	91	138	31	6	14	65	10	.305
2000 Reading	Eastern		OF	113	437	71	129	30	4	10	74	7	.295
2001 Scranton-WB..........	Int.		OF	109	418	58	109	19	3	17	69	11	.261
2001 Philadelphia a.........	N.L.		OF	6	6	0	1	0	0	0	1	0	.167
2002 Scranton-WB..........	Int.		OF	9	32	3	9	2	0	0	7	1	.281
2002 Philadelphia	N.L.		OF-3B	81	105	16	28	10	3	2	11	1	.267
2003 Clearwater	Fla.St.		OF	4	14	1	0	0	0	0	0	0	.000
2003 Philadelphia b..........	N.L.		OF	76	109	20	36	11	0	5	17	0	.330
2004 Philadelphia	N.L.		OF	115	299	44	82	12	0	10	40	2	.274
2005 Philadelphia	N.L.		OF	105	289	54	88	16	2	4	31	3	.304
2006 Buffalo	Int.		OF	2	7	1	3	0	0	1	1	0	.429
2006 Cleveland c-d.........	A.L.		OF	123	494	77	132	32	1	9	55	9	.267
2007 Cleveland	A.L.		OF	105	267	43	72	11	1	7	39	3	.270
2008 Cleveland	A.L.		OF	21	58	3	12	4	0	0	9	1	.207
2008 Pittsburgh e-f.........	N.L.		OF	102	228	25	52	9	1	8	44	1	.228
2009 Houston g	N.L.		OF	102	135	17	32	12	1	4	16	1	.237
2010 Houston	N.L.		OF	106	186	23	47	14	1	8	26	0	.253
2011 Oklahoma.............	P.C.		OF	5	20	0	6	2	0	0	2	0	.300
2011 Houston h-i..........	N.L.		OF	89	156	10	31	9	0	2	10	1	.199
Major League Totals		11 Yrs.		1031	2332	332	613	140	10	59	299	22	.263
Division Series													
2007 Cleveland	A.L.		OF	1	1	0	1	1	0	0	0	0	1.000
Championship Series													
2007 Cleveland	A.L.		PH	1	0	1	0	0	0	0	0	0	.000

a On disabled list from May 1 to 10, 2001.
b On disabled list from March 21 to April 14, 2003.
c Traded to Cleveland Indians for pitcher Arthur Rhodes, January 27, 2006.
d On disabled list from June 16 to July 4, 2006.
e Sold to Pittsburgh Pirates, May 8, 2008.
f Not offered contract, October 31, 2008. Signed with Houston Astros, December 15, 2008.
g Filed for free agency, November 5, 2009, re-signed with Houston Astros, December 14, 2009.
h On disabled list from April 26 to May 13, 2011.
i Filed for free agency, October 30, 2011. Signed with Washington Nationals organization, December 16, 2011.

MILES, AARON WADE

Born, Pittsburg, California, December 15, 1976.
Bats Both. Throws Right. Height, 5 feet, 8 inches. Weight, 175 pounds.

Year Club	Lea	Pos	G	AB	R	H	2B	3B	HR	RBI	SB	Avg
1995 Astros . . . . . .Gulf Coast		SS-2B	47	171	32	44	9	3	0	18	9	.257
1996 Astros . . . . . .Gulf Coast		2B	55	214	48	63	3	2	0	15	14	.294
1997 Quad City . . . . . Midwest		2B	97	370	55	97	13	2	1	35	18	.262
1998 Quad City . . . . . Midwest		2B-3B-OF	108	369	42	90	22	6	2	37	28	.244
1999 Michigan . . . . . Midwest		2B	112	470	72	149	28	8	10	71	17	.317
2000 Kissimmee a . . . .Fla.St.		2B	75	295	40	86	20	1	2	36	11	.292
2001 Birmingham b .Southern		3B-2B	84	343	53	89	16	3	8	42	3	.259
2002 Birmingham c .Southern		2B-3B	138	531	67	171	39	1	9	68	25	.322
2003 Charlotte . . . . Int.		2B-3B	133	546	80	166	34	5	11	50	8	.304
2003 Chicago d. . . . . .A.L.		2B	8	12	3	4	3	0	0	2	0	.333
2004 Colorado Springs. . .P.C.		2B	12	54	8	18	3	0	0	8	2	.333
2004 Colorado . . . . .N.L.		2B	134	522	75	153	15	3	6	47	12	.293
2005 Colorado Springs. . .P.C.		2B	8	32	6	7	0	1	0	1	1	.219
2005 Colorado e-f . . . . . .N.L.		2B-SS	99	324	37	91	12	3	2	28	4	.281
2006 St. Louis. . . . . .N.L.		2B-SS-3B	135	426	48	112	20	5	2	30	2	.263
2007 St. Louis g . . . . . . .N.L.		2B-SS-3B-P	133	414	55	120	16	1	2	32	2	.290
2008 St. Louis h . . . . . . .N.L.		2B-SS-3B-OF	134	379	49	120	15	2	4	31	3	.317
2009 Iowa . . . . .P.C.		2B-3B-SS	21	87	8	22	4	0	0	8	1	.253
2009 Chicago i-j . . . . . .N.L.		2B-SS-3B	74	157	17	29	7	1	0	5	3	.185
2010 Springfield . . . . . . Texas		2B-SS-3B	16	61	11	17	4	0	0	13	0	.279
2010 St. Louis k-l-m . . . . .N.L.		2B-SS-3B-P	79	139	14	39	5	0	0	9	0	.281
2011 Los Angeles n . . . . .N.L.		2B-3B-SS	136	454	49	125	17	3	3	45	4	.275
Major League Totals	9 Yrs.		932	2827	347	793	110	18	19	229	30	.281
Division Series												
2006 St. Louis. . . . . .N.L.		2B	2	2	0	1	0	0	0	0	0	.500
Championship Series												
2006 St. Louis. . . . . .N.L.		2B	3	3	0	2	0	1	0	0	0	.667
World Series Record												
2006 St. Louis. . . . . .N.L.		2B	2	6	2	1	0	0	0	0	1	.167

a Selected by Chicago White Sox organization from Houston Astros organization in Rule V draft, December 11, 2000.
b Filed for free agency, October 15, 2001, re-signed with Chicago White Sox, November 16, 2001.
c Filed for free agency, October 15, 2002, re-signed with Chicago White Sox, October 25, 2002.
d Traded to Colorado Rockies for infielder Juan Uribe, December 2, 2003.
e On disabled list from May 26 to June 28, 2005.
f Traded to St. Louis Cardinals with outfielder Larry Bigbie for pitcher Ray King, December 7, 2005.
g Not offered contract, December 12, 2007, re-signed with St. Louis Cardinals organization, January 4, 2008.
h Not offered contract, December 12, 2008. Signed with Chicago Cubs, December 31, 2008.
i On disabled list from May 26 to June 10 and June 21 to August 5, 2009.
j Traded to Oakland Athletics with infielder Jake Fox and cash for pitcher Jeff Gray, pitcher Ronny Morla and outfielder Matt Spencer, December 3, 2009.
k Traded to Cincinnati Reds for infielder Adam Rosales and outfielder Willy Taveras, February 1, 2010.
l Released by Cincinnati Reds, April 12, 2010. Signed with St. Louis Cardinals organization, April 30, 2010.
m Filed for free agency, November 1, 2010. Signed with Los Angeles Dodgers organization, February 7, 2011.
n Filed for free agency, October 30, 2011.

MOLINA, YADIER BENJAMIN

Born, Bayamon, Puerto Rico, July 13, 1982.
Bats Right. Throws Right. Height, 5 feet, 11 inches. Weight, 225 pounds.

Year Club	Lea	Pos	G	AB	R	H	2B	3B	HR	RBI	SB	Avg
2001 Johnson City . . . . . . .Appal.		C	44	158	18	41	11	0	4	18	1	.259
2002 Peoria. . . . . .Midwest		C	112	393	39	110	20	0	7	50	2	.280
2003 Tennessee . . . . Southern		C	104	364	32	100	13	1	2	51	0	.275
2004 Memphis . . . . .P.C.		C	37	129	19	39	6	0	1	14	0	.302
2004 St. Louis. . . . . .N.L.		C	51	135	12	36	6	0	2	15	0	.267
2005 St. Louis a . . . . .N.L.		C-1B	114	385	36	97	15	1	8	49	2	.252
2006 St. Louis. . . . . .N.L.		C-1B	129	417	29	90	26	0	6	49	1	.216
2007 St. Louis b . . . . .N.L.		C-1B	111	353	30	97	15	0	6	40	1	.275
2008 St. Louis. . . . . .N.L.		C-1B	124	444	37	135	18	0	7	56	0	.304
2009 St. Louis. . . . . .N.L.		C-1B	140	481	45	141	23	1	6	54	9	.293
2010 St. Louis. . . . . .N.L.		C-1B	136	465	34	122	19	0	6	62	8	.262
2011 St. Louis. . . . . .N.L.		C-1B	139	475	55	145	32	1	14	65	4	.305
Major League Totals	8 Yrs.		944	3155	278	863	154	3	55	390	25	.274
Division Series												
2005 St. Louis. . . . . .N.L.		C	3	13	1	3	0	0	0	3	0	.231
2006 St. Louis. . . . . .N.L.		C	4	13	0	4	1	0	0	1	0	.308
2009 St. Louis. . . . . .N.L.		C	3	13	0	4	1	0	0	0	0	.308

Year Club	Lea	Pos	G	AB	R	H	2B	3B	HR	RBI	SB	Avg
2011 St. Louis............	N.L.	C	5	19	1	4	0	0	0	1	1	.211
Division Series Totals..........			15	58	2	15	2	0	0	5	1	.259
Championship Series												
2004 St. Louis.............	N.L.	C	1	4	0	1	0	0	0	0	0	.250
2005 St. Louis.............	N.L.	C	6	22	1	7	3	0	0	0	0	.318
2006 St. Louis.............	N.L.	C	7	23	2	8	1	0	2	6	0	.348
2011 St. Louis.............	N.L.	C-1B	6	24	5	8	3	0	0	2	0	.333
Championship Series Totals......			20	73	8	24	7	0	2	8	0	.329
World Series Record												
2004 St. Louis.............	N.L.	C	3	3	0	0	0	0	0	0	0	.000
2006 St. Louis.............	N.L.	C	5	17	3	7	2	0	0	1	0	.412
2011 St. Louis.............	N.L.	C	7	24	1	8	2	0	0	9	0	.333
World Series Totals............			15	44	4	15	4	0	0	10	0	.341

a On disabled list from July 9 to August 18, 2005.
b On disabled list from May 30 to June 28, 2007.

MONTERO (LOPEZ), JESUS ALEJANDRO

Born, Guacara, Venezuela, November 28, 1989.
Bats Right. Throws Right. Height, 6 feet, 3 inches. Weight, 235 pounds.

Year Club	Lea	Pos	G	AB	R	H	2B	3B	HR	RBI	SB	Avg
2007 Yankees........	Gulf Coast	C	33	107	13	30	6	0	3	19	0	.280
2008 Charleston.........	So.Atl.	C	132	525	86	171	34	1	17	87	2	.326
2009 Tampa.............	Fla.St.	C	48	180	26	64	15	1	8	37	0	.356
2009 Trenton............	Eastern	C	44	167	19	53	10	0	9	33	0	.317
2010 Scranton-WB..........	Int.	C	123	453	66	131	34	3	21	75	0	.289
2011 Scranton-WB..........	Int.	C	109	420	52	121	19	1	18	67	0	.288
2011 New York a...........	A.L.	DH-C	18	61	9	20	4	0	4	12	0	.328
Division Series												
2011 New York............	A.L.	PH	1	2	1	2	0	0	0	1	0	1.000

a Traded to Seattle Mariners with pitcher Hector Noesi for pitcher Michael Pineda and pitcher Jose Campos, January 17, 2012.

MONTERO, MIGUEL ANGEL

Born, Caracas, Venezuela, July 9, 1983.
Bats Left. Throws Right. Height, 5 feet, 11 inches. Weight, 195 pounds.

Year Club	Lea	Pos	G	AB	R	H	2B	3B	HR	RBI	SB	Avg
2002 Missoula.........Pioneer		C-3B-1B	50	152	21	40	10	1	3	14	2	.263
2003 Missoula.........Pioneer		C	59	196	24	59	10	2	4	32	2	.301
2004 South Bend.......Midwest		C-1B-SS	115	403	47	106	22	2	11	59	8	.263
2005 Lancaster..........Calif.		C-1B	85	355	73	124	24	1	24	82	1	.349
2005 Tennessee.......	Southern	C-1B	30	108	13	27	1	2	2	13	1	.250
2006 Tennessee.......	Southern	C	81	289	24	78	18	0	10	46	0	.270
2006 Tucson..............	P.C.	C	36	134	21	43	5	0	7	29	1	.321
2006 Arizona.............	N.L.	C	6	16	0	4	1	0	0	3	0	.250
2007 Arizona.............	N.L.	C	84	214	30	48	7	0	10	37	0	.224
2008 Tucson..............	P.C.	C	11	32	3	9	2	0	1	5	0	.281
2008 Arizona a...........	N.L.	C	70	184	24	47	16	1	5	18	0	.255
2009 Arizona.............	N.L.	C	128	425	61	125	30	0	16	59	1	.294
2010 Reno..............	P.C.	C	4	15	1	5	0	0	0	2	0	.333
2010 Arizona b...........	N.L.	C	85	297	36	79	20	2	9	43	0	.266
2011 Arizona.............	N.L.	C	140	493	65	139	36	1	18	86	1	.282
Major League Totals............	6 Yrs.	513	1629	216	442	110	4	58	246	2	.271	
Division Series												
2007 Arizona.............	N.L.	C	1	2	1	0	0	0	0	0	0	.000
2011 Arizona.............	N.L.	C	5	20	3	6	2	0	0	2	0	.300
Division Series Totals.......			6	22	4	6	2	0	0	2	0	.273
Championship Series												
2007 Arizona.............	N.L.	C	3	5	0	2	0	0	0	0	0	.400

a On disabled list from March 23 to April 23, 2008.
b On disabled list from April 11 to June 12, 2010.

MORALES, KENDRYS (KENDRY)

Born, Fomento, Cuba, June 20, 1983.
Bats Both. Throws Right. Height, 6 feet, 1 inch. Weight, 225 pounds.

Year Club	Lea	Pos	G	AB	R	H	2B	3B	HR	RBI	SB	Avg
2005 Rancho CucamongaCalif.		1B-3B-OF	22	90	18	31	3	0	5	17	0	.344

Year	Club	Lea	Pos	G	AB	R	H	2B	3B	HR	RBI	SB	Avg
2005 Arkansas	Texas		1B-OF	74	281	47	86	12	0	17	54	2	.306
2006 Salt Lake	P.C.		1B	66	256	41	82	13	1	12	52	0	.320
2006 Los Angeles	A.L.		1B	57	197	21	46	10	1	5	22	1	.234
2007 Salt Lake	P.C.		1B	64	255	42	87	20	1	5	37	0	.341
2007 Los Angeles	A.L.		1B-OF	43	119	12	35	10	0	4	15	0	.294
2008 Angels	Arizona		OF	5	21	4	11	3	0	1	10	0	.524
2008 Salt Lake	P.C.		1B-OF	78	317	46	108	19	0	15	64	1	.341
2008 Los Angeles	A.L.		OF-1B	27	61	7	13	2	0	3	8	0	.213
2009 Los Angeles	A.L.		1B	152	566	86	173	43	2	34	108	3	.306
2010 Los Angeles a	A.L.		1B	51	193	29	56	5	0	11	39	0	.290
2011 Los Angeles b	A.L.		INJURED—Did Not Play										
Major League Totals			5 Yrs.	330	1136	155	323	70	3	57	192	4	.284
Division Series													
2007 Los Angeles	A.L.		1B-DH	3	9	1	1	0	0	0	0	0	.111
2008 Los Angeles	A.L.		PH	4	4	0	2	1	0	0	0	0	.500
2009 Los Angeles	A.L.		1B	3	10	1	2	0	0	1	3	0	.200
Division Series Totals				10	23	2	5	1	0	1	3	0	.217
Championship Series													
2009 Los Angeles	A.L.		1B	6	24	1	4	0	0	1	4	0	.167

a On disabled list from May 30 to November 2, 2010.
b On disabled list from March 22 to October 30, 2011.

MOREL, BRENT
Born, Bakersfield, California, April 21, 1987.
Bats Right. Throws Right. Height, 6 feet, 2 inches. Weight, 220 pounds.

Year	Club	Lea	Pos	G	AB	R	H	2B	3B	HR	RBI	SB	Avg
2008 Great Falls	Pioneer		3B	15	64	11	24	0	2	0	3	7	.375
2008 Kannapolis	So.Atl.		3B	45	172	26	51	6	2	6	24	5	.297
2009 Winston-Salem	Carolina		3B	128	481	82	135	33	1	16	79	25	.281
2010 Birmingham	Southern		3B	49	184	25	60	13	1	2	30	5	.326
2010 Charlotte	Int.		3B-SS	81	306	40	98	24	4	8	34	3	.320
2010 Chicago	A.L.		3B	21	65	9	15	3	0	3	7	2	.231
2011 Chicago	A.L.		3B	126	413	44	101	18	1	10	41	5	.245
Major League Totals			2 Yrs.	147	478	53	116	21	1	13	48	7	.243

MORELAND, MITCHELL AUSTIN (MITCH)
Born, Amory, Mississippi, September 6, 1985.
Bats Left. Throws Left. Height, 6 feet, 2 inches. Weight, 230 pounds.

Year	Club	Lea	Pos	G	AB	R	H	2B	3B	HR	RBI	SB	Avg
2007 Spokane	Northwest		1B-OF	27	108	10	28	7	1	2	15	1	.259
2008 Clinton	Midwest		1B-OF	123	466	64	151	37	4	18	99	2	.324
2009 Bakersfield	Calif.		1B-OF	43	170	34	58	19	0	8	26	1	.341
2009 Frisco	Texas		OF-1B	73	301	51	98	19	3	8	59	1	.326
2010 Oklahoma	P.C.		OF-1B	95	353	52	102	29	2	12	65	2	.289
2010 Texas	A.L.		1B-OF	47	145	20	37	4	0	9	25	3	.255
2011 Texas	A.L.		1B-OF	134	464	60	120	22	1	16	51	2	.259
Major League Totals			2 Yrs.	181	609	80	157	26	1	25	76	5	.258
Division Series													
2010 Texas	A.L.		1B	4	15	1	3	3	0	0	1	0	.200
2011 Texas	A.L.		1B	3	10	1	1	0	0	1	2	0	.100
Division Series Totals				7	25	2	4	3	0	1	3	0	.160
Championship Series													
2010 Texas	A.L.		1B	6	18	3	7	0	0	0	3	0	.389
2011 Texas	A.L.		1B	3	9	0	1	0	0	0	0	0	.111
Championship Series Totals				9	27	3	8	0	0	0	3	0	.296
World Series Record													
2010 Texas	A.L.		1B	5	13	1	6	1	0	1	3	0	.462
2011 Texas	A.L.		1B	3	10	1	1	0	0	1	1	0	.100
World Series Totals				8	23	2	7	1	0	2	4	0	.304

MORGAN, NYJER JAMID
Born, San Francisco, California, July 2, 1980.
Bats Left. Throws Left. Height, 6 feet. Weight, 170 pounds.

Year	Club	Lea	Pos	G	AB	R	H	2B	3B	HR	RBI	SB	Avg
2003 Williamsport.....	N.Y.-Penn.	OF	72	268	49	92	7	4	0	23	26	.343
2004 Hickory...........	So.Atl.	OF	134	514	83	131	16	7	4	41	55	.255
2005 Lynchburg	Carolina	OF	60	252	36	72	12	3	0	24	24	.286
2006 Lynchburg	Carolina	OF	61	228	43	69	7	3	0	22	38	.303
2006 Altoona..........	Eastern	OF	56	219	39	67	6	5	1	10	21	.306
2007 Pirates	Gulf Coast	OF	4	13	3	4	0	0	1	1	0	.308
2007 Indianapolis	Int.	OF	44	164	30	50	4	2	0	10	26	.305
2007 Pittsburgh a	N.L.	OF	28	107	15	32	3	4	1	7	7	.299
2008 Indianapolis	Int.	OF	82	322	54	96	13	4	1	33	44	.298
2008 Pittsburgh	N.L.	OF	58	160	26	47	13	0	0	7	9	.294
2009 Pittsburgh-Washington b-c	N.L.	OF	120	469	74	144	15	7	3	39	42	.307
2010 Hagerstown	So.Atl.	OF	1	3	0	0	0	0	0	0	0	.000
2010 Potomac...........	Carolina	DH	1	3	0	0	0	0	0	0	0	.000
2010 Washington d.........	N.L.	OF	136	509	60	129	17	7	0	24	34	.253
2011 Nashville	P.C.	OF	2	4	1	2	0	0	0	0	1	.500
2011 Milwaukee e-f........	N.L.	OF	119	378	61	115	20	6	4	37	13	.304
Major League Totals		5 Yrs.	461	1623	236	467	68	24	8	114	105	.288
Division Series												
2011 Milwaukee	N.L.	OF	4	16	1	3	1	0	0	3	0	.188
Championship Series												
2011 Milwaukee	N.L.	OF	6	12	1	2	1	0	0	0	0	.167

a On minor league disabled list from May 14 through August 23, 2007.
b Traded to Washington Nationals with pitcher Sean Burnett for outfielder Lastings Milledge and pitcher Joel Hanrahan, June 30, 2009.
c On disabled list from August 28 to October 13, 2009.
d On disabled list from August 4 to August 19, 2010.
e Traded to Milwaukee Brewers for infielder Cutter Dykstra, March 27, 2011.
f On disabled list from April 18 to May 3 and May 6 to May 27, 2011.

MORNEAU, JUSTIN ERNEST GEORGE
Born, New Westminster, British Columbia, Canada, May 15, 1981.
Bats Left. Throws Right. Height, 6 feet, 4 inches. Weight, 225 pounds.

Year	Club	Lea	Pos	G	AB	R	H	2B	3B	HR	RBI	SB	Avg
1999 Twins	Gulf Coast	DH	17	53	3	16	5	0	0	9	0	.302
2000 Twins	Gulf Coast	1B-C-OF	52	194	47	78	21	0	10	58	3	.402
2000 Elizabethton	Appal.	C	6	23	4	5	0	0	1	3	0	.217
2001 Quad Cities........	Midwest	1B	64	236	50	84	17	2	12	53	0	.356
2001 Fort Myers	Fla.St.	1B	53	197	25	58	10	3	4	40	0	.294
2001 New Britain	Eastern	1B	10	38	3	6	1	0	0	4	0	.158
2002 New Britain	Eastern	1B	126	494	72	147	31	4	16	80	7	.298
2003 New Britain	Eastern	1B	20	79	14	26	3	1	6	13	0	.329
2003 Rochester............	Int.	1B	71	265	39	71	11	1	16	42	0	.268
2003 Minnesota...........	A.L.	DH-1B	40	106	14	24	4	0	4	16	0	.226
2004 Rochester...........	Int.	1B	72	288	51	88	23	0	22	63	1	.306
2004 Minnesota...........	A.L.	1B	74	280	39	76	17	0	19	58	0	.271
2005 Minnesota a	A.L.	1B	141	490	62	117	23	4	22	79	0	.239
2006 Minnesota b.........	A.L.	1B	157	592	97	190	37	1	34	130	3	.321
2007 Minnesota...........	A.L.	1B	157	590	84	160	31	3	31	111	1	.271
2008 Minnesota...........	A.L.	1B	*163	623	97	187	47	4	23	129	0	.300
2009 Minnesota...........	A.L.	1B	135	508	85	139	31	1	30	100	0	.274
2010 Minnesota c.........	A.L.	1B	81	296	53	102	25	1	18	56	0	.345
2011 Rochester...........	Int.	1B	7	30	8	11	4	0	1	8	0	.367
2011 Minnesota d.........	A.L.	1B	69	264	19	60	16	0	4	30	0	.227
Major League Totals		9 Yrs.	1017	3749	550	1055	231	14	185	709	4	.281
Division Series												
2004 Minnesota	A.L.	1B	4	17	1	4	2	0	0	2	0	.235
2006 Minnesota	A.L.	1B	3	12	3	5	1	0	2	2	0	.417
Division Series Totals			7	29	4	9	3	0	2	4	0	.310

a On disabled list from April 7 to April 22, 2005.
b Selected Most Valuable Player in American League for 2006.
c On disabled list from July 8 to November 2, 2010.
d On disabled list from June 10 to August 12 and September 12 to October 3, 2011.

MORRISON, JUSTIS LOGAN (LOGAN)

Born, Kansas City, Missouri, August 25, 1987.
Bats Left. Throws Left. Height, 6 feet, 3 inches. Weight, 235 pounds.

Year	Club	Lea	Pos	G	AB	R	H	2B	3B	HR	RBI	SB	Avg
2006 Marlins	Gulf Coast		1B	26	89	10	24	4	0	1	7	1	.270
2006 Jamestown	N.Y.-Penn.		1B	23	74	6	15	3	0	1	11	0	.203
2007 Greensboro	So.Atl.		1B	128	453	71	121	22	2	24	86	2	.267
2008 Jupiter	Fla.St.		1B	130	488	71	162	38	1	13	74	9	.332
2009 Jupiter	Fla.St.		1B	3	11	0	3	1	0	0	2	0	.273
2009 Jacksonville	Southern		1B-OF	79	278	48	77	18	2	8	47	9	.277
2010 Jupiter	Fla.St.		1B	5	21	3	8	2	2	0	2	0	.381
2010 New Orleans	P.C.		1B-OF	68	238	36	73	17	4	6	45	1	.307
2010 Florida	N.L.		OF	62	244	43	69	20	7	2	18	0	.283
2011 Jupiter	Fla.St.		OF	3	10	2	2	0	0	1	3	0	.200
2011 New Orleans	P.C.		OF	6	24	3	4	2	0	1	5	0	.167
2011 Florida a	N.L.		OF-1B	123	462	54	114	25	4	23	72	2	.247
Major League Totals			2 Yrs.	185	706	97	183	45	11	25	90	2	.259

a On disabled list from April 20 to May 13, 2011.

MORSE, MICHAEL JOHN (MIKE)

Born, Fort Lauderdale, Florida, March 22, 1982.
Bats Right. Throws Right. Height, 6 feet, 4 inches. Weight, 230 pounds.

Year	Club	Lea	Pos	G	AB	R	H	2B	3B	HR	RBI	SB	Avg
2000 White Sox	Arizona		SS	45	180	32	46	6	1	2	24	5	.256
2001 Bristol	Appal.		SS	57	181	23	41	7	3	4	27	6	.227
2002 Kannapolis	So.Atl.		SS-3B	113	417	43	107	30	4	2	56	7	.257
2003 Winston-Salem	Carolina		SS	122	432	45	106	30	2	10	55	4	.245
2004 Birmingham	Southern		SS	54	209	30	60	9	5	11	38	0	.287
2004 San Antonio a	Texas		SS	41	157	18	43	10	1	6	33	0	.274
2005 Tacoma	P.C.		SS	49	182	20	46	12	2	4	23	1	.253
2005 Seattle	A.L.		SS-OF	72	230	27	64	10	1	3	23	3	.278
2006 Tacoma	P.C.		1B-3B-SS-OF	57	206	23	51	15	1	5	34	0	.248
2006 Seattle	A.L.		OF-3B-1B-SS	21	43	5	16	5	0	0	11	1	.372
2007 Mariners	Arizona		3B-SS	5	15	2	3	1	0	0	2	0	.200
2007 Tacoma	P.C.		3B-SS-OF	76	291	48	90	26	0	6	39	5	.309
2007 Seattle	A.L.		1B-3B-SS-OF	9	18	1	8	2	0	0	3	0	.444
2008 Seattle b			OF	5	9	0	2	1	0	0	0	0	.222
2009 Tacoma	P.C.		SS-2B-3B-OF	66	260	38	81	14	0	10	52	0	.312
2009 Syracuse	Int.		1B-3B-OF-SS	44	165	21	56	12	3	6	34	2	.339
2009 Washington c	N.L.		1B-OF-3B	32	52	4	13	3	0	3	10	0	.250
2010 Syracuse	Int.		1B	15	51	12	13	2	0	3	8	0	.255
2010 Washington d	N.L.		OF-1B	98	266	36	77	12	2	15	41	0	.289
2011 Washington	N.L.		1B-OF	146	522	73	158	36	0	31	95	2	.303
Major League Totals			7 Yrs.	383	1140	146	338	69	3	52	183	6	.296

a Traded by Chicago White Sox to Seattle Mariners with catcher Miguel Olivo and outfielder Jeremy Reed for pitcher
Freddy Garcia, catcher Ben Davis and cash, June 27, 2004.

b On disabled list from April 14 to September 29, 2008.

c Traded to Washington Nationals for outfielder Ryan Langerhans, June 28, 2009.

d On disabled list from April 11 to May 16, 2010.

MOUSTAKAS, MICHAEL CHRISTOPHER (MIKE)

Born, Los Angeles, California, September 11, 1988.
Bats Left. Throws Right. Height, 5 feet, 11 inches. Weight, 230 pounds.

Year	Club	Lea	Pos	G	AB	R	H	2B	3B	HR	RBI	SB	Avg
2007 Idaho Falls	Pioneer		SS	11	41	6	12	4	1	0	10	0	.293
2008 Burlington	Midwest		3B-SS	126	496	77	135	25	3	22	71	8	.272
2009 Wilmington	Carolina		3B	129	492	66	123	32	2	16	86	10	.250
2010 Omaha	P.C.		3B	52	225	36	66	16	0	15	48	2	.293
2010 NW Arkansas	Texas		3B	66	259	58	90	25	0	21	76	0	.347
2011 Omaha	P.C.		3B	55	223	38	64	15	1	10	44	1	.287
2011 Kansas City	A.L.		3B	89	338	26	89	18	1	5	30	2	.263

MURPHY, DANIEL THOMAS
Born, Jacksonville, Florida, April 1, 1985.
Bats Left. Throws Right. Height, 6 feet, 3 inches. Weight, 205 pounds.

Year Club	Lea	Pos	G	AB	R	H	2B	3B	HR	RBI	SB	Avg
2006 Mets.......Gulf Coast		DH	8	18	2	1	0	0	0	0	0	.056
2006 Kingsport.......Appal.		DH	9	33	2	9	0	0	2	7	0	.273
2006 Brooklyn.....N.Y.-Penn.		DH	8	29	2	7	1	0	0	3	0	.241
2007 St. Lucie........Fla.St.		3B	135	502	68	143	34	3	11	78	6	.285
2008 Brooklyn.....N.Y.-Penn.		DH	3	14	1	7	0	0	0	2	0	.500
2008 Binghamton....Eastern	3B-2B-1B-OF		95	357	56	110	26	1	13	67	14	.308
2008 New Orleans.......P.C.		3B	1	4	2	1	0	0	0	0	0	.250
2008 New York.........N.L.		OF	49	131	24	41	9	3	2	17	0	.313
2009 New York.........N.L.	1B-OF		155	508	60	135	38	4	12	63	4	.266
2010 St. Lucie........Fla.St.		1B	3	11	2	8	1	0	1	6	0	.727
2010 Buffalo a.........Int.	1B-2B		8	34	4	10	3	0	1	8	1	.294
2011 New York b.......N.L.	1B-3B-2B-OF		109	391	49	125	28	2	6	49	5	.320
Major League Totals	3 Yrs.		313	1030	133	301	75	9	20	129	9	.292

a On disabled list from March 31 to May 24, 2010.
b On disabled list from August 8 to October 24, 2011.

MURPHY, DAVID MATTHEW
Born, Houston, Texas, October 18, 1981.
Bats Left. Throws Left. Height, 6 feet, 4 inches. Weight, 205 pounds.

Year Club	Lea	Pos	G	AB	R	H	2B	3B	HR	RBI	SB	Avg
2003 Sarasota...........Fla.St.		OF	45	153	18	37	5	1	1	18	6	.242
2003 Lowell ..........N.Y.-Penn.		OF	21	78	13	27	4	0	0	13	4	.346
2004 Sarasota...........Fla.St.		OF	73	272	35	71	11	0	4	38	3	.261
2004 Red Sox........ Gulf Coast		OF	5	18	3	5	1	0	0	1	1	.278
2005 Portland...........Eastern		OF	135	484	71	133	25	4	14	75	13	.275
2006 Portland...........Eastern		OF	42	172	22	47	17	1	3	25	4	.273
2006 Pawtucket ....Int.		OF	84	318	45	85	23	5	8	44	3	.267
2006 Boston ..............A.L.		OF	20	22	4	5	1	0	1	2	0	.227
2007 Oklahoma...........P.C.		OF	2	7	0	2	0	0	0	0	0	.286
2007 Pawtucket ....Int.		OF	100	400	50	112	20	5	9	47	8	.280
2007 Boston-Texas a.......A.L.		OF	46	105	17	36	12	2	2	14	0	.343
2008 Texas b..............A.L.		OF	108	415	64	114	28	3	15	74	7	.275
2009 Texas ...............A.L.		OF	128	432	61	116	24	1	17	57	9	.269
2010 Texas ...............A.L.		OF	138	419	54	122	26	2	12	65	14	.291
2011 Texas ...............A.L.		OF	120	404	46	111	14	2	11	46	11	.275
Major League Totals	6 Yrs.		560	1797	246	504	105	10	58	258	41	.280
Division Series												
2010 Texas ...............A.L.		OF	2	7	0	1	0	0	0	0	0	.143
2011 Texas ...............A.L.		OF	3	6	0	2	0	0	0	0	0	.333
Division Series Totals			5	13	0	3	0	0	0	0	0	.231
Championship Series												
2010 Texas ...............A.L.		OF	6	13	6	3	1	0	1	2	0	.231
2011 Texas ...............A.L.		OF-DH	5	17	4	7	2	1	0	3	1	.412
Championship Series Totals			11	30	10	10	3	1	1	5	1	.333
World Series Record												
2010 Texas ...............A.L.		OF	3	7	0	1	0	0	0	1	0	.143
2011 Texas ...............A.L.		OF	7	18	1	4	1	0	0	0	0	.222
World Series Totals			10	25	1	5	1	0	0	1	0	.200

a Traded to Texas Rangers with pitcher Kason Gabbard and outfielder Engle Beltre for pitcher Eric Gagne, July 31, 2007.
b On disabled list from August 7 to October 2, 2008.

NADY, XAVIER CLIFFORD
Born, Salinas, California, November 14, 1978.
Bats Right. Throws Right. Height, 6 feet, 2 inches. Weight, 220 pounds.

Year Club	Lea	Pos	G	AB	R	H	2B	3B	HR	RBI	SB	Avg
2000 San Diego ...........N.L.		PH	1	1	1	1	0	0	0	0	0	1.000
2001 Lake Elsinore ..... California		1B	137	524	96	158	38	1	26	100	6	.302
2002 Lake Elsinore ..... California		OF	45	169	41	47	6	3	13	37	2	.278
2002 Portland..............P.C.		OF	85	315	46	89	12	1	10	43	0	.283
2003 Portland..............P.C.		OF	37	136	19	36	7	0	7	23	0	.265
2003 San Diego ...........N.L.		OF	110	371	50	99	17	1	9	39	6	.267
2004 Portland..............P.C.		OF-1B	74	291	52	96	19	1	22	70	3	.330

Year Club	Lea	Pos	G	AB	R	H	2B	3B	HR	RBI	SB	Avg
2004 San Diego	N.L.	OF	34	77	7	19	4	0	3	9	0	.247
2005 San Diego a	N.L.	OF-1B-3B	124	326	40	85	15	2	13	43	2	.261
2006 Norfolk................	Int.	OF	3	11	2	4	1	0	0	3	0	.364
2006 New York-Pittsburgh b-c .	N.L.	OF-1B	130	468	57	131	28	1	17	63	3	.280
2007 Pittsburgh	N.L.	OF	125	431	55	120	23	1	20	72	3	.278
2008 Pittsburgh	N.L.	OF	89	327	50	108	26	1	13	57	1	.330
2008 New York d..........	A.L.	OF-1B	59	228	26	61	11	0	12	40	1	.268
2009 Scranton/WB	Int.	OF	2	5	0	1	1	0	0	0	0	.200
2009 New York e-f	A.L.	OF	7	28	4	8	4	0	0	2	0	.286
2010 Chicago g............	N.L.	1B-OF	119	317	33	81	13	0	6	33	0	.256
2011 Arizona h-i	N.L.	1B-OF	82	206	26	51	11	0	4	35	2	.248
Major League Totals		10 Yrs.	880	2780	349	764	152	6	97	393	18	.275
Division Series												
2005 San Diego	N.L.	1B	2	3	0	1	0	0	0	2	0	.333

a Traded to New York Mets for outfielder Mike Cameron, November 18, 2005.

b On disabled list from May 30 to June 18, 2006.

c Traded to Pittsburgh Pirates for pitcher Oliver Perez and pitcher Roberto Hernandez, July 31, 2006.

d Traded to New York Yankees with pitcher Damaso Marte for outfielder Jose Tabata, pitcher Ross Ohlendorf, pitcher Jeff Karstens and pitcher Dan McCutchen, July 26, 2008.

e On disabled list from April 15 to November 9, 2009.

f Filed for free agency, November 9, 2009. Signed with Chicago Cubs, January 29, 2010.

g Filed for free agency, November 1, 2010. Signed with Arizona Diamondbacks, December 17, 2010.

h On disabled list from August 13 to October 11, 2011.

i Filed for free agency, October 31, 2011.

NAPOLI, MICHAEL ANTHONY (MIKE)

Born, Hollywood, Florida, October 31, 1981.
Bats Right. Throws Right. Height, 6 feet. Weight, 205 pounds.

Year Club	Lea	Pos	G	AB	R	H	2B	3B	HR	RBI	SB	Avg
2000 Butte	Pioneer	1B-C	10	26	3	6	2	0	0	3	1	.231
2001 Rancho Cucamonga...	Calif.	C	7	20	3	4	0	0	1	4	0	.200
2001 Cedar Rapids	Midwest	C-1B	43	155	23	36	10	1	5	18	3	.232
2002 Cedar Rapids	Midwest	C-1B-3B	106	362	57	91	19	1	10	50	6	.251
2003 Rancho Cucamonga...	Calif.	C-1B	47	165	28	44	10	1	4	26	5	.267
2004 Rancho Cucamonga...	Calif.	C-1B-3B	132	482	94	136	29	4	29	118	9	.282
2005 Arkansas	Texas	C-1B	131	439	96	104	22	2	31	99	12	.237
2006 Salt Lake	P.C.	C-1B	21	78	12	19	6	0	3	10	1	.244
2006 Los Angeles	A.L.	C	99	268	47	61	13	0	16	42	2	.228
2007 Los Angeles a	A.L.	C	75	219	40	54	11	1	10	34	5	.247
2008 Rancho Cucamonga...	Calif.	C	5	14	3	8	3	0	1	4	0	.571
2008 Los Angeles b	A.L.	C	78	227	39	62	9	1	20	49	7	.273
2009 Los Angeles	A.L.	C	114	382	60	104	22	1	20	56	3	.272
2010 Los Angeles	A.L.	1B-C	140	453	60	108	24	1	26	68	4	.238
2011 Round Rock..........	P.C.	C-1B	4	15	3	4	1	0	3	9	0	.267
2011 Texas c-d-e..........	A.L.	C-1B	113	369	72	118	25	0	30	75	4	.320
Major League Totals		6 Yrs.	619	1918	318	507	104	4	122	324	25	.264
Division Series												
2007 Los Angeles	A.L.	C	3	6	0	1	0	0	0	0	0	.167
2008 Los Angeles	A.L.	C	4	12	3	3	0	0	2	4	0	.250
2009 Los Angeles	A.L.	C	2	4	1	1	1	0	0	0	0	.250
2011 Texas	A.L.	C	4	14	3	5	0	0	1	4	1	.357
Division Series Totals			13	36	7	10	1	0	3	8	1	.278
Championship Series												
2009 Los Angeles	A.L.	C	5	9	0	1	0	0	0	0	0	.111
2011 Texas	A.L.	C-1B-DH	6	24	6	7	0	0	0	1	0	.292
Championship Series Totals			11	33	6	8	0	0	0	1	0	.242
World Series Record												
2011 Texas	A.L.	C-1B	7	20	2	7	1	0	2	10	0	.350

a On disabled list from July 2 to July 18 and July 28 to September 1, 2007.

b On disabled list from July 6 to August 8, 2008.

c Traded to Toronto Blue Jays with outfielder Juan Rivera for outfielder Vernon Wells, January 21, 2011.

d Traded to Texas Rangers for pitcher Frank Francisco, January 25, 2011.

e On disabled list from June 12 to July 4, 2011.

NAVARRO (VIVAS), DIONER FAVIAN
Born, Caracas, Venezuela, February 9, 1984.
Bats Both. Throws Right. Height, 5 feet, 10 inches. Weight, 205 pounds.

Year	Club	Lea	Pos	G	AB	R	H	2B	3B	HR	RBI	SB	Avg
2001	Yankees	Gulf Coast	C	43	143	27	40	10	1	2	22	6	.280
2002	Greensboro	So.Atl.	C	92	328	41	78	12	2	8	36	1	.238
2002	Tampa	Fla.St.	C	1	2	1	1	0	0	0	0	0	.500
2003	Tampa	Fla.St.	C	52	197	28	59	16	4	3	28	1	.299
2003	Trenton	Eastern	C	58	208	28	71	15	0	4	37	2	.341
2004	Trenton	Eastern	C	70	255	32	69	14	1	3	29	1	.271
2004	Columbus	Int.	C	40	136	18	34	8	2	1	16	1	.250
2004	New York	A.L.	C	5	7	2	3	0	0	0	1	0	.429
2005	Las Vegas	P.C.	C	75	241	31	64	12	0	6	29	2	.266
2005	Los Angeles a-b	N.L.	C	50	176	21	48	9	0	3	14	0	.273
2006	Los Angeles	N.L.	C	25	75	5	21	2	0	2	8	1	.280
2006	Las Vegas	P.C.	C	11	40	3	7	2	0	0	2	1	.175
2006	Tampa Bay c-d	A.L.	C	56	193	23	47	7	0	4	20	1	.244
2007	Tampa Bay	A.L.	C	119	388	46	88	19	2	9	44	3	.227
2008	Vero Beach	Fla.St.	C	4	10	4	4	1	0	1	4	1	.400
2008	Tampa Bay e	A.L.	C	120	427	43	126	27	0	7	54	0	.295
2009	Tampa Bay	A.L.	C	115	376	38	82	15	0	8	32	5	.218
2010	Durham	Int.	C	43	141	19	40	9	0	2	21	3	.284
2010	Tampa Bay f	A.L.	C	48	124	11	24	5	0	1	7	0	.194
2011	Chattanooga	Southern	C-1B	5	14	0	2	0	0	0	1	2	.143
2011	Los Angeles g-h-j	N.L.	C	64	176	13	34	6	1	5	17	0	.193
Major League Totals			8 Yrs.	602	1942	202	473	90	3	39	197	10	.244
Division Series													
2008	Tampa Bay	A.L.	C	4	15	1	6	3	0	0	3	0	.400
Championship Series													
2008	Tampa Bay	A.L.	C	7	26	1	5	0	0	0	2	0	.192
World Series Record													
2008	Tampa Bay	A.L.	C	5	17	2	6	1	0	0	0	0	.353

a Traded to Arizona Diamondbacks with pitcher Javier Vazquez, pitcher Brad Halsey and cash for pitcher Randy Johnson, January 11, 2005.
b Traded to Los Angeles Dodgers with pitcher Danny Muegge, pitcher Beltran Perez and pitcher William Juarez for outfielder Shawn Green, January 11, 2005.
c On disabled list from May 5 to June 15, 2006.
d Traded to Tampa Bay Devil Rays with pitcher Jae Seo and outfielder Justin Ruggiano for pitcher Mark Hendrickson, catcher Toby Hall and cash, June 27, 2006.
e On disabled list from April 5 to April 22, 2008.
f Not offered contract, December 2, 2010. Signed with Los Angeles Dodgers, December 14, 2010.
g On disabled list from March 22 to April 25, 2011.
h Released by Los Angeles Dodgers, August 30, 2011.
j Signed with Cincinnati Reds organization, January 16, 2012.

NELSON, CHRISTOPHER L. (CHRIS)
Born, Escondido, California, September 3, 1985.
Bats Right. Throws Right. Height, 5 feet, 11 inches. Weight, 175 pounds.

Year	Club	Lea	Pos	G	AB	R	H	2B	3B	HR	RBI	SB	Avg
2004	Casper	Pioneer	SS	38	147	36	51	6	3	4	20	6	.347
2005	Asheville	So.Atl.	SS	79	315	51	76	13	3	3	38	7	.241
2006	Asheville	So.Atl.	SS	118	466	69	121	38	1	11	76	14	.260
2007	Modesto	Calif.	SS	133	529	97	153	42	7	19	99	27	.289
2008	Modesto	Calif.	SS	8	30	2	5	1	0	1	5	0	.167
2008	Tulsa	Texas	SS	73	283	38	67	18	2	3	42	6	.237
2009	Tulsa	Texas	SS-2B	29	107	21	30	5	2	4	17	5	.280
2010	Colorado Springs	P.C.	SS-2B-3B-OF	85	319	60	100	15	3	12	55	7	.313
2010	Colorado	N.L.	2B-3B	17	25	7	7	1	0	0	0	1	.280
2011	Colorado Springs	P.C.	SS-2B-3B	73	289	52	95	20	5	11	65	3	.329
2011	Colorado	N.L.	2B-3B-SS	63	180	20	45	10	1	4	16	3	.250
Major League Totals			2 Yrs.	80	205	27	52	11	1	4	16	4	.254

NISHIOKA, TSUYOSHI
Born, Osaka, Japan, July 27, 1984.
Bats Both. Throws Right. Height, 6 feet, 1 inch. Weight, 175 pounds.

Year	Club	Lea	Pos	G	AB	R	H	2B	3B	HR	RBI	SB	Avg
2003	Chiba Lotte	Japan Pac.	2B	7	9	3	3	2	0	0	1	0	.333
2004	Chiba Lotte	Japan Pac.	2B	63	212	32	54	8	2	6	35	8	.255
2005	Chiba Lotte	Japan Pac.	SS-2B	122	447	80	120	22	11	4	48	41	.268
2006	Chiba Lotte	Japan Pac.	SS	115	426	58	120	20	7	4	27	33	.282

Year	Club	Lea	Pos	G	AB	R	H	2B	3B	HR	RBI	SB	Avg
2007 Chiba Lotte......	Japan	Pac.	SS	130	494	76	148	31	3	3	40	27	.300
2008 Chiba Lotte......	Japan	Pac.	SS	116	473	78	142	26	6	13	49	18	.300
2009 Chiba Lotte......	Japan	Pac.	SS	120	454	70	118	24	5	14	41	26	.260
2010 Chiba Lotte a	Japan	Pac.	SS	144	596	121	206	32	8	11	59	22	.346
2011 Fort Myers.........	Fla.St.		SS	4	12	4	4	1	0	0	1	1	.333
2011 Rochester.........	Int.		SS	3	12	0	4	1	0	0	1	0	.333
2011 Minnesota b.........	A.L.		SS-2B	68	221	14	50	5	0	0	19	2	.226

a Signed with Minnesota Twins, December 17, 2010.
b On disabled list from April 8 to June 15 and September 12 to October 3, 2011.

NIX, LAYNCE MICHAEL
Born, Houston, Texas, October 30, 1980.
Bats Left. Throws Left. Height, 6 feet. Weight, 220 pounds.

Year	Club	Lea	Pos	G	AB	R	H	2B	3B	HR	RBI	SB	Avg
2000 Rangers........	Gulf Coast		OF	51	199	34	45	7	1	2	25	4	.226
2001 Charlotte	Fla.St.		OF	9	37	4	11	3	1	0	2	0	.297
2001 Savannah	So.Atl.		OF	104	407	50	113	26	8	8	59	9	.278
2002 Charlotte	Fla.St.		OF	137	512	86	146	27	3	21	110	17	.285
2003 Frisco..............	Texas		OF	87	335	52	95	23	0	15	63	9	.284
2003 Texas	A.L.		OF	53	184	25	47	10	0	8	30	3	.255
2004 Frisco..............	Texas		OF	7	26	2	7	1	0	0	2	0	.269
2004 Texas a...........	A.L.		OF	115	371	58	92	20	4	14	46	1	.248
2005 Oklahoma........	P.C.		OF	10	36	8	12	1	1	3	6	0	.333
2005 Texas b..........	A.L.		OF	63	229	28	55	12	3	6	32	2	.240
2006 Texas	A.L.		OF	9	32	1	3	1	0	0	4	0	.094
2006 Oklahoma........	P.C.		OF	77	286	39	77	14	1	10	55	4	.269
2006 Nashville	P.C.		OF	18	68	16	28	5	1	7	13	0	.412
2006 Milwaukee c-d	N.L.		OF	10	35	2	8	1	0	1	6	0	.229
2007 Huntsville	Southern		OF	4	11	2	4	1	0	1	6	0	.364
2007 Nashville	P.C.		OF	95	347	60	93	20	1	24	74	5	.268
2007 Milwaukee e.........	N.L.		OF	10	12	0	0	0	0	0	0	0	.000
2008 Nashville	P.C.		OF	103	380	63	108	22	3	23	60	5	.284
2008 Milwaukee f.........	N.L.		OF	10	12	1	1	0	0	0	0	0	.083
2009 Cincinnati g-h.....	N.L.		OF	116	309	42	74	26	1	15	46	0	.239
2010 Cincinnati i-j.....	N.L.		OF	97	165	16	48	11	2	4	18	0	.291
2011 Washington k........	N.L.		OF-1B	124	324	38	81	15	1	16	44	2	.250
Major League Totals			9 Yrs.	607	1673	211	409	96	11	64	226	8	.244
Division Series													
2010 Cincinnati............	N.L.		OF	1	3	1	0	0	0	0	0	0	.000

a On disabled list from June 14 to July 10, 2004.
b On disabled list from July 15 to October 12, 2005.
c Traded to Milwaukee Brewers with pitcher Francisco Cordero, outfielder Kevin Mench and pitcher Julian Cordero for outfielder Carlos Lee and outfielder Nelson Cruz, July 28, 2006.
d On disabled list from September 9 to October 2, 2006.
e On disabled list from March 23 to May 14, 2007.
f Filed for free agency, October 9, 2008. Signed with Cincinnati Reds organization, December 15, 2008.
g On disabled list from August 31 to September 15, 2009.
h Filed for free agency, November 20, 2009, re-signed with Cincinnati Reds organization, December 18, 2009.
i On disabled list from August 26 to September 18, 2010.
j Filed for free agency, November 9, 2010. Signed with Washington Nationals organization, February 3, 2011.
k Filed for free agency, October 30, 2011. Signed with Philadelphia Phillies, December 5, 2011.

NUNEZ (MENDEZ), EDUARDO MICHELLE
Born, Santo Domingo, Dominican Republic, June 15, 1987.
Bats Right. Throws Right. Height, 6 feet. Weight, 155 pounds.

Year	Club	Lea	Pos	G	AB	R	H	2B	3B	HR	RBI	SB	Avg
2005 Staten Island .N.Y.-Penn.			SS	73	281	37	88	11	6	3	46	6	.313
2006 Tampa	Fla.St.		SS	37	147	17	27	5	3	4	26	6	.184
2006 Charleston	So.Atl.		SS-2B-3B	90	344	36	78	11	3	2	40	16	.227
2007 Charleston	So.Atl.		SS	91	328	36	78	10	2	1	28	20	.238
2007 Tampa	Fla.St.		SS	30	123	16	35	5	0	1	13	9	.285
2008 Tampa	Fla.St.		SS	94	373	45	101	18	3	6	42	14	.271
2009 Trenton........	Eastern		SS	123	497	70	160	26	1	9	55	19	.322
2010 Scranton-WB	Int.		SS-3B-2B	118	464	55	134	25	3	4	50	23	.289
2010 New York..........	A.L.		3B-SS-2B	30	50	12	14	1	0	1	7	5	.280
2011 New York..........	A.L.		SS-3B-2B-OF	112	309	38	82	18	2	5	30	22	.265
Major League Totals			2 Yrs.	142	359	50	96	19	2	6	37	27	.267
Division Series													
2011 New York.........	A.L.		PH	1	0	0	0	0	0	0	0	1	.000

OELTJEN, TRENT CARL WAYNE

Born, Sydney, Australia, February 28, 1983.
Bats Left. Throws Left. Height, 6 feet, 1 inch. Weight, 190 pounds.

Year Club	Lea	Pos	G	AB	R	H	2B	3B	HR	RBI	SB	Avg
2001 Twins	Gulf Coast	OF	45	134	21	43	7	3	0	18	10	.321
2001 Elizabethton	Appal.	OF	9	30	4	7	1	0	0	4	2	.233
2002 Elizabethton	Appal.	OF	54	215	36	64	7	2	3	18	7	.298
2002 Quad Cities	Midwest	OF	10	25	4	6	1	0	0	1	1	.240
2003 Quad Cities	Midwest	OF	123	466	73	139	12	8	4	44	29	.298
2004 Fort Myers	Fla.St.	OF	90	324	45	90	8	5	2	28	25	.278
2005 Fort Myers	Fla.St.	OF	98	341	44	98	17	4	4	43	21	.287
2006 New Britain	Eastern	OF	113	401	61	120	16	10	3	44	23	.299
2007 Rochester a	Int.	OF	97	244	33	58	9	5	2	23	14	.238
2008 Tucson	P.C.	OF	127	442	75	140	28	10	6	60	15	.317
2009 Reno	P.C.	OF	114	442	78	134	29	14	10	64	22	.303
2009 Arizona b	N.L.	OF	24	70	11	17	4	1	3	4	3	.243
2010 Nashville	P.C.	OF	70	266	47	80	24	2	8	38	13	.301
2010 Albuquerque	P.C.	OF	49	199	40	69	18	5	5	33	14	.347
2010 Los Angeles c-d	N.L.	OF	14	23	5	5	1	1	0	1	0	.217
2011 Albuquerque	P.C.	OF	56	180	33	61	14	3	8	34	7	.339
2011 Los Angeles	N.L.	OF	61	71	10	14	1	1	2	6	6	.197
Major League Totals	3 Yrs.		99	164	26	36	6	3	5	11	9	.220

a Field for free agency from Minnesota Twins, October 29, 2007. Signed with Arizona Diamondbacks organization, November 28, 2007.
b Filed for free agency, November 9, 2009. Signed with Milwaukee Brewers organization, December 4, 2009.
c Filed for free agency, July 1, 2010. Signed with Los Angeles Dodgers organization, July 6, 2010.
d Not offered contract, December 2, 2010, re-signed with Los Angeles Dodgers organization, December 7, 2010.

OLIVO (PENA), MIGUEL EDUARDO

Born, Villa Vasquez, Dominican Republic, July 15, 1978.
Bats Right. Throws Right. Height, 6 feet. Weight, 220 pounds.

Year Club	Lea	Pos	G	AB	R	H	2B	3B	HR	RBI	SB	Avg
1997 Oakland-East	Dominican	C	63	221	37	60	11	4	6	57	6	.271
1998 Athletics	Arizona	C-OF	46	164	30	51	11	3	2	23	2	.311
1999 Modesto	California	C	73	243	46	74	13	6	9	42	4	.305
2000 Modesto	California	C	58	227	40	64	11	5	5	35	5	.282
2000 Midland a-b-c	Texas	C	19	59	8	14	2	0	1	9	0	.237
2001 Birmingham d	Southern	C	93	316	45	82	23	1	14	55	6	.259
2002 Birmingham	Southern	C	106	359	51	110	24	10	6	49	29	.306
2002 Chicago e	A.L.	C	6	19	2	4	1	0	1	5	0	.211
2003 Chicago	A.L.	C	114	317	37	75	19	1	6	27	6	.237
2004 Everett	Northwest	C	2	6	0	0	0	0	0	0	0	.000
2004 Chicago-Seattle f-g	A.L.	C	96	301	46	70	15	4	13	40	7	.233
2005 Tacoma	P.C.	C	24	90	13	21	4	1	3	21	8	.233
2005 Seattle	A.L.	C	54	152	14	23	4	0	5	18	1	.151
2005 San Diego h	N.L.	C	37	115	16	35	7	1	4	16	6	.304
2006 Florida i	N.L.	C-1B	127	430	52	113	22	3	16	58	2	.263
2007 Florida j	N.L.	C	122	452	43	107	20	4	16	60	3	.237
2008 Kansas City	A.L.	C	84	306	29	78	22	0	12	41	7	.255
2009 Kansas City k	A.L.	C	114	390	51	97	15	5	23	65	5	.249
2010 Colorado l-m	N.L.	C	112	394	55	106	17	6	14	58	7	.269
2011 Seattle	A.L.	C	130	477	54	107	19	1	19	62	6	.224
Major League Totals	10 Yrs.		996	3353	399	815	161	25	129	450	50	.243
Division Series												
2005 San Diego	N.L.	PH	1	1	0	0	0	0	0	0	0	.000

a On disabled list from August 8 to September 29, 2000.
b Chicago White Sox traded pitcher Chad Bradford to Oakland Athletics for player to be named later, December 7, 2000.
c Sent by Oakland Athletics to Chicago White Sox to complete trade, December 12, 2000.
d On disabled list from April 22 to May 2, 2001.
e On disabled list from June 4 to 11, 2002.
f Traded to Seattle Mariners with outfielder Jeremy Reed and infielder Michael Morse for pitcher Freddy Garcia, catcher Ben Davis and cash, June 27, 2004.
g On disabled list from June 30 to July 15, 2004.
h Traded to San Diego Padres for catcher Miguel Ojeda and pitcher Nathaniel Mateo, July 31, 2005.
i Filed for free agency, December 21, 2005. Signed with Florida Marlins, January 3, 2006.
j Not offered contract, December 12, 2007. Signed with Kansas City Royals, December 27, 2007.
k Filed for free agency, November 6, 2009. Signed with Colorado Rockies, January 4, 2010.
l Traded to Toronto Blue Jays for player to be named later, November 4, 2010.
m Filed for free agency, November 4, 2010. Signed with Seattle Mariners, December 10, 2010.

ORDONEZ, MAGGLIO JOSE

Born, Caracas, Venezuela, January 28, 1974.
Bats Right. Throws Right. Height, 6 feet. Weight, 215 pounds.

Year	Club	Lea	Pos	G	AB	R	H	2B	3B	HR	RBI	SB	Avg
1993 Hickory	So. Atl.		OF	84	273	32	59	14	4	3	20	5	.216
1994 Hickory	So. Atl.		OF	132	490	86	144	24	5	11	69	16	.294
1995 Pr William	Carolina		OF	131	487	61	116	24	2	12	65	11	.238
1996 Birmingham	Southern		OF	130	479	66	126	41	0	18	67	9	.263
1997 Nashville	A.A.		OF	135	523	65	172	29	3	14	90	14	.329
1997 Chicago	A.L.		OF	21	69	12	22	6	0	4	11	1	.319
1998 Chicago	A.L.		OF	145	535	70	151	25	2	14	65	9	.282
1999 Chicago	A.L.		OF	157	624	100	188	34	3	30	117	13	.301
2000 Chicago	A.L.		OF	153	588	102	185	34	3	32	126	18	.315
2001 Chicago	A.L.		OF	160	593	97	181	40	1	31	113	25	.305
2002 Chicago	A.L.		OF	153	590	116	189	47	1	38	135	7	.320
2003 Chicago	A.L.		OF	160	606	95	192	46	3	29	99	9	.317
2004 Chicago a-b	A.L.		OF	52	202	32	59	8	2	9	37	0	.292
2005 Toledo	Int.		OF	4	14	3	3	1	0	1	2	0	.214
2005 Detroit c	A.L.		OF	82	305	38	92	17	0	8	46	0	.302
2006 Detroit	A.L.		OF	155	593	82	177	32	1	24	104	1	.298
2007 Detroit	A.L.		OF	157	595	117	216	*54	0	28	139	4	*.363
2008 West Michigan	Midwest		DH	1	4	1	1	0	0	0	0	0	.250
2008 Detroit d	A.L.		OF	146	561	72	178	32	2	21	103	1	.317
2009 Detroit	A.L.		OF	131	465	54	144	24	2	9	50	3	.310
2010 Detroit e-f	A.L.		OF	84	323	56	98	17	1	12	59	1	.303
2011 Toledo	Int.		OF	9	37	3	11	1	0	2	6	0	.297
2011 Detroit g-h	A.L.		OF	92	329	33	84	10	0	5	32	2	.255
Major League Totals		15 Yrs.		1848	6978	1076	2156	426	21	294	1236	94	.309
Division Series													
2000 Chicago	A.L.		OF	3	11	0	2	0	1	0	1	1	.182
2006 Detroit	A.L.		OF	4	15	3	4	1	0	1	2	0	.267
2011 Detroit	A.L.		OF	4	11	1	5	1	0	0	0	0	.455
Division Series Totals				11	37	4	11	2	1	1	3	1	.297
Championship Series													
2006 Detroit	A.L.		OF	4	17	3	4	0	0	2	6	0	.235
2011 Detroit	A.L.		OF	1	2	0	0	0	0	0	0	0	.000
Championship Series Totals				5	19	3	4	0	0	2	6	0	.211
World Series Record													
2006 Detroit	A.L.		OF	5	19	2	2	0	0	0	0	0	.105

a On disabled list from May 26 to July 8 and from July 22 to October 12, 2004.
b Filed for free agency, October 28, 2004. Signed with Detroit Tigers organization, February 7, 2005.
c On disabled list from April 13 to July 1, 2005.
d On disabled list from June 29 to July 17, 2008.
e On disabled list from July 25 to October 6, 2010.
f Filed for free agency, November 1, 2010, re-signed with Detroit Tigers, December 17, 2010.
g On disabled list from May 11 to June 13, 2011.
h Filed for free agency, October 30, 2011.

ORTIZ (ARIAS), DAVID AMERICO

Born, Santo Domingo, Dominican Republic, November 18, 1975.
Bats Left. Throws Left. Height, 6 feet, 4 inches. Weight, 230 pounds.

Year	Club	Lea	Pos	G	AB	R	H	2B	3B	HR	RBI	SB	Avg
1993 Seattle	Dominican		1B	61	201	37	53	17	1	7	31	1	.264
1994 Mariners	Arizona		1B	53	167	14	41	10	1	2	20	1	.246
1995 Mariners	Arizona		1B	48	184	30	61	18	4	4	37	2	.332
1996 Wisconsin a	Midwest		1B	129	485	89	156	34	2	18	93	3	.322
1997 Salt Lake	P.C.		1B	10	42	5	9	1	0	4	10	0	.214
1997 New Britain	Eastern		DH-1B	69	258	40	83	22	2	14	56	2	.322
1997 Ft. Myers	Fla.St.		1B	61	239	45	79	15	0	13	58	2	.331
1997 Minnesota	A.L.		1B	15	49	10	16	3	0	1	6	0	.327
1998 Salt Lake	P.C.		1B	11	37	5	9	3	0	2	6	0	.243
1998 Minnesota b	A.L.		1B	86	278	47	77	20	0	9	46	1	.277
1999 Salt Lake	P.C.		1B	130	476	85	150	35	3	30	110	2	.315
1999 Minnesota	A.L.		1B	10	20	1	0	0	0	0	0	0	.000
2000 Minnesota	A.L.		DH-1B	130	415	59	117	36	1	10	63	1	.282
2001 Twins	Gulf Coast		DH	4	10	3	4	0	0	0	1	0	.400
2001 Fort Myers	Fla.St.		1B	1	3	0	0	0	0	0	0	0	.000
2001 New Britain	Eastern		1B	9	37	3	9	4	0	0	1	0	.243
2001 Minnesota c	A.L.		DH-1B	89	303	46	71	17	1	18	48	1	.234

Year	Club	Lea	Pos	G	AB	R	H	2B	3B	HR	RBI	SB	Avg
2002 Minnesota d-e	A.L.	DH-1B	125	412	52	112	32	1	20	75	1	.272
2003 Boston	A.L.	DH-1B	128	448	79	129	39	2	31	101	0	.288
2004 Boston	A.L.	DH-1B	150	582	94	175	47	3	41	139	0	.301
2005 Boston	A.L.	DH-1B	159	601	119	180	40	1	47	*148	1	.300
2006 Boston	A.L.	DH-1B	151	558	115	160	29	2	*54	*137	1	.287
2007 Boston	A.L.	DH-1B	149	549	116	182	52	1	35	117	3	.332
2008 Portland	Eastern	DH	3	8	2	2	0	0	0	1	0	.250
2008 Pawtucket	Int.	DH	3	9	4	3	0	0	3	5	0	.333
2008 Boston f	A.L.	DH	109	416	74	110	30	1	23	89	1	.264
2009 Boston	A.L.	DH-1B	150	541	77	129	35	1	28	99	1	.238
2010 Boston	A.L.	DH-1B	145	518	86	140	36	1	32	102	0	.270
2011 Boston g	A.L.	DH-1B	146	525	84	162	40	1	29	96	1	.309
Major League Totals	15 Yrs.		1742	6215	1059	1760	456	16	378	1266	11	.283
Division Series												
2002 Minnesota	A.L.	DH	4	13	0	3	2	0	0	2	0	.231
2003 Boston	A.L.	DH	5	21	0	2	1	0	0	2	0	.095
2004 Boston	A.L.	DH	3	11	4	6	2	0	1	4	0	.545
2005 Boston	A.L.	DH	3	12	2	4	2	0	1	1	0	.333
2007 Boston	A.L.	DH	3	7	5	5	0	0	2	3	0	.714
2008 Boston	A.L.	DH	4	17	1	4	1	0	0	1	0	.235
2009 Boston	A.L.	DH	3	12	0	1	0	0	0	0	0	.083
Division Series Totals			25	93	12	25	8	0	4	13	0	.269
Championship Series												
2002 Minnesota	A.L.	DH	5	16	0	5	1	0	0	2	0	.313
2003 Boston	A.L.	DH	7	26	4	7	1	0	2	6	0	.269
2004 Boston	A.L.	DH	7	31	6	12	0	1	3	11	0	.387
2007 Boston	A.L.	DH	7	24	7	7	3	0	1	3	0	.292
2008 Boston	A.L.	DH	7	26	3	4	1	1	1	4	0	.154
Championship Series Totals			33	123	20	35	6	2	7	26	0	.285
World Series Record												
2004 Boston	A.L.	1B-DH	4	13	3	4	1	0	1	4	0	.308
2007 Boston	A.L.	1B-DH	4	15	4	5	3	0	0	4	0	.333
World Series Totals			8	28	7	9	4	0	1	8	0	.321

a Sent to Minnesota Twins by Seattle Mariners to complete trade for infielder Dave Hollins, September 13, 1996.
b On disabled list from May 10 to July 9, 1998.
c On disabled list from May 5 to July 21, 2001.
d On disabled list from April 20 to May 13, 2002.
e Released by Minnesota Twins, December 16, 2002. Signed with Boston Red Sox, January 22, 2003.
f On disabled list from June 1 to July 25, 2008.
g Filed for free agency, October 30, 2011. Accepted arbitration, December 7, 2011.

OVERBAY, LYLE STEFAN
Born, Centralia, Washington, January 28, 1977.
Bats Left. Throws Left. Height, 6 feet, 2 inches. Weight, 235 pounds.

Year	Club	Lea	Pos	G	AB	R	H	2B	3B	HR	RBI	SB	Avg
1999 Missoula	Pioneer	1B	75	306	66	105	25	7	12	101	10	.343
2000 South Bend	Midwest	1B	71	259	47	86	19	3	6	47	9	.332
2000 El Paso	Texas	1B	62	244	43	86	16	2	8	49	3	.352
2001 El Paso	Texas	1B-OF	138	532	82	187	49	3	13	100	5	.352
2001 Arizona	N.L.	PH	2	2	0	1	0	0	0	0	0	.500
2002 Tucson	P.C.	1B	134	525	83	180	40	0	19	109	0	.343
2002 Arizona	N.L.	PH	10	10	0	1	0	0	0	1	0	.100
2003 Tucson	P.C.	1B	35	119	24	34	11	0	4	16	0	.286
2003 Arizona a	N.L.	1B	86	254	23	70	20	0	4	28	1	.276
2004 Milwaukee	N.L.	1B	159	579	83	174	*53	1	16	87	2	.301
2005 Milwaukee b	N.L.	1B	158	537	80	148	34	1	19	72	1	.276
2006 Toronto	A.L.	1B	157	581	82	181	46	1	22	92	5	.312
2007 New Hampshire	Eastern	1B	4	15	2	4	1	0	1	5	0	.267
2007 Toronto c	A.L.	1B	122	425	49	102	30	2	10	44	2	.240
2008 Toronto	A.L.	1B	158	544	74	147	32	2	15	69	1	.270
2009 Toronto	A.L.	1B	132	423	57	112	35	1	16	64	0	.265
2010 Toronto d	A.L.	1B	154	534	75	130	37	2	20	67	1	.243
2011 Pittsburgh-Arizona e-f	N.L.	1B	121	394	43	92	21	1	9	47	2	.234
Major League Totals	11 Yrs.		1259	4283	566	1158	308	11	131	571	15	.270
Division Series												
2011 Arizona	N.L.	1B	2	4	0	0	0	0	0	0	0	.000

a Traded to Milwaukee Brewers with infielder Junior Spivey, infielder Craig Counsell, catcher Chad Moeller, pitcher Chris Capuano and pitcher Jorge De La Rosa for infielder Richie Sexson, pitcher Shane Nance and player to be named later, December 1, 2003. Arizona Diamondbacks received outfielder Gary Varner to complete trade, December 15, 2003.

b Traded to Toronto Blue Jays with pitcher Ty Taubenheim for pitcher Dave Bush, outfielder Gabe Gross and pitcher Zach Jackson, December 7, 2005.

c On disabled list from June 4 to July 12, 2007.

d Filed for free agency, November 1, 2010. Signed with Pittsburgh Pirates, December 14, 2010.

e Released by Toronto Blue Jays, August 5, 2011. Signed with Arizona Diamondbacks, August 13, 2011.

f Filed for free agency, October 31, 2011, re-signed with Arizona Diamondbacks, December 9, 2011.

PAGAN, ANGEL ANTHONY

Born, Rio Piedras, Puerto Rico, July 2, 1981.
Bats Both. Throws Right. Height, 6 feet, 1 inch. Weight, 195 pounds.

Year	Club	Lea	Pos	G	AB	R	H	2B	3B	HR	RBI	SB	Avg
2000 Kingsport	Appal.	OF	19	72	13	26	5	1	0	8	6	.361
2001 Brooklyn	N.Y.-Penn.	OF	62	238	46	75	10	2	0	15	30	.315
2001 Columbia	So.Atl.	OF	15	57	4	17	1	1	0	5	3	.298
2002 St. Lucie	Fla.St.	OF	16	67	12	23	2	1	1	7	10	.343
2002 Columbia	So.Atl.	OF	108	458	79	128	14	5	1	36	52	.279
2003 St. Lucie	Fla.St.	OF	113	441	64	110	15	5	1	33	35	.249
2004 Binghamton	Eastern	OF	112	448	71	129	25	8	4	63	29	.288
2004 Norfolk	Int.	OF	12	45	13	13	3	3	0	1	4	.289
2005 Norfolk	Int.	OF	129	516	69	140	20	10	8	40	27	.271
2006 Cubs	Arizona	OF	3	9	1	1	0	0	0	0	1	.111
2006 Iowa	P.C.	OF	4	15	2	4	1	0	0	0	1	.267
2006 Chicago a-b	N.L.	OF	77	170	28	42	6	2	5	18	4	.247
2007 Iowa	P.C.	OF	33	116	18	29	4	3	3	9	6	.250
2007 Chicago c-d	N.L.	OF	71	148	21	39	10	2	4	21	4	.264
2008 Mets	Gulf Coast	OF	2	5	1	3	1	0	0	0	2	.600
2008 Brooklyn	N.Y.-Penn.	OF	4	13	0	4	0	0	0	1	3	.308
2008 St. Lucie	Fla.St.	OF	1	4	1	0	0	0	0	0	0	.000
2008 New York e	N.L.	OF	31	91	12	25	7	1	0	13	4	.275
2009 St. Lucie	Fla.St.	OF	4	12	4	5	2	0	0	3	2	.417
2009 Buffalo	Int.	OF	3	14	2	4	0	2	0	2	0	.286
2009 New York f	N.L.	OF	88	343	54	105	22	11	6	32	14	.306
2010 New York	N.L.	OF	151	579	80	168	31	7	11	69	37	.290
2011 St. Lucie	Fla.St.	OF	8	31	6	7	1	1	1	2	0	.226
2011 New York g-h	N.L.	OF	123	478	68	125	24	4	7	56	32	.262
Major League Totals		6 Yrs.	541	1809	263	504	100	27	33	209	95	.279	

a Sold to Chicago by New York Mets, January 25, 2006.

b On disabled list from April 16 to June 30, 2006.

c On disabled list from August 8 to November 1, 2007.

d Traded to New York Mets for pitcher Ryan Meyers and outfielder Corey Coles, January 5, 2008.

e On disabled list from May 13 to November 3, 2008.

f On disabled list from March 27 to May 16 and June 1 to July 10, 2009.

g On disabled list from April 22 to May 27, 2011.

h Traded to San Francisco Giants for pitcher Ramon Ramirez and outfielder Andres Torres, December 7, 2011.

PAREDES, JIMMY SANTIAGO

Born, Haina, Dominican Republic, November 25, 1988.
Bats Both. Throws Right. Height, 6 feet, 1 inch. Weight, 200 pounds.

Year	Club	Lea	Pos	G	AB	R	H	2B	3B	HR	RBI	SB	Avg
2008 Yankees	Gulf Coast	3B-SS	47	161	23	45	9	2	1	15	6	.280
2009 Staten Island	N.Y.-Penn.	2B-3B	54	205	36	62	8	4	2	17	23	.302
2010 Charleston	So.Atl.	2B-SS-3B	99	404	59	114	24	6	5	48	36	.282
2010 Lexington a	So.Atl.	2B	34	147	24	44	10	1	3	17	14	.299
2011 Corpus Christi	Texas	2B-3B	93	385	69	104	22	4	10	41	29	.270
2011 Houston	N.L.	3B	46	168	16	48	8	2	2	18	5	.286

a Traded by New York Yankees to Houston Astros with pitcher Mark Melancon for infielder Lance Berkman and cash, July 31, 2010.

PARRA, GERARDO ENRIQUE

Born, Santa Barbara Del Zulia, Venezuela, May 6, 1987.
Bats Left. Throws Left. Height, 5 feet, 11 inches. Weight, 195 pounds.

Year	Club	Lea	Pos	G	AB	R	H	2B	3B	HR	RBI	SB	Avg
2006 Missoula	Pioneer	OF	69	271	46	89	18	4	4	43	23	.328
2007 Visalia	Calif.	OF	24	102	11	29	2	1	2	14	2	.284
2007 South Bend	Midwest	OF	110	444	64	142	25	4	6	57	24	.320
2008 Visalia	Calif.	OF	50	196	26	59	8	4	2	19	12	.301
2008 Mobile	Southern	OF	73	265	35	73	14	6	4	33	16	.275

Year Club	Lea	Pos	G	AB	R	H	2B	3B	HR	RBI	SB	Avg
2009 Mobile .... Southern		OF	29	108	23	39	3	1	3	12	7	.361
2009 Arizona............. N.L.		OF	120	455	59	132	21	8	5	60	5	.290
2010 Reno .... P.C.		OF	9	36	8	15	4	0	1	7	3	.417
2010 Arizona............. N.L.		OF	133	364	31	95	19	6	3	30	1	.261
2011 Arizona............. N.L.		OF	141	445	55	130	20	8	8	46	15	.292
Major League Totals	3 Yrs.		394	1264	145	357	60	22	16	136	21	.282
Division Series												
2011 Arizona............. N.L.		OF	5	18	1	1	1	0	0	0	0	.056

PATTERSON, DONALD COREY (COREY)
Born, Atlanta, Georgia, August 13, 1979.
Bats Left. Throws Right. Height, 5 feet, 10 inches. Weight, 180 pounds.

Year Club	Lea	Pos	G	AB	R	H	2B	3B	HR	RBI	SB	Avg
1999 Lansing .... Midwest		OF	112	475	94	152	35	17	20	79	33	.320
2000 West Tenn .... Southern		OF	118	444	73	116	26	5	22	82	27	.261
2000 Chicago .... N.L.		OF	11	42	9	7	1	0	2	2	1	.167
2001 Iowa................. P.C.		OF	89	367	63	93	22	3	7	32	19	.253
2001 Chicago .... N.L.		OF	59	131	26	29	3	0	4	14	4	.221
2002 Chicago .... N.L.		OF	153	592	71	150	30	5	14	54	18	.253
2003 Chicago a .... N.L.		OF	83	329	49	98	17	7	13	55	16	.298
2004 Chicago .... N.L.		OF	157	631	91	168	33	6	24	72	32	.266
2005 Iowa................. P.C.		OF	24	91	16	27	4	0	5	12	6	.297
2005 Chicago .... N.L.		OF	126	451	47	97	15	3	13	34	15	.215
2006 Baltimore b .... A.L.		OF	135	463	75	128	19	5	16	53	45	.276
2007 Baltimore .... A.L.		OF	132	461	65	124	26	2	8	45	37	.269
2008 Louisville .... Int.		OF	5	22	3	9	2	0	0	0	1	.409
2008 Cincinnati c-d........ N.L.		OF	135	366	46	75	17	2	10	34	14	.205
2009 Syracuse .... Int.		OF	84	263	30	72	16	1	7	40	14	.274
2009 Nashville .... P.C.		OF	29	124	24	41	12	3	5	22	7	.331
2009 Washington-Milwaukee e-f N.L.		OF	16	29	0	3	0	0	0	0	2	.103
2010 Norfolk .... Int.		OF	14	57	6	21	5	1	0	2	3	.368
2010 Baltimore g-h......... A.L.		OF	90	308	43	83	16	1	8	32	21	.269
2011 Dunedin .... Fla.St.		OF	4	15	1	5	0	0	0	0	3	.333
2011 Toronto .... A.L.		OF	89	317	44	80	16	3	6	33	13	.252
2011 St. Louis i-j-k .... N.L.		OF	44	51	5	8	4	0	0	3	0	.157
Major League Totals	12 Yrs.		1230	4171	571	1050	197	34	118	431	218	.252

a On disabled list from July 7 to October 31, 2003.
b Traded to Baltimore Orioles for infielder Nate Spears and pitcher Carlos Perez, January 9, 2006.
c Filed for free agency, October 31, 2007. Signed with Cincinnati Reds organization, March 3, 2008.
d Filed for free agency, November 3, 2008. Signed with Washington Nationals organization, December 18, 2008.
e Released by Washington Nationals, July 29, 2009. Signed with Milwaukee Brewers organization, August 1, 2009.
f Filed for free agency, November 5, 2009. Signed with Seattle Mariners organization, December 10, 2009.
g Released by Seattle Mariners, April 1, 2010. Signed with Baltimore Orioles organization, April 21, 2010.
h Filed for free agency, November 1, 2010. Signed with Toronto Blue Jays organization, December 21, 2010.
i On disabled list from March 27 to April 11, 2011.
j Traded to St. Louis Cardinals with pitcher Edwin Jackson, pitcher Octavio Dotel, pitcher Marc Rzepczynski and cash for outfielder Colby Rasmus, pitcher Trever Miller, pitcher Brian Tallet and pitcher P.J. Walters, July 27, 2011.
k Filed for free agency, October 31, 2011.

PAUL, XAVIER BROOKS
Born, Slidell, Louisiana, February 25, 1985.
Bats Left. Throws Right. Height, 6 feet. Weight, 205 pounds.

Year Club	Lea	Pos	G	AB	R	H	2B	3B	HR	RBI	SB	Avg
2003 Ogden .... Pioneer		OF	69	264	60	81	15	6	7	47	11	.307
2004 Columbus.......... So.Atl.		OF	126	460	69	122	26	6	9	72	10	.265
2005 Vero Beach......... Fla.St.		OF	85	288	42	71	15	3	7	41	1	.247
2006 Vero Beach......... Fla.St.		OF	120	470	62	134	23	3	13	49	22	.285
2007 Jacksonville ...... Southern		OF	118	422	64	123	21	2	11	50	17	.291
2008 Las Vegas............ P.C.		OF	115	443	82	140	28	5	9	68	17	.316
2009 Los Angeles .... N.L.		OF	11	14	3	3	1	0	1	1	0	.214
2009 Albuquerque a .... P.C.		OF	31	116	13	38	10	2	2	16	8	.328
2010 Los Angeles .... N.L.		OF	44	121	16	28	8	1	0	11	3	.231
2010 Albuquerque.......... P.C.		OF	57	228	46	74	20	1	12	38	7	.325
2011 Los Angeles-Pittsburgh b-c..N.L.		OF	128	243	30	62	6	5	2	20	16	.255
Major League Totals	3 Yrs.		183	378	49	93	15	6	3	32	19	.246

a On disabled list from May 21 to November 9, 2009.
b Claimed on waivers by Pittsburgh Pirates, April 26, 2011.
c Filed for free agency, November 30, 2011. Signed with Washington Nationals organization, December 20, 2011.

PAULINO, RONNY LEONEL

Born, Santo Domingo, Dominican Republic, April 21, 1981.
Bats Right. Throws Right. Height, 6 feet, 3 inches. Weight, 245 pounds.

Year	Club	Lea	Pos	G	AB	R	H	2B	3B	HR	RBI	SB	Avg
1998 Pittsburgh	Dominican		C	53	170	18	40	5	0	4	26	6	.235
1999 Pirates	Gulf Coast		C	29	83	6	21	2	4	1	13	1	.253
2000 Hickory	So.Atl.	C-1B-3B	88	301	38	87	16	2	6	39	3	.289	
2001 Lynchburg	Carolina		C	103	352	30	102	16	1	6	51	4	.290
2002 Lynchburg	Carolina	C-1B	119	442	63	116	26	2	12	55	2	.262	
2003 Lynchburg	Carolina		C	23	81	8	19	3	0	1	12	1	.235
2003 Altoona a	Eastern		C	46	159	19	36	6	1	6	19	0	.226
2004 Altoona	Eastern	C-1B	99	369	54	105	23	2	15	60	3	.285	
2005 Altoona	Eastern		C	43	168	24	49	6	0	6	20	3	.292
2005 Indianapolis	Int.		C	77	273	49	86	18	2	13	42	3	.315
2005 Pittsburgh	N.L.		C	2	4	1	2	0	0	0	0	0	.500
2006 Indianapolis	Int.		C	8	29	2	7	3	0	0	4	1	.241
2006 Pittsburgh	N.L.		C	129	442	37	137	19	0	6	55	0	.310
2007 Pittsburgh	N.L.		C	133	457	56	120	25	0	11	55	2	.263
2008 Pirates	Gulf Coast		C	8	28	3	8	1	0	1	6	0	.286
2008 Indianapolis	Int.		C	30	111	16	34	13	1	4	18	0	.306
2008 Pittsburgh b	N.L.		C	40	118	8	25	5	0	2	18	0	.212
2009 Florida c-d	N.L.		C	80	239	24	65	10	1	8	27	1	.272
2010 Florida e	N.L.		C	91	316	31	82	18	0	4	37	1	.259
2011 St. Lucie	Fla.St.		C	5	17	1	3	1	0	0	2	0	.176
2011 Buffalo	Int.		C	7	25	2	5	1	0	0	2	0	.200
2011 New York f-g	N.L.		C	78	228	19	61	13	0	2	19	0	.268
Major League Totals			7 Yrs.	553	1804	176	492	90	1	33	211	4	.273

a Selected by Kansas City Royals from Pittsburgh Pirates in Rule V draft, December 16, 2002. Returned to Pittsburgh Pirates, March 13, 2003.

b Traded to Philadelphia Phillies for catcher Jason Jaramillo, December 10, 2008.

c Traded to San Francisco Giants for pitcher Jack Taschner, March 27, 2009.

d Traded to Florida Marlins for pitcher Hector Correa, March 28, 2009.

e Not offered contract, December 2, 2010. Signed with New York Mets, December 9, 2010.

f On disabled list from April 10 to April 29, 2011.

g Not offered contract, December 12, 2011.

PEDROIA, DUSTIN LUIS

Born, Woodland, California, August 17, 1983.
Bats Right. Throws Right. Height, 5 feet, 9 inches. Weight, 180 pounds.

Year	Club	Lea	Pos	G	AB	R	H	2B	3B	HR	RBI	SB	Avg
2004 Sarasota	Fla.St.		SS	30	107	23	36	8	3	2	14	0	.336
2004 Augusta	So.Atl.		SS	12	50	11	20	5	0	1	5	2	.400
2005 Portland	Eastern	2B-SS	66	256	39	83	19	2	8	40	7	.324	
2005 Pawtucket	Int.	2B-SS	51	204	39	52	9	1	5	24	1	.255	
2006 Pawtucket	Int.	SS-2B-3B	111	423	55	129	30	3	5	50	1	.305	
2006 Boston	A.L.	2B-SS	31	89	5	17	4	0	2	7	0	.191	
2007 Boston a	A.L.		2B	139	520	86	165	39	1	8	50	7	.317
2008 Boston b	A.L.		2B	157	653	*118	*213	*54	2	17	83	20	.326
2009 Boston	A.L.		2B	154	626	*115	185	48	1	15	72	20	.296
2010 Pawtucket	Int.		2B	2	6	1	1	0	0	0	0	0	.167
2010 Boston c	A.L.		2B	75	302	53	87	24	1	12	41	9	.288
2011 Boston	A.L.		2B	159	635	102	195	37	3	21	91	26	.307
Major League Totals			6 Yrs.	715	2825	479	862	206	8	75	344	82	.305
Division Series													
2007 Boston	A.L.		2B	3	13	2	2	2	0	0	1	0	.154
2008 Boston	A.L.		2B	4	17	0	1	1	0	0	1	0	.059
2009 Boston	A.L.		2B	3	12	1	2	1	0	0	2	0	.167
Division Series Totals				10	42	3	5	4	0	0	4	0	.119
Championship Series													
2007 Boston	A.L.		2B	7	29	8	10	3	0	1	5	0	.345
2008 Boston	A.L.		2B	7	26	9	9	1	0	3	5	2	.346
Championship Series Totals				14	55	17	19	4	0	4	10	2	.345
World Series Record													
2007 Boston	A.L.		2B	4	18	2	5	1	0	1	4	0	.278

a Selected Rookie of the Year in American League for 2007.

b Selected Most Valuable Player in American League for 2008.

c On disabled list from June 26 to August 17 and August 19 to October 13, 2010.

PENA, BRAYAN EDUARDO

Born, Havana, Cuba, January 7, 1982.
Bats Both. Throws Right. Height, 5 feet, 11 inches. Weight, 245 pounds.

Year	Club	Lea	Pos	G	AB	R	H	2B	3B	HR	RBI	SB	Avg
2001 Danville		Appal.	C	64	235	39	87	16	2	1	33	3	.370
2002 Myrtle Beach		Carolina	C	6	19	3	4	1	0	0	1	0	.211
2002 Macon		So.Atl.	C	81	271	26	62	10	0	3	25	0	.229
2003 Myrtle Beach		Carolina	C	82	286	24	84	14	1	2	27	2	.294
2004 Greenville		Southern	C	77	277	30	87	10	4	2	30	3	.314
2005 Richmond		Int.	C-1B	81	282	27	92	21	2	0	25	3	.326
2005 Atlanta		N.L.	C	18	39	2	7	2	0	0	4	0	.179
2006 Richmond		Int.	C	87	325	32	98	18	1	1	33	6	.302
2006 Atlanta		N.L.	C-3B	23	41	9	11	2	0	1	5	0	.268
2007 Richmond		Int.	C-1B-OF-3B	94	345	42	104	20	2	6	48	5	.301
2007 Atlanta a		N.L.	C	16	33	2	7	0	0	1	3	0	.212
2008 Atlanta		N.L.	PH	14	14	3	4	1	0	0	0	0	.286
2008 Omaha b-c		P.C.	C-OF-3B	60	234	33	71	17	1	6	31	7	.303
2009 Omaha		P.C.	OF-C	22	88	11	27	6	1	4	18	2	.307
2009 Kansas City		A.L.	C	64	165	17	45	10	0	6	18	0	.273
2010 Kansas City		A.L.	C	60	158	11	40	10	0	1	19	2	.253
2011 Kansas City		A.L.	C	72	222	17	55	11	0	3	24	0	.248
Major League Totals			7 Yrs.	267	672	61	169	36	0	12	73	2	.251

a On disabled list from May 2 to May 17, 2007.
b On disabled list from May 5 to May 23, 2008.
c Claimed on waivers by Kansas City Royals, May 30, 2008.

PENA, CARLOS FELIPE

Born, Santo Domingo, Dominican Republic, May 17, 1978.
Bats Left. Throws Left. Height, 6 feet, 2 inches. Weight, 210 pounds.

Year	Club	Lea	Pos	G	AB	R	H	2B	3B	HR	RBI	SB	Avg
1998 Rangers		Gulf Coast	1B	2	5	1	2	0	0	0	0	1	.400
1998 Savannah		So.Atl.	1B-OF	30	117	22	38	14	0	6	20	3	.325
1998 Charlotte		Fla.St.	1B	7	22	1	6	1	0	0	3	0	.273
1999 Charlotte		Fla.St.	1B	136	501	85	128	31	8	18	103	2	.255
2000 Tulsa		Texas	1B	138	529	117	158	36	2	28	105	12	.299
2001 Oklahoma		P.C.	1B	119	431	71	124	38	3	23	74	11	.288
2001 Texas		A.L.	1B	22	62	6	16	4	1	3	12	0	.258
2002 Sacramento		P.C.	1B	44	175	30	42	10	1	10	33	3	.240
2002 Oakland-Detroit a-b		A.L.	1B	115	397	43	96	17	4	19	52	2	.242
2003 Toledo		Int.	1B	8	30	4	10	4	1	0	5	0	.333
2003 Detroit c		A.L.	1B	131	452	51	112	21	6	18	50	4	.248
2004 Detroit		A.L.	1B	142	481	89	116	22	4	27	82	7	.241
2005 Toledo		Int.	1B	71	257	43	80	17	1	12	45	3	.311
2005 Detroit		A.L.	1B	79	260	37	61	9	0	18	44	0	.235
2006 Columbus		Int.	1B	105	381	65	99	17	0	19	66	4	.260
2006 Pawtucket		Int.	1B	11	37	7	17	3	0	4	8	0	.459
2006 Boston d-e-f		A.L.	1B-OF	18	33	3	9	2	0	1	3	0	.273
2007 Tampa Bay		A.L.	1B	148	490	99	138	29	1	46	121	1	.282
2008 Vero Beach		Fla.St.	DH	1	4	0	0	0	0	0	1	0	.000
2008 Tampa Bay g		A.L.	1B	139	490	76	121	24	2	31	102	1	.247
2009 Tampa Bay h		A.L.	1B	135	471	91	107	25	2	*39	100	3	.227
2010 Charlotte		Fla.St.	DH	1	3	1	2	0	0	0	1	0	.667
2010 Tampa Bay i-j		A.L.	1B	144	484	64	95	18	0	28	84	5	.196
2011 Chicago k		N.L.	1B	153	493	72	111	27	3	28	80	2	.225
Major League Totals			11 Yrs.	1226	4113	631	982	198	23	258	730	25	.239
Division Series													
2008 Tampa Bay		A.L.	1B	3	10	0	5	0	0	0	2	2	.500
2010 Tampa Bay		A.L.	1B	4	14	4	4	1	1	1	4	0	.286
Division Series Totals				7	24	4	9	1	1	1	6	2	.375
Championship Series													
2008 Tampa Bay		A.L.	1B	7	26	8	7	1	0	3	6	1	.269
World Series Record													
2008 Tampa Bay		A.L.	1B	5	17	1	2	1	0	0	2	0	.118

a Traded to Oakland Athletics with pitcher Mike Venafro for pitcher Mario Ramos, outfielder Ryan Ludwick, infielder Jason Hart and catcher Gerald Laird, January 14, 2002.
b Traded to Detroit Tigers with pitcher Franklyn German and player to be named later for pitcher Jeff Weaver, July 5, 2002. Detroit Tigers received pitcher Jeremy Bonderman to complete trade, August 22, 2002.
c On disabled list from June 2 to June 27, 2003.
d Released by Detroit Tigers, March 26, 2006. Signed with New York Yankees organization, April 15, 2006.

e Filed for free agency, August 16, 2006. Signed with Boston Red Sox organization, August 17, 2006.
f Filed for free agency, October 13, 2006. Signed with Tampa Bay Devil Rays organization, February 1, 2007.
g On disabled list from June 4 to June 27, 2008.
h On disabled list from September 7 to November 19, 2009.
i On disabled list from August 1 to August 16, 2010.
j Filed for free agency, November 1, 2010. Signed with Chicago Cubs, December 8, 2010.
k Filed for free agency, October 30, 2011.

PENCE, HUNTER ANDREW

Born, Arlington, Texas, April 13, 1983.
Bats Right. Throws Right. Height, 6 feet, 4 inches. Weight, 210 pounds.

Year	Club	Lea	Pos	G	AB	R	H	2B	3B	HR	RBI	SB	Avg
2004 Tri-City	N.Y.-Penn.	OF	51	199	36	59	18	1	8	37	3	.296
2005 Lexington	So.Atl.	OF	80	302	59	102	14	3	25	60	8	.338
2005 Salem	Carolina	OF	41	151	24	46	8	1	6	30	1	.305
2006 Corpus Christi	Texas	OF	136	523	97	148	31	8	28	95	17	.283
2007 Round Rock	P.C.	OF	25	95	17	31	11	1	3	21	2	.326
2007 Houston a	N.L.	OF	108	456	57	147	30	9	17	69	11	.322
2008 Houston	N.L.	OF	157	595	78	160	34	4	25	83	11	.269
2009 Houston	N.L.	OF	159	585	76	165	26	5	25	72	14	.282
2010 Houston	N.L.	OF	156	614	93	173	29	3	25	91	18	.282
2011 Houston-Philadelphia b	N.L.	OF	154	606	84	190	38	5	22	97	8	.314
Major League Totals		5 Yrs.	734	2856	388	835	157	26	114	412	62	.292
Division Series												
2011 Philadelphia	N.L.	OF	5	19	3	4	0	0	0	4	0	.211

a On disabled list from July 23 to August 21, 2007.
b Traded to Philadelphia Phillies with cash for infielder Jonathan Singleton, pitcher Jarred Cosart, pitcher Josh Zeid and player to be named later, July 30, 2011. Houston Astros received pitcher Domingo Santana to complete trade, August 15, 2011.

PENNINGTON, CLIFTON RANDOLPH (CLIFF)

Born, Corpus Christi, Texas, June 15, 1984.
Bats Both. Throws Right. Height, 5 feet, 11 inches. Weight, 190 pounds.

Year	Club	Lea	Pos	G	AB	R	H	2B	3B	HR	RBI	SB	Avg
2005 Kane County	Midwest	SS	69	290	49	80	15	0	3	29	25	.276
2006 Athletics	Arizona	SS	9	28	3	13	3	1	0	6	0	.464
2006 Stockton	Calif.	SS	46	177	36	36	7	0	2	21	7	.203
2007 Stockton	Calif.	SS-2B	68	286	50	73	17	3	6	36	9	.255
2007 Midland	Texas	SS-2B	70	271	41	68	13	2	2	21	8	.251
2008 Midland	Texas	SS-2B	50	204	42	53	7	2	0	18	20	.260
2008 Sacramento	P.C.	SS-2B-3B	65	236	47	70	9	3	2	16	11	.297
2008 Oakland	A.L.	2B-SS-3B	36	99	14	24	5	0	0	9	4	.242
2009 Sacramento	P.C.	SS-2B-3B-OF	99	360	48	95	22	3	3	40	27	.264
2009 Oakland	A.L.	SS	60	208	27	58	11	3	4	21	7	.279
2010 Oakland	A.L.	SS	156	508	64	127	26	8	6	46	29	.250
2011 Oakland	A.L.	SS	148	515	57	136	26	2	8	58	14	.264
Major League Totals		4 Yrs.	400	1330	162	345	68	13	18	134	54	.259

PERALTA, JHONNY ANTONIO

Born, Santiago, Dominican Republic, May 28, 1982.
Bats Right. Throws Right. Height, 6 feet, 1 inch. Weight, 210 pounds.

Year	Club	Lea	Pos	G	AB	R	H	2B	3B	HR	RBI	SB	Avg
2001 Kinston	Carolina	SS	125	441	57	106	24	2	7	47	4	.240
2002 Akron	Eastern	SS	130	470	62	132	28	5	15	62	4	.281
2003 Buffalo	Int.	SS-3B	63	237	25	61	12	1	1	21	1	.257
2003 Cleveland	A.L.	SS-3B	77	242	24	55	10	1	4	21	1	.227
2004 Buffalo	Int.	SS-3B	138	556	109	181	44	2	15	86	8	.326
2004 Cleveland	A.L.	SS-3B	8	25	2	6	1	0	0	2	0	.240
2005 Cleveland	A.L.	SS	141	504	82	147	35	4	24	78	0	.292
2006 Cleveland	A.L.	SS	149	569	84	146	28	3	13	68	0	.257
2007 Cleveland	A.L.	SS	152	574	87	155	27	1	21	72	4	.270
2008 Cleveland	A.L.	SS-3B	154	605	104	167	42	4	23	89	3	.276
2009 Cleveland	A.L.	3B-SS	151	582	59	148	35	1	11	83	0	.254
2010 Cleveland-Detroit a-b	A.L.	3B-SS-1B	148	551	60	137	30	2	15	81	1	.249
2011 Detroit	A.L.	SS-1B	146	525	68	157	25	3	21	86	0	.299
Major League Totals		9 Yrs.	1126	4177	568	1118	233	19	132	580	9	.268

Year	Club	Lea	Pos	G	AB	R	H	2B	3B	HR	RBI	SB	Avg
	Division Series												
2007 Cleveland	....	A.L.	SS	4	15	2	7	3	0	0	2	1	.467
2011 Detroit	....	A.L.	SS	5	18	0	4	2	0	0	1	0	.222
Division Series Totals	....			9	33	2	11	5	0	0	3	1	.333
	Championship Series												
2007 Cleveland	....	A.L.	SS	7	27	4	7	2	0	2	8	0	.259
2011 Detroit	....	A.L.	SS	6	23	2	5	1	0	2	2	0	.217
Championship Series Totals	.....			13	50	6	12	3	0	4	10	0	.240

a Traded to Detroit Tigers for pitcher Giovanni Soto, July 28, 2010.
b Filed for free agency, November 2, 2010, re-signed with Detroit Tigers, November 8, 2010.

PEREZ (DIAZ), SALVADOR
Born, Valencia, Venezuela, May 10, 1990.
Bats Right. Throws Right. Height, 6 feet, 3 inches. Weight, 230 pounds.

Year	Club	Lea	Pos	G	AB	R	H	2B	3B	HR	RBI	SB	Avg
2007 Royals	....	Arizona	C	30	86	10	21	3	0	0	10	1	.244
2008 Burlington	....	Appal.	C-2B	13	40	4	13	0	1	0	10	0	.325
2008 Idaho Falls	....	Pioneer	C	12	43	7	17	3	1	1	6	0	.395
2009 Burlington	....	Midwest	C	36	127	10	24	6	0	0	7	0	.189
2009 Idaho Falls	....	Pioneer	C	57	226	33	71	14	3	2	37	0	.314
2010 Wilmington	......	Carolina	C	99	365	35	106	21	1	7	53	1	.290
2011 NW Arkansas	....	Texas	C	79	286	35	81	14	0	9	43	0	.283
2011 Omaha	....	P.C.	C	12	48	5	16	5	0	1	10	0	.333
2011 Kansas City	....	A.L.	C	39	148	20	49	8	2	3	21	0	.331

PETERSEN, BRYAN E.
Born, Agoura, California, April 9, 1986.
Bats Left. Throws Right. Height, 6 feet. Weight, 205 pounds.

Year	Club	Lea	Pos	G	AB	R	H	2B	3B	HR	RBI	SB	Avg
2007 Jamestown	......	N.Y.-Penn.	OF	57	216	27	54	13	1	5	24	11	.250
2008 Greensboro	....	So.Atl.	OF	79	296	60	89	10	2	19	58	15	.301
2008 Carolina	....	Southern	OF	12	37	5	13	2	0	1	10	1	.351
2008 Jupiter	....	Fla.St.	OF	40	155	23	41	5	0	3	12	7	.265
2009 Jacksonville	......	Southern	OF	121	431	64	128	15	7	7	49	13	.297
2010 Florida	....	N.L.	OF	23	24	1	2	0	0	0	2	0	.083
2010 New Orleans	....	P.C.	OF	91	322	47	82	13	2	5	27	5	.255
2011 New Orleans	....	P.C.	OF	67	248	47	87	21	0	11	26	6	.351
2011 Florida	....	N.L.	OF-P	74	204	18	54	13	3	2	10	7	.265
Major League Totals	....	2 Yrs.		97	228	19	56	13	3	2	12	7	.246

PHILLIPS, BRANDON EMIL
Born, Raleigh, North Carolina, June 28, 1981.
Bats Right. Throws Right. Height, 6 feet. Weight, 195 pounds.

Year	Club	Lea	Pos	G	AB	R	H	2B	3B	HR	RBI	SB	Avg
1999 Expos	....	Gulf Coast	SS	47	169	23	49	11	3	1	21	12	.290
2000 Cape Fear	....	So.Atl.	SS-2B	126	484	74	117	17	8	11	72	23	.242
2001 Harrisburg	....	Eastern	SS-2B-3B	67	265	35	79	19	0	7	36	13	.298
2001 Jupiter	....	Fla.St.	SS	55	194	36	55	12	2	4	23	17	.284
2002 Harrisburg	....	Eastern	SS	60	245	40	80	13	2	9	35	6	.327
2002 Ottawa	....	Int.	SS	10	35	1	9	4	0	1	5	0	.257
2002 Buffalo	....	Int.	SS-2B	55	223	30	63	14	0	8	27	8	.283
2002 Cleveland a-b	....	A.L.	2B	11	31	5	8	3	1	0	4	0	.258
2003 Cleveland	....	A.L.	2B	112	370	36	77	18	1	6	33	4	.208
2003 Buffalo	....	Int.	2B	43	154	14	27	7	0	3	13	7	.175
2004 Buffalo	....	Int.	2B-SS	135	521	83	158	34	4	8	50	14	.303
2004 Cleveland	....	A.L.	2B	6	22	1	4	2	0	0	1	0	.182
2005 Cleveland	....	A.L.	2B-SS	6	9	1	0	0	0	0	0	0	.000
2005 Buffalo	....	Int.	SS	112	465	79	119	24	1	15	46	7	.256
2006 Cincinnati c-d	....	N.L.	2B-SS	149	536	65	148	28	1	17	75	25	.276
2007 Cincinnati	....	N.L.	2B-SS	158	650	107	187	26	6	30	94	32	.288
2008 Cincinnati e	....	N.L.	2B	141	559	80	146	24	7	21	78	23	.261
2009 Cincinnati	....	N.L.	2B	153	584	78	161	30	5	20	98	25	.276
2010 Cincinnati	....	N.L.	2B	155	626	100	172	33	5	18	59	16	.275
2011 Cincinnati	....	N.L.	2B	150	610	94	183	38	2	18	82	14	.300
Major League Totals	....	10 Yrs.	1041	3997	567	1086	202	28	130	524	139	.272

Year	Club	Lea	Pos	G	AB	R	H	2B	3B	HR	RBI	SB	Avg
	Division Series												
2010 Cincinnati...........	N.L.		2B	3	12	2	4	1	0	1	1	0	.333

a Traded to Cleveland Indians with infielder Lee Stevens, outfielder Grady Sizemore and pitcher Cliff Lee for pitcher Bartolo Colon and player to be named later, June 27, 2002.
b Montreal Expos received pitcher Tim Drew to complete trade, June 28, 2002.
c Traded to Cincinnati Reds for player to be named later, April 7, 2006.
d Cleveland Indians received pitcher Jeff Stevens to complete trade, June 13, 2006.
e On disabled list from September 12 to November 6, 2008.

PIE, FELIX

Born, LaRomana, Dominican Republic, February 8, 1985.
Bats Left. Throws Left. Height, 6 feet, 2 inches. Weight, 170 pounds.

Year	Club	Lea	Pos	G	AB	R	H	2B	3B	HR	RBI	SB	Avg
2002 Cubs.............	Arizona	OF	55	218	42	70	16	13	4	37	17	.321
2002 Boise........	Northwest	OF	2	8	1	1	1	0	0	1	0	.125
2003 Lansing.........	Midwest	OF	124	505	72	144	22	9	4	47	19	.285
2004 Daytona...........	Fla.St.	OF	105	412	79	123	17	9	8	47	31	.299
2005 West Tenn.......	Southern	OF	59	240	41	73	17	5	11	25	13	.304
2006 Iowa................	P.C.	OF	141	559	78	158	33	8	15	57	17	.283
2007 Iowa................	P.C.	OF	55	229	51	83	9	5	9	43	9	.362
2007 Chicago..........	N.L.	OF	87	177	26	38	9	3	2	20	8	.215
2008 Cubs.............	Arizona	OF	1	3	3	2	0	0	1	5	0	.667
2008 Iowa................	P.C.	OF	85	335	57	96	20	5	10	55	11	.287
2008 Chicago..........	N.L.	OF	43	83	9	20	2	1	1	10	3	.241
2009 Baltimore a..........	A.L.	OF	101	252	38	67	10	3	9	29	1	.266
2010 Orioles.........	Gulf Coast	DH	2	8	1	1	0	0	0	0	0	.125
2010 Frederick........	Carolina	OF	3	12	3	5	0	0	0	2	0	.417
2010 Bowie.............	Eastern	OF	6	23	2	8	2	1	0	1	1	.348
2010 Baltimore b..........	A.L.	OF	82	288	39	79	15	5	5	31	5	.274
2011 Norfolk...........	Int.	OF	7	24	6	6	2	1	0	1	3	.250
2011 Baltimore c..........	A.L.	OF	85	164	15	36	8	1	0	7	3	.220
Major League Totals		5 Yrs.	398	964	127	240	44	13	17	97	20	.249
	Division Series												
2007 Chicago...........	N.L.	PH	1	1	0	0	0	0	0	0	0	.000
2008 Chicago..............	N.L.	PH	1	0	0	0	0	0	0	0	0	.000
Division Series Totals			2	1	0	0	0	0	0	0	0	.000

a Traded to Baltimore Orioles for pitcher Garrett Olson and pitcher Hank Williamson, January 18, 2009.
b On disabled list from April 16 to July 6, 2010.
c Filed for free agency, November 2, 2011. Signed with Cleveland Indians organization, December 16, 2011.

PIERRE, JUAN D'VAUGHN

Born, Mobile, Alabama, August 14, 1977.
Bats Left. Throws Left. Height, 6 feet. Weight, 180 pounds.

Year	Club	Lea	Pos	G	AB	R	H	2B	3B	HR	RBI	SB	Avg
1998 Portland........	Northwest	OF	64	264	55	93	9	2	0	30	38	.352
1999 Asheville........	So.Atl.	OF	140	585	93	187	28	5	1	55	66	.320
2000 Carolina.........	Southern	OF	107	439	63	143	16	4	0	32	46	.326
2000 Colorado Spgs.........	P.C.	OF	4	17	3	8	0	1	0	1	1	.471
2000 Colorado	N.L.	OF	51	200	26	62	2	0	0	20	7	.310
2001 Colorado	N.L.	OF	156	617	108	202	26	11	2	55	*46	.327
2002 Colorado a............	N.L.	OF	152	592	90	170	20	5	1	35	47	.287
2003 Florida..............	N.L.	OF	*162	*668	100	204	28	7	1	41	*65	.305
2004 Florida.............	N.L.	OF	*162	*678	100	*221	22	*12	3	49	45	.326
2005 Florida b............	N.L.	OF	*162	656	96	181	19	13	2	47	57	.276
2006 Chicago c..........	N.L.	OF	*162	*699	87	*204	32	13	3	40	58	.292
2007 Los Angeles..........	N.L.	OF	*162	668	96	196	24	8	0	41	64	.293
2008 Las Vegas............	P.C.	OF	2	6	2	3	1	0	0	0	0	.500
2008 Los Angeles d..........	N.L.	OF	119	375	44	106	10	2	1	28	40	.283
2009 Los Angeles e........	N.L.	OF	145	380	57	117	16	8	0	31	30	.308
2010 Chicago	A.L.	OF	160	651	96	179	18	3	1	47	*68	.275
2011 Chicago f..............	A.L.	OF	158	639	80	178	17	4	2	50	27	.279
Major League Totals		12 Yrs.	1751	6823	980	2020	234	86	16	484	554	.296
	Division Series												
2003 Florida..............	N.L.	OF	4	19	5	5	1	0	0	3	1	.263
2008 Los Angeles	N.L.	OF	1	1	1	0	0	0	0	0	0	.000
2009 Los Angeles	N.L.	OF	3	0	1	0	0	0	0	0	0	.000
Division Series Totals			8	20	7	5	1	0	0	3	1	.250

Year	Club	Lea	Pos	G	AB	R	H	2B	3B	HR	RBI	SB	Avg
Championship Series													
2003 Florida	N.L.	OF	7	33	5	10	1	2	0	1	1	.303
2008 Los Angeles	N.L.	OF	1	3	1	2	1	0	0	0	0	.667
2009 Los Angeles	N.L.	OF	4	2	1	0	0	0	0	0	0	.000
Championship Series Totals			12	38	7	12	2	2	0	1	1	.316
World Series Record													
2003 Florida	N.L.	OF	6	21	2	7	2	0	0	3	1	.333

a Traded to Florida Marlins with pitcher Mike Hampton for outfielder Preston Wilson, catcher Charles Johnson, pitcher Vic Darensbourg and infielder Pablo Ozuna, November 16, 2002.

b Traded to Chicago Cubs for pitcher Sergio Mitre, pitcher Ricky Nolasco and pitcher Renyel Pinto, December 7, 2005.

c Filed for free agency, October 29, 2006. Signed with Los Angeles Dodgers, November 22, 2006.

d On disabled list from June 30 to July 25, 2008.

e Traded with cash to Chicago White Sox for pitcher John Ely and pitcher Jon Link, December 15, 2009.

f Filed for free agency, October 30, 2011.

PIERZYNSKI, ANTHONY JOHN (A.J.)
Born, Bridgehampton, New York, December 30, 1976.
Bats Left. Throws Right. Height, 6 feet, 3 inches. Weight, 235 pounds.

Year	Club	Lea	Pos	G	AB	R	H	2B	3B	HR	RBI	SB	Avg
1994 Twins	Gulf Coast	C	43	152	21	44	8	1	1	19	0	.289
1995 Ft. Wayne	Midwest	C	22	84	10	26	5	1	2	14	0	.310
1995 Elizabethtn	Appal.	C-1B	56	205	29	68	13	1	7	45	0	.332
1996 Ft. Wayne	Midwest	C-OF	114	431	48	118	30	3	7	70	0	.274
1997 Ft. Myers	Fla.St.	C-1B	118	412	49	115	23	1	9	64	2	.279
1998 New Britain	Eastern	C	59	212	30	63	11	0	3	17	0	.297
1998 Salt Lake	P.C.	C	59	208	29	53	7	2	7	30	3	.255
1998 Minnesota	A.L.	C	7	10	1	3	0	0	0	1	0	.300
1999 Salt Lake	P.C.	C	67	228	29	59	10	0	1	25	0	.259
1999 Minnesota a	A.L.	C	9	22	3	6	2	0	0	3	0	.273
2000 New Britain	Eastern	C	62	228	36	68	17	2	4	34	0	.298
2000 Salt Lake	P.C.	C	41	155	22	52	14	1	4	25	1	.335
2000 Minnesota	A.L.	C	33	88	12	27	5	1	2	11	1	.307
2001 Minnesota	A.L.	C	114	381	51	110	33	2	7	55	1	.289
2002 Minnesota	A.L.	C	130	440	54	132	31	6	6	49	1	.300
2003 Minnesota b	A.L.	C	137	487	63	152	35	3	11	74	3	.312
2004 San Francisco c	N.L.	C	131	471	45	128	28	2	11	77	0	.272
2005 Chicago	A.L.	C	128	460	61	118	21	0	18	56	0	.257
2006 Chicago	A.L.	C	140	509	65	150	24	0	16	64	1	.295
2007 Chicago	A.L.	C	136	472	54	124	24	0	14	50	1	.263
2008 Chicago	A.L.	C	134	534	66	150	31	1	13	60	1	.281
2009 Chicago	A.L.	C	138	504	57	151	22	1	13	49	1	.300
2010 Chicago d	A.L.	C	128	474	43	128	29	0	9	56	3	.270
2011 Charlotte	Int.	C	3	10	2	2	0	0	0	1	0	.200
2011 Chicago e	A.L.	C	129	464	38	133	29	1	8	48	0	.287
Major League Totals		14 Yrs.	1494	5316	613	1512	314	17	128	653	13	.284
Division Series													
2002 Minnesota	A.L.	C	5	16	4	7	0	1	1	4	0	.438
2003 Minnesota	A.L.	C	4	13	1	3	0	0	1	1	0	.231
2005 Chicago	A.L.	C	3	9	5	4	2	0	2	4	1	.444
2008 Chicago	A.L.	C	4	13	1	5	1	0	0	1	0	.385
Division Series Totals			16	51	11	19	3	1	4	10	1	.373
Championship Series													
2002 Minnesota	A.L.	C	5	16	1	4	0	0	0	2	0	.250
2005 Chicago	A.L.	C	5	18	1	3	0	0	1	2	0	.167
Championship Series Totals			10	34	2	7	0	0	1	4	0	.206
World Series Record													
2005 Chicago	A.L.	C	4	15	3	4	2	0	0	3	1	.267

a On disabled list from August 24 to September 30, 1999.

b Traded to San Francisco Giants with cash for pitcher Joe Nathan, pitcher Boof Bonser and pitcher Francisco Liriano, November 14, 2003.

c Released by San Francisco Giants, December 16, 2004. Signed with Chicago White Sox, January 5, 2005.

d Filed for free agency, November 1, 2010, re-signed with Chicago White Sox, December 3, 2010.

e On disabled list from August 13 to September 2, 2011.

PLOUFFE, TREVOR PATRICK

Born, West Hills, California, June 15, 1986.
Bats Right. Throws Right. Height, 6 feet, 2 inches. Weight, 200 pounds.

Year	Club	Lea	Pos	G	AB	R	H	2B	3B	HR	RBI	SB	Avg
2004	Elizabethton	Appal.	SS	60	237	29	67	7	2	4	28	3	.283
2005	Beloit	Midwest	SS	127	466	58	104	18	0	13	60	8	.223
2006	Fort Myers	Fla.St.	SS-3B	125	455	60	112	26	4	4	45	8	.246
2007	New Britain	Eastern	SS	126	497	75	136	37	2	9	50	12	.274
2008	New Britain	Eastern	SS-3B	58	227	32	61	17	3	3	21	4	.269
2008	Rochester	Int.	3B-2B-SS	66	250	34	64	17	3	6	39	1	.256
2009	Rochester	Int.	SS	118	430	53	112	23	5	10	60	3	.260
2010	Rochester	Int.	SS-3B-2B	102	402	53	98	22	4	15	49	5	.244
2010	Minnesota	A.L.	SS-2B	22	41	7	6	1	0	2	6	0	.146
2011	Rochester	Int.	SS-2B-1B-OF	51	192	33	60	11	3	15	33	3	.313
2011	Minnesota	A.L.	SS-2B-OF-1B	81	286	47	68	18	1	8	31	3	.238
Major League Totals			2 Yrs.	103	327	54	74	19	1	10	37	3	.226

POLANCO, PLACIDO ENRIQUE

Born, Santo Domingo, Dominican Republic, October 10, 1975.
Bats Right. Throws Right. Height, 5 feet, 10 inches. Weight, 195 pounds.

Year	Club	Lea	Pos	G	AB	R	H	2B	3B	HR	RBI	SB	Avg
1994	Cardinals	Arizona	SS-2B	32	127	17	27	4	0	1	10	4	.213
1995	Peoria	Midwest	SS-2B	103	361	43	96	7	4	2	41	7	.266
1996	St. Pete	Fla.St.	2B	137	540	65	157	29	5	0	51	4	.291
1997	Arkansas	Texas	2B	129	508	71	148	16	3	2	51	19	.291
1998	Memphis	P.C.	2B-SS	70	246	36	69	19	1	1	21	6	.280
1998	St. Louis	N.L.	SS-2B	45	114	10	29	3	2	1	11	2	.254
1999	Memphis	P.C.	2B	29	120	18	33	4	1	0	10	2	.275
1999	St. Louis	N.L.	2B-3B-SS	88	220	24	61	9	3	1	19	1	.277
2000	St. Louis a	N.L.	2B-3B-SS-1B	118	323	50	102	12	3	5	39	4	.316
2001	St. Louis	N.L.	3B-SS-2B	144	564	87	173	26	4	3	38	12	.307
2002	St. Louis-Phil. b	N.L.	3B-SS-2B	147	548	75	158	32	2	9	49	5	.288
2003	Philadelphia c	N.L.	2B-3B	122	492	87	142	30	3	14	63	14	.289
2004	Reading	Eastern	2B	1	3	0	2	0	0	0	0	0	.667
2004	Scranton/WB	Int.	2B	1	3	1	0	0	0	0	0	0	.000
2004	Philadelphia d-e	N.L.	2B-3B	126	503	74	150	21	0	17	55	7	.298
2005	Philadelphia	N.L.	2B-3B-OF-SS	43	158	26	50	7	0	3	20	0	.316
2005	Detroit f-g	A.L.	2B-3B	86	343	58	116	20	2	6	36	4	.338
2006	Detroit h	A.L.	2B	110	461	58	136	18	1	4	52	1	.295
2007	Detroit	A.L.	2B	142	587	105	200	36	3	9	67	7	.341
2008	Detroit	A.L.	2B	141	580	90	178	34	3	8	58	7	.307
2009	Detroit i	A.L.	2B	153	618	82	176	31	4	10	72	7	.285
2010	Phillies	Gulf Coast	2B	1	3	1	3	1	0	0	2	0	1.000
2010	Clearwater	Fla.St.	3B	1	4	1	1	0	0	0	0	0	.250
2010	Philadelphia j	N.L.	3B-2B	132	554	76	165	27	2	6	52	5	.298
2011	Lehigh Valley	Int.	3B	2	6	0	0	0	0	0	0	0	.000
2011	Philadelphia k	N.L.	3B-2B	122	469	46	130	14	0	5	50	3	.277
Major League Totals			14 Yrs.	1719	6534	948	1966	320	32	101	681	79	.301
Division Series													
2000	St. Louis	N.L.	3B	3	10	1	3	0	0	0	3	1	.300
2001	St. Louis	N.L.	3B	5	15	1	4	0	0	0	1	1	.267
2006	Detroit	A.L.	2B	4	17	3	7	1	0	0	2	0	.412
2010	Philadelphia	N.L.	3B	2	9	1	1	0	0	0	0	0	.111
2011	Philadelphia	N.L.	3B	5	19	0	2	0	0	0	0	0	.105
Division Series Totals				19	70	6	17	1	0	0	6	2	.243
Championship Series													
2000	St. Louis	N.L.	3B	4	5	0	1	0	0	0	0	0	.200
2006	Detroit	A.L.	2B	4	17	2	9	1	0	0	2	0	.529
2010	Philadelphia	N.L.	3B	6	20	3	5	2	0	0	5	1	.250
Championship Series Totals				14	42	5	15	3	0	0	7	1	.357
World Series Record													
2006	Detroit	A.L.	2B	5	17	0	0	0	0	0	0	0	.000

a On disabled list from July 1 to July 15, 2000.
b Traded to Philadelphia Phillies with pitcher Bud Smith and pitcher Mike Timlin for infielder Scott Rolen and pitcher
   Doug Nickle, July 29, 2002.
c On disabled list from April 16 to May 1, 2003.
d On disabled list from May 8 to June 7, 2004.
e Filed for free agency, October 29, 2004, re-signed with Philadelphia Phillies, December 19, 2004.
f Traded to Detroit Tigers for pitcher Ugueth Urbina and infielder Ramon Martinez, June 8, 2005.

g On disabled list from July 12 to July 27, 2005.
h On disabled list from August 16 to September 22, 2006.
i Filed for free agency, November 5, 2009. Signed with Philadelphia Phillies, December 3, 2009.
j On disabled list from June 26 to July 17, 2010.
k On disabled list from July 5 to July 30 and August 7 to August 22, 2011.

POSADA, JORGE RAFAEL

Born, Santurce, Puerto Rico, August 17, 1971.
Bats Both. Throws Right. Height, 6 feet, 2 inches. Weight, 205 pounds

Year	Club	Lea	Pos	G	AB	R	H	2B	3B	HR	RBI	SB	Avg
1991	Oneonta	N.Y.-Penn	2B-C	71	217	34	51	5	5	4	33	6	.235
1992	Greensboro	So. Atl.	DH-C-3B	101	339	60	94	22	4	12	58	11	.277
1993	Pr William	Carolina	C-3B	118	410	71	106	27	2	17	61	17	.259
1993	Albany	Eastern	C	7	25	3	7	0	0	0	0	0	.280
1994	Columbus.	Int.	C-OF	92	313	46	75	13	3	11	48	5	.240
1995	Columbus.	Int.	C	108	368	60	94	32	5	8	51	4	.255
1995	New York	A.L.	C	1	0	0	0	0	0	0	0	0	.000
1996	Columbus.	Int.	C-OF	106	354	76	96	22	6	11	62	3	.271
1996	New York	A.L.	C	8	14	1	1	0	0	0	0	0	.071
1997	New York	A.L.	C	60	188	29	47	12	0	6	25	1	.250
1998	New York	A.L.	C-1B	111	358	56	96	23	0	17	63	0	.268
1999	New York	A.L.	C-1B	112	379	50	93	19	2	12	57	1	.245
2000	New York	A.L.	C-1B	151	505	92	145	35	1	28	86	2	.287
2001	New York	A.L.	C-1B	138	484	59	134	28	1	22	95	2	.277
2002	New York	A.L.	C	143	511	79	137	40	1	20	99	1	.268
2003	New York	A.L.	C	142	481	83	135	24	0	30	101	2	.281
2004	New York	A.L.	C	137	449	72	122	31	0	21	81	1	.272
2005	New York	A.L.	C	142	474	67	124	23	0	19	71	1	.262
2006	New York	A.L.	C-1B	143	465	65	129	27	2	23	93	3	.277
2007	New York a.	A.L.	C-1B	144	506	91	171	42	1	20	90	2	.338
2008	New York b.	A.L.	C-1B	51	168	18	45	13	1	3	22	0	.268
2009	New York c.	A.L.	C-1B	111	383	55	109	25	0	22	81	1	.285
2010	New York d.	A.L.	C-1B	120	383	49	95	23	1	18	57	3	.248
2011	New York e.	A.L.	DH-1B-C-2B	115	344	34	81	14	0	14	44	0	.235
Major League Totals		17 Yrs.	1829	6092	900	1664	379	10	275	1065	20	.273
Division Series													
1995	New York	A.L.	C	1	0	1	0	0	0	0	0	0	.000
1997	New York	A.L.	C	2	2	0	0	0	0	0	0	0	.000
1998	New York	A.L.	C	1	2	1	0	0	0	0	0	0	.000
1999	New York	A.L.	C	1	4	0	1	1	0	0	0	0	.250
2000	New York	A.L.	C	5	17	2	4	2	0	0	1	0	.235
2001	New York	A.L.	C	5	18	3	8	1	0	1	2	1	.444
2002	New York	A.L.	C	4	17	2	4	0	0	1	3	0	.235
2003	New York	A.L.	C	4	17	1	3	1	0	0	0	0	.176
2004	New York	A.L.	C	4	18	2	4	0	0	0	0	0	.222
2005	New York	A.L.	C	5	13	3	3	1	0	1	2	0	.231
2006	New York	A.L.	C	4	14	2	7	1	0	1	2	0	.500
2007	New York	A.L.	C	4	15	1	2	1	0	0	0	0	.133
2009	New York	A.L.	C	3	11	1	4	0	0	1	2	0	.364
2010	New York	A.L.	C	3	11	2	3	0	0	0	2	0	.273
2011	New York	A.L.	DH	5	14	4	6	0	1	0	0	0	.429
Division Series Totals			51	173	25	49	8	1	5	14	1	.283
Championship Series													
1998	New York	A.L.	C	5	11	1	2	0	0	1	2	0	.182
1999	New York	A.L.	C	3	10	1	1	0	0	1	2	0	.100
2000	New York	A.L.	C	6	19	2	3	1	0	0	3	0	.158
2001	New York	A.L.	C	5	14	4	3	1	0	0	0	0	.214
2003	New York	A.L.	C	7	27	5	8	4	0	1	6	0	.296
2004	New York	A.L.	C	7	27	4	7	1	0	0	2	0	.259
2009	New York	A.L.	C	6	20	3	4	1	0	1	1	1	.200
2010	New York	A.L.	C	6	19	1	5	2	0	0	1	0	.263
Championship Series Totals			45	147	21	33	10	0	4	17	1	.224
World Series Record													
1998	New York	A.L.	C	3	9	2	3	0	0	1	2	0	.333
1999	New York	A.L.	C	2	8	0	2	1	0	0	1	0	.250
2000	New York	A.L.	C	5	18	2	4	1	0	0	1	0	.222
2001	New York	A.L.	C	7	23	2	4	1	0	1	1	0	.174
2003	New York	A.L.	C	6	19	0	3	1	0	0	1	1	.158
2009	New York	A.L.	C	6	19	1	5	1	0	0	5	0	.263
World Series Totals			29	96	7	21	5	0	2	11	1	.219

a Filed for free agency, October 29, 2007, re-signed with New York Yankees, November 29, 2007.
b On disabled list from April 27 to June 4 and July 21 to November 14, 2008.
c On disabled list from May 5 to May 29, 2009.
d On disabled list from May 17 to June 2, 2010.
e Filed for free agency, October 30, 2011.

POSEY, GERALD DEMP (BUSTER)
Born, Leesburg, Georgia, March 27, 1987.
Bats Right. Throws Right. Height, 6 feet, 1 inch. Weight, 205 pounds.

Year Club	Lea	Pos	G	AB	R	H	2B	3B	HR	RBI	SB	Avg
2008 Giants.............	Arizona	C	7	26	8	10	3	1	1	4	0	.385
2008 Salem-Keizer	Northwest	C	3	11	2	3	2	0	0	2	0	.273
2009 San Jose	Calif.	C	80	291	63	95	23	0	13	58	6	.326
2009 Fresno	P.C.	C	35	131	21	42	8	1	5	22	0	.321
2009 San Francisco ...	N.L.	C	7	17	1	2	0	0	0	0	0	.118
2010 Fresno	P.C.	C-1B	47	172	31	60	13	2	6	32	1	.349
2010 San Francisco a	N.L.	C-1B	108	406	58	124	23	2	18	67	0	.305
2011 San Francisco b	N.L.	C-1B	45	162	17	46	5	0	4	21	3	.284
Major League Totals		3 Yrs.	160	585	76	172	28	2	22	88	3	.294
Division Series												
2010 San Francisco	N.L.	C	4	16	3	6	1	0	0	0	1	.375
Championship Series												
2010 San Francisco	N.L.	C	6	23	1	5	2	0	0	3	0	.217
World Series Record												
2010 San Francisco	N.L.	C	5	20	2	6	0	0	1	2	0	.300

a Selected Rookie of the Year in National League for 2010.
b On disabled list from May 26 to October 31, 2011.

PRADO, MARTIN MANUEL
Born, Maracay, Venezuela, October 27, 1983.
Bats Right. Throws Right. Height, 6 feet, 1 inch. Weight, 170 pounds.

Year Club	Lea	Pos	G	AB	R	H	2B	3B	HR	RBI	SB	Avg
2003 Braves	Gulf Coast	2B-3B	59	220	28	63	2	6	0	23	9	.286
2004 Rome	So.Atl.	2B	107	429	68	135	25	6	3	38	14	.315
2005 Myrtle Beach ...	Carolina	2B	75	297	44	91	13	3	4	34	9	.306
2005 Mississippi ...	Southern	2B	39	143	17	40	7	1	1	11	3	.280
2006 Richmond	Int.	2B-3B	60	241	30	68	12	1	2	23	2	.282
2006 Mississippi	Southern	2B-3B	43	176	17	49	6	2	1	15	2	.278
2006 Atlanta	N.L.	2B-3B	24	42	3	11	1	1	1	9	0	.262
2007 Richmond	Int.	2B-3B-SS	103	395	61	125	23	3	4	41	5	.316
2007 Atlanta	N.L.	2B-3B	28	59	5	17	3	0	0	2	0	.288
2008 Mississippi	Southern	2B-3B-SS-OF	5	19	2	5	2	0	0	3	0	.263
2008 Atlanta a	N.L.	3B-1B-2B-OF	78	228	36	73	18	4	2	33	3	.320
2009 Atlanta	N.L.	2B-3B-1B-OF	128	450	64	138	38	0	11	49	1	.307
2010 Gwinnett.	Int.	2B-3B	1	4	0	1	0	0	0	0	0	.250
2010 Atlanta b	N.L.	2B-3B-1B	140	599	100	184	40	3	15	66	5	.307
2011 Mississippi	Southern	3B	2	9	2	2	0	0	0	2	0	.222
2011 Gwinnett.	Int.	3B-OF	6	17	2	3	0	0	0	1	0	.176
2011 Atlanta c	N.L.	OF-3B-1B	129	551	66	143	26	2	13	57	4	.260
Major League Totals		6 Yrs.	527	1929	274	566	126	10	42	216	13	.293

a On disabled list from May 5 to July 3, 2008.
b On disabled list from July 31 to August 17, 2010.
c On disabled list from June 8 to July 15, 2011.

PRESLEY, ALEXANDER CRAWFORD (ALEX)
Born, Monroe, Louisiana, July 25, 1985.
Bats Left. Throws Left. Height, 5 feet, 9 inches. Weight, 190 pounds.

Year Club	Lea	Pos	G	AB	R	H	2B	3B	HR	RBI	SB	Avg
2006 Williamsport.....	N.Y.-Penn.	OF	61	223	26	58	7	8	3	23	3	.260
2007 Hickory............	So.Atl.	OF	121	495	79	145	22	8	11	63	18	.293
2008 Lynchburg	Carolina	OF	82	287	39	74	15	1	6	35	13	.258
2009 Lynchburg	Carolina	OF	115	417	51	107	17	11	4	37	9	.257
2010 Altoona............	Eastern	OF	67	246	42	86	13	7	6	47	5	.350
2010 Indianapolis	Int.	OF	69	272	44	80	15	6	6	38	8	.294
2010 Pittsburgh	N.L.	OF	19	23	2	6	1	0	0	0	1	.261
2011 Bradenton	Fla.St.	OF	2	6	2	1	0	0	0	0	0	.167
2011 Indianapolis	Int.	OF	87	342	58	114	18	5	8	41	22	.333

Year	Club	Lea	Pos	G	AB	R	H	2B	3B	HR	RBI	SB	Avg
2011 Pittsburgh a	N.L.		OF	52	215	27	64	12	6	4	20	9	.298
Major League Totals			2 Yrs.	71	238	29	70	13	6	4	20	10	.294

a On disabled list from July 23 to August 25, 2011.

PRIDIE, JASON ORVILLE

Born, Phoenix, Arizona, October 9, 1983.
Bats Left. Throws Right. Height, 6 feet, 1 inch. Weight, 205 pounds.

Year	Club	Lea	Pos	G	AB	R	H	2B	3B	HR	RBI	SB	Avg
2002 Princeton	Appal.		OF	67	285	60	105	12	9	7	33	13	.368
2002 Hudson Valley ...	N.Y.-Penn.		OF	8	32	4	11	1	1	1	1	0	.344
2003 Charleston	So.Atl.		OF-3B	128	530	75	138	28	10	7	48	26	.260
2004 Charleston	So.Atl.		OF	128	515	103	142	27	11	17	86	17	.276
2005 Visalia	Calif.		OF	1	2	0	1	0	0	0	0	0	.500
2005 Montgomery	Southern		OF	28	94	15	20	4	2	3	8	5	.213
2006 Montgomery a	Southern		OF	132	460	39	106	11	4	5	34	16	.230
2007 Montgomery b	Southern		OF	71	279	42	81	16	7	4	27	14	.290
2007 Durham	Int.		OF	63	245	47	78	16	4	10	39	12	.318
2008 Rochester.	Int.		OF	138	559	84	151	21	16	13	61	25	.270
2008 Minnesota	A.L.		OF	10	4	3	0	0	0	0	0	0	.000
2009 Minnesota	A.L.		PH	1	0	0	0	0	0	0	0	0	.000
2009 Rochester.	Int.		OF	121	513	69	136	23	5	9	53	25	.265
2010 Mets.	Gulf Coast		OF	4	11	3	4	1	0	0	0	0	.364
2010 Buffalo c.	Int.		OF	40	164	17	46	6	1	3	19	9	.280
2011 Buffalo	Int.		OF	14	59	8	11	1	0	3	6	1	.186
2011 New York d.	N.L.		OF	101	208	28	48	11	3	4	20	7	.231
Major League Totals			3 Yrs.	112	212	31	48	11	3	4	20	7	.226

a Selected by Minnesota Twins from Tampa Bay Devil Rays in Rule V draft, December 8, 2005. Returned to Tampa Bay Devil Rays, March 29, 2006.
b Traded by Tampa Bat Devil Rays to Minnesota Twins with infielder Brendan Harris and outfielder Delmon Young for infielder Jason Bartlett, pitcher Matt Garza and pitcher Eduardo Morlan, November 28, 2007.
c Claimed on waivers by New York Mets, February 9, 2010.
d Filed for free agency, November 13, 2011. Signed with Oakland Athletics organization, November 18, 2011.

PUJOLS, JOSE ALBERTO (ALBERT)

Born, Santo Domingo, Dominican Republic, January 16, 1980.
Bats Right. Throws Right. Height, 6 feet, 3 inches. Weight, 225 pounds.

Year	Club	Lea	Pos	G	AB	R	H	2B	3B	HR	RBI	SB	Avg
2000 Potomac.	Carolina		3B	21	81	11	23	8	1	2	10	1	.284
2000 Peoria.	Midwest		3B	109	395	62	128	32	6	17	84	2	.324
2000 Memphis	P.C.		3B-OF	3	14	1	3	1	0	0	2	1	.214
2001 St. Louis a	N.L.		OF-3B-1B	161	590	112	194	47	4	37	130	1	.329
2002 St. Louis.	N.L.		OF-3B-1B-SS	157	590	118	185	40	2	34	127	2	.314
2003 St. Louis.	N.L.		OF-1B	157	591	*137	*212	*51	1	43	124	5	*.359
2004 St. Louis.	N.L.		1B	154	592	*133	196	51	2	46	123	5	.331
2005 St. Louis b	N.L.		1B	161	591	*129	195	38	2	41	117	16	.330
2006 St. Louis c	N.L.		1B	143	535	119	177	33	1	49	137	7	.331
2007 St. Louis.	N.L.		1B	158	565	99	185	38	1	32	103	2	.327
2008 St. Louis d-e	N.L.		1B-2B	148	524	100	187	44	0	37	116	7	.357
2009 St. Louis f	N.L.		1B	160	568	*124	186	45	1	*47	135	16	.327
2010 St. Louis.	N.L.		1B	159	587	*115	183	39	1	*42	*118	14	.312
2011 St. Louis g-h	N.L.		1B-3B	147	579	105	173	29	0	37	99	9	.299
Major League Totals			11 Yrs.	1705	6312	1291	2073	455	15	445	1329	84	.328
Division Series													
2001 St. Louis.	N.L.		1B-OF	5	18	1	2	0	0	1	2	0	.111
2002 St. Louis.	N.L.		OF-1B-3B	3	10	3	3	0	1	0	3	0	.300
2004 St. Louis.	N.L.		1B	4	15	4	5	0	0	2	5	0	.333
2005 St. Louis.	N.L.		1B	3	9	4	5	2	0	0	2	0	.556
2006 St. Louis.	N.L.		1B	4	15	3	5	1	0	1	3	0	.333
2009 St. Louis.	N.L.		1B	3	10	0	3	0	0	0	1	0	.300
2011 St. Louis.	N.L.		1B	5	20	2	7	3	0	0	1	1	.350
Division Series Totals				27	97	17	30	6	1	4	17	1	.309
Championship Series													
2002 St. Louis.	N.L.		OF-3B-1B	5	19	2	5	1	0	1	2	0	.263
2004 St. Louis.	N.L.		1B	7	28	10	14	2	0	4	9	0	.500
2005 St. Louis.	N.L.		1B	6	23	3	7	0	0	2	6	0	.304
2006 St. Louis.	N.L.		1B	7	22	5	7	1	0	1	1	0	.318
2011 St. Louis.	N.L.		1B	6	23	5	11	4	0	2	9	0	.478

Year	Club	Lea	Pos	G	AB	R	H	2B	3B	HR	RBI	SB	Avg
Championship Series Totals				31	115	25	44	8	0	10	27	0	.383
World Series Record													
2004 St. Louis . . . . .N.L.			1B	4	15	1	5	2	0	0	0	0	.333
2006 St. Louis . . . . .N.L.			1B	5	15	3	3	1	0	1	2	0	.200
2011 St. Louis . . . . .N.L.			1B	7	25	8	6	1	0	3	6	0	.240
World Series Totals				16	55	12	14	4	0	4	8	0	.255

a Selected Rookie of the Year in National League for 2001.
b Selected Most Valuable Player in National League for 2005.
c On disabled list from June 4 to June 22, 2006.
d On disabled list from June 11 to June 26, 2008.
e Selected Most Valuable Player in National League for 2008.
f Selected Most Valuable Player in National League for 2009.
g On disabled list from June 20 to July 5, 2011.
h Filed for free agency, October 30, 2011. Signed with Los Angeles Angels, December 10, 2011.

PUNTO, NICHOLAS PAUL (NICK)

Born, San Diego, California, November 8, 1977.
Bats Both. Throws Right. Height, 5 feet, 9 inches. Weight, 185 pounds.

Year	Club	Lea	Pos	G	AB	R	H	2B	3B	HR	RBI	SB	Avg
1998 Batavia . . . . . .N.Y.-Penn.			SS-2B	72	279	51	69	9	4	1	20	19	.247
1999 Clearwater . . . . . .Fla.St.			SS	106	400	65	122	18	6	1	48	16	.305
2000 Reading . . . . . . .Eastern			SS	121	456	77	116	15	4	5	47	33	.254
2001 Scranton-WB . . . . . . Int.			SS	123	463	57	106	19	5	1	39	33	.229
2001 Philadelphia . . . . .N.L.			SS	4	5	0	2	0	0	0	0	0	.400
2002 Philadelphia . . . . .N.L.			2B-SS	9	6	0	1	0	0	0	0	0	.167
2002 Scranton-WB . . . . . . Int.			SS	115	443	74	120	12	5	1	29	42	.271
2003 Philadelphia . . . . .N.L.			2B-3B-SS	64	92	14	20	2	0	1	4	2	.217
2003 Scranton/WB a . . . . . . Int.			SS	25	111	19	35	7	1	0	9	7	.315
2004 Minnesota . . . . .A.L.			2B-SS-3B-OF	38	91	17	23	0	0	2	12	6	.253
2004 Quad Cities b . . Midwest			SS-2B-3B	4	16	4	7	1	0	1	6	1	.438
2005 Rochester . . . . Int.			2B	4	15	2	3	1	0	0	1	0	.200
2005 Minnesota c . . . . . .A.L.			2B-SS-3B-OF	112	394	45	94	18	4	4	26	13	.239
2006 Minnesota . . . . .A.L.			3B-SS-2B-OF	135	459	73	133	21	7	1	45	17	.290
2007 Minnesota . . . . .A.L.			3B-SS-2B	150	472	53	99	18	4	1	25	16	.210
2008 Fort Myers . . . . . .Fla.St.			SS	3	12	0	3	0	0	0	1	1	.250
2008 Minnesota d-e . . . . .A.L.			SS-2B-3B-OF	99	338	43	96	19	4	2	28	15	.284
2009 Minnesota f . . . . . . .A.L.			2B-SS-3B	125	359	56	82	15	1	1	38	16	.228
2010 Minnesota g-h . . . . .A.L.			3B-SS-2B	88	252	24	60	11	1	1	20	6	.238
2011 Springfield . . . . .Texas			2B	7	24	3	8	1	0	0	2	1	.333
2011 Memphis . . . . .P.C.			2B-3B	5	15	2	3	0	0	0	0	0	.200
2011 St. Louis i-j . . . . . . .N.L.			2B-SS-3B	63	133	21	37	8	4	1	20	1	.278
Major League Totals	11 Yrs.			887	2601	346	647	112	25	14	218	92	.249
Division Series													
2006 Minnesota . . . . . .A.L.			3B	3	12	0	2	0	0	0	0	0	.167
2009 Minnesota . . . . . . .A.L.			2B	3	9	0	4	1	0	0	1	0	.444
2011 St. Louis. . . . . . . .N.L.			2B	3	6	0	1	0	0	0	0	0	.167
Division Series Totals				9	27	0	7	1	0	0	1	0	.259
Championship Series													
2011 St. Louis. . . . . .N.L.			2B	6	15	0	2	0	0	0	3	0	.133
World Series Record													
2011 St. Louis. . . . . .N.L.			2B	6	14	0	3	0	0	0	0	0	.214

a Traded to Minnesota Twins with pitcher Carlos Silva and cash for pitcher Eric Milton, December 3, 2003.
b On disabled list from May 9 to June 30 and July 27 to October 28, 2004.
c On disabled list from June 3 to July 3, 2005.
d On disabled list from May 8 to May 31 and June 6 to June 24, 2008.
e Filed for free agency, October 30, 2008, re-signed with Minnesota Twins, December 11, 2008.
f On disabled list from May 28 to June 12, 2009.
g On disabled list from April 16 to May 1 and July 29 to August 17 and August 20 to September 10, 2010.
h Filed for free agency, November 1, 2010. Signed with St. Louis Cardinals, January 21, 2011.
i On disabled list from March 22 to April 19 and May 18 to June 27 and July 29 to September 6, 2011.
j Filed for free agency, October 30, 2011. Signed with Boston Red Sox, December 14, 2011.

QUENTIN, CARLOS JOSE

Born, Bellflower, California, August 28, 1982.
Bats Right. Throws Right. Height, 6 feet, 1 inch. Weight, 225 pounds.

Year	Club	Lea	Pos	G	AB	R	H	2B	3B	HR	RBI	SB	Avg
2004 Lancaster . . . . .Calif.			OF	65	242	64	75	14	1	15	51	5	.310
2004 El Paso . . . . .Texas			OF	60	210	39	75	19	0	6	38	0	.357

Year Club	Lea	Pos	G	AB	R	H	2B	3B	HR	RBI	SB	Avg
2005 Tucson ..............P.C.		OF	136	452	98	136	28	4	21	89	9	.301
2006 Tucson ..............P.C.		OF	85	318	66	92	30	3	9	52	5	.289
2006 Arizona.............N.L.		OF	57	166	23	42	13	3	9	32	1	.253
2007 Tucson..............P.C.		OF	33	115	30	40	12	1	4	27	0	.348
2007 Arizona a-b...........N.L.		OF	81	229	29	49	16	0	5	31	2	.214
2008 Chicago ............A.L.		OF	130	480	96	138	26	1	36	100	7	.287
2009 Kannapolis ....So.Atl.		OF	2	3	0	1	1	0	0	1	0	.333
2009 Charlotte ....Int.		OF	12	37	10	14	3	0	.1	9	0	.378
2009 Chicago c............A.L.		OF	99	351	47	83	14	0	21	56	3	.236
2010 Chicago ............A.L.		OF	131	453	73	110	25	2	26	87	2	.243
2011 Chicago d-e .........A.L.		OF	118	421	53	107	31	0	24	77	1	.254
Major League Totals		6 Yrs.	616	2100	321	529	125	6	121	383	16	.252

a On disabled list from March 23 to April 16 and August 2 to September 1, 2007.
b Traded to Chicago White Sox for infielder Chris Carter, December 3, 2007.
c On disabled list from May 26 to July 20, 2009.
d On disabled list from August 21 to September 12, 2011.
e Traded to San Diego Padres for pitcher Simon Castro and pitcher Pedro Hernandez, December 31, 2011.

QUINTERO, HUMBERTO
Born, Maracaibo, Venezuela, August 2, 1979.
Bats Right. Throws Right. Height, 5 feet, 9 inches. Weight, 205 pounds.

Year Club	Lea	Pos	G	AB	R	H	2B	3B	HR	RBI	SB	Avg
1997 Guacara-1 .....Venzuelan		C	24	42	4	11	2	0	0	0	1	.262
1998 Miranda ......Venzuelan		C	30	73	6	15	1	0	0	1	0	.205
1999 Bristol ....Appal.		C	48	155	30	43	5	2	0	15	11	.277
2000 White Sox ....Arizona		C-OF	15	56	13	22	2	2	0	8	1	.393
2000 Burlington ....Midwest		C	75	248	23	59	12	2	0	24	10	.238
2001 Winston-Salem .... Carolina		C	43	154	15	37	6	0	0	12	9	.240
2001 Kannapolis .... So.Atl.		C	60	197	32	53	7	1	1	20	7	.269
2001 Birmingham ...... Southern		C	5	19	0	4	0	0	0	2	0	.211
2002 Winston-Salem .... Carolina		C	52	160	15	31	1	1	0	12	2	.194
2002 Charlotte ....Int.		C	15	41	2	9	1	0	0	5	0	.220
2002 Birmingham ...... Southern		C	4	12	1	6	0	0	0	3	1	.500
2002 Mobile a........ Southern		C	37	125	11	30	8	0	1	14	0	.240
2003 Mobile .... Southern		C	110	386	37	115	26	0	3	52	0	.298
2003 San Diego .... N.L.		C	12	23	1	5	0	0	0	2	0	.217
2004 Portland .............P.C.		C	68	259	36	82	25	0	5	30	0	.317
2004 San Diego .... N.L.		C	23	72	7	18	3	0	2	10	0	.250
2005 Corpus Christi .... Texas		C	4	11	0	2	1	0	0	1	0	.182
2005 Round Rock.........P.C.		C	52	191	23	55	13	0	8	31	2	.288
2005 Houston b-c........... N.L.		C-1B	18	54	6	10	1	0	1	8	0	.185
2006 Round Rock.........P.C.		C	82	292	39	87	21	2	4	37	4	.298
2006 Houston .... N.L.		C	11	21	2	7	2	0	0	2	0	.333
2007 Round Rock.........P.C.		C-1B	53	177	22	59	12	1	5	22	0	.333
2007 Houston .... N.L.		C	29	53	2	12	2	0	0	1	0	.226
2008 Round Rock.........P.C.		C-1B	32	118	13	28	2	2	3	18	0	.237
2008 Corpus Christi .... Texas		C	3	12	0	3	2	0	0	1	0	.250
2008 Houston d .... N.L.		C	59	168	16	38	6	0	2	12	0	.226
2009 Round Rock.........P.C.		C	4	10	0	1	1	0	0	1	0	.100
2009 Houston e .... N.L.		C	60	157	11	37	8	1	4	14	0	.236
2010 Houston .... N.L.		C	88	265	13	62	10	0	4	20	0	.234
2011 Oklahoma............P.C.		C	4	14	1	4	1	0	0	0	0	.286
2011 Houston f............ N.L.		C	79	262	22	63	12	1	2	25	1	.240
Major League Totals		9 Yrs.	379	1075	80	252	44	2	15	94	1	.234

a Traded by Chicago White Sox to San Diego Padres with outfielder Alex Fernandez for infielder D'Angelo Jimenez, July 12, 2002.
b Traded to Houston Astros for pitcher Tim Redding and cash, March 28, 2005.
c On disabled list from June 19 to July 16, 2005.
d On disabled list from July 2 to July 22, 2008.
e On disabled list from April 25 to May 12, 2009.
f On disabled list from May 28 to July 7, 2011.

RABURN, RYAN NEIL
Born, Tampa, Florida, April 17, 1981.
Bats Right. Throws Right. Height, 6 feet. Weight, 185 pounds.

Year Club	Lea	Pos	G	AB	R	H	2B	3B	HR	RBI	SB	Avg
2001 Tigers.......Gulf Coast		3B	19	58	4	9	2	0	1	5	2	.155
2001 Oneonta .....N.Y.-Penn.		3B-2B	44	171	25	62	17	8	8	42	1	.363
2002 Tigers.......Gulf Coast		3B	8	30	4	9	3	1	1	5	0	.300

Year	Club	Lea	Pos	G	AB	R	H	2B	3B	HR	RBI	SB	Avg
2002 West Michigan .. Midwest			3B	40	150	27	33	10	1	6	28	0	.220
2003 Lakeland....... Fla.St.			3B	95	325	52	72	14	3	12	56	2	.222
2003 West Michigan .. Midwest			3B	16	57	14	20	7	0	3	12	1	.351
2004 Lakeland....... Fla.St.			2B	3	11	1	3	1	0	1	3	0	.273
2004 Erie.......... Eastern			2B	98	366	66	110	29	4	16	63	3	.301
2004 Detroit.........A.L.			2B	12	29	4	4	1	0	0	1	1	.138
2005 Toledo .... Int.			2B-OF	130	471	62	119	22	4	19	64	8	.253
2006 Toledo .... Int.			OF-2B	118	451	68	124	29	4	20	79	16	.275
2007 Toledo .... Int.			OF-2B	85	315	60	92	21	3	17	64	12	.292
2007 Detroit.........A.L.			OF-2B-3B	49	138	28	42	12	2	4	27	3	.304
2008 Toledo .... Int.			OF	5	19	6	6	2	0	2	6	0	.316
2008 Detroit.........A.L.			OF-3B-2B	92	182	26	43	10	1	4	20	3	.236
2009 Toledo .... Int.			OF	12	47	11	12	3	0	5	9	2	.255
2009 Detroit.........A.L.			OF-1B-3B	113	261	44	76	11	2	16	45	5	.291
2010 Toledo .... Int.			OF	7	27	5	12	6	0	0	2	1	.444
2010 Detroit.........A.L.			OF-2B-3B-1B	113	371	54	104	25	1	15	62	2	.280
2011 Detroit.........A.L.			OF-2B-3B-1B	121	387	53	99	22	2	14	49	1	.256
Major League Totals			6 Yrs.	500	1368	209	368	81	8	53	204	15	.269
Division Series													
2011 Detroit.........A.L.			OF-2B	3	5	0	2	0	0	0	1	0	.400
Championship Series													
2011 Detroit.........A.L.			OF	6	23	4	6	1	0	2	4	0	.261

RAMIREZ, ALEXEI FERNANDO
Born, Pinar Del Rio, Cuba, September 22, 1981.
Bats Right. Throws Right. Height, 6 feet, 3 inches. Weight, 185 pounds.

Year	Club	Lea	Pos	G	AB	R	H	2B	3B	HR	RBI	SB	Avg
2008 Chicago a-b .......A.L.			2B-SS-OF-3B	136	480	65	139	22	2	21	77	13	.290
2009 Chicago .........A.L.			SS	148	542	71	150	14	1	15	68	14	.277
2010 Chicago .........A.L.			SS	156	585	83	165	29	2	18	70	13	.282
2011 Chicago .........A.L.			SS	158	614	81	165	31	2	15	70	7	.269
Major League Totals			4 Yrs.	598	2221	300	619	96	7	69	285	47	.279
Division Series													
2008 Chicago .........A.L.			2B	4	12	1	3	0	0	0	2	0	.250

a Played in Cuba 2001-2007.
b Signed with Chicago White Sox, January 1, 2008.

RAMIREZ (NIN), ARAMIS
Born, Santo Domingo, Dominican Republic, June 25, 1978.
Bats Right. Throws Right. Height, 6 feet, 1 inch. Weight, 215 pounds.

Year	Club	Lea	Pos	G	AB	R	H	2B	3B	HR	RBI	SB	Avg
1995 Pittsburgh ......Dominican			3B	64	214	41	63	13	0	11	54	2	.294
1996 Erie............. N.Y.-Penn.			3B	61	223	37	68	14	4	9	42	0	.305
1996 Augusta .... So.Atl.			3B	6	20	3	4	1	0	1	2	0	.200
1997 Lynchburg .... Carolina			3B	137	482	85	134	24	2	29	114	5	.278
1998 Nashville .............P.C.			3B-SS	47	168	19	46	10	0	5	18	0	.274
1998 Pittsburgh a.........N.L.			3B	72	251	23	59	9	1	6	24	0	.235
1999 Nashville ..........P.C.			3B	131	460	92	151	35	1	21	74	5	.328
1999 Pittsburgh ........N.L.			3B	18	56	2	10	2	1	0	7	0	.179
2000 Nashville ..........P.C.			3B	44	167	28	59	12	2	4	26	2	.353
2000 Pittsburgh b..........N.L.			3B	73	254	19	65	15	2	6	35	0	.256
2001 Pittsburgh .........N.L.			3B	158	603	83	181	40	0	34	112	5	.300
2002 Pittsburgh .........N.L.			3B	142	522	51	122	26	0	18	71	2	.234
2003 Pittsburgh-Chicago c-d . N.L.			3B	159	607	75	165	32	2	27	106	2	.272
2004 Chicago ..........N.L.			3B	145	547	99	174	32	1	36	103	0	.318
2005 Chicago e.........N.L.			3B	123	463	72	140	30	0	31	92	0	.302
2006 Chicago f.........N.L.			3B	157	594	93	173	38	4	38	119	2	.291
2007 Chicago g.........N.L.			3B	132	506	72	157	35	4	26	101	0	.310
2008 Chicago ..........N.L.			3B	149	554	97	160	44	1	27	111	2	.289
2009 Peoria...........Midwest			3B	3	6	2	3	1	0	0	1	0	.500
2009 Chicago h.........N.L.			3B	82	306	46	97	14	1	15	65	2	.317
2010 Peoria...........Midwest			3B	2	6	1	1	0	0	0	1	0	.167
2010 Chicago i.........N.L.			3B	124	465	61	112	21	1	25	83	0	.241
2011 Chicago j.........N.L.			3B	149	565	80	173	35	1	26	93	1	.306
Major League Totals			14 Yrs.	1683	6293	873	1788	373	19	315	1122	16	.284
Division Series													
2003 Chicago .............N.L.			3B	5	18	2	5	1	0	1	3	0	.278

Year	Club	Lea	Pos	G	AB	R	H	2B	3B	HR	RBI	SB	Avg
2007 Chicago	N.L.	3B	3	12	0	0	0	0	0	0	0	.000
2008 Chicago	N.L.	3B	3	11	1	2	1	0	0	0	0	.182
Division Series Totals...........			11	41	3	7	2	0	1	3	0	.171
Championship Series												
2003 Chicago	N.L.	3B	7	26	4	6	0	1	3	7	0	.231

a On disabled list from August 10 to September 4, 1998.
b On disabled list from August 29 to October 1, 2000.
c Traded to Chicago Cubs with outfielder Kenny Lofton for infielder Jose Hernandez, pitcher Matt Bruback and player to be named later, July 22, 2003.
d Pittsburgh Pirates received infielder Bobby Hill to complete trade, August 15, 2003.
e On disabled list from August 25 to October 3, 2005.
f Filed for free agency, October 30, 2006, re-signed with Chicago Cubs, November 12, 2006.
g On disabled list from June 7 to June 22, 2007.
h On disabled list from May 9 to July 6, 2009.
i On disabled list from June 8 to June 25, 2010.
j Filed for free agency, November 1, 2011. Signed with Milwaukee Brewers, December 12, 2011.

RAMIREZ, HANLEY
Born, Samana, Dominican Republic, December 23, 1983.
Bats Right. Throws Right. Height, 6 feet, 3 inches. Weight, 195 pounds.

Year	Club	Lea	Pos	G	AB	R	H	2B	3B	HR	RBI	SB	Avg
2002 Red Sox	Gulf Coast	SS-2B-3B	45	164	29	56	11	3	6	26	8	.341
2002 Lowell	N.Y.-Penn.	SS	22	97	17	36	9	2	1	19	4	.371
2003 Augusta	So.Atl.	SS	111	422	69	116	24	3	8	50	36	.275
2004 Portland	Eastern	SS	32	129	26	40	7	2	5	15	12	.310
2004 Sarasota........	Fla.St.	SS	62	239	33	74	8	4	1	24	12	.310
2004 Red Sox	Gulf Coast	SS-2B	6	20	5	8	0	1	0	7	1	.400
2005 Portland	Eastern	SS-2B-3B	122	465	66	126	21	7	6	52	26	.271
2005 Boston a..........	A.L.	SS	2	2	0	0	0	0	0	0	0	.000
2006 Florida b........	N.L.	SS	158	633	119	185	46	11	17	59	51	.292
2007 Florida	N.L.	SS	154	639	125	212	48	6	29	81	51	.332
2008 Florida	N.L.	SS	153	589	*125	177	34	4	33	67	35	.301
2009 Florida	N.L.	SS	151	576	101	197	42	1	24	106	27	*.342
2010 Florida	N.L.	SS	142	543	92	163	28	2	21	76	32	.300
2011 Jupiter	Fla.St.	SS	6	21	6	10	1	1	0	4	1	.476
2011 Florida c........	N.L.	SS	92	338	55	82	16	0	10	45	20	.243
Major League Totals			7 Yrs.	852	3320	617	1016	214	24	134	434	216	.306

a Traded to Florida Marlins with pitcher Anibal Sanchez and pitcher Jesus Delgado for pitcher Josh Beckett, infielder Mike Lowell and pitcher Guillermo Mota, November 24, 2005.
b Selected Rookie of the Year in National League for 2006.
c On disabled list from May 30 to June 14 and August 3 to October 31, 2011.

RAMOS (CAMPOS), WILSON ABRAHAM
Born, Valencia, Venezuela, August 10, 1987.
Bats Right. Throws Right. Height, 6 feet. Weight, 220 pounds.

Year	Club	Lea	Pos	G	AB	R	H	2B	3B	HR	RBI	SB	Avg
2006 Twins	Gulf Coast	C-1B	46	154	18	44	12	1	3	26	4	.286
2007 Beloit	Midwest	C	73	292	40	85	17	1	8	42	1	.291
2008 Fort Myers	Fla.St.	C	126	452	50	130	23	2	13	78	0	.288
2009 Twins	Gulf Coast	C	5	19	4	6	1	1	3	6	0	.316
2009 New Britain	Eastern	C	54	205	31	65	16	0	4	29	0	.317
2010 Minnesota	A.L.	C	7	27	2	8	3	0	0	1	0	.296
2010 Rochester.............	Int.	C	71	278	25	67	14	0	5	30	1	.241
2010 Syracuse	Int.	C	20	79	14	25	3	1	3	8	0	.316
2010 Washington a.........	N.L.	C	15	52	3	14	4	0	1	4	0	.269
2011 Washington	N.L.	C	113	389	48	104	22	1	15	52	0	.267
Major League Totals			2 Yrs.	135	468	53	126	29	1	16	57	0	.269

a Traded to Washington Nationals with pitcher Joe Testa and cash for pitcher Matt Capps, July 30, 2010.

RASMUS, COLBY RYAN
Born, Columbus, Georgia, August 11, 1986.
Bats Left. Throws Left. Height, 6 feet, 2 inches. Weight, 200 pounds.

Year	Club	Lea	Pos	G	AB	R	H	2B	3B	HR	RBI	SB	Avg
2005 Johnson City	Appal.	OF	62	216	47	64	16	5	7	27	13	.296
2006 Palm Beach	Fla.St.	OF	53	193	22	49	4	5	5	35	11	.254
2006 Quad Cities........	Midwest	OF	78	303	49	94	22	3	11	50	17	.310

Year	Club	Lea	Pos	G	AB	R	H	2B	3B	HR	RBI	SB	Avg
2007 Springfield	Texas		OF	128	472	93	130	37	3	29	72	18	.275
2008 Palm Beach	Fla.St.		OF	3	9	1	0	0	0	0	0	0	.000
2008 Cardinals	Gulf Coast		OF	3	9	1	5	1	0	1	2	0	.556
2008 Memphis	P.C.		OF	90	331	56	83	15	0	11	36	15	.251
2009 St. Louis	N.L.		OF	147	474	72	119	22	2	16	52	3	.251
2010 St. Louis	N.L.		OF	144	464	85	128	28	3	23	66	12	.276
2011 St. Louis	N.L.		OF	94	338	61	83	14	6	11	40	5	.246
2011 Toronto a-b	A.L.		OF	35	133	14	23	10	0	3	13	0	.173
Major League Totals			3 Yrs.	420	1409	232	353	74	11	53	171	20	.251
Division Series													
2009 St. Louis	N.L.		OF	3	9	1	4	3	0	1	1	0	.444

a Traded to Toronto Blue Jays with pitcher Trever Miller, pitcher Brian Tallet and pitcher P.J. Walters for pitcher Edwin Jackson, pitcher Octavio Dotel, pitcher Marc Rzepczynski, outfielder Corey Patterson and cash, July 27, 2011.
b On disabled list from August 24 to September 16, 2011.

REDDICK, WILLIAM JOSHUA (JOSH)
Born, Savannah, Georgia, February 19, 1987.
Bats Left. Throws Right. Height, 6 feet, 2 inches. Weight, 180 pounds.

Year	Club	Lea	Pos	G	AB	R	H	2B	3B	HR	RBI	SB	Avg
2007 Greenville	So.Atl.		OF	94	369	60	113	17	6	18	72	8	.306
2007 Portland	Eastern		PH	1	1	0	0	0	0	0	0	0	.000
2008 Greenville	So.Atl.		OF	14	53	7	18	4	2	0	9	2	.340
2008 Lancaster	Calif.		OF	76	312	60	107	11	8	17	57	9	.343
2008 Portland	Eastern		OF	34	117	22	25	4	2	6	25	3	.214
2009 Portland	Eastern		OF	63	256	47	71	17	3	13	29	5	.277
2009 Pawtucket	Int.		OF	18	71	1	9	0	2	0	6	0	.127
2009 Boston	A.L.		OF	27	59	5	10	4	0	2	4	0	.169
2010 Pawtucket	Int.		OF	114	451	59	120	28	4	18	65	4	.266
2010 Boston	A.L.		OF	29	62	5	12	3	1	1	5	1	.194
2011 Pawtucket	Int.		OF	52	191	37	44	9	1	14	36	4	.230
2011 Boston a	A.L.		OF	87	254	41	71	18	3	7	28	1	.280
Major League Totals			3 Yrs.	143	375	51	93	25	4	10	37	2	.248

a Traded to Oakland Athletics with infielder Miles Head and pitcher Raul Alcantara for pitcher Andrew Bailey and outfielder Ryan Sweeney, December 28, 2011.

REIMOLD, NOLAN GALLAGHER
Born, Greenville, Pennsylvania, October 12, 1983.
Bats Right. Throws Right. Height, 6 feet, 4 inches. Weight, 215 pounds.

Year	Club	Lea	Pos	G	AB	R	H	2B	3B	HR	RBI	SB	Avg
2005 Aberdeen	N.Y.-Penn.		OF-1B	50	180	33	53	15	2	9	30	2	.294
2005 Frederick	Carolina		OF	23	83	17	22	6	0	6	11	3	.265
2006 Frederick	Carolina		OF	119	415	73	106	26	0	19	75	14	.255
2007 Orioles	Gulf Coast		OF	9	30	4	7	4	1	0	8	0	.233
2007 Bowie	Eastern		OF	50	186	30	57	15	0	11	34	2	.306
2008 Bowie	Eastern		OF	139	507	87	144	29	3	25	84	7	.284
2009 Norfolk	Int.		OF	31	109	21	43	11	0	9	27	6	.394
2009 Baltimore a	A.L.		OF	104	358	49	100	18	2	15	45	8	.279
2010 Norfolk	Int.		OF-1B	94	337	52	84	12	0	10	37	9	.249
2010 Baltimore	A.L.		OF	39	116	9	24	5	0	3	14	0	.207
2011 Norfolk	Int.		OF	39	139	16	33	6	0	6	22	2	.237
2011 Baltimore	A.L.		OF	87	267	40	66	10	3	13	45	7	.247
Major League Totals			3 Yrs.	230	741	98	190	33	5	31	104	15	.256

a On disabled list from September 18 to October 13, 2009.

RENTERIA, EDGAR ENRIQUE
Born, Barranquilla, Colombia, August 7, 1976.
Bats Right. Throws Right. Height, 6 feet, 1 inch. Weight, 200 pounds.

Year	Club	Lea	Pos	G	AB	R	H	2B	3B	HR	RBI	SB	Avg
1992 Marlins	Gulf Coast		SS	43	163	25	47	8	1	0	9	10	.288
1993 Kane County	Midwest		SS	116	384	40	78	8	0	1	35	7	.203
1994 Brevard Cty	Fla. St.		SS	128	439	46	111	15	1	0	36	6	.253
1995 Portland	Eastern		SS	135	508	70	147	15	7	7	68	30	.289
1996 Charlotte	Int.		SS	35	132	17	37	8	0	2	16	10	.280
1996 Florida a	N.L.		SS	106	431	68	133	18	3	5	31	16	.309
1997 Florida	N.L.		SS	154	617	90	171	21	3	4	52	32	.277
1998 Florida b-c	N.L.		SS	133	517	79	146	18	2	3	31	41	.282
1999 St. Louis	N.L.		SS	154	585	92	161	36	2	11	63	37	.275

145

Year	Club	Lea	Pos	G	AB	R	H	2B	3B	HR	RBI	SB	Avg
2000 St. Louis.............	N.L.	SS	150	562	94	156	32	1	16	76	21	.278
2001 St. Louis.............	N.L.	SS-1B	141	493	54	128	19	3	10	57	17	.260
2002 St. Louis.............	N.L.	SS	152	544	77	166	36	2	11	83	22	.305
2003 St. Louis.............	N.L.	SS	157	587	96	194	47	1	13	100	34	.330
2004 St. Louis d..........	N.L.	SS	149	586	84	168	37	0	10	72	17	.287
2005 Boston e.............	A.L.	SS	153	623	100	172	36	4	8	70	9	.276
2006 Atlanta.............	N.L.	SS	149	598	100	175	40	2	14	70	17	.293
2007 Atlanta f-g.........	N.L.	SS	124	494	87	164	30	1	12	57	11	.332
2008 Detroit h...........	A.L.	SS	138	503	69	136	22	2	10	55	6	.270
2009 San Francisco........	N.L.	SS	124	460	50	115	19	1	5	48	7	.250
2010 Fresno..............	P.C.	SS	2	4	2	3	0	0	0	3	0	.750
2010 San Francisco i-j......	N.L.	SS	72	243	26	67	11	2	3	22	3	.276
2011 Cincinnati k..........	N.L.	SS-2B	96	299	34	75	14	0	5	36	4	.251
Major League Totals...........	16 Yrs.	2152	8142	1200	2327	436	29	140	923	294	.286

Division Series													
1997 Florida..............	N.L.	SS	3	13	1	2	0	0	0	1	0	.154
2000 St. Louis.............	N.L.	SS	3	10	5	2	0	0	0	0	2	.200
2001 St. Louis.............	N.L.	SS	5	17	2	4	1	0	1	1	0	.235
2002 St. Louis.............	N.L.	SS	3	12	3	3	0	0	0	0	2	.250
2004 St. Louis.............	N.L.	SS	4	11	4	5	2	0	0	4	1	.455
2005 Boston..............	A.L.	SS	3	13	1	3	2	0	0	0	0	.231
2010 San Francisco	N.L.	SS	2	2	0	2	0	0	0	0	0	1.000
Division Series Totals..........	23	78	16	21	5	0	1	6	5	.269

Championship Series													
1997 Florida..............	N.L.	SS	6	22	4	5	1	0	0	0	1	.227
2000 St. Louis.............	N.L.	SS	5	20	4	6	1	0	0	4	3	.300
2002 St. Louis.............	N.L.	SS	5	19	0	3	0	0	0	1	0	.158
2004 St. Louis.............	N.L.	SS	7	24	1	4	0	0	0	2	0	.167
2010 San Francisco........	N.L.	SS	4	16	1	1	0	0	0	0	0	.063
Championship Series Totals......	27	101	10	19	2	0	0	7	4	.188

World Series Record													
1997 Florida..............	N.L.	SS	7	31	3	9	2	0	0	3	0	.290
2004 St. Louis.............	N.L.	SS	4	15	2	5	3	0	0	1	0	.333
2010 San Francisco........	N.L.	SS	5	17	6	7	0	0	2	6	0	.412
World Series Totals.............	16	63	11	21	5	0	2	10	0	.333

a On disabled list from June 24 to July 11, 1996.
b On disabled list from August 25 to September 9, 1998.
c Traded to St. Louis Cardinals for infielder Pablo Ozuna, pitcher Armando Almanza and pitcher Braden Looper, December 14, 1998.
d Filed for free agency, October 29, 2004. Signed with Boston Red Sox, December 17, 2004.
e Traded to Atlanta Braves with cash for infielder Andy Marte, December 7, 2005.
f On disabled list from August 3 to August 22 and from August 23 to September 7, 2007.
g Traded to Detroit Tigers for pitcher Jair Jurrjens and outfielder Gorkys Hernandez, October 29, 2007.
h Not offered contract, October 30, 2008. Signed with San Francisco Giants, December 4, 2008.
i On disabled list from May 7 to May 22 and May 26 to June 16 and August 11 to September 1, 2010.
j Filed for free agency, November 4, 2010. Signed with Cincinnati Reds, January 10, 2011.
k Filed for free agency, October 30, 2011.

REVERE, BEN DANIEL

Born, Atlanta, Georgia, May 3, 1988.
Bats Left. Throws Right. Height, 5 feet, 9 inches. Weight, 170 pounds.

Year	Club	Lea	Pos	G	AB	R	H	2B	3B	HR	RBI	SB	Avg
2007 Twins..........	Gulf Coast	OF	50	191	46	62	6	10	0	29	21	.325
2008 Beloit...........	Midwest	OF	83	340	51	129	17	10	1	43	44	.379
2009 Fort Myers.........	Fla.St.	OF	121	466	75	145	13	4	2	48	45	.311
2010 New Britain.......	Eastern	OF	94	361	44	110	10	4	1	23	36	.305
2010 Minnesota...........	A.L.	OF	13	28	1	5	0	0	0	2	0	.179
2011 Rochester.............	Int.	OF	32	132	15	40	3	1	1	9	8	.303
2011 Minnesota...........	A.L.	OF	117	450	56	120	9	5	0	30	34	.267
Major League Totals...........	2 Yrs.	130	478	57	125	9	5	0	32	34	.262

REYES, JOSE BERNABE

Born, Villa Gonzalez, Dominican Republic, June 11, 1983.
Bats Both. Throws Right. Height, 6 feet. Weight, 200 pounds.

Year	Club	Lea	Pos	G	AB	R	H	2B	3B	HR	RBI	SB	Avg
2000 Kingsport.......	Appal.	SS-3B-2B-OF	49	132	22	33	3	3	0	8	10	.250
2001 Columbia.......	So.Atl.	SS	108	407	71	125	22	15	5	48	30	.307

Year	Club	Lea	Pos	G	AB	R	H	2B	3B	HR	RBI	SB	Avg
2002 Binghamton	. . . . Eastern		SS	65	275	46	79	16	8	2	24	27	.287
2002 St. Lucie	. . . . Fla.St.		SS	69	288	58	83	10	11	6	38	31	.288
2003 Norfolk	. . . . Int.		SS	42	160	28	43	6	4	0	13	26	.269
2003 New York a	. . . . N.L.		SS	69	274	47	84	12	4	5	32	13	.307
2004 St. Lucie	. . . . Fla.St.		2B	6	23	3	6	2	0	0	1	2	.261
2004 Binghamton	. . . . Eastern		2B	4	18	2	2	0	0	0	3	3	.111
2004 New York b	. . . . . . N.L.		2B-SS	53	220	33	56	16	2	2	14	19	.255
2005 New York	. . . . N.L.		SS	161	*696	99	190	24	*17	7	58	*60	.273
2006 New York	. . . . N.L.		SS	153	647	*122	194	30	17	19	81	*64	.300
2007 New York	. . . . N.L.		SS	160	681	119	191	36	12	12	57	*78	.280
2008 New York	. . . . N.L.		SS	159	*688	113	*204	37	*19	16	68	56	.297
2009 New York c	. . . . N.L.		SS	36	147	18	41	7	2	2	15	11	.279
2010 St. Lucie	. . . . . . Fla.St.		SS	1	4	0	0	0	0	0	1	0	.000
2010 New York d	. . . . . . N.L.		SS	133	563	83	159	29	10	11	54	30	.282
2011 Brooklyn	. . . . N.Y.-Penn.		SS	1	3	1	1	1	0	0	0	0	.333
2011 Binghamton	. . . . Eastern		SS	3	9	3	3	0	0	1	1	0	.333
2011 New York e-f	. . . . . N.L.		SS	126	537	101	181	31	*16	7	44	39	*.337
Major League Totals			9 Yrs.	1050	4453	735	1300	222	99	81	423	370	.292
Division Series													
2006 New York	. . . . N.L.		SS	3	12	2	2	0	0	0	3	1	.167
Championship Series													
2006 New York	. . . . N.L.		SS	7	32	5	9	1	1	1	2	2	.281

a On disabled list from September 1 to November 6, 2003.
b On disabled list from March 26 to June 19 and August 12 to September 24, 2004.
c On disabled list from May 21 to October 14, 2009.
d On disabled list from March 26 to April 8, 2010.
e On disabled list from July 3 to July 19 and August 8 to August 29, 2011.
f Filed for free agency, October 30, 2011. Signed with Florida Marlins, December 7, 2011.

REYNOLDS, MARK ANDREW
Born, Pikeville, Kentucky, August 3, 1983.
Bats Right. Throws Right. Height, 6 feet, 1 inch. Weight, 220 pounds.

Year	Club	Lea	Pos	G	AB	R	H	2B	3B	HR	RBI	SB	Avg
2004 Lancaster	. . . . Calif.		3B-SS	4	12	1	1	0	0	0	1	0	*.083
2004 South Bend	. . . Midwest		3B	4	15	0	1	1	0	0	0	0	.067
2004 Yakima	. . . . . . Northwest		SS-3B-2B	64	234	58	64	19	1	12	41	5	.274
2005 South Bend	. . . Midwest		SS-3B	118	434	65	110	26	2	19	76	4	.253
2006 Lancaster	. . . . Calif.		SS-3B-2B-1B	76	273	64	92	18	2	23	77	1	.337
2006 Tennessee	. . . . Southern		OF-3B-2B	30	114	23	31	7	0	8	21	0	.272
2007 Mobile	. . . . . . Southern		3B-2B	37	134	28	41	9	2	6	22	2	.306
2007 Arizona	. . . . N.L.		3B-2B-OF	111	366	62	102	20	4	17	62	0	.279
2008 Arizona	. . . . N.L.		3B-1B	152	539	87	129	28	3	28	97	11	.239
2009 Arizona	. . . . N.L.		3B-1B	155	578	98	150	30	1	44	102	24	.260
2010 Arizona a	. . . . N.L.		3B-1B	145	499	79	99	17	2	32	85	7	.198
2011 Baltimore	. . . . A.L.		3B-1B	155	534	84	118	27	1	37	86	6	.221
Major League Totals			5 Yrs.	718	2516	410	598	122	11	158	432	48	.238
Division Series													
2007 Arizona	. . . . N.L.		3B	3	10	2	2	0	0	1	1	0	.200
Championship Series													
2007 Arizona	. . . . N.L.		3B	4	16	1	2	0	0	1	1	0	.125

a Traded to Baltimore Orioles with player to be named later for pitcher Kam Mickolio and pitcher David Hernandez, December 6, 2010.

RIOS, ALEXIS ISRAEL
Born, Coffee County, Alabama, February 18, 1981.
Bats Right. Throws Right. Height, 6 feet, 5 inches. Weight, 195 pounds.

Year	Club	Lea	Pos	G	AB	R	H	2B	3B	HR	RBI	SB	Avg
1999 Medicine Hat	. . . . . . .Pioneer		OF	67	234	35	63	7	3	0	13	8	.269
2000 Hagerstown	. . . . So.Atl.		DH	22	74	5	17	3	1	0	5	2	.230
2000 Queens	. . . . . . N.Y.-Penn.		OF	50	206	22	55	9	2	1	25	5	.267
2001 Charleston-WV	. . . . . So.Atl.		OF	130	480	40	126	20	9	2	58	22	.262
2002 Dunedin	. . . . .Fla.St.		OF	111	456	60	139	22	8	3	61	14	.305
2003 New Haven	. . . . Eastern		OF	127	514	86	181	32	11	11	82	11	.352
2004 Syracuse	. . . . Int.		OF	46	185	14	48	10	1	3	23	2	.259
2004 Toronto	. . . . A.L.		OF	111	426	55	122	24	7	1	28	15	.286
2005 Toronto	. . . . A.L.		OF	146	481	71	126	23	6	10	59	14	.262
2006 Syracuse	. . . . Int.		OF	3	10	0	3	1	0	0	1	0	.300
2006 Toronto a	. . . . A.L.		OF	128	450	68	136	33	6	17	82	15	.302

Year	Club	Lea	Pos	G	AB	R	H	2B	3B	HR	RBI	SB	Avg
2007 Toronto	A.L.	OF	161	643	114	191	43	7	24	85	17	.297
2008 Toronto	A.L.	OF	155	635	91	185	47	8	15	79	32	.291
2009 Toronto-Chicago b	A.L.	OF	149	582	63	144	31	2	17	71	24	.247
2010 Chicago	A.L.	OF	147	567	89	161	29	3	21	88	34	.284
2011 Chicago	A.L.	OF	145	537	64	122	22	2	13	44	11	.227
Major League Totals	8 Yrs.	1142	4321	615	1187	252	41	118	536	162	.275		

a On disabled list from June 28 to July 28, 2006.

b Claimed on waivers by Chicago White Sox, August 10, 2009.

RIVERA, JUAN LUIS

Born, Guarenas, Venezuela, July 3, 1978.
Bats Right. Throws Right. Height, 6 feet, 2 inches. Weight, 225 pounds.

Year	Club	Lea	Pos	G	AB	R	H	2B	3B	HR	RBI	SB	Avg
1996 NY Yankees	Dominican	OF	10	18	0	3	0	0	0	2	0	.167
1997 Maracay-2	Venzuelan	OF	52	142	25	40	9	0	0	14	12	.282
1998 Yankees	Gulf Coast	OF	57	210	43	70	9	1	12	45	8	.333
1998 Oneonta	N.Y.-Penn.	OF	6	18	2	5	0	0	1	3	1	.278
1999 Tampa	Fla.St.	OF	109	427	50	112	20	2	14	77	5	.262
1999 Yankees	Gulf Coast	OF	5	18	7	6	0	0	1	4	0	.333
2000 Norwich	Eastern	OF	17	62	9	14	5	0	2	12	0	.226
2000 Tampa	Fla.St.	OF-1B	115	409	62	113	26	1	14	69	11	.276
2001 Norwich	Eastern	OF	77	316	50	101	18	3	14	58	5	.320
2001 Columbus...........	Int.	OF	55	199	39	65	11	1	14	40	4	.327
2001 New York	A.L.	OF	3	4	0	0	0	0	0	0	0	.000
2002 Columbus...........	Int.	OF	65	265	40	86	21	1	8	47	5	.325
2002 New York a...........	A.L.	OF	28	83	9	22	5	0	1	6	1	.265
2003 Columbus...........	Int.	OF	79	308	47	100	21	0	7	37	1	.325
2003 New York b...........	A.L.	OF	57	173	22	46	14	0	7	26	0	.266
2004 Montreal c	N.L.	OF	134	391	48	120	24	1	12	49	6	.307
2005 Los Angeles	A.L.	OF	106	350	46	95	17	1	15	59	1	.271
2006 Salt Lake	P.C.	OF	2	9	3	5	3	0	1	6	0	.556
2006 Los Angeles d	A.L.	OF	124	448	65	139	27	0	23	85	0	.310
2007 Rancho Cucamonga....	Calif.	OF	3	10	3	4	1	0	0	2	0	.400
2007 Salt Lake	P.C.	OF	15	61	4	16	8	0	0	17	0	.262
2007 Los Angeles e........	A.L.	OF	14	43	3	12	1	0	2	8	0	.279
2008 Los Angeles f........	A.L.	OF-1B-2B	89	256	31	63	13	0	12	45	1	.246
2009 Los Angeles	A.L.	OF	138	529	72	152	24	1	25	88	0	.287
2010 Los Angeles	A.L.	OF-1B	124	416	53	105	20	0	15	52	2	.252
2011 Toronto	A.L.	OF-1B	70	247	22	60	11	0	6	28	3	.243
2011 Los Angeles g-h-i...	N.L.	OF-1B	62	219	24	60	12	1	5	46	2	.274
Major League Totals	11 Yrs.	949	3159	395	874	168	4	123	492	16	.277		
Division Series													
2002 New York	A.L.	OF	4	12	2	3	0	0	0	3	0	.250
2003 New York	A.L.	OF	4	12	2	4	0	0	0	0	0	.333
2005 Los Angeles	A.L.	DH	5	17	3	6	1	0	1	1	0	.353
2007 Los Angeles	A.L.	DH	2	3	0	1	0	0	0	0	0	.333
2008 Los Angeles	A.L.	OF	3	8	1	1	0	0	0	1	0	.125
2009 Los Angeles	A.L.	OF	3	11	1	3	1	0	0	2	1	.273
Division Series Totals		21	63	9	18	2	0	1	7	1	.286		
Championship Series													
2003 New York	A.L.	OF	2	2	0	0	0	0	0	0	0	.000
2005 Los Angeles	A.L.	OF-DH	3	9	1	1	1	0	0	0	0	.111
2009 Los Angeles	A.L.	OF	6	25	0	5	1	0	0	0	0	.200
Championship Series Totals		11	36	1	6	2	0	0	0	0	.167		
World Series Record													
2003 New York	A.L.	OF	4	6	0	1	1	0	0	1	0	.167

a On disabled list from June 8 to August 19, 2002.

b Traded to Montreal Expos with infielder Nick Johnson and pitcher Randy Choate for pitcher Javier Vazquez, December 4, 2003.

c Traded to Anaheim Angels with infielder Maicer Izturis for outfielder Jose Guillen, November 19, 2004.

d On disabled list from April 17 to May 8, 2006.

e On disabled list from March 23 to September 2, 2007.

f Filed for free agency, October 31, 2008, re-signed with Los Angeles Angels, December 19, 2008.

g Traded to Toronto Blue Jays with catcher Mike Napoli for outfielder Vernon Wells, January 21, 2011.

h Sold to Los Angeles Dodgers, July 12, 2011.

i Filed for free agency, October 30, 2011, re-signed with Los Angeles Dodgers, November 3, 2011.

ROBERTS, BRIAN MICHAEL

Born, Durham, North Carolina, October 9, 1977.
Bats Both. Throws Right. Height, 5 feet, 9 inches. Weight, 175 pounds.

Year	Club	Lea	Pos	G	AB	R	H	2B	3B	HR	RBI	SB	Avg
1999 Delmarva a	So.Atl.		SS	47	167	22	40	12	1	0	21	17	.240
2000 Frederick	Carolina		SS	48	163	27	49	6	3	0	16	13	.301
2000 Orioles b	Gulf Coast		SS	9	29	8	9	1	2	1	3	7	.310
2001 Bowie	Eastern		2B-SS	22	81	12	24	7	0	1	7	10	.296
2001 Rochester	Int.		SS	44	161	16	43	4	1	1	12	23	.267
2001 Baltimore	A.L.		SS-2B	75	273	42	69	12	3	2	17	12	.253
2002 Rochester	Int.		2B	78	313	49	86	9	7	3	30	22	.275
2002 Baltimore	A.L.		2B	38	128	18	29	6	0	.1	11	9	.227
2003 Ottawa	Int.		2B-SS	44	178	36	56	13	1	0	15	19	.315
2003 Baltimore	A.L.		2B-SS	112	460	65	124	22	4	5	41	23	.270
2004 Baltimore	A.L.		2B	159	641	107	175	*50	2	4	53	29	.273
2005 Baltimore	A.L.		2B	143	561	92	176	45	7	18	73	27	.314
2006 Bowie	Eastern		2B	2	5	0	1	0	0	0	0	0	.200
2006 Baltimore c	A.L.		2B	138	563	85	161	34	3	10	55	36	.286
2007 Baltimore	A.L.		2B	156	621	103	180	42	5	12	57	*50	.290
2008 Baltimore	A.L.		2B	155	611	107	181	51	6	9	57	40	.296
2009 Baltimore	A.L.		2B	159	632	110	179	*56	1	16	79	30	.283
2010 Orioles	Gulf Coast		2B	5	15	1	8	1	0	0	0	0	.533
2010 Bowie	Eastern		2B	3	14	3	6	2	0	0	3	0	.429
2010 Baltimore d	A.L.		2B	59	230	28	64	14	0	4	15	12	.278
2011 Baltimore e	A.L.		2B	39	163	18	36	7	1	3	19	6	.221
Major League Totals			11 Yrs.	1233	4883	775	1374	339	34	84	477	274	.281

a Drafted by Baltimore Orioles with choice received for Texas Rangers signing infielder Rafael Palmeiro, June 2, 1999.
b On disabled list from April 19 to July 13, 2000.
c On disabled list from April 30 to May 24, 2006.
d On disabled list from April 10 to July 23, 2010.
e On disabled list from May 17 to May 31 and May 31 to November 2, 2011.

ROBERTS, RYAN ALAN

Born, Fort Worth, Texas, September 19, 1980.
Bats Right. Throws Right. Height, 5 feet, 11 inches. Weight, 185 pounds.

Year	Club	Lea	Pos	G	AB	R	H	2B	3B	HR	RBI	SB	Avg
2003 Auburn	N.Y.-Penn.		3B-SS	66	248	52	69	10	3	8	36	7	.278
2004 Charleston	So.Atl.		2B	64	225	38	64	9	0	13	39	0	.284
2004 Dunedin	Fla.St.		2B	59	205	29	49	1	1	7	25	0	.239
2005 Dunedin	Fla.St.		2B	42	164	33	47	9	0	9	35	6	.287
2005 New Hampshire	Eastern		2B	92	338	54	92	19	3	15	44	5	.272
2006 Toronto	A.L.		2B	9	13	1	1	0	0	1	1	0	.077
2006 Syracuse	Int.		2B-3B	98	362	44	99	28	1	10	49	5	.273
2007 Toronto	A.L.		3B-2B-OF	8	13	2	1	0	0	0	0	0	.077
2007 Syracuse a	Int.		3B-2B-SS-1B	100	337	46	84	16	1	12	47	1	.249
2008 Texas	A.L.		DH	1	1	0	0	0	0	0	0	0	.000
2008 Oklahoma b	P.C.		2B-3B-SS-OF	130	453	71	136	28	8	10	66	15	.300
2009 Reno	P.C.		2B-SS	10	42	10	13	1	1	1	10	7	.310
2009 Arizona	N.L.		2B-3B-OF	110	305	41	85	17	2	7	25	7	.279
2010 Reno	P.C.		2B-OF-3B-SS	94	347	62	92	25	2	11	55	16	.265
2010 Arizona	N.L.		OF-2B-3B	36	66	8	13	4	0	2	9	0	.197
2011 Arizona	N.L.		3B-2B-OF-SS	143	482	86	120	25	2	19	65	18	.249
Major League Totals			6 Yrs.	307	880	138	220	46	4	29	100	25	.250
Division Series													
2011 Arizona	N.L.		3B	5	20	2	7	1	0	2	6	0	.350

a Filed for free agency, October 10, 2007. Signed with Texas Rangers organization, November 21, 2007.
b Filed for free agency, September 29, 2008. Signed with Arizona Diamondbacks organization, November 6, 2008.

ROBINSON, TRAYVON ANDREW DWAYNE

Born, Los Angeles, California, September 1, 1987.
Bats Both. Throws Right. Height, 5 feet, 10 inches. Weight, 200 pounds.

Year	Club	Lea	Pos	G	AB	R	H	2B	3B	HR	RBI	SB	Avg
2005 Dodgers	Gulf Coast		OF-2B	40	115	19	34	7	2	3	15	6	.296
2005 Ogden	Pioneer		OF	8	23	2	5	0	0	1	2	0	.217
2006 Dodgers	Gulf Coast		OF-3B	39	134	24	34	7	2	2	20	5	.254
2006 Vero Beach	Fla.St.		OF	3	5	1	2	0	0	0	1	1	.400
2007 Great Lakes	Midwest		OF	110	396	50	100	9	4	2	31	22	.253
2008 Inland Empire	Calif.		OF	112	439	67	121	20	8	4	42	22	.276

149

Year	Club	Lea	Pos	G	AB	R	H	2B	3B	HR	RBI	SB	Avg
2009 Inland Empire	Calif.	OF	117	470	82	144	28	9	15	54	43	.306
2009 Chattanooga	Southern	OF	19	57	8	14	1	2	2	10	4	.246
2010 Chattanooga	Southern	OF	120	434	80	130	23	5	9	57	38	.300
2011 Albuquerque	P.C.	OF	100	368	70	108	9	6	26	71	8	.293
2011 Tacoma	P.C.	OF	3	9	1	1	0	0	0	0	1	.111
2011 Seattle a-b	A.L.	OF	44	143	12	30	12	0	2	14	1	.210

a Traded to Boston Red Sox for catcher Tim Federowicz, pitcher Stephen Fife and pitcher Juan Rodriguez, July 31, 2011.

b Traded to Seattle Mariners with outfielder Chih-Hsien Chiang for pitcher Erik Bedard and pitcher Josh Fields, July 31, 2011.

RODRIGUEZ, ALEXANDER EMMANUEL (ALEX)
Born, New York, New York, July 27, 1975.
Bats Right. Throws Right. Height, 6 feet, 3 inches. Weight, 225 pounds.

Year	Club	Lea	Pos	G	AB	R	H	2B	3B	HR	RBI	SB	Avg
1994 Appleton	Midwest	SS	65	248	49	79	17	6	14	55	16	.319
1994 Jacksonville	Southern	SS	17	59	7	17	4	1	1	8	2	.288
1994 Seattle	A.L.	SS	17	54	4	11	0	0	0	2	3	.204
1994 Calgary	P.C.	SS	32	119	22	37	7	4	6	21	2	.311
1995 Tacoma	P.C.	SS	54	214	37	77	12	3	15	45	2	.360
1995 Seattle	A.L.	SS	48	142	15	33	6	2	5	19	4	.232
1996 Tacoma a	P.C.	SS	2	5	0	1	0	0	0	0	0	.200
1996 Seattle	A.L.	SS	146	601	*141	215	*54	1	36	123	15	*.358
1997 Seattle b	A.L.	SS	141	587	100	176	40	3	23	84	29	.300
1998 Seattle	A.L.	SS	161	*686	123	*213	35	5	42	124	46	.310
1999 Seattle c	A.L.	SS	129	502	110	143	25	0	42	111	21	.285
2000 Seattle d-e	A.L.	SS	148	554	134	175	34	2	41	132	15	.316
2001 Texas	A.L.	SS	*162	632	*133	201	34	1	*52	135	18	.318
2002 Texas	A.L.	SS	*162	624	125	187	27	2	*57	*142	9	.300
2003 Texas	A.L.	SS	161	607	*124	181	30	6	*47	118	17	.298
2004 New York f-g	A.L.	3B-SS	155	601	112	172	24	2	36	106	28	.286
2005 New York h	A.L.	3B-SS	*162	605	*124	194	29	1	*48	130	21	.321
2006 New York	A.L.	3B	154	572	113	166	26	1	35	121	15	.290
2007 New York i-j	A.L.	3B	158	583	*143	183	31	0	*54	*156	24	.314
2008 New York k	A.L.	3B	138	510	104	154	33	0	35	103	18	.302
2009 New York l	A.L.	3B	124	444	78	127	17	1	30	100	14	.286
2010 New York m	A.L.	3B	137	522	74	141	29	2	30	125	4	.270
2011 Tampa	Fla.St.	DH	2	6	2	2	1	0	1	2	0	.333
2011 Scranton-WB	Int.	3B	2	5	0	2	0	0	0	1	0	.400
2011 New York n	A.L.	3B	99	373	67	103	21	0	16	62	4	.276
Major League Totals		18 Yrs.	2402	9199	1824	2775	495	29	629	1893	305	.302
Division Series												
1995 Seattle	A.L.	SS	1	1	1	0	0	0	0	0	0	.000
1997 Seattle	A.L.	SS	4	16	1	5	1	0	1	1	0	.313
2000 Seattle	A.L.	SS	3	13	0	4	0	0	0	2	0	.308
2004 New York	A.L.	3B	4	19	3	8	3	0	1	3	2	.421
2005 New York	A.L.	3B	5	15	2	2	1	0	0	0	1	.133
2006 New York	A.L.	3B	4	14	0	1	0	0	0	0	0	.071
2007 New York	A.L.	3B	4	15	2	4	0	0	1	1	0	.267
2009 New York	A.L.	3B	3	11	4	5	0	0	2	6	0	.455
2010 New York	A.L.	3B	3	11	1	3	0	0	0	1	1	.273
2011 New York	A.L.	3B	5	18	1	2	0	0	0	3	0	.111
Division Series Totals			36	133	15	34	5	0	5	17	4	.256
Championship Series												
1995 Seattle	A.L.	PH	1	1	0	0	0	0	0	0	0	.000
2000 Seattle	A.L.	SS	6	22	4	9	2	0	2	5	1	.409
2004 New York	A.L.	3B	7	31	8	8	2	0	2	5	0	.258
2009 New York	A.L.	3B	6	21	6	9	2	0	3	6	1	.429
2010 New York	A.L.	3B	6	21	4	4	2	0	0	2	1	.190
Championship Series Totals			26	96	22	30	8	0	7	18	3	.313
World Series Record												
2009 New York	A.L.	3B	6	20	5	5	3	0	1	6	1	.250

a On disabled list from April 22 to May 7, 1996.

b On disabled list from June 12 to June 27, 1997.

c On disabled list from April 7 to May 14, 1999.

d On disabled list from July 8 to July 23, 2000.

e Filed for free agency, October 30, 2000. Signed with Texas Rangers, December 11, 2000.

f Traded to New York Yankees for infielder Alfonso Soriano and player to be named later, February 16, 2004.

g Texas Rangers received infielder Joaquin Arias to complete trade, March 23, 2004.

RODRIGUEZ (TORRES), IVAN

Born, Manati, Puerto Rico, November 27, 1971.
Bats Right. Throws Right. Height, 5 feet, 9 inches. Weight, 195 pounds.

Year	Club	Lea	Pos	G	AB	R	H	2B	3B	HR	RBI	SB	Avg
1989 Gastonia	So. Atl.		C	112	386	38	92	22	1	7	42	2	.238
1990 Charlotte	Fla. St.		C	109	408	48	117	17	7	2	55	1	.287
1991 Tulsa	Texas		C	50	175	16	48	7	2	3	28	1	.274
1991 Texas	A.L.		C	88	280	24	74	16	0	3	27	0	.264
1992 Texas a	A.L.		C	123	420	39	109	16	1	8	37	0	.260
1993 Texas	A.L.		C	137	473	56	129	28	4	10	66	8	.273
1994 Texas	A.L.		C	99	363	56	108	19	1	16	57	6	.298
1995 Texas	A.L.		C	130	492	56	149	32	2	12	67	0	.303
1996 Texas	A.L.		C	153	639	116	192	47	3	19	86	5	.300
1997 Texas	A.L.		C	150	597	98	187	34	4	20	77	7	.313
1998 Texas	A.L.		C	145	579	88	186	40	4	21	91	9	.321
1999 Texas b	A.L.		C	144	600	116	199	29	1	35	113	25	.332
2000 Texas c	A.L.		C	91	363	66	126	27	4	27	83	5	.347
2001 Texas	A.L.		C	111	442	70	136	24	2	25	65	10	.308
2002 Charlotte	Fla.St.		C	3	9	1	3	0	0	0	0	0	.333
2002 Texas e-f	A.L.		C	108	408	67	128	32	2	19	60	5	.314
2003 Florida g	N.L.		C	144	511	90	152	36	3	16	85	10	.297
2004 Detroit	A.L.		C	135	527	72	176	32	2	19	86	7	.334
2005 Detroit	A.L.		C	129	504	71	139	33	5	14	50	7	.276
2006 Detroit	A.L.		C-1B-2B	136	547	74	164	28	4	13	69	8	.300
2007 Detroit	A.L.		C	129	502	50	141	31	3	11	63	2	.281
2008 Detroit-New York h-i	A.L.		C	115	398	44	110	20	3	7	35	10	.276
2009 Houston	N.L.		C	93	327	41	82	15	2	8	34	0	.251
2009 Texas j-k	A.L.		C	28	98	14	24	8	0	2	13	1	.245
2010 Potomac	Carolina		C	1	3	0	0	0	0	0	0	0	.000
2010 Washington l	N.L.		C	111	398	32	106	18	1	4	49	2	.266
2011 Potomac	Carolina		C	1	3	1	1	0	0	1	1	0	.333
2011 Harrisburg	Eastern		C	3	9	2	2	1	0	0	0	0	.222
2011 Washington m-n	N.L.		C-1B	44	124	14	27	7	0	2	19	0	.218
Major League Totals			21 Yrs.	2543	9592	1354	2844	572	51	311	1332	127	.296
Division Series													
1996 Texas	A.L.		C	4	16	1	6	1	0	0	2	0	.375
1998 Texas	A.L.		C	3	10	0	1	0	0	0	1	0	.100
1999 Texas	A.L.		C	3	12	0	3	1	0	0	0	1	.250
2003 Florida	N.L.		C	4	17	3	6	1	0	1	6	0	.353
2006 Detroit	A.L.		C	4	13	3	3	1	0	0	3	0	.231
Division Series Totals				18	68	7	19	4	0	1	12	1	.279
Championship Series													
2003 Florida	N.L.		C	7	28	5	9	2	0	2	10	0	.321
2006 Detroit	A.L.		C	4	16	2	2	0	0	1	1	0	.125
Championship Series Totals				11	44	7	11	2	0	3	11	0	.250
World Series Record													
2003 Florida	N.L.		C	6	22	2	6	2	0	0	1	0	.273
2006 Detroit	A.L.		C	5	19	1	3	1	0	0	1	0	.158
World Series Totals				11	41	3	9	3	0	0	2	0	.220

l On disabled list from May 23 to June 8, 2010.
m On disabled list from July 7 to September 3, 2011.
n Filed for free agency, October 30, 2011.

RODRIGUEZ, SEAN JOHN

Born, Miami, Florida, April 26, 1985.
Bats Right. Throws Right. Height, 6 feet, 1 inch. Weight, 215 pounds.

Year	Club	Lea	Pos	G	AB	R	H	2B	3B	HR	RBI	SB	Avg
2003	Angels	Arizona	SS-3B-2B-OF	54	216	30	58	8	5	2	25	11	.269
2004	Cedar Rapids	Midwest	2B-OF-3B-SS	57	196	35	49	8	4	4	17	14	.250
2004	Provo	Pioneer	SS-OF	64	225	64	76	14	4	10	55	9	.338
2005	Cedar Rapids	Midwest	SS-3B-OF-2B	124	448	86	112	29	3	14	45	27	.250
2006	Rancho Cucamonga	Calif.	SS-OF	116	455	78	137	29	5	24	77	15	.301
2006	Salt Lake	P.C.	SS	1	2	0	0	0	0	0	0	0	.000
2006	Arkansas	Texas	SS	18	65	16	23	5	0	5	9	0	.354
2007	Arkansas	Texas	SS-OF	136	508	84	129	31	2	17	73	15	.254
2008	Salt Lake	P.C.	2B-SS-OF	66	248	68	76	19	1	21	52	4	.306
2008	Los Angeles	A.L.	2B-SS-3B	59	167	18	34	8	1	3	10	3	.204
2009	Los Angeles	A.L.	OF-2B	12	25	4	5	0	0	2	4	0	.200
2009	Salt Lake	P.C.	2B-SS-OF	103	365	81	109	17	6	29	93	9	.299
2009	Durham a	Int.	2B-3B	5	20	6	4	2	0	1	5	0	.200
2010	Tampa Bay	A.L.	2B-OF-3B-SS	118	343	53	86	19	2	9	40	13	.251
2011	Tampa Bay	A.L.	SS-2B-3B-1B	131	373	45	83	20	3	8	36	11	.223
Major League Totals			4 Yrs.	320	908	120	208	47	6	22	90	27	.229
Division Series													
2010	Tampa Bay	A.L.	2B	4	10	2	2	0	0	0	0	0	.200
2011	Tampa Bay	A.L.	SS-2B	4	12	3	2	1	0	0	1	0	.167
Division Series Totals				8	22	5	4	1	0	0	1	0	.182

a Sent to Tampa Bay Rays as player to be named later for pitcher Scott Kazmir, September 1, 2009.

ROLEN, SCOTT BRUCE

Born, Evansville, Indiana, April 4, 1975.
Bats Right. Throws Right. Height, 6 feet, 4 inches. Weight, 240 pounds.

Year	Club	Lea	Pos	G	AB	R	H	2B	3B	HR	RBI	SB	Avg
1993	Martinsville	Appal.	3B	25	80	8	25	5	0	0	12	3	.313
1994	Spartanburg	So.Atl.	3B	138	513	83	151	34	5	14	72	6	.294
1995	Clearwater	Fla.St.	3B	66	238	45	69	13	2	10	39	4	.290
1995	Reading	Eastern	3B	20	76	16	22	3	0	3	15	1	.289
1996	Reading	Eastern	3B	61	230	44	83	22	2	9	42	8	.361
1996	Scranton-WB	Int.	3B	45	168	23	46	17	0	2	19	4	.274
1996	Philadelphia	N.L.	3B	37	130	10	33	7	0	4	18	0	.254
1997	Philadelphia a	N.L.	3B	156	561	93	159	35	3	21	92	16	.283
1998	Philadelphia	N.L.	3B	160	601	120	174	45	4	31	110	14	.290
1999	Philadelphia	N.L.	3B	112	421	74	113	28	1	26	77	12	.268
2000	Philadelphia b	N.L.	3B	128	483	88	144	32	6	26	89	8	.298
2001	Philadelphia	N.L.	3B	151	554	96	160	39	1	25	107	16	.289
2002	Philadelphia-St. Louis c	N.L.	3B	155	580	89	154	29	8	31	110	8	.266
2003	St. Louis	N.L.	3B	154	559	98	160	49	1	28	104	13	.286
2004	St. Louis	N.L.	3B	142	500	109	157	32	4	34	124	4	.314
2005	St. Louis d	N.L.	3B	56	196	28	46	12	1	5	28	1	.235
2006	St. Louis	N.L.	3B	142	521	94	154	48	1	22	95	7	.296
2007	St. Louis e-f	N.L.	3B	112	392	55	104	24	2	8	58	5	.265
2008	Dunedin	Fla.St.	3B	3	9	0	0	0	0	0	0	0	.000
2008	Toronto g	A.L.	3B	115	408	58	107	30	3	11	50	5	.262
2009	Louisville	Int.	3B	2	6	1	2	0	0	0	1	0	.333
2009	Toronto	A.L.	3B	88	338	52	108	29	0	8	43	4	.320
2009	Cincinnati h-i	N.L.	3B	40	137	24	37	7	1	3	24	1	.270
2010	Cincinnati	N.L.	3B	133	471	66	134	34	3	20	83	1	.285
2011	Cincinnati j	N.L.	3B	65	252	31	61	20	2	5	36	1	.242
Major League Totals			16 Yrs.	1946	7104	1185	2005	500	41	308	1248	116	.282
Division Series													
2002	St. Louis	N.L.	3B	2	7	1	3	0	0	1	2	0	.429
2004	St. Louis	N.L.	3B	4	12	1	0	0	0	0	0	0	.000
2006	St. Louis	N.L.	3B	3	11	0	1	1	0	0	0	0	.091
2010	Cincinnati	N.L.	3B	3	11	0	1	0	0	0	0	0	.091
Division Series Totals				12	41	2	5	1	0	1	2	0	.122

Year	Club	Lea	Pos	G	AB	R	H	2B	3B	HR	RBI	SB	Avg
	Championship Series												
2004 St. Louis.............	N.L.		3B	7	29	6	9	2	0	3	6	0	.310
2006 St. Louis.............	N.L.		3B	7	21	4	5	1	0	0	0	0	.238
Championship Series Totals......				14	50	10	14	3	0	3	6	0	.280
	World Series Record												
2004 St. Louis.............	N.L.		3B	4	15	0	0	0	0	0	1	0	.000
2006 St. Louis.............	N.L.		3B	5	19	5	8	3	0	1	2	0	.421
World Series Totals............				9	34	5	8	3	0	1	3	0	.235

a Selected Rookie of the Year in National League for 1997.
b On disabled list from May 24 to June 8, 2000.
c Traded to St. Louis Cardinals with pitcher Doug Nickle for infielder Placido Polanco, pitcher Bud Smith and pitcher Mike Timlin, July 29, 2002.
d On disabled list from May 11 to June 18 and July 22 to October 31, 2005.
e On disabled list from August 29 to November 2, 2007.
f Traded to Toronto Blue Jays for infielder Troy Glaus, January 14, 2008.
g On disabled list from March 21 to April 25 and from August 11 to August 26, 2008.
h Traded to Cincinnati Reds for infielder Edwin Encarnacion, pitcher Josh Roenicke and pitcher Zach Stewart, July 31, 2009.
i On disabled list from August 8 to August 23, 2009.
j On disabled list from April 21 to May 13 and July 22 to October 3, 2011.

ROLLINS, JAMES CALVIN (JIMMY)

Born, Oakland, California, November 27, 1978.
Bats Both. Throws Right. Height, 5 feet, 8 inches. Weight, 170 pounds.

Year	Club	Lea	Pos	G	AB	R	H	2B	3B	HR	RBI	SB	Avg
1996 Martinsville.........	Appal.	SS	49	172	22	41	3	1	1	16	11	.238
1997 Piedmont..........	So.Atl.	SS	139	560	94	151	22	8	6	59	46	.270
1998 Clearwater.........	Fla.St.	SS	119	495	72	121	18	9	6	35	23	.244
1999 Reading..........	Eastern	SS	133	532	81	145	21	8	11	56	24	.273
1999 Scranton-WB..........	Int.	SS	4	13	0	1	1	0	0	0	1	.077
2000 Scranton-WB..........	Int.	SS	133	470	67	129	28	11	12	69	24	.274
2000 Philadelphia..........	N.L.	SS	14	53	5	17	1	1	0	5	3	.321
2001 Philadelphia..........	N.L.	SS	158	*656	97	180	29	*12	14	54	*46	.274
2002 Philadelphia..........	N.L.	SS-2B	154	*637	82	156	33	*10	11	60	31	.245
2003 Philadelphia..........	N.L.	SS	156	628	85	165	42	6	8	62	20	.263
2004 Philadelphia..........	N.L.	SS	154	657	119	190	43	*12	14	73	30	.289
2005 Philadelphia..........	N.L.	SS	158	677	115	196	38	11	12	54	41	.290
2006 Philadelphia..........	N.L.	SS	158	689	127	191	45	9	25	83	36	.277
2007 Philadelphia a........	N.L.	SS	*162	*716	*139	212	38	*20	30	94	41	.296
2008 Clearwater........	Fla.St.	SS	1	3	2	0	0	0	0	0	0	.000
2008 Philadelphia b........	N.L.	SS	137	556	76	154	38	9	11	59	47	.277
2009 Philadelphia..........	N.L.	SS	155	*672	100	168	43	5	21	77	31	.250
2010 Clearwater........	Fla.St.	SS	5	14	2	2	0	0	0	2	0	.143
2010 Philadelphia c........	N.L.	SS	88	350	48	85	16	3	8	41	17	.243
2011 Philadelphia d-e.......	N.L.	SS	142	567	87	152	22	2	16	63	30	.268
Major League Totals............	12 Yrs.	1636	6858	1080	1866	388	100	170	725	373	.272		
	Division Series												
2007 Philadelphia..........	N.L.	SS	3	11	1	2	0	1	1	4	1	.182
2008 Philadelphia..........	N.L.	SS	4	16	2	6	2	0	1	1	1	.375
2009 Philadelphia..........	N.L.	SS	4	19	1	5	1	0	0	0	0	.263
2010 Philadelphia..........	N.L.	SS	3	11	1	1	0	0	0	0	0	.091
2011 Philadelphia..........	N.L.	SS	5	20	6	9	4	0	0	0	2	.450
Division Series Totals...........				19	77	11	23	7	1	2	5	4	.299
	Championship Series												
2008 Philadelphia..........	N.L.	SS	5	21	4	3	0	0	1	1	2	.143
2009 Philadelphia..........	N.L.	SS	5	22	5	5	2	0	0	3	0	.227
2010 Philadelphia..........	N.L.	SS	6	23	0	6	1	0	0	4	2	.261
Championship Series Totals......				16	66	9	14	3	0	1	8	4	.212
	World Series Record												
2008 Philadelphia..........	N.L.	SS	5	22	4	5	2	0	0	0	0	.227
2009 Philadelphia..........	N.L.	SS	6	23	3	5	0	0	0	2	3	.217
World Series Totals............				11	45	7	10	2	0	0	2	3	.222

a Selected Most Valuable Player in National League for 2007.
b On disabled list from April 20 to May 9, 2008.
c On disabled list from April 13 to May 17 and May 22 to June 22, 2010.
d On disabled list from August 22 to September 8, 2011.
e Filed for free agency, October 30, 2011, re-signed with Philadelphia Phillies, December 19, 2011.

ROSS, CODY JOSEPH

Born, Portales, New Mexico, December 23, 1980.
Bats Right. Throws Left. Height, 5 feet, 9 inches. Weight, 205 pounds.

Year	Club	Lea	Pos	G	AB	R	H	2B	3B	HR	RBI	SB	Avg
1999 Tigers	Gulf Coast		OF	42	142	19	31	8	3	4	18	3	.218
2000 West Michigan	Midwest		OF	122	434	71	116	17	9	7	68	11	.267
2001 Lakeland	Fla.St.		OF	127	482	84	133	34	5	15	80	28	.276
2002 Erie	Eastern		OF	105	400	73	112	28	3	19	72	16	.280
2003 Toledo	Int.		OF	124	470	74	135	35	6	20	61	15	.287
2003 Detroit	A.L.		OF	6	19	1	4	1	0	1	5	0	.211
2004 Las Vegas a	P.C.		OF	60	238	44	65	17	2	14	49	2	.273
2005 Los Angeles	N.L.		OF	14	25	1	4	1	0	0	1	0	.160
2005 Las Vegas	P.C.		OF	115	393	79	105	21	4	22	63	4	.267
2006 L.A.-Cin.-Florida b-c-d-e	N.L.		OF	101	269	34	61	12	2	13	46	1	.227
2007 Jupiter	Fla.St.		OF	7	23	2	6	1	0	2	3	0	.261
2007 Florida f	N.L.		OF	66	173	35	58	19	0	12	39	2	.335
2008 Florida	N.L.		OF	145	461	59	120	29	5	22	73	6	.260
2009 Florida	N.L.		OF-P	151	559	73	151	37	1	24	90	5	.270
2010 Florida-San Francisco g	N.L.		OF	153	525	71	141	28	3	14	65	9	.269
2011 Fresno	P.C.		OF	2	6	1	3	1	0	0	2	0	.500
2011 San Francisco h-i	N.L.		OF	121	405	54	97	25	0	14	52	5	.240
Major League Totals			8 Yrs.	757	2436	328	636	152	11	100	371	28	.261
Division Series													
2010 San Francisco	N.L.		OF	4	14	2	4	1	0	1	3	0	.286
Championship Series													
2010 San Francisco	N.L.		OF	6	20	4	7	3	0	3	5	0	.350
World Series Record													
2010 San Francisco	N.L.		OF	5	17	5	4	1	0	1	2	0	.235

a Traded to Los Angeles Dodgers for pitcher Steve Colyer and cash, April 1, 2004.
b Traded to Cincinnati Reds for player to be named later, April 24, 2006.
c Los Angeles Dodgers received pitcher Ben Kozlowski to complete trade, June 1, 2006.
d On disabled list from April 29 to May 23, 2006.
e Sold to Florida Marlins, May 27, 2006.
f On disabled list from May 6 to July 19, 2007.
g Claimed on waivers by San Francisco Giants, August 22, 2010.
h On disabled list from March 22 to April 20, 2011.
i Filed for free agency, October 30, 2011.

ROSS, DAVID WADE

Born, Bainbridge, Georgia, March 19, 1977.
Bats Right. Throws Right. Height, 6 feet, 2 inches. Weight, 240 pounds.

Year	Club	Lea	Pos	G	AB	R	H	2B	3B	HR	RBI	SB	Avg
1998 Yakima	Northwest		C	59	191	31	59	14	1	6	25	2	.309
1999 Vero Beach	Fla.St.		C-1B-OF	114	375	47	85	19	1	7	39	5	.227
2000 San Bernardino	Calif.		C	51	191	27	49	11	1	7	21	3	.257
2000 San Antonio	Texas		C	24	67	11	14	2	1	3	12	1	.209
2001 Jacksonville	Southern		C	74	246	35	65	13	1	11	45	1	.264
2002 Las Vegas	P.C.		C	92	293	48	87	16	2	15	68	1	.297
2002 Los Angeles	N.L.		C	8	10	2	2	1	0	1	2	0	.200
2003 Las Vegas	P.C.		C	24	86	12	19	4	0	5	16	0	.221
2003 Los Angeles	N.L.		C	40	124	19	32	7	0	10	18	0	.258
2004 Los Angeles	N.L.		C	70	165	13	28	3	1	5	15	0	.170
2005 Indianapolis	Int.		C	6	19	1	4	1	0	0	1	0	.211
2005 Portland	P.C.		C	6	21	3	3	1	0	0	1	0	.143
2005 Pittsburgh-San Diego a-b	N.L.		C	51	125	11	30	8	1	3	15	0	.240
2006 Chattanooga	Southern		C	2	6	0	2	0	0	0	2	0	.333
2006 Cincinnati c-d	N.L.		C	90	247	37	63	15	1	21	52	0	.255
2007 Louisville	Int.		C	3	9	0	2	1	0	0	0	0	.222
2007 Cincinnati e	N.L.		C	112	311	32	63	10	0	17	39	0	.203
2008 Sarasota	Fla.St.		C	4	11	2	2	0	0	0	1	0	.182
2008 Louisville	Int.		C	9	30	4	5	1	1	1	2	0	.167
2008 Cincinnati	N.L.		C	52	134	17	31	9	0	3	13	0	.231
2008 Pawtucket	Int.		C	6	28	4	7	1	0	1	3	0	.250
2008 Boston f-g-h	A.L.		C	8	8	1	1	0	0	0	0	0	.125
2009 Rome	So.Atl.		C	2	6	1	3	0	0	1	4	0	.500
2009 Atlanta i	N.L.		C	54	128	18	35	9	0	7	20	0	.273
2010 Atlanta	N.L.		C	59	121	15	35	13	2	2	28	0	.289
2011 Atlanta	N.L.		C	52	152	14	40	7	0	6	23	0	.263
Major League Totals			10 Yrs.	596	1525	179	360	82	5	75	225	0	.236

154

Year	Club	Lea	Pos	G	AB	R	H	2B	3B	HR	RBI	SB	Avg
	Division Series												
2004 Los Angeles	N.L.		C	2	3	0	0	0	0	0	0	0	.000
2008 Boston	A.L.		C	1	0	0	0	0	0	0	0	0	.000
2010 Atlanta	N.L.		C	2	0	0	0	0	0	0	0	0	.000
Division Series Totals				5	3	0	0	0	0	0	0	0	.000

a Sold to Pittsburgh Pirates, March 30, 2005.
b Traded to San Diego Padres for infielder J.J. Furmaniak, July 28, 2005.
c Traded to Cincinnati Reds for pitcher Bobby Basham, March 21, 2006.
d On disabled list from July 8 to July 26, 2006.
e On disabled list from August 13 to August 28, 2007.
f On disabled list from March 30 to April 23, 2008.
g Released by Cincinnati Reds, August 19, 2008. Signed with Boston Red Sox organization, August 22, 2008.
h Filed for free agency, October 30, 2008. Signed with Atlanta Braves, December 5, 2008.
i On disabled list from April 1 to April 16, 2009.

ROWAND, AARON RYAN

Born, Portland, Oregon, August 29, 1977.
Bats Right. Throws Right. Height, 6 feet. Weight, 220 pounds.

Year	Club	Lea	Pos	G	AB	R	H	2B	3B	HR	RBI	SB	Avg
1998 Hickory a	So.Atl.	OF	60	218	42	75	13	3	5	32	7	.344
1999 Winston-Salem	Carolina	OF	133	512	96	143	37	3	24	88	15	.279
2000 Birmingham	Southern	OF	139	532	80	137	26	5	20	98	22	.258
2001 Charlotte	Int.	OF	82	329	54	97	28	0	16	48	8	.295
2001 Chicago	A.L.	OF	63	123	21	36	5	0	4	20	5	.293
2002 Chicago	A.L.	OF	126	302	41	78	16	2	7	29	0	.258
2003 Charlotte	Int.	OF	32	120	15	29	9	0	3	13	0	.242
2003 Chicago	A.L.	OF	93	157	22	45	8	0	6	24	0	.287
2004 Chicago	A.L.	OF	140	487	94	151	38	2	24	69	17	.310
2005 Chicago b..........	A.L.	OF	157	578	77	156	30	5	13	69	16	.270
2006 Philadelphia c..........	N.L.	OF	109	405	59	106	24	3	12	47	10	.262
2007 Philadelphia d	N.L.	OF	161	612	105	189	45	0	27	89	6	.309
2008 San Francisco	N.L.	OF	152	549	57	149	37	0	13	70	2	.271
2009 San Francisco	N.L.	OF	144	499	61	130	30	2	15	64	4	.261
2010 San Francisco e	N.L.	OF	105	331	42	76	12	2	11	34	5	.230
2011 San Francisco f	N.L.	OF	108	331	34	77	22	2	4	21	2	.233
Major League Totals	11 Yrs.	1358	4374	613	1193	267	18	136	536	67	.273
	Division Series											
2005 Chicago	A.L.	OF	3	10	3	4	2	0	0	2	1	.400
2007 Philadelphia	N.L.	OF	3	12	1	1	0	0	1	1	0	.083
2010 San Francisco	N.L.	PH	2	2	0	1	0	0	0	0	0	.500
Division Series Totals				8	24	4	6	2	0	1	3	1	.250
	Championship Series											
2005 Chicago	A.L.	OF	5	18	3	3	3	0	0	1	0	.167
2010 San Francisco	N.L.	OF	3	5	1	1	1	0	0	0	0	.200
Championship Series Totals				8	23	4	4	4	0	0	1	0	.174
	World Series Record											
2005 Chicago	A.L.	OF	4	17	2	5	1	0	0	0	0	.294
2010 San Francisco	N.L.	OF	2	4	1	1	0	1	0	2	0	.250
World Series Totals............				6	21	3	6	1	1	0	2	0	.286

a Drafted by Chicago White Sox with choice received for Tampa Bay Devil Rays signing of outfielder Dave Martinez, June 2, 1998.
b Traded to Philadelphia Phillies with pitcher Dan Haigwood and player to be named later for infielder Jim Thome, November 25, 2005. Philadelphia Phillies received pitcher Giovany Gonzalez to complete trade, December 8, 2005.
c On disabled list from May 12 to May 27 and August 22 to October 4, 2006.
d Filed for free agency, October 29, 2007. Signed with San Francisco Giants, December 12, 2007.
e On disabled list from April 17 to May 2, 2010.
f Released by San Francisco Giants, September 8, 2011. Signed with Florida Marlins organization, December 12, 2011.

RUIZ, CARLOS JOAQUIN

Born, David, Panama, January 22, 1979.
Bats Right. Throws Right. Height, 5 feet, 10 inches. Weight, 200 pounds.

Year	Club	Lea	Pos	G	AB	R	H	2B	3B	HR	RBI	SB	Avg
2000 Phillies.........	Gulf Coast	C	38	130	11	36	7	1	1	22	3	.277
2001 Lakewood..........	So.Atl.	C-OF	73	249	21	65	14	3	4	32	5	.261
2002 Clearwater	Fla.St.	C	92	342	35	73	18	3	5	32	3	.213

Year	Club	Lea	Pos	G	AB	R	H	2B	3B	HR	RBI	SB	Avg
2003 Reading . . . . Eastern			C-OF	52	169	22	45	6	0	2	16	1	.266
2003 Clearwater . . . . Fla.St.			C	15	54	5	17	0	0	2	9	2	.315
2004 Reading . . . . Eastern			C	101	349	45	99	15	2	17	50	8	.284
2005 Scranton-WB . . . . Int.			C-1B	100	347	50	104	25	9	4	40	4	.300
2006 Scranton-WB . . . . Int.			C	100	368	56	113	25	0	16	69	4	.307
2006 Philadelphia . . . . N.L.			C	27	69	5	18	1	1	3	10	0	.261
2007 Philadelphia . . . . N.L.			C	115	374	42	97	29	2	6	54	6	.259
2008 Philadelphia . . . . N.L.			C-3B	117	320	47	70	14	0	4	31	1	.219
2009 Lehigh Valley . . . . Int.			C	4	13	1	3	1	0	0	2	0	.231
2009 Philadelphia a . . . . N.L.			C	107	322	32	82	26	1	9	43	3	.255
2010 Lakewood . . . . So.Atl.			C	2	8	1	4	2	0	0	1	0	.500
2010 Lehigh Valley . . . . Int.			C	1	2	0	0	0	0	0	0	0	.000
2010 Philadelphia b . . . . N.L.			C	121	371	43	112	28	1	8	53	0	.302
2011 Clearwater . . . . Fla.St.			C	1	3	1	1	0	0	0	0	0	.333
2011 Philadelphia c . . . . N.L.			C-3B	132	410	49	116	23	0	6	40	1	.283
Major League Totals			6 Yrs.	619	1866	218	495	121	5	36	231	11	.265
Division Series													
2007 Philadelphia . . . . N.L.			C	3	9	1	3	1	0	0	0	1	.333
2008 Philadelphia . . . . N.L.			C	4	14	1	1	0	0	0	0	0	.071
2009 Philadelphia . . . . N.L.			C	4	13	0	4	0	0	0	3	0	.308
2010 Philadelphia . . . . N.L.			C	3	8	1	2	1	0	0	1	0	.250
2011 Philadelphia . . . . N.L.			C	5	17	1	1	0	0	0	0	0	.059
Division Series Totals				19	61	4	11	2	0	0	4	1	.180
Championship Series													
2008 Philadelphia . . . . N.L.			C	5	16	3	5	1	0	0	1	0	.313
2009 Philadelphia . . . . N.L.			C	5	13	4	5	1	0	1	4	1	.385
2010 Philadelphia . . . . N.L.			C	6	18	2	3	0	0	1	1	0	.167
Championship Series Totals				16	47	9	13	2	0	2	6	1	.277
World Series Record													
2008 Philadelphia . . . . N.L.			C	5	16	2	6	2	0	1	3	1	.375
2009 Philadelphia . . . . N.L.			C	6	18	4	6	2	1	1	2	0	.333
World Series Totals				11	34	6	12	4	1	2	5	1	.353

a On disabled list from April 11 to May 2, 2009.

b On disabled list from June 19 to July 10, 2010.

c On disabled list from April 28 to May 13, 2011.

RYAN, BRENDAN WOOD

Born, Los Angeles, California, March 26, 1982.
Bats Right. Throws Right. Height, 6 feet, 2 inches. Weight, 195 pounds.

Year	Club	Lea	Pos	G	AB	R	H	2B	3B	HR	RBI	SB	Avg
2003 New Jersey . . N.Y.-Penn.			SS-3B	53	193	20	60	14	4	0	13	11	.311
2004 Peoria. . . . . Midwest			SS	105	426	72	137	21	4	2	59	30	.322
2005 Palm Beach . . . . . Fla.St.			SS	49	188	29	57	17	0	1	16	8	.303
2005 Springfield . . . . . . Texas			SS	43	154	28	42	8	1	2	9	6	.273
2006 Palm Beach . . . . . Fla.St.			SS	3	14	2	6	1	0	0	1	1	.429
2006 State College . . N.Y.-Penn.			SS	8	34	5	8	0	0	0	3	1	.235
2006 Memphis . . . . P.C.			SS	7	26	4	4	0	0	1	6	1	.154
2006 Springfield . . . . . . Texas			SS	10	43	6	13	1	0	0	3	1	.302
2007 Memphis . . . . P.C.			SS	81	323	55	88	9	5	1	15	17	.272
2007 St. Louis. . . . . N.L.			SS-3B-2B	67	180	30	52	9	0	4	12	7	.289
2008 Palm Beach . . . . . Fla.St.			SS	3	12	1	3	1	0	0	0	1	.250
2008 Springfield . . . . . . Texas			3B-2B-SS	4	19	5	7	3	0	1	3	1	.368
2008 Memphis . . . . P.C.			OF-2B-SS	21	80	13	19	5	0	3	10	1	.237
2008 St. Louis a . . . . N.L.			SS-2B-3B-OF	80	197	30	48	9	0	0	10	7	.244
2009 Memphis . . . . P.C.			SS	3	11	0	0	0	0	0	0	0	.000
2009 St. Louis b . . . . N.L.			SS-2B	129	390	55	114	19	7	3	37	14	.292
2010 St. Louis c . . . . N.L.			SS	139	439	50	98	19	3	2	36	11	.223
2011 Seattle d . . . . A.L.			SS	123	436	51	108	19	3	3	39	13	.248
Major League Totals			5 Yrs.	538	1642	216	420	75	13	12	134	52	.256
Division Series													
2009 St. Louis. . . . . N.L.			SS	3	12	0	1	1	0	0	0	0	.083

a On disabled list from March 21 to April 23, 2008.

b On disabled list from April 30 to May 15, 2009.

c Traded to Seattle Mariners for pitcher Maikel Cleto, December 12, 2010.

d On disabled list from August 4 to August 19, 2011.

SALTALAMACCHIA, JARROD SCOTT

Born, West Palm Beach, Florida, May 2, 1985.
Bats Both. Throws Right. Height, 6 feet, 4 inches. Weight, 235 pounds.

Year	Club	Lea	Pos	G	AB	R	H	2B	3B	HR	RBI	SB	Avg
2003	Braves	Gulf Coast	C-3B	46	134	23	32	11	2	2	14	0	.239
2004	Rome	So.Atl.	C	91	323	42	88	19	2	10	51	1	.272
2005	Myrtle Beach	Carolina	C	129	459	70	144	35	1	19	81	4	.314
2006	Mississippi	Southern	C	92	313	30	72	18	1	9	39	0	.230
2007	Mississippi	Southern	C	22	81	18	25	7	0	6	13	2	.309
2007	Atlanta	N.L.	C-1B	47	141	11	40	6	0	4	12	0	.284
2007	Texas a	A.L.	1B-C	46	167	28	42	7	1	7	21	0	.251
2008	Oklahoma	P.C.	C	15	55	10	16	3	1	2	13	0	.291
2008	Texas	A.L.	C	61	198	27	50	13	0	3	26	0	.253
2009	Frisco	Texas	C	2	4	1	0	0	0	0	0	0	.000
2009	Texas b	A.L.	C	84	283	34	66	12	0	9	34	0	.233
2010	Oklahoma	P.C.	C	63	238	37	58	11	2	11	33	1	.244
2010	Pawtucket	Int.	C-1B	9	36	5	10	5	0	1	6	0	.278
2010	Texas-Boston c-d	A.L.	C-1B	12	24	2	4	3	0	0	2	0	.167
2011	Boston	A.L.	C	103	358	52	84	23	3	16	56	1	.235
Major League Totals			5 Yrs.	353	1171	154	286	64	4	39	151	1	.244

a Traded to Texas Rangers with infielder Elvis Andrews, pitcher Neftali Feliz, pitcher Matt Harrison and pitcher Beau
   James for infielder Mark Teixeira and pitcher Ron Mahay, July 31, 2007.
b On disabled list from August 16 to September 2, 2009.
c On disabled list from August 16 to September 1 and April 8 to April 27, 2010.
d Traded to Boston Red Sox for pitcher Roman Mendez, infielder Chris McGuiness, player to be named later and
   cash, July 31, 2010. Texas Rangers received catcher Michael Thomas to complete trade, August 14, 2010.

SANCHEZ, ANGEL LUIS

Born, Humacao, Puerto Rico, September 20, 1983.
Bats Right. Throws Right. Height, 6 feet, 2 inches. Weight, 205 pounds.

Year	Club	Lea	Pos	G	AB	R	H	2B	3B	HR	RBI	SB	Avg
2001	Royals	Gulf Coast	SS-3B-2B	30	95	10	23	4	0	0	6	3	.242
2002	Royals	Gulf Coast	2B-SS-3B	49	175	21	44	4	0	0	12	9	.251
2003	Burlington	Midwest	SS-2B	106	408	54	110	8	1	2	35	14	.270
2004	Burlington	Midwest	SS	96	357	37	90	13	1	2	25	16	.252
2005	High Desert	Calif.	SS	133	585	102	183	33	4	5	70	10	.313
2006	Wichita	Texas	SS	133	542	105	153	24	1	4	57	8	.282
2006	Kansas City	A.L.	2B-SS	8	27	2	6	0	0	0	1	0	.222
2007	Kansas City a	A.L.			INJURED—Did Not Play								
2008	Omaha	P.C.	SS	38	131	13	29	7	1	1	13	1	.221
2008	NW Arkansas b-c	Texas	SS	63	241	28	63	7	2	1	23	4	.261
2009	Las Vegas	P.C.	SS-2B	126	449	67	137	29	4	6	60	1	.305
2010	Pawtucket	Int.	SS-2B-3B	62	223	26	61	10	1	0	17	6	.274
2010	Boston d-e	A.L.	SS	1	3	0	0	0	0	0	0	0	.000
2010	Houston	N.L.	SS-2B	65	250	30	70	9	4	0	25	0	.280
2011	Houston	N.L.	SS-2B-3B	110	288	35	69	10	0	1	28	3	.240
Major League Totals			3 Yrs.	184	568	67	145	19	4	1	54	3	.255

a On disabled list from March 28 to November 13, 2007.
b On disabled list from September 2 to September 29, 2008.
c Claimed on waivers by Toronto Blue Jays, November 3, 2008.
d Filed for free agency, November 9, 2009. Signed with Boston Red Sox organization, January 15, 2010.
e Traded to Houston Astros for catcher Kevin Cash, July 1, 2010.

SANCHEZ, FREDERICK PHILLIP (FREDDY)

Born, Hollywood, California, December 21, 1977.
Bats Right. Throws Right. Height, 5 feet, 10 inches. Weight, 185 pounds.

Year	Club	Lea	Pos	G	AB	R	H	2B	3B	HR	RBI	SB	Avg
2000	Lowell	N.Y.-Penn.	SS	34	132	24	38	13	2	1	14	2	.288
2000	Augusta	So.Atl.	SS	30	109	17	33	7	0	0	15	4	.303
2001	Trenton	Eastern	SS	44	178	25	58	20	0	2	19	3	.326
2001	Sarasota	Fla.St.	SS	69	280	40	95	19	4	1	24	5	.339
2002	Trenton	Eastern	SS-2B	80	311	60	102	23	1	3	38	19	.328
2002	Pawtucket	Int.	SS-2B	45	183	25	55	10	1	4	28	5	.301
2002	Boston	A.L.	2B-SS	12	16	3	3	0	0	0	2	0	.188
2003	Pawtucket	Int.	SS-2B-3B	58	211	46	72	17	0	5	25	8	.341
2003	Boston	A.L.	3B-SS-2B	20	34	6	8	2	0	0	2	0	.235
2003	Nashville a	P.C.	2B	1	5	1	2	1	0	0	0	0	.400
2004	Nashville	P.C.	2B-SS	44	125	10	33	7	1	1	11	4	.264

Year	Club	Lea	Pos	G	AB	R	H	2B	3B	HR	RBI	SB	Avg
2004 Pittsburgh b......N.L.			SS-2B-3B	9	19	2	3	0	0	0	2	0	.158
2005 Pittsburgh........N.L.			3B-2B-SS	132	453	54	132	26	4	5	35	2	.291
2006 Pittsburgh........N.L.			3B-SS-2B	157	582	85	200	*53	2	6	85	3	*.344
2007 Indianapolis.......Int.			2B	1	2	1	1	1	0	0	0	0	.500
2007 Pittsburgh c.......N.L.			2B-SS	147	602	77	183	42.	4	11	81	0	.304
2008 Pittsburgh........N.L.			2B	145	569	75	154	26	2	9	52	0	.271
2009 Fresno...........P.C.			2B	3	9	1	3	1	0	0	0	0	.333
2009 Pittsburgh-San Fran. d-e N.L.			2B	111	457	56	134	29	3	7	41	5	.293
2010 San Jose.......Calif.			2B	3	9	6	6	5	0	0	4	0	.667
2010 Fresno...........P.C.			2B	4	11	1	3	0	0	0	0	0	.273
2010 San Francisco f ...N.L.			2B	111	431	55	126	22	1	7	47	3	.292
2011 San Francisco g ...N.L.			2B	60	239	21	69	15	1	3	24	0	.289
Major League Totals............	10 Yrs.			904	3402	434	1012	215	17	48	371	13	.297
Division Series													
2010 San Francisco .....N.L.			2B	4	16	2	2	0	0	0	0	0	.125
Championship Series													
2010 San Francisco .....N.L.			2B	6	25	1	9	1	0	0	1	0	.360
World Series Record													
2010 San Francisco .....N.L.			2B	5	22	2	6	3	0	0	3	0	.273

a Traded to Pittsburgh Pirates with pitcher Mike Gonzalez and cash for pitcher Jeff Suppan, pitcher Brandon Lyon and pitcher Anastacio Martinez, July 31, 2003.
b On disabled list from March 26 to July 9, 2004.
c On disabled list from March 23 to April 8, 2007.
d Traded to San Francisco Giants for pitcher Tim Alderson, July 30, 2009.
e On disabled list from August 18 to September 7, 2009.
f On disabled list from March 26 to May 19, 2010.
g On disabled list from June 11 to October 31, 2011.

SANCHEZ, GABRIEL (GABY)
Born, Miami, Florida, September 2, 1983.
Bats Right. Throws Right. Height, 6 feet, 2 inches. Weight, 225 pounds.

Year	Club	Lea	Pos	G	AB	R	H	2B	3B	HR	RBI	SB	Avg
2005 Jamestown......	N.Y.-Penn.		3B-1B-C	62	234	34	83	16	0	5	42	11	.355
2006 Jupiter.........	Fla.St.		1B-3B-C	16	55	13	10	3	1	1	7	1	.182
2006 Marlins........	Gulf Coast		1B	3	6	1	2	1	0	0	3	0	.333
2006 Greensboro........	So.Atl.		1B-C	55	189	43	60	12	0	14	40	6	.317
2007 Jupiter.........	Fla.St.		1B-3B-C	133	473	89	132	40	3	9	70	6	.279
2008 Carolina........	Southern		1B-3B	133	478	70	150	42	1	17	92	17	.314
2008 Florida........	N.L.		1B	5	8	0	3	2	0	0	1	0	.375
2009 New Orleans...........	P.C.		1B-3B	85	318	55	92	11	0	16	56	5	.289
2009 Florida........	N.L.		1B	21	21	2	5	0	0	2	3	0	.238
2010 Florida........	N.L.		1B	151	572	72	156	37	3	19	85	5	.273
2011 Florida........	N.L.		1B	159	572	72	152	35	0	19	78	3	.266
Major League Totals............	4 Yrs.			336	1173	146	316	74	3	40	167	8	.269

SANDOVAL, PABLO E.
Born, Puerto Cabello, Venezuela, August 11, 1986.
Bats Both. Throws Right. Height, 5 feet, 11 inches. Weight, 245 pounds.

Year	Club	Lea	Pos	G	AB	R	H	2B	3B	HR	RBI	SB	Avg
2004 Giants............	Arizona		C	46	177	21	47	9	5	0	26	4	.266
2005 Salem-Keizer....	Northwest		3B-1B-C	75	294	46	97	15	2	3	50	2	.330
2006 Augusta...........	So.Atl.		1B-3B	117	438	43	116	20	1	1	49	3	.265
2007 San Jose...........	Calif.		C-1B	102	401	56	115	33	5	11	52	3	.287
2008 San Jose...........	Calif.		C-1B	68	273	61	98	25	2	12	59	2	.359
2008 Connecticut........	Eastern		C-1B	44	175	29	59	13	0	8	37	0	.337
2008 San Francisco........	N.L.		1B-3B-C	41	145	24	50	10	1	3	24	0	.345
2009 San Francisco........	N.L.		3B-1B-C	153	572	79	189	44	5	25	90	5	.330
2010 San Francisco........	N.L.		3B-1B	152	563	61	151	34	3	13	63	3	.268
2011 San Jose...........	Calif.		3B	1	3	1	0	0	0	0	0	0	.000
2011 Fresno..............	P.C.		3B-1B	5	18	4	5	0	0	2	7	0	.278
2011 San Francisco a.......	N.L.		3B-1B	117	426	55	134	26	3	23	70	2	.315
Major League Totals............	4 Yrs.			463	1706	219	524	114	12	64	247	10	.307
Division Series													
2010 San Francisco	N.L.		3B	2	6	0	1	0	0	0	0	0	.167
Championship Series													
2010 San Francisco	N.L.		3B	3	8	0	2	1	0	0	2	0	.250

Year	Club	Lea	Pos	G	AB	R	H	2B	3B	HR	RBI	SB	Avg
	World Series Record												
2010 San Francisco	N.L.		DH	1	3	0	0	0	0	0	0	0	.000

a On disabled list from April 30 to June 14, 2011.

SANDS, GERALD ROBERT (JERRY)

Born, Middletown, New York, September 28, 1987.
Bats Right. Throws Right. Height, 6 feet, 4 inches. Weight, 220 pounds.

Year	Club	Lea	Pos	G	AB	R	H	2B	3B	HR	RBI	SB	Avg
2008 Dodgers........	Gulf Coast	OF	46	146	29	30	4	0	10	33	5	.205
2009 Great Lakes	Midwest	1B-OF	32	104	22	27	7	2	5	19	1	.260
2009 Ogden	Pioneer	OF	41	163	41	57	9	2	14	39	0	.350
2010 Great Lakes	Midwest	1B-OF	69	243	48	81	16	3	18	46	14	.333
2010 Chattanooga......	Southern	OF-1B-3B	68	259	54	70	12	2	17	47	4	.270
2011 Albuquerque...........	P.C.	OF-1B-3B	94	370	78	103	21	3	29	88	3	.278
2011 Los Angeles	N.L.	OF-1B	61	198	20	50	15	0	4	26	3	.253

SANTANA, CARLOS

Born, Santo Domingo, Dominican Republic, April 8, 1986.
Bats Both. Throws Right. Height, 5 feet, 11 inches. Weight, 190 pounds.

Year	Club	Lea	Pos	G	AB	R	H	2B	3B	HR	RBI	SB	Avg
2005 Dodgers.....	Gulf Coast	3B-OF-C-2B	32	78	14	23	4	1	1	14	0	.295
2006 Vero Beach.......	Fla.St.	3B-OF	54	198	16	53	10	2	3	18	0	.268
2006 Ogden	Pioneer	OF-3B	37	132	31	40	5	1	7	27	4	.303
2007 Great Lakes	Midwest	C-3B-OF	86	292	32	65	20	1	7	36	5	.223
2008 Inland Empire.....	Calif.	C-OF-1B-2B	99	350	88	113	34	4	14	96	7	.323
2008 Kinston.......	Carolina	C	29	105	34	37	5	1	6	19	3	.352
2008 Akron a	Eastern	C	2	8	3	1	0	0	1	2	0	.125
2009 Akron........	Eastern	C	130	428	91	124	30	2	23	97	2	.290
2010 Columbus.........	Int.	C	57	196	39	62	14	1	13	51	6	.316
2010 Cleveland b	A.L.	C	46	150	23	39	13	0	6	22	3	.260
2011 Cleveland	A.L.	C-1B	155	552	84	132	35	2	27	79	5	.239
Major League Totals		2 Yrs.	201	702	107	171	48	2	33	101	8	.244

a Traded by Los Angeles Dodgers to Cleveland Indians with pitcher Jonathan Meloan for infielder Casey Blake, July 26, 2008.

b On disabled list from August 3 to November 9, 2010.

SANTIAGO, RAMON D.

Born, Las Matas de Farfan, Dominican Republic, August 31, 1979.
Bats Both. Throws Right. Height, 5 feet, 11 inches. Weight, 150 pounds.

Year	Club	Lea	Pos	G	AB	R	H	2B	3B	HR	RBI	SB	Avg
1999 Tigers.......	Gulf Coast	SS	35	134	25	43	9	2	0	11	20	.321
1999 Oneonta	N.Y.-Penn.	SS	12	50	9	17	1	2	1	8	5	.340
2000 West Michigan.	Midwest	SS	98	379	69	103	15	1	1	42	39	.272
2001 Lakeland........	Fla.St.	DH	120	429	64	115	15	3	2	46	34	.268
2002 Erie..........	Eastern	SS	22	75	9	21	0	2	1	7	6	.280
2002 Toledo	Int.	SS	9	28	8	12	1	0	2	6	0	.429
2002 Detroit	A.L.	SS	65	222	33	54	5	5	4	20	8	.243
2003 Detroit	A.L.	SS-2B	141	444	41	100	18	1	2	29	10	.225
2004 Tacoma	P.C.	SS-2B	71	243	35	47	7	2	1	24	9	.193
2004 Seattle a	A.L.	SS	19	39	8	7	1	0	0	2	0	.179
2005 Tacoma	P.C.	2B-SS-3B-C	129	441	68	111	22	3	10	50	18	.252
2005 Seattle	A.L.	2B-SS	8	8	2	1	0	0	0	0	0	.125
2006 Toledo	Int.	2B-SS	25	83	13	21	6	0	2	12	2	.253
2006 Detroit b	A.L.	SS-2B-3B	43	80	9	18	1	1	0	3	2	.225
2007 Toledo	Int.	SS-2B	91	365	40	96	19	4	3	30	8	.263
2007 Detroit	A.L.	SS	32	67	10	19	5	1	0	7	3	.284
2008 Toledo	Int.	SS	8	28	3	6	2	0	0	3	0	.214
2008 Detroit c	A.L.	SS-2B-3B	58	124	30	35	6	2	4	18	1	.282
2009 Detroit	A.L.	SS-2B-3B	93	262	29	70	6	2	7	35	1	.267
2010 Detroit	A.L.	SS-2B	112	320	38	84	9	1	3	22	2	.262
2011 Detroit d	A.L.	2B-SS-3B	101	258	29	67	11	3	5	30	0	.260
Major League Totals		10 Yrs.	672	1824	229	455	62	16	25	166	27	.249
	Division Series												
2011 Detroit	A.L.	2B	4	14	0	2	1	0	0	2	0	.143
	Championship Series												
2006 Detroit	A.L.	SS	3	7	0	0	0	0	0	0	0	.000

Year	Club	Lea	Pos	G	AB	R	H	2B	3B	HR	RBI	SB	Avg
Championship Series Totals				9	31	1	9	1	0	0	0	0	.290
World Series Record													
2006 Detroit . . . . .A.L.			SS	3	5	0	1	0	0	0	0	0	.200

a Traded to Seattle Mariners with infielder Juan Gonzalez for infielder Carlos Guillen, January 8, 2004.
b Released by Seattle Mariners, November 18, 2005. Signed with Detroit Tigers organization, January 4, 2006.
c On disabled list from June 5 to July 8, 2008.
d Filed for free agency, October 30, 2011, re-signed with Detroit Tigers November 30, 2011.

SAUNDERS, MICHAEL EDWARD BRETT
Born, Victoria, British Columbia, Canada, November 19, 1986.
Bats Left. Throws Right. Height, 6 feet, 4 inches. Weight, 210 pounds.

Year	Club	Lea	Pos	G	AB	R	H	2B	3B	HR	RBI	SB	Avg
2005 Everett	Northwest		OF	56	196	24	53	13	3	7	39	2	.270
2006 Wisconsin	Midwest		OF	104	359	48	86	10	8	4	39	22	.240
2007 High Desert	Calif.		OF	108	431	91	129	25	4	14	77	27	.299
2007 West Tenn	Southern		OF	15	52	8	15	1	2	1	7	2	.288
2008 Tacoma . . . . .P.C.			OF	24	95	12	23	4	1	3	16	1	.242
2008 West Tenn	Southern		OF	67	248	46	72	18	3	8	30	11	.290
2009 Tacoma . . . . .P.C.			OF	64	248	58	77	15	2	13	32	6	.310
2009 Seattle . . . . .A.L.			OF	46	122	13	27	1	3	0	4	4	.221
2010 Tacoma . . . . .P.C.			OF	21	80	6	16	1	0	0	5	4	.200
2010 Seattle . . . . .A.L.			OF	100	289	29	61	11	2	10	33	6	.211
2011 Tacoma . . . . .P.C.			OF	64	236	51	68	11	3	7	38	10	.288
2011 Seattle . . . . .A.L.			OF	58	161	16	24	5	0	2	8	6	.149
Major League Totals		3 Yrs.		204	572	58	112	17	5	12	45	16	.196

SCHAFER, JORDAN JAMES
Born, Hammond, Indiana, September 4, 1986.
Bats Left. Throws Left. Height, 6 feet, 1 inch. Weight, 200 pounds.

Year	Club	Lea	Pos	G	AB	R	H	2B	3B	HR	RBI	SB	Avg
2005 Braves	Gulf Coast		OF	49	182	18	37	12	3	3	19	13	.203
2006 Rome	So.Atl.		OF	114	388	49	93	15	7	8	60	15	.240
2007 Rome	So.Atl.		OF	30	129	16	48	15	2	5	20	4	.372
2007 Myrtle Beach	Carolina		OF	106	436	70	128	34	8	10	43	19	.294
2008 Mississippi	Southern		OF	84	297	46	80	18	6	10	51	12	.269
2009 Atlanta	N.L.		OF	50	167	18	34	8	0	2	8	2	.204
2009 Gwinnett a	Int.		OF	9	35	6	8	0	0	2	3	3	.229
2010 Gwinnett	Int.		OF	52	189	16	38	5	1	1	8	9	.201
2010 Rome	So.Atl.		OF	6	22	4	6	2	0	0	1	2	.273
2010 Mississippi b	Southern		OF	18	63	7	11	3	0	0	5	1	.175
2011 Oklahoma . . . . .P.C.			OF	5	20	4	10	2	0	0	3	3	.500
2011 Gwinnett	Int.		OF	42	164	21	42	8	0	1	21	6	.256
2011 Atlanta-Houston c-d	N.L.		OF	82	302	46	73	10	3	2	13	22	.242
Major League Totals		2 Yrs.		132	469	64	107	18	3	4	21	24	.228

a On disabled list from September 4 to October 9, 2009.
b On disabled list from March 26 to May 17, 2010.
c Traded to Houston Astros with pitcher Juan Abreu, pitcher Paul Clemens and pitcher Brett Oberholtzer for outfielder Michael Bourn and cash, July 31, 2011.
d On disabled list from July 27 to August 22, 2011.

SCHIERHOLTZ, NATHAN JOHN (NATE)
Born, Reno, Nevada, February 15, 1984.
Bats Left. Throws Right. Height, 6 feet, 2 inches. Weight, 215 pounds.

Year	Club	Lea	Pos	G	AB	R	H	2B	3B	HR	RBI	SB	Avg
2003 Giants	Arizona		3B-1B	11	45	5	18	0	2	0	5	4	.400
2003 Salem-Keizer	Northwest		3B	35	124	23	38	6	2	3	29	0	.306
2004 San Jose . . . . .Calif.			3B-OF	62	258	39	76	18	9	3	31	3	.295
2004 Hagerstown	So.Atl.		3B	59	235	41	70	22	0	15	54	1	.298
2005 San Jose . . . . .Calif.			OF	128	502	83	160	37	8	15	86	5	.319
2006 Connecticut	Eastern		OF	125	470	55	127	25	7	14	54	8	.270
2007 Fresno . . . . .P.C.			OF	109	411	67	137	31	7	16	68	10	.333
2007 San Francisco	N.L.		OF	39	112	9	34	5	3	0	10	3	.304
2008 Fresno . . . . .P.C.			OF	93	350	62	112	22	10	18	73	9	.320
2008 San Francisco	N.L.		OF	19	75	12	24	8	1	1	5	0	.320
2009 Fresno . . . . .P.C.			OF	5	18	2	4	1	0	0	1	1	.222
2009 San Francisco a	N.L.		OF	116	285	33	76	19	2	5	29	3	.267

Year	Club	Lea	Pos	G	AB	R	H	2B	3B	HR	RBI	SB	Avg
2011 San Francisco b	N.L.		OF	115	335	42	93	22	1	9	41	7	.278
Major League Totals		5 Yrs.		426	1034	130	282	67	10	18	102	17	.273
Division Series													
2010 San Francisco	N.L.		OF	4	4	0	1	0	0	0	0	0	.250
Championship Series													
2010 San Francisco	N.L.		OF	4	3	1	0	0	0	0	0	0	.000
World Series Record													
2010 San Francisco	N.L.		OF	3	5	1	1	0	0	0	1	0	.200

a On disabled list from July 27 to August 12, 2009.
b On disabled list from August 22 to September 29, 2011.

SCHUMAKER, JARED MICHAEL (SKIP)

Born, Torrance, California, February 3, 1980.
Bats Left. Throws Right. Height, 5 feet, 10 inches. Weight, 195 pounds.

Year	Club	Lea	Pos	G	AB	R	H	2B	3B	HR	RBI	SB	Avg
2001 New Jersey	N.Y.-Penn.		OF	49	162	22	41	10	1	0	14	11	.253
2002 Potomac	Carolina		OF	136	551	71	158	22	4	2	44	26	.287
2003 Tennessee	Southern		OF	91	342	43	86	20	3	2	22	6	.251
2004 Tennessee	Southern		OF-3B	138	516	78	163	29	6	4	43	19	.316
2005 Memphis	P.C.		OF	115	443	66	127	24	3	7	34	14	.287
2005 St. Louis	N.L.		OF	27	24	9	6	1	0	0	1	1	.250
2006 Memphis	P.C.		OF	95	369	47	113	13	3	3	27	11	.306
2006 St. Louis	N.L.		OF	28	54	3	10	1	0	1	2	2	.185
2007 Memphis	P.C.		OF	59	232	34	71	16	0	7	31	2	.306
2007 St. Louis	N.L.		OF	88	177	19	59	12	2	2	19	1	.333
2008 St. Louis	N.L.		OF	153	540	87	163	22	5	8	46	8	.302
2009 St. Louis	N.L.		2B-OF	153	532	85	161	34	1	4	35	2	.303
2010 St. Louis	N.L.		2B-OF	137	476	66	126	18	1	5	42	5	.265
2011 St. Louis a-b	N.L.		2B-OF-P	117	367	34	104	19	0	2	38	0	.283
Major League Totals		7 Yrs.		703	2170	303	629	107	9	22	183	19	.290
Division Series													
2009 St. Louis	N.L.		2B-OF	2	6	1	2	1	0	0	1	0	.333
2011 St. Louis	N.L.		OF-2B	5	10	1	6	2	0	0	3	0	.600
Division Series Totals				7	16	2	8	3	0	0	4	0	.500
World Series Record													
2011 St. Louis	N.L.		OF	6	11	1	2	0	0	0	1	0	.182

a On disabled list from April 16 to May 23, 2011.
b Not offered contract, December 12, 2011, re-signed with St. Louis Cardinals, December 12, 2011.

SCOTT, LUKE BRANDON

Born, DeLeon Springs, Florida, June 25, 1978.
Bats Left. Throws Right. Height, 6 feet. Weight, 210 pounds.

Year	Club	Lea	Pos	G	AB	R	H	2B	3B	HR	RBI	SB	Avg
2001 Kinston a	Carolina					INJURED — Did Not Play							
2002 Kinston	Carolina		OF-1B	48	163	22	39	7	1	8	30	2	.239
2002 Columbus	So.Atl.		OF	49	171	28	44	15	4	7	32	9	.257
2003 Kinston	Carolina		OF	67	241	37	67	12	1	13	44	6	.278
2003 Akron	Eastern		OF	50	183	21	50	13	1	7	37	0	.273
2004 Salem	Carolina		OF	66	241	45	67	20	1	8	35	6	.278
2004 Round Rock b	Texas		OF	63	208	45	62	17	0	19	62	0	.298
2005 Round Rock	P.C.		OF	103	398	69	114	25	4	31	87	2	.286
2005 Houston	N.L.		OF	34	80	6	15	4	2	0	4	1	.188
2006 Round Rock	P.C.		OF	87	318	63	95	15	1	20	63	6	.299
2006 Houston	N.L.		OF	65	214	31	72	19	6	10	37	2	.336
2007 Houston c	N.L.		OF	132	369	49	94	28	5	18	64	3	.255
2008 Baltimore	A.L.		OF	148	475	67	122	29	2	23	65	2	.257
2009 Delmarva	So.Atl.		OF	2	4	1	3	0	0	1	1	0	.750
2009 Baltimore d	A.L.		DH-OF-1B	128	449	61	116	26	1	25	77	0	.258
2010 Orioles	Gulf Coast		OF	3	9	1	2	0	0	0	2	0	.222
2010 Baltimore e	A.L.		DH-1B-OF	131	447	70	127	29	1	27	72	2	.284
2011 Bowie	Eastern		DH	3	10	5	5	1	0	3	7	0	.500
2011 Baltimore f-g	A.L.		OF-1B	64	209	24	46	11	0	9	22	1	.220
Major League Totals		7 Yrs.		702	2243	308	592	146	17	112	341	11	.264
Division Series													
2005 Houston	N.L.		OF	2	2	1	0	0	0	0	0	0	.000
World Series Record													
2005 Houston	N.L.		PH	0	0	0	0	0	0	0	0	0	.000

a On disabled list from June 21 to September 14, 2001.
b Traded by Cleveland Indians to Houston Astros with outfielder Willy Taveras for pitcher Jeriome Robertston, March 31, 2004.
c Traded to Baltimore Orioles with pitcher Troy Patton, pitcher Matt Albers, pitcher Dennis Sarfate and infielder Michael Costanzo for infielder Miguel Tejada, December 12, 2007.
d On disabled list from May 11 to May 27, 2009.
e On disabled list from July 1 to July 19, 2010.
f On disabled list from July 3 to July 22 and July 23 to November 2, 2011.
g Not offered contract, December 12, 2011. Signed with Tampa Bay Rays, January 12, 2012.

SCUTARO, MARCOS (MARCO)
Born, San Felipe, Venezuela, October 30, 1975.
Bats Right. Throws Right. Height, 5 feet, 10 inches. Weight, 190 pounds.

Year Club	Lea	Pos	G	AB	R	H	2B	3B	HR	RBI	SB	Avg
1995 Cleveland . . .	Dominican	3B	66	262	71	103	18	6	0	38	32	.393
1996 Columbus.	So.Atl.	2B-SS-3B	85	315	66	79	12	3	10	45	6	.251
1997 Buffalo	A.A.	2B-3B-SS	21	57	8	15	3	0	1	6	0	.263
1997 Kinston.	Carolina	2B-3B	97	378	58	103	17	6	10	59	23	.272
1998 Buffalo	Int.	2B-3B	8	26	3	6	3	0	0	4	0	.231
1998 Akron	Eastern	2B-SS	124	462	68	146	27	6	11	62	33	.316
1999 Buffalo	Int.	2B-SS	129	462	76	126	24	2	8	51	21	.273
2000 Buffalo	Int.	2B-SS	124	425	67	117	20	5	5	54	9	.275
2000 Indianapolis a.	Int.	2B-SS	4	13	5	7	1	1	1	3	1	.538
2001 Indianapolis	Int.	2B-3B-SS	132	495	87	146	29	3	11	50	11	.295
2002 Norfolk.	Int.	2B-SS-OF-3B	97	354	48	113	22	6	7	28	7	.319
2002 New York b.	N.L.	2B-SS-3B-OF	27	36	2	8	0	1	1	6	0	.222
2003 Norfolk.	Int.	3B-2B-SS-OF	70	244	42	76	18	3	9	32	11	.311
2003 New York c.	N.L.	2B-SS	48	75	10	16	4	0	2	6	2	.213
2004 Oakland	A.L.	2B-SS-3B	137	455	50	124	32	1	7	43	0	.273
2005 Oakland	A.L.	SS-2B-3B-OF	118	381	48	94	22	3	9	37	5	.247
2006 Oakland	A.L.	2B-SS-3B-OF	117	365	52	97	21	6	5	41	5	.266
2007 Oakland d.	A.L.	SS-3B-2B-OF	104	338	49	88	13	0	7	41	2	.260
2008 Toronto	A.L.	SS-2B-3B-1B	145	517	76	138	23	1	7	60	7	.267
2009 Toronto e	A.L.	SS-2B	144	574	100	162	35	1	12	60	14	.282
2010 Boston	A.L.	SS-2B	150	632	92	174	38	0	11	56	5	.275
2011 Pawtucket	Int.	2B-SS	3	11	4	5	1	0	0	0	0	.455
2011 Boston f.	A.L.	SS-2B	113	395	59	118	26	1	7	54	4	.299
Major League Totals	10 Yrs.		1103	3768	538	1019	214	14	68	404	44	.270
Division Series												
2006 Oakland	A.L.	SS	3	12	1	4	4	0	0	6	0	.333
Championship Series												
2006 Oakland	A.L.	SS	4	15	0	1	0	0	0	0	0	.067

a Sent by Cleveland Indians to Milwaukee Brewers as player to be named later in Richie Sexson trade, August 30, 2000.
b Claimed on waivers by New York Mets, April 3, 2002.
c Claimed on waivers by Oakland Athletics, October 9, 2003.
d Traded to Toronto Blue Jays for pitcher Kristian Bell and pitcher Graham Godfrey, November 18, 2007.
e Filed for free agency, November 6, 2009. Signed with Boston Red Sox, December 4, 2009.
f On disabled list from May 8 to June 7, 2011.

SEAGER, KYLE DUERR
Born, Charlotte, North Carolina, November 3, 1987.
Bats Left. Throws Right. Height, 5 feet, 10 inches. Weight, 175 pounds.

Year Club	Lea	Pos	G	AB	R	H	2B	3B	HR	RBI	SB	Avg
2009 Mariners.	Arizona	2B	1	3	0	0	0	0	0	0	0	.000
2009 Clinton	Midwest	2B-3B-SS	41	153	17	42	8	0	1	22	4	.275
2009 High Desert	Calif.	2B	2	5	1	0	0	0	0	0	0	.000
2010 High Desert	Calif.	2B-3B-SS	135	557	126	192	40	3	14	74	13	.345
2011 Jackson	Southern	2B-SS-3B	66	266	33	83	25	1	4	37	8	.312
2011 Tacoma	P.C.	3B-2B-SS	24	106	24	41	8	2	3	17	3	.387
2011 Seattle	A.L.	3B-SS-2B	53	182	22	47	13	0	3	13	3	.258

SHOPPACH, KELLY BRIAN
Born, Fort Worth, Texas, April 29, 1980.
Bats Right. Throws Right. Height, 6 feet, 1 inch. Weight, 210 pounds.

Year Club	Lea	Pos	G	AB	R	H	2B	3B	HR	RBI	SB	Avg
2002 Sarasota.	Fla.St.	C	116	414	54	112	35	1	10	66	2	.271
2003 Portland	Eastern	C	92	340	45	96	30	2	12	60	0	.282

Year Club	Lea	Pos	G	AB	R	H	2B	3B	HR	RBI	SB	Avg
2004 Pawtucket	Int.	C	113	399	62	93	25	0	22	64	0	.233
2005 Pawtucket	Int.	C	102	371	60	94	16	0	26	75	0	.253
2005 Boston	A.L.	C	9	15	1	0	0	0	0	0	0	.000
2006 Buffalo	Int.	C	21	78	11	22	8	0	4	9	0	.282
2006 Cleveland a	A.L.	C	41	110	7	27	6	0	3	16	0	.245
2007 Cleveland	A.L.	C	59	161	26	42	13	0	7	30	0	.261
2008 Cleveland	A.L.	C	112	352	67	92	27	0	21	55	0	.261
2009 Cleveland b	A.L.	C	89	271	33	58	14	0	12	40	0	.214
2010 Durham	Int.	C	4	13	0	4	0	0	0	2	0	.308
2010 Tampa Bay c	A.L.	C	63	158	17	31	8	0	5	17	0	.196
2011 Tampa Bay d	A.L.	C	87	221	23	39	3	0	11	22	0	.176
Major League Totals		7 Yrs.	460	1288	174	289	71	0	59	180	0	.224
Division Series												
2007 Cleveland	A.L.	C	1	3	1	2	2	0	0	0	0	.667
2010 Tampa Bay	A.L.	C	3	9	0	0	0	0	0	0	0	.000
2011 Tampa Bay	A.L.	C	4	10	3	4	0	0	2	6	0	.400
Division Series Totals			8	22	4	6	2	0	2	6	0	.273
Championship Series												
2007 Cleveland	A.L.	C	1	3	0	1	0	0	0	0	0	.333

a Traded to Cleveland Indians with infielder Andy Marte and pitcher Guillermo Mota for outfielder Coco Crisp, pitcher David Riske and catcher Josh Bard, January 27, 2006.
b Traded to Tampa Bay Rays for player to be named later, December 1, 2009. Cleveland Indians received pitcher Mitch Talbot to complete the trade, December 21, 2009.
c On disabled list from April 11 to June 4, 2010.
d Filed for free agency, October 31, 2011. Signed with Boston Red Sox, December 12, 2011.

SIZEMORE, GRADY

Born, Seattle, Washington, August 2, 1982.
Bats Left. Throws Left. Height, 6 feet, 2 inches. Weight, 200 pounds.

Year Club	Lea	Pos	G	AB	R	H	2B	3B	HR	RBI	SB	Avg
2000 Expos	Gulf Coast	OF	55	205	31	60	8	3	1	14	16	.293
2001 Clinton	Midwest	OF	123	451	64	121	16	4	2	61	32	.268
2002 Kinston	Carolina	OF	47	172	31	59	9	3	3	20	14	.343
2002 Brevard County a	Fla.St.	OF	75	256	37	66	15	4	0	26	9	.258
2003 Akron	Eastern	OF-2B	128	496	96	151	26	11	13	78	10	.304
2004 Buffalo	Int.	OF	101	418	73	120	23	8	8	51	15	.287
2004 Cleveland	A.L.	OF	43	138	15	34	6	2	4	24	2	.246
2005 Cleveland	A.L.	OF	158	640	111	185	37	11	22	81	22	.289
2006 Cleveland	A.L.	OF	*162	655	*134	190	*53	11	28	76	22	.290
2007 Cleveland	A.L.	OF	*162	628	118	174	34	5	24	78	33	.277
2008 Cleveland	A.L.	OF	157	634	101	170	39	5	33	90	38	.268
2009 Cleveland b	A.L.	OF	106	436	73	108	20	6	18	64	13	.248
2010 Cleveland c	A.L.	OF	33	128	15	27	6	2	0	13	4	.211
2011 Akron	Eastern	OF	6	20	1	8	3	0	0	3	0	.400
2011 Columbus	Int.	OF	2	8	1	2	0	0	1	2	0	.250
2011 Cleveland d-e	A.L.	OF	71	268	34	60	21	1	10	32	0	.224
Major League Totals		8 Yrs.	892	3527	601	948	216	43	139	458	134	.269
Division Series												
2007 Cleveland	A.L.	OF	4	16	3	6	0	1	1	1	1	.375
Championship Series												
2007 Cleveland	A.L.	OF	7	27	6	6	2	0	2	3	1	.222

a Traded by Montreal Expos to Cleveland Indians with infielder Lee Stevens, infielder Brandon Phillips and pitcher Cliff Lee for pitcher Bartolo Colon and player to be named later, June 27, 2002. Montreal Expos received pitcher Tim Drew to complete trade, June 28, 2002.
b On disabled list from May 31 to June 23 and September 4 to October 14, 2009.
c On disabled list from May 17 to November 9, 2010.
d On disabled list from March 29 to April 17 and May 11 to May 27 and July 18 to September 5, 2011.
e Filed for free agency, October 31, 2011, re-signed with Cleveland Indians, November 23, 2011.

SIZEMORE, SCOTT DANIEL

Born, Virginia Beach, Virginia, January 4, 1985.
Bats Right. Throws Right. Height, 6 feet. Weight, 185 pounds.

Year Club	Lea	Pos	G	AB	R	H	2B	3B	HR	RBI	SB	Avg
2006 Oneonta	N.Y.-Penn.	SS-2B	70	294	49	96	15	4	3	37	7	.327
2007 West Michigan .	Midwest	2B	125	438	78	116	33	5	4	48	16	.265
2008 Lakeland	Fla.St.	2B	53	203	32	58	11	1	4	20	14	.286
2009 Erie	Eastern	2B	59	228	39	70	17	4	9	33	7	.307
2009 Toledo	Int.	2B-3B-SS	71	292	49	90	22	1	8	33	14	.308

Year Club	Lea	Pos	G	AB	R	H	2B	3B	HR	RBI	SB	Avg
2010 Toledo .... Int.		2B-3B-SS	76	299	49	89	23	1	9	37	2	.298
2010 Detroit .... A.L.		2B-3B	48	143	19	32	7	0	3	14	0	.224
2011 Sacramento .... P.C.		3B-2B	9	30	11	8	2	0	1	3	2	.267
2011 Toledo .... Int.		2B	23	76	17	31	7	1	2	15	3	.408
2011 Detroit-Oakland a ... A.L.		3B-2B	110	368	50	90	22	1	11	56	5	.245
Major League Totals		2 Yrs.	158	511	69	122	29	1	14	70	5	.239

a Traded to Oakland Athletics for pitcher David Purcey, May 27, 2011.

SMITH, GARRY SETH (SETH)
Born, Jackson, Mississippi, September 30, 1982.
Bats Left. Throws Left. Height, 6 feet, 3 inches. Weight, 215 pounds.

Year Club	Lea	Pos	G	AB	R	H	2B	3B	HR	RBI	SB	Avg
2004 Tri-Cities........ Northwest		OF	9	27	6	7	1	1	2	5	0	.259
2004 Casper .... Pioneer		OF	56	233	46	86	21	3	9	61	9	.369
2005 Modesto............ Calif.		OF	129	533	87	160	45	6	9	72	5	.300
2006 Tulsa .... Texas		OF	130	524	79	154	46	4	15	71	4	.294
2007 Colorado Springs....... P.C.		OF	129	451	68	143	32	6	17	82	7	.317
2007 Colorado .... N.L.		OF	7	8	4	5	0	1	0	0	0	.625
2008 Colorado Springs....... P.C.		OF	68	248	55	80	16	2	10	53	11	.323
2008 Colorado .... N.L.		OF	67	108	13	28	7	0	4	15	1	.259
2009 Colorado a .... N.L.		OF	133	335	61	98	20	4	15	55	4	.293
2010 Colorado .... N.L.		OF	133	358	55	88	19	5	17	52	2	.246
2011 Colorado .... N.L.		OF	147	476	67	135	32	9	15	59	10	.284
Major League Totals		5 Yrs.	487	1285	200	354	78	19	51	181	17	.275
Division Series												
2007 Colorado .... N.L.		PH	2	2	1	1	0	0	0	0	0	.500
2009 Colorado .... N.L.		OF	3	5	0	1	0	0	0	0	0	.200
Division Series Totals			5	7	1	2	0	0	0	0	0	.286
Championship Series												
2007 Colorado .... N.L.		PH	2	2	1	1	1	0	0	2	0	.500
World Series Record												
2007 Colorado .... N.L.		PH	2	2	0	1	0	0	0	0	0	.500

a On disabled list from September 1 to November 13, 2009.

SMOAK, JUSTIN KYLE
Born, Goose Creek, South Carolina, December 5, 1986.
Bats Both. Throws Left. Height, 6 feet, 4 inches. Weight, 220 pounds.

Year Club	Lea	Pos	G	AB	R	H	2B	3B	HR	RBI	SB	Avg
2008 Clinton .... Midwest		1B	14	56	9	17	3	0	3	6	0	.304
2009 Rangers .... Arizona		1B	2	6	3	4	0	1	2	5	0	.667
2009 Okla.................. P.C.		1B	54	197	25	48	11	0	4	23	0	.244
2009 Frisco .... Texas		1B	50	183	30	60	10	0	6	29	0	.328
2010 Oklahoma........... P.C.		1B	15	50	10	15	6	0	2	5	0	.300
2010 Tacoma .... P.C.		1B	35	133	23	36	7	0	7	25	0	.271
2010 Texas-Seattle a ...... A.L.		1B	100	348	40	76	14	0	13	48	1	.218
2011 Tacoma .... P.C.		1B	4	11	1	0	0	0	0	0	0	.000
2011 Seattle b............. A.L.		1B	123	427	38	100	24	0	15	55	0	.234
Major League Totals		2 Yrs.	223	775	78	176	38	0	28	103	1	.227

a Traded to Seattle Mariners with pitcher Blake Beavan, pitcher Josh Lueke and infielder Matt Lawson for pitcher Cliff Lee, pitcher Mark Lowe and cash, July 9, 2010.
b On disabled list from August 13 to September 1, 2011.

SNIDER, TRAVIS JAMES
Born, Kirkland, Washington, February 2, 1988.
Bats Left. Throws Left. Height, 5 feet, 11 inches. Weight, 245 pounds.

Year Club	Lea	Pos	G	AB	R	H	2B	3B	HR	RBI	SB	Avg
2006 Pulaski .... Appal.		OF	54	194	36	63	12	1	11	41	6	.325
2007 Lansing .... Midwest		OF	118	457	72	143	35	7	16	93	3	.313
2008 Dunedin .... Fla.St.		DH	17	61	15	17	5	0	4	7	1	.279
2008 New Hampshire ..... Eastern		OF	98	362	65	95	21	0	17	67	1	.262
2008 Syracuse .... Int.		OF	18	64	9	22	5	0	2	17	1	.344
2008 Toronto .... A.L.		OF	24	73	9	22	6	0	2	13	0	.301
2009 Las Vegas............ P.C.		OF	48	175	32	59	13	1	14	40	2	.337
2009 Toronto .... A.L.		OF	77	241	34	58	14	1	9	29	1	.241
2010 Blue Jays .... Gulf Coast		OF	4	14	2	4	0	0	0	1	1	.286
2010 Dunedin .... Fla.St.		DH	1	4	0	0	0	0	0	0	0	.000

Year	Club	Lea	Pos	G	AB	R	H	2B	3B	HR	RBI	SB	Avg
2010 New Hampshire	Eastern	OF	20	81	14	24	5	0	5	17	3	.296
2010 Toronto a	A.L.	OF	82	298	36	76	20	0	14	32	6	.255
2011 Las Vegas.	P.C.	OF	61	248	47	81	22	2	4	42	12	.327
2011 Toronto	A.L.	OF	49	187	23	42	14	0	3	30	9	.225
Major League Totals		4 Yrs.	232	799	102	198	54	1	28	104	16	.248

a On disabled list from May 15 to July 17, 2010.

SNYDER, CHRISTOPHER RYAN (CHRIS)
Born, Houston, Texas, February 12, 1981.
Bats Right. Throws Right. Height, 6 feet, 3 inches. Weight, 245 pounds.

Year	Club	Lea	Pos	G	AB	R	H	2B	3B	HR	RBI	SB	Avg
2002 Lancaster	Calif.	C	60	217	32	56	16	0	9	44	0	.258
2003 Lancaster	Calif.	C	69	245	53	77	16	2	10	53	0	.314
2003 El Paso	Texas	C	53	188	21	38	14	0	4	26	0	.202
2004 El Paso	Texas	C-1B	99	346	66	104	31	0	15	57	3	.301
2004 Arizona.	N.L.	C	29	96	10	23	6	0	5	15	0	.240
2005 Arizona.	N.L.	C	115	326	24	66	14	0	6	28	0	.202
2006 Arizona.	N.L.	C	61	184	19	51	9	0	6	32	0	.277
2007 Arizona.	N.L.	C-1B-OF	110	326	37	82	20	0	13	47	0	.252
2008 Visalia	Calif.	C	1	5	1	2	0	0	1	4	0	.400
2008 Arizona a	N.L.	C	115	334	47	79	22	1	16	64	0	.237
2009 Visalia	Calif.	C	3	7	1	1	0	0	0	0	0	.143
2009 Reno	P.C.	C	3	13	2	4	1	0	1	4	0	.308
2009 Arizona b	N.L.	C-1B	61	165	20	33	7	0	6	22	0	.200
2010 Arizona-Pittsburgh c . . .	N.L.	C	105	319	34	66	9	0	15	48	0	.207
2011 Bradenton	Fla.St.	C	6	20	6	8	2	0	1	8	0	.400
2011 Pittsburgh d-e	N.L.	C	34	96	13	26	3	0	3	17	0	.271
Major League Totals		8 Yrs.	630	1846	204	426	90	1	70	273	0	.231
Division Series													
2007 Arizona.	N.L.	C	3	7	2	1	0	0	0	0	0	.143
Championship Series													
2007 Arizona.	N.L.	C	3	12	1	4	2	0	1	3	0	.333

a On disabled list from July 1 to July 20, 2008.
b On disabled list from June 21 to July 28 and August 27 to October 15, 2009.
c Traded to Pittsburgh Pirates with infielder Pedro Ciriaco and cash for infielder Bobby Crosby, outfielder Ryan Church and pitcher D.J. Carrasco, July 31, 2010.
d On disabled list from March 25 to April 14 and June 9 to October 31, 2011.
e Filed for free agency, October 31, 2011.

SORIANO, ALFONSO GUILLEARD
Born, San Pedro de Macoris, Dominican Republic, January 7, 1976.
Bats Right. Throws Right. Height, 6 feet, 1 inch. Weight, 180 pounds.

Year	Club	Lea	Pos	G	AB	R	H	2B	3B	HR	RBI	SB	Avg
1995 Hiroshima	Dominican	SS	63	227	52	83	12	3	4	55	8	.366
1996 Hiroshima	Japan East	SS	57	131	11	28	0	0	0	13	0	.214
1997 Hiroshima	Japan Cent.	SS	9	17	2	2	0	0	0	2	0	.118
1998 a			Did Not Play									
1999 Norwich	Eastern	SS	89	361	57	110	20	3	15	68	24	.305
1999 Yankees	Gulf Coast	SS	5	19	7	5	2	0	1	5	0	.263
1999 Columbus.	Int.	SS	20	82	8	15	5	1	2	11	1	.183
1999 New York b	A.L.	SS	9	8	2	1	0	0	1	1	0	.125
2000 Columbus.	Int.	SS-2B	111	459	90	133	32	6	12	66	14	.290
2000 New York	A.L.	3B-SS-2B	22	50	5	9	3	0	2	3	2	.180
2001 New York	A.L.	2B	158	574	77	154	34	3	18	73	43	.268
2002 New York	A.L.	2B	156	*696	*128	*209	51	2	39	102	41	.300
2003 New York	A.L.	2B	156	*682	114	198	36	5	38	91	35	.290
2004 Texas c-d	A.L.	2B	145	608	77	170	32	4	28	91	18	.280
2005 Texas e	A.L.	2B	156	637	102	171	43	2	36	104	30	.268
2006 Washington f	N.L.	OF	159	647	119	179	41	2	46	95	41	.277
2007 Chicago g	N.L.	OF-2B	135	579	97	173	42	5	33	70	19	.299
2008 Azl Cubs	Arizona	DH	1	2	1	0	0	0	0	0	0	.000
2008 Iowa.	P.C.	OF	1	3	0	1	0	0	0	0	0	.333
2008 Chicago h	N.L.	OF-2B	109	453	76	127	27	0	29	75	19	.280
2009 Chicago i	N.L.	OF-2B-3B	117	477	64	115	25	1	20	55	9	.241
2010 Chicago	N.L.	OF	147	496	67	128	40	3	24	79	5	.258
2011 Iowa	P.C.	OF	3	13	3	1	0	0	0	0	0	.077
2011 Chicago j	N.L.	OF	137	475	50	116	27	1	26	88	2	.244
Major League Totals		13 Yrs.	1606	6382	978	1750	401	28	340	927	264	.274

Year	Club	Lea	Pos	G	AB	R	H	2B	3B	HR	RBI	SB	Avg
Division Series													
2001 New York	A.L.	2B	5	18	2	4	0	0	0	3	2	.222
2002 New York	A.L.	2B	4	17	2	2	1	0	1	2	1	.118
2003 New York	A.L.	2B	4	19	2	7	1	0	0	4	2	.368
2007 Chicago	N.L.	OF	3	14	0	2	0	0	0	0	0	.143
2008 Chicago	N.L.	OF	3	14	0	1	0	0	0	0	0	.071
Division Series Totals			19	82	6	16	2	0	1	9	5	.195
Championship Series													
2001 New York	A.L.	2B	5	15	5	6	0	0	1	2	2	.500
2003 New York	A.L.	2B	7	30	0	4	1	0	0	3	2	.133
Championship Series Totals			12	45	5	10	1	0	1	5	4	.222
World Series Record													
2001 New York	A.L.	2B	7	25	1	6	0	0	1	2	0	.240
2003 New York	A.L.	2B-OF	6	22	2	5	0	0	1	2	1	.227
World Series Totals			13	47	3	11	0	0	2	4	1	.234

a Signed by New York Yankees as free agent, September 29, 1998.

b On disabled list from July 15 to August 15, 1999.

c Traded to Texas Rangers with player to be named later for infielder Alex Rodriguez, February 16, 2004.

d Texas Rangers received infielder Joaquin Arias to complete trade, March 23, 2004.

e Traded to Washington Nationals for outfielder Brad Wilkerson, outfielder Terrmel Sledge and pitcher Armando Galarraga, December 13, 2005.

f Filed for free agency, October 29, 2006. Signed with Chicago Cubs, November 20, 2006.

g On disabled list from August 6 to August 28, 2007.

h On disabled list from April 16 to May 1 and June 12 to July 23, 2008.

i On disabled list from September 4 to October 14, 2009.

j On disabled list from May 31 to June 15, 2011.

SOTO, GEOVANY

Born, San Juan, Puerto Rico, January 20, 1983.
Bats Right. Throws Right. Height, 6 feet, 1 inch. Weight, 230 pounds.

Year	Club	Lea	Pos	G	AB	R	H	2B	3B	HR	RBI	SB	Avg
2001 Cubs	Arizona	C-1B-3B-OF	41	150	18	39	16	0	1	20	1	.260
2002 Cubs	Arizona	C-1B	44	156	24	42	10	2	3	24	0	.269
2002 Boise	Northwest	C	1	5	1	2	0	0	0	0	0	.400
2003 Daytona	Fla.St.	C-3B	89	297	26	72	12	2	2	38	0	.242
2004 West Tenn	Southern	C-1B	104	332	47	90	16	0	9	48	1	.271
2005 Iowa	P.C.	C	91	292	30	74	14	0	4	39	0	.253
2005 Chicago	N.L.	PH	1	0	0	0	0	0	0	0	0	.000
2006 Iowa	P.C.	C	108	342	34	93	21	0	6	38	0	.272
2006 Chicago	N.L.	C	11	25	1	5	1	0	0	2	0	.200
2007 Iowa	P.C.	C-1B	110	385	75	136	31	3	26	109	0	.353
2007 Chicago	N.L.	C	18	54	12	21	6	0	3	8	0	.389
2008 Chicago a	N.L.	C	141	494	66	141	35	2	23	86	0	.285
2009 Azl Cubs	Arizona	DH	1	3	0	1	1	0	0	2	0	.333
2009 Tennessee	Southern	C	3	9	2	3	0	0	2	4	0	.333
2009 Chicago b	N.L.	C	102	331	27	72	19	1	11	47	1	.218
2010 Chicago c	N.L.	C	105	322	47	90	19	0	17	53	0	.280
2011 Tennessee	Southern	C	2	7	0	0	0	0	0	0	0	.000
2011 Chicago d	N.L.	C	125	421	46	96	26	0	17	54	0	.228
Major League Totals		7 Yrs.	503	1648	199	425	106	3	71	250	1	.258
Division Series													
2007 Chicago	N.L.	C	2	6	1	1	0	0	1	2	0	.167
2008 Chicago	N.L.	C	3	11	0	2	1	0	0	0	0	.182
Division Series Totals			5	17	1	3	1	0	1	2	0	.176

a Selected Rookie of the Year in National League for 2008.

b On disabled list from July 7 to August 7, 2009.

c On disabled list from August 7 to August 23 and September 19 to October 6, 2010.

d On disabled list from May 11 to May 29, 2011.

SPAN, KEIUNTA DENARD (DENARD)

Born, Tampa, Florida, February 17, 1984.
Bats Left. Throws Left. Height, 6 feet. Weight, 205 pounds.

Year	Club	Lea	Pos	G	AB	R	H	2B	3B	HR	RBI	SB	Avg
2003 Elizabethton	Appal.	OF	50	207	34	56	5	1	1	18	14	.271
2004 Twins	Gulf Coast	OF	5	16	1	6	2	0	0	1	0	.375
2004 Quad Cities	Midwest	OF	64	240	29	64	4	3	0	14	15	.267

166

Year	Club	Lea	Pos	G	AB	R	H	2B	3B	HR	RBI	SB	Avg
2005 New Britain		Eastern	OF	68	267	47	76	6	5	0	26	10	.285
2005 Fort Myers		Fla.St.	OF	49	186	38	63	3	3	1	19	13	.339
2006 New Britain		Eastern	OF	134	536	80	153	16	6	2	45	24	.285
2007 Rochester		Int.	OF	139	487	59	130	20	7	3	55	25	.267
2008 Rochester		Int.	OF	40	156	32	53	11	1	3	14	15	.340
2008 Minnesota		A.L.	OF	93	347	70	102	16	7	6	47	18	.294
2009 Rochester		Int.	OF	2	6	1	2	1	0	0	0	1	.333
2009 Minnesota a		A.L.	OF	145	578	97	180	16	*10	8	68	23	.311
2010 Minnesota		A.L.	OF	153	629	85	166	24	10	3	58	26	.264
2011 Rochester		Int.	OF	10	39	4	8	1	0	0	2	3	.205
2011 Minnesota b		A.L.	OF	70	284	37	75	11	5	2	16	6	.264
Major League Totals	4 Yrs.			461	1838	289	523	67	32	19	189	73	.285
Division Series													
2009 Minnesota		A.L.	OF	3	15	1	6	1	0	0	1	1	.400
2010 Minnesota		A.L.	OF	3	13	0	4	0	0	0	0	0	.308
Division Series Totals				6	28	1	10	1	0	0	1	1	.357

a On disabled list from June 10 to June 25, 2009.
b On disabled list from June 10 to June 23 and June 23 to August 2 and August 14 to September 21, 2011.

SPILBORGHS, RYAN ADAM

Born, Santa Barbara, California, September 5, 1979.
Bats Right. Throws Right. Height, 6 feet, 1 inch. Weight, 190 pounds.

Year	Club	Lea	Pos	G	AB	R	H	2B	3B	HR	RBI	SB	Avg
2002 Tri-City		Northwest	OF	71	261	34	60	11	1	4	34	11	.230
2003 Asheville		So.Atl.	OF	119	434	78	122	22	2	15	61	10	.281
2004 Visalia		Calif.	OF-SS	125	444	59	115	26	3	8	57	8	.259
2005 Tulsa		Texas	OF	71	255	52	87	23	3	6	54	10	.341
2005 Colorado		N.L.	OF	1	4	0	2	0	0	0	1	0	.500
2005 Colorado Springs a		P.C.	OF	60	227	49	77	23	5	5	30	7	.339
2006 Colorado Springs		P.C.	OF	68	269	50	91	20	1	5	34	8	.338
2006 Colorado		N.L.	OF	67	167	26	48	6	3	4	21	5	.287
2007 Colorado Springs		P.C.	OF-1B	34	124	25	40	7	1	5	17	4	.323
2007 Colorado		N.L.	OF	97	264	40	79	14	1	11	51	4	.299
2008 Colorado Springs		P.C.	OF	11	30	9	9	1	0	1	4	0	.300
2008 Colorado b		N.L.	OF	89	233	38	73	14	2	6	36	7	.313
2009 Colorado		N.L.	OF	133	352	55	85	24	3	8	48	9	.241
2010 Colorado		N.L.	OF	134	341	41	95	20	2	10	39	4	.279
2011 Colorado Springs		P.C.	OF	10	45	8	20	3	0	3	10	0	.444
2011 Colorado c-d		N.L.	OF	98	200	22	42	8	1	3	22	2	.210
Major League Totals	7 Yrs.			619	1561	222	424	86	12	42	218	31	.272
Division Series													
2007 Colorado		N.L.	OF	3	8	2	2	0	0	0	0	0	.250
2009 Colorado		N.L.	OF	4	9	1	2	1	0	0	0	0	.222
Division Series Totals				7	17	3	4	1	0	0	0	0	.235
Championship Series													
2007 Colorado		N.L.	OF	2	2	1	1	0	0	0	0	0	.500
World Series Record													
2007 Colorado		N.L.	OF-DH	4	10	0	0	0	0	0	0	0	.000

a Not offered contract, December 21, 2005, re-signed with Colorado Rockies organization, December 22, 2005.
b On disabled list from July 9 to September 1, 2008.
c On disabled list from August 6 to September 2 and September 11 to October 31, 2011.
d Not offered contract, December 12, 2011.

STAIRS, MATTHEW WADE (MATT)

Born, St. John, New Brunswick, Canada, February 27, 1969.
Bats Left. Throws Right. Height, 5 feet, 9 inches. Weight, 215 pounds.

Year	Club	Lea	Pos	G	AB	R	H	2B	3B	HR	RBI	SB	Avg
1989 Jamestown		N.Y.Penn.	2B-3B	14	43	8	11	1	0	1	5	1	.256
1989 West Palm Bch.		Fla. St.	3B-SS-2B	36	111	12	21	3	1	1	9	0	.189
1989 Rockford		Midwest	3B	44	141	20	40	9	2	2	14	5	.284
1990 West Palm Bch.		Fla. St.	3B-SS	55	183	30	62	9	3	3	30	15	.339
1990 Jacksonville		Southern	3B-OF-2B	79	280	26	71	17	0	3	34	5	.254
1991 Harrisburg		Eastern	2B-3B-OF	129	505	87	168	30	10	13	78	23	.333
1992 Montreal		N.L.	OF	13	30	2	5	2	0	0	5	0	.167
1992 Indianapolis		A.A.	OF	110	401	57	107	23	4	11	56	11	.267
1993 Ottawa a - b		Int.	OF	34	125	18	35	4	2	3	20	4	.280
1993 Montreal		N.L.	OF	6	8	1	3	1	0	0	2	0	.375

Year	Club	Lea	Pos	G	AB	R	H	2B	3B	HR	RBI	SB	Avg
1993 Chunichi.......	Japan Cent.		OF	60	132	10	33	6	0	6	23	1	.250
1994 New Britain	Eastern		OF-1B	93	317	44	98	25	2	9	61	10	.309
1995 Pawtucket	Int.		OF	75	271	40	77	17	0	13	56	3	.284
1995 Boston c............	A.L.		OF	39	88	8	23	7	1	1	17	0	.261
1996 Edmonton	P.C.	DH-OF-1B	51	180	35	62	16	1	8	41	0	.344	
1996 Oakland	A.L.		OF-1B	61	137	21	38	5	1	10	23	1	.277
1997 Oakland	A.L.		OF-1B	133	352	62	105	19	0	27	73	3	.298
1998 Oakland	A.L.	DH-OF-1B	149	523	88	154	33	1	26	106	8	.294	
1999 Oakland	A.L.		OF-1B	146	531	94	137	26	3	38	102	2	.258
2000 Oakland d...........	A.L.		OF-1B	143	476	74	108	26	0	21	81	5	.227
2001 Chicago e...........	N.L.	1B-OF-2B	128	340	48	85	21	0	17	61	2	.250	
2002 Milwaukee f-g	N.L.		OF	107	270	41	66	15	0	16	41	2	.244
2003 Nashville	P.C.		OF-1B	7	18	4	3	0	0	2	3	0	.167
2003 Pittsburgh h-i......	N.L.		OF-1B	121	305	49	89	20	1	20	57	0	.292
2004 Kansas City j	A.L.		OF-1B	126	439	48	117	21	3	18	66	1	.267
2005 Kansas City	A.L.		1B-OF	127	396	55	109	26	1	13	66	1	.275
2006 K.C.-Texas-Detroit k-l-m.	A.L.	DH-OF-1B	117	348	42	86	21	0	13	51	0	.247	
2007 Toronto n...........	A.L.		OF-1B	125	357	58	103	28	1	21	64	2	.289
2008 Toronto	A.L.		DH-OF	105	320	42	80	11	1	11	44	1	.250
2008 Philadelphia o	N.L.		OF	16	17	4	5	1	0	2	5	0	.294
2009 Philadelphia p........	N.L.		OF	99	103	15	20	4	0	5	17	0	.194
2010 San Diego q-r........	N.L.		OF-1B	78	99	14	23	6	0	6	16	2	.232
2011 Washington s........	N.L.		1B	56	65	4	10	1	0	0	2	0	.154
Major League Totals			19 Yrs.	1895	5204	770	1366	294	13	265	899	30	.262

Division Series

Year	Club	Lea	Pos	G	AB	R	H	2B	3B	HR	RBI	SB	Avg
1995 Boston	A.L.	PH	1	1	0	0	0	0	0	0	0	.000	
2000 Oakland	A.L.	OF	3	9	0	1	1	0	0	0	0	.111	
2008 Philadelphia	N.L.	PH	2	2	0	0	0	0	0	0	0	.000	
2009 Philadelphia	N.L.	PH	2	1	0	0	0	0	0	0	0	.000	
Division Series Totals				8	13	0	1	1	0	0	0	0	.077

Championship Series

Year	Club	Lea	Pos	G	AB	R	H	2B	3B	HR	RBI	SB	Avg
2008 Philadelphia	N.L.	PH	1	1	1	1	0	0	1	2	0	1.000	
2009 Philadelphia	N.L.	PH	2	1	0	0	0	0	0	0	0	.000	
Championship Series Totals				3	2	1	1	0	0	1	2	0	.500

World Series Record

Year	Club	Lea	Pos	G	AB	R	H	2B	3B	HR	RBI	SB	Avg
2008 Philadelphia	N.L.	PH	1	1	0	0	0	0	0	0	0	.000	
2009 Philadelphia	N.L.	DH	5	8	0	1	0	0	0	1	0	.125	
World Series Totals				6	9	0	1	0	0	0	1	0	.111

a Released, June 8, 1993, played in Japan, re-signed by Montreal Expos organization, December 15, 1993.
b Sold to Boston Red Sox, February 18, 1994.
c Filed for free agency, October 14, 1995. Signed by Oakland Athletics organization, December 1, 1995.
d Traded to Chicago Cubs for pitcher Eric Ireland, November 20, 2000.
e Filed for free agency, November 5, 2001. Signed with Milwaukee Brewers, January 25, 2002.
f On disabled list from May 16 to June 3, 2002.
g Filed for free agency, October 28, 2002. Signed with Pittsburgh Pirates, December 15, 2002.
h On disabled list from May 19 to June 10, 2003.
i Filed for free agency, October 31, 2003. Signed with Kansas City Royals, December 9, 2003.
j On disabled list from August 7 to August 22, 2004.
k Traded to Texas Rangers for pitcher Joselo Diaz, July 31, 2006.
l Claimed on waivers by Detroit Tigers, September 15, 2006.
m Filed for free agency, October 30, 2006. Signed with Toronto Blue Jays organization, December 12, 2006.
n Filed for free agency, October 29, 2007, re-signed with Toronto Blue Jays, November 2, 2007.
o Traded to Philadelphia Phillies August 30, 2008. Toronto Blue Jays received pitcher Fabio Castro to complete trade, September 29, 2008.
p Filed for free agency, November 9, 2009. Signed with San Diego Padres organization, January 26, 2010.
q On disabled list from June 7 to July 1, 2010.
r Filed for free agency, November 1, 2010. Signed with Washington Nationals organization, December 14, 2010.
s Released by Washington Nationals, August 1, 2011.

STANTON, GIANCARLO CRUZ-MICHAEL (MIKE)
Born, Panorama, California, November 8, 1989.
Bats Right. Throws Right. Height, 6 feet, 5 inches. Weight, 235 pounds.

Year	Club	Lea	Pos	G	AB	R	H	2B	3B	HR	RBI	SB	Avg
2007 Marlins........	Gulf Coast		OF	8	26	6	7	2	0	0	1	0	.269
2007 Jamestown......	N.Y.-Penn.		OF	9	30	2	2	1	0	1	2	0	.067
2008 Greensboro	So.Atl.		OF	125	468	89	137	26	3	39	97	4	.293
2009 Jupiter	Fla.St.		OF	50	180	27	53	9	3	12	39	2	.294
2009 Jacksonville	Southern		OF	79	299	49	69	15	2	16	53	1	.231

Year	Club	Lea	Pos	G	AB	R	H	2B	3B	HR	RBI	SB	Avg
2010 Jacksonville	Southern		OF	53	192	42	60	13	2	21	52	1	.313
2010 Florida	N.L.		OF	100	359	45	93	21	1	22	59	5	.259
2011 Florida	N.L.		OF	150	516	79	135	30	5	34	87	5	.262
Major League Totals			2 Yrs.	250	875	124	228	51	6	56	146	10	.261

STUBBS, ANDREW ROBERT (DREW)
Born, Texarkana, Texas, October 4, 1984.
Bats Right. Throws Right. Height, 6 feet, 4 inches. Weight, 205 pounds.

Year	Club	Lea	Pos	G	AB	R	H	2B	3B	HR	RBI	SB	Avg
2006 Billings	Pioneer		OF	56	210	39	53	7	3	6	24	19	.252
2007 Dayton	Midwest		OF	129	497	93	134	29	5	12	43	23	.270
2008 Sarasota	Fla.St.		OF	86	303	49	79	21	4	5	38	27	.261
2008 Louisville	Int.		OF	19	75	14	22	4	2	2	10	3	.293
2008 Chattanooga	Southern		OF	26	92	12	29	8	0	0	9	3	.315
2009 Louisville	Int.		OF	107	411	57	110	25	2	3	39	46	.268
2009 Cincinnati	N.L.		OF	42	180	27	48	5	1	8	17	10	.267
2010 Cincinnati	N.L.		OF	150	514	91	131	19	6	22	77	30	.255
2011 Cincinnati	N.L.		OF	158	604	92	147	22	3	15	44	40	.243
Major League Totals			3 Yrs.	350	1298	210	326	46	10	45	138	80	.251
Division Series													
2010 Cincinnati	N.L.		OF	3	9	0	1	0	0	0	0	0	.111

SUZUKI, ICHIRO
Born, Kasugai, Japan, October 22, 1973.
Bats Left. Throws Right. Height, 5 feet, 9 inches. Weight, 170 pounds.

Year	Club	Lea	Pos	G	AB	R	H	2B	3B	HR	RBI	SB	Avg
1992 Orix	Japan Pac.		OF	40	95	9	24	5	0	0	5	3	.253
1993 Orix	Japan Pac.		OF	43	64	4	12	2	0	1	2	0	.188
1994 Orix	Japan Pac.		OF	130	546	111	210	41	5	13	54	29	.385
1995 Orix	Japan Pac.		OF	130	524	104	179	23	4	25	80	49	.342
1996 Orix	Japan Pac.		OF	130	542	104	193	24	4	16	84	35	.356
1997 Orix	Japan Pac.		OF	135	536	94	185	31	4	17	91	39	.345
1998 Orix	Japan Pac.		OF	135	506	79	181	36	3	13	71	11	.358
1999 Orix	Japan Pac.		OF	103	411	80	141	27	2	21	68	12	.343
2000 Orix a	Japan Pac.		OF	105	395	73	153	22	1	12	73	21	.387
2001 Seattle b-c	A.L.		OF	157	*692	127	*242	34	8	8	69	*56	*.350
2002 Seattle	A.L.		OF	157	647	111	208	27	8	8	51	31	.321
2003 Seattle	A.L.		OF	159	679	111	212	29	8	13	62	34	.312
2004 Seattle	A.L.		OF	161	*704	101	*262	24	5	8	60	36	*.372
2005 Seattle	A.L.		OF	*162	679	111	206	21	12	15	68	33	.303
2006 Seattle	A.L.		OF	161	*695	110	*224	20	9	9	49	45	.322
2007 Seattle	A.L.		OF	161	*678	111	*238	22	7	6	68	37	.351
2008 Seattle	A.L.		OF	162	*686	103	*213	20	7	6	42	43	.310
2009 Seattle d	A.L.		OF	146	639	88	*225	31	4	11	46	26	.352
2010 Seattle	A.L.		OF	*162	*680	74	*214	30	3	6	43	42	.315
2011 Seattle	A.L.		OF	*161	*677	80	184	22	3	5	47	40	.272
Major League Totals			11 Yrs.	1749	7456	1127	2428	280	74	95	605	423	.326
Division Series													
2001 Seattle	A.L.		OF	5	20	4	12	1	0	0	2	1	.600
Championship Series													
2001 Seattle	A.L.		OF	5	18	3	4	1	0	0	1	2	.222

a Signed by Seattle Mariners as free agent, November 18, 2000.
b Selected Rookie of the Year in American League for 2001.
c Selected Most Valuable Player in American League for 2001.
d On disabled list from March 31 to April 15, 2009.

SUZUKI, KURT KIYOSHI
Born, Wailuku, Hawaii, October 4, 1983.
Bats Right. Throws Right. Height, 6 feet. Weight, 205 pounds.

Year	Club	Lea	Pos	G	AB	R	H	2B	3B	HR	RBI	SB	Avg
2004 Vancouver	Northwest		C	46	175	27	52	10	3	3	31	0	.297
2005 Stockton	Calif.		C	114	441	85	122	26	5	12	65	5	.277
2006 Midland	Texas		C-1B	99	376	64	107	26	1	7	55	5	.285
2007 Sacramento	P.C.		C	55	211	32	59	9	0	3	27	0	.280
2007 Oakland	A.L.		C	68	213	27	53	13	0	7	39	0	.249
2008 Oakland	A.L.		C	148	530	54	148	25	1	7	42	2	.279
2009 Oakland	A.L.		C	147	570	74	156	37	1	15	88	8	.274

Year	Club	Lea	Pos	G	AB	R	H	2B	3B	HR	RBI	SB	Avg
2010 Sacramento	. . . .	P.C.	C	3	8	4	3	2	0	1	5	0	.375
2010 Oakland a	. . . .	A.L.	C	131	495	55	120	18	2	13	71	3	.242
2011 Oakland	. . . .	A.L.	C	134	460	54	109	26	0	14	44	2	.237
Major League Totals	. . . .		5 Yrs.	628	2268	264	586	119	4	56	284	15	.258

a On disabled list from April 24 to May 16, 2010.

SWEENEY, RYAN JOSEPH

Born, Cedar Rapids, Iowa, February 20, 1985.
Bats Left. Throws Left. Height, 6 feet, 4 inches. Weight, 200 pounds.

Year	Club	Lea	Pos	G	AB	R	H	2B	3B	HR	RBI	SB	Avg
2003 Bristol	. . . .	Appal.	OF	19	67	11	21	3	0	2	5	3	.313
2003 Great Falls	. . . .	Pioneer	OF	10	34	0	12	2	0	0	4	0	.353
2004 Winston-Salem	. . . .	Carolina	OF	134	515	71	146	22	3	7	66	8	.283
2005 Birmingham	. . . . . .	Southern	OF	113	429	64	128	22	3	1	47	6	.298
2006 Charlotte	. . . .	Int.	OF	118	449	64	133	25	3	13	70	7	.296
2006 Chicago	. . . .	A.L.	OF	18	35	1	8	0	0	0	5	0	.229
2007 Chicago	. . . .	A.L.	OF	15	45	5	9	3	0	1	5	0	.200
2007 Charlotte	. . . .	Int.	OF	105	397	50	107	17	2	10	47	8	.270
2008 Azl Athletics	. . . .	Arizona	DH	1	3	0	0	0	0	0	0	0	.000
2008 Sacramento	. . . .	P.C.	OF	8	34	5	14	4	0	1	5	0	.412
2008 Oakland a-b	. . . .	A.L.	OF	115	384	53	110	18	2	5	45	9	.286
2009 Oakland c	. . . .	A.L.	OF	134	484	68	142	31	3	6	53	6	.293
2010 Oakland d	. . . .	A.L.	OF	82	303	41	89	20	2	1	36	1	.294
2011 Oakland e	. . . .	A.L.	OF	108	264	34	70	11	3	1	25	1	.265
Major League Totals	. . . .		6 Yrs.	472	1515	202	428	83	10	14	169	17	.283

a Traded to Oakland Athletics with pitcher Gio Gonzalez and pitcher Fautino de los Santos for outfielder Nick Swisher, January 3, 2008.

b On disabled list from May 29 to June 13 and August 13 to August 28, 2008.

c On disabled list from June 3 to June 18, 2009.

d On disabled list from July 12 to November 4, 2010.

e Traded to Boston Red Sox with pitcher Andrew Bailey for outfielder Josh Reddick, infielder Miles Head and pitcher Raul Alcantara, December 28, 2011.

SWISHER, NICHOLAS THOMPSON (NICK)

Born, Columbus, Ohio, January 25, 1980.
Bats Both. Throws Left. Height, 6 feet. Weight, 215 pounds.

Year	Club	Lea	Pos	G	AB	R	H	2B	3B	HR	RBI	SB	Avg
2002 Visalia	. . . .	California	OF	49	183	22	44	13	2	4	23	3	.240
2002 Vancouver	. . . . . .	Northwest	OF	13	44	10	11	3	0	2	12	3	.250
2003 Modesto	. . . .	California	OF-1B	51	189	38	56	14	2	10	43	0	.296
2003 Midland	. . . .	Texas	OF-1B	76	287	36	66	24	2	5	43	0	.230
2004 Sacramento	. . . .	P.C.	OF-1B	125	443	109	119	28	2	29	92	3	.269
2004 Oakland	. . . .	A.L.	OF-1B	20	60	11	15	4	0	2	8	0	.250
2005 Sacramento	. . . .	P.C.	OF-1B	6	23	4	9	3	0	0	1	0	.391
2005 Oakland a	. . . .	A.L.	OF-1B	131	462	66	109	32	1	21	74	0	.236
2006 Oakland	. . . .	A.L.	1B-OF	157	556	106	141	24	2	35	95	1	.254
2007 Oakland b	. . . .	A.L.	OF-1B	150	539	84	141	36	1	22	78	3	.262
2008 Chicago c	. . . .	A.L.	OF-1B	153	497	86	109	21	1	24	69	3	.219
2009 New York	. . . .	A.L.	OF-1B-P	150	498	84	124	35	1	29	82	0	.249
2010 New York	. . . .	A.L.	OF-1B	150	566	91	163	33	3	29	89	1	.288
2011 New York	. . . .	A.L.	OF-1B	150	526	81	137	30	0	23	85	2	.260
Major League Totals	. . . .		8 Yrs.	1061	3704	609	939	215	9	185	580	10	.254
Division Series													
2006 Oakland	. . . .	A.L.	1B	3	10	3	3	2	0	0	1	0	.300
2008 Chicago	. . . .	A.L.	OF-1B	3	4	1	1	0	0	0	0	0	.250
2009 New York	. . . .	A.L.	OF	3	12	0	1	1	0	0	1	0	.083
2010 New York	. . . .	A.L.	OF	3	12	3	4	2	0	1	1	0	.333
2011 New York	. . . .	A.L.	OF	5	19	1	4	0	0	1	1	0	.211
Division Series Totals	. . . .			17	57	8	13	5	0	2	4	0	.228
Championship Series													
2006 Oakland	. . . .	A.L.	1B	4	10	0	1	0	0	0	0	0	.100
2009 New York	. . . .	A.L.	OF	6	20	2	3	0	0	0	0	0	.150
2010 New York	. . . .	A.L.	OF-1B	6	22	3	2	1	0	1	1	0	.091
Championship Series Totals	. . . . . .			16	52	5	6	1	0	1	1	0	.115
World Series Record													
2009 New York	. . . .	A.L.	OF	5	15	3	2	1	0	1	1	0	.133

b Traded to Chicago White Sox for pitcher Gio Gonzalez, pitcher Fautino de los Santos and outfielder Ryan Sweeney, January 3, 2008.
c Traded to New York Yankees with pitcher Kaneoka Texeira for infielder Wilson Betemit, pitcher Jeff Marquez and pitcher Jhonny Nunez, November 13, 2008.

TABATA, JOSE NICOLAS
Born, El Tigre, Venezuela, August 12, 1988.
Bats Right. Throws Right. Height, 5 feet, 11 inches. Weight, 210 pounds.

Year	Club	Lea	Pos	G	AB	R	H	2B	3B	HR	RBI	SB	Avg
2005 Yankees	Gulf Coast	OF	44	156	30	49	5	1	3	25	22	.314
2006 Charleston	So.Atl.	OF	86	319	50	95	22	1	5	51	15	.298
2007 Tampa	.Fla.St.	OF	103	411	56	126	16	2	5	54	15	.307
2008 Altoona...........	.Eastern	OF	22	89	16	31	6	2	3	13	8	.348
2008 Trenton...........	.Eastern	OF	79	294	40	73	9	0	3	36	10	.248
2008 Pirates a.........	Gulf Coast	OF	4	11	4	5	1	0	2	7	0	.455
2009 Altoona..........	.Eastern	OF	61	228	31	69	15	1	2	25	7	.303
2009 Indianapolis	Int.	OF	32	134	21	37	7	1	3	10	4	.276
2010 Indianapolis	Int.	OF	53	224	42	69	13	2	3	19	25	.308
2010 Pittsburgh	N.L.	OF	102	405	61	121	21	4	4	35	19	.299
2011 Bradenton	.Fla.St.	OF	4	8	1	1	1	0	0	1	0	.125
2011 Indianapolis	Int.	OF	9	33	6	11	6	0	0	2	0	.333
2011 Pittsburgh b.........	N.L.	OF	91	334	53	89	18	1	4	21	16	.266
Major League Totals		2 Yrs.	193	739	114	210	39	5	8	56	35	.284

a Traded by New York Yankees to Pittsburgh Pirates with pitcher Ross Ohlendorf, pitcher Jeff Karstens and pitcher Dan McCutchen for outfielder Xavier Nady and pitcher Damaso Marte, July 26, 2008.
b On disabled list from June 27 to August 16, 2011.

TEAHEN, MARK THOMAS
Born, Redlands, California, September 6, 1981.
Bats Left. Throws Right. Height, 6 feet, 3 inches. Weight, 220 pounds.

Year	Club	Lea	Pos	G	AB	R	H	2B	3B	HR	RBI	SB	Avg
2002 Modesto.....	California	3B	59	234	25	56	9	1	1	26	1	.239
2002 Vancouver ...	Northwest	3B	13	57	10	23	5	1	0	6	4	.404
2003 Modesto.....	California	3B	121	453	68	128	27	4	3	71	4	.283
2004 Omaha.........	P.C.	3B	66	246	33	69	15	1	8	31	0	.280
2004 Sacramento	P.C.	3B	20	69	9	19	8	0	0	10	0	.275
2004 Midland a.......	Texas	3B	53	197	31	66	15	4	6	36	0	.335
2005 Omaha.........	P.C.	3B	8	27	4	7	2	0	0	4	0	.259
2005 Kansas City b......	A.L.	3B	130	447	60	110	29	4	7	55	7	.246
2006 Omaha.........	P.C.	3B	24	79	14	30	8	4	2	14	0	.380
2006 Kansas City	A.L.	3B	109	393	70	114	21	7	18	69	10	.290
2007 Kansas City c......	A.L.	OF-1B	144	544	78	155	31	8	7	60	13	.285
2008 Kansas City ......A.L.		OF-3B-1B	149	572	66	146	31	4	15	59	4	.255
2009 Kansas City d......	A.L.	3B-OF-1B-2B	144	524	69	142	34	1	12	50	8	.271
2010 Charlotte	Int.	3B-OF-1B	11	33	7	12	2	0	0	4	0	.364
2010 Chicago e.........	A.L.	3B-OF-1B	77	233	31	60	13	2	4	25	3	.258
2011 Charlotte ...	Int.	3B-1B-OF	8	31	1	6	1	0	0	3	0	.194
2011 Chicago-Toronto f-g A.L.		3B-1B-OF	78	160	14	32	4	0	4	14	0	.200
Major League Totals		7 Yrs.	831	2873	388	759	163	26	67	332	45	.264

a Traded by Oakland Athletics to Kansas City Royals with pitcher Mike Wood for pitcher Octavio Dotel and cash, June 24, 2004.
b On disabled list from April 12 to May 3, 2005.
c On disabled list from August 19 to September 3, 2007.
d Traded to Chicago White Sox for infielder Josh Fields and infielder Chris Getz, November 6, 2009.
e On disabled list from May 31 to August 13, 2010.
f On disabled list from May 12 to June 5, 2011.
g Traded to Toronto Blue Jays with pitcher Edwin Jackson for pitcher Jason Frasor and pitcher Zach Stewart, July 27, 2011.

TEIXEIRA, MARK CHARLES
Born, Annapolis, Maryland, April 11, 1980.
Bats Both. Throws Right. Height, 6 feet, 3 inches. Weight, 220 pounds.

Year	Club	Lea	Pos	G	AB	R	H	2B	3B	HR	RBI	SB	Avg
2002 Charlotte	.Fla.St.	3B	38	150	32	48	10	2	9	41	2	.320
2002 Tulsa	Texas	3B	48	171	31	54	11	3	10	28	3	.316
2003 Texas	A.L.	1B-OF-3B	146	529	66	137	29	5	26	84	1	.259
2004 Frisco..............	Texas	1B	1	3	0	0	0	0	0	0	0	.000

Year	Club	Lea	Pos	G	AB	R	H	2B	3B	HR	RBI	SB	Avg
2004 Texas a	A.L.	1B-OF	145	545	101	153	34	2	38	112	4	.281
2005 Texas	A.L.	1B	*162	644	112	194	41	3	43	144	4	.301
2006 Texas	A.L.	1B	*162	628	99	177	45	1	33	110	2	.282
2007 Frisco	Texas	1B	1	2	0	0	0	0	0	0	0	.000
2007 Texas	A.L.	1B	78	286	48	85	24	1	13	49	0	.297
2007 Atlanta b-c	N.L.	1B	54	208	38	66	9	1	17	56	0	.317
2008 Atlanta	N.L.	1B	103	381	63	108	27	0	20	78	0	.283
2008 Los Angeles d-e	A.L.	1B	54	193	39	69	14	0	13	43	2	.358
2009 New York	A.L.	1B	156	609	103	178	43	3	*39	*122	2	.292
2010 New York	A.L.	1B	158	601	*113	154	36	0	33	108	0	.256
2011 New York	A.L.	1B	156	589	90	146	26	1	39	111	4	.248
Major League Totals		9 Yrs.	1374	5213	872	1467	328	17	314	1017	19	.281
Division Series												
2008 Los Angeles	A.L.	1B	4	15	4	7	0	0	0	1	0	.467
2009 New York	A.L.	1B	3	12	3	2	0	0	1	1	0	.167
2010 New York	A.L.	1B	3	13	2	4	1	0	1	3	0	.308
2011 New York	A.L.	1B	5	18	2	3	2	0	0	1	0	.167
Division Series Totals			15	58	11	16	3	0	2	6	0	.276
Championship Series												
2009 New York	A.L.	1B	6	27	2	6	1	0	0	4	0	.222
2010 New York	A.L.	1B	4	14	1	0	0	0	0	0	0	.000
Championship Series Totals			10	41	3	6	1	0	0	4	0	.146
World Series Record												
2009 New York	A.L.	1B	6	22	5	3	1	0	1	3	0	.136

a On disabled list from April 13 to April 29, 2004.
b On disabled list from June 9 to July 13, 2007.
c Traded to Atlanta Braves with pitcher Ron Mahay for catcher Jarrod Saltalamacchia, infielder Elvis Andrus, pitcher Neftali Feliz, pitcher Matt Harrison and pitcher Beau James, July 31, 2007.
d Traded to Los Angeles Angels for infielder Casey Kotchman and pitcher Steve Marek, July 29, 2008.
e Filed for free agency, October 30, 2008. Signed with New York Yankees, January 6, 2009.

TEJADA, MIGUEL ODALIS

Born, Bani, Dominican Republic, May 25, 1976.
Bats Right. Throws Right. Height, 5 feet, 9 inches. Weight, 215 pounds.

Year	Club	Lea	Pos	G	AB	R	H	2B	3B	HR	RBI	SB	Avg
1994 Oakland	Dominican	2B	74	218	51	64	9	1	18	62	13	.294
1995 Sou. Oregon	Northwest	SS	74	269	45	66	15	5	8	44	19	.245
1996 Modesto	California	SS-3B	114	458	97	128	12	5	20	72	27	.279
1997 Huntsville	Southern	SS	128	502	85	138	20	3	22	97	15	.275
1997 Oakland	A.L.	SS	26	99	10	20	3	2	2	10	2	.202
1998 Edmonton	P.C.	SS	1	3	0	0	0	0	0	0	0	.000
1998 Huntsville	Southern	SS	15	52	9	17	6	0	2	7	1	.327
1998 Oakland a	A.L.	SS	105	365	53	85	20	1	11	45	5	.233
1999 Oakland	A.L.	SS	159	593	93	149	33	4	21	84	8	.251
2000 Oakland	A.L.	SS	160	607	105	167	32	1	30	115	6	.275
2001 Oakland	A.L.	SS	*162	622	107	166	31	3	31	113	11	.267
2002 Oakland b	A.L.	SS	*162	662	108	204	30	0	34	131	7	.308
2003 Oakland c	A.L.	SS	162	636	98	177	42	0	27	106	10	.278
2004 Baltimore	A.L.	SS	*162	653	107	203	40	2	34	*150	4	.311
2005 Baltimore	A.L.	SS	*162	654	89	199	*50	5	26	98	5	.304
2006 Baltimore	A.L.	SS	*162	648	99	214	37	0	24	100	6	.330
2007 Frederick	Carolina	3B	1	2	1	2	0	0	1	1	0	1.000
2007 Bowie	Eastern	SS	1	3	0	0	0	0	0	1	0	.000
2007 Baltimore d-e	A.L.	SS	133	514	72	152	19	1	18	81	2	.296
2008 Houston	N.L.	SS	158	632	92	179	38	3	13	66	7	.283
2009 Houston f	N.L.	SS	158	635	83	199	*46	1	14	86	5	.313
2010 Baltimore	A.L.	3B	97	401	40	108	16	0	7	39	0	.269
2010 San Diego g-h	N.L.	SS-3B	59	235	31	63	10	0	8	32	2	.268
2011 San Francisco i-j	N.L.	3B-SS-2B	91	322	28	77	16	0	4	26	4	.239
Major League Totals		15 Yrs.	2118	8278	1215	2362	463	23	304	1282	84	.285
Division Series												
2000 Oakland	A.L.	SS	5	20	5	7	2	0	0	1	1	.350
2001 Oakland	A.L.	SS	5	21	1	6	3	0	0	1	0	.286
2002 Oakland	A.L.	SS	5	21	3	3	1	0	1	4	0	.143
2003 Oakland	A.L.	SS	5	23	0	2	1	0	0	2	0	.087
Division Series Totals			20	85	9	18	7	0	1	8	1	.212

a On disabled list from March 31 to May 20, 1998.
b Selected Most Valuable Player in American League for 2002.

c Filed for free agency, October 27, 2003. Signed with Baltimore Orioles, December 14, 2003.
d On disabled list from June 22 to July 27, 2007.
e Traded to Houston Astros for pitcher Troy Patton, outfielder Luke Scott, pitcher Matt Albers, pitcher Dennis Sarfate and infielder Michael Costanzo, December 12, 2007.
f Filed for free agency, November 6, 2009. Signed with Baltimore Orioles, January 26, 2010.
g Traded to San Diego Padres with cash for pitcher Wynn Pelzer, July 29, 2010.
h Filed for free agency, November 1, 2010. Signed with San Francisco Giants, November 30, 2010.
i On disabled list from July 19 to August 16, 2011.
j Released by San Francisco Giants, September 8, 2011.

TEJADA, RUBEN DARIO

Born, Veraguas, Panama, September 1, 1989.
Bats Right. Throws Right. Height, 5 feet, 11 inches. Weight, 160 pounds.

Year	Club	Lea	Pos	G	AB	R	H	2B	3B	HR	RBI	SB	Avg
2007 Mets	Gulf Coast	SS-2B	35	120	13	34	4	3	0	16	2	.283
2008 St. Lucie	Fla.St.	SS	131	497	55	114	19	4	2	37	8	.229
2009 Binghamton	Eastern	SS-2B	134	488	59	141	24	3	5	46	19	.289
2010 Buffalo	Int.	SS-2B	65	218	25	61	11	0	1	16	1	.280
2010 New York	N.L.	2B-SS	78	216	28	46	12	0	1	15	2	.213
2011 Buffalo	Int.	SS-2B	54	207	26	51	7	3	3	21	4	.246
2011 New York	N.L.	2B-SS	96	328	31	93	15	1	0	36	5	.284
Major League Totals			2 Yrs.	174	544	59	139	27	1	1	51	7	.256

THAMES, ERIC ALLYN

Born, Santa Clara, California, November 10, 1986.
Bats Left. Throws Right. Height, 6 feet, 1 inch. Weight, 205 pounds.

Year	Club	Lea	Pos	G	AB	R	H	2B	3B	HR	RBI	SB	Avg
2008 a			INJURED—Did Not Play										
2009 Blue Jays	Gulf Coast	OF	7	21	4	6	3	0	0	1	0	.286
2009 Dunedin	Fla.St.	OF	52	195	33	61	15	5	3	38	1	.313
2010 New Hampshire	Eastern	OF	130	496	95	143	25	6	27	104	8	.288
2011 Las Vegas	P.C.	OF	53	210	38	74	25	4	7	45	5	.352
2011 Toronto	A.L.	OF	95	362	58	95	24	5	12	37	2	.262

a On minor league disabled list from June 19 to September 17, 2008.

THERIOT, RYAN STEWART

Born, Baton Rouge, Louisiana, December 7, 1979.
Bats Right. Throws Right. Height, 5 feet, 11 inches. Weight, 175 pounds.

Year	Club	Lea	Pos	G	AB	R	H	2B	3B	HR	RBI	SB	Avg
2001 Daytona	Fla.St.	SS	30	103	20	21	5	0	0	9	2	.204
2002 Lansing	Midwest	2B-SS	130	489	75	123	19	4	1	37	32	.252
2003 Lansing	Midwest	2B-SS	58	220	29	57	8	1	1	17	21	.259
2003 West Tenn	Southern	SS	53	178	20	42	3	0	1	9	9	.236
2004 Daytona	Fla.St.	2B-SS-3B	103	330	47	90	14	3	1	34	13	.273
2005 West Tenn	Southern	2B-SS-3B	120	448	52	136	28	4	1	53	24	.304
2005 Chicago	N.L.	2B	9	13	3	2	1	0	0	0	0	.154
2006 Iowa	P.C.	SS-2B-OF-3B	73	280	41	85	11	5	0	22	14	.304
2006 Chicago	N.L.	2B-SS-3B	53	134	34	44	11	3	3	16	13	.328
2007 Chicago	N.L.	SS-2B-3B-OF	148	537	80	143	30	2	3	45	28	.266
2008 Chicago	N.L.	SS	149	580	85	178	19	4	1	38	22	.307
2009 Chicago	N.L.	SS	154	602	81	171	20	5	7	54	21	.284
2010 Chicago-Los Angeles a-b	N.L.	2B-SS	150	586	72	158	15	2	2	29	20	.270
2011 St. Louis c	N.L.	SS-2B	132	442	46	120	26	1	1	47	4	.271
Major League Totals			7 Yrs.	795	2894	401	816	122	17	17	229	108	.282
Division Series													
2007 Chicago	N.L.	SS	3	12	0	3	0	0	0	1	1	.250
2008 Chicago	N.L.	SS	3	11	0	3	0	0	0	0	0	.273
2011 St. Louis	N.L.	2B	3	10	2	6	2	0	0	1	1	.600
Division Series Totals				9	33	2	12	2	0	0	2	2	.364
Championship Series													
2011 St. Louis	N.L.	2B	4	10	0	1	0	0	0	0	0	.100
World Series Record													
2011 St. Louis	N.L.	2B	5	13	1	1	0	0	0	2	0	.077

a Traded to Los Angeles Dodgers with pitcher Ted Lilly and cash for infielder Blake Dewitt, pitcher Kyle Smit and pitcher Brett Wallach, July 31, 2010.
b Traded to St. Louis Cardinals for pitcher Blake Hawksworth, November 30, 2010.
c Not offered contract, December 12, 2011.

THOLE, JOSHUA MICHAEL (JOSH)
Born, Breese, Illinois, October 28, 1986.
Bats Left. Throws Right. Height, 6 feet, 1 inch. Weight, 205 pounds.

Year	Club	Lea	Pos	G	AB	R	H	2B	3B	HR	RBI	SB	Avg
2005 Mets	Gulf Coast	1B-C	35	104	14	28	2	1	1	12	1	.269
2006 Kingsport	Appal.	1B-C	36	98	13	23	4	0	1	12	1	.235
2007 Savannah	So.Atl.	1B-C	117	389	46	104	17	0	0	36	4	.267
2008 St. Lucie	Fla.St.	C-1B	111	347	49	104	25	2	5	56	2	.300
2009 Binghamton	Eastern	C-1B	103	384	48	126	29	2	1	46	8	.328
2009 New York	N.L.	C	17	53	2	17	2	1	0	9	1	.321
2010 Buffalo	Int.	C	48	165	20	44	19	1	2	17	0	.267
2010 New York	N.L.	C	73	202	17	56	7	1	3	17	1	.277
2011 New York	N.L.	C	114	340	22	91	17	0	3	40	1	.268
Major League Totals		3 Yrs.	204	595	41	164	26	2	6	66	2	.276

THOME, JAMES HOWARD (JIM)
Born, Peoria, Illinois, August 27, 1970.
Bats Left. Throws Right. Height, 6 feet, 4 inches. Weight, 245 pounds.

Year	Club	Lea	Pos	G	AB	R	H	2B	3B	HR	RBI	SB	Avg
1989 Indians	Gulf Coast	SS-3B	55	186	22	44	5	3	0	22	6	.237
1990 Burlington	Appal.	3B	34	118	31	44	7	1	12	34	6	.373
1990 Kinston	Carolina	3B	33	117	19	36	4	1	4	16	4	.308
1991 Canton	Eastern	3B	84	294	47	99	20	2	5	45	8	.337
1991 Colorado Springs	P.C.	3B	41	151	20	43	7	3	2	28	0	.285
1991 Cleveland	A.L.	3B	27	98	7	25	4	2	1	9	1	.255
1992 Colorado Springs	P.C.	3B	12	48	11	15	4	1	2	14	0	.313
1992 Cleveland a	A.L.	3B	40	117	8	24	3	1	2	12	2	.205
1993 Charlotte	Int.	3B	115	410	85	136	21	4	25	*102	1	*.332
1993 Cleveland	A.L.	3B	47	154	28	41	11	0	7	22	2	.266
1994 Cleveland	A.L.	3B	98	321	58	86	20	1	20	52	3	.268
1995 Cleveland	A.L.	3B	137	452	92	142	29	3	25	73	4	.314
1996 Cleveland	A.L.	3B	151	505	122	157	28	5	38	116	2	.311
1997 Cleveland	A.L.	1B	147	496	104	142	25	0	40	102	1	.286
1998 Cleveland b	A.L.	1B	123	440	89	129	34	2	30	85	1	.293
1999 Cleveland	A.L.	1B	146	494	101	137	27	2	33	108	0	.277
2000 Cleveland	A.L.	1B	158	557	106	150	33	1	37	106	1	.269
2001 Cleveland	A.L.	1B	156	526	101	153	26	1	49	124	0	.291
2002 Cleveland c	A.L.	1B	147	480	101	146	19	2	52	118	1	.304
2003 Philadelphia	N.L.	1B	159	578	111	154	30	3	*47	131	0	.266
2004 Philadelphia	N.L.	1B	143	508	97	139	28	1	42	105	0	.274
2005 Clearwater	Fla.St.	DH	5	12	2	4	0	0	1	3	0	.333
2005 Philadelphia d-e	N.L.	1B	59	193	26	40	7	0	7	30	0	.207
2006 Chicago	A.L.	DH-1B	143	490	108	141	26	0	42	109	0	.288
2007 Charlotte	Int.	DH	5	14	2	3	1	0	0	5	0	.214
2007 Chicago f	A.L.	DH-1B	130	432	79	119	19	0	35	96	0	.275
2008 Chicago	A.L.	DH	149	503	93	123	28	0	34	90	1	.245
2009 Chicago	A.L.	DH	107	345	55	86	15	0	23	74	0	.249
2009 Los Angeles g-h	N.L.	PH	17	17	0	4	0	0	0	3	0	.235
2010 Minnesota i	A.L.	DH	108	276	48	78	16	2	25	59	0	.283
2011 Minnesota-Cleveland j-k-l	A.L.	DH-3B	93	277	32	71	16	0	15	50	0	.256
Major League Totals		21 Yrs.	2485	8259	1566	2287	444	26	604	1674	19	.277

Division Series

Year	Club	Lea	Pos	G	AB	R	H	2B	3B	HR	RBI	SB	Avg
1995 Cleveland	A.L.	3B	3	13	1	2	0	0	1	3	0	.154
1996 Cleveland	A.L.	3B	4	10	1	3	0	0	0	0	0	.300
1997 Cleveland	A.L.	1B	5	15	1	3	0	0	0	1	0	.200
1998 Cleveland	A.L.	1B-DH	4	15	2	2	0	0	2	2	0	.133
1999 Cleveland	A.L.	1B	5	17	7	6	0	0	4	10	0	.353
2001 Cleveland	A.L.	1B	5	19	2	3	0	0	1	1	0	.158
2008 Chicago	A.L.	DH	4	16	1	2	1	0	0	1	0	.125
2009 Los Angeles	N.L.	PH	3	2	0	0	0	0	0	0	0	.000
2010 Minnesota	A.L.	DH	3	10	2	1	0	0	0	0	0	.100
Division Series Totals			35	117	17	22	1	0	8	18	0	.188

Championship Series

Year	Club	Lea	Pos	G	AB	R	H	2B	3B	HR	RBI	SB	Avg
1995 Cleveland	A.L.	3B	5	15	2	4	0	0	2	5	0	.267
1997 Cleveland	A.L.	1B	6	14	3	1	0	0	0	0	0	.071
1998 Cleveland	A.L.	1B-DH	6	23	4	7	0	0	4	8	0	.304
2009 Los Angeles	N.L.	PH	2	1	0	1	0	0	0	0	0	1.000
Championship Series Totals			19	53	9	13	0	0	6	13	0	.245

Year	Club	Lea	Pos	G	AB	R	H	2B	3B	HR	RBI	SB	Avg
	World Series Record												
1995 Cleveland	A.L.		3B	6	19	1	4	1	0	1	2	0	.211
1997 Cleveland	A.L.		1B	7	28	8	8	0	1	2	4	0	.286
World Series Totals.				13	47	9	12	1	1	3	6	0	.255

a On disabled list from March 28 to May 18 and May 29 to June 15, 1992.
b On disabled list from August 8 to September 16, 1998.
c Filed for free agency, October 28, 2002. Signed with Philadelphia Phillies, December 3, 2002.
d On disabled list from May 1 to May 21 and July 1 to November 1, 2005.
e Traded to Chicago White Sox for outfielder Aaron Rowand, pitcher Dan Haigwood and player to be named later, November 25, 2005. Philadelphia Phillies received pitcher Giovany Gonzalez to complete trade, December 8, 2005.
f On disabled list from April 28 to May 20, 2007.
g Traded to Los Angeles Dodgers with cash for infielder Justin Fuller, August 31, 2009.
h Filed for free agency, November 6, 2009. Signed with Minnesota Twins, February 5, 2010.
i Filed for free agency, November 1, 2010, re-signed with Minnesota Twins, January 14, 2011.
j On disabled list from May 1 to May 23 and June 2 to June 25, 2011.
k Traded to Cleveland Indians for player to be named later, August 26, 2011.
l Filed for free agency, October 30, 2011. Signed with Philadelphia Phillies, November 12, 2011.

TOLBERT, CHRISTOPHER MATTHEW (MATT)
Born, McComb, Mississippi, May 4, 1982.
Bats Both. Throws Right. Height, 6 feet. Weight, 185 pounds.

Year	Club	Lea	Pos	G	AB	R	H	2B	3B	HR	RBI	SB	Avg
2004 Elizabethton	Appal.		2B-3B	33	104	23	32	7	2	3	18	3	.308
2005 Fort Myers	Fla.St.		2B-SS	111	417	55	111	20	6	3	46	11	.266
2006 Fort Myers	Fla.St.		2B-OF-SS-3B	40	155	20	47	6	3	4	24	7	.303
2006 New Britain	Eastern		2B-3B-SS	72	248	33	64	15	1	3	35	5	.258
2007 Rochester.	Int.		2B-3B-SS	121	417	65	122	24	7	6	53	11	.293
2008 New Britain	Eastern		SS-2B-3B-OF	14	56	6	14	3	0	0	6	3	.250
2008 Minnesota a	A.L.		3B-SS-2B	41	113	18	32	6	3	0	6	7	.283
2009 Rochester.	Int.		2B-OF-SS-3B	56	236	35	68	11	6	3	22	7	.288
2009 Minnesota	A.L.		2B-3B-SS-1B	71	198	28	46	7	1	2	19	6	.232
2010 Twins	Gulf Coast		SS-2B-3B	4	12	4	4	2	0	0	0	1	.333
2010 Rochester.	Int.		2B-SS-OF-3B	42	173	19	49	9	3	1	11	6	.283
2010 Minnesota b	A.L.		2B-3B-1B-SS	48	87	8	20	4	3	1	18	1	.230
2011 Rochester.	Int.		SS-2B	17	59	7	8	1	1	0	3	5	.136
2011 Minnesota	A.L.		2B-SS-3B	87	207	22	41	10	2	0	11	3	.198
Major League Totals		4 Yrs.		247	605	76	139	27	9	3	54	17	.230
	Division Series												
2009 Minnesota	A.L.		3B	2	5	0	1	0	0	0	0	0	.200
2010 Minnesota	A.L.		3B	1	0	0	0	0	0	0	0	0	.000
Division Series Totals				3	5	0	1	0	0	0	0	0	.200

a On disabled list from May 16 to September 2, 2008.
b On disabled list from July 3 to August 15, 2010.

TORREALBA, YORVIT ADOLFO
Born, Caracas, Venezuela, July 19, 1978.
Bats Right. Throws Right. Height, 5 feet, 11 inches. Weight, 200 pounds.

Year	Club	Lea	Pos	G	AB	R	H	2B	3B	HR	RBI	SB	Avg
1995 Bellingham	Northwest		C	26	71	2	11	3	0	0	8	0	.155
1996 San Jose	California		C	2	5	0	0	0	0	0	0	0	.000
1996 Burlington	Midwest		C	1	4	0	0	0	0	0	0	0	.000
1996 Bellingham	Northwest		C	48	150	23	40	4	0	1	10	4	.267
1997 Bakersfield	California		C	119	446	52	122	15	3	4	40	4	.274
1998 San Jose	California		C	21	70	10	20	2	0	0	10	2	.286
1998 Shreveport	Texas		C	59	196	18	46	7	0	0	13	0	.235
1998 Fresno	.P.C.		C	4	11	1	2	1	0	0	1	0	.182
1999 San Jose	California		C	19	73	10	23	3	0	2	14	0	.315
1999 Fresno	.P.C.		C	17	63	9	16	2	0	2	10	0	.254
1999 Shreveport	Texas		C	65	217	25	53	10	1	4	19	0	.244
2000 Shreveport	Texas		C	108	398	50	114	21	1	4	32	2	.286
2001 Fresno	.P.C.		C	115	394	56	108	23	3	8	36	2	.274
2001 San Francisco	N.L.		C	3	4	0	2	0	0	0	0	0	.500
2002 San Francisco	N.L.		C	53	136	17	38	10	0	2	14	0	.279
2003 San Francisco	N.L.		C-OF	66	200	22	52	10	2	4	29	1	.260
2004 San Francisco	N.L.		C	64	172	19	39	7	3	6	23	2	.227
2005 San Francisco	N.L.		C	34	93	18	21	8	0	1	7	1	.226

Year	Club	Lea	Pos	G	AB	R	H	2B	3B	HR	RBI	SB	Avg
2005 Seattle a-b	A.L.	C	42	108	14	26	4	0	2	8	0	.241
2006 Colorado Springs	P.C.	C	10	36	0	6	2	0	0	2	0	.167
2006 Colorado c	N.L.	C	65	223	23	55	16	3	7	43	4	.247
2007 Colorado d	N.L.	C	113	396	47	101	22	1	8	47	2	.255
2008 Colorado e	N.L.	C	70	236	19	58	17	0	6	31	0	.246
2009 Colorado Springs	P.C.	C-1B	4	15	1	4	0	0	0	1	0	.267
2009 Colorado f	N.L.	C	64	213	27	62	11	1	2	31	1	.291
2010 San Diego g	N.L.	C	95	325	31	88	14	0	7	37	7	.271
2011 Texas	A.L.	C	113	396	40	108	27	1	7	37	0	.273
Major League Totals		11 Yrs.	782	2502	277	650	146	12	52	309	18	.260
Division Series												
2003 San Francisco	N.L.	C	2	3	0	0	0	0	0	1	0	.000
2007 Colorado	N.L.	C	3	10	3	5	1	0	0	3	0	.500
2009 Colorado	N.L.	C	4	14	1	5	2	0	1	4	0	.357
2011 Texas	A.L.	DH	1	3	0	0	0	0	0	0	0	.000
Division Series Totals			10	30	4	10	3	0	1	8	0	.333
Championship Series												
2007 Colorado	N.L.	C	4	15	2	3	1	0	1	4	0	.200
2011 Texas	A.L.	C-DH	3	9	1	4	1	0	0	0	0	.444
Championship Series Totals			7	24	3	7	2	0	1	4	0	.292
World Series Record												
2007 Colorado	N.L.	C	4	14	0	2	0	0	0	1	0	.143
2011 Texas	A.L.	C	3	5	0	2	0	0	0	0	0	.400
World Series Totals			7	19	0	4	0	0	0	1	0	.211

a Traded to Seattle Mariners with pitcher Jesse Foppert for outfielder Randy Winn, July 31, 2005.

b Traded to Colorado Rockies for player to be named later, December 7, 2005. Seattle Mariners received pitcher Marcos Carvajal to complete trade, December 8, 2005.

c On disabled list from March 24 to June 2 and September 10 to November 1, 2006.

d Filed for free agency, October 31, 2007, re-signed with Colorado Rockies, November 29, 2007.

e On disabled list from August 26 to October 1, 2008.

f Filed for free agency, November 6, 2009. Signed with San Diego Padres, February 9, 2010.

g Filed for free agency, November 1, 2010. Signed with Texas Rangers, December 19, 2010.

TORRES, ANDRES VUNGO

Born, Aguadilla, Puerto Rico, January 26, 1978.
Bats Both. Throws Right. Height, 5 feet, 10 inches. Weight, 190 pounds.

Year	Club	Lea	Pos	G	AB	R	H	2B	3B	HR	RBI	SB	Avg
1998 Jamestown	N.Y.-Penn.	OF	48	192	28	45	2	6	1	21	13	.234
1999 West Michigan	Midwest	OF	117	407	72	96	20	5	2	34	39	.236
2000 Lakeland	Fla.St.	OF	108	398	82	118	11	11	3	33	65	.296
2000 Jacksonville	Southern	OF	14	54	3	8	0	0	0	0	2	.148
2001 Erie	Eastern	OF	64	252	54	74	16	3	1	23	19	.294
2002 Toledo	Int.	OF	115	462	80	123	17	8	4	42	42	.266
2002 Detroit	A.L.	OF	19	70	7	14	1	1	0	3	2	.200
2003 Toledo	Int.	OF	70	271	36	69	13	3	2	16	27	.255
2003 Detroit	A.L.	OF	59	168	23	37	4	3	1	9	5	.220
2004 Detroit	A.L.	OF	3	0	1	0	0	0	0	0	1	.000
2004 Charlotte	Int.	OF	87	322	49	95	11	4	8	26	23	.295
2004 Bristol a-b	Appal.	OF	6	22	8	8	0	0	1	2	5	.364
2005 Oklahoma	P.C.	OF	15	63	12	19	3	1	0	1	6	.302
2005 Texas c	A.L.	OF	8	19	2	3	1	0	0	1	1	.158
2006 Rochester	Int.	OF	116	348	46	82	17	9	2	30	19	.236
2007 Erie	Eastern	OF	85	305	53	89	15	11	6	35	17	.292
2007 Toledo d-e	Int.	OF	42	168	23	49	6	9	4	17	5	.292
2008 Iowa f	P.C.	OF	118	409	91	125	27	10	11	51	29	.306
2009 Azl Giants	Arizona	OF	3	6	1	2	1	0	0	1	1	.333
2009 San Jose	Calif.	OF	3	10	0	1	1	0	0	0	0	.100
2009 Fresno	P.C.	OF	11	43	7	13	1	1	1	2	1	.302
2009 San Francisco g	N.L.	OF	75	152	30	41	6	8	6	23	6	.270
2010 San Francisco	N.L.	OF	139	507	84	136	43	8	16	63	26	.268
2011 Fresno	P.C.	OF	13	55	10	15	2	2	4	11	1	.273
2011 San Francisco h-i	N.L.	OF	112	348	50	77	24	1	4	19	19	.221
Major League Totals		7 Yrs.	415	1264	197	308	79	21	27	118	60	.244
Division Series												
2010 San Francisco	N.L.	OF	4	16	0	2	0	0	0	0	1	.125
Championship Series												
2010 San Francisco	N.L.	OF	6	20	2	7	0	0	0	0	0	.350

Year	Club	Lea	Pos	G	AB	R	H	2B	3B	HR	RBI	SB	Avg
World Series Record													
2010 San Francisco	N.L.		OF	5	22	4	7	4	0	1	3	1	.318

a Filed for free agency, April 22, 2004. Signed with Chicago White Sox organization, April 26, 2004.
b Field for free agency, October 15, 2004. Signed with Texas Rangers organization, November 19, 2004.
c Filed for free agency, October 6, 2005. Signed with Minnesota Twins organization, December 20, 2005.
d Filed for free agency, October 15, 2006. Signed with Detroit Tigers organization, March 2, 2007.
e Filed for free agency, October 29, 2007. Signed with Chicago Cubs organization, November 20, 2007.
f Filed for free agency, November 3, 2008. Signed with San Francisco Giants organization, January 9, 2009.
g On disabled list from April 28 to May 26 July 31 to September 1, 2009.
h On disabled list from April 10 to May 10 and August 13 to August 28, 2011.
i Traded to New York Mets with pitcher Ramon Ramirez for outfielder Angel Pagan, December 7, 2011.

TOSONI, RENE MICHEAL

Born, Toronto, Ontario, Canada, July 2, 1986.
Bats Left. Throws Right. Height, 6 feet. Weight, 195 pounds.

Year	Club	Lea	Pos	G	AB	R	H	2B	3B	HR	RBI	SB	Avg
2007 Elizabethton	Appal.		OF-2B	63	236	58	71	13	4	3	31	13	.301
2007 Beloit	Midwest		OF	2	11	1	3	1	0	0	1	0	.273
2008 Twins	Gulf Coast		OF	2	6	3	4	0	0	1	3	0	.667
2008 Fort Myers	Fla.St.		OF	42	140	27	42	7	3	1	19	3	.300
2009 New Britain	Eastern		OF	122	425	64	115	25	4	15	71	8	.271
2010 New Britain	Eastern		OF-1B	52	185	22	50	8	4	4	24	3	.270
2011 Rochester	Int.		OF	73	274	30	62	14	0	6	32	4	.226
2011 Minnesota	A.L.		OF	60	172	20	35	7	1	5	22	0	.203

TREANOR, MATTHEW AARON (MATT)

Born, Garden Grove, California, March 3, 1976.
Bats Right. Throws Right. Height, 6 feet, 2 inches. Weight, 220 pounds.

Year	Club	Lea	Pos	G	AB	R	H	2B	3B	HR	RBI	SB	Avg
1994 Royals	Gulf Coast		C-2B-OF	46	99	17	18	5	0	1	12	1	.182
1995 Springfield	Midwest		C	75	211	17	39	6	2	3	19	1	.185
1996 Lansing	Midwest		C-OF	119	384	56	100	18	2	6	33	5	.260
1997 Wilmington	Carolina		C	80	257	22	51	6	1	5	25	1	.198
1997 Brevard Cty a	Fla.St.		C	23	70	11	15	4	1	0	3	0	.214
1998 Brevard Cty	Fla.St.		C-1B-3B	80	243	24	57	8	0	3	28	3	.235
1999 Kane County	Midwest		C	86	308	56	88	21	1	10	53	4	.286
2000 Brevard County b	Fla.St.		C-1B	109	350	51	86	17	0	3	37	3	.246
2001 Portland	Eastern		C-1B	35	89	7	14	2	0	2	8	1	.157
2001 Marlins	Gulf Coast		C	11	34	10	14	4	0	1	4	3	.412
2001 Kane County	Midwest		C	1	1	2	1	0	0	0	0	0	1.000
2002 Portland	Eastern		C	50	156	24	39	5	1	9	28	3	.250
2002 Calgary c	P.C.		C-1B	36	95	10	27	8	0	1	18	1	.284
2003 Albuquerque d	P.C.		C	98	315	45	86	18	1	11	40	9	.273
2004 Albuquerque.	P.C.		C	62	198	32	51	8	0	8	38	2	.258
2004 Florida	N.L.		C	29	55	7	13	2	0	0	1	0	.236
2005 Florida	N.L.		C	58	134	10	27	8	0	0	13	0	.201
2006 Florida e	N.L.		C	67	157	12	36	6	1	2	14	0	.229
2007 Florida	N.L.		C	55	171	16	46	7	1	4	19	0	.269
2008 Jupiter	Fla.St.		C	5	16	7	5	1	0	1	5	0	.313
2008 Florida f-g	N.L.		C	65	206	18	49	7	0	2	23	1	.238
2009 Detroit h-i	A.L.		C	4	13	0	0	0	0	0	0	0	.000
2010 Oklahoma.	P.C.		C	5	15	2	3	0	0	0	2	0	.200
2010 Texas j-k-l.	A.L.		C	82	237	22	50	6	1	5	27	1	.211
2011 Northwest	Texas		C	7	19	2	5	1	0	0	5	0	.263
2011 Kansas City-Texas m-n-o-p	A.L.		C	72	196	24	42	6	0	3	22	2	.214
Major League Totals		8 Yrs.		432	1169	109	263	42	3	16	119	4	.225
Division Series													
2010 Texas	A.L.		C	1	1	1	0	0	0	0	0	0	.000
Championship Series													
2010 Texas	A.L.		C	2	6	2	2	0	0	1	2	0	.333
World Series Record													
2010 Texas	A.L.		C	1	3	0	0	0	0	0	0	0	.000

a Traded by Kansas City Royals to Florida Marlins for pitcher Matt Whisenant, July 29, 1997.
b Filed for free agency, October 15, 2000, re-signed with Florida Marlins, November 13, 2000.
c Filed for free agency, October 15, 2002, re-signed with Florida Marlins organization, November 25, 2002.
d Filed for free agency, October 15, 2003, re-signed with Florida Marlins, December 4, 2003.
e On disabled list from August 2 to August 16, 2006.
f On disabled list from July 8 to August 6, 2008.

g Released by Florida Marlins, December 10, 2008. Signed with Detroit Tigers, December 18, 2008.
h On disabled list from April 24 to November 6, 2009.
i Filed for free agency, November 9, 2009. Signed with Milwaukee Brewers organization, December 18, 2009.
j Traded to Texas Rangers for infielder Ray Olmedo, March 22, 2010.
k On disabled list from July 24 to August 23, 2010.
l Filed for free agency, November 1, 2010. Re-signed with Texas Rangers, December 13, 2010.
m Sold to Kansas City Royals, March 28, 2011.
n On disabled list from July 31 to August 14 and August 14 to August 31, 2011.
o Sold to Texas Rangers, August 31, 2011.
p Filed for free agency, October 30, 2011. Signed with Los Angeles Dodgers, November 15, 2011.

TROUT, MICHAEL NELSON (MIKE)
Born, Vineland, New Jersey, August 7, 1991.
Bats Right. Throws Right. Height, 6 feet, 1 inch. Weight, 200 pounds.

Year	Club	Lea	Pos	G	AB	R	H	2B	3B	HR	RBI	SB	Avg
2009 Angels	....	Arizona	OF	39	164	29	59	7	7	1	25	13	.360
2009 Cedar Rapids	......	Midwest	OF	5	15	1	4	0	0	0	0	0	.267
2010 Rancho Cucamonga	....	Calif.	OF	50	196	30	60	9	2	4	19	11	.306
2010 Cedar Rapids	......	Midwest	OF	81	312	76	113	19	7	6	39	45	.362
2011 Arkansas	....	Texas	OF	91	353	82	115	18	13	11	38	33	.326
2011 Los Angeles	....	A.L.	OF	40	123	20	27	6	0	5	16	4	.220

TRUMBO, MARK DANIEL
Born, Anaheim, California, January 16, 1986.
Bats Right. Throws Right. Height, 6 feet, 4 inches. Weight, 220 pounds.

Year	Club	Lea	Pos	G	AB	R	H	2B	3B	HR	RBI	SB	Avg
2005 Orem	....	Pioneer	1B	71	299	45	82	23	1	10	45	2	.274
2006 Cedar Rapids	......	Midwest	1B	118	428	43	94	19	0	13	59	5	.220
2007 Cedar Rapids	......	Midwest	1B	128	471	57	128	27	2	14	76	10	.272
2008 Rancho Cucamonga	....	Calif.	1B	103	407	70	115	28	2	26	68	7	.283
2008 Arkansas	....	Texas	1B	32	123	13	34	7	1	6	25	1	.276
2009 Arkansas	....	Texas	1B-OF	137	533	54	155	35	3	15	88	6	.291
2010 Salt Lake	....	P.C.	1B-OF	139	532	103	160	29	5	36	122	3	.301
2010 Los Angeles	....	A.L.	1B-OF	8	15	2	1	0	0	0	2	0	.067
2011 Los Angeles	....	A.L.	1B-OF	149	539	65	137	31	1	29	87	9	.254
Major League Totals	....		2 Yrs.	157	554	67	138	31	1	29	89	9	.249

TULOWITZKI, TROY TREVER
Born, Santa Clara, California, October 10, 1984.
Bats Right. Throws Right. Height, 6 feet, 3 inches. Weight, 205 pounds.

Year	Club	Lea	Pos	G	AB	R	H	2B	3B	HR	RBI	SB	Avg
2005 Modesto	....	Calif.	SS	22	94	17	25	6	0	4	14	1	.266
2006 Tulsa	....	Texas	SS	104	423	75	123	34	2	13	61	6	.291
2006 Colorado	....	N.L.	SS	25	96	15	23	2	0	1	6	3	.240
2007 Colorado	....	N.L.	SS	155	609	104	177	33	5	24	99	7	.291
2008 Modesto	....	Calif.	SS	5	12	3	4	3	0	0	1	0	.333
2008 Tulsa	....	Texas	SS	5	21	5	7	0	0	2	3	0	.333
2008 Colorado Springs	....	P.C.	SS	2	7	2	3	1	0	0	1	1	.429
2008 Colorado a	....	N.L.	SS	101	377	48	99	24	2	8	46	1	.263
2009 Colorado	....	N.L.	SS	151	543	101	161	25	9	32	92	20	.297
2010 Tulsa	....	Texas	SS	2	7	1	1	1	0	0	1	0	.143
2010 Colorado Springs	....	P.C.	SS	2	4	1	1	0	0	0	0	0	.250
2010 Colorado b	....	N.L.	SS	122	470	89	148	32	3	27	95	11	.315
2011 Colorado	....	N.L.	SS	143	537	81	162	36	2	30	105	9	.302
Major League Totals	....		6 Yrs.	697	2632	438	770	152	21	122	443	51	.293
Division Series													
2007 Colorado	....	N.L.	SS	3	12	1	2	1	0	1	2	0	.167
2009 Colorado	....	N.L.	SS	4	16	0	4	2	0	0	3	0	.250
Division Series Totals	....			7	28	1	6	3	0	1	5	0	.214
Championship Series													
2007 Colorado	....	N.L.	SS	4	16	1	3	0	0	0	0	0	.188
World Series Record													
2007 Colorado	....	N.L.	SS	4	13	1	3	2	0	0	1	0	.231

a On disabled list from April 30 to June 20 and July 5 to July 21, 2008.
b On disabled list from June 18 to July 27, 2010.

TURNER, JUSTIN MATTHEW

Born, Long Beach, California, November 23, 1984.
Bats Right. Throws Right. Height, 5 feet, 11 inches. Weight, 210 pounds.

Year	Club	Lea	Pos	G	AB	R	H	2B	3B	HR	RBI	SB	Avg
2006 Billings	Pioneer	2B-OF-3B-SS	60	231	53	78	16	3	6	41	12	.338
2007 Dayton	Midwest	2B-SS-3B	117	466	70	145	25	4	10	59	12	.311
2007 Sarasota	Fla.St.	2B	6	20	2	4	0	0	0	0	0	.200
2008 Sarasota	Fla.St.	2B	33	136	23	43	8	1	0	11	3	.316
2008 Chattanooga	Southern	2B-3B	78	280	45	81	14	1	8	42	2	.289
2009 Norfolk	Int.	2B-3B-SS	108	387	54	116	28	0	2	43	9	.300
2009 Baltimore	A.L.	3B-2B	12	18	2	3	0	0	0	3	0	.167
2010 Baltimore	A.L.	2B-SS	5	9	0	0	0	0	0	0	0	.000
2010 Norfolk	Int.	2B-3B-SS	23	84	11	21	8	0	1	8	2	.250
2010 New York	N.L.	2B-3B	4	8	1	1	1	0	0	0	0	.125
2010 Buffalo b	Int.	2B-SS-3B	78	312	58	104	22	1	11	35	5	.333
2011 Buffalo	Int.	2B-3B	10	40	6	12	3	2	0	2	0	.300
2011 New York	N.L.	2B-3B-SS	117	435	49	113	30	0	4	51	7	.260
Major League Totals			3 Yrs.	138	470	52	117	31	0	4	54	7	.249

a Traded by Cincinnati Reds to Baltimore Orioles with outfielder Ryan Freel and infielder Brandon Waring for catcher Ramon Hernandez and cash, December 9, 2008.
b Claimed on waivers by New York Mets, May 25, 2010.

UGGLA, DANIEL COOLEY (DAN)

Born, Louisville, Kentucky, March 11, 1980.
Bats Right. Throws Right. Height, 5 feet, 11 inches. Weight, 200 pounds.

Year	Club	Lea	Pos	G	AB	R	H	2B	3B	HR	RBI	SB	Avg
2001 Yakima	Northwest	2B	72	278	39	77	21	0	5	40	8	.277
2002 Lancaster	Calif.	2B-3B	54	184	21	42	7	2	3	16	3	.228
2002 South Bend	Midwest	3B-2B	53	171	16	34	5	1	2	10	0	.199
2003 Lancaster	Calif.	3B-2B	134	534	104	155	31	7	23	90	24	.290
2004 Lancaster	Calif.	2B-3B-SS-1B	37	140	29	47	13	3	6	38	2	.336
2004 El Paso	Texas	3B-OF-2B	83	295	29	76	12	2	4	30	10	.258
2005 Tennessee a	Southern	2B-3B-1B-SS	135	498	88	148	33	3	21	87	15	.297
2006 Florida	N.L.	2B	154	611	105	172	26	7	27	90	6	.282
2007 Florida	N.L.	2B	159	632	113	155	49	3	31	88	2	.245
2008 Florida	N.L.	2B	146	531	97	138	37	1	32	92	5	.260
2009 Florida	N.L.	2B	158	564	84	137	27	1	31	90	2	.243
2010 Florida b	N.L.	2B	159	589	100	169	31	0	33	105	4	.287
2011 Atlanta	N.L.	2B	161	600	88	140	22	1	36	82	1	.233
Major League Totals			6 Yrs.	937	3527	587	911	192	13	190	547	20	.258

a Selected by Florida Marlins from Arizona Diamondbacks in Rule V draft, December 8, 2005.
b Traded to Atlanta Braves for infielder Omar Infante and pitcher Michael Dunn, November 16, 2010.

UPTON, JUSTIN IRVIN

Born, Norfolk, Virginia, August 25, 1987.
Bats Right. Throws Right. Height, 6 feet, 3 inches. Weight, 205 pounds.

Year	Club	Lea	Pos	G	AB	R	H	2B	3B	HR	RBI	SB	Avg
2006 South Bend	Midwest	OF	113	438	71	115	28	1	12	66	15	.263
2007 Visalia	Calif.	OF	32	126	27	43	6	2	5	17	9	.341
2007 Mobile	Southern	OF	71	259	48	80	17	4	13	53	10	.309
2007 Arizona	N.L.	OF	43	140	17	31	8	3	2	11	2	.221
2008 Tucson	P.C.	OF	15	61	13	17	3	1	3	10	2	.279
2008 Arizona a	N.L.	OF	108	356	52	89	19	6	15	42	1	.250
2009 Visalia	Calif.	OF	2	8	1	2	0	0	1	6	1	.250
2009 Arizona b	N.L.	OF	138	526	84	158	30	7	26	86	20	.300
2010 Arizona	N.L.	OF	133	495	73	135	27	3	17	69	18	.273
2011 Arizona	N.L.	OF	159	592	105	171	39	5	31	88	21	.289
Major League Totals			5 Yrs.	581	2109	331	584	123	24	91	296	62	.277
Division Series													
2007 Arizona	N.L.	OF	2	5	2	3	0	0	0	1	1	.600
2011 Arizona	N.L.	OF	5	20	3	4	0	0	2	3	0	.200
Division Series Totals				7	25	5	7	0	0	2	4	1	.280
Championship Series													
2007 Arizona	N.L.	OF	4	9	0	2	1	1	0	0	0	.222

a On disabled list from July 9 to August 29, 2008.
b On disabled list from August 6 to August 26, 2009.

UPTON, MELVIN EMANUEL (B.J.)
Born, Norfolk, Virginia, August 21, 1984.
Bats Right. Throws Right. Height, 6 feet, 3 inches. Weight, 180 pounds.

Year	Club	Lea	Pos	G	AB	R	H	2B	3B	HR	RBI	SB	Avg
2003 Charleston		So.Atl.	SS	101	384	70	116	22	6	7	46	38	.302
2003 Orlando		Southern	SS	29	105	14	29	8	0	1	16	2	.276
2004 Montgomery		Southern	SS	29	104	21	34	7	1	2	15	3	.327
2004 Durham		Int.	SS	69	264	65	82	17	1	12	36	17	.311
2004 Tampa Bay		A.L.	SS-3B-OF	45	159	19	41	8	2	4	12	4	.258
2005 Durham		Int.	SS	139	545	98	165	36	6	18	74	44	.303
2006 Durham		Int.	SS-3B	106	398	72	107	18	4	8	41	46	.269
2006 Tampa Bay		A.L.	3B	50	175	20	43	5	0	1	10	11	.246
2007 Vero Beach		Fla.St.	2B-OF	7	17	4	4	0	0	1	3	0	.235
2007 Durham		Int.	2B	2	7	1	3	0	0	1	1	0	.429
2007 Tampa Bay a		A.L.	OF-2B	129	474	86	142	25	1	24	82	22	.300
2008 Tampa Bay		A.L.	OF	145	531	85	145	37	2	9	67	44	.273
2009 Charlotte		Fla.St.	OF	3	9	1	4	0	0	0	2	4	.444
2009 Tampa Bay b		A.L.	OF	144	560	79	135	33	4	11	55	42	.241
2010 Tampa Bay		A.L.	OF	154	536	89	127	38	4	18	62	42	.237
2011 Tampa Bay		A.L.	OF	153	560	82	136	27	4	23	81	36	.243
Major League Totals			7 Yrs.	820	2995	460	769	173	17	90	369	201	.257
Division Series													
2008 Tampa Bay		A.L.	OF	4	18	5	5	0	1	3	4	0	.278
2010 Tampa Bay		A.L.	OF	5	21	0	4	2	0	0	2	2	.190
2011 Tampa Bay		A.L.	OF	4	14	3	4	3	0	0	0	1	.286
Division Series Totals				13	53	8	13	5	1	3	6	3	.245
Championship Series													
2008 Tampa Bay		A.L.	OF	7	28	8	9	1	0	4	11	2	.321
World Series Record													
2008 Tampa Bay		A.L.	OF	5	20	3	5	0	0	0	1	4	.250

a On disabled list from June 9 to July 13, 2007.

b On disabled list from March 27 to April 13, 2009.

URIBE (TENA), JUAN C.
Born, Bani, Dominican Republic, July 22, 1979.
Bats Right. Throws Right. Height, 6 feet. Weight, 220 pounds.

Year	Club	Lea	Pos	G	AB	R	H	2B	3B	HR	RBI	SB	Avg
1997 Colorado		Dominican	SS	65	234	32	63	12	0	0	29	7	.269
1998 Rockies		Arizona	SS	40	148	25	41	5	3	0	17	8	.277
1999 Asheville		So.Atl.	SS	125	430	57	115	28	3	9	46	11	.267
2000 Salem		Carolina	SS	134	485	64	124	22	7	13	65	22	.256
2001 Carolina		Southern	SS	3	13	1	3	1	0	0	1	1	.231
2001 Colo Sprngs		P.C.	SS	74	281	40	87	27	7	7	48	11	.310
2001 Colorado		N.L.	SS	72	273	32	82	15	11	8	53	3	.300
2002 Colorado		N.L.	SS	155	566	69	136	25	7	6	49	9	.240
2003 Visalia		California	2B-SS	2	9	4	5	1	0	0	1	0	.556
2003 Tulsa		Texas	2B-3B-SS-OF	5	20	3	5	2	0	1	4	0	.250
2003 Colorado a-b		N.L.	SS-2B-OF	87	316	45	80	19	3	10	33	7	.253
2004 Chicago		A.L.	2B-SS-3B	134	502	82	142	31	6	23	74	9	.283
2005 Chicago		A.L.	SS	146	481	58	121	23	3	16	71	4	.252
2006 Chicago		A.L.	SS	132	463	53	109	28	2	21	71	1	.235
2007 Chicago		A.L.	SS	150	513	55	120	18	2	20	68	1	.234
2008 Charlotte		Int.	2B-SS	3	11	0	2	0	0	0	2	0	.182
2008 Chicago c-d		A.L.	3B-2B-SS	110	324	38	80	22	1	7	40	1	.247
2009 San Francisco e		N.L.	3B-SS-2B	122	398	50	115	26	4	16	55	3	.289
2010 San Francisco f		N.L.	SS-3B-2B	148	521	64	129	24	2	24	85	1	.248
2011 Rancho Cucamonga		Calif.	2B	3	8	2	4	1	0	0	0	0	.500
2011 Los Angeles g		N.L.	3B-2B-SS	77	270	21	55	12	0	4	28	2	.204
Major League Totals			11 Yrs.	1333	4627	567	1169	243	41	155	627	41	.253
Division Series													
2005 Chicago		A.L.	SS	3	10	4	4	1	0	1	4	0	.400
2008 Chicago		A.L.	3B	4	12	0	2	0	0	0	1	1	.167
2010 San Francisco		N.L.	SS-3B	4	14	0	1	0	0	0	1	0	.071
Division Series Totals				11	36	4	7	1	0	1	6	1	.194
Championship Series													
2005 Chicago		A.L.	SS	5	16	1	4	1	0	0	0	0	.250
2010 San Francisco		N.L.	SS-3B	5	14	1	3	0	0	1	3	0	.214
Championship Series Totals				10	30	2	7	1	0	1	3	0	.233

Year	Club	Lea	Pos	G	AB	R	H	2B	3B	HR	RBI	SB	Avg
	World Series Record												
2005 Chicago .........A.L.			SS	4	16	2	4	3	0	0	2	1	.250
2010 San Francisco .....N.L.			3B	5	19	3	3	0	0	1	5	0	.158
World Series Totals............				9	35	5	7	3	0	1	7	1	.200

a On disabled list from March 18 to June 3, 2003.
b Traded to Chicago White Sox for infielder Aaron Miles, December 2, 2003.
c On disabled list from May 16 to May 31, 2008.
d Filed for free agency, October 30, 2008. Signed with San Francisco Giants organization, January 29, 2009.
e Filed for free agency, November 5, 2009, re-signed with San Francisco Giants, January 5, 2010.
f Filed for free agency, November 1, 2010. Signed with Los Angeles Dodgers, November 30, 2010.
g On disabled list from May 21 to June 6 and July 24 to September 30, 2011.

UTLEY, CHASE CAMERON

Born, Pasadena, California, December 17, 1978.
Bats Left. Throws Right. Height, 6 feet, 1 inch. Weight, 200 pounds.

Year	Club	Lea	Pos	G	AB	R	H	2B	3B	HR	RBI	SB	Avg
2000 Batavia........	N.Y.-Penn.		2B	40	153	21	47	13	1	2	22	5	.307
2001 Clearwater ....Fla.St.			2B	122	467	65	120	25	2	16	59	19	.257
2002 Scranton/W.B. ....Int.			3B	125	464	73	122	39	1	17	70	8	.263
2003 Scranton/W.B.	Int.		2B	113	431	80	139	26	2	18	77	10	.323
2003 Philadelphia	N.L.		2B	43	134	13	32	10	1	2	21	2	.239
2004 Scranton/WB	Int.		2B	33	123	23	35	8	1	6	25	4	.285
2004 Philadelphia	N.L.		2B-1B	94	267	36	71	11	2	13	57	4	.266
2005 Philadelphia	N.L.		2B-1B	147	543	93	158	39	6	28	105	16	.291
2006 Philadelphia	N.L.		2B-1B	160	658	*131	203	40	4	32	102	15	.309
2007 Reading	Eastern		2B	3	10	0	1	0	0	0	0	0	.100
2007 Philadelphia a.	N.L.		2B-1B	132	530	104	176	48	5	22	103	9	.332
2008 Philadelphia	N.L.		2B-1B	159	607	113	177	41	4	33	104	14	.292
2009 Philadelphia	N.L.		2B	156	571	112	161	28	4	31	93	23	.282
2010 Clearwater ....Fla.St.			2B	4	12	1	3	0	2	0	1	0	.250
2010 Philadelphia b	N.L.		2B	115	425	75	117	20	2	16	65	13	.275
2011 Clearwater ....Fla.St.			2B	9	32	4	9	2	0	1	4	1	.281
2011 Philadelphia c.	N.L.		2B	103	398	54	103	21	6	11	44	14	.259
Major League Totals		9 Yrs.		1109	4133	731	1198	258	34	188	694	110	.290
	Division Series												
2007 Philadelphia	N.L.		2B	3	11	0	2	0	0	0	0	0	.182
2008 Philadelphia	N.L.		2B	4	15	1	2	1	0	0	2	0	.133
2009 Philadelphia	N.L.		2B	4	14	5	6	0	0	1	1	2	.429
2010 Philadelphia	N.L.		2B	3	11	3	3	0	0	1	4	1	.273
2011 Philadelphia	N.L.		2B	5	16	5	7	2	1	0	1	0	.438
Division Series Totals				19	67	14	20	3	1	2	8	3	.299
	Championship Series												
2008 Philadelphia	N.L.		2B	5	17	4	6	2	0	1	3	0	.353
2009 Philadelphia	N.L.		2B	5	19	3	4	0	0	0	1	0	.211
2010 Philadelphia	N.L.		2B	6	22	5	4	1	0	0	1	3	.182
Championship Series Totals				16	58	12	14	3	0	1	5	3	.241
	World Series Record												
2008 Philadelphia	N.L.		2B	5	18	5	3	0	0	2	4	3	.167
2009 Philadelphia	N.L.		2B	6	21	7	6	1	0	5	8	1	.286
World Series Totals............				11	39	12	9	1	0	7	12	4	.231

a On disabled list from July 27 to August 27, 2007.
b On disabled list from June 29 to August 17, 2010.
c On disabled list from March 22 to May 23, 2011.

VALDEZ, WILSON ANTONIO

Born, Nizao, Dominican Republic, May 20, 1978.
Bats Right. Throws Right. Height, 5 feet, 11 inches. Weight, 170 pounds.

Year	Club	Lea	Pos	G	AB	R	H	2B	3B	HR	RBI	SB	Avg
1997 Montreal....	Dominican		SS	62	244	39	74	13	1	2	29	19	.303
1998 Montreal....	Dominican		SS	64	247	42	74	9	0	3	30	15	.300
1999 Expos.......	Gulf Coast		SS-2B	22	82	12	24	2	0	0	7	10	.293
1999 Vermont.....N.Y.-Penn.			SS-2B	36	130	19	32	7	0	1	10	4	.246
2000 Vermont.....N.Y.-Penn.			SS	65	248	32	66	8	1	1	30	16	.266
2000 Cape Fear.......So.Atl.			2B-SS-C	15	49	6	12	2	0	0	3	3	.245
2001 Jupiter ....Fla.St.			SS	64	233	34	58	13	2	2	19	7	.249
2001 Clinton	Midwest		SS	59	214	31	54	8	1	0	11	6	.252

Year Club	Lea	Pos	G	AB	R	H	2B	3B	HR	RBI	SB	Avg
2002 Portland a ..... Eastern		SS	114	375	51	98	19	5	1	30	18	.261
2003 Albuquerque....... P.C.		SS-2B	90	338	45	97	12	4	0	18	33	.287
2003 Carolina ..... Southern		2B-SS	37	144	28	45	6	2	0	14	16	.313
2004 Albuquerque....... P.C.		SS	66	285	36	91	11	3	2	25	19	.319
2004 Charlotte .... Int.		SS	70	281	37	85	7	2	2	15	13	.302
2004 Chicago b .... A.L.		SS-2B	19	43	8	10	1	0	1	4	1	.233
2005 Seattle .... A.L.		SS	42	126	9	25	5	1	0	8	2	.198
2005 Tacoma .... P.C.		SS	1	4	0	0	0	0	0	0	0	.000
2005 San Diego .... N.L.		SS	9	13	0	3	2	0	0	1	0	.231
2005 Portland c-d-e-f ... P.C.		SS	50	155	14	38	5	3	1	15	8	.245
2006 Las Vegas g .... P.C.		SS-OF-2B	137	528	94	157	24	1	6	53	26	.297
2007 Las Vegas......... P.C.		SS-OF-2B-3B	90	361	81	124	19	1	4	29	14	.343
2007 Los Angeles....... N.L.		2B-SS-3B-OF	41	74	.12	16	2	1	0	7	1	.216
2008 Kia .... Korea		SS	47	156	17	34	9	1	1	16	13	.218
2008 Yakult h-i ... Japan Pac.		SS	29	78	8	20	1	0	1	8	4	.256
2009 Columbus .... Int.		SS-OF-2B	41	121	17	24	1	0	0	6	5	.198
2009 Buffalo .... Int.		SS-2B-OF	36	114	13	34	4	0	0	6	1	.298
2009 New York j-k ..... N.L.		SS-OF-2B-3B	41	86	11	22	3	2	0	7	0	.256
2010 Lehigh Valley ...... Int.		2B-SS	5	22	2	10	0	0	0	5	2	.455
2010 Philadelphia .... N.L.		SS-2B-3B	111	333	37	86	16	3	4	35	7	.258
2011 Philadelphia .... N.L.		2B-SS-3B-P	99	273	39	68	14	4	1	30	3	.249
Major League Totals		6 Yrs.	362	948	116	230	43	11	6	92	14	.243
Division Series												
2010 Philadelphia .... N.L.		3B	1	3	1	1	0	0	0	0	0	.333
Championship Series												
2010 Philadelphia .... N.L.		PH	2	0	0	0	0	0	0	0	0	.000

a Claimed on waivers from Montreal Expos by Florida Marlins, March 29, 2002.
b Traded to Chicago White Sox for pitcher Billy Koch and cash, June 17, 2004.
c Claimed on waivers by New York Mets, March 29, 2005.
d Claimed on waivers by Seattle Mariners, April 1, 2005.
e Traded to San Diego Padres for pitcher Mike Bumstead and pitcher R.D. Spiehs, June 9, 2005.
f Filed for free agency, October 3, 2005. Signed with Kansas City Royals organization, November 18, 2005.
g Traded to Los Angeles Dodgers for pitcher Jarod Plummer, March 31, 2006.
h Sold to Kia (Korea) January 8, 2008. Signed with Yakult (Japan), 2008.
i Signed with Cleveland Indians organization, December 15, 2008.
j Sold to New York Mets, May 26, 2009.
k Filed for free agency, October 27, 2009. Signed with Philadelphia Phillies organization, November 25, 2009.

VALENCIA, DANIEL PAUL (DANNY)

Born, Miami, Florida, September 19, 1984.
Bats Right. Throws Right. Height, 6 feet, 2 inches. Weight, 210 pounds.

Year Club	Lea	Pos	G	AB	R	H	2B	3B	HR	RBI	SB	Avg
2006 Elizabethton .... Appal.		1B-3B	48	190	30	59	13	0	8	29	0	.311
2007 Fort Myers .... Fla.St.		3B	61	230	28	67	8	2	6	31	1	.291
2007 Beloit .... Midwest		3B-1B	66	242	44	73	15	0	11	35	3	.302
2008 New Britain .... Eastern		3B-1B	69	266	40	77	18	2	10	32	2	.289
2008 Fort Myers .... Fla.St.		3B-SS	60	220	35	74	19	3	5	44	2	.336
2009 New Britain .... Eastern		3B	57	218	44	62	14	4	7	29	0	.284
2009 Rochester............. Int.		3B	71	269	35	77	24	0	7	41	0	.286
2010 Rochester............. Int.		3B	49	185	22	54	15	0	0	24	2	.292
2010 Minnesota .... A.L.		3B	85	299	30	93	18	1	7	40	2	.311
2011 Minnesota .... A.L.		3B	154	564	63	139	28	2	15	72	2	.246
Major League Totals		2 Yrs.	239	863	93	232	46	3	22	112	4	.269
Division Series												
2010 Minnesota .... A.L.		3B	3	9	1	2	1	0	0	2	0	.222

VARITEK, JASON ANDREW

Born, Rochester, Minnesota, April 11, 1972.
Bats Both. Throws Right. Height, 6 feet, 2 inches. Weight, 230 pounds.

Year Club	Lea	Pos	G	AB	R	H	2B	3B	HR	RBI	SB	Avg
1995 Port City .... Southern		C	104	352	42	79	14	2	10	44	0	.224
1996 Port City .... Southern		C-3B-OF	134	503	63	132	34	1	12	67	7	.262
1997 Tacoma .... P.C.		C	87	307	54	78	13	0	15	48	0	.254
1997 Pawtucket .... Int.		C	20	66	6	13	5	0	1	5	0	.197
1997 Boston a............. A.L.		C	1	1	0	1	0	0	0	0	0	1.000
1998 Boston .... A.L.		C	86	221	31	56	13	0	7	33	2	.253
1999 Boston .... A.L.		C	144	483	70	130	39	2	20	76	1	.269

Year	Club	Lea	Pos	G	AB	R	H	2B	3B	HR	RBI	SB	Avg
2000 Boston		A.L.	C	139	448	55	111	31	1	10	65	1	.248
2001 Boston b		A.L.	C	51	174	19	51	11	1	7	25	0	.293
2002 Boston		A.L.	C	132	467	58	124	27	1	10	61	4	.266
2003 Boston		A.L.	C	142	451	63	123	31	1	25	85	3	.273
2004 Boston c		A.L.	C	137	463	67	137	30	1	18	73	10	.296
2005 Boston		A.L.	C	133	470	70	132	30	1	22	70	2	.281
2006 Pawtucket		Int.	C	2	7	2	3	0	0	1	1	0	.429
2006 Boston d		A.L.	C	103	365	46	87	19	2	12	55	1	.238
2007 Boston		A.L.	C	131	435	57	111	15	3	17	68	1	.255
2008 Boston e		A.L.	C	131	423	37	93	20	0	13	43	0	.220
2009 Boston		A.L.	C	109	364	41	76	24	0	14	51	0	.209
2010 Pawtucket		Int.	C	2	5	0	2	0	0	0	1	0	.400
2010 Boston f-g		A.L.	C	39	112	18	26	6	0	7	16	0	.232
2011 Boston h		A.L.	C	68	222	32	49	10	1	11	36	0	.221
Major League Totals		15 Yrs.		1546	5099	664	1307	306	14	193	757	25	.256
Division Series													
1998 Boston		A.L.	C	1	4	0	1	0	0	0	1	0	.250
1999 Boston		A.L.	C	5	21	7	5	3	0	1	3	0	.238
2003 Boston		A.L.	C	5	14	4	4	0	0	2	2	0	.286
2004 Boston		A.L.	C	3	12	3	2	0	0	1	2	0	.167
2005 Boston		A.L.	C	3	10	1	3	0	0	0	1	0	.300
2007 Boston		A.L.	C	3	11	1	2	1	0	0	1	0	.182
2008 Boston		A.L.	C	4	14	2	3	0	0	0	0	0	.214
Division Series Totals				24	86	18	20	4	0	4	10	0	.233
Championship Series													
1999 Boston		A.L.	C	5	20	1	4	1	1	1	1	0	.200
2003 Boston		A.L.	C	6	20	4	6	2	0	2	3	0	.300
2004 Boston		A.L.	C	7	28	5	9	1	0	2	7	0	.321
2007 Boston		A.L.	C	7	26	3	7	3	0	1	4	0	.269
2008 Boston		A.L.	C	6	20	2	1	0	0	1	1	0	.050
Championship Series Totals				31	114	15	27	7	1	7	16	0	.237
World Series Record													
2004 Boston		A.L.	C	4	13	2	2	0	1	0	2	0	.154
2007 Boston		A.L.	C	4	15	2	5	1	0	0	5	0	.333
World Series Totals				8	28	4	7	1	1	0	7	0	.250

a Traded to Boston Red Sox by Seattle Mariners with pitcher Derek Lowe for pitcher Heathcliff Slocumb, July 31, 1997.

b On disabled list from June 8 to November 7, 2001.

c Filed for free agency, November 1, 2004, re-signed with Boston Red Sox, December 24, 2004.

d On disabled list from August 1 to September 3, 2006.

e Filed for free agency, October 30, 2008, re-signed with Boston Red Sox, February 6, 2009.

f On disabled list from July 1 to September 6, 2010.

g Filed for free agency, November 1, 2010, re-signed with Boston Red Sox, December 10, 2010.

h Filed for free agency, October 30, 2011.

VENABLE, WILLIAM DION (WILL)

Born, Greenbrae, California, October 29, 1982.
Bats Left. Throws Left. Height, 6 feet, 2 inches. Weight, 205 pounds.

Year	Club	Lea	Pos	G	AB	R	H	2B	3B	HR	RBI	SB	Avg
2005 Padres		Arizona	OF	15	59	13	19	4	2	1	12	4	.322
2005 Eugene		Northwest	OF	42	139	17	30	5	2	2	14	2	.216
2006 Fort Wayne		Midwest	OF	124	472	86	148	34	5	11	91	18	.314
2007 San Antonio		Texas	OF	134	515	66	143	19	3	8	68	21	.278
2008 Portland		P.C.	OF	120	442	70	129	26	4	14	58	7	.292
2008 San Diego		N.L.	OF	28	110	16	29	4	2	2	10	1	.264
2009 Portland		P.C.	OF	53	200	33	52	10	3	12	30	1	.260
2009 San Diego		N.L.	OF	95	293	38	75	14	2	12	38	6	.256
2010 Lake Elsinore		Calif.	OF	5	14	0	1	1	0	0	0	1	.071
2010 San Antonio		Texas	OF	2	6	2	2	0	0	0	1	2	.333
2010 San Diego a		N.L.	OF-1B	131	392	60	96	11	7	13	51	29	.245
2011 Tucson		P.C.	OF	14	58	14	16	3	2	3	11	3	.276
2011 San Diego		N.L.	OF	121	370	49	91	14	7	9	44	26	.246
Major League Totals		4 Yrs.		375	1165	163	291	43	18	36	143	62	.250

a On disabled list from July 2 to July 21, 2010.

VICIEDO (PEREZ), DAYAN
Born, Remedios, Cuba, March 10, 1989.
Bats Right. Throws Right. Height, 5 feet, 11 inches. Weight, 240 pounds.

Year	Club	Lea	Pos	G	AB	R	H	2B	3B	HR	RBI	SB	Avg
2009 Birmingham a		Southern	3B-1B	130	504	72	141	20	0	12	78	5	.280
2010 Charlotte		Int.	1B-3B	86	343	42	94	15	0	20	47	1	.274
2010 Chicago		A.L.	3B-1B	38	104	17	32	7	0	5	13	1	.308
2011 Charlotte		Int.	OF-1B	119	452	60	134	28	0	20	78	2	.296
2011 Chicago b		A.L.	OF-1B	29	102	11	26	3	0	1	6	1	.255
Major League Totals			2 Yrs.	67	206	28	58	10	0	6	19	2	.282

a Played in Cuba 2006 and 2007.

b On disabled list from March 22 to April 6, 2011.

VICTORINO, SHANE PATRICK
Born, Wailuku, Hawaii, November 30, 1980.
Bats Both. Throws Right. Height, 5 feet, 9 inches. Weight, 180 pounds.

Year	Club	Lea	Pos	G	AB	R	H	2B	3B	HR	RBI	SB	Avg
1999 Great Falls		Pioneer	OF	55	225	53	63	7	6	2	25	20	.280
2000 Yakima		Northwest	2B-SS	61	236	32	58	7	2	2	20	21	.246
2001 Vero Beach		Fla.St.	OF	2	6	2	1	0	0	0	0	0	.167
2001 Wilmington		So.Atl.	OF	112	435	71	123	21	9	4	32	47	.283
2002 Jacksonville		Southern	OF	122	481	61	124	15	1	4	34	45	.258
2003 Jacksonville		Southern	OF	66	266	37	75	9	4	2	15	16	.282
2003 Las Vegas		P.C.	OF	11	41	6	16	1	2	1	9	0	.390
2003 San Diego a		N.L.	OF	36	73	8	11	2	0	0	4	7	.151
2004 Las Vegas		P.C.	OF-2B	55	200	28	47	9	1	3	20	7	.235
2004 Jacksonville b		Southern	OF	75	293	70	96	13	7	16	43	9	.328
2005 Scranton/WB		Int.	OF	126	494	93	153	25	16	18	70	17	.310
2005 Philadelphia		N.L.	OF	21	17	5	5	0	0	2	8	0	.294
2006 Philadelphia		N.L.	OF	153	415	70	119	19	8	6	46	4	.287
2007 Lakewood		So.Atl.	DH	1	5	1	1	0	0	0	0	0	.200
2007 Reading		Eastern	OF	2	6	0	2	0	0	0	1	1	.333
2007 Philadelphia c		N.L.	OF	131	456	78	128	23	3	12	46	37	.281
2008 Clearwater		Fla.St.	OF	2	5	1	2	0	0	0	1	0	.400
2008 Reading		Eastern	OF	1	3	0	1	0	0	0	0	0	.333
2008 Lehigh Valley		Int.	OF	2	8	0	3	0	0	0	0	0	.375
2008 Philadelphia d		N.L.	OF	146	570	102	167	30	8	14	58	36	.293
2009 Philadelphia		N.L.	OF	156	620	102	181	39	*13	10	62	25	.292
2010 Lehigh Valley		Int.	OF	2	6	1	4	0	1	1	3	0	.667
2010 Philadelphia e		N.L.	OF	147	587	84	152	26	10	18	69	34	.259
2011 Lakewood		So.Atl.	OF	2	6	1	1	0	0	0	2	0	.167
2011 Reading		Eastern	OF	4	15	2	5	1	0	1	3	1	.333
2011 Philadelphia f		N.L.	OF	132	519	95	145	27	*16	17	61	19	.279
Major League Totals			8 Yrs.	922	3257	544	908	166	58	79	354	162	.279
Division Series													
2007 Philadelphia		N.L.	OF	3	9	2	2	0	0	1	1	1	.222
2008 Philadelphia		N.L.	OF	4	14	2	5	3	0	1	5	3	.357
2009 Philadelphia		N.L.	OF	4	17	4	6	1	0	1	1	1	.353
2010 Philadelphia		N.L.	OF	3	13	2	3	1	0	0	3	1	.231
2011 Philadelphia		N.L.	OF	5	19	2	6	1	0	0	2	0	.316
Division Series Totals				19	72	12	22	6	0	3	12	6	.306
Championship Series													
2008 Philadelphia		N.L.	OF	5	18	2	4	0	1	1	6	0	.222
2009 Philadelphia		N.L.	OF	5	19	4	7	1	1	2	6	1	.368
2010 Philadelphia		N.L.	OF	6	24	3	5	1	0	0	2	1	.208
Championship Series Totals				16	61	9	16	2	2	3	14	2	.262
World Series Record													
2008 Philadelphia		N.L.	OF	5	20	1	5	0	0	0	2	0	.250
2009 Philadelphia		N.L.	OF	6	22	3	4	1	0	0	2	0	.182
World Series Totals				11	42	4	9	1	0	0	4	0	.214

a Selected by San Diego Padres from Los Angeles Dodgers in Rule V draft, December 16, 2002. Returned to Los Angeles Dodgers, May 28, 2003.

b Selected by Philadelphia Phillies in Rule V draft, December 13, 2004.

c On disabled list from July 31 to August 22, 2007.

d On disabled list from April 13 to April 29, 2008.

e On disabled list from July 28 to August 12, 2010.

f On disabled list from May 20 to June 3 and July 4 to July 19, 2011.

VIZQUEL, OMAR ENRIQUE

Born, Caracas, Venezuela, April 24, 1967.
Bats Both. Throws Right. Height, 5 feet, 9 inches. Weight, 175 pounds.

Year	Club	Lea	Pos	G	AB	R	H	2B	3B	HR	RBI	SB	Avg
1984	Butte a	Pioneer	SS-2B	15	45	7	14	2	0	0	4	2	.311
1985	Bellingham	Northwest	SS-2B	50	187	24	42	9	0	5	17	4	.225
1986	Wausau	Midwest	SS-2B	105	352	60	75	13	2	4	28	19	.213
1987	Salinas	California	SS-2B	114	407	61	107	12	8	0	38	25	.263
1988	Vermont	Eastern	SS	103	375	54	95	18	2	2	35	30	.253
1988	Calgary	P.C.	SS	33	107	10	24	2	3	1	12	2	.224
1989	Seattle	A.L.	SS	143	387	45	85	7	3	1	20	1	.220
1989	Calgary	P.C.	SS	7	28	3	6	2	0	0	3	0	.214
1990	San Bernardino	California	SS	6	28	5	7	0	0	0	3	1	.250
1990	Calgary	P.C.	SS	48	150	18	35	6	2	0	8	4	.233
1990	Seattle b	A.L.	SS	81	255	19	63	3	2	2	18	4	.247
1991	Seattle	A.L.	SS-2B	142	426	42	98	16	4	1	41	7	.230
1992	Seattle c	A.L.	SS	136	483	49	142	20	4	0	21	15	.294
1992	Calgary	P.C.	SS	6	22	0	6	1	0	0	2	0	.273
1993	Seattle d	A.L.	SS	158	560	68	143	14	2	2	31	12	.255
1994	Charlotte	Int.	SS	7	26	3	7	1	0	0	1	1	.269
1994	Cleveland e	A.L.	SS	69	286	39	78	10	1	1	33	13	.273
1995	Cleveland	A.L.	SS	136	542	87	144	28	0	6	56	29	.266
1996	Cleveland	A.L.	SS	151	542	98	161	36	1	9	64	35	.297
1997	Cleveland	A.L.	SS	153	565	89	158	23	6	5	49	43	.280
1998	Cleveland	A.L.	SS	151	576	86	166	30	6	2	50	37	.288
1999	Cleveland	A.L.	SS-OF	144	574	112	191	36	4	5	66	42	.333
2000	Cleveland	A.L.	SS	156	613	101	176	27	3	7	66	22	.287
2001	Cleveland	A.L.	SS	155	611	84	156	26	8	2	50	13	.255
2002	Cleveland	A.L.	SS	151	582	85	160	31	5	14	72	18	.275
2003	Lake County	So.Atl.	SS	4	14	0	1	0	0	0	0	1	.071
2003	Cleveland f	A.L.	SS	64	250	43	61	13	2	2	19	8	.244
2004	Cleveland g	A.L.	SS	148	567	82	165	28	3	7	59	19	.291
2005	San Francisco	N.L.	SS	152	568	66	154	28	4	3	45	24	.271
2006	San Francisco	N.L.	SS	153	579	88	171	22	10	4	58	24	.295
2007	San Francisco	N.L.	SS	145	513	54	126	18	3	4	51	14	.246
2008	San Jose	Calif.	SS	3	8	3	3	0	0	0	1	0	.375
2008	Fresno	P.C.	SS	2	5	0	1	0	0	0	0	0	.200
2008	San Francisco h-i	N.L.	SS	92	266	24	59	10	1	0	23	5	.222
2009	Texas j	A.L.	SS-3B-2B	62	177	17	47	7	2	1	14	4	.266
2010	Chicago	A.L.	3B-2B-SS	108	344	36	95	11	1	2	30	11	.276
2011	Chicago k	A.L.	3B-2B-SS-1B	58	167	18	42	7	1	0	8	1	.251
Major League Totals			23 Yrs.	2908	10433	1432	2841	451	76	80	944	401	.272

Division Series

Year	Club	Lea	Pos	G	AB	R	H	2B	3B	HR	RBI	SB	Avg
1995	Cleveland	A.L.	SS	3	12	2	2	1	0	0	4	1	.167
1996	Cleveland	A.L.	SS	4	14	4	6	1	0	0	2	4	.429
1997	Cleveland	A.L.	SS	5	18	3	9	0	0	0	1	4	.500
1998	Cleveland	A.L.	SS	4	15	1	1	0	0	0	0	0	.067
1999	Cleveland	A.L.	SS	5	21	3	5	1	1	0	3	0	.238
2001	Cleveland	A.L.	SS	5	22	2	9	1	1	0	6	1	.409
Division Series Totals				26	102	15	32	4	2	0	16	10	.314

Championship Series

Year	Club	Lea	Pos	G	AB	R	H	2B	3B	HR	RBI	SB	Avg
1995	Cleveland	A.L.	SS	6	23	2	2	1	0	0	2	3	.087
1997	Cleveland	A.L.	SS	6	25	1	1	0	0	0	0	0	.040
1998	Cleveland	A.L.	SS	6	25	2	11	0	1	0	0	4	.440
Championship Series Totals				18	73	5	14	1	1	0	2	7	.192

World Series Record

Year	Club	Lea	Pos	G	AB	R	H	2B	3B	HR	RBI	SB	Avg
1995	Cleveland	A.L.	SS	6	23	3	4	0	1	0	1	1	.174
1997	Cleveland	A.L.	SS	7	30	5	7	2	0	0	1	5	.233
World Series Totals				13	53	8	11	2	1	0	2	6	.208

a Batted righthanded only from 1984 through 1988 season.
b On disabled list from April 7 to May 14, 1990.
c On disabled list from April 13 to May 11, 1992.
d On disabled list from April 23 to June 13, 1994.
e On disabled list from April 23 to June 13, 1994.
f On disabled list from June 12 to August 26 and September 6 to October 28, 2003.
g Filed for free agency, October 29, 2004. Signed with San Francisco Giants, November 14, 2004.
h On disabled list from March 21 to May 10, 2008.
i Not offered contract, November 3, 2008. Signed with Texas Rangers organization, January 21, 2009.
j Filed for free agency, November 6, 2009. Signed with Chicago White Sox, November 23, 2009.
k Filed for free agency, October 30, 2011.

VOTTO, JOSEPH DANIEL (JOEY)

Born, Toronto, Ontario, Canada, September 10, 1983.
Bats Left. Throws Right. Height, 6 feet, 3 inches. Weight, 220 pounds.

Year	Club	Lea	Pos	G	AB	R	H	2B	3B	HR	RBI	SB	Avg
2002 Reds		Gulf Coast	3B-C-OF	50	175	29	47	13	3	9	33	7	.269
2003 Dayton		Midwest	1B	60	195	19	45	8	0	1	20	2	.231
2003 Billings		Pioneer	1B	70	240	47	76	17	3	6	37	4	.317
2004 Potomac		Carolina	1B	24	84	11	25	7	0	5	20	1	.298
2004 Dayton		Midwest	1B	111	391	60	118	26	2	14	73	9	.302
2005 Sarasota		Fla.St.	1B	124	464	64	119	23	2	17	83	4	.256
2006 Chattanooga		Southern	1B	136	508	85	162	46	2	22	77	24	.319
2007 Louisville		Int.	1B-OF	133	496	74	146	21	2	22	92	17	.294
2007 Cincinnati		N.L.	1B-OF	24	84	11	27	7	0	4	17	1	.321
2008 Cincinnati		N.L.	1B	151	526	69	156	32	3	24	84	7	.297
2009 Dayton		Midwest	1B	2	7	3	3	0	0	1	3	1	.429
2009 Sarasota		Fla.St.	1B	1	2	0	0	0	0	0	0	0	.000
2009 Cincinnati a		N.L.	1B	131	469	82	151	38	1	25	84	4	.322
2010 Cincinnati b		N.L.	1B	150	547	106	177	36	2	37	113	16	.324
2011 Cincinnati		N.L.	1B	161	599	101	185	*40	3	29	103	8	.309
Major League Totals			5 Yrs.	617	2225	369	696	153	9	119	401	36	.313
Division Series													
2010 Cincinnati		N.L.	1B	3	10	0	1	0	0	0	1	0	.100

a On disabled list from May 30 to June 23, 2009.
b Selected Most Valuable Player in National League for 2010.

WALKER, NEIL MARTIN

Born, Pittsburgh, Pennsylvania, September 10, 1985.
Bats Both. Throws Right. Height, 6 feet, 3 inches. Weight, 210 pounds.

Year	Club	Lea	Pos	G	AB	R	H	2B	3B	HR	RBI	SB	Avg
2004 Pirates		Gulf Coast	C	52	192	28	52	12	3	4	20	3	.271
2004 Williamsport		N.Y.-Penn.	C	8	33	2	10	3	0	0	7	1	.303
2005 Lynchburg		Carolina	C	9	42	4	11	2	1	0	12	0	.262
2005 Hickory		So.Atl.	C	120	485	78	146	33	2	12	68	7	.301
2006 Lynchburg		Carolina	C	72	264	32	75	22	1	3	35	3	.284
2006 Altoona		Eastern	C	10	31	5	5	0	0	2	3	0	.161
2007 Altoona		Eastern	3B	117	431	77	124	30	3	13	66	9	.288
2007 Indianapolis		Int.	3B	19	64	7	13	3	0	0	1	0	.203
2008 Indianapolis		Int.	3B	133	505	69	122	25	7	16	80	10	.242
2009 Pirates		Gulf Coast	3B	8	30	2	5	2	0	1	1	0	.167
2009 Indianapolis		Int.	3B	95	356	38	94	31	2	14	69	5	.264
2009 Pittsburgh		N.L.	3B	17	36	5	7	1	0	0	0	1	.194
2010 Indianapolis		Int.	2B-OF-1B-3B	43	168	25	54	18	2	6	26	10	.321
2010 Pittsburgh		N.L.	2B-3B	110	426	57	126	29	3	12	66	2	.296
2011 Pittsburgh		N.L.	2B	159	596	76	163	36	4	12	83	9	.273
Major League Totals			3 Yrs.	286	1058	138	296	66	7	24	149	12	.280

WALLACE, BRETT ALEXANDER

Born, Marin, California, August 26, 1986.
Bats Left. Throws Right. Height, 6 feet, 2 inches. Weight, 205 pounds.

Year	Club	Lea	Pos	G	AB	R	H	2B	3B	HR	RBI	SB	Avg
2008 Quad Cities		Midwest	3B	41	153	28	50	8	1	5	25	0	.327
2008 Springfield		Texas	3B	13	49	13	18	5	0	3	11	0	.367
2009 Memphis		P.C.	3B-1B	62	222	22	65	11	0	6	19	0	.293
2009 Sacramento		P.C.	3B-1B	44	182	32	55	10	0	9	28	1	.302
2009 Springfield a-b		Texas	3B	32	128	22	36	5	0	5	16	0	.281
2010 Las Vegas		P.C.	1B	95	385	64	116	24	1	18	61	1	.301
2010 Houston c		N.L.	1B	51	144	14	32	6	1	2	13	0	.222
2011 Oklahoma		P.C.	1B	28	104	16	37	10	0	1	24	1	.356
2011 Houston		N.L.	1B	115	336	37	87	22	0	5	29	1	.259
Major League Totals			2 Yrs.	166	480	51	119	28	1	7	42	1	.248

a Traded by St. Louis Cardinals to Oakland Athletics with pitcher Clayton Mortensen and outfielder Shane Peterson for outfielder Matt Holliday, July 24, 2009.
b Traded to Philadelphia Phillies for pitcher Michael Taylor, December 16, 2009.
c Traded to Houston Astros for outfielder Anthony Gose, July 29, 2010.

WEEKS, JEMILE NYKIWA

Born, Orlando, Florida, January 26, 1987.
Bats Both. Throws Right. Height, 5 feet, 9 inches. Weight, 160 pounds.

Year Club	Lea	Pos	G	AB	R	H	2B	3B	HR	RBI	SB	Avg
2008 Kane County	Midwest	2B	19	74	11	22	3	1	1	8	6	.297
2009 Stockton	Calif.	2B	50	201	29	60	9	2	7	31	5	.299
2009 Midland	Texas	2B	30	105	10	25	5	0	2	13	4	.238
2010 Athletics	Arizona	2B	10	36	9	11	2	1	0	1	5	.306
2010 Midland	Texas	2B	67	273	43	73	14	7	3	33	11	.267
2011 Sacramento	P.C.	2B	45	184	30	59	6	4	3	22	10	.321
2011 Oakland	A.L.	2B	97	406	50	123	26	8	2	36	22	.303

WEEKS, RICKIE DARNELL

Born, Altamonte Springs, Florida, September 13, 1982.
Bats Right. Throws Right. Height, 6 feet. Weight, 205 pounds.

Year Club	Lea	Pos	G	AB	R	H	2B	3B	HR	RBI	SB	Avg
2003 Brewers	Arizona	DH	1	4	0	2	0	0	0	4	1	.500
2003 Beloit	Midwest	2B	20	63	13	22	8	1	1	16	2	.349
2003 Milwaukee	N.L.	2B	7	12	1	2	1	0	0	0	0	.167
2004 Huntsville	Southern	2B	133	479	67	124	35	6	8	42	11	.259
2005 Nashville	P.C.	2B	55	203	43	65	14	9	12	48	10	.320
2005 Milwaukee	N.L.	2B	96	360	56	86	13	2	13	42	15	.239
2006 Milwaukee a	N.L.	2B	95	359	73	100	15	3	8	34	19	.279
2007 Nashville	P.C.	2B	6	22	5	10	3	1	0	3	1	.455
2007 Milwaukee b	N.L.	2B	118	409	87	96	21	6	16	36	25	.235
2008 Milwaukee c	N.L.	2B	129	475	89	111	22	7	14	46	19	.234
2009 Milwaukee d	N.L.	2B	37	147	28	40	5	2	9	24	2	.272
2010 Milwaukee	N.L.	2B	160	*651	112	175	32	4	29	83	11	.269
2011 Milwaukee e	N.L.	2B	118	453	77	·122	26	2	20	49	9	.269
Major League Totals		8 Yrs.	760	2866	523	732	135	26	109	314	100	.255
Division Series												
2008 Milwaukee	N.L.	2B	3	4	0	0	0	0	0	0	0	.000
2011 Milwaukee	N.L.	2B	5	18	0	1	0	1	0	1	0	.056
Division Series Totals			8	22	0	1	0	1	0	1	0	.045
Championship Series												
2011 Milwaukee	N.L.	2B	6	23	5	5	1	0	2	3	0	.217

a On disabled list from July 29 to October 31, 2006.
b On disabled list from May 30 to June 18, 2007.
c On disabled list from June 7 to June 22, 2008.
d On disabled list from May 17 to November 6, 2009.
e On disabled list from July 28 to September 8, 2011.

WELLS, CASPER CHARLES

Born, Grand Rapids, Michigan, November 23, 1984.
Bats Right. Throws Right. Height, 6 feet, 2 inches. Weight, 210 pounds.

Year Club	Lea	Pos	G	AB	R	H	2B	3B	HR	RBI	SB	Avg
2005 Tigers	Gulf Coast	OF	45	141	25	31	9	5	5	20	6	.220
2006 Lakeland	Fla.St.	OF	11	33	4	5	1	0	1	4	1	.152
2006 Oneonta	N.Y.-Penn.	OF	35	105	19	24	8	0	1	14	1	.229
2007 Lakeland	Fla.St.	OF	2	2	0	1	1	0	0	0	0	.500
2007 Oneonta	N.Y.-Penn.	OF	67	260	46	69	18	11	9	47	8	.265
2008 West Michigan	Midwest	OF	50	179	30	43	7	0	10	26	17	.240
2008 Erie	Eastern	OF	75	270	60	78	18	6	17	53	8	.289
2009 Erie	Eastern	OF	86	311	52	81	18	4	15	41	8	.260
2010 Toledo	Int.	OF	103	387	56	90	22	6	21	46	7	.233
2010 Detroit	A.L.	OF	36	93	14	30	6	1	4	17	0	.323
2011 Toledo	Int.	OF	7	27	4	10	2	2	2	6	0	.370
2011 Detroit-Seattle a	A.L.	OF	95	215	30	51	11	0	11	27	3	.237
Major League Totals		2 Yrs.	131	308	44	81	17	1	15	44	3	.263

a Traded to Seattle Mariners with pitcher Charlie Furbush, infielder Francisco Martinez and player to be named later for pitcher Doug Fister and pitcher David Pauley, July 30, 2011. Seattle Mariners received pitcher Chance Ruffin to complete trade, August 17, 2011.

WELLS, VERNON M.

Born, Shreveport, Louisiana, December 8, 1978.
Bats Right. Throws Right. Height, 6 feet, 1 inch. Weight, 225 pounds.

Year Club	Lea	Pos	G	AB	R	H	2B	3B	HR	RBI	SB	Avg
1997 St.Catherines	N.Y.-Penn.	OF	66	264	52	81	20	1	10	31	8	.307
1998 Hagerstown	So.Atl.	OF	134	509	86	145	35	2	11	65	13	.285

Year	Club	Lea	Pos	G	AB	R	H	2B	3B	HR	RBI	SB	Avg
1999 Dunedin . . . . .Fla.St.			OF	70	265	43	91	16	2	11	43	13	.343
1999 Knoxville . . . . Southern			OF	26	106	18	36	6	2	3	17	6	.340
1999 Syracuse . . . . .Int.			OF	33	129	20	40	8	1	4	21	5	.310
1999 Toronto . . . . .A.L.			OF	24	88	8	23	5	0	1	8	1	.261
2000 Syracuse . . . . .Int.			OF	127	493	76	120	31	7	16	66	23	.243
2000 Toronto . . . . .A.L.			OF	3	2	0	0	0	0	0	0	0	.000
2001 Syracuse . . . . .Int.			OF	107	413	57	116	27	4	12	52	15	.281
2001 Toronto a . . . . .A.L.			OF	30	96	14	30	8	0	1	6	5	.313
2002 Toronto . . . . .A.L.			OF	159	608	87	167	34	4	23	100	9	.275
2003 Toronto . . . . .A.L.			OF	161	678	118	*215	*49	5	33	117	4	.317
2004 Toronto b . . . . .A.L.			OF	134	536	82	146	34	2	23	67	9	.272
2005 Toronto . . . . .A.L.			OF	156	620	78	167	30	3	28	97	8	.269
2006 Toronto . . . . .A.L.			OF	154	611	91	185	40	5	32	106	17	.303
2007 Toronto c . . . . .A.L.			OF	149	584	85	143	36	4	16	80	10	.245
2008 Dunedin . . . . .Fla.St.			OF	2	8	3	4	0	0	0	4	0	.500
2008 Syracuse . . . . .Int.			OF	2	6	0	0	0	0	0	0	0	.000
2008 Toronto d . . . . .A.L.			OF	108	427	63	128	22	1	20	78	4	.300
2009 Toronto . . . . .A.L.			OF	158	630	84	164	37	3	15	66	17	.260
2010 Toronto . . . . .A.L.			OF	157	590	79	161	44	3	31	88	6	.273
2011 Inland Empire. . . . . . . .Calif.			OF	2	5	3	1	1	0	0	3	0	.200
2011 Los Angeles e-f . . . . A.L.			OF	131	505	60	110	15	4	25	66	9	.218
Major League Totals		13 Yrs.		1524	5975	849	1639	354	34	248	879	99	.274

a On disabled list from April 14 to 24, 2001.
b On disabled list from June 16 to July 16, 2004.
c On disabled list from September 22 to November 13, 2007.
d On disabled list from May 10 to June 7 and July 10 to August 10, 2008.
e Traded to Los Angeles Angels for catcher Mike Napoli and outfielder Juan Rivera, January 21, 2011.
f On disabled list from May 10 to June 7, 2011.

WERTH, JAYSON RICHARD GOWAN

Born, Springfield, Illinois, May 20, 1979.
Bats Right. Throws Right. Height, 6 feet, 5 inches. Weight, 220 pounds.

Year	Club	Lea	Pos	G	AB	R	H	2B	3B	HR	RBI	SB	Avg
1997 Orioles . . . . Gulf Coast			C-1B-OF	32	88	16	26	6	0	1	8	7	.295
1998 Delmarva . . . . So.Atl.			C	120	408	71	108	20	3	8	53	21	.265
1998 Bowie. . . . . .Eastern			C	5	19	2	3	2	0	0	1	1	.158
1999 Frederick . . . . Carolina			C	66	236	41	72	10	1	3	30	16	.305
1999 Bowie. . . . . .Eastern			C-OF	35	121	18	33	5	1	1	11	7	.273
2000 Frederick . . . . Carolina			C	24	83	16	23	3	0	2	18	5	.277
2000 Bowie a . . . . .Eastern			C-OF	85	276	47	63	16	2	5	26	9	.228
2001 Dunedin . . . . .Fla.St.			C	21	70	9	14	3	0	2	14	1	.200
2001 Tennessee . . . . Southern			C-1B	104	369	51	105	23	1	18	69	12	.285
2002 Syracuse . . . . .Int.			OF-C	127	443	65	114	25	2	18	82	24	.257
2002 Toronto . . . . .A.L.			OF	15	46	4	12	2	1	0	6	1	.261
2003 Dunedin . . . . .Fla.St.			OF	18	62	10	23	5	0	4	18	1	.371
2003 Toronto . . . . .A.L.			OF	26	48	7	10	4	0	2	10	1	.208
2003 Syracuse b . . . . .Int.			OF	64	236	37	56	19	1	9	34	11	.237
2004 Los Angeles . . . . .N.L.			OF	89	290	56	76	11	3	16	47	4	.262
2004 Las Vegas c-d . . . . .P.C.			OF	14	51	13	21	2	1	5	20	2	.412
2005 Las Vegas. . . . . .P.C.			OF	15	49	9	18	0	0	3	10	6	.367
2005 Los Angeles e . . . . .N.L.			OF	102	337	46	79	22	2	7	43	11	.234
2006 Los Angeles f-g . . . . N.L.					INJURED—Did Not Play								
2007 Clearwater . . . . .Fla.St.			OF	4	13	3	1	0	0	0	0	0	.077
2007 Philadelphia h . . . . .N.L.			OF-1B	94	255	43	76	11	3	8	49	7	.298
2008 Clearwater . . . . .Fla.St.			OF	2	6	0	1	0	0	0	0	0	.167
2008 Philadelphia i . . . . .N.L.			OF	134	418	73	114	16	3	24	67	20	.273
2009 Philadelphia . . . . .N.L.			OF	159	571	98	153	26	1	36	99	20	.268
2010 Philadelphia j . . . . .N.L.			OF	156	554	106	164	*46	2	27	85	13	.296
2011 Washington . . . . .N.L.			OF	150	561	69	130	26	1	20	58	19	.232
Major League Totals		9 Yrs.		925	3080	502	814	164	16	140	464	96	.264
Division Series													
2004 Los Angeles . . . . .N.L.			OF	4	14	3	4	1	0	2	3	0	.286
2007 Philadelphia . . . . .N.L.			OF	2	3	0	0	0	0	0	0	0	.000
2008 Philadelphia . . . . .N.L.			OF	4	16	3	5	3	1	1	1	1	.313
2009 Philadelphia . . . . .N.L.			OF	4	14	5	5	0	1	2	4	0	.357
2010 Philadelphia . . . . .N.L.			OF	3	12	2	2	0	0	0	1	1	.167
Division Series Totals				17	59	13	16	4	2	5	9	2	.271
Championship Series													
2008 Philadelphia . . . . .N.L.			OF	5	21	2	4	1	0	0	0	0	.190

Year Club	Lea	Pos	G	AB	R	H	2B	3B	HR	RBI	SB	Avg
2009 Philadelphia	N.L.	OF	5	18	5	4	0	0	3	6	0	.222
2010 Philadelphia	N.L.	OF	6	18	3	4	1	0	2	5	0	.222
Championship Series Totals			16	57	10	12	2	0	5	11	0	.211
World Series Record												
2008 Philadelphia	N.L.	OF	5	18	4	8	3	0	1	3	3	.444
2009 Philadelphia	N.L.	OF	6	19	3	5	0	0	2	3	0	.263
World Series Totals			11	37	7	13	3	0	3	6	3	.351

a Traded to Toronto Blue Jays by Baltimore Orioles for pitcher John Bale, December 11, 2000.
b On disabled list from March 21 to April 11, 2003.
c On disabled list from April 6 to June 4, 2004.
d Traded to Los Angeles Dodgers for pitcher Jason Frasor, March 30, 2004.
e On disabled list from March 25 to May 25 and from July 27 to August 11, 2005.
f On disabled list from April 1 to November 2, 2006.
g Not offered contract, December 12, 2006. Signed with Philadelphia Phillies, December 19, 2006.
h On disabled list from June 29 to August 1, 2007.
i On disabled list from May 23 to June 7, 2008.
j Filed for free agency, November 1, 2010. Signed with Washington Nationals, December 5, 2010.

WHITESIDE, DUSTIN ELI (ELI)

Born, New Albany, Mississippi, October 22, 1979.
Bats Right. Throws Right. Height, 6 feet, 2 inches. Weight, 220 pounds.

Year Club	Lea	Pos	G	AB	R	H	2B	3B	HR	RBI	SB	Avg
2001 Delmarva	So.Atl.	C	61	212	30	53	11	0	7	28	1	.250
2002 Frederick	Carolina	C	80	313	34	81	19	0	8	42	0	.259
2002 Bowie	Eastern	C	27	99	11	26	5	0	2	11	0	.263
2003 Bowie	Eastern	C	81	265	25	54	13	1	1	23	0	.204
2003 Orioles	Gulf Coast	C	1	3	0	1	1	0	0	0	0	.333
2003 Aberdeen	N.Y.-Penn.	C	2	10	0	7	3	0	0	4	1	.700
2004 Bowie	Eastern	C	90	297	41	75	18	0	18	60	2	.253
2005 Ottawa	Int.	C-3B	95	317	28	74	22	1	4	27	1	.233
2005 Baltimore	A.L.	C	9	12	1	3	0	0	0	1	0	.250
2006 Ottawa	Int.	C	92	315	37	77	18	1	11	47	1	.244
2007 Norfolk a	Int.	C	18	61	5	11	1	0	2	6	1	.180
2007 Bowie	Eastern	C	42	141	18	41	7	4	4	30	0	.291
2008 Rochester	Int.	C	8	24	2	4	0	0	1	1	0	.167
2008 Fresno b-c	P.C.	C-OF	49	151	13	36	7	0	2	22	2	.238
2009 Fresno	P.C.	C	34	116	16	28	7	1	6	24	0	.241
2009 San Francisco	N.L.	C	49	127	15	29	6	1	2	13	0	.228
2010 San Francisco	N.L.	C	56	126	19	30	6	1	4	10	1	.238
2011 San Francisco d-e	N.L.	C	82	213	14	42	8	2	4	17	2	.197
Major League Totals		4 Yrs.	196	478	49	104	20	4	10	41	3	.218

a Filed for free agency, October 29, 2007. Signed with Minnesota Twins organization, November 24, 2007.
b Released by Minnesota Twins, April 30, 2008. Signed with San Francisco Giants organization, May 5, 2008.
c Filed for free agency, November 3, 2008, re-signed with San Francisco Giants organization, November 21, 2008.
d On disabled list from August 19 to August 25, 2011.
e Not offered contract, December 12, 2011, re-signed with San Francisco Giants, December 15, 2011.

WIETERS, MATTHEW RICHARD (MATT)

Born, Goose Creek, South Carolina, May 21, 1986.
Bats Both. Throws Right. Height, 6 feet, 5 inches. Weight, 230 pounds.

Year Club	Lea	Pos	G	AB	R	H	2B	3B	HR	RBI	SB	Avg
2008 Frederick	Carolina	C	69	229	48	79	8	0	15	40	1	.345
2008 Bowie	Eastern	C	61	208	41	76	14	2	12	51	1	.365
2009 Norfolk	Int.	C	39	141	25	43	9	2	5	30	0	.305
2009 Baltimore	A.L.	C	96	354	35	102	15	1	9	43	0	.288
2010 Baltimore a	A.L.	C	130	446	37	111	22	1	11	55	0	.249
2011 Baltimore	A.L.	C-1B	139	500	72	131	28	0	22	68	1	.262
Major League Totals		3 Yrs.	365	1300	144	344	65	2	42	166	1	.265

a On disabled list from July 10 to July 25, 2010.

WIGGINTON, TY ALLEN (TY)

Born, San Diego, California, October 11, 1977.
Bats Right. Throws Right. Height, 6 feet. Weight, 225 pounds.

Year Club	Lea	Pos	G	AB	R	H	2B	3B	HR	RBI	SB	Avg
1998 Pittsfield	N.Y.-Penn.	2B-3B-OF	70	272	39	65	14	4	8	29	11	.239
1999 St. Lucie	Fla.St.	2B	123	456	69	133	23	5	21	73	9	.292

Year	Club	Lea	Pos	G	AB	R	H	2B	3B	HR	RBI	SB	Avg
2000 Binghamton	. . . . Eastern		2B-3B	122	453	64	129	27	3	20	77	5	.285
2001 Binghamton	. . . . Eastern		2B-3B	8	28	5	8	3	0	0	0	1	.286
2001 St. Lucie	. . . . Fla.St.		2B	3	9	1	3	1	0	0	1	0	.333
2001 Norfolk	. . . . Int.		3B-2B-1B-OF	78	260	29	65	12	0	7	24	3	.250
2002 Norfolk	. . . . Int.		3B-2B-OF-1B	104	383	49	115	26	3	6	48	5	.300
2002 New York	. . . . . . .N.L.		3B-1B-2B-OF	46	116	18	35	8	0	6	18	2	.302
2003 New York	. . . . .N.L.		3B	156	573	73	146	36	6	11	71	12	.255
2004 St. Lucie	. . . . Fla.St.		3B	2	8	1	3	0	0	0	0	0	.375
2004 N.Y.-Pittsburgh a-b	.N.L.		3B-2B-1B	144	494	63	129	30	2	17	66	7	.261
2005 Indianapolis	. . . . Int.		3B-1B-2B	72	280	53	82	18	0	14	52	8	.293
2005 Pittsburgh c	. . . . .N.L.		3B-1B-2B	57	155	20	40	9	1	7	25	0	.258
2006 Durham	. . . . Int.		1B	2	8	2	3	2	0	1	2	0	.375
2006 Tampa Bay d	. . . . . .A.L.		1B-2B-3B-OF	122	444	55	122	25	1	24	79	4	.275
2007 Tampa Bay	. . . . .A.L.		2B-3B-1B	98	378	47	104	21	0	16	49	1	.275
2007 Houston e	. . . . .N.L.		3B-OF-1B	50	169	24	48	12	0	6	18	2	.284
2008 Round Rock	. . . . P.C.		3B	3	9	1	1	0	1	0	1	0	.111
2008 Houston f-g	. . . .N.L.		3B-OF	111	386	50	110	22	1	23	58	4	.285
2009 Baltimore	. . . . .A.L.		1B-3B-SS	122	410	44	112	19	0	11	41	1	.273
2010 Baltimore h	. . . . . . .A.L.		1B-2B-3B	154	581	63	144	29	1	22	76	0	.248
2011 Colorado Springs	. . . P.C.		3B	2	7	1	2	0	0	0	1	0	.286
2011 Colorado i-j	. . . . .N.L.		3B-1B-OF	130	401	52	97	21	2	15	47	8	.242
Major League Totals	. . . .	10 Yrs.		1190	4107	509	1087	232	14	158	548	41	.265

a On disabled list from April 21 to May 7, 2004.
b Traded to Pittsburgh Pirates with pitcher Matt Peterson and infielder Jose Bautista for pitcher Kris Benson and infielder Jeff Keppinger, July 30, 2004.
c Released by Pittsburgh Pirates, December 8, 2005. Signed with Tampa Bay Devil Rays, January 10, 2006.
d On disabled list from July 31 to September 1, 2006.
e Traded to Houston Astros for pitcher Dan Wheeler, July 28, 2007.
f On disabled list from April 6 to May 2, 2008.
g Not offered contract, December 12, 2008. Signed with Baltimore Orioles, February 10, 2009.
h Filed for free agency, November 1, 2010. Signed with Colorado Rockies, December 7, 2010.
i On disabled list from April 27 to May 13, 2011.
j Sold to Philadelphia Phillies, November 20, 2011.

WILLINGHAM, JOSHUA DAVID (JOSH)
Born, Florence, Alabama, February 17, 1979.
Bats Right. Throws Right. Height, 6 feet, 1 inch. Weight, 215 pounds.

Year	Club	Lea	Pos	G	AB	R	H	2B	3B	HR	RBI	SB	Avg
2000 Utica	. . . . .N.Y.-Penn.		OF-2B-3B-SS	65	205	37	54	16	0	6	29	9	.263
2001 Kane County	. . . Midwest		3B-OF-2B	97	320	57	83	20	2	7	36	24	.259
2002 Jupiter	. . . . Fla.St.		1B-3B-OF	107	376	72	103	21	4	17	69	18	.274
2003 Jupiter	. . . . Fla.St.		C-1B-OF-3B	59	193	46	51	17	1	12	34	9	.264
2003 Marlins	. . . . . Gulf Coast		DH	2	7	3	3	1	0	1	3	0	.429
2003 Carolina	. . . . . . .Southern		1B-C-3B-OF	22	67	15	20	2	1	5	14	0	.299
2004 Carolina	. . . . . Southern		C-1B-OF-3B	112	338	81	95	24	0	24	76	6	.281
2004 Florida	. . . . .N.L.		C-OF	12	25	2	5	0	0	1	1	0	.200
2005 Jupiter	. . . . Fla.St.		C	2	9	1	2	1	0	0	1	0	.222
2005 Albuquerque	. . . . P.C.		C-3B	66	219	56	71	14	3	19	54	5	.324
2005 Florida a	. . . . .N.L.		C-OF	16	23	3	7	1	0	0	4	0	.304
2006 Carolina	. . . . .Southern		OF	2	8	0	2	0	0	0	0	0	.250
2006 Florida b	. . . . .N.L.		OF-C-1B	142	502	62	139	28	2	26	74	2	.277
2007 Florida	. . . . .N.L.		OF	144	521	75	138	32	4	21	89	8	.265
2008 Carolina	. . . . . . .Southern		OF	8	26	6	6	2	0	0	5	0	.231
2008 Florida c-d	. . . . .N.L.		OF	102	351	54	89	21	5	15	51	3	.254
2009 Washington	. . . . .N.L.		OF-1B	133	427	70	111	29	0	24	61	4	.260
2010 Washington e-f	. . .N.L.		OF	114	370	54	99	19	2	16	56	8	.268
2011 Sacramento	. . . . . . .P.C.		DH	2	5	1	1	0	0	1	2	0	.200
2011 Oakland g-h	. . . . . . .A.L.		OF	136	488	69	120	26	0	29	98	4	.246
Major League Totals	. . . .	8 Yrs.		799	2707	389	708	156	13	132	434	29	.262

a On disabled list from June 30 to September 2, 2005.
b On disabled list from June 7 to June 22, 2006.
c On disabled list from April 28 to June 23, 2008.
d Traded to Washington Nationals with pitcher Scott Olsen for infielder Emilio Bonifacio, pitcher P.J. Dean and infielder Jake Smolinkski, November 11, 2008.
e On disabled list from August 18 to November 10, 2010.
f Traded to Oakland Athletics for pitcher Henry Rodriguez and outfielder Corey Brown, December 16, 2010.
g On disabled list from June 18 to July 7, 2011.
h Filed for free agency, October 30, 2011. Signed with Minnesota Twins, December 15, 2011.

WILSON, JACK EUGENE
Born, Westlake Village, California, December 29, 1977.
Bats Right. Throws Right. Height, 6 feet. Weight, 185 pounds.

Year	Club	Lea	Pos	G	AB	R	H	2B	3B	HR	RBI	SB	Avg
1998 Johnson Cty	Appal.	SS	61	241	50	90	18	4	4	29	22	.373
1999 Potomac	Carolina	SS	64	257	44	76	10	1	2	18	7	.296
1999 Peoria	Midwest	SS	64	251	47	86	22	4	3	28	11	.343
2000 Potomac	Carolina	SS	13	47	7	13	0	1	2	7	2	.277
2000 Altoona	Eastern	SS	33	139	17	35	7	2	1	16	1	.252
2000 Arkansas a	Texas	SS	88	343	65	101	20	8	6	34	2	.294
2001 Nashville	P.C.	SS	27	103	20	38	6	1	1	6	2	.369
2001 Pittsburgh	N.L.	SS	108	390	44	87	17	1	3	25	1	.223
2002 Pittsburgh	N.L.	SS	147	527	77	133	22	4	4	47	5	.252
2003 Pittsburgh	N.L.	SS	150	558	58	143	21	3	9	62	5	.256
2004 Pittsburgh	N.L.	SS	157	652	82	201	41	*12	11	59	8	.308
2005 Pittsburgh	N.L.	SS	158	587	60	151	24	7	8	52	7	.257
2006 Pittsburgh	N.L.	SS	142	543	70	148	27	1	8	35	4	.273
2007 Pittsburgh	N.L.	SS	135	477	67	141	29	2	12	56	2	.296
2008 Altoona	Eastern	SS	7	19	1	6	0	0	0	0	1	.316
2008 Indianapolis	Int.	SS	4	12	2	4	1	0	0	2	0	.333
2008 Pittsburgh b	N.L.	SS	87	305	24	83	18	1	1	22	2	.272
2009 Indianapolis	Int.	SS	2	6	0	2	2	0	0	3	0	.333
2009 Pittsburgh	N.L.	SS	75	266	26	71	18	1	4	31	2	.267
2009 Seattle c-d	A.L.	SS	31	107	11	24	5	0	1	8	1	.224
2010 West Tenn	Southern	DH	1	2	1	1	0	0	0	0	0	.500
2010 Tacoma	P.C.	SS	9	33	3	10	2	0	1	4	2	.303
2010 Seattle e	A.L.	SS	61	193	17	48	11	1	0	14	1	.249
2011 Seattle	A.L.	2B-SS-3B	62	173	22	43	8	0	0	11	5	.249
2011 Atlanta f-g-h	N.L.	SS-3B	17	41	3	9	1	0	0	0	0	.220
Major League Totals			11 Yrs.	1330	4819	561	1282	242	33	61	422	43	.266

a Traded by St. Louis Cardinals to Pittsburgh Pirates for pitcher Jason Christiansen, July 30, 2000.
b On disabled list from April 4 to May 27, 2008.
c On disabled list from April 25 to May 12, 2009.
d Traded to Seattle Mariners with pitcher Ian Snell for outfielder Jeff Clement, infielder Ronny Cedeno, pitcher
  Aaron Pribanic, pitcher Brett Lorin and pitcher Nathan Adcock, July 29, 2009.
e On disabled list from May 6 to June 20 and August 8 to October 8, 2010.
f Traded to Atlanta Braves with cash for player to be named later, August 31, 2011. Seattle Mariners received
  infielder Luis Caballero to complete trade, September 30, 2011.
g On disabled list from August 18 to September 2, 2011.
h Filed for free agency, October 30, 2011. Signed with Atlanta Braves, January 13, 2012.

WILSON, JOSHUA AARON (JOSH)
Born, Pittsburgh, Pennsylvania, March 26, 1981.
Bats Right. Throws Right. Height, 6 feet, 1 inch. Weight, 175 pounds.

Year	Club	Lea	Pos	G	AB	R	H	2B	3B	HR	RBI	SB	Avg
1999 Marlins	Gulf Coast	SS	53	203	29	54	9	4	0	27	14	.266
2000 Kane County	Midwest	SS-2B-3B	13	52	2	14	3	1	1	6	0	.269
2000 Utica	N.Y.-Penn.	SS	66	259	43	89	13	6	3	43	9	.344
2001 Kane County	Midwest	2B-SS-3B	123	506	65	144	28	5	4	61	17	.285
2002 Portland	Eastern	SS	12	41	5	14	3	0	2	5	0	.341
2002 Jupiter	Fla.St.	SS-2B-3B	111	398	51	102	17	1	11	50	7	.256
2003 Carolina	Southern	SS-2B	118	434	53	110	30	6	3	58	6	.253
2004 Albuquerque	P.C.	SS	56	240	32	67	12	2	5	23	6	.279
2004 Carolina	Southern	SS	81	311	63	98	21	1	10	41	8	.315
2005 Albuquerque	P.C.	SS-2B	143	526	88	135	31	6	17	82	17	.257
2005 Florida	N.L.	SS-2B	11	10	2	1	1	0	0	0	0	.100
2006 Colorado Springs a-b-c	P.C.	SS-3B-2B	89	335	61	103	18	4	10	45	15	.307
2007 Washington	N.L.	SS	15	19	3	1	0	0	0	0	0	.053
2007 Tampa Bay d-e	A.L.	SS-2B-3B-P	90	263	25	66	15	3	2	24	6	.251
2008 Indianapolis	Int.	SS-2B-3B-OF	97	293	28	81	18	1	5	32	11	.276
2008 Pawtucket f-g	Int.	SS-2B-3B	27	112	16	25	6	0	2	10	2	.223
2009 Reno	P.C.	SS	15	50	5	13	3	1	1	10	1	.260
2009 Arizona-San Diego	N.L.	SS-P-3B	27	64	3	10	3	0	0	3	0	.156
2009 Tacoma	P.C.	SS-2B	16	53	10	13	2	0	1	3	1	.245
2009 Seattle h-i-j	A.L.	SS-3B-2B	45	128	16	32	8	1	3	10	1	.250
2010 Tacoma	P.C.	SS-2B	20	81	7	27	11	1	0	11	0	.333
2010 Seattle	A.L.	SS-3B-1B-2B	108	361	20	82	14	2	2	25	5	.227
2011 Reno	P.C.	SS-2B	16	57	11	20	5	2	1	12	2	.351
2011 Arizona-Milwaukee k-l-m	N.L.	3B-SS-2B-OF	60	85	13	19	5	0	2	5	1	.224
Major League Totals			5 Yrs.	356	930	84	211	46	6	9	67	13	.227

a Sold to Colorado Rockies, January 6, 2006.
b On disabled list from March 28 to June 7, 2006.

c Filed for free agency, November 1, 2006. Signed with Washington Nationals, November 6, 2006.
d Claimed on waivers by Tampa Bay Devil Rays, May 10, 2007.
e Claimed on waivers by Pittsburgh Pirates, December 3, 2007.
f Sold to Boston Red Sox, August 2, 2008.
g Filed for free agency, October 14, 2008, signed with Arizona Diamondbacks organization, December 5, 2008.
h Claimed on waivers by San Diego Padres, May 15, 2009.
i Claimed on waivers by Seattle Mariners, June 19, 2009.
j Filed for free agency, November 23, 2009, re-signed with Seattle Mariners organization, December 10, 2009.
k Released by Seattle Mariners, March 28, 2011. Signed with Arizona Diamondbacks organization, April 1, 2011.
l Claimed on waivers by Milwaukee Brewers, May 25, 2011.
m Filed for free agency, November 15, 2011. Signed with Atlanta Braves organization, November 22, 2011.

WOOD, RICHARD BRANDON (BRANDON)
Born, Austin, Texas, March 2, 1985.
Bats Right. Throws Right. Height, 6 feet, 3 inches. Weight, 210 pounds.

Year Club	Lea	Pos	G	AB	R	H	2B	3B	HR	RBI	SB	Avg
2003 Angels	Arizona	SS-3B	19	78	14	24	8	2	0	13	3	.308
2003 Provo	Pioneer	SS-3B	42	162	25	45	13	2	5	31	1	.278
2004 Cedar Rapids	Midwest	SS	125	478	65	120	30	5	11	64	21	.251
2005 Rancho Cucamonga	Calif.	SS	130	536	109	172	51	4	43	115	7	.321
2005 Salt Lake	P.C.	SS	4	19	1	6	2	1	0	1	0	.316
2006 Arkansas	Texas	SS	118	453	74	125	42	4	25	83	19	.276
2007 Salt Lake	P.C.	3B-SS	111	437	73	119	27	1	23	77	10	.272
2007 Los Angeles	A.L.	3B-SS	13	33	2	5	1	0	1	3	0	.152
2008 Salt Lake	P.C.	SS-3B	103	395	82	117	21	2	31	84	6	.296
2008 Los Angeles	A.L.	3B-SS	55	150	12	30	4	0	5	13	4	.200
2009 Salt Lake	P.C.	3B-SS-1B	99	386	65	113	28	4	22	72	1	.293
2009 Los Angeles	A.L.	3B-SS-1B	18	41	5	8	1	0	1	3	0	.195
2010 Salt Lake	P.C.	3B-1B-SS	13	51	4	10	0	0	1	2	0	.196
2010 Los Angeles a.	A.L.	3B-SS-1B	81	226	20	33	2	0	4	14	1	.146
2011 Los Angeles	A.L.	SS-1B	6	14	1	2	1	0	0	0	0	.143
2011 Pittsburgh b-c	N.L.3B-SS-1B-2B	99	236	25	52	9	0	7	31	0	.220
Major League Totals	5 Yrs.	272	700	65	130	18	0	18	64	5	.186

a On disabled list from May 24 to June 15, 2010.
b Claimed on waivers by Pittsburgh Pirates, April 22, 2011.
c Filed for free agency, November 2, 2011. Signed with Colorado Rockies organization, November 17, 2011.

WRIGHT, DAVID ALLEN
Born, Norfolk, Virginia, December 20, 1982.
Bats Right. Throws Right. Height, 6 feet. Weight, 215 pounds.

Year Club	Lea	Pos	G	AB	R	H	2B	3B	HR	RBI	SB	Avg
2001 Kingsport	Appal.	3B	35	116	27	35	7	0	4	16	9	.302
2002 Columbia	So.Atl.	3B	135	496	85	132	30	2	11	93	21	.266
2003 St. Lucie	Fla.St.	3B	133	466	69	126	39	2	15	75	19	.270
2004 Binghamton	Eastern	3B	60	223	44	81	27	0	10	40	20	.363
2004 Norfolk	Int.	3B	31	114	18	34	8	0	8	17	2	.298
2004 New York	N.L.	3B	69	263	41	77	17	1	14	40	6	.293
2005 New York	N.L.	3B	160	575	99	176	42	1	27	102	17	.306
2006 New York	N.L.	3B	154	582	96	181	40	5	26	116	20	.311
2007 New York	N.L.	3B	160	604	113	196	42	1	30	107	34	.325
2008 New York	N.L.	3B	160	626	115	189	42	2	33	124	15	.302
2009 New York a.	N.L.	3B	144	535	88	164	39	3	10	72	27	.307
2010 New York	N.L.	3B	157	587	87	166	36	3	29	103	19	.283
2011 St. Lucie	Fla.St.	3B	6	21	9	10	3	0	0	2	1	.476
2011 New York b.	N.L.	3B-SS	102	389	60	99	23	1	14	61	13	.254
Major League Totals	8 Yrs.	1106	4161	699	1248	281	17	183	725	151	.300
Division Series												
2006 New York	N.L.	3B	3	12	1	4	2	0	0	4	0	.333
Championship Series												
2006 New York	N.L.	3B	7	25	2	4	1	0	1	2	0	.160

a On disabled list from August 16 to September 1, 2009.
b On disabled list from May 16 to July 22, 2011.

YOUKILIS, KEVIN EDMUND
Born, Cincinnati, Ohio, March 15, 1979.
Bats Right. Throws Right. Height, 6 feet, 1 inch. Weight, 220 pounds.

Year Club	Lea	Pos	G	AB	R	H	2B	3B	HR	RBI	SB	Avg
2001 Lowell	N.Y.-Penn.	3B	59	183	52	58	14	2	3	28	4	.317
2001 Augusta	So.Atl.	3B	5	12	0	2	0	0	0	0	0	.167

Year	Club	Lea	Pos	G	AB	R	H	2B	3B	HR	RBI	SB	Avg
2002 Augusta	So.Atl.		3B	15	53	5	15	5	0	0	6	0	.283
2002 Sarasota	Fla.St.		1B-3B	76	268	45	79	16	0	3	48	0	.295
2002 Trenton	Eastern		3B	44	160	34	55	10	0	5	26	5	.344
2003 Portland	Eastern		3B	94	312	74	102	23	1	6	37	7	.327
2003 Pawtucket	Int.		3B	32	109	9	18	3	0	2	15	0	.165
2004 Lowell	N.Y.-Penn.		3B	2	4	1	3	1	1	0	0	0	.750
2004 Pawtucket	Int.		3B-1B	38	154	25	41	12	0	3	18	2	.266
2004 Boston a	A.L.		3B	72	208	38	54	11	0	7	35	0	.260
2005 Pawtucket	Int.		3B-1B-2B	43	152	30	49	15	1	8	27	1	.322
2005 Boston	A.L.		3B-1B-2B	44	79	11	22	7	0	1	9	0	.278
2006 Boston	A.L.		1B-OF-3B	147	569	100	159	42	2	13	72	5	.279
2007 Boston	A.L.		1B-3B	145	528	85	152	35	2	16	83	4	.288
2008 Boston	A.L.		1B-3B-OF	145	538	91	168	43	4	29	115	3	.312
2009 Pawtucket	Int.		1B	2	6	0	0	0	0	0	0	0	.000
2009 Boston b	A.L.		1B-3B-OF	136	491	99	150	36	1	27	94	7	.305
2010 Boston c	A.L.		1B-3B	102	362	77	111	26	5	19	62	4	.307
2011 Pawtucket	Int.		3B	2	8	2	2	0	0	1	1	0	.250
2011 Boston d	A.L.		3B-1B	120	431	68	111	32	2	17	80	3	.258
Major League Totals		8 Yrs.		911	3206	569	927	232	16	129	550	26	.289
Division Series													
2004 Boston	A.L.		3B	1	2	0	0	0	0	0	0	0	.000
2007 Boston	A.L.		1B	3	12	3	3	1	0	1	2	0	.250
2008 Boston	A.L.		1B-3B	4	18	2	4	1	0	0	1	0	.222
2009 Boston	A.L.		1B-3B	3	12	0	1	1	0	0	0	0	.083
Division Series Totals				11	44	5	8	3	0	1	3	0	.182
Championship Series													
2007 Boston	A.L.		1B	7	28	10	14	1	1	3	7	0	.500
2008 Boston	A.L.		3B	7	30	4	10	3	0	2	6	0	.333
Championship Series Totals				14	58	14	24	4	1	5	13	0	.414
World Series Record													
2007 Boston	A.L.		1B	4	9	3	2	2	0	0	1	0	.222

a On disabled list from August 16 to September 1, 2004.
b On disabled list from May 5 to May 21, 2009.
c On disabled list from August 3 to November 8, 2010.
d On disabled list from August 18 to September 2 and September 28 to October 31, 2011.

YOUNG, CHRISTOPHER BRANDON (CHRIS)

Born, Houston, Texas, September 5, 1983.
Bats Right. Throws Right. Height, 6 feet, 2 inches. Weight, 200 pounds.

Year	Club	Lea	Pos	G	AB	R	H	2B	3B	HR	RBI	SB	Avg
2002 White Sox	Arizona		OF	55	184	26	40	13	1	5	17	7	.217
2003 Bristol	Appal.		OF	64	238	47	69	18	3	7	28	21	.290
2003 Great Falls	Pioneer		OF	10	34	5	6	3	0	0	0	0	.176
2004 Kannapolis	So.Atl.		OF	136	467	83	122	31	5	24	56	31	.261
2005 Birmingham a	Southern		OF	126	466	100	129	41	3	26	77	32	.277
2006 Tucson	P.C.		OF	100	402	78	111	32	4	21	77	17	.276
2006 Arizona	N.L.		OF	30	70	10	17	4	0	2	10	2	.243
2007 Arizona	N.L.		OF	148	569	85	135	29	3	32	68	27	.237
2008 Arizona	N.L.		OF	160	625	85	155	42	7	22	85	14	.248
2009 Reno	P.C.		OF	13	54	17	20	5	1	3	9	2	.370
2009 Arizona	N.L.		OF	134	433	54	92	28	4	15	42	11	.212
2010 Arizona	N.L.		OF	156	584	94	150	33	0	27	91	28	.257
2011 Arizona	N.L.		OF	156	567	89	134	38	3	20	71	22	.236
Major League Totals		6 Yrs.		784	2848	417	683	174	17	118	367	104	.240
Division Series													
2007 Arizona	N.L.		OF	3	11	3	3	0	0	2	4	1	.273
2011 Arizona	N.L.		OF	5	18	5	7	1	0	3	4	2	.389
Division Series Totals				8	29	8	10	1	0	5	8	3	.345
Championship Series													
2007 Arizona	N.L.		OF	4	14	1	4	1	0	0	1	0	.286

a Traded to Arizona Diamondbacks by Chicago White Sox with pitcher Orlando Hernandez and pitcher Luis Vizcaino for pitcher Javier Vazquez, December 20, 2005.

YOUNG, DELMON DAMARCUS

Born, Birmingham, Alabama, September 14, 1985.
Bats Right. Throws Right. Height, 6 feet, 3 inches. Weight, 205 pounds.

Year	Club	Lea	Pos	G	AB	R	H	2B	3B	HR	RBI	SB	Avg
2004 Charleston	So.Atl.		OF	131	513	95	165	26	5	25	116	21	.322

Year Club	Lea	Pos	G	AB	R	H	2B	3B	HR	RBI	SB	Avg
2005 Durham	Int.	OF	52	228	33	65	13	3	6	28	7	.285
2005 Montgomery	Southern	OF	84	330	59	111	13	4	20	71	25	.336
2006 Durham	Int.	OF	86	342	50	108	22	4	8	59	22	.316
2006 Tampa Bay	A.L.	OF	30	126	16	40	9	1	3	10	2	.317
2007 Tampa Bay a	A.L.	OF	*162	645	65	186	38	0	13	93	10	.288
2008 Minnesota	A.L.	OF	152	575	80	167	28	4	10	69	14	.290
2009 Minnesota	A.L.	OF	108	395	50	112	16	2	12	60	2	.284
2010 Minnesota	A.L.	OF	153	570	77	170	46	1	21	112	5	.298
2011 Rochester.	Int.	OF	9	31	5	9	3	0	2	5	0	.290
2011 Minnesota-Detroit b-c . .	A.L.	OF	124	473	54	127	21	1	12	64	1	.268
Major League Totals		6 Yrs.	729	2784	342	802	158	9	71	408	34	.288
Division Series												
2009 Minnesota	A.L.	OF	3	12	1	1	1	0	0	0	1	.083
2010 Minnesota	A.L.	OF	3	12	1	4	0	1	0	0	0	.333
2011 Detroit	A.L.	OF	5	19	4	6	0	0	3	3	0	.316
Division Series Totals			11	43	6	11	1	1	3	3	1	.256
Championship Series												
2011 Detroit	A.L.	OF	4	15	2	2	0	0	2	3	0	.133

a Traded to Minnesota Twins with infielder Brendan Harris and outfielder Jason Pridie for infielder Jason Bartlett, pitcher Matt Garza and pitcher Eduardo Morlan, November 28, 2007.

b On disabled list from April 19 to May 13 and June 26 to July 11, 2011.

c Traded to Detroit Tigers for pitcher Cole Nelson and player to be named later, August 15, 2011. Minnesota Twins received pitcher Lester Oliveros to complete trade, August 16, 2011.

YOUNG, ERIC ORLANDO JR.

Born, New Brunswick, New Jersey, May 25, 1985.
Bats Both. Throws Right. Height, 5 feet, 10 inches. Weight, 180 pounds.

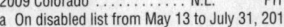

Year Club	Lea	Pos	G	AB	R	H	2B	3B	HR	RBI	SB	Avg
2004 Casper	Pioneer	2B	23	87	20	23	5	1	0	7	14	.264
2005 Casper	Pioneer	2B	63	219	48	66	7	7	3	25	25	.301
2006 Asheville.	So.Atl.	2B	128	482	92	142	28	6	5	49	87	.295
2007 Modesto	Calif.	2B	130	540	113	157	29	11	8	63	73	.291
2008 Tulsa	Texas	2B-OF	105	403	74	117	24	4	3	33	46	.290
2009 Colorado Springs.	P.C.	2B-OF	119	472	118	141	21	10	7	43	58	.299
2009 Colorado	N.L.	2B-OF	30	57	7	14	1	0	1	1	4	.246
2010 Tulsa	Texas	2B	4	13	2	3	0	0	0	0	0	.231
2010 Colorado Springs.	P.C.	2B-OF	33	123	20	31	5	1	1	9	10	.252
2010 Colorado a	N.L.	2B-OF	51	172	26	42	5	1	0	8	17	.244
2011 Colorado Springs	P.C.	OF-2B	58	223	61	81	18	9	2	28	17	.363
2011 Colorado	N.L.	OF-2B	77	198	34	49	4	3	0	10	27	.247
Major League Totals		3 Yrs.	158	427	67	105	10	4	1	19	48	.246
Division Series												
2009 Colorado	N.L.	PH	2	1	0	0	0	0	0	0	0	.000

a On disabled list from May 13 to July 31, 2010.

YOUNG, MICHAEL BRIAN

Born, Covina, California, October 19, 1976.
Bats Right. Throws Right. Height, 6 feet, 1 Inch. Weight, 200 pounds.

Year Club	Lea	Pos	G	AB	R	H	2B	3B	HR	RBI	SB	Avg
1997 St.Catherines .	N.Y.-Penn.	SS-2B	74	276	49	85	18	3	9	48	9	.308
1998 Hagerstown . . .	So.Atl.	2B-SS-OF	140	522	86	147	33	5	16	87	16	.282
1999 Dunedin	Fla.St.	2B	129	495	86	155	36	3	5	83	30	.313
2000 Tennessee	Southern	2B-SS	91	345	51	95	24	5	6	47	16	.275
2000 Tulsa	Texas	SS	43	188	30	60	13	5	1	32	9	.319
2000 Texas a	A.L.	2B	2	2	0	0	0	0	0	0	0	.000
2001 Oklahoma.	P.C.	2B-SS	47	189	28	55	8	0	8	28	3	.291
2001 Texas	A.L.	2B	106	386	57	96	18	4	11	49	3	.249
2002 Texas	A.L.	2B-SS-3B	156	573	77	150	26	8	9	62	6	.262
2003 Texas	A.L.	2B-SS	160	666	106	204	33	9	14	72	13	.306
2004 Texas	A.L.	SS	160	690	114	216	33	9	22	99	12	.313
2005 Texas	A.L.	SS	159	668	*114	*221	40	5	24	91	5	*.331
2006 Texas	A.L.	SS	*162	691	93	217	52	3	14	103	7	.314
2007 Texas	A.L.	SS	156	639	80	201	37	1	9	94	13	.315
2008 Texas	A.L.	SS	155	645	102	183	36	2	12	82	10	.284
2009 Texas	A.L.	3B	135	541	76	174	36	2	22	68	8	.322
2010 Texas	A.L.	3B	157	656	99	186	36	3	21	91	4	.284
2011 Texas	A.L.	DH-3B-1B-2B	159	631	88	*213	41	6	11	106	6	.338
Major League Totals		12 Yrs.	1667	6788	1006	2061	388	52	169	917	87	.304

Year	Club	Lea	Pos	G	AB	R	H	2B	3B	HR	RBI	SB	Avg
	Division Series												
2010 Texas		A.L.	3B	5	20	1	3	0	0	1	3	0	.150
2011 Texas		A.L.	DH-1B	4	15	1	2	0	0	0	0	0	.133
Division Series Totals				9	35	2	5	0	0	1	3	0	.143
	Championship Series												
2010 Texas		A.L.	3B	6	27	3	9	3	0	0	4	0	.333
2011 Texas		A.L.	1B-DH	6	28	3	7	3	0	1	7	0	.250
Championship Series Totals				12	55	6	16	6	0	1	11	0	.291
	World Series Record												
2010 Texas		A.L.	3B	5	20	0	5	0	0	0	0	0	.250
2011 Texas		A.L.	1B-DH	7	27	3	7	4	0	1	5	0	.259
World Series Totals............				12	47	3	12	4	0	1	5	0	.255

a Traded by Toronto Blue Jays to Texas Rangers with pitcher Darwin Cubillan for pitcher Esteban Loaiza, July 19, 2000.

ZIMMERMAN, RYAN WALLACE

Born, Washington, North Carolina, September 28, 1984.
Bats Right. Throws Right. Height, 6 feet, 3 inches. Weight, 230 pounds.

Year	Club	Lea	Pos	G	AB	R	H	2B	3B	HR	RBI	SB	Avg
2005 Savannah	So.Atl.	1B-SS	4	17	5	8	2	1	2	6	0	.471	
2005 Harrisburg	Eastern	3B-SS	63	233	40	76	20	0	9	32	1	.326	
2005 Washington	N.L.	3B-SS	20	58	6	23	10	0	0	6	0	.397	
2006 Washington	N.L.	3B	157	614	84	176	47	3	20	110	11	.287	
2007 Washington	N.L.	3B	*162	653	99	174	43	5	24	91	4	.266	
2008 Potomac.	Carolina	DH	2	10	1	3	0	0	0	0	0	.300	
2008 Columbus.............	Int.	3B	4	15	4	4	1	0	1	3	0	.267	
2008 Washington a.........	N.L.	3B	106	428	51	121	24	1	14	51	1	.283	
2009 Washington	N.L.	3B	157	610	110	178	37	3	33	106	2	.292	
2010 Washington	N.L.	3B	142	525	85	161	32	0	25	85	4	.307	
2011 Hagerstown	So.Atl.	2B	1	2	2	2	1	1	0	1	0	1.000	
2011 Potomac.	Carolina	3B	3	10	0	4	2	0	0	1	0	.400	
2011 Syracuse	Int.	3B	2	9	1	2	0	0	0	1	0	.222	
2011 Washington b.........	N.L.	3B	101	395	52	114	21	2	12	49	3	.289	
Major League Totals		7 Yrs.	845	3283	487	947	214	14	128	498	25	.288	

a On disabled list from May 26 to July 22, 2008.
b On disabled list from April 10 to June 14, 2011.

ZOBRIST, BENJAMIN THOMAS (BEN)

Born, Eureka, Illinois, May 26, 1981.
Bats Both. Throws Right. Height, 6 feet, 3 inches. Weight, 200 pounds.

Year	Club	Lea	Pos	G	AB	R	H	2B	3B	HR	RBI	SB	Avg
2004 Tri-City .....N.Y.-Penn.		SS	68	257	50	87	14	3	4	45	15	.339	
2005 Salem........ Carolina		SS	42	141	25	47	12	1	3	13	2	.333	
2005 Lexington....... So.Atl.		SS	68	247	45	75	17	2	2	32	16	.304	
2006 Corpus Christi ... Texas		SS-3B	83	315	57	103	25	6	3	30	9	.327	
2006 Durham .... Int.		SS	18	69	12	21	3	1	0	6	4	.304	
2006 Tampa Bay a........A.L.		SS	52	183	10	41	6	2	2	18	2	.224	
2007 Durham .... Int.		SS	61	222	42	62	14	2	7	22	8	.279	
2007 Tampa Bay b ......A.L.		SS	31	97	8	15	2	0	1	9	2	.155	
2008 Vero Beach...... Fla.St.		2B-3B-SS	4	14	1	4	1	0	0	2	0	.286	
2008 Durham .... Int.		SS-3B-2B	20	71	15	26	3	0	4	13	4	.366	
2008 Tampa Bay c.......A.L.		SS-OF-2B-3B	62	198	32	50	10	2	12	30	3	.253	
2009 Tampa Bay ........A.L.		2B-OF-SS-1B	152	501	91	149	28	7	27	91	17	.297	
2010 Tampa Bay ........A.L.		OF-2B-1B-3B	151	541	77	129	28	2	10	75	24	.238	
2011 Tampa Bay ........A.L.		2B-OF	156	588	99	158	46	6	20	91	19	.269	
Major League Totals		6 Yrs.	604	2108	317	542	120	19	72	314	67	.257	
	Division Series												
2010 Tampa Bay ........A.L.		OF-2B-1B	5	20	2	6	2	0	1	2	0	.300	
2011 Tampa Bay ........A.L.		2B	4	17	2	4	0	0	0	0	0	.235	
Division Series Totals				9	37	4	10	2	0	1	2	0	.270
	Championship Series												
2008 Tampa Bay ........A.L.		OF-SS	3	4	0	0	0	0	0	0	0	.000	
	World Series Record												
2008 Tampa Bay ........A.L.		OF	4	7	0	1	0	0	0	0	0	.143	

a Traded by Houston Astros to Tampa Bay Devil Rays with pitcher Mitch Talbot for infielder Aubrey Huff and cash, July 12, 2006.
b On disabled list from August 19 to November 12, 2007.
c On disabled list from March 25 to May 13, 2008.

ACEVES, ALFREDO
Born, San Luis Rio Colorado, Mexico, December 8, 1982.
Bats Right. Throws Right. Height, 6 feet, 3 inches. Weight, 220 pounds.

Year	Club	Lea	G	IP	W	L	Pct	SO	BB	H	ERA	SAVES
2002	Yucatan a	Mexican	23	45	1	2	.333	25	20	42	3.00	0
2003	Yucatan	Mexican	27	43	1	1	.500	29	18	49	3.35	1
2004	Yucatan	Mexican	17	65^{1}/3	4	2	.667	37	37	64	4.55	0
2005	Yucatan	Mexican	22	145^{2}/3	9	8	.529	101	44	155	4.32	0
2006	Monterrey	Mexican	19	124	8	5	.615	95	26	126	4.50	0
2007	Monterrey	Mexican	18	106^{1}/3	11	5	.688	70	33	96	3.64	0
2008	Trenton...........	Eastern	7	50	2	2	.500	35	6	37	1.80	0
2008	Tampa	Fla.St.	8	47	4	1	.800	37	8	32	2.11	0
2008	Scranton-WB	Int.	10	43^{2}/3	2	3	.400	42	13	42	4.12	0
2008	New York b...........	A.L.	6	30	1	0	1.000	16	10	25	2.40	0
2009	Scranton-WB	Int.	4	23^{2}/3	2	0	1.000	18	5	18	3.80	0
2009	New York	A.L.	43	84	10	1	.909	69	16	69	3.54	1
2010	New York	A.L.	10	12	3	0	1.000	2	4	10	3.00	1
2010	Trenton............	Eastern	4	8	0	0	.000	7	1	10	5.63	0
2010	Scranton-WB c-d	Int.	3	3^{2}/3	0	0	.000	4	5	4	7.36	0
2011	Pawtucket	Int.	2	8	0	1	.000	6	4	6	5.63	0
2011	Boston	A.L.	55	114	10	2	.833	80	42	84	2.61	2
Major League Totals		4 Yrs.	114	240	24	3	.889	167	72	188	2.93	4
Division Series												
2009	New York	A.L.	1	1	0	0	.000	1	1	1	0.00	0
Championship Series												
2009	New York	A.L.	2	1^{1}/3	0	1	.000	0	2	3	13.50	0
World Series Record												
2009	New York	A.L.	1	2	0	0	.000	1	0	1	0.00	0

a Sold by Toronto Blue Jays to Yucatan (Mexican), April 24, 2002.
b Signed with New York Yankees organization, March 10, 2008.
c On disabled list from May 9 to November 3, 2010.
d Not offered contract, December 2, 2010. Signed with Boston Red Sox, February 9, 2011.

ACOSTA, MANUEL ALCIDES (MANNY)
Born, Colon, Panama, May 1, 1981.
Bats Right. Throws Right. Height, 6 feet, 4 inches. Weight, 215 pounds.

Year	Club	Lea	G	IP	W	L	Pct	SO	BB	H	ERA	SAVES
1998	NY Yankees	Dominican	9	7^{2}/3	0	1	.000	5	10	20	16.43	1
2000	Yankees	Gulf Coast	12	62^{1}/3	4	2	.667	46	21	64	3.47	0
2001	Tampa	Fla.St.	2	7	0	1	.000	8	6	7	7.71	0
2001	Greensboro	So.Atl.	10	65^{2}/3	5	2	.714	67	37	37	1.51	0
2002	Staten Island ...	N.Y.-Penn.	3	15^{1}/3	2	1	.667	12	8	20	4.11	0
2002	Greensboro	So.Atl.	13	52	2	5	.286	35	44	65	6.40	0
2003	Battle Creek a	Midwest	15	61	0	8	.000	45	29	80	6.64	0
2003	Myrtle Beach	Carolina	8	12^{2}/3	2	0	1.000	10	11	19	6.39	1
2004	Myrtle Beach	Carolina	11	23^{1}/3	4	0	1.000	21	11	20	4.24	0
2004	Braves	Gulf Coast	2	2^{2}/3	0	0	.000	2	2	5	3.38	0
2005	Danville	Appal.	3	6	0	0	.000	8	1	3	3.00	0
2005	Myrtle Beach	Carolina	18	22^{1}/3	2	2	.500	18	9	22	4.43	7
2006	Mississippi.......	Southern	13	15^{1}/3	0	0	.000	13	15	7	2.35	4
2006	Richmond	Int.	38	44^{2}/3	1	6	.143	44	32	38	3.63	17
2007	Richmond	Int.	40	59^{2}/3	9	3	.750	56	35	46	2.26	12
2007	Atlanta	N.L.	21	23^{2}/3	1	1	.500	22	14	13	2.28	0
2008	Richmond	Int.	4	3^{2}/3	0	0	.000	4	2	4	0.00	0
2008	Atlanta b............	N.L.	46	53	3	5	.375	31	26	48	3.57	3
2009	Gwinnett.............	Int.	18	27^{1}/3	1	3	.250	25	13	21	2.63	2
2009	Atlanta	N.L.	36	37^{1}/3	1	1	.500	32	19	45	4.34	0
2010	Buffalo	Int.	28	36^{1}/3	2	3	.400	36	15	28	3.47	5
2010	New York c...........	N.L.	41	39^{2}/3	3	2	.600	42	18	30	2.95	1
2011	Buffalo	Int.	20	20^{1}/3	1	0	1.000	27	17	13	1.77	4
2011	New York	N.L.	44	47	4	1	.800	46	15	50	3.45	4
Major League Totals		5 Yrs.	188	200^{2}/3	12	10	.545	173	92	186	3.41	8

a Released by New York Yankees, July 24, 2003. Signed with Atlanta Braves organization, July 29, 2003.
b On disabled list from July 7 to August 23, 2008.
c Claimed on waivers by New York Mets, March 30, 2010.

ADAMS, JON MICHAEL (MIKE)
Born, Corpus Christi, Texas, July 29, 1978.
Bats Right. Throws Right. Height, 6 feet, 5 inches. Weight, 190 pounds.

Year	Club	Lea	G	IP	W	L	Pct	SO	BB	H	ERA	SAVES
2001	Ogden	Pioneer	23	32	2	2	.500	44	6	26	2.81	12
2002	High Desert	Calif.	10	14	2	1	.667	23	7	9	2.57	5
2002	Beloit	Midwest	11	15⅓	0	0	.000	21	2	13	2.93	5
2002	Huntsville	Southern	13	18⅔	1	0	1.000	17	12	14	3.38	1
2003	Huntsville	Southern	45	74⅓	3	7	.300	83	33	58	3.15	14
2004	Indianapolis	Int.	10	31	2	0	1.000	37	4	23	2.61	0
2004	Milwaukee	N.L.	46	53	2	3	.400	39	14	50	3.40	0
2005	Milwaukee	N.L.	13	13⅓	0	1	.000	14	10	12	2.70	1
2005	Nashville	P.C.	26	36	3	4	.429	45	12	35	5.75	2
2006	Milwaukee	N.L.	2	2⅓	0	0	.000	1	2	4	11.57	0
2006	Nashville	P.C.	15	16⅓	1	1	.500	18	8	17	3.31	2
2006	Norfolk	Int.	13	14⅔	0	0	.000	12	7	13	4.91	0
2006	Buffalo	Int.	3	4⅔	0	0	.000	3	0	4	1.93	0
2006	Portland a-b-c	P.C.	17	23⅔	0	2	.000	15	7	29	4.18	0
2007							INJURED—Did Not Play					
2008	Portland	P.C.	12	14⅔	3	1	.750	16	9	21	5.52	0
2008	San Diego d	N.L.	54	65⅓	2	3	.400	74	19	49	2.48	0
2009	San Antonio	Texas	4	4	1	0	1.000	6	2	3	2.25	0
2009	Portland	P.C.	4	5	0	0	.000	0	1	4	5.40	0
2009	San Diego e	N.L.	37	37	0	0	.000	45	8	14	0.73	0
2010	San Antonio	Texas	1	1	0	0	.000	1	0	0	0.00	0
2010	San Diego f	N.L.	70	66⅔	4	1	.800	73	23	48	1.75	0
2011	San Diego	N.L.	48	48	3	1	.750	49	9	26	1.13	1
2011	Texas g	A.L.	27	25⅔	2	3	.400	25	5	18	2.10	1
Major League Totals	7 Yrs.		297	311⅓	13	12	.520	320	90	221	2.11	3
Division Series												
2011	Texas	A.L.	3	2	0	0	.000	1	3	1	4.50	0
Championship Series												
2011	Texas	A.L.	5	4⅓	1	0	1.000	4	1	5	2.08	0
World Series Record												
2011	Texas	A.L.	3	2	0	0	1.000	1	2	5	4.50	0

a Traded to New York Mets for pitcher Jeremi Gonzalez, May 26, 2006.
b Claimed on waivers by Cleveland Indians, July 6, 2006.
c Traded to San Diego Padres for pitcher Brian Sikorski, July 18, 2006.
d Released by San Diego Padres, March 14, 2007, re-signed with San Diego Padres organization, April 12, 2007.
e On disabled list from April 1 to June 8 and August 22 to September 17, 2009.
f On disabled list from July 12 to August 7, 2010.
g Traded to Texas Rangers for pitcher Robert Erlin and pitcher Joseph Wieland, July 31, 2011.

AFFELDT, JEREMY DAVID
Born, Phoenix, Arizona, June 6, 1979.
Bats Left. Throws Left. Height, 6 feet, 4 inches. Weight, 225 pounds.

Year	Club	Lea	G	IP	W	L	Pct	SO	BB	H	ERA	SAVES
1997	Royals	Gulf Coast	10	40	2	0	1.000	36	21	34	4.50	0
1998	Royals	Gulf Coast	12	56	4	3	.571	67	24	50	2.89	0
1998	Lansing	Midwest	6	17	0	3	.000	8	12	27	9.53	0
1999	Charleston-WV	So.Atl.	27	143⅓	7	7	.500	111	80	140	3.83	0
2000	Wilmington	Carolina	27	147¼	5	15	.250	92	59	158	4.09	0
2001	Wichita	Texas	25	145⅓	10	6	.625	128	46	153	3.90	0
2002	Wichita	Texas	3	6	0	0	.000	3	3	1	1.50	0
2002	Kansas City a	A.L.	34	77⅔	3	4	.429	67	37	85	4.64	0
2003	Kansas City b	A.L.	36	126	7	6	.538	98	38	126	3.93	4
2004	Omaha	P.C.	4	4	0	0	.000	5	0	2	0.00	3
2004	Kansas City c	A.L.	38	76⅓	3	4	.429	49	32	91	4.95	13
2005	Omaha	P.C.	9	8⅓	0	1	.000	9	6	9	6.48	0
2005	Kansas City d	A.L.	49	49⅔	0	2	.000	39	29	56	5.26	0
2006	Kansas City	A.L.	27	70	4	6	.400	28	42	71	5.91	0
2006	Colorado e	N.L.	27	27⅓	4	2	.667	20	13	30	6.91	1
2007	Colorado f	N.L.	75	59	4	3	.571	46	33	47	3.51	0
2008	Cincinnati g	N.L.	74	78⅓	1	1	.500	80	25	78	3.33	0
2009	San Francisco	N.L.	74	62⅓	2	2	.500	55	31	42	1.73	0
2010	San Jose	Calif.	2	3	0	0	.000	4	1	2	0.00	0
2010	San Francisco h	N.L.	53	50	4	3	.571	44	24	56	4.14	4
2011	San Francisco	N.L.	67	61⅔	3	2	.600	54	24	47	2.63	3
Major League Totals	10 Yrs.		554	738⅓	35	35	.500	580	328	730	4.12	25

Year	Club	Lea	G	IP	W	L	Pct	SO	BB	H	ERA	SAVES
Division Series												
2007 Colorado	N.L.		1	1	0	0	.000	2	0	1	9.00	0
Championship Series												
2007 Colorado	N.L.		2	1⅓	0	0	.000	0	0	0	0.00	0
2010 San Francisco	N.L.		3	2⅔	0	0	.000	4	1	0	3.38	0
Championship Series Totals			5	4	0	0	.000	4	1	0	2.25	0
World Series Record												
2007 Colorado	N.L.		4	3	0	0	.000	2	1	2	0.00	0
2010 San Francisco	N.L.		2	1⅓	0	0	.000	0	1	1	6.75	0
World Series Totals.............			6	4⅓	0	0	.000	2	2	3	2.08	0

a On disabled list from June 9 to August 1, 2002.
b On disabled list from April 20 to May 6, 2003.
c On disabled list from June 27 to August 21, 2004.
d On disabled list from April 16 to June 4 and June 19 to July 7, 2005.
e Traded to Colorado Rockies with pitcher Denny Bautista for infielder Ryan Shealy and pitcher Scott Dohmann, July 31, 2006.
f Filed for free agency, October 29, 2007. Signed with Cincinnati Reds, January 23, 2008.
g Filed for free agency, October 30, 2008. Signed with San Francisco Giants, November 17, 2008.
h On disabled list from July 21 to August 18, 2010.

ALBERS, MATTHEW JAMES (MATT)
Born, Houston, Texas, January 20, 1983.
Bats Left. Throws Right. Height, 6 feet. Weight, 205 pounds.

Year	Club	Lea	G	IP	W	L	Pct	SO	BB	H	ERA	SAVES
2002 Martinsville	Appal.	13	59⅔	2	3	.400	72	38	61	5.13	0
2003 Tri-City	N.Y.-Penn.	15	86⅓	5	4	.556	94	25	69	2.92	0
2004 Lexington...........	So.Atl.	22	111⅓	8	3	.727	140	57	95	3.31	0
2005 Salem.............	Carolina	28	148⅔	8	12	.400	146	62	161	4.66	0
2006 Corpus Christi	Texas	19	116	10	2	.833	95	47	96	2.17	0
2006 Round Rock...........	P.C.	4	25	2	1	.667	26	10	24	3.96	0
2006 Houston..............	N.L.	4	15	0	2	.000	11	7	17	6.00	0
2007 Round Rock...........	P.C.	9	53	2	3	.400	43	22	50	3.74	0
2007 Houston a	N.L.	31	110⅔	4	11	.267	71	50	127	5.86	0
2008 Aberdeen	N.Y.-Penn.	2	2	0	0	.000	4	1	1	0.00	0
2008 Baltimore b	A.L.	28	49	3	3	.500	26	22	43	3.49	0
2009 Norfolk...............	Int.	10	12⅔	1	0	1.000	12	5	19	5.68	0
2009 Baltimore.............	A.L.	56	67	3	6	.333	49	36	80	5.51	0
2010 Baltimore c...........	A.L.	62	75⅔	5	3	.625	49	34	78	4.52	0
2011 Pawtucket	Int.	2	3	0	0	.000	2	0	1	0.00	0
2011 Boston d	A.L.	56	64⅔	4	4	.500	68	31	62	4.73	0
Major League Totals ....6 Yrs.		237	382	19	29	.396	274	180	407	5.04	0

a Traded to Baltimore Orioles with pitcher Troy Patton, outfielder Luke Scott, pitcher Dennis Sarfate and infielder Michael Costanzo for infielder Miguel Tejada, December 12, 2007.
b On disabled list from June 26 to October 21, 2008.
c Not offered contract, December 2, 2010. Signed with Boston Red Sox, December 16, 2010.
d On disabled list from April 8 to April 21, 2011.

ALBURQUERQUE, ALBERTO JOSE (AL)
Born, San Pedro de Macoris, Dominican Republic, June 10, 1986.
Bats Right. Throws Right. Height, 6 feet. Weight, 195 pounds.

Year	Club	Lea	G	IP	W	L	Pct	SO	BB	H	ERA	SAVES
2005					INJURED—Did Not Play							
2006 Cubs..............	Arizona	8	12⅔	0	2	.000	15	10	10	5.68	0
2007 Boise	Northwest	10	41	3	2	.600	49	17	42	3.73	1
2007 Peoria...........	Midwest	11	25⅓	1	4	.200	20	12	36	9.24	0
2008 a					INJURED—Did Not Play							
2009 Daytona b...........	Fla.St.	24	34⅔	1	0	1.000	44	14	26	2.08	2
2009 Tulsa	Texas	23	26⅓	1	3	.250	31	13	23	3.76	0
2010 Tulsa c	Texas	25	34⅓	2	4	.333	32	19	32	4.98	3
2011 Toledo	Int.	4	4⅔	0	0	.000	10	2	5	1.93	0
2011 Detroit d..............	A.L.	41	43⅓	6	1	.857	67	29	21	1.87	0
Division Series												
2011 Detroit	A.L.	2	0⅓	0	0	.000	0	1	2	81.00	0
Championship Series												
2011 Detroit	A.L.	2	1⅔	0	0	.000	2	2	0	0.00	0

a On minor league disabled list from June 28 to September 1, 2008.
b Traded to Colorado Rockies for outfielder Jeff Baker, July 2, 2009.

c Filed for free agency, November 6, 2010. Signed with Detroit Tigers organization, November 19, 2010.
d On disabled list from June 30 to July 16 and August 12 to September 4, 2011.

ARREDONDO, JOSE JUAN

Born, San Pedro de Macoris, Dominican Republic, March 30, 1984.
Bats Right. Throws Right. Height, 6 feet. Weight, 175 pounds.

Year	Club	Lea	G	IP	W	L	Pct	SO	BB	H	ERA	SAVES
2004	Angels	Arizona	8	12¹/₃	0	0	.000	14	4	14	2.92	1
2005	Arkansas	Texas	5	5¹/₃	0	0	.000	4	4	5	3.38	0
2005	Orem	Pioneer	15	68²/₃	5	0	1.000	60	20	76	4.19	0
2006	Rancho Cucamonga	Calif.	15	90	5	6	.455	115	35	62	2.30	0
2006	Arkansas	Texas	11	60²/₃	2	3	.400	48	22	80	6.53	0
2007	Arkansas	Texas	23	25	0	1	.000	28	12	16	2.52	10
2007	Rancho Cucamonga	Calif.	28	35	2	4	.333	34	11	46	6.43	4
2007	Salt Lake	P.C.	2	3	0	0	.000	1	2	2	3.00	0
2008	Salt Lake	P.C.	15	17	1	1	.500	15	4	12	2.12	10
2008	Los Angeles	A.L.	52	61	10	2	.833	55	22	42	1.62	0
2009	Salt Lake	P.C.	19	20²/₃	1	1	.500	24	14	13	2.18	1
2009	Los Angeles	A.L.	43	45	2	3	.400	47	23	47	6.00	0
2010	Cincinnati a-b	N.L.					INJURED—Did Not Play					
2011	Carolina	Southern	6	7²/₃	1	0	1.000	11	4	4	2.35	0
2011	Louisville	Int.	6	8	1	1	.500	10	2	6	2.25	0
2011	Cincinnati c	N.L.	53	53	4	4	.500	48	31	43	3.23	0
Major League Totals		3 Yrs.	148	159	16	9	.640	150	76	132	3.40	0

Division Series

Year	Club	Lea	G	IP	W	L	Pct	SO	BB	H	ERA	SAVES
2008	Los Angeles	A.L.	3	3²/₃	0	0	.000	4	2	2	0.00	0

a Not offered contract, December 12, 2009. Signed with Cincinnati Reds organization, January 22, 2010.
b On disabled list from July 22 to November 2, 2010.
c On disabled list from March 25 to May 14 and July 7 to July 22, 2011.

ARRIETA, JACOB JOSEPH (JAKE)

Born, Farmington, Missouri, March 6, 1986.
Bats Right. Throws Right. Height, 6 feet, 4 inches. Weight, 225 pounds.

Year	Club	Lea	G	IP	W	L	Pct	SO	BB	H	ERA	SAVES
2008	Frederick	Carolina	20	113	6	5	.545	120	51	80	2.87	0
2009	Bowie	Eastern	11	59	6	3	.667	70	23	45	2.59	0
2009	Norfolk	Int.	17	91²/₃	5	8	.385	78	33	97	3.93	0
2010	Norfolk	Int.	12	73	6	2	.750	64	34	48	1.85	0
2010	Baltimore	A.L.	18	100¹/₃	6	6	.500	52	48	106	4.66	0
2011	Baltimore b	A.L.	22	119¹/₃	10	8	.556	93	59	115	5.05	0
Major League Totals		2 Yrs.	40	219²/₃	16	14	.533	145	107	221	4.88	0

b On disabled list from August 1 to November 2, 2011.

ARROYO, BRONSON ANTHONY

Born, Key West, Florida, February 24, 1977.
Bats Right. Throws Right. Height, 6 feet, 5 inches. Weight, 190 pounds.

Year	Club	Lea	G	IP	W	L	Pct	SO	BB	H	ERA	SAVES
1995	Pirates	Gulf Coast	13	61¹/₃	5	4	.556	48	9	72	4.26	1
1996	Augusta	So.Atl.	26	135²/₃	8	6	.571	107	36	123	3.52	0
1997	Lynchburg	Carolina	24	160¹/₃	12	4	.750	121	33	154	3.31	0
1998	Carolina a	Southern	23	127	9	8	.529	90	51	158	5.46	0
1999	Altoona	Eastern	25	153	15	4	.789	100	58	167	3.65	0
1999	Nashville	P.C.	3	13	0	2	.000	11	10	22	10.38	0
2000	Nashville	P.C.	13	88²/₃	8	2	.800	52	25	82	3.65	0
2000	Pittsburgh	N.L.	20	71²/₃	2	6	.250	50	36	88	6.40	0
2000	Lynchburg	Carolina	1	7	0	0	.000	3	2	8	3.86	0
2001	Pittsburgh	N.L.	24	88¹/₃	5	7	.417	39	34	99	5.09	0
2001	Nashville	P.C.	9	66¹/₃	6	2	.750	49	15	63	3.93	0
2002	Nashville	P.C.	22	143	8	6	.571	116	28	126	2.96	0
2002	Pittsburgh	N.L.	9	27	2	1	.667	22	15	30	4.00	0
2003	Pawtucket	Int.	24	149²/₃	12	6	.667	155	23	148	3.43	0
2003	Boston b	A.L.	6	17¹/₃	0	0	.000	14	4	10	2.08	1
2004	Boston	A.L.	32	178²/₃	10	9	.526	142	47	171	4.03	0
2005	Boston	A.L.	35	205¹/₃	14	10	.583	100	54	213	4.51	0
2006	Cincinnati c	N.L.	35	*240²/₃	14	11	.560	184	64	222	3.29	0
2007	Cincinnati	N.L.	34	210²/₃	9	15	.375	156	63	232	4.23	0
2008	Cincinnati	N.L.	34	200	15	11	.577	163	68	219	4.77	0

Year Club	Lea	G	IP	W	L	Pct	SO	BB	H	ERA	SAVES
2009 Cincinnati............	N.L.	33	220^{1}/$_{3}$	15	13	.536	127	65	214	3.84	0
2010 Cincinnati............	N.L.	33	215^{2}/$_{3}$	17	10	.630	121	59	188	3.88	0
2011 Cincinnati............	N.L.	32	199	9	12	.429	108	45	227	5.07	0
Major League Totals ....12 Yrs.		327	1874^{2}/$_{3}$	112	105	.516	1226	554	1913	4.28	1
Division Series											
2004 Boston..............	A.L.	1	6	0	0	.000	7	2	3	3.00	0
2005 Boston..............	A.L.	1	1	0	0	.000	1	2	2	18.00	0
2010 Cincinnati............	N.L.	1	5^{1}/$_{3}$	0	0	.000	2	3	4	1.69	0
Division Series Totals		3	12^{1}/$_{3}$	0	0	.000	10	7	9	3.65	0
Championship Series											
2003 Boston..............	A.L.	3	3^{1}/$_{3}$	0	0	.000	5	2	2	2.70	0
2004 Boston..............	A.L.	3	4	0	0	.000	3	2	8	15.75	0
Championship Series Totals		6	7^{1}/$_{3}$	0	0	.000	8	4	10	9.82	0
World Series Record											
2004 Boston..............	A.L.	2	2^{2}/$_{3}$	0	0	.000	4	1	4	6.75	0

a On minor league disabled list from May 18 to June 7 and June 18 to July 4, 1998.
b Claimed on waivers by Boston Red Sox, February 4, 2003.
c Traded to Cincinnati Reds for outfielder Wily Mo Pena, March 20, 2006.

AXFORD, JOHN BERTON
Born, Simcoe, Ontario, Canada, April 1, 1983.
Bats Right. Throws Right. Height, 6 feet, 5 inches. Weight, 195 pounds.

Year Club	Lea	G	IP	W	L	Pct	SO	BB	H	ERA	SAVES
2007 Tampa	Fla.St.	5	11^{1}/$_{3}$	0	0	.000	15	7	6	2.38	2
2007 Scranton/WB	Int.	1	0^{2}/$_{3}$	0	0	.000	1	1	2	13.50	0
2007 Staten Island ..... N.Y.-Penn.		8	24^{1}/$_{3}$	1	1	.500	30	15	13	2.22	2
2007 Charleston	So.Atl.	13	26^{2}/$_{3}$	0	3	.000	21	22	29	4.39	0
2008 Brevard County a	Fla.St.	26	95	5	10	.333	89	73	86	4.55	0
2009 Brevard County	Fla.St.	19	27^{2}/$_{3}$	4	1	.800	43	16	14	1.63	0
2009 Huntsville.........	Southern	4	7^{2}/$_{3}$	0	0	.000	9	3	7	3.52	1
2009 Nashville	P.C.	22	33	5	0	1.000	37	19	23	3.55	0
2009 Milwaukee	N.L.	7	7^{2}/$_{3}$	0	0	.000	9	6	5	3.52	1
2010 Nashville	P.C.	12	13^{1}/$_{3}$	3	2	.600	19	5	14	2.03	2
2010 Milwaukee	N.L.	50	58	8	2	.800	76	27	42	2.48	24
2011 Milwaukee	N.L.	74	73^{2}/$_{3}$	2	2	.500	86	25	59	1.95	*46
Major League Totals ....3 Yrs.		131	139^{1}/$_{3}$	10	4	.714	171	58	106	2.26	71
Division Series											
2011 Milwaukee	N.L.	3	4	1	0	1.000	5	2	3	2.25	1
Championship Series											
2011 Milwaukee	N.L.	3	3	0	0	.000	4	0	2	0.00	2

a Released by New York Yankees, December 14, 2007. Signed with Milwaukee Brewers organization, March 4, 2008.

AYALA, LUIS IGNACIO
Born, Los Mochis, Mexico, January 12, 1978.
Bats Right. Throws Right. Height, 6 feet, 2 inches. Weight, 190 pounds.

Year Club	Lea	G	IP	W	L	Pct	SO	BB	H	ERA	SAVES
1997 Saltillo	Mexican	37	62	7	5	.583	30	21	76	4.62	0
1998 Saltillo	Mexican	47	83	7	8	.467	29	45	105	5.62	7
1999 Saltillo a	Mexican	61	79	7	3	.700	28	22	54	1.71	41
2000 Saltillo	Mexican	55	65	5	3	.625	38	13	69	2.76	25
2001 Salem............	Carolina	13	13^{1}/$_{3}$	0	1	.000	10	5	19	4.05	7
2001 Saltillo b	Mexican	33	40	1	2	.333	34	11	34	2.03	21
2002 Saltillo	Mexican	49	54	3	5	.375	43	15	43	1.68	23
2002 Ottawa c-d-e	Int.	6	7^{2}/$_{3}$	0	0	.000	6	4	7	3.52	0
2003 Expos..........	Gulf Coast	2	3^{2}/$_{3}$	0	0	.000	2	2	2	0.00	0
2003 Montreal f	N.L.	65	71	10	3	.769	46	13	65	2.92	5
2004 Montreal	N.L.	81	90^{1}/$_{3}$	6	12	.333	63	15	92	2.69	2
2005 Washington	N.L.	68	71	8	7	.533	40	14	75	2.66	1
2006 Washington g........	N.L.					INJURED—Did Not Play					
2007 Potomac	Carolina	3	2^{2}/$_{3}$	0	0	.000	1	1	1	0.00	0
2007 Columbus..........	Int.	5	7	0	0	.000	5	2	4	1.29	0
2007 Washington h........	N.L.	44	42^{1}/$_{3}$	2	2	.500	28	12	43	3.19	1
2008 Washington-New York i ..	N.L.	81	75^{2}/$_{3}$	2	10	.167	50	24	86	5.71	9
2009 Minnesota	A.L.	28	32^{1}/$_{3}$	1	2	.333	21	8	38	4.18	0
2009 New Orleans..........	P.C.	9	10	0	0	.000	10	3	4	0.00	4
2009 Florida j-k-l..........	N.L.	10	7^{2}/$_{3}$	0	3	.000	7	6	12	11.74	0

Year	Club	Lea	G	IP	W	L	Pct	SO	BB	H	ERA	SAVES
2010	Albuquerque.	P.C.	14	14	1	3	.250	10	7	14	4.50	4
2010	Colorado Springs.	P.C.	4	7$^{1}/_{3}$	1	1	.500	4	0	8	4.91	0
2010	Reno m-n-o	P.C.	18	26$^{1}/_{3}$	0	6	.000	17	11	38	7.86	0
2011	Scranton-WB	Int.	3	5	0	0	.000	7	0	6	1.80	0
2011	New York p-q	A.L.	52	56	2	2	.500	39	20	51	2.09	0
Major League Totals . . . . . . .7 Yrs.			429	446$^{1}/_{3}$	31	41	.431	294	112	462	3.47	18
Division Series												
2011	New York	A.L.	2	1$^{1}/_{3}$	0	0	.000	0	0	3	6.75	0

a Sold to Colorado Rockies by Saltillo (Mexican), October 14, 1999.
b Sold to Saltillo (Mexican), May 15, 2001.
c Sold to Montreal Expos, August 18, 2002.
d Filed for free agency, October 15, 2002. Signed with Arizona Diamondbacks organization, October 23, 2002.
e Selected by Montreal Expos organization in Rule V draft, December 16, 2002.
f On disabled list from June 22 to July 21, 2003.
g On disabled list from March 24 to October 9, 2006.
h On disabled list from March 28 to June 20, 2007.
i Traded to New York Mets for player to be named later, August 17, 2008. Washington Nationals received infielder Anderson Hernandez to complete trade, August 20, 2008.
j Filed for free agency, October 31, 2008. Signed with Minnesota Twins, February 18, 2009.
k Released by Minnesota Twins, June 30, 2009. Signed with Florida Marlins organization, July 2, 2009.
l Filed for free agency, September 4, 2009. Signed with Los Angeles Dodgers organization, December 17, 2009.
m Released by Los Angeles Dodgers, May 17, 2010. Signed with Arizona Diamondbacks organization, May 20, 2010.
n Released by Arizona Diamondbacks, July 16, 2010. Signed with Colorado Rockies organization, August 27, 2010.
o Released by Colorado Rockies, November 22, 2010. Signed with New York Yankees organization, February 11, 2011.
p On disabled list from April 13 to May 11, 2011.
q Filed for free agency, October 30, 2011.

BADENHOP, BURKE HEINRICH
Born, Atlanta, Georgia, February 8, 1983.
Bats Right. Throws Right. Height, 6 feet, 5 inches. Weight, 220 pounds.

Year	Club	Lea	G	IP	W	L	Pct	SO	BB	H	ERA	SAVES
2005	Oneonta	N.Y.-Penn.	14	77	6	4	.600	55	26	69	2.92	0
2006	West Michigan	Midwest	27	171	14	3	.824	124	31	170	2.84	0
2007	Erie	Eastern	3	18$^{2}/_{3}$	2	0	1.000	12	3	8	1.45	0
2007	Lakeland a	Fla.St.	23	135$^{1}/_{3}$	10	6	.625	78	34	130	3.13	0
2008	Carolina	Southern	1	6$^{1}/_{3}$	1	0	1.000	3	0	6	0.00	0
2008	Florida	N.L.	13	47$^{1}/_{3}$	2	3	.400	35	21	55	6.08	0
2008	Marlins	Gulf Coast	1	3	0	0	.000	2	0	1	0.00	0
2009	Marlins	Gulf Coast	2	3	0	1	.000	4	0	2	0.00	0
2009	Jupiter	Fla.St.	2	8	0	0	.000	8	1	2	0.00	0
2009	New Orleans	P.C.	2	9$^{1}/_{3}$	0	1	.000	6	4	14	6.75	0
2009	Florida b	N.L.	35	72	7	4	.636	57	24	71	3.75	0
2010	New Orleans	P.C.	12	16	0	1	.000	9	7	16	2.81	0
2010	Florida	N.L.	53	67$^{2}/_{3}$	2	5	.286	47	21	62	3.99	0
2011	New Orleans	P.C.	11	14$^{2}/_{3}$	1	1	.500	10	7	20	6.75	1
2011	Florida c	N.L.	50	63$^{2}/_{3}$	2	3	.400	51	24	65	4.10	1
Major League Totals . . . . .4 Yrs.			151	250$^{2}/_{3}$	13	15	.464	190	90	253	4.34	2

a Traded by Detroit Tigers to Florida Marlins with pitcher Eulogio De La Cruz, pitcher Andrew Miller, catcher Mike Rabelo and outfielder Cameron Maybin for pitcher Dontrelle Willis and infielder Miguel Cabrera, December 5, 2007.
b On disabled list from August 2 to September 1, 2009.
c Traded to Tampa Bay Rays for catcher Jake Jefferies, December 12, 2011.

BAILEY, ANDREW SCOTT
Born, Voorhees, New Jersey, May 31, 1984.
Bats Right. Throws Right. Height, 6 feet, 3 inches. Weight, 235 pounds.

Year	Club	Lea	G	IP	W	L	Pct	SO	BB	H	ERA	SAVES
2006	Vancouver	Northwest	13	58	2	5	.286	53	20	39	2.02	0
2007	Stockton.	Calif.	11	66	3	4	.429	72	31	56	3.82	0
2007	Kane County	Midwest	11	51	1	4	.200	74	22	42	3.35	0
2007	Sacramento	P.C.	1	8	1	0	1.000	4	1	3	1.13	0
2008	Midland	Texas	37	110$^{1}/_{3}$	5	9	.357	110	56	99	4.32	0
2009	Oakland a	A.L.	68	83$^{1}/_{3}$	6	3	.667	91	24	49	1.84	26
2010	Sacramento	P.C.	1	0$^{2}/_{3}$	0	0	.000	1	0	3	27.00	0
2010	Oakland b	A.L.	47	49	1	3	.250	42	13	34	1.47	25
2011	Sacramento	P.C.	4	4	0	0	.000	3	1	3	0.00	0
2011	Oakland c-d	A.L.	42	41$^{2}/_{3}$	0	4	.000	41	12	34	3.24	24
Major League Totals . . . . .3 Yrs.			157	174	7	10	.412	174	49	117	2.07	75

a Selected Rookie of the Year in American League for 2009.
b On disabled list from July 21 to August 22, 2010.
c On disabled list from March 22 to May 29, 2011.
d Traded to Boston Red Sox with outfielder Ryan Sweeney for outfielder Josh Reddick, infielder Miles Head and pitcher Raul Alcantara, December 28, 2011.

BAILEY, DAVID DEWITT (HOMER)
Born, LaGrange, Texas, May 3, 1986.
Bats Right. Throws Right. Height, 6 feet, 4 inches. Weight, 210 pounds.

Year	Club	Lea	G	IP	W	L	Pct	SO	BB	H	ERA	SAVES
2004 Reds		Gulf Coast	6	12⅓	0	1	.000	9	3	14	4.38	0
2005 Dayton		Midwest	28	103⅔	8	4	.667	125	62	89	4.43	0
2006 Sarasota		Fla.St.	13	70⅔	3	5	.375	79	22	49	3.31	0
2006 Chattanooga		Southern	13	68	7	1	.875	77	28	50	1.59	0
2007 Louisville		Int.	12	67⅓	6	3	.667	59	32	49	3.07	0
2007 Sarasota		Fla.St.	2	8	0	1	.000	7	5	15	10.13	0
2007 Cincinnati		N.L.	9	45⅓	4	2	.667	28	28	43	5.76	0
2008 Cincinnati		N.L.	8	36⅓	0	6	.000	18	17	59	7.93	0
2008 Louisville		Int.	19	111⅓	4	7	.364	96	46	118	4.77	0
2009 Louisville		Int.	14	89⅔	8	5	.615	82	27	87	2.71	0
2009 Cincinnati		N.L.	20	113⅓	8	5	.615	86	52	115	4.53	0
2010 Dayton		Midwest	1	4	0	1	.000	5	1	4	6.75	0
2010 Louisville		Int.	4	19	2	0	1.000	15	5	15	2.37	0
2010 Cincinnati a		N.L.	19	109	4	3	.571	100	40	109	4.46	0
2011 Louisville		Int.	6	30	2	1	.667	22	6	34	3.00	0
2011 Cincinnati b		N.L.	22	132	9	7	.563	106	33	136	4.43	0
Major League Totals	5 Yrs.		78	436	25	23	.521	338	170	462	4.89	0
Division Series												
2010 Cincinnati		N.L.	1	2	0	0	.000	2	0	2	0.00	0

a On disabled list from May 24 to August 15, 2010.
b On disabled list from March 24 to May 5 and May 27 to June 26, 2011.

BAKER, TIMOTHY SCOTT (SCOTT)
Born, Shreveport, Louisiana, September 19, 1981.
Bats Right. Throws Right. Height, 6 feet, 4 inches. Weight, 210 pounds.

Year	Club	Lea	G	IP	W	L	Pct	SO	BB	H	ERA	SAVES
2003 Quad Cities		Midwest	11	50⅔	3	1	.750	47	8	45	2.49	0
2004 New Britain		Eastern	10	70⅓	5	3	.625	72	13	44	2.43	0
2004 Fort Myers		Fla.St.	7	45	4	2	.667	37	6	40	2.40	0
2004 Rochester		Int.	9	54⅓	1	3	.250	36	15	65	4.97	0
2005 Rochester		Int.	22	134⅔	5	8	.385	107	26	123	3.01	0
2005 Minnesota		A.L.	10	53⅔	3	3	.500	32	14	48	3.35	0
2006 Rochester		Int.	12	84⅓	5	4	.556	68	25	77	2.67	0
2006 Minnesota		A.L.	16	83⅓	5	8	.385	62	16	114	6.37	0
2007 Rochester		Int.	7	42⅔	3	2	.600	41	4	34	3.16	1
2007 Minnesota		A.L.	24	143⅔	9	9	.500	102	29	162	4.26	0
2008 Fort Myers		Fla.St.	1	5	1	0	1.000	4	0	7	5.40	0
2008 Minnesota a		A.L.	28	172⅓	11	4	.733	141	42	161	3.45	0
2009 Fort Myers		Fla.St.	1	7	1	0	1.000	3	1	5	1.29	0
2009 Minnesota b		A.L.	33	200	15	9	.625	162	48	190	4.36	0
2010 Minnesota		A.L.	29	170⅓	12	9	.571	148	43	186	4.49	0
2011 Minnesota c		A.L.	23	134⅔	8	6	.571	123	32	126	3.14	0
Major League Totals	7 Yrs.		163	958	63	48	.568	770	224	987	4.15	0
Division Series												
2010 Minnesota		A.L.	1	2⅓	0	0	.000	2	0	3	3.86	0

a On disabled list from May 4 to June 5, 2008.
b On disabled list from March 28 to April 15, 2009.
c On disabled list from July 7 to July 23 and August 9 to September 20, 2011.

BALFOUR, GRANT ROBERT
Born, Sydney, New South Wales, Australia, December 30, 1977.
Bats Right. Throws Right. Height, 6 feet, 2 inches. Weight, 190 pounds.

Year	Club	Lea	G	IP	W	L	Pct	SO	BB	H	ERA	SAVES
1997 Twins		Gulf Coast	13	67	2	4	.333	43	20	73	3.76	0
1998 Elizabethtn		Appal.	13	77⅔	7	2	.778	75	27	70	3.36	0
1999 Quad Cities		Midwest	19	91⅔	8	5	.615	95	37	66	3.53	1
2000 Fort Myers		Fla.St.	35	89	8	5	.615	90	34	91	4.25	6
2001 New Britain		Eastern	35	50	2	1	.667	72	22	26	1.08	13

Year	Club	Lea	G	IP	W	L	Pct	SO	BB	H	ERA	SAVES
2001	Minnesota	A.L.	2	2⅔	0	0	.000	2	3	3	13.50	0
2001	Edmonton	P.C.	11	16⅓	2	2	.500	17	10	18	5.51	0
2002	Edmonton	P.C.	58	71⅓	2	4	.333	88	30	60	4.16	8
2003	Rochester	Int.	21	71	5	2	.714	87	16	48	2.41	5
2003	Minnesota a	A.L.	17	26	1	0	1.000	30	14	23	4.15	0
2004	Minnesota a	A.L.	36	39⅓	4	1	.800	42	21	35	4.35	0
2005	Minnesota b	A.L.		INJURED—Did Not Play								
2006	Sarasota	Fla.St.	5	5⅔	0	0	.000	7	3	8	7.94	0
2006	Reds	Gulf Coast	2	1⅓	0	0	.000	2	3	1	13.50	0
2006	Dayton c-d	Midwest	2	2	0	0	.000	3	0	0	0.00	0
2007	Huntsville	Southern	8	11⅓	0	0	.000	21	4	8	2.38	2
2007	Nashville	P.C.	24	32	1	1	.500	47	11	17	1.69	5
2007	Milwaukee e-f	N.L.	3	2⅔	0	2	.000	3	4	4	20.25	0
2007	Tampa Bay	A.L.	22	22	1	0	1.000	27	16	26	6.14	0
2008	Durham	Int.	15	23⅔	1	0	1.000	39	10	5	0.38	4
2008	Tampa Bay	A.L.	51	58⅓	6	2	.750	82	24	28	1.54	4
2009	Tampa Bay	A.L.	73	67⅓	5	4	.556	69	33	59	4.81	4
2010	Charlotte	Fla.St.	2	1⅔	0	1	.000	2	3	2	10.80	0
2010	Tampa Bay g-h	A.L.	57	55⅓	2	1	.667	56	17	43	2.28	0
2011	Sacramento	P.C.	1	1	0	0	.000	0	1	2	9.00	0
2011	Oakland i	A.L.	62	62	5	2	.714	59	20	44	2.47	2
Major League Totals	8 Yrs.		323	335⅔	24	12	.667	370	152	265	3.57	10
Division Series												
2004	Minnesota	A.L.	2	2⅔	0	0	.000	2	0	0	0.00	0
2008	Tampa Bay	A.L.	3	3⅓	0	0	.000	4	1	2	0.00	0
2010	Tampa Bay	A.L.	3	3⅔	0	0	.000	1	0	2	0.00	0
Division Series Totals			8	9⅔	0	0	.000	7	1	4	0.00	0
Championship Series												
2008	Tampa Bay	A.L.	4	2⅓	0	0	.000	1	4	5	19.29	0
World Series Record												
2008	Tampa Bay	A.L.	3	3	0	0	.000	2	3	4	3.00	0

a On disabled list from April 4 to May 14 and August 2 to August 17, 2004.
b On disabled list from March 25 to October 14, 2005.
c Filed for free agency, October 15, 2005. Signed with Cincinnati Reds organization, January 12, 2006.
d On disabled list from March 31 to October 3, 2006.
e Claimed on waivers by Milwaukee Brewers, October 5, 2006.
f Traded to Tampa Bay Devil Rays for pitcher Seth McClung, July 27, 2007.
g On disabled list from July 30 to September 1, 2010.
h Filed for free agency, November 1, 2010. Signed with Oakland Athletics, January 18, 2011.
i On disabled list from June 22 to July 7, 2011.

BARD, DANIEL PAUL

Born, Houston, Texas, June 25, 1985.
Bats Right. Throws Right. Height, 6 feet, 4 inches. Weight, 200 pounds.

Year	Club	Lea	G	IP	W	L	Pct	SO	BB	H	ERA	SAVES
2007	Lancaster	Calif.	5	13⅓	0	2	.000	9	22	21	10.13	0
2007	Greenville	So.Atl.	17	61⅔	3	5	.375	38	56	55	6.42	0
2008	Portland	Eastern	31	49⅔	4	1	.800	64	26	30	1.99	7
2008	Greenville	So.Atl.	15	28	1	0	1.000	43	4	12	0.64	0
2009	Pawtucket	Int.	11	16	1	0	1.000	29	5	6	1.13	6
2009	Boston	A.L.	49	49⅓	2	2	.500	63	22	41	3.65	1
2010	Boston	A.L.	73	74⅔	1	2	.333	76	30	45	1.93	3
2011	Boston	A.L.	70	73	2	9	.182	74	24	46	3.33	1
Major League Totals	3 Yrs.		192	197	5	13	.278	213	76	132	2.88	5
Division Series												
2009	Boston	A.L.	2	3	0	0	.000	4	0	0	0.00	0

BASTARDO, ANTONIO FRANCISCO

Born, Hato Mayor, Dominican Republic, September 21, 1985.
Bats Right. Throws Left. Height, 5 feet, 11 inches. Weight, 195 pounds.

Year	Club	Lea	G	IP	W	L	Pct	SO	BB	H	ERA	SAVES
2006	Phillies	Gulf Coast	9	23	1	2	.333	27	14	20	3.91	0
2007	Lakewood	So.Atl.	15	91⅔	9	0	1.000	98	42	63	1.87	0
2007	Clearwater	Fla.St.	1	5	1	0	1.000	12	3	5	7.20	0
2008	Clearwater	Fla.St.	5	30⅔	2	0	1.000	47	10	20	1.17	0
2008	Reading	Eastern	14	67	2	5	.286	62	37	56	3.76	0
2009	Lehigh Valley	Int.	2	13	1	0	1.000	12	3	11	2.08	0
2009	Phillies	Gulf Coast	3	4⅓	0	0	.000	3	2	2	0.00	0

Year	Club	Lea	G	IP	W	L	Pct	SO	BB	H	ERA	SAVES
2009 Clearwater	Fla.St.	1	1	0	0	.000	0	0	4	27.00	0	
2009 Reading	Eastern	11	36	2	2	.500	41	7	22	1.75	3	
2009 Philadelphia a	N.L.	6	23²/₃	2	3	.400	19	9	26	6.46	0	
2010 Clearwater	Fla.St.	3	3	0	0	.000	6	0	3	0.00	0	
2010 Lehigh Valley	Int.	20	17¹/₃	1	1	.500	27	6	12	2.08	3	
2010 Philadelphia b	N.L.	25	18²/₃	2	0	1.000	26	9	19	4.34	0	
2011 Philadelphia	N.L.	64	58	6	1	.857	70	26	28	2.64	8	
Major League Totals	3 Yrs.	95	100¹/₃	10	4	.714	115	44	73	3.86	8	
Division Series												
2009 Philadelphia	N.L.	1	0¹/₃	0	0	.000	1	0	0	0.00	0	
2011 Philadelphia	N.L.	2	1	0	0	.000	1	1	0	0.00	0	
Division Series Totals		3	1¹/₃	0	0	.000	2	1	0	0.00	0	
Championship Series												
2009 Philadelphia	N.L.	1	0	0	0	.000	0	0	1	INF	0	
2010 Philadelphia	N.L.	1	0¹/₃	0	0	.000	0	0	1	0.00	0	
Championship Series Totals		2	0¹/₃	0	0	.000	0	0	2	0.00	0	

a On disabled list from June 26 to September 3, 2009.

b On disabled list from June 16 to July 15, 2010.

BEACHY, BRANDON ALAN

Born, Kokomo, Indiana, September 3, 1986.

Bats Right. Throws Right. Height, 6 feet, 3 inches. Weight, 215 pounds.

Year	Club	Lea	G	IP	W	L	Pct	SO	BB	H	ERA	SAVES
2008 Danville	Appal.	6	12	2	0	1.000	16	2	12	2.25	0	
2009 Rome	So.Atl.	12	17²/₃	0	0	.000	17	4	20	5.60	0	
2009 Mississippi	Southern	1	1	0	0	.000	0	0	1	0.00	0	
2009 Myrtle Beach	Carolina	22	58	4	3	.571	47	15	59	3.41	1	
2010 Mississippi	Southern	27	73²/₃	3	1	.750	100	22	53	1.47	1	
2010 Gwinnett	Int.	8	45²/₃	2	0	1.000	48	6	40	2.17	1	
2010 Atlanta	N.L.	3	15	0	2	.000	15	7	16	3.00	0	
2011 Gwinnett	Int.	1	5	1	0	1.000	8	2	4	1.80	0	
2011 Atlanta a	N.L.	25	141²/₃	7	3	.700	169	46	125	3.68	0	
Major League Totals	2 Yrs.	28	156²/₃	7	5	.583	184	53	141	3.62	0	

a On disabled list from May 14 to June 22, 2011.

BEATO, PEDRO

Born, Santo Domingo, Dominican Republic, October 27, 1986.

Bats Right. Throws Right. Height, 6 feet, 4 inches. Weight, 220 pounds.

Year	Club	Lea	G	IP	W	L	Pct	SO	BB	H	ERA	SAVES
2006 Aberdeen	N.Y.-Penn.	14	57	3	2	.600	52	23	47	3.63	0	
2007 Delmarva	So.Atl.	27	142¹/₃	7	8	.467	106	59	139	4.05	0	
2008 Frederick	Carolina	19	97	4	10	.286	51	33	119	5.85	0	
2008 Orioles	Gulf Coast	2	10²/₃	0	0	.000	3	1	10	2.53	0	
2009 Frederick	Carolina	20	105¹/₃	5	7	.417	70	40	125	4.53	0	
2009 Bowie	Eastern	6	32	1	3	.250	18	7	33	4.50	0	
2010 Bowie a	Eastern	43	59²/₃	4	0	1.000	50	19	49	2.11	16	
2011 Buffalo	Int.	1	1¹/₃	1	0	1.000	0	1	2	0.00	0	
2011 New York b	N.L.	60	67	2	1	.667	39	27	59	4.30	0	

a Selected by New York Mets from Baltimore Orioles in Rule V draft, December 9, 2010.

b On disabled list from May 2 to May 17, 2011.

BEAVAN, BLAKE WILLIAM

Born, Irving, Texas, January 17, 1989.

Bats Right. Throws Right. Height, 6 feet, 7 inches. Weight, 240 pounds.

Year	Club	Lea	G	IP	W	L	Pct	SO	BB	H	ERA	SAVES
2008 Clinton	Midwest	23	121²/₃	10	6	.625	73	20	105	2.37	0	
2009 Bakersfield	Calif.	12	73¹/₃	5	4	.556	51	16	75	4.30	0	
2009 Frisco	Texas	15	89²/₃	4	4	.500	34	13	113	4.01	0	
2010 Tacoma	P.C.	7	40¹/₃	2	2	.500	22	8	56	6.47	0	
2010 West Tenn	Southern	3	18	2	1	.667	11	1	18	5.00	0	
2010 Frisco a	Texas	17	110	10	5	.667	68	12	100	2.78	0	
2011 Tacoma	P.C.	16	93	5	3	.625	64	20	118	4.45	0	
2011 Seattle	A.L.	15	97	5	6	.455	42	15	106	4.27	0	

a Traded by Texas Rangers to Seattle Mariners with infielder Justin Smoak, pitcher Josh Lueke and infielder Matt Lawson for pitcher Cliff Lee, pitcher Mark Lowe and cash, July 9, 2010.

BECKETT, JOSHUA PATRICK (JOSH)
Born, Spring, Texas, May 15, 1980.
Bats Right. Throws Right. Height, 6 feet, 5 inches. Weight, 220 pounds.

Year	Club	Lea	G	IP	W	L	Pct	SO	BB	H	ERA	SAVES
2000 Kane County	Midwest		13	59$^1/_3$	2	3	.400	61	15	45	2.12	0
2001 Brevard County	Fla.St.		13	65$^2/_3$	6	0	1.000	101	15	32	1.23	0
2001 Portland	Eastern		13	74$^1/_3$	8	1	.889	102	19	50	1.82	0
2001 Florida	N.L.		4	24	2	2	.500	24	11	14	1.50	0
2002 Marlins	Gulf Coast		1	4	0	0	.000	7	1	5	4.50	0
2002 Jupiter	Fla.St.		1	6	1	0	1.000	12	1	4	0.00	0
2002 Florida a	N.L.		23	107$^2/_3$	6	7	.462	113	44	93	4.10	0
2003 Carolina	Southern		1	4	0	0	.000	7	0	4	4.50	0
2003 Jupiter	Fla.St.		1	3	0	0	.000	5	0	2	0.00	0
2003 Florida b	N.L.		24	142	9	8	.529	152	56	132	3.04	0
2004 Florida c	N.L.		26	156$^2/_3$	9	9	.500	152	54	137	3.79	0
2005 Florida d-e	N.L.		29	178$^2/_3$	15	8	.652	166	58	153	3.38	0
2006 Boston	A.L.		33	204$^2/_3$	16	11	.593	158	74	191	5.01	0
2007 Boston f	A.L.		30	200$^2/_3$	*20	7	.741	194	40	189	3.27	0
2008 Boston g	A.L.		27	174$^1/_3$	12	10	.545	172	34	173	4.03	0
2009 Boston	A.L.		32	212$^1/_3$	17	6	.739	199	55	198	3.86	0
2010 Pawtucket	Int.		2	8	0	0	.000	7	1	7	4.50	0
2010 Boston h	A.L.		21	127$^2/_3$	6	6	.500	116	45	151	5.78	0
2011 Boston	A.L.		30	193	13	7	.650	175	52	146	2.89	0
Major League Totals	11 Yrs.		279	1721$^2/_3$	125	81	.607	1621	523	1577	3.84	0
Division Series												
2003 Florida	N.L.		1	7	0	1	.000	9	5	2	1.29	0
2007 Boston	A.L.		1	9	1	0	1.000	8	0	4	0.00	0
2008 Boston	A.L.		1	5	0	0	.000	6	4	9	7.20	0
2009 Boston	A.L.		1	6$^2/_3$	0	1	.000	3	1	5	5.40	0
Division Series Totals			4	27$^2/_3$	1	2	.333	26	10	20	2.93	0
Championship Series												
2003 Florida	N.L.		3	19$^1/_3$	1	0	1.000	19	2	11	3.26	0
2007 Boston	A.L.		2	14	2	0	1.000	18	1	9	1.93	0
2008 Boston	A.L.		2	9$^1/_3$	1	0	1.000	8	2	13	9.64	0
Championship Series Totals			7	42$^2/_3$	4	0	1.000	45	5	33	4.22	0
World Series Record												
2003 Florida	N.L.		2	16$^1/_3$	1	1	.500	19	5	8	1.10	0
2007 Boston	A.L.		1	7	1	0	1.000	9	1	6	1.29	0
World Series Totals			3	23$^1/_3$	2	1	.667	28	6	14	1.16	0

a On disabled list from April 29 to May 14 and June 5 to July 16 and August 23 to September 11, 2002.
b On disabled list from May 8 to July 1, 2003.
c On disabled list from May 31 to June 17 and from June 18 to July 5 and July 6 to July 30, 2004.
d On disabled list from June 15 to June 30 and July 6 to July 23, 2005.
e Traded to Boston Red Sox with infielder Mike Lowell and pitcher Guillermo Mota for infielder Hanley Ramirez, pitcher Anibal Sanchez and pitcher Jesus Delgado, November 24, 2005.
f On disabled list from May 14 to May 29, 2007.
g On disabled list from March 19 to April 6 and August 18 to September 5, 2008.
h On disabled list from May 19 to July 23, 2010.

BEDARD, ERIK JOSEPH
Born, Navan, Ontario, Canada, March 5, 1979.
Bats Left. Throws Left. Height, 6 feet, 1 inch. Weight, 200 pounds.

Year	Club	Lea	G	IP	W	L	Pct	SO	BB	H	ERA	SAVES
1999 Orioles	Gulf Coast		8	29	2	1	.667	41	13	20	1.86	0
2000 Delmarva	So.Atl.		29	111	9	4	.692	131	35	98	3.57	2
2001 Orioles	Gulf Coast		2	6	0	1	.000	7	3	4	3.00	0
2001 Frederick	Carolina		17	96$^1/_3$	9	2	.818	130	26	68	2.15	0
2002 Baltimore	A.L.		2	0$^2/_3$	0	0	.000	1	0	2	13.50	0
2002 Bowie	Eastern		13	68$^2/_3$	6	3	.667	66	30	43	1.97	0
2003 Orioles	Gulf Coast		3	8	0	0	.000	11	2	4	1.13	0
2003 Aberdeen a	N.Y.-Penn.		2	7$^1/_3$	0	0	.000	13	1	7	2.35	0
2003 Frederick	Carolina		1	3$^2/_3$	0	1	.000	2	1	5	7.36	0
2004 Ottawa	Int.		2	5	0	1	.000	3	3	8	7.20	0
2004 Baltimore	A.L.		27	137$^1/_3$	6	10	.375	121	71	149	4.59	0
2005 Bowie	Eastern		1	2	0	1	.000	4	1	2	9.00	0
2005 Delmarva	So.Atl.		1	5	1	0	1.000	9	1	3	0.00	0
2005 Baltimore b	A.L.		24	141$^2/_3$	6	8	.429	125	57	139	4.00	0
2006 Baltimore	A.L.		33	196$^1/_3$	15	11	.577	171	69	196	3.76	0
2007 Baltimore c	A.L.		28	182	13	5	.722	221	57	141	3.16	0

Year	Club	Lea	G	IP	W	L	Pct	SO	BB	H	ERA	SAVES
2008 Seattle d-e	A.L.	15	81	6	4	.600	72	37	70	3.67	0
2009 Seattle f	A.L.	15	83	5	3	.625	90	34	65	2.82	0
2010 Mariners	Arizona	2	6²/₃	0	0	.000	11	0	7	2.70	0
2010 Tacoma g-h	P.C.	1	4¹/₃	0	0	.000	3	3	3	0.00	0
2011 Seattle-Boston i-j-k	A.L.	24	129¹/₃	5	9	.357	125	48	118	3.62	0
Major League Totals	8 Yrs.	168	951¹/₃	56	50	.528	926	373	880	3.70	0

a On disabled list from March 28 to September 29, 2003.
b On disabled list from May 22 to July 18, 2005.
c On disabled list from September 9 to October 23, 2007.
d On disabled list from April 9 to April 26 and July 5 to October 1, 2008.
e Traded to Seattle Mariners for pitcher Tony Butler, outfielder Adam Jones, pitcher Kam Mickolio, pitcher George Sherrill and pitcher Chris Tillman, February 8, 2008.
f On disabled list from June 8 to July 7 and July 26 to November 6, 2009.
g Filed for free agency, November 6, 2009, re-signed with Seattle Mariners, February 6, 2010.
h On disabled list from March 26 to November 3, 2010.
i On disabled list from June 29 to July 29, 2011.
j Traded to Boston Red Sox with pitcher Josh Fields for outfielder Trayvon Robinson and outfielder Chih-Hsien Chiang, July 31, 2011.
k Filed for free agency, October 30, 2011. Signed with Pittsburgh Pirates, December 7, 2011.

BELISLE, MATTHEW THOMAS (MATT)

Born, Austin, Texas, June 6, 1980.

Bats Right. Throws Right. Height, 6 feet, 3 inches. Weight, 225 pounds.

Year	Club	Lea	G	IP	W	L	Pct	SO	BB	H	ERA	SAVES
1999 Danville	Appal.	14	71¹/₃	2	5	.286	60	23	86	4.67	0
2000 Myrtle Beach	Carolina	12	78²/₃	3	4	.429	71	11	72	3.43	0
2000 Macon	So.Atl.	15	102¹/₃	9	5	.643	97	18	79	2.37	0
2001 a....................			INJURED—Did Not Play								
2002 Greenville.........	Southern	26	159¹/₃	5	9	.357	123	39	162	4.35	0
2003 Greenville.........	Southern	21	125¹/₃	6	8	.429	94	42	128	3.52	0
2003 Richmond	Int.	3	20	1	1	.500	10	0	17	2.25	0
2003 Louisville	Int.	4	26	1	3	.250	15	5	31	3.81	0
2003 Cincinnati b	N.L.	5	8²/₃	1	1	.500	6	2	10	5.19	0
2004 Louisville	Int.	28	162²/₃	9	11	.450	106	51	192	5.26	0
2005 Cincinnati............	N.L.	60	85²/₃	4	8	.333	59	26	101	4.41	1
2006 Dayton	Midwest	2	4	1	0	1.000	3	0	3	0.00	1
2006 Chattanooga.......	Southern	2	3¹/₃	0	0	.000	4	0	3	0.00	0
2006 Louisville	Int.	8	9	1	0	1.000	9	1	4	0.00	0
2006 Cincinnati c	N.L.	30	40	2	0	1.000	26	19	43	3.60	0
2007 Louisville	Int.	1	6	0	1	.000	7	2	7	3.00	0
2007 Cincinnati............	N.L.	30	177²/₃	8	9	.471	125	43	212	5.32	0
2008 Sarasota............	Fla.St.	1	8²/₃	1	0	1.000	3	0	2	0.00	0
2008 Chattanooga.......	Southern	1	9	1	0	1.000	3	0	7	2.00	0
2008 Cincinnati............	N.L.	6	29²/₃	1	4	.200	14	6	47	7.28	0
2008 Louisville d-e	Int.	26	38	5	1	.833	27	11	43	4.26	4
2009 Colorado Springs.......	P.C.	33	58¹/₃	1	1	.500	47	15	58	3.09	9
2009 Colorado f	N.L.	24	31	3	1	.750	22	5	35	5.52	0
2010 Colorado	N.L.	76	92	7	5	.583	91	16	84	2.93	1
2011 Colorado	N.L.	74	72	10	4	.714	58	14	77	3.25	0
Major League Totals	8 Yrs.	306	536²/₃	36	32	.529	401	131	609	4.48	2
Division Series											
2009 Colorado	N.L.	2	2	0	0	.000	2	1	0	0.00	0

a On minor league disabled list from April 6 to September 18, 2001.
b Sent by Atlanta Braves to Cincinnati Reds as player to be named later for pitcher Kent Mercker, August 14, 2003.
c On disabled list from May 28 to June 27 and July 10 to August 20, 2006.
d On disabled list from March 21 to April 21, 2008.
e On disabled list from September 9 to November 6, 2008.
f Not offered contract, December 12, 2008. Signed with Colorado Rockies organization, January 14, 2009.

BELL, HEATH JUSTIN

Born, Oceanside, California, September 29, 1977.

Bats Right. Throws Right. Height, 6 feet, 3 inches. Weight, 240 pounds.

Year	Club	Lea	G	IP	W	L	Pct	SO	BB	H	ERA	SAVES
1998 Kingsport	Appal.	22	46	1	0	1.000	61	11	40	2.54	8
1999 Columbia	So.Atl.	55	62¹/₃	1	7	.125	68	17	47	2.60	25
2000 St. Lucie............	Fla.St.	48	60	5	1	.833	75	21	43	2.55	23
2001 Binghamton	Eastern	43	61¹/₃	3	1	.750	55	19	82	6.02	4
2002 Binghamton	Eastern	24	38	1	0	1.000	49	6	22	1.18	6

Year	Club	Lea	G	IP	W	L	Pct	SO	BB	H	ERA	SAVES
2002 Norfolk	Int.	22	31²/₃	3	4	.429	28	9	38	4.26	5	
2003 Norfolk	Int.	40	49²/₃	2	3	.400	54	8	54	4.71	3	
2004 Binghamton	Eastern	1	2	0	0	.000	0	0	2	0.00	0	
2004 Norfolk	Int.	45	55²/₃	3	1	.750	68	24	42	3.23	16	
2004 New York	N.L.	17	24¹/₃	0	2	.000	27	6	22	3.33	0	
2005 Norfolk	Int.	13	26²/₃	1	0	1.000	29	5	15	1.69	6	
2005 New York	N.L.	42	46²/₃	1	3	.250	43	13	56	5.59	0	
2006 Norfolk	Int.	30	35	3	3	.500	56	8	27	1.29	12	
2006 New York a	N.L.	22	37	0	0	.000	35	11	51	5.11	0	
2007 San Diego	N.L.	81	93²/₃	6	4	.600	102	30	60	2.02	2	
2008 San Diego	N.L.	74	78	6	6	.500	71	28	66	3.58	0	
2009 San Diego	N.L.	68	69²/₃	6	4	.600	79	24	54	2.71	*42	
2010 San Diego	N.L.	67	70	6	1	.857	86	28	56	1.93	47	
2011 San Diego b	N.L.	64	62²/₃	3	4	.429	51	21	51	2.44	43	
Major League Totals ....8 Yrs.	435	482	28	24	.538	494	161	416	3.06	134		

a Traded to San Diego Padres with pitcher Royce Ring for pitcher Jon Adkins and outfielder Ben Johnson, November 15, 2006.

b Filed for free agency, October 30, 2011. Signed with Florida Marlins, December 5, 2011.

BENOIT (PENA), JOAQUIN ANTONIO

Born, Santiago, Dominican Republic, July 26, 1977.
Bats Right. Throws Right. Height, 6 feet, 3 inches. Weight, 220 pounds.

Year	Club	Lea	G	IP	W	L	Pct	SO	BB	H	ERA	SAVES
1996 Texas	Dominican	14	75	6	5	.545	63	23	63	2.28	0	
1997 Rangers	Gulf Coast	10	44	3	3	.500	38	11	40	2.05	0	
1998 Savannah	So.Atl.	15	80	4	3	.571	68	18	79	3.83	0	
1999 Charlotte	Fla.St.	22	105	7	4	.636	83	50	117	5.31	0	
2000 Tulsa	Texas	16	82¹/₃	4	4	.500	72	30	73	3.83	0	
2001 Tulsa	Texas	4	21²/₃	1	0	1.000	23	6	23	3.32	0	
2001 Oklahoma	P.C.	24	131	9	5	.643	142	73	113	4.19	0	
2001 Texas	A.L.	1	5	0	0	.000	4	3	8	10.80	0	
2002 Oklahoma	P.C.	16	98²/₃	8	4	.667	103	37	74	3.56	0	
2002 Texas	A.L.	17	84²/₃	4	5	.444	59	58	91	5.31	1	
2002 Charlotte	Fla.St.	1	5	0	0	.000	8	3	1	0.00	0	
2003 Oklahoma	P.C.	6	33	2	1	.667	31	11	28	3.82	0	
2003 Texas a	A.L.	25	105	8	5	.615	87	51	99	5.49	0	
2004 Texas	A.L.	28	103	3	5	.375	95	31	113	5.68	0	
2004 Frisco b	Texas	1	2	0	0	.000	6	0	0	0.00	0	
2005 Oklahoma	P.C.	3	5	0	1	.000	2	4	4	5.40	0	
2005 Rangers	Arizona	1	2	0	0	.000	4	1	0	0.00	0	
2005 Texas c	A.L.	32	87	4	4	.500	78	38	69	3.72	0	
2006 Texas	A.L.	56	79²/₃	1	1	.500	85	38	68	4.86	0	
2007 Texas	A.L.	70	82	7	4	.636	87	28	68	2.85	6	
2008 Frisco	Texas	3	1²/₃	0	0	.000	2	4	4	16.20	0	
2008 Oklahoma	P.C.	2	3	1	0	1.000	3	0	1	0.00	0	
2008 Texas d	A.L.	44	45	3	2	.600	43	35	40	5.00	1	
2009 Texas e-f	A.L.			INJURED—Did Not Play								
2010 Durham	Int.	8	9²/₃	0.	1	.000	17	3	8	2.79	2	
2010 Tampa Bay g		63	60¹/₃	1	2	.333	75	11	30	1.34	1	
2011 Detroit	A.L.	66	61	4	3	.571	63	17	47	2.95	2	
Major League Totals ....10 Yrs.	402	712²/₃	35	31	.530	676	310	633	4.34	11		
Division Series												
2010 Tampa Bay	A.L.	3	3²/₃	1	0	1.000	3	0	0	0.00	0	
2011 Detroit	A.L.	2	3²/₃	0	0	.000	6	1	4	2.45	0	
Division Series Totals	5	7¹/₃	1	0	1.000	9	1	4	1.23	0		
Championship Series												
2011 Detroit	A.L.	3	4	0	0	.000	3	2	0	0.00	0	

a On disabled list from June 1 to June 22, 2003.

b On disabled list from August 23 to September 7, 2004.

c On disabled list from March 25 to May 2 and June 9 to June 28, 2005.

d On disabled list from July 3 to August 6, 2008.

e On disabled list from April 5 to November 5, 2009.

f Filed for free agency, November 5, 2009. Signed with Tampa Bay Rays organization, February 15, 2010.

g Filed for free agency, November 1, 2010. Signed with Detroit Tigers, November 19, 2010.

BERGESEN, BRADLEY STEVEN (BRAD)
Born, Fairfield, California, September 25, 1985.
Bats Left. Throws Right. Height, 6 feet, 2 inches. Weight, 215 pounds.

Year	Club	Lea	G	IP	W	L	Pct	SO	BB	H	ERA	SAVES
2004 Bluefield	Appal.	5	7$^{1}/_{3}$	0	0	.000	6	3	7	6.14	0
2005 Aberdeen	N.Y.-Penn.	15	71	1	3	.250	54	14	89	4.82	0
2006 Delmarva	So.Atl.	18	86$^{1}/_{3}$	5	4	.556	49	10	97	4.27	0
2007 Frederick	Carolina	10	56$^{1}/_{3}$	3	6	.333	35	9	78	5.75	0
2007 Delmarva	So.Atl.	15	94$^{1}/_{3}$	7	3	.700	73	17	75	2.19	0
2008 Frederick	Carolina	4	17$^{1}/_{3}$	1	1	.500	15	6	15	2.08	0
2008 Bowie	Eastern	24	148	15	6	.714	72	27	143	3.22	0
2009 Norfolk	Int.	2	11	1	1	.500	9	3	6	2.45	0
2009 Baltimore a	A.L.	19	123$^{1}/_{3}$	7	5	.583	65	32	126	3.43	0
2010 Norfolk	Int.	3	14$^{2}/_{3}$	1	0	1.000	10	3	17	4.30	0
2010 Baltimore	A.L.	30	170	8	12	.400	81	51	193	4.98	0
2011 Norfolk	Int.	3	22	2	1	.667	18	8	14	1.64	0
2011 Baltimore	A.L.	34	101	2	7	.222	61	32	119	5.70	0
Major League Totals	3 Yrs.	83	394$^{1}/_{3}$	17	24	.415	207	115	438	4.68	0

a On disabled list from July 31 to November 6, 2009.

BERKEN, JASON THOMAS
Born, Green Bay, Wisconsin, November 27, 1983.
Bats Right. Throws Right. Height, 6 feet. Weight, 175 pounds.

Year	Club	Lea	G	IP	W	L	Pct	SO	BB	H	ERA	SAVES
2006 Aberdeen	N.Y.-Penn.	9	45	1	4	.200	46	5	39	2.80	0
2007 Frederick	Carolina	27	151	9	9	.500	124	49	160	4.53	0
2008 Bowie	Eastern	26	145$^{2}/_{3}$	12	4	.750	125	38	141	3.58	0
2009 Bowie	Eastern	2	8	1	1	.500	8	6	4	5.63	0
2009 Norfolk	Int.	5	25$^{2}/_{3}$	2	0	1.000	16	6	19	1.05	0
2009 Baltimore	A.L.	24	119$^{2}/_{3}$	6	12	.333	66	44	164	6.54	0
2010 Baltimore a	A.L.	41	62$^{1}/_{3}$	3	3	.500	45	19	64	3.03	0
2011 Norfolk	Int.	5	18	0	1	.000	16	7	20	3.50	0
2011 Baltimore b	A.L.	40	47	1	2	.333	41	21	63	5.36	0
Major League Totals	3 Yrs.	105	229	10	17	.370	152	84	291	5.34	0

a On disabled list from August 13 to November 4, 2010.
b On disabled list from August 18 to September 12, 2011.

BETANCOURT, RAFAEL JOSE
Born, Cumana, Venezuela, April 29, 1975.
Bats Right. Throws Right. Height, 6 feet, 2 inches. Weight, 200 pounds.

Year	Club	Lea	G	IP	W	L	Pct	SO	BB	H	ERA	SAVES
1997 Michigan	Midwest	27	32$^{1}/_{3}$	0	3	.000	52	2	26	1.95	11
1998 Red Sox	Gulf Coast	4	5	0	2	.000	4	1	6	7.20	0
1998 Sarasota	Fla.St.	20	28	3	1	.750	33	6	22	3.54	2
1998 Trenton	Eastern	7	9$^{1}/_{3}$	0	0	.000	9	3	9	6.75	0
1999 Sarasota	Fla.St.	6	7	0	0	.000	6	1	5	0.00	4
1999 Trenton a	Eastern	39	54$^{2}/_{3}$	6	2	.750	57	10	50	3.62	13
2000 Yokohama	Japan Cen.	11	29	1	2	.333	16	11	30	4.08	0
2000 Searex b	Japan East	20	23	1	0	1.000	29	6	17	1.17	6
2001 Trenton	Eastern	16	24	0	1	.000	27	3	28	5.63	4
2002					INJURED—Did Not Play							
2003 Akron	Eastern	31	45$^{1}/_{3}$	0	0	.000	75	13	33	1.39	16
2003 Buffalo	Int.	4	6$^{2}/_{3}$	0	0	.000	6	2	6	4.05	1
2003 Cleveland c	A.L.	33	38	2	2	.500	36	13	27	2.13	1
2004 Akron	Eastern	1	1	0	0	.000	2	1	0	0.00	0
2004 Cleveland d	A.L.	68	66$^{2}/_{3}$	5	6	.455	76	18	71	3.92	4
2005 Cleveland e	A.L.	54	67$^{2}/_{3}$	4	3	.571	73	17	57	2.79	1
2006 Akron f	Eastern	1	1	0	0	.000	2	1	0	0.00	0
2007 Cleveland	A.L.	68	79$^{1}/_{3}$	5	1	.833	80	9	51	1.47	3
2008 Cleveland	A.L.	69	71	3	4	.429	64	25	76	5.07	4
2009 Columbus	Int.	3	3$^{1}/_{3}$	1	0	1.000	4	1	0	0.00	0
2009 Cleveland g-h-i	A.L.	29	30$^{2}/_{3}$	1	2	.333	32	15	25	3.52	1
2009 Colorado	N.L.	32	25$^{1}/_{3}$	3	1	.750	29	5	17	1.78	1
2010 Colorado	N.L.	72	62$^{1}/_{3}$	5	1	.833	89	8	52	3.61	1
2011 Colorado	N.L.	68	62$^{1}/_{3}$	2	1	1.000	73	8	46	2.89	8
Major League Totals	9 Yrs.	543	560	33	24	.579	600	129	474	3.18	27
Division Series												
2007 Cleveland	A.L.	2	2	0	0	.000	3	0	1	0.00	0

Year	Club	Lea	G	IP	W	L	Pct	SO	BB	H	ERA	SAVES
2009 Colorado	N.L.	3	2^1/$_3$	0	0	.000	3	1	2	3.86	0	
Division Series Totals		5	4^1/$_3$	0	0	.000	6	1	3	2.08	0	
Championship Series												
2007 Cleveland	A.L.	5	8	0	0	.000	6	1	6	6.75	0	

a Sold by Boston Red Sox to Yokohama, November 18,1999.
b Sold to Boston Red Sox, December 13, 2000.
c Filed for free agency, October 15, 2001. Signed with Cleveland Indians organization, January 20, 2003.
d On disabled list from June 26 to July 11, 2004.
e On disabled list from June 30 to July 18, 2005.
f On disabled list from April 20 to May 16, 2006.
g On disabled list from June 1 to July 9, 2009.
h Traded to Colorado Rockies for pitcher Connor Graham, July 23, 2009.
i Filed for free agency, November 14, 2009. Accepted arbitration, December 7, 2009.

BILLINGSLEY, CHAD RYAN

Born, Defiance, Ohio, July 29, 1984.
Bats Right. Throws Right. Height, 6 feet. Weight, 245 pounds.

Year	Club	Lea	G	IP	W	L	Pct	SO	BB	H	ERA	SAVES
2003 Ogden	Pioneer	11	54	5	4	.556	62	15	49	2.83	0	
2004 Vero Beach..........	Fla.St.	18	92	7	4	.636	111	49	68	2.35	0	
2004 Jacksonville	Southern	8	42^1/$_3$	4	0	1.000	47	22	32	2.98	0	
2005 Jacksonville	Southern	28	146	13	6	.684	162	50	116	3.51	0	
2006 Las Vegas............	P.C.	13	70^2/$_3$	6	3	.667	78	32	57	3.95	0	
2006 Los Angeles	N.L.	18	90	7	4	.636	59	58	92	3.80	0	
2007 Los Angeles	N.L.	43	147	12	5	.706	141	64	131	3.31	0	
2008 Los Angeles	N.L.	35	200^2/$_3$	16	10	.615	201	80	188	3.14	0	
2009 Los Angeles	N.L.	33	196^1/$_3$	12	11	.522	179	86	173	4.03	0	
2010 Los Angeles a........	N.L.	31	191^2/$_3$	12	11	.522	171	69	176	3.57	0	
2011 Los Angeles	N.L.	32	188	11	11	.500	152	84	189	4.21	0	
Major League Totals ...... .6 Yrs.		192	1013^2/$_3$	70	52	.574	903	441	949	3.68	0	
Division Series												
2006 Los Angeles	N.L.	2	2	0	0	.000	3	0	1	0.00	0	
2008 Los Angeles	N.L.	1	6^2/$_3$	1	0	1.000	7	1	5	1.35	0	
Division Series Totals		3	8^2/$_3$	1	0	1.000	10	1	6	1.04	0	
Championship Series												
2008 Los Angeles	N.L.	2	5	0	2	.000	9	7	12	18.00	0	
2009 Los Angeles	N.L.	1	3^1/$_3$	0	0	.000	3	2	2	5.40	0	
Championship Series Totals		3	8^1/$_3$	0	2	.000	12	9	14	12.96	0	

a On disabled list from June 12 to June 28, 2010.

BLACKBURN, ROBERT NICHOLAS (NICK)

Born, Ada, Oklahoma, February 24, 1982.
Bats Right. Throws Right. Height, 6 feet, 4 inches. Weight, 225 pounds.

Year	Club	Lea	G	IP	W	L	Pct	SO	BB	H	ERA	SAVES
2002 Elizabethton	Appal.	13	66^2/$_3$	3	3	.500	62	21	70	4.99	0	
2003 Quad Cities..........	Midwest	16	76	2	9	.182	40	18	78	4.86	1	
2004 Fort Myers	Fla.St.	9	37^1/$_3$	3	3	.500	21	7	51	6.27	0	
2004 Quad Cities........	Midwest	20	84^1/$_3$	6	4	.600	66	23	69	2.77	1	
2005 New Britain	Eastern	7	49	2	4	.333	27	10	35	1.84	0	
2005 Fort Myers	Fla.St.	15	93^2/$_3$	7	5	.583	55	16	95	3.36	0	
2005 Rochester.............	Int.	3	14	0	0	.000	7	3	20	5.14	0	
2006 New Britain	Eastern	30	132^1/$_3$	7	8	.467	81	37	141	4.42	0	
2007 New Britain	Eastern	8	38	3	1	.750	18	7	36	3.08	0	
2007 Rochester.............	Int.	17	110^2/$_3$	7	3	.700	57	12	96	2.11	0	
2007 Minnesota	A.L.	6	11^2/$_3$	0	2	.000	8	2	19	7.71	0	
2008 Minnesota	A.L.	33	193^1/$_3$	11	11	.500	96	39	224	4.05	0	
2009 Minnesota	A.L.	33	205^2/$_3$	11	11	.500	98	41	*240	4.03	0	
2010 Rochester.............	Int.	4	21^2/$_3$	1	0	1.000	13	6	19	2.49	0	
2010 Minnesota	A.L.	28	161	10	12	.455	68	40	194	5.42	0	
2011 Minnesota a...........	A.L.	26	148^1/$_3$	7	10	.412	76	54	183	4.49	0	
Major League Totals .... .5 Yrs.		126	720	39	46	.459	346	176	860	4.50	0	
Division Series												
2009 Minnesota	A.L.	1	5^2/$_3$	0	0	.000	3	2	3	1.59	0	

a On disabled list from August 22 to October 14, 2011.

BLANTON, JOSEPH MATTHEW (JOE)

Born, Bowling Green, Kentucky, December 11, 1980.
Bats Right. Throws Right. Height, 6 feet, 3 inches. Weight, 255 pounds.

Year Club	Lea	G	IP	W	L	Pct	SO	BB	H	ERA	SAVES
2002 Modesto.........	California	2	6	0	1	.000	6	6	8	7.50	0
2002 Vancouver	Northwest	4	14^1/$_3$	1	1	.500	15	2	11	3.14	0
2003 Kane County.......	Midwest	21	133	8	7	.533	144	19	110	2.57	0
2003 Midland	Texas	7	35^2/$_3$	3	1	.750	30	7	21	1.26	1
2004 Sacramento	P.C.	28	176^1/$_3$	11	8	.579	143	34	199	4.19	0
2004 Oakland	A.L.	3	8	0	0	.000	6	2	6	5.63	0
2005 Oakland	A.L.	33	201^1/$_3$	12	12	.500	116	67	178	3.53	0
2006 Oakland	A.L.	32	194^1/$_3$	16	12	.571	107	58	241	4.82	0
2007 Oakland	A.L.	34	230	14	10	.583	140	40	*240	3.95	0
2008 Oakland	A.L.	20	127	5	12	.294	62	35	145	4.96	0
2008 Philadelphia a.......	N.L.	13	70^2/$_3$	4	0	1.000	49	31	66	4.20	0
2009 Philadelphia	N.L.	31	195^1/$_3$	12	8	.600	163	59	198	4.05	0
2010 Lakewood..........	So.Atl.	1	2	0	0	.000	2	0	0	0.00	0
2010 Reading	Eastern	2	8	0	1	.000	5	2	9	5.63	0
2010 Philadelphia b	N.L.	29	175^2/$_3$	9	6	.600	134	43	206	4.82	0
2011 Lakewood...........	So.Atl.	1	1	0	0	.000	0	0	0	0.00	0
2011 Philadelphia c.........	N.L.	11	41^1/$_3$	1	2	.333	35	9	52	5.01	0
Major League Totals .... 8 Yrs.		206	1243^2/$_3$	73	62	.541	812	344	1332	4.32	0
Division Series											
2008 Philadelphia...........	N.L.	1	6	1	0	1.000	7	0	5	1.50	0
2009 Philadelphia	N.L.	2	3^2/$_3$	0	0	.000	1	0	4	4.91	0
2011 Philadelphia..........	N.L.	1	1	0	0	.000	0	0	0	0.00	0
Division Series Totals		4	10^2/$_3$	1	0	1.000	8	0	9	2.53	0
Championship Series											
2006 Oakland	A.L.	1	2	0	0	.000	2	2	0	0.00	0
2008 Philadelphia..........	N.L.	1	5	0	0	.000	4	4	7	5.40	0
2009 Philadelphia	N.L.	1	6	0	0	.000	2	2	6	4.50	0
2010 Philadelphia	N.L.	1	4^2/$_3$	0	0	.000	3	1	5	5.79	0
Championship Series Totals		4	17^2/$_3$	0	0	.000	11	9	18	4.58	0
World Series Record											
2008 Philadelphia...........	N.L.	1	6	1	0	1.000	7	2	4	3.00	0
2009 Philadelphia	N.L.	1	6	0	0	.000	7	2	5	4.50	0
World Series Totals.............		2	12	1	0	1.000	14	4	9	4.50	0

a Traded to Philadelphia Phillies for pitcher Josh Outman, infielder Adrian Cardenas and outfielder Matt
Spencer, July 17, 2008.

b On disabled list from March 26 to May 3, 2010.

c On disabled list from April 4 to May 9 and May 16 to September 5, 2011.

BOGGS, MITCHELL THOMAS

Born, Dalton, Georgia, February 15, 1984.
Bats Right. Throws Right. Height, 6 feet, 4 inches. Weight, 215 pounds.

Year Club	Lea	G	IP	W	L	Pct	SO	BB	H	ERA	SAVES
2005 New Jersey	N.Y.-Penn.	15	71^2/$_3$	4	4	.500	61	24	77	3.89	0
2006 Palm Beach	Fla.St.	27	145	10	6	.625	126	51	153	3.41	0
2007 Springfield	Texas	26	152^1/$_3$	11	7	.611	117	62	167	3.84	0
2008 St. Louis..............	N.L.	8	34	3	2	.600	13	22	42	7.41	0
2008 Memphis	P.C.	21	125^1/$_3$	9	3	.750	81	46	107	3.45	0
2009 Memphis	P.C.	14	76^1/$_3$	6	4	.600	58	32	90	4.83	0
2009 St. Louis.............	N.L.	16	58	2	3	.400	46	33	71	4.19	0
2010 St. Louis.............	N.L.	61	67^1/$_3$	2	3	.400	52	27	60	3.61	0
2011 Memphis	P.C.	4	14^2/$_3$	0	2	.000	14	5	12	2.45	0
2011 St. Louis..............	N.L.	51	60^2/$_3$	2	3	.400	48	21	62	3.56	4
Major League Totals .... 4 Yrs.		136	220	9	11	.450	159	103	235	4.34	4
Division Series											
2009 St. Louis.............	N.L.	1	1	0	0	.000	1	2	0	0.00	0
2011 St. Louis.............	N.L.	2	2	0	0	.000	1	1	4	9.00	0
Division Series Totals		3	3	0	0	.000	2	3	4	6.00	0
Championship Series											
2011 St. Louis.............	N.L.	3	3	0	0	.000	0	1	4	6.00	0
World Series Record											
2011 St. Louis..............	N.L.	2	2^2/$_3$	0	0	.000	4	0	2	3.38	0

BOWDEN, MICHAEL MATTHEW
Born, Winfield, Illinois, September 9, 1986.
Bats Right. Throws Right. Height, 6 feet, 3 inches. Weight, 215 pounds.

Year	Club	Lea	G	IP	W	L	Pct	SO	BB	H	ERA	SAVES
2005	Red Sox	Gulf Coast	4	6	1	0	1.000	10	4	4	0.00	0
2006	Greenville	So.Atl.	24	107²/₃	9	6	.600	118	31	91	3.51	0
2006	Wilmington	Carolina	1	5	0	0	.000	3	1	9	9.00	0
2007	Lancaster	Calif.	8	46	2	0	1.000	46	8	35	1.37	0
2007	Portland	Eastern	19	96²/₃	8	6	.571	82	33	105	4.28	0
2008	Portland	Eastern	19	104¹/₃	9	4	.692	101	24	72	2.33	0
2008	Pawtucket	Int.	7	40	0	3	.000	29	5	40	3.38	0
2008	Boston	A.L.	1	5	1	0	1.000	3	1	7	3.60	0
2009	Pawtucket	Int.	24	126¹/₃	4	6	.400	88	47	106	3.13	0
2009	Boston	A.L.	8	16	1	1	.500	12	6	23	9.56	0
2010	Pawtucket	Int.	31	105²/₃	6	4	.600	77	37	84	3.66	1
2010	Boston	A.L.	14	15¹/₃	0	1	.000	13	4	20	4.70	0
2011	Pawtucket	Int.	41	52²/₃	3	3	.500	61	18	43	2.73	16
2011	Boston	A.L.	14	20	0	0	.000	17	11	19	4.05	0
Major League Totals	4 Yrs.		37	56¹/₃	2	2	.500	45	22	69	5.75	0

BRAY, WILLIAM PAUL (BILL)
Born, Virginia Beach, Virginia, June 5, 1983.
Bats Left. Throws Left. Height, 6 feet, 3 inches. Weight, 225 pounds.

Year	Club	Lea	G	IP	W	L	Pct	SO	BB	H	ERA	SAVES
2004	Brevard County	Fla.St.	6	7¹/₃	0	2	.000	6	1	9	4.91	1
2005	Potomac	Carolina	8	12²/₃	1	0	1.000	18	3	8	2.13	3
2005	Harrisburg	Eastern	3	5²/₃	1	0	1.000	6	1	10	6.35	1
2005	New Orleans	P.C.	23	21¹/₃	1	4	.200	25	9	23	5.06	2
2006	New Orleans	P.C.	21	31²/₃	4	1	.800	45	9	26	3.98	5
2006	Washington-Cincinnati a	N.L.	48	50²/₃	3	2	.600	39	18	57	4.09	2
2007	Sarasota	Fla.St.	2	2	0	0	.000	2	1	0	0.00	0
2007	Louisville	Int.	18	19	1	2	.333	29	6	19	4.26	0
2007	Cincinnati b	N.L.	19	14¹/₃	3	3	.500	14	5	16	6.28	1
2008	Louisville	Int.	9	5	0	0	.000	15	5	3	3.00	1
2008	Cincinnati	N.L.	63	47	2	2	.500	54	24	50	2.87	0
2009	Louisville	Int.	3	5	0	0	.000	6	1	2	0.00	0
2010	Lynchburg	Carolina	4	4²/₃	0	0	.000	9	2	1	0.00	0
2010	Louisville	Int.	6	5²/₃	0	0	.000	7	1	2	0.00	1
2010	Cincinnati	N.L.	35	28¹/₃	0	2	.000	30	10	21	4.13	0
2011	Cincinnati	N.L.	79	48¹/₃	5	3	.625	44	17	35	2.98	0
Major League Totals	5 Yrs.		244	188²/₃	13	12	.520	181	74	179	3.67	3
Division Series												
2010	Cincinnati	N.L.	2	1²/₃	0	0	.000	2	0	0	0.00	0

a Traded to Cincinnati Reds with pitcher Gary Majewski, infielder Royce Clayton, infielder Brendan Harris and pitcher Daryl Thompson for outfielder Austin Kearns, infielder Felipe Lopez and pitcher Ryan Wagner, July 13, 2006.
b On disabled list from March 23 to July 20, 2007.

BRESLOW, CRAIG ANDREW
Born, New Haven, Connecticut, August 8, 1980.
Bats Left. Throws Left. Height, 6 feet, 1 inch. Weight, 185 pounds.

Year	Club	Lea	G	IP	W	L	Pct	SO	BB	H	ERA	SAVES
2002	Ogden	Pioneer	23	54¹/₃	6	2	.750	56	24	42	1.82	2
2003	Beloit	Midwest	33	65	3	4	.429	80	27	64	5.12	2
2004	High Desert	Calif.	23	41¹/₃	1	3	.250	41	24	54	7.19	0
2004	New Jersey a	Northeast	19	26¹/₃	3	1	.750	37	13	19	4.10	0
2005	Mobile	Southern	40	52¹/₃	2	1	.667	47	17	38	2.75	0
2005	Portland	P.C.	7	9	0	1	.000	9	1	11	4.00	0
2005	San Diego b	N.L.	14	16¹/₃	0	0	.000	14	13	15	2.20	0
2006	Pawtucket	Int.	39	67	7	1	.875	77	24	49	2.69	7
2006	Boston c	A.L.	13	12	0	2	.000	12	6	12	3.75	0
2007	Pawtucket	Int.	49	68²/₃	2	3	.400	73	25	70	4.06	1
2008	Cleveland-Minnesota d-e	A.L.	49	47	0	2	.000	39	19	34	1.91	1
2009	Minnesota-Oakland f	A.L.	77	69²/₃	8	7	.533	55	29	48	3.36	0
2010	Oakland	A.L.	75	74²/₃	4	4	.500	71	29	53	3.01	5
2011	Oakland g	A.L.	67	59¹/₃	0	0	.000	44	21	69	3.79	0
Major League Totals	6 Yrs.		295	279	12	17	.414	235	117	231	3.06	6

a Released by Milwaukee Brewers, July 6, 2004. Signed with independent New Jersey (Northeast), July 2004.
b Signed with San Diego Padres organization, March 6, 2005.

c Not offered contract, December 21, 2005. Signed with Boston Red Sox organization, February 1, 2006.
d Claimed on waivers by Cleveland Indians, March 23, 2008.
e Claimed on waivers by Minnesota Twins, May 29, 2008.
f Claimed on waivers by Oakland Athletics, May 20, 2009.
g Traded to Arizona Diamondbacks with pitcher Trevor Cahill for outfielder Collin Cowgill, pitcher Jarrod Parker and pitcher Ryan Cook, December 9, 2011.

BRITTON, ZACHARY GRANT (ZACH)
Born, Panorama City, California, December 22, 1987.
Bats Left. Throws Left. Height, 6 feet, 3 inches. Weight, 195 pounds.

Year Club	Lea	G	IP	W	L	Pct	SO	BB	H	ERA	SAVES
2006 Bluefield	Appal.	11	34	0	4	.000	21	20	35	5.29	0
2007 Aberdeen	N.Y.-Penn.	15	63²/₃	6	4	.600	45	22	64	3.68	0
2008 Delmarva	So.Atl.	27	147¹/₃	12	7	.632	114	49	118	3.12	0
2009 Frederick	Carolina	25	140	9	6	.600	131	55	123	2.70	0
2010 Bowie	Eastern	15	87	7	3	.700	68	28	76	2.48	0
2010 Norfolk	Int.	12	66¹/₃	3	4	.429	56	23	63	2.98	0
2011 Bowie	Eastern	3	11²/₃	2	0	.000	15	2	14	5.40	0
2011 Norfolk	Int.	1	5	0	1	.000	3	1	3	1.80	0
2011 Baltimore a	A.L.	28	154¹/₃	11	11	.500	97	62	162	4.61	0

a On disabled list from August 5 to August 22, 2011.

BROTHERS, REX COLEMAN
Born, Murfreesboro, Tennessee, December 18, 1987.
Bats Left. Throws Left. Height, 6 feet. Weight, 205 pounds.

Year Club	Lea	G	IP	W	L	Pct	SO	BB	H	ERA	SAVES
2009 Tri-City	Northwest	8	10²/₃	2	0	1.000	18	5	10	3.38	0
2009 Asheville	So.Atl.	9	10²/₃	0	0	.000	10	3	6	3.38	0
2010 Modesto	Calif.	33	37	0	2	.000	43	19	20	2.68	3
2010 Tulsa	Texas	24	23	2	1	.667	27	18	14	3.91	4
2011 Colorado Springs	P.C.	25	28	3	2	.600	45	15	29	2.89	0
2011 Colorado	N.L.	48	40²/₃	1	2	.333	59	20	33	2.88	1

BROXTON, JONATHAN ROY
Born, Augusta, Georgia, June 16, 1984.
Bats Right. Throws Right. Height, 6 feet, 4 inches. Weight, 290 pounds.

Year Club	Lea	G	IP	W	L	Pct	SO	BB	H	ERA	SAVES
2002 Great Falls	Pioneer	11	29¹/₃	2	0	1.000	33	16	22	2.76	2
2003 South Bend	So.Atl.	9	37¹/₃	4	2	.667	30	22	27	3.13	0
2004 Vero Beach	Fla.St.	23	128¹/₃	11	6	.647	144	43	110	3.23	0
2005 Jacksonville	Southern	33	96²/₃	5	3	.625	107	31	79	3.17	5
2005 Los Angeles	N.L.	14	13²/₃	1	0	1.000	22	12	13	5.93	0
2006 Las Vegas	P.C.	11	11¹/₃	1	0	1.000	18	3	6	0.00	5
2006 Los Angeles	N.L.	68	76¹/₃	4	1	.800	97	33	61	2.59	3
2007 Los Angeles	N.L.	83	82	4	4	.500	99	25	69	2.85	2
2008 Los Angeles	N.L.	70	69	3	5	.375	88	27	54	3.13	14
2009 Los Angeles	N.L.	73	76	7	2	.778	114	29	44	2.61	36
2010 Los Angeles	N.L.	64	62¹/₃	5	6	.455	73	28	64	4.04	22
2011 Albuquerque	P.C.	2	2	0	0	.000	5	1	2	4.50	0
2011 Los Angeles a-b	N.L.	14	12²/₃	1	2	.333	10	9	15	5.68	7
Major League Totals ... 7 Yrs.		386	392	25	20	.556	503	163	320	3.19	84
Division Series											
2006 Los Angeles	N.L.	2	2	0	1	.000	3	2	5	13.50	0
2008 Los Angeles	N.L.	3	3¹/₃	0	0	.000	5	2	0	0.00	1
2009 Los Angeles	N.L.	3	3²/₃	0	0	.000	4	0	4	2.45	1
Division Series Totals		8	9	0	1	.000	12	4	9	4.00	2
Championship Series											
2008 Los Angeles	N.L.	2	2¹/₃	0	0	.000	2	1	3	3.86	0
2009 Los Angeles	N.L.	3	3	0	1	.000	1	1	2	6.00	1
Championship Series Totals		5	5¹/₃	0	1	.000	3	2	5	5.06	1

a On disabled list from May 4 to September 30, 2011.
b Filed for free agency, October 30, 2011. Signed with Kansas City Royals, November 29, 2011.

BUCHHOLZ, CLAY DANIEL

Born, Nederland, Texas, August 14, 1984.
Bats Left. Throws Right. Height, 6 feet, 3 inches. Weight, 190 pounds.

Year	Club	Lea	G	IP	W	L	Pct	SO	BB	H	ERA	SAVES
2005 Lowell	N.Y.-Penn.	15	41⅓	0	1	.000	45	9	34	2.61	0
2006 Wilmington	Carolina	3	16	2	0	1.000	23	4	10	1.13	0
2006 Greenville	So.Atl.	21	103	9	4	.692	117	29	78	2.62	0
2007 Portland	Eastern	16	86²/₃	7	2	.778	116	22	55	1.77	0
2007 Pawtucket	Int.	8	38²/₃	1	3	.250	55	13	32	3.96	0
2007 Boston a	A.L.	4	22²/₃	3	1	.750	22	10	14	1.59	0
2008 Portland	Eastern	2	15	1	0	1.000	18	1	7	1.80	0
2008 Pawtucket	Int.	9	43²/₃	4	2	.667	43	17	36	2.47	0
2008 Boston b	A.L.	16	76	2	9	.182	72	41	93	6.75	0
2009 Pawtucket	Int.	17	99	7	2	.778	89	30	67	2.36	0
2009 Boston	A.L.	16	92	7	4	.636	68	36	91	4.21	0
2010 Pawtucket	Int.	1	3²/₃	0	0	.000	2	1	4	4.91	0
2010 Boston c	A.L.	28	173²/₃	17	7	.708	120	67	142	2.33	0
2011 Boston d	A.L.	14	82²/₃	6	3	.667	60	31	76	3.48	0
Major League Totals ....5 Yrs.		78	447	35	24	.593	342	185	416	3.64	0
Division Series											
2009 Boston	A.L.	1	5	0	0	.000	3	1	6	3.60	0

a Pitched no-hit, no-run game against Baltimore Orioles, September 1, 2007.
b On disabled list from May 13 to May 31, 2008.
c On disabled list from June 27 to July 21, 2010.
d On disabled list from June 17 to September 28, 2011.

BUEHRLE, MARK ANTHONY

Born, St. Charles, Missouri, March 23, 1979.
Bats Left. Throws Left. Height, 6 feet, 2 inches. Weight, 225 pounds.

Year	Club	Lea	G	IP	W	L	PCT	SO	BB	H	ERA	SAVES
1999 Burlington	Midwest	20	98²/₃	7	4	.636	91	16	105	4.10	3
2000 Birmingham	Southern	16	118²/₃	8	4	.667	68	17	95	2.28	0
2000 Chicago	A.L.	28	51¹/₃	4	1	.800	37	19	55	4.21	0
2001 Chicago	A.L.	32	221¹/₃	16	8	.667	126	48	188	3.29	0
2002 Chicago	A.L.	34	239	19	12	.613	134	61	236	3.58	0
2003 Chicago	A.L.	35	230¹/₃	14	14	.500	119	61	250	4.14	0
2004 Chicago	A.L.	35	*245¹/₃	16	10	.615	165	51	257	3.89	0
2005 Chicago	A.L.	33	*236²/₃	16	8	.667	149	40	*240	3.12	0
2006 Chicago	A.L.	32	204	12	13	.480	98	48	*247	4.99	0
2007 Chicago a	A.L.	30	201	10	9	.526	115	45	208	3.63	0
2008 Chicago	A.L.	34	218²/₃	15	12	.556	140	52	*240	3.79	0
2009 Chicago b	A.L.	33	213¹/₃	13	10	.565	105	45	222	3.84	0
2010 Chicago	A.L.	33	210¹/₃	13	13	.500	99	49	*246	4.28	0
2011 Chicago c	A.L.	31	205¹/₃	13	9	.591	109	45	221	3.59	0
Major League Totals ...... .12 Yrs.		390	2476²/₃	161	119	.575	1396	564	2610	3.83	0
Division Series											
2000 Chicago	A.L.	1	0¹/₃	0	0	.000	1	0	2	0.00	0
2005 Chicago	A.L.	1	7	1	0	1.000	2	1	8	5.14	0
2008 Chicago	A.L.	1	7	0	1	.000	3	0	10	6.43	0
Division Series Totals		3	14¹/₃	1	1	.500	6	1	20	5.65	0
Championship Series											
2005 Chicago	A.L.	1	9	1	0	1.000	4	0	5	1.00	0
World Series Record											
2005 Chicago	A.L.	2	7¹/₃	0	0	.000	6	0	7	4.91	1

a Pitched no-hit, no-run game against Texas Rangers, April 18, 2007.
b Pitched no-hit, no-run perfect game against Tampa Bay Rays, July 23, 2009.
c Filed for free agency, October 30, 2011. Signed with Florida Marlins, December 9, 2011.

BUMGARNER, MADISON K.

Born, Hickory, North Carolina, August 1, 1989.
Bats Right. Throws Left. Height, 6 feet, 4 inches. Weight, 215 pounds.

Year	Club	Lea	G	IP	W	L	Pct	SO	BB	H	ERA	SAVES
2008 Augusta	So.Atl.	24	141²/₃	15	3	.833	164	21	111	1.46	0
2009 San Jose	Calif.	5	24¹/₃	3	1	.750	23	4	20	1.48	0
2009 Connecticut	Eastern	20	107	9	1	.900	69	30	80	1.93	0
2009 San Francisco	N.L.	4	10	0	0	.000	10	3	8	1.80	0
2010 Fresno	P.C.	14	82²/₃	7	1	.875	59	22	88	3.16	0
2010 San Francisco	N.L.	18	111	7	6	.538	86	26	119	3.00	0

Year Club	Lea	G	IP	W	L	Pct	SO	BB	H	ERA	SAVES
2011 San Francisco	N.L.	33	204²/₃	13	13	.500	191	46	202	3.21	0
Major League Totals .... 3 Yrs.		55	325²/₃	20	19	.513	287	75	329	3.10	0
Division Series											
2010 San Francisco	N.L.	1	6	1	0	1.000	5	1	6	3.00	0
Championship Series											
2010 San Francisco	N.L.	2	6²/₃	0	0	.000	7	2	9	4.05	0
World Series Record											
2010 San Francisco	N.L.	1	8	1	0	1.000	6	2	3	0.00	0

BURNETT, ALEX JAMES

Born, Anaheim, California, July 26, 1987.
Bats Right. Throws Right. Height, 6 feet. Weight, 210 pounds.

Year Club	Lea	G	IP	W	L	Pct	SO	BB	H	ERA	SAVES
2005 Twins .... Gulf Coast		13	48¹/₃	4	2	.667	33	14	50	4.10	0
2006 Elizabethton .... Appal.		13	71¹/₃	4	3	.571	71	13	66	4.04	0
2007 Beloit .... Midwest		27	155	9	8	.529	117	38	140	3.02	0
2008 Fort Myers .... Fla.St.		28	143²/₃	8	6	.571	84	36	151	3.76	0
2009 New Britain .... Eastern		40	55¹/₃	1	2	.333	52	19	36	1.79	9
2009 Fort Myers .... Fla.St.		18	22²/₃	2	1	.667	26	7	14	1.99	4
2010 Rochester .... Int.		14	19²/₃	0	2	.000	18	8	26	5.49	2
2010 Minnesota .... A.L.		41	47²/₃	2	2	.500	37	23	52	5.29	0
2011 Rochester .... Int.		4	3²/₃	0	0	.000	3	1	5	7.36	1
2011 Minnesota .... A.L.		66	50²/₃	2	5	.286	33	21	50	5.51	0
Major League Totals .... 2 Yrs.		107	98¹/₃	4	7	.364	70	44	102	5.40	0

BURNETT, ALLAN JAMES (A.J.)

Born, North Little Rock, Arkansas, January 3, 1977.
Bats Right. Throws Right. Height, 6 feet, 4 inches. Weight, 230 pounds.

Year Club	Lea	G	IP	W	L	Pct	SO	BB	H	ERA	SAVES
1995 Mets .... Gulf Coast		9	33²/₃	2	3	.400	26	23	27	4.28	0
1996 Kingsport .... Appal.		12	58	4	0	1.000	68	54	31	3.88	0
1997 Mets .... Gulf Coast		3	11¹/₃	0	1	.000	15	8	8	3.18	0
1997 Pittsfield .... N.Y.-Penn.		9	44	3	1	.750	48	35	28	4.70	0
1998 Kane County a ..... Midwest		20	119	10	4	.714	186	45	74	1.97	0
1999 Portland .... Eastern		26	120²/₃	6	12	.333	121	71	132	5.52	0
1999 Florida .... N.L.		7	41¹/₃	4	2	.667	33	25	37	3.48	0
2000 Brevard County ...... Fla.St.		2	7¹/₃	0	0	.000	6	6	4	3.68	0
2000 Calgary .... P.C.		1	5	0	0	.000	6	3	0	0.00	0
2000 Florida b .... N.L.		13	82²/₃	3	7	.300	57	44	80	4.79	0
2001 Brevard County ...... Fla.St.		2	9¹/₃	0	0	.000	10	4	4	1.93	0
2001 Florida c-d .... N.L.		27	173¹/₃	11	12	.478	128	83	145	4.05	0
2002 Florida e .... N.L.		31	204¹/₃	12	9	.571	203	90	153	3.30	0
2003 Florida f .... N.L.		4	23	0	2	.000	21	18	18	4.70	0
2004 Jupiter .... Fla.St.		1	4	0	0	.000	4	2	2	0.00	0
2004 Albuquerque........... P.C.		1	3¹/₃	0	0	.000	6	2	7	10.80	0
2004 Florida g .... N.L.		20	120	7	6	.538	113	38	102	3.68	0
2005 Florida h .... N.L.		32	209	12	12	.500	198	79	184	3.44	0
2006 Dunedin .... Fla.St.		2	8	0	0	.000	6	2	9	3.38	0
2006 New Hampshire ..... Eastern		1	6	1	0	1.000	9	3	2	1.50	0
2006 Syracuse .... Int.		1	5	0	0	.000	7	1	0	0.00	0
2006 Toronto i .... A.L.		21	135²/₃	10	8	.556	118	39	138	3.98	0
2007 Syracuse .... Int.		1	5	0	0	.000	7	1	3	1.80	0
2007 Toronto j .... A.L.		25	165²/₃	10	8	.556	176	66	131	3.75	0
2008 Toronto k .... A.L.		35	221¹/₃	18	10	.643	*231	86	211	4.07	0
2009 New York .... A.L.		33	207	13	9	.591	195	*97	193	4.04	0
2010 New York .... A.L.		33	186²/₃	10	15	.400	145	78	204	5.26	0
2011 New York .... A.L.		33	190¹/₃	11	11	.500	173	83	190	5.15	0
Major League Totals .... 13 Yrs.		314	1960¹/₃	121	111	.522	1791	826	1786	4.10	0
Division Series											
2009 New York .... A.L.		1	6	0	0	.000	6	5	3	1.50	0
2011 New York .... A.L.		1	5²/₃	1	0	1.000	3	4	4	1.59	0
Division Series Totals		2	11²/₃	1	0	1.000	9	9	7	1.54	0
Championship Series											
2009 New York .... A.L.		2	12¹/₃	0	0	.000	7	5	11	5.84	0
2010 New York .... A.L.		1	6	0	1	.000	4	3	6	7.50	0
Championship Series Totals		3	18¹/₃	0	1	.000	11	8	17	6.38	0

Year	Club	Lea	G	IP	W	L	Pct	SO	BB	H	ERA	SAVES
	World Series Record											
2009 New York	A.L.	2	9	1	1	.500	11	6	8	7.00	0

a Traded to Florida Marlins by New York Mets with pitcher Jesus Sanchez and outfielder Robert Stratton for pitcher Al Leiter and infielder Ralph Milliard, February 6, 1998.
b On disabled list from March 17 to July 19, 2000.
c On disabled list from March 23 to May 7, 2001.
d Pitched no-hit, no-run game against San Diego Padres, May 12, 2001.
e On disabled list from August 19 to September 14, 2002.
f On disabled list from March 21 to April 9 and April 26 to September 29, 2003.
g On disabled list from March 26 to June 3, 2004.
h Filed for free agency, October 27, 2005. Signed with Toronto Blue Jays, December 6, 2005.
i On disabled list from March 24 to April 15 and April 22 to June 22, 2006.
j On disabled list from June 13 to June 28 and June 29 to August 12, 2007.
k Filed for free agency, November 13, 2008. Signed with New York Yankees, December 18, 2008.

BURNETT, SEAN RICHARD
Born, Dunedin, Florida, September 17, 1982.
Bats Left. Throws Left. Height, 5 feet, 11 inches. Weight, 190 pounds.

Year	Club	Lea	G	IP	W	L	Pct	SO	BB	H	ERA	SAVES
2000 Pirates	Gulf Coast	8	31	2	1	.667	24	3	31	4.06	0
2001 Hickory	So.Atl.	26	161⅓	11	8	.579	134	33	164	2.62	0
2002 Lynchburg	Carolina	26	155⅓	13	4	.765	96	33	118	1.80	0
2003 Altoona.	Eastern	27	159²⁄₃	14	6	.700	86	29	158	3.21	0
2004 Nashville	P.C.	10	47	1	5	.167	25	17	58	5.36	0
2004 Pittsburgh a	N.L.	13	71²⁄₃	5	5	.500	30	28	86	5.02	0
2005 Pittsburgh b	N.L.			INJURED—Did Not Play							
2006 Indianapolis	.Int.	25	120⅓	8	11	.421	46	46	136	5.16	0
2007 Indianapolis	.Int.	15	70⅓	4	5	.444	31	39	83	4.48	0
2008 Indianapolis	.Int.	12	17⅓	1	1	.500	15	8	9	1.04	3
2008 Pittsburgh	N.L.	58	56²⁄₃	1	1	.500	42	34	57	4.76	0
2009 Pittsburgh-Washington c	N.L.	71	57²⁄₃	2	3	.400	43	28	36	3.12	1
2010 Washington	N.L.	73	63	1	7	.125	62	20	52	2.14	3
2011 Washington	N.L.	69	56²⁄₃	5	5	.500	33	21	54	3.81	4
Major League Totals . . . . .5 Yrs.		284	305²⁄₃	14	21	.400	210	131	285	3.80	8

a On disabled list from August 22 to October 4, 2004.
b On disabled list from April 2 to October 3, 2005.
c Traded to Washington Nationals with outfielder Nyjer Morgan for outfielder Lastings Milledge and pitcher Joel Hanrahan, June 30, 2009.

BYRDAK, TIMOTHY CHRISTOPHER (TIM)
Born, Oak Lawn, Illinois, October 31, 1973.
Bats Left. Throws Left. Height, 5 feet, 11 inches. Weight, 195 pounds.

Year	Club	Lea	G	IP	W	L	Pct	SO	BB	H	ERA	SAVES
1994 Eugene.	Northwest	15	73⅓	4	5	.444	77	20	60	3.07	0
1995 Wilmington	Carolina	27	166⅓	11	5	.688	127	45	118	2.16	0
1996 Wichita.	Texas	15	84²⁄₃	5	7	.417	47	44	112	6.91	0
1997 Wilmington	Carolina	22	41	4	3	.571	47	12	34	3.51	3
1998 Wichita.	Texas	34	52	3	5	.375	37	28	58	4.15	2
1998 Kansas City	A.L.	3	1²⁄₃	0	0	.000	1	0	5	5.40	0
1998 Omaha.	P.C.	26	36²⁄₃	2	1	.667	32	20	31	2.45	1
1999 Omaha.	P.C.	33	49²⁄₃	3	1	.750	51	28	39	1.81	4
1999 Kansas City	A.L.	33	24²⁄₃	0	3	.000	17	20	32	7.66	1
2000 Omaha.	P.C.	34	52²⁄₃	6	2	.750	47	29	59	4.44	4
2000 Kansas City	A.L.	12	6⅓	0	1	.000	8	4	11	11.37	0
2000 Wichita a	Texas	4	6²⁄₃	0	0	.000	1	3	9	5.40	0
2001 Buffalo	.Int.	4	17⅓	2	0	1.000	17	5	18	4.67	0
2002 Kinston.	Carolina	2	4	1	0	1.000	3	4	3	4.50	0
2002 Akron	Eastern	9	13	0	0	.000	8	11	16	6.23	1
2003 Joliet	Northern	5	34	2	1	.667	18	10	31	2.67	0
2003 Gary	Northern	10	66	2	4	.333	58	25	60	4.34	0
2004 Ottawa	.Int.	33	34⅓	2	1	.667	43	12	46	4.19	2
2004 Portland b-c-d	P.C.	20	38	3	0	1.000	25	17	47	5.45	0
2005 Ottawa	.Int.	37	38²⁄₃	3	2	.600	44	15	23	2.09	11
2005 Baltimore	A.L.	41	26²⁄₃	0	1	.000	31	21	27	4.05	1
2006 Aberdeen	N.Y.-Penn.	1	1	0	0	.000	3	0	2	9.00	0
2006 Frederick	Carolina	1	1⅓	0	0	.000	0	1	4	13.50	0
2006 Bowie.	Eastern	3	4	0	0	.000	7	2	4	2.25	0
2006 Baltimore e-f	A.L.	16	7	1	0	1.000	2	8	14	12.86	0

Year	Club	Lea	G	IP	W	L	Pct	SO	BB	H	ERA	SAVES
2007	Toledo	Int.	17	24⅓	1	0	1.000	30	8	22	2.59	0
2007	Detroit g	A.L.	39	45	3	0	1.000	49	26	38	3.20	1
2008	Round Rock	P.C.	7	7⅓	0	0	.000	10	0	8	3.68	0
2008	Houston h	N.L.	59	55⅓	2	1	.667	47	29	45	3.90	0
2009	Houston	N.L.	76	61⅓	1	2	.333	58	36	39	3.23	0
2010	Round Rock	P.C.	2	2	0	0	.000	1	2	1	4.50	0
2010	Houston i-j	N.L.	64	38⅔	2	2	.500	29	20	40	3.49	0
2011	New York k	N.L.	72	37⅔	2	1	.667	47	19	34	3.82	1
Major League Totals	10 Yrs.		415	304⅓	11	11	.500	289	183	285	4.29	4

a Not offered contract, December 1, 2000. Signed with Cleveland Indians organization, December 24, 2000.
b Released by Cleveland Indians, June 28, 2002. Signed with San Diego Padres organization, January 30, 2004.
c Sold to Baltimore Orioles, June 22, 2004.
d Filed for free agency, October 15, 2004, re-signed with Baltimore Orioles organization, November 16, 2004.
e On disabled list from April 19 to July 30, 2006.
f Filed for free agency, October 15, 2006. Signed with Detroit Tigers organization, November 18, 2006.
g On disabled list from June 27 to July 25, 2007.
h Released by Detroit Tigers, March 26, 2008. Signed with Houston Astros organization, April 3, 2008.
i On disabled list from May 4 to May 24, 2010.
j Filed for free agency, November 29, 2010.
k Signed with New York Mets organization, January 25, 2011.

CAHILL, TREVOR JOHN
Born, Oceanside, California, March 1, 1988.
Bats Right. Throws Right. Height, 6 feet, 3 inches. Weight, 210 pounds.

Year	Club	Lea	G	IP	W	L	Pct	SO	BB	H	ERA	SAVES
2006	Athletics...........	Arizona	4	9	0	0	.000	11	7	2	3.00	0
2007	Kane County.......	Midwest	20	105⅓	11	4	.733	117	40	85	2.73	0
2008	Stockton............	Calif.	14	87⅓	5	4	.556	103	31	52	2.78	0
2008	Midland	Texas	7	37	6	1	.857	33	19	24	2.19	0
2009	Oakland	A.L.	32	178⅔	10	13	.435	90	72	185	4.63	0
2010	Sacramento	P.C.	2	8⅔	1	0	1.000	8	5	7	1.04	0
2010	Oakland a...........	A.L.	30	196⅔	18	8	.692	118	63	155	2.97	0
2011	Oakland b...........	A.L.	34	207⅔	12	14	.462	147	82	214	4.16	0
Major League Totals	3 Yrs.		96	583	40	35	.533	355	217	554	3.91	0

a On disabled list from April 4 to April 20, 2010.
b Traded to Arizona Diamondbacks with pitcher Craig Breslow for outfielder Collin Cowgill, pitcher Jarrod Parker and pitcher Ryan Cook, December 9, 2011.

CAIN, MATTHEW THOMAS (MATT)
Born, Dothan, Alabama, October 1, 1984.
Bats Right. Throws Right. Height, 6 feet, 3 inches. Weight, 235 pounds.

Year	Club	Lea	G	IP	W	L	Pct	SO	BB	H	ERA	SAVES
2002	Giants.............	Arizona	8	19⅓	0	1	.000	20	11	13	3.72	0
2003	Hagerstown	So.Atl.	14	74	4	4	.500	90	24	57	2.55	0
2004	San Jose	Calif.	13	72⅔	7	1	.875	89	17	58	1.86	0
2004	Norwich...........	Eastern	15	86	6	4	.600	72	40	73	3.35	0
2005	Fresno	P.C.	26	145⅔	10	5	.667	176	73	118	4.39	0
2005	San Francisco	N.L.	7	46⅓	2	1	.667	30	19	24	2.33	0
2006	San Francisco	N.L.	32	190⅔	13	12	.520	179	87	157	4.15	0
2007	San Francisco	N.L.	32	200	7	16	.304	163	79	173	3.65	0
2008	San Francisco	N.L.	34	217⅔	8	14	.364	186	91	206	3.76	0
2009	San Francisco	N.L.	33	217⅔	14	8	.636	171	73	184	2.89	0
2010	San Francisco	N.L.	33	223⅓	13	11	.542	177	61	181	3.14	0
2011	San Francisco	N.L.	33	221⅔	12	11	.522	179	63	177	2.88	0
Major League Totals	7 Yrs.		204	1317⅓	69	73	.486	1085	473	1102	3.35	0
Division Series												
2010 San Francisco	N.L.		1	6⅔	0	0	.000	6	2	7	0.00	0
Championship Series												
2010 San Francisco	N.L.		1	7	1	0	1.000	5	3	2	0.00	0
World Series Record												
2010 San Francisco	N.L.		1	7⅔	1	0	1.000	2	2	4	0.00	0

CAMP, SHAWN ANTHONY

Born, Fairfax, Virginia, November 18, 1975.
Bats Right. Throws Right. Height, 6 feet, 1 inch. Weight, 205 pounds.

Year	Club	Lea	G	IP	W	L	Pct	SO	BB	H	ERA	SAVES
1997	Idaho Falls	Pioneer	30	32²/₃	2	1	.667	41	14	41	5.51	12
1998	Clinton	Midwest	47	55	3	5	.375	62	20	48	2.62	13
1999	Rancho Cucamonga	Calif.	53	66	1	5	.167	78	25	68	3.95	6
2000	Rancho Cucamonga	Calif.	14	18²/₃	1	0	1.000	18	5	10	1.45	6
2000	Mobile	Southern	45	59¹/₃	3	3	.500	53	30	47	2.43	1
2001	Altoona	Eastern	8	23¹/₃	4	0	1.000	19	8	25	4.24	0
2001	Nashville	P.C.	11	17	0	0	.000	15	8	11	2.12	0
2001	Portland	P.C.	4	7	1	0	1.000	6	1	2	0.00	0
2001	Mobile a	Southern	35	48²/₃	6	2	.750	55	15	46	4.44	0
2002	Nashville	P.C.	39	58¹/₃	4	1	.800	59	15	50	3.24	2
2003	Altoona	Eastern	18	29	0	2	.000	35	11	26	4.34	0
2003	Nashville b	P.C.	33	43¹/₃	0	1	.000	36	15	50	4.98	0
2004	Kansas City	A.L.	42	66²/₃	2	2	.500	51	16	74	3.92	2
2004	Omaha	P.C.	15	22	1	1	.500	21	6	26	5.32	1
2005	Omaha	P.C.	21	67²/₃	3	6	.333	42	22	71	3.86	1
2005	Kansas City	A.L.	29	49	1	4	.200	28	13	69	6.43	0
2006	Tampa Bay c	A.L.	75	75	7	4	.636	53	19	93	4.68	4
2007	Tampa Bay	A.L.	50	40	0	3	.000	36	18	63	7.20	0
2007	Durham	Int.	12	15¹/₃	1	0	1.000	16	2	13	1.17	4
2008	Syracuse	Int.	7	10	1	0	1.000	13	0	4	0.00	4
2008	Toronto d	A.L.	40	39¹/₃	3	1	.750	31	11	40	4.12	0
2009	Toronto	A.L.	59	79²/₃	2	6	.250	58	29	73	3.50	1
2010	Toronto	A.L.	70	72¹/₃	4	3	.571	46	18	71	2.99	2
2011	Toronto e	A.L.	67	66¹/₃	6	3	.667	32	22	79	4.21	1
Major League Totals		8 Yrs.	432	488¹/₃	25	26	.490	335	146	562	4.40	10

a Traded by San Diego Padres to Pittsburgh Pirates for outfielder Emil Brown, July 10, 2001.
b Filed for free agency, October 15, 2003. Signed with Kansas City Royals organization, October 29, 2003.
c Not offered contract, December 21, 2005. Signed with Tampa Bay Devil Rays, January 17, 2006.
d Filed for free agency, October 31, 2007. Signed with Toronto Blue Jays organization, January 7, 2008.
e Filed for free agency, October 30, 2011.

CAPPS, MATTHEW DICUS (MATT)

Born, Douglasville, Georgia, September 3, 1983.
Bats Right. Throws Right. Height, 6 feet, 2 inches. Weight, 240 pounds.

Year	Club	Lea	G	IP	W	L	Pct	SO	BB	H	ERA	SAVES
2002	Pirates	Gulf Coast	7	13	1	0	1.000	8	6	13	0.69	1
2003	Lynchburg	Carolina	1	5	0	0	.000	5	4	3	5.40	0
2003	Pirates	Gulf Coast	10	62²/₃	5	1	.833	54	9	40	1.87	0
2004	Williamsport	N.Y.-Penn.	11	65	3	5	.375	33	4	84	4.85	0
2004	Hickory	So.Atl.	12	42	2	3	.400	27	16	82	10.07	0
2005	Hickory	So.Atl.	35	53²/₃	3	4	.429	39	5	47	2.52	14
2005	Altoona	Eastern	17	20	0	2	.000	26	1	21	2.70	7
2005	Pittsburgh	N.L.	4	4	0	0	.000	3	0	5	4.50	0
2006	Pittsburgh	N.L.	85	80²/₃	9	1	.900	56	12	81	3.79	1
2007	Pittsburgh	N.L.	76	79	4	7	.364	64	16	64	2.28	18
2008	Pirates	Gulf Coast	2	2	0	0	.000	2	0	2	0.00	0
2008	Altoona	Eastern	3	3	0	0	.000	5	1	0	0.00	0
2008	Indianapolis	Int.	1	1²/₃	0	0	.000	1	3	0	0.00	0
2008	Pittsburgh a	N.L.	49	53²/₃	2	3	.400	39	5	47	3.02	21
2009	Pittsburgh b	N.L.	57	54¹/₃	4	8	.333	46	17	73	5.80	27
2010	Washington	N.L.	47	46	3	3	.500	38	9	51	2.74	26
2010	Minnesota c	A.L.	27	27	2	0	1.000	21	8	24	2.00	16
2011	Minnesota d	A.L.	69	65²/₃	4	7	.364	34	13	66	4.25	15
Major League Totals		7 Yrs.	414	410¹/₃	28	29	.491	301	80	411	3.51	124
Division Series												
2010	Minnesota	A.L.	1	1	0	0	.000	0	0	2	9.00	0

a On disabled list from July 2 to August 23, 2008.
b Not offered contract, December 12, 2009. Signed with Washington Nationals, December 24, 2009.
c Traded to Minnesota Twins for catcher Wilson Ramos, pitcher Joe Testa and cash, July 30, 2010.
d Filed for free agency, October 30, 2011, re-signed with Minnesota Twins, December 7, 2011.

CAPUANO, CHRISTOPHER FRANK (CHRIS)

Born, Springfield, Massachusetts, August 19, 1978.
Bats Left. Throws Left. Height, 6 feet, 3 inches. Weight, 225 pounds.

Year	Club	Lea	G	IP	W	L	Pct	SO	BB	H	ERA	SAVES
2000 South Bend		Midwest	18	101²/₃	10	4	.714	105	45	68	2.21	0
2001 El Paso		Texas	28	159¹/₃	10	11	.476	167	75	184	5.31	0
2002 Tucson		P.C.	6	36¹/₃	4	1	.800	29	11	30	2.72	0
2003 Tucson		P.C.	23	142²/₃	9	5	.643	108	43	133	3.34	0
2003 Arizona a		N.L.	9	33	2	4	.333	23	11	27	4.64	0
2004 Milwaukee		N.L.	17	88¹/₃	6	8	.429	80	37	91	4.99	0
2004 Beloit		Midwest	1	2²/₃	0	0	.000	4	1	3	3.38	0
2004 Indianapolis		Int.	2	8²/₃	0	1	.000	9	5	10	8.31	0
2004 High Desert b		Calif.	1	2	0	1	.000	2	3	6	27.00	0
2005 Milwaukee		N.L.	35	219	18	12	.600	176	91	212	3.99	0
2006 Milwaukee		N.L.	34	221¹/₃	11	12	.478	174	47	229	4.03	0
2007 Milwaukee c		N.L.	29	150	5	12	.294	132	54	170	5.10	0
2008 Milwaukee d-e		N.L.					INJURED—Did Not Play					
2009 Brewers		Arizona	3	3	0	0	.000	4	2	5	6.00	0
2009 Helena		Pioneer	2	4	0	0	.000	3	0	2	0.00	0
2010 Brevard County		Fla.St.	3	14²/₃	2	0	1.000	17	0	12	1.23	0
2010 Nashville		P.C.	4	25	1	1	.500	16	4	21	1.80	0
2010 Milwaukee f		N.L.	24	66	4	4	.500	54	21	65	3.95	0
2011 New York g		N.L.	33	186	11	12	.478	168	53	198	4.55	0
Major League Totals		7 Yrs.	181	963²/₃	57	64	.471	807	314	992	4.39	0

a Traded to Milwaukee Brewers with infielder Junior Spivey, infielder Craig Counsell, infielder Lyle Overbay, catcher Chad Moeller and pitcher Jorge DeRosa for infielder Richie Sexson, pitcher Shane Nance and player to be named later, December 1, 2003. Arizona Diamondbacks received outfielder Noochie Varner to complete trade, December 15, 2003.
b On disabled list from April 19 to May 26 and May 27 to June 12 and August 25 to October 6, 2004.
c On disabled list from June 9 to July 1, 2007.
d Not offered contract, December 12, 2008, re-signed with Milwaukee Brewers organization, December 16, 2008.
e On disabled list from March 21 to September 29, 2008.
f Filed for free agency, November 1, 2010. Signed with New York Mets, January 3, 2011.
g Filed for free agency, October 30, 2011. Signed with Los Angeles Dodgers, December 2, 2011.

CARMONA, FAUSTO C.

Born, Santo Domingo, Dominican Republic, December 7, 1983.
Bats Right. Throws Right. Height, 6 feet, 4 inches. Weight, 220 pounds.

Year	Club	Lea	G	IP	W	L	Pct	SO	BB	H	ERA	SAVES
2002 Burlington		Appal.	13	76¹/₃	2	4	.333	42	10	89	3.30	1
2002 Mahoning Valley		N.Y.-Penn.	3	4	0	0	.000	0	1	2	0.00	0
2003 Akron		Eastern	1	6	0	0	.000	3	0	8	4.50	0
2003 Lake County		So.Atl.	24	148¹/₃	17	4	.810	83	14	117	2.06	0
2004 Kinston		Carolina	13	70	5	2	.714	57	20	68	2.83	0
2004 Akron		Eastern	15	87	4	8	.333	63	21	114	4.97	0
2004 Buffalo		Int.	1	6	1	0	1.000	2	3	6	6.00	0
2005 Akron		Eastern	14	90²/₃	6	5	.545	57	20	100	4.07	0
2005 Buffalo		Int.	13	83	7	4	.636	49	15	76	3.25	0
2006 Buffalo		Int.	6	27²/₃	1	3	.250	28	8	28	5.53	0
2006 Cleveland		A.L.	38	74²/₃	1	10	.091	58	31	88	5.42	0
2007 Cleveland		A.L.	32	215	19	8	.704	137	61	199	3.06	0
2008 Lake County		So.Atl.	1	4	0	0	.000	3	0	1	0.00	0
2008 Akron		Eastern	1	5	1	0	1.000	2	1	9	1.80	0
2008 Cleveland a		A.L.	22	120²/₃	8	7	.533	58	70	126	5.44	0
2009 Lake County		So.Atl.	1	6¹/₃	1	0	1.000	7	1	1	0.00	0
2009 Akron		Eastern	1	7	1	0	1.000	5	0	4	1.29	0
2009 Columbus		Int.	5	33	1	3	.250	27	6	32	3.55	0
2009 Cleveland		A.L.	24	125¹/₃	5	12	.294	79	70	151	6.32	0
2010 Cleveland		A.L.	33	210¹/₃	13	14	.481	124	72	203	3.77	0
2011 Cleveland b		A.L.	32	188²/₃	7	15	.318	109	60	205	5.25	0
Major League Totals		6 Yrs.	181	934²/₃	53	66	.445	565	364	972	4.59	0
Division Series												
2007 Cleveland		A.L.	1	9	0	0	.000	5	2	3	1.00	0
Championship Series												
2007 Cleveland		A.L.	2	6	0	1	.000	7	9	10	16.50	0

a On disabled list from May 24 to July 26, 2008.
b On disabled list from July 3 to July 18, 2011.

CARPENTER, CHRISTOPHER JOHN (CHRIS)
Born, Exeter, New Hampshire, April 27, 1975.
Bats Right. Throws Right. Height, 6 feet, 6 inches. Weight, 230 pounds.

Year	Club	Lea	G	IP	W	L	Pct	SO	BB	H	ERA	SAVES
1994	Medicne Hat	Pioneer	15	84^{2}/3	6	3	.667	80	39	76	2.76	0
1995	Dunedin	Fla.St.	15	99^{1}/3	3	5	.375	56	50	83	2.17	0
1995	Knoxville	Southern	12	64^{1}/3	3	7	.300	53	31	71	5.18	0
1996	Knoxville	Southern	28	171^{1}/3	7	9	.438	150	91	161	3.94	0
1997	Syracuse	Int.	19	120	4	9	.308	97	53	113	4.50	0
1997	Toronto	A.L.	14	81^{1}/3	3	7	.300	55	37	108	5.09	0
1998	Toronto	A.L.	33	175	12	7	.632	136	61	177	4.37	0
1999	Toronto	A.L.	24	150	9	8	.529	106	48	177	4.38	0
1999	St. Catharines a	N.Y.-Penn.	1	4	0	0	.000	6	1	5	4.50	0
2000	Toronto	A.L.	34	175^{1}/3	10	12	.455	113	83	204	6.26	0
2001	Toronto	A.L.	34	215^{2}/3	11	11	.500	157	75	229	4.09	0
2002	Toronto	A.L.	13	73^{1}/3	4	5	.444	45	27	89	5.28	0
2002	Tennessee	Southern	5	18^{2}/3	0	1	.000	9	8	26	8.20	0
2002	Syracuse b-c	Int.	1	6	0	1	.000	6	2	8	4.50	0
2003	Palm Beach	Fla.St.	4	7	0	1	.000	6	1	6	1.29	0
2003	Memphis	P.C.	3	8^{1}/3	0	0	.000	4	2	11	5.40	0
2003	Tennessee d-e	Southern	1	3^{1}/3	0	1	.000	2	2	7	13.50	0
2004	St. Louis	N.L.	28	182	15	5	.750	152	38	169	3.46	0
2005	St. Louis f	N.L.	33	241^{2}/3	21	5	*.808	213	51	204	2.83	0
2006	St. Louis g	N.L.	32	221^{2}/3	15	8	.652	184	43	194	3.09	0
2007	Palm Beach	Fla.St.	2	4^{1}/3	0	1	.000	4	1	7	6.23	0
2007	St. Louis h	N.L.	1	6	0	1	.000	3	1	9	7.50	0
2008	Springfield	Texas	1	4	0	0	.000	4	4	1	0.00	0
2008	Memphis	P.C.	1	5^{2}/3	0	1	.000	5	1	4	3.18	0
2008	St. Louis i	N.L.	4	15^{1}/3	0	1	.000	7	4	16	1.76	0
2009	St. Louis j	N.L.	28	192^{2}/3	17	4	*.810	144	38	156	*2.24	0
2010	St. Louis	N.L.	35	235	16	9	.640	179	63	214	3.22	0
2011	St. Louis	N.L.	34	*237^{1}/3	11	9	.550	191	55	243	3.45	0
Major League Totals	14 Yrs.		347	2202^{1}/3	144	92	.610	1685	624	2189	3.76	0
	Division Series											
2005	St. Louis	N.L.	1	6	1	0	1.000	3	3	3	0.00	0
2006	St. Louis	N.L.	2	13^{1}/3	2	0	1.000	12	4	12	2.03	0
2009	St. Louis	N.L.	1	5	0	1	.000	3	4	9	7.20	0
2011	St. Louis	N.L.	2	12	1	0	1.000	5	3	8	3.00	0
Division Series Totals			6	36^{1}/3	4	1	.800	23	14	32	2.72	0
	Championship Series											
2005	St. Louis	N.L.	2	15	1	0	1.000	9	4	14	3.00	0
2006	St. Louis	N.L.	2	11	0	1	.000	5	4	13	5.73	0
2011	St. Louis	N.L.	1	5	1	0	1.000	3	3	6	5.40	0
Championship Series Totals			5	31	2	1	.667	17	11	33	4.35	0
	World Series Record											
2006	St. Louis	N.L.	1	8	1	0	1.000	6	0	3	0.00	0
2011	St. Louis	N.L.	3	19	2	0	1.000	13	5	17	2.84	0
World Series Totals			4	27	3	0	1.000	19	5	20	2.00	0

a On disabled list from June 3 to June 28, 1999.
b On disabled list from April 2 to April 20 and April 22 to June 21 and August 14 to October 7, 2002.
c Filed for free agency, October 9, 2002. Signed with St. Louis Cardinals, December 15, 2002.
d On disabled list from March 27 to September 30, 2003.
e Filed for free agency, November 3, 2003, re-signed with St. Louis Cardinals, December 1, 2003.
f Selected Cy Young Award Winner in National League for 2005.
g On disabled list from May 22 to June 6, 2006.
h On disabled list from April 2 to November 2, 2007.
i On disabled list from March 21 to July 30 and August 11 to September 1, 2008.
j On disabled list from April 15 to May 20, 2009.

CARRASCO, CARLOS LUIS
Born, Barquisimeto, Venezuela, March 21, 1987.
Bats Right. Throws Right. Height, 6 feet, 3 inches. Weight, 220 pounds.

Year	Club	Lea	G	IP	W	L	Pct	SO	BB	H	ERA	SAVES
2004	Phillies	Gulf Coast	11	48	5	4	.556	34	15	53	3.56	0
2005	Phillies	Gulf Coast	2	5	0	0	.000	2	1	3	1.80	0
2005	Batavia	N.Y.-Penn.	4	15^{1}/3	0	3	.000	12	5	29	13.50	0
2005	Lakewood	So.Atl.	13	62^{2}/3	1	7	.125	46	28	78	7.04	0
2006	Lakewood	So.Atl.	26	159^{1}/3	12	6	.667	159	65	103	2.26	0
2007	Reading	Eastern	14	70^{1}/3	6	4	.600	49	46	65	4.86	0

Year	Club	Lea	G	IP	W	L	Pct	SO	BB	H	ERA	SAVES
2007	Clearwater	Fla.St.	12	69²/₃	6	2	.750	53	22	49	2.84	0
2008	Reading	Eastern	20	114²/₃	7	7	.500	109	45	109	4.32	0
2008	Lehigh Valley	Int.	6	36²/₃	2	2	.500	46	13	37	1.72	0
2009	Lehigh Valley	Int.	20	114²/₃	6	9	.400	112	38	118	5.18	0
2009	Columbus..............	Int.	6	42¹/₃	5	1	.833	36	7	31	3.19	0
2009	Cleveland a...........	A.L.	5	22¹/₃	0	4	.000	11	11	40	8.87	0
2010	Columbus.............	Int.	25	150¹/₃	10	6	.625	133	46	139	3.65	0
2010	Cleveland	A.L.	7	44²/₃	2	2	.500	38	14	47	3.83	0
2011	Akron	Eastern	1	3²/₃	0	0	.000	3	3	4	9.82	0
2011	Cleveland b	A.L.	21	124²/₃	8	9	.471	85	40	130	4.62	0
Major League Totals	3 Yrs.		33	191²/₃	10	15	.400	134	65	217	4.93	0

a Traded by Philadelphia Phillies to Cleveland Indians with catcher Lou Marson, pitcher Jason Knapp and infielder Jason Donald for pitcher Cliff Lee and outfielder Ben Francisco, July 29, 2009.

b On disabled list from April 25 to May 11 and August 4 to November 2, 2011.

CARRASCO, DANIEL (D.J.)

Born, Safford, Arizona, April 12, 1977.

Bats Right. Throws Right. Height, 6 feet, 1 inch. Weight, 220 pounds.

Year	Club	Lea	G	IP	W	L	Pct	SO	BB	H	ERA	SAVES
1998	Watertown a......	N.Y.-Penn.	13	31²/₃	1	1	.500	38	14	36	5.40	2
1999	Lynchburg	Carolina	2	5²/₃	0	1	.000	4	3	9	6.35	0
1999	Williamsport b	N.Y.-Penn.	18	51²/₃	4	2	.667	49	23	43	2.96	0
2000	Lynchburg	Carolina	8	10¹/₃	1	0	1.000	10	8	8	3.48	2
2000	Altoona...........	Eastern	9	14	1	1	.500	10	13	16	8.36	0
2000	Hickory............	So.Atl.	27	40¹/₃	5	4	.556	40	20	35	1.34	6
2001	Lynchburg	Carolina	22	36	4	0	1.000	40	14	18	1.50	7
2001	Altoona...........	Eastern	27	37	2	2	.500	35	25	34	4.14	1
2002	Lynchburg c	Carolina	55	72²/₃	4	4	.500	83	18	52	1.61	29
2003	Kansas City	A.L.	50	80¹/₃	6	5	.545	57	40	82	4.82	2
2004	Omaha	P.C.	32	56¹/₃	2	1	.667	50	18	60	3.20	3
2004	Kansas City	A.L.	30	35¹/₃	2	2	.500	22	15	41	4.84	0
2005	Omaha	P.C.	11	27²/₃	3	2	.600	21	11	24	2.28	0
2005	Kansas City	A.L.	21	114²/₃	6	8	.429	49	51	129	4.79	0
2006	Fukuoka d-e	Japan Pac.	3	10¹/₃	0	3	.000	9	10	22	14.81	0
2007	Tucson	P.C.	34	137¹/₃	5	14	.263	103	60	185	6.68	0
2008	Charlotte	Int.	8	25	2	1	.667	24	7	24	2.88	1
2008	Chicago f	N.L.	31	38²/₃	1	0	1.000	30	14	30	3.96	0
2009	Chicago g.........	A.L.	49	93¹/₃	5	1	.833	62	29	103	3.76	0
2010	Pittsburgh-Arizona h-i ..	N.L.	63	78¹/₃	3	2	.600	65	34	68	3.68	0
2011	Buffalo...............	Int.	9	46²/₃	2	3	.400	37	17	46	3.47	0
2011	New York	N.L.	42	49¹/₃	1	3	.250	27	16	67	6.02	0
Major League Totals	7 Yrs.		286	490	24	21	.533	312	199	520	4.48	2

a Released by Baltimore Orioles organization, June 14, 1998. Signed with Cleveland Indians organization, June 18, 1998.

b Released by Cleveland Indians organization, August 21, 1998. Signed with Pittsburgh Pirates organization, March 29, 1999.

c Selected by Kansas City Royals in Rule V draft, December 16, 2002.

d Released by Kansas City Royals, December 7, 2005. Signed with Fukoka (Japan) for 2006.

e Signed with Arizona Diamondbacks organization, December 22, 2006.

f Filed for free agency, October 29, 2007. Signed with Chicago White Sox organization, January 11, 2008.

g Not offered contract, December 12, 2009. Signed with Pittsburgh Pirates organization, January 16, 2010.

h Traded to Arizona Diamondbacks with infielder Bobby Crosby and outfielder Ryan Church for catcher Chris Snyder, infielder Pedro Ciriaco and cash, July 31, 2010.

i Not offered contract, December 2, 2010. Signed with New York Mets organization, December 9, 2010.

CASHNER, ANDREW BURTON

Born, Conroe, Texas, September 11, 1986.

Bats Right. Throws Right. Height, 6 feet, 6 inches. Weight, 210 pounds.

Year	Club	Lea	G	IP	W	L	Pct	SO	BB	H	ERA	SAVES
2008	Cubs................	Arizona	1	1	0	0	.000	2	0	1	0.00	0
2008	Daytona	Fla.St.	1	2²/₃	0	1	.000	1	4	4	13.50	0
2008	Boise	Northwest	6	16¹/₃	1	1	.500	16	19	19	4.96	0
2009	Daytona	Fla.St.	12	42	0	0	.000	34	15	31	1.50	0
2009	Tennessee	Southern	12	58¹/₃	3	4	.429	41	27	45	3.39	0
2010	Tennessee	Southern	6	36	3	1	.750	42	13	22	2.75	0
2010	Iowa.................	P.C.	5	21	3	0	1.000	17	2	17	0.86	0
2010	Chicago	N.L.	53	54¹/₃	2	6	.250	50	30	55	4.80	0

Year	Club	Lea	G	IP	W	L	Pct	SO	BB	H	ERA	SAVES
2011 Tennessee	Southern	3	2²/₃	0	1	.000	6	0	3	6.75	0
2011 Iowa................	P.C.	2	2	0	0	.000	2	0	0	0.00	0
2011 Chicago a-b	N.L.	7	10²/₃	0	0	.000	8	4	3	1.69	0
Major League Totals	.2 Yrs.	60	65	2	6	.250	58	34	58	4.29	0

a On disabled list from April 8 to September 5, 2011.
b Traded to San Diego Padres with outfielder Kyung-Min Na for infielder Anthony Rizzo and pitcher Xach Cates, January 6, 2012.

CASILLA, SANTIAGO
Born, Don Gregorio, Dominican Republic, June 25, 1980.
Bats Right. Throws Right. Height, 6 feet. Weight, 200 pounds.

Year	Club	Lea	G	IP	W	L	Pct	SO	BB	H	ERA	SAVES
2001 Athletics...........	Arizona	12	47¹/₃	4	2	.667	50	6	37	2.85	0
2002 Athletics...........	Arizona	13	59	2	1	.667	66	17	56	2.44	1
2002 Vancouver	Northwest	3	12¹/₃	0	3	.000	16	7	15	7.30	0
2003 Kane County.......	Midwest	14	42¹/₃	0	1	.000	28	19	40	2.55	0
2004 Kane County.......	Midwest	25	30	1	0	1.000	49	6	16	0.30	16
2004 Midland	Texas	13	18	2	0	1.000	32	15	10	1.50	2
2004 Sacramento	P.C.	11	13²/₃	1	2	.333	21	9	10	3.95	1
2004 Oakland	A.L.	4	5²/₃	0	0	.000	5	9	5	12.71	0
2005 Midland	Texas	10	16²/₃	0	0	.000	30	9	9	1.08	6
2005 Sacramento	P.C.	44	48¹/₃	3	6	.333	73	20	45	4.47	20
2005 Oakland a.........	A.L.	3	3	0	0	.000	1	1	2	3.00	0
2006 Oakland	A.L.	2	2¹/₃	0	0	.000	2	2	2	11.57	0
2006 Sacramento	P.C.	25	33	2	0	1.000	32	10	25	3.27	4
2007 Sacramento	P.C.	22	24	2	1	.667	29	14	18	4.13	3
2007 Oakland	A.L.	46	50²/₃	3	1	.750	52	23	43	4.44	2
2008 Stockton...........	Calif.	1	1	0	0	.000	2	0	0	0.00	0
2008 Sacramento	P.C.	2	2²/₃	0	0	.000	5	1	3	3.38	0
2008 Oakland b..........	A.L.	51	50¹/₃	2	1	.667	43	20	60	3.93	2
2009 Stockton...........	Calif.	1	1	0	0	.000	0	0	0	0.00	0
2009 Sacramento	P.C.	1	1	0	0	.000	0	0	0	0.00	0
2009 Oakland c..........	A.L.	46	48¹/₃	1	2	.333	35	25	61	5.96	0
2010 Fresno	P.C.	4	4	0	0	.000	7	2	2	0.00	2
2010 San Francisco	N.L.	52	55¹/₃	7	2	.778	56	26	40	1.95	2
2011 San Jose	Calif.	2	3	0	0	.000	1	2	3	0.00	0
2011 Fresno	P.C.	4	5	0	0	.000	4	1	3	1.80	0
2011 San Francisco	N.L.	49	51²/₃	2	2	.500	45	25	33	1.74	6
Major League Totals	.8 Yrs.	253	267¹/₃	15	8	.652	239	131	246	3.80	12
Division Series											
2010 San Francisco	N.L.	1	1²/₃	0	0	.000	2	0	1	0.00	0
Championship Series											
2010 San Francisco	N.L.	2	1²/₃	0	0	.000	2	1	2	5.40	0
World Series Record											
2010 San Francisco	N.L.	1	1¹/₃	0	0	.000	1	0	0	0.00	0

a Played under name of Jairo Garcia 2001-2005.
b On disabled list from May 16 to June 19, 2008.
c Released by Oakland Athletics, December 10, 2009. Signed with San Francisco Giants organization, January 21, 2010.

CECIL, BRETT AARION
Born, Dunkirk, Maryland, July 2, 1986.
Bats Right. Throws Left. Height, 6 feet, 2 inches. Weight, 225 pounds.

Year	Club	Lea	G	IP	W	L	Pct	SO	BB	H	ERA	SAVES
2007 Auburn...........	N.Y.-Penn.	14	49²/₃	1	0	1.000	56	11	36	1.27	0
2008 New Hampshire	Eastern	18	77²/₃	6	2	.750	87	23	66	2.55	0
2008 Dunedin	Fla.St.	4	10¹/₃	0	0	.000	11	2	6	1.74	0
2008 Syracuse	Int.	6	30²/₃	2	3	.400	31	16	28	4.11	0
2009 Las Vegas...........	P.C.	9	49	1	5	.167	32	19	53	5.69	0
2009 Toronto	A.L.	18	93¹/₃	7	4	.636	69	38	116	5.30	0
2010 Las Vegas...........	P.C.	2	11	2	0	1.000	11	2	13	2.45	0
2010 Toronto	A.L.	28	172²/₃	15	7	.682	117	54	175	4.22	0
2011 Las Vegas...........	P.C.	12	78²/₃	8	2	.800	63	24	89	5.26	0
2011 Toronto	A.L.	20	123²/₃	4	11	.267	87	42	122	4.73	0
Major League Totals	.3 Yrs.	66	389²/₃	26	22	.542	273	134	413	4.64	0

CHACIN (MOLINA), JHOULYS JOSE

Born, Maracaibo, Venezuela, January 7, 1988.
Bats Right. Throws Right. Height, 6 feet, 3 inches. Weight, 215 pounds.

Year Club	Lea	G	IP	W	L	Pct	SO	BB	H	ERA	SAVES
2007 Casper	Pioneer	16	73	6	5	.545	77	26	85	3.13	0
2008 Asheville.	So.Atl.	16	111⅓	10	1	.909	98	30	82	1.86	0
2008 Modesto.	Calif.	12	66⅓	8	2	.800	62	12	61	2.31	0
2009 Tulsa	Texas	18	103⅓	8	6	.571	86	35	87	3.14	0
2009 Colorado Springs	P.C.	4	14⅓	1	2	.333	11	13	11	3.77	0
2009 Colorado	N.L.	9	11	0	1	.000	13	11	6	4.91	0
2010 Colorado Springs	P.C.	7	35⅔	3	2	.600	34	17	27	1.51	0
2010 Colorado	N.L.	28	137⅓	9	11	.450	138	61	114	3.28	0
2011 Colorado	N.L.	31	194	11	14	.440	150	*87	168	3.62	0
Major League Totals . . . . .3 Yrs.		68	342⅓	20	26	.435	301	159	288	3.52	0

CHAMBERLAIN, JUSTIN LOUIS (JOBA)

Born, Lincoln, Nebraska, September 23, 1985.
Bats Right. Throws Right. Height, 6 feet, 2 inches. Weight, 230 pounds.

Year Club	Lea	G	IP	W	L	Pct	SO	BB	H	ERA	SAVES
2007 Tampa	Fla.St.	7	40	4	0	1.000	51	11	25	2.03	0
2007 Trenton.	Eastern	8	40⅓	4	2	.667	66	15	32	3.35	0
2007 Scranton-WB	Int.	3	8	1	0	1.000	18	1	5	0.00	0
2007 New York	A.L.	19	24	2	0	1.000	34	6	12	0.38	1
2008 New York a.	A.L.	42	100⅓	4	3	.571	118	39	87	2.60	0
2009 New York	A.L.	32	157⅓	9	6	.600	133	76	167	4.75	0
2010 New York	A.L.	73	71⅓	3	4	.429	77	22	71	4.40	3
2011 New York b.	A.L.	27	28⅔	2	0	1.000	24	7	23	2.83	0
Major League Totals . . . . .5 Yrs.		193	382	20	13	.606	386	150	360	3.70	4
Division Series											
2007 New York	A.L.	2	3⅔	0	0	.000	4	3	3	4.91	0
2009 New York	A.L.	3	1⅔	0	0	.000	1	0	2	0.00	0
Division Series Totals		5	5⅓	0	0	.000	5	3	5	3.38	0
Championship Series											
2009 New York	A.L.	4	1⅔	0	0	.000	2	0	5	5.40	0
2010 New York	A.L.	3	3⅓	0	0	.000	3	2	4	2.70	0
Championship Series Totals		7	5	0	0	.000	5	2	9	3.60	0
World Series Record											
2009 New York	A.L.	3	3	1	0	1.000	4	1	2	3.00	0

a On disabled list from August 5 to September 2, 2008.
b On disabled list from June 8 to October 12, 2011.

CHAPMAN, ALBERTIN AROLDIS (AROLDIS)

Born, Holguin, Cuba, February 28, 1988.
Bats Left. Throws Left. Height, 6 feet, 4 inches. Weight, 185 pounds.

Year Club	Lea	G	IP	W	L	Pct	SO	BB	H	ERA	SAVES
2010 Louisville	Int.	39	95⅔	9	6	.600	125	52	77	3.57	8
2010 Cincinnati a	N.L.	15	13⅓	2	2	.500	19	5	9	2.03	0
2011 Cincinnati b	N.L.	54	50	4	1	.800	71	41	24	3.60	1
Major League Totals . . . . .2 Yrs.		69	63⅓	6	3	.667	90	46	33	3.27	1
Division Series											
2010 Cincinnati	N.L.	2	1⅔	0	1	.000	1	0	3	0.00	0

a Played in Cuba 2005 through 2009. Signed with Cincinnati Reds, January 12, 2010.
b On disabled list from May 16 to June 24, 2011.

CHATWOOD, TYLER COLE

Born, Fontana, California, December 16, 1989.
Bats Right. Throws Right. Height, 6 feet. Weight, 185 pounds.

Year Club	Lea	G	IP	W	L	Pct	SO	BB	H	ERA	SAVES
2008 Angels	Arizona	11	38	1	2	.333	48	36	25	3.08	0
2009 Cedar Rapids	Midwest	24	116⅓	8	7	.533	106	66	99	4.02	0
2010 Rancho Cucamonga. . . .	Calif.	14	81⅓	8	3	.727	70	36	71	1.77	0
2010 Salt Lake	P.C.	1	5⅓	1	0	1.000	3	0	9	6.35	0
2010 Arkansas	Texas	12	68⅓	4	6	.400	36	27	72	3.82	0
2011 Salt Lake	P.C.	4	16	1	2	.333	11	11	21	5.06	0
2011 Los Angeles a.	A.L.	27	142	6	11	.353	74	71	166	4.75	0

a Traded to Colorado Rockies for catcher Chris Iannetta, November 30, 2011.

CHEN, BRUCE KASTULO

Born, Panama City, Panama, June 19, 1977.
Bats Left. Throws Left. Height, 6 feet, 2 inches. Weight, 215 pounds.

Year	Club	Lea	G	IP	W	L	Pct	SO	BB	H	ERA	SAVES
1994	Braves	Gulf Coast	9	42¹/₃	1	4	.200	26	3	42	3.80	1
1995	Danville	Appal.	14	70¹/₃	4	4	.500	56	19	78	3.97	0
1996	Eugene	Northwest	11	35²/₃	4	1	.800	55	14	23	2.27	0
1997	Macon	So.Atl.	28	146¹/₃	12	7	.632	182	44	120	3.51	0
1998	Greenville	Southern	24	139¹/₃	13	7	.650	164	48	106	3.29	0
1998	Richmond	Int.	4	24	2	1	.667	29	19	17	1.88	0
1998	Atlanta	N.L.	4	20¹/₃	2	0	1.000	17	9	23	3.98	0
1999	Richmond	Int.	14	78	6	3	.667	90	26	73	3.81	0
1999	Atlanta	N.L.	16	51	2	2	.500	45	27	38	5.47	0
2000	Richmond	Int.	1	6	1	0	1.000	6	1	5	0.00	0
2000	Atlanta-Philadelphia a	N.L.	37	134	7	4	.636	112	46	116	3.29	0
2001	Reading	Eastern	1	6	1	0	1.000	7	0	3	0.00	0
2001	Scranton-WB	Int.	3	18²/₃	1	0	1.000	14	5	14	3.86	0
2001	Philadelphia-New York b	N.L.	27	146	7	7	.500	126	59	146	4.87	0
2002	NY-Montreal-Cincinnati c-d	N.L.	55	77²/₃	2	5	.286	80	43	85	5.56	0
2003	Houston	N.L.	11	12	0	0	.000	8	8	14	6.00	0
2003	Boston	A.L.	5	12¹/₃	0	1	.000	12	2	12	5.11	0
2003	Pawtucket e-f-g	Int.	16	85	5	5	.500	73	15	80	4.24	1
2004	Syracuse	Int.	3	10¹/₃	0	1	.000	8	5	17	8.71	0
2004	Ottawa	Int.	22	95	4	3	.571	108	30	85	3.22	0
2004	Baltimore h	A.L.	8	47²/₃	2	1	.667	32	16	39	3.02	0
2005	Baltimore	A.L.	34	197¹/₃	13	10	.565	133	63	187	3.83	0
2006	Baltimore	A.L.	40	98²/₃	0	7	.000	70	35	137	6.93	0
2007	Texas	A.L.	5	10	0	0	.000	7	6	11	7.20	0
2007	Oklahoma i	P.C.	4	16	1	1	.500	12	3	17	5.63	0
2008					Did Not Play							
2009	Omaha	P.C.	14	82	4	2	.667	69	23	57	3.40	0
2009	Kansas City j-k-l	A.L.	17	62¹/₃	1	6	.143	45	25	74	5.78	0
2010	Omaha	P.C.	3	20²/₃	0	1	.000	20	5	13	1.31	0
2010	Kansas City m	A.L.	33	140¹/₃	12	7	.632	98	57	136	4.17	1
2011	NW Arkansas	Texas	1	2	0	1	.000	2	0	5	18.00	0
2011	Omaha	P.C.	2	9	0	0	.000	8	1	11	6.00	0
2011	Kansas City n-o	A.L.	25	155	12	8	.600	97	50	152	3.77	0
Major League Totals	13 Yrs.		317	1164²/₃	60	58	.508	882	446	1170	4.52	1

a Traded to Philadelphia Phillies with pitcher Jim Osting for pitcher Andy Ashby, July 12, 2000.
b Traded to New York Mets with pitcher Adam Walker for pitcher Turk Wendell and pitcher Dennis Cook, July 27, 2001.
c Traded to Montreal Expos with pitcher Dicky Gonzalez, infielder Luis Figueroa and player to be named later for pitcher Scott Strickland, pitcher Paul Seubel and outfielder Matt Watson, April 5, 2002. Montreal Expos received pitcher Saul Rivera to complete trade, July 14, 2002.
d Traded to Cincinnati Reds for pitcher Jim Brower, June 14, 2002.
e Released by Cincinnati Reds, March 12, 2003. Signed with Houston Astros organization, March 14, 2003.
f Claimed on waivers by Boston Red Sox, May 7, 2003.
g Filed for free agency, October 3, 2003. Signed with Toronto Blue Jays organization, November 26, 2003.
h Sold to Baltimore Orioles, May 1, 2004.
i Filed for free agency, October 29, 2006. Signed with Texas Rangers organization, February 6, 2007.
j Filed for free agency, October 15, 2007. Signed with Kansas City Royals organization, March 1, 2009.
k On disabled list from September 23 to November 6, 2009.
l Filed for free agency, November 6, 2009, re-signed with Kansas City Royals organization, December 11, 2009.
m On disabled list, November 1, 2010, re-signed with Kansas City Royals, January 15, 2011.
n On disabled list from May 6 to June 24, 2011.
o Filed for free agency, October 30, 2011, re-signed with Kansas City Royals, November 22, 2011.

CHOATE, RANDOL DOYLE (RANDY)

Born, San Antonio, Texas, September 5, 1975.
Bats Left. Throws Left. Height, 6 feet, 3 inches. Weight, 200 pounds.

Year	Club	Lea	G	IP	W	L	Pct	SO	BB	H	ERA	SAVES
1997	Oneonta	N.Y.-Penn.	10	62¹/₃	5	1	.833	61	12	49	1.73	0
1998	Tampa	Fla.St.	13	70	1	8	.111	55	22	83	5.27	0
1998	Greensboro	So.Atl.	8	39	1	5	.167	32	7	46	3.00	0
1999	Tampa	Fla.St.	47	50	2	2	.500	62	24	51	4.50	1
2000	Columbus	Int.	33	35¹/₃	2	0	1.000	37	14	34	2.04	1
2000	New York	A.L.	22	17	0	0	.000	12	8	14	4.76	0
2001	New York	A.L.	37	48¹/₃	3	1	.750	35	27	34	3.35	0
2001	Columbus	Int.	4	.4¹/₃	1	1	.500	4	3	7	2.08	0
2002	New York	A.L.	18	22¹/₃	0	0	.000	17	15	18	6.04	0
2002	Columbus	Int.	31	36²/₃	3	2	.600	32	15	25	1.72	1

Year	Club	Lea	G	IP	W	L	Pct	SO	BB	H	ERA	SAVES
2003	Columbus..............	Int.	54	71⅓	3	5	.375	56	24	75	3.91	1
2003	New York a............	A.L.	5	3⅔	0	0	.000	0	1	7	7.36	0
2004	Arizona................	N.L.	74	50⅔	2	4	.333	49	28	52	4.62	0
2004	Tucson b	P.C.	15	12⅔	0	0	.000	7	8	10	5.68	1
2005	Arizona................	N.L.	8	7	0	0	.000	4	5	8	9.00	0
2005	Tucson..............	P.C.	47	40	1	1	.500	20	22	44	3.38	3
2006	Tucson..............	P.C.	43	45⅔	6	0	1.000	44	10	39	2.17	8
2006	Arizona................	N.L.	30	16	0	1	.000	12	3	21	3.94	0
2007	Arizona................	N.L.	2	0	0	0 ·	.000	0	0	3	0.00	0
2007	Tucson c-d-e	P.C.	55	63⅓	3	1	.750	61	16	68	2.98	3
2008	Brevard County	Fla.St.	1	1	0	0	.000	1	0	0	0.00	0
2008	Nashville f-g..........	P.C.	26	39	0	4	.000	31	20	42	5.08	2
2009	Durham..............	Int.	21	19⅓	3	0	1.000	15	9	16	3.72	0
2009	Tampa Bay............	A.L.	61	36⅓	1	0	1.000	28	11	28	3.47	5
2010	Tampa Bay h	A.L.	*85	44⅔	4	3	.571	40	17	41	4.23	0
2011	Florida i	N.L.	54	24⅔	1	1	.500	31	13	13	1.82	0
Major League Totals ....11 Yrs.			396	270⅔	11	11	.500	228	128	239	4.16	5
Division Series												
2000	New York.............	A.L.	1	1⅓	0	0	.000	1	1	0	6.75	0
2010	Tampa Bay............	A.L.	3	1	0	0	.000	0	0	0	0.00	0
Division Series Totals			4	2⅓	0	0	.000	1	1	0	3.86	0
Championship Series												
2000	New York.............	A.L.	1	0⅓	0	0	.000	1	0	0	0.00	0
World Series Record												
2001	New York.............	A.L.	2	3⅔	0	0	.000	2	1	7	2.45	0

a Traded to Montreal Expos with infielder Nick Johnson and outfielder Juan Rivera for pitcher Javier Vazquez, December 4, 2003.
b Traded to Arizona Diamondbacks for pitcher John Patterson, March 25, 2004.
c Filed for free agency, October 31, 2006. Signed with Minnesota Twins organization, January 29, 2007.
d Released by Minnesota Twins, March 23, 2007. Signed with Arizona Diamondbacks organization, April 17, 2007.
e Filed for free agency, October 4, 2007. Signed with Milwaukee Brewers, November 13, 2007.
f On disabled list from March 21 to July 10, 2008.
g Filed for free agency, October 1, 2008. Signed with Tampa Bay Rays organization, December 23, 2008.
h Filed for free agency, November 1, 2010. Signed with Florida Marlins organization, December 15, 2010.
i On disabled list from August 16 to October 31, 2011.

CLIPPARD, TYLER LEE

Born, Lexington, Kentucky, February 14, 1985.
Bats Right. Throws Right. Height, 6 feet, 4 inches. Weight, 200 pounds.

Year	Club	Lea	G	IP	W	L	Pct	SO	BB	H	ERA	SAVES
2003	Yankees	Gulf Coast	11	43⅔	3	3	.500	56	5	33	2.89	0
2004	Battle Creek	Midwest	26	149	10	10	.500	145	32	153	3.44	0
2005	Tampa	Fla.St.	26	147⅓	10	9	.526	169	34	118	3.18	0
2005	Columbus.............	Int.	1	1	0	0	.000	2	0	0	0.00	0
2005	Charleston	So.Atl.	1	6	0	1	.000	10	0	9	7.50	0
2006	Trenton............	Eastern	28	166⅓	12	10	.545	175	55	118	3.35	0
2007	New York	A.L.	6	27	3	1	.750	18	17	29	6.33	0
2007	Scranton/WB	Int.	14	69⅓	4	4	.500	55	35	82	4.15	0
2007	Trenton a	Eastern	6	26⅔	2	1	.667	28	12	22	5.40	0
2008	Washington	N.L.	2	10⅓	1	1	.500	8	7	12	4.35	0
2008	Columbus.............	Int.	27	143	6	13	.316	125	66	129	4.66	0
2009	Syracuse	Int.	24	39	4	1	.800	42	15	20	0.92	1
2009	Washington	N.L.	41	60⅓	4	2	.667	67	32	36	2.69	0
2010	Washington	N.L.	78	91	11	8	.579	112	41	69	3.07	1
2011	Washington	N.L.	72	88⅓	3	0	1.000	104	26	48	1.83	0
Major League Totals ....5 Yrs.			199	277	22	12	.647	309	123	194	2.96	1

a Traded to Washington Nationals for pitcher Jonathan Albaladejo, December 5, 2007.

COFFEY, JUSTIN TODD (TODD)

Born, Shelby, North Carolina, September 9, 1980.
Bats Right. Throws Right. Height, 6 feet, 5 inches. Weight, 240 pounds.

Year	Club	Lea	G	IP	W	L	Pct	SO	BB	H	ERA	SAVES
1998	Billings.............	Pioneer	3	12	0	0	.000	8	1	13	3.00	0
1999	Reds............	Gulf Coast	5	16	1	1	.500	14	14	9	3.38	0
2000 a	....		INJURED—Did Not Play									
2001	Reds............	Gulf Coast	3	12⅔	0	1	.000	15	5	11	4.26	0
2001	Billings.............	Pioneer	14	33⅓	2	2	.500	33	15	34	3.51	1

Year	Club	Lea	G	IP	W	L	Pct	SO	BB	H	ERA	SAVES
2002 Dayton	Midwest	38	$80^{1}/_3$	6	4	.600	62	25	78	3.59	2
2003 Potomac.	Carolina	11	23	0	2	.000	21	3	16	1.96	2
2003 Dayton	Midwest	39	56	3	3	.500	53	14	61	2.25	9
2004 Louisville	Int.	15	$13^{2}/_3$	1	0	1.000	11	2	15	5.27	4
2004 Chattanooga.	Southern	40	$45^{1}/_3$	4	1	.800	53	4	36	2.38	20
2005 Louisville	Int.	8	$8^{2}/_3$	0	0	.000	5	2	8	5.19	3
2005 Cincinnati.	N.L.	57	58	4	1	.800	26	11	84	4.50	1
2006 Cincinnati.	N.L.	81	78	6	7	.462	60	27	85	3.58	8
2007 Louisville	Int.	19	27	2	0	1.000	25	5	17	1.33	1
2007 Cincinnati.	N.L.	58	51	2	1	.667	43	19	70	5.82	0
2008 Louisville	Int.	34	$39^{1}/_3$	3	3	.500	43	15	49	4.35	2
2008 Cincinnati-Milwaukee b .	N.L.	26	$26^{2}/_3$	1	0	1.000	15	8	31	4.39	0
2009 Milwaukee	N.L.	78	$83^{2}/_3$	4	4	.500	65	21	76	2.90	2
2010 Nashville	P.C.	1	1	0	0	.000	1	0	0	0.00	0
2010 Milwaukee c-d	N.L.	69	$62^{1}/_3$	2	4	.333	56	23	65	4.76	0
2011 Washington e-f.	N.L.	69	$59^{2}/_3$	5	1	.833	46	20	55	3.62	0
Major League Totals . . . . .7 Yrs.		438	$419^{1}/_3$	24	18	.571	311	129	466	4.08	11

a On minor league disabled list, June 19 to September 27, 2000.
b Claimed on waivers by Milwaukee Brewers, September 10, 2008.
c On disabled list from May 30 to June 20, 2010.
d Not offered contract, December 2, 2010. Signed with Washington Nationals, January 24, 2011.
e On disabled list from April 9 to April 24, 2011.
f Filed for free agency, October 30, 2011.

COKE, PHILLIP DOUGLAS (PHIL)

Born, Sonora, California, July 19, 1982.
Bats Left. Throws Left. Height, 6 feet, 1 inch. Weight, 210 pounds.

Year	Club	Lea	G	IP	W	L	Pct	SO	BB	H	ERA	SAVES
2003 Yankees	Gulf Coast	10	12	0	0	.000	5	3	13	3.75	0
2004 Yankees	Gulf Coast	7	$11^{1}/_3$	0	1	.000	13	3	18	3.97	0
2004 Staten Island	N.Y.-Penn.	3	8	0	0	.000	7	3	9	6.75	0
2005 Charleston	So.Atl.	24	103	8	11	.421	68	34	122	5.42	0
2006 Tampa	Fla.St.	22	110	5	7	.417	88	35	101	3.60	0
2006 Charleston	So.Atl.	5	17	0	1	.000	19	4	10	0.53	1
2007 Tampa	Fla.St.	17	99	7	3	.700	76	37	93	3.09	5
2008 Trenton	Eastern	23	$118^{1}/_3$	9	4	.692	115	39	105	2.51	0
2008 Scranton-WB	Int.	14	$17^{1}/_3$	2	2	.500	22	5	19	4.67	0
2008 New York	A.L.	12	$14^{2}/_3$	1	0	1.000	14	2	8	0.61	0
2009 New York a	A.L.	72	60	4	3	.571	49	20	44	4.50	2
2010 Detroit	A.L.	74	$64^{2}/_3$	7	5	.583	53	26	67	3.76	2
2011 Toledo	Int.	1	$5^{1}/_3$	0	0	.000	6	2	8	5.06	0
2011 Detroit b	A.L.	48	$108^{2}/_3$	3	9	.250	69	40	118	4.47	1
Major League Totals . . . . .4 Yrs.		206	248	15	17	.469	185	88	237	4.06	5
Division Series											
2009 New York	A.L.	2	$0^{2}/_3$	0	0	.000	1	0	0	0.00	0
2011 Detroit	A.L.	1	1	0	0	.000	1	1	3	27.00	0
Division Series Totals		3	$1^{2}/_3$	0	0	.000	2	1	3	16.20	0
Championship Series											
2009 New York	A.L.	2	$0^{2}/_3$	0	0	.000	1	1	1	0.00	0
2011 Detroit	A.L.	4	$3^{1}/_3$	0	0	.000	2	1	3	2.70	1
Championship Series Totals		6	4	0	0	.000	3	2	4	2.25	1
World Series Record											
2009 New York	A.L.	2	$1^{1}/_3$	0	0	.000	1	0	3	13.50	0

a Traded to Detroit Tigers with outfielder Austin Jackson and pitcher Ian Kennedy for outfielder Curtis Granderson, December 9, 2009.
b On disabled list from May 24 to June 8, 2011.

COLEMAN, HAROLD LOUIS (LOUIS)

Born, Greenwood, Mississippi, April 4, 1986.
Bats Right. Throws Right. Height, 6 feet, 4 inches. Weight, 200 pounds.

Year	Club	Lea	G	IP	W	L	Pct	SO	BB	H	ERA	SAVES
2009 Burlington	Midwest	4	$7^{1}/_3$	1	0	1.000	6	1	2	2.45	1
2009 Wilmington	Carolina	10	$14^{1}/_3$	3	1	.750	16	3	8	1.26	1
2010 Omaha	P.C.	21	$40^{1}/_3$	5	2	.714	48	11	31	2.23	1
2010 NW Arkansas	Texas	21	$51^{2}/_3$	2	1	.667	55	14	31	2.09	6
2011 Omaha	P.C.	6	7	0	1	.000	16	4	4	3.86	2
2011 Kansas City	A.L.	48	$59^{2}/_3$	1	4	.200	64	26	44	2.87	1

COLEMAN, JOSEPH CASEY (CASEY)
Born, Fort Myers, Florida, July 3, 1987.
Bats Left. Throws Right. Height, 6 feet. Weight, 180 pounds.

Year	Club	Lea	G	IP	W	L	Pct	SO	BB	H	ERA	SAVES
2008 Daytona	Fla.St.	1	5	1	0	1.000	2	2	4	0.00	0
2008 Peoria	Midwest	5	23⅓	2	2	.500	18	4	25	2.70	0
2008 Boise	Northwest	7	26⅔	1	1	.500	24	7	27	4.05	0
2009 Tennessee	Southern	27	149	14	6	.700	84	58	142	3.68	0
2010 Iowa	P.C.	20	117⅓	10	7	.588	59	35	106	4.07	0
2010 Chicago	N.L.	12	57	4	2	.667	27	25	56	4.11	0
2011 Iowa	P.C.	12	74	5	2	.714	54	22	69	3.65	0
2011 Chicago	N.L.	19	84⅓	3	9	.250	75	46	102	6.40	0
Major League Totals	2 Yrs.	31	141⅓	7	11	.389	102	71	158	5.48	0

COLLINS, TIMOTHY M. (TIM)
Born, Worcester, Massachusetts, August 21, 1989.
Bats Left. Throws Left. Height, 5 feet, 7 inches. Weight, 170 pounds.

Year	Club	Lea	G	IP	W	L	Pct	SO	BB	H	ERA	SAVES
2007 Blue Jays	Gulf Coast	7	6	0	0	.000	7	2	6	4.50	0
2008 Lansing	Midwest	39	68⅓	4	2	.667	98	32	36	1.58	14
2009 Dunedin	Fla.St.	40	64⅔	7	4	.636	99	28	47	2.37	3
2009 New Hampshire	Eastern	9	12⅔	2	3	.400	17	7	12	5.68	0
2010 New Hampshire	Eastern	35	43	1	0	1.000	73	16	27	2.51	9
2010 Mississippi a-b	Southern	6	8	0	0	.000	14	3	4	1.13	2
2010 Omaha	P.C.	15	20⅓	2	1	.667	21	8	9	1.33	4
2011 Kansas City	A.L.	68	67	4	4	.500	60	48	52	3.63	0

a Traded to Atlanta Braves with infielder Alex Gonzalez and infielder Tyler Pastornicky for infielder Yunel Escobar and pitcher Jo-Jo Reyes, July 14, 2010.
b Traded to Kansas City Royals with outfielder Gregor Blanco and pitcher Jesse Chavez for outfielder Rick Ankiel, pitcher Kyle Farnsworth and cash, July 31, 2010.

COLLMENTER, JOSHUA MICHAEL (JOSH)
Born, Homer, Michigan, February 7, 1986.
Bats Right. Throws Right. Height, 6 feet, 2 inches. Weight, 235 pounds.

Year	Club	Lea	G	IP	W	L	Pct	SO	BB	H	ERA	SAVES
2007 Yakima	Northwest	14	66⅓	6	3	.667	57	21	60	2.71	0
2008 South Bend	Midwest	27	145⅓	12	8	.600	123	47	126	3.41	0
2009 Visalia	Calif.	27	145⅓	8	10	.444	152	55	127	4.15	0
2010 Visalia	Calif.	3	15	2	0	1.000	21	3	11	2.40	0
2010 Reno	P.C.	10	57⅔	4	3	.571	39	26	64	5.77	0
2010 Mobile	Southern	12	79⅓	8	3	.727	73	22	61	1.82	0
2011 Reno	P.C.	1	6	1	0	1.000	7	2	2	1.50	0
2011 Arizona	N.L.	31	154⅓	10	10	.500	100	28	137	3.38	0
Division Series											
2011 Arizona	N.L.	1	7	1	0	1.000	6	2	2	1.29	0

COLON, BARTOLO
Born, Altamira, Dominican Republic, May 24, 1973.
Bats Right. Throws Right. Height, 6 feet. Weight, 265 pounds.

Year	Club	Lea	G	IP	W	L	Pct	SO	BB	H	ERA	SAVES
1993 Cleveland	Dominican	11	66	6	1	.857	43	33	44	2.59	1
1994 Burlington	Appal.	12	66	7	4	.636	84	44	46	3.14	0
1995 Kinston	Carolina	21	128⅔	13	3	.813	152	39	91	1.96	0
1996 Canton-Akrn.	Eastern	13	62	2	2	.500	56	25	44	1.74	0
1996 Buffalo	A.A.	8	15	0	0	.000	19	8	16	6.00	0
1997 Buffalo	A.A.	10	56⅔	7	1	.875	54	23	45	2.22	0
1997 Cleveland	A.L.	19	94	4	7	.364	66	45	107	5.65	0
1998 Cleveland	A.L.	31	204	14	9	.609	158	79	205	3.71	0
1999 Cleveland	A.L.	32	205	18	5	.783	161	76	185	3.95	0
2000 Cleveland	A.L.	30	188	15	8	.652	212	98	163	3.88	0
2000 Buffalo a	Int.	1	5	1	0	1.000	4	0	6	1.80	0
2001 Cleveland	A.L.	34	222⅓	14	12	.538	201	90	220	4.09	0
2002 Cleveland	A.L.	16	116⅓	10	4	.714	75	31	104	2.55	0
2002 Montreal b	N.L.	17	117	10	4	.714	74	39	115	3.31	0
2003 Chicago c	A.L.	34	242	15	13	.536	173	67	223	3.87	0
2004 Anaheim	A.L.	34	208⅓	18	12	.600	158	71	215	5.01	0
2005 Los Angeles	A.L.	33	222⅔	*21	8	.724	157	43	215	3.48	0
2006 Rancho Cucamonga	Calif.	1	4	0	0	.000	3	1	2	0.00	0

226

Year	Club	Lea	G	IP	W	L	Pct	SO	BB	H	ERA	SAVES
2006 Salt Lake	P.C.	2	11$\frac{2}{3}$	0	1	.000	3	2	14	6.17	0
2006 Los Angeles d-e	A.L.	10	56$\frac{1}{3}$	1	5	.167	31	11	71	5.11	0
2007 Rancho Cucamonga	Calif.	2	9$\frac{2}{3}$	1	0	1.000	10	1	6	1.86	0
2007 Salt Lake	P.C.	3	15	2	0	1.000	8	3	12	2.40	0
2007 Los Angeles f-g	A.L.	19	99$\frac{1}{3}$	6	8	.429	76	29	132	6.34	0
2008 Pawtucket	Int.	9	31$\frac{2}{3}$	3	1	.750	21	6	23	2.27	0
2008 Boston h-i	A.L.	7	39	4	2	.667	27	10	44	3.92	0
2009 Kannapolis	So.Atl.	1	7	0	1	.000	8	1	7	2.57	0
2009 Charlotte	Int.	2	12	1	1	.500	1	4	10	3.75	0
2009 Chicago j-k	A.L.	12	62$\frac{1}{3}$	3	6	.333	38	21	69	4.19	0
2010						Did not play					
2011 New York l-m-n	A.L.	29	164$\frac{1}{3}$	8	10	.444	135	40	172	4.00	0
Major League Totals ...... 14 Yrs.		357	2241	161	113	.588	1742	750	2240	4.09	0
Division Series											
1998 Cleveland	A.L.	1	5$\frac{2}{3}$	0	0	.000	3	3	5	1.59	0
1999 Cleveland	A.L.	2	9	0	1	.000	12	4	11	9.00	0
2001 Cleveland	A.L.	2	14$\frac{2}{3}$	1	1	.500	13	6	12	1.84	0
2004 Anaheim	A.L.	1	6	0	0	.000	3	3	7	4.50	0
2005 Los Angeles	A.L.	2	8	0	1	.000	7	1	10	4.50	0
Division Series Totals		8	43$\frac{1}{3}$	1	3	.250	38	17	45	4.15	0
Championship Series											
1998 Cleveland	A.L.	1	9	1	0	1.000	3	4	4	1.00	0

a On disabled list from April 16 to May 11, 2000.

b Traded to Montreal Expos with player to be named later for infielder Lee Stevens, infielder Brandon Phillips, outfielder Grady Sizemore and pitcher Cliff Lee, June 27, 2002. Montreal Expos received pitcher Tim Drew to complete trade, June 28, 2002.

c Filed for free agency, October 27, 2003. Signed with Anaheim Angels, December 9, 2003.

d On disabled list from April 16 to June 18, 2006.

e On disabled list from July 30 to October 2, 2006.

f On disabled list from March 23 to April 21, 2007.

g On disabled list from July 24 to September 9, 2007.

h Filed for free agency, October 29, 2007. Signed with Boston Red Sox organization, February 25, 2008.

i On disabled list from June 17 to September 7, 2008.

j Filed for free agency, October 31, 2008. Signed with Chicago White Sox, January 15, 2009.

k On disabled list from June 8 to July 23, 2009.

l Released by Chicago White Sox, September 16, 2009. Signed with New York Yankees organization, January 26, 2011.

m On disabled list from June 12 to July 2, 2011.

n Filed for free,agency, October 30, 2011.

CONTRERAS, JOSE ARIEL
Born, Las Martinas, Cuba, December 6, 1971.
Bats Right. Throws Right. Height, 6 feet, 4 inches. Weight, 245 pounds.

Year	Club	Lea	G	IP	W	L	Pct	SO	BB	H	ERA	SAVES
2003 Staten Island	N.Y.-Penn.	1	7	0	0	.000	15	0	2	0.00	0
2003 Tampa	Fla.St.	1	4	0	0	.000	5	3	4	4.50	0
2003 Trenton	Eastern	1	1$\frac{2}{3}$	0	0	.000	3	2	1	0.00	0
2003 Columbus	Int.	3	15	2	0	1.000	18	2	10	1.20	0
2003 New York a-b-c	A.L.	18	71	7	2	.778	72	30	52	3.30	0
2004 New York-Chicago d	A.L.	31	170$\frac{1}{3}$	13	9	.591	150	84	166	5.50	0
2005 Chicago	A.L.	32	204$\frac{2}{3}$	15	7	.682	154	75	177	3.61	0
2006 Chicago e	A.L.	30	196	13	9	.591	134	55	194	4.27	0
2007 Chicago	A.L.	32	189	10	17	.370	113	62	232	5.57	0
2008 Charlotte	Int.	1	5	0	0	.000	4	3	4	5.40	0
2008 Chicago f	A.L.	20	121	7	6	.538	70	35	130	4.54	0
2009 Charlotte	Int.	5	33$\frac{1}{3}$	3	1	.750	27	16	19	2.70	0
2009 Chicago	A.L.	21	114$\frac{2}{3}$	5	13	.278	89	45	121	5.42	0
2009 Colorado g-h	N.L.	7	17	1	0	1.000	17	8	20	1.59	0
2010 Philadelphia i	N.L.	67	56$\frac{2}{3}$	6	4	.600	57	16	53	3.34	4
2011 Clearwater	Fla.St.	1	0$\frac{2}{3}$	0	1	.000	0	0	4	40.50	0
2011 Reading	Eastern	1	1	0	0	.000	1	1	2	0.00	0
2011 Lehigh Valley	Int.	1	2	0	0	.000	0	0	2	0.00	0
2011 Philadelphia j	N.L.	17	14	0	0	.000	13	8	11	3.86	5
Major League Totals .... 9 Yrs.		275	1154$\frac{1}{3}$	77	67	.535	869	418	1156	4.54	9
Division Series											
2005 Chicago	A.L.	1	7$\frac{2}{3}$	1	0	1.000	6	0	8	2.35	0
2009 Colorado	N.L.	2	2	0	0	.000	3	2	3	4.50	0
2010 Philadelphia	N.L.	1	1	1	0	1.000	1	0	0	0.00	0
Division Series Totals		4	10$\frac{2}{3}$	2	0	1.000	10	2	11	2.53	0

Year	Club	Lea	G	IP	W	L	Pct	SO	BB	H	ERA	SAVES
	Championship Series											
2003 New York	A.L.	4	4²/₃	0	1	.000	7	2	6	5.79	0
2005 Chicago	A.L.	2	17¹/₃	1	1	.500	6	2	12	3.12	0
2010 Philadelphia	N.L.	3	3	0	0	.000	3	0	1	0.00	0
Championship Series Totals		9	25	1	2	.333	16	4	19	3.24	0
	World Series Record											
2003 New York	A.L.	4	6¹/₃	0	1	.000	10	5	5	5.68	0
2005 Chicago	A.L.	1	7	1	0	1.000	2	0	6	3.86	0
World Series Totals		5	13¹/₃	1	1	.500	12	5	11	4.72	0

a Played in Cuba 1996 through 2002.
b Signed as free agent by New York Yankees, February 6, 2003.
c On disabled list from June 7 to August 24, 2003.
d Traded to Chicago White Sox for pitcher Esteban Loaiza, July 31, 2004.
e On disabled list from May 5 to May 21, 2006.
f On disabled list from July 18 to August 9 and August 10 to October 17, 2008.
g Traded to Colorado Rockies with cash for pitcher Brandon Hynick, August 31, 2009.
h Filed for free agency, November 9, 2009. Signed with Philadelphia Phillies, January 28, 2010.
i Filed for free agency, November 1, 2010, re-signed with Philadelphia Phillies, November 16, 2010.
j On disabled list from April 22 to May 26 and June 20 to October 19, 2011.

COOK, AARON LANE
Born, Fort Campbell, Kentucky, February 8, 1979.
Bats Right. Throws Right. Height, 6 feet, 3 inches. Weight, 215 pounds.

Year	Club	Lea	G	IP	W	L	Pct	SO	BB	H	ERA	SAVES
1997 Rockies	Arizona	9	46	1	3	.250	35	17	48	3.13	0
1998 Portland	Northwest	15	79¹/₃	5	8	.385	38	39	87	4.88	0
1999 Asheville	So.Atl.	25	121²/₃	4	12	.250	73	42	157	6.44	0
2000 Salem	Carolina	7	43	1	6	.143	37	12	52	5.44	0
2000 Asheville	So.Atl.	21	142²/₃	10	7	.588	118	23	130	2.96	0
2001 Salem	Carolina	27	155	11	11	.500	122	38	157	3.08	0
2002 Carolina	Southern	14	95	7	2	.778	58	19	73	1.42	0
2002 Colorado Springs	P.C.	10	64¹/₃	4	4	.500	32	18	67	3.78	0
2002 Colorado	N.L.	9	35²/₃	2	1	.667	14	13	41	4.54	0
2003 Colorado Springs	P.C.	2	16	1	1	.500	12	4	10	2.25	0
2003 Colorado	N.L.	43	124	4	6	.400	43	57	160	6.02	0
2004 Colorado Springs	P.C.	7	46	3	1	.750	25	8	34	2.74	0
2004 Colorado a	N.L.	16	96²/₃	6	4	.600	40	39	112	4.28	0
2005 Tri-City	Northwest	2	7	0	0	.000	0	0	1	0.00	0
2005 Modesto	California	1	5	1	0	1.000	5	0	5	1.80	0
2005 Tulsa	Texas	1	3²/₃	0	1	.000	1	1	10	17.18	0
2005 Colorado Springs	P.C.	3	16¹/₃	1	0	1.000	11	7	18	5.51	0
2005 Colorado b	N.L.	13	83¹/₃	7	2	.778	24	16	101	3.67	0
2006 Colorado	N.L.	32	212²/₃	9	15	.375	92	55	242	4.23	0
2007 Colorado Springs	P.C.	1	1	0	1	.000	0	1	4	27.00	0
2007 Colorado c	N.L.	25	166	8	7	.533	61	44	178	4.12	0
2008 Colorado	N.L.	32	211¹/₃	16	9	.640	96	48	*236	3.96	0
2009 Colorado d	N.L.	27	158	11	6	.647	78	47	175	4.16	0
2010 Tulsa	Texas	2	10²/₃	1	1	.500	10	3	8	2.53	0
2010 Colorado e	N.L.	23	127²/₃	6	8	.429	62	52	147	5.08	0
2011 Tulsa	Texas	3	14	0	1	.000	13	3	16	5.79	0
2011 Colorado Springs	P.C.	2	14²/₃	1	0	1.000	5	2	13	5.52	0
2011 Colorado f-g	N.L.	18	97	3	10	.231	48	37	127	6.03	0
Major League Totals	10 Yrs.	238	1312¹/₃	72	68	.514	558	408	1519	4.53	0
	Division Series											
2009 Colorado	N.L.	1	5	1	0	1.000	4	2	7	5.40	0
	World Series Record											
2007 Colorado	N.L.	1	6	0	1	.000	2	0	6	4.50	0

a On disabled list from August 8 to November 3, 2004.
b On disabled list from March 25 to July 30, 2005.
c On disabled list from August 16 to October 10, 2007.
d On disabled list from August 22 to September 25, 2009.
e On disabled list from August 4 to September 3 and September 9 to October 4, 2010.
f On disabled list from March 22 to June 8, 2011.
g Filed for free agency, October 31, 2011. Signed with Boston Red Sox organization, January 9, 2012.

CORDERO, FRANCISCO JAVIER

Born, Santo Domingo, Dominican Republic, May 11, 1975.
Bats Right. Throws Right. Height, 6 feet, 2 inches. Weight, 235 pounds.

Year	Club	Lea	G	IP	W	L	Pct	SO	BB	H	ERA	SAVES
1994 Detroit	Dominican		12	60	4	3	.571	36	27	65	3.90	0
1995 Fayettevlle	So.Atl.		4	20	0	3	.000	19	12	26	6.30	0
1995 Jamestown	N.Y.-Penn.		15	88	4	7	.364	54	37	96	5.22	0
1996 Fayettevlle	So.Atl.		2	7	0	0	.000	7	6	2	2.57	0
1996 Jamestown a	N.Y.-Penn.		2	11	0	0	.000	10	2	5	0.82	0
1997 W Michigan	Midwest		50	54¹/₃	6	1	.857	67	15	36	0.99	35
1998 Jacksnville	Southern		17	16²/₃	1	1	.500	18	9	19	4.86	8
1998 Lakeland b	Fla.St.		1	0	0	0	.000	0	0	1	0.00	0
1999 Jacksonville	Southern		47	52¹/₃	4	1	.800	58	22	35	1.38	27
1999 Detroit c	A.L.		20	19	2	2	.500	19	18	19	3.32	0
2000 Texas	A.L.		56	77¹/₃	1	2	.333	49	48	87	5.35	0
2000 Oklahoma	P.C.		3	4¹/₃	0	0	.000	5	3	7	4.15	1
2001 Oklahoma	P.C.		12	15¹/₃	0	1	.000	20	3	8	0.59	6
2001 Texas d	A.L.		3	2¹/₃	0	1	.000	1	2	3	3.86	0
2002 Oklahoma	P.C.		11	12¹/₃	0	2	.000	21	7	15	5.84	2
2002 Texas e	A.L.		39	45¹/₃	2	0	1.000	41	13	33	1.79	10
2003 Texas	A.L.		73	82²/₃	5	8	.385	90	38	70	2.94	15
2004 Texas	A.L.		67	71²/₃	3	4	.429	79	32	60	2.13	49
2005 Texas	A.L.		69	69	3	1	.750	79	30	61	3.39	37
2006 Texas	A.L.		49	48²/₃	7	4	.636	54	16	49	4.81	6
2006 Milwaukee f	N.L.		28	26²/₃	3	1	.750	30	16	20	1.69	16
2007 Milwaukee g	N.L.		66	63¹/₃	0	4	.000	86	18	52	2.98	44
2008 Cincinnati	N.L.		72	70¹/₃	5	4	.556	78	38	61	3.33	34
2009 Cincinnati	N.L.		68	66²/₃	2	6	.250	58	30	58	2.16	39
2010 Cincinnati	N.L.		75	72²/₃	6	5	.545	59	36	68	3.84	40
2011 Cincinnati h	N.L.		68	69²/₃	5	3	.625	42	22	49	2.45	37
Major League Totals	13 Yrs.		753	785¹/₃	44	45	.494	765	357	690	3.17	327

a On disabled list from June 28 to September 30, 1996.
b On disabled list from May 22 to June 18 and June 26 to September 30, 1998.
c Traded to Texas Rangers with pitcher Justin Thompson, pitcher Alan Webb, outfielder Gabe Kapler, catcher Bill Haselman and infielder Frank Catalanotto for outfielder Juan Gonzalez, pitcher Danny Patterson and catcher Gregg Zaun, November 2, 1999.
d On disabled list from March 23 to June 22 and June 26 to October 11, 2001.
e On disabled list from June 25 to July 27, 2002.
f Traded to Milwaukee Brewers with outfielder Kevin Mench, outfielder Laynce Nix and pitcher Julian Cordero for outfielder Carlos Lee and outfielder Nelson Cruz, July 28, 2006.
g Filed for free agency, October 29, 2007. Signed with Cincinnati Reds, November 28, 2007.
h Filed for free agency, October 31, 2011.

CORREIA, KEVIN JOHN

Born, San Diego, California, August 24, 1980.
Bats Right. Throws Right. Height, 6 feet, 3 inches. Weight, 200 pounds.

Year	Club	Lea	G	IP	W	L	Pct	SO	BB	H	ERA	SAVES
2002 Salem-Keizer	Northwest		10	37²/₃	2	2	.500	31	14	37	4.54	0
2003 Norwich	Eastern		16	86¹/₃	6	6	.500	73	30	80	3.65	0
2003 San Francisco	N.L.		10	39¹/₃	3	1	.750	28	18	41	3.66	0
2003	P.C.		3	19	1	0	1.000	23	2	16	2.84	0
2004 Fresno	P.C.		29	105¹/₃	3	7	.300	70	35	118	4.53	0
2004 San Francisco	N.L.		12	19	0	1	.000	14	10	25	8.05	0
2005 San Jose	California		1	7	0	1	.000	7	5	5	2.57	0
2005 Fresno	P.C.		31	46	3	2	.600	35	23	50	6.07	7
2005 San Francisco	N.L.		16	58¹/₃	2	5	.286	44	31	61	4.63	0
2006 San Francisco	N.L.		48	69²/₃	2	0	1.000	57	22	64	3.49	0
2007 San Francisco	N.L.		59	101²/₃	4	7	.364	80	40	94	3.45	0
2008 San Jose	Calif.		1	3¹/₃	0	0	.000	1	1	1	0.00	0
2008 Fresno	P.C.		2	12	1	0	1.000	15	0	8	1.50	0
2008 San Francisco a-b	N.L.		25	110	3	8	.273	66	47	141	6.05	0
2009 San Diego	N.L.		33	198	12	11	.522	142	64	194	3.91	0
2010 San Diego c	N.L.		28	145	10	10	.500	115	64	152	5.40	0
2011 Pittsburgh d	N.L.		27	154	12	11	.522	77	39	175	4.79	0
Major League Totals	9 Yrs.		258	895	48	54	.471	623	335	947	4.61	0

a On disabled list from April 27 to June 15, 2008.
b Filed for free agency, October 14, 2008. Signed with San Diego Padres organization, December 24, 2008.
c Filed for free agency, November 1, 2010. Signed with Pittsburgh Pirates, December 7, 2010.
d On disabled list from August 20 to November 1, 2011.

CRAIN, JESSE ALAN
Born, Toronto, Ontario, Canada, July 5, 1981.
Bats Right. Throws Right. Height, 6 feet, 1 inch. Weight, 205 pounds.

Year	Club	Lea	G	IP	W	L	Pct	SO	BB	H	ERA	SAVES
2002 Elizabethton	Appal.	9	$15^{1}/_{3}$	2	1	.667	18	7	4	0.57	2
2002 Quad Cities	Midwest	9	12	1	1	.500	11	4	6	1.50	1
2003 New Britain	Eastern	22	39	1	1	.500	56	10	13	0.69	9
2003 Fort Myers	Fla.St.	10	19	2	1	.667	25	5	10	2.84	0
2003 Rochester	Int.	23	26	3	1	.750	33	10	24	3.12	10
2004 Rochester	Int.	41	$50^{2}/_{3}$	3	2	.600	64	17	38	2.49	19
2004 Minnesota	A.L.	22	27	3	0	1.000	14	12	17	2.00	0
2005 Minnesota	A.L.	75	$79^{2}/_{3}$	12	5	.706	25	29	61	2.71	1
2006 Minnesota	A.L.	68	$76^{2}/_{3}$	4	5	.444	60	18	79	3.52	1
2007 Minnesota a	A.L.	18	$16^{1}/_{3}$	1	2	.333	10	4	19	5.51	0
2008 Minnesota	A.L.	66	$62^{2}/_{3}$	5	4	.556	50	24	62	3.59	0
2009 Rochester	Int.	12	$17^{2}/_{3}$	1	0	1.000	22	8	13	2.55	1
2009 Minnesota b	A.L.	56	$51^{2}/_{3}$	7	4	.636	43	27	48	4.70	0
2010 Minnesota	A.L.	71	68	1	1	.500	62	27	53	3.04	1
2011 Chicago	A.L.	67	$65^{1}/_{3}$	8	3	.727	70	31	50	2.62	1
Major League Totals	8 Yrs.	443	$447^{1}/_{3}$	41	24	.631	334	172	389	3.30	4
Division Series											
2004 Minnesota	A.L.	1	$0^{1}/_{3}$	0	0	.000	0	0	1	0.00	0
2006 Minnesota	A.L.	2	1	0	0	.000	1	1	3	9.00	0
2010 Minnesota	A.L.	1	$0^{1}/_{3}$	0	1	.000	0	0	3	54.00	0
Division Series Totals		4	$1^{2}/_{3}$	0	1	.000	1	1	7	16.20	0

a On disabled list from May 16 to October 10, 2007.
b On disabled list from April 18 to May 4, 2009.
c Filed for free agency, November 1, 2010. Signed with Chicago White Sox, December 20, 2010.

CROW, AARON J.
Born, Topeka, Kansas, November 10, 1986.
Bats Right. Throws Right. Height, 6 feet, 3 inches. Weight, 190 pounds.

Year	Club	Lea	G	IP	W	L	Pct	SO	BB	H	ERA	SAVES
2008 Fort Worth	Amer. Assoc.	1	1	0	0	.000	0	0	1	0.00	0
2009 Fort Worth	Amer. Assoc.	3	17	3	0	1.000	17	5	11	1.06	0
2010 Wilmington	Carolina	7	44	2	3	.400	53	6	51	5.93	0
2010 NW Arkansas	Texas	22	$119^{1}/_{3}$	7	7	.500	90	59	130	5.66	0
2011 Kansas City	A.L.	57	62	4	4	.500	65	31	55	2.76	0

CRUZ, JUAN CARLOS
Born, Bonao, Dominican Republic, October 15, 1978.
Bats Right. Throws Right. Height, 6 feet, 2 inches. Weight, 165 pounds.

Year	Club	Lea	G	IP	W	L	Pct	SO	BB	H	ERA	SAVES
1998 Cubs	Arizona	12	$41^{1}/_{3}$	2	4	.333	36	14	61	6.10	0
1999 Eugene	Northwest	15	$80^{1}/_{3}$	5	6	.455	65	33	97	5.94	0
2000 Lansing	Midwest	17	96	5	5	.500	106	60	75	3.28	0
2000 Daytona	Fla.St.	8	$44^{1}/_{3}$	3	0	1.000	54	18	30	3.25	0
2001 West Tenn	Southern	23	$121^{1}/_{3}$	9	6	.600	137	60	107	4.01	0
2001 Chicago	N.L.	8	$44^{2}/_{3}$	3	1	.750	39	17	40	3.22	0
2002 Chicago a	N.L.	45	$97^{1}/_{3}$	3	11	.214	81	59	84	3.98	1
2003 Chicago	N.L.	25	61	2	7	.222	65	28	66	6.05	0
2003 Iowa	P.C.	9	$50^{2}/_{3}$	4	0	1.000	47	11	37	1.95	0
2004 Atlanta b-c	N.L.	50	72	6	2	.750	70	30	59	2.75	0
2005 Sacramento	P.C.	13	75	5	1	.833	90	28	51	2.40	0
2005 Oakland	A.L.	28	$32^{2}/_{3}$	0	3	.000	34	22	38	7.44	0
2006 Tucson	P.C.	1	$3^{1}/_{3}$	0	0	.000	4	1	4	2.70	0
2006 Arizona d-e	N.L.	31	$94^{2}/_{3}$	5	6	.455	88	47	80	4.18	0
2007 Tucson	P.C.	1	2	0	0	.000	5	0	1	0.00	0
2007 Arizona f	N.L.	53	61	6	1	.857	87	32	45	3.10	0
2008 Tucson	P.C.	2	3	0	0	.000	4	0	3	3.00	0
2008 Arizona g	N.L.	57	$51^{2}/_{3}$	4	0	1.000	71	31	34	2.61	0
2009 Kansas City h-i	A.L.	46	$50^{1}/_{3}$	3	4	.429	38	29	46	5.72	2
2010 Kansas City	A.L.	11	$5^{1}/_{3}$	0	0	.000	7	4	9	3.38	0
2011 Charlotte	Fla.St.	1	1	0	0	.000	2	0	2	0.00	0
2011 Tampa Bay j-k-l	A.L.	56	$48^{2}/_{3}$	5	0	1.000	46	28	36	3.88	0
Major League Totals	11 Yrs.	404	$619^{1}/_{3}$	37	35	.514	626	327	537	4.13	3
Division Series											
2003 Chicago	N.L.	1	1	0	0	.000	2	1	0	0.00	0

Year Club	Lea	G	IP	W	L	Pct	SO	BB	H	ERA	SAVES
2004 Atlanta	N.L.	3	3²/₃	0	0	.000	4	4	6	9.82	0
2007 Arizona.	N.L.	1	0¹/₃	0	0	.000	1	0	1	0.00	0
2011 Tampa Bay	A.L.	2	2	0	0	.000	2	2	1	0.00	0
Division Series Totals		7	7	0	0	.000	9	7	8	5.14	0
Championship Series											
2007 Arizona.	N.L.	3	4	0	0	.000	8	3	0	0.00	0

a On disabled list from August 10 to August 25, 2002.
b Traded to Atlanta Braves with pitcher Steve Smyth for pitcher Andy Pratt and infielder Richard Lewis, March 25, 2004.
c Traded to Oakland Athletics with pitcher Dan Meyer and outfielder Charles Thomas for pitcher Tim Hudson, December 16, 2004.
d Traded to Arizona Diamondbacks, for pitcher Brad Halsey, March 26, 2006.
e On disabled list from June 4 to July 3, 2006.
f On disabled list from April 21 to May 11, 2007.
g On disabled list from July 6 to August 1, 2008.
h Filed for free agency, October 30, 2008. Signed with Kansas City Royals organization, February 28, 2009.
i On disabled list from August 6 to September 23, 2009.
j Released by Kansas City Royals, April 23, 2010. Signed with Tampa Bay Rays organization, February 3, 2011.
k On disabled list from July 18 to August 2, 2011.
l Filed for free agency, October 30, 2011.

CUETO (ORTIZ), JOHNNY
Born, San Pedro de Macoris, Dominican Republic, February 15, 1985.
Bats Right. Throws Right. Height, 5 feet, 10 inches. Weight, 185 pounds.

Year Club	Lea	G	IP	W	L	Pct	SO	BB	H	ERA	SAVES
2005 Sarasota.	Fla.St.	2	6	0	1	.000	6	2	5	3.00	0
2005 Reds.	Gulf Coast	13	43	2	2	.500	38	8	49	5.02	1
2006 Sarasota.	Fla.St.	12	61²/₃	7	2	.778	61	23	48	3.50	0
2006 Dayton	Midwest	14	76¹/₃	8	1	.889	82	15	52	2.59	0
2007 Sarasota.	Fla.St.	14	78¹/₃	4	5	.444	72	21	72	3.33	0
2007 Louisville	Int.	4	22	2	1	.667	21	2	22	2.05	0
2007 Chattanooga	Southern	10	61	6	3	.667	77	11	52	3.10	0
2008 Cincinnati.	N.L.	31	174	9	14	.391	158	68	178	4.81	0
2009 Cincinnati a	N.L.	30	171¹/₃	11	11	.500	132	61	172	4.41	0
2010 Cincinnati.	N.L.	31	185²/₃	12	7	.632	138	56	181	3.64	0
2011 Louisville	Int.	4	14¹/₃	0	2	.000	13	6	19	6.28	0
2011 Cincinnati b	N.L.	24	156	9	5	.643	104	47	123	2.31	0
Major League Totals . . . . .4 Yrs.		116	687	41	37	.526	532	232	654	3.83	0
Division Series											
2010 Cincinnati.	N.L.	1	5	0	1	.000	2	1	5	1.80	0

a On disabled list from August 16 to August 31, 2009.
b On disabled list from March 22 to May 8, 2011.

DANKS, JOHN WILLIAM
Born, Austin, Texas, April 15, 1985.
Bats Left. Throws Left. Height, 6 feet, 1 inch. Weight, 200 pounds.

Year Club	Lea	G	IP	W	L	Pct	SO	BB	H	ERA	SAVES
2003 Rangers	Arizona	5	13	1	0	1.000	22	4	6	0.69	0
2003 Spokane.	Northwest	5	12²/₃	0	2	.000	13	7	12	8.53	0
2004 Stockton.	Calif.	13	55	1	4	.200	48	26	62	5.24	0
2004 Clinton.	Midwest	14	49²/₃	3	2	.600	64	14	38	2.17	0
2005 Bakersfield	Calif.	10	57²/₃	3	3	.500	53	16	50	2.50	0
2005 Frisco.	Texas	18	98¹/₃	4	10	.286	85	34	117	5.49	0
2006 Oklahoma.	P.C.	14	70²/₃	4	5	.444	72	34	67	4.33	0
2006 Frisco a	Texas	13	69¹/₃	5	4	.556	82	22	74	4.15	0
2007 Chicago	A.L.	26	139	6	13	.316	109	54	160	5.50	0
2008 Chicago	A.L.	33	195	12	9	.571	159	57	182	3:32	0
2009 Chicago	A.L.	32	200¹/₃	13	11	.542	149	73	184	3.77	0
2010 Chicago	A.L.	32	213	15	11	.577	162	70	189	3.72	0
2011 Charlotte	Int.	2	9	1	0	1.000	6	2	9	2.00	0
2011 Chicago b.	A.L.	27	170¹/₃	8	12	.400	135	46	182	4.33	0
Major League Totals . . . . .5 Yrs.		150	917²/₃	54	56	.491	714	300	897	4.03	0
Division Series											
2008 Chicago	A.L.	1	6²/₃	1	0	1.000	7	3	7	4.05	0

a Traded to Chicago White Sox by Texas Rangers with pitcher Nick Masset and pitcher Jacob Rasner for pitcher Brandon McCarthy and outfielder David Paisano, December 23, 2006.
b On disabled list from June 26 to July 20, 2011.

DARVISH, SEFAT FARID YU (YU)
Born, Osaka, Japan, August 16, 1986.
Bats Right. Throws Right. Height 6 feet, 5 inches. Weight, 187 pounds.

Year	Club	Lea	G	IP	W	L	Pct	SO	BB	H	ERA	SAVES
2005	Nippon Ham......Japan	Pac.	14	94¹/₃	5	5	.500	52	48	97	3.53	0
2006	Nippon Ham......Japan	Pac.	25	149²/₃	12	5	.706	115	64	128	2.89	0
2007	Nippon Ham......Japan	Pac.	26	207²/₃	15	5	.750	210	49	123	1.82	0
2008	Nippon Ham......Japan	Pac.	25	200²/₃	16	4	.800	208	44	136	1.80	0
2009	Nippon Ham......Japan	Pac.	23	182	15	5	.750	167	45	118	1.73	0
2010	Nippon Ham......Japan	Pac.	26	202	12	8	.600	222	47	158	1.78	0
2011	Nippon Ham......Japan	Pac.	28	232	18	6	.750	276	36	156	1.44	0

DAVIS, WADE ALLEN
Born, Lake Wales, Florida, September 7, 1985.
Bats Right. Throws Right. Height, 6 feet, 5 inches. Weight, 220 pounds.

Year	Club	Lea	G	IP	W	L	Pct	SO	BB	H	ERA	SAVES
2004	Princeton	Appal.	13	57²/₃	3	5	.375	38	19	71	5.93	0
2005	Hudson Valley	N.Y.-Penn.	15	86	7	4	.636	97	23	75	2.72	0
2006	SW Michigan	Midwest	27	146	7	12	.368	165	64	124	3.02	0
2007	Vero Beach.........	Fla.St.	13	78¹/₃	3	0	1.000	88	21	54	1.84	0
2007	Montgomery	Southern	14	80	7	3	.700	81	30	74	3.15	0
2008	Durham	Int.	9	53	4	2	.667	55	24	39	2.72	0
2008	Montgomery	Southern	19	107²/₃	9	6	.600	81	42	104	3.85	0
2009	Durham	Int.	28	158²/₃	10	8	.556	140	60	139	3.40	0
2009	Tampa Bay	A.L.	6	36¹/₃	2	2	.500	36	13	33	3.72	0
2010	Tampa Bay a.......	A.L.	29	168	12	10	.545	113	62	165	4.07	0
2011	Tampa Bay b	A.L.	29	184	11	10	.524	105	63	190	4.45	0
Major League Totals	3 Yrs.		64	388¹/₃	25	22	.532	254	138	388	4.22	0
Division Series												
2010	Tampa Bay	A.L.	1	5	1	0	1.000	7	3	7	3.60	0
2011	Tampa Bay	A.L.	2	2¹/₃	0	0	.000	1	1	1	0.00	0
Division Series Totals			3	7¹/₃	1	0	1.000	8	4	8	2.45	0

a On disabled list from August 6 to August 24, 2010.
b On disabled list from July 7 to July 22, 2011.

DELGADO, RANDALL ENRIQUE
Born, Las Tablas, Panama, February 9, 1990.
Bats Right. Throws Right. Height, 6 feet, 3 inches. Weight, 200 pounds.

Year	Club	Lea	G	IP	W	L	Pct	SO	BB	H	ERA	SAVES
2008	Danville	Appal.	14	69	3	8	.273	81	30	63	3.13	0
2009	Rome	So.Atl.	25	124	5	10	.333	141	49	123	4.35	0
2010	Myrtle Beach	Carolina	20	117¹/₃	4	7	.364	120	32	89	2.76	0
2010	Mississippi.......	Southern	8	43²/₃	3	5	.375	42	20	36	4.74	0
2011	Mississippi.......	Southern	21	117¹/₃	5	5	.500	110	46	116	3.84	0
2011	Gwinnett.............	Int.	4	21²/₃	2	2	.500	25	11	19	4.15	0
2011	Atlanta	N.L.	7	35	1	1	.500	18	14	29	2.83	0

DEL ROSARIO, ENERIO
Born, Santa Lucia, Dominican Republic, October 16, 1985.
Bats Right. Throws Right. Height, 6 feet, 2 inches. Weight, 180 pounds.

Year	Club	Lea	G	IP	W	L	Pct	SO	BB	H	ERA	SAVES
2007	Billings............	Pioneer	15	70¹/₃	5	4	.556	40	30	77	3.97	0
2008	Sarasota............	Fla.St.	13	44¹/₃	1	4	.200	32	23	57	6.09	0
2008	Dayton	Midwest	19	70	5	2	.714	49	11	52	1.16	5
2009	Sarasota............	Fla.St.	31	50	2	1	.667	33	6	40	1.98	7
2009	Carolina	Southern	4	5²/₃	0	0	.000	9	0	2	1.59	1
2009	Louisville	Int.	15	24²/₃	1	0	1.000	12	6	24	1.09	4
2010	Louisville	Int.	50	64	4	4	.500	34	17	61	3.09	4
2010	Cincinnati-Houston a	N.L.	11	10	1	1	.500	4	4	17	4.50	0
2011	Astros	Gulf Coast	1	1	0	0	.000	2	0	2	9.00	0
2011	Oklahoma	P.C.	3	3	0	0	.000	0	0	3	0.00	0
2011	Houston b	N.L.	54	53	0	3	.000	31	31	59	4.58	0
Major League Totals	2 Yrs.		65	63	1	4	.200	35	35	76	4.57	0

a Sold to Houston Astros, September 16, 2010.
b On disabled list from August 6 to September 2, 2011.

DEMPSTER, RYAN SCOTT

Born, Sechelt, British Columbia, Canada, May 3, 1977.
Bats Right. Throws Right. Height, 6 feet, 2 inches. Weight, 215 pounds.

Year	Club	Lea	G	IP	W	L	Pct	SO	BB	H	ERA	SAVES
1995	Rangers	Gulf Coast	8	34$\frac{1}{3}$	3	1	.750	37	17	34	2.36	0
1995	Hudson Val.	N.Y.-Penn.	1	5$\frac{2}{3}$	1	0	1.000	6	1	7	3.18	0
1996	Chston-SC	So.Atl.	23	144$\frac{1}{3}$	7	11	.389	141	58	120	3.30	0
1996	Kane County a	Midwest	4	26$\frac{1}{3}$	2	1	.667	16	18	18	2.73	0
1997	Brevard Cty	Fla.St.	28	165$\frac{1}{3}$	10	9	.526	131	46	190	4.90	0
1998	Portland	Eastern	7	44$\frac{2}{3}$	4	3	.571	33	15	34	3.22	0
1998	Florida	N.L.	14	54$\frac{2}{3}$	1	5	.167	35	38	72	7.08	0
1998	Charlotte	Int.	5	33	3	1	.750	24	12	33	3.27	0
1999	Calgary	P.C.	5	30$\frac{2}{3}$	1	1	.500	29	10	30	4.99	0
1999	Florida	N.L.	25	147	7	8	.467	126	93	146	4.71	0
2000	Florida	N.L.	33	226$\frac{1}{3}$	14	10	.583	209	97	210	3.66	0
2001	Florida	N.L.	34	211$\frac{1}{3}$	15	12	.556	171	112	218	4.94	0
2002	Florida-Cincinnati b	N.L.	33	209	10	13	.435	153	93	228	5.38	0
2003	Cincinnati	N.L.	22	115$\frac{2}{3}$	3	7	.300	84	70	134	6.54	0
2003	Louisville c	Int.	2	13$\frac{2}{3}$	1	1	.500	9	3	13	3.29	0
2004	Lansing	Midwest	5	18$\frac{1}{3}$	0	0	.000	21	2	20	1.96	0
2004	Iowa	P.C.	6	21	1	1	.500	20	10	19	3.86	0
2004	Chicago d-e	N.L.	23	20$\frac{2}{3}$	1	1	.500	18	13	16	3.92	2
2005	Chicago	N.L.	63	92	5	3	.625	89	49	83	3.13	33
2006	Chicago	N.L.	74	75	1	9	.100	67	36	77	4.80	24
2007	Iowa	P.C.	2	2	0	0	.000	4	1	1	0.00	0
2007	Chicago f	N.L.	66	66$\frac{2}{3}$	2	7	.222	55	30	59	4.72	28
2008	Chicago g	N.L.	33	206$\frac{2}{3}$	17	6	.739	187	76	174	2.96	0
2009	Chicago h	N.L.	31	200	11	9	.550	172	65	196	3.65	0
2010	Chicago	N.L.	34	215$\frac{1}{3}$	15	12	.556	208	86	198	3.85	0
2011	Chicago	N.L.	34	202$\frac{1}{3}$	10	14	.417	191	82	211	4.80	0
Major League Totals	14 Yrs.		519	2042$\frac{2}{3}$	112	116	.491	1765	940	2022	4.41	87

Division Series

Year	Club	Lea	G	IP	W	L	Pct	SO	BB	H	ERA	SAVES
2007	Chicago	N.L.	1	1	0	0	.000	2	0	0	0.00	0
2008	Chicago	N.L.	1	4$\frac{2}{3}$	0	1	.000	2	7	4	7.71	0
Division Series Totals			2	5$\frac{2}{3}$	0	1	.000	4	7	4	6.35	0

a Traded by Texas Rangers to Florida Marlins with player to be named later for pitcher John Burkett, August 8, 1996. Florida Marlins received pitcher Rick Helling to complete trade, September 3, 1996.
b Traded to Cincinnati Reds for outfielder Juan Encarnacion, infielder Wilton Guerrero and pitcher Ryan Snare, July 11, 2002.
c On disabled list from May 23 to June 7 and July 29 to November 3, 2003.
d Waived by Cincinnati Reds, November 4, 2003. Signed with Chicago Cubs, January 21, 2004.
e On disabled list from March 26 to August 1, 2004.
f On disabled list from June 23 to July 20, 2007.
g Filed for free agency, October 30, 2008, re-signed with Chicago Cubs, November 18, 2008.
h On disabled list from July 7 to July 28, 2009.

DETWILER, ROSS EMERY

Born, St.Louis, Missouri, March 6, 1986.
Bats Right. Throws Right. Height, 6 feet, 5 inches. Weight, 185 pounds.

Year	Club	Lea	G	IP	W	L	Pct	SO	BB	H	ERA	SAVES
2007	Nationals	Gulf Coast	4	12	0	0	.000	15	3	11	2.25	0
2007	Potomac	Carolina	5	21$\frac{1}{3}$	2	2	.500	13	9	27	4.22	0
2007	Washington	N.L.	1	1	0	0	.000	1	0	0	0.00	0
2008	Potomac	Carolina	26	124	8	8	.500	114	57	140	4.86	0
2009	Harrisburg	Eastern	6	27$\frac{1}{3}$	0	3	.000	28	10	28	2.96	0
2009	Syracuse	Int.	10	49$\frac{1}{3}$	4	2	.667	42	20	56	3.10	0
2009	Washington	N.L.	15	75$\frac{2}{3}$	1	6	.143	43	33	87	5.00	0
2010	Potomac	Carolina	2	6	0	0	.000	6	1	6	1.50	0
2010	Harrisburg	Eastern	7	32$\frac{2}{3}$	2	2	.500	31	7	38	2.48	0
2010	Syracuse	Int.	1	5	1	0	1.000	2	1	5	1.80	0
2010	Washington a	N.L.	8	29$\frac{2}{3}$	1	3	.250	17	14	34	4.25	0
2011	Syracuse	Int.	16	87$\frac{1}{3}$	6	6	.500	63	32	98	4.53	0
2011	Washington	N.L.	15	66	4	5	.444	41	20	63	3.00	0
Major League Totals	4 Yrs.		39	172$\frac{1}{3}$	6	14	.300	102	67	184	4.07	0

a On disabled list from April 4 to June 21 and August 6 to September 7, 2010.

DICKEY, ROBERT ALAN (R.A.)
Born, Nashville, Tennessee, October 29, 1974.
Bats Right. Throws Right. Height, 6 feet, 3 inches. Weight, 220 pounds.

Year	Club	Lea	G	IP	W	L	Pct	SO	BB	H	ERA	SAVES
1997	Charlotte	Fla.St.	8	35	1	4	.200	32	12	51	6.94	0
1998	Charlotte	Fla.St.	57	60	1	5	.167	53	22	58	3.30	38
1999	Oklahoma	P.C.	6	22²/₃	2	2	.500	17	7	23	4.37	0
1999	Tulsa	Texas	35	95	6	7	.462	59	40	105	4.55	10
2000	Oklahoma	P.C.	30	158¹/₃	8	9	.471	85	65	167	4.49	1
2001	Oklahoma	P.C.	24	163	11	7	.611	120	45	164	3.75	0
2001	Texas	A.L.	4	12	0	1	.000	4	7	13	6.75	0
2002	Oklahoma	P.C.	37	154	8	7	.533	109	47	176	4.09	0
2003	Oklahoma	P.C.	3	15	1	1	.500	4	3	14	1.20	0
2003	Texas	A.L.	38	116²/₃	9	8	.529	94	38	135	5.09	1
2004	Frisco	Texas	4	13²/₃	1	1	.500	9	1	16	1.98	0
2004	Texas a	A.L.	25	104¹/₃	6	7	.462	57	33	136	5.61	1
2005	Oklahoma	P.C.	19	121²/₃	10	6	.625	81	39	152	5.99	0
2005	Texas b	A.L.	9	29²/₃	1	2	.333	15	17	29	6.67	0
2006	Texas	A.L.	1	3¹/₃	0	1	.000	1	1	8	18.90	0
2006	Oklahoma	P.C.	22	131²/₃	9	8	.529	61	46	134	4.92	1
2007	Nashville c-d-e	P.C.	31	169¹/₃	13	6	.684	119	60	159	3.72	0
2008	Tacoma	P.C.	7	49²/₃	2	5	.286	30	8	58	3.44	0
2008	Seattle f-g	A.L.	32	112¹/₃	5	8	.385	58	51	124	5.21	0
2009	Rochester	Int.	5	33¹/₃	2	1	.667	18	9	39	5.13	0
2009	Minnesota h	A.L.	35	64¹/₃	1	1	.500	42	30	74	4.62	0
2010	Buffalo	Int.	8	60²/₃	4	2	.667	37	8	55	2.23	0
2010	New York	N.L.	27	174¹/₃	11	9	.550	104	42	165	2.84	0
2011	New York	N.L.	33	208²/₃	8	13	.381	134	54	202	3.28	0
Major League Totals		9 Yrs.	204	825²/₃	41	50	.451	509	273	886	4.34	2

a On disabled list from June 25 to July 19 and July 30 to August 23, 2004.
b On disabled list from April 13 to May 25, 2005.
c Filed for free agency, October 11, 2006. Signed with Milwaukee Brewers organization, January 10, 2007.
d Filed for free agency, October 29, 2007. Signed with Minnesota Twins organization, November 29, 2007.
e Selected by Seattle Mariners in Rule V draft, December 6, 2007.
f Seattle retained rights to Dickey for catcher Jair Fernandez, March 29, 2008.
g Filed for free agency, December 9, 2008. Signed with Minnesota Twins organization, December 26, 2008.
h Filed for free agency, October 6, 2009. Signed with New York Mets organization, December 23, 2009.

DOTEL (DIAZ), OCTAVIO EDUARDO
Born, Santo Domingo, Dominican Republic, November 25, 1973.
Bats Right. Throws Right. Height, 6 feet. Weight, 215 pounds.

Year	Club	Lea	G	IP	W	L	Pct	SO	BB	H	ERA	SAVES
1993	Mets	Dominican	15	59¹/₃	6	2	.750	48	38	46	4.10	0
1994	Mets	Dominican	15	81¹/₃	5	0	1.000	95	31	84	4.32	0
1995	Mets	Gulf Coast	13	74¹/₃	7	4	.636	86	17	48	2.18	0
1995	St. Lucie	Fla.St.	3	8	1	0	1.000	9	4	10	5.63	0
1996	Columbia	So.Atl.	22	115¹/₃	11	3	.786	142	49	89	3.59	0
1997	Mets	Gulf Coast	3	9¹/₃	0	0	.000	7	2	9	0.96	1
1997	St. Lucie	Fla.St.	9	50	5	2	.714	39	23	44	2.52	0
1997	Binghamton	Eastern	12	55²/₃	3	4	.429	40	38	66	5.98	0
1998	Binghamton	Eastern	10	68²/₃	4	2	.667	82	24	41	1.97	0
1998	Norfolk	Int.	17	99	8	6	.571	118	43	82	3.45	0
1999	Norfolk	Int.	13	70¹/₃	5	2	.714	90	34	52	3.84	0
1999	New York a	N.L.	19	85¹/₃	8	3	.727	85	49	69	5.38	0
2000	Houston	N.L.	50	125	3	7	.300	142	61	127	5.40	16
2001	Houston	N.L.	61	105	7	5	.583	145	47	79	2.66	2
2002	Houston	N.L.	83	97¹/₃	6	4	.600	118	27	58	1.85	6
2003	Houston	N.L.	76	87	6	4	.600	97	31	53	2.48	4
2004	Houston	N.L.	32	34²/₃	0	0	.000	50	15	27	3.12	14
2004	Oakland b-c	A.L.	45	50²/₃	6	2	.750	72	18	41	4.09	22
2005	Oakland d-e	A.L.	15	15¹/₃	1	2	.333	16	11	10	3.52	7
2006	Staten Island	N.Y.-Penn.	1	1	0	0	.000	1	0	2	0.00	0
2006	Yankees	Gulf Coast	3	3	0	0	.000	6	1	0	0.00	0
2006	Tampa	Fla.St.	2	2	0	0	.000	2	0	1	0.00	0
2006	Trenton	Eastern	2	2	0	0	.000	3	0	1	0.00	0
2006	Columbus	Int.	5	5¹/₃	0	0	.000	8	0	6	3.38	0
2006	New York f-g	A.L.	14	10	0	0	.000	7	11	18	10.80	0
2007	Wichita	Texas	3	3	0	1	.000	4	0	2	3.00	1
2007	Kansas City	A.L.	24	23	2	1	.667	29	11	24	3.91	11
2007	Atlanta h-i-j	N.L.	9	7²/₃	0	0	.000	12	1	5	4.70	0

Year	Club	Lea	G	IP	W	L	Pct	SO	BB	H	ERA	SAVES
2008 Chicago	A.L.	72	67	4	4	.500	92	29	52	3.76	1
2009 Chicago k	A.L.	62	62^{1}/$_{3}$	3	3	.500	75	36	54	3.32	0
2010 Pitt-LA-Col l-m-n	N.L.	68	64	3	4	.429	75	32	52	4.08	22
2011 Toronto	A.L.	36	29^{1}/$_{3}$	2	1	.667	30	12	20	3.68	1
2011 St. Louis o-p-q	N.L.	29	24^{2}/$_{3}$	3	3	.500	32	5	16	3.28	2
Major League Totals . . . . 13 Yrs.			695	888^{1}/$_{3}$	54	47	.535	1077	396	705	3.74	108
Division Series												
1999 New York	N.L.	1	0^{1}/$_{3}$	0	0	.000	0	2	1	54.00	0
2001 Houston	N.L.	2	3^{1}/$_{3}$	0	0	.000	5	0	5	5.40	0
2008 Chicago	A.L.	4	1^{1}/$_{3}$	0	0	.000	3	0	2	13.50	0
2011 St. Louis	N.L.	3	2^{2}/$_{3}$	1	0	1.000	4	0	0	0.00	0
Division Series Totals			10	7^{2}/$_{3}$	1	0	1.000	12	2	8	7.04	0
Championship Series												
1999 New York	N.L.	1	3	1	0	1.000	5	2	4	3.00	0
2011 St. Louis	N.L.	4	4	1	0	1.000	5	1	2	2.25	0
Championship Series Totals			5	7	2	0	1.000	10	3	6	2.57	0
World Series Record												
2011 St. Louis	N.L.	5	3^{2}/$_{3}$	0	1	.000	5	1	3	4.91	0

a Traded with Roger Cedeno and Kyle Kessel to Houston for Mike Hampton and Derek Bell December 23, 1999.
b Traded to Kansas City Royals with catcher John Buck for outfielder Carlos Beltran, June 24, 2004.
c Traded to Oakland Athletics with cash for pitcher Mike Wood and infielder Mark Teahen, June 24, 2004.
d On disabled list from May 19 to October 28, 2005.
e Filed for free agency, October 28, 2005. Signed with New York Yankees, December 29, 2005.
f On disabled list from March 24 to August 16, 2006.
g Filed for free agency, October 28, 2006. Signed with Kansas City Royals, December 8, 2006.
h On disabled list from March 30 to May 22, 2007 and August 8 to September 20, 2007.
i Traded to Atlanta Braves for pitcher Kyle Davies, July 31, 2007.
j Filed for free agency, November 6, 2007. Signed with Chicago White Sox, January 22, 2008.
k Filed for free agency, November 9, 2009. Signed with Pittsburgh Pirates, January 21, 2010.
l Traded to Los Angeles Dodgers for pitcher James McDonald and outfielder Andrew Lambo, July 31, 2010.
m Traded to Colorado Rockies for player to be named later, September 18, 2010. Los Angeles Dodgers received outfielder Anthony Jackson to complete trade, November 15, 2010.
n Filed for free agency, November 3, 2010. Signed with Toronto Blue Jays, January 4, 2011.
o On disabled list from March 22 to April 8, 2011.
p Traded to St. Louis Cardinals with pitcher Edwin Jackson, pitcher Marc Rzepczynski, outfielder Corey Patterson and cash for outfielder Colby Rasmus, pitcher Trever Miller, pitcher Brian Tallet and pitcher P.J. Walters, July 27, 2011.
q Filed for free agency, October 31, 2011. Signed with Detroit Tigers, December 9, 2011.

DOWNS, SCOTT JEREMY

Born, Louisville, Kentucky, March 17, 1976.
Bats Left. Throws Left. Height, 6 feet, 2 inches. Weight, 210 pounds.

Year	Club	Lea	G	IP	W	L	Pct	SO	BB	H	ERA	SAVES
1997 Williamsprt.	N.Y.-Penn.	5	23	0	2	.000	28	7	15	2.74	0
1997 Rockford	Midwest	5	36	3	0	1.000	43	8	17	1.25	0
1998 Daytona a	Fla.St.	27	161^{2}/$_{3}$	8	9	.471	117	55	179	3.90	0
1999 New Britain	Eastern	6	19^{2}/$_{3}$	0	0	.000	22	10	33	8.69	0
1999 Daytona	Fla.St.	7	48	5	0	1.000	41	11	41	1.88	0
1999 Fort Myers	Fla.St.	2	9^{2}/$_{3}$	0	1	.000	9	6	7	0.00	0
1999 West Tenn b	Southern	13	80	8	1	.889	101	28	56	1.35	0
2000 Chicago-Montreal c-d	N.L.	19	97	4	3	.571	63	40	122	5.29	0
2001 Montreal e	N.L.	INJURED—Did Not Play									
2002 Brevard County	Fla.St.	7	9	0	0	.000	7	2	7	3.00	1
2002 Ottawa f	Int.	17	23^{1}/$_{3}$	2	1	.667	15	3	31	5.79	0
2003 Edmonton	P.C.	21	121^{2}/$_{3}$	8	9	.471	54	39	119	4.29	0
2003 Montreal	N.L.	1	3	0	1	.000	4	3	5	15.00	0
2004 Edmonton	P.C.	22	135^{1}/$_{3}$	10	6	.625	67	26	143	3.52	0
2004 Montreal g	N.L.	12	63	3	6	.333	38	23	79	5.14	0
2005 Syracuse	Int.	7	39^{1}/$_{3}$	2	3	.400	35	3	45	4.81	0
2005 Toronto	A.L.	26	94	4	3	.571	75	34	93	4.31	0
2006 Toronto	A.L.	59	77	6	2	.750	61	30	73	4.09	1
2007 Toronto	A.L.	*81	58	4	2	.667	57	24	47	2.17	1
2008 Toronto h	A.L.	66	70^{2}/$_{3}$	0	3	.000	57	27	54	1.78	5
2009 Dunedin	Fla.St.	3	2^{1}/$_{3}$	0	0	.000	2	1	3	3.86	0
2009 Toronto i.	A.L.	48	46^{2}/$_{3}$	1	3	.250	43	13	46	3.09	9
2010 Toronto j.	A.L.	67	61^{1}/$_{3}$	5	5	.500	48	14	47	2.64	0
2011 Inland Empire.	Calif.	2	2	1	1	.500	1	1	5	9.00	0
2011 Los Angeles k	A.L.	60	53^{2}/$_{3}$	6	3	.667	35	15	39	1.34	1
Major League Totals . . . . 10 Yrs.			439	624^{1}/$_{3}$	33	31	.516	481	223	605	3.58	17

a Sent by Chicago Cubs to Minnesota Twins as player to be named later for pitcher Mike Morgan, November 3, 1998.
b Traded to Chicago Cubs with pitcher Rick Aguilera for pitcher Jason Ryan and pitcher Kyle Lohse, May 21, 1999.
c On disabled list from August 9 to October 1, 2000.
d Traded to Montreal Expos for outfielder Rondell White, July 31, 2000.
e On disabled list from March 23 to November 14, 2001.
f On disabled list from March 27 to June 10, 2002.
g Released by Montreal Expos, November 29, 2004. Signed with Toronto Blue Jays organization, December 16, 2004.
h On disabled list from September 20 to October 2, 2008.
i On disabled list from June 17 to July 8 and August 1 to August 24, 2009.
j Filed for free agency, November 1, 2010. Signed with Los Angeles Angels, December 10, 2010.
k On disabled list from March 22 to April 11 and April 14 to April 29, 2011.

DRABEK, KYLE JORDAN
Born, The Woodlands, Texas, December 8, 1987.
Bats Right. Throws Right. Height, 6 feet, 1 inch. Weight, 190 pounds.

Year Club	Lea	G	IP	W	L	Pct	SO	BB	H	ERA	SAVES
2006 Phillies	Gulf Coast	6	23⅓	1	3	.250	14	11	33	7.71	0
2007 Lakewood	So.Atl.	11	54	5	1	.833	46	23	50	4.33	0
2008 Phillies	Gulf Coast	4	12	0	1	.000	6	6	6	2.25	0
2008 Williamsport	N.Y.-Penn.	4	20⅓	1	2	.333	10	6	11	2.21	0
2009 Reading	Eastern	15	96⅓	8	2	.800	76	31	92	3.64	0
2009 Clearwater a	Fla.St.	10	61⅔	4	1	.800	74	19	49	2.48	0
2010 New Hampshire	Eastern	27	162	14	9	.609	132	68	126	2.94	0
2010 Toronto	A.L.	3	17	0	3	.000	12	5	18	4.76	0
2011 Las Vegas	P.C.	15	75	5	4	.556	45	41	111	7.44	0
2011 Toronto	A.L.	18	78⅔	4	5	.444	51	55	87	6.06	0
Major League Totals ....2 Yrs.		21	95⅔	4	8	.333	63	60	105	5.83	0

a Traded by Philadelphia Phillies to Toronto Blue Jays with pitcher Michael Taylor and catcher Travis D'Arnaud for pitcher Roy Halladay, December 16, 2009.

DUENSING, BRIAN MATTHEW
Born, Marysville, Kansas, February 22, 1983.
Bats Left. Throws Left. Height, 5 feet, 11 inches. Weight, 195 pounds.

Year Club	Lea	G	IP	W	L	Pct	SO	BB	H	ERA	SAVES
2005 Elizabethton	Appal.	12	50⅓	4	3	.571	55	16	49	2.32	0
2006 New Britain	Eastern	10	49⅓	1	2	.333	30	18	51	3.65	0
2006 Fort Myers	Fla.St.	7	40⅓	2	5	.286	33	8	47	4.24	0
2006 Beloit	Midwest	11	70⅓	2	3	.400	55	14	68	2.94	0
2007 New Britain	Eastern	9	50⅔	4	1	.800	38	7	47	2.66	0
2007 Rochester	Int.	19	116⅔	11	5	.688	86	30	115	3.24	0
2008 Rochester	Int.	25	138⅔	5	11	.313	77	34	150	4.28	0
2009 Rochester	Int.	13	75⅓	4	6	.400	44	19	87	4.66	0
2009 Minnesota	A.L.	24	84	5	2	.714	53	31	84	3.64	0
2010 Minnesota	A.L.	53	130⅔	10	3	.769	78	35	122	2.62	0
2011 Minnesota	A.L.	32	161⅔	9	14	.391	115	52	193	5.23	0
Major League Totals ....3 Yrs.		109	376⅓	24	19	.558	246	118	399	3.97	0
Division Series											
2009 Minnesota	A.L.	1	4⅔	0	1	.000	3	1	7	9.64	0
2010 Minnesota	A.L.	1	3⅓	0	1	.000	1	1	7	13.50	0
Division Series Totals		2	8	0	2	.000	4	2	14	11.25	0

DUFFY, DANIEL RICHARD (DANNY)
Born, Goleta, California, December 21, 1988.
Bats Left. Throws Left. Height, 6 feet, 3 inches. Weight, 200 pounds.

Year Club	Lea	G	IP	W	L	Pct	SO	BB	H	ERA	SAVES
2007 Royals	Arizona	11	37⅓	2	3	.400	63	17	24	1.45	0
2008 Burlington	Midwest	17	81⅔	8	4	.667	102	25	56	2.20	0
2009 Wilmington	Carolina	24	126⅔	9	3	.750	125	41	108	2.98	0
2010 Royals	Arizona	2	2⅔	0	0	.000	4	1	2	3.38	0
2010 Wilmington	Carolina	3	14	0	0	.000	18	7	8	2.57	0
2010 Idaho Falls	Pioneer	2	6	0	1	.000	6	0	4	1.50	0
2010 NW Arkansas	Texas	7	39⅔	5	2	.714	41	9	38	2.95	0
2011 Omaha	P.C.	8	42	3	1	.750	48	10	37	3.43	0
2011 Kansas City	A.L.	20	105⅓	4	8	.333	87	51	119	5.64	0

DUKE, ZACHARY THOMAS (ZACH)

Born, Clifton, Texas, April 19, 1983.
Bats Left. Throws Left. Height, 6 feet, 2 inches. Weight, 220 pounds.

Year	Club	Lea	G	IP	W	L	Pct	SO	BB	H	ERA	SAVES
2002	Pirates	Gulf Coast	11	60	8	1	.889	48	18	38	1.95	0
2003	Hickory	So.Atl.	26	141²/₃	8	7	.533	113	46	124	3.11	0
2004	Lynchburg	Carolina	17	97	10	5	.667	106	20	73	1.39	0
2004	Altoona	Eastern	9	51¹/₃	5	1	.833	36	10	41	1.58	0
2005	Indianapolis	Int.	16	108	12	3	.800	66	23	108	2.92	0
2005	Pittsburgh a	N.L.	14	84²/₃	8	2	.800	58	23	79	1.81	0
2006	Pittsburgh	N.L.	34	215¹/₃	10	15	.400	117	68	*255	4.47	0
2007	Pirates	Gulf Coast	2	6²/₃	0	0	.000	3	2	5	1.35	0
2007	State College	NY-Penn	1	5²/₃	1	0	1.000	3	2	3	1.59	0
2007	Indianapolis	Int.	1	3²/₃	0	1	.000	1	2	7	4.91	0
2007	Pittsburgh b	N.L.	20	107¹/₃	3	8	.273	41	25	161	5.53	0
2008	Pittsburgh	N.L.	31	185	5	14	.263	87	47	230	4.82	0
2009	Pittsburgh	N.L.	32	213	11	*16	.407	106	49	231	4.06	0
2010	Altoona	Eastern	2	7	0	0	.000	1	1	5	2.57	0
2010	Pittsburgh c-d	N.L.	29	159	8	15	.348	96	51	212	5.72	0
2011	Visalia	Calif.	1	5	1	0	1.000	4	0	5	1.80	0
2011	Reno	P.C.	1	5¹/₃	1	0	1.000	2	1	7	8.44	0
2011	Arizona e-f	N.L.	21	76²/₃	3	4	.429	32	19	101	4.93	1
Major League Totals	7 Yrs.		181	1041	48	74	.393	537	282	1269	4.56	1

a On disabled list from August 24 to September 16, 2005.
b On disabled list from June 29 to September 11, 2007.
c On disabled list from June 17 to July 12, 2010.
d Traded to Arizona Diamondbacks for player to be named later, November 24, 2010. Pittsburgh Pirates received pitcher Cesar Valdez to complete trade, December 9, 2010.
e On disabled list from March 22 to May 28, 2011.
f Filed for free agency, October 31, 2011.

DUNN, MICHAEL G.

Born, Farmington, New Mexico, May 23, 1985.
Bats Left. Throws Left. Height, 6 feet, 1 inch. Weight, 195 pounds.

Year	Club	Lea	G	IP	W	L	Pct	SO	BB	H	ERA	SAVES
2006	Yankees	Gulf Coast	11	24²/₃	3	0	1.000	26	9	13	0.73	4
2006	Staten Island	N.Y.-Penn.	3	6¹/₃	0	0	.000	7	7	3	5.68	0
2007	Charleston	So.Atl.	27	144²/₃	12	5	.706	138	45	136	3.42	0
2008	Trenton	Eastern	1	1²/₃	1	0	1.000	2	1	1	0.00	0
2008	Tampa	Fla.St.	30	124²/₃	4	7	.364	118	58	124	4.55	1
2009	Trenton	Eastern	26	53¹/₃	3	3	.500	76	32	41	3.71	2
2009	Scranton/WB	Int.	12	20	1	0	1.000	23	14	17	2.25	0
2009	New York a	A.L.	4	4	0	0	.000	5	5	3	6.75	0
2010	Gwinnett	Int.	38	47¹/₃	2	0	1.000	64	25	31	1.52	7
2010	Atlanta b	N.L.	25	19	2	0	1.000	27	17	15	1.89	0
2011	Florida	N.L.	72	63	5	6	.455	68	31	51	3.43	0
Major League Totals	3 Yrs.		101	86	7	6	.538	100	53	69	3.24	0
Division Series												
2010	Atlanta	N.L.	3	1¹/₃	0	0	.000	2	0	2	0.00	0

a Traded to Atlanta Braves with outfielder Melky Cabrera, pitcher Arodys Vizcaino and cash for pitcher Javier Vazquez and pitcher Boone Logan, December 22, 2009.
b Traded to Florida Marlins with infielder Omar Infante for infielder Dan Uggla, November 16, 2010.

DURBIN, CHAD GRIFFIN

Born, Spring Valley, Illinois, December 3, 1977.
Bats Both. Throws Right. Height, 6 feet, 2 inches. Weight, 200 pounds.

Year	Club	Lea	G	IP	W	L	Pct	SO	BB	H	ERA	SAVES
1996	Royals	Gulf Coast	11	44¹/₃	3	2	.600	43	25	34	4.26	0
1997	Lansing	Midwest	26	144²/₃	5	8	.385	116	53	157	4.79	0
1998	Wilmington	Carolina	26	147²/₃	10	7	.588	162	59	126	2.93	0
1999	Wichita	Texas	28	157	8	10	.444	122	49	154	4.64	0
1999	Kansas City	A.L.	1	2¹/₃	0	0	.000	3	1	1	0.00	0
2000	Kansas City	A.L.	16	72¹/₃	2	5	.286	37	43	91	8.21	0
2000	Omaha	P.C.	12	72²/₃	4	4	.500	53	22	75	4.46	0
2001	Omaha	P.C.	5	27	2	2	.500	35	6	22	3.33	0
2001	Kansas City	A.L.	29	179	9	16	.360	95	58	201	4.93	0
2002	Omaha	P.C.	1	1²/₃	0	1	.000	2	0	4	10.80	0
2002	Royals	Gulf Coast	3	6	0	0	.000	5	1	4	0.00	0

Year	Club	Lea	G	IP	W	L	Pct	SO	BB	H	ERA	SAVES
2002 Wichita.............Texas			3	5 1/3	0	0	.000	6	4	5	5.06	0
2002 Kansas City...........A.L.			2	8 1/3	0	1	.000	5	4	13	11.88	0
2003 Mahoning Valley...N.Y.-Penn.			2	12	1	1	.500	8	3	9	2.25	0
2003 Akron.............Eastern			3	12	2	0	1.000	11	1	7	1.50	0
2003 Buffalo................Int.			10	58 2/3	3	6	.333	64	16	51	4.60	0
2003 Cleveland a............A.L.			3	8 2/3	0	1	.000	8	3	18	7.27	0
2004 Cleveland.............A.L.			17	51 1/3	5	6	.455	38	24	63	6.66	0
2004 Buffalo................Int.			9	52	3	3	.500	40	16	55	3.46	0
2004 Arizona b-c............N.L.			7	9 1/3	1	1	.500	10	11	9	8.68	0
2005 New Orleans..........P.C.			26	115 1/3	4	5	.444	99	48	121	5.77	0
2006 Toledo................Int.			28	185	11	8	.579	149	46	169	3.11	0
2006 Detroit d..............A.L.			3	6	0	0	.000	3	0	6	1.50	0
2007 Detroit e..............A.L.			36	127 2/3	8	7	.533	66	49	133	4.72	1
2008 Philadelphia...........N.L.			71	87 2/3	5	4	.556	63	35	81	2.87	1
2009 Clearwater.........Fla.St.			2	3	0	0	.000	4	1	3	0.00	0
2009 Lehigh Valley..........Int.			1	1	0	0	.000	1	0	1	0.00	0
2009 Philadelphia f..........N.L.			59	69 2/3	2	2	.500	62	47	56	4.39	2
2010 Clearwater.........Fla.St.			2	3	1	0	1.000	3	0	0	0.00	0
2010 Philadelphia g-h.......N.L.			64	68 2/3	4	1	.800	63	27	63	3.80	0
2011 Cleveland i............A.L.			56	68 1/3	2	2	.500	59	26	86	5.53	0
Major League Totals.......12 Yrs.			364	759 1/3	38	46	.452	512	328	821	5.10	4
Division Series												
2008 Philadelphia...........N.L.			1	0 2/3	0	0	.000	1	0	3	0.00	0
2009 Philadelphia...........N.L.			1	1	1	0	1.000	0	0	0	0.00	0
2010 Philadelphia...........N.L.			1	0 1/3	0	0	.000	0	1	0	0.00	0
Division Series Totals...........			3	2	1	0	1.000	1	1	3	0.00	0
Championship Series												
2008 Philadelphia...........N.L.			3	2	0	0	.000	2	2	3	4.50	0
2009 Philadelphia...........N.L.			4	3	1	0	1.000	1	0	0	0.00	0
2010 Philadelphia...........N.L.			1	1	0	0	.000	1	2	2	18.00	0
Championship Series Totals......			8	6	1	0	1.000	4	4	5	4.50	0
World Series Record												
2008 Philadelphia...........N.L.			2	0 2/3	0	0	.000	0	1	1	0.00	0
2009 Philadelphia...........N.L.			2	1 1/3	0	0	.000	2	2	3	27.00	0
World Series Totals............			4	2	0	0	.000	2	3	4	18.00	0

a Not offered contract, December 20, 2002. Signed with Cleveland Indians organization, February 17, 2003.
b Claimed on waivers by Arizona Diamondbacks, August 13, 2004.
c Filed for free agency, October 11, 2004. Signed with Washington Nationals organization, December 23, 2004.
d Filed for free agency, October 28, 2005. Signed with Detroit Tigers organization, January 10, 2006.
e Not offered contract, December 12, 2007. Signed with Philadelphia Phillies, December 20, 2007.
f On disabled list from July 23 to August 10, 2009.
g On disabled list from June 24 to July 13, 2010.
h Filed for free agency, November 1, 2010. Signed with Cleveland Indians, March 1, 2011.
i Filed for free agency, October 30, 2011.

EOVALDI, NATHAN EDWARD

Born, Houston, Texas, February 13, 1990.
Bats Right. Throws Right. Height, 6 feet, 3 inches. Weight, 195 pounds.

Year	Club	Lea	G	IP	W	L	Pct	SO	BB	H	ERA	SAVES
2008 Dodgers.........Gulf Coast			6	8	0	1	.000	9	3	6	1.13	1
2008 Ogden............Pioneer			1	2 2/3	0	0	.000	2	0	1	0.00	0
2009 Great Lakes........Midwest			26	96 1/3	3	5	.375	71	41	95	3.27	1
2010 Dodgers...........Arizona			3	8 1/3	0	1	.000	10	4	6	4.32	0
2010 Inland Empire.........Calif.			16	85	3	5	.375	58	33	99	4.45	0
2010 Ogden............Pioneer			1	5	1	0	1.000	4	0	3	1.80	0
2011 Chattanooga.......Southern			20	103	6	5	.545	99	46	76	2.62	0
2011 Los Angeles...........N.L.			10	34 2/3	1	2	.333	23	20	28	3.63	0

ESTRADA, MARCO RENE

Born, Sonora, Mexico, July 5, 1983.
Bats Right. Throws Right. Height, 6 feet. Weight, 180 pounds.

Year	Club	Lea	G	IP	W	L	Pct	SO	BB	H	ERA	SAVES
2005 Vermont........N.Y.-Penn.			9	33 2/3	1	3	.250	37	16	31	5.08	1
2006 Nationals........Gulf Coast			5	23 2/3	2	0	1.000	27	6	14	1.52	0
2006 Savannah...........So.Atl.			8	37	1	4	.200	29	14	44	5.59	0
2007 Hagerstown.........So.Atl.			8	36	1	5	.167	35	17	39	5.25	0
2007 Nationals........Gulf Coast			4	11 1/3	0	0	.000	13	3	19	3.18	0

Year	Club	Lea	G	IP	W	L	Pct	SO	BB	H	ERA	SAVES
2007 Potomac..........	Carolina	11	58 1/3	5	3	.625	54	17	67	4.94	0
2008 Harrisburg	Eastern	13	74 1/3	6	3	.667	67	32	62	2.66	0
2008 Columbus.............	Int.	12	65 1/3	3	3	.500	52	21	73	3.58	0
2008 Washington	N.L.	11	12 2/3	0	0	.000	10	5	17	7.82	0
2009 Syracuse	Int.	27	136 1/3	9	5	.643	98	33	133	3.63	0
2009 Washington	N.L.	4	7 1/3	0	1	.000	9	4	6	6.14	0
2010 Nashville	P.C.	7	40	1	2	.333	33	11	30	3.15	0
2010 Milwaukee a-b	N.L.	7	11 1/3	0	0	.000	13	6	14	9.53	0
2011 Milwaukee	N.L.	43	92 2/3	4	8	.333	88	29	83	4.08	0
Major League Totals	4 Yrs.	65	124	4	9	.308	120	44	120	5.08	0
Division Series											
2011 Milwaukee	N.L.	2	3	0	0	.000	5	0	3	0.00	0
Championship Series											
2011 Milwaukee	N.L.	2	3	0	0	.000	4	2	4	12.00	0

a Claimed on waivers by Milwaukee Brewers, February 3, 2010.
b On disabled list from June 1 to October 5, 2010.

FARNSWORTH, KYLE LYNN

Born, Wichita, Kansas, April 14, 1976.
Bats Right. Throws Right. Height, 6 feet, 4 inches. Weight, 230 pounds.

Year	Club	Lea	G	IP	W	L	Pct	SO	BB	H	ERA	SAVES
1995 Cubs...........	Gulf Coast	16	31	3	2	.600	18	11	22	0.87	1
1996 Rockford.........	Midwest	20	112	9	6	.600	82	35	122	3.70	0
1997 Daytona	Fla.St.	27	156 1/3	10	10	.500	105	47	178	4.09	0
1998 West Tenn	Southern	13	81 1/3	8	2	.800	73	21	70	2.77	0
1998 Iowa.................	P.C.	18	102 2/3	5	9	.357	79	36	129	6.93	0
1999 Iowa.................	P.C.	6	39 1/3	2	2	.500	29	9	38	3.20	0
1999 Chicago	N.L.	27	130	5	9	.357	70	52	140	5.05	0
2000 Chicago	N.L.	46	77	2	9	.182	74	50	90	6.43	1
2000 Iowa.................	P.C.	22	25 1/3	0	2	.000	22	18	24	3.20	9
2001 Chicago	N.L.	76	82	4	6	.400	107	29	65	2.74	2
2002 Iowa.................	P.C.	2	3	0	1	.000	2	0	3	6.00	0
2002 Chicago a.............	N.L.	45	46 2/3	4	6	.400	46	24	53	7.33	1
2003 Chicago	N.L.	77	76 1/3	3	2	.600	92	36	53	3.30	0
2004 Chicago b.............	N.L.	72	66 2/3	4	5	.444	78	33	67	4.72	0
2005 Detroit	A.L.	46	42 2/3	1	1	.500	55	20	29	2.32	6
2005 Atlanta c-d-e	N.L.	26	27 1/3	0	0	.000	32	7	15	1.98	10
2006 New York	A.L.	72	66	3	6	.333	75	28	62	4.36	6
2007 New York	A.L.	64	60	2	1	.667	48	27	60	4.80	0
2008 New York-Detroit f-g .	A.L.	61	60 1/3	2	3	.400	61	22	70	4.48	1
2009 Omaha...............	P.C.	2	2	0	0	.000	2	0	0	0.00	0
2009 NW Arkansas	Texas	3	3 2/3	0	0	.000	3	1	1	0.00	0
2009 Kansas City h..........	A.L.	41	37 1/3	1	5	.167	42	14	43	4.58	0
2010 Kansas City	A.L.	37	44 2/3	3	0	1.000	36	12	40	2.42	0
2010 Atlanta i-j.............	N.L.	23	20	0	2	.000	25	7	15	5.40	0
2011 Tampa Bay	A.L.	63	57 2/3	5	1	.833	51	12	45	2.18	25
Major League Totals	13 Yrs.	776	894 2/3	39	56	.411	892	373	847	4.25	52
Division Series											
2003 Chicago	N.L.	3	2 2/3	0	0	.000	2	1	1	0.00	0
2005 Atlanta	N.L.	2	3	0	0	.000	4	1	2	9.00	0
2006 New York	A.L.	2	2	0	0	.000	1	1	1	0.00	0
2007 New York	A.L.	1	1	0	0	.000	2	0	1	0.00	0
2010 Atlanta	N.L.	2	2	1	0	1.000	1	1	1	0.00	0
Division Series Totals		10	10 2/3	1	0	1.000	10	4	6	2.53	0
Championship Series											
2003 Chicago	N.L.	5	5 1/3	0	0	.000	7	2	6	10.13	0

a On disabled list from April 10 to June 4, 2002.
b On disabled list from August 28 to September 12, 2004.
c Traded to Detroit Tigers for pitcher Roberto Novoa, infielder Scott Moore and outfielder Clarence Flowers, February 9, 2005.
d Traded to Atlanta Braves for pitcher Roman Colon and pitcher Zach Miner, July 26, 2005.
e Filed for free agency, October 31, 2005. Signed with New York Yankees, December 5, 2005.
f Traded to Detroit Tigers for catcher Ivan Rodriguez, July 30, 2008.
g Filed for free agency, November 3, 2008. Signed with Kansas City Royals, December 13, 2008.
h On disabled list from June 25 to August 18, 2009.
i Traded to Atlanta Braves with outfielder Rick Ankiel and cash for outfielder Gregor Blanco, pitcher Jesse Chavez and pitcher Tim Collins, July 31, 2010.
j Filed for free agency, November 1, 2010. Signed with Tampa Bay Rays, January 15, 2011.

FELDMAN, SCOTT WAYNE

Born, Kailua, Hawaii, February 7, 1983.
Bats Left. Throws Right. Height, 6 feet, 5 inches. Weight, 210 pounds.

Year	Club	Lea	G	IP	W	L	Pct	SO	BB	H	ERA	SAVES
2003 Rangers	Arizona		3	6⅓	1	1	.500	7	1	4	4.26	0
2004 Rangers	Arizona		4	7	0	0	.000	5	1	2	0.00	0
2005 Bakersfield	Calif.		6	9	0	0	.000	11	2	5	0.00	3
2005 Frisco	Texas		46	61	1	2	.333	41	23	43	2.36	14
2005 Texas	A.L.		8	9⅓	0	1	.000	4	2	9	0.96	0
2006 Oklahoma	P.C.		23	27⅓	2	2	.500	24	9	20	1.98	4
2006 Texas	A.L.		36	41⅓	0	2	.000	30	10	42	3.92	0
2007 Oklahoma	P.C.		21	30	1	1	.500	24	12	28	4.50	2
2007 Texas	A.L.		29	39	1	2	.333	19	32	44	5.77	0
2008 Frisco	Texas		2	12⅔	2	0	1.000	4	2	11	4.26	0
2008 Texas	A.L.		28	151⅓	6	8	.429	74	56	161	5.29	0
2009 Texas	A.L.		34	189⅔	17	8	.680	113	65	178	4.08	0
2010 Oklahoma	P.C.		1	4	0	0	.000	3	0	5	4.50	0
2010 Texas a	A.L.		29	141⅓	7	11	.389	75	45	181	5.48	0
2011 Frisco	Texas		2	9	1	0	1.000	8	2	5	3.00	0
2011 Round Rock	P.C.		8	40⅔	2	1	.667	24	9	48	4.43	0
2011 Texas b	A.L.		11	32	2	1	.667	22	10	25	3.94	0
Major League Totals	7 Yrs.		175	604	33	33	.500	337	220	640	4.75	0
Division Series												
2011 Texas	A.L.		1	3	0	0	.000	4	0	2	0.00	0
Championship Series												
2011 Texas	A.L.		3	5⅔	1	0	1.000	5	0	1	0.00	0
World Series Record												
2011 Texas	A.L.		5	5	0	0	.000	2	6	5	9.00	0

a On disabled list from August 22 to September 7, 2010.
b On disabled list from March 22 to July 14, 2011.

FELIZ (ANTONIO), NEFTALI

Born, Azua, Dominican Republic, May 2, 1988.
Bats Right. Throws Right. Height, 6 feet, 3 inches. Weight, 190 pounds.

Year	Club	Lea	G	IP	W	L	Pct	SO	BB	H	ERA	SAVES
2006 Braves	Gulf Coast		11	29	0	2	.000	42	14	20	4.03	2
2007 Danville	Appal.		8	27⅓	2	0	1.000	28	12	18	1.98	0
2007 Spokane a	Northwest		8	15	0	2	.000	27	12	13	3.60	0
2008 Clinton	Midwest		17	82	6	3	.667	106	28	55	2.52	0
2008 Frisco	Texas		10	45⅓	4	3	.571	47	23	34	2.98	0
2009 Okla.	P.C.		25	77⅓	4	6	.400	75	30	69	3.49	0
2009 Texas	A.L.		20	31	1	0	1.000	39	8	13	1.74	2
2010 Texas b	A.L.		70	69⅓	4	3	.571	71	18	43	2.73	40
2011 Frisco	Texas		1	1	0	0	.000	3	0	1	0.00	0
2011 Texas c	A.L.		64	62⅓	2	3	.400	54	30	42	2.74	32
Major League Totals	3 Yrs.		154	162⅔	7	6	.538	164	56	98	2.55	74
Division Series												
2010 Texas	A.L.		2	1⅓	0	0	.000	2	3	2	6.75	0
2011 Texas	A.L.		3	3⅓	0	0	.000	2	2	2	2.70	3
Division Series Totals			5	4⅔	0	0	.000	4	5	4	3.86	3
Championship Series												
2010 Texas	A.L.		3	3	0	0	.000	5	2	0	0.00	0
2011 Texas	A.L.		4	4⅓	0	0	.000	3	2	1	0.00	1
Championship Series Totals			7	7⅓	0	0	.000	8	4	1	0.00	1
World Series Record												
2010 Texas	A.L.		2	3	0	0	.000	4	0	1	0.00	1
2011 Texas	A.L.		4	3⅔	0	0	.000	7	4	2	4.91	2
World Series Totals			6	6⅔	0	0	.000	11	4	3	2.70	3

a Traded by Atlanta Braves to Texas Rangers with catcher Jarrod Saltalamacchia, infielder Elvis Andrus, pitcher Matt Harrison and pitcher Beau James for infielder Mark Teixeira and pitcher Ron Mahay, July 31, 2007.
b Selected Rookie of the Year in American League for 2010.
c On disabled list from April 21 to May 6, 2011.

FISTER, DOUGLAS WILDES (DOUG)

Born, Merced, California, February 4, 1984.
Bats Left. Throws Right. Height, 6 feet, 8 inches. Weight, 200 pounds.

Year	Club	Lea	G	IP	W	L	Pct	SO	BB	H	ERA	SAVES
2006 Everett	Northwest		20	40	3	5	.375	35	11	35	2.25	4
2007 West Tenn	Southern		24	131	7	8	.467	85	32	156	4.60	0
2008 West Tenn	Southern		31	134$^{1}/_{3}$	6	14	.300	104	45	155	5.43	0
2009 West Tenn	Southern		2	5$^{2}/_{3}$	1	0	1.000	5	1	2	0.00	0
2009 Tacoma	P.C.		22	106$^{1}/_{3}$	6	4	.600	79	11	132	3.81	0
2009 Seattle	A.L.		11	61	3	4	.429	36	15	63	4.13	0
2010 Tacoma	P.C.		1	4	0	0	.000	3	0	4	4.50	0
2010 Seattle a	A.L.		28	171	6	14	.300	93	32	187	4.11	0
2011 Seattle-Detroit b	A.L.		32	216$^{1}/_{3}$	11	13	.458	146	37	193	2.83	0
Major League Totals	3 Yrs.		71	448$^{1}/_{3}$	20	31	.392	275	84	443	3.49	0
Division Series												
2011 Detroit	A.L.		2	9$^{2}/_{3}$	1	1	.500	10	4	12	6.52	0
Championship Series												
2011 Detroit	A.L.		1	7$^{1}/_{3}$	1	0	1.000	3	0	7	2.45	0

a On disabled list from June 1 to June 25, 2010.

b Traded to Detroit Tigers with pitcher David Pauley for pitcher Charlie Furbush, outfielder Casper Wells, infielder Francisco Martinez and player to be named later, July 30, 2011. Seattle Mariners received pitcher Chance Ruffin to complete trade, August 17, 2011.

FLOYD, GAVIN CHRISTOPHER

Born, Annapolis, Maryland, January 27, 1983.
Bats Right. Throws Right. Height, 6 feet, 4 inches. Weight, 230 pounds.

Year	Club	Lea	G	IP	W	L	Pct	SO	BB	H	ERA	SAVES
2002 Lakewood	So.Atl.		27	166	11	10	.524	140	64	119	2.77	0
2003 Clearwater	Fla.St.		24	138	7	8	.467	115	45	128	3.00	0
2004 Reading	Eastern		20	119	6	6	.500	94	46	93	2.57	0
2004 Scranton-WB	Int.		5	30$^{2}/_{3}$	1	3	.250	18	9	39	4.99	0
2004 Philadelphia	N.L.		6	28$^{1}/_{3}$	2	0	1.000	24	16	25	3.49	0
2005 Scranton-WB	Int.		24	137$^{1}/_{3}$	6	9	.400	97	66	155	6.16	0
2005 Philadelphia	N.L.		7	26	1	2	.333	17	16	30	10.04	0
2006 Philadelphia	N.L.		11	54$^{1}/_{3}$	4	3	.571	34	32	70	7.29	0
2006 Scranton-WB a	Int.		17	115	7	4	.636	85	38	117	4.23	0
2007 Charlotte	Int.		17	106$^{2}/_{3}$	7	3	.700	96	35	93	3.12	0
2007 Chicago	A.L.		16	70	1	5	.167	49	19	85	5.27	0
2008 Chicago	A.L.		33	206$^{1}/_{3}$	17	8	.680	145	70	190	3.84	0
2009 Chicago	A.L.		30	193	11	11	.500	163	59	178	4.06	0
2010 Chicago	A.L.		31	187$^{1}/_{3}$	10	13	.435	151	58	199	4.08	0
2011 Chicago	A.L.		31	193$^{2}/_{3}$	12	13	.480	151	45	180	4.37	0
Major League Totals	8 Yrs.		165	959	58	55	.513	734	315	957	4.50	0
Division Series												
2008 Chicago	A.L.		1	3	0	1	.000	4	2	5	12.00	0

a Traded to Chicago White Sox with player to be named later for pitcher Freddy Garcia, December 6, 2006. Chicago White Sox received pitcher Gio Gonzalez to complete trade, December 7, 2006.

FRANCIS, JEFFREY WILLIAM (JEFF)

Born, Vancouver, British Columbia, Canada, January 8, 1981.
Bats Left. Throws Left. Height, 6 feet, 5 inches. Weight, 220 pounds.

Year	Club	Lea	G	IP	W	L	Pct	SO	BB	H	ERA	SAVES
2002 Tri-City	Northwest		4	10$^{2}/_{3}$	0	0	.000	16	4	5	0.00	0
2002 Asheville	So.Atl.		4	20	0	0	.000	23	4	16	1.80	0
2003 Visalia	Calif.		27	160$^{2}/_{3}$	12	9	.571	153	45	135	3.47	0
2004 Tulsa	Texas		17	113$^{2}/_{3}$	13	1	.929	147	22	73	1.98	0
2004 Colorado Springs	P.C.		7	41	3	2	.600	49	7	35	2.85	0
2004 Colorado	N.L.		7	36$^{2}/_{3}$	3	2	.600	32	13	42	5.15	0
2005 Colorado	N.L.		33	183$^{2}/_{3}$	14	12	.538	128	70	228	5.68	0
2006 Colorado	N.L.		32	199	13	11	.542	117	69	187	4.16	0
2007 Colorado	N.L.		34	215$^{1}/_{3}$	17	9	.654	165	63	234	4.22	0
2008 Tulsa	Texas		3	14$^{1}/_{3}$	1	0	1.000	19	2	12	0.63	0
2008 Colorado a	N.L.		24	143$^{2}/_{3}$	4	10	.286	94	49	164	5.01	0
2009 Colorado b	N.L.					INJURED—Did Not Play						
2010 Tulsa	Texas		2	11$^{2}/_{3}$	0	0	.000	5	2	11	1.54	0
2010 Colorado Springs	P.C.		1	3	0	0	.000	3	1	1	0.00	0
2010 Colorado c-d	N.L.		20	104$^{1}/_{3}$	4	6	.400	67	23	119	5.00	0
2011 Kansas City e	A.L.		31	183	6	16	.273	91	39	224	4.82	0
Major League Totals	7 Yrs.		181	1065$^{2}/_{3}$	61	66	.480	694	326	1198	4.78	0

Year	Club	Lea	G	IP	W	L	Pct	SO	BB	H	ERA	SAVES
	Division Series											
2007	Colorado	N.L.	1	6	1	0	1.000	8	2	4	3.00	0
	Championship Series											
2007	Colorado	N.L.	1	6²/₃	1	0	1.000	4	1	7	1.35	0
	World Series Record											
2007	Colorado	N.L.	1	4	0	1	.000	3	3	10	13.50	0

a On disabled list from June 29 to August 6, 2008.
b On disabled list from March 27 to November 13, 2009.
c On disabled list from April 2 to May 16 and August 12 to September 7, 2010.
d Filed for free agency, November 3, 2010. Signed with Kansas City Royals, January 14, 2011.
e Filed for free agency, October 30, 2011.

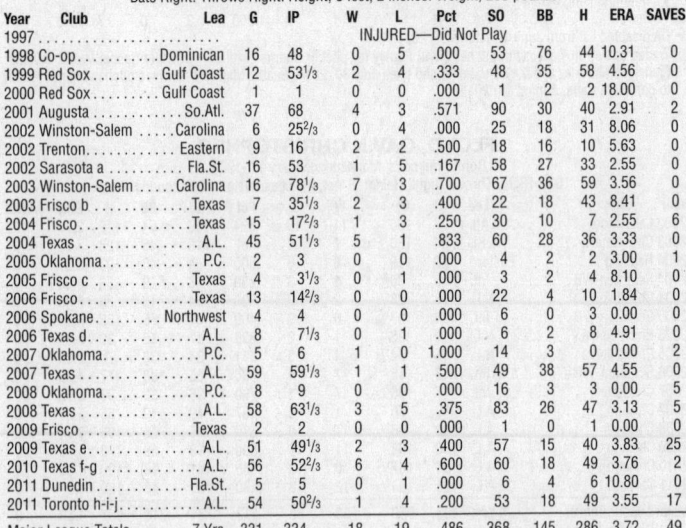

FRANCISCO, FRANKLIN (FRANK)

Born, Santo Domingo, Dominican Republic, September 11, 1979.
Bats Right. Throws Right. Height, 6 feet, 2 inches. Weight, 235 pounds.

Year	Club	Lea	G	IP	W	L	Pct	SO	BB	H	ERA	SAVES
1997	. . . .			INJURED—Did Not Play								
1998	Co-op	Dominican	16	48	0	5	.000	53	76	44	10.31	0
1999	Red Sox	Gulf Coast	12	53¹/₃	2	4	.333	48	35	58	4.56	0
2000	Red Sox	Gulf Coast	1	1	0	0	.000	1	2	2	18.00	0
2001	Augusta	So.Atl.	37	68	4	3	.571	90	30	40	2.91	2
2002	Winston-Salem	Carolina	6	25²/₃	0	4	.000	25	18	31	8.06	0
2002	Trenton	Eastern	9	16	2	2	.500	18	16	10	5.63	0
2002	Sarasota a	Fla.St.	16	53	1	5	.167	58	27	33	2.55	0
2003	Winston-Salem	Carolina	16	78¹/₃	7	3	.700	67	36	59	3.56	0
2003	Frisco b	Texas	7	35¹/₃	2	3	.400	22	18	43	8.41	0
2004	Frisco	Texas	15	17²/₃	1	3	.250	30	10	7	2.55	6
2004	Texas	A.L.	45	51¹/₃	5	1	.833	60	28	36	3.33	0
2005	Oklahoma	P.C.	2	3	0	0	.000	4	2	2	3.00	1
2005	Frisco c	Texas	4	3¹/₃	0	1	.000	3	2	4	8.10	0
2006	Frisco	Texas	13	14²/₃	0	0	.000	22	4	10	1.84	0
2006	Spokane	Northwest	4	4	0	0	.000	6	0	3	0.00	0
2006	Texas d	A.L.	8	7¹/₃	0	1	.000	6	2	8	4.91	0
2007	Oklahoma	P.C.	5	6	1	0	1.000	14	3	0	0.00	2
2007	Texas	A.L.	59	59¹/₃	1	1	.500	49	38	57	4.55	0
2008	Oklahoma	P.C.	8	9	0	0	.000	16	3	3	0.00	5
2008	Texas	A.L.	58	63¹/₃	3	5	.375	83	26	47	3.13	5
2009	Frisco	Texas	2	2	0	0	.000	1	0	1	0.00	0
2009	Texas e	A.L.	51	49¹/₃	2	3	.400	57	15	40	3.83	25
2010	Texas f-g	A.L.	56	52²/₃	6	4	.600	60	18	49	3.76	2
2011	Dunedin	Fla.St.	5	5	0	1	.000	6	4	6	10.80	0
2011	Toronto h-i-j	A.L.	54	50²/₃	1	4	.200	53	18	49	3.55	17

Major League Totals . . . . .7 Yrs. 331 334 18 19 .486 368 145 286 3.72 49

a Traded to Chicago White Sox by Boston Red Sox with pitcher Byeong An for pitcher Bob Howry, July 31, 2002.
b Sent to Texas Rangers as one of the players to be named later for outfielder Carl Everett, July 23, 2003.
c On disabled list from March 25 to October 12, 2005.
d On disabled list from March 24 to June 19, 2006.
e On disabled list from May 7 to May 22 and June 4 to June 20 and July 11 to August 2, 2009.
f On disabled list from August 28 to November 1, 2010.
g Filed for free agency, November 1, 2010, accepted arbitration to remain with Texas Rangers, November 30, 2010.
h Traded to Toronto Blue Jays for catcher Mike Napoli, January 25, 2011.
i On disabled list from March 22 to April 19, 2011.
j Filed for free agency, October 30, 2011. Signed with New York Mets, December 19, 2011.

FRASOR, JASON ANDREW

Born, Chicago, Illinois, August 9, 1977.
Bats Right. Throws Right. Height, 5 feet, 10 inches. Weight, 170 pounds.

Year	Club	Lea	G	IP	W	L	Pct	SO	BB	H	ERA	SAVES
1999	Oneonta	N.Y.-Penn.	12	58²/₃	3	3	.500	69	22	36	1.69	0
1999	West Michigan	Midwest	4	24	2	1	.667	33	9	17	2.63	0
2000	West Michigan	Midwest	14	71¹/₃	5	3	.625	65	29	55	3.28	0
2001	West Michigan a . . .	Midwest		INJURED—Did Not Play								
2002	Lakeland b	Fla.St.	24	117	5	6	.455	87	46	112	3.54	0
2003	Vero Beach	Fla.St.	15	24¹/₃	1	0	1.000	36	4	16	1.85	6
2003	Jacksonville	Southern	35	36²/₃	1	0	1.000	50	14	33	2.95	17
2004	Syracuse	Int.	3	4	0	0	.000	6	5	1	2.25	0
2004	Toronto c	A.L.	63	68¹/₃	4	6	.400	54	36	64	4.08	17
2005	Toronto	A.L.	67	74²/₃	3	5	.375	62	28	67	3.25	1

Year Club	Lea	G	IP	W	L	Pct	SO	BB	H	ERA	SAVES
2006 Syracuse ....Int.	18	$20^{1/3}$	3	1	.750	33	13	21	3.98	1
2006 Toronto ...............A.L.	51	50	3	2	.600	51	17	47	4.32	0
2007 Toronto ...............A.L.	51	57	1	5	.167	59	23	47	4.58	3
2008 Toronto ...............A.L.	49	$47^{1/3}$	1	2	.333	42	32	36	4.18	0
2009 Toronto ...............A.L.	61	$57^{2/3}$	7	3	.700	56	16	43	2.50	11
2010 Toronto d ..............A.L.	69	$63^{2/3}$	3	4	.429	65	27	61	3.68	4
2011 Toronto-Chicago e-f.....A.L.	64	60	3	3	.500	57	26	58	3.60	0
Major League Totals ....8 Yrs.	475	$478^{2/3}$	25	30	.455	446	205	423	3.74	36

a On minor league disabled list, April 5 to September 14, 2001.
b Sent by Detroit Tigers to Los Angeles Dodgers as player to be named later for infielder Hiram Bocachica, September 18, 2002.
c Traded to Toronto Blue Jays for outfielder Jayson Werth, March 30, 2004.
d Filed for free agency, November 1, 2010, accepted arbitration to remain with Toronto Blue Jays, November 30, 2010.
e Traded to Chicago White Sox with pitcher Zach Stewart for pitcher Edwin Jackson and infielder Mark Teahen, July 27, 2011.
f Traded to Toronto Blue Jays for pitcher Daniel Webb and pitcher Myles Jaye, January 1, 2012.

FRIERI (GUTIERREZ), ERNESTO

Born, Bolivar, Colombia, July 19, 1985.
Bats Right. Throws Right. Height, 6 feet, 2 inches. Weight, 200 pounds.

Year Club	Lea	G	IP	W	L	Pct	SO	BB	H	ERA	SAVES
2005 Lake Elsinore .... Calif.	2	$3^{1/3}$	0	0	.000	3	1	3	2.70	0
2005 Padres .... Arizona	17	$46^{1/3}$	7	1	.875	59	29	21	1.17	0
2006 Fort Wayne......... Midwest	1	1	0	0	.000	1	5	1	9.00	0
2006 Lake Elsinore .... Calif.	2	6	0	0	.000	4	3	8	6.00	0
2006 Eugene.......... Northwest	27	$37^{2/3}$	3	3	.500	38	15	31	3.82	2
2007 Fort Wayne......... Midwest	40	$64^{1/3}$	1	2	.333	65	23	48	2.64	0
2007 Lake Elsinore .... Calif.	13	$21^{2/3}$	1	0	1.000	27	6	11	1.25	1
2008 Portland .... P.C.	1	6	1	0	1.000	7	2	2	1.50	0
2008 Lake Elsinore .... Calif.	33	$123^{2/3}$	8	6	.571	108	32	125	4.00	0
2008 San Antonio ....Texas	2	11	1	0	1.000	10	2	7	4.09	0
2009 San Antonio ....Texas	27	$140^{1/3}$	10	9	.526	118	62	125	3.59	0
2009 San Diego .............N.L.	2	2	0	0	.000	2	1	0	0.00	0
2010 Portland .... P.C.	34	$37^{2/3}$	3	1	.750	49	18	14	1.43	17
2010 San Diego .............N.L.	33	$31^{2/3}$	1	1	.500	41	17	18	1.71	0
2011 Tucson................ P.C.	4	$3^{1/3}$	1	0	1.000	5	2	3	2.70	0
2011 San Diego a ...........N.L.	59	63	1	3	.333	76	34	51	2.71	0
Major League Totals ....3 Yrs.	94	$96^{2/3}$	2	3	.400	119	52	69	2.33	0

a On disabled list from August 8 to August 21, 2011.

FUENTES, BRIAN CHRISTOPHER

Born, Merced, California, August 9, 1975.
Bats Left. Throws Left. Height, 6 feet, 4 inches. Weight, 230 pounds.

Year Club	Lea	G	IP	W	L	Pct	SO	BB	H	ERA	SAVES
1996 Everett .... Northwest	13	$26^{2/3}$	0	1	.000	26	13	23	4.39	0
1997 Wisconsin .... Midwest	22	$118^{2/3}$	6	7	.462	153	59	84	3.56	0
1998 Lancaster a ......California	24	$118^{2/3}$	7	7	.500	137	81	121	4.17	0
1999 New Haven b .... Eastern	15	60	3	3	.500	66	46	53	4.95	0
2000 New Haven........ Eastern	26	$139^{2/3}$	7	12	.368	152	70	127	4.51	0
2001 Tacoma .... P.C.	35	52	3	2	.600	70	25	35	2.94	6
2001 Seattle c-d ............A.L.	10	$11^{2/3}$	1	1	.500	10	8	6	4.63	0
2002 Colorado Springs....... P.C.	41	$49^{1/3}$	3	3	.500	62	32	44	3.65	1
2002 Colorado .............N.L.	31	$26^{2/3}$	2	0	1.000	38	13	25	4.72	0
2003 Colorado .............N.L.	75	$75^{1/3}$	3	3	.500	82	34	64	2.75	4
2004 Colorado Springs....... P.C.	5	5	0	0	.000	6	3	1	0.00	0
2004 Colorado e ...........N.L.	47	$44^{2/3}$	2	4	.333	48	19	46	5.64	0
2005 Colorado .............N.L.	78	$74^{1/3}$	2	5	.286	91	34	59	2.91	31
2006 Colorado .............N.L.	66	$65^{1/3}$	3	4	.429	73	26	50	3.44	30
2007 Asheville........ So.Atl.	1	1	0	0	.000	2	0	0	0.00	0
2007 Colorado Springs....... P.C.	2	2	0	0	.000	2	0	2	0.00	0
2007 Colorado f ............N.L.	64	$61^{1/3}$	3	5	.375	56	23	46	3.08	20
2008 Colorado g ...........N.L.	67	$62^{2/3}$	1	5	.167	82	22	47	2.73	30
2009 Los Angeles ...........A.L.	65	55	1	5	.167	46	24	53	3.93	*48
2010 Rancho Cucamonga ..... Calif.	1	1	0	0	.000	1	0	0	0.00	0
2010 LA-Minnesota h-i-j......A.L.	48	48	4	1	.800	47	20	31	2.81	24
2011 Oakland ...............A.L.	67	$58^{1/3}$	2	8	.200	42	20	52	3.70	12
Major League Totals ....11 Yrs.	618	$583^{1/3}$	24	41	.369	615	243	479	3.44	199

Year Club	Lea	G	IP	W	L	Pct	SO	BB	H	ERA	SAVES
Division Series											
2007 Colorado .... N.L.		3	2⅓	1	0	1.000	4	3	1	0.00	0
2009 Los Angeles .... A.L.		2	1⅔	0	0	.000	0	1	0	0.00	2
2010 Minnesota .... A.L.		2	2⅔	0	0	.000	2	0	1	0.00	0
Division Series Totals		7	6⅔	1	0	1.000	6	4	2	0.00	2
Championship Series											
2007 Colorado .... N.L.		4	3⅔	0	0	.000	6	0	7	7.36	0
2009 Los Angeles .... A.L.		3	3	0	0	.000	3	3	1	3.00	1
Championship Series Totals		7	6⅔	0	0	.000	9	3	8	5.40	1
World Series Record											
2007 Colorado .... N.L.		3	3⅔	0	0	.000	1	2	6	9.82	0

a On disabled list from April 2 to 20, 1998.
b On disabled list from June 9 to August 22, 1999.
c On disabled list from August 26 to September 29, 2001.
d Traded to Colorado Rockies with pitcher Dennis Stark and pitcher Jose Paniagua for infielder Jeff Cirillo, December 15, 2001.
e On disabled list from June 7 to August 15, 2004.
f On disabled list from July 4 to August 14, 2007.
g Filed for free agency, November 1, 2008. Signed with Los Angeles Angels, December 31, 2008.
h On disabled list from April 6 to April 21, 2010.
i Traded to Minnesota Twins for player to be named later, August 27, 2010. Los Angeles Angels received pitcher Loek Van Mil to complete trade, September 1, 2010.
j Filed for free agency, November 1, 2010. Signed with Oakland Athletics, January 19, 2011.

FURBUSH, CHARLES R. (CHARLIE)
Born, South Portland, Maine, April 11, 1986.
Bats Left. Throws Left. Height, 6 feet, 5 inches. Weight, 215 pounds.

Year Club	Lea	G	IP	W	L	Pct	SO	BB	H	ERA	SAVES
2007 Tigers.......... Gulf Coast		4	16	2	0	1.000	23	3	11	2.81	0
2007 West Michigan...... Midwest		8	45⅔	4	1	.800	46	11	40	2.17	0
2008 a					INJURED—Did Not Play						
2009 Lakeland............ Fla.St.		24	111⅓	6	7	.462	93	32	111	3.96	0
2010 Erie............... Eastern		5	33⅓	1	0	1.000	37	10	31	3.24	0
2010 Lakeland............ Fla.St.		13	77	4	5	.444	109	14	68	3.39	0
2010 Toledo .... Int.		9	48⅔	3	4	.429	37	16	59	6.29	0
2011 Toledo .... Int.		10	54	5	3	.625	61	16	35	3.17	0
2011 Detroit-Seattle b........ A.L.		28	85⅓	4	10	.286	67	30	97	5.48	0
Major League Totals ....1 Yrs.		28	85⅓	4	10	.286	67	30	97	5.48	0

a On minor league disabled list from April 3 to September 8, 2008.
b Traded to Seattle Mariners with outfielder Casper Wells, infielder Francisco Martinez and player to be named later for pitcher Doug Fister and pitcher David Pauley, July 30, 2011. Seattle Mariners received pitcher Chance Ruffin to complete trade, August 17, 2011.

GALLARDO, YOVANI
Born, La Piedad, Mexico, February 27, 1986.
Bats Right. Throws Right. Height, 6 feet, 1 inch. Weight, 210 pounds.

Year Club	Lea	G	IP	W	L	Pct	SO	BB	H	ERA	SAVES
2004 Brewers .... Arizona		6	19⅓	0	0	.000	23	4	14	0.47	0
2004 Beloit .... Midwest		2	7⅓	0	1	.000	8	4	12	12.27	0
2005 West Virginia .... So.Atl.		26	121⅓	8	3	.727	110	51	100	2.74	1
2006 Brevard County ..... Fla.St.		13	77⅔	6	3	.667	103	23	54	2.09	0
2006 Huntsville........ Southern		13	77⅓	5	2	.714	85	28	50	1.63	0
2007 Nashville .... P.C.		13	77⅔	8	3	.727	110	28	53	2.90	0
2007 Milwaukee .... N.L.		20	110⅓	9	5	.643	101	37	103	3.67	0
2008 Nashville .... P.C.		3	15⅔	0	1	.000	18	5	20	5.17	0
2008 Milwaukee a.......... N.L.		4	24	0	0	.000	20	8	22	1.88	0
2009 Milwaukee .... N.L.		30	185⅔	13	12	.520	204	94	150	3.73	0
2010 Milwaukee b.......... N.L.		31	185	14	7	.667	200	75	178	3.84	0
2011 Milwaukee .... N.L.		33	207⅓	17	10	.630	207	59	193	3.52	0
Major League Totals ....5 Yrs.		118	712⅓	53	34	.609	732	273	646	3.63	0
Division Series											
2008 Milwaukee .... N.L.		2	7	0	1	.000	4	5	4	0.00	0
2011 Milwaukee .... N.L.		2	14	1	0	1.000	14	3	10	1.29	0
Division Series Totals..........		4	21	1	1	.500	18	8	14	0.86	0
Championship Series											
2011 Milwaukee .... N.L.		1	5	0	1	.000	2	5	8	7.20	0

a On disabled list from March 21 to April 20 and May 2 to September 23, 2008.
b On disabled list from July 5 to July 22, 2010.

GARCIA, FREDDY ANTONIO

Born, Caracas, Venezuela, October 6, 1976.
Bats Right. Throws Right. Height, 6 feet, 4 inches. Weight, 250 pounds.

Year	Club	Lea	G	IP	W	L	Pct	SO	BB	H	ERA	SAVES
1994	Hou/Mil	Dominican	16	85	4	6	.400	68	38	80	5.29	0
1995	Astros	Gulf Coast	11	58$^{1/3}$	6	3	.667	58	14	60	4.47	0
1996	Quad City	Midwest	13	60$^{2/3}$	5	4	.556	50	27	57	3.12	0
1997	Kissimmee	Fla.St.	27	179	10	8	.556	131	49	165	2.56	0
1998	Jackson	Texas	19	119$^{1/3}$	6	7	.462	115	58	94	3.24	0
1998	New Orleans	P.C.	2	14$^{1/3}$	1	0	1.000	13	1	14	3.14	0
1998	Tacoma a	P.C.	5	32$^{2/3}$	3	1	.750	30	13	30	3.86	0
1999	Seattle	A.L.	33	201$^{1/3}$	17	8	.680	170	90	205	4.07	0
2000	Seattle	A.L.	21	124$^{1/3}$	9	5	.643	79	64	112	3.91	0
2000	Everett	Northwest	2	10	0	0	.000	15	2	11	4.50	0
2000	Tacoma b	P.C.	1	7	1	0	1.000	11	2	5	2.57	0
2001	Seattle	A.L.	34	*238$^{2/3}$	18	6	.750	163	69	199	*3.05	0
2002	Seattle	A.L.	34	223$^{2/3}$	16	10	.615	181	63	227	4.39	0
2003	Seattle	A.L.	33	201$^{1/3}$	12	14	.462	144	71	196	4.51	0
2004	Seattle-Chicago c	A.L.	31	210	13	11	.542	184	64	192	3.81	0
2005	Chicago	A.L.	33	228	14	8	.636	146	60	225	3.87	0
2006	Chicago d	A.L.	33	216$^{1/3}$	17	9	.654	135	48	228	4.53	0
2007	Philadelphia	N.L.	11	58	1	5	.167	50	19	74	5.90	0
2007	Phillies	Gulf Coast	1	2	0	0	.000	2	0	2	4.50	0
2007	Clearwater e	Fla.St.	2	6$^{1/3}$	0	0	.000	8	1	5	0.00	0
2008	Lakeland	Fla.St.	1	2	0	0	.000	1	1	3	0.00	0
2008	Toledo	Int.	1	3	0	0	.000	4	0	2	0.00	0
2008	Detroit f	A.L.	3	15	1	1	.500	12	6	11	4.20	0
2009	Buffalo	Int.	2	11	0	2	.000	6	5	12	8.18	0
2009	Kannapolis	So.Atl.	1	3	0	0	.000	3	1	2	0.00	0
2009	Bristol	Appal.	2	11	0	0	.000	7	0	6	1.64	0
2009	Charlotte	Int.	1	6	0	1	.000	9	0	8	3.00	0
2009	Chicago g-h	A.L.	9	56	3	4	.429	37	12	56	4.34	0
2010	Chicago i	A.L.	28	157	12	6	.667	89	45	171	4.64	0
2011	Scranton-WB	Int.	1	4	1	0	1.000	0	1	8	4.50	0
2011	New York j-k.	A.L.	26	146$^{2/3}$	12	8	.600	96	45	152	3.62	0
Major League Totals	13 Yrs.		329	2076$^{1/3}$	145	95	.604	1486	656	2048	4.09	0
Division Series												
2000	Seattle	A.L.	1	3$^{1/3}$	0	0	.000	2	3	6	10.80	0
2001	Seattle	A.L.	2	11$^{2/3}$	1	1	.500	13	3	13	3.86	0
2005	Chicago	A.L.	1	5	1	0	1.000	1	4	5	5.40	0
2011	New York	A.L.	1	5$^{1/3}$	0	1	.000	6	0	6	5.06	0
Division Series Totals			5	25$^{1/3}$	2	2	.500	22	10	30	5.33	0
Championship Series												
2000	Seattle	A.L.	2	11$^{2/3}$	2	0	1.000	11	4	10	1.54	0
2001	Seattle	A.L.	1	7$^{1/3}$	0	1	.000	6	4	7	3.68	0
2005	Chicago	A.L.	1	9	1	0	1.000	5	1	6	2.00	0
Championship Series Totals			4	28	3	1	.750	22	9	23	2.25	0
World Series Record												
2005	Chicago	A.L.	1	7	1	0	1.000	7	3	4	0.00	0

a Traded by Houston Astros to Seattle Mariners with infielder Carlos Guillen and player to be named later for pitcher Randy Johnson, July 31, 1998. Seattle Mariners received pitcher John Halama to complete trade, October 1, 1998.

b On disabled list from April 22 to July 6, 2000.

c Traded to Chicago White Sox with catcher Ben Davis and cash for catcher Miguel Olivo, outfielder Jeremy Reed and infielder Michael Morse, June 27, 2004.

d Traded to Philadelphia Phillies for pitcher Gavin Floyd and player to be named later, December 6, 2006. Chicago White Sox received pitcher Gio Gonzalez to complete trade, December 7, 2006.

e On disabled list from March 23 to April 16 and June 9 to October 31, 2007.

f Filed for free agency, October 31, 2007. Signed with Detroit Tigers organization, August 12, 2008.

g Filed for free agency, October 30, 2008. Signed with New York Mets organization, January 22, 2009.

h Released by New York Mets, April 28, 2009. Signed with Chicago White Sox organization, June 9, 2009.

i Filed for free agency, November 1, 2010. Signed with New York Yankees organization, February 1, 2011.

j On disabled list from August 8 to August 29, 2011.

k Filed for free agency, October 30, 2011, re-signed with New York Yankees, December 9, 2011.

GARCIA, JAIME OMAR

Born, Reynosa, Mexico, July 8, 1986.
Bats Left. Throws Left. Height, 6 feet, 2 inches. Weight, 215 pounds.

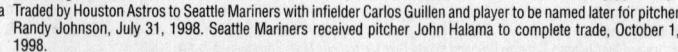

Year	Club	Lea	G	IP	W	L	Pct	SO	BB	H	ERA	SAVES
2006	Palm Beach	Fla.St.	12	77$^{1/3}$	5	4	.556	51	16	84	3.84	0

Year	Club	Lea	G	IP	W	L	Pct	SO	BB	H	ERA	SAVES
2006 Quad Cities........	Midwest	13	77²/₃	5	4	.556	80	18	67	2.90	0
2007 Springfield	Texas	18	103¹/₃	5	9	.357	97	45	93	3.75	0
2008 Springfield	Texas	6	35	3	2	.600	41	16	26	2.06	0
2008 Memphis	P.C.	13	71	4	4	.500	59	26	74	4.44	0
2008 St. Louis a	N.L.	10	16	1	1	.500	8	8	14	5.63	0
2009 Palm Beach	Fla.St.	3	12²/₃	0	1	.000	16	4	4	0.71	0
2009 Cardinals	Gulf Coast	2	4	0	1	.000	3	1	4	4.50	0
2009 Memphis b...........	P.C.	4	21	2	0	1.000	22	9	17	3.86	0
2010 St. Louis.............	N.L.	28	163¹/₃	13	8	.619	132	64	151	2.70	0
2011 St. Louis.............	N.L.	32	194²/₃	13	7	.650	156	50	207	3.56	0
Major League Totals ....3 Yrs.		70	374	27	16	.628	296	122	372	3.27	0
Division Series											
2011 St. Louis.............	N.L.	1	7	0	1	.000	3	2	6	3.86	0
Championship Series											
2011 St. Louis.............	N.L.	2	8²/₃	0	1	.000	8	3	13	7.27	0
World Series Record											
2011 St. Louis.............	N.L.	2	10	0	0	.000	10	3	8	1.80	0

a On disabled list from August 27 to October 8, 2008.
b On disabled list from March 27 to August 20, 2009.

GARLAND, JON STEVEN
Born, Valencia, California, September 27, 1979.
Bats Right. Throws Right. Height, 6 feet, 6 inches. Weight, 215 pounds.

Year	Club	Lea	G	IP	W	L	Pct	SO	BB	H	ERA	SAVES
1997 Cubs..............	Arizona	10	40	3	2	.600	39	10	37	2.70	0
1998 Rockford	Midwest	19	107¹/₃	4	7	.364	70	45	124	5.03	0
1998 Hickory a	So.Atl.	5	26²/₃	1	4	.200	19	13	36	5.40	0
1999 Winston-Salem	Carolina	19	119	5	7	.417	84	39	109	3.33	0
1999 Birmingham	Southern	7	39	3	1	.750	27	18	39	4.38	0
2000 Charlotte	Int.	16	103²/₃	9	2	.818	63	32	99	2.26	0
2000 Birmingham	Southern	1	6	0	0	.000	10	1	4	0.00	0
2000 Chicago b...........	A.L.	15	69²/₃	4	8	.333	42	40	82	6.46	0
2001 Charlotte	Int.	5	33	0	3	.000	26	11	31	2.73	0
2001 Chicago	A.L.	35	117	6	7	.462	61	55	123	3.69	1
2002 Chicago	A.L.	33	192²/₃	12	12	.500	112	83	188	4.58	0
2003 Chicago	A.L.	32	191²/₃	12	13	.480	108	74	188	4.51	0
2004 Chicago	A.L.	34	217	12	11	.522	113	76	223	4.89	0
2005 Chicago	A.L.	32	221	18	10	.643	115	47	212	3.50	0
2006 Chicago	A.L.	33	211¹/₃	18	7	.720	112	41	*247	4.51	0
2007 Chicago c...........	A.L.	32	208¹/₃	10	13	.435	98	57	219	4.23	0
2008 Los Angeles d	A.L.	32	196²/₃	14	8	.636	90	59	237	4.90	0
2009 Arizona-Los Angeles e-f..	N.L.	33	204	11	13	.458	109	61	225	4.01	0
2010 San Diego g	N.L.	33	200	14	12	.538	136	87	176	3.46	0
2011 Rancho Cucamonga	Calif.	1	4²/₃	0	0	.000	3	0	6	5.79	0
2011 Los Angeles h-i	N.L.	9	54	1	5	.167	28	20	55	4.33	0
Major League Totals ....12 Yrs.		353	2083¹/₃	132	119	.526	1124	700	2175	4.32	1
Championship Series											
2005 Chicago	A.L.	1	9	1	0	1.000	7	1	4	2.00	0
World Series Record											
2005 Chicago	A.L.	1	7	0	0	.000	4	2	7	2.57	0

a Traded by Chicago Cubs to Chicago White Sox for pitcher Matt Karchner, July 29, 1998.
b On disabled list from August 19 to September 2, 2000.
c Traded to Los Angeles Angels for infielder Orlando Cabrera, November 19, 2007.
d Filed for free agency, October 30, 2008. Signed with Arizona Diamondbacks, January 29, 2009.
e Traded to Los Angeles Dodgers for player to be named later, August 31, 2009. Arizona Diamondbacks received infielder Tony Abreu to complete trade, October 9, 2009.
f Filed for free agency, November 5, 2009. Signed with San Diego Padres, January 26, 2010.
g Filed for free agency, November 1, 2010. Signed with Los Angeles Dodgers, November 26, 2010.
h On disabled list from March 22 to April 15 and June 2 to September 30, 2011.
i Filed for free agency, October 30, 2011.

GARZA, MATTHEW SCOTT (MATT)
Born, Selma, California, November 11, 1983.
Bats Right. Throws Right. Height, 6 feet, 4 inches. Weight, 205 pounds.

Year	Club	Lea	G	IP	W	L	Pct	SO	BB	H	ERA	SAVES
2005 Elizabethton	Appal.	4	19²/₃	1	1	.500	25	6	14	3.66	0
2006 Fort Myers	Fla.St.	8	44¹/₃	5	1	.833	53	11	27	1.42	0
2006 New Britain	Eastern	10	57¹/₃	6	2	.750	68	14	40	2.51	0
2006 Rochester............	Int.	5	34	3	1	.750	33	7	20	1.85	0

Year Club	Lea	G	IP	W	L	Pct	SO	BB	H	ERA	SAVES
2006 Minnesota . . . . A.L.		10	50	3	6	.333	38	23	62	5.76	0
2007 Rochester. . . . . .Int.		16	92	4	6	.400	95	31	93	3.62	0
2007 Minnesota a . . . . A.L.		16	83	5	7	.417	67	32	96	3.69	0
2008 Vero Beach. . . . . Fla.St.		1	3²/₃	0	0	.000	4	3	8	9.82	0
2008 Tampa Bay b . . . . .A.L.		30	184²/₃	11	9	.550	128	59	170	3.70	0
2009 Tampa Bay . . . . A.L.		32	203	8	12	.400	189	79	177	3.95	0
2010 Tampa Bay c-d . . . . .A.L.		33	204²/₃	15	10	.600	150	63	193	3.91	1
2011 Chicago e . . . . .N.L.		31	198	10	10	.500	197	63	186	3.32	0
Major League Totals . . . . .6 Yrs.		152	923¹/₃	52	54	.491	769	319	884	3.83	1
Division Series											
2008 Tampa Bay . . . . A.L.		1	6	0	1	.000	4	4	7	7.50	0
2010 Tampa Bay . . . . A.L.		1	6	0	0	.000	4	2	5	1.50	0
Division Series Totals		2	12	0	1	.000	8	6	12	4.50	0
Championship Series											
2008 Tampa Bay . . . . A.L.		2	13	2	0	1.000	14	6	8	1.38	0
World Series Record											
2008 Tampa Bay . . . . A.L.		1	6	0	0	.000	7	2	6	6.00	0

a Traded to Tampa Bay Devil Rays with infielder Jason Bartlett and pitcher Eduardo Morlan for infielder Brendan Harris, outfielder Jason Pridie and outfielder Delmon Young, November 28, 2007.

b On disabled list from April 9 to April 25, 2008.

c Pitched no-hit, no-run game against Detroit Tigers, July 26, 2010.

d Traded to Chicago Cubs with outfielder Fernando Perez and pitcher Zachary Russcup for infielder Hak-Ju Lee, outfielder Brandon Guyer, pitcher Chris Archer, catcher Robinson Chirinos and outfielder Sam Fuld, January 8, 2011.

e On disabled list from May 24 to June 6, 2011.

GEE, DILLON KYLE
Born, Cleburne, Texas, April 28, 1986.
Bats Right. Throws Right. Height, 6 feet, 1 inch. Weight, 205 pounds.

Year Club	Lea	G	IP	W	L	Pct	SO	BB	H	ERA	SAVES
2007 Brooklyn. . . . . N.Y.-Penn.		14	62	3	1	.750	56	9	57	2.47	0
2008 St. Lucie. . . . . Fla.St.		21	127¹/₃	8	6	.571	94	19	117	3.25	0
2008 Binghamton . . . . Eastern		4	27	2	0	1.000	20	5	18	1.33	0
2009 Buffalo . . . . .Int.		9	48¹/₃	1	3	.250	42	16	47	4.10	0
2010 Buffalo . . . . .Int.		28	161¹/₃	13	8	.619	165	41	174	4.96	0
2010 New York . . . . .N.L.		5	33	2	2	.500	17	15	25	2.18	0
2011 Buffalo . . . . .Int.		2	11²/₃	1	1	.500	8	5	7	4.63	0
2011 New York . . . . .N.L.		30	160²/₃	13	6	.684	114	71	150	4.43	0
Major League Totals . . . . .2 Yrs.		35	193²/₃	15	8	.652	131	86	175	4.04	0

GONZALEZ, GIOVANY A. (GIO)
Born, Hialeah, Florida, September 19, 1985.
Bats Right. Throws Left. Height, 5 feet, 11 inches. Weight, 195 pounds.

Year Club	Lea	G	IP	W	L	Pct	SO	BB	H	ERA	SAVES
2004 Bristol . . . . Appal.		7	24	1	2	.333	36	8	17	2.25	0
2004 Kannapolis . . . . So.Atl.		8	40²/₃	1	2	.333	34	20	39	3.76	0
2005 Winston-Salem . . . . .Carolina		13	73¹/₃	8	3	.727	79	25	61	3.56	0
2005 Kannapolis a . . . . So.Atl.		11	57²/₃	5	3	.625	84	22	36	1.87	0
2006 Reading b . . . . Eastern		27	154²/₃	7	12	.368	166	81	140	4.66	0
2007 Birmingham . . . . Southern		27	150	9	7	.563	185	57	116	3.18	0
2008 Sacramento . . . . .P.C.		23	123	8	7	.533	128	61	106	4.24	0
2008 Oakland c . . . . .A.L.		10	34	1	4	.200	34	25	32	7.68	0
2009 Sacramento . . . . .P.C.		12	61	4	1	.800	71	34	42	2.51	0
2009 Oakland . . . . .A.L.		20	98²/₃	6	7	.462	109	56	113	5.75	0
2010 Oakland . . . . .A.L.		33	200²/₃	15	9	.625	171	92	171	3.23	0
2011 Oakland d . . . . .A.L.		32	202	16	12	.571	197	*91	175	3.12	0
Major League Totals . . . . .4 Yrs.		95	535¹/₃	38	32	.543	511	264	491	3.93	0

a Sent by Chicago White Sox to Philadelphia as player to be named later for infielder Jim Thome, December 8, 2005.

b Sent to Chicago White Sox as player to be named later for pitcher Freddy Garcia, December 7, 2006.

c Traded to Oakland Athletics with pitcher Fautino de los Santos and outfielder Ryan Sweeney for outfielder Nick Swisher, January 3, 2008.

d Traded to Washington Nationals with pitcher Robert Gilliam for pitcher A.J. Cole, pitcher Brad Peacock, pitcher Derek Norris and pitcher Tom Milone, December 23, 2011.

GONZALEZ, MICHAEL VELA (MIKE)
Born, Corpus Christi, Texas, May 23, 1978.
Bats Right. Throws Left. Height, 6 feet, 2 inches. Weight, 215 pounds.

Year Club	Lea	G	IP	W	L	Pct	SO	BB	H	ERA	SAVES
1997 Pirates . . . . Gulf Coast		7	29	2	0	1.000	33	8	21	2.48	0

Year	Club	Lea	G	IP	W	L	Pct	SO	BB	H	ERA	SAVES
1997 Augusta	So.Atl.	4	$19^{1/3}$	1	1	.500	22	8	11	1.86	0
1998 Lynchburg	Carolina	7	$28^{1/3}$	0	3	.000	22	13	40	6.67	0
1998 Augusta	So.Atl.	11	$50^{2/3}$	4	2	.667	72	26	43	2.84	0
1999 Lynchburg	Carolina	20	112	10	4	.714	119	63	98	4.02	0
1999 Altoona	Eastern	7	$26^{2/3}$	2	3	.400	31	19	34	8.10	0
2000 Pirates	Gulf Coast	2	6	1	0	1.000	7	4	8	4.50	0
2000 Lynchburg	Carolina	12	56	4	3	.571	53	34	57	4.66	0
2001 Lynchburg	Carolina	14	$30^{2/3}$	2	2	.500	32	7	28	2.93	0
2001 Altoona	Eastern	14	$87^{1/3}$	5	4	.556	66	36	81	3.71	0
2002 Altoona	Eastern	16	$85^{1/3}$	8	4	.667	82	47	77	3.80	0
2002 Pirates	Gulf Coast	2	$13^{1/3}$	2	0	1.000	14	3	5	0.00	0
2003 Lynchburg	Carolina	5	7	0	1	.000	9	5	7	5.14	0
2003 Altoona	Eastern	5	$7^{1/3}$	0	0	.000	10	2	4	1.23	1
2003 Pawtucket	Int.	2	$1^{2/3}$	0	0	.000	2	1	2	0.00	1
2003 Nashville	P.C.	7	10	0	0	.000	10	4	9	4.50	2
2003 Pittsburgh a-b	N.L.	16	$8^{1/3}$	0	1	.000	6	6	7	7.56	0
2004 Nashville	P.C.	14	20	2	0	1.000	35	7	12	0.90	2
2004 Pittsburgh	N.L.	47	$43^{1/3}$	3	1	.750	55	6	32	1.25	1
2005 Indianapolis	Int.	2	$3^{1/3}$	0	0	.000	5	0	0	0.00	0
2005 Pittsburgh c	N.L.	51	50	1	3	.250	58	31	35	2.70	3
2006 Pittsburgh d	N.L.	54	54	3	4	.429	64	31	42	2.17	24
2007 Atlanta e-f	N.L.	18	17	2	0	1.000	13	8	15	1.59	2
2008 Mississippi	Southern	4	5	0	0	.000	4	0	7	0.00	0
2008 Richmond	Int.	5	6	1	0	1.000	8	1	5	1.50	1
2008 Atlanta g	N.L.	36	$33^{2/3}$	0	3	.000	44	14	26	4.28	14
2009 Atlanta h	N.L.	80	$74^{1/3}$	5	4	.556	90	33	56	2.42	10
2010 Orioles	Gulf Coast	2	2	0	0	.000	3	0	1	0.00	0
2010 Bowie	Eastern	4	4	1	0	1.000	4	1	2	2.25	0
2010 Aberdeen	N.Y.-Penn.	4	5	0	1	.000	5	0	7	5.40	0
2010 Norfolk	Int.	2	$1^{2/3}$	0	0	.000	4	2	3	10.80	0
2010 Baltimore i	A.L.	29	$24^{2/3}$	1	3	.250	31	14	18	4.01	1
2011 Baltimore-Texas j-k	A.L.	56	$53^{1/3}$	2	2	.500	51	21	51	4.39	1
Major League Totals ......9 Yrs.		387	$358^{2/3}$	17	21	.447	412	164	282	2.94	56
Division Series											
2011 Texas	A.L.	2	$0^{2/3}$	0	0	.000	2	0	1	0.00	0
Championship Series											
2011 Texas	A.L.	3	$0^{2/3}$	0	0	.000	0	0	1	0.00	0
World Series Record											
2011 Texas	A.L.	3	3	0	0	.000	2	1	6	6.00	0

a Traded to Boston Red Sox with pitcher Scott Sauerbeck for pitcher Brandon Lyon and pitcher Anastacio Martinez, July 22, 2003.

b Traded to Pittsburgh Pirates with infielder Freddy Sanchez and cash for pitcher Jeff Suppan, pitcher Brandon Lyon and pitcher Anastacio Martinez, July 31, 2003.

c On disabled list from June 23 to August 16, 2005.

d On disabled list from August 25 to October 3, 2006.

e Traded to Atlanta Braves with infielder Brent Lillibridge for infielder Adam LaRoche and outfielder Jamie Romak, January 17, 2007.

f On disabled list from May 16 to November 13, 2007.

g On disabled list from March 21 to June 18, 2008.

h Filed for free agency, November 5, 2009. Signed with Baltimore Orioles, December 18, 2009.

i On disabled list from April 10 to July 21, 2010.

j Traded to Texas Rangers for player to be named later, August 31, 2011. Baltimore Orioles received pitcher Pedro Strop to complete trade, September 1, 2011.

k Filed for free agency, October 30, 2011.

GORZELANNY, THOMAS STEPHEN (TOM)
Born, Evergreen Park, Illinois, July 12, 1982.
Bats Left. Throws Left. Height, 6 feet, 2 inches. Weight, 205 pounds.

Year	Club	Lea	G	IP	W	L	Pct	SO	BB	H	ERA	SAVES
2003 Williamsport	N.Y.-Penn.	8	$30^{1/3}$	1	2	.333	22	10	23	1.78	0
2004 Lynchburg	Carolina	10	$55^{2/3}$	3	5	.375	61	19	54	4.85	0
2004 Hickory	So.Atl.	16	93	7	2	.778	106	34	63	2.23	0
2005 Altoona	Eastern	23	$129^{2/3}$	8	5	.615	124	46	114	3.26	0
2005 Pittsburgh	N.L.	3	6	0	1	.000	3	3	10	12.00	0
2006 Indianapolis	Int.	16	$99^{2/3}$	6	5	.545	94	27	67	2.35	0
2006 Pittsburgh a	N.L.	11	$61^{2/3}$	2	5	.286	40	31	50	3.79	0
2007 Pittsburgh	N.L.	32	$201^{2/3}$	14	10	.583	135	68	214	3.88	0
2008 Indianapolis	Int.	7	35	3	1	.750	33	4	28	2.06	0
2008 Pittsburgh b	N.L.	21	$105^{1/3}$	6	9	.400	67	70	120	6.66	0
2009 Indianapolis	Int.	15	87	4	3	.571	85	30	73	2.48	0
2009 Pittsburgh-Chicago c	N.L.	22	47	7	3	.700	47	17	45	5.55	0

Year	Club	Lea	G	IP	W	L	Pct	SO	BB	H	ERA	SAVES
2010 Chicago d	N.L.	29	136⅓	7	9	.438	119	68	136	4.09	1
2011 Syracuse	Int.	1	4	0	1	.000	3	1	5	9.00	0
2011 Washington e	N.L.	30	105	4	6	.400	95	33	102	4.03	0
Major League Totals ....7 Yrs.		148	663	40	43	.482	506	290	677	4.57	1

a On disabled list from August 18 to September 16, 2006.
b On disabled list from September 24 to November 13, 2008.
c Traded to Chicago Cubs with pitcher John Grabow for pitcher Kevin Hart, pitcher Jose Ascanio and infielder Josh Harrison, July 30, 2009.
d Traded to Washington Nationals for outfielder Michael Burgess, pitcher Graham Hicks and pitcher A.J. Morris, January 19, 2011.
e On disabled list from May 24 to June 19, 2011.

GRABOW, JOHN WILLIAM

Born, Arcadia, California, November 4, 1978.
Bats Left. Throws Left. Height, 6 feet, 2 inches. Weight, 205 pounds.

Year	Club	Lea	G	IP	W	L	Pct	SO	BB	H	ERA	SAVES
1997 Pirates	Gulf Coast	11	45⅓	2	7	.222	28	14	57	4.57	0
1998 Augusta	So.Atl.	17	71⅔	6	3	.667	67	34	84	5.78	0
1999 Hickory	So.Atl.	26	156⅓	9	10	.474	164	32	152	3.80	0
2000 Altoona	Eastern	24	145⅓	8	7	.533	109	65	145	4.33	0
2001 Pirates	Gulf Coast	6	12	0	1	.000	9	4	11	3.75	0
2001 Lynchburg	Carolina	7	36⅔	1	3	.250	35	26	42	6.38	0
2001 Altoona	Eastern	10	50⅔	2	5	.286	42	39	30	3.38	0
2002 Altoona	Eastern	28	146⅓	8	13	.381	97	47	181	5.47	0
2003 Altoona	Eastern	24	83	6	1	.857	73	19	87	3.36	1
2003 Nashville	P.C.	17	24⅔	0	2	.000	26	7	31	4.74	0
2003 Pittsburgh	N.L.	5	5	0	0	.000	9	0	6	3.60	0
2004 Pittsburgh	N.L.	68	61⅔	2	5	.286	64	28	81	5.11	1
2005 Pittsburgh	N.L.	63	52	2	3	.400	42	25	46	4.85	0
2006 Pittsburgh	N.L.	72	69⅔	4	2	.667	66	30	68	4.13	0
2007 Indianapolis	Int.	4	4	0	0	.000	4	2	4	2.25	0
2007 Pittsburgh a	N.L.	63	51⅔	3	2	.600	42	19	56	4.53	1
2008 Pittsburgh	N.L.	74	76	6	3	.667	62	37	60	2.84	4
2009 Pittsburgh-Chicago b-c	N.L.	75	72⅓	3	0	1.000	57	40	62	3.36	0
2010 Iowa	P.C.	4	4	0	0	.000	2	1	6	6.75	0
2010 Chicago d	N.L.	28	25⅔	1	3	.250	20	13	35	7.36	0
2011 Chicago e	N.L.	58	62⅓	3	1	.750	38	28	67	4.76	0
Major League Totals ....9 Yrs.		506	476⅓	24	19	.558	400	220	481	4.31	6

a On disabled list from March 23 to April 23, 2007.
b Traded to Chicago Cubs with pitcher Tom Gorzelanny for pitcher Kevin Hart, pitcher Jose Ascanio and infielder Josh Harrison, July 30, 2009.
c Filed for free agency, November 16, 2009, re-signed with Chicago Cubs, November 20, 2009.
d On disabled list from May 31 to June 15 and June 29 to November 9, 2010.
e Filed for free agency, October 30, 2011. Signed with Los Angeles Dodgers organization, December 19, 2011.

GREGERSON, LUKAS JOHN (LUKE)

Born, Park Ridge, Illinois, May 14, 1984.
Bats Left. Throws Right. Height, 6 feet, 3 inches. Weight, 200 pounds.

Year	Club	Lea	G	IP	W	L	Pct	SO	BB	H	ERA	SAVES
2006 Johnson City	Appal.	15	16⅓	0	1	.000	24	6	14	3.86	5
2006 State College	N.Y.-Penn.	12	15⅔	6	1	.857	22	9	9	1.72	4
2007 Palm Beach	Fla.St.	53	64	3	4	.429	69	20	42	1.97	29
2007 Springfield	Texas	1	1	0	0	.000	3	0	1	0.00	0
2008 Springfield	Texas	57	75⅓	7	6	.538	78	26	62	3.35	10
2009 San Diego a-b	N.L.	72	75	2	4	.333	93	31	62	3.24	1
2010 San Diego	N.L.	80	78⅓	4	7	.364	89	18	47	3.22	2
2011 Tucson	P.C.	2	1⅓	0	0	.000	2	2	3	20.25	0
2011 San Diego c	N.L.	61	55⅔	3	3	.500	34	19	57	2.75	0
Major League Totals ....3 Yrs.		213	209	9	14	.391	216	68	166	3.10	3

a Sent by St. Louis Cardinals to San Diego Padres as player to be named later for Khalil Greene, March 23, 2009.
b On disabled list from June 8 to July 6, 2009.
c On disabled list from June 9 to July 5, 2011.

GREGG, KEVIN MARSCHALL

Born, Corvallis, Oregon, June 20, 1978.
Bats Right. Throws Right. Height, 6 feet, 6 inches. Weight, 235 pounds.

Year	Club	Lea	G	IP	W	L	Pct	SO	BB	H	ERA	SAVES
1996 Athletics	Arizona	11	40⅔	3	3	.500	48	21	30	3.10	0

Year Club	Lea	G	IP	W	L	Pct	SO	BB	H	ERA	SAVES
1997 Visalia ....California		25	115⅓	6	8	.429	136	74	116	5.70	0
1998 Modesto..........California		30	144	8	7	.533	141	76	139	3.81	1
1999 Visalia ....California		13	64	4	4	.500	48	23	60	3.80	1
1999 Midland ....Texas		16	91⅓	4	7	.364	66	31	75	3.74	0
1999 Vancouver ...........P.C.		1	5	1	0	1.000	4	2	6	3.60	0
2000 Midland ....Texas		28	140⅔	5	14	.263	97	73	171	6.40	0
2001 Midland ....Texas		44	81⅓	5	5	.500	72	40	88	4.54	1
2002 Midland ....Texas		11	37⅔	3	3	.500	45	18	31	4.30	0
2002 Sacramento ...........P.C.		16	58⅔	2	5	.286	45	23	82	7.52	0
2002 Visalia a ....California		3	17⅓	2	1	.667	11	9	8	2.08	0
2003 Arkansas ....Texas		15	66⅓	4	3	.571	60	19	60	3.53	0
2003 Salt Lake ...........P.C.		15	91⅔	7	4	.636	75	18	90	4.03	0
2003 Anaheim............A.L.		5	24⅔	2	0	1.000	14	8	18	3.28	0
2004 Anaheim.............A.L.		55	87⅔	5	2	.714	84	28	86	4.21	1
2005 Salt Lake ...........P.C.		7	34⅔	3	1	.750	36	10	36	3.89	0
2005 Los Angeles...........A.L.		33	64⅓	1	2	.333	52	29	70	5.04	0
2006 Salt Lake .............P.C.		3	10	1	0	1.000	8	4	5	0.00	0
2006 Los Angeles b ........A.L.		32	78⅓	3	4	.429	71	21	88	4.14	0
2007 Florida ...............N.L.		74	84	0	5	.000	87	40	63	3.54	32
2008 Florida c.............N.L.		72	68⅔	7	8	.467	58	37	51	3.41	29
2009 Chicago d.............N.L.		72	68⅔	5	6	.455	71	30	60	4.72	23
2010 Toronto e.............A.L.		63	59	2	6	.250	58	30	52	3.51	37
2011 Baltimore.............A.L.		63	59⅔	0	3	.000	53	40	58	4.37	22
Major League Totals ....9 Yrs.		469	595	25	36	.410	548	263	546	4.07	144
Division Series											
2004 Anaheim.............A.L.		1	2	0	0	.000	0	1	3	0.00	0
Championship Series											
2005 Los Angeles ...........A.L.		1	2	0	0	.000	3	1	1	0.00	0

a Filed for free agency from Oakland Athletics, October 15, 2002. Signed with Anaheim Angels organization, November 20, 2002.
b Traded to Florida Marlins for pitcher Chris Resop, November 20, 2006.
c Traded to Chicago Cubs for pitcher Jose Ceda, November 13, 2008.
d Filed for free agency, November 9, 2009. Signed with Toronto Blue Jays, February 5, 2010.
e Filed for free agency, November 4, 2010. Signed with Baltimore Orioles, January 5, 2011.

GREINKE, DONALD ZACKARY (ZACK)

Born, Orlando, Florida, October 21, 1983.
Bats Right. Throws Right. Height, 6 feet, 2 inches. Weight, 185 pounds.

Year Club	Lea	G	IP	W	L	Pct	SO	BB	H	ERA	SAVES
2002 Wilmington ....Carolina		1	2	0	0	.000	0	0	1	0.00	0
2002 Royals ....Gulf Coast		3	4⅔	0	0	.000	4	3	3	1.93	0
2002 Spokane........Northwest		2	4⅔	0	0	.000	5	0	9	7.71	0
2003 Wilmington ....Carolina		14	87	11	1	.917	78	13	56	1.14	0
2003 Wichita..............Texas		9	53	4	3	.571	34	5	58	3.23	0
2004 Omaha...............P.C.		6	28⅔	1	1	.500	23	6	25	2.51	0
2004 Kansas City ...........A.L.		24	145	8	11	.421	100	26	143	3.97	0
2005 Kansas City ...........A.L.		33	183	5	17	.227	114	53	233	5.80	0
2006 Wichita..............Texas		18	105⅔	8	3	.727	94	27	96	4.34	0
2006 Kansas City a ..........A.L.		3	6⅓	1	0	1.000	5	3	7	4.26	0
2007 Kansas City ...........A.L.		52	122	7	7	.500	106	36	122	3.69	1
2008 Kansas City ...........A.L.		32	202⅓	13	10	.565	183	56	202	3.47	0
2009 Kansas City b .........A.L.		33	229⅓	16	8	.667	242	51	195	*2.16	0
2010 Kansas City c .........A.L.		33	220	10	14	.417	181	55	219	4.17	0
2011 Brevard County ......Fla.St.		1	3	0	0	.000	4	0	1	0.00	0
2011 Nashville ............P.C.		2	7⅔	0	1	.000	9	2	10	4.70	0
2011 Milwaukee d...........N.L.		28	171⅔	16	6	.727	201	45	161	3.83	0
Major League Totals ....8 Yrs.		238	1279⅔	76	73	.510	1132	325	1282	3.82	1
Division Series											
2011 Milwaukee ...........N.L.		1	5	0	0	.000	7	0	8	7.20	0
Championship Series											
2011 Milwaukee ...........N.L.		2	11⅔	1	1	.500	6	4	15	6.17	0

a On disabled list from April 1 to June 21, 2006.
b Selected Cy Young Award Winner in American League for 2009.
c Traded to Milwaukee Brewers with outfielder Yuniesky Betancourt for outfielder Lorenzo Cain, infielder Alcides Escobar, pitcher Jeremy Jeffress and pitcher Jake Odorizzi, December 19, 2010.
d On disabled list from March 26 to May 3, 2011.

GUERRA, LUIS JAVIER (JAVY)

Born, Denton, Texas, October 31, 1985.
Bats Right. Throws Right. Height, 6 feet. Weight, 205 pounds.

Year	Club	Lea	G	IP	W	L	Pct	SO	BB	H	ERA	SAVES
2004 Dodgers	Gulf Coast	11	40	4	1	.800	36	19	31	3.38	0
2005 Columbus	So.Atl.	11	52²/₃	2	5	.286	40	23	51	4.96	0
2006 Dodgers	Gulf Coast	4	8²/₃	0	1	.000	11	4	10	4.15	0
2006 Ogden	Pioneer	7	28	1	3	.250	22	20	37	4.82	0
2007 Inland Empire	Calif.	27	117²/₃	6	9	.400	121	80	139	6.27	1
2008 Inland Empire	Calif.	31	66¹/₃	5	4	.556	63	44	68	4.07	2
2009 Great Lakes	Midwest	28	41	3	1	.750	55	15	23	1.54	16
2009 Chattanooga	Southern	23	28¹/₃	3	1	.750	29	16	32	4.13	0
2010 Dodgers	Arizona	2	2	0	1	.000	3	0	2	4.50	0
2010 Chattanooga	Southern	28	27	2	0	1.000	27	22	24	2.33	5
2011 Chattanooga	Southern	14	17	1	0	1.000	15	5	8	1.06	3
2011 Los Angeles	N.L.	47	46²/₃	2	2	.500	38	18	37	2.31	21

GUERRIER, MATTHEW OLSON (MATT)

Born, Cleveland, Ohio, August 2, 1978.
Bats Right. Throws Right. Height, 6 feet, 3 inches. Weight, 195 pounds.

Year	Club	Lea	G	IP	W	L	Pct	SO	BB	H	ERA	SAVES
1999 Bristol	Appal.	21	25²/₃	5	0	1.000	37	14	18	1.05	10
1999 Winston-Salem	Carolina	4	3¹/₃	0	0	.000	5	0	3	5.40	2
2000 Winston-Salem	Carolina	30	34²/₃	0	3	.000	35	12	25	1.30	19
2000 Birmingham	Southern	23	23¹/₃	3	1	.750	19	12	17	2.70	7
2001 Charlotte	Int.	12	81¹/₃	7	1	.875	43	18	75	3.54	0
2001 Birmingham	Southern	15	98²/₃	11	3	.786	75	32	85	3.10	0
2002 Nashville a	P.C.	27	157	7	12	.368	130	47	154	4.59	0
2003 Nashville b	P.C.	20	105¹/₃	4	6	.400	78	18	108	4.53	0
2004 Rochester	Int.	24	144	5	10	.333	97	25	135	3.19	0
2004 Minnesota	A.L.	9	19	0	1	.000	11	6	22	5.68	0
2005 Minnesota	A.L.	43	71²/₃	0	3	.000	46	24	71	3.39	0
2006 New Britain	Eastern	4	8²/₃	2	0	1.000	10	3	3	1.04	0
2006 Minnesota c	A.L.	39	69²/₃	1	0	1.000	37	21	78	3.36	1
2007 Minnesota	A.L.	73	88	2	4	.333	68	21	71	2.35	1
2008 Minnesota	A.L.	*76	76¹/₃	6	9	.400	59	37	84	5.19	1
2009 Minnesota	A.L.	*79	76¹/₃	5	1	.833	47	16	58	2.36	1
2010 Minnesota d	A.L.	74	71	5	7	.417	42	22	56	3.17	1
2011 Los Angeles	N.L.	70	66¹/₃	4	3	.571	50	25	59	4.07	1
Major League Totals ....8 Yrs.		463	538¹/₃	23	28	.451	360	172	499	3.46	6
Division Series											
2006 Minnesota	A.L.	1	1	0	0	.000	0	0	0	0.00	0
2009 Minnesota	A.L.	2	2	0	0	.000	2	0	0	0.00	0
2010 Minnesota	A.L.	2	1²/₃	0	0	.000	2	1	1	0.00	0
Division Series Totals		5	4²/₃	0	0	.000	4	1	1	0.00	0

a Traded by Chicago White Sox to Pittsburgh Pirates for pitcher Damaso Marte and infielder Edwin Yan, March 27, 2002.

b Claimed on waivers by Minnesota Twins, November 20, 2003.

c On disabled list from June 9 to August 1, 2006.

d Filed for free agency, November 1, 2010. Signed with Los Angeles Dodgers, December 16, 2010.

GUTHRIE, JEREMY SHANE

Born, Roseburg, Oregon, April 8, 1979.
Bats Right. Throws Right. Height, 6 feet, 1 inch. Weight, 200 pounds.

Year	Club	Lea	G	IP	W	L	Pct	SO	BB	H	ERA	SAVES
2003 Akron	Eastern	10	62²/₃	6	2	.750	35	14	44	1.44	0
2003 Buffalo	Int.	18	96²/₃	4	9	.308	62	30	129	6.52	0
2004 Buffalo	Int.	4	19¹/₃	1	2	.333	10	18	23	7.91	0
2004 Akron	Eastern	23	130¹/₃	8	8	.500	94	42	145	4.21	0
2004 Cleveland	A.L.	6	11²/₃	0	0	.000	7	6	9	4.63	0
2005 Cleveland	A.L.	1	6	0	0	.000	3	2	9	6.00	0
2005 Buffalo	Int.	25	136¹/₃	12	10	.545	100	49	152	5.08	0
2006 Buffalo	Int.	21	123¹/₃	9	5	.643	88	48	104	3.14	0
2006 Cleveland	A.L.	9	19¹/₃	0	0	.000	14	15	24	6.98	0
2007 Baltimore a	A.L.	32	175¹/₃	7	5	.583	123	47	165	3.70	0
2008 Baltimore b	A.L.	30	190²/₃	10	12	.455	120	58	176	3.63	0
2009 Baltimore	A.L.	33	200	10	*17	.370	110	60	224	5.04	0
2010 Baltimore	A.L.	32	209¹/₃	11	14	.440	119	50	193	3.83	0

Year Club	Lea	G	IP	W	L	Pct	SO	BB	H	ERA	SAVES
2011 Baltimore	A.L.	34	208	9	*17	.346	130	66	213	4.33	0
Major League Totals	8 Yrs.	177	1020⅓	47	65	.420	626	304	1013	4.19	0

a Claimed on waivers by Baltimore Orioles, January 29, 2007.
b On disabled list from September 6 to September 27, 2008.

HALLADAY, HARRY LEROY (ROY)
Born, Denver, Colorado, May 14, 1977.
Bats Right. Throws Right. Height, 6 feet, 6 inches. Weight, 225 pounds.

Year Club	Lea	G	IP	W	L	Pct	SO	BB	H	ERA	SAVES
1995 Blue Jays	Gulf Coast	10	50⅓	3	5	.375	48	16	35	3.40	0
1996 Dunedin	Fla.St.	27	164⅔	15	7	.682	109	46	158	2.73	0
1997 Knoxville	Southern	7	36⅔	2	3	.400	30	11	46	5.40	0
1997 Syracuse	Int.	22	125⅔	7	10	.412	64	53	132	4.58	0
1998 Syracuse	Int.	21	116⅓	9	5	.643	71	53	107	3.79	0
1998 Toronto	A.L.	2	14	1	0	1.000	13	2	9	1.93	0
1999 Toronto	A.L.	36	149⅓	8	7	.533	82	79	156	3.92	1
2000 Syracuse	Int.	11	73⅔	2	3	.400	38	21	85	5.50	0
2000 Toronto	A.L.	19	67⅔	4	7	.364	44	42	107	10.64	0
2001 Dunedin	Fla.St.	13	22⅔	0	1	.000	15	3	28	3.97	2
2001 Tennessee	Southern	5	34	2	1	.667	29	6	25	2.12	0
2001 Syracuse	Int.	2	14	1	0	1.000	13	0	12	3.21	0
2001 Toronto	A.L.	17	105⅓	5	3	.625	96	25	97	3.16	0
2002 Toronto	A.L.	34	*239⅓	19	7	.731	168	62	223	2.93	0
2003 Toronto a	A.L.	36	*266	*22	7	*.759	204	32	*253	3.25	0
2004 Toronto b	A.L.	21	133	8	8	.500	95	39	140	4.20	0
2005 Toronto c	A.L.	19	141⅔	12	4	.750	108	18	118	2.41	0
2006 Toronto	A.L.	32	220	16	5	*.762	132	34	208	3.19	0
2007 Toronto d	A.L.	31	225⅓	16	7	.696	139	48	232	3.71	0
2008 Toronto	A.L.	34	*246	20	11	.645	206	39	220	2.78	0
2009 Toronto e-f	A.L.	32	239	17	10	.630	208	35	234	2.79	0
2010 Philadelphia g-h-i . .	N.L.	33	*250⅔	*21	10	.677	219	30	*231	2.44	0
2011 Philadelphia	N.L.	32	233⅔	19	6	.760	220	35	208	2.35	0
Major League Totals	14 Yrs.	378	2531	188	92	.671	1934	520	2436	3.23	1
Division Series											
2010 Philadelphia	N.L.	1	9	1	0	1.000	8	1	0	0.00	0
2011 Philadelphia	N.L.	2	16	1	1	.500	15	2	9	2.25	0
Division Series Totals		3	25	2	1	.667	23	3	9	1.44	0
Championship Series											
2010 Philadelphia	N.L.	2	13	1	1	.500	12	2	14	4.15	0

a Selected Cy Young Award Winner in American League for 2003.
b On disabled list from May 28 to June 12 and from July 17 to September 21, 2004.
c On disabled list from July 9 to October 3, 2005.
d On disabled list from May 11 to May 31, 2007.
e On disabled list from June 13 to June 28, 2009.
f Traded to Philadelphia Phillies for pitcher Kyle Drabek, pitcher Michael Taylor and catcher Travis D'Arnaud, December 16, 2009.
g Pitched no-hit, no-run perfect game against Florida Marlins, May 29, 2010.
h Pitched no-hit, no-run game against Cincinnati Reds in divisional playoff, October 6, 2010.
i Selected Cy Young Award Winner in National League for 2010.

HAMELS, COLBERT RICHARD (COLE)
Born, San Diego, California, December 27, 1983.
Bats Left. Throws Left. Height, 6 feet, 4 inches. Weight, 195 pounds.

Year Club	Lea	G	IP	W	L	Pct	SO	BB	H	ERA	SAVES
2003 Clearwater	Fla.St.	5	26⅓	0	2	.000	32	14	29	2.73	0
2003 Lakewood	So.Atl.	13	74⅔	6	1	.857	115	25	32	0.84	0
2004 Clearwater	Fla.St.	4	16	1	0	1.000	24	4	10	1.13	0
2005 Reading	Eastern	3	19	2	0	1.000	19	12	10	2.37	0
2005 Clearwater	Fla.St.	3	16	2	0	1.000	18	7	7	2.25	0
2006 Lakewood	So.Atl.	1	5⅔	0	0	.000	3	2	3	1.59	0
2006 Clearwater	Fla.St.	4	20⅓	1	1	.500	29	9	16	1.77	0
2006 Scranton/WB	Int.	3	23	2	0	1.000	36	1	10	0.39	0
2006 Philadelphia a	N.L.	23	132⅓	9	8	.529	145	48	117	4.08	0
2007 Philadelphia b	N.L.	28	183⅓	15	5	.750	177	43	163	3.39	0
2008 Philadelphia	N.L.	33	227⅓	14	10	.583	196	53	193	3.09	0
2009 Philadelphia	N.L.	32	193⅔	10	11	.476	168	43	206	4.32	0
2010 Philadelphia	N.L.	33	208⅔	12	11	.522	211	61	185	3.06	0

Year	Club	Lea	G	IP	W	L	Pct	SO	BB	H	ERA	SAVES
2011 Philadelphia c	N.L.	32	216	14	9	.609	194	44	169	2.79	0
Major League Totals	6 Yrs.	181	1161⅓	74	54	.578	1091	292	1033	3.39	0
Division Series											
2007 Philadelphia	N.L.	1	6⅔	0	1	.000	7	4	3	4.05	0
2008 Philadelphia	N.L.	1	8	1	0	1.000	9	1	2	0.00	0
2009 Philadelphia	N.L.	1	5	0	1	.000	5	0	7	7.20	0
2010 Philadelphia	N.L.	1	9	1	0	1.000	9	0	5	0.00	0
2011 Philadelphia	N.L.	1	6	1	0	1.000	8	3	5	0.00	0
Division Series Totals		5	34⅔	3	2	.600	38	8	22	1.82	0
Championship Series											
2008 Philadelphia	N.L.	2	14	2	0	1.000	13	5	11	1.93	0
2009 Philadelphia	N.L.	2	9⅔	1	0	1.000	7	2	13	6.52	0
2010 Philadelphia	N.L.	1	6	0	1	.000	8	1	5	4.50	0
Championship Series Totals		5	29⅔	3	1	.750	28	8	29	3.94	0
World Series Record											
2008 Philadelphia	N.L.	2	13	1	0	1.000	8	3	10	2.77	0
2009 Philadelphia	N.L.	2	4⅓	0	1	.000	3	2	5	10.38	0
World Series Totals		3	17⅓	1	1	.500	11	5	15	4.67	0

a On disabled list from May 19 to June 6, 2006.
b On disabled list from August 17 to September 18, 2007.
c On disabled list from August 13 to August 29, 2011.

HAMMEL, JASON AARON

Born, Greenville, South Carolina, September 2, 1982.
Bats Right. Throws Right. Height, 6 feet, 6 inches. Weight, 220 pounds.

Year	Club	Lea	G	IP	W	L	Pct	SO	BB	H	ERA	SAVES
2002 Princeton	Appal.	2	5⅓	0	0	.000	5	0	7	0.00	1
2002 Hudson Valley	N.Y.-Penn.	13	51⅔	1	5	.167	38	14	71	5.23	1
2003 Charleston	So.Atl.	14	76⅔	6	2	.750	50	27	70	3.40	0
2004 Bakersfield	Calif.	11	71⅓	6	2	.750	65	20	52	1.89	0
2004 Charleston	So.Atl.	18	94⅔	4	7	.364	88	27	94	3.23	0
2005 Durham	Int.	10	54⅔	3	2	.600	48	27	57	4.12	0
2005 Montgomery	Southern	12	81⅓	8	2	.800	76	19	70	2.66	0
2006 Durham	Int.	24	127⅔	5	9	.357	117	36	133	4.23	0
2006 Tampa Bay	A.L.	9	44	0	6	.000	32	21	61	7.77	0
2007 Durham	Int.	13	76⅓	4	5	.444	75	28	61	3.42	0
2007 Tampa Bay	A.L.	24	85	3	5	.375	64	40	100	6.14	0
2008 Tampa Bay	A.L.	40	78⅓	4	4	.500	44	35	83	4.60	2
2009 Colorado a	N.L.	34	176⅔	10	8	.556	133	42	203	4.33	0
2010 Colorado Springs	P.C.	1	7	1	0	1.000	6	1	9	5.14	0
2010 Colorado b	N.L.	30	177⅔	10	9	.526	141	47	201	4.81	0
2011 Colorado	N.L.	32	170⅓	7	13	.350	94	68	175	4.76	1
Major League Totals	6 Yrs.	169	732	34	45	.430	508	253	823	4.99	3
Division Series											
2009 Colorado	N.L.	1	3⅔	0	0	.000	5	3	4	9.82	0

a Traded to Colorado Rockies for pitcher Aneury Rodriguez, April 4, 2009.
b On disabled list from April 27 to May 15, 2010.

HAND, BRAD

Born, Minneapolis, Minnesota, March 20, 1990.
Bats Left. Throws Left. Height, 6 feet, 3 inches. Weight, 200 pounds.

Year	Club	Lea	G	IP	W	L	Pct	SO	BB	H	ERA	SAVES
2008 Marlins	Gulf Coast	9	32⅔	2	0	1.000	34	11	25	2.48	0
2008 Jamestown	N.Y.-Penn.	3	15	1	2	.333	12	10	11	3.00	0
2009 Greensboro	So.Atl.	26	127⅔	7	13	.350	122	66	130	4.86	0
2010 Jupiter	Fla.St.	26	140⅔	8	8	.500	134	49	153	3.33	0
2010 Jacksonville	Southern	1	6	1	0	1.000	4	3	3	3.00	0
2011 Jupiter	Fla.St.	1	5	0	1	.000	4	5	5	7.20	0
2011 Jacksonville	Southern	19	108⅔	11	4	.733	71	50	90	3.40	0
2011 Florida	N.L.	12	60	1	8	.111	38	35	53	4.20	0

HANRAHAN, JOEL RYAN
Born, Des Moines, Iowa, October 6, 1981.
Bats Right. Throws Right. Height, 6 feet, 3 inches. Weight, 250 pounds.

Year	Club	Lea	G	IP	W	L	Pct	SO	BB	H	ERA	SAVES
2000	Great Falls	Pioneer	12	55	3	1	.750	40	23	49	4.75	0
2001	Wilmington	So.Atl.	27	144	9	11	.450	116	55	136	3.38	0
2002	Vero Beach	Fla.St.	25	143²/₃	10	6	.625	139	51	129	4.20	0
2002	Jacksonville	Southern	3	11	1	1	.500	10	7	15	10.64	0
2003	Las Vegas	P.C.	5	25	1	2	.333	13	20	36	10.08	0
2003	Jacksonville	Southern	23	133¹/₃	10	4	.714	130	53	117	2.43	0
2004	Las Vegas	P.C.	25	119¹/₃	7	7	.500	97	75	128	5.05	0
2005	Vero Beach	Fla.St.	5	21¹/₃	1	0	1.000	25	11	25	5.91	0
2005	Jacksonville	Southern	23	111²/₃	9	8	.529	102	55	118	4.92	0
2006	Las Vegas	P.C.	14	74¹/₃	4	3	.571	46	39	70	4.48	0
2006	Jacksonville a	Southern	12	66¹/₃	7	2	.778	67	38	49	2.58	0
2007	Columbus	Int.	15	75¹/₃	5	4	.556	71	36	65	3.70	0
2007	Washington	N.L.	12	51	5	3	.625	43	38	59	6.00	0
2008	Washington	N.L.	69	84¹/₃	6	3	.667	93	42	73	3.95	9
2009	Washington-Pittsburgh b	N.L.	67	64	1	4	.200	72	34	73	4.78	5
2010	Bradenton	Fla.St.	2	2	0	0	.000	3	0	0	0.00	0
2010	Pittsburgh c	N.L.	72	69²/₃	4	1	.800	100	26	58	3.62	6
2011	Pittsburgh	N.L.	70	68²/₃	1	4	.200	61	16	56	1.83	40
Major League Totals	5 Yrs.		290	337²/₃	17	15	.531	369	156	319	3.92	60

a Filed for free agency from Los Angeles Dodgers, October 15, 2006. Signed with Washington Nationals organization, November 6, 2006.

b Traded to Pittsburgh Pirates with outfielder Lastings Milledge for outfielder Nyjer Morgan and pitcher Sean Burnett, June 30, 2009.

c On disabled list from March 26 to April 12, 2010.

HANSON, THOMAS J. (TOMMY)
Born, Tulsa, Oklahoma, August 28, 1986.
Bats Right. Throws Right. Height, 6 feet, 6 inches. Weight, 220 pounds.

Year	Club	Lea	G	IP	W	L	Pct	SO	BB	H	ERA	SAVES
2006	Danville	Appal.	13	51²/₃	4	1	.800	56	9	42	2.09	0
2007	Myrtle Beach	Carolina	11	60	3	3	.500	64	32	53	4.20	0
2007	Rome	So.Atl.	15	73	2	6	.250	90	26	51	2.59	0
2008	Myrtle Beach	Carolina	7	40	3	1	.750	49	11	15	0.90	0
2008	Mississippi	Southern	18	98	8	4	.667	114	41	70	3.03	0
2009	Gwinnett	Int.	11	66¹/₃	3	3	.500	90	17	40	1.49	0
2009	Atlanta	N.L.	21	127²/₃	11	4	.733	116	46	105	2.89	0
2010	Atlanta	N.L.	34	202²/₃	10	11	.476	173	56	182	3.33	0
2011	Atlanta a	N.L.	22	130	11	7	.611	142	46	106	3.60	0
Major League Totals	3 Yrs.		77	460¹/₃	32	22	.593	431	148	393	3.28	0
Division Series												
2010	Atlanta	N.L.	1	4	0	0	.000	5	1	5	9.00	0

a On disabled list from June 13 to June 28 and August 7 to September 30, 2011.

HAPP, JAMES ANTHONY (J.A.)
Born, Spring Valley, Illinois, October 19, 1982.
Bats Left. Throws Left. Height, 6 feet, 6 inches. Weight, 200 pounds.

Year	Club	Lea	G	IP	W	L	Pct	SO	BB	H	ERA	SAVES
2004	Batavia	N.Y.-Penn.	11	35²/₃	1	2	.333	37	18	22	2.02	0
2005	Reading	Eastern	1	6	1	0	1.000	8	2	3	1.50	0
2005	Lakewood	So.Atl.	14	72¹/₃	4	4	.500	70	26	57	2.36	0
2006	Reading	Eastern	12	74²/₃	6	2	.750	81	29	58	2.65	0
2006	Clearwater	Fla.St.	13	80	3	7	.300	77	19	63	2.81	0
2006	Scranton/WB	Int.	1	6	1	0	1.000	4	1	3	1.50	0
2007	Philadelphia	N.L.	1	4	0	1	.000	5	2	7	11.25	0
2007	Ottawa	Int.	24	118¹/₃	4	6	.400	117	62	118	5.02	0
2008	Lehigh Valley	Int.	24	135	8	7	.533	151	48	116	3.60	0
2008	Philadelphia	N.L.	8	31²/₃	1	0	1.000	26	14	28	3.69	0
2009	Philadelphia	N.L.	35	166	12	4	.750	119	56	149	2.93	0
2010	Clearwater	Fla.St.	1	3	0	1	.000	2	0	3	6.00	0
2010	Reading	Eastern	3	12¹/₃	1	0	1.000	10	4	18	8.03	0
2010	Lehigh Valley	Int.	5	22¹/₃	0	1	.000	22	15	26	4.84	0
2010	Philadelphia-Houston a-b	N.L.	16	87¹/₃	6	4	.600	70	47	73	3.40	0
2011	Oklahoma	P.C.	3	18	1	0	1.000	16	9	11	1.50	0
2011	Houston	N.L.	28	156¹/₃	6	15	.286	134	83	157	5.35	0
Major League Totals	5 Yrs.		88	445¹/₃	25	24	.510	354	202	414	4.00	0

Year	Club	Lea	G	IP	W	L	Pct	SO	BB	H	ERA	SAVES
	Division Series											
2009 Philadelphia	N.L.	2	3	0	0	.000	4	2	6	9.00	0
	Championship Series											
2008 Philadelphia	N.L.	1	3	0	0	.000	2	2	4	3.00	0
2009 Philadelphia	N.L.	3	0²/₃	0	0	.000	0	3	0	0.00	0
Championship Series Totals		4	3²/₃	0	0	.000	2	5	4	2.45	0
	World Series Record											
2009 Philadelphia	N.L.	2	2²/₃	0	0	.000	4	1	2	3.38	0

a On disabled list from April 16 to July 6, 2010.
b Traded to Houston Astros with outfielder Anthony Gose and infielder Jonathan Villar for pitcher Roy Oswalt and cash, July 29, 2010.

HARANG, AARON MICHAEL
Born, San Diego, California, May 9, 1978.
Bats Right. Throws Right. Height, 6 feet, 7 inches. Weight, 270 pounds.

Year	Club	Lea	G	IP	W	L	Pct	SO	BB	H	ERA	SAVES
1999 Pulaski	Appal.	16	78¹/₃	9	2	.818	87	17	64	2.30	1
2000 Charlotte a	Fla.St.	28	157	13	5	.722	136	50	128	3.32	0
2001 Midland	Texas	27	150	10	8	.556	112	37	173	4.14	0
2002 Midland	Texas	3	16²/₃	2	0	1.000	21	7	12	1.08	0
2002 Sacramento	P.C.	8	38²/₃	3	3	.500	39	9	41	3.26	0
2002 Oakland	A.L.	16	78¹/₃	5	4	.556	64	45	78	4.83	0
2003 Louisville	Int.	1	3	0	1	.000	4	2	5	15.00	0
2003 Sacramento	P.C.	12	69²/₃	8	2	.800	60	17	62	2.71	0
2003 Oakland	A.L.	7	30¹/₃	1	3	.250	16	9	41	5.34	0
2003 Cincinnati b	N.L.	9	46	4	3	.571	26	10	48	5.28	0
2004 Louisville	Int.	1	3	0	1	.000	3	3	9	12.00	0
2004 Cincinnati c	N.L.	28	161	10	9	.526	125	53	177	4.86	0
2005 Cincinnati	N.L.	32	211²/₃	11	13	.458	163	51	217	3.83	0
2006 Cincinnati	N.L.	36	234¹/₃	*16	11	.593	*216	56	242	3.76	0
2007 Cincinnati	N.L.	34	231²/₃	16	6	.727	218	52	213	3.73	0
2008 Louisville	Int.	1	6	1	0	1.000	6	0	5	0.00	0
2008 Cincinnati d	N.L.	30	184¹/₃	6	*17	.261	153	50	205	4.78	0
2009 Cincinnati e	N.L.	26	162¹/₃	6	14	.300	142	43	186	4.21	0
2010 Louisville	Int.	2	11	0	2	.000	10	2	14	9.00	0
2010 Cincinnati f-g	N.L.	22	111²/₃	6	7	.462	82	38	139	5.32	0
2011 Lake Elsinore	Calif.	1	4	0	1	.000	7	1	5	6.75	0
2011 San Diego h-i	N.L.	28	170²/₃	14	7	.667	124	58	175	3.64	0
Major League Totals . . . . 10 Yrs.		268	1622¹/₃	95	94	.503	1329	465	1721	4.25	0

a Traded by Texas Rangers to Oakland Athletics with pitcher Ryan Cullen for infielder Randy Velarde, November 17, 2000.
b Traded to Cincinnati Reds with pitcher Joe Valentine and pitcher Jeff Bruksch for outfielder Jose Guillen, July 30, 2003.
c On disabled list from June 2 to June 26, 2004.
d On disabled list from July 9 to August 10, 2008.
e On disabled list from August 21 to October 14, 2009.
f On disabled list from July 1 to August 31, 2010.
g Filed for free agency, November 3, 2010. Signed with San Diego Padres, December 6, 2010.
h On disabled list from June 10 to July 9, 2011.
i Filed for free agency, October 31, 2011. Signed with Los Angeles Dodgers, December 8, 2011.

HARDEN, JAMES RICHARD (RICH)
Born, Victoria, British Columbia, Canada, November 30, 1981.
Bats Left. Throws Right. Height, 6 feet, 1 inch. Weight, 195 pounds.

Year	Club	Lea	G	IP	W	L	Pct	SO	BB	H	ERA	SAVES
2001 Vancouver	Northwest	18	74¹/₃	2	4	.333	100	38	47	3.39	0
2002 Visalia	California	12	68	4	3	.571	85	24	49	2.91	0
2002 Midland	Texas	16	85¹/₃	8	3	.727	102	52	67	2.95	0
2003 Midland	Texas	2	13	2	0	1.000	17	0	0	0.00	0
2003 Sacramento	P.C.	16	88²/₃	9	4	.692	91	35	72	3.15	0
2003 Oakland	A.L.	15	74¹/₃	5	4	.556	67	40	72	4.46	0
2004 Sacramento	P.C.	1	5	0	0	.000	6	3	6	5.40	0
2004 Oakland	A.L.	31	189²/₃	11	7	.611	167	81	171	3.99	0
2005 Sacramento	P.C.	1	3	0	0	.000	7	0	1	0.00	0
2005 Oakland a	A.L.	22	128	10	5	.667	121	43	93	2.53	0
2006 Sacramento	P.C.	1	2	0	0	.000	3	0	1	0.00	0

Year	Club	Lea	G	IP	W	L	Pct	SO	BB	H	ERA	SAVES
2006 Oakland b............	A.L.	9	46²/₃	4	0	1.000	49	26	31	4.24	0
2007 Sacramento...........	P.C.	1	1	0	0	.000	1	0	1	0.00	0
2007 Oakland c.............	A.L.	7	25²/₃	1	2	.333	27	11	18	2.45	0
2008 Stockton............	Calif.	1	6	1	0	1.000	9	0	3	0.00	0
2008 Sacramento..........	P.C.	1	3²/₃	0	0	.000	4	0	3	2.45	0
2008 Oakland.............	A.L.	13	77	5	1	.833	92	31	57	2.34	0
2008 Chicago d-e..........	N.L.	12	71	5	1	.833	89	30	39	1.77	0
2009 Iowa................	P.C.	1	4²/₃	0	0	.000	6	2	3	1.93	0
2009 Chicago f-g..........	N.L.	26	141	9	9	.500	171	67	122	4.09	0
2010 Oklahoma............	P.C.	5	23¹/₃	0	2	.000	34	8	21	3.86	0
2010 Texas h-i............	A.L.	20	92	5	5	.500	75	62	91	5.58	0
2011 Sacramento..........	P.C.	2	7²/₃	0	0	.000	12	3	3	3.52	0
2011 Oakland k-l..........	A.L.	15	82²/₃	4	4	.500	91	31	87	5.12	0
Major League Totals........9 Yrs.		170	928¹/₃	59	38	.608	949	422	781	3.76	0
Division Series											
2003 Oakland.............	A.L.	2	1¹/₃	1	1	.500	1	2	2	13.50	0
2008 Chicago.............	N.L.	1	4¹/₃	0	1	.000	4	3	5	6.23	0
Division Series Totals...........		3	5²/₃	1	2	.333	5	5	7	7.94	0
Championship Series											
2006 Oakland.............	A.L.	1	5²/₃	0	1	.000	4	5	5	4.76	0

a On disabled list from May 14 to June 21, 2005.
b On disabled list from April 27 to June 4 and June 5 to September 21, 2006.
c On disabled list from April 16 to June 22 and July 8 to October 8, 2007.
d On disabled list from April 3 to May 11, 2008.
e Traded to Chicago Cubs with pitcher Chad Gaudin for pitcher Sean Gallagher, outfielder Matt Murton, outfielder Eric Patterson and catcher Josh Donaldson, July 8, 2008.
f On disabled list from May 18 to June 13, 2009.
g Filed for free agency, November 5, 2009. Signed with Texas Rangers, December 10, 2009.
h On disabled list from June 12 to July 31 and August 15 to August 23, 2010.
i Released by Texas Rangers, October 8, 2010. Signed with Oakland Athletics, December 21, 2010.
k On disabled list from March 22 to July 1, 2011.
l Filed for free agency, October 30, 2011.

HAREN, DANIEL JOHN (DANNY)
Born, Monterey Park, California, September 17, 1980.
Bats Right. Throws Right. Height, 6 feet, 5 inches. Weight, 220 pounds.

Year	Club	Lea	G	IP	W	L	Pct	SO	BB	H	ERA	SAVES
2001 New Jersey......	N.Y.-Penn.	12	52¹/₃	3	3	.500	57	8	47	3.10	1
2002 Potomac..........	Carolina	14	92	3	6	.333	82	19	90	3.62	0
2002 Peoria............	Midwest	14	101²/₃	7	3	.700	89	12	89	1.95	0
2003 Memphis.........	P.C.	8	45²/₃	2	1	.667	35	8	50	4.93	0
2003 Tennessee.......	Southern	8	55	6	0	1.000	49	6	36	0.82	0
2003 St. Louis.........	N.L.	14	72²/₃	3	7	.300	43	22	84	5.08	0
2004 Memphis.........	P.C.	21	128	11	4	.733	150	33	136	4.15	0
2004 St. Louis a.......	N.L.	14	46	3	3	.500	32	17	45	4.50	0
2005 Oakland.........	A.L.	34	217	14	12	.538	163	53	212	3.73	0
2006 Oakland.........	A.L.	34	223	14	13	.519	176	45	224	4.12	0
2007 Oakland b........	A.L.	34	222²/₃	15	9	.625	192	55	214	3.07	0
2008 Arizona..........	N.L.	33	216	16	8	.667	206	40	204	3.33	0
2009 Arizona..........	N.L.	33	229¹/₃	14	10	.583	223	38	192	3.14	0
2010 Arizona..........	N.L.	21	141	7	8	.467	141	29	161	4.60	0
2010 Los Angeles c......	A.L.	14	94	5	4	.556	75	25	84	2.87	0
2011 Los Angeles......	A.L.	35	238¹/₃	16	10	.615	192	33	211	3.17	0
Major League Totals........9 Yrs.		266	1700	107	84	.560	1443	357	1631	3.59	0
Division Series											
2004 St. Louis..........	N.L.	1	2	1	0	1.000	3	1	1	0.00	0
2006 Oakland..........	A.L.	1	6	1	0	1.000	2	1	9	3.00	0
Division Series Totals...........		2	8	2	0	1.000	5	2	10	2.25	0
Championship Series											
2004 St. Louis..........	N.L.	2	1²/₃	0	0	.000	2	0	3	10.80	0
2006 Oakland..........	A.L.	1	5	0	0	.000	7	2	7	5.40	0
Championship Series Totals......		3	6²/₃	0	0	.000	9	2	10	6.75	0
World Series Record											
2004 St. Louis..........	N.L.	2	4²/₃	0	0	.000	2	3	4	0.00	0

a Traded to Oakland Athletics with pitcher Kiko Calero and catcher Daric Barton for pitcher Mark Mulder, December 18, 2004.

b Traded to Arizona Diamondbacks with pitcher Connor Robertson for pitcher Brett Anderson, pitcher Dana Eveland, pitcher Greg Smith, infielder Chris Carter, outfielder Aaron Cunningham and outfielder Carlos Gonzalez, December 14, 2007.

c Traded to Los Angeles Angels for pitcher Joe Saunders, pitcher Rafael Rodriguez, pitcher Patrick Corbin and player to be named later, July 25, 2010. Arizona Diamondbacks received pitcher Tyler Skaggs to complete trade, August 7, 2010.

HARRISON, MATTHEW REID (MATT)

Born, Durham, North Carolina, August 16, 1985.
Bats Left. Throws Left. Height, 6 feet, 4 inches. Weight, 225 pounds.

Year	Club	Lea	G	IP	W	L	Pct	SO	BB	H	ERA	SAVES
2003	Braves	Gulf Coast	11	39	3	1	.750	33	9	40	3.69	1
2004	Danville	Appal.	13	66	4	4	.500	49	10	72	4.09	0
2005	Rome	So.Atl.	27	167	12	7	.632	118	30	151	3.23	0
2006	Myrtle Beach	Carolina	13	81 1/3	8	4	.667	60	16	77	3.10	0
2006	Mississippi	Southern	13	77 1/3	3	4	.429	54	17	83	3.61	0
2007	Mississippi a	Southern	20	116 2/3	5	7	.417	78	34	118	3.39	0
2008	Frisco	Texas	9	46	3	2	.600	35	14	49	3.33	0
2008	Oklahoma	P.C.	6	38	3	1	.750	20	14	40	3.55	0
2008	Texas	A.L.	15	83 2/3	9	3	.750	42	31	100	5.49	0
2009	Frisco	Texas	3	9	0	1	.000	7	4	9	3.00	0
2009	Texas b	A.L.	11	63 1/3	4	5	.444	34	23	81	6.11	0
2010	Frisco	Texas	2	3	0	0	.000	4	0	3	3.00	1
2010	Oklahoma	P.C.	1	4 1/3	0	1	.000	4	1	9	6.23	0
2010	Texas c	A.L.	37	78 1/3	3	2	.600	46	39	80	4.71	2
2011	Texas	A.L.	31	185 2/3	14	9	.609	126	57	180	3.39	0
Major League Totals ....4 Yrs.			94	411	30	19	.612	248	150	441	4.49	2

Division Series

Year	Club	Lea	G	IP	W	L	Pct	SO	BB	H	ERA	SAVES
2011	Texas	A.L.	2	5 2/3	1	0	1.000	9	3	6	4.76	0

Championship Series

Year	Club	Lea	G	IP	W	L	Pct	SO	BB	H	ERA	SAVES
2011	Texas	A.L.	1	5	0	0	.000	3	3	3	3.60	0

World Series Record

Year	Club	Lea	G	IP	W	L	Pct	SO	BB	H	ERA	SAVES
2011	Texas	A.L.	2	7 2/3	0	2	.000	4	3	11	7.04	0

a Traded to Texas Rangers with catcher Jarrod Saltalamacchia, infielder Elvis Andrus, pitcher Neftali Feliz and pitcher Beau James for infielder Mark Teixeira and pitcher Ron Mahay, July 31, 2007.

b On disabled list from May 26 to June 17 and June 24 to November 13, 2009.

c On disabled list from May 7 to May 29, 2010.

HAWKINS, LA TROY (LA TROY)

Born, Gary, Indiana, December 21, 1972.
Bats Right. Throws Right. Height, 6 feet, 5 inches. Weight, 220 pounds.

Year	Club	Lea	G	IP	W	L	Pct	SO	BB	H	ERA	SAVES
1991	Twins	Gulf Coast	11	55	4	3	.571	47	26	62	4.75	0
1992	Twins	Gulf Coast	6	36 1/3	3	2	.600	35	10	36	3.22	0
1992	Elizabethtn	Appal.	5	26 2/3	0	1	.000	36	11	21	3.38	0
1993	Ft. Wayne	Midwest	26	157 1/3	15	5	.750	179	41	110	2.06	0
1994	Ft. Myers	Fla.St.	6	38 2/3	4	0	1.000	36	6	32	2.33	0
1994	Nashville	Southern	11	73 1/3	9	2	.818	53	28	50	2.33	0
1994	Salt Lake	P.C.	12	81 2/3	5	4	.556	37	33	92	4.08	0
1995	Salt Lake	P.C.	22	144 1/3	9	7	.563	74	40	150	3.55	0
1995	Minnesota	A.L.	6	27	2	3	.400	9	12	39	8.67	0
1996	Minnesota	A.L.	7	26 1/3	1	1	.500	24	9	42	8.20	0
1996	Salt Lake	P.C.	20	137 2/3	9	8	.529	99	31	138	3.92	0
1997	Salt Lake	P.C.	14	76	9	4	.692	53	16	100	5.45	0
1997	Minnesota	A.L.	20	103 1/3	6	12	.333	58	47	134	5.84	0
1998	Minnesota	A.L.	33	190 1/3	7	14	.333	105	61	227	5.25	0
1999	Minnesota	A.L.	33	174 1/3	10	14	.417	103	60	238	6.66	0
2000	Minnesota	A.L.	66	87 2/3	2	5	.286	59	32	85	3.39	14
2001	Minnesota	A.L.	62	51 1/3	1	5	.167	36	39	59	5.96	28
2002	Minnesota	A.L.	65	80 1/3	6	0	1.000	63	15	63	2.13	0
2003	Minnesota a	A.L.	74	77 1/3	9	3	.750	75	15	69	1.86	2
2004	Chicago	N.L.	77	82	5	4	.556	69	14	72	2.63	25
2005	Fresno	P.C.	2	2	0	0	.000	1	0	2	0.00	0
2005	Chicago-San Fran. b-c-d	N.L.	66	56 1/3	2	8	.200	43	24	58	3.83	6
2006	Baltimore e	A.L.	60	60 1/3	3	2	.600	27	15	73	4.48	0
2007	Colorado Springs	P.C.	4	4	1	0	1.000	5	2	2	2.25	0
2007	Colorado f-g	N.L.	62	55 1/3	2	5	.286	29	16	52	3.42	0
2008	New York	A.L.	33	41	1	1	.500	23	17	42	5.71	0
2008	Houston h-i	N.L.	24	21	2	0	1.000	25	5	11	0.43	1

Year	Club	Lea	G	IP	W	L	Pct	SO	BB	H	ERA	SAVES
2009 Houston j-k	N.L.	65	63⅓	1	4	.200	45	16	60	2.13	11
2010 Brewers	Arizona	2	3⅔	0	0	.000	5	0	4	2.45	0
2010 Nashville	P.C.	4	6⅓	0	0	.000	1	0	4	0.00	1
2010 Milwaukee l	N.L.	18	16	0	3	.000	18	6	21	8.44	0
2011 Brevard County	Fla.St.	3	3⅔	0	0	.000	5	0	6	4.91	0
2011 Nashville	P.C.	2	1⅓	0	0	.000	1	2	1	0.00	0
2011 Milwaukee m-n	N.L.	52	48⅓	3	1	.750	28	10	50	2.42	0
Major League Totals 17 Yrs.		823	1261⅔	63	85	.426	839	413	1395	4.48	87
Division Series											
2002 Minnesota	A.L.	3	2⅓	0	0	.000	5	0	0	0.00	0
2003 Minnesota	A.L.	3	3	1	0	1.000	5	0	5	6.00	0
2007 Colorado	N.L.	1	1	0	0	.000	0	1	0	0.00	0
2011 Milwaukee	N.L.	1	1	0	0	.000	1	2	0	0.00	0
Division Series Totals		8	7⅓	1	0	1.000	11	3	5	2.45	0
Championship Series											
2002 Minnesota	A.L.	4	1⅓	0	0	.000	1	1	4	20.25	0
2007 Colorado	N.L.	2	2	0	0	.000	1	0	1	0.00	0
2011 Milwaukee	N.L.	3	3	0	0	.000	2	2	2	0.00	0
Championship Series Totals		9	6⅓	0	0	.000	4	3	7	4.26	0
World Series Record											
2007 Colorado	N.L.	2	2	0	0	.000	2	0	1	4.50	0

a Filed for free agency, October 27, 2003. Signed with Chicago Cubs, December 3, 2003.
b On disabled list from June 10 to July 4, 2005.
c Traded to San Francisco Giants for pitcher Jerome Williams and pitcher David Aardsma, May 28, 2005.
d Traded to Baltimore Orioles for pitcher Steve Kline, December 6, 2005.
e Filed for free agency, October 31, 2006. Signed with Colorado Rockies, December 5, 2006.
f On disabled list from April 21 to May 22, 2007.
g Filed for free agency, November 1, 2007. Signed with New York Yankees, December 21, 2007.
h Traded to Houston Astros for infielder Matt Cusick and cash, July 30, 2008.
i Filed for free agency, October 31, 2008, re-signed with Houston Astros, November 11, 2008.
j On disabled list from July 28 to August 12, 2009.
k Filed for free agency, November 6, 2009. Signed with Milwaukee Brewers, December 16, 2009.
l On disabled list from May 7 to July 29 and August 11 to October 5, 2010.
m On disabled list from March 22 to April 21, 2011.
n Filed for free agency, October 30, 2011. Signed with Los Angeles Dodgers, December 8, 2011.

HAWKSWORTH, BLAKE EDWARD
Born, N.Vancouver, British Columbia, Canada, March 1, 1983.
Bats Right. Throws Right. Height, 6 feet, 3 inches. Weight, 195 pounds.

Year	Club	Lea	G	IP	W	L	Pct	SO	BB	H	ERA	SAVES
2002 Johnson City	Appal.	13	66	2	4	.333	61	18	58	3.14	0
2002 New Jersey	N.Y.-Penn.	2	9⅔	1	0	1.000	8	2	6	0.00	0
2003 Palm Beach	Fla.St.	6	32	1	3	.250	32	11	28	3.94	0
2003 Peoria	Midwest	10	54⅔	5	1	.833	57	12	37	2.30	0
2004 Palm Beach	Fla.St.	2	10⅔	1	0	1.000	11	3	10	5.91	0
2005 New Jersey	N.Y.-Penn.	7	14⅔	0	3	.000	12	10	18	7.98	0
2006 Palm Beach	Fla.St.	14	83⅔	7	2	.778	55	19	75	2.47	0
2006 Springfield	Texas	13	79⅔	4	2	.667	66	31	72	3.39	0
2007 Memphis	P.C.	25	129⅔	4	13	.235	88	41	150	5.28	0
2008 Cardinals	Gulf Coast	2	7	0	0	.000	6	2	2	0.00	0
2008 Memphis	P.C.	18	88⅔	5	7	.417	83	38	111	6.09	0
2009 Memphis	P.C.	12	73	5	4	.556	57	20	61	3.58	0
2009 St. Louis a	N.L.	30	40	4	0	1.000	20	15	29	2.03	0
2010 St. Louis	N.L.	45	90⅓	4	8	.333	61	35	113	4.98	0
2011 Rancho Cucamonga	Calif.	4	4	0	0	.000	5	1	2	2.25	0
2011 Los Angeles b	N.L.	49	53	2	5	.286	43	17	45	4.08	0
Major League Totals 3 Yrs.		124	183⅓	10	13	.435	124	67	187	4.07	0
Division Series											
2009 St. Louis	N.L.	1	1	0	0	.000	1	1	1	0.00	0

a Traded to Los Angeles Dodgers for infielder Ryan Theriot, November 30, 2010.
b On disabled list from May 11 to June 6, 2011.

HELLICKSON, JEREMY ROBERT
Born, Des Moines, Iowa, April 8, 1987.
Bats Right. Throws Right. Height, 6 feet, 1 inch. Weight, 185 pounds.

Year	Club	Lea	G	IP	W	L	Pct	SO	BB	H	ERA	SAVES
2005 Princeton	Appal.	4	6	0	0	.000	11	1	6	6.00	0

Year	Club	Lea	G	IP	W	L	Pct	SO	BB	H	ERA	SAVES
2006 Hudson Valley	N.Y.-Penn.	15	77²/₃	3	3	.500	96	16	55	2.43	0
2007 Columbus	So.Atl.	21	111¹/₃	13	3	.813	106	34	87	2.67	0
2008 Vero Beach	Fla.St.	14	76²/₃	7	1	.875	83	5	64	2.00	0
2008 Montgomery	Southern	13	75¹/₃	4	4	.500	79	15	84	3.94	0
2009 Durham	Int.	9	57¹/₃	6	1	.857	70	15	31	2.51	0
2009 Montgomery	Southern	11	56²/₃	3	1	.750	62	14	41	2.38	0
2010 Charlotte	Fla.St.	1	1²/₃	0	0	.000	4	2	4	21.60	0
2010 Durham	Int.	21	117²/₃	12	3	.800	123	35	103	2.45	0
2010 Tampa Bay	A.L.	10	36¹/₃	4	0	1.000	33	8	32	3.47	0
2011 Tampa Bay a	A.L.	29	189	13	10	.565	117	72	146	2.95	0
Major League Totals ....2 Yrs.		39	225¹/₃	17	10	.630	150	80	178	3.04	0
Division Series											
2011 Tampa Bay	A.L.	1	4	0	1	.000	1	1	4	6.75	0

a Selected Rookie of the Year in American League for 2011.

HENSLEY, CLAYTON ALLEN (CLAY)

Born, Tomball, Texas, August 31, 1979.
Bats Right. Throws Right. Height, 5 feet, 11 inches. Weight, 190 pounds.

Year	Club	Lea	G	IP	W	L	Pct	SO	BB	H	ERA	SAVES
2002 Salem-Keizer	Northwest	15	81²/₃	7	0	1.000	84	25	72	2.53	0
2003 Lake Elsinore	Calif.	8	44¹/₃	3	4	.429	40	14	51	3.45	0
2003 San Jose	Calif.	5	29¹/₃	2	3	.400	25	9	38	5.83	0
2003 Hagerstown	So.Atl.	12	68	4	3	.571	74	20	56	3.18	0
2004 Mobile	Southern	27	159	11	10	.524	125	48	167	4.30	0
2005 Portland	P.C.	15	90¹/₃	2	2	.500	71	22	63	2.99	0
2005 San Diego	N.L.	24	47²/₃	1	1	.500	28	17	33	1.70	0
2006 San Diego	N.L.	37	187	11	12	.478	122	76	174	3.71	0
2007 Portland	P.C.	13	71	2	7	.222	50	34	102	6.72	0
2007 San Diego a	N.L.	13	50	2	3	.400	30	32	62	6.84	0
2008 Lake Elsinore	Calif.	1	1	1	0	1.000	1	0	1	0.00	0
2008 Portland	P.C.	16	48	1	1	.500	34	16	46	3.94	0
2008 San Diego b	N.L.	32	39	1	2	.333	26	25	36	5.31	0
2009 New Orleans	P.C.	19	114	8	4	.667	82	38	105	3.24	0
2009 Round Rock c-d-e	P.C.	6	10	1	0	1.000	5	7	12	7.20	0
2010 Jupiter	Fla.St.	2	2²/₃	0	0	.000	2	1	1	0.00	0
2010 Florida f	N.L.	68	75	3	4	.429	77	29	54	2.16	7
2011 Marlins	Gulf Coast	1	3¹/₃	0	0	.000	6	0	2	2.70	0
2011 Jupiter	Fla.St.	1	4	0	1	.000	2	0	2	4.50	0
2011 Jacksonville	Southern	1	4¹/₃	0	0	.000	7	1	5	2.08	0
2011 Florida g-h	N.L.	37	67²/₃	6	7	.462	46	30	62	5.19	0
Major League Totals ....6 Yrs.		211	466¹/₃	24	29	.453	329	209	421	3.94	7
Division Series											
2005 San Diego	N.L.	3	4²/₃	0	0	.000	1	3	4	3.86	0
2006 San Diego	N.L.	2	2²/₃	0	0	.000	0	1	2	0.00	0
Division Series Totals		5	7¹/₃	0	0	.000	1	4	6	2.45	0

a On disabled list from May 3 to June 1 and September 25 to November 1, 2007.
b On disabled list from March 21 to June 6, 2008.
c Not offered contract, December 12, 2008. Signed with Houston Astros organization, January 5, 2009.
d Released by Houston Astros, April 28, 2009. Signed with Florida Marlins organization, May 25, 2009.
e Filed for free agency, November 9, 2009, re-signed with Florida Marlins, December 14, 2009.
f On disabled list from June 12 to July 2, 2010.
g On disabled list from May 7 to May 22 and June 2 to July 17, 2011.
h Not offered contract, December 12, 2011.

HERNANDEZ, DAVID JESUS

Born, Sacramento, California, May 13, 1985.
Bats Right. Throws Right. Height, 6 feet, 3 inches. Weight, 215 pounds.

Year	Club	Lea	G	IP	W	L	Pct	SO	BB	H	ERA	SAVES
2005 Aberdeen	N.Y.-Penn.	12	41²/₃	1	2	.333	47	17	41	3.89	0
2006 Delmarva	So.Atl.	28	145¹/₃	7	8	.467	154	71	134	4.15	0
2007 Frederick	Carolina	28	145¹/₃	7	11	.389	168	47	139	4.95	0
2008 Bowie	Eastern	27	141	10	4	.714	166	71	112	2.68	0
2009 Bowie	Eastern	1	4	0	0	.000	4	1	2	2.25	0
2009 Norfolk	Int.	11	57¹/₃	3	2	.600	79	18	42	3.30	0
2009 Baltimore	A.L.	20	101¹/₃	4	10	.286	68	46	118	5.42	0
2010 Bowie	Eastern	2	2	0	0	.000	3	0	1	0.00	0
2010 Baltimore a-b	A.L.	41	79¹/₃	8	8	.500	72	42	72	4.31	2

Year Club	Lea	G	IP	W	L	Pct	SO	BB	H	ERA	SAVES
2011 Arizona..............	N.L.	74	69⅓	5	3	.625	77	30	49	3.38	11
Major League Totals ....3 Yrs.		135	250	17	21	.447	217	118	239	4.50	13
Division Series											
2011 Arizona..............	N.L.	4	5	0	0	.000	5	0	2	3.60	0

a On disabled list from August 5 to September 7, 2010.
b Traded to Baltimore Orioles with pitcher Kam Mickolio for infielder Mark Reynolds and player to be named later, December 6, 2010. Baltimore Orioles received catcher John Hester to complete trade, April 30, 2011.

HERNANDEZ, EISLER LIVAN
Born, Villa Clara, Cuba, February 20, 1975.
Bats Right. Throws Right. Height, 6 feet, 2 inches. Weight, 245 pounds.

Year Club	Lea	G	IP	W	L	Pct	SO	BB	H	ERA	SAVES
1996 Charlotte	Int.	10	49	2	4	.333	45	34	61	5.14	0
1996 Portland	Eastern	15	93⅓	9	2	.818	95	34	81	4.34	0
1996 Florida	N.L.	1	3	0	0	.000	2	2	3	0.00	0
1997 Portland	Eastern	1	4	0	0	.000	2	7	2	2.25	0
1997 Charlotte	Int.	14	81⅓	5	3	.625	58	38	76	3.98	0
1997 Florida	N.L.	17	96⅓	9	3	.750	72	38	81	3.18	0
1998 Florida	N.L.	33	234⅓	10	12	.455	162	104	*265	4.72	0
1999 Florida-San Francisco a ..	N.L.	30	199⅔	8	12	.400	144	76	227	4.64	0
2000 San Francisco	N.L.	33	240	17	11	.607	165	73	*254	3.75	0
2001 San Francisco	N.L.	34	226⅔	13	15	.464	138	85	*266	5.24	0
2002 San Francisco	N.L.	33	216	12	*16	.429	134	71	233	4.38	0
2003 Montreal b-c	N.L.	33	*233⅓	15	10	.600	178	57	225	3.20	0
2004 Montreal..............	N.L.	35	*255	11	15	.423	186	83	234	3.60	0
2005 Washington	N.L.	35	*246⅓	15	10	.600	147	84	*268	3.98	0
2006 Washington-Arizona d ...	N.L.	34	216	13	13	.500	128	78	246	4.83	0
2007 Arizona e	N.L.	33	204⅓	11	11	.500	90	79	*247	4.93	0
2008 Minnesota	A.L.	23	139⅔	10	8	.556	54	29	199	5.48	0
2008 Colorado f-g.........	N.L.	8	40⅓	3	3	.500	13	14	58	8.03	0
2009 New York-Washington h-i	N.L.	31	183⅔	9	12	.429	102	67	220	5.44	0
2010 Washington	N.L.	33	211⅔	10	12	.455	114	64	216	3.66	0
2011 Washington j	N.L.	29	175⅓	8	13	.381	99	46	199	4.47	0
Major League Totals ....16 Yrs.		475	3121⅔	174	176	.497	1928	1050	3441	4.39	0
Division Series											
1997 Florida	N.L.	1	4	0	0	.000	3	0	3	2.25	0
2000 San Francisco	N.L.	1	7⅔	1	0	1.000	5	5	5	1.17	0
2002 San Francisco	N.L.	1	8⅓	1	0	1.000	6	2	8	3.24	0
2007 Arizona...............	N.L.	1	6	1	0	1.000	2	5	5	1.50	0
Division Series Totals		4	26	3	0	1.000	16	12	21	2.08	0
Championship Series											
1997 Florida	N.L.	2	10⅔	2	0	1.000	16	2	5	0.84	0
2002 San Francisco	N.L.	1	6⅓	0	0	.000	0	1	9	2.84	0
2007 Arizona...............	N.L.	1	5⅔	0	1	.000	4	2	8	6.35	0
Championship Series Totals		4	22⅔	2	1	.667	20	5	22	2.78	0
World Series Record											
1997 Florida	N.L.	2	13⅔	2	0	1.000	7	10	15	5.27	0
2002 San Francisco	N.L.	2	5⅔	0	2	.000	4	9	9	14.29	0
World Series Totals..............		4	19⅓	2	2	.500	11	19	24	7.91	0

a Traded to San Francisco Giants for pitcher Jason Grilli and pitcher Nathan Bump, July 24, 1999.
b Traded to Montreal Expos with catcher Edwards Guzman for pitcher Jim Brower and player to be named later, March 24, 2003.
c San Francisco Giants received pitcher Matt Blank to complete trade, April 30, 2003.
d Traded to Arizona Diamondbacks with cash for pitcher Garrett Mock and pitcher Matt Chico, August 7, 2006.
e Filed for free agency, October 29, 2007. Signed with Minnesota Twins, February 12, 2008.
f Claimed on waivers by Colorado Rockies, August 6, 2008.
g Filed for free agency, November 1, 2008. Signed with New York Mets organization, February 14, 2009.
h Released by New York Mets, August 20, 2009. Signed with Washington Nationals, August 26, 2009.
i Filed for free agency, November 5, 2009, re-signed with Washington Nationals organization, February 24, 2010.
j Filed for free agency, October 30, 2011.

HERNANDEZ, FELIX ABRAHAM
Born, Valencia, Venezuela, April 8, 1986.
Bats Right. Throws Right. Height, 6 feet, 3 inches. Weight, 230 pounds.

Year Club	Lea	G	IP	W	L	Pct	SO	BB	H	ERA	SAVES
2003 Wisconsin	Midwest	2	14	0	0	.000	18	3	9	1.93	0
2003 Everett	Northwest	11	55	7	2	.778	73	24	43	2.29	0

Year	Club	Lea	G	IP	W	L	Pct	SO	BB	H	ERA	SAVES
2004 Inland Empire......California			16	92	9	3	.750	114	26	85	2.74	0
2004 San Antonio..........Texas			10	57¹/₃	5	1	.833	58	21	47	3.30	0
2005 Tacoma..............P.C.			19	88	9	4	.692	100	48	62	2.25	0
2005 Seattle .............A.L.			12	84¹/₃	4	4	.500	77	23	61	2.67	0
2006 Seattle .............A.L.			31	191	12	14	.462	176	60	195	4.52	0
2007 Seattle a............A.L.			30	190¹/₃	14	7	.667	165	53	209	3.92	0
2008 Seattle b............A.L.			31	200²/₃	9	11	.450	175	80	198	3.45	0
2009 Seattle .............A.L.			34	238²/₃	*19	5	*.792	217	71	200	2.49	0
2010 Seattle c............A.L.			34	*249²/₃	13	12	.520	232	70	194	*2.27	0
2011 Seattle .............A.L.			33	233²/₃	14	14	.500	222	67	218	3.47	0
Major League Totals ....7 Yrs.			205	1388¹/₃	85	67	.559	1264	424	1275	3.24	0

a On disabled list from April 19 to May 15, 2007.
b On disabled list from June 24 to July 11, 2008.
c Selected Cy Young Award Winner in American League for 2010.

HERNDON, KENNETH DAVID (DAVID)

Born, Panama City, Florida, September 4, 1985.
Bats Right. Throws Right. Height, 6 feet, 5 inches. Weight, 230 pounds.

Year	Club	Lea	G	IP	W	L	Pct	SO	BB	H	ERA	SAVES
2006 Orem .... Pioneer			14	69¹/₃	5	2	.714	36	10	65	2.21	0
2007 Cedar Rapids ....Midwest			25	152¹/₃	13	8	.619	83	20	175	4.02	0
2008 Rancho Cucamonga.... Calif.			43	100²/₃	3	7	.300	70	16	120	5.01	17
2009 Arkansas a...........Texas			50	65¹/₃	5	6	.455	35	14	70	3.03	11
2010 Philadelphia ....,N.L.			47	52¹/₃	1	3	.250	29	17	67	4.30	0
2011 Lehigh Valley ....Int.			8	14²/₃	2	0	1.000	14	2	15	2.45	1
2011 Philadelphia ..........N.L.			45	57	1	4	.200	39	24	54	3.32	1
Major League Totals ....2 Yrs.			92	109¹/₃	2	7	.222	68	41	121	3.79	1

a Selected by Philadelphia Phillies from Los Angeles Angels in Rule V draft, December 20, 2009.

HERRMANN, FRANK JOSEPH

Born, Rutherford, New Jersey, May 30, 1984.
Bats Left. Throws Right. Height, 6 feet, 4 inches. Weight, 220 pounds.

Year	Club	Lea	G	IP	W	L	Pct	SO	BB	H	ERA	SAVES
2006 Lake County........So.Atl.			26	122¹/₃	4	6	.400	89	47	122	3.90	0
2007 Kinston............Carolina			26	146	11	5	.688	88	28	163	4.01	0
2008 Kinston............Carolina			1	5¹/₃	0	0	.000	4	1	8	11.81	0
2008 Buffalo................Int.			2	13	0	2	.000	14	6	11	1.38	0
2008 Akron..............Eastern			23	131²/₃	11	6	.647	86	36	142	4.10	0
2009 Akron..............Eastern			5	30²/₃	2	1	.667	12	5	27	2.93	0
2009 Columbus.............Int.			44	76	2	3	.400	50	13	83	2.96	2
2010 Columbus.............Int.			19	28²/₃	3	0	1.000	22	8	15	0.31	2
2010 Cleveland.............A.L.			40	44²/₃	0	1	.000	24	9	48	4.03	1
2011 Columbus.............Int.			9	10²/₃	0	0	.000	12	4	13	5.91	0
2011 Cleveland.............A.L.			40	56¹/₃	4	0	1.000	34	16	71	5.11	0
Major League Totals ....2 Yrs.			80	101	4	1	.800	58	25	119	4.63	1

HOCHEVAR, LUKE ANTHONY

Born, Denver, Colorado, September 15, 1983.
Bats Right. Throws Right. Height, 6 feet, 5 inches. Weight, 205 pounds.

Year	Club	Lea	G	IP	W	L	Pct	SO	BB	H	ERA	SAVES
2006 Burlington ....Midwest			4	15¹/₃	0	1	.000	16	2	8	1.17	0
2007 Wichita..............Texas			17	94	3	6	.333	94	26	110	4.69	0
2007 Omaha...............P.C.			10	58	1	3	.250	44	21	53	5.12	0
2007 Kansas City ...........A.L.			4	12²/₃	0	1	.000	5	4	11	2.13	0
2008 Omaha...............P.C.			3	17¹/₃	1	1	.500	12	6	11	2.60	0
2008 Kansas City a..........A.L.			22	129	6	12	.333	72	47	143	5.51	0
2009 Omaha...............P.C.			8	48	5	1	.833	36	12	41	1.50	0
2009 Kansas City ..........A.L.			25	143	7	13	.350	106	46	167	6.55	0
2010 Omaha...............P.C.			2	5	0	0	.000	4	1	3	1.80	0
2010 Kansas City b..........A.L.			18	103	6	6	.500	76	37	110	4.81	0
2011 Kansas City ..........A.L.			31	198	11	11	.500	128	62	192	4.68	0
Major League Totals ....5 Yrs.			100	585²/₃	30	43	.411	387	196	623	5.29	0

a On disabled list from August 20 to November 14, 2008.
b On disabled list from June 12 to September 3, 2010.

HOLLAND, DEREK LANE

Born, Newark, Ohio, October 9, 1986.
Bats Both. Throws Left. Height, 6 feet, 2 inches. Weight, 185 pounds.

Year	Club	Lea	G	IP	W	L	Pct	SO	BB	H	ERA	SAVES
2007 Spokane	Northwest		16	67	4	5	.444	83	21	57	3.22	0
2008 Bakersfield	Calif.		5	31	3	1	.750	37	5	20	3.19	0
2008 Clinton	Midwest		17	93⅔	7	0	1.000	91	29	77	2.40	0
2008 Frisco	Texas		4	26	3	0	1.000	29	6	14	0.69	0
2009 Okla.	P.C.		1	4	0	1	.000	5	3	5	9.00	0
2009 Texas	A.L.		33	138⅓	8	13	.381	107	47	160	6.12	0
2010 Rangers	Arizona		1	3	0	0	.000	6	0	0	0.00	0
2010 Oklahoma	P.C.		11	62⅔	6	2	.750	51	18	50	1.87	0
2010 Texas a	A.L.		14	57⅓	3	4	.429	54	24	55	4.08	0
2011 Texas	A.L.		32	198	16	5	.762	162	67	201	3.95	0
Major League Totals	3 Yrs.		79	393⅔	27	22	.551	323	138	416	4.73	0
Division Series												
2010 Texas	A.L.		2	4⅔	0	0	.000	4	1	6	5.79	0
2011 Texas	A.L.		2	6⅓	1	0	1.000	2	2	7	1.42	0
Division Series Totals			4	11	1	0	1.000	6	3	13	3.27	0
Championship Series												
2010 Texas	A.L.		2	5⅔	1	0	1.000	4	2	3	0.00	0
2011 Texas	A.L.		2	7⅓	0	0	.000	5	4	11	8.59	0
Championship Series Totals			4	13	1	0	1.000	9	6	14	4.85	0
World Series Record												
2010 Texas	A.L.		2	1	0	0	.000	1	4	0	27.00	0
2011 Texas	A.L.		2	10⅓	1	0	1.000	7	2	4	0.87	0
World Series Totals			4	11⅓	1	0	1.000	8	6	4	3.18	0

a On disabled list from May 31 to August 1, 2010.

HOLLAND, GREGORY SCOTT (GREG)

Born, Morganton, North Carolina, November 20, 1985.
Bats Right. Throws Right. Height, 5 feet, 11 inches. Weight, 200 pounds.

Year	Club	Lea	G	IP	W	L	Pct	SO	BB	H	ERA	SAVES
2007 Idaho Falls	Pioneer		22	33⅔	6	1	.857	37	15	28	3.48	6
2008 Wilmington	Carolina		32	84⅓	4	5	.444	96	35	70	3.42	4
2009 NW Arkansas	Texas		29	45⅓	3	2	.600	49	19	46	3.18	8
2009 Omaha	P.C.		6	9	1	1	.500	1	5	12	7.00	2
2010 Omaha	P.C.		36	56⅔	3	3	.500	60	30	40	3.81	3
2010 Kansas City	A.L.		15	18⅔	0	1	.000	23	8	23	6.75	0
2011 Omaha	P.C.		13	21⅔	2	0	1.000	27	11	13	2.08	2
2011 Kansas City	A.L.		46	60	5	1	.833	74	19	37	1.80	4
Major League Totals	2 Yrs.		61	78⅔	5	2	.714	97	27	60	2.97	4

HUDSON, DANIEL CLAIRBORNE

Born, Lynchburg, Virginia, March 9, 1987.
Bats Right. Throws Right. Height, 6 feet, 4 inches. Weight, 220 pounds.

Year	Club	Lea	G	IP	W	L	Pct	SO	BB	H	ERA	SAVES
2008 Great Falls	Pioneer		14	69⅔	5	4	.556	90	22	52	3.36	0
2009 Kannapolis	So.Atl.		4	22	1	2	.333	30	2	15	1.23	0
2009 Winston-Salem	Carolina		8	45	4	3	.571	49	13	31	3.40	0
2009 Birmingham	Southern		9	56⅓	7	0	1.000	63	10	37	1.60	0
2009 Charlotte	Int.		5	24	2	0	1.000	24	9	22	3.00	0
2009 Chicago	A.L.		6	18⅔	1	1	.500	14	9	16	3.38	0
2010 Charlotte	Int.		17	93⅓	11	4	.733	108	31	81	3.47	0
2010 Chicago	A.L.		3	15⅔	1	1	.500	14	11	17	6.32	0
2010 Arizona a	N.L.		11	79⅔	7	1	.875	70	16	51	1.69	0
2011 Arizona	N.L.		33	222	16	12	.571	169	50	217	3.49	0
Major League Totals	3 Yrs.		53	336	25	15	.625	267	86	301	3.19	0
Division Series												
2011 Arizona	N.L.		1	5⅓	0	1	.000	6	0	9	8.44	0

a Traded to Arizona Diamondbacks with pitcher David Holmberg for pitcher Edwin Jackson, July 30, 2010.

HUDSON, TIMOTHY ADAM (TIM)

Born, Columbus, Georgia, July 14, 1975.
Bats Right. Throws Right. Height, 6 feet, 1 Inch. Weight, 170 pounds.

Year	Club	Lea	G	IP	W	L	Pct	SO	BB	H	ERA	SAVES
1997	Sou Oregon	Northwest	8	28²/₃	3	1	.750	37	15	12	2.51	0
1998	Modesto	California	8	37²/₃	4	0	1.000	48	18	19	1.67	0
1998	Huntsville	Southern	22	134²/₃	10	9	.526	104	71	136	4.54	0
1999	Midland	Texas	3	18	3	0	1.000	18	3	9	0.50	0
1999	Vancouver	P.C.	8	49	4	0	1.000	61	21	38	2.20	0
1999	Oakland	A.L.	21	136¹/₃	11	2	.846	132	62	121	3.23	0
2000	Oakland	A.L.	32	202¹/₃	*20	6	*.769	169	82	169	4.14	0
2001	Oakland	A.L.	35	235	18	9	.667	181	71	216	3.37	0
2002	Oakland	A.L.	34	238¹/₃	15	9	.625	152	62	237	2.98	0
2003	Oakland	A.L.	34	240	16	7	.696	162	61	197	2.70	0
2004	Sacramento	P.C.	1	3	0	0	.000	3	2	2	6.00	0
2004	Oakland a-b	A.L.	27	188²/₃	12	6	.667	103	44	194	3.53	0
2005	Atlanta c	N.L.	29	192	14	9	.609	115	65	194	3.52	0
2006	Atlanta	N.L.	35	218¹/₃	13	12	.520	141	79	235	4.86	0
2007	Atlanta	N.L.	34	224¹/₃	16	10	.615	132	53	221	3.33	0
2008	Atlanta d	N.L.	23	142	11	7	.611	85	40	125	3.17	0
2009	Myrtle Beach	Carolina	2	4²/₃	0	1	.000	3	2	5	5.79	0
2009	Gwinnett	Int.	4	18²/₃	1	0	1.000	11	2	24	3.38	0
2009	Atlanta e	N.L.	7	42¹/₃	2	1	.667	30	13	49	3.61	0
2010	Atlanta	N.L.	34	228²/₃	17	9	.654	139	74	189	2.83	0
2011	Atlanta	N.L.	33	215	16	10	.615	158	56	189	3.22	0
Major League Totals	13 Yrs.		378	2503¹/₃	181	97	.651	1699	762	2336	3.40	0
Division Series												
2000	Oakland	A.L.	1	8	0	1	.000	5	4	6	3.38	0
2001	Oakland	A.L.	2	9²/₃	1	0	1.000	5	1	8	0.93	0
2002	Oakland	A.L.	2	8²/₃	0	1	.000	8	4	13	6.23	0
2003	Oakland	A.L.	2	7²/₃	0	0	.000	6	1	10	3.52	0
2005	Atlanta	N.L.	2	13²/₃	0	1	.000	8	6	13	5.27	0
2010	Atlanta	N.L.	1	7	0	0	.000	5	4	4	0.00	0
Division Series Totals			10	54²/₃	1	3	.250	37	20	54	3.46	0

a On disabled list from June 23 to August 7, 2004.
b Traded to Atlanta Braves for pitcher Juan Cruz, pitcher Dan Meyer and outfielder Charles Thomas, December 16, 2004.
c On disabled list from June 14 to July 16, 2005.
d On disabled list from July 27 to November 3, 2008.
e On disabled list from February 24 to September 1, 2009.

HUGHES, PHILIP JOSEPH

Born, Mission Viejo, California, June 24, 1986.
Bats Right. Throws Right. Height, 6 feet, 5 inches. Weight, 220 pounds.

Year	Club	Lea	G	IP	W	L	Pct	SO	BB	H	ERA	SAVES
2004	Yankees	Gulf Coast	3	5	0	0	.000	8	0	4	0.00	0
2005	Tampa	Fla.St.	5	17²/₃	2	0	1.000	21	4	8	3.06	0
2005	Charleston	So.Atl.	12	68²/₃	7	1	.875	72	16	46	1.97	0
2006	Trenton	Eastern	21	116	10	3	.769	138	32	73	2.25	0
2006	Tampa	Fla.St.	5	30	2	3	.400	30	2	19	1.80	0
2007	Tampa	Fla.St.	1	2	0	0	.000	3	2	0	0.00	0
2007	Trenton	Eastern	2	7	0	0	.000	11	2	5	1.29	0
2007	Scranton-WB	Int.	5	28²/₃	4	1	.800	28	8	16	2.20	0
2007	New York a	A.L.	13	72²/₃	5	3	.625	58	29	64	4.46	0
2008	Charleston	So.Atl.	2	6²/₃	2	0	1.000	6	2	3	0.00	0
2008	Scranton-WB	Int.	6	29	1	0	1.000	31	9	34	5.90	0
2008	New York b	A.L.	8	34	0	4	.000	23	15	43	6.62	0
2009	Scranton/WB	Int.	3	19¹/₃	3	0	1.000	19	3	17	1.86	0
2009	New York	A.L.	51	86	8	3	.727	96	28	68	3.03	3
2010	New York	A.L.	31	176¹/₃	18	8	.692	146	58	162	4.19	0
2011	Staten Island	N.Y.-Penn.	1	4¹/₃	0	0	.000	7	1	3	2.08	0
2011	Trenton	Eastern	2	9²/₃	1	0	1.000	11	4	6	1.86	0
2011	New York c	A.L.	17	74²/₃	5	5	.500	47	27	84	5.79	0
Major League Totals	5 Yrs.		120	443²/₃	36	23	.610	370	157	421	4.46	3
Division Series												
2007	New York	A.L.	2	5²/₃	1	0	1.000	6	0	3	1.59	0
2009	New York	A.L.	3	2	0	0	.000	3	1	5	9.00	0
2010	New York	A.L.	1	7	1	0	1.000	6	1	4	0.00	0
2011	New York	A.L.	2	2¹/₃	0	0	.000	4	0	2	0.00	0
Division Series Totals			8	17	2	0	1.000	19	2	14	1.59	0

Year	Club	Lea	G	IP	W	L	Pct	SO	BB	H	ERA	SAVES
	Championship Series											
2009	New York	A.L.	3	$2\frac{2}{3}$	0	1	.000	3	1	4	3.38	0
2010	New York	A.L.	2	$8\frac{2}{3}$	0	2	.000	6	7	14	11.42	0
Championship Series Totals			5	$11\frac{1}{3}$	0	3	.000	9	8	18	9.53	0
	World Series Record											
2009	New York	A.L.	3	$1\frac{2}{3}$	0	0	.000	1	2	2	16.20	0

a On disabled list from May 2 to August 4, 2007.
b On disabled list from April 30 to July 30, 2008.
c On disabled list from April 15 to July 6, 2011.

HUMBER, PHILIP GREGORY

Born, Nacogdoches, Texas, December 21, 1982.
Bats Right. Throws Right. Height, 6 feet, 4 inches. Weight, 210 pounds.

Year	Club	Lea	G	IP	W	L	Pct	SO	BB	H	ERA	SAVES
2005	St. Lucie	Fla.St.	14	$70\frac{1}{3}$	2	6	.250	65	18	74	4.99	0
2005	Binghamton	Eastern	1	4	0	1	.000	2	2	4	6.75	0
2006	Mets	Gulf Coast	1	4	0	0	.000	7	1	7	6.75	0
2006	St. Lucie	Fla.St.	7	38	3	1	.750	36	9	24	2.37	0
2006	Binghamton	Eastern	6	$34\frac{1}{3}$	2	2	.500	36	10	25	2.88	0
2006	New York	N.L.	2	2	0	0	.000	2	1	0	0.00	0
2007	New Orleans	P.C.	25	139	11	9	.550	120	44	129	4.27	0
2007	New York	N.L.	3	7	0	0	.000	2	2	9	7.71	0
2008	Rochester	Int.	31	$136\frac{1}{3}$	10	8	.556	106	49	145	4.56	0
2008	Minnesota a	A.L.	5	$11\frac{2}{3}$	0	0	.000	6	5	11	4.63	0
2009	Minnesota	A.L.	8	9	0	0	.000	9	9	17	8.00	0
2009	Rochester b	Int.	23	$119\frac{2}{3}$	7	9	.438	87	45	135	5.34	0
2010	Omaha	P.C.	21	$118\frac{2}{3}$	5	6	.455	80	20	131	4.47	0
2010	Kansas City c	A.L.	8	$21\frac{2}{3}$	2	1	.667	16	7	22	4.15	0
2011	Charlotte	Int.	1	5	0	0	.000	5	1	7	7.20	0
2011	Chicago d-e	A.L.	28	163	9	9	.500	116	41	151	3.75	0
Major League Totals	6 Yrs.		54	$214\frac{1}{3}$	11	10	.524	151	65	210	4.12	0

a Traded to Minnesota Twins with outfielder Carlos Gomez, pitcher Kevin Mulvey and pitcher Deolis Garcia for pitcher Johan Santana, February 2, 2008.
b Filed for free agency, October 6, 2009. Signed with Kansas City Royals organization, December 15, 2009.
c Claimed on waivers by Oakland Athletics, December 17, 2010.
d Claimed on waivers by Chicago White Sox, January 18, 2011.
e On disabled list from August 19 to September 3, 2011.

HUNTER, RAYMOND THOMAS (TOMMY)

Born, Tuscaloosa, Alabama, July 3, 1986.
Bats Right. Throws Right. Height, 6 feet, 3 inches. Weight, 255 pounds.

Year	Club	Lea	G	IP	W	L	Pct	SO	BB	H	ERA	SAVES
2007	Spokane	Northwest	10	$17\frac{2}{3}$	2	3	.400	13	1	15	2.55	1
2008	Bakersfield	Calif.	9	$58\frac{1}{3}$	5	4	.556	50	8	63	3.55	0
2008	Frisco	Texas	8	$52\frac{1}{3}$	4	2	.667	28	17	52	3.78	0
2008	Texas	A.L.	3	11	0	2	.000	9	3	23	16.36	0
2008	Oklahoma	P.C.	8	53	4	2	.667	28	9	55	2.89	0
2009	Frisco	Texas	5	$21\frac{2}{3}$	1	0	1.000	16	4	30	4.98	0
2009	Okla.	P.C.	8	$49\frac{1}{3}$	3	2	.600	35	16	53	3.83	0
2009	Texas	A.L.	19	112	9	6	.600	64	33	113	4.10	0
2010	Oklahoma	P.C.	6	$26\frac{2}{3}$	1	2	.333	14	11	28	4.05	0
2010	Texas a	A.L.	23	128	13	4	.765	68	33	126	3.73	0
2011	Frisco	Texas	1	4	0	0	.000	5	1	3	4.50	0
2011	Round Rock	P.C.	8	$26\frac{2}{3}$	2	2	.500	16	3	37	5.06	1
2011	Texas-Baltimore b-c	A.L.	20	$84\frac{2}{3}$	4	4	.500	45	15	100	4.68	0
Major League Totals	4 Yrs.		65	$335\frac{2}{3}$	26	16	.619	186	84	362	4.50	0
	Division Series											
2010	Texas	A.L.	1	4	0	1	.000	7	0	6	4.50	0
	Championship Series											
2010	Texas	A.L.	1	$3\frac{1}{3}$	0	0	.000	5	0	5	8.10	0
	World Series Record											
2010	Texas	A.L.	1	4	0	1	.000	1	1	5	4.50	0

a On disabled list from March 26 to April 28, 2010.
b On disabled list from March 25 to July 1, 2011.
c Traded to Baltimore Orioles with infielder Chris Davis for pitcher Koji Uehara and cash, July 30, 2011.

ISRINGHAUSEN, JASON DERIK

Born, Brighton, Illinois, September 7, 1972.
Bats Right. Throws Right. Height, 6 feet, 3 inches. Weight, 235 pounds.

Year	Club	Lea	G	IP	W	L	Pct	SO	BB	H	ERA	SAVES
1992 Mets	Gulf Coast		6	29	2	4	.333	25	17	26	4.34	0
1992 Kingsport	Appal.		7	36	4	1	.800	24	12	32	3.25	0
1993 Pittsfield	N.Y.-Penn.		15	90⅓	7	4	.636	104	28	68	3.29	0
1994 St. Lucie	Fla.St.		14	101	6	4	.600	59	27	76	2.23	0
1994 Binghamton	Eastern		14	92⅓	5	4	.556	69	23	78	3.02	0
1995 Binghamton	Eastern		6	41	2	1	.667	59	12	26	2.85	0
1995 Norfolk	Int.		12	87	9	1	.900	75	24	64	1.55	0
1995 New York	N.L.		14	93	9	2	.818	55	31	88	2.81	0
1996 New York a	N.L.		27	171⅔	6	14	.300	114	73	190	4.77	0
1997 Mets	Gulf Coast		1	4⅔	1	0	1.000	7	1	2	1.93	0
1997 St. Lucie	Fla.St.		2	12	1	0	1.000	15	5	8	0.00	0
1997 Norfolk	Int.		3	20	0	2	.000	17	8	20	4.05	0
1997 New York b	N.L.		6	29⅔	2	2	.500	25	22	40	7.58	0
1998 c							INJURED—Did Not Play					
1999 Norfolk	Int.		12	51	3	1	.750	51	20	33	2.29	0
1999 New York	N.L.		13	39⅓	1	3	.250	31	22	43	6.41	1
1999 Oakland d	A.L.		20	25⅓	0	1	.000	20	12	21	2.13	8
2000 Oakland	A.L.		66	69	6	4	.600	57	32	67	3.78	33
2001 Oakland e	A.L.		65	71⅓	4	3	.571	74	23	54	2.65	34
2002 St. Louis	N.L.		60	65⅓	3	2	.600	68	18	46	2.48	32
2003 Tennessee	Southern		2	2	0	0	.000	3	0	1	0.00	0
2003 St. Louis f	N.L.		40	42	0	1	.000	41	18	31	2.36	22
2004 St. Louis	N.L.		74	75⅓	4	2	.667	71	23	55	2.87	*47
2005 St. Louis g	N.L.		63	59	1	2	.333	51	27	43	2.14	39
2006 St. Louis	N.L.		59	58⅓	4	8	.333	52	38	47	3.55	33
2007 St. Louis	N.L.		63	65⅓	4	0	1.000	54	28	42	2.48	32
2008 Palm Beach	Fla.St.		1	2	0	0	.000	1	0	1	0.00	0
2008 Springfield	Texas		1	1⅔	0	0	.000	2	0	1	0.00	0
2008 St. Louis h	N.L.		42	42⅔	1	5	.167	36	22	48	5.70	12
2009 Montgomery	Southern		4	4	0	0	.000	3	4	2	2.25	0
2009 Durham	Int.		6	7	0	0	.000	0	2	7	5.14	0
2009 Tampa Bay i-j	A.L.		9	8	0	1	.000	6	5	6	2.25	0
2010 Louisville k	Int.		7	5⅔	1	0	1.000	5	7	4	9.53	0
2011 New York l-m	N.L.		53	46⅔	3	3	.500	44	24	36	4.05	7
Major League Totals 15 Yrs.			674	962	48	53	.475	799	418	857	3.62	300
Division Series												
2000 Oakland	A.L.		2	2	0	0	.000	3	0	1	0.00	1
2001 Oakland	A.L.		2	2	0	0	.000	3	1	1	0.00	2
2002 St. Louis	N.L.		2	2	0	0	.000	1	0	0	0.00	2
2004 St. Louis	N.L.		2	2	0	0	.000	2	2	1	4.50	0
2005 St. Louis	N.L.		3	3	0	0	.000	4	1	5	3.00	1
Division Series Totals			11	11	0	0	.000	13	4	8	1.64	6
Championship Series												
2002 St. Louis	N.L.		2	2	0	0	.000	3	3	1	4.50	1
2004 St. Louis	N.L.		6	7⅔	0	1	.000	3	4	4	4.70	3
2005 St. Louis	N.L.		3	4	1	0	1.000	2	0	3	0.00	1
Championship Series Totals			11	13⅔	1	1	.500	8	7	8	3.29	5
World Series Record												
2004 St. Louis	N.L.		1	2	0	0	.000	2	1	1	0.00	0

a On disabled list from August 13 to September 1, 1996.
b On disabled list from April 1 to August 27, 1997.
c On disabled list from March 31 to September 28, 1998.
d Traded to Oakland Athletics with pitcher Greg McMichael for pitcher Billy Taylor, July 31, 1999.
e Filed for free agency, November 5, 2001. Signed with St. Louis Cardinals, December 10, 2001.
f On disabled list from March 21 to June 10, 2003.
g On disabled list from April 27 to May 13, 2005
h On disabled list from May 16 to June 14 and August 17 to November 1, 2008.
i Filed for free agency, November 1, 2008. Signed with Tampa Bay Rays organization, February 20, 2009.
j On disabled list from March 31 to May 18 and June 14 to November 9, 2009.
k Filed for free agency, November 9, 2009. Signed with Cincinnati Reds organization, July 22, 2010.
l Signed with New York Mets organization, February 16, 2011.
m Filed for free agency, October 30, 2011.

JACKSON, EDWIN
Born, Neu-Ulm, West Germany, September 9, 1983.
Bats Right. Throws Right. Height, 6 feet, 3 inches. Weight, 210 pounds.

Year	Club	Lea	G	IP	W	L	Pct	SO	BB	H	ERA	SAVES
2001 Dodgers	Gulf Coast		12	22	2	1	.667	23	19	14	2.45	0
2002 South Bend	So.Atl.		19	104²/₃	5	2	.714	85	33	79	1.98	0
2003 Jacksonville	Southern		27	148¹/₃	7	7	.500	157	53	121	3.70	0
2003 Los Angeles	N.L.		4	22	2	1	.667	19	11	17	2.45	0
2004 Las Vegas	P.C.		19	90²/₃	6	4	.600	70	55	90	5.86	0
2004 Los Angeles a	N.L.		8	24²/₃	2	1	.667	16	11	31	7.30	0
2005 Jacksonville	Southern		11	62	6	4	.600	44	18	52	3.48	0
2005 Las Vegas	P.C.		12	55¹/₃	3	7	.300	33	37	76	8.62	0
2005 Los Angeles	N.L.		7	28²/₃	2	2	.500	13	17	31	6.28	0
2006 Durham	Int.		22	73	3	7	.300	66	35	84	5.55	5
2006 Tampa Bay b	A.L.		23	36¹/₃	0	0	.000	27	25	42	5.45	0
2007 Tampa Bay	A.L.		32	161	5	15	.250	128	88	195	5.76	0
2008 Tampa Bay c	A.L.		32	183¹/₃	14	11	.560	108	77	199	4.42	0
2009 Detroit d	A.L.		33	214	13	9	.591	161	70	200	3.62	0
2010 Chicago	A.L.		11	75	4	2	.667	77	18	73	3.24	0
2010 Arizona e-f	N.L.		21	134¹/₃	6	10	.375	104	60	141	5.16	0
2011 Chicago	A.L.		19	121²/₃	7	7	.500	97	39	134	3.92	0
2011 St. Louis g-h-i	N.L.		13	78	5	2	.714	51	23	91	3.58	0
Major League Totals	9 Yrs.		203	1079	60	60	.500	801	439	1154	4.46	0
Division Series												
2011 St. Louis	N.L.		1	6	1	0	1.000	4	1	5	3.00	0
Championship Series												
2008 Tampa Bay	N.L.		2	2¹/₃	0	0	.000	4	2	0	0.00	0
2011 St. Louis	N.L.		2	6¹/₃	0	0	.000	5	1	11	8.53	0
Championship Series Totals			4	8²/₃	0	0	.000	9	3	11	6.23	0
World Series Record												
2008 Tampa Bay c	N.L.		1	2	0	0	.000	1	1	2	4.50	0
2011 St. Louis	N.L.		1	5¹/₃	0	1	.000	3	7	3	5.06	0
World Series Totals			2	7¹/₃	0	1	.000	4	8	5	4.91	0

a On disabled list from July 9 to September 7, 2004.
b Traded to Tampa Bay Devil Rays with pitcher Chuck Tiffany for pitcher Danys Baez and pitcher Lance Carter, January 14, 2006.
c Traded to Detroit Tigers for outfielder Matt Joyce, December 10, 2008.
d Traded to Arizona Diamondbacks with pitcher Ian Kennedy for pitcher Daniel Schlereth and pitcher Max Scherzer, December 9, 2009.
e Pitched no-hit, no-run game against Tampa Bay Rays, June 25, 2010.
f Traded to Chicago White Sox for pitcher Dan Hudson and pitcher David Holmberg, July 30, 2010.
g Traded to Toronto Blue Jays with infielder Mark Teahen for pitcher Jason Frasor and pitcher Zach Stewart, July 27, 2011.
h Traded to St. Louis Cardinals with pitcher Octavio Dotel, pitcher Marc Rzepczynski, outfielder Corey Patterson and cash for outfielder Colby Rasmus, pitcher Trever Miller, pitcher Brian Tallet and pitcher P.J. Walters, July 27, 2011.
i Filed for free agency, October 30, 2011.

JAKUBAUSKAS, CHRIS
Born, Anaheim, California, December 22, 1978.
Bats Left. Throws Right. Height, 6 feet, 2 inches. Weight, 215 pounds.

Year	Club	Lea	G	IP	W	L	Pct	SO	BB	H	ERA	SAVES
2003 Florence	Frontier		16	100¹/₃	4	9	.308	57	38	120	5.11	0
2004 Florence	Frontier		7	34	0	2	.000	18	9	34	7.50	0
2005 Ohio Valley	Frontier		12	70	5	4	.556	48	30	74	3.34	0
2006 Fullerton	Golden		15	96	8	1	.889	76	21	89	3.09	0
2007 Lincoln	Amer. Assoc.		7	44²/₃	6	0	1.000	44	18	29	2.42	0
2007 West Tenn a	Southern		16	51	0	4	.000	39	21	53	4.94	0
2008 West Tenn	Southern		6	32²/₃	3	0	1.000	24	7	25	0.83	0
2008 Everett	Northwest		1	2²/₃	0	0	.000	7	0	1	0.00	0
2008 Tacoma	P.C.		12	55²/₃	5	1	.833	48	14	52	2.59	0
2009 Tacoma	P.C.		1	1	0	0	.000	1	1	0	0.00	0
2009 Seattle b	A.L.		35	93	6	7	.462	47	27	91	5.32	0
2010 Pittsburgh	N.L.		1	0²/₃	0	1	.000	0	0	2	27.00	0
2010 Bradenton	Fla.St.		1	4¹/₃	0	0	.000	3	2	7	6.23	0
2010 Pirates	Gulf Coast		2	6	0	2	.000	6	3	9	7.50	0
2010 Indianapolis c-d	Int.		8	30¹/₃	1	4	.200	24	10	35	4.45	0
2011 Norfolk	Int.		5	20	0	1	.000	14	7	23	4.05	0
2011 Baltimore e-f	A.L.		33	72¹/₃	2	2	.500	52	29	93	5.72	0
Major League Totals	3 Yrs.		69	166	8	10	.444	99	56	186	5.58	0

a Signed by Seattle Mariners organization, June 13, 2007.
b Claimed on waivers by Pittsburgh Pirates, November 20, 2009.
c On disabled list from April 25 to August 18, 2010.
d Released by Pittsburgh Pirates, November 1, 2010. Signed with Baltimore Orioles organization, February 1, 2011.
e Filed for free agency, October 30, 2011. Signed with Arizona Diamondbacks organization, November 8, 2011.

JANSEN, KENLEY JERONIMO
Born, Curacao, Netherlands Antilles, September 30, 1987.
Bats Both. Throws Right. Height, 6 feet, 6 inches. Weight, 220 pounds.

Year	Club	Lea	G	IP	W	L	Pct	SO	BB	H	ERA	SAVES
2009 Inland Empire a	Calif.	12	11²/₃	0	0	.000	19	11	14	4.63	0
2010 Inland Empire	Calif.	11	18	1	1	.500	28	6	15	1.50	0
2010 Chattanooga	Southern	22	27	4	0	1.000	50	17	14	1.67	8
2010 Los Angeles	N.L.	25	27	1	0	1.000	41	15	12	0.67	4
2011 Rancho Cucamonga	Calif.	2	2	0	0	.000	4	0	0	0.00	0
2011 Chattanooga	Southern	5	6	0	1	.000	9	3	2	4.50	0
2011 Los Angeles b	N.L.	51	53²/₃	2	1	.667	96	26	30	2.85	5
Major League Totals 2 Yrs.		76	80²/₃	3	1	.750	137	41	42	2.12	9

a Played catcher in the Dodger organzation, 2005-2008.
b On disabled list from May 29 to June 17 and July 27 to August 25, 2011.

JANSSEN, ROBERT CASEY (CASEY)
Born, Orange, California, September 17, 1981.
Bats Right. Throws Right. Height, 6 feet, 4 inches. Weight, 205 pounds.

Year	Club	Lea	G	IP	W	L	Pct	SO	BB	H	ERA	SAVES
2004 Auburn	N.Y.-Penn.	10	50	3	1	.750	45	10	47	3.60	0
2005 New Hampshire	Eastern	9	43	3	3	.500	47	4	49	2.93	0
2005 Dunedin	Fla.St.	10	59²/₃	6	1	.857	51	12	46	2.26	0
2005 Lansing	Midwest	7	46	4	0	1.000	38	4	27	1.37	0
2006 Syracuse	Int.	9	42²/₃	1	5	.167	32	8	47	4.85	0
2006 Toronto	A.L.	19	94	6	10	.375	44	21	103	5.07	0
2007 Toronto	A.L.	70	72²/₃	2	3	.400	39	20	67	2.35	6
2008 Toronto a	A.L.				INJURED—Did Not Play						
2009 Blue Jays	Gulf Coast	1	1	0	0	.000	0	0	2	9.00	0
2009 Dunedin	Fla.St.	4	13	0	0	.000	10	2	6	0.69	0
2009 New Hampshire	Eastern	6	15	1	0	1.000	12	5	12	2.40	0
2009 Las Vegas	P.C.	7	6²/₃	0	0	.000	7	1	4	5.40	0
2009 Toronto b	A.L.	21	40	2	4	.333	24	14	59	5.85	1
2010 Toronto	A.L.	56	68²/₃	5	2	.714	63	21	74	3.67	0
2011 New Hampshire	Eastern	5	5	0	0	.000	7	1	1	0.00	0
2011 Las Vegas	P.C.	1	2	0	0	.000	3	0	1	0.00	0
2011 Toronto c	A.L.	55	55²/₃	6	0	1.000	53	14	47	2.26	2
Major League Totals 5 Yrs.		221	331	21	19	.525	223	90	350	3.81	9

a On disabled list from March 17 to November 14, 2008.
b On disabled list from March 27 to April 30 and June 14 to July 23, 2009.
c On disabled list from June 16 to July 19, 2011.

JENKS, ROBERT SCOTT (BOBBY)
Born, Mission Hills, California, March 14, 1981.
Bats Right. Throws Right. Height, 6 feet, 3 inches. Weight, 280 pounds.

Year	Club	Lea	G	IP	W	L	Pct	SO	BB	H	ERA	SAVES
2000 Butte	Pioneer	14	52²/₃	1	7	.125	42	44	61	7.86	0
2001 Cedar Rapids	Midwest	21	99	3	7	.300	98	64	90	5.27	0
2001 Arkansas	Texas	2	10	1	0	1.000	10	5	8	3.60	0
2002 Rancho Cucamonga	California	11	65¹/₃	3	5	.375	64	46	50	4.82	0
2002 Arkansas	Texas	10	58	3	6	.333	58	44	49	4.66	0
2003 Angels	Arizona	1	4	0	0	.000	5	0	2	0.00	0
2003 Arkansas	Texas	16	83	7	2	.778	103	51	56	2.17	0
2004 Angels	Arizona	1	3¹/₃	0	0	.000	5	3	2	8.10	0
2004 Rancho Cucamonga	California	1	3²/₃	0	1	.000	3	7	5	19.64	0
2004 Salt Lake a	P.C.	3	12¹/₃	0	1	.000	13	6	19	8.76	0
2005 Birmingham	Southern	35	41	1	2	.333	48	20	34	2.85	19
2005 Chicago	A.L.	32	39¹/₃	1	1	.500	50	15	34	2.75	6
2006 Chicago	A.L.	67	69²/₃	3	4	.429	80	31	66	4.00	41
2007 Chicago	A.L.	66	65	3	5	.375	56	13	45	2.77	40
2008 Winston-Salem	Carolina	1	1	0	0	.000	0	0	3	9.00	0
2008 Birmingham	Southern	1	1	0	0	.000	3	0	0	0.00	0

Year	Club	Lea	G	IP	W	L	Pct	SO	BB	H	ERA	SAVES
2008 Chicago b	A.L.	57	61²/₃	3	1	.750	38	17	51	2.63	30	
2009 Chicago	A.L.	52	53¹/₃	3	4	.429	49	16	52	3.71	29	
2010 Chicago c	A.L.	55	52²/₃	1	3	.250	61	18	54	4.44	27	
2011 Portland	Eastern	1	1	0	0	.000	1	0	1	0.00	0	
2011 Pawtucket	Int.	2	2	0	0	.000	2	1	2	4.50	0	
2011 Boston d	A.L.	19	15²/₃	2	2	.500	17	13	22	6.32	0	
Major League Totals .... 7 Yrs.		348	357¹/₃	16	20	.444	351	123	324	3.53	173	
Division Series												
2005 Chicago	A.L.	2	3	0	0	.000	1	1	1	0.00	2	
2008 Chicago	A.L.	1	1	0	0	.000	1	0	1	0.00	1	
Division Series Totals		3	4	0	0	.000	2	1	2	0.00	3	
World Series Record												
2005 Chicago	A.L.	4	5	0	0	.000	7	2	3	3.60	2	

a Claimed on waivers by Chicago White Sox from Anaheim Angels, December 17, 2004.
b On disabled list from June 30 to July 18, 2008.
c Not offered contract, December 2, 2010. Signed with Boston Red Sox, December 21, 2010.
d On disabled list from May 2 to May 31 and June 8 to June 28 and July 8 to October 31, 2011.

JIMENEZ, UBALDO

Born, Nagua, Dominican Republic, January 22, 1984.
Bats Right. Throws Right. Height, 6 feet, 4 inches. Weight, 200 pounds.

Year	Club	Lea	G	IP	W	L	Pct	SO	BB	H	ERA	SAVES
2002 Casper	Pioneer	14	62	3	5	.375	65	29	72	6.53	0	
2003 Visalia	Calif.	1	5	1	0	1.000	7	1	3	0.00	0	
2003 Asheville	So.Atl.	27	153²/₃	10	6	.625	138	67	129	3.46	0	
2004 Visalia	Calif.	9	44¹/₃	4	1	.800	61	12	29	2.23	0	
2005 Modesto	Calif.	14	72¹/₃	5	3	.625	78	40	61	3.98	0	
2005 Tulsa	Texas	12	63	2	5	.286	53	31	58	5.43	0	
2006 Tulsa	Texas	13	73¹/₃	9	2	.818	86	40	49	2.45	0	
2006 Colorado Springs	P.C.	13	78¹/₃	5	2	.714	64	43	74	5.06	0	
2006 Colorado	N.L.	2	7²/₃	0	0	.000	3	3	5	3.52	0	
2007 Colorado Springs	P.C.	19	103	8	5	.615	89	62	110	5.85	0	
2007 Colorado	N.L.	15	82	4	4	.500	68	37	70	4.28	0	
2008 Colorado	N.L.	34	198²/₃	12	12	.500	172	103	182	3.99	0	
2009 Colorado	N.L.	33	218	15	12	.556	198	85	183	3.47	0	
2010 Colorado	N.L.	33	221²/₃	19	8	*.704	214	92	164	2.88	0	
2011 Colorado	N.L.	21	123	6	9	.400	118	51	118	4.46	0	
2011 Cleveland a-b	A.L.	11	65¹/₃	4	4	.500	62	27	68	5.10	0	
Major League Totals .... 6 Yrs.		149	916¹/₃	60	49	.550	835	398	790	3.76	0	
Division Series												
2007 Colorado	N.L.	1	6¹/₃	0	0	.000	5	4	3	1.42	0	
2009 Colorado	N.L.	2	12	0	1	.000	11	3	15	5.25	0	
Division Series Totals		3	18¹/₃	0	1	.000	16	7	18	3.93	0	
Championship Series												
2007 Colorado	N.L.	1	5	0	0	.000	6	4	5	1.80	0	
World Series Record												
2007 Colorado	N.L.	1	4²/₃	0	1	.000	2	5	3	3.86	0	

a On disabled list from April 2 to April 19, 2011.
b Traded to Cleveland Indians for pitcher Alex White, pitcher Joseph Gardner, outfielder Matt McBride and player to be named later, July 31, 2011. Colorado Rockies received pitcher Drew Pomeranz to complete trade, August 17, 2011.

JOHNSON, JAMES ROBERT (JIM)

Born, Johnson City, New York, June 27, 1983.
Bats Right. Throws Right. Height, 6 feet, 5 inches. Weight, 230 pounds.

Year	Club	Lea	G	IP	W	L	Pct	SO	BB	H	ERA	SAVES
2001 Orioles	Gulf Coast	7	18²/₃	0	1	.000	19	7	17	3.86	0	
2002 Bluefield	Appal.	11	55²/₃	4	2	.667	36	16	52	4.37	0	
2003 Bluefield	Appal.	11	51¹/₃	3	2	.600	46	18	62	3.68	0	
2004 Frederick	Carolina	1	3	0	0	.000	6	1	6	9.00	0	
2004 Delmarva	So.Atl.	20	106²/₃	8	7	.533	93	30	97	3.29	0	
2005 Frederick	Carolina	28	159²/₃	12	9	.571	168	64	139	3.49	1	
2005 Bowie	Eastern	1	7	0	0	.000	6	2	3	0.00	0	
2006 Baltimore	A.L.	1	3	0	1	.000	0	3	9	24.00	0	
2006 Bowie	Eastern	27	156	13	6	.684	124	57	165	4.44	0	
2007 Baltimore	A.L.	1	2	0	0	.000	1	2	3	9.00	0	
2007 Norfolk	Int.	26	148	6	12	.333	109	48	164	4.07	0	
2008 Norfolk	Int.	1	4	0	1	.000	2	1	2	2.25	0	

Year Club	Lea	G	IP	W	L	Pct	SO	BB	H	ERA	SAVES
2008 Baltimore a	A.L.	54	68²/₃	2	4	.333	38	28	54	2.23	1
2009 Baltimore	A.L.	64	70	4	6	.400	49	23	73	4.11	10
2010 Orioles	Gulf Coast	4	4	0	0	.000	5	1	5	6.75	0
2010 Frederick	Carolina	2	3	0	0	.000	1	0	6	3.00	0
2010 Bowie	Eastern	4	5	0	0	.000	6	0	2	1.80	0
2010 Norfolk	Int.	1	1	0	0	.000	0	0	1	0.00	0
2010 Baltimore b	A.L.	26	26¹/₃	1	1	.500	22	5	32	3.42	1
2011 Baltimore	A.L.	69	91	6	5	.545	58	21	80	2.67	9
Major League Totals ....6 Yrs.		215	261	13	17	.433	168	82	251	3.31	21

a On disabled list from September 1 to October 2, 2008.
b On disabled list from May 28 to August 27, 2010.

JOHNSON, JOSHUA MICHAEL (JOSH)

Born, Minneapolis, Minnesota, January 31, 1984.
Bats Left. Throws Right. Height, 6 feet, 7 inches. Weight, 230 pounds.

Year Club	Lea	G	IP	W	L	Pct	SO	BB	H	ERA	SAVES
2002 Marlins	Gulf Coast	4	15	2	0	1.000	11	3	8	0.60	0
2003 Greensboro	So.Atl.	17	82¹/₃	4	7	.364	59	29	69	3.61	0
2004 Jupiter	Fla.St.	23	114¹/₃	5	12	.294	103	47	124	3.38	0
2005 Carolina	Southern	26	139²/₃	12	4	.750	113	50	139	3.87	0
2005 Florida	N.L.	4	12¹/₃	0	0	.000	10	10	11	3.65	0
2006 Florida	N.L.	31	157	12	7	.632	133	68	136	3.10	0
2007 Carolina	Southern	2	10¹/₃	0	0	.000	9	5	8	1.74	0
2007 Florida	N.L.	4	15²/₃	0	3	.000	14	12	26	7.47	0
2007 Jupiter a	Fla.St.	3	11¹/₃	0	0	.000	13	0	9	0.79	0
2008 Greensboro	So.Atl.	1	5	0	1	.000	7	0	8	3.60	0
2008 Jupiter	Fla.St.	1	5¹/₃	0	0	.000	2	2	6	5.06	0
2008 Carolina	Southern	3	19	1	1	.500	14	3	22	3.32	0
2008 Florida b	N.L.	14	87¹/₃	7	1	.875	77	27	91	3.61	0
2009 Florida	N.L.	33	209	15	5	.750	191	58	184	3.23	0
2010 Florida	N.L.	28	183²/₃	11	6	.647	186	48	155	*2.30	0
2011 Florida c	N.L.	9	60¹/₃	3	1	.750	56	20	39	1.64	0
Major League Totals ....7 Yrs.		123	725¹/₃	48	23	.676	667	243	642	2.98	0

a On disabled list from March 23 to June 18 and July 5 to November 12, 2007.
b On disabled list from March 21 to July 10, 2008.
c On disabled list from May 17 to October 31, 2011.

JURRJENS, JAIR FRANCOISE

Born, Santa Maria, Curacao,Netherlands Antilles, January 29, 1986.
Bats Right. Throws Right. Height, 6 feet, 1 inch. Weight, 200 pounds.

Year Club	Lea	G	IP	W	L	Pct	SO	BB	H	ERA	SAVES
2003 Tigers	Gulf Coast	7	28	2	1	.667	20	3	33	3.21	0
2004 Tigers	Gulf Coast	6	39²/₃	4	2	.667	39	10	25	2.27	0
2004 Oneonta	N.Y.-Penn.	7	39	1	5	.167	31	10	50	5.31	0
2005 West Michigan	Midwest	26	142²/₃	12	6	.667	108	36	132	3.41	0
2006 Erie	Eastern	12	67	4	3	.571	53	21	71	3.36	0
2006 Lakeland	Fla.St.	12	73²/₃	5	0	1.000	59	10	53	2.08	0
2007 Erie	Eastern	19	112²/₃	7	5	.583	94	31	112	3.20	0
2007 Detroit a-b	A.L.	7	30²/₃	3	1	.750	13	11	24	4.70	0
2008 Atlanta	N.L.	31	188¹/₃	13	10	.565	139	70	188	3.68	0
2009 Atlanta	N.L.	34	215	14	10	.583	152	75	186	2.60	0
2010 Gwinnett	Int.	3	13	1	1	.500	9	6	20	5.54	0
2010 Atlanta c	N.L.	20	116¹/₃	7	6	.538	86	42	120	4.64	0
2011 Gwinnett	Int.	1	6	1	0	1.000	3	2	4	3.00	0
2011 Atlanta d	N.L.	23	152	13	6	.684	90	44	142	2.96	0
Major League Totals ....5 Yrs.		115	702¹/₃	50	33	.602	480	242	660	3.40	0

a On disabled list from August 27 to September 11, 2007.
b Traded to Atlanta Braves with outfielder Gorkys Hernandez for infielder Edgar Renteria, October 29, 2007.
c On disabled list from April 30 to June 30, 2010.
d On disabled list from April 3 to April 16 and August 1 to August 17, 2011.

KARSTENS, JEFFREY WAYNE (JEFF)

Born, San Diego, California, September 24, 1982.
Bats Right. Throws Right. Height, 6 feet, 3 inches. Weight, 185 pounds.

Year Club	Lea	G	IP	W	L	Pct	SO	BB	H	ERA	SAVES
2003 Staten Island	N.Y.-Penn.	14	67¹/₃	4	2	.667	53	16	63	2.54	0

Year	Club	Lea	G	IP	W	L	Pct	SO	BB	H	ERA	SAVES
2004 Tampa	Fla.St.	24	138²/₃	6	9	.400	116	31	151	4.02	0
2005 Trenton	Eastern	28	169	12	11	.522	147	42	192	4.15	0
2006 Trenton	Eastern	11	74	6	0	1.000	67	14	54	2.31	0
2006 Columbus	Int.	14	73²/₃	5	5	.500	48	30	80	4.28	0
2006 New York	A.L.	8	42²/₃	2	1	.667	16	11	40	3.80	0
2007 Tampa	Fla.St.	1	4	0	0	.000	5	1	3	0.00	0
2007 Yankees	Gulf Coast	1	3¹/₃	0	0	.000	2	1	3	0.00	0
2007 Staten Island	N.Y.-Penn.	1	5	1	0	1.000	8	0	4	1.80	0
2007 Trenton	Eastern	1	5	1	0	1.000	5	2	4	1.80	0
2007 Scranton/WB	Int.	6	31	3	0	1.000	27	9	25	1.74	0
2007 New York a	A.L.	7	14²/₃	1	4	.200	5	9	27	11.05	0
2008 Scranton/WB	Int.	12	68²/₃	6	4	.600	55	15	66	3.80	0
2008 Pittsburgh b-c	N.L.	9	51¹/₃	2	6	.250	23	13	56	4.03	0
2009 Indianapolis	Int.	3	6	0	0	.000	7	0	4	0.00	0
2009 Pittsburgh d	N.L.	39	108	4	6	.400	52	45	115	5.42	0
2010 Indianapolis	Int.	5	16	1	2	.333	12	2	21	7.31	0
2010 Pittsburgh	N.L.	26	122²/₃	3	10	.231	72	27	146	4.92	0
2011 Pittsburgh	N.L.	30	162¹/₃	9	9	.500	96	33	163	3.38	0
Major League Totals	6 Yrs.	119	501²/₃	21	36	.368	264	138	547	4.52	0

a On disabled list from March 26 to April 21 and April 29 to August 1, 2007.
b On disabled list from March 28 to May 20, 2008.
c Traded to Pittsburgh Pirates with outfielder Jose Tabata, pitcher Ross Ohlendorf and pitcher Dan McCutchen for outfielder Xavier Nady and pitcher Damaso Marte, July 26, 2008.
d On disabled list from August 25 to September 9, 2009.

KELLEY, SHAWN ANDREW

Born, Louisville, Kentucky, April 26, 1984.
Bats Right. Throws Right. Height, 6 feet, 2 inches. Weight, 215 pounds.

Year	Club	Lea	G	IP	W	L	Pct	SO	BB	H	ERA	SAVES
2007 Wisconsin	Midwest	9	12	1	1	.500	14	4	16	2.25	0
2007 Everett	Northwest	3	3	1	0	1.000	4	0	2	3.00	0
2008 High Desert	Calif.	12	12	0	0	.000	12	3	8	0.00	3
2008 Wisconsin	Midwest	8	7²/₃	0	0	.000	12	2	10	3.52	3
2008 West Tenn	Southern	29	42²/₃	3	1	.750	44	17	31	2.11	9
2009 Azl Mariners	Arizona	2	2	0	0	.000	3	0	0	0.00	0
2009 Tacoma	P.C.	1	1	0	0	.000	0	0	0	0.00	0
2009 Seattle a	A.L.	41	46	5	4	.556	41	9	45	4.50	0
2010 Tacoma	P.C.	3	3²/₃	0	0	.000	6	3	1	4.91	1
2010 Seattle b	A.L.	22	25	3	1	.750	26	12	26	3.96	0
2011 Jackson	Southern	3	3	0	1	.000	3	0	4	0.00	0
2011 Tacoma	P.C.	12	14²/₃	1	0	1.000	15	6	11	1.84	0
2011 Seattle c	A.L.	10	12²/₃	0	0	.000	10	3	7	0.00	0
Major League Totals	3 Yrs.	73	83²/₃	8	5	.615	77	24	78	3.66	0

a On disabled list from May 6 to July 3, 2009.
b On disabled list from June 16 to October 8, 2010.
c On disabled list from March 2 to August 9, 2011.

KENDRICK, KYLE RODNEY

Born, Houston, Texas, August 26, 1984.
Bats Right. Throws Right. Height, 6 feet, 3 inches. Weight, 190 pounds.

Year	Club	Lea	G	IP	W	L	Pct	SO	BB	H	ERA	SAVES
2003 Phillies	Gulf Coast	9	31¹/₃	0	4	.000	26	12	40	5.46	0
2004 Batavia	N.Y.-Penn.	13	70²/₃	2	8	.200	53	18	94	5.48	0
2004 Lakewood	So.Atl.	15	66²/₃	3	8	.273	36	33	85	6.07	0
2005 Clearwater	Fla.St.	1	4	0	1	.000	1	2	5	0.00	0
2005 Batavia	N.Y.-Penn.	14	91¹/₃	5	4	.556	70	22	94	3.74	0
2005 Lakewood	So.Atl.	5	22²/₃	0	3	.000	11	10	38	9.13	0
2006 Clearwater	Fla.St.	21	130	9	7	.563	79	37	117	3.53	0
2006 Lakewood	So.Atl.	7	46	3	2	.600	54	15	34	2.15	0
2007 Reading	Eastern	12	81¹/₃	4	7	.364	50	18	82	3.21	0
2007 Philadelphia	N.L.	20	121	10	4	.714	49	25	129	3.87	0
2008 Philadelphia	N.L.	31	155²/₃	11	9	.550	68	57	194	5.49	0
2009 Lehigh Valley	Int.	24	143	9	7	.563	62	35	133	3.34	0
2009 Philadelphia	N.L.	9	26¹/₃	3	1	.750	15	9	27	3.42	0
2010 Philadelphia	N.L.	33	180²/₃	11	10	.524	84	49	199	4.73	0
2011 Philadelphia	N.L.	34	114²/₃	8	6	.571	59	30	110	3.22	0
Major League Totals	5 Yrs.	127	598¹/₃	43	30	.589	275	170	659	4.41	0

Year Club	Lea	G	IP	W	L	Pct	SO	BB	H	ERA	SAVES
Division Series											
2007 Philadelphia . . . . N.L.	1	3²/₃	0	1	.000	2	2	5	12.27	0	

KENNEDY, IAN PATRICK
Born, Huntington Beach, California, December 19, 1984.
Bats Right. Throws Right. Height, 6 feet. Weight, 195 pounds.

Year Club	Lea	G	IP	W	L	Pct	SO	BB	H	ERA	SAVES
2006 Staten Island . . . . . N.Y.-Penn.	1	2²/₃	0	0	.000	2	2	2	0.00	0	
2007 Tampa . . . . Fla.St.	11	63	6	1	.857	72	22	39	1.29	0	
2007 Trenton. . . . . Eastern	9	48²/₃	5	1	.833	57	17	27	2.59	0	
2007 Scranton/WB . . . . Int.	6	34²/₃	1	1	.500	34	11	25	2.08	0	
2007 New York . . . . A.L.	3	19	1	0	1.000	15	9	13	1.89	0	
2008 Yankees . . . . Gulf Coast	1	3	1	0	1.000	7	0	3	3.00	0	
2008 Tampa . . . . Fla.St.	1	5	0	0	.000	4	1	2	0.00	0	
2008 New York . . . . A.L.	10	39²/₃	0	4	.000	27	26	50	8.17	0	
2008 Scranton/WB a . . . . Int.	13	69	5	3	.625	72	17	52	2.35	0	
2009 Scranton/WB . . . . Int.	4	22²/₃	1	0	1.000	25	7	18	1.59	0	
2009 New York b-c . . . . A.L.	1	1	0	0	.000	1	2	0	0.00	0	
2010 Arizona. . . . . N.L.	32	194	9	10	.474	168	70	163	3.80	0	
2011 Arizona. . . . . N.L.	33	222	*21	4	*.840	198	55	186	2.88	0	
Major League Totals . . . . .5 Yrs.	79	475²/₃	31	18	.633	409	162	412	3.65	0	
Division Series											
2011 Arizona. . . . . N.L.	2	12²/₃	0	1	.000	8	3	13	4.26	0	

a On disabled list from May 28 to June 24, 2008.
b Traded to Detroit Tigers with outfielder Austin Jackson and pitcher Phil Coke for outfielder Curtis Granderson, December 9, 2009.
c Traded to Arizona Diamondbacks with pitcher Edwin Jackson for pitcher Daniel Schlereth and pitcher Max Scherzer, December 9, 2009.

KERSHAW, CLAYTON EDWARD
Born, Dallas, Texas, March 19, 1988.
Bats Left. Throws Left. Height, 6 feet, 3 inches. Weight, 220 pounds.

Year Club	Lea	G	IP	W	L	Pct	SO	BB	H	ERA	SAVES
2006 Dodgers . . . . Gulf Coast	10	37	2	0	1.000	54	5	28	1.95	1	
2007 Great Lakes . . . . Midwest	20	97¹/₃	7	5	.583	134	50	72	2.77	0	
2007 Jacksonville . . . . Southern	5	24²/₃	1	2	.333	29	17	17	3.65	0	
2008 Jacksonville . . . . . . Southern	13	61¹/₃	2	3	.400	59	19	39	1.91	0	
2008 Los Angeles . . . . N.L.	22	107²/₃	5	5	.500	100	52	109	4.26	0	
2009 Los Angeles . . . . N.L.	31	171	8	8	.500	185	91	119	2.79	0	
2010 Los Angeles . . . . N.L.	32	204¹/₃	13	10	.565	212	81	160	2.91	0	
2011 Los Angeles a . . . . N.L.	33	233¹/₃	*21	5	.808	*248	54	174	*2.28	0	
Major League Totals . . . . .4 Yrs.	118	716¹/₃	47	28	.627	745	278	562	2.88	0	
Division Series											
2009 Los Angeles . . . . N.L.	1	6²/₃	0	0	.000	4	1	9	2.70	0	
Championship Series											
2008 Los Angeles . . . . N.L.	2	2	0	0	.000	1	2	1	4.50	0	
2009 Los Angeles . . . . N.L.	2	6²/₃	0	1	.000	6	6	5	9.45	0	
Championship Series Totals	4	8²/₃	0	1	.000	7	8	6	8.31	0	

a Selected Cy Young Award Winner in National League for 2011.

KIMBREL, CRAIG MICHAEL
Born, Huntsville, Alabama, May 28, 1988.
Bats Right. Throws Right. Height, 5 feet, 11 inches. Weight, 205 pounds.

Year Club	Lea	G	IP	W	L	Pct	SO	BB	H	ERA	SAVES
2008 Danville . . . . Appal.	12	19	1	2	.333	27	10	5	0.47	6	
2008 Myrtle Beach . . . . Carolina	2	3²/₃	0	0	.000	3	1	5	0.00	0	
2008 Rome . . . . So.Atl.	10	12²/₃	2	0	1.000	26	4	6	0.71	4	
2009 Myrtle Beach . . . . Carolina	19	26¹/₃	0	2	.000	45	28	18	5.47	2	
2009 Gwinnett. . . . . Int.	2	2	0	0	.000	3	4	0	0.00	0	
2009 Rome . . . . So.Atl.	16	20	0	0	.000	38	6	9	0.90	10	
2009 Mississippi. . . . . Southern	12	11²/₃	2	1	.667	17	7	3	0.77	6	
2010 Gwinnett. . . . . Int.	48	55²/₃	3	2	.600	83	35	28	1.62	23	
2011 Atlanta a. . . . . N.L.	79	77	4	3	.571	127	32	48	2.10	*46	
Major League Totals . . . . .2 Yrs.	100	97²/₃	8	3	.727	167	48	57	1.75	47	

Year	Club	Lea	G	IP	W	L	Pct	SO	BB	H	ERA	SAVES
	Division Series											
2010 Atlanta	....	N.L.	4	4¹/₃	0	1	.000	7	1	1	2.08	0

a Selected Rookie of the Year in National League for 2011.

KUO, HONG-CHIH
Born, Tainan City, Taiwan, July 23, 1981.
Bats Left. Throws Left. Height, 6 feet. Weight, 235 pounds.

Year	Club	Lea	G	IP	W	L	Pct	SO	BB	H	ERA	SAVES
2000 San Bernardino	....	Calif.	1	3	0	0	.000	7	0	0	0.00	0
2001 Dodgers	....	Gulf Coast	7	19¹/₃	0	0	.000	21	4	13	2.33	0
2002 Vero Beach	....	Fla.St.	4	8	0	1	.000	8	2	11	6.75	0
2002 Dodgers	....	Gulf Coast	3	6	0	0	.000	9	1	4	4.50	0
2003 Columbus a	....	So.Atl			INJURED—Did Not Play							
2004 Columbus	....	So.Atl.	3	6	1	0	1.000	10	4	8	4.50	0
2005 Vero Beach	....	Fla.St.	11	26	1	1	.500	42	10	19	2.08	0
2005 Jacksonville	....	Southern	17	28¹/₃	1	1	.500	44	11	22	1.91	3
2005 Los Angeles	....	N.L.	9	5¹/₃	0	1	.000	10	5	5	6.75	0
2006 Las Vegas	....	P.C.	23	53	4	3	.571	63	22	52	3.06	1
2006 Los Angeles	....	N.L.	28	59²/₃	1	5	.167	71	33	54	4.22	0
2007 Las Vegas	....	P.C.	7	20	0	1	.000	28	8	18	3.60	0
2007 Los Angeles b	....	N.L.	8	30¹/₃	1	4	.200	27	14	35	7.42	0
2008 Los Angeles	....	N.L.	42	80	5	3	.625	96	21	60	2.14	1
2009 Azl Dodgers	....	Arizona	3	3	0	0	.000	5	1	2	0.00	0
2009 Inland Empire	....	Calif.	4	4	0	0	.000	6	0	3	0.00	0
2009 Albuquerque	....	P.C.	2	2	0	0	.000	1	1	2	4.50	0
2009 Los Angeles c	....	N.L.	35	30	2	0	1.000	32	13	21	3.00	0
2010 Inland Empire	....	Calif.	2	2	0	0	.000	3	0	0	0.00	0
2010 Los Angeles d	....	N.L.	56	60	3	2	.600	73	18	29	1.20	12
2011 Rancho Cucamonga	..	Calif.	5	4¹/₃	0	1	.000	7	1	7	6.23	0
2011 Albuquerque	....	P.C.	2	1²/₃	0	0	.000	3	1	0	0.00	0
2011 Los Angeles e-f	....	N.L.	40	27	1	2	.333	36	23	24	9.00	0
Major League Totals	....	7 Yrs.	218	292¹/₃	13	17	.433	345	127	228	3.73	13
	Division Series											
2006 Los Angeles	....	N.L.	1	4¹/₃	0	1	.000	4	2	4	4.15	0
2009 Los Angeles	....	N.L.	1	1	0	0	.000	2	0	2	0.00	0
Division Series Totals	....		2	5¹/₃	0	1	.000	6	2	6	3.38	0
	Championship Series											
2008 Los Angeles	....	N.L.	3	3	0	0	.000	3	0	2	3.00	0
2009 Los Angeles	....	N.L.	4	4	1	0	1.000	6	0	2	2.25	0
Championship Series Totals	......		7	7	1	0	1.000	9	0	4	2.57	0

a On minor league disabled list from April 3 to September 8, 2003.

b On disabled list from March 23 to May 3 and June 30 to October 31, 2007.

c On disabled list from April 30 to July 27, 2009.

d On disabled list from March 26 to April 22, 2010.

e On disabled list from April 14 to May 1 and May 10 to June 19, 2011.

f Not offered contract, December 12, 2011.

KURODA, HIROKI
Born, Osaka, Japan, February 10, 1975.
Bats Right. Throws Right. Height, 6 feet, 1 inch. Weight, 210 pounds.

Year	Club	Lea	G	IP	W	L	Pct	SO	BB	H	ERA	SAVES
1997 Hiroshima	.....	Japan Cent.	23	135	6	9	.400	64	63	147	4.40	0
1998 Hiroshima	.....	Japan Cent.	18	45	1	4	.200	25	24	53	6.60	0
1999 Hiroshima	.....	Japan Cent.	21	87²/₃	5	8	.385	55	39	106	6.78	0
2000 Hiroshima	.....	Japan Cent.	29	144	9	6	.600	116	61	147	4.31	0
2001 Hiroshima	.....	Japan Cent.	27	190	12	8	.600	146	45	175	3.03	0
2002 Hiroshima	.....	Japan Cent.	23	164¹/₃	10	10	.500	144	34	166	3.67	0
2003 Hiroshima	.....	Japan Cent.	28	205²/₃	13	9	.591	137	45	197	3.11	0
2004 Hiroshima	.....	Japan Cent.	21	147	7	9	.438	138	29	187	4.65	0
2005 Hiroshima	.....	Japan Cent.	29	212²/₃	15	12	.556	165	42	183	3.17	0
2006 Hiroshima	.....	Japan Cent.	26	189¹/₃	13	6	.684	144	21	169	1.85	1
2007 Hiroshima a	.....	Japan Cent.	26	179²/₃	12	8	.600	123	42	176	3.56	0
2008 Los Angeles b	....	N.L.	31	183¹/₃	9	10	.474	116	42	181	3.73	0
2009 Los Angeles c	....	N.L.	21	117¹/₃	8	7	.533	87	24	110	3.76	0
2010 Los Angeles d	....	N.L.	31	196¹/₃	11	13	.458	159	48	180	3.39	0
2011 Los Angeles e	....	N.L.	32	202	13	16	.448	161	49	196	3.07	0
Major League Totals	....	4 Yrs.	115	699	41	46	.471	523	163	667	3.45	0

Year	Club	Lea	G	IP	W	L	Pct	SO	BB	H	ERA	SAVES
	Division Series											
2008 Los Angeles	N.L.	1	6¹/₃	1	0	1.000	4	2	6	0.00	0
	Championship Series											
2008 Los Angeles	N.L.	1	6	1	0	1.000	3	1	5	3.00	0
2009 Los Angeles	N.L.	1	1¹/₃	0	1	.000	1	0	6	40.50	0
Championship Series Totals		2	7¹/₃	1	1	.500	4	1	11	9.82	0

a Signed with Los Angeles Dodgers, December 16, 2007.
b On disabled list from June 13 to July 2, 2008.
c On disabled list from April 7 to June 1 and August 16 to September 6, 2009.
d Filed for free agency, November 1, 2010, re-signed with Los Angeles Dodgers, November 15, 2010.
e Filed for free agency, October 30, 2011. Signed with New York Yankees, January 14, 2012.

LACKEY, JOHN DERRAN

Born, Abilene, Texas, October 23, 1978.
Bats Right. Throws Right. Height, 6 feet, 6 inches. Weight, 235 pounds.

Year	Club	Lea	G	IP	W	L	Pct	SO	BB	H	ERA	SAVES
1999 Boise	Northwest	15	81¹/₃	6	2	.750	77	50	81	4.98	0
2000 Lake Elsinore	California	15	100²/₃	6	6	.500	74	42	94	3.40	0
2000 Erie	Eastern	8	57¹/₃	6	1	.857	43	9	58	3.30	0
2000 Cedar Rapids	Midwest	5	30¹/₃	3	2	.600	21	5	20	2.08	0
2001 Salt Lake	P.C.	10	57²/₃	3	4	.429	42	16	75	6.71	0
2001 Arkansas	Texas	18	127¹/₃	9	7	.563	94	29	106	3.46	0
2002 Salt Lake	P.C.	16	101²/₃	8	2	.800	82	28	89	2.57	0
2002 Anaheim	A.L.	18	108¹/₃	9	4	.692	69	33	113	3.66	0
2003 Anaheim	A.L.	33	204	10	16	.385	151	66	223	4.63	0
2004 Anaheim	A.L.	33	198¹/₃	14	13	.519	144	60	215	4.67	0
2005 Los Angeles	A.L.	33	209	14	5	.737	199	71	208	3.44	0
2006 Los Angeles	A.L.	33	217²/₃	13	11	.542	190	72	203	3.56	0
2007 Los Angeles	A.L.	33	224	19	9	.679	179	52	219	*3.01	0
2008 Rancho Cucamonga	Calif.	3	9	0	0	.000	11	2	8	4.00	0
2008 Los Angeles a	A.L.	24	163¹/₃	12	5	.706	130	40	161	3.75	0
2009 Salt Lake	P.C.	2	9²/₃	0	1	.000	8	1	6	2.79	0
2009 Los Angeles b-c	A.L.	27	176¹/₃	11	8	.579	139	47	177	3.83	0
2010 Boston	A.L.	33	215	14	11	.560	156	72	233	4.40	0
2011 Pawtucket	Int.	1	5²/₃	0	0	.000	4	0	3	1.59	0
2011 Boston d	A.L.	28	160	12	12	.500	108	56	203	6.41	0
Major League Totals	10 Yrs.	295	1876	128	94	.577	1465	569	1955	4.10	0
	Division Series											
2002 Anaheim	A.L.	1	3	0	0	.000	3	1	3	0.00	0
2005 Los Angeles	A.L.	2	11¹/₃	0	0	.000	9	9	7	2.38	0
2007 Los Angeles	A.L.	1	6	0	1	.000	4	2	9	6.00	0
2008 Los Angeles	A.L.	2	13²/₃	0	1	.000	6	4	11	2.63	0
2009 Los Angeles	A.L.	1	7¹/₃	1	0	1.000	4	1	4	0.00	0
Division Series Totals		7	41¹/₃	1	2	.333	26	17	34	2.40	0
	Championship Series											
2002 Anaheim	A.L.	1	7	1	0	1.000	7	0	3	0.00	0
2005 Los Angeles	A.L.	1	5	0	1	.000	3	1	8	9.00	0
2009 Los Angeles	A.L.	2	12¹/₃	0	1	.000	10	6	15	3.65	0
Championship Series Totals		4	24¹/₃	1	2	.333	20	7	26	3.70	0
	World Series Record											
2002 Anaheim	A.L.	3	12¹/₃	1	0	1.000	7	5	15	4.38	0

a On disabled list from March 21 to May 14, 2008.
b On disabled list from March 27 to May 16, 2009.
c Filed for free agency, November 5, 2009. Signed with Boston Red Sox, December 16, 2009.
d On disabled list from May 12 to June 5, 2011.

LAFFEY, AARON STEVEN

Born, Cumberland, Maryland, April 15, 1985.
Bats Left. Throws Left. Height, 6 feet. Weight, 185 pounds.

Year	Club	Lea	G	IP	W	L	Pct	SO	BB	H	ERA	SAVES
2003 Burlington	Appal.	9	34	3	1	.750	46	15	22	2.91	0
2004 Mahoning Valley	N.Y.-Penn.	8	43²/₃	3	1	.750	30	10	38	1.24	0
2004 Lake County	So.Atl.	19	74	3	7	.300	69	44	79	6.45	1
2005 Akron	Eastern	1	5	1	0	1.000	6	2	8	3.60	0
2005 Lake County	So.Atl.	25	142¹/₃	7	7	.500	69	52	123	3.22	1
2006 Kinston	Carolina	10	41¹/₃	4	1	.800	24	6	38	2.18	1
2006 Akron	Eastern	19	112¹/₃	8	3	.727	61	33	121	3.53	0
2007 Akron	Eastern	6	35	4	1	.800	24	7	29	2.31	0

Year Club	Lea	G	IP	W	L	Pct	SO	BB	H	ERA	SAVES
2007 Buffalo . . . . .Int.	Int.	16	96¹/₃	9	3	.750	75	23	89	3.08	0
2007 Cleveland . . . . .A.L.	A.L.	9	49¹/₃	4	2	.667	25	12	54	4.56	0
2008 Buffalo . . . . .Int.	Int.	11	61²/₃	6	2	.750	47	18	72	4.38	0
2008 Cleveland . . . . .A.L.	A.L.	16	93²/₃	5	7	.417	43	31	103	4.23	0
2009 Akron . . . . Eastern	Eastern	2	7¹/₃	0	0	.000	6	7	6	3.68	0
2009 Columbus. . . . . .Int.	Int.	3	10¹/₃	0	2	.000	4	5	21	11.32	0
2009 Cleveland a. . . . . .A.L.	A.L.	25	121²/₃	7	9	.438	59	57	140	4.44	1
2010 Lake County . . . . So.Atl.	So.Atl.	2	2	0	0	.000	3	0	2	4.50	0
2010 Akron . . . . Eastern	Eastern	1	1	0	0	.000	0	0	1	0.00	0
2010 Columbus. . . . . .Int.	Int.	10	27	0	1	.000	12	16	29	3.67	0
2010 Cleveland b . . . . .A.L.	A.L.	29	55²/₃	2	3	.400	28	28	62	4.53	0
2011 Scranton-WB . . . . .Int.	Int.	2	3²/₃	0	1	.000	1	2	5	7.36	0
2011 Seattle-New York c-d-e-f A.L.	A.L.	47	53¹/₃	3	2	.600	30	21	67	3.88	0
Major League Totals . . . . .5 Yrs.		126	373²/₃	21	23	.477	185	149	426	4.34	1
Championship Series											
2007 Cleveland . . . . .A.L.	A.L.	1	4²/₃	0	0	.000	3	1	1	0.00	0

a On disabled list from May 23 to July 8, 2009.
b On disabled list from July 20 to August 31, 2010.
c Traded to Seattle Mariners for infielder Matt Lawson, March 2, 2011.
d Claimed on waivers by New York Yankees, August 19, 2011.
e Claimed on waivers by Kansas City Royals, October 11, 2011.
f Not offered contract, December 12, 2011. Signed with Toronto Blue Jays organization, December 31, 2011.

LANNAN, JOHN EDWARD

Born, Long Beach, New York, September 27, 1984.
Bats Left. Throws Left. Height, 6 feet, 5 inches. Weight, 225 pounds.

Year Club	Lea	G	IP	W	L	Pct	SO	BB	H	ERA	SAVES
2005 Vermont. . . . . N.Y.-Penn.	N.Y.-Penn.	14	63¹/₃	3	5	.375	41	31	74	5.26	0
2006 Savannah . . . . .So.Atl.	So.Atl.	27	138	6	8	.429	114	54	149	4.76	0
2007 Potomac. . . . . .Carolina	Carolina	8	50²/₃	6	0	1.000	35	15	31	2.13	0
2007 Harrisburg . . . . Eastern	Eastern	6	36	3	2	.600	20	15	31	3.25	0
2007 Columbus. . . . . .Int.	Int.	7	38	3	1	.750	19	12	30	1.66	0
2007 Washington . . . . .N.L.	N.L.	6	34²/₃	2	2	.500	10	17	36	4.15	0
2008 Washington . . . . .N.L.	N.L.	31	182	9	15	.375	117	72	172	3.91	0
2009 Washington . . . . .N.L.	N.L.	33	206¹/₃	9	13	.409	89	68	210	3.88	0
2010 Harrisburg . . . . Eastern	Eastern	7	40²/₃	1	4	.200	28	10	49	4.20	0
2010 Washington . . . . .N.L.	N.L.	25	143¹/₃	8	8	.500	71	49	175	4.65	0
2011 Washington . . . . .N.L.	N.L.	33	184²/₃	10	13	.435	106	76	194	3.70	0
Major League Totals . . . . .5 Yrs.		128	751	38	51	.427	393	282	787	4.00	0

LATOS, MATHEW ADAM (MAT)

Born, Alexandria, Virginia, December 9, 1987.
Bats Right. Throws Right. Height, 6 feet, 6 inches. Weight, 225 pounds.

Year Club	Lea	G	IP	W	L	Pct	SO	BB	H	ERA	SAVES
2007 Eugene. . . . . Northwest	Northwest	16	56¹/₃	1	4	.200	74	22	58	3.83	0
2008 Padres . . . . Arizona	Arizona	5	14	1	0	1.000	23	2	12	3.21	0
2008 Fort Wayne. . . . . . . .Midwest	Midwest	7	24²/₃	0	3	.000	23	8	24	3.28	0
2008 Eugene. . . . . Northwest	Northwest	3	17¹/₃	2	0	1.000	23	3	13	1.04	0
2009 Fort Wayne. . . . . . . .Midwest	Midwest	4	25¹/₃	3	0	1.000	27	3	10	0.36	0
2009 San Antonio . . . . .Texas	Texas	9	47	5	1	.833	46	9	32	1.91	0
2009 San Diego . . . . .N.L.	N.L.	10	50²/₃	4	5	.444	39	23	43	4.62	0
2010 San Diego a . . . . .N.L.	N.L.	31	184²/₃	14	10	.583	189	50	150	2.92	0
2011 San Diego b-c . . . . .N.L.	N.L.	31	194¹/₃	9	14	.391	185	62	168	3.47	0
Major League Totals . . . . .3 Yrs.		72	429²/₃	27	29	.482	413	135	361	3.37	0

a On disabled list from July 9 to July 24, 2010.
b On disabled list from March 22 to April 11, 2011.
c Traded to Cincinnati Reds for pitcher Edinson Volquez, pitcher Brad Boxberger, catcher Yasmani Grandal and infielder Yonder Alonso, December 17, 2011.

LEAGUE, BRANDON PAUL

Born, Sacramento, California, March 16, 1983.
Bats Right. Throws Right. Height, 6 feet, 3 inches. Weight, 200 pounds.

Year Club	Lea	G	IP	W	L	Pct	SO	BB	H	ERA	SAVES
2001 Medicine Hat . . . . Pioneer	Pioneer	9	38²/₃	2	2	.500	38	11	36	4.66	0
2002 Auburn. . . . . N.Y.-Penn.	N.Y.-Penn.	16	85²/₃	7	2	.778	72	23	80	3.15	0
2003 Dunedin . . . . Fla.St.	Fla.St.	13	66¹/₃	4	3	.571	34	20	76	4.75	0
2003 Charleston . . . . So.Atl.	So.Atl.	12	70²/₃	2	4	.400	61	18	58	1.91	0

Year	Club	Lea	G	IP	W	L	Pct	SO	BB	H	ERA	SAVES
2004 New Hampshire	Eastern	41	104	6	4	.600	90	41	92	3.38	2
2004 Toronto	A.L.	3	4²/₃	1	0	1.000	2	1	3	0.00	0
2005 Syracuse	Int.	19	63	4	4	.500	35	18	78	5.71	0
2005 Toronto	A.L.	20	35²/₃	1	0	1.000	17	20	42	6.56	0
2006 Syracuse	Int.	31	54²/₃	3	2	.600	43	15	57	2.14	8
2006 Toronto	A.L.	33	42²/₃	1	2	.333	29	9	34	2.53	1
2007 Syracuse	Int.	11	12	0	0	.000	10	6	12	3.00	0
2007 Blue Jays	Gulf Coast	1	1	0	0	.000	1	0	1	0.00	0
2007 Dunedin	Fla.St.	4	6	0	0	.000	6	2	5	4.50	0
2007 New Hampshire	Eastern	6	7²/₃	1	1	.500	7	7	5	3.52	0
2007 Toronto a	A.L.	14	11²/₃	0	0	.000	7	7	19	6.17	0
2008 Syracuse	Int.	20	34¹/₃	2	3	.400	32	10	36	3.93	2
2008 Toronto	A.L.	31	33	1	2	.333	23	15	28	2.18	1
2009 Louisville b	A.L.	67	74²/₃	3	6	.333	76	21	72	4.58	0
2010 Seattle	A.L.	70	79	9	7	.563	56	27	67	3.42	6
2011 Seattle	A.L.	65	61¹/₃	1	5	.167	45	10	56	2.79	37
Major League Totals ...... 8 Yrs.		303	342²/₃	17	22	.436	255	110	321	3.70	45

a On disabled list from March 31 to July 15 and August 5 to September 4, 2007.

b Traded to Seattle Mariners with outfielder Johermyn Chavez for pitcher Brandon Morrow, December 23, 2009.

LEAKE, MICHAEL RAYMOND (MIKE)
Born, San Diego, California, November 12, 1987.
Bats Right. Throws Right. Height, 6 feet, 1 inch. Weight, 190 pounds.

Year	Club	Lea	G	IP	W	L	Pct	SO	BB	H	ERA	SAVES
2010 Cincinnati a	N.L.	24	138¹/₃	8	4	.667	91	49	158	4.23	0
2011 Louisville	Int.	2	7¹/₃	0	1	.000	5	0	12	9.82	0
2011 Cincinnati	N.L.	29	167²/₃	12	9	.571	118	38	159	3.86	0
Major League Totals ...... 2 Yrs.		53	306	20	13	.606	209	87	317	4.03	0

a On disabled list from August 25 to September 10, 2010.

LE CURE, SAMUEL R. (SAM)
Born, Jefferson City, Missouri, May 4, 1984.
Bats Right. Throws Right. Height, 6 feet, 1 inch. Weight, 205 pounds.

Year	Club	Lea	G	IP	W	L	Pct	SO	BB	H	ERA	SAVES
2005 Billings	Pioneer	13	41¹/₃	5	1	.833	44	15	43	3.27	0
2006 Sarasota	Fla.St.	27	141²/₃	7	12	.368	115	46	130	3.43	0
2007 Sarasota	Fla.St.	1	5	1	0	1.000	8	0	2	1.80	0
2007 Chattanooga	Southern	21	110	7	5	.583	104	46	119	4.17	0
2008 Chattanooga	Southern	27	155¹/₃	9	7	.563	128	58	147	3.42	0
2009 Louisville	Int.	25	143¹/₃	10	8	.556	125	44	143	4.46	0
2010 Louisville	Int.	15	98	8	3	.727	87	23	98	3.67	0
2010 Cincinnati	N.L.	15	48	2	5	.286	37	25	50	4.50	0
2011 Louisville	Int.	4	6²/₃	0	1	.000	6	2	5	1.35	1
2011 Cincinnati a	N.L.	43	77²/₃	2	1	.667	73	21	57	3.71	0
Major League Totals ...... 2 Yrs.		58	125²/₃	4	6	.400	110	46	107	4.01	0

a On disabled list from May 29 to June 22, 2011.

LEE, CLIFTON PHIFER (CLIFF)
Born, Benton, Arkansas, August 30, 1978.
Bats Left. Throws Left. Height, 6 feet, 3 inches. Weight, 190 pounds.

Year	Club	Lea	G	IP	W	L	Pct	SO	BB	H	ERA	SAVES
2000 Cape Fear	So.Atl.	11	44²/₃	1	4	.200	63	36	50	5.24	0
2001 Jupiter	Fla.St.	21	109²/₃	6	7	.462	179	46	78	2.79	0
2002 Harrisburg	Eastern	15	86¹/₃	7	2	.778	105	23	61	3.23	0
2002 Akron	Eastern	3	16²/₃	2	1	.667	18	10	11	5.40	0
2002 Buffalo	Int.	8	43	3	2	.600	30	22	36	3.77	0
2002 Cleveland a-b	A.L.	2	10¹/₃	0	1	.000	6	8	6	1.74	0
2003 Buffalo	Int.	11	63¹/₃	6	1	.857	61	31	62	3.27	0
2003 Kinston	Carolina	1	4¹/₃	0	0	.000	4	3	0	0.00	0
2003 Akron	Eastern	2	12	1	0	1.000	13	4	7	1.50	0
2003 Cleveland c	A.L.	9	52¹/₃	3	3	.500	44	20	41	3.61	0
2004 Cleveland	A.L.	33	179	14	8	.636	161	81	188	5.43	0
2005 Cleveland	A.L.	32	202	18	5	*.783	143	52	194	3.79	0
2006 Cleveland	A.L.	33	200²/₃	14	11	.560	129	58	224	4.40	0
2007 Kinston	Carolina	1	2	0	0	.000	4	0	1	0.00	0
2007 Akron	Eastern	1	5	1	0	1.000	7	1	2	0.00	0
2007 Buffalo	Int.	8	41	1	3	.250	50	25	32	3.51	0

Year Club	Lea	G	IP	W	L	Pct	SO	BB	H	ERA	SAVES
2007 Cleveland d	A.L.	20	97⅓	5	8	.385	66	36	112	6.29	0
2008 Cleveland e............	A.L.	31	223⅓	*22	3	*.880	170	34	214	*2.54	0
2009 Philadelphia	N.L.	12	79⅔	7	4	.636	74	10	80	3.39	0
2009 Cleveland f-g	A.L.	22	152	7	9	.438	107	33	165	3.14	0
2010 Tacoma	P.C.	1	6	0	0	.000	4	0	3	0.00	0
2010 Seattle-Texas h-i-j	A.L.	28	212⅓	12	9	.571	185	18	·195	3.18	0
2011 Philadelphia	N.L.	32	232⅔	17	8	.680	238	42	197	2.40	0
Major League Totals ....10 Yrs.		254	1641⅔	119	69	.633	1323	392	1616	3.65	0
Division Series											
2009 Philadelphia	N.L.	2	16⅓	1	0	1.000	10	3	11	1.10	0
2010 Texas	A.L.	2	16	2	0	1.000	21	0	11	1.13	0
2011 Philadelphia	N.L.	1	6	0	1	.000	9	2	12	7.50	0
Division Series Totals		5	38⅓	3	1	.750	40	5	34	2.11	0
Championship Series											
2009 Philadelphia	N.L.	1	8	1	0	1.000	10	0	3	0.00	0
2010 Texas	A.L.	1	8	1	0	1.000	13	1	2	0.00	0
Championship Series Totals		2	16	2	0	1.000	23	1	5	0.00	0
World Series Record											
2009 Philadelphia	N.L.	2	16	2	0	1.000	13	3	13	2.81	0
2010 Texas	A.L.	2	11⅔	0	2	.000	13	1	14	6.94	0
World Series Totals............		4	27⅔	2	2	.500	26	4	27	4.55	0

a Traded to Cleveland Indians with infielder Lee Stevens, infielder Brandon Phillips and outfielder Grady Sizemore for pitcher Bartolo Colon and player to be named later, June 27, 2002.

b Montreal Expos received pitcher Tim Drew to complete trade, June 28, 2002.

c On disabled list from March 29 to May 30, 2003.

d On disabled list from March 23 to May 3, 2007.

e Selected Cy Young Award Winner in American League for 2008.

f Traded to Philadelphia Phillies with outfielder Ben Francisco for catcher Lou Marson, pitcher Jason Knapp, infielder Jason Donald and pitcher Carlos Carrasco, July 29, 2009.

g Traded to Seattle Mariners for outfielder J.C. Ramirez, pitcher Phillippe Aumont and outfielder Tyson Gillies, December 16, 2009.

h On disabled list from March 26 to April 30, 2010.

i Traded to Texas Rangers with pitcher Mark Lowe and cash for infielder Justin Smoak, pitcher Blake Beavan, pitcher Josh Lueke and infielder Matt Lawson, July 9, 2010.

j Filed for free agency, November 1, 2010. Signed with Philadelphia Phillies, December 15, 2010.

LESTER, JONATHAN TYLER (JON)
Born, Tacoma, Washington, January 7, 1984.
Bats Left. Throws Left. Height, 6 feet, 2 inches. Weight, 190 pounds.

Year Club	Lea	G	IP	W	L	Pct	SO	BB	H	ERA	SAVES
2002 Red Sox	Gulf Coast	1	0⅔	0	1	.000	1	1	5	13.50	0
2003 Augusta	So.Atl.	24	106	6	9	.400	71	44	102	3.65	0
2004 Sarasota...........	Fla.St.	21	90⅓	7	6	.538	97	37	82	4.28	0
2004 Red Sox	Gulf Coast	1	1	1	0	.000	1	2	0	0.00	0
2005 Portland	Eastern	26	148⅓	11	6	.647	163	57	114	2.61	0
2006 Pawtucket	Int.	11	46⅔	3	4	.429	43	25	43	2.70	0
2006 Boston a...........	A.L.	15	81⅓	7	2	.778	60	43	91	4.76	0
2007 Greenville...........	So.Atl.	3	13	0	0	.000	15	2	11	2.08	0
2007 Portland	Eastern	1	6	1	0	1.000	4	4	5	1.50	0
2007 Pawtucket	Int.	14	71⅔	4	5	.444	51	31	67	3.89	0
2007 Boston b	A.L.	12	63	4	0	1.000	50	31	61	4.57	0
2008 Boston c...........	A.L.	33	210⅓	16	6	.727	152	66	202	3.21	0
2009 Boston	A.L.	32	203⅓	15	8	.652	225	64	186	3.41	0
2010 Boston	A.L.	32	208	19	9	.679	225	83	167	3.25	0
2011 Boston d	A.L.	31	191⅔	15	9	.625	182	75	166	3.47	0
Major League Totals .... 6 Yrs.		155	957⅔	76	34	.691	894	362	873	3.53	0
Division Series											
2008 Boston	A.L.	2	14	1	0	1.000	11	3	10	0.00	0
2009 Boston	A.L.	1	6	0	1	.000	5	4	4	4.50	0
Division Series Totals		3	20	1	1	.500	16	7	14	1.35	0
Championship Series											
2007 Boston	A.L.	2	3⅔	0	0	.000	5	1	3	4.91	0
2008 Boston	A.L.	2	12⅔	0	2	.000	15	2	14	4.97	0
Championship Series Totals		4	16⅓	0	2	.000	20	3	17	4.96	0
World Series Record											
2007 Boston	A.L.	1	5⅔	1	0	1.000	3	3	3	0.00	0

a On disabled list from August 24 to November 6, 2006.

LEWIS, COLBY PRESTON

Born, Bakersfield, California, August 2, 1979.
Bats Right. Throws Right. Height, 6 feet, 4 inches. Weight, 230 pounds.

Year	Club	Lea	G	IP	W	L	Pct	SO	BB	H	ERA	SAVES
1999	Pulaski	Appal.	14	64⅔	7	3	.700	84	27	46	1.95	0
2000	Charlotte	Fla.St.	28	163⅔	11	10	.524	153	45	169	4.07	0
2001	Charlotte	Fla.St.	1	4⅓	1	0	1.000	8	0	0	0.00	0
2001	Tulsa	Texas	25	156	10	10	.500	162	62	150	4.50	0
2002	Texas	A.L.	15	34⅓	1	3	.250	28	26	42	6.29	0
2002	Oklahoma	P.C.	20	106⅔	5	6	.455	99	28	100	3.63	0
2003	Texas	A.L.	26	127	10	9	.526	88	70	163	7.30	0
2003	Oklahoma	P.C.	7	47⅔	5	1	.833	43	19	36	3.02	0
2004	Texas a-b	A.L.	3	15⅓	1	1	.500	11	13	13	4.11	0
2005	Detroit c	A.L.		INJURED—Did Not Play								
2006	Toledo	Int.	24	147⅔	6	7	.462	104	36	154	3.96	0
2006	Detroit d	A.L.	2	3	0	0	.000	5	1	8	3.00	0
2007	Sacramento	P.C.	15	95⅔	8	3	.727	97	23	70	1.88	0
2007	Oakland e-f	A.L.	26	37⅔	0	2	.000	23	14	44	6.45	0
2008	Hiroshima g	Japan Cent.	26	178	15	8	.652	183	27	151	2.68	0
2009	Hiroshima	Japan Cent.	29	176⅓	11	9	.550	186	19	156	2.96	0
2010	Texas h	A.L.	32	201	12	13	.480	196	65	174	3.72	0
2011	Texas	A.L.	32	200⅓	14	10	.583	169	56	187	4.40	0
Major League Totals		7 Yrs.	136	618⅔	38	38	.500	520	245	631	4.99	0
Division Series												
2010	Texas	A.L.	1	5	0	0	.000	5	5	2	0.00	0
2011	Texas	A.L.	1	6	1	0	1.000	6	2	1	1.50	0
Division Series Totals			2	11	1	0	1.000	11	7	3	0.82	0
Championship Series												
2010	Texas	A.L.	2	13⅔	2	0	1.000	13	6	9	1.98	0
2011	Texas	A.L.	1	5⅔	0	1	.000	6	2	8	6.35	0
Championship Series Totals			3	19⅓	2	1	.667	19	8	17	3.26	0
World Series Record												
2010	Texas	A.L.	1	7⅔	1	0	1.000	6	2	5	2.35	0
2011	Texas	A.L.	2	12	0	0	.000	8	5	7	2.25	0
World Series Totals			3	19⅔	1	0	1.000	14	7	12	2.29	0

a On disabled list from April 18 to October 6, 2004.
b Claimed on waivers by Detroit Tigers, October 8, 2004.
c On disabled list from April 2 to October 31, 2005.
d Filed for free agency, October 2, 2006. Signed with Washington Nationals organization, November 6, 2006.
e Released by Washington Nationals, March 19, 2007. Signed with Oakland Athletics organization, March 29, 2007.
f Claimed on waivers by Kansas City Royals, November 2, 2007.
g Released by Kansas City Royals, December 4, 2007. Signed with Hiroshima (Japan) for 2008.
h Signed with Texas Rangers, January 14, 2010.

LIDGE, BRADLEY THOMAS (BRAD)

Born, Sacramento, California, December 23, 1976.
Bats Right. Throws Right. Height, 6 feet, 5 inches. Weight, 210 pounds.

Year	Club	Lea	G	IP	W	L	Pct	SO	BB	H	ERA	SAVES
1998	Quad City a-b	Midwest	4	11	0	1	.000	6	5	10	3.27	0
1999	Kissimmee c	Fla.St.	6	21⅓	0	2	.000	19	11	13	3.38	0
2000	Kissimmee d	Fla.St.	8	41⅔	2	1	.667	46	15	28	2.81	0
2001	Round Rock e	Texas	5	26	2	0	1.000	42	7	21	1.73	0
2002	Round Rock	Texas	5	11	1	1	.500	18	3	9	2.45	0
2002	Houston	N.L.	6	8⅔	1	0	1.000	12	9	12	6.23	0
2002	New Orleans	P.C.	24	111⅔	5	5	.500	110	47	83	3.39	0
2003	Houston	N.L.	78	85	6	3	.667	97	42	60	3.60	1
2004	Houston	N.L.	80	94⅔	6	5	.545	157	30	57	1.90	29
2005	Houston	N.L.	70	70⅔	4	4	.500	103	23	58	2.29	42
2006	Houston	N.L.	78	75	1	5	.167	104	36	69	5.28	32
2007	Corpus Christi	Texas	1	1	0	0	.000	0	0	0	0.00	0
2007	Houston f-g	N.L.	66	67	5	3	.625	88	30	54	3.36	19
2008	Clearwater	Fla.St.	1	1	0	0	.000	2	1	2	9.00	0
2008	Philadelphia h	N.L.	72	69⅓	2	0	1.000	92	35	50	1.95	41
2009	Clearwater	Fla.St.	1	1	0	0	.000	0	1	0	0.00	0

Year Club	Lea	G	IP	W	L	Pct	SO	BB	H	ERA	SAVES
2009 Reading	Eastern	1	1	0	0	.000	2	0	1	0.00	0
2009 Philadelphia i	N.L.	67	58²/₃	0	8	.000	61	34	72	7.21	31
2010 Clearwater	Fla.St.	6	5²/₃	0	1	.000	5	2	5	7.94	0
2010 Reading	Eastern	2	3	0	0	.000	4	1	1	0.00	0
2010 Lehigh Valley	Int.	1	1	0	0	.000	0	1	0	0.00	0
2010 Philadelphia j	N.L.	50	45²/₃	1	1	.500	52	24	32	2.96	27
2011 Lakewood	So.Atl.	4	4	0	0	.000	5	0	5	2.25	0
2011 Reading	Eastern	4	3²/₃	0	0	.000	5	1	3	4.91	0
2011 Philadelphia k-l	N.L.	25	19¹/₃	0	2	.000	23	13	16	1.40	1
Major League Totals . . . . . . .10 Yrs.		592	594	26	31	.456	789	276	480	3.44	223
Division Series											
2004 Houston	N.L.	3	4¹/₃	0	0	.000	6	1	4	2.08	1
2005 Houston	N.L.	3	4	0	0	.000	5	4	2	0.00	0
2008 Philadelphia	N.L.	3	3	0	0	.000	4	1	3	3.00	2
2009 Philadelphia	N.L.	2	1¹/₃	0	0	.000	1	2	0	0.00	2
2010 Philadelphia	N.L.	1	1	0	0	.000	0	1	0	0.00	1
2011 Philadelphia	N.L.	3	2	0	0	.000	1	1	2	0.00	0
Division Series Totals		15	15²/₃	0	0	.000	17	10	11	1.15	6
Championship Series											
2004 Houston	N.L.	4	8	1	0	1.000	14	2	1	0.00	2
2005 Houston	N.L.	4	5	0	1	.000	7	2	6	7.20	3
2008 Philadelphia	N.L.	4	4¹/₃	0	0	.000	6	2	2	0.00	3
2009 Philadelphia	N.L.	3	2²/₃	1	0	1.000	3	1	1	0.00	1
2010 Philadelphia	N.L.	3	3	0	0	.000	5	2	3	0.00	1
Championship Series Totals		18	23	2	1	.667	35	9	13	1.57	10
World Series Record											
2005 Houston	N.L.	3	3²/₃	0	2	.000	6	0	4	4.91	0
2008 Philadelphia	N.L.	2	2	0	0	.000	3	0	1	0.00	2
2009 Philadelphia	N.L.	1	1	0	1	.000	1	0	3	27.00	0
World Series Totals		6	6²/₃	0	3	.000	10	0	8	6.75	2

a Drafted by Texas Rangers with choice received for Colorado Rockies signing pitcher Darryl Kile, June 2, 1998.
b On disabled list from August 18 to September 29, 1998.
c On disabled list from April 1 to June 1 and July 10 to September 29, 1999.
d On disabled list from April 24 to June 13 and July 1 to September 29, 2000.
e On disabled list from May 5 to September 29, 2001.
f On disabled list from June 16 to July 13, 2007.
g Traded to Philadelphia Phillies with infielder Eric Bruntlett for pitcher Geoff Geary, outfielder Michael Bourn and infielder Mike Costanzo, November 12, 2007.
h On disabled list from March 21 to April 5, 2008.
i On disabled list from June 7 to June 25, 2009.
j On disabled list from March 26 to April 30 and May 10 to May 31, 2010.
k On disabled list from March 25 to July 22, 2011.
l Filed for free agency, October 30, 2011.

LILLY, THEODORE ROOSEVELT (TED)

Born, Lamita, California, January 4, 1976.
Bats Left. Throws Left. Height, 6 feet, 1 inch. Weight, 190 pounds.

Year Club	Lea	G	IP	W	L	Pct	SO	BB	H	ERA	SAVES
1996 Yakima	Northwest	13	53²/₃	4	0	1.000	75	14	25	0.84	0
1997 San Bernardino	California	23	134²/₃	7	8	.467	158	32	116	2.81	0
1998 San Antonio	Texas	17	111²/₃	8	4	.667	96	37	114	3.30	0
1998 Albuquerque.	P.C.	5	31	1	3	.250	25	9	39	4.94	0
1998 Ottawa a	Int.	7	39	2	2	.500	49	19	45	4.85	0
1999 Ottawa	Int.	16	89	8	5	.615	78	23	81	3.84	0
1999 Montreal b-c	N.L.	9	23²/₃	0	1	.000	28	9	30	7.61	0
2000 Tampa	Fla.St.	1	6²/₃	0	0	.000	6	1	5	1.35	0
2000 Columbus.	Int.	22	137¹/₃	8	11	.421	127	48	157	4.19	0
2000 New York d-e	A.L.	7	8	0	0	.000	11	5	8	5.63	0
2001 Columbus	Int.	5	25¹/₃	0	0	.000	30	8	16	2.84	0
2001 New York	A.L.	26	120²/₃	5	6	.455	112	51	126	5.37	0
2002 New York-Oakland f-g	A.L.	22	100	5	7	.417	77	31	80	3.69	0
2003 Oakland h	A.L.	32	178¹/₃	12	10	.545	147	58	179	4.34	0
2004 Toronto	A.L.	32	197¹/₃	12	10	.545	168	89	171	4.06	0
2005 Syracuse	Int.	2	8²/₃	0	1	.000	9	5	5	3.12	0
2005 Toronto i	A.L.	25	126¹/₃	10	11	.476	96	58	135	5.56	0
2006 Toronto j	A.L.	32	181²/₃	15	13	.536	160	81	179	4.31	0
2007 Chicago	N.L.	34	207	15	8	.652	174	55	181	3.83	0
2008 Chicago	N.L.	34	204²/₃	17	9	.654	184	64	187	4.09	0

Year	Club	Lea	G	IP	W	L	Pct	SO	BB	H	ERA	SAVES
2009 Peoria............	Midwest	1	5	1	0	1.000	2	1	2	0.00	0
2009 Chicago k............	N.L.	27	177	12	9	.571	151	36	151	3.10	0
2010 Peoria............	Midwest	1	7	1	0	1.000	9	1	3	1.29	0
2010 Iowa.................	P.C.	1	4	0	0	.000	4	1	1	2.25	0
2010 Chicago-Los Angeles l-m	N.L.	30	193²/₃	4	12	.455	166	44	165	3.62	0
2011 Los Angeles............	N.L.	33	192²/₃	12	14	.462	158	51	172	3.97	0
Major League Totals.......13 Yrs.		343	1911	125	110	.532	1632	632	1764	4.16	0
Division Series											
2002 Oakland...............	A.L.	2	4	0	1	.000	3	1	10	13.50	0
2003 Oakland...............	A.L.	2	9	0	0	.000	7	2	2	0.00	0
2007 Chicago...............	N.L.	1	3¹/₃	0	1	.000	4	4	7	16.20	0
Division Series Totals...........		5	16¹/₃	0	2	.000	14	7	19	6.61	0

a Traded by Los Angeles Dodgers to Montreal Expos with infielder Wilton Guerrero, outfielder Peter Bergeron and infielder Jonathan Tucker for infielder Mark Grudzielanek, outfielder Hiram Bocachica and pitcher Carlos Perez, July 31, 1998.
b On disabled list from June 21 to September 30, 1999.
c Montreal Expos traded pitcher Jake Westbrook and two players to be named later to New York Yankees for pitcher Hideki Irabu, December 22, 1999.
d Sent to New York Yankees with pitcher Christian Parker as players to be named later for Jake Westbrook, March 17 and March 22, 2000.
e On disabled list from March 25 to May 22, 2000.
f Traded to Oakland Athletics with pitcher Jason Arnold and outfielder John-Ford Griffin for pitcher Jeff Weaver, July 5, 2002.
g On disabled list from July 23 to September 10, 2002.
h Traded to Toronto Blue Jays for outfielder Bobby Kielty and cash, November 18, 2003.
i On disabled list from March 25 to April 10 and July 25 to September 6, 2005.
j Filed for free agency, October 28, 2006. Signed with Chicago Cubs, December 15, 2006.
k On disabled list from July 21 to August 17, 2009.
l On disabled list from March 26 to April 24, 2010.
m Traded to Los Angeles Dodgers with infielder Ryan Theriot and cash for infielder Blake Dewitt, pitcher Kyle Smit and pitcher Brett Wallach, July 31, 2010.

LINCECUM, TIMOTHY LEROY (TIM)

Born, Bellevue, Washington, June 15, 1984.
Bats Left. Throws Right. Height, 5 feet, 11 inches. Weight, 160 pounds.

Year	Club	Lea	G	IP	W	L	Pct	SO	BB	H	ERA	SAVES
2006 San Jose............	Calif.	6	27²/₃	2	0	1.000	48	12	13	1.95	0
2006 Salem-Keizer.....	Northwest	2	4	0	0	.000	10	0	1	0.00	0
2007 Fresno...............	P.C.	5	31	4	0	1.000	46	11	12	0.29	0
2007 San Francisco..........	N.L.	24	146¹/₃	7	5	.583	150	65	122	4.00	0
2008 San Francisco a.........	N.L.	34	227	18	5	*.783	*265	84	182	2.62	0
2009 San Francisco b.........	N.L.	32	225¹/₃	15	7	.682	*261	68	168	2.48	0
2010 San Francisco..........	N.L.	33	212¹/₃	16	10	.615	*231	76	194	3.43	0
2011 San Francisco..........	N.L.	33	217	13	14	.481	220	86	176	2.74	0
Major League Totals........5 Yrs.		156	1028	69	41	.627	1127	379	842	2.98	0
Division Series											
2010 San Francisco.........N.L.		1	9	1	0	1.000	14	1	2	0.00	0
Championship Series											
2010 San Francisco.........N.L.		3	14¹/₃	1	1	.500	16	4	12	3.14	0
World Series Record											
2010 San Francisco.........N.L.		2	13²/₃	2	0	1.000	13	4	11	3.29	0

a Selected Cy Young Award Winner in National League for 2008.
b Selected Cy Young Award Winner in National League for 2009.

LINCOLN, BRAD ERIC

Born, Lake Jackson, Texas, May 25, 1985.
Bats Left. Throws Right. Height, 6 feet. Weight, 210 pounds.

Year	Club	Lea	G	IP	W	L	Pct	SO	BB	H	ERA	SAVES
2006 Pirates..........	Gulf Coast	2	7²/₃	0	0	.000	9	1	6	0.00	0
2006 Hickory.............	So.Atl.	4	16	1	2	.333	10	6	25	6.75	0
2007 a...................					INJURED—Did Not Play						
2008 Hickory.............	So.Atl.	11	62	5	5	.500	46	6	72	4.65	0
2008 Lynchburg.........	Carolina	8	41²/₃	1	5	.167	29	11	42	4.75	0
2009 Altoona.............	Eastern	13	75	1	5	.167	65	18	63	2.28	0
2009 Indianapolis............	Int.	12	61¹/₃	6	2	.750	42	10	72	4.70	0
2010 Indianapolis............	Int.	17	94	7	5	.583	84	24	83	4.12	0
2010 Pittsburgh............	N.L.	11	52²/₃	1	4	.200	25	15	66	6.66	0
2011 Indianapolis............	Int.	19	111²/₃	7	8	.467	94	21	115	4.19	0

279

Year	Club	Lea	G	IP	W	L	Pct	SO	BB	H	ERA	SAVES
2011 Pittsburgh b...........N.L.			12	47²/₃	2	3	.400	29	16	54	4.72	0
Major League Totals........2 Yrs.			23	100¹/₃	3	7	.300	54	31	120	5.74	0

a On minor league disabled list from April 5 to September 7, 2007.
b On disabled list from March 22 to April 11, 2011.

LINDSTROM, MATTHEW JAMES (MATT)
Born, Rexburg, Idaho, February 11, 1980.
Bats Right. Throws Right. Height, 6 feet, 4 inches. Weight, 210 pounds.

Year	Club	Lea	G	IP	W	L	Pct	SO	BB	H	ERA	SAVES
2002 Kingsport...........Appal.			12	48¹/₃	0	6	.000	39	21	56	4.84	0
2003 Brooklyn.........N.Y.-Penn.			14	65¹/₃	7	3	.700	52	27	61	3.44	0
2003 Capital City.........So.Atl.			12	56²/₃	2	3	.400	50	33	46	2.86	0
2004 St. Lucie............Fla.St.			14	79²/₃	5	5	.500	50	20	83	3.73	0
2004 Capital City.........So.Atl.			12	56	3	2	.600	64	10	47	3.21	0
2005 Binghamton......Eastern			35	73¹/₃	2	5	.286	58	55	90	5.40	0
2006 Binghamton.......Eastern			35	40²/₃	2	4	.333	54	14	42	3.76	11
2006 St. Lucie a..........Fla.St.			11	18	1	0	1.000	16	7	14	2.50	2
2007 Florida.............N.L.			71	67	3	4	.429	62	21	66	3.09	0
2008 Albuquerque..........P.C.			3	4	0	0	.000	4	1	5	9.00	0
2008 Florida..............N.L.			66	57¹/₃	3	3	.500	43	26	57	3.14	5
2009 Jupiter...........Fla.St.			2	2	0	0	.000	1	0	1	0.00	0
2009 Jacksonville......Southern			2	2	0	1	.000	3	0	2	9.00	0
2009 Florida b-c...........N.L.			54	47¹/₃	2	1	.667	39	24	54	5.89	15
2010 Corpus Christi.......Texas			1	1	0	0	.000	1	0	0	0.00	0
2010 Houston d-e..........N.L.			58	53¹/₃	2	5	.286	43	20	68	4.39	23
2011 Colorado Springs.......P.C.			2	2	0	0	.000	4	0	4	13.50	0
2011 Colorado f............N.L.			63	54	2	2	.500	36	14	52	3.00	2
Major League Totals.......5 Yrs.			312	279	12	15	.444	223	105	297	3.81	45

a Traded to Florida Marlins by New York Mets with pitcher Henry Owens for pitcher Adam Bostick and pitcher Jason Vargas, November 20, 2006.
b On disabled list from June 24 to August 1, 2009.
c Traded to Houston Astros for infielder Luis Bryan and pitcher Robert Bono, December 9, 2009.
d On disabled list from August 17 to September 1, 2010.
e Traded to Colorado Rockies for pitcher Wes Musick and pitcher Jonnathan Aristil, December 23, 2010.
f On disabled list from August 10 to August 26, 2011.

LINEBRINK, SCOTT CAMERON
Born, Austin, Texas, August 4, 1976.
Bats Right. Throws Right. Height, 6 feet, 2 inches. Weight, 215 pounds.

Year	Club	Lea	G	IP	W	L	Pct	SO	BB	H	ERA	SAVES
1997 Salem-Keizr......Northwest			3	10	0	0	.000	6	6	7	4.50	0
1997 San Jose........California			6	28¹/₃	2	1	.667	40	10	29	3.18	0
1998 Shreveport..........Texas			21	113	10	8	.556	128	58	101	5.02	0
1999 Shreveport..........Texas			10	43¹/₃	1	8	.111	33	14	48	6.44	0
2000 Fresno.............P.C.			28	62	1	4	.200	49	12	54	5.23	4
2000 San Francisco-Houston..N.L.			11	12	0	0	.000	6	8	18	6.00	0
2000 New Orleans a.........P.C.			11	15	2	0	1.000	22	7	15	1.80	1
2001 New Orleans..........P.C.			50	72	7	6	.538	72	24	52	3.50	8
2001 Houston.............N.L.			9	10¹/₃	0	0	.000	9	6	6	2.61	0
2002 Houston.............N.L.			22	24¹/₃	0	0	.000	24	13	31	7.03	0
2002 New Orleans..........P.C.			13	15	1	1	.500	16	11	17	6.00	0
2002 Round Rock b........Texas			2	2	0	0	.000	1	2	2	0.00	0
2003 New Orleans..........P.C.			2	10	0	2	.000	6	5	8	2.70	0
2003 Houston-San Diego c-d..N.L.			52	92¹/₃	3	2	.600	68	36	93	3.31	0
2004 San Diego..........N.L.			73	84	7	3	.700	83	26	61	2.14	0
2005 San Diego..........N.L.			73	73²/₃	8	1	.889	70	23	55	1.83	1
2006 San Diego..........N.L.			73	75²/₃	7	4	.636	68	22	70	3.57	2
2007 San Diego-Milwaukee e-f N.L.			71	70¹/₃	5	6	.455	50	25	68	3.71	1
2008 Chicago g............A.L.			50	46¹/₃	2	2	.500	40	9	41	3.69	1
2009 Chicago.............A.L.			57	56	3	7	.300	55	23	70	4.66	2
2010 Chicago h...........A.L.			52	57¹/₃	3	2	.600	52	17	59	4.40	0
2011 Atlanta i-j...........N.L.			64	54¹/₃	4	4	.500	42	21	58	3.64	1
Major League Totals.......12 Yrs.			607	656²/₃	42	31	.575	567	229	630	3.51	8
Division Series												
2005 San Diego..........N.L.			1	1	0	0	.000	1	0	2	0.00	0
2006 San Diego..........N.L.			2	1¹/₃	0	0	.000	0	1	1	6.75	0
2008 Chicago.............A.L.			1	1	0	0	.000	1	1	1	0.00	0
Division Series Totals...........			4	3¹/₃	0	0	.000	2	2	4	2.70	0

a Traded to Houston Astros for pitcher Doug Henry, July 30, 2000.
b On disabled list from May 20 to June 17, 2002.
c Filed for free agency, October 29, 2002, re-signed with Houston Astros, January 31, 2003.
d Claimed on waivers by San Diego Padres, May 29, 2003.
e Traded to Milwaukee Brewers for pitcher Will Inman, pitcher Joe Thatcher and pitcher Steve Garrison, July 25, 2007.
f Filed for free agency, October 29, 2007. Signed with Chicago White Sox, November 28, 2007.
g On disabled list from July 23 to September 1, 2008.
h Traded to Atlanta Braves for pitcher Kyle Cofield, December 3, 2010.
i On disabled list from July 30 to August 14, 2011.
j Filed for free agency, October 30, 2011.

LIRIANO, FRANCISCO CASILLAS

Born, San Cristobal, Dominican Republic, October 26, 1983.
Bats Left. Throws Left. Height, 6 feet, 2 inches. Weight, 225 pounds.

Year	Club	Lea	G	IP	W	L	Pct	SO	BB	H	ERA	SAVES
2001 Giants	. . . .	Arizona	13	62	5	4	.556	67	24	51	3.63	0
2001 Salem-Keizer	. . . . .	Northwest	2	9	0	0	.000	12	1	7	5.00	0
2002 Hagerstown	. . . .	So.Atl.	16	80	3	6	.333	85	31	61	3.49	0
2003 Giants	. . . .	Arizona	4	8$^{1}/_{3}$	0	1	.000	9	6	5	4.32	0
2003 San Jose	. . . .	Calif.	1	0$^{2}/_{3}$	0	0	.000	0	2	5	54.00	0
2004 New Britain	. . . .	Eastern	7	39$^{2}/_{3}$	3	2	.600	49	17	45	3.18	0
2004 Fort Myers	. . . .	Fla.St.	21	117	6	7	.462	125	43	118	4.00	0
2005 New Britain	. . . .	Eastern	13	76$^{2}/_{3}$	3	5	.375	92	26	70	3.64	0
2005 Rochester	. . . .	.Int.	14	91	9	2	.818	112	24	56	1.78	0
2005 Minnesota	. . . .	A.L.	6	23$^{2}/_{3}$	1	2	.333	33	7	19	5.70	0
2006 Minnesota b	. . . .	A.L.	28	121	12	3	.800	144	32	89	2.16	1
2007 Minnesota c	. . . .	A.L.				INJURED—Did Not Play						
2008 Fort Myers	. . . .	Fla.St.	1	5$^{1}/_{3}$	0	1	.000	8	2	6	6.75	0
2008 Rochester	. . . .	.Int.	19	118	10	2	.833	113	31	102	3.28	0
2008 Minnesota	. . . .	A.L.	14	76	6	4	.600	67	32	74	3.91	0
2009 Minnesota d	. . . .	A.L.	29	136$^{2}/_{3}$	5	13	.278	122	65	147	5.80	0
2010 Minnesota	. . . .	A.L.	31	191$^{2}/_{3}$	14	10	.583	201	58	184	3.62	0
2011 Minnesota e-f	. . . .	A.L.	26	134$^{1}/_{3}$	9	10	.474	112	75	125	5.09	0
Major League Totals	. . . .	.6 Yrs.	134	683$^{1}/_{3}$	47	42	.528	679	269	638	4.19	1
Division Series												
2009 Minnesota	. . . .	A.L.	1	2	0	0	.000	1	1	1	4.50	0
2010 Minnesota	. . . .	A.L.	1	5$^{2}/_{3}$	0	0	.000	7	3	6	6.35	0
Division Series Totals	. . . .		2	7$^{2}/_{3}$	0	0	.000	8	4	7	5.87	0

a Traded by San Francisco Giants to Minnesota Twins with pitcher Joe Nathan and pitcher Boof Bonser for catcher A.J. Pierzynski, November 14, 2003.
b On disabled list from August 8 to September 11, 2006.
c On disabled list from March 24 to October 10, 2007.
d On disabled list from August 18 to September 9, 2009.
e Pitched no-hit, no-run game against Chicago White Sox, May 3, 2011.
f On disabled list from August 26 to September 16 and May 30 to June 7, 2011.

LITSCH, JESSE ALLEN

Born, Pinellas Park, Florida, March 9, 1985.
Bats Right. Throws Right. Height, 6 feet, 1 inch. Weight, 225 pounds.

Year	Club	Lea	G	IP	W	L	Pct	SO	BB	H	ERA	SAVES
2005 Pulaski	. . . .	Appal.	11	65$^{2}/_{3}$	5	1	.833	67	10	51	2.74	0
2005 Auburn	. . . .	N.Y.-Penn.	4	10	0	1	.000	7	6	11	3.60	0
2006 New Hampshire	. . . . .	Eastern	12	69$^{1}/_{3}$	3	4	.429	54	13	85	5.06	0
2006 Dunedin	. . . .	Fla.St.	16	89$^{1}/_{3}$	6	6	.500	81	8	94	3.53	0
2007 New Hampshire	. . . . .	Eastern	10	61$^{1}/_{3}$	7	2	.778	46	14	51	2.35	0
2007 Syracuse	. . . .	.Int.	2	15	1	0	1.000	10	3	12	1.80	0
2007 Toronto	. . . .	A.L.	20	111	7	9	.438	50	36	116	3.81	0
2008 Syracuse	. . . .	.Int.	3	20	1	1	.500	18	4	18	3.60	0
2008 Toronto	. . . .	A.L.	29	176	13	9	.591	99	39	178	3.58	0
2009 Toronto a	. . . .	A.L.	2	9	0	1	.000	8	1	14	9.00	0
2010 Dunedin	. . . .	Fla.St.	2	15	1	1	.500	10	4	9	1.80	0
2010 Las Vegas	. . . .	P.C.	4	22	0	3	.000	13	3	34	8.18	0
2010 Toronto b	. . . .	A.L.	9	46$^{2}/_{3}$	1	5	.167	16	15	53	5.79	0
2011 Lansing	. . . .	.Midwest	1	2	0	0	.000	3	1	3	9.00	0
2011 New Hampshire	. . . . .	Eastern	2	8$^{2}/_{3}$	0	0	.000	9	0	6	1.04	0
2011 Las Vegas	. . . .	P.C.	6	28$^{2}/_{3}$	1	2	.333	27	11	41	8.16	0
2011 Toronto c	. . . .	A.L.	28	75	6	3	.667	66	28	69	4.44	1
Major League Totals	. . . .	.5 Yrs.	88	417$^{2}/_{3}$	27	27	.500	239	119	430	4.16	1

a On disabled list from April 14 to October 13, 2009.
b On disabled list from February 26 to June 9 and August 6 to November 10, 2010.
c On disabled list from May 19 to July 18, 2011.

LOE, KAMERON DAVID

Born, Simi Valley, California, September 10, 1981.
Bats Right. Throws Right. Height, 6 feet, 8 inches. Weight, 240 pounds.

Year	Club	Lea	G	IP	W	L	Pct	SO	BB	H	ERA	SAVES
2002	Pulaski	Appal.	14	58$\frac{1}{3}$	4	4	.500	55	17	64	4.47	1
2003	Stockton	Calif.	9	37$\frac{2}{3}$	3	0	1.000	31	6	26	0.96	1
2003	Clinton	Midwest	23	97	4	3	.571	94	19	78	1.95	2
2004	Frisco	Texas	19	113$\frac{1}{3}$	7	7	.500	97	29	122	3.10	0
2004	Oklahoma	P.C.	8	52$\frac{1}{3}$	5	2	.714	42	13	52	3.27	0
2004	Texas	A.L.	2	6$\frac{2}{3}$	0	0	.000	3	6	6	5.40	0
2005	Oklahoma	P.C.	5	28$\frac{1}{3}$	2	1	.667	23	10	32	5.08	0
2005	Texas	A.L.	48	92	9	6	.600	45	31	89	3.42	1
2006	Texas	A.L.	15	78$\frac{1}{3}$	3	6	.333	34	22	105	5.86	0
2006	Frisco	Texas	2	7	0	1	.000	4	4	8	5.14	0
2006	Oklahoma a	P.C.	13	22$\frac{2}{3}$	1	2	.333	21	13	32	9.13	1
2007	Frisco	Texas	1	3	0	0	.000	1	5	1	6.00	0
2007	Texas b	A.L.	28	136	6	11	.353	78	56	162	5.36	0
2008	Oklahoma	P.C.	26	58	3	5	.375	31	20	70	5.59	1
2008	Texas	A.L.	14	30$\frac{2}{3}$	1	0	1.000	20	8	36	3.23	0
2009	Fukuoka c-d	Japan Pac.	5	27	0	4	.000	18	12	36	6.33	0
2010	Nashville	P.C.	10	62$\frac{2}{3}$	4	3	.571	39	19	57	3.16	0
2010	Milwaukee	N.L.	53	58$\frac{1}{3}$	3	5	.375	46	15	54	2.78	0
2011	Milwaukee	N.L.	72	72	4	7	.364	61	16	65	3.50	1
Major League Totals	7 Yrs.		232	474	26	35	.426	287	154	517	4.33	2
Division Series												
2011 Milwaukee	N.L.		2	2	0	0	.000	1	0	3	0.00	0
Championship Series												
2011 Milwaukee	N.L.		3	2$\frac{1}{3}$	0	0	.000	2	1	10	15.43	0

a On disabled list from June 19 to August 3, 2006.
b On disabled list from July 30 to August 18, 2007.
c Released by Texas Rangers, November 28, 2008. Signed with Fukuoka (Japan) for 2009.
d Signed with Milwaukee Brewers organization, December 18, 2009.

LOGAN, BOONE

Born, San Antonio, Texas, August 13, 1984.
Bats Right. Throws Left. Height, 6 feet, 5 inches. Weight, 215 pounds.

Year	Club	Lea	G	IP	W	L	Pct	SO	BB	H	ERA	SAVES
2003	Great Falls	Pioneer	16	67	3	3	.500	48	31	76	6.58	0
2004	Great Falls	Pioneer	18	64$\frac{1}{3}$	3	7	.300	48	31	74	5.60	1
2005	Winston-Salem	Carolina	4	5$\frac{1}{3}$	0	0	.000	5	4	7	5.06	0
2005	Great Falls	Pioneer	21	35$\frac{1}{3}$	1	1	.500	29	4	34	3.31	2
2006	Charlotte	Int.	38	42$\frac{2}{3}$	3	1	.750	57	12	35	3.38	11
2006	Chicago	A.L.	21	17$\frac{1}{3}$	0	0	.000	15	15	21	8.31	1
2007	Charlotte	Int.	4	8$\frac{1}{3}$	0	1	.000	11	4	8	2.16	1
2007	Chicago	A.L.	68	50$\frac{2}{3}$	2	1	.667	35	20	59	4.97	0
2008	Charlotte	Int.	5	9	0	1	.000	7	6	10	6.00	0
2008	Chicago a	A.L.	55	42$\frac{1}{3}$	2	3	.400	42	14	57	5.95	0
2009	Gwinnett	Int.	29	35$\frac{2}{3}$	4	2	.667	39	17	26	3.28	2
2009	Atlanta b	N.L.	20	17$\frac{1}{3}$	1	1	.500	10	9	21	5.19	0
2010	Scranton/WB	Int.	14	21$\frac{1}{3}$	0	1	.000	23	4	18	2.11	0
2010	New York	A.L.	51	40	2	0	1.000	38	20	34	2.93	0
2011	New York	A.L.	64	41$\frac{2}{3}$	5	3	.625	46	13	43	3.46	0
Major League Totals	6 Yrs.		279	209$\frac{1}{3}$	12	8	.600	186	91	235	4.77	1
Division Series												
2010 New York	A.L.		2	1	0	0	.000	0	0	1	0.00	0
2011 New York	A.L.		3	2$\frac{1}{3}$	0	0	.000	6	0	1	0.00	0
Division Series Totals			5	3$\frac{1}{3}$	0	0	.000	6	0	2	0.00	0
Championship Series												
2010 New York	A.L.		3	0$\frac{2}{3}$	0	0	.000	1	1	2	27.00	0

a Traded to Atlanta Braves with pitcher Javier Vazquez for catcher Tyler Flowers, infielder Jonathan Gilmore, infielder Brent Lillibridge and pitcher Santos Rodriguez, December 4, 2008.
b Traded to New York Yankees with pitcher Javier Vazquez for outfielder Melky Cabrera, pitcher Arodys Vizcaino, pitcher Michael Dunn and cash, December 22, 2009.

LOHSE, KYLE MATTHEW

Born, Chico, California, October 4, 1978.
Bats Right. Throws Right. Height, 6 feet, 2 inches. Weight, 210 pounds.

Year	Club	Lea	G	IP	W	L	Pxt	SO	BB	H	ERA	SAVES
1997	Cubs	Arizona	12	47²/₃	2	2	.500	49	22	46	3.02	0
1998	Rockford	Midwest	28	170²/₃	13	8	.619	121	45	158	3.22	0
1999	New Britain	Eastern	11	70¹/₃	3	4	.429	41	23	87	5.89	0
1999	Daytona	Fla.St.	9	53	5	3	.625	41	16	48	2.89	0
1999	Fort Myers a	Fla.St.	7	41²/₃	2	3	.400	33	9	47	5.18	0
2000	New Britain	Eastern	28	167	3	18	.143	124	55	196	6.04	0
2001	New Britain	Eastern	6	38	3	1	.750	32	4	32	2.37	0
2001	Edmonton	P.C.	8	49	4	2	.667	48	13	50	3.12	0
2001	Minnesota	A.L.	19	90¹/₃	4	7	.364	64	29	102	5.68	0
2002	Minnesota	A.L.	32	180²/₃	13	8	.619	124	70	181	4.23	0
2003	Minnesota	A.L.	33	201	14	11	.560	130	45	211	4.61	0
2004	Minnesota	A.L.	35	194	9	13	.409	111	76	240	5.34	0
2005	Minnesota	A.L.	31	178²/₃	9	13	.409	86	44	211	4.18	0
2006	Rochester	Int.	4	24	2	1	.667	12	6	15	1.50	0
2006	Minnesota	A.L.	22	63²/₃	2	5	.286	46	25	80	7.07	0
2006	Cincinnati b	N.L.	12	63	3	5	.375	51	19	70	4.57	0
2007	Cincinnati-Philadelphia c-d	N.L.	34	192²/₃	9	12	.429	122	57	207	4.62	0
2008	St. Louis	N.L.	33	200	15	6	.714	119	49	211	3.78	0
2009	Springfield	Texas	1	4²/₃	0	0	.000	3	4	3	3.86	0
2009	Memphis	P.C.	1	6	1	0	1.000	6	2	2	0.00	0
2009	St. Louis e	N.L.	23	117²/₃	6	10	.375	77	36	125	4.74	0
2010	Springfield	Texas	1	5	0	1	.000	4	0	12	9.00	0
2010	Memphis	P.C.	3	14	1	0	1.000	14	2	9	3.21	0
2010	St. Louis f	N.L.	18	92	4	8	.333	54	35	129	6.55	0
2011	St. Louis	N.L.	30	188¹/₃	14	8	.636	111	42	178	3.39	0
Major League Totals		11 Yrs.	322	1762	102	106	.490	1095	527	1945	4.64	0

Division Series

Year	Club	Lea	G	IP	W	L	Pxt	SO	BB	H	ERA	SAVES
2002	Minnesota	A.L.	2	4	0	0	.000	5	0	2	0.00	0
2003	Minnesota	A.L.	1	5	0	1	.000	5	2	6	5.40	0
2004	Minnesota	A.L.	1	2	0	1	.000	3	0	1	4.50	0
2007	Philadelphia	N.L.	1	1²/₃	0	0	.000	1	0	1	6.75	0
2011	St. Louis	N.L.	1	5¹/₃	0	1	.000	4	1	7	8.44	0
Division Series Totals			6	17²/₃	0	3	.000	18	3	17	5.09	0

Championship Series

Year	Club	Lea	G	IP	W	L	Pxt	SO	BB	H	ERA	SAVES
2002	Minnesota	A.L.	1	1	0	0	.000	1	0	0	0.00	0
2011	St. Louis	N.L.	1	4¹/₃	0	1	.000	3	0	6	6.23	0
Championship Series Totals			2	5¹/₃	0	1	.000	4	0	6	5.06	0

World Series Record

Year	Club	Lea	G	IP	W	L	Pxt	SO	BB	H	ERA	SAVES
2011	St. Louis	N.L.	1	3	0	0	.000	3	2	5	9.00	0

a Traded by Chicago Cubs to Minnesota Twins with pitcher Jason Ryan for pitcher Rick Aguilera and pitcher Scott Downs, May 21, 1999.
b Traded to Cincinnati Reds for pitcher Zach Ward, July 31, 2006.
c Traded to Philadelphia Phillies for pitcher Matt Maloney, July 30, 2007.
d Filed for free agency, October 31, 2007. Signed with St. Louis Cardinals, March 14, 2008.
e On disabled list from June 4 to July 12 and August 22 to September 6, 2009.
f On disabled list from May 23 to August 15, 2010.

LOPEZ, JAVIER ALFONSO

Born, San Juan, Puerto Rico, July 11, 1977.
Bats Left. Throws Left. Height, 6 feet, 4 inches. Weight, 225 pounds.

Year	Club	Lea	G	IP	W	L	Pct	SO	BB	H	ERA	SAVES
1998	South Bend	Midwest	16	44	2	4	.333	31	30	60	6.55	0
1999	South Bend	Midwest	20	99	4	6	.400	70	43	122	6.00	0
2000	High Desert	Calif.	30	136¹/₃	8	4	.333	98	57	152	5.22	2
2001	Lancaster	Calif.	17	24	1	3	.250	18	5	30	2.63	1
2001	El Paso	Texas	22	40	1	0	1.000	21	14	64	7.43	0
2002	El Paso a	Texas	61	46¹/₃	2	2	.500	47	16	34	2.72	6
2003	Colorado b	N.L.	75	58¹/₃	4	1	.800	40	12	58	3.70	1
2004	Colorado Springs	P.C.	8	9	0	1	.000	9	2	10	4.00	0
2004	Colorado	N.L.	64	40²/₃	1	2	.333	20	26	45	7.52	0
2005	Tucson	P.C.	27	24¹/₃	0	1	.000	16	12	17	2.22	2
2005	Colorado-Arizona c	N.L.	32	16¹/₃	1	1	.500	12	11	26	11.02	2
2006	Charlotte	Int.	26	33	2	1	.667	26	6	28	0.55	14
2006	Pawtucket	Int.	13	16²/₃	0	0	.000	12	8	20	4.86	4
2006	Boston d-e	A.L.	27	16²/₃	1	0	1.000	11	10	13	2.70	1

Year Club	Lea	G	IP	W	L	Pct	SO	BB	H	ERA	SAVES
2007 Pawtucket ....Int.		17	16²/₃	2	1	.667	15	8	19	3.78	0
2007 Boston ..............A.L.		61	40²/₃	2	1	.667	26	18	36	3.10	0
2008 Boston ..............A.L.		70	59¹/₃	2	0	1.000	38	27	53	2.43	0
2009 Boston ..............A.L.		14	11²/₃	0	2	.000	5	9	20	9.26	0
2009 Pawtucket f ....Int.		38	39²/₃	1	1	.500	23	13	35	3.18	0
2010 Pittsburgh-San Francisco g .N.L.		77	57²/₃	4	2	.667	38	20	50	2.34	0
2011 San Francisco .........N.L.		70	53	5	2	.714	40	26	42	2.72	1
Major League Totals ....9 Yrs.		490	354¹/₃	20	11	.645	230	159	343	3.96	5
Division Series											
2007 Boston ..............A.L.		1	0¹/₃	0	0	.000	0	0	0	0.00	0
2008 Boston ..............A.L.		1	1	0	1	.000	1	0	3	9.00	0
2010 San Francisco .........N.L.		2	0²/₃	0	0	.000	2	0	0	0.00	0
Division Series Totals		4	2	0	1	.000	3	0	3	4.50	0
Championship Series											
2007 Boston ..............A.L.		3	2	0	0	.000	0	2	3	18.00	0
2008 Boston ..............A.L.		2	1²/₃	0	0	.000	0	0	3	0.00	0
2010 San Francisco .........N.L.		5	4¹/₃	1	0	1.000	4	1	1	2.08	0
Championship Series Totals		10	8	1	0	1.000	4	3	7	5.63	0
World Series Record											
2007 Boston ..............A.L.		1	0	0	0	.000	0	0	2	INF	0
2010 San Francisco .........N.L.		2	0²/₃	0	0	.000	0	0	0	0.00	0
World Series Totals.............		3	0²/₃	0	0	.000	0	0	2	27.00	0

a Selected by Boston Red Sox from Arizona Diamondbacks in Rule V draft, December 16, 2002.

b Traded to Colorado Rockies for player to be named later, March 28, 2003. Boston Red Sox received pitcher Ryan Cameron to complete trade, March 29, 2003.

c Claimed on waivers by Arizona Diamondbacks, April 14, 2005.

d Filed for free agency, October 15, 2005. Signed with Chicago White Sox organization, January 19, 2006.

e Traded to Boston Red Sox for pitcher David Riske, June 15, 2006.

f Filed for free agency, October 5, 2009. Signed with Pittsburgh Pirates, December 18, 2009.

g Traded to San Francisco Giants for pitcher Joe Martinez and outfielder John Bowker, July 31, 2010.

LOPEZ (MUNOZ), RODRIGO
Born, Tlalnepantla, Mexico, December 14, 1975.
Bats Right. Throws Right. Height, 6 feet, 1 inch. Weight, 185 pounds.

Year Club	Lea	G	IP	W	L	Pct	SO	BB	H	ERA	SAVES
1993 Veracruz ....Mexican		2	1	0	0	.000	0	3	3	0.00	0
1994 Aguila............Mexican		10	12²/₃	0	0	.000	5	3	15	4.97	0
1995 Padres a..........Arizona		11	34²/₃	1	1	.500	33	14	41	5.45	1
1996 Poza Rica ....Mexican		7	20¹/₃	1	1	.500	22	16	15	3.54	1
1996 Idaho Falls ....Pioneer		15	71	4	4	.500	72	34	76	5.70	1
1997 Clinton...........Midwest		37	121²/₃	6	8	.429	123	42	103	3.18	9
1998 Mexico ....Mexican		26	163²/₃	10	6	.625	95	79	165	3.35	0
1998 Mobile ....Southern		4	25²/₃	3	0	1.000	20	4	21	1.40	0
1999 Mobile ....Southern		28	169¹/₃	10	8	.556	138	58	187	4.41	0
2000 Las Vegas.............P.C.		20	109¹/₃	8	7	.533	100	45	123	4.69	0
2000 San Diego ...........N.L.		6	24²/₃	0	3	.000	17	13	40	8.76	0
2001 Lake Elsinore ....Calif.		9	13	0	1	.000	9	4	15	0.69	0
2001 Portland b ............P.C.		11	52¹/₃	2	2	.500	37	15	45	3.44	0
2002 Baltimore ............A.L.		33	196²/₃	15	9	.625	136	62	172	3.57	0
2003 Bowie ....Eastern		1	6¹/₃	1	0	1.000	13	0	3	0.00	0
2003 Baltimore c...........A.L.		26	147	7	10	.412	103	43	188	5.82	0
2004 Baltimore ............A.L.		37	170²/₃	14	9	.609	121	54	164	3.59	0
2005 Baltimore ............A.L.		35	209¹/₃	15	12	.556	118	63	232	4.90	0
2006 Baltimore ............A.L.		36	189	9	*18	.333	136	59	234	5.90	0
2007 Colorado Springs.......P.C.		2	11¹/₃	1	0	1.000	4	3	4	2.38	0
2007 Colorado d-e .........N.L.		14	79¹/₃	5	4	.556	43	21	83	4.42	0
2008 Braves ....Gulf Coast		2	3	0	0	.000	4	0	2	0.00	0
2008 Rome f.............So.Atl.		1	2	0	1	.000	1	2	8	40.50	0
2009 Philadelphia...........N.L.		7	30	3	1	.750	19	11	42	5.70	0
2009 Lehigh Valley g-h........Int.		18	100¹/₃	7	5	.583	71	14	122	4.31	0
2010 Arizona i.............N.L.		33	200	7	*16	.304	116	56	227	4.99	0
2011 Gwinnett..............Int.		9	59	6	1	.857	44	14	59	2.59	0
2011 Chicago j-k............N.L.		26	97²/₃	6	6	.500	54	29	116	4.42	0
Major League Totals ....10 Yrs.		253	1344¹/₃	81	88	.479	863	411	1498	4.82	0

a Signed by Veracruz (Mexico) for 1993. Sold to San Diego Padres, March 21, 1995.

b Filed for free agency, October 15, 2001. Signed with Baltimore Orioles organization, November 23, 2001.

c On disabled list from May 2 to June 15, 2003.

d Traded to Colorado Rockies for pitcher Jason Burch and pitcher Jim Miller, January 12, 2007.

e On disabled list from April 19 to May 29 and July 27 to October 31, 2007.
f Filed for free agency, October 31, 2007. Signed with Atlanta Braves organization, August 22, 2008.
g Released by Atlanta Braves, November 12, 2008. Signed with Philadelphia Phillies organization, March 6, 2009.
h Released by Philadelphia Phillies, September 8, 2009. Signed with Arizona Diamondbacks, December 16, 2009.
i Filed for free agency, November 1, 2010. Signed with Atlanta Braves organization, January 31, 2011.
j Traded to Chicago Cubs for pitcher Ryan Buchter, May 26, 2011.
k Filed for free agency, October 30, 2011.

LOPEZ, WILTON

Born, Leon, Nicaragua, July 19, 1983.
Bats Right. Throws Right. Height, 6 feet. Weight, 190 pounds.

Year	Club	Lea	G	IP	W	L	Pct	SO	BB	H	ERA	SAVES
2002-03	. . . .						Did Not Play					
2004	Tampa	Fla.St.	1	2	0	0	.000	2	1	2	4.50	0
2004	Yankees	Gulf Coast	4	5²/₃	1	0	1.000	6	0	2	0.00	1
2004	Battle Creek	Midwest	2	1²/₃	0	1	.000	2	1	4	0.00	0
2004	Staten Island	N.Y.-Penn.	2	3	0	0	.000	2	1	5	12.00	0
2005-06	. . . .						Did Not Play					
2007	Lake Elsinore	Calif.	22	20²/₃	2	1	.667	19	1	35	6.10	3
2007	Fort Wayne a	Midwest	22	30	1	0	1.000	17	2	34	3.30	0
2008	Lake Elsinore	Calif.	30	30²/₃	2	1	.667	26	4	34	2.64	12
2008	Portland	P.C.	1	1	0	0	.000	1	2	1	9.00	0
2008	San Antonio	Texas	27	38¹/₃	0	2	.000	24	9	41	4.93	0
2009	Corpus Christi	Texas	29	110¹/₃	4	5	.444	69	13	133	4.73	0
2009	Houston b	N.L.	8	19¹/₃	0	2	.000	9	8	32	8.38	0
2010	Round Rock	P.C.	3	5	2	1	.667	2	0	8	5.40	0
2010	Houston	N.L.	68	67	5	2	.714	50	5	66	2.96	1
2011	Houston c	N.L.	73	71	2	6	.250	56	18	72	2.79	0
Major League Totals		3 Yrs.	149	157¹/₃	7	10	.412	115	31	170	3.55	1

a Released by New York Yankees, March 1, 2007. Signed with San Diego Padres organization, March 3, 2007.
b Claimed on waivers by Houston Astros, April 10, 2009.
c On disabled list from April 14 to May 3, 2011.

LOWE, DEREK CHRISTOPHER

Born, Dearborn, Michigan, June 1, 1973.
Bats Right. Throws Right. Height, 6 feet, 6 inches. Weight, 230 pounds.

Year	Club	Lea	G	IP	W	L	Pct	SO	BB	H	ERA	SAVES
1991	Mariners	Arizona	12	71	5	3	.625	60	21	58	2.41	0
1992	Bellingham	Northwest	14	85²/₃	7	3	.700	66	22	69	2.42	0
1993	Riverside	California	27	154	12	9	.571	80	60	189	5.26	0
1994	Jacksnville	Southern	26	151¹/₃	7	10	.412	75	50	177	4.94	0
1995	Mariners	Arizona	2	9²/₃	1	0	1.000	11	2	5	0.93	0
1995	Port City	Southern	10	53¹/₃	1	6	.143	30	22	70	6.07	0
1996	Port City	Southern	10	65	5	3	.625	33	17	56	3.05	0
1996	Tacoma	P.C.	17	105	6	9	.400	54	37	118	4.54	0
1997	Tacoma	P.C.	10	57¹/₃	3	4	.429	49	20	53	3.45	0
1997	Pawtucket	Int.	6	30¹/₃	4	0	1.000	21	11	23	2.37	0
1997	Seattle-Boston a	A.L.	20	69	2	6	.250	52	23	74	6.13	0
1998	Boston	A.L.	63	123	3	9	.250	77	42	126	4.02	4
1999	Boston	A.L.	74	109¹/₃	6	3	.667	80	25	84	2.63	15
2000	Boston	A.L.	74	91¹/₃	4	4	.500	79	22	90	2.56	*42
2001	Boston	A.L.	67	91²/₃	5	10	.333	82	29	103	3.53	24
2002	Boston b	A.L.	32	219²/₃	21	8	.724	127	48	166	2.58	0
2003	Boston	A.L.	33	203¹/₃	17	7	.708	110	72	216	4.47	0
2004	Boston c	A.L.	33	182²/₃	14	12	.538	105	71	224	5.42	0
2005	Los Angeles	N.L.	35	222	12	15	.444	146	55	223	3.61	0
2006	Los Angeles	N.L.	35	218	*16	8	.667	123	55	221	3.63	0
2007	Los Angeles	N.L.	33	199¹/₃	12	14	.462	147	59	194	3.88	0
2008	Los Angeles d	N.L.	34	211	14	11	.560	147	45	194	3.24	0
2009	Atlanta	N.L.	34	194²/₃	15	10	.600	111	63	*232	4.67	0
2010	Atlanta	N.L.	33	193²/₃	16	12	.571	136	61	204	4.00	0
2011	Atlanta e	N.L.	34	187	9	*17	.346	137	70	212	5.05	0
Major League Totals		15 Yrs.	634	2515²/₃	166	146	.532	1659	740	2563	3.94	85
	Division Series											
1998	Boston	A.L.	2	4¹/₃	0	0	.000	2	1	3	2.08	0
1999	Boston	A.L.	3	8¹/₃	1	1	.500	7	1	6	4.32	0
2003	Boston	A.L.	3	9²/₃	1	0	.000	6	7	7	0.93	1
2004	Boston	A.L.	1	1	1	0	1.000	0	1	1	0.00	0

285

Year Club	Lea	G	IP	W	L	Pct	SO	BB	H	ERA	SAVES
2006 Los Angeles	N.L.	1	5^1/$_3$	0	0	.000	6	2	6	6.75	0
2008 Los Angeles	N.L.	1	6	1	0	1.000	6	1	7	3.00	0
2010 Atlanta	N.L.	2	11^2/$_3$	0	2	.000	14	6	6	2.31	0
Division Series Totals		13	46^1/$_3$	3	4	.429	41	19	36	2.91	1
Championship Series											
1999 Boston	A.L.	3	6^1/$_3$	0	0	.000	7	2	6	1.42	0
2003 Boston	A.L.	2	14	0	2	.000	5	7	14	6.43	0
2004 Boston	A.L.	2	11^1/$_3$	1	0	1.000	6	1	7	3.18	0
2008 Los Angeles	N.L.	2	10^1/$_3$	0	1	.000	6	2	12	3.48	0
Championship Series Totals		9	42	1	3	.250	24	12	39	4.07	0
World Series Record											
2004 Boston	A.L.	1	7	1	0	1.000	4	1	3	0.00	0

a Traded to Boston Red Sox with catcher Jason Varitek for pitcher Heathcliff Slocumb, July 31, 1997.

b Pitched no-hit, no-run game against Tampa Bay Devil Rays, April 27, 2002.

c Filed for free agency, November 1, 2004. Signed with Los Angeles Dodgers, January 11, 2005.

d Filed for free agency, October 30, 2008. Signed with Atlanta Braves, January 13, 2009.

e Traded to Cleveland Indians for pitcher Chris Jones, October 31, 2011.

LOWE, MARK CHRISTOPHER
Born, Houston, Texas, June 7, 1983.
Bats Left. Throws Right. Height, 6 feet, 3 inches. Weight, 210 pounds.

Year Club	Lea	G	IP	W	L	Pct	SO	BB	H	ERA	SAVES
2004 Everett	Northwest	18	38^1/$_3$	1	2	.333	38	14	42	4.93	7
2005 Wisconsin	Midwest	22	103^2/$_3$	6	6	.500	72	49	107	5.47	0
2006 Inland Empire.	Calif.	13	29^1/$_3$	1	0	1.000	46	11	14	1.84	2
2006 San Antonio	Texas	11	16^2/$_3$	0	2	.000	14	3	14	2.16	4
2006 Seattle a	A.L.	15	18^2/$_3$	1	0	1.000	20	9	12	1.93	0
2007 Everett	Northwest	1	1	0	0	.000	0	0	0	0.00	0
2007 West Tenn	Southern	3	2^2/$_3$	0	0	.000	1	2	2	3.38	0
2007 Seattle	A.L.	4	2^2/$_3$	0	0	.000	3	3	2	6.75	0
2007 Tacoma b	P.C.	7	6^1/$_3$	0	0	.000	5	3	12	5.68	0
2008 Seattle	A.L.	57	63^2/$_3$	1	5	.167	55	34	78	5.37	1
2009 Seattle	A.L.	75	80	2	7	.222	69	29	71	3.26	3
2010 Seattle-Texas c-d	A.L.	14	13^1/$_3$	1	3	.250	12	6	18	5.40	0
2011 Round Rock	P.C.	6	9^1/$_3$	1	0	1.000	13	4	7	2.89	0
2011 Texas	A.L.	52	45	2	3	.400	42	19	46	3.80	1
Major League Totals . . . . 6 Yrs.		217	223^1/$_3$	7	18	.280	201	100	227	4.03	5
World Series Record											
2010 Texas	A.L.	2	0^2/$_3$	0	0	.000	0	1	4	67.50	0
2011 Texas	A.L.	2	1	0	1	.000	1	0	3	18.00	0
World Series Totals		4	1^2/$_3$	0	1	.000	1	1	7	37.80	0

a On disabled list from August 20 to November 2, 2006.

b On disabled list from March 23 to July 24 and August 28 to October 25, 2007.

c On disabled list from May 3 to July 9 and July 9 to September 29, 2010.

d Traded to Texas Rangers with pitcher Cliff Lee and cash for infielder Justin Smoak, pitcher Blake Beavan, pitcher Josh Lueke and infielder Matt Lawson, July 9, 2010.

LUEBKE, CORY ROBERT
Born, Coldwater, Ohio, March 4, 1985.
Bats Right. Throws Left. Height, 6 feet, 4 inches. Weight, 205 pounds.

Year Club	Lea	G	IP	W	L	Pct	SO	BB	H	ERA	SAVES
2007 Eugene	Northwest	8	24^2/$_3$	3	0	1.000	26	2	18	1.46	0
2007 Fort Wayne	Midwest	5	27	1	2	.333	30	5	29	3.33	0
2007 Lake Elsinore	Calif.	2	7	1	1	.500	5	1	10	7.71	0
2008 Lake Elsinore	Calif.	17	72^1/$_3$	3	6	.333	60	23	97	6.84	0
2008 Fort Wayne	Midwest	10	56	3	3	.500	40	9	52	2.89	0
2009 Lake Elsinore	Calif.	14	88^1/$_3$	8	2	.800	80	17	73	2.34	0
2009 San Antonio	Texas	9	41^1/$_3$	3	2	.600	32	15	38	3.70	0
2010 San Antonio	Texas	10	56^1/$_3$	5	1	.833	44	12	41	2.40	0
2010 Portland	P.C.	9	57^2/$_3$	5	0	1.000	44	17	42	2.97	0
2010 San Diego	N.L.	4	17^2/$_3$	1	1	.500	18	6	17	4.08	0
2011 San Diego	N.L.	46	139^2/$_3$	6	10	.375	154	44	105	3.29	0
Major League Totals . . . . 2 Yrs.		50	157^1/$_3$	7	11	.389	172	50	122	3.38	0

LYLES, JORDAN HORTON

Born, Florence, North Carolina, October 19, 1990.
Bats Right. Throws Right. Height, 6 feet, 4 inches. Weight, 210 pounds.

Year Club	Lea	G	IP	W	L	Pct	SO	BB	H	ERA	SAVES
2008 Greeneville	Appal.	13	49²/₃	3	3	.500	64	10	44	3.99	0
2008 Tri-City	N.Y.-Penn.	2	5²/₃	0	0	.000	4	7	7	6.35	0
2009 Lexington	So.Atl.	26	144²/₃	7	11	.389	167	38	134	3.24	0
2010 Round Rock	P.C.	6	31²/₃	0	3	.000	22	11	48	5.40	0
2010 Corpus Christi	Texas	21	127	7	9	.438	115	35	133	3.12	0
2011 Oklahoma	P.C.	12	62¹/₃	3	3	.500	42	17	64	3.61	0
2011 Houston	N.L.	20	94	2	8	.200	67	26	107	5.36	0

MAC DOUGAL, ROBERT MEIKLEJOHN (MIKE)

Born, Las Vegas, Nevada, March 5, 1977.
Bats Both. Throws Right. Height, 6 feet, 4 inches. Weight, 185 pounds.

Year Club	Lea	G	IP	W	L	Pct	SO	BB	H	ERA	SAVES
1999 Spokane	Northwest	11	46¹/₃	2	2	.500	57	17	43	4.47	0
2000 Wilmington	Carolina	26	144²/₃	9	7	.563	129	76	115	3.92	0
2000 Wichita	Texas	2	11¹/₃	0	1	.000	9	7	16	7.71	0
2001 Omaha	P.C.	28	144¹/₃	8	8	.500	110	76	144	4.68	0
2001 Kansas City	A.L.	3	15¹/₃	1	1	.500	7	4	18	4.70	0
2002 Omaha	P.C.	12	53	3	5	.375	30	55	52	5.60	0
2002 Wichita	Texas	4	17²/₃	1	1	.500	14	24	11	3.06	0
2002 Royals	Gulf Coast	1	3	0	0	.000	3	0	3	3.00	0
2002 Wilmington	Carolina	5	8¹/₃	0	1	.000	10	5	3	1.08	2
2002 Kansas City	A.L.	6	9	0	1	.000	10	7	5	5.00	0
2003 Kansas City	A.L.	68	64	3	5	.375	57	32	64	4.08	27
2004 Omaha	P.C.	14	14¹/₃	0	1	.000	8	11	12	5.65	2
2004 Wichita	Texas	17	18¹/₃	1	0	1.000	13	14	14	1.47	1
2004 Kansas City a	A.L.	13	11¹/₃	1	1	.500	14	9	16	5.56	1
2005 Kansas City	A.L.	68	70¹/₃	5	6	.455	72	24	69	3.33	21
2006 Wichita	Texas	1	1	0	0	.000	1	0	0	0.00	0
2006 Omaha	P.C.	8	7²/₃	0	1	.000	6	5	4	4.70	1
2006 Kansas City-Chicago b-c	A.L.	29	29	1	1	.500	21	6	21	1.55	1
2007 Charlotte	Int.	8	8²/₃	2	0	1.000	11	2	7	0.00	0
2007 Chicago d	A.L.	54	42¹/₃	2	5	.286	39	33	50	6.80	0
2008 Charlotte	Int.	38	49¹/₃	0	4	.000	65	30	48	3.83	4
2008 Chicago	A.L.	16	17	0	0	.000	12	12	16	2.12	0
2009 Chicago	A.L.	5	4¹/₃	0	0	.000	3	7	7	12.46	0
2009 Syracuse	Int.	8	8¹/₃	0	0	.000	6	5	7	3.24	2
2009 Washington e	N.L.	52	50	1	1	.500	31	31	45	3.60	20
2010 Harrisburg	Eastern	8	7¹/₃	2	1	.667	4	5	11	7.36	1
2010 Syracuse	Int.	10	13²/₃	2	0	1.000	9	6	13	3.29	1
2010 Memphis	P.C.	8	9¹/₃	2	0	1.000	6	3	8	3.86	1
2010 St. Louis f-g-h	N.L.	17	18²/₃	1	1	.500	14	12	23	7.23	0
2011 Los Angeles i-j	N.L.	69	57	3	1	.750	41	29	54	2.05	1
Major League Totals	11 Yrs.	400	388¹/₃	18	23	.439	321	206	388	3.94	71

a On disabled list from March 26 to April 24, 2004.
b On disabled list from March 24 to July 13, 2006.
c Traded to Chicago White Sox for pitcher Tyler Lumsden and pitcher Daniel Cortes, July 24, 2006.
d On disabled list from July 5 to August 2, 2007.
e Released by Chicago White Sox, April 29, 2009. Signed with Washington Nationals organization, May 3, 2009.
f Not offered contract, December 12, 2009. Signed with Florida Marlins organization, February 19, 2010.
g Released by Florida Marlins, March 23, 2010. Signed with Washington Nationals organization, March 24, 2010.
h Filed for free agency, July 1, 2010. Signed with St. Louis Cardinals organization, July 8, 2010.
i Filed for free agency, November 1, 2010. Signed with Los Angeles Dodgers organization, January 28, 2011.
j Filed for free agency, October 30, 2011, re-signed with Los Angeles Dodgers, January 5, 2012.

MADSON, RYAN MICHAEL

Born, Long Beach, California, August 28, 1980.
Bats Left. Throws Right. Height, 6 feet, 6 inches. Weight, 195 pounds.

Year Club	Lea	G	IP	W	L	Pct	SO	BB	H	ERA	SAVES
1998 Martinsville	Appal.	12	54	3	3	.500	52	20	57	4.83	0
1999 Batavia	N.Y.-Penn.	15	87²/₃	5	5	.500	75	43	80	4.72	0
2000 Piedmont	So.Atl.	21	135²/₃	14	5	.737	123	45	113	2.59	0
2001 Clearwater	Fla.St.	22	117²/₃	9	9	.500	101	49	137	3.90	0
2002 Reading	Eastern	26	171¹/₃	16	4	.800	132	53	150	3.20	0
2003 Clearwater	Fla.St.	2	8	0	0	.000	9	2	11	5.63	0
2003 Scranton/WB	Int.	26	157	12	8	.600	138	42	157	3.50	0

Year	Club	Lea	G	IP	W	L	Pct	SO	BB	H	ERA	SAVES
2003 Philadelphia	N.L.	1	2	0	0	.000	0	0	0	0.00	0
2004 Reading	Eastern	2	2	0	0	.000	1	2	3	4.50	0
2004 Philadelphia	N.L.	52	77	9	3	.750	55	19	68	2.34	1
2005 Philadelphia	N.L.	78	87	6	5	.545	79	25	84	4.14	0
2006 Philadelphia	N.L.	50	134^1/$_3$	11	9	.550	99	50	176	5.69	2
2007 Reading	Eastern	2	3	0	0	.000	4	0	3	0.00	0
2007 Philadelphia a..	N.L.	38	56	2	2	.500	43	23	48	3.05	1
2008 Philadelphia	N.L.	76	82^2/$_3$	4	2	.667	67	23	79	3.05	1
2009 Philadelphia	N.L.	79	77^1/$_3$	5	5	.500	78	22	73	3.26	10
2010 Clearwater	Fla.St.	2	5	0	1	.000	3	0	1	4.50	0
2010 Reading	Eastern	1	2	0	0	.000	1	0	2	0.00	0
2010 Lehigh Valley	Int.	2	1^2/$_3$	0	0	.000	2	2	1	5.40	0
2010 Philadelphia b	N.L.	55	53	6	2	.750	64	13	42	2.55	5
2011 Clearwater	Fla.St.	1	1	0	0	.000	1	0	0	0.00	0
2011 Philadelphia c-d	N.L.	62	60^2/$_3$	4	2	.667	62	16	54	2.37	32
Major League Totals ....9 Yrs.		491	630	47	30	.610	547	191	624	3.59	52
Division Series											
2008 Philadelphia	N.L.	3	4	0	0	.000	2	0	3	2.25	0
2009 Philadelphia	N.L.	3	2^2/$_3$	1	0	1.000	4	1	2	3.38	0
2010 Philadelphia	N.L.	1	1	0	0	.000	1	0	1	0.00	0
2011 Philadelphia	N.L.	4	4^1/$_3$	0	0	.000	6	0	4	2.08	1
Division Series Totals		11	12	1	0	1.000	13	1	10	2.25	1
Championship Series											
2008 Philadelphia	N.L.	4	5	1	0	1.000	4	1	4	0.00	0
2009 Philadelphia	N.L.	4	3^1/$_3$	0	0	.000	4	3	6	5.40	0
2010 Philadelphia	N.L.	5	6^2/$_3$	0	1	.000	10	3	4	1.35	0
Championship Series Totals		13	15	1	1	.500	18	7	14	1.80	0
World Series Record											
2008 Philadelphia	N.L.	4	3^2/$_3$	0	0	.000	6	0	3	4.91	0
2009 Philadelphia	N.L.	5	4^1/$_3$	0	0	.000	6	2	6	2.08	1
World Series Totals		9	8	0	0	.000	12	2	9	3.38	1

a On disabled list from May 4 to May 22 and July 30 to November 2, 2007.
b On disabled list from April 29 to July 8, 2010.
c On disabled list from June 19 to July 15, 2011.
d Filed for free agency, October 30, 2011. Signed with Cincinnati Reds, January 11, 2012.

MAHOLM, PAUL GURNER
Born, Greenwood, Mississippi, June 25, 1982.
Bats Left. Throws Left. Height, 6 feet, 2 inches. Weight, 230 pounds.

Year	Club	Lea	G	IP	W	L	Pct	SO	BB	H	ERA	SAVES
2003 Williamsport.	N.Y.-Penn.	8	34^1/$_3$	2	1	.667	32	10	25	1.83	0
2004 Lynchburg	Carolina	8	44	1	3	.250	28	15	39	1.84	0
2004 Pirates	Gulf Coast	1	4	0	0	.000	2	1	5	2.25	0
2004 Hickory.	So.Atl.	3	12^1/$_3$	0	2	.000	12	10	17	9.49	0
2005 Altoona.	Eastern	16	81^2/$_3$	6	2	.750	75	26	73	3.20	0
2005 Indianapolis	Int.	6	35^2/$_3$	1	1	.500	21	12	40	3.53	0
2005 Pittsburgh	N.L.	6	41^1/$_3$	3	1	.750	26	17	31	2.18	0
2006 Pittsburgh	N.L.	30	176	8	10	.444	117	81	202	4.76	0
2007 Pittsburgh	N.L.	29	177^2/$_3$	10	15	.400	105	49	204	5.02	0
2008 Pittsburgh	N.L.	31	206^1/$_3$	9	9	.500	139	63	201	3.71	0
2009 Pittsburgh	N.L.	31	194^2/$_3$	8	9	.471	119	60	221	4.44	0
2010 Pittsburgh	N.L.	32	185^1/$_3$	9	15	.375	102	62	228	5.10	0
2011 Pittsburgh a-b	N.L.	26	162^1/$_3$	6	14	.300	97	50	160	3.66	0
Major League Totals ....7 Yrs.		185	1143^2/$_3$	53	73	.421	705	382	1247	4.36	0

a On disabled list from August 18 to October 31, 2011.
b Filed for free agency, October 31, 2011. Signed with Chicago Cubs organization, January 10, 2012.

MARCUM, SHAUN MICHAL
Born, Kansas City, Missouri, December 14, 1981.
Bats Right. Throws Right. Height, 6 feet. Weight, 195 pounds.

Year	Club	Lea	G	IP	W	L	Pct	SO	BB	H	ERA	SAVES
2003 Auburn.	N.Y.-Penn.	21	34	1	0	1.000	47	7	15	1.32	8
2004 Dunedin	Fla.St.	12	69^1/$_3$	3	2	.600	72	4	74	3.12	0
2004 Charleston	So.Atl.	13	79	7	4	.636	83	16	64	3.19	0
2005 New Hampshire	Eastern	9	53^1/$_3$	7	1	.875	40	10	44	2.53	0
2005 Syracuse	Int.	18	103^2/$_3$	6	4	.600	90	18	112	4.95	0

Year	Club	Lea	G	IP	W	L	Pct	SO	BB	H	ERA	SAVES
2005 Toronto	A.L.	5	8	0	0	.000	4	4	6	0.00	0
2006 Syracuse	Int.	18	52²/₃	4	0	1.000	60	9	48	3.42	0
2006 Toronto	A.L.	21	78¹/₃	3	4	.429	65	38	87	5.06	0
2007 Toronto	A.L.	38	159	12	6	.667	122	49	149	4.13	1
2008 Dunedin	Fla.St.	1	4	0	0	.000	6	0	0	0.00	0
2008 Syracuse	Int.	2	13	0	1	.000	15	3	10	2.77	0
2008 Toronto a	A.L.	25	151¹/₃	9	7	.563	123	50	126	3.39	0
2009 New Hampshire	Eastern	2	7²/₃	0	1	.000	8	2	8	1.17	0
2009 Dunedin	Fla.St.	2	6	0	1	.000	5	0	7	3.00	0
2009 Las Vegas b	P.C.	1	2	0	0	.000	0	1	2	4.50	0
2010 Toronto c-d	A.L.	31	195¹/₃	13	8	.619	165	43	181	3.64	0
2011 Milwaukee	N.L.	33	200²/₃	13	7	.650	158	57	175	3.54	0
Major League Totals ....6 Yrs.		153	792²/₃	50	32	.610	637	241	724	3.77	1
Division Series											
2011 Milwaukee	N.L.	1	4²/₃	0	1	.000	3	3	7	13.50	0
Championship Series											
2011 Milwaukee	N.L.	2	5	0	2	.000	2	2	10	16.20	0

a On disabled list from June 19 to July 22, 2008.
b On disabled list from March 27 to November 13, 2009.
c On disabled list from July 2 to July 18, 2010.
d Traded to Milwaukee Brewers for infielder Brett Lawrie, December 6, 2010.

MARMOL, CARLOS AGUSTIN

Born, Bonao, Dominican Republic, October 14, 1982.
Bats Right. Throws Right. Height, 6 feet, 2 inches. Weight, 180 pounds.

Year	Club	Lea	G	IP	W	L	Pct	SO	BB	H	ERA	SAVES
2002 Cubs	Arizona	1	1	0	0	.000	1	1	1	0.00	0
2003 Cubs	Arizona	15	64¹/₃	3	5	.375	74	37	59	4.76	0
2004 Lansing	Midwest	26	154²/₃	14	8	.636	154	53	131	3.20	0
2005 Daytona	Fla.St.	13	72¹/₃	6	2	.750	71	37	60	2.99	0
2005 West Tenn	Southern	14	81¹/₃	3	4	.429	70	40	70	3.65	0
2006 West Tenn	Southern	11	58	3	2	.600	67	25	42	2.33	0
2006 Iowa	P.C.	2	3	0	0	.000	1	1	4	9.00	0
2006 Chicago a	N.L.	19	77	5	7	.417	59	59	71	6.08	0
2007 Iowa	P.C.	8	41	4	1	.800	48	12	30	3.95	0
2007 Chicago	N.L.	59	69¹/₃	5	1	.833	96	35	41	1.43	1
2008 Chicago	N.L.	82	87¹/₃	2	4	.333	114	41	40	2.68	7
2009 Chicago	N.L.	79	74	2	4	.333	93	65	43	3.41	15
2010 Chicago	N.L.	77	77²/₃	2	3	.400	138	52	40	2.55	38
2011 Chicago	N.L.	75	74	2	6	.250	99	48	54	4.01	34
Major League Totals ....6 Yrs.		391	459¹/₃	18	25	.419	599	300	289	3.37	95
Division Series											
2007 Chicago	N.L.	2	3	0	1	.000	6	3	3	9.00	0
2008 Chicago	N.L.	2	2²/₃	0	0	.000	3	0	3	6.75	0
Division Series Totals		4	5²/₃	0	1	.000	9	3	6	7.94	0

a On disabled list from August 19 to September 4, 2006.

MARQUIS, JASON SCOTT

Born, Manhasset, New York, August 21, 1978.
Bats Left. Throws Right. Height, 6 feet, 1 inch. Weight, 210 pounds.

Year	Club	Lea	G	IP	W	L	Pct	SO	BB	H	ERA	SAVES
1996 Danville	Appal.	7	23¹/₃	1	1	.500	24	7	30	4.63	0
1997 Macon	So.Atl.	28	141²/₃	14	10	.583	121	55	156	4.38	0
1998 Danville	Carolina	22	114²/₃	2	12	.143	135	41	120	4.87	0
1999 Myrtle Beach	Carolina	6	32	3	0	1.000	41	17	22	0.28	0
1999 Greenville a	Southern	12	55	3	4	.429	35	29	52	4.58	0
2000 Greenville	Southern	11	68	4	2	.667	49	23	68	3.57	0
2000 Atlanta	N.L.	15	23¹/₃	1	0	1.000	17	12	23	5.01	0
2000 Richmond	Int.	6	20	0	3	.000	18	13	26	9.00	0
2001 Atlanta	N.L.	38	129¹/₃	5	6	.455	98	59	113	3.48	0
2002 Richmond	Int.	1	5	0	1	.000	6	1	5	3.60	0
2002 Atlanta b	N.L.	22	114¹/₃	8	9	.471	84	49	127	5.04	0
2003 Richmond	Int.	15	94	8	4	.667	75	34	93	3.35	0
2003 Atlanta c	N.L.	21	40²/₃	0	0	.000	19	18	43	5.53	1
2004 St. Louis	N.L.	32	201¹/₃	15	7	.682	138	70	215	3.71	0
2005 St. Louis	N.L.	33	207	13	14	.481	100	69	206	4.13	0
2006 St. Louis d	N.L.	33	194¹/₃	14	*16	.467	96	75	221	6.02	0

Year Club	Lea	G	IP	W	L	Pct	SO	BB	H	ERA	SAVES
2007 Chicago	N.L.	34	191²/₃	12	9	.571	109	76	190	4.60	0
2008 Chicago e.............	N.L.	29	167	11	9	.550	91	70	172	4.53	0
2009 Colorado	N.L.	33	216	15	13	.536	115	80	218	4.04	0
2010 Nationals	Gulf Coast	1	3	0	0	.000	4	0	2	0.00	0
2010 Potomac..........	Carolina	1	3²/₃	0	0	.000	3	1	6	7.36	0
2010 Harrisburg	Eastern	1	3¹/₃	0	0	.000	3	1	5	8.10	0
2010 Syracuse	Int.	2	11	0	0	.000	11	3	7	4.09	0
2010 Washington	N.L.	13	58²/₃	2	9	.182	31	24	76	6.60	0
2011 Washington-Arizona h-i-j.	N.L.	23	132	8	6	.571	76	43	154	4.43	0
Major League Totals ....12 Yrs.		326	1675²/₃	104	98	.515	974	645	1758	4.55	1
Division Series											
2004 St. Louis..............	N.L.	1	3¹/₃	0	0	.000	0	4	4	8.10	0
2008 Chicago	N.L.	1	1	0	0	.000	1	0	1	9.00	0
2009 Colorado	N.L.	1	1	0	0	.000	0	0	1	0.00	0
Division Series Totals		3	5¹/₃	0	0	.000	1	4	6	6.75	0
Championship Series											
2001 Atlanta	N.L.	2	2	0	0	.000	3	2	2	0.00	0
2004 St. Louis..............	N.L.	1	4	0	0	.000	2	2	5	6.75	0
2005 St. Louis..............	N.L.	3	5¹/₃	0	1	.000	4	3	6	3.38	0
Championship Series Totals		6	11¹/₃	0	1	.000	9	7	13	3.97	0
World Series Record											
2004 St. Louis..............	N.L.	2	7	0	1	.000	4	7	6	3.86	0

a On disabled list from July 5 to 31, 1999.
b On disabled list from April 15 to May 11, 2002.
c Traded to St. Louis Cardinals with pitcher Ray King and pitcher Adam Wainwright for catcher Eli Marrero and outfielder J.D. Drew, December 13, 2003.
d Filed for free agency, October 30, 2006. Signed with Chicago Cubs, December 19, 2006.
e Traded to Colorado Rockies for pitcher Luis Vizcaino, January 6, 2009.
f Filed for free agency, November 5, 2009. Signed with Washington Nationals, December 22, 2009.
g On disabled list from April 19 to August 8, 2010.
h Traded to Arizona Diamondbacks for infielder Zachary Walters, July 30, 2011.
i On disabled list from August 15 to October 30, 2011.
j Filed for free agency, October 31, 2011. Signed with Minnesota Twins, December 22, 2011.

MARSHALL, SEAN CHRISTOPHER
Born, Richmond, Virginia, August 30, 1982.
Bats Left. Throws Left. Height, 6 feet, 7 inches. Weight, 220 pounds.

Year Club	Lea	G	IP	W	L	Pct	SO	BB	H	ERA	SAVES
2003 Lansing	Midwest	1	7	1	0	1.000	11	0	5	0.00	0
2003 Boise	Northwest	14	73²/₃	5	6	.455	88	23	66	2.57	0
2004 Lansing	Midwest	7	48²/₃	2	0	1.000	51	4	29	1.11	0
2004 West Tenn	Southern	6	29	2	2	.500	23	12	36	5.90	0
2005 Daytona	Fla.St.	12	69	4	4	.500	61	26	63	2.74	0
2005 West Tenn	Southern	4	25	0	1	.000	24	5	16	2.52	0
2006 Iowa	P.C.	4	21²/₃	0	2	.000	21	14	17	3.32	0
2006 Chicago a...........	N.L.	24	125²/₃	6	9	.400	77	59	132	5.59	0
2007 Daytona	Fla.St.	1	6	1	0	1.000	4	1	7	3.00	0
2007 Iowa	P.C.	4	24²/₃	2	0	1.000	15	8	17	1.82	0
2007 Chicago	N.L.	21	103¹/₃	7	8	.467	67	35	107	3.92	0
2008 Iowa...............	P.C.	7	31²/₃	1	1	.500	25	6	26	3.41	0
2008 Chicago	N.L.	34	65¹/₃	3	5	.375	58	23	60	3.86	1
2009 Chicago	N.L.	55	85¹/₃	3	7	.300	68	32	91	4.32	0
2010 Chicago	N.L.	80	74²/₃	7	5	.583	90	25	58	2.65	1
2011 Chicago b..........	N.L.	78	75²/₃	6	6	.500	79	17	66	2.26	5
Major League Totals ....6 Yrs.		292	530	32	40	.444	439	191	514	3.96	7
Division Series											
2008 Chicago	N.L.	2	3¹/₃	0	0	.000	5	1	2	2.70	0

a On disabled list from July 23 to September 1, 2006.
b Traded to Cincinnati Reds for pitcher Travis Wood, outfielder Dave Sappell and infielder Ronald Torreyes, December 23, 2011.

MARTINEZ (MERCEDES), CRISTHIAN A.
Born, Santo Domingo, Dominican Republic, March 6, 1982.
Bats Right. Throws Right. Height, 6 feet, 1 inch. Weight, 185 pounds.

Year Club	Lea	G	IP	W	L	Pct	SO	BB	H	ERA	SAVES
2003 Tigers...........	Gulf Coast	9	36²/₃	4	2	.667	39	13	35	5.65	0
2004 Oneonta	N.Y.-Penn.	2	13	1	0	1.000	12	1	9	2.08	0

Year	Club	Lea	G	IP	W	L	Pct	SO	BB	H	ERA	SAVES
2004 West Michigan	Midwest	12	73²/₃	5	2	.714	45	20	59	2.44	0
2005 Lakeland	Fla.St.	3	11	2	0	1.000	9	4	11	4.91	0
2006 Lakeland	Fla.St.	5	21²/₃	1	1	.500	15	5	27	4.98	0
2006 Tigers	Gulf Coast	7	35	3	2	.600	27	4	30	1.54	0
2006 Oneonta a	N.Y.-Penn.	7	41²/₃	1	2	.333	30	5	38	2.16	0
2007 Greensboro	So.Atl.	18	97	9	5	.643	74	18	97	4.08	0
2008 Greensboro	So.Atl.	8	44¹/₃	4	1	.800	14	9	44	4.67	0
2008 Jupiter	Fla.St.	20	109¹/₃	2	7	.222	78	16	117	3.79	0
2009 Jacksonville	Southern	17	104	9	3	.750	62	22	96	2.94	0
2009 Florida	N.L.	15	26¹/₃	1	1	.500	18	8	27	5.13	0
2010 Gwinnett	Int.	23	52²/₃	5	1	.833	49	8	45	3.08	0
2010 Atlanta b	N.L.	18	26	0	0	.000	22	6	28	4.85	0
2011 Gwinnett	Int.	4	22	2	1	.667	18	2	26	2.86	0
2011 Atlanta	N.L.	46	77²/₃	1	3	.250	58	19	56	3.36	0
Major League Totals	3 Yrs.	79	130	2	4	.333	98	33	111	4.02	0

a Selected by Florida Marlin from Detroit Tigers in Rule V draft, December 7, 2006.
b Claimed on waivers by Atlanta Braves, April 8, 2010.

MASSET, NICHOLAS ALLEN (NICK)
Born, St. Petersburg, Florida, May 17, 1982.
Bats Right. Throws Right. Height, 6 feet, 4 inches. Weight, 235 pounds.

Year	Club	Lea	G	IP	W	L	Pct	SO	BB	H	ERA	SAVES
2001 Rangers	Gulf Coast	15	31	0	6	.000	32	7	34	4.35	0
2002 Savannah	So.Atl.	33	120¹/₃	5	8	.385	93	47	129	4.56	0
2003 Clinton	Midwest	30	123²/₃	7	7	.500	63	43	144	4.08	2
2004 Stockton	Calif.	16	77	6	5	.545	43	19	71	3.51	0
2004 Frisco	Texas	2	10	1	0	1.000	8	4	8	1.80	0
2005 Frisco	Texas	29	157¹/₃	7	12	.368	105	61	197	6.18	0
2006 Frisco	Texas	8	48	2	2	.500	40	20	38	2.06	0
2006 Oklahoma	P.C.	24	67¹/₃	4	5	.444	65	28	79	4.81	3
2006 Texas a	A.L.	8	8²/₃	0	0	.000	4	2	9	4.15	0
2007 Chicago	A.L.	27	39¹/₃	2	3	.400	21	26	52	7.09	0
2007 Charlotte	Int.	11	45¹/₃	0	4	.000	33	9	51	4.57	0
2008 Chicago	A.L.	32	44²/₃	1	0	1.000	32	21	55	4.63	1
2008 Cincinnati b	N.L.	10	17¹/₃	1	0	1.000	11	5	16	2.08	0
2009 Cincinnati c	N.L.	74	76	5	1	.833	70	24	54	2.37	0
2010 Cincinnati	N.L.	82	76²/₃	4	4	.500	85	33	64	3.40	2
2011 Cincinnati	N.L.	75	70¹/₃	3	6	.333	62	31	76	3.71	1
Major League Totals	6 Yrs.	308	333	16	14	.533	285	142	326	3.78	4
Division Series											
2010 Cincinnati	N.L.	2	2	0	0	.000	1	2	2	4.50	0

a Traded to Chicago White Sox by Texas Rangers with pitcher John Danks and pitcher Jacob Rasner for pitcher Brandon McCarthy and outfielder David Paisano, December 23, 2006.
b Traded to Cincinnati Reds with infielder Danny Richar for outfielder Ken Griffey, July 31, 2008.
c On disabled list from May 11 to May 26, 2009.

MASTERSON, JUSTIN DANIEL
Born, Kingston, Jamaica, March 22, 1985.
Bats Right. Throws Right. Height, 6 feet, 6 inches. Weight, 250 pounds.

Year	Club	Lea	G	IP	W	L	Pct	SO	BB	H	ERA	SAVES
2006 Lowell	N.Y.-Penn.	14	31²/₃	3	1	.750	33	2	20	0.85	0
2007 Lancaster	Calif.	17	95²/₃	8	5	.615	56	22	103	4.33	0
2007 Portland	Eastern	10	58	4	3	.571	59	18	49	4.34	0
2008 Portland	Eastern	8	38¹/₃	1	3	.250	37	16	37	4.23	0
2008 Pawtucket	Int.	4	9¹/₃	1	0	1.000	8	1	6	2.89	0
2008 Boston	A.L.	36	88¹/₃	6	5	.545	68	40	68	3.16	0
2009 Boston-Cleveland a	A.L.	42	129¹/₃	4	10	.286	119	60	128	4.52	0
2010 Cleveland	A.L.	34	180	6	13	.316	140	73	197	4.70	0
2011 Cleveland	A.L.	34	216	12	10	.545	158	65	211	3.21	0
Major League Totals	4 Yrs.	146	613²/₃	28	38	.424	485	238	604	3.92	0
Division Series											
2008 Boston	A.L.	4	4	0	0	.000	3	3	6	2.25	0
Championship Series											
2008 Boston	A.L.	5	5²/₃	1	0	1.000	6	2	4	1.59	0

a Traded to Cleveland Indians with pitcher Nick Hagadone and pitcher Bryan Price for catcher Victor Martinez, July 31, 2009.

MATUSZ, BRIAN ROBERT

Born, Grand Junction, Colorado, February 11, 1987.
Bats Left. Throws Left. Height, 6 feet, 5 inches. Weight, 200 pounds.

Year	Club	Lea	G	IP	W	L	Pct	SO	BB	H	ERA	SAVES
2009 Frederick	Carolina		11	66²/₃	4	2	.667	75	21	56	2.16	0
2009 Bowie	Eastern		8	46¹/₃	7	0	1.000	46	11	31	1.55	0
2009 Baltimore	A.L.		8	44²/₃	5	2	.714	38	14	52	4.63	0
2010 Baltimore	A.L.		32	175²/₃	10	12	.455	143	63	173	4.30	0
2011 Frederick	Carolina		1	4	0	0	.000	2	2	2	2.25	0
2011 Bowie	Eastern		1	6	0	0	.000	1	1	3	0.00	0
2011 Norfolk	Int.		9	54²/₃	2	3	.400	41	19	51	3.46	0
2011 Baltimore a	A.L.		12	49²/₃	1	9	.100	38	24	81	10.69	0
Major League Totals	3 Yrs.		52	270	16	23	.410	219	101	306	5.53	0

a On disabled list from April 3 to June 1, 2011.

MC CARTHY, BRANDON PATRICK

Born, Glendale, California, July 7, 1983.
Bats Right. Throws Right. Height, 6 feet, 7 inches. Weight, 200 pounds.

Year	Club	Lea	G	IP	W	L	Pct	SO	BB	H	ERA	SAVES
2002 White Sox	Arizona		14	78¹/₃	4	4	.500	79	15	78	2.76	0
2003 Great Falls	Pioneer		16	101	9	4	.692	125	15	105	3.65	0
2004 Kannapolis	So.Atl.		15	94	8	5	.615	113	21	80	3.64	0
2004 Winston-Salem	Carolina		8	52	6	0	1.000	60	3	31	2.08	0
2004 Birmingham	Southern		4	26	3	1	.750	29	6	23	3.46	0
2005 Charlotte	Int.		20	119¹/₃	7	7	.500	130	32	104	3.92	0
2005 Chicago	A.L.		12	67	3	2	.600	48	17	62	4.03	0
2006 Chicago a	A.L.		53	84²/₃	4	7	.364	69	33	77	4.68	0
2007 Oklahoma	P.C.		1	4¹/₃	0	0	.000	6	0	3	0.00	0
2007 Texas b	A.L.		23	101²/₃	5	10	.333	59	48	111	4.87	0
2008 Rangers	Arizona		2	5	0	0	.000	5	1	7	3.60	0
2008 Oklahoma	P.C.		5	26²/₃	1	1	.500	23	8	21	3.38	0
2008 Texas c	A.L.		5	22	1	1	.500	10	8	20	4.09	0
2009 Okla.	P.C.		5	21²/₃	0	1	.000	22	9	20	4.15	0
2009 Texas d	A.L.		17	97¹/₃	7	4	.636	65	36	96	4.62	0
2010 Oklahoma e-f	P.C.		11	56¹/₃	4	2	.667	44	11	51	3.36	0
2011 Stockton	Calif.		2	10	1	0	1.000	8	0	7	0.00	0
2011 Oakland g	A.L.		25	170²/₃	9	9	.500	123	25	168	3.32	0
Major League Totals	6 Yrs.		135	543¹/₃	29	33	.468	374	167	534	4.17	0

a Traded to Texas Rangers with outfielder David Paisano for pitcher John Danks, pitcher Jacob Rasner and pitcher Nick Massett, December 23, 2006.
b On disabled list from June 10 to July 2 and August 11 to September 11, 2007.
c On disabled list from March 30 to August 7, 2008.
d On disabled list from June 5 to September 1, 2009.
e On disabled list from July 29 to November 3, 2010.
f Filed for free agency, November 5, 2010. Signed with Oakland Athletics, December 14, 2010.
g On disabled list from May 19 to July 3, 2011.

MC CLELLAN, KYLE WILLIAM

Born, Florissant, Missouri, June 12, 1984.
Bats Right. Throws Right. Height, 6 feet, 4 inches. Weight, 205 pounds.

Year	Club	Lea	G	IP	W	L	Pct	SO	BB	H	ERA	SAVES
2002 Johnson City	Appal.		7	12	0	2	.000	8	7	17	11.25	0
2003 Johnson City	Appal.		12	67²/₃	3	6	.333	44	16	74	3.99	0
2004 Peoria	Midwest		24	128	4	12	.250	84	34	143	5.34	0
2005 Quad Cities	Midwest		17	54	1	4	.200	36	26	59	4.83	1
2006 Johnson City	Appal.		3	6²/₃	0	1	.000	4	3	7	9.45	0
2007 Palm Beach	Fla.St.		16	29	4	1	.800	24	4	22	1.24	0
2007 Springfield	Texas		24	30²/₃	2	0	1.000	30	6	24	2.35	0
2008 St. Louis	N.L.		68	75²/₃	2	7	.222	59	26	79	4.04	1
2009 St. Louis	N.L.		66	66²/₃	4	4	.500	51	34	56	3.38	3
2010 St. Louis	N.L.		68	75¹/₃	1	4	.200	60	23	58	2.27	2
2011 St. Louis a	N.L.		43	141²/₃	12	7	.632	76	43	143	4.19	0
Major League Totals	4 Yrs.		245	359¹/₃	19	22	.463	246	126	336	3.61	6
Division Series												
2009 St. Louis	N.L.		1	0²/₃	0	0	.000	0	1	1	0.00	0
Championship Series												
2011 St. Louis	N.L.		1	0¹/₃	0	0	.000	0	0	2	27.00	0

a On disabled list from May 31 to June 15, 2011.

MC CUTCHEN, DANIEL THOMAS

Born, McKinney, Texas, September 26, 1982.
Bats Right. Throws Right. Height, 6 feet, 2 inches. Weight, 215 pounds.

Year	Club	Lea	G	IP	W	L	Pct	SO	BB	H	ERA	SAVES
2006	Staten Island	N.Y.-Penn.	2	8	1	0	1.000	11	1	4	1.13	0
2006	Charleston	So.Atl.	7	21	1	0	1.000	18.	5	13	2.14	1
2007	Trenton............	Eastern	7	41	3	2	.600	36	12	30	2.41	0
2007	Tampa	Fla.St.	17	101	11	2	.846	67	21	86	2.50	0
2008	Trenton............	Eastern	9	53	4	3	.571	52	18	43	2.55	0
2008	Indianapolis	Int.	8	48	3	3	.500	41	7	49	4.69	0
2008	Scranton/WB a.........	Int.	11	70$\frac{1}{3}$	4	6	.400	58	11	73	3.58	0
2009	Indianapolis	Int.	24	142$\frac{2}{3}$	13	6	.684	110	29	145	3.47	0
2009	Pittsburgh	N.L.	6	36$\frac{1}{3}$	1	2	.333	19	11	38	4.21	0
2010	Indianapolis	Int.	13	79	4	8	.333	39	19	71	3.99	0
2010	Pittsburgh	N.L.	28	67$\frac{2}{3}$	2	5	.286	38	28	83	6.12	0
2011	Pittsburgh	N.L.	73	84$\frac{2}{3}$	5	3	.625	47	33	87	3.72	0
Major League Totals		3 Yrs.	107	188$\frac{2}{3}$	8	10	.444	104	72	208	4.67	0

a Traded by New York Yankees to Pittsburgh Pirates with outfielder Jose Tabata, pitcher Ross Ohlendorf and pitcher Jeff Karstens for outfielder Xavier Nady and pitcher Damaso Marte, July 26, 2008.

MC DONALD, JAMES ZELL

Born, Long Beach, California, October 19, 1984.
Bats Left. Throws Right. Height, 6 feet, 5 inches. Weight, 195 pounds.

Year	Club	Lea	G	IP	W	L	Pct	SO	BB	H	ERA	SAVES
2003	Dodgers	Gulf Coast	12	48$\frac{2}{3}$	2	4	.333	47	15	39	3.33	0
2004	a......................						Did Not Pitch					
2005	Ogden	Pioneer	4	6	0	0	.000	9	2	4	1.50	0
2006	Columbus..........	So.Atl.	30	142$\frac{1}{3}$	5	10	.333	146	65	119	3.98	0
2007	Inland Empire........	Calif.	16	82	6	7	.462	104	21	79	3.95	0
2007	Jacksonville	Southern	10	52$\frac{2}{3}$	7	2	.778	64	16	42	1.71	0
2008	Jacksonville	Southern	22	118$\frac{2}{3}$	5	3	.625	113	46	98	3.19	0
2008	Las Vegas...........	P.C.	5	22$\frac{1}{3}$	2	1	.667	28	7	17	3.63	0
2008	Los Angeles...........	N.L.	4	6	0	0	.000	2	1	5	0.00	0
2009	Albuquerque...........	P.C.	6	30$\frac{1}{3}$	1	0	1.000	40	14	21	3.26	0
2009	Los Angeles...........	N.L.	45	63	5	5	.500	54	34	60	4.00	0
2010	Dodgers...........	Arizona	2	5$\frac{2}{3}$	0	0	.000	8	3	3	1.59	0
2010	Albuquerque...........	P.C.	12	63$\frac{1}{3}$	6	1	.857	57	24	64	4.41	0
2010	Los Angeles-Pittsburgh b	N.L.	15	71$\frac{2}{3}$	4	6	.400	68	29	70	4.02	0
2011	Pittsburgh	N.L.	31	171	9	9	.500	142	78	176	4.21	0
Major League Totals		4 Yrs.	95	311$\frac{2}{3}$	18	20	.474	266	142	311	4.04	0
Championship Series												
2008	Los Angeles...........	N.L.	2	5$\frac{1}{3}$	0	0	.000	7	2	3	0.00	0

a Played outfield for Dodgers in the Gulf Coast League.
b Traded to Pittsburgh Pirates with outfielder Andrew Lambo for pitcher Octavio Dotel, July 31, 2010.

MEDLEN, KRISTOPHER ALLEN (KRIS)

Born, Artesia, California, October 7, 1985.
Bats Both. Throws Right. Height, 5 feet, 10 inches. Weight, 190 pounds.

Year	Club	Lea	G	IP	W	L	Pct	SO	BB	H	ERA	SAVES
2006	Danville	Appal.	20	22	1	0	1.000	36	2	14	0.41	10
2007	Myrtle Beach	Carolina	18	24	2	0	1.000	28	7	22	1.13	2
2007	Rome..............	So.Atl.	17	20$\frac{2}{3}$	0	1	.000	33	3	13	0.87	8
2007	Mississippi........	Southern	3	2$\frac{1}{3}$	0	0	.000	2	2	4	11.57	1
2008	Mississippi........	Southern	36	120$\frac{1}{3}$	7	8	.467	120	27	121	3.52	1
2009	Gwinnett..............	Int.	8	37$\frac{2}{3}$	5	0	1.000	44	10	20	1.19	0
2009	Atlanta..............	N.L.	37	67$\frac{2}{3}$	3	5	.375	72	30	65	4.26	0
2010	Atlanta a...........	N.L.	31	107$\frac{2}{3}$	6	2	.750	83	21	108	3.68	0
2011	Atlanta b..............	N.L.	2	29$\frac{1}{3}$	0	0	.000	2	0	1	0.00	0
Major League Totals		3 Yrs.	70	179$\frac{2}{3}$	9	7	.563	157	51	174	3.85	0

a On disabled list from August 5 to November 4, 2010.
b On disabled list from March 27 to September 24, 2011.

MEEK, EVAN DAVID

Born, Bellevue, Washington, May 12, 1983.
Bats Right. Throws Right. Height, 6 feet. Weight, 220 pounds.

Year	Club	Lea	G	IP	W	L	Pct	SO	BB	H	ERA	SAVES
2003 Elizabethton	. . . .	Appal.	14	51	7	1	.875	47	24	33	2.47	1
2004 Elizabethton	. . . .	Appal.	11	21⅓	1	2	.333	23	25	18	8.44	0
2004 Quad Cities	. . . .	Midwest	3	5⅔	0	0	.000	3	15	7	11.12	0
2005 Beloit a	. . . .	Midwest	13	18	0	1	.000	11	36	15	10.00	0
2006 Lake Elsinore	. . . .	Calif.	26	119⅓	6	6	.500	113	62	136	4.98	0
2006 Visalia b	. . . .	Calif.	2	5	0	1	.000	7	4	6	9.00	0
2007 Montgomery c	. . . . .	Southern	44	67	2	1	.667	69	34	74	4.30	1
2008 Pittsburgh	. . . .	N.L.	9	13	0	1	.000	7	12	11	6.92	0
2008 Altoona	. . . .	Eastern	9	16	1	1	.500	17	3	14	2.81	2
2008 Indianapolis	. . . .	Int.	23	41⅓	0	0	.000	34	14	30	2.40	2
2009 Indianapolis	. . . .	Int.	6	8⅔	0	0	.000	7	7	3	1.04	0
2009 Pittsburgh d	. . . .	N.L.	41	47	1	1	.500	42	29	34	3.45	0
2010 Pittsburgh	. . . .	N.L.	70	80	5	4	.556	70	31	53	2.14	4
2011 Bradenton	. . . .	Fla.St.	2	2	0	0	.000	2	0	1	0.00	0
2011 Indianapolis	. . . .	Int.	8	8	0	0	.000	8	1	6	2.25	1
2011 Pittsburgh e	. . . .	N.L.	24	20⅔	1	1	.500	17	12	27	3.48	0
Major League Totals	. . . . 4 Yrs.		144	160⅔	7	7	.500	136	84	125	3.08	4

a Released by Minnesota Twins, June 22, 2005. Signed with San Diego Padres organization, September 17, 2005.

b Traded to Tampa Bay Devil Rays with player to be named later for infielder Russell Branyan, August 24, 2006. Tampa Bay Devil Rays received pitcher Dale Thayer to complete trade, September 15, 2006.

c Selected by Pittsburgh Pirates in Rule V draft, December 6, 2007.

d On disabled list from August 12 to November 17, 2009.

e On disabled list from April 27 to May 23 and June 8 to September 6, 2011.

MELANCON, MARK DAVID

Born, Wheat Ridge, Colorado, March 28, 1985.
Bats Right. Throws Right. Height, 6 feet, 2 inches. Weight, 215 pounds.

Year	Club	Lea	G	IP	W	L	Pct	SO	BB	H	ERA	SAVES
2006 Staten Island	. . . . .	N.Y.-Penn.	7	7⅔	0	1	.000	8	2	9	3.52	2
2007 a	. . . .				INJURED—Did Not Play								
2008 Trenton	. . . .	Eastern	19	49⅔	6	0	1.000	47	12	32	1.81	2
2008 Tampa	. . . .	Fla.St.	13	25⅓	1	0	1.000	20	6	26	2.84	0
2008 Scranton/WB	. . . .	Int.	12	20	1	1	.500	22	4	11	2.70	1
2009 Scranton/WB	. . . .	Int.	32	53	4	0	1.000	54	11	37	2.89	3
2009 New York	. . . .	A.L.	13	16⅓	0	1	.000	10	10	13	3.86	0
2010 Round Rock	. . . .	P.C.	3	4⅓	1	0	1.000	2	1	5	0.00	1
2010 Scranton/WB	. . . .	Int.	40	56⅓	6	1	.857	58	31	63	3.67	6
2010 New York	. . . .	A.L.	2	4	0	0	.000	3	0	7	9.00	0
2010 Houston b	. . . .	N.L.	20	17⅓	2	0	1.000	19	8	12	3.12	0
2011 Houston c	. . . .	N.L.	71	74⅓	8	4	.667	66	26	65	2.78	20
Major League Totals	. . . . 3 Yrs.		106	112	10	5	.667	98	44	97	3.21	20

a On minor league disabled list from April 5 to September 16, 2007.

b Traded to Houston Astros with infielder Jimmy Paredes for infielder Lance Berkman and cash, July 31, 2010.

c Traded to Boston Red Sox for infielder Jed Lowrie and pitcher Kyle Weiland, December 14, 2011.

MIJARES, JOSE MANUEL

Born, Caracas, Venezuela, October 29, 1984.
Bats Left. Throws Left. Height, 6 feet. Weight, 230 pounds.

Year	Club	Lea	G	IP	W	L	Pct	SO	BB	H	ERA	SAVES
2004 Twins	. . . .	Gulf Coast	19	29⅔	4	0	1.000	25	15	22	2.43	5
2005 Fort Myers	. . . .	Fla.St.	5	12	0	0	.000	17	5	5	1.50	0
2005 Beloit	. . . .	Midwest	20	54⅓	6	3	.667	78	40	43	4.31	2
2006 Fort Myers	. . . .	Fla.St.	27	63	3	5	.375	77	27	52	3.57	0
2007 New Britain	. . . .	Eastern	46	61	5	3	.625	75	48	40	3.54	9
2007 Rochester	. . . .	Int.	9	8⅔	0	1	.000	6	5	9	6.23	0
2008 Twins	. . . .	Gulf Coast	7	11	2	1	.667	16	1	10	2.45	0
2008 Fort Myers	. . . .	Fla.St.	5	10⅓	0	0	.000	8	3	7	2.61	0
2008 New Britain	. . . .	Eastern	11	15⅓	1	1	.500	17	7	16	2.93	2
2008 Minnesota	. . . .	A.L.	10	10⅓	0	1	.000	5	0	3	0.87	0
2009 Rochester	. . . .	Int.	5	6⅓	1	0	1.000	4	1	2	0.00	1
2009 Minnesota	. . . .	A.L.	71	61⅔	2	2	.500	55	23	50	2.34	0
2010 Rochester	. . . .	Int.	2	1⅔	0	0	.000	2	1	6	27.00	0
2010 Minnesota a	. . . .	A.L.	47	32⅔	1	1	.500	28	9	34	3.31	0

Year	Club	Lea	G	IP	W	L	Pct	SO	BB	H	ERA	SAVES
2011 Minnesota b-c		A.L.	58	49	0	2	.000	30	30	53	4.59	0
Major League Totals	4 Yrs.		186	153²/₃	3	6	.333	118	62	140	3.16	0
Division Series												
2009 Minnesota		A.L.	2	0²/₃	0	1	.000	0	1	1	13.50	0
2010 Minnesota		A.L.	3	1¹/₃	0	0	.000	0	1	0	0.00	0
Division Series Totals			5	2	0	1	.000	0	2	1	4.50	0

a On disabled list from April 16 to May 14 and August 12 to September 11, 2010.

b On disabled list from May 15 to May 30, 2011.

c Not offered contract, December 12, 2011. Signed with Kansas City Royals, December 21, 2011.

MILLER, ANDREW MARK

Born, Gainesville, Florida, May 21, 1985.
Bats Left. Throws Left. Height, 6 feet, 6 inches. Weight, 210 pounds.

Year	Club	Lea	G	IP	W	L	Pct	SO	BB	H	ERA	SAVES
2006 Lakeland	Fla.St.	3	5	0	0	.000	9	1	2	0.00	0	
2006 Detroit	A.L.	8	10¹/₃	0	1	.000	6	10	8	6.10	0	
2007 Lakeland	Fla.St.	7	41¹/₃	1	4	.200	28	15	43	3.48	0	
2007 Erie	Eastern	4	30²/₃	2	0	1.000	24	5	22	0.59	0	
2007 Toledo	Int.	2	6	0	0	.000	9	5	6	9.00	0	
2007 Detroit a-b	A.L.	13	64	5	5	.500	56	39	73	5.63	0	
2008 Marlins	Gulf Coast	1	1	0	1	.000	0	1	2	18.00	0	
2008 Carolina	Southern	1	5²/₃	0	0	.000	6	4	2	3.18	0	
2008 Jupiter	Fla.St.	4	12²/₃	1	0	1.000	11	1	10	0.71	0	
2008 Florida c	N.L.	29	107¹/₃	6	10	.375	89	56	120	5.87	0	
2009 Jupiter	Fla.St.	1	4	0	0	.000	5	1	3	2.25	0	
2009 Jacksonville	Southern	1	6	0	0	.000	5	2	5	1.50	0	
2009 Marlins	Gulf Coast	2	7	0	0	.000	10	4	8	2.57	0	
2009 New Orleans	P.C.	3	11²/₃	1	2	.333	16	13	9	7.71	0	
2009 Florida d	N.L.	20	80	3	5	.375	59	43	85	4.84	0	
2010 Jupiter	Fla.St.	3	15²/₃	1	1	.500	23	15	8	1.72	0	
2010 Jacksonville	Southern	18	85¹/₃	1	8	.111	66	61	98	6.01	0	
2010 Florida e	N.L.	9	32²/₃	1	5	.167	28	26	51	8.54	0	
2011 Pawtucket	Int.	13	65²/₃	3	3	.500	61	35	42	2.47	0	
2011 Boston f	A.L.	17	65	6	3	.667	50	41	77	5.54	0	
Major League Totals	6 Yrs.	96	359¹/₃	21	29	.420	288	215	414	5.79	0	

a On disabled list from August 4 to August 24, 2007.

b Traded to Florida Marlins with pitcher Burke Badenhop, pitcher Eulogio De La Cruz, catcher Mike Rabelo and outfielder Cameron Maybin for pitcher Dontrelle Willis and infielder Miguel Cabrera, December 5, 2007.

c On disabled list from July 14 to September 1, 2008.

d On disabled list from April 21 to May 16, 2009.

e Traded to Boston Red Sox for pitcher Dustin Richardson, November 12, 2010.

f Not offered contract, December 2, 2010, re-signed with Boston Red Sox organization, December 16, 2010.

MOORE, MATTHEW CODY (MATT)

Born, Fort Walton Beach, Florida, June 18, 1989.
Bats Left. Throws Left. Height, 6 feet, 2 inches. Weight, 205 pounds.

Year	Club	Lea	G	IP	W	L	Pct	SO	BB	H	ERA	SAVES
2007 Princeton	Appal.	8	20¹/₃	0	0	.000	29	16	12	2.66	0	
2008 Princeton	Appal.	12	54¹/₃	2	2	.500	77	19	30	1.66	0	
2009 Bowling	So.Atl.	26	123	8	5	.615	176	70	86	3.15	0	
2010 Charlotte	Fla.St.	26	144²/₃	6	11	.353	208	61	109	3.36	0	
2011 Montgomery	Southern	18	102¹/₃	8	3	.727	131	28	68	2.20	0	
2011 Durham	Int.	9	52²/₃	4	0	1.000	79	18	33	1.37	0	
2011 Tampa Bay	A.L.	3	9¹/₃	1	0	1.000	15	3	9	2.89	0	
Division Series												
2011 Tampa Bay	A.L.	2	10	1	0	1.000	8	3	3	0.90	0	

MORALES, FRANKLIN MIGUEL

Born, San Juan de los Morros, Venezuela, January 24, 1986.
Bats Left. Throws Left. Height, 6 feet. Weight, 210 pounds.

Year	Club	Lea	G	IP	W	L	Pct	SO	BB	H	ERA	SAVES
2004 Casper	Pioneer	15	65	6	4	.600	82	39	92	7.62	0	
2005 Asheville	So.Atl.	21	96¹/₃	8	4	.667	108	48	73	3.08	1	
2006 Modesto	Calif.	27	154	10	9	.526	179	89	126	3.68	0	
2007 Tulsa	Texas	17	95²/₃	3	4	.429	77	45	77	3.48	0	
2007 Colorado Springs	P.C.	3	17	2	0	1.000	16	13	20	3.71	0	

Year	Club	Lea	G	IP	W	L	Pct	SO	BB	H	ERA	SAVES
2007 Colorado		N.L.	8	39⅓	3	2	.600	26	14	34	3.43	0
2008 Colorado		N.L.	5	25⅓	1	2	.333	9	17	28	6.39	0
2008 Colorado Springs		P.C.	21	110⅓	10	5	.667	83	82	108	5.47	0
2009 Colorado Springs		P.C.	8	41⅓	2	2	.500	37	19	39	3.48	0
2009 Colorado a		N.L.	40	40	3	2	.600	41	23	38	4.50	7
2010 Colorado Springs		P.C.	24	30⅓	3	0	1.000	34	19	20	2.67	1
2010 Colorado b		N.L.	35	28⅔	0	4	.000	27	24	28	6.28	3
2011 Pawtucket		Int.	6	6⅓	0	0	.000	6	3	3	1.42	0
2011 Colorado		N.L.	14	14	0	1	.000	11	8	10	3.86	0
2011 Boston c-d		A.L.	36	32⅓	1	1	.500	31	11	30	3.62	0
Major League Totals	5 Yrs.		138	179⅔	8	12	.400	145	97	168	4.61	10
Division Series												
2009 Colorado		N.L.	4	2⅔	0	0	.000	1	3	0	0.00	0

a On disabled list from April 22 to June 12, 2009.
b On disabled list from May 6 to June 2, 2010.
c Sold to Boston Red Sox, May 20, 2011.
d On disabled list from May 26 to June 28, 2011.

MORROW, BRANDON JOHN

Born, Santa Rosa, California, July 26, 1984.
Bats Right. Throws Right. Height, 6 feet, 3 inches. Weight, 190 pounds.

Year	Club	Lea	G	IP	W	L	Pct	SO	BB	H	ERA	SAVES
2006 Mariners		Arizona	7	13	0	2	.000	13	9	10	2.77	0
2006 Inland Empire		Calif.	1	3	0	0	.000	4	0	0	0.00	0
2007 Seattle		A.L.	60	63⅓	3	4	.429	66	50	56	4.12	0
2008 West Tenn		Southern	6	7⅓	0	0	.000	8	6	3	0.00	0
2008 Tacoma		P.C.	6	23⅓	1	2	.333	26	11	17	5.01	0
2008 Seattle		A.L.	45	64⅔	3	4	.429	75	34	40	3.34	10
2009 Tacoma		P.C.	10	55	5	3	.625	40	23	50	3.60	0
2009 Seattle a-b		A.L.	26	69⅔	2	4	.333	63	44	66	4.39	6
2010 Toronto		A.L.	26	146⅓	10	7	.588	178	66	136	4.49	0
2011 Dunedin		Fla.St.	3	9⅓	0	2	.000	11	6	13	7.71	0
2011 Toronto c		A.L.	30	179⅓	11	11	.500	203	69	162	4.72	0
Major League Totals	5 Yrs.		187	523⅓	29	30	.492	585	263	460	4.37	16

a On disabled list from April 24 to May 9, 2009.
b Traded to Toronto Blue Jays for pitcher Brandon League and outfielder Johermyn Chavez, December 23, 2009.
c On disabled list from March 22 to April 21, 2011.

MORTON, CHARLES A. (CHARLIE)

Born, Flemington, New Jersey, October 12, 1983.
Bats Right. Throws Right. Height, 6 feet, 4 inches. Weight, 190 pounds.

Year	Club	Lea	G	IP	W	L	Pct	SO	BB	H	ERA	SAVES
2002 Braves		Gulf Coast	11	39⅔	1	7	.125	32	30	37	4.54	0
2003 Danville		Appal.	14	54	2	5	.286	46	25	65	4.67	0
2004 Rome		So.Atl.	27	116⅔	7	9	.438	102	67	140	4.86	2
2005 Rome		So.Atl.	26	124⅔	5	9	.357	86	62	124	5.20	1
2006 Myrtle Beach		Carolina	30	100	6	7	.462	75	54	116	5.40	2
2007 Mississippi		Southern	41	79⅔	4	6	.400	67	37	80	4.29	0
2008 Richmond		Int.	13	79	5	2	.714	72	27	51	2.05	0
2008 Atlanta		N.L.	16	74⅔	4	8	.333	48	41	80	6.15	0
2009 Gwinnett		Int.	10	64⅔	7	2	.778	55	16	52	2.51	0
2009 Indianapolis		Int.	1	7	0	0	.000	7	1	4	0.00	0
2009 Pittsburgh a-b		N.L.	18	97	5	9	.357	62	40	102	4.55	0
2010 Indianapolis		Int.	14	80	4	4	.500	53	30	83	3.83	0
2010 Pittsburgh c		N.L.	17	79⅔	2	12	.143	59	26	112	7.57	0
2011 Pittsburgh		N.L.	29	171⅔	10	10	.500	110	77	186	3.83	0
Major League Totals	4 Yrs.		80	423	21	39	.350	279	184	480	5.11	0

a On disabled list from March 27 to April 11, 2009.
b Traded to Pittsburgh Pirates with outfielder Gorkys Hernandez and pitcher Jeff Locke for outfielder Nate McLouth, June 3, 2009.
c On disabled list from May 28 to July 2, 2010.

MOSCOSO, GUILLERMO A.

Born, Maracay, Venezuela, November 14, 1983.
Bats Right. Throws Right. Height, 6 feet, 1 inch. Weight, 200 pounds.

Year	Club	Lea	G	IP	W	L	Pct	SO	BB	H	ERA	SAVES
2005 Oneonta		N.Y.-Penn.	11	47⅓	2	2	.500	44	11	49	4.37	0

Year Club	Lea	G	IP	W	L	Pct	SO	BB	H	ERA	SAVES
2006 Tigers...........	Gulf Coast	13	36	3	2	.600	33	8	37	2.50	0
2007 Lakeland............	Fla.St.	1	3	0	0	.000	4	1	2	0.00	0
2007 West Michigan......	Midwest	1	8	0	0	.000	7	0	5	1.13	0
2007 Oneonta.........	N.Y.-Penn.	14	79²/₃	8	2	.800	68	15	75	2.37	0
2008 Lakeland a..........	Fla.St.	15	52	2	3	.400	72	13	36	2.42	1
2008 Erie............	Eastern	6	34²/₃	3	1	.750	50	8	24	3.12	0
2009 Frisco...............	Texas	9	42¹/₃	3	1	.750	36	14	41	4.46	0
2009 Okla...............	P.C.	12	70	5	4	.556	60	15	56	2.31	0
2009 Texas..............	A.L.	10	14	0	0	.000	12	6	15	3.21	0
2010 Texas..............	A.L.	1	0²/₃	0	0	.000	2	2	2	27.00	0
2010 Oklahoma b-c..........	P.C.	23	123¹/₃	7	7	.500	107	49	142	5.18	0
2011 Sacramento.........	P.C.	9	46¹/₃	3	3	.500	52	16	41	3.88	0
2011 Oakland d...........	A.L.	23	128	8	10	.444	74	38	102	3.38	0
Major League Totals........3 Yrs.		34	142²/₃	8	10	.444	88	46	119	3.47	0

a Traded by Detroit Tigers to Texas Rangers with pitcher Carlos Melo for catcher Gerald Laird, December 9, 2008.
b On disabled list from September 29 to November 10, 2010.
c Traded to Oakland Athletics for pitcher Ryan Kelly, January 8, 2011.
d Traded to Colorado Rockies with pitcher Josh Outman for outfielder Seth Smith, January 16, 2012.

MOSELEY, DUSTIN AARON
Born, Texarkana, Texas, December 26, 1981.
Bats Right. Throws Right. Height, 6 feet, 4 inches. Weight, 215 pounds.

Year Club	Lea	G	IP	W	L	Pct	SO	BB	H	ERA	SAVES
2001 Dayton............	Midwest	25	148	10	8	.556	108	42	158	4.20	0
2002 Stockton............	Calif.	14	88²/₃	6	3	.667	80	21	60	2.74	0
2002 Chattanooga......	Southern	13	80²/₃	5	6	.455	52	37	91	4.13	0
2003 Louisville..............	Int.	8	50	2	3	.400	27	14	46	2.70	0
2003 Chattanooga......	Southern	18	112³/₈	5	6	.455	73	28	116	3.83	0
2004 Louisville..............	Int.	12	71²/₃	2	4	.333	48	34	78	4.65	0
2004 Chattanooga a.....	Southern	8	47¹/₃	3	2	.600	40	10	33	2.66	0
2005 Salt Lake..........	P.C.	17	82¹/₃	4	6	.400	38	30	102	5.03	0
2006 Salt Lake..........	P.C.	26	149²/₃	13	8	.619	114	51	164	4.69	0
2006 Los Angeles..........	A.L.	3	11	1	0	1.000	3	2	22	9.00	0
2007 Los Angeles..........	A.L.	46	92	4	3	.571	50	27	97	4.40	0
2008 Rancho Cucamonga....	Calif.	1	3²/₃	0	0	.000	6	2	3	0.00	0
2008 Salt Lake...........	P.C.	20	116²/₃	7	10	.412	83	34	150	6.94	0
2008 Los Angeles b........	A.L.	12	50¹/₃	2	4	.333	37	20	70	6.79	0
2009 Los Angeles c........	A.L.	3	14²/₃	1	0	1.000	8	3	20	4.30	0
2010 Scranton-WB...........	Int.	12	72²/₃	4	4	.500	55	18	83	4.21	0
2010 New York d-e..........	A.L.	16	65¹/₃	4	4	.500	33	27	66	4.96	0
2011 San Diego f...........	N.L.	20	120	3	10	.231	64	36	117	3.30	0
Major League Totals........6 Yrs.		100	353¹/₃	15	21	.417	195	115	392	4.61	0
Division Series											
2007 Los Angeles...........	A.L.	1	1	0	0	.000	1	0	1	0.00	0
Championship Series											
2010 New York............	A.L.	1	2	1	0	1.000	4	0	0	0.00	0

a Traded by Cincinnati Reds to Anaheim Angels for pitcher Ramon Ortiz, December 14, 2004.
b On disabled list from May 2 to May 30, 2008.
c On disabled list from April 18 to November 12, 2009.
d Not offered contract, December 12, 2009. Signed with New York Yankees organization, February 16, 2010.
e Not offered contract, December 2, 2010. Signed with San Diego Padres, December 13, 2010.
f On disabled list from July 31 to October 28, 2011.

MOTA, GUILLERMO
Born, San Pedro de Macoris, Dominican Republic, July 25, 1973.
Bats Right. Throws Right. Height, 6 feet, 6 inches. Weight, 210 pounds.

Year Club	Lea	G	IP	W	L	Pct	SO	BB	H	ERA	SAVES
1997 Cape Fear a-b........	So.Atl.	25	126	5	10	.333	112	33	135	4.36	0
1998 Jupiter.............	Fla.St.	20	41	3	2	.600	27	6	18	0.66	2
1998 Harrisburg.........	Eastern	12	17	2	0	1.000	19	2	10	1.06	4
1999 Ottawa.............	Int.	14	19	2	0	1.000	17	5	16	1.89	5
1999 Montreal............	N.L.	51	55¹/₃	2	4	.333	27	25	54	2.93	0
2000 Ottawa..............	Int.	35	63	4	5	.444	35	31	49	2.29	7
2000 Montreal............	N.L.	29	30	1	1	.500	24	12	27	6.00	0
2001 Ottawa..............	Int.	4	4	0	0	.000	4	0	1	2.25	0
2001 Montreal c.........	N.L.	53	49²/₃	1	3	.250	31	18	51	5.26	0
2002 Las Vegas..........	P.C.	20	36²/₃	1	3	.250	38	8	34	2.95	1
2002 Los Angeles d........	N.L.	43	60²/₃	1	3	.250	49	27	45	4.15	0

Year	Club	Lea	G	IP	W	L	Pct	SO	BB	H	ERA	SAVES
2003	Los Angeles	N.L.	76	105	6	3	.667	99	26	78	1.97	1
2004	Los Angeles-Florida e. . . .	N.L.	78	96²/₃	9	8	.529	85	37	75	3.07	4
2005	Jupiter	Fla.St.	2	2²/₃	0	0	.000	4	0	3	0.00	0
2005	Florida f-g	N.L.	56	67	2	2	.500	60	32	65	4.70	2
2006	Cleveland h	A.L.	34	37²/₃	1	3	.250 .	27	19	45	6.21	0
2006	New York i-j	N.L.	18	18	3	0	1.000	19	5	10	1.00	0
2007	New Orleans.	P.C.	7	7²/₃	0	1	.000	7	5	11	7.04	0
2007	New York k.	N.L.	52	59¹/₃	2	2	.500	47	18	63	5.76	0
2008	Milwaukee l	N.L.	58	57	5	6	.455	50	28	52	4.11	1
2009	Los Angeles m-n	N.L.	61	65¹/₃	3	4	.429	39	24	53	3.44	0
2010	San Francisco o-p	N.L.	56	54	1	3	.250	38	22	49	4.33	1
2011	San Francisco q	N.L.	52	80¹/₃	2	2	.500	77	30	71	3.81	1
Major League Totals	13 Yrs.		717	836	39	44	.470	672	323	738	3.91	10
Division Series												
2006	New York	N.L.	2	4	1	0	1.000	5	0	6	6.75	0
2008	Milwaukee	N.L.	2	1²/₃	0	0	.000	0	0	2	5.40	0
Division Series Totals			4	5²/₃	1	0	1.000	5	0	8	6.35	0
Championship Series												
2006	New York	N.L.	5	4¹/₃	0	0	.000	2	2	4	4.15	0
World Series Record												
2010	San Francisco	N.L.	2	2¹/₃	0	0	.000	0	2	1	0.00	0

a Played infield, starting in the Dominican Summer League and finishing in the Florida State League, from 1991 to 1996.

b Selected by Montreal Expos from New York Mets in Rule V draft, December 9, 1996.

c On disabled list from July 13 to September 1, 2001.

d Traded to Los Angeles Dodgers with outfielder Wilkin Ruan for pitcher Matt Herges and infielder Jorge Nunez, March 23, 2002.

e Traded to Florida Marlins with catcher Paul LoDuca and outfielder Juan Encarnacion for pitcher Brad Penny, pitcher Bill Murphy and infielder Hee Seop Choi, July 30, 2004.

f On disabled list from May 1 to May 27, 2005.

g Traded to Boston Red Sox with pitcher Josh Beckett and infielder Mike Lowell for infielder Hanley Ramirez, pitcher Anibal Sanchez and pitcher Jesus Delgado, November 24, 2005.

h Traded to Cleveland Indians with infielder Andy Marte and catcher Kelly Shoppach for outfielder Coco Crisp, pitcher David Riske and catcher Josh Bard, January 27, 2006.

i Traded to New York Mets for player to be named later, August 20, 2006.

j Filed for free agency, October 30, 2006, re-signed with New York Mets, December 7, 2006.

k Traded to Milwaukee Brewers for catcher Johnny Estrada, November 20, 2007.

l Filed for free agency, November 3, 2008. Signed with Los Angeles Dodgers, January 14, 2009.

m On disabled list from August 30 to September 14, 2009.

n Filed for free agency, November 6, 2009. Signed with San Francisco Giants organization, February 21, 2010.

o On disabled list from August 23 to September 7, 2010.

p Filed for free agency, November 1, 2010, re-signed with San Francisco Giants organization, December 20, 2010.

q Filed for free agency, October 30, 2011, re-signed with San Francisco Giants, December 15, 2011.

MOTTE, JASON LOUIS

Born, Port Huron, Michigan, June 22, 1982.
Bats Right. Throws Right. Height, 6 feet. Weight, 195 pounds.

Year	Club	Lea	G	IP	W	L	Pct	SO	BB	H	ERA	SAVES
2006	Quad Cities	Midwest	8	12²/₃	1	1	.500	13	3	16	4.97	0
2006	State College a	N.Y.-Penn.	21	26¹/₃	1	2	.333	25	4	30	3.08	8
2007	Palm Beach	Fla.St.	9	10	1	0	1.000	6	1	7	0.90	3
2007	Springfield	Texas	44	49	3	3	.500	63	22	36	2.20	8
2008	Memphis	P.C.	63	66²/₃	4	3	.571	110	26	64	3.24	9
2008	St. Louis.	N.L.	12	11	0	0	.000	16	3	5	0.82	1
2009	St. Louis.	N.L.	69	56²/₃	4	4	.500	54	23	57	4.76	0
2010	Memphis	P.C.	2	2²/₃	0	0	.000	2	1	2	3.38	0
2010	St. Louis b	N.L.	56	52¹/₃	4	2	.667	54	18	41	2.24	2
2011	St. Louis.	N.L.	78	68	5	2	.714	63	16	49	2.25	9
Major League Totals	4 Yrs.		215	188	13	8	.619	187	60	152	2.92	12
Division Series												
2009	St. Louis.	N.L.	1	1	0	0	.000	0	0	0	0.00	0
2011	St. Louis.	N.L.	3	3¹/₃	0	0	.000	3	0	1	0.00	2
Division Series Totals			4	4¹/₃	0	0	.000	3	0	1	0.00	2
Championship Series												
2011	St. Louis.	N.L.	4	4²/₃	0	0	.000	4	0	0	0.00	2
World Series Record												
2011	St. Louis.	N.L.	5	4¹/₃	0	1	.000	1	1	4	6.23	1

a Played catcher 2003-2006.

b On disabled list from August 3 to August 30, 2010.

MUJICA, EDWARD JOSE

Born, Valencia, Venezuela, May 10, 1984.
Bats Right. Throws Right. Height, 6 feet, 2 inches. Weight, 215 pounds.

Year	Club	Lea	G	IP	W	L	Pct	SO	BB	H	ERA	SAVES
2003	Burlington	Appal.	14	55²/₃	2	6	.250	41	20	57	4.37	0
2004	Lake County	So.Atl.	26	124	7	7	.500	89	32	130	4.65	2
2005	Kinston	Carolina	25	26	1	0	1.000	32	2	17	2.08	14
2005	Akron	Eastern	27	34¹/₃	2	1	.667	33	5	36	2.88	10
2006	Akron	Eastern	12	19	1	0	1.000	17	9	11	0.00	8
2006	Buffalo	Int.	22	32²/₃	3	1	.750	29	5	31	2.48	5
2006	Cleveland	A.L.	10	18¹/₃	0	1	.000	12	0	25	2.95	0
2007	Buffalo	Int.	34	37²/₃	2	1	.667	44	9	35	5.02	14
2007	Cleveland	A.L.	10	13	0	0	.000	7	2	19	8.31	0
2008	Buffalo	Int.	18	26	0	2	.000	27	10	29	4.15	4
2008	Cleveland	A.L.	33	38²/₃	3	2	.600	27	10	46	6.75	0
2009	San Diego a	N.L.	67	93²/₃	3	5	.375	76	19	101	3.94	2
2010	San Diego b	N.L.	59	69²/₃	2	1	.667	72	6	59	3.62	0
2011	Florida	N.L.	67	76	9	6	.600	63	14	64	2.96	0
Major League Totals	6 Yrs.		246	309¹/₃	17	15	.531	257	51	314	4.10	2

a Sold to San Diego Padres, April 1, 2009.
b Traded to Florida Marlins with pitcher Ryan Webb for outfielder Cameron Maybin, November 13, 2010.

MYERS, BRETT ALLEN

Born, Jacksonville, Florida, August 17, 1980.
Bats Right. Throws Right. Height, 6 feet, 4 inches. Weight, 240 pounds.

Year	Club	Lea	G	IP	W	L	Pct	SO	BB	H	ERA	SAVES
1999	Phillies	Gulf Coast	7	27	2	1	.667	30	7	17	2.33	0
2000	Piedmont	So.Atl.	27	175¹/₃	13	7	.650	140	69	165	3.18	0
2001	Reading	Eastern	26	156	13	4	.765	130	43	156	3.87	0
2002	Scranton-WB	Int.	19	128	9	6	.600	97	20	121	3.59	0
2002	Philadelphia	N.L.	12	72	4	5	.444	34	29	73	4.25	0
2003	Philadelphia	N.L.	32	193	14	9	.609	143	76	205	4.43	0
2004	Philadelphia	N.L.	32	176	11	11.	.500	116	62	196	5.52	0
2005	Philadelphia	N.L.	34	215¹/₃	13	8	.619	208	68	193	3.72	0
2006	Philadelphia	N.L.	31	198	12	7	.632	189	63	194	3.91	0
2007	Clearwater	Fla.St.	3	3¹/₃	0	0	.000	4	1	2	0.00	0
2007	Philadelphia a	N.L.	51	68²/₃	5	7	.417	83	27	61	4.33	21
2008	Clearwater	Fla.St.	1	6²/₃	0	1	.000	6	1	7	2.70	0
2008	Reading	Eastern	1	8	0	1	.000	10	2	5	2.25	0
2008	Lehigh	Int.	2	12¹/₃	1	1	.500	12	4	12	3.65	0
2008	Philadelphia	N.L.	30	190	10	13	.435	163	65	197	4.55	0
2009	Lakewood	So.Atl.	1	1	0	0	.000	1	1	0	0.00	0
2009	Clearwater	Fla.St.	1	1	0	0	.000	3	0	2	0.00	0
2009	Reading	Eastern	2	4	0	1	.000	7	1	2	2.25	0
2009	Lehigh Valley	Int.	2	2	0	0	.000	3	0	0	0.00	1
2009	Philadelphia b-c	N.L.	18	70²/₃	4	3	.571	50	23	74	4.84	0
2010	Houston	N.L.	33	223²/₃	14	8	.636	180	66	212	3.14	0
2011	Houston	N.L.	34	216	7	14	.333	160	57	226	4.46	0
Major League Totals	10 Yrs.		307	1623¹/₃	94	85	.525	1326	536	1631	4.24	21
Division Series												
2007	Philadelphia	N.L.	2	1¹/₃	0	0	.000	3	0	2	0.00	0
2008	Philadelphia	N.L.	1	7	1	0	1.000	4	3	2	2.57	0
2009	Philadelphia	N.L.	1	0²/₃	0	0	.000	0	2	0	0.00	0
Division Series Totals			4	9	1	0	1.000	7	5	4	2.00	0
Championship Series												
2008	Philadelphia	N.L.	1	5	1	0	1.000	6	4	6	9.00	0
World Series Record												
2008	Philadelphia	N.L.	1	7	0	1	.000	2	3	7	3.86	0
2009	Philadelphia	N.L.	1	1	0	0	.000	2	0	1	9.00	0
World Series Totals			2	8	0	1	.000	4	3	8	4.50	0

a On disabled list from May 24 to July 27, 2007.
b On disabled list from May 28 to September 4, 2009.
c Filed for free agency, November 6, 2009. Signed with Houston Astros, January 9, 2010.

NARVESON, CHRISTOPHER GREGG (CHRIS)

Born, Englewood, Colorado, December 20, 1981.
Bats Left. Throws Left. Height, 6 feet, 3 inches. Weight, 205 pounds.

Year Club	Lea	G	IP	W	L	Pct	SO	BB	H	ERA	SAVES
2000 Johnson City	Appal.	12	55	2	4	.333	63	25	57	3.27	0
2001 Potomac	Carolina	11	66 2/3	4	3	.571	53	13	52	2.57	0
2001 Peoria	Midwest	8	50	3	3	.500	53	11	32	1.98	0
2002 Johnson City	Appal.	6	18 1/3	0	2	.000	16	6	23	4.91	0
2002 Peoria	Midwest	9	42 1/3	2	1	.667	36	8	49	4.46	0
2003 Palm Beach	Fla.St.	15	91 1/3	7	7	.500	65	19	83	2.86	0
2003 Tennessee	Southern	10	57	4	3	.571	34	26	56	3.00	0
2004 Tennessee	Southern	23	127 2/3	5	10	.333	121	51	114	4.16	0
2004 Tulsa a	Texas	4	20	0	3	.000	14	13	16	3.15	0
2005 Pawtucket	Int.	21	111 1/3	4	5	.444	66	46	109	4.77	0
2005 Memphis b-c	P.C.	2	6 2/3	0	1	.000	8	7	11	12.15	0
2006 Palm Beach	Fla.St.	3	17	0	0	.000	13	1	9	2.12	0
2006 Memphis	P.C.	15	80	8	5	.615	58	33	70	2.81	0
2006 St. Louis	N.L.	5	9 1/3	0	0	.000	12	5	6	4.82	0
2007 Palm Beach	Fla.St.	3	10	0	0	.000	6	3	10	2.70	0
2007 Memphis d	P.C.	9	45 2/3	3	2	.600	35	21	41	5.72	0
2008 Nashville	P.C.	28	136	6	13	.316	125	57	140	5.43	0
2009 Nashville	P.C.	26	75 1/3	4	4	.500	76	26	59	3.70	5
2009 Milwaukee	N.L.	21	47	2	0	1.000	46	16	45	3.83	0
2010 Milwaukee	N.L.	37	167 2/3	12	9	.571	137	59	172	4.99	0
2011 Milwaukee e	N.L.	30	161 2/3	11	8	.579	126	65	160	4.45	0
Major League Totals ....4 Yrs.		93	385 2/3	25	17	.595	321	145	383	4.62	0
Division Series											
2011 Milwaukee	N.L.	2	2 1/3	0	0	.000	5	1	2	11.57	0
Championship Series											
2011 Milwaukee	N.L.	4	5	0	0	.000	8	1	5	10.80	0

a Sent by St. Louis Cardinals to Colorado Rockies as player to be named later for outfielder Larry Walker, August 11, 2004.
b Traded to Boston Red Sox with catcher Charles Johnson and cash for pitcher Byung-Hyun Kim, March 30, 2005.
c Claimed on waivers by St. Louis Cardinals, August 9, 2005.
d Filed for free agency, October 29, 2007. Signed with Milwaukee Brewers organization, December 4, 2007.
e On disabled list from August 7 to August 22, 2011.

NATHAN, JOSEPH MICHAEL (JOE)

Born, Houston, Texas, November 22, 1974.
Bats Right. Throws Right. Height, 6 feet, 4 inches. Weight, 220 pounds.

Year Club	Lea	G	IP	W	L	Pct	SO	BB	H	ERA	SAVES
1995 San Francisco a	N.L.					Did Not Pitch					
1996						Did Not Play					
1997 Salem-Keizer	Northwest	18	62	2	1	.667	44	26	53	2.47	2
1998 Shreveport	Texas	4	15 1/3	1	3	.250	10	9	20	8.80	0
1998 San Jose	California	22	122	8	6	.571	118	48	100	3.32	0
1999 Shreveport	Texas	2	8 2/3	0	1	.000	7	7	5	3.12	0
1999 San Francisco	N.L.	19	90 1/3	7	4	.636	54	46	84	4.18	1
1999 Fresno	P.C.	13	74 2/3	6	4	.600	82	36	68	4.46	0
2000 San Francisco	N.L.	20	93 1/3	5	2	.714	61	63	89	5.21	0
2000 San Jose	California	1	5	0	1	.000	2	1	4	3.60	0
2000 Bakersfield	California	1	5 1/3	1	0	1.000	6	7	2	5.06	0
2000 Fresno b	P.C.	3	14 1/3	0	2	.000	9	7	15	4.40	0
2001 Fresno	P.C.	10	46 1/3	0	5	.000	21	33	63	7.77	0
2001 Shreveport	Texas	21	62 1/3	3	6	.333	33	37	73	6.93	0
2002 Fresno	P.C.	31	146 1/3	6	12	.333	117	74	167	5.60	0
2002 San Francisco	N.L.	4	3 2/3	0	0	.000	2	0	1	0.00	0
2003 San Francisco c	N.L.	78	79	12	4	.750	83	33	51	2.96	0
2004 Minnesota	A.L.	73	72 1/3	1	2	.333	89	23	48	1.62	44
2005 Minnesota	A.L.	69	70	7	4	.636	94	22	46	2.70	43
2006 Minnesota	A.L.	64	68 1/3	7	0	1.000	95	16	38	1.58	36
2007 Minnesota	A.L.	68	71 2/3	4	2	.667	77	19	54	1.88	37
2008 Minnesota	A.L.	68	67 2/3	1	2	.333	74	18	43	1.33	39
2009 Minnesota	A.L.	70	68 2/3	2	2	.500	89	22	42	2.10	47
2010 Minnesota d	A.L.					INJURED—Did Not Play					
2011 Rochester	Int.	3	3	0	0	.000	5	1	2	0.00	0
2011 Minnesota e-f	A.L.	48	44 2/3	2	1	.667	43	14	38	4.84	14
Major League Totals ....11 Yrs.		581	729 2/3	48	23	.676	761	276	534	2.87	261
Division Series											
2003 San Francisco	N.L.	2	0 1/3	0	1	.000	1	1	4	81.00	0
2004 Minnesota	A.L.	3	5	0	1	.000	6	5	2	3.60	1

Year	Club	Lea	G	IP	W	L	Pct	SO	BB	H	ERA	SAVES
2006 Minnesota	....	A.L.	1	0²/₃	0	0	.000	1	0	1	0.00	0
2009 Minnesota	....	A.L.	2	2	0	0	.000	2	1	5	9.00	0
Division Series Totals	....		8	8	0	2	.000	10	7	12	7.88	1

a Played shortstop in 1995.

b On disabled list from May 13 to June 5 and July 14 to August 18, 2000.

c Traded to Minnesota Twins with pitcher Boof Bonser and pitcher Francisco Liriano for catcher A.J. Pierzynski, November 14, 2003.

d On disabled list from March 26 to November 3, 2010.

e On disabled list from May 28 to June 24, 2011.

f Filed for free agency, October 30, 2011. Signed with Pittsburgh Pirates, November 21, 2011.

NIEMANN, JEFFREY WARREN (JEFF)
Born, Houston, Texas, February 28, 1983.
Bats Right. Throws Right. Height, 6 feet, 9 inches. Weight, 280 pounds.

Year	Club	Lea	G	IP	W	L	Pct	SO	BB	H	ERA	SAVES
2005 Visalia	....	Calif.	5	20¹/₃	0	1	.000	28	10	12	3.98	0
2005 Montgomery	......	Southern	6	10¹/₃	0	1	.000	14	5	7	4.35	0
2006 Montgomery	......	Southern	14	77¹/₃	5	5	.500	84	29	56	2.68	0
2007 Durham	....	Int.	25	131	12	6	.667	123	46	144	3.98	0
2008 Durham	....	Int.	24	133	9	5	.643	128	50	101	3.59	0
2008 Tampa Bay	....	A.L.	5	16	2	2	.500	14	8	18	5.06	0
2009 Tampa Bay	....	A.L.	31	180²/₃	13	6	.684	125	59	185	3.94	0
2010 Tampa Bay a	....	A.L.	30	174¹/₃	12	8	.600	131	61	159	4.39	0
2011 Charlotte	....	Fla.St.	1	4	0	0	.000	2	0	1	0.00	0
2011 Durham	....	Int.	2	9¹/₃	1	1	.500	8	3	10	3.86	0
2011 Tampa Bay b	....	A.L.	23	135¹/₃	11	7	.611	105	37	131	4.06	0
Major League Totals	....	4 Yrs.	89	506¹/₃	38	23	.623	375	165	493	4.16	0
Division Series												
2010 Tampa Bay	....	A.L.	1	3	0	0	.000	4	1	1	0.00	0

a On disabled list from August 4 to August 25, 2010.

b On disabled list from May 6 to June 19, 2011.

NIESE, JONATHON JOSEPH
Born, Lima, Ohio, October 27, 1986.
Bats Left. Throws Left. Height, 6 feet, 4 inches. Weight, 215 pounds.

Year	Club	Lea	G	IP	W	L	Pct	SO	BB	H	ERA	SAVES
2005 Mets	....	Gulf Coast	7	24²/₃	1	0	1.000	24	10	23	3.65	0
2006 St. Lucie	....	Fla.St.	2	10	0	2	.000	10	5	8	4.50	0
2006 Hagerstown	....	So.Atl.	25	123²/₃	11	9	.550	132	62	121	3.93	0
2007 St. Lucie	....	Fla.St.	27	134¹/₃	11	7	.611	110	31	151	4.29	0
2008 Binghamton	....	Eastern	22	124¹/₃	6	7	.462	112	44	118	3.04	0
2008 New Orleans	....	P.C.	7	39²/₃	5	1	.833	32	14	34	3.40	0
2008 New York	....	N.L.	3	14	1	1	.500	11	8	20	7.07	0
2009 Buffalo	....	Int.	16	94¹/₃	5	6	.455	82	26	95	3.82	0
2009 New York a	....	N.L.	5	25²/₃	1	1	.500	18	9	27	4.21	0
2010 Buffalo	....	Int.	1	6	0	0	.000	3	0	8	3.00	0
2010 New York b	....	N.L.	30	173²/₃	9	10	.474	148	62	192	4.20	0
2011 New York c	....	N.L.	27	157¹/₃	11	11	.500	138	44	178	4.40	0
Major League Totals	....	4 Yrs.	65	370²/₃	22	23	.489	315	123	417	4.39	0

a On disabled list from August 6 to November 12, 2009.

b On disabled list from May 17 to June 5, 2010.

c On disabled list from August 24 to September 30, 2011.

NOESI, HECTOR
Born, Esperanza, Dominican Republic, January 26, 1987.
Bats Right. Throws Right. Height, 6 feet, 3 inches. Weight, 200 pounds.

Year	Club	Lea	G	IP	W	L	Pct	SO	BB	H	ERA	SAVES
2006 Yankees	....	Gulf Coast	5	7	0	0	.000	11	1	5	1.29	1
2007 Charleston	....	So.Atl.	5	20	1	1	.500	11	8	25	4.50	0
2008 Yankees	....	Gulf Coast	9	24²/₃	2	1	.667	24	3	23	3.65	0
2008 Staten Island	......	N.Y.-Penn.	5	24	1	1	.500	31	7	20	3.00	0
2009 Charleston	....	So.Atl.	17	75²/₃	3	4	.429	78	11	62	2.38	0
2009 Tampa	....	Fla.St.	9	41¹/₃	3	0	1.000	40	6	34	3.92	0
2010 Trenton	....	Eastern	17	98²/₃	8	4	.667	86	18	90	3.10	0
2010 Tampa	....	Fla.St.	8	43	5	2	.714	53	6	35	2.72	0
2010 Scranton-WB	....	Int.	3	18²/₃	1	1	.500	14	4	23	4.82	0

Year	Club	Lea	G	IP	W	L	Pct	SO	BB	H	ERA	SAVES
2011 Scranton-WB	Int.	6	24²/₃	1	1	.500	17	9	28	3.28	0	
2011 New York a	A.L.	30	56¹/₃	2	2	.500	45	22	63	4.47	0	

a Traded to Seattle Mariners with catcher Jesus Montero for pitcher Michael Pineda and pitcher Jose Campos, January 17, 2012.

NOLASCO, CARLOS ENRIQUE (RICKY)
Born, Corona, California, December 13, 1982.
Bats Right. Throws Right. Height, 6 feet, 2 inches. Weight, 220 pounds.

Year	Club	Lea	G	IP	W	L	Pct	SO	BB	H	ERA	SAVES
2001 Cubs.............	Arizona	5	18	1	0	1.000	23	5	11	1.50	0
2002 Boise	Northwest	15	90²/₃	7	2	.778	92	25	72	2.48	0
2003 Daytona	Fla.St.	26	149	11	5	.688	136	48	129	2.96	0
2004 Iowa................	P.C.	9	40²/₃	2	3	.400	28	16	68	9.30	0
2004 West Tenn	Southern	19	107	6	4	.600	115	37	104	3.70	0
2005 West Tenn a	Southern	27	161²/₃	14	3	.824	173	46	151	2.89	0
2006 Florida	N.L.	35	140	11	11	.500	99	41	157	4.82	0
2007 Florida	N.L.	5	21¹/₃	1	2	.333	11	9	26	5.48	0
2007 Marlins........	Gulf Coast	2	3¹/₃	0	0	.000	8	0	4	2.70	0
2007 Jupiter	Fla.St.	5	12	1	1	.500	9	1	10	0.75	0
2007 Carolina	Southern	1	3	0	1	.000	2	1	2	6.00	0
2007 Albuquerque b	P.C.	4	15¹/₃	0	2	.000	15	4	29	14.09	0
2008 Florida	N.L.	34	212¹/₃	15	8	.652	186	42	192	3.52	0
2009 New Orleans..........	P.C.	2	15	1	1	.500	12	3	12	2.40	0
2009 Florida	N.L.	31	185	13	9	.591	195	44	188	5.06	0
2010 Florida c.............	N.L.	26	157²/₃	14	9	.609	147	33	169	4.51	0
2011 Florida	N.L.	33	206	10	12	.455	148	44	*244	4.67	0
Major League Totals ....6 Yrs.		164	922¹/₃	64	51	.557	786	213	976	4.50	0

a Traded by Chicago Cubs to Florida Marlins with pitcher Sergio Mitre and pitcher Renyel Pinto for outfielder Juan Pierre, December 7, 2005.

b On disabled list from April 7 to May 1 and May 18 to August 20, 2007.

c On disabled list from September 1 to November 5, 2010.

NORRIS, DAVID STEFAN (BUD)
Born, Greenbrae, California, March 2, 1985.
Bats Right. Throws Right. Height, 6 feet. Weight, 225 pounds.

Year	Club	Lea	G	IP	W	L	Pct	SO	BB	H	ERA	SAVES
2006 Tri-City	N.Y.-Penn.	15	38	2	0	1.000	46	13	28	3.79	2
2007 Salem.............	Carolina	1	6	1	0	1.000	2	1	4	1.50	0
2007 Lexington	So.Atl.	22	96²/₃	2	8	.200	117	41	85	4.75	0
2008 Corpus Christi	Texas	19	80	3	8	.273	84	31	89	4.05	0
2009 Round Rock...........	P.C.	19	120	4	9	.308	112	53	104	2.63	0
2009 Houston.............	N.L.	11	55²/₃	6	3	.667	54	25	59	4.53	0
2010 Round Rock...........	P.C.	3	14²/₃	1	0	1.000	14	6	16	3.07	0
2010 Houston a	N.L.	27	153²/₃	9	10	.474	158	77	151	4.92	0
2011 Houston	N.L.	31	186	6	11	.353	176	70	177	3.77	0
Major League Totals ....3 Yrs.		69	395¹/₃	21	24	.467	388	172	387	4.33	0

a On disabled list from May 24 to June 27, 2010.

NOVA (GUANCE), IVAN MANUEL
Born, San Cristobal, Dominican Republic, January 12, 1987.
Bats Right. Throws Right. Height, 6 feet, 4 inches. Weight, 225 pounds.

Year	Club	Lea	G	IP	W	L	Pct	SO	BB	H	ERA	SAVES
2006 Yankees	Gulf Coast	10	43	3	0	1.000	36	7	36	2.72	1
2007 Charleston	So.Atl.	21	99¹/₃	6	8	.429	54	31	121	4.98	0
2008 Tampa	Fla.St.	26	148²/₃	8	13	.381	109	46	168	4.36	0
2009 Trenton............	Eastern	12	72¹/₃	5	4	.556	47	31	65	2.36	0
2009 Scranton-WB a..........	Int.	12	67	1	4	.200	43	28	72	5.10	0
2010 Scranton-WB	Int.	23	145	12	3	.800	115	48	135	2.86	0
2010 New York	A.L.	10	42	1	2	.333	26	17	44	4.50	0
2011 Scranton-WB	Int.	3	16	1	2	.333	18	2	16	3.38	0
2011 New York	A.L.	28	165¹/₃	16	4	.800	98	57	163	3.70	0
Major League Totals ....2 Yrs.		38	207¹/₃	17	6	.739	124	74	207	3.86	0
Division Series											
2011 New York	A.L.	2	8¹/₃	1	1	.500	8	4	7	4.32	0

a Selected by San Diego Padres from New York Yankees in Rule V draft, December 11, 2008. Returned to New York Yankees, March 25, 2009.

NUNEZ (MORALES), LEONEL (LEO)

Born, Bonao, Dominican Republic, March 15, 1982.
Bats Right. Throws Right. Height, 6 feet, 1 inch. Weight, 165 pounds.

Year	Club	Lea	G	IP	W	L	Pct	SO	BB	H	ERA	SAVES
2001	Pirates	Gulf Coast	10	53⅓	2	2	.500	34	9	62	4.39	0
2002	Pirates	Gulf Coast	11	60⅓	4	2	.667	52	5	54	3.43	0
2002	Hickory	So.Atl.	1	4	0	0	.000	1	3	5	0.00	0
2003	Williamsport	N.Y.-Penn.	8	38⅓	4	3	.571	41	12	31	3.05	0
2003	Hickory	So.Atl.	13	48⅓	2	1	.667	37	14	59	5.59	0
2004	Hickory a	So.Atl.	27	144	10	4	.714	140	46	121	3.13	1
2005	High Desert	Calif.	8	13	0	0	.000	15	3	23	9.00	0
2005	Wichita	Texas	12	13	1	0	1.000	14	2	8	0.69	4
2005	Kansas City	A.L.	41	53⅔	3	2	.600	32	18	73	7.55	0
2006	Wichita	Texas	15	21	1	2	.333	22	12	18	4.29	3
2006	Kansas City	A.L.	7	13⅓	0	0	.000	7	5	15	4.72	0
2006	Omaha	P.C.	23	38	2	2	.500	33	13	37	2.13	5
2007	Wichita	Texas	6	20⅔	1	0	1.000	13	6	10	0.87	0
2007	Omaha	P.C.	5	23	1	2	.333	19	4	16	2.74	0
2007	Kansas City b	A.L.	13	43⅔	2	4	.333	37	10	44	3.92	0
2008	NW Arkansas	Texas	1	2	0	0	.000	2	0	0	0.00	0
2008	Omaha	P.C.	4	4	0	0	.000	3	1	7	6.75	0
2008	Kansas City c-d	A.L.	45	48⅓	4	1	.800	26	15	45	2.98	0
2009	Florida	N.L.	75	68⅔	4	6	.400	60	27	59	4.06	26
2010	Florida	N.L.	68	65	4	3	.571	71	21	62	3.46	30
2011	Florida	N.L.	68	64⅓	1	4	.200	55	21	57	4.06	36
Major League Totals	7 Yrs.	317	357	18	20	.474	288	117	355	4.34	92

a Traded to Kansas City Royals by Pittsburgh Pirates for catcher Benito Santiago, December 16, 2004.
b On disabled list from April 1 to June 10, 2007.
c On disabled list from May 28 to July 21, 2008.
d Traded to Florida Marlins for infielder Mike Jacobs, October 30, 2008.

O'DAY, DARREN CHRISTOPHER

Born, Jacksonville, Florida, October 22, 1982.
Bats Right. Throws Right. Height, 6 feet, 4 inches. Weight, 225 pounds.

Year	Club	Lea	G	IP	W	L	Pct	SO	BB	H	ERA	SAVES
2006	Cedar Rapids	Midwest	17	23⅓	3	1	.750	14	2	20	2.70	1
2006	Orem	Pioneer	14	14⅓	0	1	.000	15	5	11	2.51	7
2007	Rancho Cucamonga	Calif.	24	24	4	0	1.000	26	6	10	0.75	11
2007	Arkansas	Texas	29	29⅓	3	4	.429	22	14	27	3.99	10
2008	Salt Lake	P.C.	21	33	2	2	.500	30	7	29	3.27	7
2008	Los Angeles a	A.L.	30	43⅓	0	1	.000	29	14	49	4.57	0
2009	New York	N.L.	4	3	0	0	.000	2	1	5	0.00	0
2009	Texas b	A.L.	64	55⅔	2	1	.667	54	17	36	1.94	2
2010	Texas	A.L.	72	62	6	2	.750	45	12	43	2.03	0
2011	Frisco	Texas	1	1	0	0	.000	1	0	1	9.00	0
2011	Round Rock	P.C.	17	20⅓	1	0	1.000	26	4	16	2.21	1
2011	Texas c-d	A.L.	16	16⅔	0	1	.000	18	5	17	5.40	0
Major League Totals	4 Yrs.	186	180⅔	8	5	.615	148	49	150	2.89	2
Division Series											
2010 Texas	A.L.	4	2	0	0	.000	4	0	2	0.00	0
Championship Series											
2010 Texas	A.L.	3	0⅔	0	1	.000	1	1	1	13.50	0
World Series Record											
2010 Texas	A.L.	4	2	0	0	.000	3	0	3	13.50	0

a Selected by New York Mets in Rule V draft, December 11, 2008.
b Claimed on waivers by Texas Rangers, April 22, 2009.
c On disabled list from April 27 to July 2 and August 25 to September 13, 2011.
d Claimed on waivers by Baltimore Orioles, November 2, 2011.

O'FLAHERTY, ERIC GEORGE

Born, Walla Walla, Washington, February 5, 1985.
Bats Left. Throws Left. Height, 6 feet, 2 inches. Weight, 220 pounds.

Year	Club	Lea	G	IP	W	L	Pct	SO	BB	H	ERA	SAVES
2003	Mariners	Arizona	13	27⅔	3	0	1.000	20	7	17	1.95	0
2003	Everett	Northwest	3	10⅔	1	0	1.000	7	3	8	3.38	0
2004	Wisconsin	Midwest	12	57⅓	3	3	.500	38	23	83	6.12	0
2005	Wisconsin	Midwest	45	69⅔	4	4	.500	51	30	73	3.75	13
2006	Inland Empire	Calif.	16	28⅔	0	1	.000	33	6	31	3.45	1

Year Club	Lea	G	IP	W	L	Pct	SO	BB	H	ERA	SAVES
2006 San Antonio . . . . Texas	Texas	25	39$\frac{1}{3}$	2	2	.500	36	15	45	1.14	7
2006 Tacoma . . . . P.C.	P.C.	2	3$\frac{2}{3}$	1	0	1.000	4	1	3	0.00	0
2006 Seattle . . . . A.L.	A.L.	15	11	0	0	.000	6	6	18	4.09	0
2007 Tacoma . . . . P.C.	P.C.	6	8	0	0	.000	8	4	5	1.13	3
2007 Seattle . . . . A.L.	A.L.	56	52$\frac{1}{3}$	7	1	.875	36	20	45	4.47	0
2008 Seattle . . . . A.L.	A.L.	7	6$\frac{2}{3}$	0	1	.000	4	4	16	20.25	0
2008 West Tenn . . . . Southern	Southern	1	2	0	0	.000	2	0	1	0.00	0
2008 Tacoma a . . . . P.C.	P.C.	14	16$\frac{1}{3}$	1	0	1.000	19	9	23	4.96	2
2009 Atlanta . . . . N.L.	N.L.	78	56$\frac{1}{3}$	2	1	.667	39	18	52	3.04	0
2010 Gwinnett . . . . Int.	Int.	3	4	0	0	.000	5	1	1	0.00	0
2010 Atlanta b . . . . N.L.	N.L.	56	44	3	2	.600	36	18	37	2.45	0
2011 Atlanta . . . . N.L.	N.L.	78	73$\frac{2}{3}$	2	4	.333	67	21	59	0.98	0
Major League Totals . . . . . . 6 Yrs.		290	244	14	9	.609	188	87	227	3.14	

a Claimed on waivers by Atlanta Braves, November 20, 2008.
b On disabled list from July 10 to August 20, 2010.

OGANDO, ALEXI

Born, San Pedro de Macoris, Dominican Republic, October 5, 1983.
Bats Right. Throws Right. Height, 6 feet, 4 inches. Weight, 185 pounds.

Year Club	Lea	G	IP	W	L	Pct	SO	BB	H	ERA	SAVES
2010 Texas a-b-c . . . . A.L.	A.L.	44	41$\frac{2}{3}$	4	1	.800	39	16	31	1.30	0
2011 Texas . . . . A.L.	A.L.	31	169	13	8	.619	126	43	149	3.51	0
Major League Totals . . . . 2 Yrs.		75	210$\frac{2}{3}$	17	9	.654	165	59	180	3.08	0
Division Series											
2010 Texas . . . . A.L.	A.L.	1	0$\frac{1}{3}$	0	0	.000	0	0	1	0.00	0
2011 Texas . . . . A.L.	A.L.	3	2$\frac{2}{3}$	0	0	.000	2	0	1	0.00	0
Division Series Totals		4	3	0	0	.000	2	0	2	0.00	0
Championship Series											
2010 Texas . . . . A.L.	A.L.	2	2	0	0	.000	2	1	3	4.50	0
2011 Texas . . . . A.L.	A.L.	4	7$\frac{2}{3}$	2	0	1.000	10	2	3	1.17	0
Championship Series Totals		6	9$\frac{1}{3}$	2	0	1.000	12	3	6	1.86	0
World Series Record											
2010 Texas . . . . A.L.	A.L.	2	3$\frac{2}{3}$	0	0	.000	6	0	1	0.00	0
2011 Texas . . . . A.L.	A.L.	6	2$\frac{2}{3}$	0	0	.000	3	7	7	10.13	0
World Series Totals		8	6$\frac{1}{3}$	0	0	.000	9	7	8	4.26	0

a Played as an outfielder in the Arizona and Northern Leagues in 2003-2004.
b Confined to the Dominican Republic with visa problems 2005-2009.
c Selected by Texas Rangers from Oakland Athletics in Rule V draft. December 8, 2005.

OHMAN, WILLIAM MC DANIEL (WILL)

Born, Frankfurt, West Germany, August 13, 1977.
Bats Left. Throws Left. Height, 6 feet, 2 inches. Weight, 190 pounds.

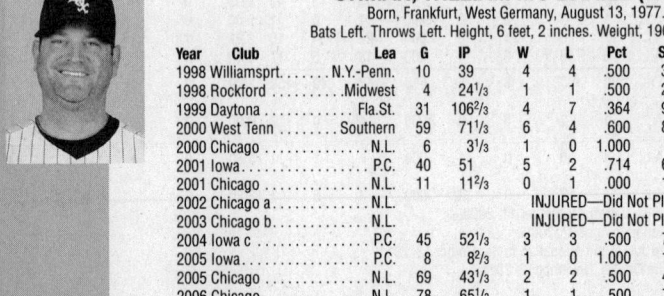

Year Club	Lea	G	IP	W	L	Pct	SO	BB	H	ERA	SAVES
1998 Williamsprt. . . . . . . N.Y.-Penn.	N.Y.-Penn.	10	39	4	4	.500	35	13	39	6.46	0
1998 Rockford . . . . Midwest	Midwest	4	24$\frac{1}{3}$	1	1	.500	21	7	25	4.44	0
1999 Daytona . . . . Fla.St.	Fla.St.	31	106$\frac{2}{3}$	4	7	.364	97	41	102	3.46	5
2000 West Tenn . . . . Southern	Southern	59	71$\frac{1}{3}$	6	4	.600	85	36	53	1.89	3
2000 Chicago . . . . N.L.	N.L.	6	3$\frac{1}{3}$	1	0	1.000	2	4	8	8.10	0
2001 Iowa . . . . P.C.	P.C.	40	51	5	2	.714	66	18	51	4.06	4
2001 Chicago . . . . N.L.	N.L.	11	11$\frac{2}{3}$	0	1	.000	12	6	14	7.71	0
2002 Chicago a . . . . N.L.	N.L.					INJURED—Did Not Play					
2003 Chicago b . . . . N.L.	N.L.					INJURED—Did Not Play					
2004 Iowa c . . . . P.C.	P.C.	45	52$\frac{1}{3}$	3	3	.500	75	29	53	4.30	0
2005 Iowa . . . . P.C.	P.C.	8	8$\frac{2}{3}$	1	0	1.000	12	2	4	4.15	1
2005 Chicago . . . . N.L.	N.L.	69	43$\frac{1}{3}$	2	2	.500	45	24	32	2.91	0
2006 Chicago . . . . N.L.	N.L.	78	65$\frac{1}{3}$	1	1	.500	74	34	51	4.13	0
2007 Iowa . . . . P.C.	P.C.	9	6$\frac{2}{3}$	0	0	.000	9	5	7	2.70	0
2007 Chicago d . . . . N.L.	N.L.	56	36$\frac{1}{3}$	2	4	.333	33	16	42	4.95	1
2008 Atlanta . . . . N.L.	N.L.	83	58$\frac{2}{3}$	4	1	.800	53	22	51	3.68	1
2009 Los Angeles . . . . N.L.	N.L.	21	12$\frac{1}{3}$	1	0	1.000	7	8	12	5.84	1
2009 Inland Empire. . . . . Calif.	Calif.	3	2$\frac{2}{3}$	0	0	.000	2	1	5	13.50	0
2009 Albuquerque e-f-g . . . . . P.C.	P.C.	8	7$\frac{2}{3}$	0	0	.000	9	3	3	1.17	0
2010 Baltimore . . . . A.L.	A.L.	51	30	0	0	.000	29	18	30	3.30	0
2010 Florida h-i-j . . . . N.L.	N.L.	17	12	0	2	.000	14	5	10	3.00	0
2011 Chicago . . . . A.L.	A.L.	59	53$\frac{1}{3}$	1	3	.250	54	17	53	4.22	0
Major League Totals . . . . . . 9 Yrs.		451	326$\frac{1}{3}$	12	14	.462	323	154	299	4.11	3

a On disabled list from March 15 to October 9, 2002.
b On disabled list from March 28 to September 29, 2003.
c Released by Chicago Cubs, October 20, 2003, re-signed with Chicago Cubs organization, February 11, 2004.
d Traded to Atlanta Braves with infielder Omar Infante for pitcher Jose Ascanio, December 4, 2007.
e Filed for free agency, October 30, 2008. Signed with Los Angeles Dodgers, March 30, 2009.
f On disabled list from May 28 to November 9, 2009.
g Filed for free agency, November 9, 2009.
h Signed with Baltimore Orioles organization, February 9, 2010.
i Traded to Florida Marlins for pitcher Rick Vanden Hurk, July 31, 2010.
j Filed for free agency, November 1, 2010. Signed with Chicago White Sox, January 10, 2011

OLIVER, DARREN CHRISTOPHER

Born, Rio Linda, California, October 6, 1970.
Bats Right. Throws Left. Height, 6 feet, 2 inches. Weight, 200 pounds.

Year Club	Lea	G	IP	W	L	Pct	SO	BB	H	ERA	SAVES
1988 Rangers	Gulf Coast	12	54$\frac{1}{3}$	5	1	.833	59	18	39	2.15	0
1989 Gastonia	So.Atl.	24	122$\frac{1}{3}$	8	7	.533	108	82	86	3.16	0
1990 Rangers	Gulf Coast	3	6	0	0	.000	7	1	1	0.00	0
1990 Gastonia	So.Atl.	1	2	0	0	.000	2	4	1	13.50	0
1991 Charlotte	Fla.St.	2	8	0	1	.000	12	3	6	4.50	0
1992 Charlotte	Fla.St.	8	25	1	0	1.000	33	10	11	0.72	2
1992 Tulsa	Texas	3	14$\frac{1}{3}$	0	1	.000	14	4	15	3.14	0
1993 Tulsa	Texas	46	73$\frac{1}{3}$	7	5	.583	77	41	51	1.96	6
1993 Texas	A.L.	2	3$\frac{1}{3}$	0	0	.000	4	1	2	2.70	0
1994 Okla City	A.A.	6	7$\frac{1}{3}$	0	0	.000	6	3	1	0.00	1
1994 Texas	A.L.	43	50	4	0	1.000	50	35	40	3.42	2
1995 Texas a	A.L.	17	49	4	2	.667	39	32	47	4.22	0
1996 Charlotte	Fla.St.	2	12	0	1	.000	9	3	8	3.00	0
1996 Texas	A.L.	30	173$\frac{2}{3}$	14	6	.700	112	76	190	4.66	0
1997 Texas	A.L.	32	201$\frac{1}{3}$	13	12	.520	104	82	213	4.20	0
1998 Oklahoma	P.C.	1	5	0	0	.000	1	1	2	0.00	0
1998 Texas b	A.L.	19	103$\frac{1}{3}$	6	7	.462	58	43	140	6.53	0
1998 St. Louis c	N.L.	10	57	4	4	.500	29	23	64	4.26	0
1999 St. Louis	N.L.	30	196$\frac{1}{3}$	9	9	.500	119	74	197	4.26	0
2000 Texas	A.L.	21	108	2	9	.182	49	42	151	7.42	0
2000 Oklahoma	P.C.	7	32	2	1	.667	28	14	22	1.97	0
2000 Tulsa d-e	Texas	1	4$\frac{2}{3}$	1	0	1.000	5	2	10	11.57	0
2001 Texas	A.L.	28	154	11	11	.500	104	65	189	6.02	0
2001 Oklahoma	P.C.	1	3	0	0	.000	3	0	3	0.00	0
2001 Tulsa f-g	Texas	1	5	0	1	.000	5	2	4	5.40	0
2002 Memphis	P.C.	5	16	0	2	.000	9	17	17	7.87	0
2002 Boston h	A.L.	14	58	4	5	.444	32	27	70	4.66	0
2003 Colorado i	N.L.	33	180$\frac{1}{3}$	13	11	.542	88	61	201	5.04	0
2004 Florida-Houston j-k-l	N.L.	27	72$\frac{2}{3}$	3	3	.500	46	21	87	5.94	0
2005 Iowa	P.C.	3	13$\frac{1}{3}$	0	3	.000	10	5	28	13.50	0
2005 Tucson m-n-o-p	P.C.	4	18$\frac{1}{3}$	1	0	1.000	8	3	33	6.38	0
2006 New York q	N.L.	45	81	4	1	.800	60	21	70	3.44	0
2007 Los Angeles	A.L.	61	64$\frac{1}{3}$	3	1	.750	51	23	58	3.78	0
2008 Los Angeles r	A.L.	54	72	7	1	.875	48	16	67	2.88	0
2009 Los Angeles s-t	A.L.	63	73	5	1	.833	65	22	61	2.71	0
2010 Texas	A.L.	64	61$\frac{2}{3}$	1	2	.333	65	15	53	2.48	1
2011 Texas u	A.L.	61	51	5	5	.500	44	11	47	2.29	2
Major League Totals ...18 Yrs.		654	1810	112	90	.554	1167	690	1947	4.60	5
Division Series											
1996 Texas	A.L.	1	8	0	1	.000	3	2	6	3.38	0
2006 New York	N.L.	1	1$\frac{1}{3}$	0	0	.000	0	0	3	20.25	0
2007 Los Angeles	A.L.	1	0$\frac{2}{3}$	0	0	.000	0	0	2	27.00	0
2008 Los Angeles	A.L.	2	1$\frac{1}{3}$	0	0	.000	1	1	0	0.00	0
2009 Los Angeles	A.L.	3	2$\frac{1}{3}$	1	0	1.000	2	0	1	0.00	0
2010 Texas	A.L.	3	4$\frac{1}{3}$	0	1	.000	5	1	3	4.15	0
2011 Texas	A.L.	2	1$\frac{1}{3}$	0	0	.000	1	0	3	6.75	0
Division Series Totals		13	19$\frac{1}{3}$	1	2	.333	12	4	18	5.12	0
Championship Series											
2006 New York	N.L.	1	6	0	0	.000	3	1	3	0.00	0
2009 Los Angeles	A.L.	5	6$\frac{1}{3}$	0	0	.000	6	4	6	4.26	0
2010 Texas	A.L.	3	2$\frac{1}{3}$	0	0	.000	1	3	1	7.71	1
2011 Texas	A.L.	3	2$\frac{1}{3}$	0	0	.000	2	0	0	0.00	0
Championship Series Totals		12	17$\frac{1}{3}$	0	0	.000	12	8	10	2.60	1
World Series Record											
2010 Texas	A.L.	2	2$\frac{2}{3}$	0	0	.000	4	0	3	3.38	0

Year Club	Lea	G	IP	W	L	Pct	SO	BB	H	ERA	SAVES
2011 Texas	A.L.	3	2¹/₃	1	0	1.000	3	0	3	11.57	0
World Series Totals............		5	5	1	0	1.000	7	0	6	7.20	0

a On disabled list from June 27 to October 2, 1995.
b On disabled list from June 11 to June 26, 1998.
c Traded to St. Louis Cardinals with infielder Fernando Tatis and player to be named later for infielder Royce Clayton and pitcher Todd Stottlemyre, July 31, 1998. St. Louis Cardinals received infielder Mark Little to complete trade, August 9, 1998.
d Filed for free agency, October 29, 1999. Signed with Texas Rangers, January 27, 2000.
e On disabled list from June 17 to July 19 and July 31 to August 31, 2000.
f On disabled list from May 8 to June 6, 2001.
g Traded to Boston Red Sox for outfielder Carl Everett, December 12, 2001.
h Released by Boston Red Sox, July 2, 2002. Signed with St. Louis Cardinals organization, July 20, 2002.
i Released by St. Louis Cardinals, August 13, 2002. Signed with Colorado Rockies organization, January 29, 2003.
j Filed for free agency, October 26, 2003. Signed with Florida Marlins, January 28, 2004.
k Sold to Houston Astros, July 22, 2004.
l On disabled list from August 6 to September 6, 2004.
m Filed for free agency, November 8, 2004. Signed with Colorado Rockies organization, January 22, 2005.
n Released by Colorado Rockies, March 31, 2005. Signed with Arizona Diamondbacks organization, April 12, 2005.
o Released by Arizona Diamondbacks, May 3, 2005. Signed with Chicago Cubs organization, May 7, 2005.
p Released by Chicago Cubs, May 20, 2005. Signed with New York Mets organization, December 16, 2005.
q Filed for free agency, October 31, 2006. Signed with Los Angeles Angels, December 11, 2006.
r Filed for free agency, October 31, 2008, re-signed with Los Angeles Angels, January 17, 2009.
s On disabled list from April 19 to May 4, 2009.
t Filed for free agency, November 5, 2009. Signed with Texas Rangers, December 22, 2009.
u Filed for free agency, October 30, 2011. Signed with Toronto Blue Jays, January 9, 2012.

ONDRUSEK, LOGAN JARED
Born, Hallettsville, Texas, February 13, 1985.
Bats Right. Throws Right. Height, 6 feet, 8 inches. Weight, 225 pounds.

Year Club	Lea	G	IP	W	L	Pct	SO	BB	H	ERA	SAVES
2005 Billings...........	Pioneer	15	55¹/₃	1	6	.143	46	19	72	6.02	0
2006 Dayton	Midwest	27	52²/₃	4	5	.444	47	19	48	3.42	0
2006 Billings...........	Pioneer	1	1	0	1	.000	3	1	4	27.00	0
2006 Chattanooga.......	Southern	1	4	0	0	.000	7	3	0	0.00	0
2007 Sarasota...........	Fla.St.	31	124	7	10	.412	86	48	131	4.43	1
2008 Sarasota...........	Fla.St.	40	79²/₃	1	7	.125	58	32	93	4.97	1
2008 Louisville	Int.	1	1¹/₃	0	0	.000	1	2	1	0.00	0
2009 Sarasota...........	Fla.St.	13	18²/₃	2	0	1.000	12	7	7	0.96	0
2009 Louisville	Int.	19	20²/₃	0	0	.000	11	2	16	1.74	12
2009 Carolina	Southern	24	32²/₃	2	1	.667	24	12	21	1.65	7
2010 Louisville	Int.	14	19²/₃	0	1	.000	14	3	21	4.12	1
2010 Cincinnati.............	N.L.	60	58²/₃	5	0	1.000	39	20	49	3.68	0
2011 Cincinnati a	N.L.	66	61¹/₃	5	5	.500	41	28	55	3.23	0
Major League Totals ....2 Yrs.		126	120	10	5	.667	80	48	104	3.45	0
Division Series											
2010 Cincinnati.............	N.L.	2	2	0	0	.000	0	1	0	0.00	0

a On disabled list from August 8 to August 26, 2011.

OSWALT, ROY EDWARD
Born, Kosciusko, Mississippi, August 29, 1977.
Bats Right. Throws Right. Height, 6 feet. Weight, 185 pounds.

Year Club	Lea	G	IP	W	L	Pct	SO	BB	H	ERA	SAVES
1997 Astros	Gulf Coast	5	28¹/₃	1	1	.500	28	7	25	0.64	0
1997 Auburn..........	N.Y.-Penn.	9	51²/₃	2	4	.333	44	15	50	4.53	0
1998 Astros	Gulf Coast	4	16	1	1	.500	27	1	10	2.25	0
1998 Auburn..........	N.Y.-Penn.	11	70¹/₃	4	5	.444	67	31	49	2.18	0
1999 Michigan	Midwest	22	151¹/₃	13	4	.765	143	54	144	4.46	0
2000 Kissimmee..........	Fla.St.	8	45¹/₃	4	3	.571	47	11	52	2.98	0
2000 Round Rock.........	Texas	19	129²/₃	11	4	.733	141	22	106	1.94	2
2001 New Orleans..........	P.C.	5	31	2	3	.400	34	6	32	4.35	0
2001 Houston	N.L.	28	141²/₃	14	3	.824	144	24	126	2.73	0
2002 Houston	N.L.	35	233	19	9	.679	208	62	215	3.01	0
2003 New Orleans..........	P.C.	3	3	0	0	.000	2	0	3	3.00	0
2003 Houston a	N.L.	21	127¹/₃	10	5	.667	108	29	116	2.97	0
2004 Houston	N.L.	36	237	*20	10	.667	206	62	233	3.49	0
2005 Houston	N.L.	35	241²/₃	20	12	.625	184	48	243	2.94	0
2006 Houston b	N.L.	33	220²/₃	15	8	.652	166	38	220	*2.98	0

Year	Club	Lea	G	IP	W	L	Pct	SO	BB	H	ERA	SAVES
2007 Houston.............	N.L.	33	212	14	7	.667	154	60	221	3.18	0
2008 Houston c	N.L.	32	208²/₃	17	10	.630	165	47	199	3.54	0
2009 Houston d	N.L.	30	181¹/₃	8	6	.571	138	42	183	4.12	0
2010 Houston-Philadelphia e ..	N.L.	33	211²/₃	13	13	.500	193	55	162	2.76	0
2011 Clearwater	Fla.St.	1	5	0	0	.000	5	1	7	5.40	0
2011 Lehigh Valley	Int.	2	10	0	0	.000	8	4	8	2.70	0
2011 Philadelphia f-g	N.L.	23	139	9	10	.474	93	33	153	3.69	0
Major League Totals ....11 Yrs.		339	2154	159	93	.631	1759	500	2071	3.21	0

Division Series

Year	Club	Lea	G	IP	W	L	Pct	SO	BB	H	ERA	SAVES
2004 Houston..............	N.L.	2	11¹/₃	1	0	1.000	8	4	15	2.38	0
2005 Houston..............	N.L.	1	7¹/₃	1	0	1.000	7	2	6	3.68	0
2010 Philadelphia	N.L.	1	5	0	0	.000	5	1	5	5.40	0
2011 Philadelphia	N.L.	1	6	0	1	.000	5	1	6	7.50	0
Division Series Totals		5	29²/₃	2	1	.667	25	8	32	4.25	0

Championship Series

Year	Club	Lea	G	IP	W	L	Pct	SO	BB	H	ERA	SAVES
2004 Houston..............	N.L.	2	8	0	0	.000	2	4	11	6.75	0
2005 Houston..............	N.L.	2	14	2	0	1.000	12	4	8	1.29	0
2010 Philadelphia	N.L.	3	14²/₃	1	1	.500	14	3	14	1.84	0
Championship Series Totals		7	36²/₃	3	1	.750	28	11	33	2.70	0

World Series Record

Year	Club	Lea	G	IP	W	L	Pct	SO	BB	H	ERA	SAVES
2005 Houston..............	N.L.	1	6	0	0	.000	3	5	8	7.50	0

a On disabled list from May 16 to May 31 and June 19 to July 7 and July 30 to September 8, 2003.
b On disabled list from May 30 to June 14, 2006.
c On disabled list from July 12 to July 28, 2008.
d On disabled list from September 16 to October 13, 2009.
e Traded to Philadelphia Phillies with cash for pitcher J.A.Happ, outfielder Anthony Gose and infielder Jonathan Villar, July 29, 2010.
f On disabled list from April 27 to May 16 and June 24 to August 7, 2011.
g Filed for free agency, October 30, 2011.

OUTMAN, JOSHUA S. (JOSH)
Born, St.Louis, Missouri, September 14, 1984.
Bats Left. Throws Left. Height, 6 feet, 1 inch. Weight, 185 pounds.

Year	Club	Lea	G	IP	W	L	Pct	SO	BB	H	ERA	SAVES
2005 Batavia..........	N.Y.-Penn.	11	29¹/₃	2	1	.667	31	14	23	2.76	0
2006 Lakewood.........	So.Atl.	27	155¹/₃	14	6	.700	161	75	119	2.95	0
2007 Clearwater	Fla.St.	20	117¹/₃	10	4	.714	117	54	104	2.45	0
2007 Reading	Eastern	7	42	2	3	.400	34	23	38	4.50	0
2008 Reading	Eastern	33	70¹/₃	5	4	.556	66	37	68	3.20	1
2008 Midland	Texas	4	12²/₃	1	0	1.000	5	3	13	4.26	0
2008 Sacramento	P.C.	5	15¹/₃	1	0	1.000	15	5	9	1.76	0
2008 Oakland a...........	A.L.	6	25²/₃	1	2	.333	19	8	34	4.56	0
2009 Oakland b...........	A.L.	14	67¹/₃	4	1	.800	53	25	53	3.48	0
2010 Oakland c...........	A.L.				INJURED —Did Not Play						
2011 Sacramento	P.C.	17	78¹/₃	8	3	.727	72	47	77	3.91	0
2011 Oakland d...........	A.L.	13	58¹/₃	3	5	.375	35	23	62	3.70	0
Major League Totals ....3 Yrs.		33	151¹/₃	8	8	.500	107	56	149	3.75	0

a Traded by Philadelphia Phillies to Oakland Athletics with infielder Adrian Cardenas and outfielder Matt Spencer for pitcher Joe Blanton, July 17, 2008.
b On disabled list from June 20 to November 4, 2009.
c On disabled list from March 26 to November 4, 2010.
d Traded to Colorado Rockies with pitcher Guillermo Moscoso for outfielder Seth Smith, January 16, 2012.

OWINGS, MICAH BURTON
Born, Gainesville, Georgia, September 28, 1982.
Bats Right. Throws Right. Height, 6 feet, 5 inches. Weight, 220 pounds.

Year	Club	Lea	G	IP	W	L	Pct	SO	BB	H	ERA	SAVES
2005 Lancaster............	Calif.	16	22	1	1	.500	30	4	17	2.45	0
2006 Tennessee	Southern	12	74¹/₃	6	2	.750	69	17	66	2.91	0
2006 Tucson..............	P.C.	15	87²/₃	10	0	1.000	61	34	96	3.70	0
2007 Tucson..............	P.C.	1	5	0	0	.000	7	1	4	0.00	0
2007 Arizona a	N.L.	29	152²/₃	8	8	.500	106	50	146	4.30	0
2008 Arizona.............	N.L.	22	104²/₃	6	9	.400	87	41	104	5.93	0
2008 Tucson..............	P.C.	2	11	0	0	.000	9	6	8	4.09	0
2008 Cincinnati b	N.L.				Used as pinch hitter only						
2009 Louisville	Int.	2	10¹/₃	1	0	1.000	5	7	8	0.87	0
2009 Cincinnati c	N.L.	26	119²/₃	7	12	.368	68	64	126	5.34	1

Year	Club	Lea	G	IP	W	L	Pct	SO	BB	H	ERA	SAVES
2010 Cincinnati	N.L.	22	33⅓	3	2	.600	35	25	28	5.40	0
2010 Louisville d.	Int.	8	20⅓	0	0	.000	13	10	20	2.21	0
2011 Reno	P.C.	7	39	3	1	.750	27	9	41	4.85	0
2011 Arizona e-f	N.L.	33	63	8	0	1.000	44	23	56	3.57	0
Major League Totals 5 Yrs.		132	473⅓	32	31	.508	340	203	460	4.91	1
Division Series											
2011 Arizona	N.L.	2	3	1	0	1.000	1	0	2	0.00	0
Championship Series											
2007 Arizona	N.L.	1	3⅔	0	1	.000	2	2	6	4.91	0

a On disabled list from April 18 to May 3, 2007.
b Sent to Cincinnati Reds as player to be named later for outfielder Adam Dunn, September 10, 2008.
c On disabled list from July 27 to August 20, 2009.
d Filed for free agency, October 5, 2010.
e Signed with Arizona Diamondbacks organization, January 24, 2011.
f Not offered contract, December 12, 2011.

PADILLA, VICENTE DE LA CRUZ

Born, Chinandega, Nicaragua, September 27, 1977.
Bats Right. Throws Right. Height, 6 feet, 2 inches. Weight, 220 pounds.

Year	Club	Lea	G	IP	W	L	Pct	SO	BB	H	ERA	SAVES
1999 High Desert	California	9	50⅔	4	1	.800	55	17	50	3.73	0
1999 Tucson	P.C.	18	93⅓	7	4	.636	58	24	107	3.75	0
1999 Arizona	N.L.	5	2⅔	0	1	.000	0	3	7	16.88	0
2000 Tucson	P.C.	12	18⅓	0	1	.000	22	8	22	4.42	1
2000 Arizona-Philadelphia a	N.L.	55	65⅓	4	7	.364	51	28	72	3.72	2
2001 Scranton-WB	Int.	16	81⅔	7	0	1.000	75	11	64	2.42	0
2001 Philadelphia b	N.L.	23	34	3	1	.750	29	12	36	4.24	0
2002 Philadelphia	N.L.	32	206	14	11	.560	128	53	198	3.28	0
2003 Philadelphia	N.L.	32	208⅔	14	12	.538	133	62	196	3.62	0
2004 Clearwater	Fla.St.	1	2	0	1	.000	1	1	3	9.00	0
2004 Scranton/WB	Int.	2	4⅔	0	0	.000	6	5	6	13.50	0
2004 Philadelphia c	N.L.	20	115⅓	7	7	.500	82	36	119	4.53	0
2005 Clearwater	Fla.St.	1	5	0	1	.000	3	1	4	1.80	0
2005 Scranton/WB	Int.	1	5	1	0	1.000	4	2	6	3.60	0
2005 Philadelphia d-e	N.L.	27	147	9	12	.429	103	74	146	4.71	0
2006 Texas f	A.L.	33	200	15	10	.600	156	70	206	4.50	0
2007 Frisco	Texas	6	12	0	1	.000	12	9	14	8.25	0
2007 Texas g	A.L.	23	120⅓	6	10	.375	71	50	146	5.76	0
2008 Texas h	A.L.	29	171	14	8	.636	127	65	185	4.74	0
2009 Albuquerque	P.C.	1	5	1	0	1.000	5	3	3	3.60	0
2009 Texas	A.L.	18	108	8	6	.571	59	42	120	4.92	0
2009 Los Angeles i-j-k	N.L.	8	39⅓	4	0	1.000	38	12	36	3.20	0
2010 Inland Empire	Calif.	3	10⅔	0	0	.000	10	1	6	0.84	0
2010 Albuquerque	P.C.	1	5⅔	0	1	.000	5	0	8	6.35	0
2010 Los Angeles l-m	N.L.	16	95	6	5	.545	84	24	79	4.07	0
2011 Rancho Cucamonga	Calif.	4	6⅓	0	0	.000	5	1	4	1.42	0
2011 Los Angeles n-o	N.L.	9	8⅔	0	0	.000	9	5	7	4.15	3
Major League Totals 13 Yrs.		330	1521⅓	104	90	.536	1070	536	1553	4.31	5
Division Series											
2009 Los Angeles	N.L.	1	7	1	0	1.000	4	1	4	0.00	0
Championship Series											
2009 Los Angeles	N.L.	2	10⅓	0	1	.000	9	3	8	6.10	0

a Traded to Philadelphia Phillies with infielder Travis Lee, pitcher Omar Daal and pitcher Nelson Figueroa for pitcher Curt Schilling, July 26, 2000.
b On disabled list from May 4 to May 30, 2001.
c On disabled list from May 30 to August 10, 2004.
d On disabled list from March 25 to April 19, 2005.
e Traded to Texas Rangers for player to be named later, December 12, 2005. Philadelphia Phillies received pitcher Ricardo Rodriguez to complete trade, December 19, 2005.
f Filed for free agency, October 30, 2006, re-signed with Texas Rangers, December 9, 2006.
g On disabled list from June 22 to August 15, 2007.
h On disabled list from July 5 to July 20 and August 25 to September 9, 2008.
i On disabled list from May 17 to June 2, 2009.
j Released by Texas Rangers, August 17, 2009. Signed with Los Angeles Dodgers organization, August 19, 2009.
k Filed for free agency, November 6, 2009, Re-signed with Los Angeles Dodgers, January 21, 2010.
l On disabled list from April 23 to June 19 and August 16 to September 3, 2010.
m Filed for free agency, November 1, 2010, re-signed with Los Angeles Dodgers, December 9, 2010.
n Filed for free agency, October 30, 2011.
o On disabled list from March 22 to April 22 and May 14 to October 30, 2011.

PAPELBON, JONATHAN ROBERT

Born, Baton Rouge, Louisiana, November 23, 1980.
Bats Right. Throws Right. Height, 6 feet, 4 inches. Weight, 230 pounds.

Year	Club	Lea	G	IP	W	L	Pct	SO	BB	H	ERA	SAVES
2003 Lowell	N.Y.-Penn.	13	32²/₃	1	2	.333	36	9	43	6.34	0
2004 Sarasota	Fla.St.	24	129²/₃	12	7	.632	153	43	97	2.64	0
2005 Portland	Eastern	14	87	5	2	.714	83	23	59	2.48	0
2005 Pawtucket	Int.	7	27²/₃	1	2	.333	27	3	21	2.93	1
2005 Boston	A.L.	17	34	3	1	.750	34	17	33	2.65	0
2006 Boston	A.L.	59	68¹/₃	4	2	.667	75	13	40	0.92	35
2007 Boston	A.L.	59	58¹/₃	1	3	.250	84	15	30	1.85	37
2008 Boston	A.L.	67	69¹/₃	5	4	.556	77	8	58	2.34	41
2009 Boston	A.L.	66	68	1	1	.500	76	24	54	1.85	38
2010 Boston	A.L.	65	67	5	7	.417	76	28	57	3.90	37
2011 Boston a	A.L.	63	64¹/₃	4	1	.800	87	10	50	2.94	31
Major League Totals	7 Yrs.	396	429¹/₃	23	19	.548	509	115	322	2.33	219
Division Series											
2005 Boston	A.L.	2	4	0	0	.000	2	0	2	0.00	0
2007 Boston	A.L.	1	1¹/₃	1	0	1.000	1	2	0	0.00	0
2008 Boston	A.L.	3	5	1	0	1.000	7	1	2	0.00	1
2009 Boston	A.L.	2	2	0	1	.000	1	2	4	13.50	0
Division Series Totals		8	12¹/₃	2	1	.667	11	5	8	2.19	1
Championship Series											
2007 Boston	A.L.	3	5	0	0	.000	3	3	3	0.00	1
2008 Boston	A.L.	4	5¹/₃	0	0	.000	6	1	1	0.00	2
Championship Series Totals		7	10¹/₃	0	0	.000	9	3	4	0.00	3
World Series Record											
2007 Boston	A.L.	3	4¹/₃	0	0	.000	3	0	2	0.00	3

a Filed for free agency, October 30, 2011. Signed with Philadelphia Phillies, November 14, 2011.

PARNELL, ROBERT ALLEN (BOBBY)

Born, Salisbury, North Carolina, September 8, 1984.
Bats Right. Throws Right. Height, 6 feet, 4 inches. Weight, 200 pounds.

Year	Club	Lea	G	IP	W	L	Pct	SO	BB	H	ERA	SAVES
2005 Brooklyn	N.Y.-Penn.	15	73	2	3	.400	67	29	48	1.73	0
2006 St. Lucie	Fla.St.	3	11²/₃	0	1	.000	13	9	16	9.26	0
2006 Hagerstown	So.Atl.	18	93²/₃	5	10	.333	84	40	84	4.04	0
2007 Binghamton	Eastern	17	88²/₃	5	5	.500	74	38	98	4.77	0
2007 St. Lucie	Fla.St.	12	55¹/₃	3	3	.500	62	22	56	3.25	0
2008 Binghamton	Eastern	24	127²/₃	10	6	.625	91	57	126	4.30	0
2008 New Orleans	P.C.	5	20¹/₃	2	2	.500	23	9	25	6.64	0
2008 New York	N.L.	6	5	0	0	.000	3	2	3	5.40	0
2009 New York	N.L.	68	88¹/₃	4	8	.333	74	46	101	5.30	1
2010 Buffalo	Int.	24	41¹/₃	1	1	.500	42	17	36	4.14	4
2010 New York	N.L.	41	35	0	1	.000	33	8	41	2.83	0
2011 St. Lucie	Fla.St.	1	1	0	0	.000	0	1	0	0.00	0
2011 Buffalo	Int.	8	8	0	0	.000	11	2	7	3.38	1
2011 New York a	N.L.	60	59¹/₃	4	6	.400	64	27	60	3.64	6
Major League Totals	4 Yrs.	175	187²/₃	8	15	.348	174	83	205	4.32	7

a On disabled list from April 20 to May 30, 2011.

PATERSON, JOSEPH MICHAEL (JOE)

Born, Oakland, California, May 19, 1986.
Bats Right. Throws Left. Height, 6 feet, 1 inch. Weight, 210 pounds.

Year	Club	Lea	G	IP	W	L	Pct	SO	BB	H	ERA	SAVES
2007 Giants	Arizona	4	5	1	0	1.000	8	0	1	0.00	0
2007 Salem-Keizer	Northwest	9	9²/₃	1	0	1.000	13	2	15	5.59	0
2008 Augusta	So.Atl.	20	31¹/₃	5	1	.833	37	13	23	2.30	1
2008 San Jose	Calif.	34	37²/₃	3	2	.600	41	15	28	3.11	7
2009 Connecticut	Eastern	55	69	5	6	.455	69	24	47	1.96	5
2010 San Jose	Calif.	7	11	1	0	1.000	15	2	9	0.82	1
2010 Fresno a	P.C.	46	54¹/₃	4	3	.571	49	24	55	3.48	2
2011 Arizona	N.L.	62	34	0	3	.000	28	15	28	2.91	1
Division Series											
2011 Arizona	N.L.	1	0¹/₃	0	0	.000	1	0	0	0.00	0

a Selected by Arizona Diamondbacks from San Francisco Giants in Rule V draft, December 9, 2010.

PAULEY, DAVID WAYNE
Born, Longmont, Colorado, June 17, 1983.
Bats Right. Throws Right. Height, 6 feet, 2 inches. Weight, 210 pounds.

Year	Club	Lea	G	IP	W	L	Pct	SO	BB	H	ERA	SAVES
2001	Idaho Falls	Pioneer	15	68²/₃	4	9	.308	53	24	88	6.03	0
2002	Eugene	Northwest	15	80	6	1	.857	62	18	81	2.81	0
2003	Fort Wayne	Midwest	22	117²/₃	7	7	.500	117	38	109	3.29	1
2004	Lake Elsinore a	Calif.	27	153¹/₃	7	12	.368	128	60	155	4.17	0
2005	Portland	Eastern	27	156	9	7	.563	104	34	169	3.81	0
2006	Portland	Eastern	10	60¹/₃	2	3	.400	47	17	54	2.39	0
2006	Boston	A.L.	3	16	0	2	.000	10	6	31	7.87	0
2006	Pawtucket b	Int.	9	50¹/₃	1	3	.250	25	18	60	5.54	0
2007	Pawtucket	Int.	27	153²/₃	6	6	.500	110	49	164	4.33	0
2008	Pawtucket	Int.	25	147	14	4	.778	103	41	147	3.55	0
2008	Boston	A.L.	6	12¹/₃	0	1	.000	11	5	23	11.68	0
2009	Norfolk c-d	Int.	27	152¹/₃	9	12	.429	108	45	171	4.37	0
2010	Tacoma	P.C.	15	85²/₃	1	6	.143	56	26	82	3.68	0
2010	Seattle	A.L.	19	90²/₃	4	9	.308	51	30	89	4.07	0
2011	Seattle-Detroit e	A.L.	53	74	5	6	.455	44	22	64	3.16	0
Major League Totals	4 Yrs.		81	193	9	18	.333	116	63	207	4.52	0

a Traded by San Diego Padres to Boston Red Sox with outfielder Jay Payton, infielder Ramon Vazquez and cash for outfielder Dave Roberts, December 20, 2004.

b On disabled list from August 29 to November 6, 2006.

c Traded to Baltimore Orioles for pitcher Randor Bierd, January 19, 2009.

d Filed for free agency, November 9, 2009. Signed with Seattle Mariners organization, December 14, 2009.

e Traded to Detroit Tigers with pitcher Doug Fister for pitcher Charlie Furbush, outfielder Casper Wells, infielder Francisco Martinez and player to be named later, July 30, 2011. Seattle Mariners received pitcher Chance Ruffin to complete trade, August 17, 2011.

PAULINO (DEL GUIDICE), FELIPE ADOLFO
Born, Santo Domingo, Dominican Republic, October 5, 1983.
Bats Right. Throws Right. Height, 6 feet, 2 inches. Weight, 260 pounds.

Year	Club	Lea	G	IP	W	L	Pct	SO	BB	H	ERA	SAVES
2003	Martinsville	Appal.	16	25²/₃	2	2	.500	27	19	23	5.61	1
2004	Greenville	Appal.	10	32	1	3	.250	37	22	30	7.59	0
2005	Tri-City	N.Y.-Penn.	13	30²/₃	2	2	.500	34	11	21	3.82	1
2005	Lexington	So.Atl.	7	24¹/₃	1	1	.500	30	6	21	1.85	0
2006	Salem	Carolina	27	126¹/₃	9	7	.563	91	59	119	4.35	0
2007	Corpus Christi	Texas	22	112	6	9	.400	110	49	103	3.62	0
2007	Houston	N.L.	5	19	2	1	.667	11	7	22	7.11	0
2008	Round Rock a	P.C.	1	0²/₃	0	0	.000	1	1	1	0.00	0
2009	Round Rock	P.C.	7	34²/₃	2	1	.667	29	23	30	3.12	0
2009	Houston b	N.L.	23	97²/₃	3	11	.214	93	37	126	6.27	0
2010	Corpus Christi	Texas	1	4	0	0	.000	3	1	2	0.00	0
2010	Houston c-d	N.L.	19	91²/₃	1	9	.100	83	46	95	5.11	0
2011	Colorado	N.L.	18	14²/₃	0	4	.000	14	7	23	7.36	0
2011	Kansas City e	A.L.	21	124²/₃	4	6	.400	119	48	123	4.11	0
Major League Totals	4 Yrs.		86	347²/₃	10	31	.244	320	145	389	5.28	0

a On disabled list from March 21 to September 30, 2008.

b On disabled list from June 8 to June 27, 2009.

c On disabled list from June 21 to September 12, 2010.

d Traded to Colorado Rockies for infielder Clint Barmes, November 18, 2010.

e Sold to Kansas City Royals, May 26, 2011.

PAVANO, CARL ANTHONY
Born, New Britain, Connecticut, January 8, 1976.
Bats Right. Throws Right. Height, 6 feet, 5 inches. Weight, 240 pounds.

Year	Club	Lea	G	IP	W	L	Pct	SO	BB	H	ERA	SAVES
1994	Red Sox	Gulf Coast	9	44	4	3	.571	47	7	31	1.84	0
1995	Michigan	Midwest	22	141¹/₃	6	6	.500	138	52	118	3.44	0
1996	Trenton	Eastern	27	185	16	5	.762	146	47	154	2.63	0
1997	Pawtucket a	Int.	23	161²/₃	11	6	.647	147	34	148	3.12	0
1998	Jupiter	Fla.St.	4	15	0	0	.000	14	3	20	6.60	0
1998	Ottawa	Int.	3	18²/₃	1	0	1.000	14	7	12	2.41	0
1998	Montreal	N.L.	24	134²/₃	6	9	.400	83	43	130	4.21	0
1999	Montreal	N.L.	19	104	6	8	.429	70	35	117	5.63	0
1999	Ottawa b	Int.	2	5	0	1	.000	3	0	7	9.00	0
2000	Montreal c	N.L.	15	97	8	4	.667	64	34	89	3.06	0
2001	Jupiter	Fla.St.	3	12¹/₃	1	1	.500	11	2	10	2.19	0

310

Year	Club	Lea	G	IP	W	L	Pct	SO	BB	H	ERA	SAVES
2001	Ottawa	Int.	4	27²/₃	2	1	.667	19	5	27	3.58	0
2001	Montreal d	N.L.	8	42²/₃	1	6	.143	36	16	59	6.33	0
2002	Ottawa	Int.	3	20¹/₃	3	0	1.000	9	2	23	3.10	0
2002	Montreal-Florida e	N.L.	37	136	6	10	.375	92	45	174	5.16	0
2003	Florida	N.L.	33	201	12	13	.480	133	49	204	4.30	0
2004	Florida f	N.L.	31	222¹/₃	18	8	.692	139	49	212	3.00	0
2005	Yankees	Gulf Coast	1	5	0	0	.000	5	0	2	1.80	0
2005	Tampa	Fla.St.	1	6	0	1	.000	3	0	6	4.50	0
2005	New York g	A.L.	17	100	4	6	.400	56	18	129	4.77	0
2006	Trenton	Eastern	3	11	1	0	1.000	12	0	6	1.64	0
2006	Tampa	Fla.St.	3	11²/₃	0	2	.000	10	3	10	2.31	0
2006	Columbus h	Int.	1	6	1	0	1.000	5	1	8	3.00	0
2007	New York i	A.L.	2	11¹/₃	1	0	1.000	4	2	12	4.76	0
2008	Charleston	So.Atl.	2	5	0	0	.000	6	1	6	1.80	0
2008	Trenton	Eastern	3	14	1	1	.500	13	3	14	3.86	0
2008	New York j-k	A.L.	7	34¹/₃	4	2	.667	15	10	41	5.77	0
2009	Cleveland-Minnesota l-m .	A.L.	33	199¹/₃	14	12	.538	147	39	235	5.10	0
2010	Minnesota n	A.L.	32	221	17	11	.607	117	37	227	3.75	0
2011	Minnesota	A.L.	33	222	9	13	.409	102	40	*262	4.30	0
Major League Totals	13 Yrs.		291	1725²/₃	106	102	.510	1058	417	1891	4.33	0
Division Series												
2003	Florida	N.L.	1	2²/₃	2	0	1.000	1	1	1	0.00	0
2009	Minnesota	A.L.	1	7	0	1	.000	9	0	5	2.57	0
2010	Minnesota	A.L.	1	6	0	1	.000	3	1	10	6.00	0
Division Series Totals			5	15²/₃	2	2	.500	13	2	16	3.45	0
Championship Series												
2003	Florida	N.L.	3	7²/₃	0	0	.000	8	1	8	2.35	0
World Series Record												
2003	Florida	N.L.	2	9	0	0	.000	6	1	8	1.00	0

a Traded by Boston Red Sox to Montreal Expos with player to be named later for pitcher Pedro Martinez, November 18, 1997. Montreal Expos received pitcher Tony Armas to complete trade, December 18, 1997.

b On disabled list from July 12 to September 11, 1999.

c On disabled list from June 25 to November 13, 2000.

d On disabled list from March 23 to August 15, 2001.

e Traded to Florida Marlins with pitcher Graeme Lloyd, infielder Mike Mordecai and pitcher Justin Wayne for outfielder Cliff Floyd, infielder Wilton Guerrero and cash, July 11, 2002.

f Filed for free agency, November 3, 2004. Signed with New York Yankees, December 22, 2004.

g On disabled list from June 28 to October 31, 2005.

h On disabled list from March 29 to October 31, 2006.

i On disabled list from April 10 to October 31, 2007.

j On disabled list from March 21 to August 23, 2008.

k Filed for free agency, November 5, 2008. Signed with Cleveland Indians, January 6, 2009.

l Traded to Minnesota Twins for player to be named later, August 7, 2009. Cleveland Indians received pitcher Yohan Pinto to complete trade, August 28, 2009.

m Filed for free agency, November 7, 2009. Accepted arbitration, December 7, 2009.

n Filed for free agency, November 1, 2010, re-signed with Minnesota Twins, January 19, 2011.

PEAVY, JACOB EDWARD (JAKE)

Born, Mobile, Alabama, May 3, 1981.
Bats Right. Throws Right. Height, 6 feet, 1 inch. Weight, 195 pounds.

Year	Club	Lea	G	IP	W	L	Pct	SO	BB	H	ERA	SAVES
1999	Padres	Arizona	13	73²/₃	7	1	.875	90	23	52	1.34	0
1999	Idaho Falls	Pioneer	2	11	2	0	1.000	13	1	5	0.00	0
2000	Fort Wayne	Midwest	26	133²/₃	13	8	.619	164	53	107	2.90	0
2001	Mobile	Southern	5	28	2	1	.667	44	12	19	2.57	0
2002	Mobile	Southern	14	80¹/₃	4	5	.444	89	30	65	2.80	0
2002	San Diego	N.L.	17	97²/₃	6	7	.462	90	33	106	4.52	0
2003	San Diego	N.L.	32	194²/₃	12	11	.522	156	82	173	4.11	0
2004	Mobile	Southern	1	4²/₃	0	0	.000	4	2	7	5.79	0
2004	San Diego a	N.L.	27	166¹/₃	15	6	.714	173	53	146	*2.27	0
2005	San Diego	N.L.	30	203	13	7	.650	*216	50	162	2.88	0
2006	San Diego	N.L.	32	202¹/₃	11	14	.440	215	62	187	4.09	0
2007	San Diego b	N.L.	34	223¹/₃	*19	6	.760	*240	68	169	*2.54	0
2008	San Diego c	N.L.	27	173²/₃	10	11	.476	166	59	146	2.85	0
2009	Charlotte	Int.	4	15¹/₃	1	1	.500	17	4	14	2.93	0
2009	San Diego	N.L.	13	81²/₃	6	6	.500	92	28	69	3.97	0
2009	Chicago d-e	A.L.	3	20	3	0	1.000	18	6	11	1.35	0
2010	Chicago f	A.L.	17	107	7	6	.538	93	34	98	4.63	0
2011	Birmingham	Southern	2	4¹/₃	0	0	.000	4	1	9	6.23	0

Year Club	Lea	G	IP	W	L	Pct	SO	BB	H	ERA	SAVES
2011 Charlotte . . . . .Int.		4	24⅔	1	1	.500	26	1	21	3.65	0
2011 Chicago g . . . . A.L.		19	111⅔	7	7	.500	95	24	117	4.92	0
Major League Totals . . . . . . .10 Yrs.		251	1581⅓	109	81	.574	1554	499	1384	3.47	0
Division Series											
2005 San Diego . . . . N.L.		1	4⅓	0	1	.000	3	3	8	16.62	0
2006 San Diego . . . . N.L.		1	5⅓	0	1	.000	2	1	11	8.44	0
Division Series Totals		2	9⅔	0	2	.000	5	4	19	12.10	0

a On disabled list from May 20 to July 2, 2004.
b Selected Cy Young Award Winner in National League for 2007.
c On disabled list from May 15 to June 12, 2008.
d Traded to Chicago White Sox for pitcher Aaron Poreda, pitcher Clayton Richard, pitcher Adam Russell and pitcher Dexter Carter, July 31, 2009.
e On disabled list from June 9 to September 19, 2009.
f On disabled list from July 7 to November 2, 2010.
g On disabled list from March 22 to May 11, 2011.

PELFREY, MICHAEL ALAN (MIKE)

Born, Wright-Patterson AFB, Ohio, January 14, 1984.
Bats Right. Throws Right. Height, 6 feet, 7 inches. Weight, 230 pounds.

Year Club	Lea	G	IP	W	L	Pct	SO	BB	H	ERA	SAVES
2006 St. Lucie. . . . . Fla.St.		4	22	2	1	.667	26	2	17	1.64	0
2006 Binghamton . . . . Eastern		12	66⅓	4	2	.667	77	26	60	2.71	0
2006 New York . . . . N.L.		4	21⅓	2	1	.667	13	12	25	5.48	0
2006 Norfolk. . . . . .Int.		2	8	1	0	1.000	6	5	4	2.25	0
2007 St. Lucie . . . . Fla.St.		1	6	0	0	.000	2	3	5	3.00	0
2007 New Orleans. . . . . P.C.		14	74	3	6	.333	56	26	74	4.01	0
2007 New York . . . . N.L.		15	72⅔	3	8	.273	45	39	85	5.57	0
2008 New York . . . . N.L.		32	200⅔	13	11	.542	110	64	209	3.72	0
2009 New York . . . . N.L.		31	184⅓	10	12	.455	107	66	213	5.03	0
2010 New York . . . . N.L.		34	204	15	9	.625	113	68	213	3.66	1
2011 New York . . . . N.L.		34	193⅔	7	13	.350	105	65	220	4.74	0
Major League Totals . . . . .6 Yrs.		150	876⅔	50	54	.481	493	314	965	4.40	1

PENNY, BRADLEY WAYNE (BRAD)

Born, Broken Arrow, Oklahoma, May 24, 1978.
Bats Right. Throws Right. Height, 6 feet, 4 inches. Weight, 260 pounds.

Year Club	Lea	G	IP	W	L	Pct	SO	BB	H	ERA	SAVES
1996 Diamondbcks. . . . . . . Arizona		11	49⅔	2	2	.500	52	14	36	2.36	0
1997 South Bend . . . . . . .Midwest		25	118⅔	10	5	.667	116	43	91	2.73	0
1998 High Desert . . . . . . .California		28	164	14	5	.737	207	35	138	2.96	0
1999 El Paso a-b-c . . . . Texas		17	90	2	7	.222	100	25	109	4.80	0
1999 Portland . . . . Eastern		6	32⅓	1	0	1.000	35	14	28	3.90	0
2000 Brevard County . . . . . . Fla.St.		2	8	0	1	.000	11	4	5	1.13	0
2000 Calgary. . . . . P.C.		3	15	2	0	1.000	16	10	8	1.80	0
2000 Florida d . . . . N.L.		23	119⅔	8	7	.533	80	60	120	4.81	0
2001 Florida . . . . N.L.		31	205	10	10	.500	154	54	183	3.69	0
2002 Jupiter . . . . Fla.St.		2	7⅔	0	0	.000	9	0	5	0.00	0
2002 Florida e . . . . N.L.		24	129⅓	8	7	.533	93	50	148	4.66	0
2003 Florida . . . . N.L.		32	196⅓	14	10	.583	138	56	195	4.13	0
2004 Florida-Los Angeles f-g . . N.L.		24	143	9	10	.474	111	45	130	3.15	0
2005 Vero Beach. . . . . Fla.St.		1	5	1	0	1.000	3	1	2	1.80	0
2005 Las Vegas. . . . . P.C.		1	6	1	0	1.000	9	2	5	3.00	0
2005 Los Angeles h . . . . N.L.		29	175⅓	7	9	.438	122	41	185	3.90	0
2006 Los Angeles . . . . N.L.		34	189	*16	9	.640	148	54	206	4.33	0
2007 Los Angeles . . . . N.L.		33	208	16	4	*.800	135	73	199	3.03	0
2008 Las Vegas . . . . P.C.		1	4	0	0	.000	4	1	6	4.50	0
2008 Los Angeles i-j . . . . N.L.		19	94⅔	6	9	.400	51	42	112	6.27	0
2009 Boston . . . . A.L.		24	131⅔	7	8	.467	89	42	160	5.61	0
2009 San Francisco k-l . . . . . . N.L.		6	41⅔	4	1	.800	20	9	31	2.59	0
2010 St. Louis m-n . . . . N.L.		9	55⅔	3	4	.429	35	9	63	3.23	0
2011 Detroit o . . . . A.L.		31	181⅔	11	11	.500	74	62	222	5.30	0
Major League Totals . . . . . . .12 Yrs.		319	1871	119	99	.546	1250	597	1954	4.23	0
2011 Detroit . . . . A.L.		1	1⅔	0	0	.000	1	1	7	27.00	0
Championship Series Totals		4	5⅔	1	1	.500	1	5	16	19.06	0
Division Series											
2003 Florida . . . . N.L.		2	5⅔	0	0	.000	6	1	5	6.35	0
2006 Los Angeles . . . . N.L.		1	1	0	1	.000	1	2	2	18.00	0

Year	Club	Lea	G	IP	W	L	Pct	SO	BB	H	ERA	SAVES
Division Series Totals			3	6^2/$_3$	0	1	.000	7	3	7	8.10	0
Championship Series												
2003 Florida		N.L.	3	4	1	1	.500	0	3	9	15.75	0
World Series Record												
2003 Florida		N.L.	2	12^1/$_3$	2	0	1.000	7	5	15	2.19	0

a On disabled list from April 20 to 30, 1999.
b Traded by Arizona Diamondbacks to Florida Marlins with pitcher Vladimir Nunez and player to be named later for pitcher Matt Mantei, July 9, 1999.
c Florida Marlins received outfielder Abraham Nunez to complete trade, December 13, 1999.
d On disabled list from July 20 to September 1, 2000.
e On disabled list from May 19 to July 2, 2002.
f Traded to Los Angeles Dodgers with pitcher Bill Murphy and infielder Hee Seop Choi for catcher Paul LoDuca, outfielder Juan Encarnacion and pitcher Guillermo Mota, July 30, 2004.
g On disabled list from August 9 to September 22, 2004.
h On disabled list from March 25 to April 24, 2005.
i On disabled list from June 15 to August 8 and August 14 to September 10 and September 24 to November 4, 2008.
j Not offered contract, November 5, 2008. Signed with Boston Red Sox, January 9, 2009.
k Released by Boston Red Sox, August 27, 2009. Signed with San Francisco Giants organization, August 31, 2009.
l Filed for free agency, November 5, 2009. Signed with St. Louis Cardinals, December 9, 2009.
m On disabled list from May 22 to November 1, 2010.
n Filed for free agency, November 1, 2010. Signed with Detroit Tigers, January 18, 2011.
o Filed for free agency, October 30, 2011.

PERALTA (GUTIERREZ), JOEL

Born, Bonao, Dominican Republic, March 23, 1976.
Bats Right. Throws Right. Height, 5 feet, 11 inches. Weight, 195 pounds.

Year	Club	Lea	G	IP	W	L	Pct	SO	BB	H	ERA	SAVES
2000 Boise	Northwest		4	8^1/$_3$	0	0	.000	9	5	12	6.48	0
2000 Butte a	Pioneer		10	19	2	1	.667	17	10	24	6.63	1
2001 Cedar Rapids	Midwest		41	42^1/$_3$	0	0	.000	53	5	27	2.13	23
2001 Arkansas	Texas		9	10	0	1	.000	14	5	15	6.30	2
2002 Cedar Rapids	Midwest		41	47^1/$_3$	5	0	1.000	53	11	28	0.95	21
2002 Arkansas	Texas		12	17^2/$_3$	0	0	.000	11	10	25	6.62	0
2003 Salt Lake	P.C.		1	0	0	0	.000	0	1	0	0.00	0
2003 Arkansas	Texas		47	52^1/$_3$	5	4	.556	48	12	39	2.24	20
2004 Angels	Arizona		2	4^1/$_3$	0	0	.000	9	0	1	2.08	0
2004 Rancho Cucamonga	Calif.		1	2	0	0	.000	1	1	5	9.00	0
2004 Salt Lake	P.C.		39	56	4	2	.667	68	18	64	4.98	1
2005 Los Angeles	A.L.		28	34^2/$_3$	1	0	1.000	30	14	28	3.89	0
2005 Salt Lake b	P.C.		19	20	4	1	.800	18	6	11	2.70	10
2006 Omaha	P.C.		6	7^2/$_3$	1	0	1.000	8	3	8	2.35	2
2006 Kansas City	A.L.		64	73^2/$_3$	1	3	.250	57	17	74	4.40	1
2007 Kansas City	A.L.		62	87^2/$_3$	1	3	.250	66	19	93	3.80	1
2008 Omaha	P.C.		10	18^2/$_3$	1	0	1.000	19	6	9	0.00	2
2008 Kansas City	A.L.		40	52^2/$_3$	1	2	.333	38	14	56	5.98	0
2009 Colorado Springs	P.C.		31	36^2/$_3$	6	0	1.000	32	11	31	2.45	4
2009 Colorado c-d	N.L.		27	24^2/$_3$	0	3	.000	22	12	27	6.20	0
2010 Syracuse	Int.		28	33^1/$_3$	2	0	1.000	38	7	24	1.08	20
2010 Washington e..........	N.L.		39	49	1	0	1.000	49	9	30	2.02	0
2011 Tampa Bay	A.L.		71	67^2/$_3$	3	4	.429	61	18	44	2.93	6
Major League Totals	7 Yrs.		331	390	8	15	.348	323	103	352	3.99	8
Division Series												
2011 Tampa Bay	A.L.		3	2^1/$_3$	0	0	.000	0	2	1	0.00	0

a Released by Oakland Athletics, July 4, 1998. Signed with Anaheim Angels organization, February 25, 1999.
b Claimed on waivers by Kansas City Royals, October 7, 2005.
c Released by Kansas City Royals, March 31, 2009. Signed with Colorado Rockies organization, April 8, 2009.
d Filed for free agency, October 26, 2009. Signed with Washington Nationals organization, December 15, 2009.
e Not offered contract, December 2, 2010. Signed with Tampa Bay Rays, December 17, 2010.

PEREZ, CHRISTOPHER RALPH (CHRIS)

Born, Bradenton, Florida, July 1, 1985.
Bats Right. Throws Right. Height, 6 feet, 4 inches. Weight, 225 pounds.

Year	Club	Lea	G	IP	W	L	Pct	SO	BB	H	ERA	SAVES
2006 Quad Cities.........	Midwest		25	29^1/$_3$	2	0	1.000	32	19	20	1.84	12
2007 Memphis	P.C.		15	14	0	1	.000	15	13	6	4.50	8
2007 Springfield	Texas		39	40^2/$_3$	2	0	1.000	62	28	17	2.43	27
2008 Memphis	P.C.		26	25^1/$_3$	1	1	.500	38	12	18	3.20	11
2008 St. Louis	N.L.		41	41^2/$_3$	3	3	.500	42	22	34	3.46	7
2009 Memphis	P.C.		3	4	1	0	1.000	4	3	0	0.00	2

Year	Club	Lea	G	IP	W	L	Pct	SO	BB	H	ERA	SAVES
2009 St. Louis..............	N.L.	29	23²/₃	1	1	.500	30	15	17	4.18	1
2009 Cleveland a............	A.L.	32	33¹/₃	0	1	.000	38	12	24	4.32	1
2010 Cleveland..............	A.L.	63	63	2	2	.500	61	28	40	1.71	23
2011 Cleveland..............	A.L.	64	59²/₃	4	7	.364	39	26	46	3.32	36
Major League Totals........4 Yrs.		229	221¹/₃	10	14	.417	210	103	161	3.13	68

a Traded to Cleveland Indians with player to be named later for infielder Mark DeRosa, June 27, 2009. Cleveland Indians received pitcher Jess Todd to complete trade, July 26, 2009.

PEREZ (GONZALEZ), LUIS MANUEL
Born, Guayubin, Dominican Republic, January 20, 1985.
Bats Left. Throws Left. Height, 6 feet. Weight, 160 pounds.

Year	Club	Lea	G	IP	W	L	Pct	SO	BB	H	ERA	SAVES
2007 Auburn..........	N.Y.-Penn.	16	75¹/₃	3	3	.500	71	38	73	3.70	0
2008 Lansing..........	Midwest	28	137¹/₃	5	12	.294	137	51	136	3.60	0
2009 New Hampshire.....	Eastern	28	162¹/₃	9	11	.450	112	67	145	3.55	0
2010 New Hampshire.....	Eastern	13	73¹/₃	5	6	.455	49	37	67	4.54	0
2010 Las Vegas.............	P.C.	15	86²/₃	5	5	.500	56	47	107	6.13	0
2011 Las Vegas.............	P.C.	8	45	2	2	.500	43	23	37	4.60	0
2011 Toronto..............	A.L.	37	65	3	3	.500	54	27	74	5.12	0

PEREZ, RAFAEL JEROME
Born, Santo Domingo, Dominican Republic, May 15, 1982.
Bats Left. Throws Left. Height, 6 feet, 3 inches. Weight, 185 pounds.

Year	Club	Lea	G	IP	W	L	Pct	SO	BB	H	ERA	SAVES
2003 Burlington..........	Appal.	13	69	9	3	.750	63	16	56	1.70	0
2004 Kinston............	Carolina	1	4²/₃	0	0	.000	3	2	10	11.57	0
2004 Lake County........	So.Atl.	23	115	7	6	.538	99	47	121	4.85	0
2005 Kinston............	Carolina	14	77²/₃	8	5	.615	48	32	54	3.36	0
2005 Akron.............	Eastern	15	66²/₃	4	3	.571	46	12	53	1.75	1
2006 Akron.............	Eastern	12	67¹/₃	4	5	.444	53	22	53	2.81	0
2006 Buffalo.............	Int.	13	27¹/₃	0	3	.000	33	8	20	2.63	0
2006 Cleveland..........	A.L.	18	12¹/₃	0	0	.000	15	6	10	4.38	0
2007 Buffalo.............	Int.	8	46²/₃	3	3	.500	31	11	53	3.66	0
2007 Cleveland..........	A.L.	44	60²/₃	1	2	.333	62	15	41	1.78	1
2008 Cleveland..........	A.L.	73	76¹/₃	4	4	.500	86	23	67	3.54	2
2009 Columbus..........	Int.	16	21²/₃	1	0	1.000	23	5	23	0.83	3
2009 Cleveland..........	A.L.	54	48	4	3	.571	32	25	66	7.31	0
2010 Cleveland..........	A.L.	70	61	6	1	.857	36	25	72	3.25	0
2011 Cleveland..........	A.L.	71	63	5	2	.714	33	19	59	3.00	0
Major League Totals........6 Yrs.		330	321¹/₃	20	12	.625	264	113	315	3.64	3
Division Series											
2007 Cleveland..........	A.L.	3	6	1	0	1.000	6	1	3	1.50	0
Championship Series											
2007 Cleveland..........	A.L.	3	1	0	0	.000	0	2	7	45.00	0

PERKINS, GLEN WESTON
Born, St.Paul, Minnesota, March 2, 1983.
Bats Left. Throws Left. Height, 5 feet, 11 inches. Weight, 210 pounds.

Year	Club	Lea	G	IP	W	L	Pct	SO	BB	H	ERA	SAVES
2004 Elizabethton........	Appal.	3	12	1	0	1.000	22	4	8	2.25	0
2004 Quad Cities........	Midwest	9	48¹/₃	2	1	.667	49	12	33	1.30	0
2005 Fort Myers..........	Fla.St.	10	55	3	2	.600	66	13	41	2.13	0
2005 New Britain........	Eastern	14	79	4	4	.500	67	35	80	4.90	0
2006 New Britain........	Eastern	23	117¹/₃	4	11	.267	131	45	109	3.91	0
2006 Rochester..........	Int.	1	4¹/₃	0	1	.000	3	5	6	2.08	0
2006 Minnesota..........	A.L.	4	5²/₃	0	0	.000	6	0	3	1.59	0
2007 Rochester..........	Int.	1	6	0	0	.000	2	1	2	1.50	0
2007 Fort Myers..........	Fla.St.	1	1	0	0	.000	0	0	3	27.00	0
2007 Twins...........	Gulf Coast	3	5	0	0	.000	6	2	3	1.80	0
2007 New Britain........	Eastern	3	7¹/₃	0	2	.000	7	7	11	11.05	0
2007 Minnesota a..........	A.L.	19	28²/₃	0	0	.000	20	12	23	3.14	0
2008 Rochester..........	Int.	7	33¹/₃	2	1	.667	27	19	28	2.97	0
2008 Minnesota..........	A.L.	26	151	12	4	.750	74	39	183	4.41	0
2009 Fort Myers..........	Fla.St.	2	11	1	0	1.000	9	1	8	2.45	0
2009 Minnesota..........	A.L.	18	96¹/₃	6	7	.462	45	23	120	5.89	0
2009 Twins b..........	Gulf Coast	1	1	0	0	.000	0	0	0	0.00	0

Year Club	Lea	G	IP	W	L	Pct	SO	BB	H	ERA	SAVES
2010 Rochester..............	Int.	26	124	4	9	.308	98	36	160	5.81	0
2010 Minnesota	A.L.	13	$21\frac{2}{3}$	1	1	.500	14	5	29	5.82	0
2011 Rochester..............	Int.	2	3	0	0	.000	2	0	4	0.00	0
2011 Minnesota c.............	A.L.	65	$61\frac{2}{3}$	4	4	.500	65	21	55	2.48	2
Major League Totals	6 Yrs.	145	365	23	16	.590	224	100	413	4.41	2
Division Series											
2006 Minnesota	A.L.	1	$0\frac{1}{3}$	0	0	.000	0	0	2	0.00	0

a On disabled list from May 22 to September 11, 2007.
b On disabled list from May 19 to June 16 and August 9 to August 30, 2009.
c On disabled list from May 22 to June 17, 2011.

PESTANO, VINCENT WILLIAM (VINNIE)
Born, Huntington Beach, California, February 20, 1985.
Bats Right. Throws Right. Height, 6 feet, 1 inch. Weight, 200 pounds.

Year Club	Lea	G	IP	W	L	Pct	SO	BB	H	ERA	SAVES
2007 Mahoning Valley...	N.Y.-Penn.	21	$22\frac{2}{3}$	1	1	.500	27	7	17	3.57	6
2008 Lake County.........	So.Atl.	29	29	1	1	.500	23	13	25	1.55	15
2008 Kinston.............	Carolina	25	27	1	2	.333	27	11	23	4.00	9
2009 Akron..............	Eastern	34	$34\frac{2}{3}$	2	3	.400	31	13	30	2.86	24
2010 Akron..............	Eastern	14	$13\frac{1}{3}$	1	1	.500	18	2	12	2.70	3
2010 Columbus..............	Int.	43	$46\frac{1}{3}$	1	2	.333	59	14	35	1.55	14
2010 Cleveland.............	A.L.	5	5	0	0	.000	8	5	4	3.60	1
2011 Cleveland.............	A.L.	67	62	1	2	.333	84	24	41	2.32	2
Major League Totals	2 Yrs.	72	67	1	2	.333	92	29	45	2.42	3

PINEDA, MICHAEL FRANCISCO
Born, Yaguate, Dominican Republic, January 18, 1989.
Bats Right. Throws Right. Height, 6 feet, 7 inches. Weight, 260 pounds.

Year Club	Lea	G	IP	W	L	Pct	SO	BB	H	ERA	SAVES
2008 Wisconsin	Midwest	26	$138\frac{1}{3}$	8	6	.571	128	35	109	1.95	0
2009 Mariners...........	Arizona	2	3	0	0	.000	4	0	2	0.00	0
2009 High Desert	Calif.	10	$44\frac{1}{3}$	4	2	.667	48	6	29	2.84	0
2010 Tacoma	P.C.	12	$62\frac{1}{3}$	3	3	.500	76	17	54	4.76	0
2010 West Tenn	Southern	13	77	8	1	.889	78	17	67	2.22	0
2011 Seattle a.............	A.L.	28	171	9	10	.474	173	55	133	3.74	0

a Traded to New York Yankees with pitcher Jose Campos for catcher Jesus Montero and pitcher Hector Noesi, January 17, 2012.

PINEIRO, JOEL ALBERTO
Born, Rio Piedras, Puerto Rico, September 25, 1978.
Bats Right. Throws Right. Height, 6 feet, 1 inch. Weight, 200 pounds.

Year Club	Lea	G	IP	W	L	Pct	SO	BB	H	ERA	SAVES
1997 Mariners...........	Arizona	1	3	1	0	1.000	4	0	1	0.00	0
1997 Everett..........	Northwest	18	49	4	2	.667	59	18	54	5.33	2
1998 Wisconsin	Midwest	16	96	8	4	.667	84	28	92	3.19	0
1998 Lancaster...........	California	9	45	2	0	1.000	48	22	58	7.80	0
1998 Orlando	Southern	1	5	1	0	1.000	2	2	7	5.40	0
1999 New Haven........	Eastern	28	166	10	15	.400	116	52	190	4.72	0
2000 New Haven........	Eastern	9	$52\frac{1}{3}$	2	1	.667	43	12	42	4.13	0
2000 Tacoma	P.C.	10	61	7	1	.875	41	22	53	2.80	0
2000 Seattle	A.L.	8	$19\frac{1}{3}$	1	0	1.000	10	13	25	5.59	0
2001 Tacoma	P.C.	18	77	6	3	.667	64	33	68	3.62	0
2001 Seattle	A.L.	17	$75\frac{1}{3}$	6	2	.750	56	21	50	2.03	0
2002 Seattle	A.L.	37	$194\frac{1}{3}$	14	7	.667	136	54	189	3.24	0
2003 Seattle	A.L.	32	$211\frac{2}{3}$	16	11	.593	151	76	192	3.78	0
2004 Seattle a.............	A.L.	21	$140\frac{2}{3}$	6	11	.353	111	43	144	4.67	0
2005 Tacoma	P.C.	1	7	0	0	.000	6	0	5	1.29	0
2005 Seattle b.............	A.L.	30	189	7	11	.389	107	56	224	5.62	0
2006 Seattle c.............	A.L.	40	$165\frac{2}{3}$	8	13	.381	87	64	209	6.36	1
2007 Lowell	N.Y.-Penn.	1	1	0	0	.000	2	0	0	0.00	0
2007 Pawtucket	Int.	2	8	0	0	.000	3	4	3	2.25	0
2007 Boston	A.L.	31	34	1	1	.500	20	14	41	5.03	0
2007 St. Louis d-e-f	N.L.	11	$63\frac{2}{3}$	6	4	.600	40	12	69	3.96	0
2008 Memphis	P.C.	1	6	0	0	.000	5	1	6	3.00	0
2008 St. Louis g	N.L.	26	$148\frac{2}{3}$	7	7	.500	81	35	180	5.15	1
2009 St. Louis h	N.L.	32	214	15	12	.556	105	27	218	3.49	0

Year	Club	Lea	G	IP	W	L	Pct	SO	BB	H	ERA	SAVES
2010 Los Angeles i	A.L.	23	152⅓	10	7	.588	92	34	155	3.84	0
2011 Inland Empire	Calif.	1	5⅔	0	0	.000	2	2	6	0.00	0
2011 Los Angeles j	A.L.	27	145⅔	7	7	.500	62	38	182	5.13	0
Major League Totals . . . . 12 Yrs.		335	1754⅓	104	93	.528	1058	487	1878	4.41	2
Division Series											
2009 St. Louis.	N.L.	1	4	0	1	.000	3	0	7	9.00	0
Championship Series											
2001 Seattle	A.L.	1	2	0	0	.000	5	2	4	4.50	0

a On disabled list from July 26 to November 1, 2004.
b On disabled list from March 27 to April 15, 2005.
c Not offered contract, December 12, 2006. Signed with Boston Red Sox, January 4, 2007.
d On disabled list from June 28 to July 13, 2007.
e Traded to St. Louis Cardinals for player to be named later, July 31, 2007.
f Boston Red Sox received outfielder Sean Danielson to complete trade, November 2, 2007.
g On disabled list from March 21 to April 13 and May 21 to June 12, 2008.
h Filed for free agency, November 6, 2009. Signed with Los Angeles Angels, February 4, 2010.
i On disabled list from July 30 to September 14, 2010.
j Filed for free agency, October 30, 2011.

POMERANZ, THOMAS ANDREW (DREW)
Born, Collierville, Tennessee, November 22, 1988.
Bats Right. Throws Left. Height, 6 feet, 5 inches. Weight, 230 pounds.

Year	Club	Lea	G	IP	W	L	Pct	SO	BB	H	ERA	SAVES
2011 Kinston	Carolina	15	77	3	2	.600	95	32	56	1.87	0
2011 Tulsa	Texas	2	10	1	0	1.000	7	0	2	0.00	0
2011 Akron	Eastern	3	14	0	1	.000	17	6	10	2.57	0
2011 Colorado a	N.L.	4	18⅓	2	1	.667	13	5	19	5.40	0

a Sent to Colorado Rockies as player to be named later for pitcher Ubaldo Jimenez, August 17, 2011.

PORCELLO, FREDERICK ALFRED (RICK)
Born, Morristown, New Jersey, December 27, 1988.
Bats Right. Throws Right. Height, 6 feet, 5 inches. Weight, 200 pounds.

Year	Club	Lea	G	IP	W	L	Pct	SO	BB	H	ERA	SAVES
2008 Lakeland	Fla.St.	24	125	8	6	.571	72	33	116	2.66	0
2009 Detroit	A.L.	31	170⅔	14	9	.609	89	52	176	3.96	0
2010 Toledo	Int.	4	28	1	2	.333	19	10	24	3.21	0
2010 Detroit	A.L.	27	162⅔	10	12	.455	84	38	188	4.92	0
2011 Detroit	A.L.	31	182	14	9	.609	104	46	210	4.75	0
Major League Totals . . . . 3 Yrs.		89	515⅓	38	30	.559	277	136	574	4.54	0
Division Series											
2011 Detroit	A.L.	1	6	0	1	.000	5	1	5	6.00	0
Championship Series											
2011 Detroit	A.L.	3	9	0	0	.000	7	1	10	4.00	0

PRICE, DAVID TAYLOR
Born, Murfreesboro, Tennessee, August 26, 1985.
Bats Left. Throws Left. Height, 6 feet, 6 inches. Weight, 225 pounds.

Year	Club	Lea	G	IP	W	L	Pct	SO	BB	H	ERA	SAVES
2008 Vero Beach	Fla.St.	6	34⅔	4	0	1.000	37	7	28	1.82	0
2008 Montgomery	Southern	9	57	7	0	1.000	55	16	42	1.89	0
2008 Durham	Int.	4	18	1	1	.500	17	9	22	4.50	0
2008 Tampa Bay	A.L.	5	14	0	0	.000	12	4	9	1.93	0
2009 Durham	Int.	8	34⅓	1	4	.200	35	18	28	3.93	0
2009 Tampa Bay	A.L.	23	128⅓	10	7	.588	102	54	119	4.42	0
2010 Tampa Bay	A.L.	32	208⅔	19	6	*.760	188	79	170	2.72	0
2011 Tampa Bay	A.L.	34	224⅓	12	13	.480	218	63	192	3.49	0
Major League Totals . . . . 4 Yrs.		94	575⅓	41	26	.612	520	200	490	3.38	0
Division Series											
2010 Tampa Bay	A.L.	2	12⅔	0	2	.000	14	0	17	4.97	0
2011 Tampa Bay	A.L.	1	6⅔	0	1	.000	3	1	7	4.05	0
Division Series Totals		3	19⅓	0	3	.000	17	1	24	4.66	0
Championship Series											
2008 Tampa Bay	A.L.	3	2⅓	1	0	1.000	4	2	0	0.00	1
World Series Record											
2008 Tampa Bay	A.L.	2	3⅓	0	0	.000	4	2	2	2.70	0

PUTZ, JOSEPH JASON (J.J.)
Born, Trenton, Michigan, February 2, 1977.
Bats Right. Throws Right. Height, 6 feet, 5 inches. Weight, 250 pounds.

Year	Club	Lea	G	IP	W	L	Pct	SO	BB	H	ERA	SAVES
1999 Everett	Northwest	10	22⅓	0	0	.000	17	11	23	4.84	2
2000 Wisconsin	Midwest	26	142⅔	12	6	.667	105	63	130	3.15	0
2001 San Antonio	Texas	27	148	7	9	.438	135	59	145	3.83	0
2002 San Antonio	Texas	15	84	3	10	.231	60	28	84	3.64	0
2002 Tacoma	P.C.	9	54	2	4	.333	39	21	51	3.83	0
2003 Tacoma	P.C.	41	86	0	3	.000	60	34	69	2.51	11
2003 Seattle	A.L.	3	3⅔	0	0	.000	3	3	4	4.91	0
2004 Tacoma	P.C.	7	8⅓	0	0	.000	13	3	10	4.32	3
2004 Seattle	A.L.	54	63	0	3	.000	47	24	66	4.71	9
2005 Seattle	A.L.	64	60	6	5	.545	45	23	58	3.60	1
2006 Seattle	A.L.	72	78⅓	4	1	.800	104	13	59	2.30	36
2007 Seattle	A.L.	68	71⅔	6	1	.857	82	13	37	1.38	40
2008 Azl Mariners	Arizona	2	3	0	0	.000	4	0	2	0.00	0
2008 Tacoma	P.C.	1	1⅔	0	0	.000	1	0	0	0.00	0
2008 Seattle a-b	A.L.	47	46⅓	6	5	.545	56	28	46	3.88	15
2009 New York c-d	N.L.	29	29⅓	1	4	.200	19	19	29	5.22	2
2010 Chicago e-f	A.L.	60	54	7	5	.583	65	15	41	2.83	3
2011 Diamondbacks	Arizona	2	2	0	0	.000	0	0	1	0.00	0
2011 Reno	P.C.	2	2	0	0	.000	3	0	1	0.00	0
2011 Arizona g	N.L.	60	58	2	2	.500	61	12	41	2.17	45
Major League Totals 9 Yrs.		457	464⅓	32	26	.552	482	150	381	3.06	151
Division Series											
2011 Arizona	N.L.	3	2⅓	0	1	.000	0	1	3	3.86	0

a On disabled list from April 2 to April 22 and June 12 to July 20, 2008.
b Traded to New York Mets with pitcher Sean Green and outfielder Jeremy Reed for pitcher Aaron Heilman, outfielder Endy Chavez, pitcher Jason Vargas, infielder Mike Carp, outfielder Ezequiel Carrera and pitcher Maikel Cleto, December 10, 2008.
c On disabled list from June 5 to November 7, 2009.
d Filed for free agency, November 7, 2009. Signed with Chicago White Sox, December 11, 2009.
e On disabled list from August 25 to September 9, 2010.
f Filed for free agency, November 1, 2010. Signed with Arizona Diamondbacks, December 7, 2010.
g On disabled list from June 29 to July 26, 2011.

QUALLS, CHAD MICHAEL
Born, Lomita, California, August 17, 1978.
Bats Right. Throws Right. Height, 6 feet, 5 inches. Weight, 220 pounds.

Year	Club	Lea	G	IP	W	L	Pct	SO	BB	H	ERA	SAVES
2001 Michigan	Midwest	26	162	15	6	.714	125	31	149	3.72	0
2002 Round Rock	Texas	29	163	6	13	.316	142	67	174	4.36	0
2003 Round Rock	Texas	28	175⅓	8	11	.421	132	61	174	3.85	0
2004 New Orleans	P.C.	32	106⅔	3	6	.333	72	30	134	5.57	1
2004 Houston	N.L.	25	33	4	0	1.000	24	8	34	3.55	1
2005 Houston	N.L.	77	79⅔	6	4	.600	60	23	73	3.28	0
2006 Houston	N.L.	81	88⅔	7	3	.700	56	28	76	3.76	0
2007 Houston a	N.L.	79	82⅔	6	5	.545	78	25	84	3.05	5
2008 Arizona	N.L.	77	73⅔	4	8	.333	71	18	61	2.81	9
2009 Arizona b	N.L.	51	52	2	2	.500	45	7	53	3.63	24
2010 Arizona	N.L.	43	38	1	4	.200	34	15	61	8.29	12
2010 Tampa Bay c-d-e	A.L.	27	21	2	0	1.000	15	6	24	5.57	0
2011 San Diego f	N.L.	77	74⅓	6	8	.429	43	20	73	3.51	0
Major League Totals 8 Yrs.		537	543	38	34	.528	426	150	539	3.78	51
Division Series											
2004 Houston c-d	N.L.	4	4	0	0	.000	3	1	4	6.75	0
2005 Houston	N.L.	2	3	0	0	.000	1	2	5	6.00	0
2010 Tampa Bay	A.L.	2	1⅔	0	0	.000	0	0	4	10.80	0
Division Series Totals		8	8⅔	0	0	.000	4	3	13	7.27	0
Championship Series											
2004 Houston	N.L.	2	4	0	1	.000	4	2	8	11.25	0
2005 Houston	N.L.	4	4⅔	1	0	1.000	4	0	0	0.00	0
Championship Series Totals		6	8⅔	1	1	.500	8	2	8	5.19	0
World Series Record											
2005 Houston	N.L.	3	5⅓	0	0	.000	5	3	3	1.69	0

a Traded to Arizona Diamondbacks with pitcher Juan Gutierrez and outfielder Chris Burke for pitcher Jose Valverde, December 14, 2007.
b On disabled list from August 31 to November 20, 2009.

c Traded to Tampa Bay Rays for player to be named later, July 31, 2010.
d Arizona Diamondbacks received pitcher Matt Gorgen to complete trade, September 9, 2010.
e Filed for free agency, November 1, 2010. Signed with San Diego Padres, January 19, 2011.
f Filed for free agency, October 31, 2011.

RAMIREZ, RAMON SANTO
Born, Puerto Plata, Dominican Republic, August 31, 1981.
Bats Right. Throws Right. Height, 5 feet, 11 inches. Weight, 190 pounds.

Year	Club	Lea	G	IP	W	L	Pct	SO	BB	H	ERA	SAVES
2002 Hiroshima a-b	...	Japan Cent.	2	3	0	0	.000	3	2	3	3.00	0
2003 Tampa	....	Fla.St.	14	74⅓	2	8	.200	70	20	88	5.21	0
2003 Trenton	....	Eastern	4	21⅓	1	1	.500	21	8	18	1.69	0
2003 Columbus c	....	Int.	2	6	0	1	.000	5	1	5	4.50	0
2004 Trenton	....	Eastern	18	114	4	6	.400	128	32	116	4.66	0
2004 Columbus	....	Int.	4	18	0	3	.000	17	8	25	8.50	0
2005 Columbus	....	Int.	6	27	1	3	.250	26	9	32	5.33	0
2005 Trenton	....	Eastern	15	89	6	5	.545	82	35	79	3.84	0
2005 Tulsa d	....	Texas	9	25⅓	2	1	.667	23	8	27	5.33	0
2006 Colorado Springs	....	P.C.	1	1	0	0	.000	1	0	0	0.00	0
2006 Colorado	....	N.L.	61	67⅔	4	3	.571	61	27	58	3.46	0
2007 Colorado Springs	....	P.C.	25	27⅔	4	0	1.000	35	16	18	2.28	0
2007 Colorado e	....	N.L.	22	17⅓	2	2	.500	15	6	21	8.31	0
2008 Kansas City f-g	....	A.L.	71	71⅔	3	2	.600	70	31	57	2.64	1
2009 Boston	....	A.L.	70	69⅔	7	4	.636	52	32	61	2.84	0
2010 Boston	....	A.L.	44	42⅓	0	3	.000	31	16	39	4.46	2
2010 San Francisco h	....	N.L.	25	27	1	0	1.000	15	11	13	0.67	1
2011 San Francisco i	....	N.L.	66	68⅔	3	3	.500	66	26	54	2.62	4
Major League Totals	....	6 Yrs.	359	364⅓	20	17	.541	310	149	303	3.16	8
Division Series												
2009 Boston	....	A.L.	1	0	0	0	.000	0	1	1	INF	0
2010 San Francisco	....	N.L.	1	2	0	1	.000	1	0	1	4.50	0
Division Series Totals	....		2	2	0	1	.000	1	1	2	13.50	0
Championship Series												
2010 San Francisco	....	N.L.	2	1	0	0	.000	0	1	3	27.00	0
World Series Record												
2010 San Francisco	....	N.L.	2	1	0	0	.000	1	1	1	18.00	0

a Played for Texas Rangers in the Dominican Summer League as an infielder 1997. Did not play 1998 through 2001.
b Released by Texas Rangers, June 4, 1998. Signed with Hiroshima (Japan) 2002.
c Signed with New York Yankees organization, March 5, 2003.
d Traded to Colorado Rockies with pitcher Eduardo Sierra for pitcher Shawn Chacon, July 28, 2005.
e On disabled list from April 18 to May 15 and September 8 to October 31, 2007.
f Traded to Kansas City Royals for player to be named later, March 26, 2008. Colorado Rockies received pitcher Jorge De La Rosa to complete trade, April 30, 2008.
g Traded to Boston Red Sox for outfielder Coco Crisp, November 19, 2008.
h Traded to San Francisco Giants for pitcher Daniel Turpen, July 31, 2010.
i Traded to New York Mets with outfielder Andres Torres for outfielder Angel Pagan, December 7, 2011.

RAMOS, CESAR
Born, Los Angeles, California, June 22, 1984.
Bats Left. Throws Left. Height, 6 feet, 2 inches. Weight, 205 pounds.

Year	Club	Lea	G	IP	W	L	Pct	SO	BB	H	ERA	SAVES
2005 Eugene	....	Northwest	6	20⅔	0	1	.000	13	7	27	6.53	0
2005 Fort Wayne	....	Midwest	7	38⅔	3	2	.600	32	7	42	4.19	0
2006 Lake Elsinore	....	Calif.	26	141	7	8	.467	70	44	161	3.70	0
2007 San Antonio	....	Texas	27	163⅔	13	9	.591	90	43	153	3.41	0
2008 Portland	....	P.C.	28	149⅔	9	11	.450	105	57	183	5.29	0
2009 Padres	....	Arizona	4	8	0	1	.000	8	0	8	2.25	0
2009 Lake Elsinore	....	Calif.	2	9	1	0	1.000	6	5	9	1.00	0
2009 Portland	....	P.C.	15	76⅔	5	6	.455	45	31	84	3.99	0
2009 San Diego	....	N.L.	5	14⅔	0	1	.000	10	4	19	3.07	0
2010 Portland	....	P.C.	30	96	6	7	.462	63	43	90	3.28	0
2010 San Diego a	....	N.L.	14	8⅓	0	1	.000	9	4	18	11.88	0
2011 Durham	....	Int.	4	4	2	0	1.000	1	2	5	4.50	0
2011 Tampa Bay	....	A.L.	59	43⅔	0	1	.000	31	25	36	3.92	0
Major League Totals	....	3 Yrs.	78	66⅔	0	3	.000	50	33	73	4.72	0

a Traded to Tampa Bay Rays with pitcher Adam Russell, pitcher Brandon Gomes and infielder Cole Figueroa for infielder Jason Bartlett and player to be named later, December 17, 2010. Tampa Bay Rays sent cash to complete trade, May 24, 2011.

RAUCH, JON ERICH

Born, Louisville, Kentucky, September 27, 1978.
Bats Right. Throws Right. Height, 6 feet, 11 inches. Weight, 290 pounds.

Year	Club	Lea	G	IP	W	L	Pct	SO	BB	H	ERA	SAVES
1999	Bristol	Appal.	14	56²/₃	4	4	.500	66	16	65	4.45	2
1999	Winston-Salem	Carolina	1	6	0	0	.000	7	3	4	3.00	0
2000	Winston-Salem	Carolina	18	110	11	3	.786	124	33	102	2.86	0
2000	Birmingham	Southern	8	56	5	1	.833	63	16	36	2.25	0
2001	Charlotte	Int.	6	28	1	3	.250	27	7	28	5.79	0
2002	Chicago	A.L.	8	28²/₃	2	1	.667	19	14	28	6.59	0
2002	Charlotte	Int.	19	109¹/₃	7	8	.467	97	42	91	4.28	0
2003	Charlotte	Int.	24	124²/₃	7	1	.875	94	35	121	4.11	0
2004	Charlotte	Int.	14	72¹/₃	6	3	.667	61	25	57	3.11	0
2004	Chicago	A.L.	2	8²/₃	1	1	.500	4	4	16	6.23	0
2004	Edmonton	P.C.	3	18	1	1	.500	13	2	17	4.50	0
2004	Montreal a-b	N.L.	9	23¹/₃	3	0	1.000	18	7	14	1.54	0
2005	New Orleans	P.C.	7	21¹/₃	1	1	.500	25	2	19	2.53	0
2005	Washington c	N.L.	15	30	2	4	.333	23	11	24	3.60	0
2006	Washington	N.L.	85	91¹/₃	4	5	.444	86	36	78	3.35	2
2007	Washington	N.L.	*88	87¹/₃	8	4	.667	71	21	75	3.61	4
2008	Washington-Arizona d	N.L.	74	71²/₃	4	8	.333	66	16	69	4.14	18
2009	Arizona	N.L.	58	54¹/₃	2	2	.500	35	17	57	4.14	2
2009	Minnesota e	A.L.	17	15²/₃	5	1	.833	14	6	13	1.72	0
2010	Minnesota f	A.L.	59	57²/₃	3	1	.750	46	14	61	3.12	21
2011	Toronto g-h	A.L.	53	52	5	4	.556	36	14	56	4.85	11
Major League Totals	9 Yrs.		468	520²/₃	39	31	.557	418	160	491	3.82	58
Division Series												
2009	Minnesota	A.L.	3	1¹/₃	0	0	.000	0	2	1	6.75	0
2010	Minnesota	A.L.	2	1²/₃	0	0	.000	1	0	0	0.00	0
Division Series Totals			5	3	0	0	.000	1	2	1	3.00	0

a Traded to Montreal Expos with pitcher Gary Majewski for outfielder Carl Everett, July 18, 2004.
b On disabled list from August 14 to September 14, 2004.
c On disabled list from May 26 to September 6, 2005.
d Traded to Arizona Diamondbacks for infielder Emilio Bonifacio, July 22, 2008.
e Traded to Minnesota Twins for player to be named later, August 28, 2009. Arizona Diamondbacks received pitcher Kevin Mulvey to complete trade, September 1, 2009.
f Filed for free agency, November 1, 2010. Signed with Toronto Blue Jays, January 17, 2011.
g On disabled list from September 5 to September 29 and August 16 to September 1, 2011.
h Filed for free agency, October 31, 2011. Signed with New York Mets, December 14, 2011.

RESOP, CHRISTOPHER PAUL (CHRIS)

Born, Naples, Florida, November 4, 1982.
Bats Right. Throws Right. Height, 6 feet, 3 inches. Weight, 225 pounds.

Year	Club	Lea	G	IP	W	L	Pct	SO	BB	H	ERA	SAVES
2003	Greensboro	So.Atl.	11	12²/₃	0	1	.000	15	5	11	4.97	0
2004	Greensboro	So.Atl.	42	42²/₃	3	1	.750	71	8	28	2.11	13
2005	Carolina	Southern	43	49	3	2	.600	56	16	47	2.57	24
2005	Florida	N.L.	15	17	2	0	1.000	15	9	22	8.47	0
2006	Albuquerque	P.C.	40	49²/₃	4	0	1.000	43	15	49	3.81	2
2006	Florida a	N.L.	22	21¹/₃	1	2	.333	10	16	26	3.38	0
2007	Salt Lake	P.C.	27	45¹/₃	1	3	.250	39	16	50	4.57	0
2007	Los Angeles b-c	A.L.	4	4¹/₃	0	0	.000	2	1	4	4.15	0
2008	Atlanta	N.L.	16	18¹/₃	0	1	.000	13	10	16	5.89	0
2008	Richmond d	Int.	9	18	2	0	1.000	22	12	14	1.50	0
2009	Hanshin	Japan Pac.	8	21¹/₃	0	2	.000	6	7	29	6.75	0
2010	Mississippi	Southern	2	4¹/₃	0	0	.000	2	1	5	4.15	0
2010	Gwinnett	Int.	15	82	6	3	.667	91	32	53	2.09	0
2010	Atlanta-Pittsburgh e-f	N.L.	23	21	0	0	.000	26	13	15	3.86	0
2011	Pittsburgh	N.L.	76	69²/₃	5	4	.556	79	30	73	4.39	1
Major League Totals	6 Yrs.		156	151²/₃	8	7	.533	145	79	156	4.81	1

a Traded to Los Angeles Angels for pitcher Kevin Gregg, November 20, 2006.
b On disabled list from July 9 to October 25, 2007.
c Claimed on waivers by Atlanta Braves, October 25, 2007.
d Released by Atlanta Braves, July 24, 2008. Signed with Atlanta Braves organization, February 17, 2010.
e On disabled list from June 16 to August 5, 2010.
f Claimed on waivers by Pittsburgh Pirates, August 4, 2010.

REYES, JOSEPH ALBERT (JO-JO)
Born, West Covina, California, November 20, 1984.
Bats Left. Throws Left. Height, 6 feet, 2 inches. Weight, 230 pounds.

Year	Club	Lea	G	IP	W	L	Pct	SO	BB	H	ERA	SAVES
2003 Braves	Gulf Coast	11	45²/₃	5	3	.625	55	14	34	2.56	0
2004 Rome	So.Atl.	15	74	2	4	.333	71	25	84	5.35	0
2005 Braves	Gulf Coast	3	5¹/₃	0	1	.000	6	1	6	1.69	0
2005 Danville	Appal.	9	43¹/₃	3	0	1.000	27	6	37	3.53	0
2006 Rome	So.Atl.	13	75¹/₃	8	1	.889	84	25	62	2.99	0
2006 Myrtle Beach	Carolina	14	65²/₃	4	4	.500	58	36	52	4.11	0
2007 Mississippi	Southern	13	73¹/₃	8	1	.889	71	35	63	3.56	0
2007 Richmond	Int.	6	36	4	0	1.000	39	12	25	1.00	0
2007 Atlanta	N.L.	11	50²/₃	2	2	.500	27	30	55	6.22	0
2008 Richmond	Int.	8	39	1	1	.500	38	16	31	2.31	0
2008 Atlanta	N.L.	23	113	3	11	.214	78	52	134	5.81	0
2009 Atlanta	N.L.	6	27	0	2	.000	21	13	27	7.00	0
2009 Gwinnett a	Int.	15	66	4	2	.667	32	24	68	2.86	0
2010 Atlanta	N.L.	1	3¹/₃	0	0	.000	2	3	10	24.30	0
2010 Gwinnett	Int.	12	47¹/₃	1	5	.167	50	15	57	5.70	0
2010 New Hampshire b-c	Eastern	2	14	1	1	.500	10	4	7	2.57	0
2011 Toronto-Baltimore d-e	A.L.	29	140²/₃	7	11	.389	87	48	176	5.57	0
Major League Totals	5 Yrs.	70	334²/₃	12	26	.316	215	146	402	6.05	0

a On disabled list from May 21 to July 12, 2009.
b On disabled list from April 13 to May 15, 2010.
c Traded to Toronto Blue Jays with infielder Yunel Escobar for infielder Alex Gonzalez, pitcher Tim Collins and infielder Tyler Pastornicky, July 14, 2010.
d Claimed on waivers by Baltimore Orioles, August 2, 2011.
e Not offered contract, December 12, 2011. Signed with Pittsburgh Pirates organization, January 4, 2012.

REYNOLDS, MATTHEW PAUL (MATT)
Born, Knoxville, Tennessee, October 2, 1984.
Bats Left. Throws Left. Height, 6 feet, 5 inches. Weight, 240 pounds.

Year	Club	Lea	G	IP	W	L	Pct	SO	BB	H	ERA	SAVES
2007 Tri-City	Northwest	20	35	1	4	.200	27	4	37	3.60	0
2008 Asheville	So.Atl.	42	57	6	2	.750	53	14	49	2.53	2
2009 Modesto	Calif.	39	49	5	3	.625	58	8	32	1.29	3
2009 Tulsa	Texas	21	25²/₃	1	2	.333	29	9	23	4.21	1
2010 Colorado Springs	P.C.	50	55	1	3	.250	67	16	49	2.62	7
2010 Colorado	N.L.	21	18	1	0	1.000	17	5	10	2.00	0
2011 Colorado	N.L.	73	50²/₃	1	2	.333	50	18	48	4.09	0
Major League Totals	2 Yrs.	94	68²/₃	2	2	.500	67	23	58	3.54	0

RHODES, ARTHUR LEE
Born, Waco, Texas, October 24, 1969.
Bats Left. Throws Left. Height, 6 feet, 2 inches. Weight, 210 pounds.

Year	Club	Lea	G	IP	W	L	Pct	SO	BB	H	ERA	SAVES
1988 Bluefield	Appal.	11	35¹/₃	3	4	.429	44	15	29	3.31	0
1989 Erie	N.Y.-Penn.	5	31	2	0	1.000	45	10	13	1.16	0
1989 Frederick	Carolina	7	24¹/₃	2	2	.500	28	19	19	5.18	0
1990 Frederick	Carolina	13	80²/₃	4	6	.400	103	21	62	2.12	0
1990 Hagerstown	Eastern	12	72²/₃	3	4	.429	60	39	62	3.73	0
1991 Hagerstown	Eastern	19	106²/₃	7	4	.636	115	47	73	2.70	0
1991 Baltimore	A.L.	8	36	0	3	.000	23	23	47	8.00	0
1992 Rochester	Int.	17	101²/₃	6	6	.500	115	46	84	3.72	0
1992 Baltimore	A.L.	15	94¹/₃	7	5	.583	77	38	87	3.63	0
1993 Rochester	Int.	6	26²/₃	1	1	.500	33	15	26	4.05	0
1993 Baltimore	A.L.	17	85²/₃	5	6	.455	49	49	91	6.51	0
1994 Frederick	Carolina	1	5	0	0	.000	7	0	3	0.00	0
1994 Baltimore	A.L.	10	52²/₃	3	5	.375	47	30	51	5.81	0
1994 Rochester	Int.	15	90¹/₃	7	5	.583	86	34	70	2.79	0
1995 Rochester	Int.	4	30	2	1	.667	33	8	27	2.70	0
1995 Baltimore	A.L.	19	75¹/₃	2	5	.286	77	48	68	6.21	0
1996 Baltimore	A.L.	28	53	9	1	.900	62	23	48	4.08	1
1997 Baltimore	A.L.	53	95¹/₃	10	3	.769	102	26	75	3.02	1
1998 Rochester	Int.	1	2	0	0	.000	1	1	3	4.50	0
1998 Baltimore a	A.L.	45	77	4	4	.500	83	34	65	3.51	4
1999 Baltimore b	A.L.	43	53	3	4	.429	59	45	43	5.43	3
2000 Seattle	A.L.	72	69¹/₃	5	8	.385	77	29	51	4.28	0
2001 Seattle	A.L.	71	68	8	0	1.000	83	12	46	1.72	3

Year	Club	Lea	G	IP	W	L	Pct	SO	BB	H	ERA	SAVES
2002 Seattle	A.L.	66	69²/₃	10	4	.714	81	13	45	2.33	2
2003 Seattle c.............	A.L.	67	54	3	3	.500	48	18	53	4.17	3
2004 Sacramento	P.C.	2	2	0	0	.000	3	1	0	0.00	0
2004 Oakland d-e-f	A.L.	37	38²/₃	3	3	.500	34	21	46	5.12	9
2005 Akron	Eastern	1	1	0	0	.000	0	0	0	0.00	0
2005 Cleveland g	A.L.	47	43¹/₃	3	1	.750	43	12	33	2.08	0
2006 Philadelphia h	N.L.	55	45²/₃	0	5	.000	48	30	47	5.32	4
2007 Seattle i-j	A.L.					INJURED—Did Not Play					
2008 West Tenn	Southern	1	0¹/₃	0	1	.000	1	1	2	27.00	0
2008 Seattle	A.L.	36	22	2	1	.667	26	13	17	2.86	1
2008 Florida k-l.............	N.L.	25	13¹/₃	2	0	1.000	14	3	11	0.68	1
2009 Cincinnati.............	N.L.	66	53¹/₃	1	1	.500	48	20	37	2.53	0
2010 Cincinnati m...........	N.L.	69	55	4	4	.500	50	18	38	2.29	0
2011 Texas	A.L.	32	24¹/₃	3	3	.500	15	8	28	4.81	1
2011 St. Louis n-o	N.L.	19	8²/₃	0	1	.000	6	3	6	4.15	0
Major League Totals	20 Yrs.	900	1187²/₃	87	70	.554	1152	516	1033	4.08	33
Division Series											
1996 Baltimore	A.L.	2	1	0	0	.000	1	1	1	9.00	0
1997 Baltimore	A.L.	1	2¹/₃	0	0	.000	4	0	0	0.00	0
2000 Seattle	A.L.	3	2²/₃	0	0	.000	2	2	0	0.00	0
2001 Seattle	A.L.	3	2²/₃	0	0	.000	1	0	1	0.00	0
2010 Cincinnati..............	N.L.	1	0¹/₃	0	0	.000	1	0	0	0.00	0
2011 St. Louis..............	N.L.	3	1	0	0	.000	2	0	0	0.00	0
Division Series Totals		13	10	0	0	.000	11	3	2	0.90	0
Championship Series											
1996 Baltimore	A.L.	3	2	0	0	.000	2	0	2	0.00	0
1997 Baltimore	A.L.	2	2¹/₃	0	0	.000	2	3	2	0.00	0
2000 Seattle	A.L.	4	2	0	0	.000	5	4	8	31.50	0
2001 Seattle	A.L.	2	2	0	0	.000	2	0	2	4.50	0
2011 St. Louis..............	N.L.	2	0²/₃	0	0	.000	1	1	0	0.00	0
Championship Series Totals		13	9	0	1	.000	12	8	14	8.00	0
World Series Record											
2011 St. Louis..............	N.L.	3	1	0	0	.000	0	0	0	0.00	0

a On disabled list from July 5 to August 17, 1998.
b Filed for free agency, November 1, 1999. Signed with Seattle Mariners, December 21, 1999.
c Filed for free agency, October 27, 2003. Signed with Oakland Athletics, December 22, 2003.
d On disabled list from June 28 to August 18, 2004.
e Traded to Pittsburgh Pirates with pitcher Mark Redman for catcher Jason Kendall and cash, November 25, 2004.
f Traded to Cleveland Indians for outfielder Matt Lawton, December 11, 2004.
g On disabled list from August 12 to September 2, 2005.
h Traded to Philadelphia Phillies for outfielder Jason Michaels, January 27, 2006.
i Filed for free agency, October 28, 2006. Signed with Seattle Mariners, January 25, 2007.
j On disabled list from April 2 to October 24, 2007.
k Traded to Florida Marlins for pitcher Gaby Hernandez, July 31, 2008.
l Filed for free agency, November 1, 2008. Signed with Cincinnati Reds, December 12, 2008.
m Filed for free agency, November 1, 2010. Signed with Texas Rangers, January 3, 2011.
n Released by Texas Rangers, August 8, 2011. Signed with St. Louis Cardinals, August 12, 2011.
o Filed for free agency, October 30, 2011.

RICHARD, CLAYTON COLBY

Born, Lafayette, Indiana, September 12, 1983.
Bats Left. Throws Left. Height, 6 feet, 5 inches. Weight, 240 pounds.

Year	Club	Lea	G	IP	W	L	Pct	SO	BB	H	ERA	SAVES
2005 Great Falls	Pioneer	10	41	2	1	.667	39	12	37	2.85	0
2005 Kannapolis..........	So.Atl.	3	10¹/₃	0	1	.000	8	1	14	5.23	0
2006 Winston-Salem	Carolina	4	23²/₃	1	3	.250	12	6	29	4.56	0
2006 Kannapolis..........	So.Atl.	18	95²/₃	6	6	.500	54	28	117	3.67	0
2007 Winston-Salem	Carolina	28	161¹/₃	8	12	.400	99	59	159	3.63	0
2008 Birmingham	Southern	13	83²/₃	6	6	.500	53	16	66	2.47	0
2008 Charlotte	Int.	7	44	6	0	1.000	33	4	33	2.45	0
2008 Chicago a.............	A.L.	13	47²/₃	2	5	.286	29	13	61	6.04	0
2009 Chicago	A.L.	26	89	4	3	.571	66	37	94	4.65	0
2009 San Diego b	N.L.	12	64	5	2	.714	48	34	60	4.08	0
2010 San Diego	N.L.	33	201²/₃	14	9	.609	153	78	206	3.75	0
2011 San Diego c	N.L.	18	99²/₃	5	9	.357	53	38	104	3.88	0
Major League Totals	4 Yrs.	102	502	30	28	.517	349	200	525	4.20	0
Division Series											
2008 Chicago	A.L.	2	6¹/₃	0	0	.000	6	3	5	1.42	0

a On disabled list from March 22 to May 29, 2008.
b Traded to San Diego Padres with pitcher Aaron Poreda, pitcher Adam Russell and pitcher Dexter Carter for pitcher Jake Peavy, July 31, 2009.
c On disabled list from July 5 to October 28, 2011.

RIVERA, MARIANO
Born, Panama City, Panama, November 29, 1969.
Bats Right. Throws Right. Height, 6 feet, 2 inches. Weight, 195 pounds.

Year Club	Lea	G	IP	W	L	Pct	SO	BB	H	ERA	SAVES
1990 Yankees . . . . Gulf Coast		22	52	5	1	.833	58	7	17	0.17	1
1991 Greensboro . . . . So. Atl.		29	114⅔	4	9	.308	123	36	103	2.75	0
1992 Ft. Lauderdale . . . . . . Fla. St.		10	59⅓	5	3	.625	42	5	40	2.28	0
1993 Yankees . . . . Gulf Coast		2	4	0	1	.000	6	1	2	2.25	0
1993 Greensboro . . . . So. Atl.		10	39⅓	1	0	1.000	32	15	31	2.06	0
1994 Tampa . . . . Fla. St.		7	36⅔	3	0	1.000	27	12	34	2.21	0
1994 Albany . . . . Eastern		9	63⅓	3	0	1.000	39	8	58	2.27	0
1994 Columbus. . . . . .Int.		6	31	4	2	.667	23	10	34	5.81	0
1995 Columbus. . . . . .Int.		7	30	2	2	.500	30	3	25	2.10	0
1995 New York . . . . A.L.		19	67	5	3	.625	51	30	71	5.51	0
1996 New York . . . . A.L.		61	107⅔	8	3	.727	130	34	73	2.09	5
1997 New York . . . . A.L.		66	71⅓	6	4	.600	68	20	65	1.88	43
1998 New York a . . . . A.L.		54	61⅓	3	0	1.000	36	17	48	1.91	36
1999 New York . . . . A.L.		66	69	4	3	.571	52	18	43	1.83	*45
2000 New York . . . . A.L.		66	75⅔	7	4	.636	58	25	58	2.85	36
2001 New York . . . . A.L.		71	80⅔	4	6	.400	83	12	61	2.34	*50
2002 Yankees . . . . Gulf Coast		1	2	0	0	.000	2	1	2	0.00	0
2002 New York b. . . . . A.L.		45	46	1	4	.200	41	11	35	2.74	28
2003 New York c. . . . . A.L.		64	70⅔	5	2	.714	63	10	61	1.66	40
2004 New York . . . . A.L.		74	78⅔	4	2	.667	66	20	65	1.94	*53
2005 New York . . . . A.L.		71	78⅓	7	4	.636	80	18	50	1.38	43
2006 New York . . . . A.L.		63	75	5	5	.500	55	11	61	1.80	34
2007 New York d. . . . . A.L.		67	71⅓	3	4	.429	74	12	68	3.15	30
2008 New York . . . . A.L.		64	70⅔	6	5	.545	77	6	41	1.40	39
2009 New York . . . . A.L.		66	66⅓	3	3	.500	72	12	48	1.76	44
2010 New York e. . . . . A.L.		61	60	3	3	.500	45	11	39	1.80	33
2011 New York . . . . A.L.		64	61⅓	1	2	.333	60	8	47	1.91	44
Major League Totals . . . . . . .17 Yrs.		1042	1211⅓	75	57	.568	1111	275	934	2.21	603
Division Series											
1995 New York . . . . A.L.		3	5⅓	1	0	1.000	8	1	3	0.00	0
1996 New York . . . . A.L.		2	4⅔	0	0	.000	1	1	0	0.00	0
1997 New York . . . . A.L.		2	2	0	0	.000	1	0	2	4.50	1
1998 New York . . . . A.L.		3	3⅓	0	0	.000	2	1	1	0.00	2
1999 New York . . . . A.L.		2	3	0	0	.000	3	0	1	0.00	2
2000 New York . . . . A.L.		3	5	0	0	.000	2	0	2	0.00	3
2001 New York . . . . A.L.		3	5	0	0	.000	4	0	4	0.00	2
2002 New York . . . . A.L.		1	1	0	0	.000	0	0	1	0.00	1
2003 New York . . . . A.L.		2	4	0	0	.000	4	0	0	0.00	2
2004 New York . . . . A.L.		4	5⅔	1	0	1.000	2	0	2	0.00	0
2005 New York . . . . A.L.		2	3	0	0	.000	2	1	1	3.00	2
2006 New York . . . . A.L.		1	1	0	0	.000	0	0	1	0.00	0
2007 New York . . . . A.L.		3	4⅔	0	0	.000	6	1	2	0.00	0
2009 New York . . . . A.L.		3	3⅔	0	0	.000	7	1	4	0.00	1
2010 New York . . . . A.L.		3	3⅓	0	0	.000	1	0	2	0.00	2
2011 New York . . . . A.L.		2	1⅓	0	0	.000	1	0	0	0.00	0
Division Series Totals		39	56	2	0	1.000	44	6	26	0.32	18
Championship Series											
1996 New York . . . . A.L.		2	4	1	0	1.000	5	1	6	0.00	0
1998 New York . . . . A.L.		4	5⅔	0	0	.000	5	1	0	0.00	1
1999 New York . . . . A.L.		3	4⅔	1	0	1.000	3	0	5	0.00	2
2000 New York . . . . A.L.		3	4⅔	0	0	.000	1	0	4	1.93	1
2001 New York . . . . A.L.		4	4⅔	1	0	1.000	3	1	2	1.93	2
2003 New York . . . . A.L.		4	8	1	0	1.000	6	0	5	1.13	2
2004 New York . . . . A.L.		5	7	0	0	.000	6	2	6	1.29	2
2009 New York . . . . A.L.		5	7	0	0	.000	4	2	3	1.29	2
2010 New York . . . . A.L.		3	3	0	0	.000	1	0	2	0.00	1
Championship Series Totals		33	48⅔	4	0	1.000	34	7	33	0.92	13
World Series Record											
1996 New York . . . . A.L.		4	5⅔	0	0	.000	4	3	4	1.59	0
1998 New York . . . . A.L.		3	4⅓	0	0	.000	4	0	5	0.00	3
1999 New York . . . . A.L.		3	4⅔	1	0	1.000	3	1	3	0.00	2

Year Club	Lea	G	IP	W	L	Pct	SO	BB	H	ERA	SAVES
2000 New York	A.L.	4	6	0	0	.000	7	1	4	3.00	2
2001 New York	A.L.	4	6$\frac{1}{3}$	1	1	.500	7	1	6	1.42	0
2003 New York	A.L.	2	4	0	0	.000	4	0	2	0.00	1
2009 New York	A.L.	4	5$\frac{1}{3}$	0	0	.000	3	2	3	0.00	2
World Series Totals		24	36$\frac{1}{3}$	2	1	.667	32	8	27	0.99	11

a On disabled list from April 6 to April 24, 1998.
b On disabled list from June 9 to June 25 and July 21 to August 8 and August 18 to September 20, 2002.
c On disabled list from March 25 to April 29, 2003.
d Filed for free agency, October 30, 2007, re-signed with New York Yankees, December 17, 2007.
e Filed for free agency, November 1, 2010, re-signed with New York Yankees, December 14, 2010.

ROBERTSON, DAVID

Born, Birmingham, Alabama, April 9, 1985.
Bats Right. Throws Right. Height, 5 feet, 11 inches. Weight, 190 pounds.

Year Club	Lea	G	IP	W	L	Pct	SO	BB	H	ERA	SAVES
2007 Trenton............	Eastern	2	4	0	0	.000	9	2	2	2.25	0
2007 Tampa	Fla.St.	18	33$\frac{1}{3}$	3	1	.750	37	15	18	1.08	1
2007 Charleston	So.Atl.	24	47	5	2	.714	67	15	25	0.77	3
2008 Trenton............	Eastern	9	18$\frac{2}{3}$	0	0	.000	26	6	8	0.96	2
2008 Scranton/WB ....Int.		21	35	4	0	1.000	51	17	20	2.06	1
2008 New York	A.L.	25	30$\frac{1}{3}$	4	0	1.000	36	15	29	5.34	0
2009 Scranton/WB ....Int.		8	14$\frac{2}{3}$	0	3	.000	25	6	10	1.84	2
2009 New York	A.L.	45	43$\frac{2}{3}$	2	1	.667	63	23	36	3.30	1
2010 New York	A.L.	64	61$\frac{1}{3}$	4	5	.444	71	33	59	3.82	1
2011 New York	A.L.	70	66$\frac{2}{3}$	4	0	1.000	100	35	40	1.08	1
Major League Totals ....4 Yrs.		204	202	14	6	.700	270	106	164	3.03	3
Division Series											
2009 New York	A.L.	1	1	1	0	1.000	0	0	1	0.00	0
2010 New York	A.L.	2	0$\frac{2}{3}$	0	0	.000	1	1	0	0.00	0
2011 New York	A.L.	2	2	0	0	.000	2	0	0	0.00	0
Division Series Totals		5	3$\frac{2}{3}$	1	0	1.000	3	1	1	0.00	0
Championship Series											
2009 New York	A.L.	2	2	1	0	1.000	1	2	1	0.00	0
2010 New York	A.L.	4	2$\frac{2}{3}$	0	0	.000	4	1	8	20.25	0
Championship Series Totals		6	4$\frac{2}{3}$	1	0	1.000	5	3	9	11.57	0
World Series Record											
2009 New York	A.L.	2	2$\frac{1}{3}$	0	0	.000	2	1	2	0.00	0

RODNEY, FERNANDO

Born, Samana, Dominican Republic, March 17, 1977.
Bats Right. Throws Right. Height, 5 feet, 11 inches. Weight, 220 pounds.

Year Club	Lea	G	IP	W	L	Pct	SO	BB	H	ERA	SAVES
1998 Detroit	Dominican	11	32	1	3	.250	37	19	25	3.38	1
1999 Lakeland............	Fla.St.	4	6$\frac{1}{3}$	1	0	1.000	5	1	7	1.42	2
1999 Tigers...........	Gulf Coast	22	30	3	3	.500	39	21	20	2.40	9
2000 West Michigan.....	Midwest	22	82$\frac{2}{3}$	6	4	.600	56	35	74	2.94	0
2001 Erie...............	Eastern	4	6$\frac{1}{3}$	0	0	.000	8	3	7	4.26	1
2001 Lakeland............	Fla.St.	16	55$\frac{1}{3}$	4	2	.667	44	19	53	3.42	0
2001 Tigers............	Gulf Coast	1	1	0	0	.000	1	1	0	0.00	0
2002 Erie............	Eastern	21	20$\frac{1}{3}$	1	0	1.000	18	5	14	1.33	11
2002 Detroit	A.L.	20	18	1	3	.250	10	10	25	6.00	0
2002 Toledo	Int.	20	22$\frac{1}{3}$	1	1	.500	25	9	13	0.81	4
2003 Toledo	Int.	38	40$\frac{2}{3}$	1	1	.500	58	13	22	1.33	23
2003 Detroit	A.L.	27	29$\frac{2}{3}$	1	3	.250	33	17	35	6.07	3
2004 Detroit a.............	A.L.			INJURED—Did Not Play							
2005 Toledo	Int.	3	3	0	0	.000	4	1	2	3.00	0
2005 Detroit b.............	A.L.	39	44	2	0	.400	42	17	39	2.86	9
2006 Detroit	A.L.	63	71$\frac{2}{3}$	7	4	.636	65	34	51	3.52	7
2007 Toledo	Int.	4	3	0	0	.000	4	2	4	0.00	0
2007 Detroit c.............	A.L.	48	50$\frac{2}{3}$	2	6	.250	54	21	46	4.26	1
2008 Toledo	Int.	4	5$\frac{1}{3}$	1	0	1.000	8	5	3	6.75	0
2008 Detroit d.............	A.L.	38	40$\frac{1}{3}$	0	6	.000	49	30	34	4.91	13
2009 Detroit e.............	A.L.	73	75$\frac{2}{3}$	2	5	.286	61	41	70	4.40	37
2010 Los Angeles	A.L.	72	68	4	3	.571	53	35	70	4.24	14
2011 Inland Empire.........	Calif.	2	2	0	0	.000	3	1	2	9.00	0
2011 Los Angeles f-g	A.L.	39	32	3	5	.375	26	28	26	4.50	3
Major League Totals ....9 Yrs.		419	430	22	38	.367	393	233	396	4.29	87

Year	Club	Lea	G	IP	W	L	Pct	SO	BB	H	ERA	SAVES
Championship Series												
2006 Detroit		A.L.	3	3⅔	0	0	.000	4	1	1	0.00	0
World Series Record												
2006 Detroit		A.L.	4	4	0	0	.000	5	4	5	4.50	0

a On disabled list from March 26 to October 4, 2004.
b On disabled list from March 29 to June 9, 2005.
c On disabled list from May 21 to June 5 and June 24 to August 4, 2007.
d On disabled list from March 30 to June 16, 2008.
e Filed for free agency, November 5, 2009. Signed with Los Angeles Angels, December 24, 2009.
f On disabled list from June 9 to July 22, 2011.
g Filed for free agency, October 30, 2011. Signed with Tampa Bay Rays, January 4, 2012.

RODRIGUEZ, ANEURY
Born, Higuey, Dominican Republic, December 13, 1987.
Bats Right. Throws Right. Height, 6 feet, 4 inches. Weight, 200 pounds.

Year	Club	Lea	G	IP	W	L	Pct	SO	BB	H	ERA	SAVES
2005 Casper	Pioneer	15	62	3	4	.429	47	26	77	7.55	0
2006 Tri-City	Northwest	15	76	4	4	.500	69	30	78	4.14	0
2007 Asheville	So.Atl.	28	152	9	9	.500	160	48	182	5.15	0
2008 Modesto	Calif.	27	156⅓	9	10	.474	139	40	148	3.74	0
2009 Montgomery a	Southern	27	142	9	11	.450	111	59	122	4.50	0
2010 Durham	Int.	27	113⅔	6	5	.545	94	49	104	3.80	0
2010 Montgomery	Southern	2	10	1	0	1.000	6	2	9	2.70	0
2011 Houston	N.L.	43	85⅓	1	6	.143	64	32	83	5.27	0

a Traded by Colorado Rockies to Tampa Bay Rays for pitcher Jason Hammel, April 4, 2009.

RODRIGUEZ, FERNANDO
Born, El Paso, Texas, June 18, 1984.
Bats Right. Throws Right. Height, 6 feet, 3 inches. Weight, 215 pounds.

Year	Club	Lea	G	IP	W	L	Pct	SO	BB	H	ERA	SAVES
2003 Angels	Arizona	15	25	0	2	.000	27	14	29	6.48	0
2003 Provo	Pioneer	4	6	0	0	.000	9	1	9	1.50	1
2004 Provo	Pioneer	14	58⅔	4	3	.571	54	18	64	4.14	0
2005 Cedar Rapids	Midwest	28	157⅓	8	10	.444	128	49	161	4.18	0
2006 Rancho Cucamonga	Calif.	28	163⅓	11	8	.579	112	49	188	4.57	0
2007 Arkansas	Texas	22	125⅓	8	4	.667	61	46	138	4.52	0
2008 Arkansas	Texas	33	136⅔	7	11	.389	85	62	153	5.53	0
2009 Los Angeles	A.L.	1	0⅔	0	0	.000	1	2	1	27.00	0
2009 Salt Lake	P.C.	23	37	1	1	.500	25	23	44	7.54	0
2009 Arkansas	Texas	26	42⅓	3	1	.750	52	22	20	1.28	4
2010 Salt Lake a	P.C.	31	97⅓	4	6	.400	84	42	134	5.92	0
2011 Oklahoma	P.C.	16	24	2	3	.400	33	11	16	1.50	2
2011 Houston	N.L.	47	52⅓	2	3	.400	57	30	51	3.96	0
Major League Totals	2 Yrs.	48	53	2	3	.400	58	32	52	4.25	0

a Filed for free agency, November 6, 2010. Signed with Houston Astros organization, November 10, 2010.

RODRIGUEZ, FRANCISCO JOSE
Born, Caracas, Venezuela, January 7, 1982.
Bats Right. Throws Right. Height, 6 feet. Weight, 195 pounds.

Year	Club	Lea	G	IP	W	L	Pct	SO	BB	H	ERA	SAVES
1999 Boise	Northwest	1	5	1	0	1.000	6	1	3	5.40	0
1999 Butte	Pioneer	12	51⅔	1	1	.500	69	21	33	3.31	0
2000 Lake Elsinore	California	13	64	4	4	.500	79	32	43	2.81	0
2001 Rancho Cucamonga	California	20	113⅔	5	7	.417	147	55	127	5.38	0
2002 Arkansas	Texas	23	41⅓	3	3	.500	61	15	32	1.96	9
2002 Salt Lake	P.C.	27	42	2	3	.400	59	13	30	2.57	6
2002 Anaheim	A.L.	5	5⅔	0	0	.000	13	2	3	0.00	0
2003 Anaheim	A.L.	59	86	8	3	.727	95	35	50	3.03	2
2004 Anaheim	A.L.	69	84	4	1	.800	123	33	51	1.82	12
2005 Los Angeles a	A.L.	66	67⅓	2	5	.286	91	32	45	2.67	*45
2006 Los Angeles	A.L.	69	73	2	3	.400	98	28	52	1.73	*47
2007 Los Angeles	A.L.	64	67⅓	5	2	.714	90	34	50	2.81	40
2008 Los Angeles b	A.L.	*76	68⅓	2	3	.400	77	34	54	2.24	*62
2009 New York	N.L.	70	68	3	6	.333	73	38	51	3.71	35
2010 New York	N.L.	53	57⅓	4	2	.667	67	21	45	2.20	25
2011 New York-Milwaukee	N.L.	73	71⅔	6	2	.750	79	26	67	2.64	23
Major League Totals	10 Yrs.	604	648⅔	36	27	.571	806	283	468	2.51	291

Year	Club	Lea	G	IP	W	L	Pct	SO	BB	H	ERA	SAVES
	Division Series											
2002 Anaheim.............	A.L.	3	$5^2/3$	2	0	1.000	8	2	2	3.18	0	
2004 Anaheim.............	A.L.	2	$4^2/3$	0	0	.000	5	3	4	3.86	0	
2005 Los Angeles...........	A.L.	3	$3^1/3$	0	0	.000	2	0	5	2.70	2	
2007 Los Angeles...........	A.L.	1	$0^1/3$	0	0	.000	1	1	1	54.00	0	
2008 Los Angeles...........	A.L.	2	$2^1/3$	0	1	.000	2	2	5	7.71	0	
2011 Milwaukee	N.L.	2	2	0	0	.000	4	3	2	0.00	0	
Division Series Totals		13	$18^1/3$	2	3	.400	22	11	19	4.42	2	
	Championship Series											
2002 Anaheim.............	A.L.	4	$4^1/3$	2	0	1.000	7	2	2	0.00	0	
2005 Los Angeles...........	A.L.	2	$2^1/3$	0	0	.000	3	3	2	0.00	1	
2011 Milwaukee	N.L.	3	3	0	0	.000	4	1	3	3.00	0	
Championship Series Totals		9	$9^2/3$	2	0	1.000	14	6	7	0.93	1	
	World Series Record											
2002 Anaheim.............	A.L.	4	$8^2/3$	1	1	.500	13	1	6	2.08	0	

a On disabled list from May 15 to June 1, 2005.
b Filed for free agency, November 3, 2008. Signed with New York Mets, December 10, 2008.

RODRIGUEZ, HENRY ALBERTO
Born, Santa Barbara, Venezuela, February 25, 1987.
Bats Right. Throws Right. Height, 6 feet. Weight, 220 pounds.

Year	Club	Lea	G	IP	W	L	Pct	SO	BB	H	ERA	SAVES
2006 Athletics..........	Arizona	15	$43^2/3$	5	2	.714	59	50	46	7.42	1	
2007 Kane County........	Midwest	20	$99^2/3$	6	8	.429	106	58	75	3.07	0	
2008 Stockton............	Calif.	20	75	2	3	.400	104	40	57	3.96	2	
2008 Midland	Texas	14	41	2	7	.222	43	44	51	7.46	0	
2009 Stockton............	Calif.	3	5	0	0	.000	11	1	3	0.00	0	
2009 Sacramento	P.C.	37	$43^2/3$	2	1	.667	71	38	38	5.77	4	
2009 Oakland	A.L.	3	4	0	0	.000	4	2	4	2.25	0	
2010 Sacramento	P.C.	20	$21^1/3$	0	2	.000	31	9	10	1.69	11	
2010 Oakland a	A.L.	29	$27^2/3$	1	0	1.000	33	13	25	4.55	0	
2011 Harrisburg	Eastern	3	4	0	0	.000	7	0	3	0.00	0	
2011 Syracuse	Int.	6	$8^1/3$	0	0	.000	9	6	5	1.08	0	
2011 Washington b.........	N.L.	59	$65^2/3$	3	3	.500	70	45	54	3.56	2	
Major League Totals	3 Yrs.	91	$97^1/3$	4	3	.571	107	60	83	3.79	2	

a Traded to Washington Nationals with outfielder Corey Brown for outfielder Josh Willingham, December 16, 2010.
b On disabled list from March 28 to April 27, 2011.

RODRIGUEZ, WANDY FULTON
Born, Santiago Rodriguez, Dominican Republic, January 18, 1979.
Bats Both. Throws Left. Height, 5 feet, 11 inches. Weight, 160 pounds.

Year	Club	Lea	G	IP	W	L	Pct	SO	BB	H	ERA	SAVES
2001 Martinsville	Appal.	12	74	4	3	.571	67	20	54	1.58	0	
2002 Lexington...........	So.Atl.	28	$159^1/3$	11	4	.733	137	44	167	3.78	0	
2003 Salem.............	Carolina	20	111	8	7	.533	72	41	102	3.49	0	
2004 Round Rock..........	Texas	26	$142^2/3$	11	6	.647	115	57	159	4.48	0	
2005 Corpus Christi	Texas	1	$3^1/3$	0	0	.000	3	2	3	2.70	0	
2005 Round Rock...........	P.C.	8	$46^1/3$	4	2	.667	48	16	43	3.69	0	
2005 Houston.............	N.L.	25	$128^2/3$	10	10	.500	80	53	135	5.53	0	
2006 Round Rock...........	P.C.	5	26	2	2	.500	13	13	32	6.92	0	
2006 Houston.............	N.L.	30	$135^2/3$	9	10	.474	98	63	154	5.64	0	
2007 Houston.............	N.L.	31	$182^2/3$	9	13	.409	158	62	179	4.58	0	
2008 Corpus Christi	Texas	1	6	0	0	.000	0	1	4	1.50	0	
2008 Houston a	N.L.	25	$137^1/3$	9	7	.563	131	44	136	3.54	0	
2009 Houston.............	N.L.	33	$205^2/3$	14	12	.538	193	63	192	3.02	0	
2010 Houston.............	N.L.	32	195	11	12	.478	178	68	183	3.60	0	
2011 Corpus Christi	Texas	1	4	0	0	.000	2	1	6	2.25	0	
2011 Houston b	N.L.	30	191	11	11	.500	166	69	182	3.49	0	
Major League Totals	7 Yrs.	206	1176	73	75	.493	1004	422	1161	4.07	0	
	Division Series											
2005 Houston.............	N.L.	1	1	0	0	.000	2	0	1	9.00	0	
	World Series Record											
2005 Houston.............	N.L.	2	$3^2/3$	0	1	.000	2	5	4	2.45	0	

a On disabled list from April 20 to May 28, 2008.
b On disabled list from May 23 to June 13, 2011.

ROGERS, ESMIL ANTONIO
Born, Santo Domingo, Dominican Republic, August 14, 1985.
Bats Right. Throws Right. Height, 6 feet, 1 inch. Weight, 190 pounds.

Year	Club	Lea	G	IP	W	L	Pct	SO	BB	H	ERA	SAVES
2006 Casper	Pioneer	15	63⅓	3	6	.333	40	24	78	6.96	0
2007 Asheville	So.Atl.	19	117⅔	7	4	.636	90	42	125	3.75	0
2008 Modesto	Calif.	25	143⅔	9	7	.563	116	45	146	3.95	0
2009 Tulsa	Texas	15	94⅓	8	2	.800	83	19	87	2.48	0
2009 Colorado Springs	P.C.	12	60⅔	3	5	.375	46	35	77	7.42	0
2009 Colorado	N.L.	1	4	0	0	.000	3	2	3	4.50	0
2010 Colorado Springs	P.C.	12	61	3	3	.500	53	19	62	5.75	0
2010 Colorado	N.L.	28	72	2	3	.400	66	26	94	6.13	0
2011 Tulsa	Texas	1	4	0	1	.000	2	1	5	2.25	0
2011 Colorado Springs	P.C.	5	23	1	2	.333	15	5	36	6.26	0
2011 Colorado a	N.L.	18	83	6	6	.500	63	47	110	7.05	0
Major League Totals ....3 Yrs.		47	159	8	9	.471	132	75	207	6.57	0

a On disabled list from May 2 to July 25, 2011.

ROMERO, RICARDO (RICKY)
Born, Los Angeles, California, November 6, 1984.
Bats Right. Throws Left. Height, 6 feet. Weight, 215 pounds.

Year	Club	Lea	G	IP	W	L	Pct	SO	BB	H	ERA	SAVES
2005 Dunedin	Fla.St.	8	30⅔	1	0	1.000	22	7	36	3.82	0
2005 Auburn	N.Y.-Penn.	1	2	0	0	.000	2	1	2	0.00	0
2006 New Hampshire	Eastern	12	67⅓	2	7	.222	41	26	65	5.08	0
2006 Dunedin	Fla.St.	10	58⅓	2	1	.667	61	14	48	2.47	0
2007 New Hampshire	Eastern	18	88⅓	3	6	.333	80	51	98	4.89	0
2007 Dunedin	Fla.St.	1	4⅔	0	0	.000	2	1	4	3.86	0
2008 New Hampshire	Eastern	21	121⅔	5	5	.500	78	55	139	4.96	0
2008 Syracuse	Int.	7	42⅔	3	3	.500	38	20	42	3.38	0
2009 Dunedin	Fla.St.	1	4	0	1	.000	5	1	6	13.50	0
2009 New Hampshire	Eastern	1	5⅓	0	0	.000	4	5	3	1.69	0
2009 Las Vegas	P.C.	1	5	0	0	.000	3	2	8	7.20	0
2009 Toronto a	A.L.	29	178	13	9	.591	141	79	192	4.30	0
2010 Toronto	A.L.	32	210	14	9	.609	174	82	189	3.73	0
2011 Toronto	A.L.	32	225	15	11	.577	178	80	176	2.92	0
Major League Totals ....3 Yrs.		93	613	42	29	.592	493	241	557	3.60	0

a On disabled list from April 20 to May 15, 2009.

ROMO, SERGIO FRANCISCO
Born, Brawley, California, March 4, 1983.
Bats Right. Throws Right. Height, 5 feet, 11 inches. Weight, 190 pounds.

Year	Club	Lea	G	IP	W	L	Pct	SO	BB	H	ERA	SAVES
2005 Salem-Keizer	Northwest	15	68⅔	7	1	.875	65	9	70	2.75	0
2006 Augusta	So.Atl.	31	103⅓	10	2	.833	95	19	78	2.53	4
2007 San Jose	Calif.	41	66⅓	6	2	.750	106	15	35	1.36	9
2008 Connecticut	Eastern	24	27	1	3	.250	30	7	22	4.00	11
2008 Fresno	P.C.	3	6	0	0	.000	7	2	3	0.00	0
2008 San Francisco	N.L.	29	34	3	1	.750	33	8	16	2.12	0
2009 San Jose	Calif.	3	4⅔	0	0	.000	6	2	2	0.00	0
2009 Fresno	P.C.	3	3	0	0	.000	3	0	2	0.00	0
2009 San Francisco a	N.L.	45	34	5	2	.714	41	11	30	3.97	2
2010 San Francisco	N.L.	68	62	5	3	.625	70	14	46	2.18	0
2011 Giants	Arizona	1	1	0	0	.000	3	0	1	0.00	0
2011 San Francisco b	N.L.	65	48	3	1	.750	70	5	29	1.50	1
Major League Totals ....4 Yrs.		207	178	16	7	.696	214	38	121	2.33	3
Division Series											
2010 San Francisco	N.L.	2	0⅔	1	0	1.000	0	0	3	40.50	0
Championship Series											
2010 San Francisco	N.L.	3	2⅓	0	0	.000	3	1	2	0.00	0
World Series Record											
2010 San Francisco	N.L.	1	0⅔	0	0	.000	1	0	1	0.00	0

a On disabled list from March 26 to May 30, 2009.
b On disabled list from August 10 to August 28, 2011.

RUFFIN, CHANCE KRAIG

Born, Philadelphia, Pennsylvania, September 8, 1988.
Bats Right. Throws Right. Height, 6 feet. Weight, 185 pounds.

Year	Club	Lea	G	IP	W	L	Pct	SO	BB	H	ERA	SAVES
2011	Erie...............	Eastern	31	34	3	3	.500	43	16	23	2.12	10
2011	Toledo	Int.	13	14²/₃	0	0	.000	17	6	14	1.84	9
2011	Detroit-Seattle a........	A.L.	15	17²/₃	1	0	1.000	18	9	18	4.08	0

a Sent to Seattle Mariners as player to be named later for pitcher Doug Fister and pitcher David Pauley, August 17, 2011.

RUSSELL, JAMES CLAYTON

Born, Cincinnati, Ohio, January 8, 1986.
Bats Left. Throws Left. Height, 6 feet, 4 inches. Weight, 205 pounds.

Year	Club	Lea	G	IP	W	L	Pct	SO	BB	H	ERA	SAVES
2007	Cubs.............	Arizona	1	2	0	0	.000	2	0	0	0.00	0
2007	Peoria............	Midwest	2	7	0	0	.000	9	4	3	0.00	0
2008	Daytona	Fla.St.	8	41	2	2	.500	24	13	36	3.51	0
2008	Tennessee	Southern	18	86¹/₃	4	8	.333	62	25	111	6.36	0
2009	Iowa.................	P.C.	26	65²/₃	3	3	.500	46	19	71	3.43	0
2009	Tennessee	Southern	11	37	2	3	.400	26	9	45	5.11	0
2010	Iowa.................	P.C.	5	11	0	0	.000	10	4	11	5.73	0
2010	Chicago	N.L.	57	49	1	1	.500	42	11	55	4.96	0
2011	Chicago	N.L.	64	67²/₃	1	6	.143	43	14	76	4.12	0
Major League Totals ....2 Yrs.			121	116²/₃	2	7	.222	85	25	131	4.47	0

RZEPCZYNSKI, MARC WALTER

Born, Yorba Linda, California, August 29, 1985.
Bats Left. Throws Left. Height, 6 feet, 1 inch. Weight, 205 pounds.

Year	Club	Lea	G	IP	W	L	Pct	SO	BB	H	ERA	SAVES
2007	Auburn..........	N.Y.-Penn.	11	45²/₃	5	0	1.000	49	17	33	2.76	0
2008	Lansing	Midwest	22	121	7	6	.538	124	42	100	2.83	0
2009	New Hampshire	Eastern	14	76²/₃	7	5	.583	88	36	80	2.93	0
2009	Las Vegas.............	P.C.	2	11¹/₃	2	0	1.000	16	4	7	0.79	0
2009	Toronto	A.L.	11	61¹/₃	2	4	.333	60	30	51	3.67	0
2010	Las Vegas.............	P.C.	12	67	5	5	.500	61	27	81	6.04	0
2010	Toronto a.............	A.L.	14	63²/₃	4	4	.500	57	30	72	4.95	0
2011	Toronto	A.L.	43	39¹/₃	2	3	.400	33	15	28	2.97	0
2011	St. Louis b............	N.L.	28	22²/₃	0	3	.000	28	11	22	3.97	0
Major League Totals ....3 Yrs.			96	187	8	14	.364	178	86	173	3.99	0
Division Series												
2011	St. Louis.............	N.L.	3	1	0	0	.000	1	0	4	27.00	0
Championship Series												
2011	St. Louis.............	N.L.	5	4²/₃	1	0	1.000	4	1	1	1.93	0
World Series Record												
2011	St. Louis.............	N.L.	4	2²/₃	0	0	.000	4	0	2	0.00	0

a On disabled list from March 31 to May 19, 2010.

b Traded to St. Louis Cardinals with pitcher Edwin Jackson, pitcher Octavio Dotel, outfielder Corey Patterson and cash for outfielder Colby Rasmus, pitcher Trever Miller, pitcher Brian Tallet and pitcher P.J. Walters, July 27, 2011.

SABATHIA, CARSTEN CHARLES (C.C.)

Born, Vallejo, California, July 21, 1980.
Bats Left. Throws Left. Height, 6 feet, 7 inches. Weight, 290 pounds.

Year	Club	Lea	G	IP	W	L	Pct	SO	BB	H	ERA	SAVES
1998	Burlington	Appal.	5	18	1	0	1.000	35	8	20	4.50	0
1999	Kinston............	Carolina	7	32	3	3	.500	29	19	30	5.34	0
1999	Mahoning Valley.....	N.Y.-Penn.	6	19²/₃	0	0	.000	27	12	9	1.83	0
1999	Columbus a.......	So.Atl.	3	16²/₃	2	0	1.000	20	5	8	1.08	0
2000	Kinston............	Carolina	10	56	3	2	.600	69	24	48	3.54	0
2000	Akron............	Eastern	17	90¹/₃	3	7	.300	90	48	75	3.59	0
2001	Cleveland	A.L.	33	180¹/₃	17	5	.773	171	95	149	4.39	0
2002	Cleveland	A.L.	33	210	13	11	.542	149	88	198	4.37	0
2003	Cleveland	A.L.	30	197²/₃	13	9	.591	141	66	190	3.60	0
2004	Cleveland	A.L.	30	188	11	10	.524	139	72	176	4.12	0
2005	Akron............	Eastern	2	9	0	1	.000	9	2	4	1.00	0
2005	Cleveland b	A.L.	31	196²/₃	15	10	.600	161	62	185	4.03	0
2006	Buffalo................	Int.	1	5	1	0	1.000	5	1	6	1.80	0

Year	Club	Lea	G	IP	W	L	Pct	SO	BB	H	ERA	SAVES
2006 Cleveland c...........A.L.		A.L.	28	$192\frac{2}{3}$	12	11	.522	172	44	182	3.22	0
2007 Cleveland d ...........A.L.		A.L.	34	*241	19	7	.731	209	37	238	3.21	0
2008 Cleveland.............A.L.		A.L.	18	$122\frac{1}{3}$	6	8	.429	123	34	117	3.83	0
2008 Milwaukee e-f.........N.L.		N.L.	17	$130\frac{2}{3}$	11	2	.846	128	25	106	1.65	0
2009 New York.............A.L.		A.L.	34	230	*19	8	.704	197	67	197	3.37	0
2010 New York.............A.L.		A.L.	34	$237\frac{2}{3}$	*21	7	.750	197	74	209	3.18	0
2011 New York.............A.L.		A.L.	33	$237\frac{1}{3}$	19	8	.704	230	61	230	3.00	0
Major League Totals ....11 Yrs.			355	$2364\frac{1}{3}$	176	96	.647	2017	725	2177	3.51	0
Division Series												
2001 Cleveland.............A.L.		A.L.	1	6	1	0	1.000	5	5	6	3.00	0
2007 Cleveland.............A.L.		A.L.	1	5	1	0	1.000	5	6	4	5.40	0
2008 Milwaukee............N.L.		N.L.	1	$3\frac{2}{3}$	0	1	.000	5	4	6	12.27	0
2009 New York.............A.L.		A.L.	1	$6\frac{2}{3}$	1	0	1.000	8	0	8	1.35	0
2010 New York.............A.L.		A.L.	1	6	1	0	1.000	5	3	5	4.50	0
2011 New York.............A.L.		A.L.	3	$8\frac{2}{3}$	0	0	.000	11	8	10	6.23	0
Division Series Totals			8	36	4	1	.800	39	26	39	5.00	0
Championship Series												
2007 Cleveland.............A.L.		A.L.	2	$10\frac{1}{3}$	0	2	.000	9	7	.17	10.45	0
2009 New York.............A.L.		A.L.	2	16	2	0	1.000	12	3	9	1.13	0
2010 New York.............A.L.		A.L.	2	10	1	0	1.000	10	4	17	6.30	0
Championship Series Totals			6	$36\frac{1}{3}$	3	2	.600	31	14	43	5.20	0
World Series Record												
2009 New York.............A.L.		A.L.	2	$13\frac{2}{3}$	0	1	.000	12	6	11	3.29	0

a On disabled list from April 1 through June 20, 1999.

b On disabled list from March 25 to April 17, 2005.

c On disabled list from April 3 to May 2, 2006.

d Selected Cy Young Award Winner in American League for 2007.

e Traded to Milwaukee Brewers for outfielder Matt LaPorta, pitcher Zach Jackson, pitcher Rob Bryson and player to be named later, July 7, 2008. Cleveland Indians received outfielder Michael Brantley to complete trade, October 3, 2008.

f Filed for free agency, November 1, 2008. Signed with New York Yankees, December 18, 2008.

SAITO, TAKASHI
Born, Miyagi, Japan, February 14, 1970.
Bats Left. Throws Right. Height, 6 feet, 2 inch. Weight, 215 pounds.

Year	Club	Lea	G	IP	W	L	Pct	SO	BB	H	ERA	SAVES
1992 Yokohama	Japan Cent.		6	16	0	2	.000	21	10	18	8.44	0
1993 Yokohama	Japan Cent.		29	149	8	10	.444	125	61	127	3.81	0
1994 Yokohama	Japan Cent.		28	181	9	12	.429	169	69	175	3.13	0
1995 Yokohama	Japan Cent.		26	162	8	9	.471	132	45	166	3.94	0
1996 Yokohama	Japan Cent.		28	$196\frac{2}{3}$	10	10	.500	206	63	157	3.29	0
1997							INJURED—Did Not Play					
1998 Yokohama	Japan Cent.		34	$143\frac{2}{3}$	13	5	.722	101	23	131	2.94	1
1999 Yokohama	Japan Cent.		26	$184\frac{2}{3}$	14	3	.824	125	31	178	3.95	0
2000 Yokohama	Japan Cent.		19	$115\frac{2}{3}$	6	10	.375	97	36	123	5.52	0
2001 Yokohama	Japan Cent.		50	$64\frac{2}{3}$	7	1	.857	60	14	51	1.67	27
2002 Yokohama	Japan Cent.		39	$47\frac{2}{3}$	1	2	.333	46	15	37	2.45	20
2003 Yokohama	Japan Cent.		17	$103\frac{1}{3}$	6	7	.462	72	22	103	4.18	0
2004 Yokohama	Japan Cent.		16	44	2	5	.286	37	13	64	7.71	0
2005 Yokohama	Japan Cent.		21	106	3	4	.429	93	29	111	3.82	0
2006 Los Angeles a.	N.L.		72	$78\frac{1}{3}$	6	2	.750	107	23	48	2.07	24
2007 Los Angeles ...	N.L.		63	$64\frac{1}{3}$	2	1	.667	78	13	33	1.40	39
2008 Los Angeles b-c.	N.L.		45	47	4	4	.500	60	16	40	2.49	18
2009 Boston d	A.L.		56	$55\frac{2}{3}$	3	3	.500	52	25	50	2.43	2
2010 Gwinnett........	Int.		1	1	0	0	.000	1	0	1	0.00	0
2010 Atlanta e-f ...	N.L.		56	54	2	3	.400	69	17	41	2.83	1
2011 Nashville	P.C.		6	$5\frac{2}{3}$	0	0	.000	7	0	3	0.00	0
2011 Milwaukee g-h.	N.L.		30	$26\frac{2}{3}$	4	2	.667	23	9	21	2.03	0
Major League Totals ....6 Yrs.			322	326	21	15	.583	389	103	233	2.18	84
Division Series												
2006 Los Angeles ...........N.L.			2	$2\frac{2}{3}$	0	0	.000	4	0	0	0.00	0
2008 Los Angeles ...........N.L.			1	0	0	0	.000	0	0	3	INF	0
2009 Boston ...............A.L.			1	1	0	0	.000	0	0	2	0.00	0
2011 Milwaukee ............N.L.			3	3	1	0	1.000	2	0	2	0.00	0
Division Series Totals			7	$6\frac{2}{3}$	1	0	1.000	6	0	7	2.70	0
Championship Series												
2011 Milwaukee ............N.L.			3	4	0	0	.000	3	0	2	0.00	0

a Signed with Los Angeles Dodgers organization, February 7, 2006.

b On disabled list from July 13 to September 13, 2008.
c Not offered contract, December 12, 2008. Signed with Boston Red Sox, January 10, 2009.
d Filed for free agency, October 19, 2009. Signed with Atlanta Braves, December 3, 2009.
e On disabled list from June 4 to June 22, 2010.
f Released by Atlanta Braves, October 18, 2010. Signed with Milwaukee Brewers, January 5, 2011.
g On disabled list from April 5 to July 2, 2011.
h Filed for free agency, October 30, 2011. Signed with Arizona Diamondbacks, December 14, 2011.

SALAS, NOEL FERNANDO (FERNANDO)

Born, Huatabampo, Mexico, May 30, 1985.
Bats Right. Throws Right. Height, 6 feet, 2 inches. Weight, 200 pounds.

Year	Club	Lea	G	IP	W	L	Pct	SO	BB	H	ERA	SAVES
2005 Saltillo	Mexican		14	16²/₃			.000	12	10	21	2.08	0
2006 Saltillo	Mexican		29	47²/₃	8	2	.800	38	20	40	3.02	0
2007 Palm Beach	Fla.St.		16	39¹/₃	2	3	.400	25	10	39	5.26	0
2007 Saltillo a	Mexican		3	2²/₃	0	0	.000	2	2	5	6.75	0
2008 Springfield	Texas		60	74	7	3	.700	100	16	65	3.65	25
2009 Cardinals	Gulf Coast		1	1	0	0	.000	1	0	0	0.00	0
2009 Springfield	Texas		10	11¹/₃	1	0	1.000	7	2	10	3.18	0
2009 Memphis	P.C.		24	27	3	2	.600	24	10	22	3.67	0
2010 Memphis	P.C.		34	35²/₃	1	0	1.000	44	9	26	3.79	19
2010 St. Louis	N.L.		27	30²/₃	0	0	.000	29	15	28	3.52	0
2011 Memphis	P.C.		3	3	0	0	.000	4	0	2	0.00	2
2011 St. Louis	N.L.		68	75	5	6	.455	75	21	50	2.28	24
Major League Totals	2 Yrs.		95	105²/₃	5	6	.455	104	36	78	2.64	24
Division Series												
2011 St. Louis	N.L.		3	3²/₃	0	0	.000	2	0	2	2.45	0
Championship Series												
2011 St. Louis	N.L.		4	6	0	0	.000	6	1	3	1.50	0
World Series Record												
2011 St. Louis	N.L.		4	3²/₃	0	0	.000	4	3	7	7.36	0

a Sold to St. Louis Cardinals, April 5, 2007. Loaned back to Saltillo (Mexican), July 29, 2007.

SALE, CHRISTOPHER (CHRIS)

Born, Lakeland, Florida, March 30, 1989.
Bats Left. Throws Left. Height, 6 feet, 5 inches. Weight, 170 pounds.

Year	Club	Lea	G	IP	W	L	Pct	SO	BB	H	ERA	SAVES
2010 Winston-Salem	Carolina		4	4	0	0	.000	4	2	3	2.25	0
2010 Charlotte	Int.		7	6¹/₃	0	0	.000	15	4	3	2.84	0
2010 Chicago	A.L.		21	23¹/₃	2	1	.667	32	10	15	1.93	4
2011 Chicago	A.L.		58	71	2	2	.500	79	27	52	2.79	8
Major League Totals	2 Yrs.		79	94¹/₃	4	3	.571	111	37	67	2.58	12

SAMARDZIJA, JEFFREY ALAN (JEFF)

Born, Merrillville, Indiana, January 23, 1985.
Bats Right. Throws Right. Height, 6 feet, 5 inches. Weight, 225 pounds.

Year	Club	Lea	G	IP	W	L	Pct	SO	BB	H	ERA	SAVES
2006 Boise	Northwest		5	19	1	1	.500	13	6	18	2.37	0
2006 Peoria	Midwest		2	11	0	1	.000	4	6	6	3.27	0
2007 Daytona	Fla.St.		24	107¹/₃	3	8	.273	45	35	142	4.95	0
2007 Tennessee	Southern		6	34¹/₃	3	3	.500	20	9	33	3.41	0
2008 Tennessee	Southern		16	76	3	5	.375	44	42	71	4.86	0
2008 Iowa	P.C.		6	37¹/₃	4	1	.800	40	16	32	3.13	0
2008 Chicago	N.L.		26	27²/₃	1	0	1.000	25	15	24	2.28	1
2009 Iowa	P.C.		18	89	6	6	.500	71	27	98	4.35	0
2009 Chicago	N.L.		20	34²/₃	1	3	.250	21	15	46	7.53	0
2010 Iowa	P.C.		35	111¹/₃	11	3	.786	102	67	86	4.37	0
2010 Chicago	N.L.		7	19¹/₃	2	2	.500	9	20	21	8.38	0
2011 Chicago	N.L.		75	88	8	4	.667	87	50	64	2.97	0
Major League Totals	4 Yrs.		128	169²/₃	12	9	.571	142	100	155	4.40	1
Division Series												
2008 Chicago	N.L.		1	1	0	0	.000	0	0	2	9.00	0

SANCHES, BRIAN LEE

Born, Beaumont, Texas, August 8, 1978.
Bats Right. Throws Right. Height, 6 feet. Weight, 195 pounds.

Year	Club	Lea	G	IP	W	L	Pct	SO	BB	H	ERA	SAVES
1999 Spokane	Northwest	9	34	1	1	.500	51	12	32	4.76	0
2000 Wilmington	Carolina	28	158	6	12	.333	122	69	132	3.53	0
2001 Wichita	Texas	29	134	7	9	.438	95	61	152	5.98	0
2002 Wichita	Texas	33	116²/₃	10	6	.625	101	43	111	4.40	0
2003 Wichita a	Texas	38	85¹/₃	1	5	.167	73	17	84	3.16	2
2004 Reading	Eastern	41	69²/₃	4	2	.667	60	25	55	2.71	3
2004 Scranton/WB b	Int.	4	6	0	0	.000	4	3	9	7.50	0
2005 Scranton/WB	Int.	51	83	5	3	.625	75	27	81	3.69	1
2006 Scranton/WB	Int.	36	43²/₃	3	2	.600	52	13	24	1.85	19
2006 Philadelphia	N.L.	18	21¹/₃	0	0	.000	22	13	23	5.91	0
2007 Ottawa	Int.	36	47¹/₃	2	3	.400	52	8	57	4.75	16
2007 Philadelphia c	N.L.	12	14²/₃	1	1	.500	9	12	13	5.52	0
2008 Washington	N.L.	12	11	2	0	1.000	10	5	16	7.36	0
2008 Columbus d	Int.	32	33²/₃	2	1	.667	45	9	24	2.41	13
2009 New Orleans	P.C.	16	17²/₃	1	1	.500	22	4	13	2.04	4
2009 Florida	N.L.	47	56¹/₃	4	2	.667	51	26	50	2.56	0
2010 Jupiter	Fla.St.	3	4	0	1	.000	6	0	2	2.25	0
2010 Florida e	N.L.	61	63²/₃	2	2	.500	54	27	43	2.26	0
2011 Jupiter	Fla.St.	1	2²/₃	0	1	.000	1	0	2	6.75	0
2011 Florida f-g	N.L.	39	61²/₃	4	1	.800	53	36	52	3.94	0
Major League Totals	6 Yrs.	189	228²/₃	13	6	.684	199	119	197	3.58	0

a Traded by Kansas City Royals to San Diego Padres with pitcher Chris Tierney for outfielder Rondell White, August 26, 2003.

b Traded to Philadelphia Phillies for player named later, April 1, 2004. San Diego Padres received catcher Mauber Lopez to complete trade, August 2, 2004.

c Filed for free agency, October 29, 2007. Signed with Washington Nationals organization, December 21, 2007.

d Filed for free agency, September 29, 2008. Signed with Florida Marlins organization, November 17, 2008.

e On disabled list from April 3 to April 26, 2010.

f On disabled list from August 10 to September 3, 2011.

g Filed for free agency, November 2, 2011. Signed with Philadelphia Phillies organization, November 30, 2011.

SANCHEZ, ANIBAL ALEJANDRO

Born, Maracay, Venezuela, February 27, 1984.
Bats Right. Throws Right. Height, 6 feet. Weight, 180 pounds.

Year	Club	Lea	G	IP	W	L	Pct	SO	BB	H	ERA	SAVES
2004 Lowell a	N.Y.-Penn.	15	76¹/₃	4	4	.500	101	29	43	1.77	0
2005 Wilmington	Carolina	14	78²/₃	6	1	.857	95	24	53	2.40	0
2005 Portland b	Eastern	11	57¹/₃	3	5	.375	63	16	53	3.45	0
2006 Carolina	Southern	15	85²/₃	6	3	.333	92	27	82	3.15	0
2006 Florida c	N.L.	18	114¹/₃	10	3	.769	72	46	90	2.83	0
2007 Florida d	N.L.	6	30	2	1	.667	14	19	43	4.80	0
2008 Marlins	Gulf Coast	1	5	1	0	1.000	4	1	4	3.60	0
2008 Jupiter	Fla.St.	2	10	0	0	.000	9	4	7	1.80	0
2008 Carolina	Southern	2	13	1	0	1.000	12	5	12	3.46	0
2008 Florida e	N.L.	10	51²/₃	2	5	.286	50	27	54	5.57	0
2009 Marlins	Gulf Coast	1	2²/₃	0	0	.000	2	0	3	3.38	0
2009 Jupiter	Fla.St.	3	13¹/₃	1	0	1.000	12	3	7	0.68	0
2009 Jacksonville	Southern	2	10¹/₃	1	0	1.000	8	3	5	2.61	0
2009 Florida f	N.L.	16	86	4	8	.333	71	46	84	3.87	0
2010 Florida	N.L.	32	195	13	12	.520	157	70	192	3.55	0
2011 Florida	N.L.	32	196¹/₃	8	9	.471	202	64	187	3.67	0
Major League Totals	6 Yrs.	114	673¹/₃	39	38	.506	566	272	650	3.72	0

a On minor league disabled list July 1 to September 16, 2003.

b Traded by Boston Red Sox to Florida Marlins with infielder Hanley Ramirez and pitcher Jesus Delgado for pitcher Josh Beckett, infielder Mike Lowell and pitcher Guillermo Mota, November 24, 2005.

c Pitched no-hit, no-run game against Arizona Diamondbacks, September 6, 2006.

d On minor league disabled list May 7 to September 30, 2007.

e On disabled list from March 21 to July 31, 2008.

f On disabled list from May 8 to June 2 and June 3 to August 21, 2009.

SANCHEZ, JONATHAN O.

Born, Mayaguez, Puerto Rico, November 19, 1982.
Bats Left. Throws Left. Height, 6 feet, 2 inches. Weight, 190 pounds.

Year	Club	Lea	G	IP	W	L	Pct	SO	BB	H	ERA	SAVES
2004 Giants	Arizona	9	26	5	0	1.000	27	9	22	2.77	1

Year	Club	Lea	G	IP	W	L	Pct	SO	BB	H	ERA	SAVES
2004 Salem-Keizer	Northwest		6	22¹/₃	2	1	.667	34	19	16	4.84	0
2005 Augusta	So.Atl.		25	125²/₃	5	7	.417	166	39	122	4.08	0
2006 Connecticut	Eastern		13	31¹/₃	2	1	.667	46	9	14	1.15	2
2006 Fresno	P.C.		6	23²/₃	2	2	.500	28	13	13	3.80	0
2006 San Francisco	N.L.		27	40	3	1	.750	33	23	39	4.95	0
2007 San Jose	Calif.		2	3	0	0	.000	5	1	0	0.00	0
2007 Fresno	P.C.		6	20²/₃	0	0	.000	27	8	15	2.18	0
2007 San Francisco a	N.L.		33	52	1	5	.167	62	28	57	5.88	0
2008 San Francisco b	N.L.		29	158	9	12	.429	157	75	154	5.01	0
2009 San Francisco c	N.L.		32	163¹/₃	8	12	.400	177	88	135	4.24	0
2010 San Francisco	N.L.		34	193¹/₃	13	9	.591	205	*96	142	3.07	0
2011 San Jose	Calif.		1	2²/₃	0	0	.000	3	2	6	20.25	0
2011 Fresno	P.C.		2	11	1	0	1.000	13	5	10	3.27	0
2011 San Francisco d-e	N.L.		19	101¹/₃	4	7	.364	102	66	80	4.26	0
Major League Totals	6 Yrs.		174	708	38	46	.452	736	376	607	4.26	0
Division Series												
2010 San Francisco	N.L.		1	7¹/₃	0	0	.000	11	1	2	1.23	0
Championship Series												
2010 San Francisco	N.L.		2	8	0	1	.000	8	5	8	4.50	0
World Series Record												
2010 San Francisco	N.L.		1	4²/₃	0	1	.000	3	3	6	7.71	0

a On disabled list from June 25 to July 19, 2007.
b On disabled list from August 12 to September 1, 2008.
c Pitched no-hit, no-run game against San Diego Padres, July 10, 2009.
d On disabled list from June 25 to August 1 and August 17 to September 29, 2011.
e Traded to Kansas City Royals with pitcher Ryan Verdugo for outfielder Melky Cabrera, November 7, 2011.

SANTANA, ERVIN RAMON

Born, La Romana, Dominican Republic, January 10, 1983.
Bats Right. Throws Right. Height, 6 feet, 2 inches. Weight, 185 pounds.

Year	Club	Lea	G	IP	W	L	Pct	SO	BB	H	ERA	SAVES
2001 Angels	Arizona		10	58²/₃	3	2	.600	69	35	40	3.22	0
2001 Provo	Pioneer		4	18²/₃	2	1	.667	22	12	19	7.71	0
2002 Cedar Rapids	Midwest		27	147	14	8	.636	146	48	133	4.16	0
2003 Rancho Cucamonga	California		20	124²/₃	10	2	.833	130	36	98	2.53	0
2003 Arkansas	Texas		6	29²/₃	1	1	.500	23	12	23	3.94	0
2004 Arkansas	Texas		8	43²/₃	2	1	.667	48	18	41	3.30	0
2005 Arkansas	Texas		7	39	5	1	.833	32	15	34	2.31	0
2005 Salt Lake	P.C.		3	19¹/₃	1	0	1.000	17	2	19	4.19	0
2005 Los Angeles	A.L.		23	133²/₃	12	8	.600	99	47	139	4.65	0
2006 Los Angeles	A.L.		33	204	16	8	.667	141	70	181	4.28	0
2007 Salt Lake	P.C.		5	32¹/₃	2	1	.667	32	10	39	5.01	0
2007 Los Angeles	A.L.		28	150	7	14	.333	126	58	174	5.76	0
2008 Los Angeles	A.L.		32	219	16	7	.696	214	47	198	3.49	0
2009 Azl Angels	Arizona		1	3¹/₃	0	0	.000	7	0	3	0.00	0
2009 Rancho Cucamonga	Calif.		1	4²/₃	0	0	.000	3	0	4	5.79	0
2009 Salt Lake	P.C.		1	5	1	0	1.000	4	1	3	3.60	0
2009 Los Angeles a	A.L.		24	139²/₃	8	8	.500	107	47	159	5.03	0
2010 Los Angeles	A.L.		33	222²/₃	17	10	.630	169	73	221	3.92	0
2011 Los Angeles b	A.L.		33	228²/₃	11	12	.478	178	72	207	3.38	0
Major League Totals	7 Yrs.		206	1297²/₃	87	67	.565	1034	414	1279	4.22	0
Division Series												
2005 Los Angeles	A.L.		1	5¹/₃	1	0	1.000	2	3	5	5.06	0
2007 Los Angeles	A.L.		1	2	0	0	.000	2	0	0	0.00	0
2008 Los Angeles	A.L.		1	5¹/₃	0	0	.000	3	0	8	8.44	0
Division Series Totals			3	12²/₃	1	0	1.000	7	3	13	5.68	0
Championship Series												
2005 Los Angeles	A.L.		1	4¹/₃	0	1	.000	2	3	3	10.38	0
2009 Los Angeles	A.L.		4	5²/₃	1	1	.500	5	4	5	1.59	0
Championship Series Totals			5	10	1	2	.333	7	7	8	5.40	0

a On disabled list from March 27 to May 14 and June 17 to July 3, 2009.
b Pitched no-hit, no-run game against Cleveland Indians, July 27, 2011.

SANTANA, JOHAN ALEXANDER
Born, Tovar, Venezuela, March 13, 1979.
Bats Left. Throws Left. Height, 6 feet. Weight, 210 pounds.

Year Club	Lea	G	IP	W	L	Pct	SO	BB	H	ERA	SAVES
1996 Houston/Bos	Dominican	23	40	4	3	.571	51	22	26	2.70	3
1997 Auburn	N.Y.-Penn.	1	4	0	0	.000	5	6	1	2.25	0
1997 Astros	Gulf Coast	9	36⅓	0	4	.000	25	18	49	7.93	0
1998 Quad City	Midwest	2	6⅔	0	1	.000	6	3	14	9.45	0
1998 Auburn	N.Y.-Penn.	15	86⅔	7	5	.583	88	21	81	4.36	0
1999 Michigan a-b	Midwest	27	160⅓	8	8	.500	150	55	162	4.66	0
2000 Minnesota	A.L.	30	86	2	3	.400	64	54	102	6.49	0
2001 Minnesota	A.L.	15	43⅔	1	0	1.000	28	16	50	4.74	0
2002 Edmonton	P.C.	11	48⅔	5	2	.714	75	27	37	3.14	0
2002 Minnesota	A.L.	27	108⅓	8	6	.571	137	49	84	2.99	1
2003 Minnesota	A.L.	45	158⅓	12	3	.800	169	47	127	3.07	0
2004 Minnesota c	A.L.	34	228	20	6	.769	*265	54	156	*2.61	0
2005 Minnesota	A.L.	33	231⅔	16	7	.696	*238	45	180	2.87	0
2006 Minnesota d	A.L.	34	*233⅔	*19	6	.760	*245	47	186	*2.77	0
2007 Minnesota	A.L.	33	219	15	13	.536	235	52	183	3.33	0
2008 New York e	N.L.	34	*234⅓	16	7	.696	206	63	206	*2.53	0
2009 New York f	N.L.	25	166⅔	13	9	.591	146	46	156	3.13	0
2010 New York	N.L.	29	199	11	9	.550	144	55	179	2.98	0
2011 New York g	N.L.					INJURED—Did Not Play					
Major League Totals	11 Yrs.	339	1908⅔	133	69	.658	1877	528	1609	3.10	1
Division Series											
2002 Minnesota	A.L.	2	3	0	0	.000	2	2	3	6.00	0
2003 Minnesota	A.L.	2	7⅔	0	1	.000	6	3	9	7.04	0
2004 Minnesota	A.L.	2	12	1	0	1.000	12	4	14	0.75	0
2006 Minnesota	A.L.	1	8	0	1	.000	8	1	5	2.25	0
Division Series Totals		7	30⅔	1	2	.333	28	10	31	3.23	0
Championship Series											
2002 Minnesota	A.L.	4	3⅓	0	1	.000	4	0	4	10.80	0

a Selected by Florida Marlins from Houston Astros in Rule V draft, December 13, 1999.
b Traded to Minnesota Twins with cash for pitcher Jared Camp, December 13, 1999.
c Selected Cy Young Award Winner in American League for 2004.
d Selected Cy Young Award Winner in American League for 2006.
e Traded to New York Mets for outfielder Carlos Gomez, pitcher Philip Humber, pitcher Kevin Mulvey and pitcher Deolis Garcia, February 2, 2008.
f On disabled list from August 25 to October 14, 2009.
g On disabled list from March 22 to October 24, 2011.

SANTOS, SERGIO JOSE
Born, Bellflower, California, July 4, 1983.
Bats Right. Throws Right. Height, 6 feet, 3 inches. Weight, 240 pounds.

Year Club	Lea	G	IP	W	L	Pct	SO	BB	H	ERA	SAVES
2009 Winston-Salem a-b-c-d-e	Carolina	8	7⅔	0	0	.000	7	3	9	5.87	0
2009 Charlotte	Int.	3	5	0	1	.000	7	7	5	9.00	0
2009 Kannapolis	So.Atl.	8	7⅓	0	1	.000	10	3	8	7.36	0
2009 Birmingham	Southern	7	8⅔	0	1	.000	6	7	15	10.38	0
2010 Chicago	A.L.	56	51⅔	2	2	.500	56	26	53	2.96	1
2011 Chicago f	A.L.	63	63⅓	4	5	.444	92	29	41	3.55	30
Major League Totals	2 Yrs.	119	115	6	7	.462	148	55	94	3.29	31

a Played infield in the minors for 2003 through 2008.
b Traded by Arizona Diamondbacks to Toronto Blue Jays with infielder Troy Glaus for infielder Orlando Hudson and pitcher Miguel Batista, December 27, 2005.
c Claimed on waivers by Minnesota Twins, May 16, 2008.
d Filed for free agency, November 3, 2008. Signed with Chicago White Sox organization, January 12, 2009.
e Sold to San Francisco Giants, March 20, 2009. Sold to Chicago White Sox, April 1, 2009.
f Traded to Toronto Blue Jays for pitcher Nestor Molina, December 6, 2011.

SAUNDERS, JOSEPH FRANCIS (JOE)
Born, Falls Church, Virginia, June 16, 1981.
Bats Left. Throws Left. Height, 6 feet, 3 inches. Weight, 210 pounds.

Year Club	Lea	G	IP	W	L	Pct	SO	BB	H	ERA	SAVES
2002 Cedar Rapids	Midwest	5	28⅔	3	1	.750	27	9	16	1.88	0
2002 Provo	Pioneer	8	32⅓	2	1	.667	21	11	40	3.62	0
2003 Provo a	Pioneer					INJURED—Did Not Play					
2004 Rancho Cucamonga	Calif.	19	105⅔	9	7	.563	76	23	106	3.41	0

Year	Club	Lea	G	IP	W	L	Pct	SO	BB	H	ERA	SAVES
2004 Arkansas	Texas	8	39	4	3	.571	25	14	51	5.77	0
2005 Arkansas	Texas	18	105²/₃	7	4	.636	80	32	107	3.49	0
2005 Salt Lake	P.C.	9	55	3	3	.500	29	21	65	4.58	0
2005 Los Angeles	A.L.	2	9¹/₃	0	0	.000	4	4	10	7.71	0
2006 Salt Lake	P.C.	21	135	10	4	.714	97	38	117	2.67	0
2006 Los Angeles	A.L.	13	70²/₃	7	3	.700	51	29	71	4.71	0
2007 Salt Lake	P.C.	14	86¹/₃	4	7	.364	84	20	89	5.11	0
2007 Los Angeles	A.L.	18	107¹/₃	8	5	.615	69	34	129	4.44	0
2008 Los Angeles	A.L.	31	198	17	7	.708	103	53	187	3.41	0
2009 Los Angeles b	A.L.	31	186	16	7	.696	101	64	202	4.60	0
2010 Los Angeles	A.L.	20	120²/₃	6	10	.375	64	45	135	4.62	0
2010 Arizona c	N.L.	13	82²/₃	3	7	.300	50	19	97	4.25	0
2011 Arizona d	N.L.	33	212	12	13	.480	108	67	210	3.69	0
Major League Totals ....7 Yrs.		161	986²/₃	69	52	.570	550	315	1041	4.16	0
Division Series											
2008 Los Angeles	A.L.	1	4²/₃	0	0	.000	2	4	5	7.71	0
2011 Arizona	N.L.	1	3	0	0	.000	1	2	5	9.00	0
Division Series Totals		2	7²/₃	0	0	.000	3	6	10	8.22	0
Championship Series											
2009 Los Angeles	A.L.	2	10¹/₃	0	1	.000	5	6	13	4.35	0

a On minor league disabled list from April 3 to September 18, 2003.
b On disabled list from August 8 to August 26, 2009.
c Traded to Arizona Diamondbacks with pitcher Rafael Rodriguez, pitcher Patrick Corbin and player to be named later for pitcher Danny Haren, July 25, 2010. Arizona Diamondbacks received pitcher Tyler Skaggs to complete trade, August 7, 2010.
d Not offered contract, December 12, 2011.

SCHERZER, MAXWELL M. (MAX)
Born, St. Louis, Missouri, July 27, 1984.
Bats Right. Throws Right. Height, 6 feet, 3 inches. Weight, 215 pounds.

Year	Club	Lea	G	IP	W	L	Pct	SO	BB	H	ERA	SAVES
2007 Fort Worth	Amer.Assoc.	3	16	1	0	1.000	25	4	9	0.56	0
2007 Visalia	Calif.	3	17	2	0	1.000	30	2	5	0.53	0
2007 Mobile a-b	Southern	14	73²/₃	4	4	.500	76	40	64	3.91	0
2008 Tucson	P.C.	13	53	1	1	.500	79	22	35	2.72	0
2008 Arizona	N.L.	16	56	0	4	.000	66	21	48	3.05	0
2009 Visalia	Calif.	1	4²/₃	0	0	.000	5	4	1	1.93	0
2009 Arizona c-d.	N.L.	30	170¹/₃	9	11	.450	174	63	166	4.12	0
2010 Toledo	Int.	2	15	2	0	1.000	17	2	4	0.60	0
2010 Detroit	A.L.	31	195²/₃	12	11	.522	184	70	174	3.50	0
2011 Detroit	A.L.	33	195	15	9	.625	174	56	207	4.43	0
Major League Totals ....4 Yrs.		110	617	36	35	.507	598	210	595	3.92	0
Division Series											
2011 Detroit	A.L.	2	7¹/₃	1	0	1.000	7	4	4	1.23	0
Championship Series											
2011 Detroit	A.L.	2	8¹/₃	0	1	.000	7	5	11	9.72	0

a Signed by independent Fort Worth (American Association), 2007.
b Signed by Arizona Diamondbacks, May 31, 2007.
c On disabled list from March 29 to April 14, 2009.
d Traded to Detroit Tigers with pitcher Daniel Schlereth for pitcher Edwin Jackson and pitcher Ian Kennedy, December 9, 2009.

SCHLERETH, DANIEL ROBERT
Born, Anchorage, Alaska, May 9, 1986.
Bats Left. Throws Left. Height, 6 feet. Weight, 210 pounds.

Year	Club	Lea	G	IP	W	L	Pct	SO	BB	H	ERA	SAVES
2008 South Bend	Midwest	7	9	1	0	1.000	14	4	3	2.00	0
2008 Missoula	Pioneer	3	3	0	0	.000	6	2	3	0.00	0
2009 Mobile	Southern	21	26²/₃	0	0	.000	39	16	14	1.01	4
2009 Reno	P.C.	1	1	0	0	.000	1	1	1	0.00	0
2009 Arizona a	N.L.	21	18¹/₃	1	4	.200	22	15	15	5.89	0
2010 Toledo	Int.	38	49¹/₃	1	3	.250	60	34	40	2.37	0
2010 Detroit	A.L.	18	18²/₃	2	0	1.000	19	10	20	2.89	1
2011 Toledo	Int.	8	11²/₃	1	0	1.000	18	5	6	0.77	0
2011 Detroit	A.L.	49	49	2	2	.500	44	31	36	3.49	0
Major League Totals ....3 Yrs.		88	86	5	6	.455	85	56	71	3.87	1
Division Series											
2011 Detroit	A.L.	2	1²/₃	0	0	.000	4	0	4	10.80	0

Year	Club	Lea	G	IP	W	L	Pct	SO	BB	H	ERA	SAVES
Championship Series												
2011 Detroit	A.L.	1	0		0	0	.000	0	0	1	INF	0

a Traded to Detroit Tigers with pitcher Max Scherzer for pitcher Edwin Jackson and pitcher Ian Kennedy, December 9, 2009.

SHERRILL, GEORGE FRIEDERICH
Born, Memphis, Tennessee, April 19, 1977.
Bats Left. Throws Left. Height, 6 feet. Weight, 225 pounds.

Year	Club	Lea	G	IP	W	L	Pct	SO	BB	H	ERA	SAVES
1999 Evansville (Ind)	Frontier	22	40	2	4	.333	33	18	40	3.15	2
2000 Evansville (Ind)	Frontier	13	75⅓	3	5	.375	61	35	71	4.66	2
2001 Sioux Falls (Ind)....	Northern	48	58⅔	4	4	.500	45	14	53	2.45	2
2002 Winnipeg (Ind).....	Northern	38	41	3	5	.375	61	13	35	3.07	2
2003 Winnipeg (Ind).....	Northern	16	16	1	0	1.000	30	4	8	1.13	2
2003 San Antonio a........	Texas	16	27⅓	3	0	1.000	31	12	19	0.33	0
2004 Tacoma	P.C.	36	50⅓	4	2	.667	62	9	42	2.32	13
2004 Seattle	A.L.	21	23⅔	2	1	.667	16	9	24	3.80	0
2005 Mariners...........	Arizona	3	4	0	0	.000	5	0	0	0.00	0
2005 Tacoma	P.C.	22	23⅔	1	3	.250	38	6	19	2.28	7
2005 Seattle	A.L.	29	19	4	3	.571	24	7	13	5.21	0
2006 Seattle	A.L.	72	40	2	4	.333	42	27	30	4.28	1
2007 Seattle	A.L.	73	45⅔	2	0	1.000	56	17	28	2.36	3
2008 Baltimore b-c........	A.L.	57	53⅓	3	5	.375	58	33	47	4.72	31
2009 Baltimore	A.L.	42	41⅓	0	1	.000	39	13	34	2.40	20
2009 Los Angeles d.......	N.L.	30	27⅔	1	0	1.000	22	11	19	0.65	1
2010 Inland Empire........	Calif.	2	2	0	0	.000	2	0	3	4.50	0
2010 Albuquerque..........	P.C.	2	1⅔	0	0	.000	3	0	2	0.00	0
2010 Los Angeles e-f.......	N.L.	65	36⅓	2	2	.500	25	24	46	6.69	0
2011 Atlanta g-h..........	N.L.	51	36	3	1	.750	38	12	33	3.00	0
Major League Totals .... 8 Yrs.		440	323	19	17	.528	320	153	274	3.68	56
Division Series											
2009 Los Angeles...........	N.L.	3	2⅓	1	0	1.000	0	1	1	3.86	0
Championship Series											
2009 Los Angeles...........	N.L.	3	2	0	0	.000	2	3	2	13.50	0

a Signed with Seattle Mariners, July 2, 2003.
b Traded to Baltimore Orioles with pitcher Tony Butler, outfielder Adam Jones, pitcher Kam Mickolio and pitcher Chris Tillman for pitcher Erik Bedard, February 8, 2008.
c On disabled list from August 16 to September 11, 2008.
d Traded to Los Angeles Dodgers for infielder Joshua Bell and pitcher Steve Johnson, July 30, 2009.
e On disabled list from May 24 to June 8, 2010.
f Not offered contract, December 2, 2010. Signed with Atlanta Braves, December 10, 2010.
g On disabled list from August 27 to September 26, 2011.
h Filed for free agency, October 30, 2011. Signed with Seattle Mariners, December 30, 2011.

SHIELDS, JAMES ANTHONY (JAMIE)
Born, Newhall, California, December 20, 1981.
Bats Right. Throws Right. Height, 6 feet, 4 inches. Weight, 215 pounds.

Year	Club	Lea	G	IP	W	L	Pct	SO	BB	H	ERA	SAVES
2001 Hudson Valley	N.Y.-Penn.	5	27⅓	2	1	.667	25	5	27	2.30	0
2001 Charleston-SC	So.Atl.	10	71⅓	4	5	.444	60	10	63	2.65	0
2002 Charleston-SC a...........				INJURED—Did Not Play							
2003 Bakersfield..........	Calif.	26	143⅔	10	10	.500	119	38	161	4.45	1
2004 Bakersfield..........	Calif.	20	117	8	5	.615	92	33	119	4.23	0
2004 Montgomery	Southern	4	18⅓	0	3	.000	14	8	24	7.85	0
2005 Durham	Int.	1	6	1	0	1.000	6	3	9	6.00	0
2005 Montgomery	Southern	17	109⅓	7	5	.583	104	31	95	2.80	0
2006 Durham	Int.	10	61⅓	3	2	.600	64	6	60	2.64	0
2006 Tampa Bay	A.L.	21	124⅔	6	8	.429	104	38	141	4.84	0
2007 Tampa Bay	A.L.	31	215	12	8	.600	184	36	202	3.85	0
2008 Tampa Bay	A.L.	33	215	14	8	.636	160	40	208	3.56	0
2009 Tampa Bay	A.L.	33	219⅔	11	12	.478	167	52	239	4.14	0
2010 Tampa Bay	A.L.	34	203⅓	13	15	.464	187	51	*246	5.18	0
2011 Tampa Bay	A.L.	33	249⅓	16	12	.571	225	65	195	2.82	0
Major League Totals .... 6 Yrs.		185	1227	72	63	.533	1027	282	1231	3.96	0
Division Series											
2008 Tampa Bay	A.L.	1	6⅓	1	0	1.000	4	1	6	4.26	0
2010 Tampa Bay	A.L.	1	4⅓	0	1	.000	2	0	4	8.31	0

Year	Club	Lea	G	IP	W	L	Pct	SO	BB	H	ERA	SAVES
2011 Tampa Bay	A.L.	1	5	0	1	.000	6	0	8	12.60	0	
Division Series Totals		3	15²/₃	1	2	.333	12	1	18	8.04	0	
Championship Series												
2008 Tampa Bay	A.L.	2	13	0	2	.000	9	5	15	3.46	0	
World Series Record												
2008 Tampa Bay	A.L.	1	5²/₃	1	0	1.000	4	2	7	0.00	0	

a On minor league disabled list April 4 to September 10, 2002.

SIMON (CABRERA), ALFREDO

Born, Santiago, Dominican Republic, May 8, 1981.
Bats Right. Throws Right. Height, 6 feet, 4 inches. Weight, 230 pounds.

Year	Club	Lea	G	IP	W	L	Pct	SO	BB	H	ERA	SAVES
2001 Phillies	Gulf Coast	10	43¹/₃	2	2	.500	40	23	35	2.91	0	
2002 Batavia	N.Y.-Penn.	15	90¹/₃	9	2	.818	77	46	79	3.59	0	
2003 Lakewood.	So.Atl.	14	71¹/₃	5	0	1.000	66	25	59	3.79	2	
2004 San Jose	Calif.	6	31²/₃	1	2	.333	21	12	44	5.68	0	
2004 Clearwater a	Fla.St.	22	134²/₃	7	9	.438	107	38	121	3.27	0	
2005 Norwich	Eastern	43	91¹/₃	3	8	.273	60	24	104	5.03	19	
2006 San Jose	Calif.	18	36¹/₃	2	4	.333	35	14	43	6.44	0	
2006 Fresno b-c-d	P.C.	10	52	0	6	.000	35	19	76	6.75	0	
2007 Oklahoma e	P.C.	22	119	5	10	.333	73	46	152	6.43	0	
2008 Monterrey	Mexican	15	81	7	2	.778	61	20	66	2.67	0	
2008 Norfolk f-g-h	Int.	1	4²/₃	0	1	.000	5	2	9	7.71	0	
2008 Baltimore	A.L.	4	13	0	0	.000	8	2	16	6.23	0	
2009 Baltimore i-j	A.L.	2	6¹/₃	0	1	.000	3	2	8	9.95	0	
2010 Norfolk.	Int.	4	17	1	1	.500	14	5	15	1.59	0	
2010 Baltimore k.	A.L.	49	49¹/₃	4	2	.667	37	22	54	4.93	17	
2011 Bowie.	Eastern	4	18	1	0	1.000	20	6	15	3.00	0	
2011 Baltimore l	A.L.	23	115²/₃	4	9	.308	83	40	128	4.90	0	
Major League Totals	4 Yrs.	78	184¹/₃	8	12	.400	131	66	206	5.18	17	

a Traded by Philadelphia Phillies to San Francisco Giants with outfielder Ricky Ledee for pitcher Felix Rodriguez, July 30, 2004.
b Filed for free agency, October 15,2006. Signed with Texas Rangers organization, November 3, 2006.
c Selected by Baltimore Orioles in Rule V draft, December 7, 2006.
d Traded to Philadelphia Phillies for catcher Adam Domachie and cash, December 7, 2006.
e Returned to Texas Rangers, March 17, 2007.
f Filed for free agency, October 29, 2007. Signed with Los Angeles Dodgers organization, January 20, 2008.
g Released by Los Angeles Dodgers, March 30, 2008. Signed with Monterrey (Mexican) for 2008.
h Signed with Baltimore Orioles organization, September 5, 2008.
i On disabled list from April 15 to October 30, 2009.
j Filed for free agency, November 9, 2009, re-signed with Baltimore Orioles, December 2, 2009.
k On disabled list from May 25 to June 14, 2010.
l On disabled list from June 13 to June 29, 2011.

SIPP, TONY MARCEL

Born, Pascagoula, Mississippi, July 12, 1983.
Bats Left. Throws Left. Height, 6 feet. Weight, 190 pounds.

Year	Club	Lea	G	IP	W	L	Pct	SO	BB	H	ERA	SAVES
2004 Mahoning Valley...	N.Y.-Penn.	10	42²/₃	3	1	.750	74	13	33	3.16	0	
2005 Kinston.	Carolina	22	47¹/₃	2	2	.500	59	23	34	2.66	2	
2005 Lake County	So.Atl.	13	69	4	1	.800	71	19	47	2.22	0	
2006 Akron	Eastern	29	60¹/₃	4	2	.667	80	21	44	3.13	3	
2007 a........................					INJURED—Did Not Play							
2008 Kinston.	Carolina	5	8	0	0	.000	10	3	4	1.13	0	
2008 Akron	Eastern	16	21²/₃	0	3	.000	32	7	19	3.74	1	
2008 Indians..........	Gulf Coast	3	4	0	0	.000	4	1	0	0.00	0	
2009 Columbus.	Int.	12	17	1	0	1.000	22	6	17	3.71	1	
2009 Cleveland	A.L.	46	40	2	0	1.000	68	25	27	2.93	0	
2010 Cleveland	A.L.	70	63	2	2	.500	69	39	48	4.14	1	
2011 Cleveland	A.L.	69	62¹/₃	6	3	.667	57	24	45	3.03	0	
Major League Totals	3 Yrs.	185	165¹/₃	10	5	.667	174	88	120	3.43	1	

a On minor league disabled list from April 5 to September 21, 2007.

SLATEN, DOUGLAS (DOUG)
Born, Venice, California, February 4, 1980.
Bats Left. Throws Left. Height, 6 feet, 5 inches. Weight, 215 pounds.

Year	Club	Lea	G	IP	W	L	Pct	SO	BB	H	ERA	SAVES
2000 Diamondbacks	Arizona		9	9⅓	0	0	.000	7	3	7	0.96	0
2001 Lancaster	Calif.		28	157⅔	9	8	.529	110	45	207	4.79	0
2002 Lancaster	Calif.		8	35	1	6	.143	23	12	59	9.00	0
2002 South Bend	Midwest		7	14⅓	0	0	.000	5	4	18	4.40	0
2003 Lancaster	Calif.		32	119⅓	6	7	.462	78	47	156	6.03	0
2004 South Bend	Midwest		36	44	5	2	.714	40	13	44	2.25	5
2004 El Paso	Texas		11	9	0	1	.000	6	10	16	10.00	0
2005 Tennessee	Southern		58	61⅓	2	2	.500	72	26	61	4.26	1
2006 Tennessee	Southern		40	43	2	3	.400	59	15	31	1.88	8
2006 Tucson	P.C.		18	20	2	1	.667	21	7	10	0.45	2
2006 Arizona	N.L.		9	5⅔	0	0	.000	3	2	3	0.00	0
2007 Arizona	N.L.		61	36⅓	3	2	.600	28	14	41	2.72	0
2008 Tucson	P.C.		6	6⅔	0	0	.000	9	4	6	4.05	0
2008 Arizona a	N.L.		45	32⅓	0	3	.000	20	14	33	4.73	0
2009 Arizona	N.L.		11	6⅓	0	0	.000	4	1	10	7.11	0
2009 Reno b	P.C.		39	43⅔	3	2	.600	40	15	41	3.09	9
2010 Syracuse	Int.		11	17	1	0	1.000	17	1	12	0.00	0
2010 Washington	N.L.		49	40⅔	4	1	.800	36	19	34	3.10	0
2011 Nationals	Gulf Coast		1	2	0	0	.000	1	0	0	0.00	0
2011 Hagerstown	So.Atl.		4	3⅔	0	0	.000	0	0	5	4.91	0
2011 Harrisburg	Eastern		1	2	0	0	.000	2	0	2	0.00	0
2011 Syracuse	Int.		3	2⅔	0	0	.000	5	0	2	0.00	0
2011 Washington c-d	N.L.		31	16⅓	0	2	.000	13	9	26	4.41	0
Major League Totals	6 Yrs.		206	137⅔	7	8	.467	104	59	147	3.60	0

Championship Series

Year	Club	Lea	G	IP	W	L	Pct	SO	BB	H	ERA	SAVES
2007 Arizona	N.L.		3	1⅓	0	0	.000	1	2	1	0.00	0

a On disabled list from July 19 to August 13, 2008.
b Claimed on waivers by Washington Nationals, November 5, 2009.
c On disabled list from June 4 to September 1, 2011.
d Not offered contract, December 12, 2011. Signed with Pittsburgh Pirates organization, January 11, 2012.

SLOWEY, KEVIN MICHAEL
Born, Conroe, Texas, May 4, 1984.
Bats Right. Throws Right. Height, 6 feet, 3 inches. Weight, 195 pounds.

Year	Club	Lea	G	IP	W	L	Pct	SO	BB	H	ERA	SAVES
2005 Elizabethton	Appal.		4	7⅔	0	0	.000	15	0	2	1.17	1
2006 New Britain	Eastern		9	59⅓	4	3	.571	52	13	50	3.19	0
2006 Fort Myers	Fla.St.		14	89⅓	4	2	.667	99	9	52	1.01	0
2007 Rochester	Int.		20	133⅔	10	5	.667	107	18	110	1.89	0
2007 Minnesota	A.L.		13	66⅔	4	1	.800	47	11	82	4.72	0
2008 Fort Myers	Fla.St.		2	8	0	0	.000	10	2	1	1.13	0
2008 Rochester	Int.		1	5	0	1	.000	9	2	3	3.60	0
2008 Minnesota a	A.L.		27	160⅓	12	11	.522	123	24	161	3.99	0
2009 Minnesota b	A.L.		16	90⅔	10	3	.769	75	15	113	4.86	0
2010 Minnesota c	A.L.		30	155⅔	13	6	.684	116	29	172	4.45	0
2011 Fort Myers	Fla.St.		4	12	0	1	.000	9	1	9	3.75	0
2011 Rochester	Int.		7	38	1	2	.333	29	5	44	3.55	0
2011 Minnesota d-e	A.L.		14	59⅓	0	8	.000	34	5	78	6.67	0
Major League Totals	5 Yrs.		100	532⅔	39	29	.574	395	84	606	4.66	0

a On disabled list from April 4 to May 7, 2008.
b On disabled list from July 4 to November 10, 2009.
c On disabled list from August 22 to September 6, 2010.
d On disabled list from April 5 to May 7 and May 21 to July 22, 2011.
e Traded to Colorado Rockies for player to be named later, December 6, 2011.

SMITH, JOSEPH MICHAEL (JOE)
Born, Cincinnati, Ohio, March 22, 1984.
Bats Right. Throws Right. Height, 6 feet, 2 inches. Weight, 205 pounds.

Year	Club	Lea	G	IP	W	L	Pct	SO	BB	H	ERA	SAVES
2006 Binghamton	Eastern		10	12⅔	0	2	.000	12	11	12	5.68	0
2006 Brooklyn	N.Y.-Penn.		17	20	0	1	.000	28	3	10	0.45	9
2007 New Orleans	P.C.		8	9	0	0	.000	5	4	7	2.00	2
2007 New York	N.L.		54	44⅓	3	2	.600	45	21	48	3.45	0
2008 New York a-b	N.L.		82	63⅓	6	3	.667	52	31	51	3.55	0

Year	Club	Lea	G	IP	W	L	Pct	SO	BB	H	ERA	SAVES
2009 Columbus		Int.	5	5	0	0	.000	6	1	4	0.00	0
2009 Cleveland c		A.L.	37	34	0	0	.000	30	13	30	3.44	0
2010 Columbus		Int.	20	23	2	1	.667	19	10	17	1.96	2
2010 Cleveland		A.L.	53	40	2	2	.500	32	24	30	3.83	0
2011 Akron		Eastern	4	3²/₃	0	0	.000	7	2	1	2.45	0
2011 Cleveland d		A.L.	71	67	3	3	.500	45	21	52	2.01	0
Major League Totals		5 Yrs.	297	248²/₃	14	10	.583	204	110	211	3.15	0

a Traded to Seattle Mariners with pitcher Aaron Heilman, outfielder Endy Chavez, pitcher Jason Vargas, infielder Mike Carp, outfielder Ezequiel Carrera and pitcher Maikel Cleto for pitcher J.J. Putz, pitcher Sean Green and outfielder Jeremy Reed, December 10, 2008.
b Traded to Cleveland Indians with pitcher Luis Valbuena for outfielder Franklin Gutierrez, December 10, 2008.
c On disabled list from April 29 to June 9 and September 1 to October 14, 2009.
d On disabled list from March 22 to April 15, 2011.

SORIA, JOAKIM AGUSTIN (RAMOS)
Born, Monclova, Mexico, May 18, 1984.
Bats Right. Throws Right. Height, 6 feet, 3 inches. Weight, 185 pounds.

Year	Club	Lea	G	IP	W	L	Pct	SO	BB	H	ERA	SAVES
2002 Dodgers		Gulf Coast	4	5	0	0	.000	6	0	6	3.60	0
2003						INJURED—Did Not Play						
2004 Dodgers		Dominican	4	5¹/₃	0	0	.000	4	5	3	1.69	1
2005 Mexico City a		Mexican	30	66¹/₃	5	0	1.000	60	31	75	4.48	0
2006 Mexico City		Mexican	39	37	0	0	.000	30	11	37	3.89	15
2006 Fort Wayne b		Midwest	7	11²/₃	1	0	1.000	11	2	5	2.31	0
2007 Kansas City c		A.L.	62	69	2	3	.400	75	19	46	2.48	17
2008 Kansas City		A.L.	63	67¹/₃	2	3	.400	66	19	39	1.60	42
2009 Kansas City d		A.L.	47	53	3	2	.600	69	16	44	2.21	30
2010 Kansas City		A.L.	66	65²/₃	1	2	.333	71	16	53	1.78	43
2011 Kansas City		A.L.	60	60¹/₃	5	5	.500	60	17	60	4.03	28
Major League Totals		5 Yrs.	298	315¹/₃	13	15	.464	341	87	242	2.40	160

a Released by Los Angeles Dodgers, October 12, 2004. Signed with San Diego Padres, December 20, 2005.
b Selected by Kansas City Royals from San Diego Padres in Rule V draft, December 7, 2006.
c On disabled list from May 23 to June 7, 2007.
d On disabled list from May 8 to June 2, 2009.

SORIANO, RAFAEL
Born, San Jose, Dominican Republic, December 19, 1979.
Bats Right. Throws Right. Height, 6 feet, 1 inch. Weight, 220 pounds.

Year	Club	Lea	G	IP	W	L	Pct	SO	BB	H	ERA	SAVES
1999 Everett		Northwest	14	75¹/₃	5	4	.556	83	49	56	3.11	0
2000 Wisconsin		Midwest	21	122¹/₃	8	4	.667	90	50	97	2.87	0
2001 San Bernardino		Calif.	15	89	6	3	.667	98	39	49	2.53	0
2001 San Antonio		Texas	8	48¹/₃	2	2	.500	53	14	34	3.35	0
2002 San Antonio		Texas	10	46²/₃	2	3	.400	52	15	32	2.31	0
2002 Seattle a		A.L.	10	47¹/₃	0	3	.000	32	16	45	4.56	1
2003 Tacoma		P.C.	11	62	4	3	.571	63	12	43	3.19	0
2003 Seattle		A.L.	40	53	3	0	1.000	68	12	30	1.53	1
2004 Seattle		A.L.	6	3¹/₃	0	3	.000	3	3	9	13.50	0
2004 Inland Empire		Calif.	2	8	0	0	.000	9	1	7	2.25	0
2004 San Antonio		Texas	2	8	1	0	1.000	10	0	4	1.13	0
2004 Tacoma b		P.C.	3	3²/₃	0	0	.000	5	2	2	2.45	0
2005 Inland Empire		Calif.	3	4	0	0	.000	5	0	2	0.00	0
2005 San Antonio		Texas	1	1	0	0	.000	0	0	0	0.00	0
2005 Everett		Northwest	4	6	0	0	.000	8	2	6	3.00	0
2005 Tacoma		P.C.	5	5¹/₃	1	0	1.000	11	1	3	0.00	0
2005 Seattle c		A.L.	7	7¹/₃	0	0	.000	9	1	6	2.45	0
2006 Seattle d-e		A.L.	53	60	1	2	.333	65	21	44	2.25	2
2007 Atlanta		N.L.	71	72	3	3	.500	70	15	47	3.00	9
2008 Mississippi		Southern	2	2	0	0	.000	2	1	1	0.00	0
2008 Atlanta f		N.L.	14	14	0	1	.000	16	9	7	2.57	3
2009 Atlanta g		N.L.	77	75²/₃	1	6	.143	102	27	53	2.97	27
2010 Tampa Bay h		A.L.	64	62¹/₃	3	2	.600	57	14	36	1.73	*45
2011 Tampa		Fla.St.	2	2¹/₃	0	1	.000	1	0	4	11.57	0
2011 Scranton-WB		Int.	2	2	1	0	1.000	2	0	1	4.50	0
2011 New York i		A.L.	42	39¹/₃	2	3	.400	36	18	33	4.12	2
Major League Totals		10 Yrs.	384	434¹/₃	13	23	.361	458	136	310	2.86	90

Year	Club	Lea	G	IP	W	L	Pct	SO	BB	H	ERA	SAVES
Division Series												
2011 New York	A.L.	3	4$\frac{2}{3}$	0	1	.000	4	0	1	1.93	0
Division Series Totals		6	7$\frac{2}{3}$	0	1	.000	5	0	5	4.70	1

a On disabled list from July 3 to August 2, 2002.
b On disabled list from May 10 to November 1, 2004.
c On disabled list from April 1 to September 5, 2005.
d On disabled list from July 20 to August 4, 2006.
e Traded to Atlanta Braves for pitcher Horacio Ramirez, December 7, 2006.
f On disabled list from April 7 to May 28 and June 6 to July 21 and August 3 to November 3, 2008.
g Traded to Tampa Bay Rays for pitcher Jesse Chavez, December 11, 2009.
h Filed for free agency, November 1, 2010. Signed with New York Yankees, January 18, 2011.
i On disabled list from May 17 to July 29, 2011.

STAUFFER, TIMOTHY JAMES (TIM)
Born, Portland, Maine, June 2, 1982.
Bats Right. Throws Right. Height, 6 feet, 1 inch. Weight, 205 pounds.

Year	Club	Lea	G	IP	W	L	Pct	SO	BB	H	ERA	SAVES
2004 Lake Elsinore	Calif.	6	35$\frac{1}{3}$	2	0	1.000	30	9	28	1.78	0
2004 Portland	P.C.	14	81$\frac{1}{3}$	6	3	.667	50	26	83	3.54	0
2004 Mobile	Southern	8	51$\frac{1}{3}$	3	2	.600	33	13	56	2.63	0
2005 San Diego	N.L.	15	81	3	6	.333	49	29	92	5.33	0
2005 Portland	P.C.	13	75$\frac{1}{3}$	3	5	.375	64	17	90	5.14	0
2006 San Diego	N.L.	1	6	1	0	1.000	2	1	3	1.50	0
2006 Portland	P.C.	28	153	7	12	.368	89	52	199	5.53	0
2007 San Diego	N.L.	2	7$\frac{2}{3}$	0	1	.000	6	6	15	21.13	0
2007 Portland	P.C.	25	130$\frac{2}{3}$	8	5	.615	96	36	147	4.34	0
2008 San Diego a	N.L.					INJURED—Did Not Play					
2009 San Antonio	Texas	12	19	1	0	1.000	12	4	13	1.89	1
2009 Portland	P.C.	4	23	2	1	.667	16	4	16	2.35	0
2009 San Diego	N.L.	14	73	4	7	.364	53	34	71	3.58	0
2010 Portland	P.C.	6	17$\frac{2}{3}$	0	0	.000	8	7	24	4.58	0
2010 San Diego b	N.L.	32	82$\frac{2}{3}$	6	5	.545	61	24	65	1.85	0
2011 San Diego	N.L.	31	185$\frac{2}{3}$	9	12	.429	128	53	180	3.73	0
Major League Totals ....6 Yrs.		95	436	23	31	.426	299	147	426	3.92	0

a On disabled list from March 26 to October 8, 2008.
b On disabled list from May 11 to July 1, 2010.

STOREN, DREW PATRICK
Born, Brownsburg, Indiana, August 11, 1987.
Bats Both. Throws Right. Height, 6 feet, 2 inches. Weight, 180 pounds.

Year	Club	Lea	G	IP	W	L	Pct	SO	BB	H	ERA	SAVES
2009 Potomac..........	Carolina	7	10	1	0	1.000	11	2	7	1.80	2
2009 Harrisburg	Eastern	10	12$\frac{1}{3}$	1	0	1.000	12	6	3	0.00	9
2009 Hagerstown	So.Atl.	11	14$\frac{2}{3}$	0	1	.000	26	0	11	3.68	0
2010 Harrisburg	Eastern	7	9$\frac{1}{3}$	0	0	.000	11	1	5	0.96	4
2010 Syracuse	Int.	6	7$\frac{1}{3}$	0	0	.000	4	2	7	1.23	0
2010 Washington	N.L.	54	55$\frac{1}{3}$	4	4	.500	52	22	48	3.58	5
2011 Washington	N.L.	73	75$\frac{1}{3}$	6	3	.667	74	20	57	2.75	43
Major League Totals ....2 Yrs.		127	130$\frac{2}{3}$	10	7	.588	126	42	105	3.10	48

STRASBURG, STEPHEN JAMES
Born, San Diego, California, July 20, 1988.
Bats Right. Throws Right. Height, 6 feet, 4 inches. Weight, 220 pounds.

Year	Club	Lea	G	IP	W	L	Pct	SO	BB	H	ERA	SAVES
2010 Harrisburg	Eastern	5	22	3	1	.750	27	6	13	1.64	0
2010 Syracuse	Int.	6	33$\frac{1}{3}$	4	1	.800	38	7	18	1.08	0
2010 Washington a..........	N.L.	12	68	5	3	.625	92	17	56	2.91	0
2011 Hagerstown	So.Atl.	3	6$\frac{1}{3}$	0	1	.000	13	3	9	9.95	0
2011 Potomac..........	Carolina	1	3	0	0	.000	5	0	2	0.00	0
2011 Harrisburg	Eastern	1	6	1	0	1.000	4	0	1	0.00	0
2011 Syracuse	Int.	1	5	0	0	.000	7	0	2	1.80	0
2011 Washington b..........	N.L.	5	24	1	1	.500	24	2	15	1.50	0
Major League Totals ....2 Yrs.		17	92	6	4	.600	116	19	71	2.54	0

a On disabled list from July 22 to November 10, 2010.
b On disabled list from March 23 to September 6, 2011.

STREET, HUSTON LOWELL

Born, Austin, Texas, August 2, 1983.
Bats Right. Throws Right. Height, 6 feet. Weight, 190 pounds.

Year	Club	Lea	G	IP	W	L	Pct	SO	BB	H	ERA	SAVES
2004	Kane County	Midwest	9	10²/₃	0	1	.000	14	5	9	1.69	4
2004	Sacramento	P.C.	2	2	0	0	.000	2	0	2	0.00	1
2004	Midland	Texas	10	13¹/₃	1	0	1.000	14	3	10	1.35	3
2005	Oakland a	A.L.	67	78¹/₃	5	1	.833	72	26	53	1.72	23
2006	Oakland b	A.L.	69	70²/₃	4	4	.500	67	13	64	3.31	37
2007	Sacramento	P.C.	1	1	0	0	.000	2	0	1	0.00	0
2007	Oakland c	A.L.	48	50	5	2	.714	63	12	35	2.88	16
2008	Oakland d	A.L.	63	70	7	5	.583	69	27	58	3.73	18
2009	Colorado	N.L.	64	61²/₃	4	1	.800	70	13	43	3.06	35
2010	Tulsa	Texas	2	1¹/₃	0	0	.000	2	1	1	0.00	0
2010	Colorado Springs	P.C.	7	7	1	1	.500	9	2	11	10.29	0
2010	Colorado e	N.L.	44	47¹/₃	4	4	.500	45	11	39	3.61	20
2011	Colorado Springs	P.C.	2	2	0	0	.000	2	0	0	0.00	0
2011	Colorado f-g	N.L.	62	58¹/₃	1	4	.200	55	9	62	3.86	29
Major League Totals		7 Yrs.	417	436¹/₃	30	21	.588	441	111	354	3.11	178
Division Series												
2006	Oakland	A.L.	3	3	0	0	.000	1	1	4	3.00	2
2009	Colorado	N.L.	3	2²/₃	0	2	.000	1	3	6	13.50	1
Division Series Totals			6	5²/₃	0	2	.000	2	4	10	7.94	3
Championship Series												
2006	Oakland	A.L.	2	3¹/₃	0	1	.000	3	0	4	10.80	0

a Selected Rookie of the Year in American League for 2005.
b On disabled list from August 19 to September 8, 2006.
c On disabled list from May 13 to July 23, 2007.
d Traded to Colorado Rockies with outfielder Carlos Gonzalez and pitcher Greg Smith for outfielder Matt Holliday, November 12, 2008.
e On disabled list from March 26 to June 22, 2010.
f On disabled list from August 9 to August 26, 2011.
g Traded to San Diego Padres with cash for pitcher Nick Schmidt, December 7, 2011.

STUTES, MICHAEL CHRISTOPHER

Born, Metairie, Louisiana, September 4, 1986.
Bats Right. Throws Right. Height, 6 feet, 1 inch. Weight, 185 pounds.

Year	Club	Lea	G	IP	W	L	Pct	SO	BB	H	ERA	SAVES
2008	Williamsport	N.Y.-Penn.	6	27	2	1	.667	31	11	16	1.33	0
2008	Lakewood	So.Atl.	7	42²/₃	5	1	.833	53	18	20	1.48	0
2009	Reading	Eastern	27	145¹/₃	8	8	.500	109	58	147	4.26	0
2010	Reading	Eastern	25	35²/₃	3	0	1.000	37	21	28	3.79	2
2010	Lehigh Valley	Int.	28	40²/₃	4	1	.800	42	23	29	3.10	1
2011	Lehigh Valley	Int.	7	10	2	1	.667	14	4	9	1.80	1
2011	Philadelphia	N.L.	57	62	6	2	.750	58	28	49	3.63	0
Division Series												
2011	Philadelphia	N.L.	1	0¹/₃	0	0	.000	0	1	3	81.00	0

SWARZAK, ANTHONY RAY

Born, Ft.Lauderdale, Florida, September 10, 1985.
Bats Right. Throws Right. Height, 6 feet, 4 inches. Weight, 225 pounds.

Year	Club	Lea	G	IP	W	L	Pct	SO	BB	H	ERA	SAVES
2004	Twins	Gulf Coast	11	48	5	3	.625	42	6	46	2.63	1
2005	Beloit	Midwest	18	91¹/₃	9	5	.643	101	32	81	4.04	0
2005	Fort Myers	Fla.St.	10	59	3	4	.429	55	11	72	3.66	0
2006	Fort Myers	Fla.St.	27	145²/₃	11	7	.611	131	60	131	3.27	0
2007	New Britain	Eastern	15	86¹/₃	5	4	.556	76	23	78	3.23	0
2007	Fort Myers	Fla.St.	3	15²/₃	0	0	.000	18	5	14	2.30	0
2008	New Britain	Eastern	20	101²/₃	3	8	.273	76	37	126	5.67	0
2008	Rochester	Int.	7	45	5	0	1.000	26	14	41	1.80	0
2009	Minnesota	A.L.	12	59	3	7	.300	34	20	76	6.25	0
2009	Rochester	Int.	13	79²/₃	4	5	.444	45	21	79	3.28	0
2010	Rochester	Int.	22	111²/₃	5	12	.294	69	38	143	6.21	0
2011	Rochester	Int.	6	32¹/₃	2	1	.667	25	7	35	3.90	0
2011	Minnesota	A.L.	27	102	4	7	.364	55	26	111	4.32	0
Major League Totals		2 Yrs.	39	161	7	14	.333	89	46	187	5.03	0

TAKAHASHI, HISANORI

Born, Tokyo, Japan, April 2, 1975.
Bats Left. Throws Left. Height, 5 feet, 10 inches. Weight, 170 pounds.

Year	Club	Lea	G	IP	W	L	Pct	SO	BB	H	ERA	SAVES
2000	Yomiuri	Japan Cent.	24	135⅔	9	6	.600	102	36	133	3.18	0
2001	Yomiuri	Japan Cent.	30	134⅔	9	9	.500	99	52	126	3.94	0
2002	Yomiuri	Japan Cent.	24	163⅓	10	4	.714	145	39	143	3.09	0
2003	Yomiuri	Japan Cent.	13	86⅔	4	4	.500	78	27	79	3.84	0
2004	Yomiuri	Japan Cent.	16	91	5	10	.333	61	26	107	5.44	0
2005	Yomiuri	Japan Cent.	27	163	8	12	.400	135	48	171	4.47	0
2006	Yomiuri	Japan Cent.	35	62	2	6	.250	51	15	70	4.94	15
2007	Yomiuri	Japan Cent.	28	186⅔	14	4	.778	141	50	168	2.75	0
2008	Yomiuri	Japan Cent.	23	122	8	5	.615	94	30	127	4.13	0
2009	Yomiuri	Japan Cent.	25	144	10	6	.625	126	36	147	2.94	0
2010	New York a-b	N.L.	53	122	10	6	.625	114	43	116	3.61	8
2011	Los Angeles	A.L.	61	68	4	3	.571	52	25	58	3.44	2
Major League Totals	2 Yrs.		114	190	14	9	.609	166	68	174	3.55	10

a Signed with New York Mets organization, February 11, 2010.
b Waived by New York Mets, November 5, 2010. Signed with Los Angeles Angels, December 2, 2010.

THATCHER, JOSEPH (JOE)

Born, Indianapolis, Indiana, October 4, 1981.
Bats Left. Throws Left. Height, 6 feet, 2 inches. Weight, 230 pounds.

Year	Club	Lea	G	IP	W	L	Pct	SO	BB	H	ERA	SAVES
2004	River City	Frontier	29	41⅓	2	3	.400	55	15	38	2.98	5
2005	River City	Frontier	18	21⅓	4	2	.667	27	4	18	1.27	5
2005	Brevard County a	Fla.St.	7	9	0	0	.000	14	0	6	0.00	2
2005	Helena	Pioneer	6	7⅔	2	0	1.000	10	1	8	3.52	2
2006	Brevard County	Fla.St.	16	30⅔	3	1	.750	32	9	12	0.29	2
2006	West Virginia	So.Atl.	26	29⅔	1	3	.250	42	6	28	2.43	10
2006	Huntsville	Southern	4	5⅓	1	0	1.000	6	2	2	1.69	0
2007	Huntsville	Southern	14	16⅓	1	0	1.000	20	2	11	0.55	0
2007	Nashville	P.C.	24	21⅓	2	1	.667	33	7	19	2.08	1
2007	Portland	P.C.	8	8⅔	1	0	1.000	11	1	10	1.04	0
2007	San Diego b	N.L.	22	21	2	2	.500	16	6	13	1.29	0
2008	San Diego	N.L.	25	25⅔	0	4	.000	17	13	42	8.42	0
2008	Portland	P.C.	37	39	5	2	.714	44	11	38	2.77	3
2009	Portland	P.C.	19	19	1	2	.333	22	5	18	1.89	1
2009	San Diego	N.L.	52	45	1	0	1.000	55	18	37	2.80	0
2010	Portland	P.C.	6	5	0	1	.000	3	3	6	3.60	0
2010	San Diego c	N.L.	65	35	1	0	1.000	45	7	23	1.29	0
2011	Lake Elsinore	Calif.	1	1	0	0	.000	2	0	0	0.00	0
2011	Tucson	P.C.	8	7⅓	0	0	.000	10	3	3	1.23	0
2011	San Diego d	N.L.	18	10	0	0	.000	9	7	8	4.50	0
Major League Totals	5 Yrs.		182	136⅔	4	6	.400	142	51	123	3.36	0

a Signed by Milwaukee Brewers, July 19, 2005.
b Traded to San Diego Padres with pitcher Will Inman and pitcher Steve Garrison for pitcher Scott Linebrink, July 25, 2007.
c On disabled list from March 26 to April 22, 2010.
d On disabled list from March 22 to August 4, 2011.

THOMPSON, RICHARD MICHAEL (RICH)

Born, Hornsby, New South Wales, Australia, July 1, 1984.
Bats Right. Throws Right. Height, 6 feet, 1 inch. Weight, 205 pounds.

Year	Club	Lea	G	IP	W	L	Pct	SO	BB	H	ERA	SAVES
2002	Angels	Arizona	15	23⅓	2	0	1.000	29	9	14	2.70	1
2003	Cedar Rapids	Midwest	31	37⅔	1	2	.333	54	13	18	0.24	9
2003	Rancho Cucamonga	Calif.	24	29⅓	2	2	.500	33	18	28	4.91	8
2004	Rancho Cucamonga	Calif.	41	77⅔	3	2	.600	71	33	76	3.94	4
2005	Rancho Cucamonga	Calif.	42	121⅓	6	8	.429	92	53	132	5.27	3
2006	Arkansas	Texas	42	66⅔	3	4	.429	60	27	52	5.13	10
2006	Salt Lake	P.C.	4	4⅓	0	1	.000	3	4	9	12.46	1
2007	Rancho Cucamonga	Calif.	1	2	0	0	.000	3	0	1	0.00	0
2007	Arkansas	Texas	21	49⅓	2	3	.400	50	14	34	2.01	0
2007	Salt Lake	P.C.	16	24⅔	3	0	1.000	32	6	17	2.19	1
2007	Los Angeles	A.L.	7	6⅔	0	0	.000	9	3	10	10.80	0
2008	Los Angeles	A.L.	2	2	0	0	.000	1	2	4	22.50	0
2008	Angels	Arizona	7	9	0	0	.000	13	2	6	3.00	2

Year	Club	Lea	G	IP	W	L	Pct	SO	BB	H	ERA	SAVES
2008 Salt Lake	P.C.		10	13⅓	1	0	1.000	11	9	12	4.05	0
2009 Salt Lake	P.C.		29	43⅓	3	1	.750	51	11	41	3.12	0
2009 Los Angeles	A.L.		13	19⅓	0	0	.000	21	7	27	5.12	0
2010 Salt Lake	P.C.		19	29⅔	1	1	.500	30	10	17	0.61	2
2010 Los Angeles a	A.L.		13	19⅔	2	0	1.000	15	4	12	1.37	0
2011 Los Angeles	A.L.		44	54	1	3	.250	56	20	46	3.00	0
Major League Totals ....5 Yrs.			79	101⅔	3	3	.500	102	36	99	3.98	0

a On disabled list from August 5 to August 28, 2010.

THORNTON, MATTHEW J. (MATT)

Born, Three Rivers, Michigan, September 15, 1976.
Bats Left. Throws Left. Height, 6 feet, 6 inches. Weight, 235 pounds.

Year	Club	Lea	G	IP	W	L	Pct	SO	BB	H	ERA	SAVES
1998 Everett	Northwest		2	1⅓	0	0	.000	0	3	1	27.00	0
1999 Wisconsin	Midwest		25	29⅓	0	0	.000	34	25	39	4.91	1
2000 Wisconsin	Midwest		26	103⅓	6	9	.400	88	72	94	4.01	0
2001 San Bernardino	California		27	157	14	7	.667	192	60	126	2.52	0
2002 San Antonio	Texas		12	62	1	5	.167	44	29	52	3.63	0
2003 Inland Empire	California		2	9	0	0	.000	14	4	9	4.00	0
2003 Tacoma	P.C.		2	9	0	2	.000	5	3	14	8.00	0
2003 San Antonio	Texas		4	25⅓	3	0	1.000	18	9	8	0.36	0
2004 Tacoma	P.C.		16	83	7	5	.583	74	63	85	5.20	0
2004 Seattle	A.L.		19	32⅔	1	2	.333	30	25	30	4.13	0
2005 Seattle	A.L.		55	57	0	4	.000	57	42	54	5.21	0
2006 Chicago a	A.L.		63	54	5	3	.625	49	21	46	3.33	2
2007 Chicago	A.L.		68	56⅓	4	4	.500	55	26	59	4.79	2
2008 Chicago	A.L.		74	67⅓	5	3	.625	77	19	48	2.67	1
2009 Chicago	A.L.		70	72⅓	6	3	.667	87	20	58	2.74	4
2010 Chicago b	A.L.		61	60⅔	5	4	.556	81	20	41	2.67	8
2011 Chicago	A.L.		62	59⅔	2	5	.286	63	21	60	3.32	3
Major League Totals ....8 Yrs.			472	460	28	28	.500	499	194	396	3.52	20
Division Series												
2008 Chicago	A.L.		3	3⅓	0	0	.000	2	2	2	0.00	0

a Traded to Chicago White Sox for outfielder Joe Borchard, March 20, 2006.
b On disabled list from August 18 to September 3, 2010.

TILLMAN, CHRISTOPHER STEVEN (CHRIS)

Born, Anaheim, California, April 15, 1988.
Bats Right. Throws Right. Height, 6 feet, 5 inches. Weight, 195 pounds.

Year	Club	Lea	G	IP	W	L	Pct	SO	BB	H	ERA	SAVES
2006 Mariners	Arizona		5	11	2	0	1.000	16	5	9	0.82	1
2006 Everett	Northwest		5	19⅔	1	3	.250	29	15	25	7.78	0
2007 High Desert	Calif.		20	102⅔	6	7	.462	105	48	107	5.26	0
2007 Wisconsin	Midwest		8	33	1	4	.200	34	13	31	3.55	0
2008 Bowie a	Eastern		28	135⅔	11	4	.733	154	65	115	3.18	0
2009 Norfolk	Int.		18	96⅔	8	6	.571	99	26	85	2.70	0
2009 Baltimore	A.L.		12	65	2	5	.286	39	24	77	5.40	0
2010 Norfolk	Int.		21	121⅓	11	7	.611	94	30	120	3.34	0
2010 Baltimore	A.L.		11	53⅔	2	5	.286	31	31	51	5.87	0
2011 Norfolk	Int.		15	76⅓	3	6	.333	54	38	77	5.19	0
2011 Baltimore	A.L.		13	62	3	5	.375	46	25	77	5.52	0
Major League Totals ....3 Yrs.			36	180⅔	7	15	.318	116	80	205	5.58	0

a Traded by Seattle Mariners to Baltimore Orioles with pitcher Tony Butler, outfielder Adam Jones, pitcher Kam Mickolio and pitcher George Sherrill for pitcher Erik Bedard, February 8, 2008.

TOMLIN, JOSHUA AUBRY (JOSH)

Born, Tyler, Texas, October 19, 1984.
Bats Right. Throws Right. Height, 6 feet, 1 inch. Weight, 195 pounds.

Year	Club	Lea	G	IP	W	L	Pct	SO	BB	H	ERA	SAVES
2006 Mahoning Valley	N.Y.-Penn.		15	77⅓	8	2	.800	69	15	56	2.09	0
2007 Kinston	Carolina		6	27⅔	1	1	.500	20	12	24	3.58	0
2007 Lake County	So.Atl.		26	103⅔	10	3	.769	89	19	103	3.30	0
2008 Kinston	Carolina		40	102⅔	9	5	.643	109	16	82	2.98	3
2008 Buffalo	Int.		1	7	1	0	1.000	3	1	6	3.86	0
2009 Akron	Eastern		26	145	14	9	.609	125	27	149	4.16	0
2010 Columbus	Int.		20	107⅓	8	4	.667	80	33	83	2.68	0

Year Club	Lea	G	IP	W	L	Pct	SO	BB	H	ERA	SAVES
2010 Cleveland	A.L.	12	73	6	4	.600	43	19	72	4.56	0
2011 Cleveland a	A.L.	26	165⅓	12	7	.632	89	21	157	4.25	0
Major League Totals ....2 Yrs.		38	238⅓	18	11	.621	132	40	229	4.34	0

a On disabled list from August 25 to November 2, 2011.

TURNER, JACOB EDWARD
Born, St.Charles, Missouri, May 21, 1991.
Bats Right. Throws Right. Height, 6 feet, 5 inches. Weight, 210 pounds.

Year Club	Lea	G	IP	W	L	Pct	SO	BB	H	ERA	SAVES
2010 West Michigan	Midwest	11	54	2	3	.400	51	9	53	3.67	0
2010 Lakeland.	Fla.St.	13	61⅓	4	2	.667	51	14	53	2.93	0
2011 Erie.	Eastern	17	113⅔	3	5	.375	90	32	102	3.48	0
2011 Toledo	Int.	3	17⅓	1	0	1.000	20	3	15	3.12	0
2011 Detroit	A.L.	3	12⅔	0	1	.000	8	4	17	8.53	0

UEHARA, KOJI
Born, Osaka, Japan, April 3, 1975.
Bats Right. Throws Right. Height, 6 feet, 1 inch. Weight, 190 pounds.

Year Club	Lea	G	IP	W	L	Pct	SO	BB	H	ERA	SAVES
1999 Yomiuri	Japan Cent.	25	197⅔	20	4	.833	179	24	153	2.09	0
2000 Yomiuri	Japan Cent.	20	131	9	7	.562	126	22	112	3.57	0
2001 Yomiuri	Japan Cent.	24	138⅔	10	7	.588	108	28	133	4.02	0
2002 Yomiuri	Japan Cent.	26	204	17	5	.773	182	23	173	2.60	0
2003 Yomiuri	Japan Cent.	27	207⅓	16	5	.762	194	28	190	3.17	0
2004 Yomiuri	Japan Cent.	22	163	13	5	.722	153	23	135	2.60	0
2005 Yomiuri	Japan Cent.	27	187⅓	9	12	.429	145	22	164	3.31	0
2006 Yomiuri	Japan Cent.	24	168⅓	8	9	.471	151	21	157	3.21	0
2007 Yomiuri	Japan Cent.	55	62	4	3	.571	66	4	47	1.74	32
2008 Yomiuri	Japan Cent.	26	89⅔	6	5	.545	72	16	90	3.81	1
2009 Baltimore a-b	A.L.	12	66⅔	2	4	.333	48	12	71	4.05	0
2010 Baltimore c-d	A.L.	43	44	1	2	.333	55	5	37	2.86	13
2011 Baltimore-Texas e.......	A.L.	65	65	2	3	.400	85	9	38	2.35	0
Major League Totals ....3 Yrs.		120	175⅔	5	9	.357	188	26	146	3.13	13
Division Series											
2011 Texas	A.L.	1	0	0	0	.000	0	1	2	INF	0
Championship Series											
2011 Texas	A.L.	2	1⅓	0	0	.000	1	1	3	13.50	0

a Signed with Baltimore Orioles, January 13, 2009.

b On disabled list from May 24 to June 11 and June 24 to November 6, 2009.

c On disabled list from March 26 to May 6 and May 20 to June 27, 2010.

d Filed for free agency, November 1, 2010, re-signed with Baltimore Orioles, December 9, 2010.

e Traded to Texas Rangers with cash for pitcher Tommy Hunter and infielder Chris Davis, July 30, 2011.

VALVERDE, JOSE RAFAEL
Born, San Pedro de Macoris, Dominican Republic, July 24, 1979.
Bats Right. Throws Right. Height, 6 feet, 4 inches. Weight, 255 pounds.

Year Club	Lea	G	IP	W	L	Pct	SO	BB	H	ERA	SAVES
1997 Arizona..........	Dominican	14	18⅔	0	0	.000	19	13	20	5.30	0
1998 Arizona..........	Dominican	23	51⅓	1	3	.250	56	22	31	1.75	7
1999 Diamondbacks	Arizona	20	28⅔	1	2	.333	47	10	34	4.08	8
1999 South Bend	Midwest	2	2⅔	0	0	.000	3	2	2	0.00	0
2000 South Bend	Midwest	31	31⅔	0	5	.000	39	25	31	5.40	14
2000 Missoula	Pioneer	12	11⅔	1	0	1.000	24	4	3	0.00	4
2001 El Paso..............	Texas	39	41⅓	2	2	.500	72	27	36	3.92	13
2002 Tucson ......ᵗ......	P.C.	49	47⅔	2	4	.333	65	23	45	5.85	5
2003 Tucson	P.C.	22	29	1	1	.500	26	14	26	3.10	5
2003 Arizona.............	N.L.	54	50⅓	2	1	.667	71	26	24	2.15	10
2004 Arizona.............	N.L.	29	29⅔	1	2	.333	38	17	23	4.25	8
2004 Tucson a............	P.C.	10	10⅔	1	1	.500	5	5	9	4.22	3
2005 Tucson	P.C.	2	2	0	0	.000	3	1	1	0.00	0
2005 Arizona b	N.L.	61	66⅓	3	4	.429	75	20	51	2.44	15
2006 Tucson	P.C.	15	17⅔	1	0	1.000	18	10	13	3.06	3
2006 Arizona.............	N.L.	44	49⅓	2	3	.400	69	22	50	5.84	18
2007 Arizona c	N.L.	65	64⅓	1	4	.200	78	26	46	2.66	*47
2008 Houston	N.L.	74	72	6	3	.667	83	23	62	3.38	*44
2009 Corpus Christi	Texas	2	2	0	0	.000	2	2	0	0.00	0

Year Club	Lea	G	IP	W	L	Pct	SO	BB	H	ERA	SAVES
2009 Houston d-e	N.L.	52	54	4	2	.667	56	21	40	2.33	25
2010 Detroit	A.L.	60	63	2	4	.333	63	32	41	3.00	26
2011 Detroit	A.L.	*75	72⅓	2	4	.333	69	34	52	2.24	*49
Major League Totals 9 Yrs.		514	521⅓	23	27	.460	602	221	389	3.02	242
Division Series											
2007 Arizona	N.L.	3	3	0	0	.000	6	1	1	0.00	1
2011 Detroit	A.L.	3	3	0	0	.000	3	4	2	6.00	2
Division Series Totals		6	6	0	0	.000	9	5	3	3.00	3
Championship Series											
2007 Arizona	N.L.	1	1⅔	0	1	.000	2	3	1	5.40	1
2011 Detroit	A.L.	3	4⅓	0	1	.000	3	2	5	8.31	1
Championship Series Totals		4	6	0	2	.000	5	5	6	7.50	1

a On disabled list from June 14 to October 4, 2004.
b On disabled list from March 25 to May 2, 2005.
c Traded to Houston Astros for pitcher Chad Qualls, pitcher Juan Gutierrez and outfielder Chris Burke, December 14, 2007.
d On disabled list from April 27 to June 13, 2009.
e Filed for free agency, November 9, 2009. Signed with Detroit Tigers, January 19, 2010.

VARGAS, JASON MATTHEW

Born, Apple Valley, California, February 2, 1983.
Bats Left. Throws Left. Height, 6 feet. Weight, 215 pounds.

Year Club	Lea	G	IP	W	L	Pct	SO	BB	H	ERA	SAVES
2004 Jamestown	N.Y.-Penn.	8	41⅓	3	1	.750	41	13	35	1.96	0
2004 Greensboro	So.Atl.	3	19	2	1	.667	17	2	9	2.37	0
2005 Greensboro	So.Atl.	5	33⅔	4	1	.800	33	10	16	0.80	0
2005 Jupiter	Fla.St.	9	55⅓	2	3	.400	60	14	47	3.42	0
2005 Carolina	Southern	3	19	1	0	1.000	25	7	13	2.84	0
2005 Florida	N.L.	17	73⅔	5	5	.500	59	31	71	4.03	0
2006 Florida	N.L.	12	43	1	2	.333	25	30	50	7.33	0
2006 Albuquerque a	P.C.	13	69	3	6	.333	51	28	98	7.43	0
2007 New York	N.L.	2	10⅓	0	1	.000	4	2	17	12.19	0
2007 New Orleans b	P.C.	24	125	9	7	.563	108	44	141	4.97	0
2008 New York c-d	N.L.			INJURED—Did Not Play							
2009 Tacoma	P.C.	9	51⅔	4	3	.571	46	15	48	3.14	0
2009 Seattle	A.L.	23	91⅔	3	6	.333	54	24	98	4.91	0
2010 Seattle	A.L.	31	192⅔	9	12	.429	116	54	187	3.78	0
2011 Seattle	A.L.	32	201	10	13	.435	131	59	205	4.25	0
Major League Totals 6 Yrs.		117	612⅓	28	39	.418	389	200	628	4.53	0

a Traded to New York Mets with pitcher Adam Bostick for pitcher Matt Lindstrom and pitcher Henry Owens, November 20, 2006.
b On disabled list from September 21 to November 6, 2007.
c On disabled list from March 21 to November 3, 2008.
d Traded to Seattle Mariners with pitcher Aaron Heilman, outfielder Endy Chavez, infielder Mike Carp, outfielder Ezequiel Carrera, pitcher Maikel Cleto and pitcher Joe Smith for pitcher J.J. Putz, pitcher Sean Green and outfielder Jeremy Reed, December 10, 2008.

VAZQUEZ, JAVIER CARLOS

Born, Ponce, Puerto Rico, June 25, 1976.
Bats Right. Throws Right. Height, 6 feet, 2 inches. Weight, 215 pounds.

Year Club	Lea	G	IP	W	L	Pct	SO	BB	H	ERA	SAVES
1994 Expos	Gulf Coast	15	67⅔	5	2	.714	56	15	37	2.53	0
1995 Albany	So.Atl.	21	102⅔	6	6	.500	87	47	109	5.08	0
1996 Delmarva	So.Atl.	27	164⅓	14	8	.824	173	57	138	2.68	0
1997 Wst Plm Bch	Fla.St.	19	112⅔	6	3	.667	100	28	98	2.16	0
1997 Harrisburg	Eastern	6	42	4	1	1.000	47	12	15	1.07	0
1998 Montreal	N.L.	33	172⅓	5	15	.250	139	68	196	6.06	0
1999 Ottawa	Int.	7	42⅔	4	2	.667	46	16	45	4.85	0
1999 Montreal	N.L.	26	154⅔	9	8	.529	113	52	154	5.00	0
2000 Montreal	N.L.	33	217⅔	11	9	.550	196	61	247	4.05	0
2001 Montreal	N.L.	32	223⅔	16	11	.593	208	44	197	3.42	0
2002 Montreal	N.L.	34	230⅓	10	13	.435	179	49	*243	3.91	0
2003 Montreal a	N.L.	34	230⅔	13	12	.520	241	57	198	3.24	0
2004 New York b	A.L.	32	198	14	10	.583	150	60	195	4.91	0
2005 Arizona c	N.L.	33	215⅔	11	15	.423	192	46	223	4.42	0
2006 Chicago	N.L.	33	202⅔	11	12	.478	184	56	206	4.84	0
2007 Chicago	A.L.	32	216⅔	15	8	.652	213	50	197	3.74	0

Year	Club	Lea	G	IP	W	L	Pct	SO	BB	H	ERA	SAVES
2008 Chicago d	A.L.	33	208⅓	12	16	.429	200	61	214	4.67	0	
2009 Atlanta e	N.L.	32	219⅓	15	10	.600	238	44	181	2.87	0	
2010 New York f	A.L.	31	157⅓	10	10	.500	121	65	155	5.32	0	
2011 Florida g	N.L.	32	192⅔	13	11	.542	162	50	178	3.69	0	
Major League Totals ....14 Yrs.		450	2840	165	160	.508	2536	763	2784	4.22	0	
Division Series												
2004 New York	A.L.	1	5	0	0	.000	6	2	7	9.00	0	
2008 Chicago	A.L.	1	4⅓	0	1	.000	6	1	8	12.46	0	
Division Series Totals		2	9⅓	0	1	.000	12	3	15	10.61	0	
Championship Series												
2004 New York	A.L.	2	6⅓	1	0	1.000	6	7	9	9.95	0	

a Traded to New York Yankees for infielder Nick Johnson, outfielder Juan Rivera and pitcher Randy Choate, December 4, 2003.

b Traded to Arizona Diamondbacks with pitcher Brad Halsey, catcher Dioner Navarro and cash for pitcher Randy Johnson, January 11, 2005.

c Traded to Chicago White Sox for pitcher Orlando Hernandez, pitcher Luis Vizcaino and outfielder Chris Young, December 20, 2005.

d Traded to Atlanta Braves with pitcher Boone Logan for catcher Tyler Flowers, infielder Jonathan Gilmore, infielder Brent Lillibridge and pitcher Santos Rodriguez, December 4, 2008.

e Traded to New York Yankees with pitcher Boone Logan for outfielder Melky Cabrera, pitcher Arodys Vizcaino, pitcher Michael Dunn and cash, December 22, 2009.

f Filed for free agency, November 1, 2010. Signed with Florida Marlins, December 2, 2010.

g Filed for free agency, October 30, 2011.

VENTERS, JONATHAN WILLIAM (JONNY)
Born, Pikeville, Kentucky, March 20, 1985.
Bats Left. Throws Left. Height, 6 feet, 3 inches. Weight, 195 pounds.

Year	Club	Lea	G	IP	W	L	Pct	SO	BB	H	ERA	SAVES
2004 Braves	Gulf Coast	11	42⅓	1	6	.143	54	12	53	5.74	0	
2005 Rome	So.Atl.	23	103	8	6	.571	66	52	100	3.93	3	
2006 a			INJURED—Did Not Play									
2007 Myrtle Beach	Carolina	17	79⅔	3	3	.500	64	38	60	3.39	1	
2008 Myrtle Beach	Carolina	5	17⅔	1	2	.333	7	7	21	4.08	1	
2008 Braves	Gulf Coast	4	7⅔	0	0	.000	10	2	10	4.70	0	
2008 Mississippi	Southern	3	9	1	0	1.000	7	5	10	1.00	0	
2009 Gwinnett	Int.	19	91⅓	4	7	.364	58	42	103	5.62	0	
2009 Mississippi	Southern	12	65⅓	4	4	.500	40	35	60	2.76	0	
2010 Gwinnett	Int.	2	6⅔	1	0	1.000	6	1	4	1.35	0	
2010 Atlanta	N.L.	79	83	4	4	.500	93	39	61	1.95	1	
2011 Atlanta	N.L.	*85	88	6	2	.750	96	43	53	1.84	5	
Major League Totals ....2 Yrs.		164	171	10	6	.625	189	82	114	1.89	6	
Division Series												
2010 Atlanta	N.L.	4	5⅓	0	0	.000	8	0	7	0.00	0	

a On minor league disabled list from April 6 to September 9, 2006.

VERAS, JOSE ENGER
Born, Santo Domingo, Dominican Republic, October 20, 1980.
Bats Right. Throws Right. Height, 6 feet, 5 inches. Weight, 235 pounds.

Year	Club	Lea	G	IP	W	L	Pct	SO	BB	H	ERA	SAVES
1998 Devil Rays	Gulf Coast	5	16	1	1	.500	19	12	19	6.75	0	
1999 Princeton	Appal.	14	60⅔	3	5	.375	48	50	74	7.12	0	
2000 Charleston-SC	So.Atl.	20	106⅔	8	8	.500	102	41	125	4.81	0	
2001 Bakersfield	Calif.	27	153	9	8	.529	138	55	163	4.53	0	
2002 Bakersfield	Calif.	11	59	3	4	.429	57	30	77	5.34	0	
2002 Hudson Valley	N.Y.-Penn.	2	7	0	0	.000	7	5	2	0.00	0	
2003 Durham	Int.	3	5⅓	0	0	.000	3	1	9	8.44	0	
2003 Orlando	Southern	27	130⅓	6	9	.400	118	53	108	3.45	0	
2004 Durham	Int.	30	84⅓	6	5	.545	63	33	101	5.23	0	
2004 Montgomery a	Southern	3	10	1	0	1.000	6	7	10	6.30	0	
2005 Oklahoma b	P.C.	57	61⅔	3	5	.375	72	33	63	3.79	24	
2006 Columbus	Int.	50	59⅔	5	3	.625	68	19	49	2.41	21	
2006 New York	A.L.	12	11	0	0	.000	6	5	8	4.09	1	
2007 Yankees	Gulf Coast	2	2	0	0	.000	1	0	2	0.00	0	
2007 Tampa	Fla.St.	2	3	0	0	.000	5	2	0	0.00	0	
2007 Scranton-WB	Int.	12	16	2	0	1.000	17	7	17	4.50	4	
2007 New York c	A.L.	9	9⅓	0	0	.000	7	7	6	5.79	2	
2008 Scranton-WB	Int.	13	13	0	0	.000	21	4	8	1.38	9	
2008 New York	A.L.	60	57⅔	5	3	.625	63	29	52	3.59	0	

Year	Club	Lea	G	IP	W	L	Pct	SO	BB	H	ERA	SAVES
2009 Columbus..........	Int.		7	7	0	1	.000	9	2	3	1.29	0
2009 New York-Cleveland d-e..	A.L.		47	50⅓	4	3	.571	40	28	42	5.19	0
2010 New Orleans.......	P.C.		24	29⅓	1	1	.500	37	15	34	4.60	2
2010 Florida f.............	N.L.		48	48	3	3	.500	54	29	32	3.75	0
2011 Pittsburgh g..........	N.L.		79	71	2	4	.333	79	34	54	3.80	1
Major League Totals........6 Yrs.			255	247⅓	14	13	.519	249	132	194	4.11	4
Division Series												
2007 New York.............	A.L.		2	0⅔	0	0	.000	1	1	1	0.00	0

a Filed for free agency from Tampa Bay Devil Rays, October 15, 2004. Signed with Texas Rangers organization, November 15, 2004.
b Filed for free agency, October 15, 2005. Signed with New York Yankees organization, December 12, 2005.
c On disabled list from March 23 to August 14, 2007.
d Sold to Cleveland Indians, June 24, 2009.
e Not offered contract, December 12, 2009. Signed with Florida Marlins organization, January 29, 2010.
f Not offered contract, December 2, 2010. Signed with Pittsburgh Pirates organization, January 18, 2011.
g Traded to Milwaukee Brewers for infielder Casey McGehee, December 13, 2011.

VERLANDER, JUSTIN BROOKS

Born, Manakin Sabot, Virginia, February 20, 1983.
Bats Right. Throws Right. Height, 6 feet, 5 inches. Weight, 200 pounds.

Year	Club	Lea	G	IP	W	L	Pct	SO	BB	H	ERA	SAVES
2005 Lakeland............	Fla.St.		13	86	9	2	.818	104	19	70	1.67	0
2005 Erie..............	Eastern		7	32⅔	2	0	1.000	32	7	11	0.28	0
2005 Detroit..............	A.L.		2	11⅓	0	2	.000	7	5	15	7.15	0
2006 Detroit a............	A.L.		30	186	17	9	.654	124	60	187	3.63	0
2007 Detroit b............	A.L.		32	201⅔	18	6	*.750	183	67	181	3.66	0
2008 Detroit.............	A.L.		33	201	11	*17	.393	163	87	195	4.84	0
2009 Detroit.............	A.L.		35	*240	*19	9	.679	*269	63	219	3.45	0
2010 Detroit.............	A.L.		33	224⅓	18	9	.667	219	71	190	3.37	0
2011 Detroit c-d-e..........	A.L.		34	*251	*24	5	*.828	*250	57	174	*2.40	0
Major League Totals........7 Yrs.			199	1315⅓	107	57	.652	1215	410	1161	3.54	0
Division Series												
2006 Detroit..............	A.L.		1	5⅓	0	0	.000	5	4	7	5.06	0
2011 Detroit..............	A.L.		2	9	1	0	1.000	12	5	6	5.00	0
Division Series Totals...........			3	14⅓	1	0	1.000	17	9	13	5.02	0
Championship Series												
2006 Detroit..............	A.L.		1	5⅓	1	0	1.000	6	1	7	6.75	0
2011 Detroit..............	A.L.		2	11⅓	1	1	.500	13	5	13	5.56	0
Championship Series Totals......			3	16⅔	2	1	.667	19	6	20	5.94	0
World Series Record												
2006 Detroit..............	A.L.		2	11	0	2	.000	12	5	12	5.73	0

a Selected Rookie of the Year in American League for 2006.
b Pitched no-hit, no-run game against Milwaukee Brewers, June 12, 2007.
c Pitched no-hit, no-run game against Toronto Blue Jays, May 7, 2011.
d Selected Cy Young Award Winner in American League for 2011.
e Selected Most Valuable Player in American League for 2011.

VILLANUEVA, CARLOS MANUEL

Born, Santiago, Dominican Republic, November 28, 1983.
Bats Right. Throws Right. Height, 6 feet, 2 inches. Weight, 215 pounds.

Year	Club	Lea	G	IP	W	L	Pct	SO	BB	H	ERA	SAVES
2002 Giants............	Arizona		19	30⅓	4	0	1.000	23	3	24	0.59	3
2003 Giants............	Arizona		12	59	3	6	.333	67	13	64	3.97	0
2004 Beloit a...........	Midwest		25	114⅔	8	8	.500	113	30	102	3.77	1
2005 Brevard County......	Fla.St.		21	112⅓	8	1	.889	124	32	78	2.32	0
2005 Huntsville........	Southern		4	20⅔	1	3	.250	14	9	21	7.40	0
2006 Huntsville........	Southern		11	62⅓	4	5	.444	59	14	60	3.75	0
2006 Nashville.........	P.C.		11	66⅓	7	1	.875	61	26	42	2.71	0
2006 Milwaukee..........	N.L.		10	53⅔	2	2	.500	39	11	43	3.69	0
2007 Nashville.........	P.C.		2	8⅓	0	0	.000	9	1	3	3.24	0
2007 Milwaukee..........	N.L.		59	114⅓	8	5	.615	99	53	101	3.94	1
2008 Milwaukee..........	N.L.		47	108⅓	4	7	.364	93	30	112	4.07	1
2009 Milwaukee..........	N.L.		64	96	4	10	.286	83	35	102	5.34	3
2010 Nashville.........	P.C.		11	14⅓	0	0	.000	14	7	13	3.77	1
2010 Milwaukee b..........	N.L.		50	52⅔	2	0	1.000	67	22	48	4.61	1
2011 Dunedin............	Fla.St.		1	1	0	0	.000	0	0	1	0.00	0

Year	Club	Lea	G	IP	W	L	Pct	SO	BB	H	ERA	SAVES
2011 Toronto c	A.L.	33	107	6	4	.600	68	32	103	4.04	0	

Major League Totals	6 Yrs.	263	532	26	28	.481	449	183	509	4.28	6

Division Series

Year	Club	Lea	G	IP	W	L	Pct	SO	BB	H	ERA	SAVES
2008 Milwaukee	N.L.	2	3²/₃	0	0	.000	3	0	0	0.00	0

a Traded to Milwaukee Brewers by San Francisco Giants with pitcher Glenn Woolard for pitcher Wayne Franklin and pitcher Leo Estrella, March 30, 2004.

b Traded to Toronto Blue Jays for player to be named later, December 3, 2010. Milwaukee Brewers received cash to complete the transaction, April 8, 2011.

c On disabled list from August 4 to August 31, 2011.

VOGELSONG, RYAN ANDREW

Born, Charlotte, North Carolina, July 22, 1977.
Bats Right. Throws Right. Height, 6 feet, 3 inches. Weight, 215 pounds.

Year	Club	Lea	G	IP	W	L	Pct	SO	BB	H	ERA	SAVES
1998 Salem-Keizr	Northwest	10	56	6	1	.857	66	16	37	1.77	0
1998 San Jose	Calif.	4	19	0	0	.000	26	4	23	7.58	0
1999 San Jose	Calif.	13	69²/₃	4	4	.500	86	27	37	2.45	0
1999 Shreveport	Texas	6	28¹/₃	0	2	.000	23	15	40	7.31	0
2000 Shreveport	Texas	27	155¹/₃	6	10	.375	147	69	153	4.23	0
2000 San Francisco	N.L.	4	6	0	0	.000	6	2	4	0.00	0
2001 Fresno	P.C.	10	58	3	3	.500	53	18	35	2.79	0
2001 Nashville	P.C.	6	31²/₃	2	3	.400	33	15	26	3.98	0
2001 San Fran.-Pittsburgh a	N.L.	15	34²/₃	0	5	.000	24	20	39	6.75	0
2002 Lynchburg	Carolina	4	15²/₃	1	1	.500	20	7	19	8.04	0
2002 Altoona b	Eastern	8	43²/₃	1	5	.167	35	10	47	5.56	0
2003 Nashville	P.C.	26	149	12	8	.600	146	54	142	4.29	0
2003 Pittsburgh	N.L.	6	22	2	2	.500	15	9	30	6.55	0
2004 Pittsburgh	N.L.	31	133	6	13	.316	92	67	148	6.50	0
2005 Pittsburgh	N.L.	44	81¹/₃	2	2	.500	52	40	82	4.43	0
2006 Pittsburgh	N.L.	20	38	0	0	.000	27	16	44	6.39	0
2006 Indianapolis c	Int.	11	67²/₃	4	5	.444	43	12	54	2.66	0
2007 Hanshin	Japan Pac.	20	106²/₃	7	6	.538	91	41	113	4.13	0
2008 Hanshin	Japan Pac.	12	65¹/₃	3	4	.429	50	19	65	3.99	0
2009 Orix	Japan Pac.	30	42¹/₃	1	4	.200	56	16	39	4.54	0
2010 Salt Lake	P.C.	8	36²/₃	1	3	.250	37	22	47	4.66	0
2010 Lehigh Valley d-e-f	Int.	25	58²/₃	2	5	.286	73	40	60	4.91	1
2011 Fresno	P.C.	2	11¹/₃	2	0	1.000	17	5	8	1.59	0
2011 San Francisco h	N.L.	30	179²/₃	13	7	.650	139	61	164	2.71	0

Major League Totals	7 Yrs.	150	494²/₃	23	29	.442	355	215	511	4.71	0

a Traded to Pittsburgh Pirates with outfielder Armando Rios for pitcher Jason Schmidt and outfielder John Vander Wal, July 30, 2001.

b On disabled list from March 30 to August 1, 2002.

c Filed for free agency, October 2, 2006. Signed with Hanshin Tigers for 2007.

d Signed with Philadelphia Phillies organization, January 5, 2010.

e Released by Philadelphia Phillies, July 16, 2010. Signed with Los Angeles Angels organization, July 27, 2010.

f Filed for free agency, November 6, 2010. Signed with San Francisco Giants organization, January 15, 2011.

VOLQUEZ, EDINSON

Born, Santo Domingo, Dominican Republic, July 3, 1983.
Bats Right. Throws Right. Height, 6 feet, 1 inch. Weight, 200 pounds.

Year	Club	Lea	G	IP	W	L	Pct	SO	BB	H	ERA	SAVES
2003 Rangers	Arizona	10	27	2	1	.667	28	11	24	4.00	1
2004 Stockton	Calif.	8	39²/₃	4	1	.800	34	14	31	2.95	0
2004 Clinton	Midwest	22	91	4	4	.500	77	30	83	4.05	3
2005 Bakersfield	Calif.	11	66²/₃	5	4	.556	77	12	64	4.18	0
2005 Rangers	Arizona	1	2	0	0	.000	2	0	2	0.00	0
2005 Frisco	Texas	13	58²/₃	1	5	.167	49	17	58	4.14	0
2005 Texas	A.L.	6	12²/₃	0	4	.000	11	10	25	14.21	0
2006 Oklahoma	P.C.	21	120²/₃	6	6	.500	130	72	86	3.21	0
2006 Texas	A.L.	8	33¹/₃	1	6	.143	15	17	52	7.29	0
2007 Bakersfield	Calif.	7	35¹/₃	0	4	.000	38	20	27	7.13	0
2007 Frisco	Texas	11	58¹/₃	8	1	.889	62	19	46	3.55	0
2007 Oklahoma	P.C.	8	51	6	1	.857	66	21	25	1.41	0
2007 Texas a	A.L.	6	34	2	1	.667	29	15	34	4.50	0
2008 Cincinnati	N.L.	33	196	17	6	.739	206	93	167	3.21	0
2009 Cincinnati b	N.L.	9	49²/₃	4	2	.667	47	32	34	4.35	0
2010 Dayton	Midwest	2	13	0	0	.000	19	4	11	1.38	0
2010 Lynchburg	Carolina	2	8	1	0	1.000	7	0	3	0.00	0

Year Club	Lea	G	IP	W	L	Pct	SO	BB	H	ERA	SAVES
2010 Louisville	Int.	4	23	3	0	1.000	21	8	11	1.96	0
2010 Cincinnati c	N.L.	12	62²/₃	4	3	.571	67	35	59	4.31	0
2011 Louisville	Int.	13	87¹/₃	4	2	.667	83	29	72	2.37	0
2011 Cincinnati d	N.L.	20	108²/₃	5	7	.417	104	65	106	5.71	0
Major League Totals . . . . . . .7 Yrs.		94	497	33	29	.532	479	267	477	4.65	0
Division Series											
2010 Cincinnati.	N.L.	1	1²/₃	0	1	.000	0	2	4	21.60	0

a Traded to Cincinnati Reds with pitcher Danny Herrera for outfielder Josh Hamilton, December 21, 2007.
b On disabled list from May 17 to June 1 and June 2 to November 16, 2009.
c On disabled list from February 24 to July 17, 2010.
d Traded to San Diego Padres with pitcher Brad Boxberger, catcher Yasmani Grandal and infielder Yonder Alonso for pitcher Mat Latos, December 17, 2011.

VOLSTAD, CHRISTOPHER KENNETH (CHRIS)

Born, Palm Beach Gardens, Florida, September 23, 1986.
Bats Right. Throws Right. Height, 6 feet, 8 inches. Weight, 225 pounds.

Year Club	Lea	G	IP	W	L	Pct	SO	BB	H	ERA	SAVES
2005 Marlins.	Gulf Coast	6	27	1	1	.500	26	4	25	2.33	0
2005 Jamestown.	N.Y.-Penn.	7	38	3	2	.600	29	11	43	2.13	0
2006 Greensboro	So.Atl.	26	152	11	8	.579	99	36	161	3.08	0
2007 Jupiter	Fla.St.	21	126	8	9	.471	93	37	152	4.50	0
2007 Carolina	Southern	7	42²/₃	4	2	.667	25	10	41	3.16	0
2008 Carolina	Southern	15	91	4	4	.500	56	30	86	3.36	0
2008 Florida	N.L.	15	84¹/₃	6	4	.600	52	36	76	2.88	0
2009 New Orleans.	P.C.	1	4	0	1	.000	7	2	5	6.75	0
2009 Florida	N.L.	29	159	9	13	.409	107	59	169	5.21	0
2010 New Orleans.	P.C.	3	17	1	0	1.000	13	9	13	3.18	0
2010 Florida	N.L.	30	175	12	9	.571	102	60	187	4.58	0
2011 New Orleans.	P.C.	3	18¹/₃	1	1	.500	14	9	20	4.42	0
2011 Florida a	N.L.	29	165²/₃	5	13	.278	117	49	187	4.89	0
Major League Totals . . . . . . .4 Yrs.		103	584	32	39	.451	378	204	619	4.59	0

a Traded to Chicago Cubs for pitcher Carlos Zambrano and cash, January 5, 2012.

WAINWRIGHT, ADAM PARRISH

Born, Brunswick, Georgia, August 30, 1981.
Bats Right. Throws Right. Height, 6 feet, 7 inches. Weight, 205 pounds.

Year Club	Lea	G	IP	W	L	Pct	SO	BB	H	ERA	SAVES
2000 Danville	Appal.	6	29¹/₃	2	2	.500	39	2	28	3.68	0
2000 Braves	Gulf Coast	7	32	4	0	1.000	42	10	15	1.13	0
2001 Macon	So.Atl.	28	164²/₃	10	10	.500	184	48	144	3.77	0
2002 Myrtle Beach	Carolina	28	163¹/₃	9	6	.600	167	66	149	3.31	0
2003 Greenville a	Southern	27	149²/₃	10	8	.556	128	37	133	3.37	0
2004 Memphis	P.C.	12	63²/₃	4	4	.500	64	28	68	5.37	0
2005 Memphis	P.C.	29	182	10	10	.500	147	51	204	4.40	0
2005 St. Louis.	N.L.	2	2	0	0	.000	0	1	2	13.50	0
2006 St. Louis.	N.L.	61	75	2	1	.667	72	22	64	3.12	3
2007 St. Louis.	N.L.	32	202	14	12	.538	136	70	212	3.70	0
2008 Springfield	Texas	1	4²/₃	0	0	.000	7	0	4	0.00	0
2008 Memphis	P.C.	2	3²/₃	0	1	.000	3	2	8	12.27	0
2008 St. Louis b	N.L.	20	132	11	3	.786	91	34	122	3.20	0
2009 St. Louis.	N.L.	34	*233	*19	8	.704	212	66	216	2.63	0
2010 St. Louis.	N.L.	33	230¹/₃	20	11	.645	213	56	186	2.42	0
2011 St. Louis c	N.L.					INJURED—Did Not Play					
Major League Totals . . . . . . .6 Yrs.		182	874¹/₃	66	35	.653	724	249	802	2.97	3
Division Series											
2006 St. Louis.	N.L.	3	3²/₃	0	0	.000	6	0	3	0.00	1
2009 St. Louis.	N.L.	1	8	0	0	.000	7	1	3	1.13	0
Division Series Totals		4	11²/₃	0	0	.000	13	1	6	0.77	1
Championship Series											
2006 St. Louis.	N.L.	3	3	0	0	.000	4	1	2	0.00	2
World Series Record											
2006 St. Louis.	N.L.	3	3	1	0	1.000	5	1	2	0.00	1

a Traded by Atlanta Braves to St. Louis Cardinals with pitcher Jason Marquis and pitcher Ray King for catcher Eli Marrero and outfielder J.D. Drew, December 13, 2003.
b On disabled list from June 8 to August 22, 2008.
c On disabled list from March 25 to November 1, 2011.

WAKEFIELD, TIMOTHY STEPHEN (TIM)

Born, Melborne, Florida, August 2, 1966.
Bats Right. Throws Right. Height, 6 feet, 2 inches. Weight, 230 pounds.

Year	Club	Lea	G	IP	W	L	Pct	SO	BB	H	ERA	SAVES
1989	Welland	N.Y.-Penn.	18	39²/₃	1	1	.500	42	21	30	3.40	2
1990	Salem	Carolina	28	190¹/₃	10	14	.417	127	85	187	4.73	0
1991	Buffalo	A.A.	1	4²/₃	0	1	.000	4	1	8	11.57	0
1991	Carolina	Southern	26	183	15	8	.652	123	51	155	2.90	0
1992	Buffalo	A.A.	20	135¹/₃	10	3	.769	71	51	122	3.06	0
1992	Pittsburgh	N.L.	13	92	8	1	.889	51	35	76	2.15	0
1993	Carolina	Southern	9	56²/₃	3	5	.375	36	22	68	6.99	0
1993	Pittsburgh	N.L.	24	128¹/₃	6	11	.353	59	75	145	5.61	0
1994	Buffalo	A.A.	30	175²/₃	5	15	.250	83	98	197	5.84	0
1995	Pawtucket	Int.	4	25	2	1	.667	14	9	23	2.52	0
1995	Boston a-b	A.L.	27	195¹/₃	16	8	.667	119	68	163	2.95	0
1996	Boston	A.L.	32	211²/₃	14	13	.519	140	90	238	5.14	0
1997	Boston c	A.L.	35	201¹/₃	12	*15	.444	151	87	193	4.25	0
1998	Boston	A.L.	36	216	17	8	.680	146	79	211	4.58	0
1999	Boston	A.L.	49	140	6	11	.353	104	72	146	5.08	15
2000	Boston d	A.L.	51	159¹/₃	6	10	.375	102	65	170	5.48	0
2001	Boston	A.L.	45	168²/₃	9	12	.429	148	73	156	3.90	3
2002	Boston	A.L.	45	163¹/₃	11	5	.688	134	51	121	2.81	3
2003	Boston	A.L.	35	202¹/₃	11	7	.611	169	71	193	4.09	1
2004	Boston	A.L.	32	188¹/₃	12	10	.545	116	63	197	4.87	0
2005	Boston	A.L.	33	225¹/₃	16	12	.571	151	68	210	4.15	0
2006	Boston e	A.L.	23	140	7	11	.389	90	51	135	4.63	0
2007	Boston	A.L.	31	189	17	12	.586	110	64	191	4.76	0
2008	Boston f	A.L.	30	181	10	11	.476	117	60	154	4.13	0
2009	Pawtucket	Int.	2	9¹/₃	1	1	.500	7	2	5	2.89	0
2009	Boston g	A.L.	21	129²/₃	11	5	.688	72	50	137	4.58	0
2010	Boston	A.L.	32	140	4	10	.286	84	36	153	5.34	0
2011	Boston h	A.L.	33	154²/₃	7	8	.467	93	47	163	5.12	0
Major League Totals	19 Yrs.		627	3226¹/₃	200	180	.526	2156	1205	3152	4.41	22
Division Series												
1995	Boston	A.L.	1	5¹/₃	0	1	.000	4	5	5	11.81	0
1998	Boston	A.L.	1	1¹/₃	0	1	.000	1	2	3	33.75	0
1999	Boston	A.L.	2	2	0	0	.000	4	4	3	13.50	0
2003	Boston	A.L.	2	7²/₃	0	1	.000	7	3	6	3.52	0
2005	Boston	A.L.	1	5¹/₃	0	1	.000	4	1	6	6.75	0
Division Series Totals			7	21²/₃	0	4	.000	20	15	23	9.14	0
Championship Series												
1992	Pittsburgh	N.L.	2	18	2	0	1.000	7	5	14	3.00	0
2003	Boston	A.L.	3	14	2	1	.667	10	6	8	2.57	0
2004	Boston	A.L.	3	7¹/₃	1	0	1.000	6	3	9	8.59	0
2007	Boston	A.L.	1	4²/₃	0	1	.000	7	2	5	9.64	0
2008	Boston	A.L.	1	2²/₃	0	1	.000	2	2	6	16.88	0
Championship Series Totals			10	46²/₃	5	3	.625	32	18	42	5.21	0
World Series Record												
2004	Boston	A.L.	1	3²/₃	0	0	.000	2	5	3	12.27	0

a Released by Pittsburgh Pirates, April 20, 1995.
b Signed by Boston Red Sox, April 27, 1995.
c On disabled list from April 15 to May 6, 1997.
d Filed for free agency, October 31, 2000, re-signed with Boston Red Sox, December 7, 2000.
e On disabled list from July 18 to September 13, 2006.
f On disabled list from August 7 to August 26, 2008.
g On disabled list from July 18 to August 26, 2009.
h Filed for free agency, October 30, 2011.

WALDEN, JORDAN CRAIG

Born, Fort Worth, Texas, November 16, 1987.
Bats Right. Throws Right. Height, 6 feet, 5 inches. Weight, 235 pounds.

Year	Club	Lea	G	IP	W	L	Pct	SO	BB	H	ERA	SAVES
2007	Orem	Pioneer	15	64¹/₃	1	1	.500	63	17	49	3.08	0
2008	Cedar Rapids	Midwest	18	107¹/₃	4	6	.400	91	32	80	2.18	0
2008	Rancho Cucamonga	Calif.	9	49	5	2	.714	50	24	42	4.04	0
2009	Arkansas	Texas	13	60	1	5	.167	57	29	72	5.25	0
2010	Arkansas	Texas	38	43	1	1	.500	38	22	44	3.35	8
2010	Salt Lake	P.C.	6	6²/₃	0	0	.000	3	2	8	4.05	0
2010	Los Angeles	A.L.	16	15¹/₃	0	1	.000	23	7	13	2.35	1

Year Club	Lea	G	IP	W	L	Pct	SO	BB	H	ERA	SAVES
2011 Los Angeles	A.L.	62	60⅓	5	5	.500	67	26	49	2.98	32
Major League Totals . . . . 2 Yrs.		78	75⅔	5	6	.455	90	33	62	2.85	33

WANG, CHIEN-MING

Born, Tainan City, Taiwan, March 31, 1980.
Bats Right. Throws Right. Height, 6 feet, 3 inches. Weight, 230 pounds.

Year Club	Lea	G	IP	W	L	Pct	SO	BB	H	ERA	SAVES
2000 Staten Island	N.Y.-Penn.	14	87	4	4	.500	75	21	77	2.48	0
2001 a.					INJURED—Did Not Play						
2002 Staten Island	N.Y.-Penn.	13	78⅓	6	1	.857	64	14	63	1.72	0
2003 Yankees	Gulf Coast	1	3	0	0	.000	2	0	2	0.00	0
2003 Trenton.	Eastern	21	122	7	6	.538	84	32	143	4.65	0
2004 Trenton.	Eastern	18	109	6	5	.545	90	26	112	4.05	0
2004 Columbus.	Int.	6	40⅓	5	1	.833	35	8	31	2.01	0
2005 Columbus.	Int.	6	34	2	1	.667	21	6	40	4.24	0
2005 New York b.	A.L.	18	116⅓	8	5	.615	47	32	113	4.02	0
2006 New York	A.L.	34	218	*19	6	.760	76	52	233	3.63	1
2007 Tampa	Fla.St.	1	5	0	0	.000	4	1	5	5.40	0
2007 New York c.	A.L.	30	199⅓	19	7	.731	104	59	199	3.70	0
2008 New York d.	A.L.	15	95	8	2	.800	54	35	90	4.07	0
2009 Scranton-WB	Int.	2	13	1	0	1.000	7	3	7	0.00	0
2009 New York e.	A.L.	12	42	1	6	.143	29	19	66	9.64	0
2010 Washington f-g	N.L.				INJURED—Did Not Play						
2011 Hagerstown	So.Atl.	1	3	0	0	.000	3	0	4	6.00	0
2011 Potomac.	Carolina	1	4	0	0	.000	2	2	1	0.00	0
2011 Harrisburg	Eastern	2	11	2	0	1.000	3	0	8	0.00	0
2011 Syracuse	Int.	2	10⅔	0	1	.000	9	2	15	6.75	0
2011 Washington h-i.	N.L.	11	62⅓	4	3	.571	25	13	67	4.04	0
Major League Totals . . . . 6 Yrs.		120	733	59	29	.670	335	210	768	4.15	1
Division Series											
2005 New York	A.L.	1	6⅔	0	1	.000	1	0	6	1.35	0
2006 New York	A.L.	1	6⅔	1	0	1.000	4	1	8	4.05	0
2007 New York	A.L.	2	5⅔	0	2	.000	2	4	14	19.06	0
Division Series Totals		4	19	1	3	.250	7	5	28	7.58	0

a On minor league disabled list from April 5 to September 15, 2001.
b On disabled list from July 9 to September 6, 2005.
c On disabled list from March 23 to April 24, 2007.
d On disabled list from June 16 to November 14, 2008.
e On disabled list from April 19 to May 22 and July 5 to November 12, 2009.
f Not offered contract, December 12, 2009. Signed with Washington Nationals, February 19, 2010.
g On disabled list from April 4 to November 10, 2010.
h On disabled list from March 28 to July 29, 2011.
i Filed for free agency, October 30, 2011, re-signed with Washington Nationals, November 2, 2011.

WATSON, ANTHONY M. (TONY)

Born, Sioux City, Iowa, May 30, 1985.
Bats Left. Throws Left. Height, 6 feet, 4 inches. Weight, 220 pounds.

Year Club	Lea	G	IP	W	L	Pct	SO	BB	H	ERA	SAVES
2007 State College	N.Y.-Penn.	10	53⅔	6	1	.857	40	7	47	2.52	0
2007 Hickory.	So.Atl.	3	14	1	1	.500	18	1	14	3.86	0
2008 Lynchburg	Carolina	28	151⅔	8	12	.400	104	36	149	3.56	0
2009 Altoona.	Eastern	5	15⅓	0	3	.000	14	11	22	8.22	0
2010 Altoona.	Eastern	34	111⅓	6	4	.600	105	24	82	2.67	2
2011 Indianapolis	Int.	26	34⅓	3	3	.500	35	11	24	2.36	0
2011 Pittsburgh	N.L.	43	41	2	2	.500	37	20	34	3.95	0

WEAVER, JERED DAVID

Born, Northridge, California, October 4, 1982.
Bats Right. Throws Right. Height, 6 feet, 7 inches. Weight, 205 pounds.

Year Club	Lea	G	IP	W	L	Pct	SO	BB	H	ERA	SAVES
2005 Arkansas	Texas	8	43	3	3	.500	46	19	43	3.98	0
2006 Salt Lake	P.C.	12	77	6	1	.857	93	10	63	2.10	0
2006 Los Angeles	A.L.	19	123	11	2	.846	105	33	94	2.56	0
2007 Rancho Cucamonga. . . .	Calif.	2	11	1	0	1.000	12	3	5	0.82	0
2007 Los Angeles a.	A.L.	28	161	13	7	.650	115	45	178	3.91	0
2008 Los Angeles	A.L.	30	176⅔	11	10	.524	152	54	173	4.33	0

Year Club	Lea	G	IP	W	L	Pct	SO	BB	H	ERA	SAVES
2009 Los Angeles	A.L.	33	211	16	8	.667	174	66	196	3.75	0
2010 Inland Empire	Calif.	1	3	0	0	.000	3	1	2	0.00	0
2010 Los Angeles	A.L.	34	224⅓	13	12	.520	*233	54	187	3.01	0
2011 Los Angeles	A.L.	33	235⅔	18	8	.692	198	56	182	2.41	0
Major League Totals ....6 Yrs.		177	1131⅔	82	47	.636	977	308	1010	3.31	0
Division Series											
2007 Los Angeles	A.L.	1	5	0	1	.000	5	3	4	3.60	0
2008 Los Angeles	A.L.	1	2	1	0	1.000	3	1	1	0.00	0
2009 Los Angeles	A.L.	1	7⅓	1	0	1.000	7	2	2	1.23	0
Division Series Totals		3	14⅓	2	1	.667	15	6	7	1.88	0
Championship Series											
2009 Los Angeles	A.L.	3	6⅓	0	0	.000	7	4	5	4.26	0

a On disabled list from March 23 to April 17, 2007.

WEBB, RYAN CHRISTOPHER
Born, Clearwater, Florida, February 5, 1986.
Bats Right. Throws Right. Height, 6 feet, 6 inches. Weight, 215 pounds.

Year Club	Lea	G	IP	W	L	Pct	SO	BB	H	ERA	SAVES
2004 Athletics...........	Arizona	8	20⅓	1	1	.500	23	1	18	4.87	0
2005 Kane County.......	Midwest	24	128⅔	5	11	.313	84	41	139	4.76	0
2006 Stockton............	Calif.	23	117⅔	8	9	.471	96	37	160	5.28	0
2007 Stockton............	Calif.	15	83	4	7	.364	71	22	83	5.75	0
2007 Midland	Texas	5	25⅔	0	4	.000	16	10	34	9.12	0
2008 Midland	Texas	25	130	9	8	.529	94	44	165	5.19	0
2009 Sacramento	P.C.	31	45⅔	7	1	.875	39	15	57	4.34	2
2009 Portland..............	P.C.	3	3	0	0	.000	0	1	3	3.00	0
2009 San Diego a	N.L.	28	25⅔	2	1	.667	19	11	27	3.86	0
2010 Portland..............	P.C.	17	20⅔	1	0	1.000	23	5	12	0.87	1
2010 San Diego b	N.L.	54	59	3	1	.750	44	19	64	2.90	0
2011 Marlins.........	Gulf Coast	1	2	0	0	.000	2	0	2	0.00	0
2011 Jupiter	Fla.St.	3	3⅓	1	0	1.000	3	3	4	2.70	0
2011 Florida c............	N.L.	53	50⅔	2	4	.333	31	20	48	3.20	0
Major League Totals ....3 Yrs.		135	135⅓	7	6	.538	94	50	139	3.19	0

a Traded by Oakland Athletics to San Diego Padres with pitcher Craig Italiano and player to be named later for outfielder Scott Hairston, July 5, 2009. San Diego Padres received pitcher Sean Gallagher to complete trade, July 28, 2009.

b Traded to Florida Marlins with pitcher Edward Mujica for outfielder Cameron Maybin, November 13, 2010.

c On disabled list from June 27 to August 17, 2011.

WELLS, RANDY DAVID
Born, Belleville, Illinois, August 28, 1982.
Bats Right. Throws Right. Height, 6 feet, 3 inches. Weight, 230 pounds.

Year Club	Lea	G	IP	W	L	Pct	SO	BB	H	ERA	SAVES
2003 Cubs..............	Arizona	3	5	0	0	.000	4	4	5	3.60	0
2003 Lansing	Midwest	1	1	0	0	.000	0	0	1	0.00	0
2004 Lansing	Midwest	36	107⅔	6	6	.500	121	40	112	4.43	1
2005 Daytona	Fla.St.	41	98⅔	10	2	.833	106	22	93	2.74	2
2005 West Tenn	Southern	6	9⅓	0	1	.000	4	7	13	3.86	1
2006 Iowa................	P.C.	13	69	5	5	.500	59	23	87	4.96	0
2006 West Tenn	Southern	12	62⅓	4	2	.667	54	13	45	1.59	0
2007 Iowa................	P.C.	40	95⅔	5	6	.455	101	41	100	4.52	2
2008 Toronto	A.L.	1	1	0	0	.000	0	1	0	0.00	0
2008 Iowa................	P.C.	27	118⅔	10	4	.714	102	34	127	4.02	0
2008 Chicago a...........	N.L.	3	4⅓	0	0	.000	1	2	0	0.00	0
2009 Iowa................	P.C.	5	26	3	0	1.000	21	7	19	2.77	0
2009 Chicago	N.L.	27	165⅓	12	10	.545	104	46	165	3.05	0
2010 Chicago	N.L.	32	194⅓	8	14	.364	144	63	209	4.26	0
2011 Peoria.............	Midwest	1	3⅔	1	0	1.000	1	0	6	2.45	0
2011 Iowa................	P.C.	1	4	0	1	.000	3	3	6	13.50	0
2011 Chicago b...........	N.L.	23	135⅓	7	6	.538	82	47	141	4.99	0
Major League Totals ....4 Yrs.		86	500⅓	27	30	.474	331	159	515	4.01	0

a Selected by Toronto Blue Jays from Chicago Cubs in Rule V draft, December 6, 2007. Returned to Chicago Cubs, April 16, 2008.

b On disabled list from April 8 to May 28, 2011.

WESTBROOK, JACOB CAUTHEN (JAKE)

Born, Athens, Georgia, September 29, 1977.
Bats Right. Throws Right. Height, 6 feet, 3 inches. Weight, 215 pounds.

Year	Club	Lea	G	IP	W	L	Pct	SO	BB	H	ERA	SAVES
1996	Rockies	Arizona	11	62²/₃	4	2	.667	57	14	66	2.87	0
1996	Portland	Northwest	4	24²/₃	1	1	.500	19	5	22	2.55	0
1997	Asheville a	So.Atl.	28	170	14	11	.560	92	55	176	4.29	0
1998	Jupiter	Fla.St.	27	171	11	6	.647	79	60	169	3.26	0
1999	Harrisburg b	Eastern	27	174²/₃	11	5	.688	90	63	180	3.92	0
2000	Columbus	Int.	16	89	5	7	.417	61	38	94	4.65	0
2000	New York c-d-e-f	A.L.	3	6²/₃	0	2	.000	1	4	15	13.50	0
2001	Buffalo	Int.	12	64²/₃	8	1	.889	45	23	60	3.20	0
2001	Cleveland	A.L.	23	64²/₃	4	4	.500	48	22	79	5.85	0
2002	Akron	Eastern	3	15	0	1	.000	8	1	13	4.80	0
2002	Buffalo	Int.	1	6	1	0	1.000	2	0	8	6.00	0
2002	Cleveland g	A.L.	11	41²/₃	1	3	.250	20	12	50	5.83	0
2003	Buffalo	Int.	2	10	1	0	1.000	7	4	0	0.00	0
2003	Cleveland	A.L.	34	133	7	10	.412	58	56	142	4.33	0
2004	Cleveland	A.L.	33	215²/₃	14	9	.609	116	61	208	3.38	0
2005	Cleveland	A.L.	34	210²/₃	15	15	.500	119	56	218	4.49	0
2006	Cleveland	A.L.	32	211¹/₃	15	10	.600	109	55	*247	4.17	0
2007	Lake County	So.Atl.	1	5	0	1	.000	5	0	6	7.20	0
2007	Akron	Eastern	1	2¹/₃	0	0	.000	1	3	5	15.43	0
2007	Buffalo	Int.	2	5¹/₃	0	1	.000	5	5	9	8.44	0
2007	Cleveland h	A.L.	25	152	6	9	.400	93	55	159	4.32	0
2008	Lake County	So.Atl.	1	3²/₃	0	0	.000	4	1	3	2.45	0
2008	Akron	Eastern	1	6	0	0	.000	2	4	3	0.00	0
2008	Cleveland i	A.L.	5	34²/₃	1	2	.333	19	7	33	3.12	0
2009	Akron	Eastern	3	9	0	1	.000	8	6	1	2.00	0
2009	Cleveland j	A.L.				INJURED—Did Not Play						
2010	Cleveland	A.L.	21	127²/₃	6	7	.462	73	44	133	4.65	0
2010	St. Louis k-l	N.L.	12	75	4	4	.500	55	24	70	3.48	0
2011	St. Louis	N.L.	33	183¹/₃	12	9	.571	104	73	208	4.66	0
Major League Totals		11 Yrs.	266	1456¹/₃	85	84	.503	815	469	1562	4.34	0

Division Series

Year	Club	Lea	G	IP	W	L	Pct	SO	BB	H	ERA	SAVES
2007	Cleveland	A.L.	1	5	0	1	.000	1	0	9	10.80	0

Championship Series

Year	Club	Lea	G	IP	W	L	Pct	SO	BB	H	ERA	SAVES
2007	Cleveland	A.L.	2	12²/₃	1	1	.500	7	4	16	3.55	0

World Series Record

Year	Club	Lea	G	IP	W	L	Pct	SO	BB	H	ERA	SAVES
2011	St. Louis	N.L.	2	2	1	0	1.000	0	1	2	0.00	0

a Traded to Montreal Expos by Colorado Rockies with pitcher John Nicholson and outfielder Mike Hamlin for infielder Mike Lansing, November 18, 1997.

b Traded to New York Yankees with two players to be named later for pitcher Hideki Irabu, December 22, 1999. Pitchers Ted Lilly and Christian Parker were sent to New York Yankees to complete trade, March 17 and March 22, 2000.

c On disabled list from May 5 to 23, 2000.

d Sent to Cleveland Indians by New York Yankees with pitcher Zach Day to complete trade for outfielder David Justice, July 24, 2000.

e On disabled list from July 25 to September 1, 2000.

f On disabled list from September 1 to October 31, 2000.

g On disabled list from March 30 to July 11 and August 26 to November 4, 2002.

h On disabled list from May 3 to June 24, 2007.

i On disabled list from April 20 to May 28 and May 29 to November 13, 2008.

j On disabled list from March 26 to November 18, 2009.

k Traded to St. Louis Cardinals with cash for pitcher Corey Kluber, July 31, 2010.

l File for free agency, November 1, 2010, re-signed with St. Louis Cardinals, November 16, 2010.

WHEELER, DANIEL MICHAEL (DAN)

Born, Providence, Rhode Island, December 10, 1977.
Bats Right. Throws Right. Height, 6 feet, 3 inches. Weight, 220 pounds.

Year	Club	Lea	G	IP	W	L	Pct	SO	BB	H	ERA	SAVES
1997	Hudson Valley	N.Y.-Penn.	15	84	6	7	.462	81	17	75	3.00	0
1998	Chston-SC	So.Atl.	29	181	12	14	.462	136	29	206	4.43	0
1999	Orlando	Southern	9	58	3	0	1.000	53	8	56	3.26	0
1999	Durham	Int.	14	82¹/₃	7	5	.583	58	25	103	4.92	0
1999	Tampa Bay	A.L.	6	30²/₃	0	4	.000	32	13	35	5.87	0
2000	Tampa Bay	A.L.	11	23	1	1	.500	17	11	29	5.48	0
2000	Durham	Int.	26	150¹/₃	5	11	.313	91	42	183	5.63	0
2001	Durham	Int.	18	65¹/₃	3	5	.375	39	11	72	5.23	0
2001	Tampa Bay	A.L.	13	17²/₃	1	0	1.000	12	5	30	8.66	0
2001	Orlando	Southern	3	16	0	2	.000	12	6	15	2.81	0

Year Club	Lea	G	IP	W	L	Pct	SO	BB	H	ERA	SAVES
2002 Richmond a	Int.	27	155	9	6	.600	110	42	163	4.65	0
2003 Norfolk b	Int.	22	45⅔	4	2	.667	44	16	48	3.94	4
2003 New York	N.L.	35	51	1	3	.250	35	17	49	3.71	2
2004 Norfolk	Int.	5	7⅓	1	0	1.000	10	2	8	2.45	0
2004 New York-Houston c	N.L.	46	65	3	1	.750	55	20	76	4.29	0
2005 Houston	N.L.	71	73⅓	2	3	.400	69	19	53	2.21	3
2006 Houston	N.L.	75	71⅓	3	5	.375	68	24	58	2.52	9
2007 Houston	N.L.	45	49⅔	1	4	.200	56	13	46	5.07	11
2007 Tampa Bay d	A.L.	25	25	0	5	.000	26	10	28	5.76	0
2008 Tampa Bay	A.L.	70	66⅓	5	6	.455	53	22	44	3.12	13
2009 Tampa Bay	A.L.	69	57⅔	4	5	.444	45	9	41	3.28	2
2010 Tampa Bay e	A.L.	64	48⅓	2	4	.333	46	16	36	3.35	3
2011 Pawtucket	Int.	3	4⅔	0	0	.000	7	2	3	1.93	0
2011 Boston f-g	A.L.	47	49⅓	2	2	.500	39	8	47	4.38	0
Major League Totals .... 12 Yrs.		577	628⅓	25	43	.368	553	187	572	3.88	43
Division Series											
2004 Houston	A.L.	1	1	0	0	.000	0	0	0	0.00	0
2005 Houston	A.L.	3	4⅓	0	0	.000	5	3	4	2.08	0
2008 Tampa Bay	A.L.	1	1	0	0	.000	1	0	1	9.00	1
2010 Tampa Bay	A.L.	1	1	0	0	.000	2	0	0	0.00	0
Division Series Totals		6	7⅓	0	0	.000	8	3	5	2.45	1
Championship Series											
2004 Houston	N.L.	4	7	1	0	1.000	9	0	4	0.00	0
2005 Houston	N.L.	3	2⅔	0	0	.000	2	0	2	0.00	0
2008 Tampa Bay	A.L.	3	5	0	0	.000	5	3	5	5.40	0
Championship Series Totals		10	14⅔	1	0	1.000	16	3	11	1.84	0
World Series Record											
2005 Houston	N.L.	2	2	0	0	.000	1	1	2	13.50	0
2008 Tampa Bay	A.L.	3	2⅔	0	0	.000	3	1	3	6.75	0
World Series Totals		5	4⅔	0	0	.000	4	2	9	9.64	0

a Released by Tampa Bay Devil Rays, December 13, 2001. Signed with Atlanta Braves organization, January 20, 2002.
b Filed for free agency, October 15, 2002. Signed with New York Mets organization, January 27, 2003.
c Traded to Houston Astros for outfielder Adam Seuss, August 27, 2004.
d Traded to Tampa Bay Devil Rays for infielder Ty Wigginton, July 28, 2007.
e Filed for free agency, November 3, 2010. Signed with Boston Red Sox, December 18, 2010.
f On disabled list from May 5 to May 20, 2011.
g Filed for free agency, October 31, 2011.

WHITE, ALEX BRUCE
Born, Greenville, North Carolina, August 29, 1988.
Bats Right. Throws Right. Height, 6 feet, 3 inches. Weight, 215 pounds.

Year Club	Lea	G	IP	W	L	Pct	SO	BB	H	ERA	SAVES
2010 Kinston	Carolina	8	44	2	3	.400	41	19	32	2.86	0
2010 Akron	Eastern	18	106⅔	8	7	.533	76	27	91	2.28	0
2011 Tulsa	Texas	4	16⅓	1	1	.500	10	1	10	1.65	0
2011 Columbus	Int.	4	23⅔	1	0	1.000	28	5	19	1.90	0
2011 Cleveland	A.L.	3	15	1	0	1.000	13	9	14	3.60	0
2011 Colorado a-b	N.L.	7	36⅓	2	4	.333	24	16	48	8.42	0
Major League Totals ....1 Yrs.		10	51⅓	3	4	.429	37	25	62	7.01	0

a Traded to Colorado Rockies with pitcher Joseph Gardner, outfielder Matt McBride and player to be named later for pitcher Ubaldo Jimenez, July 31, 2011. Colorado Rockies received pitcher Drew Pomeranz to complete trade, August 17, 2011.
b On disabled list from May 21 to August 23, 2011.

WILLIAMS, JEROME LEE
Born, Honolulu, Hawaii, December 4, 1981.
Bats Right. Throws Right. Height, 6 feet, 3 inches. Weight, 240 pounds.

Year Club	Lea	G	IP	W	L	Pct	SO	BB	H	ERA	SAVES
1999 Salem-Keizer	Northwest	7	37	1	1	.500	34	11	29	2.19	0
2000 San Jose	Calif.	23	125⅔	7	6	.538	115	48	89	2.94	0
2001 Shreveport	Texas	23	130	9	7	.563	84	34	116	3.95	0
2002 Fresno	P.C.	28	160⅔	6	11	.353	130	50	140	3.59	0
2003 Fresno	P.C.	10	57	4	2	.667	40	16	52	2.68	0
2003 San Francisco	N.L.	21	131	7	5	.583	88	49	116	3.30	0
2004 San Francisco a	N.L.	22	129⅓	10	7	.588	80	44	123	4.24	0
2005 Fresno	P.C.	6	30⅔	1	4	.200	15	17	47	9.39	0

Year	Club	Lea	G	IP	W	L	Pct	SO	BB	H	ERA	SAVES
2005 Iowa	P.C.		4	24⅓	1	1	.500	17	6	27	2.22	0
2005 San Francisco-Chicago b	N.L.		22	122⅔	6	10	.375	70	49	119	4.26	0
2006 Chicago	N.L.		5	12⅓	0	2	.000	5	11	15	7.30	0
2006 Iowa c	P.C.		29	111⅔	5	7	.417	52	35	145	4.76	0
2007 Columbus	Int.		1	6	0	0	.000	5	2	4	1.50	0
2007 Washington	N.L.		6	30	0	5	.000	15	18	34	7.20	0
2007 Harrisburg	Eastern		14	35⅔	0	3	.000	26	16	53	9.08	0
2007 Rochester d-e-f	Int.		8	11	0	1	.000	6	7	18	9.00	1
2008 Long Beach	Golden		6	40	3	2	.600	28	8	48	4,95	0
2008 Inland Empire	Calif.		3	10	0	1	.000	8	6	13	6.30	0
2008 Las Vegas g-h-i	P.C.		10	26	2	2	.500	21	9	23	2.08	0
2009 Sacramento	P.C.		27	101⅔	5	6	.455	52	41	116	5.58	0
2010 Uni-President	Taiwan						No Data Available					
2011 Lancaster	Atlantic		8	52⅔	7	1	.875	40	12	43	2.91	0
2011 Salt Lake	P.C.		11	73⅔	7	2	.778	60	15	78	3.91	0
2011 Los Angeles j	A.L.		10	44	4	0	1.000	28	15	45	3.68	0
Major League Totals	6 Yrs.		86	469⅓	27	29	.482	286	186	452	4.20	0
Division Series												
2003 San Francisco	N.L.		1	2	0	0	.000	1	1	5	13.50	0

a On disabled list from July 31 to September 16, 2004.

b Traded to Chicago Cubs with pitcher David Aardsma for pitcher La Troy Hawkins, May 28, 2005.

c Claimed on waivers by Oakland Athletics, September 5, 2006.

d Filed for free agency, December 12, 2006. Signed with Washington Nationals organization, January 12, 2007.

e On disabled list from April 29 to May 15 and May 16 to June 20, 2007.

f Released by Washington Nationals, August 5, 2007. Signed with Minnesota Twins organization, August 9, 2007.

g Filed for free agency, October 29, 2007. Signed with Long Beach (Golden) for 2008.

h Signed with Los Angeles Dodgers organization, June 25, 2008.

i Filed for free agency, November 3, 2008. Signed with Oakland Athletics organization, December 1, 2008.

j Filed for free agency, November 9, 2009. Signed with Los Angeles Angels organization, June 17, 2011.

WILLIS, DONTRELLE WAYNE

Born, Oakland, California, January 12, 1982.
Bats Left. Throws Left. Height, 6 feet, 4 inches. Weight, 225 pounds.

Year	Club	Lea	G	IP	W	L	Pct	SO	BB	H	ERA	SAVES
2000 Cubs	Arizona		9	28	3	1	.750	22	8	26	3.86	0
2001 Boise	Northwest		15	93⅔	8	2	.800	77	19	76	2.98	0
2002 Kane County	Midwest		19	127⅔	10	2	.833	101	21	91	1.83	0
2002 Jupiter a	Fla.St.		5	30	2	0	1.000	27	3	24	1.80	0
2003 Carolina	Southern		6	36⅓	4	0	1.000	32	9	24	1.49	0
2003 Florida b	N.L.		27	160⅔	14	6	.700	142	58	148	3.30	0
2004 Florida	N.L.		32	197	10	11	.476	139	61	210	4.02	0
2005 Florida	N.L.		34	236⅓	*22	10	.688	170	55	213	2.63	0
2006 Florida	N.L.		34	223⅓	12	12	.500	160	83	234	3.87	0
2007 Florida c	N.L.		35	205⅓	10	15	.400	146	87	241	5.17	0
2008 Lakeland	Fla.St.		6	28	0	3	.000	18	11	30	4.50	0
2008 Toledo	Int.		6	28⅓	3	1	.750	20	14	34	4.45	0
2008 Detroit d	A.L.		8	24	0	2	.000	18	35	18	9.38	0
2009 Lakeland	Fla.St.		1	7	0	1	.000	2	0	8	5.14	0
2009 Erie	Eastern		1	6	1	0	1.000	6	3	3	3.00	0
2009 Toledo	Int.		5	24⅓	1	2	.333	15	17	22	4.81	0
2009 Detroit e	A.L.		7	33⅔	1	4	.200	17	28	37	7.49	0
2010 Giants	Arizona		3	2	0	1	.000	1	1	4	9.00	0
2010 Fresno	P.C.		5	5⅓	0	0	.000	6	4	5	5.06	0
2010 Detroit	A.L.		9	43⅓	1	2	.333	33	29	48	4.98	0
2010 Arizona f-g-h	N.L.		6	22⅓	1	1	.500	14	27	24	6.85	0
2011 Louisville	Int.		13	75⅓	5	2	.714	67	20	71	2.63	0
2011 Cincinnati i	N.L.		13	75⅔	1	6	.143	57	37	78	5.00	0
Major League Totals	9 Yrs.		205	1221⅔	72	69	.511	896	500	1251	4.17	0
Division Series												
2003 Florida	N.L.		2	5⅔	0	0	.000	3	2	7	7.94	0
Championship Series												
2003 Florida	N.L.		2	3⅓	0	1	.000	4	6	4	18.90	0
World Series Record												
2003 Florida	N.L.		3	3⅔	0	0	.000	3	2	4	0.00	0

a Traded by Chicago Cubs to Florida Marlins with pitcher Julian Tavarez, pitcher Jose Cueto and catcher Ryan Jorgensen for pitcher Antonio Alfonseca and pitcher Matt Clement, March 27, 2002.

b Selected Rookie of the Year in National League for 2003.

c Traded to Detroit Tigers with infielder Miguel Cabrera for pitcher Burke Badenhop, pitcher Eulogio De La Cruz, pitcher Andrew Miller, catcher Mike Rabelo and outfielder Cameron Maybin, December 5, 2007.

d On disabled list from April 12 to May 21, 2008.
e On disabled list from March 29 to May 13 and June 15 to October 15, 2009.
f Traded to Arizona Diamondbacks with cash for pitcher Billy Buckner, June 1, 2010.
g Released by Arizona Diamondbacks, July 6, 2010. Signed with San Francisco Giants organization, July 15, 2010.
h Filed for free agency, November 6, 2010. Signed with Cincinnati Reds organization, November 23, 2010.
i Filed for free agency, October 30, 2011.

WILSON, BRIAN PATRICK

Born, Londonderry, New Hampshire, March 16, 1982.
Bats Right. Throws Right. Height, 6 feet, 1 inch. Weight, 205 pounds.

Year	Club	Lea	G	IP	W	L	Pct	SO	BB	H	ERA	SAVES
2004	Hagerstown	So.Atl.	23	57⅓	2	5	.286	41	22	63	5.34	3
2005	Norwich	Eastern	15	15⅔	0	0	.000	22	5	6	0.57	8
2005	Fresno	P.C.	9	11⅓	1	1	.500	13	8	8	3.97	0
2005	Augusta	So.Atl.	26	33	5	1	.833	30	7	23	0.82	13
2006	San Jose	Calif.	1	1	0	0	.000	1	1	1	9.00	0
2006	Fresno	P.C.	24	28	1	3	.250	30	14	20	2.89	7
2006	San Francisco	N.L.	31	30	2	3	.400	23	21	32	5.40	1
2007	San Jose	Calif.	3	3	0	0	.000	6	0	1	0.00	2
2007	Fresno	P.C.	31	34⅓	1	2	.333	37	24	24	2.10	11
2007	San Francisco	N.L.	24	23⅔	1	2	.333	18	7	16	2.28	6
2008	San Francisco	N.L.	63	62⅓	3	2	.600	67	28	62	4.62	41
2009	San Francisco	N.L.	68	72⅓	5	6	.455	83	27	60	2.74	38
2010	San Francisco	N.L.	70	74⅔	3	3	.500	93	26	62	1.81	*48
2011	San Francisco a	N.L.	57	55	6	4	.600	54	31	50	3.11	36
Major League Totals	6 Yrs.		313	318	20	20	.500	338	140	282	3.17	170
Division Series												
2010	San Francisco	N.L.	3	4	0	0	.000	5	2	2	0.00	2
Championship Series												
2010	San Francisco	N.L.	4	5	1	0	1.000	7	2	2	0.00	3
World Series Record												
2010	San Francisco	N.L.	3	2⅔	0	0	.000	4	0	1	0.00	1

a On disabled list from March 22 to April 6 and August 16 to September 18, 2011.

WILSON, CHRISTOPHER JOHN (C.J.)

Born, Newport Beach, California, November 18, 1980.
Bats Left. Throws Left. Height, 6 feet, 2 inches. Weight, 215 pounds.

Year	Club	Lea	G	IP	W	L	Pct	SO	BB	H	ERA	SAVES
2001	Pulaski	Appal.	8	37⅔	1	0	1.000	49	9	24	0.96	0
2001	Savannah	So.Atl.	5	34	1	2	.333	26	9	30	3.18	0
2002	Charlotte	Fla.St.	26	106	10	2	.833	76	41	86	3.06	1
2002	Tulsa	Texas	5	30	1	0	1.000	17	12	23	1.80	0
2003	Frisco	Texas	22	123	6	9	.400	89	38	135	5.05	0
2004							INJURED—Did Not Play					
2005	Bakersfield	Calif.	4	13⅓	0	1	.000	14	4	10	3.29	0
2005	Frisco	Texas	12	44⅔	0	4	.000	43	14	51	4.43	0
2005	Texas	A.L.	24	48	1	7	.125	30	18	63	6.94	1
2006	Frisco	Texas	4	3⅓	0	0	.000	6	2	3	2.70	0
2006	Oklahoma	P.C.	9	11	1	0	1.000	17	5	10	2.45	2
2006	Texas a	A.L.	44	44⅓	2	4	.333	43	18	39	4.06	1
2007	Texas	A.L.	66	68⅓	2	1	.667	63	33	50	3.03	12
2008	Texas b	A.L.	50	46⅓	2	2	.500	41	27	49	6.02	24
2009	Texas	A.L.	74	73⅔	5	6	.455	84	32	66	2.81	14
2010	Texas c	A.L.	33	204	15	8	.652	170	*93	161	3.35	0
2011	Texas	A.L.	34	223⅓	16	7	.696	206	74	191	2.94	0
Major League Totals	7 Yrs.		325	708	43	35	.551	637	295	619	3.60	52
Division Series												
2010	Texas	A.L.	1	6⅓	1	0	1.000	7	2	2	0.00	0
2011	Texas	A.L.	1	5	0	1	.000	6	1	7	10.80	0
Division Series Totals			2	11⅓	1	1	.500	13	3	9	4.76	0
Championship Series												
2010	Texas	A.L.	2	12	0	1	.000	6	6	12	6.00	0
2011	Texas	A.L.	2	10⅔	0	1	.000	11	7	14	6.75	0
Championship Series Totals			4	22⅔	0	2	.000	17	13	26	6.35	0
World Series Record												
2010	Texas	A.L.	1	6	0	1	.000	4	2	3	3.00	0
2011	Texas	A.L.	3	12⅓	0	1	.000	9	11	8	2.92	0
World Series Totals			4	18⅓	0	2	.000	13	13	11	2.95	0

a On disabled list from March 24 to April 14, 2006.
b On disabled list from August 6 to October 2, 2008.
c Filed for free agency, October 30, 2011. Signed with Los Angeles Angels, December 10, 2011.

WOLF, RANDALL CHRISTOPHER (RANDY)

Born, Canoga Park, California, August 22, 1976.
Bats Left. Throws Left. Height, 6 feet. Weight, 205 pounds.

Year	Club	Lea	G	IP	W	L	Pct	SO	BB	H	ERA	SAVES
1997	Batavia	N.Y.-Penn.	7	40	4	0	1.000	53	8	29	1.58	0
1998	Reading	Eastern	4	25	2	0	1.000	33	4	15	1.44	0
1998	Scranton-WB	Int.	24	148	9	7	.563	118	48	167	4.62	0
1999	Scranton-WB	Int.	12	77⅓	4	5	.444	72	29	73	3.61	0
1999	Philadelphia	N.L.	22	121⅔	6	9	.400	116	67	126	5.55	0
2000	Philadelphia	N.L.	32	206⅓	11	9	.550	160	83	210	4.36	0
2001	Scranton-WB	Int.	2	9	0	1	.000	7	5	10	5.00	0
2001	Reading	Eastern	1	6	0	0	.000	7	2	5	4.50	0
2001	Philadelphia a	N.L.	28	163	10	11	.476	152	51	150	3.70	0
2002	Clearwater	Fla.St.	1	5	0	0	.000	8	1	1	0.00	0
2002	Philadelphia b	N.L.	31	210⅔	11	9	.550	172	63	172	3.20	0
2003	Philadelphia	N.L.	33	200	16	10	.615	177	78	176	4.23	0
2004	Reading	Eastern	1	4	0	0	.000	4	0	5	2.25	0
2004	Philadelphia c	N.L.	23	136⅔	5	8	.385	89	36	145	4.28	0
2005	Philadelphia d	N.L.	13	80	6	4	.600	61	26	87	4.39	0
2006	Clearwater	Fla.St.	2	5⅔	0	0	.000	4	4	6	0.00	0
2006	Reading	Eastern	3	12	1	1	.500	11	7	15	6.75	0
2006	Lakewood	So.Atl.	2	8	0	0	.000	7	3	2	1.13	0
2006	Philadelphia e-f	N.L.	12	56⅔	4	0	1.000	44	33	63	5.56	0
2007	Inland Empire	Calif.	1	4	0	0	.000	4	1	6	6.75	0
2007	Los Angeles g-h	N.L.	18	102⅔	9	6	.600	94	39	110	4.73	0
2008	San Diego-Houston i-j	N.L.	33	190⅓	12	12	.500	162	71	191	4.30	0
2009	Los Angeles k	N.L.	34	214⅓	11	7	.611	160	58	178	3.23	0
2010	Milwaukee	N.L.	34	215⅔	13	12	.520	142	87	213	4.17	0
2011	Milwaukee	N.L.	33	212⅓	13	10	.565	134	66	214	3.69	0
Major League Totals	13 Yrs.		346	2110⅓	127	107	.543	1663	758	2035	4.09	0

Division Series

Year	Club	Lea	G	IP	W	L	Pct	SO	BB	H	ERA	SAVES
2009	Los Angeles	N.L.	1	3⅔	0	0	.000	2	5	6	4.91	0
2011	Milwaukee	N.L.	1	3	0	1	.000	2	3	8	21.00	0
Division Series Totals			2	6⅔	0	1	.000	4	8	14	12.15	0

Championship Series

Year	Club	Lea	G	IP	W	L	Pct	SO	BB	H	ERA	SAVES
2009	Los Angeles	N.L.	1	5⅓	0	0	.000	2	2	4	5.06	0
2011	Milwaukee	N.L.	1	7	1	0	1.000	6	1	6	2.57	0
Championship Series Totals			2	12⅓	1	0	1.000	8	3	10	3.65	0

a On disabled list from August 2 to September 1, 2001.
b On disabled list from March 25 to April 12, 2002.
c On disabled list from June 3 to June 26 and August 29 to October 8, 2004.
d On disabled list from June 12 to November 1, 2005.
e On disabled list from March 24 to July 30, 2006.
f Filed for free agency, October 28, 2006. Signed with Los Angeles Dodgers, November 28, 2006.
    On disabled list from July 4 to October 31, 2007.
g Filed for free agency, November 9, 2007. Signed with San Diego Padres, December 10, 2007.
h Traded to Houston Astros for pitcher Chad Reineke, July 22, 2008.
i Filed for free agency, October 31, 2008. Signed with Los Angeles Dodgers, February 6, 2009.
k Filed for free agency, November 5, 2009. Signed with Milwaukee Brewers, December 14, 2009.

WOOD, BLAKE DANIEL

Born, Atlanta, Georgia, August 8, 1985.
Bats Right. Throws Right. Height, 6 feet, 5 inches. Weight, 230 pounds.

Year	Club	Lea	G	IP	W	L	Pct	SO	BB	H	ERA	SAVES
2006	Idaho Falls	Pioneer	12	52	3	1	.750	46	15	50	4.50	0
2007	Royals	Arizona	4	9⅔	0	0	.000	15	0	9	0.00	0
2007	Wilmington	Carolina	2	9⅔	0	1	.000	11	3	9	4.66	0
2007	Burlington	Midwest	7	35⅔	2	1	.667	26	14	32	3.03	0
2008	Wilmington	Carolina	10	57⅓	3	2	.600	63	15	32	2.67	0
2008	NW Arkansas	Texas	18	86⅔	5	7	.417	76	32	96	5.30	0
2009	Royals	Arizona	3	4	0	1	.000	4	1	4	0.00	0
2009	NW Arkansas	Texas	17	78⅔	2	8	.200	49	28	92	5.83	0
2010	Omaha	P.C.	12	16⅔	2	1	.667	12	7	12	2.16	5
2010	Kansas City	A.L.	51	49⅔	1	3	.250	31	22	54	5.07	0
2011	Omaha	P.C.	3	5	0	0	.000	6	0	2	0.00	0

Year	Club	Lea	G	IP	W	L	Pct	SO	BB	H	ERA	SAVES
2011 Kansas City		A.L.	55	69²/₃	5	3	.625	62	32	66	3.75	1
Major League Totals		2 Yrs.	106	119¹/₃	6	6	.500	93	54	120	4.30	1

WOOD, KERRY LEE

Born, Irving, Texas, June 16, 1977.
Bats Right. Throws Right. Height, 6 feet, 5 inches. Weight, 210 pounds.

Year	Club	Lea	G	IP	W	L	Pct	SO	BB	H	ERA	SAVES
1995 Cubs.	Gulf Coast		1	3	0	0	.000	2	1	0	0.00	0
1995 Williamsport.	N.Y.-Penn.		2	4¹/₃	0	0	.000	5	5	5	10.38	0
1996 Daytona a	Fla.St.		22	114¹/₃	10	2	.833	136	70	72	2.91	0
1997 Orlando	Southern		19	94	6	7	.462	106	79	58	4.50	0
1997 Iowa	A.A.		10	57²/₃	4	2	.667	80	52	35	4.68	0
1998 Iowa.	P.C.		1	5	1	0	1.000	11	2	1	0.00	0
1998 Chicago b	N.L.		26	166²/₃	13	6	.684	233	85	117	3.40	0
1999 Chicago c	N.L.					INJURED—Did Not Play						
2000 Daytona	Fla.St.		2	12	2	0	1.000	17	5	3	1.50	0
2000 Iowa	P.C.		1	7	0	0	.000	7	4	4	2.57	0
2000 Chicago d	N.L.		23	137	8	7	.533	132	87	112	4.80	0
2001 Chicago e	N.L.		28	174¹/₃	12	6	.667	217	92	127	3.36	0
2002 Chicago	N.L.		33	213²/₃	12	11	.522	217	97	169	3.66	0
2003 Chicago	N.L.		32	211	14	11	.560	*266	100	152	3.20	0
2004 Iowa.	P.C.		1	5	1	0	1.000	4	1	2	0.00	0
2004 Chicago f	N.L.		22	140¹/₃	8	9	.471	144	51	127	3.72	0
2005 Peoria.	Midwest		2	2¹/₃	0	0	.000	5	0	1	0.00	0
2005 Iowa.	P.C.		3	12²/₃	0	0	.000	18	6	11	2.84	0
2005 Chicago g	N.L.		21	66	3	4	.429	77	26	52	4.23	0
2006 Peoria.	Midwest		1	5	0	0	.000	12	1	1	0.00	0
2006 Iowa.	P.C.		1	5	0	1	.000	3	2	5	1.80	0
2006 Chicago h-i.	N.L.		4	19²/₃	1	2	.333	13	8	19	4.12	0
2007 Azl Cubs	Arizona		4	4	0	1	.000	5	1	4	2.25	0
2007 Peoria.	Midwest		3	3	1	0	1.000	3	1	1	0.00	0
2007 Tennessee	Southern		1	1²/₃	0	0	.000	1	1	0	0.00	0
2007 Chicago j-k.	N.L.		22	24¹/₃	1	1	.500	24	13	18	3.33	0
2008 Chicago l-m	N.L.		65	66¹/₃	5	4	.556	84	18	54	3.26	34
2009 Cleveland	A.L.		58	55	3	3	.500	63	28	48	4.25	20
2010 Akron	Eastern		3	2²/₃	0	1	.000	2	3	4	20.25	0
2010 Cleveland-New York n-o-p.	A.L.		47	46	3	4	.429	49	29	35	3.13	8
2011 Chicago h-i.	N.L.		55	51	3	5	.375	57	21	45	3.35	1
Major League Totals		13 Yrs.	436	1371¹/₃	86	73	.541	1576	655	1075	3.64	63

Division Series

Year	Club	Lea	G	IP	W	L	Pct	SO	BB	H	ERA	SAVES
1998 Chicago	N.L.		1	5	0	1	.000	5	4	3	1.80	0
2003 Chicago	N.L.		2	15¹/₃	2	0	1.000	18	7	7	1.76	0
2007 Chicago	N.L.		2	3	0	0	.000	2	0	3	3.00	0
2008 Chicago	N.L.		1	1	0	0	.000	0	0	2	0.00	0
2010 New York	A.L.		3	2	0	0	.000	3	2	4	4.50	0
Division Series Totals			9	26¹/₃	2	1	.667	28	13	19	2.05	0

Championship Series

Year	Club	Lea	G	IP	W	L	Pct	SO	BB	H	ERA	SAVES
2003 Chicago	N.L.		2	12¹/₃	0	1	.000	13	7	14	7.30	0
2010 New York	A.L.		4	6	0	0	.000	4	3	2	1.50	0
Championship Series Totals			6	18¹/₃	0	1	.000	17	10	16	5.40	0

a On disabled list from May 24 to June 19, 1996.
b Selected Rookie of the Year in National League for 1998.
c On disabled list from March 31 to November 2, 1999.
d On disabled list from March 25 to May 1 and July 30 to August 21, 2000.
e On disabled list from August 4 to September 7, 2001.
f On disabled list from May 12 to July 11, 2004.
g On disabled list from May 1 to June 29 and July 21 to August 5 and August 30 to October 31, 2005.
h On disabled list from March 27 to May 18 and June 7 to October 29, 2006.
i Filed for free agency, October 29, 2006, re-signed with Chicago Cubs, November 15, 2006.
j On disabled list from March 29 to August 3, 2007.
k Filed for free agency, October 29, 2007, re-signed with Chicago Cubs, November 28, 2007.
l On disabled list from July 14 to August 5, 2008.
m Filed for free agency, October 31, 2008. Signed with Cleveland Indians, December 13, 2008.
n On disabled list from March 26 to May 7 and July 12 to July 31, 2010.
o Traded to New York Yankees with cash for two players to be named later, July 31, 2010. Cleveland Indians received infielder Matthew Cusick and pitcher Andrew Shive to complete trade, October 21, 2010.
p Filed for free agency, November 1, 2010. Signed with Chicago Cubs, December 17, 2010.
h On disabled list from June 13 to July 1, 2011.
i Filed for free agency, October 30, 2011, re-signed with Chicago Cubs, January 13, 2012.

WOOD, TRAVIS A.

Born, Little Rock, Arkansas, February 6, 1987.
Bats Right. Throws Left. Height, 5 feet, 11 inches. Weight, 165 pounds.

Year	Club	Lea	G	IP	W	L	Pct	SO	BB	H	ERA	SAVES
2005	Reds.............	Gulf Coast	8	24	0	0	.000	45	7	13	0.75	0
2005	Billings...........	Pioneer	6	24²/₃	2	0	1.000	22	13	15	1.82	0
2006	Dayton............	Midwest	27	140	10	5	.667	133	56	108	3.66	0
2007	Sarasota...........	Fla.St.	12	46¹/₃	3	2	.600	54	27	49	4.86	0
2008	Sarasota...........	Fla.St.	9	46²/₃	3	4	.429	41	21	39	2.70	0
2008	Chattanooga.......	Southern	17	80	4	9	.308	58	48	91	7.09	0
2009	Louisville..........	Int.	8	48²/₃	4	2	.667	32	16	43	3.14	0
2009	Carolina..........	Southern	19	119	9	3	.750	103	37	78	1.21	0
2010	Louisville..........	Int.	16	100	5	6	.455	99	24	86	3.06	0
2010	Cincinnati.........	N.L.	17	102²/₃	5	4	.556	86	26	85	3.51	0
2011	Louisville.........	Int.	10	52¹/₃	2	3	.400	47	17	64	5.33	0
2011	Cincinnati a.......	N.L.	22	106	6	6	.500	76	40	118	4.84	0
Major League Totals........2 Yrs.			39	208²/₃	11	10	.524	162	66	203	4.18	0
Division Series												
2010	Cincinnati............	N.L.	1	3¹/₃	0	0	.000	3	1	1	0.00	0

a Traded to Chicago Cubs with outfielder Dave Sappell and infielder Ronald Torreyes for pitcher Sean Marshall, December 23, 2011.

WORLEY, VANCE RICHARD

Born, Sacramento, California, September 25, 1987.
Bats Right. Throws Right. Height, 6 feet, 2 inches. Weight, 230 pounds.

Year	Club	Lea	G	IP	W	L	Pct	SO	BB	H	ERA	SAVES
2008	Williamsport......	N.Y.-Penn.	2	8	0	0	.000	8	1	3	1.13	0
2008	Lakewood.........	So.Atl.	11	61	3	2	.600	53	7	58	2.66	0
2009	Reading..........	Eastern	27	153¹/₃	7	12	.368	100	49	163	5.34	0
2010	Reading..........	Eastern	19	112²/₃	9	4	.692	83	36	114	3.20	0
2010	Lehigh Valley.........	Int.	8	45¹/₃	1	3	.250	36	10	46	3.77	0
2010	Philadelphia......	N.L.	5	13	1	1	.500	12	4	8	1.38	0
2011	Lehigh Valley......	Int.	9	50²/₃	5	2	.714	50	12	41	2.31	0
2011	Philadelphia......	N.L.	25	131²/₃	11	3	.786	119	46	116	3.01	0
Major League Totals........2 Yrs.			30	144²/₃	12	4	.750	131	50	124	2.86	0
Division Series												
2011	Philadelphia.........	N.L.	2	1¹/₃	0	0	.000	0	1	3	6.75	0

WRIGHT, JAMEY ALAN

Born, Oklahoma City, Oklahoma, December 24, 1974.
Bats Right. Throws Right. Height, 6 feet, 6 inches. Weight, 235 pounds.

Year	Club	Lea	G	IP	W	L	Pct	SO	BB	H	ERA	SAVES
1993	Rockies...........	Arizona	8	36	1	3	.250	26	9	35	4.00	0
1994	Asheville...........	So.Atl.	28	143¹/₃	7	14	.333	103	59	188	5.97	0
1995	Salem.............	Carolina	26	171	10	8	.556	95	72	160	2.47	0
1995	New Haven........	Eastern	1	3	0	1	.000	0	3	6	9.00	0
1996	New Haven........	Eastern	7	44²/₃	5	1	.833	54	12	27	0.81	0
1996	Colorado Springs.......	P.C.	9	59²/₃	4	2	.667	40	22	53	2.72	0
1996	Colorado.............	N.L.	16	91¹/₃	4	4	.500	45	41	105	4.93	0
1997	Salem............	Carolina	1	1	0	1	.000	1	1	1	9.00	0
1997	Colorado Springs.......	P.C.	2	11	1	0	1.000	11	5	9	1.64	0
1997	Colorado a............	N.L.	26	149²/₃	8	12	.400	59	71	198	6.25	0
1998	Colorado............	N.L.	34	206¹/₃	9	14	.391	86	95	235	5.67	0
1999	Colorado.............	N.L.	16	94¹/₃	4	3	.571	49	54	110	4.87	0
1999	Colorado Springs b.....	P.C.	17	100¹/₃	5	7	.417	75	38	133	6.46	0
2000	Huntsville.........	Southern	2	12¹/₃	2	0	1.000	10	5	7	0.00	0
2000	Indianapolis..........	Int.	1	5	0	0	.000	7	3	8	1.80	0
2000	Milwaukee c...........	N.L.	26	164²/₃	7	9	.438	96	88	157	4.10	0
2001	Milwaukee d...........	N.L.	33	194²/₃	11	12	.478	129	98	201	4.90	0
2002	Indianapolis..........	Int.	3	15¹/₃	1	1	.500	13	5	16	4.11	0
2002	Milwaukee-St. Louis e-f-g	N.L.	23	129¹/₃	7	13	.350	77	75	130	5.29	0
2003	Indianapolis..........	Int.	7	22	1	3	.250	17	10	32	7.36	0
2003	Oklahoma.............	P.C.	7	39¹/₃	2	1	.667	40	21	38	4.12	0
2003	Omaha.............	P.C.	13	76²/₃	3	5	.375	65	38	70	3.64	0
2003	Kansas City h-i-j-k.....	A.L.	4	25¹/₃	1	2	.333	19	11	23	4.26	0
2004	Omaha.............	P.C.	18	104²/₃	8	6	.571	70	35	111	4.21	0
2004	Colorado l-m..........	N.L.	14	78²/₃	2	3	.400	41	45	82	4.12	0
2005	Colorado n..........	N.L.	34	171¹/₃	8	16	.333	101	81	201	5.46	0
2006	San Francisco o........	N.L.	34	156	6	10	.375	79	64	167	5.19	0

Year Club	Lea	G	IP	W	L	Pct	SO	BB	H	ERA	SAVES
2007 Frisco...............	Texas	1	4	0	0	.000	2	0	6	4.50	0
2007 Oklahoma............	P.C.	3	16⅓	2	1	.667	11	3	21	4.41	0
2007 Texas p-q.............	A.L.	20	77	4	5	.444	39	41	72	3.62	0
2008 Texas r..............	A.L.	75	84⅓	8	7	.533	60	35	93	5.12	0
2009 Kansas City s..........	A.L.	65	79	3	5	.375	60	44	73	4.33	0
2010 Sacramento...........	P.C.	10	14	1	0	1.000	16	9	23	9.00	1
2010 Cleveland-Seattle t-u.....	A.L.	46	58⅓	1	3	.250	28	25	55	4.17	0
2011 Seattle v..............	A.L.	60	68⅓	2	3	.400	48	30	61	3.16	1
Major League Totals.......16 Yrs.		526	1828⅔	85	121	.413	1016	898	1963	4.93	1

a On disabled list from May 15 to June 8, 1997.

b Traded to Milwaukee Brewers with catcher Henry Blanco and pitcher Justin Miller for infielder Jeff Cirillo and pitcher Scott Karl, December 13, 1999.

c On disabled list from March 28 to May 22, 2000.

d On disabled list from May 21 to June 10, 2001.

e On disabled list from April 5 to May 24, 2002.

f Traded to St. Louis Cardinals with cash for outfielder Chris Morris and player to be named later, August 29, 2002. Milwaukee Brewers received pitcher Mike Matthews to complete trade, September 11, 2002.

g Filed for free agency, November 1, 2002. Signed with Seattle Mariners organization, January 24, 2003.

h Released by Seattle Mariners, March 18, 2003. Signed with Milwaukee Brewers organization, March 23, 2003.

i Released by Milwaukee Brewers, April 28, 2003. Signed with Texas Rangers organization, May 5, 2003.

j Released by Texas Rangers, June 16, 2003. Signed with Kansas City Royals organization, June 24, 2003.

k Filed for free agency, October 30, 2003, re-signed with Kansas City Royals organization, March 29, 2004.

l Released by Kansas City Royals, July 21, 2004. Signed with Colorado Rockies organization, July 22, 2004.

m Filed for free agency, November 1, 2004, re-signed with Colorado Rockies, December 21, 2004.

n Filed for free agency, November 2, 2005. Signed with San Francisco Giants organization, January 17, 2006.

o Filed for free agency, November 2, 2006. Signed with Texas Rangers organization, January 25, 2007.

p On disabled list from April 11 to June 16, 2007.

q Filed for free agency, November 12, 2007, re-signed with Texas Rangers organization, January 11, 2008.

r Filed for free agency, October 30, 2008. Signed with Kansas City Royals organization, February 10, 2009.

s Filed for free agency, November 5, 2009. Signed with Cleveland Indians organization, February 9, 2010.

t Released by Cleveland Indians, June 10, 2010. Signed with Seattle Mariners, July 15, 2010.

u Filed for free agency, November 1, 2010, re-signed with Seattle Mariners organization, February 1, 2011.

v Filed for free agency, October 30, 2011.

YOUNG, CHRISTOPHER RYAN (CHRIS)
Born, Dallas, Texas, May 25, 1979.
Bats Right. Throws Right. Height, 6 feet, 10 inches. Weight, 280 pounds.

Year Club	Lea	G	IP	W	L	Pct	SO	BB	H	ERA	SAVES
2001 Hickory.............	So.Atl.	12	74⅓	5	3	.625	72	20	79	4.12	0
2002 Hickory...........	So.Atl.	26	144⅔	11	9	.550	136	34	127.	3.11	0
2003 Harrisburg........	Eastern	15	83	4	4	.500	64	22	83	4.01	0
2003 Brevard County......	Fla.St.	8	50	5	2	.714	39	5	26	1.62	0
2004 Frisco..............	Texas	18	88⅓	6	5	.545	75	31	94	4.48	0
2004 Oklahoma..........	P.C.	5	30⅓	3	0	1.000	34	9	20	1.48	0
2004 Texas b..............	A.L.	7	36⅓	3	2	.600	27	10	36	4.71	0
2005 Lynchburg.........	Carolina	10	15	0	1	.000	14	5	9	3.00	2
2005 Tulsa.............	Texas	35	53	3	2	.600	35	17	53	4.75	1
2005 Texas c-d............	A.L.	31	164⅔	12	7	.632	137	45	162	4.26	0
2006 San Diego............	N.L.	31	179⅓	11	5	.688	164	69	134	3.46	0
2007 San Diego e..........	N.L.	30	173	9	8	.529	167	72	118	3.12	0
2008 Lake Elsinore.........	Calif.	2	8⅔	0	1	.000	7	1	5	3.12	0
2008 San Diego f..........	N.L.	18	102⅓	7	6	.538	93	48	84	3.96	0
2009 San Diego g..........	N.L.	14	76	4	6	.400	50	40	70	5.21	0
2010 San Antonio..........	Texas	1	0⅔	0	1	.000	1	4	2	67.50	0
2010 Portland............	P.C.	2	6⅓	0	0	.000	4	2	2	1.42	0
2010 San Diego h-i.........	N.L.	4	20	2	0	1.000	15	11	10	0.90	0
2011 New York k-l..........	N.L.	4	24	1	0	1.000	22	11	12	1.88	0
Major League Totals........8 Yrs.		139	775⅔	49	34	.590	675	306	626	3.74	0
Division Series											
2006 San Diego............	N.L.	1	6⅔	1	0	1.000	9	2	4	0.00	0

a Traded by Pittsburgh Pirates to Montreal Expos with pitcher Jon Searles for pitcher Matt Herges, December 20, 2002.

b Traded to Texas Rangers with catcher Josh McKinley for catcher Einar Diaz, April 3, 2004.

c Traded to Arizona Diamondbacks with pitcher Orlando Hernandez and pitcher Luis Vizcaino for pitcher Javier Vazquez, December 20, 2005.

d Traded to San Diego Padres with infielder Adrian Gonzalez and outfielder Terrmel Sledge for pitcher Adam Eaton, pitcher Akinori Otsuka and catcher Billy Killian, January 4, 2006.

e On disabled list from July 25 to August 9, 2007.

f On disabled list from May 22 to July 29 and August 11 to September 1, 2008.